Oracle Press™

Oracle JDeveloper 10*g* Handbook

About the Authors

Dr. Avrom Roy-Faderman is a principal technical writer in the Application Development Tools group at Oracle Corporation. He has been documenting JDeveloper since 1999 and ADF BC since 2000, and coordinating ADF business services documentation since 2003. He regularly demos JDeveloper and ADF at OracleWorld and JavaOne conferences and has delivered papers on JDeveloper and ADF at conferences of the Oracle Development Tools Users Group and the Association of Mid-Atlantic Oracle Professionals. He is a coauthor, with Peter Koletzke and Dr. Paul Dorsey, of the *Oracle9i JDeveloper Handbook,* also from Oracle Press. avromroyfaderman.com.

Before joining Oracle, Avrom served on the philosophy department faculties at Stanford University and the University of Rochester, specializing in mathematical logic and the philosophy of language. He holds a B.S. in Mathematics with a Specialization in Computer Science and a B.A. in Philosophy from UCLA, and a Ph.D. in Symbolic Systems and Philosophy from Stanford University.

Peter Koletzke is a technical director and principal instructor for the Enterprise e-Commerce Solutions practice at Quovera, in Mountain View, California, and has 20 years of industry experience. Peter has presented at various Oracle users group conferences more than 130 times and has won awards such as Pinnacle Publishing's Technical Achievement, Oracle Development Tools Users Group (ODTUG) Editor's Choice, ECO/SEOUC Oracle Designer Award, and the ODTUG Volunteer of the Year. He is an Oracle Certified Master and coauthor, with Dr. Paul Dorsey, of other Oracle Press books: *Oracle9*i *JDeveloper Handbook (also co-authored with Avrom Roy-Faderman), Oracle JDeveloper 3 Handbook, Oracle Developer Advanced Forms and Reports, Oracle Designer Handbook, 2nd Edition,* and *Oracle Designer/2000 Handbook.* ourworld.compuserve.com/homepages/Peter_Koletzke.

Quovera is a business consulting and technology integration firm that specializes in delivering solutions to the high technology, telecommunications, semiconductor, manufacturing, software and services, public sector and financial services industries. Quovera deploys solutions that deliver optimized business processes quickly and economically, driving increased productivity and improved operational efficiency. Founded in 1995, the company has a track record of delivering hundreds of strategy, design, and implementation projects to over 250 Fortune 2000 and high growth middle market companies. Quovera's client list includes notable companies such as Cisco Systems, ON Semiconductor, New York State, Sun Microsystems, Seagate, Toyota, Fujitsu, Visa, and Cendant. www.quovera.com.

Dr. Paul Dorsey is the founder and president of Dulcian, Inc., an Oracle consulting firm specializing in business rules and web-based application development. He is the chief architect of Dulcian's Business Rules Information Manager (BRIM®) tool. Paul is the co-author of six other Oracle Press books on Designer, Database Design, Developer, and JDeveloper, which have been translated into nine languages. He is on the Board of Directors of ODTUG, president of the New York Oracle Users Group and a Contributing Editor of IOUG's SELECT Journal. In 2003, Dr. Dorsey was honored by ODTUG as volunteer of the year, in 2001 by IOUG as volunteer of the year and by Oracle as one of the six initial honorary Oracle 9*i* Certified Masters. Paul is also the founder and Chairperson of the ODTUG Business Rules Symposium, now in its fifth year.

Dulcian, Inc., specializes in Oracle client/server and web custom application development using object-oriented thinking implemented in a traditional relational database. The company provides a wide variety of consulting services, customized training, and products for the Oracle development environment. Dulcian builds business rule–based systems using its business rules repository manager (BRIM®) product suite. The company website can be found at www.dulcian.com.

NOTE
Sample code for the hands-on practices in this book as well as errata are available from the websites mentioned here.

Oracle Press™

Oracle JDeveloper 10*g* Handbook

Dr. Avrom Roy-Faderman
Peter Koletzke
Dr. Paul Dorsey

McGraw-Hill/Osborne

New York Chicago San Francisco
Lisbon London Madrid Mexico City Milan
New Delhi San Juan Seoul Singapore Sydney Toronto

The McGraw-Hill Companies

McGraw-Hill/Osborne
2100 Powell Street, 10th Floor
Emeryville, California 94608
U.S.A.

To arrange bulk purchase discounts for sales promotions, premiums, or fund-raisers, please contact **McGraw-Hill/**Osborne at the above address. For information on translations or book distributors outside the U.S.A., please see the International Contact Information page immediately following the index of this book.

Oracle JDeveloper 10*g* Handbook

1234567890 CUS CUS 01987654

ISBN 0-07-225583-8

Publisher
Brandon A. Nordin

Vice President & Associate Publisher
Scott Rogers

Acquisitions Editor
Lisa McClain

Project Editors
Patty Mon, Jennifer Malnick

Acquisitions Coordinator
Athena Honore

Technical Editors
David Parker, Leslie Tierstein

Technical Reviewers
Steve Anderson, Rob Clevenger, Ted Farrell, Brian Fry, David Goering, Jonas Jacobi, Raghu Kodali, Regis Louis, Duncan Mills, Steve Muench, Frank Nimphius, Blaise Ribet, Guus Ramackers, Chris Schalk, Michael White

Technical Review Coordinators
Srinivasan Arun, Marianne Baird, Simon Day

Copy Editor
Margaret Berson

Proofreader
Judy Wilson

Indexer
Caryl Lee Fisher

Composition
Lucie Ericksen, John Patrus

Illustrators
Kathleen Edwards, Melinda Lytle

Series Design
Jani Beckwith

Cover Designer
Damore Johann Design, Inc.

This book was composed with Corel VENTURA™ Publisher.

For ina, for everything.
—Dr. Avrom Roy-Faderman

Dedicated to the memory of Charlotte Samuels McLeod,
who so loved words and Great Books.
—Peter Koletzke

For my family … my wife Ileana, who makes it all worthwhile,
and our son, whom we will always remember.
—Dr. Paul Dorsey

Contents at a Glance

PART I
Overview

1 Overview of Oracle JDeveloper 10*g* 3
2 The Integrated Development Environment Overview 33
3 IDE Tools 63
4 Introduction to the Oracle Application Development Framework 103
5 Java Language Concepts for JDeveloper Work 131
6 Naming Conventions 167
7 J2EE Architectures and Deployment Alternatives 181

PART II
Business Services

8 Introducing ADF Business Components 223
9 Creating Business Domain Components 253
10 More Complex Business Rules 287
11 Creating Data Model Components 329
12 Exposing ADF BC to Applications 369
13 Creating Custom Service Methods 407
14 Business Service Technology Alternatives 445

PART III

Java Client and Web Applications

15 Creating Java Client Applications 501

16 Layout Managers 543

17 Working with Struts 591

18 Working with JSP Pages 637

19 Working with ADF UIX Pages 685

PART IV

Appendixes

A Other Resources 715

B Java Client User Interface Components 721

C Overview of HTML, JavaScript, and Cascading Style Sheets 733

D Overview of JSP, JSTL, and EL Tags 745

Index 769

Contents

PART I
Overview

1 Overview of Oracle JDeveloper 10*g* **3**

JDeveloper: Past, Present, and Future 4

Past: Product History and Roots 4

Present: Where Is JDeveloper Now? 6

Future: The Vision 8

What Is New in JDeveloper 10*g*? 9

New Integrated Development Environment (IDE) 9

Application Development Framework 10

Struts 10

Modeling in JDeveloper 11

Business Services 12

Desupported and Deprecated Features 12

Creating Application Code in JDeveloper 13

Application Workspaces 13

Projects 14

JDeveloper Directory Structure 14

Development Steps 14

Hands-on Practice: Build a Client/Server Application Using the JDeveloper Wizards 15

I. Create the Application Workspace and Database Connection 16

II. Create the Model Project 20

III. Create the View Project 25

Hands-on Practice: Create a Simple JSP Page 29

I. Create the JSP Project 29

II. Create the JSP File 30

2 The Integrated Development Environment Overview **33**

The JDeveloper 10*g* IDE 35

IDE Window 35

About Monitor Resolution 37

Editor Window 38
Dockable Windows 40
Customizing the IDE 43
Preferences 44
Main Toolbar 44
Main Menu 45
About Javadoc 50
The Help System 54
Finding the Help Topic 56
Displaying the Help Topic 56
Locating Help Centrally 56
Software Configuration Management 57
CVS Concepts 57
Hands-on Practice: Set Up CVS Locally 58
I. Install and Set Up the CVS Server 59
II. Set Up a CVS Server Connection 60
III. Import and Check Out a Module 61

3 IDE Tools 63
Navigators 65
Application Navigator and System Navigator 65
Connection Navigator 68
Run Manager 69
Structure Window 70
Structure Window Icons 70
Other Structure Window Operations 71
Structure Window Views 71
Component Palette 72
Code Snippets 72
Property Inspector 73
Properties 73
Events 75
Log Window 76
Code Editor 76
End Tag Completion 77
Code Templates 77
Code Insight and Tag Insight 78
Other Text Editing Features 80
Editing PL/SQL 81
Code Editor Style Sheet Support 82
Debugger 84
Debugger Windows 85
Debugging Java Code 85
Debugging PL/SQL 86
Other Tools for Improving Code 86
Visual Editors 86
HTML and UIX Previewers 87

New Gallery 89
Wizards 90
New File Dialogs 91
Data Control Palette 91
Other Editors 92
XML Editor 92
Class Editor 92
EJB Module Editor 94
Viewer Windows 95
Image Viewer 95
Archive Viewer 95
Tables Viewer 96
Sequence Viewer 96
SQL Worksheet 97
Modelers and Diagrammers 98
Types of Diagrams 99
Creating a UML Diagram 99
Some Diagramming Operations 100
XML Schema Editor 101
Struts Page Flow Diagrammer 102

4 Introduction to the Oracle Application Development Framework 103
What Is a Framework? 104
Why Use a Framework? 105
What Is a Development Framework? 106
Why Use a Development Framework? 106
Support for the Framework 107
What Is Oracle Application Development Framework? 107
Who Will Use ADF? 108
ADF User Community Support 109
Development Frameworks in Previous JDeveloper Releases 109
ADF Architecture Model 110
MVC 110
ADF Layers and Components 110
ADF Code Libraries 118
Some ADF Libraries 118
ADF Development Method and IDE Support 120
The Steps 120

5 Java Language Concepts for JDeveloper Work 131
Why Java? 132
Benefits 133
Drawbacks 134
Transitioning to Java 135
Object Orientation Concepts 136
Handling and Storing Data 137
Inheritance 139
Other Primary Object-Oriented Concepts 140

Java Language Review 140
  Annotated Java Code Example 140
  Annotated Use of the Box Example Class 146
  Other Java Language Concepts 147
Hands-on Practice: Create Java Class Files 160
  I. Make an Application Workspace and Project 160
  II. Create and Test Java Class Files 161

6 Naming Conventions 167

The Importance of Using Naming Conventions 169
  The Consistency Issue 170
General Naming Convention Considerations and Guidelines 170
  Use Prefixes and Suffixes 171
  Consider the Capabilities of the Language 171
  Be Aware of Case Sensitivity 172
  Use a Dictionary of Allowable Words 172
  Use Abbreviations Carefully 172
Recognized Naming Conventions in Java 173
  Constants (Final Variables) 173
  Classes 173
  Class Instances, Exceptions, Methods, and Variables 174
  Packages 174
JDeveloper-Specific Naming Conventions 175
  Types of Objects to Name 175
  Workspaces 176
  Projects 176
  Connections 176
  Class Source Files 177
  Libraries 177
  Client Data Models 177
  UML Diagram Elements 177
  ADF Business Components 177
  Java Client Application Files 179
  Java Client UI Components 179
  Web Client Components 179

7 J2EE Architectures and Deployment Alternatives 181

An Overview of J2EE 183
  J2ME 183
  J2SE 183
  J2EE 184
Deploying a J2EE Application 186
  J2EE Archive Files 187
  Deployment Descriptor Files 187
  Deploying Archive Files 188
JDeveloper and J2EE 188
  Deploying J2EE Applications in JDeveloper 189

Java Client Architectures 189
Java Applications 189
Applets 194
Hands-on Practice: Deploy a Java Application 196
I. Prepare a Simple ADF BC Java Application 197
II. Create a Java Application JAR File 198
III. Create a Batch File and Run the JAR File 202
JavaServer Pages Architecture 204
Java Servlet Overview 204
JSP Technology Overview 205
Where Does OC4J Fit? 209
Hands-on Practice: Deploy a JSP Application 209
I. Create a JSP Application 210
II. Set Up OC4J 212
III. Deploy the JSP Application 216

PART II
Business Services

8 Introducing ADF Business Components 223
Why Use ADF BC? 225
ADF Business Components, XML, and Java 226
ADF Business Component Groups 226
Business Domain Components 227
Data Model Components 230
Hands-on Practice: Examine a Default ADF BC Layer 234
I. Create an Application Workspace with a Default ADF BC Layer 235
II. Explore the Business Domain Components 238
III. Explore the Data Model Components 242
IV. Test the Default Business Components 248

9 Creating Business Domain Components 253
Creating Default Business Domain Components 254
Entity Attributes 254
Adding and Deleting Attributes 255
Changing Datatypes 255
Representing Column Constraints 255
Synchronizing Entity Object Definitions with the Database 257
Representing Relationships Between Tables 257
Association Cardinality 258
Association Directionality and Accessor Attributes 259
Compositions 261
Representing Oracle Object Types 263
Business Components and Database Object Generation 264
Creating Entity Object Definitions for Table Generation 265
Creating Table Constraints for Generation 266
Creating Domains for Oracle Object Type Generation 268
Generating Database Objects 268

Hands-on Practice: Represent the HR Schema 269
I. Create an Application Workspace and Default Business Domain Components 270
II. Change Entity Attributes 272
III. Clean Up Accessor Attribute Names 274
IV. Create Business Domain Components for Table Generation 276
V. Generate the New Table and Constraints 278
VI. Create a Many-to-Many Association 279
VII. Test the Business Domain Components 281

10 More Complex Business Rules 287
Overview of the Entity Classes 288
Entity Object Classes 289
Entity Definition Classes 290
Entity Collection Classes 291
Manipulating Attribute Values 291
Attribute-Level Validation 293
Validation Rules 293
Validation Domains 295
Setter Method Validation 296
Choosing a Validation Style 297
Entity-Level Validation 298
Entity-Level Validation Rules 299
The validateEntity() Method 300
Choosing a Validation Style 301
Entity-Level Validation and Compositions 301
Hands-on Practice: Add Validation to the HR Business Domain Components 302
I. Remove Unneeded Entity Object Classes 303
II. Apply a Built-in Validation Rule 304
III. Create and Use a Custom Validation Rule 305
IV. Create and Use a Validation Domain 310
V. Provide Entity-Level Validation 312
Adding Default Values to Entity Attributes 314
Static Default Values 314
Dynamically Calculated Default Values 315
The SequenceImpl Class and the DBSequence Domain 315
Calculated Transient Attributes 316
Using Associations in Business Rules 317
Getting a Unique Associated Entity 317
Getting Many Associated Entities 318
Integrating with Business Logic in the Database 318
Integrating with Database Triggers 318
Using Stored Procedures to Perform DML Operations 319
Hands-on Practice: Add More Business Rules to the HR Business Domain Components 321
I. Add Defaulting Logic 322
II. Calculate an Attribute 323
III. Add Validation Logic That Uses an Association 326

11 Creating Data Model Components **329**
View Attributes, Entity Attributes, and Caching 330
How Entity-Derived View Attributes Are Populated 331
How SQL-Only Attributes Are Populated 333
Entity-Derived vs. SQL-Only View Attributes 334
Entity Object Usages and Table Aliases 337
Keys 338
Refining a View Object's Query 339
Setting the WHERE and ORDER BY Clauses 339
Expert Mode 340
Hands-on Practice: Create View Object Definitions 342
I. Create an Application Workspace for the Data Model Components 343
II. Create a Simple View Object Definition 345
III. Create a SQL-Only View Object Definition 347
IV. Create a View Object Definition with Multiple Entity Object Usages 349
V. Create a View Object Definition with an Entity Object Usage and an Expert-Mode Query 352
Representing Relationships Between Query Result Sets 357
View Link SQL 357
View Link Definition Cardinality 359
View Link Definition Directionality and Accessor Attributes 360
Aggregating Data for Applications 361
Hands-on Practice: Create View Link and Application Module Definitions 362
I. Create View Link Definitions 362
II. Create and Test an Application Module Definition 364

12 Exposing ADF BC to Applications **369**
ADF Model Layer Architecture 370
Data Controls 370
Binding Containers 371
Creating Data Controls and Bindings 372
The Data Control Palette 372
The UI Model Tab 374
Exposing a View Object Instance to an ADF Application 375
Ranges 375
Using Multiple Iterator Bindings 376
Accessing a Range of Data 376
Navigating Through Collections 378
Moving the Current Row Pointer 378
Scrolling the Range 379
Key Objects 380
Creating and Deleting Rows 381
Accessing Individual Values 381
Hands-on Practice: Create a Master-Detail JSP Application 381
I. Create a Read-Only Form with Navigation 382
II. Create a UI Table to Display Details 387

Selecting from a List 393
Navigation Mode 393
Enumeration Mode 394
LOV Mode 395
Managing Transactions 396
Hands-on Practice: Refine the JSP Application 397
I. Refine the Master-Detail Form 397
II. Create an Edit Form 400

13 Creating Custom Service Methods 407
Overview of Data Model Component Classes 409
Overview of Application Module Classes 409
Overview of View Classes 411
Custom Service Method Basics 412
Exposing and Accessing Service Methods 412
Finding View Object Instances in the Data Model 413
Finding View Object Instances in a Nested Application Module Instance 413
Retrieving View Rows 414
Stepping Through a View Cache 415
Row Keys 415
Manipulating Data 417
Reading and Changing Attribute Values 417
Creating and Deleting Rows 417
Restricting a View Object Instance's Cache 418
Using setWhereClause() 418
Parameterized WHERE Clauses 419
View Criteria Objects 420
Re-Executing the Query 421
Using View Link Definitions in Service Methods 421
Hands-on Practice: Create and Invoke Service Methods 422
I. Turn Off Batch Mode 423
II. Choose View Classes 423
III. Create a View Object Method Stub and a Service Method 425
IV. Access the Service Method from a JSP Application 427
V. Add Navigation Code to the View Object Method 431
VI. Add Code to Filter Data 432
VII. Add Code to Change Data 434
Dynamically Creating Master-Detail Relationships 436
Hands-on Practice: Create and Invoke Service Methods to Maintain a Dynamic Master-Detail Relationship 437
I. Remove a View Link Instance from an Application Module Definition 438
II. Create Service Methods to Maintain a Dynamic Master-Detail Relationship 438
III. Use the Dynamic Master-Detail Relationship 440
IV. Test the Service Methods 443

14 Business Service Technology Alternatives **445**
Enterprise JavaBeans Technology 446
EJB Technology and the Business Domain 448
EJB Technology and the Data Model 450
EJB Technology and the ADF Model Layer 454
Hands-on Practice: Build a Simple EJB Application 457
I. Create an Application Workspace and EJB Diagram 458
II. Create the Business Domain 459
III. Create the Data Model 460
IV. Create Data Control Definition Files 467
V. Create a Master-Detail Form 468
TopLink Technology 470
TopLink POJO and the Business Domain 470
TopLink POJO and the Data Model 473
TopLink Technology and the ADF Model Layer 474
Hands-on Practice: Build a Simple TopLink Application 475
I. Create an Application Workspace 476
II. Create Java Classes 478
III. Create Descriptors and Direct Mappings 480
IV. Create a Relationship Mapping 484
V. Create a TopLink Query 485
VI. Create Data Control Definition Files 486
VII. Create a Master-Detail Form 486
Web Services 488
WSDL, SOAP, and Web Service Stubs 488
Web Services and the ADF Model Layer 489
Hands-on Practice: Create an Application That Uses a Web Service 489
I. Register to Use the Google Web APIs 490
II. Create an Application Workspace 490
III. Create a Web Service Stub 491
IV. Create a Wrapper Class for the Stub 492
V. Create Data Control Definition Files 493
VI. Create a Search Application 494

PART III
Java Client and Web Applications

15 Creating Java Client Applications **501**
The JDeveloper IDE for Java Client Development 502
Building Java Client Applications 503
Directory Organization for a Java Client Application 504
Java Client Architecture Decisions 504
How Many Independent Programs Will You Use? 505
How Many Directories, Workspaces, and Projects Will You Create? 505
Where Will the Model and Data Validation Take Place? 505

What Type of Container Layout Should Be Used? 506
How Many Packages Will You Create and How Will You Name Them? 506
Other Issues 506
ADF JClient 507
Swing UI Architecture 507
Developing a Client Data Model 508
Binding Swing Components to ADF BC 508
Binding Panels 509
Working with Swing Components in JDeveloper 510
The Data Control Palette 510
The Component Palette 511
Using Swing Components 511
Adding Swing Components to a Program 512
Categories of Swing Components 512
Container Objects 513
Modifying Swing Components 517
Defining Events 517
Getting the Right Information 518
Hands-on Practice: Create a Tabbed User Interface Application 520
I. Create the ADF BC Project 520
II. Create the Java Application Project 521
III. Create a Three-Tab User Interface 524
Hands-on Practice: Customize the Component Palette and Create a JavaBean 532
I. Create and Deploy a JavaBean 533
II. Create a Library for the JavaBean 535
III. Add a Component Palette Page and Add the Custom JavaBean 536
IV. Test the Custom Component 539

16 Layout Managers 543
How Does This Work in a J2EE Web Application? 545
Layout Manager and Container Concepts 545
Laying Out a User Interface 546
The Default Layout Manager 548
Setting Layout Manager Properties 548
Java Visual Editor Tools 549
Layout Managers in JDeveloper 550
Overview of the Layout Managers 551
A Word About the "null" Layout 551
BorderLayout 551
BoxLayout2 554
CardLayout 556
FlowLayout 557
GridBagLayout 559
GridLayout 566
OverlayLayout2 568
PaneLayout 569

VerticalFlowLayout 571
XYLayout 572
Layout Manager Usage 573
Multiple Layouts 574
Hands-on Practice: Work with Layouts 577
I. Set up an Application Workspace and Two Projects 577
II. Use the BorderLayout Manager 579
III. Use the GridBagLayout Manager 583

17 Working with Struts 591
Struts Architecture 592
Struts Elements 593
ApplicationResources.properties Files 594
The struts-config.xml File 595
View-Level Struts Tag Libraries 597
JDeveloper's Implementation of Struts 598
Working in the Page Flow Diagram 599
Struts Elements in JDeveloper 600
Data Controls 604
Introduction to the Hands-on Practices 606
Hands-on Practice: Create a Simple Struts Application 607
I. Create the Application Workspace and ADF BC Project 607
II. Create Browse and Edit JSP Data Pages 608
III. Add the Ability to Save Edits 613
IV. Add the Ability to Create Records 615
V. Add Delete Functionality to the Application 617
VI. Add a Logic Tag to Highlight the Current Record 619
VII. Shade Every Other Row 622
VIII. Test for a Value in the Table 623
Hands-on Practice: Create a Struts Application with Data Actions for Custom Logic . 625
I. Create Another ViewController Project 625
II. Create a Data Action and a JSP Data Page 627
III. Add Edit and Update Functionality 631

18 Working with JSP Pages 637
JSP Development Requirements 638
Required Language Skills 639
Understanding JSP Compilation and Runtime 639
Additional Information Sources 640
JSP Application Development in JDeveloper 641
JSP/HTML Visual Editor 641
Code Editor 644
Structure Window 645
Page Flow Diagram 646
Property Inspector 647

Component Palette ... 648
Data Control Palette ... 650
Steps for Creating a Struts JSP Application ... 657
Some ADF BC JSP Coding Techniques ... 657
Find Mode ... 657
ADF Business Component Properties ... 658
Using Control Hints for Labeling and Formatting ... 659
Hands-on Practice: Build JSP Query and Results Pages ... 663
I. Create the Application Workspace and Business Services ... 664
II. Create the JSP Pages and Controller Actions ... 665
III. Modify the Data Elements ... 671
IV. Modify the Visual Aspects ... 680

19 Working with ADF UIX Pages ... 685
ADF UIX Overview ... 686
UIX Features ... 687
UIX Page Design Structure ... 689
UIX Application Development in JDeveloper ... 693
Wizards and File Creation Dialogs ... 693
UIX Visual Editor ... 694
UIX Preview ... 694
XML Editor ... 694
Structure Window ... 694
Page Flow Diagram ... 695
Property Inspector ... 695
Component Palette ... 696
Data Control Palette ... 697
Steps for Creating a Struts UIX Application ... 697
Hands-on Practice: Build a UIX Application ... 699
I. Prepare the Projects ... 699
II. Create the Browse Page Using a Wizard ... 700
III. Add Data and Action Components to the Browse Page ... 703
IV. Create and Link the Edit Page ... 706
V. Create and Link the Search Page ... 708
VI. Modify the Look-And-Feel ... 711

PART IV
Appendixes

A Other Resources ... 715
Books ... 716
Websites ... 717

B Java Client User Interface Components ... 721
AWT ... 722
Code Snippets ... 724

JClient Controls 726
Swing 728
Swing Containers 730

C Overview of HTML, JavaScript, and Cascading Style Sheets 733
HTML 734
Editing HTML 734
HTML Tags 734
Sample HTML Code 737
JavaScript in HTML 739
Cascading Style Sheets 740
Building a Cascading Style Sheet 741
Using a Cascading Style Sheet 742

D Overview of JSP, JSTL, and EL Tags 745
Basic JSP Tags 746
Where to Put the Code? 747
Beginning and Ending Tags 747
Processing of Standard Tags 747
JSP Standard Tag Library 759
JSTL Example 760
Tag Libraries 761
Expression Language 763
An Annotated Example 765

Index 769

Foreword

No problem can stand the assault of sustained thinking.

—Voltaire (Francois-Marie Arouet) (1694–1778),
French author, wit, and philosopher

Software is becoming increasingly more sophisticated and requires more powerful tools to help developers deal with its associated complexity. While most of the time these improvements are incremental, once in a while a technical revolution comes, which forces everything to be rethought and makes these advances obsolete. With the Internet, we saw one of these radical architectural shifts. Its immediate consequence has been that most of the drastic productivity advances brought by products such as Oracle Forms, PowerBuilder, Visual Basic, and so on, had to be rebuilt for a new technology stack.

Although a daunting task, this is also an incredible opportunity to solve new challenges as well as a rare chance to fix the mistakes of the past.

Nine years ago, when we started working on JDeveloper, we decided that our ideal tool would do the following:

- **Conquer the complexity of today's platform.** Between the J2EE and Web Services standards, there are thousands of APIs covering vastly different domains that need to be harnessed in order to build an application. The perfect tool would shield developers from the complexity of the platform but, unlike its client/server predecessors, would not get in the way of dealing with the underlying API when you need total control.

- **Raise developer productivity.** There are numerous best practices that need to be used in order to build a well-behaved application. Implementing these practices over and over is time consuming; a perfect tool would implement these practices automatically to let developers focus on the business problems they are trying to solve.

- **Build standard applications.** This not only means applications that can be run on any standard compliant application server, but also applications whose standard architecture is respected throughout the different steps of the development cycle. Not only do developers want an application that runs on any application server and/or any browser, they also want their application to be an MVC application, with the UI logic separated from the business logic.

With JDeveloper 10*g* and ADF (Application Development Framework) we have taken a major step toward achieving this vision.

Meanwhile, with this third iteration of the JDeveloper handbook, Avrom, Peter, and Paul have captured the essence of what makes JDeveloper different from other tools. Along with this book's focus on ADF, you will learn not only how to build an application but, more importantly, how to build an Enterprise application with all of its inherent characteristics, such as scalability, reliability, customizability, and so on. All of these have been proven in the real world by Oracle's own eBusiness suite.

By reading this book you will harness the power we have built into JDeveloper. And because, as Voltaire stated, "No problem can stand the assault of sustained thinking," find out on otn.oracle.com how Oracle will keep making your life easier with future versions of JDeveloper.

Christophe Job
Vice President, Application Development Tools
Oracle Corporation

Acknowledgments

If you read acknowledgements in the front of books with any regularity, you're surely familiar with the formula. "This book would never have existed if it had just been me. I couldn't have done it without my friends. I couldn't have done it without my family. I couldn't have done it without my colleagues. I couldn't have done it without my editors." Blah, blah. The strange thing is that it's all true. Every word.

Of course, this book would never have existed if it weren't for Peter Koletzke and Paul Dorsey, for the very simple reason that there would have been nobody to write most of it. But there's a lot more to it than that: A coauthored book isn't just a matter of a bunch of people writing separate chapters and putting them between a single set of covers; it's a truly collaborative process. Peter and Paul's tirelessly provided feedback was as vital to "my" chapters as my own by-now worn keyboard. And as for Caryl Lee Fisher, Paul's assistant, who kept us on track through snow and sleet and dead of night...well, I'd say that Caryl Lee was one of the great unsung heroes, except that we all sing her praises as loudly as possible, every chance we get.

Our technical editors, Leslie Tierstein and David Parker, went over every chapter and through each practice—sometimes more than once—and caught more inaccuracies, infelicities, and inefficiencies in the first draft than I'd care to admit to. And our editors at McGraw-Hill/Osborne—Lisa McClain, Athena Honore, Patty Mon, Jennifer Malnick, and Margaret M. Berson—shepherded this book all the way from the beginnings of an outline through the final proofs for the printer.

I count myself very fortunate to be a part of the JDeveloper team at Oracle. Not only does it put me in close proximity to the world's greatest JDeveloper experts, it's made up entirely of wonderful people. My manager, Ken Chu, his manager, Roel Stalman, and our Vice President, Christophe Job, were all extremely understanding about the demands this book put on my time. The rest of the documentation group, Mysti Berry, Orlando Cordero, David Goering, Ralph Gordon, Joe Malin, Robin Merrin, Kathryn Munn, Catherine Pickersgill, Jon Russell, Rick Sapir, Poh Lee Tan, Odile Sullivan-Tarazi, Martin Wykes, and especially Mario Korf, graciously picked up the slack when I disappeared into the Book Underworld.

As with the previous edition of this book, we got extensive assistance from the Oracle Product Management, Development, and Quality Assurance teams. I can speak specifically to those who reviewed the chapters in Part II: Steve Anderson, Steve Muench, and Blaise Ribet. Steve Anderson, in particular, reviewed *every single chapter* in Part II, which is a pretty remarkable amount of work on a project he didn't sign up for in the first place. Coordinating the reviews wouldn't have been possible without the help of Roel Stalman, Srinivasan Arun, Simon

Day, and Marianne Baird. Sung Im, Juan Oropeza, Steve Muench, Shailesh Vinayaka, and Jon Wetherbee also provided valuable technical assistance when I ran into problems I just couldn't solve.

Writing a book is exhausting. Without a lot of support, it just doesn't get done. That's why I'm exceptionally grateful to have a community of friends and family who have absolutely showered me with support. I'm fortunate in that many of the names that appear above fall into this category as well, especially Mysti, Orlando, David, Mario, Joe, Kathryn (and her husband Charles Hodgkins), Odile (and her husband Stan Tarazi), Mario, and Steve Anderson (and his wife Betsy Appell). I'd also like to thank Jon Kaplan and Sharyn Clough; Sam McCoy; Rob Hof, Margaret Young, and Devony; David Seaver; Richard Barrick and Yuni Jang; and Deb Kim. Spot and Nixie helped to stave off the tragic fluff deficiency that fells so many authors.

My parents, Lillian Faderman and Phyllis Irwin, are still my heroes. I can say, with certainty, that if it weren't for their love, support, and influence, there's no way I'd be finishing up my second book now. I'd also like to thank my new mother-in-law, Reena Roy, for welcoming me into her family.

And finally, there is my wife, ina. For one thing, she's put up with something no human being should ever be expected to tolerate—having a new spouse disappear into a book before she's been married a single month and not come out again until months later—and she's done it with graciousness and grace. She's taken care of me when I felt helpless and cheered me up when I felt grumpy. But more than that, she's been herself—her beautiful, smart, funny, sweetest self. I love you, ina. And thanks.

Avrom Roy-Faderman
Palo Alto, California
July 2004

For me, this book project had many similarities with one of the numerous cross-country flights I have taken recently. When we started writing this book, JDeveloper was still in its beta releases; keeping up with the shifting features and methods offered in the product was as challenging as trying to pin down airfare prices that shift from day to day. Some chapters required much research and the writing experienced delays not unlike those due to the long lines for check-in, security, and boarding. Like many flights, we experienced some "bumpy air" and needed to circle the connecting city's airport because of heavy traffic. Sometimes, because of unexpected weather, you need to stay overnight at a connecting city and catch the first flight the following morning. Some chapters had to wait until key information was clear. You try to keep reminding yourself of the A.R. Rahman's lyrics, "The journey home is never too long. Your heart arrives before the train." But, until you send the last chapter to the printer, you do not realize that truth.

Just as a commercial airline requires many people for a successful take off and landing, this book had many key contributors and many thanks are due.

First, much appreciation goes to the cockpit crew who successfully found the destination airport despite many versions of the outline, much unexpected weather, and the pressure from many outside forces. Thanks to Caryl Lee Fisher, Paul's assistant, who remains the best non-technical person I know, for debugging and finding problems in the hands-on practices. Caryl Lee also expertly kept Paul current on his tasks and deadlines. Fellow pilot Paul somehow managed, for our sixth book collaboration, to squeeze book time out of the demands of running a company and of volunteering for many user group events. Fellow pilot Avrom was also amazingly able to juggle the demands of his newlywed status and job at Oracle and still complete many excellent chapters about intricate J2EE matters.

Our technical editors were the in-flight crew who acted as key contributors to the quality and content of the book. As with many of our previous books, Leslie Tierstein provided not only a reality check for what readers could understand, but also provided technical information, additional sentences, and severe pruning when we used too many words. Many thanks, Leslie! David Parker added his comments and corrections from the standpoint of a non-Oracle, Java industry expert and gave us suggestions about current and future trends.

Cross-country flights cannot be undertaken without significant support from the ground crew. This role was filled by many technical reviewers from the JDeveloper product team who supplied inside information and further enhanced the technical accuracy of the book. Their names are listed on the credits page in the front of the book, but I'd like to acknowledge the assistance of Christophe Job and Roel Stalman, who allowed the JDeveloper team to play such a key role in ensuring quality of the book. Also, thanks to Christophe for writing the foreword to this edition of the book.

In addition, I'd like to thank the technical review coordinators—Srinivasan Arun, Simon Day, and Marianne Baird—who sent the chapters and our questions to the expert resources on the JDeveloper team. I'd also like to personally thank Rob Clevenger, Ted Farrell, Brian Fry, Jonas Jacobi, Raghu Kodali, Regis Louis, Steve Muench, Frank Nimphius, Guus Ramackers, Chris Schalk, and Mike White for excellent comments and corrections for my chapters.

Blaise Ribet, Odile Sullivan-Tarazi, Shailesh Vinayaka, and Juan Oropeza assisted by answering some sticky questions. David Brown supplied several paragraphs about JDeveloper's software configuration management features for the previous edition of the book that were repeated in this edition. Igor Gorbunov, another Java industry expert, gave hints about how to handle several advanced Java topics. Thanks go Quovera and my boss, Guy Wilnai, for sponsoring some book hours and providing a flexible work schedule. Also, my gratitude goes to

Quovera's client, the staff and management at New York State Office of Alcoholism and Substance Abuse Services, for their patience and flexibility in handling my abnormal work hours.

I appreciate the work and inspiring attitude of the folks at McGraw-Hill/Osborne—Lisa McClain, Patty Mon, Jennifer Malnick, Margaret M. Berson, and Athena Honore—who provided the essential guidance of the control tower so that the book's deadlines were met (mostly) and no mid-air collisions occurred.

Friends and family filled the role of, well, friends and family of those on the plane, waving us on and asking about and sympathizing with the many steps of the book process. Thanks to Alice Rischert, who was just completing her revision of another Oracle-related book and who helped me by comparing notes on the joys and frustrations of book projects. Amanda Douglas assisted by supplying strawberries to get me through a late night writing session. My parents and sister encouraged me throughout the long months of writing and editing, and I am very appreciative of that support.

Finally, to my wife, Anne, whom I love very much: Thank you for your patience and understanding on yet another book project, and now we have time before the next book project for that much-needed kitchen remodeling.

Peter Koletzke
San Carlos, California
July 2004

Each time we finish one of these projects (this is the seventh book that I have co-authored), I swear it will be the last, at least for a while. I suspect that I may have an easier time living up to that promise this time, but you never know. JDeveloper continues to evolve and become an ever more interesting product. I still want to return to UML-based data modeling and write another version of *Oracle8 Design using UML Object Modeling*.

This was, in some ways, an easier book to write in that we were preparing a third edition of our JDeveloper Handbook. However, in other ways, it was harder since we were trying to say things that are more substantive about the product. When we wrote the first JDeveloper Handbook, we were learning the product as we were writing. Now we are trying to incorporate our different experiences with the product. Each of the coauthors has worked extensively with different parts of the product and has come to different conclusions about the best way to build applications. It was a challenge to merge our respective visions of the tool.

For the sixth time, Peter Koletzke was willing to collaborate with me on another writing project. If and when he ever gets tired of doing this, I may have to retire my pen. His thoroughness and meticulous attention to detail was a huge contribution to this book. I cannot imagine undertaking a large publication project without his invaluable advice and feedback.

Since he did such a good job last time, Avrom Roy-Faderman took the lead on this writing project. Despite the distraction of getting married during our writing process, he managed to write the critical ADF Business Components portion of the book.

My brother Roger has been my research and development resource for the last several years. He spent months figuring out how to use various parts of the tool. Without his help, I would not have been able to finish my part of this project.

Once again, Leslie Tierstein undertook the difficult task of merging the voices of three authors and helped to ensure a consistent style and format for the chapters and hands-on practices. David Parker added his Java expertise to the project to help ensure its accuracy and provided valuable input to the chapters and practices.

We received unprecedented support from Oracle for this project. Christophe Job made sure that we had the right people to review each and every chapter for us. His support along with that of Roel Stalman and the JDeveloper team helped us correct many errors and misstatements that would otherwise have found their way into the finished product. Some of the people at Oracle Corp. who helped us review the chapters included Marianne Baird, Simon Day, Ted Farrell, Brian Fry, David Goering, Regis Louis, Duncan Mills, Frank Nimphius, Blaise Ribet, Chris Schalk, and Srinivasan Arun. We greatly appreciated all of the time and effort they devoted to this project. Steve Muench patiently helped me every time I got stuck trying to figure something out. His knowledge and willingness to help are greatly appreciated.

Thanks to the OMH team—Lisa McClain, Athena Honore, Patty Mon, and Jennifer Malnick—for all of their hard work on this project.

Special thanks again go to Caryl Lee Fisher. Her contribution to this book and all of my professional commitments makes my colleagues envious. "I wish I had a Caryl Lee." is a statement I hear at every conference where I speak. The OMH team should be especially thankful for her contribution. Otherwise, they would have had to work with me directly.

Dr. Paul Dorsey
Colonia, New Jersey
July 2004

Hands-on Practices at a Glance

This book contains many hands-on practices to help you learn about the myriad features and functions of Oracle JDeveloper 10*g*. The following is a quick reference list to enable you to find a specific practice:

Category	Practice Name	Chapter	Page
ADF BC	Examine a Default ADF BC Layer	8	234
ADF BC	Represent the HR Schema	9	269
ADF BC	Add Validation to the HR Business Domain Components	10	302
ADF BC	Add More Business Rules to the HR Business Domain Components	10	321
ADF BC	Create View Object Definitions	11	342
ADF BC	Create View Link and Application Module Definitions	11	362
ADF BC, JSP Pages	Create a Master-Detail JSP Application	12	381
ADF BC	Create and Invoke Service Methods	13	422
ADF BC	Create and Invoke Service Methods to Maintain a Dynamic Master-Detail Relationship	13	437
ADF BC, Java Client	Build a Client/Server Application Using the JDeveloper Wizards	1	15
ADF UIX	Build a UIX Application	19	699

Category	Practice Name	Chapter	Page
CVS	Set Up CVS Locally	2	58
EJB	Build a Simple EJB Application	14	457
Java Client	Create a Tabbed User Interface Application	15	520
Java Client	Customize the Component Palette and Create a JavaBean	15	532
Java Client	Work with Layouts	16	577
Java Client	Deploy a Java Application	7	196
Java Concepts	Create Java Class Files	5	160
JSP Pages	Create a Simple JSP Page	1	29
JSP Pages	Build JSP Query and Results Pages	18	663
JSP Pages	Deploy a JSP Application	7	209
Struts, JSP Pages	Create a Simple Struts Application	17	607
Struts, JSP Pages	Create a Struts Application with Data Actions for Custom Logic	17	625
TopLink	Build a Simple TopLink Application	14	475
Web Services	Create an Application that Uses a Web Service	14	489

Introduction

This is not a novel to be tossed aside lightly.
It should be thrown with great force.

—Dorothy Parker (1893–1967)

This is not the only book you will need to learn how to create Java-based web applications. After reading this book, you will not be able to build all types of Java applications using the full power of JDeveloper. We thought that you should know this up front.

Oracle JDeveloper's current 10*g* incarnation offers an enormous amount of functionality, and discussing all of it is beyond the scope of any one printed book. Therefore, this book is a "handbook," not in the sense of a complete guide to all areas of the tool but, as the cover indicates, a guide for creating J2EE applications using JDeveloper. It provides you with solid techniques to maximize your efficiency when developing applications using Oracle JDeveloper 10*g* (JDeveloper). The purpose of this introduction is to describe the contents of the book so you can determine whether this is the right resource for you.

NOTE
All of the material in this book has been verified with the first Oracle JDeveloper 10g production release (version 9.0.5.1, build 1605). You may need to adapt to slightly different names and features if you are using a different build or version of JDeveloper.

Should I Read This Book?

We set the scope of this book to satisfy an audience of both Oracle developers who want to make the transition to the J2EE development environment and also Java developers who want to leverage the productive tools and frameworks available in JDeveloper. In addition to chapters aimed at those new to the Java language, you will find chapters that dive into low-level techniques for interacting with data using Oracle's business services layer. The 10*g* release of JDeveloper is quite different from earlier releases and even developers with some experience with this tool will benefit from the discussion of the new architecture and additional features in this version.

Do I Have to Know Java?

Since JDeveloper generates 3GL Java code, it is important that you have a basic understanding of the Java language before beginning serious development work. This book does not explain the Java language in any detail, because the pages are filled with specific information about JDeveloper. Chapter 5 provides an overview of some of the necessary Java concepts in case you need a review or a bit of background before taking your first formal training class in Java. However, at some point in your learning process, you will also want to obtain some training or to study one or more of the basic Java books listed in Appendix A. The Sun Microsystems Java website (java.sun.com) contains a wealth of free introductory and advanced information including self-directed tutorials that you can use to become familiar with Java.

The JDeveloper wizards create a lot of code for you. This code is completely functional and well formatted. You can learn a lot by examining and analyzing the code that the wizards create. If you are new to Java, after reading through Chapter 5, you can look at the generated code and test your understanding of Java concepts.

Part II is considerably more Java-intensive than the rest of the book. Some sections of Part II (particularly Chapters 10, 13, and 14) describe features of JDeveloper that require some understanding of object-oriented programming to grasp and some hand-coding in Java to use. We expect that the background provided in Chapter 5 will be enough to make these chapters useful, but some further training in Java may make some of the subtleties expressed in those chapters clearer. Parts I and III do not rely as heavily upon fluency in Java.

What Will I Find in This Book?

We believe that the best way to learn this new tool is with a combination of overview information about JDeveloper and technologies used in JDeveloper and annotated hands-on practices. We have included these types of sections in many chapters. The overview material orients you to the tasks and the ways in which they are performed in JDeveloper. The hands-on practices help you to understand the JDeveloper environment and the basics of building applications. Although you will not be able to reach the goal of creating fully-functional production systems simply by reading the entire book or completing all of the hands-on practices, the book will take you some distance down that road and make your work much more productive.

If you just download JDeveloper and begin working, you may end up like many developers, playing with the product for weeks, if not months, trying to make it do something useful. This book will help you take the first few steps in learning about and using JDeveloper. It will provide a foundation for becoming skilled in this new environment and will point you to features that you may miss with self-directed study. We encourage you to go through the chapters and hands-on practices sequentially to help build the skills necessary to begin creating systems. The hands-on practices in Chapters 9–13 build upon one another and should be completed in order. You would even be well served to go through each practice several times.

The best way to learn a new product is to use it to solve a real problem. Once you have mastered the material well enough to make your way through the practices without difficulty, select a small project and build it using JDeveloper 10*g*.

What Is JDeveloper?

Before explaining details of the book's contents, we need to explain a bit about the tool itself. JDeveloper is a development environment designed to help you design, develop, debug, and deploy Java code of different types and build an object layer that accesses the database. The tool does these things very well. It also helps you create other types of files (such as XML) that support the Java environment. Although products such as IBM Eclipse Platform, JetBrains IntelliJ IDEA, and Borland JBuilder are also good tools, what makes JDeveloper stand head and shoulders above other Java development tools is the Oracle Application Development Framework (ADF) that wraps the entire development process in a consistent and well-supported package; the productivity tools offered by ADF are key benefits of using JDeveloper. The wizards and editors in JDeveloper allow you to quickly and easily build business services code to connect your Java applications to a relational database. Prior to ADF, building Java applications for a relational database was a challenging experience.

Book Overview

The chapters in the book build on one another and are intended to be read in order. In Part I, we introduce the JDeveloper development environment with overviews of the IDE and practices that are heavily reliant on what the wizards create for you. A typical approach for a Java development book is to describe how to create code without the complication of connecting to a database and accessing the data layer. However, in this book, you will work with database objects right away because, as a developer of Oracle-based applications, you need to access data. The hands-on practices in Part I show how to develop basic applications with the wizards. Part I also discusses the important topic of naming conventions. It provides an overview of the Java language, and J2EE architectures, and deployment alternatives. Part I also introduces Oracle Application Development Framework, which provides the structure for work in JDeveloper.

Part II builds on this overview material and explains the strategies, techniques, and best practices for working with the Application Development Framework business services layer. This part focuses on business services using ADF Business Components (ADF BC), but Chapter 14 also introduces alternative business services such as EJBs, Java classes with TopLink persistence, and web services. In this part, you learn how to represent data in ADF BC objects, how to code business rules into ADF BC, how to use the ADF model layer to declaratively expose business services, and how to create custom business service methods. Part II provides a solid background in ADF BC that will allow you to understand where and how to place business logic and database access code.

Although ADF BC offers complete support of database and business logic, it does not provide a user interface. Part III explains how to create Java client applications, work with Struts technology, create JavaServer Pages (JSP) applications, and build UIX pages. Part III explains how you would make the right decisions in structuring a Java client application. Chapter 15 also describes the ADF JClient architecture and techniques as well as some of the user interface components available in JDeveloper. To complete the application development discussion, Part III provides details about the Java client design-feature of layout managers.

The appendixes contain supplemental information about JDeveloper-related subjects. In addition to a list of additional resources, and a summary of Java client components available in

JDeveloper, the appendixes provide necessary background information about HTML, cascading style sheets and JavaScript. The last appendix discusses JSP, JSP Standard Tag Library (JSTL), and expression language (EL) tags to facilitate your development of JSP and UIX files.

What Will I Not Find in This Book?

As mentioned, this book is not a one-stop shop for all of the information that you will need to create an enterprise-class Java application. The purpose of the book is to get you started developing Java applications that use ADF business services to access a database. Each chapter contains a brief description of the contents of the chapter and the hands-on practices that demonstrate the concepts. Some of the important features of JDeveloper that are not covered in the book include the following:

- **Non–OracleAS 10*g* deployment options** The book provides some detail about deploying code to the Oracle Containers for J2EE (OC4J) feature of OracleAS 10*g*, but does not discuss in depth how to deploy to other servers.
- **Java stored procedures** The book contains no discussion about writing Java code that is stored and run in the database, even though JDeveloper is capable of writing and debugging such code.
- **XML code** The support for writing and checking XML files within JDeveloper is only briefly mentioned.
- **Security topics** The topic of security is quite important for a production application. The book does not provide material on this subject.
- **Debugging** Debugging was covered in the *Oracle JDeveloper9*i *Handbook* and has not changed much in the 10*g* release and so is not covered in detail in this book. The authors' websites mentioned at the beginning of the book offer a downloadable version of the debugging chapter from the *Oracle9*i *JDeveloper Handbook* in case you do not have a copy handy.
- **Menus and toolbars** You usually create main menus and toolbars for Java client applications (Java applications and applets). As with the subject of debugging, the current version of JDeveloper has not changed much in its support of menus and toolbars. Therefore, this subject is not included in the book but is available from the authors' websites in a downloadable version of the menus and toolbars chapter from the *Oracle9*i *JDeveloper Handbook.*
- **Code metrics and profiling tools** Since release 9*i*, JDeveloper has offered a full-featured profiler that provides information about memory usage and execution time. In addition, with the 10*g* release, JDeveloper contains CodeCoach, auditing, and metrics utilities that help you improve your code. Other than brief introductions in Chapter 3, this book does not spend time explaining these features.
- **Java Database Connectivity (JDBC) development** The authors believe that ADF BC offers the easiest solution to the problem of connecting Java to an Oracle database, and JDeveloper also provides tools to develop Enterprise JavaBeans with container-managed

persistence and Java classes with TopLink mappings as alternative connectivity options. Therefore, the book focuses on ADF BC as the connection method, with an introduction to other methods provided by ADF. ADF BC works with JDBC at a higher and easier-to-use level and pure JDBC coding is not mentioned in this book.

- **Configuration management** JDeveloper has integrated several configuration management tools, including Oracle's Software Configuration Manager (SCM) product, into JDeveloper. This topic is not discussed other than in an introduction to installing CVS support at the end of Chapter 2.
- **JavaServer Faces (JSF)** JSF technology was recently released and support is not included in JDeveloper. As mentioned in Chapter 4 and the JDeveloper help system, you can install support for JSF in JDeveloper 10*g* if needed. A future release of JDeveloper 10*g* is currently targeted to include JSF support.
- **Modeling** With the exception of the ADF BC modelers, which are discussed in Part II, the JDeveloper Modelers are still evolving and are only briefly mentioned. The book uses some of these modelers in examples of how to create code, but does not describe all features of the various modelers listed at the end of Chapter 3.

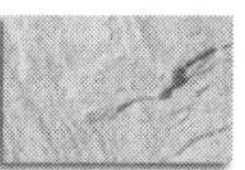

NOTE
The JDeveloper help system contains information about the topics listed above. Use the Index Search or Full Text Search tabs to find the required topic.

About the Hands-on Practices

At first glance, the hands-on practices in this book may look similar to tutorials that you have seen elsewhere. The difference with the practices in this book is that they are annotated. That is, they contain extensive explanations to help you understand the purpose of the steps you are taking. Each major section (called a "phase") contains a summary so that you can relate the instructions to the task at hand. At the end of each phase, a "What Just Happened?" section explains the code you just developed. By the time you complete the practice, with a little review, you should be able to accomplish the same task in a real work situation.

JDeveloper and the Hands-on Practices

The practices are intended to be hands-on, so it does not make sense to read through the practices without trying the steps. If you do not try the hands-on practices, you will be missing some key information, because some topics are discussed only in the context of particular hands-on steps. You learn more if you interact with something new in different ways. Since experience is the best teacher, you should follow all of the practices to receive the full benefit from this book.

As mentioned, most of the book was written using the first production release of JDeveloper 10*g* and verified with the next production patch. Since each release is slightly different, you may have to adjust some steps for the version and build you are using. The authors' websites may contain some information about changes that require adjustments for particular releases.

Installing and Running JDeveloper

JDeveloper is distributed on the Oracle Developer Suite 10*g* install CD. (At this writing, JDeveloper in the Developer Suite is at release 9.0.4.) You may also download the JDeveloper install file from the Oracle Technology Network (OTN) website at otn.oracle.com. (Navigate to the JDeveloper home page and look for the download link.) The download file is currently less than 250MB and less than 150MB if you already have a copy of the Java SDK and are willing to use documentation hosted on OTN. After downloading the file, unzip it into a new directory. (The examples in this book were built with JDeveloper installed into C:\JDev10g.) To run JDeveloper, navigate to the JDEV_HOME\jdev\bin directory and double click jdevw.exe. You can also create a shortcut that uses this executable file to start JDeveloper. The next section explains the abbreviation "JDEV_HOME" used throughout the book.

Under the "Getting Started with JDeveloper" node in the help system Table of Contents tab, you can find instructions about how to migrate existing workspaces and projects.

NOTE
The jdev.exe file in the JDEV_HOME\jdev\bin directory also starts up JDeveloper. However, this executable also opens a separate command line window, which does not appear when you run jdev.exe. If you use jdev.exe, closing this command-line window will close JDeveloper.

What Is JDEV_HOME?

When you install JDeveloper, you place all files into a single root directory such as C:\JDev10g. Since you may choose to use a different name, this book often refers to that directory as "JDEV_HOME" (as mentioned, we used "C:\JDev10g" as the JDEV_HOME). For example, if a practice instructs you to create a file in the JDEV_HOME\jdev\mywork subdirectory, and your JDeveloper installation is in the C:\JDev10g directory, the file should be created in the C:\JDev10g\jdev\mywork directory.

NOTE
All sample code in this book is created in the mywork directory under JDEV_HOME\jdev. Although this is the default directory for workspaces and projects, you can change this when you create a project or workspace.

The Sample Schema

All of the hands-on practices use a common set of human resources tables that are contained in a schema called "HR." The tables (such as Employees, Departments, and Locations) and other database objects are included with sample schemas in the Oracle9*i* Database and Oracle Database 10g. The sample tables included with Oracle8*i* database are slightly different and you will need to adjust the instructions in the practices if you need to use the Oracle8*i* tables. The reason these tables are used in this book is that they are familiar to most Oracle developers and are simple enough that no time needs to be spent explaining the data model. There are two different ways to access this sample schema:

- **Use a sample schema already installed in an Oracle9*i* or Oracle 10*g* database.** The HR schema is normally installed in these database versions. You or a database administrator (DBA) may need to unlock the account (using ALTER USER hr ACCOUNT UNLOCK). The scripts to re-create the objects are in the ORACLE_HOME\demo\schema\human_resources directory.
- **Use the SQL*Plus script.** The authors' websites, listed in the author biographies at the beginning of the book, contain sample files for the practices as well as a SQL*Plus script that you can use to create the required objects. This script is a variation of the scripts included with JDeveloper, but it only contains the objects required for this book.

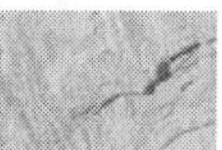

CAUTION
*The sample schema created by the Oracle9i and Oracle 10g scripts contains a trigger called "SECURE_EMPLOYEES" on the EMPLOYEES table that prevents you from committing an INSERT, UPDATE, or DELETE operation on the EMPLOYEES table after business hours. Should you want to issue these operations outside of business hours, you can disable this trigger by issuing the following statement in a SQL*Plus session:* `ALTER TRIGGER secure_employees DISABLE;`

Machine Resources

The JDeveloper website on OTN lists the JDeveloper memory requirements as 512M. A complete install of the product requires 375M of hard disk space. We have found that 1G of memory is better, if you are running a sample database and the OC4J server to display web client code. In addition, although a Pentium III, 866MHz processor is recommended, any additional processor speed that you supply to the IDE will improve your development experience. For more information about system requirements, navigate to the JDeveloper documentation on otn.oracle.com and look for the Installation Guide.

Supported Operating Systems

The authors used MS Windows 2000 and Windows XP to construct the example code, figures, and illustrations in this book. JDeveloper is also certified under Windows NT, 2000, or XP; Linux; Solaris; and HP/UX, and is being widely used under Mac OS X as well. You may need to adjust some steps in the practices if you are not using a Windows operating system.

The authors used the "classic" Windows look-and-feel for the screenshots in the book.

CAUTION
*You can switch to a different look and feel using the Environment page of the Preferences dialog (**Tools | Preferences**). If you switch to another look-and-feel and a feature is not working as documented, switch back to Windows look-and-feel and try the feature again.*

Which Database to Use?

The database drivers distributed with Oracle10g JDeveloper 9.0.3 support access to Oracle8*i* (8.1.7), Oracle9*i* Release 1 (9.0.1) and Release 2 (9.2), and Oracle Database 10*g* Release 2 (10.1). You can also connect to any database that offers a JDBC driver.

NOTE
This book uses the term "right-click menu" to mean the context menu or pop-up menu that appears when you click the alternate mouse button. Some users set the alternate mouse button as the left-hand button, and this is the button they would press when the instruction for "right-click" appears in the text.

What if the Practices Do Not Work?

Although it is not expected that you will have problems with the hands-on practices, there is always a risk in basing book material heavily on hands-on practices, because version-specific features may be added or changed. With the variable conditions that are possible in system configurations, you may experience a problem (or even a bug in the practice description) at some point. While the authors or publisher cannot personally support your work in the practices, here are some ideas for resolving any problems that you experience in the practices:

- **Slow down.** Read the instructions carefully to determine the exact operation that you need to perform. The authors and technical reviewers have run the practices many times to ensure that they work and that the instructions are clear. However, as is true with most programming languages, Java is not forgiving if you skip a step or miss a setting. If you slow down and assimilate the meaning of each step, you are more likely to succeed.
- **Start over with a new project or workspace.** Sometimes a wrong step early in the practice can cascade into a larger problem later. In some cases, you may not be able to undo a step or a series of steps by deleting mistakes. In these cases, it is better to start the practice again with a new workspace or project. You may even want to restart your system before doing this in case you have a memory area that has not been cleared correctly. Starting over is described more in the next section.
- **Step back and look at the process** to see if it makes sense from what you know. If there is a wrong step in the practice, try to skip or work around it.
- **Download the sample solution** from the authors' websites (listed in the author biographies at the beginning of the book). Compare your code with the solution (using the file comparison utility available by selecting **File | Compare With** from the menu), and determine where the differences occur.
- **Consult the list of other resources** (in the next section) for more help. Particularly helpful will be discussion forums where you can compare notes with other users.

Starting Over

At this point, you will probably not have worked through any practices. However, when you do follow the practices and experience difficulties that require starting over, it is easiest to follow these steps:

1. Close the problem workspace in the navigator by selecting the workspace node and clicking the Remove (red "x") button in the navigator toolbar. This will not delete the file system files or folders, but it will remove the workspace from the navigator view.
2. Create the workspace using the method provided in the practice. In the Create Application Workspace dialog, name the workspace as mentioned in the practice (for example, "LocationQuery". However, change the directory name so that it contains a number suffix, for example. "LocationQuery2" as shown here:

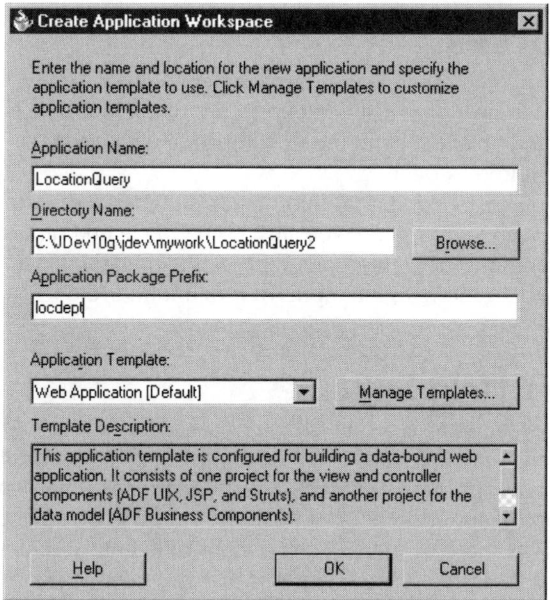

3. You can navigate to the old directory in the file system and delete the old workspace directory if desired. The instructions and screenshots in the practice will be accurate and the workspace and project names and file names will match the practice steps. Whenever the directory name is referred to, you will need to adjust to the new directory name.
4. If you want to delete a single file, select it in the navigator and select **File | Erase from Disk** from the menu (or for ADF BC nodes, select Erase from Disk from the right-click menu).

NOTE
The hands-on practices Chapters 9–13 are cumulative—that is, they build on previous practices. If you want to start over on a cumulative practice, you will need to download the previous practice's solution from the authors' websites.

CAUTION
Be aware that JDeveloper automatically writes the names of files and directories into the project and workspace files (described in Chapter 1). Therefore, if you rename a file or directory outside of JDeveloper, a reference in a JDeveloper file may no longer be valid. Therefore, use JDeveloper to rename files whenever possible.

Other Resources

By spending the time to search out what has already been written, you will probably find that others have spent many hours doing just what you want to do. With the extensibility of Java classes, you can use, modify, and extend the existing code with a fraction of the effort that would be required to develop it from scratch.

In addition to the sources of additional information summarized in Appendix A, the book contains references throughout to online websites, both Oracle and others, that you can visit, and books that you can refer to for more information about the material introduced in the text. There are several other resources generic to the topics of Java and JDeveloper that are worth special mention here.

The JDeveloper Help System

The JDeveloper help system (introduced in Chapter 2) contains a wealth of information. It contains low-level details such as Javadoc reference materials for the Java language and Oracle-created classes used in various files. There are also descriptions of the steps used to create specific components or full applications. The help system is a good companion to this book because, although there is some overlap, each contains different examples and descriptive material. You will be exposed to many of the tasks that you need to perform by using both resources.

CAUTION
References to help system topics appear throughout the book. The references often include the location or name of the help topic; however, this is subject to change as JDeveloper is upgraded. The best strategy is to use the Full Text Search or Index Search tab in the help system if you cannot find a help topic in the referenced location.

OTN JDeveloper Resources

The JDeveloper home page on OTN contains links to Product Tours, Online Demos, Tutorials, Technical Papers, Code Samples, and How-To's as well as online documentation, statements-of-direction, and lists of desupported and deprecated features. In addition, OTN contains some very active discussion forums on JDeveloper topics. From the otn.oracle.com home page, click the JDeveloper link to reach the JDeveloper home page.

JDeveloper Readme (Release Notes)

Additional notes about JDeveloper are installed with the product and are available by selecting **Help | Release Notes** from the menu. The Release Notes contain useful information that is not included in other sources, and you should be familiar with them. Some of the notes refer to limitations or workarounds that you would not know about if you tried and failed with the expected or documented method.

Oracle User Groups

One resource of which you must avail yourself is other users of Java and JDeveloper. The process of learning and using these tools is a challenging one, and it is likely that another user somewhere has already solved a problem you may be having. There are many online forums where the experts congregate, particularly, the International Oracle Users Group (IOUG) discussion forums (www.ioug.org), where users discuss Oracle web development topics. In addition, the Oracle Development Tools User Group (ODTUG) hosts list servers for a wide range of Oracle development topics, including web applications and Java (www.odtug.com). You will also want to hook up with your local Oracle users group (the IOUG office can help you locate the nearest group, or you can find one in your area at www.dbdomain.com/user_grps.htm) and discuss issues face-to-face with Oracle users in your area. As just mentioned, OTN also has an active JDeveloper forum (otn.oracle.com) that the JDeveloper product team contributes to and monitors.

PART I

Overview

CHAPTER 1

Overview of Oracle JDeveloper 10*g*

Software is like entropy. It is difficult to grasp, weighs nothing, and obeys the second law of thermodynamics; i.e., it always increases.

—Norman R. Augustine, Chairman, Exec. Comm., Lockheed Martin Corporation

racle JDeveloper 10*g* (JDeveloper) is an integrated development environment (IDE) for Java programming. It offers a rich set of features for designing, developing, debugging, and deploying Java and other related files that are part of the Java 2 Platform, Enterprise Edition (J2EE) strategy. JDeveloper is a development framework containing many wizards and code generators that make it easier to implement complex functionality in Java, enabling you to concentrate on solving business problems. It also offers strong code organization and configuration management.

The J2EE environment is quite complex, and JDeveloper strives to support the management of all of the different components including JSP pages, UIX applications, Struts, and web services. The IDE assists with XML editing and data source access and manipulation.

This part of the book provides an overview of the features and functions of JDeveloper 10*g*. This chapter offers an introduction to the main concepts needed to work with JDeveloper and includes some simple hands-on practices to give you a quick head start building applications in JDeveloper 10*g*. Chapters 2 and 3 describe the main work areas and tools of the Integrated Development Environment (IDE). Chapter 4 introduces the Oracle Application Development Framework (ADF), a rich technology environment that supports all facets of J2EE development. For those new to Java, Chapter 5 provides an overview of the Java language concepts needed to work effectively with JDeveloper. Chapter 6 discusses the importance of consistent naming conventions and provides suggestions about how to name the elements needed to develop applications with JDeveloper. Finally, Chapter 7 includes further details about J2EE architectures and outlines approaches to deploying J2EE applications.

JDeveloper: Past, Present, and Future

JDeveloper's roots go back to 1997, when Oracle licensed the JBuilder Java-development tool from Borland International to integrate it with Oracle's databases and applications tools for both Internet and traditional client/server platforms. At the time, Borland's JBuilder was a strong Java development tool. Purchasing the rights to the JBuilder source code allowed Oracle to jump-start its entry into the Java development environment. The initial JDeveloper 1.0 release (called "AppBuilder for Java") in 1998 was quite close to its JBuilder foundation. Later in 1998, it was renamed JDeveloper. The similarity between JBuilder and JDeveloper continued through the 2.0 releases in 1999. In these early versions, you can see the tool's maturation in the Java environment. While releasing only cosmetic changes to the product, behind the scenes Oracle was working on elegantly solving the problem of Java programs connecting to relational database objects.

Past: Product History and Roots

While JDeveloper releases 1.0 and 2.0 were useful Java development products, they provided little support for building applications that would interact with an Oracle database. To be fair, this was the state of the art at that time. Hardy C++ and Java programmers routinely took up the task of writing lots of code to access Oracle databases. Unfortunately, this coding required a great deal of effort, even on the part of a skilled programmer. Therefore, the early JDeveloper users were primarily Java developers who were looking for ways to create applications that would interact with Oracle databases. Oracle professionals who were accustomed to products that interacted easily with the database and who built applications efficiently using tools such as Oracle Forms Developer did not rapidly adopt this new product.

Release 3.0 of JDeveloper introduced Business Components for Java (BC4J), the forerunner of the Application Development Framework Business Components (ADF BC) included in JDeveloper 10*g*. This gave developers an easy way to connect their applications to the database without having to write hundreds of lines of code. BC4J quickly differentiated JDeveloper from other products.

The next major release (9*i*) brought a complete rewrite of the product in Java and a new way of binding components to BC4J using JClient for local Java client code and the BC4J Data Tags Library for server-run code such as servlets and JSP files. In release 3.x, Oracle supplied its own custom components to bind to BC4J; in 9*i* bindings were made to standard components.

Although JDeveloper is now Oracle's primary development tool, Oracle offers a number of other products that enable developers to build applications and deploy them over the Web:

- **Oracle Forms Developer** (sometimes called "Web Forms") has continued to mature. Since the 9*i* release, the Web is the only way to deploy Oracle forms. This tool uses applet technology that has largely been abandoned by the broader development community for Internet applications due to issues related to firewalls and performance. Oracle Forms Developer applications on the Web are still strong contenders for intra-company, rich client applications that require highly responsive and interactive user interfaces.

- **PL/SQL Web Toolkit** (mod_plsql) had its origins in the early releases of the Oracle Application Server, and Oracle Designer uses it to create applications that generate HTML client code. The PL/SQL Web Toolkit allows you to write PL/SQL in the database that can output HTML to a browser.

- **PL/SQL Server Pages (PSPs)** allow you to embed PL/SQL within HTML. PSPs leverage the concept of server pages in a similar way to JavaServer Pages files.

- **Oracle Portal** was originally designed as a simple utility to allow ad hoc access to a database and was marketed as "WebDB." Portal has evolved into a useful website development and content management tool. It is not a mainstream application development tool although it has some utilities that allow you to create simple web applications.

- **HTML DB** is Oracle's latest offering for web development. It provides an easy way to create applications of low to moderate complexity that are based directly on the database and do not require an application server. Its learning curve is less steep than that of JDeveloper, but HTML DB does not provide the robustness, flexibility, or depth of functionality of JDeveloper. HTML DB is delivered as part of the Oracle 10*g* database and is designed to be even easier to use than Portal, providing extremely rapid development for simpler web applications.

Why JDeveloper?

With all of these alternatives, why has Oracle seemingly decided to pursue JDeveloper as the primary development tool? The answer demonstrates Oracle's long-range planning strategy. Oracle JDeveloper 10*g* is built for developing J2EE applications. As such, JDeveloper sits on a strong foundation. Oracle's earlier products had to make compromises based upon existing technologies, accommodations to backward compatibility, and internal Oracle politics. JDeveloper is a development environment for J2EE, and J2EE has vast support from other vendors and the backing of recognized standards.

As JDeveloper has moved from the 1.0 release to 10*g*, it has evolved from a straightforward Java development product into a sophisticated J2EE development environment. In all prior releases, the focus seemed to be primarily on providing technical capabilities. Version 10*g* represents a maturation of both the underlying technical foundation as well as the product's ease of use. Nowhere is this more evident than in the area of web application development. The evolving WYSIWYG screen designers for JSP and ADF UIX code as well as the graphical Struts development environment provide a much more visual-graphic way to build web applications than competing products.

Oracle's direction for building Java applications to access an Oracle database became clearer through its introduction of BC4J in the 3.0 release. BC4J helped to automate most of the difficult work required to make Java code interact with relational database tables. BC4J was introduced as a framework to support Java interaction with a database. The BC4J wizards automatically generated the code necessary to allow Java applications to safely interact with the database, solving the security, locking, and performance problems that had hindered earlier efforts. The generated code utilizes an Oracle-supplied Java library. Therefore, the actual amount of code generated by the wizards is small.

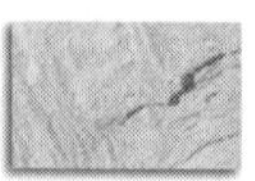

NOTE
Chapter 4 discusses the topic of frameworks and ADF in more detail.

The JDeveloper 9*i* release included improved Business Components for Java. Oracle added support for Sun's Model-View-Controller (MVC) architecture (implemented in JDeveloper as the client data model), replacing version 3's Data-Aware Components (DACs) (built on Sun's InfoBus architecture, which was abandoned by the industry). The MVC architecture allowed developers to build Java applications or JavaServer Pages to access an Oracle database with much more efficiency. In the 9*i* release, Oracle's grand vision for JDeveloper was visible, indicating a much broader scope than the earlier versions. The inclusion of some Unified Modeling Language (UML) diagrams, software configuration management (SCM) integration, and the ability to generate Data Definition Language (DDL) point to Oracle's long-term commitment to this product and technologies.

Present: Where Is JDeveloper Now?

There are two parts to the vision driving the JDeveloper product. The first is influenced by the J2EE and broader Java development communities, which strive to make JDeveloper 10*g* a full-featured J2EE development product. In this area, the JDeveloper team can take advantage of Oracle's experience with products such as Oracle Forms Developer to provide graphical or metadata-based application development, which improves the efficiency of Java and web developers. Visual editors, diagrammers, property inspectors, and component palettes have been incorporated into JDeveloper to help generate simple applications as well as to support and manage larger and more complex ones. Some portions of JDeveloper are still evolving, specifically the WYSIWYG graphical Struts designers and visual editors, which are solid efforts that continue to mature quickly. The 10*g* release deserves high marks for supporting the J2EE/Java development vision. Building J2EE applications remains a challenging task with a steep learning curve. JDeveloper 10*g* has made it easier for development organizations to make the transition from fourth-generation language (4GL) tools such as Oracle Forms Developer or Delphi into the J2EE space. Developers currently using Oracle Forms Developer and PL/SQL cannot simply replace those tools with JDeveloper and Java to create complex client/server–style applications deployed over the Web. Building fully featured web applications that allow customers to safely and efficiently interact with the database is a much more complex task.

The second part of the vision that Oracle is pursuing is that of a unified design and development environment. Here, JDeveloper is moving toward being a single point of entry for systems analysis, design, development, and deployment. JDeveloper 10*g* includes a UML Use Case Diagrammer, which allows developers to enter use cases and generate HTML documents. The product also includes the first generation of a database modeler using UML class diagrams. The modeling portions of JDeveloper are still maturing and are not yet at the point where they can be utilized for full lifecycle systems development in the same way as Oracle Designer.

Support for JSP Files

A JavaServer Page (JSP) file is compiled into a *servlet,* which is a pure Java program. The servlet produces an HTML stream that is sent to the browser. Though most of the code can be written in Java, the user interface (UI) portion is created in HTML. A JSP performs at least two functions: it renders web browser content (the results of Java processing) to the user, and reduces (or eliminates) logic code in the UI for the developer. As applications grow, the benefits of concise code are evident.

As a web application development tool for the building of JSP files, JDeveloper is almost a complete solution for traditional Oracle developers who are used to the simple "one-product development environment" of Oracle Forms Developer. A new visual editor allows users to build JSP pages using a representation of how the page will look. Elements can be dragged from the Component Palette and dropped into the work area. This visual design environment is somewhat similar to what 4GL developers are accustomed to; however, JDeveloper's support for the visual design of the HTML page is still limited compared with a tool such as Microsoft FrontPage.

Support for ADF UIX Applications

Oracle created its own alternative to JavaServer Pages technology called ADF User Interface XML (ADF UIX or just UIX). UIX pages deliver a level of functionality similar to that of JSP code but are based on Extensible Markup Language (XML) tags. The ADF UIX tag library has a better visual representation and somewhat better performance than standard JSP tag libraries. For example, by default, UIX tags can be coded to only require a portion of the screen to be refreshed when only a portion of the screen is changed, resulting in a more user-friendly interface than JSP files, where the whole screen is typically refreshed. With JSP pages, you can also use HTML and JavaScript code to specify that the screen is only partially refreshed.

ADF UIX development is one of the areas where the JDeveloper 10*g* release has made great improvements. Developers can build JSP pages or ADF UIX pages with virtually the same user-friendly interface.

NOTE
ADF UIX is described further in Chapter 19.

Support for Java Applications

JDeveloper 10*g* provides complete support for rich Java applications (Java programs running on the client machine), including visual editing and property setting in a developer-friendly interface. You can build applications of the same or greater complexity and sophistication as was possible using products such as Oracle Forms Developer. However, you will not be able to build this type of application as quickly using JDeveloper as you can with Oracle Forms Developer. The JDeveloper wizards are not sufficiently mature for JDeveloper to compete effectively with Oracle Forms Developer as a rapid application development (RAD) tool.

While Oracle Forms Developer manipulates properties of objects that are stored in an internal repository, JDeveloper is actually a code manipulator and organizer. Although you interact with the JDeveloper wizards and IDE areas as in a 4GL environment, you are really manipulating Java code. The application development process always goes beyond the capabilities of the JDeveloper wizards, and manual intervention is required to modify property settings that the wizard assigns or to add code that the wizards do not generate.

Future: The Vision

What will the JDeveloper tool encompass going forward? Tactically, JDeveloper 10*g* is a mature J2EE development environment. Developers will be pleased with the progress since the 9*i* release. In the short run, the J2EE development environment will continue to mature and add new features that enter the technological infrastructure from standards organizations such as the Java Community Process (JCP, at www.jcp.org) and Web Services Interoperability Organization (WS-I, at www.ws-i.org). For example, JavaServer Faces technology is the latest addition to the Java platform. As described in Chapter 4, you can add JSF technology support to JDeveloper now and this support will be expanded in the near future. It is also expected that the UML modeling area will evolve rapidly toward database modeling and design so that JDeveloper will match and ultimately surpass Designer. The activity, class, and use case modelers will also evolve to allow JDeveloper to more easily support complex process-based application development.

The introduction of the Application Development Framework represents a significant rethinking of the development environment. What are still lacking are advice for development best practices and a clear System Development Life Cycle (SDLC) for building J2EE systems. To be fair, the entire industry is still waiting for a coherent SDLC to emerge for building J2EE systems based on solid relational database back-ends.

JDeveloper 10*g*'s motto, "Productivity with Choice," although reflective of the tremendous flexibility of the tool, sidesteps the additional complexity that has made traditional Oracle developers reluctant to embrace J2EE. The popularity of less flexible, but potentially more productive, alternatives such as Oracle Portal and HTML DB demonstrates that, in addition to flexibility, developers also want guidance for systems development best practices.

The expected long-range vision is that JDeveloper will move closer and closer to being a unified design and development environment. However, progress toward this goal has been slower than hoped for in the last three years, mainly due to Oracle placing emphasis on creating an excellent J2EE product. In this respect, they have succeeded admirably. The question remains as to how much attention is given to the ultimate vision vs. deployment of resources toward tactical, technical J2EE topics. The 10*g* release represents significant improvement over 9*i* because of the following:

- Introduction of the Application Development Framework
- Expanded 4GL development support for Struts, JSP code, and ADF UIX pages, including drag-and-drop data binding to connect Java client and web client view layers with business services layers such as ADF BC and Enterprise JavaBeans (EJB)

As with all popular Java development tools, JDeveloper 10*g* is clearly evolving, making it an ever more user-friendly tool that offers substantive support for the J2EE architecture and is responding very well to changes in that architecture as they occur.

What Is New in JDeveloper 10*g*?

The 10*g* release of JDeveloper includes some important new features and some significant improvements of other features. Some of the new additions to the product are discussed briefly in this section with references to more in-depth information contained in other portions of the book.

New Integrated Development Environment (IDE)

There have been major changes to the JDeveloper IDE starting with the way in which applications are organized.

JDeveloper 10*g* has also provided better support for team-based development by adding to the features that integrate JDeveloper with Oracle SCM and providing additional support for external products such as Concurrent Versions System (CVS).

Chapters 2 and 3 discuss the IDE in more detail. Experienced users may be tempted to skip these chapters, but they will miss much important information and many useful tips if they do. Due to the changes in the 10*g* release, the authors recommend that even those who have used previous versions of JDeveloper read these chapters carefully.

Technology Templates

Now when you create application workspaces, you select the underlying technology scope using a technology template. The *technology template* contains default projects that are oriented toward a certain technology such as Struts. The template affects what options and objects are available by default for use in the projects. Almost all of the lists in 10*g* are context-sensitive, so inappropriate options are rarely available. As you create applications in JDeveloper 10*g*, you need to select from one of the following default templates:

- **Web Application [Default]** This template creates a Model project for ADF Business Components and a ViewController project for Struts, ADF UIX, or JSP components and is used for building web applications using Struts that need to access ADF Business Components.
- **Web Application [Default - no controller]** This template creates a Model project oriented toward ADF Business Components and a View project for ADF UIX or JSP components and is used for building web applications that need to access business services.

- **Web Application [JSP, Struts, EJB]** This template creates a Model project for the EJB data model and a ViewController project for JSP and Struts components and is used for building web applications that need to access business services based on Enterprise JavaBeans.
- **Web Application [JSP, EJB]** This template creates a Model project for the EJB data model and a View project for JSP components (with no controller) and is used for building web applications that need to access business services based on EJBs.
- **Java Application [Default]** This template creates a Model project for ADF Business Components and a View project for the client and is used for building rich client applications that need to access ADF Business Components.
- **Java Application [Java, Swing]** This template creates a Client project for the Java, Swing/JFC, or JavaBeans source code and is used for building Java applications that are not connected to a data source.

Depending upon which template you select, different projects with different default components and properties will be available by default. You can also select the "No Template" option, which creates a single project with access to all alternatives.

The inclusion of application templates is very helpful. The J2EE environment is so rich and varied that the JDeveloper templates provide important guidance. Once you have made a decision about which technology scope to use, inapplicable options will not be available unless you explicitly allow them. This is useful in many cases where you need to go outside of the bounds of the template by turning off the filters. The New Gallery includes a *Filter By* pulldown, which is either set to "Project Technologies" (filtered) or "All Technologies" (unfiltered) so that you can access items outside the technology scope of the project.

Once you evolve your unique development style, you can create and save your own technology templates in JDeveloper, which can be applied to new application workspaces.

Application Development Framework

The Application Development Framework is one area of JDeveloper that is very important but will not be obvious to most users. The benefits of ADF are evident when creating complex production applications. Even then, in order to truly appreciate ADF, you will need to have built other J2EE-compliant applications without it.

When building applications, there are numerous places where the framework will automatically take advantage of components in ADF. This greatly decreases the amount of coding required. Other benefits of ADF are evident when modifications to the applications are required. Traditionally built J2EE applications are notoriously difficult to modify. Things that should be simple such as adding an attribute to a table that then must be maintained in the applications can require hours, if not days, of effort without ADF. It is still not trivial to make these modifications using ADF, but it is much easier than the alternative.

ADF is discussed in detail in Chapter 4 and ADF Business Components are discussed in Part II.

Struts

Struts is a framework that supports the logic behind building web applications. It was developed by The Apache Software Foundation (jakarta.apache.org/struts/). Struts technology was created to bring order to the chaos of applying complex logic to the process of building and managing entire web applications including Java program files and the UI (JSP, UIX, and HTML) files.

Struts is now a popular framework for managing web application development. Despite its popularity, it has a very steep learning curve. Struts is one area where JDeveloper 10*g* has done an extraordinary job of making development much easier. The JDeveloper support of Struts through ADF greatly reduces the level of effort required to build a Struts-based application. Nowhere is the power of ADF more evident than in building Struts-based web applications.

Working with Struts still requires a great deal of skill. A thorough understanding of the Struts framework as well as Oracle's implementation of Struts is required to successfully build Struts-based applications in JDeveloper. However, once you understand the framework, using JDeveloper to build web applications is almost as rapid as the productivity that can be achieved in a 4GL. As an added benefit, the code generated is consistent and largely self-documented by JDeveloper's graphical diagramming tool, which creates page flow diagrams. Chapter 17 provides more detailed information about Struts and some hands-on practices to explore this technology.

Modeling in JDeveloper

In addition to the great strides made in J2EE development with the 10*g* release, some progress was also made in improving the modeling capabilities of the tool. JDeveloper still does not support the entire SDLC, but it continues to move in that direction.

Database Modeler

Developers want to be able to create models within JDeveloper. JDeveloper 10*g* introduces a physical database modeler that allows users to specify tables, columns, and foreign key relationships using UML class diagrams.

Full UML-based modeling including inheritance, aggregation, and composition capabilities would be a welcome addition to JDeveloper at some point. The 10*g* release includes the beginnings of a solid data modeling tool using a limited subset of the UML. Conspicuously absent is the notion of generalization.

The Database Modeler cannot be used yet for complete logical and physical database design. Oracle Designer should still be used for that purpose. JDeveloper users without access to a full-featured database design tool like Oracle Designer may find JDeveloper's modeling capabilities adequate for simpler applications. However, JDeveloper should not be considered a viable modeling environment for enterprise-level database construction.

Use Case Modeler

Use cases provide a structured method for describing analysis and design elements in a system. The core elements are Actors (people, organizations, systems) and Use Cases (functions that actors perform). Use cases are typically expressed using Scenarios that represent the steps undertaken to execute the use case. Use cases can be expressed graphically, using text, or a combination as in JDeveloper 10*g*.

The Use Case Modeler included in JDeveloper 10*g* is a graphical front-end that allows users to store an entire use case diagram as a single HTML document. Text descriptions can be entered into a document resembling a Microsoft Word document that is suitable for high-level system documentation. The Use Case Modeler provides a convenient graphical user interface for including this information in your projects. However, it has not evolved sufficiently yet to support use case–based analysis of a large project because it is too difficult to handle a large number of use cases as HTML documents without some type of repository to manage all of the information.

Business Services

In the 9*i* version of JDeveloper, even though it was possible to have persistent storage of objects in places other than BC4J (now called ADF BC), there was a clear slant toward Oracle's business components framework. In 10*g*, there is more explicit support for alternatives to ADF BC such as EJBs, web services, and Java classes (accessed with TopLink). In most cases, ADF BC is the preferred alternative and is discussed most extensively in this book; however, some discussion of EJBs, Java classes with TopLink, and web services is included in Chapter 14.

Web Services

Web Services are an important emerging area of web application development. They allow applications built in different development environments to be integrated. Developers can create reusable components that can either be called internally or published and made available over the Internet to anyone with the appropriate permissions.

This is an exciting new technology that is being adopted in a host of different contexts. JDeveloper has included a number of features to make the creation of web services much easier. For example, taking a PL/SQL program unit or Java class and turning it into a web service can be accomplished as a "one mouse-click" operation.

Desupported and Deprecated Features

As with any new release, some features of old releases are not supported or are *deprecated* (currently supported but soon to be phased out). Further discussion of these features is available on OTN (otn.oracle.com), but the following sections summarize this information.

Desupported Features

The following features do not appear in the JDeveloper 10*g* product although previous releases still support them:

- Data-Aware Controls (DAC)
- Deploying business components to a VisiBroker Object Request Broker (ORB)
- Deploying business components to an Oracle database
- Generating Java CORBA files from an Interface Definition Language (IDL) definition

Deprecated Features

The following features are still available but are planned to be desupported in future releases. Therefore, they should not be used for new applications code:

- Data Web Beans and HTML Web Beans for JSP applications
- Business Components Data Tags (BC4J Data Tags Library) for JSP applications
- UIX JSP tags, BC4J UIX JSP tags, and BC4J UIX XML tags

In addition, the plans for future releases include desupport of SQLJ (SQL embedded in Java).

Creating Application Code in JDeveloper

JDeveloper is an application development tool that can support your first steps in the Java world. It can act as a blank sheet of paper for the sophisticated do-it-yourselfer, or as a code generator for those who prefer developing applications by using 4GL techniques such as drag and drop. JDeveloper can also automatically generate basic database interface code, allowing you to customize the results to your heart's content.

Coming to an understanding of Java and JDeveloper is like trying to learn English and a computer word processing program at the same time. You should have some experience with other computer languages and application conventions before you leap into this type of effort. It is a good idea to actually build the items and structures in the hands-on practices presented in this book as you read the chapters. In this way, you can quickly get a feel for the development environment by creating real code.

The first major difference between the traditional environments and the JDeveloper environment is that in some development environments, the user interface and its interaction with the database are inseparable. However, in JDeveloper, each program will usually consist of two JDeveloper projects:

- **Model project** containing business services components built and written using Java and XML to provide the database interaction components (business services).
- **View project or ViewController project** containing components and logic for the user interface built and written mainly using Java and complementary web languages such as HTML and JavaScript. Both view and controller code are contained in this project.

JDeveloper is optimized to assist you in producing a multi-tier architecture for your database applications. This book concentrates on the power of JDeveloper to produce a multi-tier application centered around ADF BC. A multi-tier architecture encourages the logical separation of the program components.

The following sections describe the ways in which JDeveloper structures and organizes the code needed to support your applications.

Application Workspaces

An *application workspace* (or just *workspace*) is the highest-level container within JDeveloper. Its contents are projects that contain the code files. A workspace represents all related projects that you need to access in one work session, although you can have many workspaces open at the same time. It corresponds more or less in size and scope to a multi-window, multi-block .fmb file in Oracle Forms Developer. Each application workspace is implemented with a single file that has a .jws extension. This is an XML file that contains the names of the project files (containers for code files) that comprise it.

For example, an application workspace can contain a project for business services (the data sources) and another project for the user interface. The business services project can be used in other workspaces, if needed. When you use business services, the project containing the business service objects must be open in the same workspace as the project that needs to use the business services. You deploy applications a project at a time, but if the workspace contains multiple projects, you will have an option to deploy related projects at the same time.

Projects

A *project* is the next level of container in JDeveloper that contains code files. You can think of a project as a major portion of a program. As mentioned, a program is typically partitioned across two projects: one for the business services (such as ADF Business Components) and one for the UI components. The projects can reside in the same or different application workspace directories, but the business services project must be accessible in the same application workspace as the project that uses it. A project represents a number of code files that are deployed together. Usually, the files within a project are related, for example, the project contains just user interface code for your application. The project is implemented in a single XML file that has a .jpr extension and contains the names of the code files that comprise it.

JDeveloper Directory Structure

Applications built using JDeveloper will be partitioned across multiple directories. Typically, the application workspace is stored in one directory and the project files within that application workspace are stored in subdirectories underneath the application workspace directory.

As mentioned, within the application workspace directory, JDeveloper normally generates two project files, Model and View, each in its own directory for Java source code and compiled code. Within the Model directory, the source code is contained in the folder labeled "src," and compiled code is contained in the "classes" folder. Within each of these directories, additional subdirectories correspond to any defined packages, as shown here:

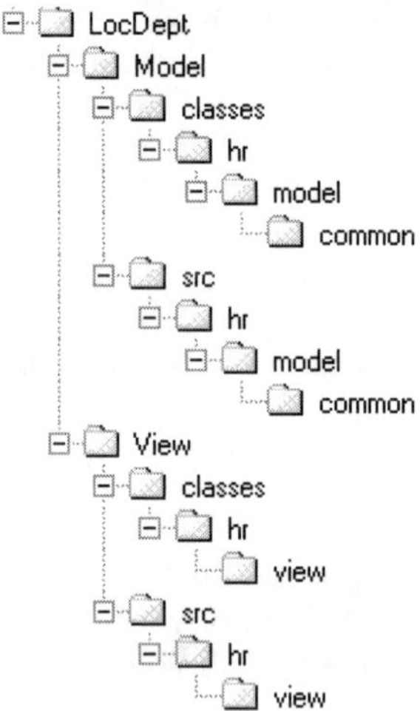

Within a business component project's model package directory, an additional folder called "common" stores the generated ADF BC configuration files.

Development Steps

The general steps you go through to create code in JDeveloper for an application that accesses the database follow:

1. Create an application workspace using a template that contains view and model (business services) projects.

2. Define and test the business services objects.
3. Add code for user interface objects. This code uses objects in the business services project.
4. Test the user interface code with the business services project.
5. Deploy the Model and View projects.

Various practices throughout the book provide specifics about each of these steps and give you experience in creating different styles of application code.

Hands-on Practice: Build a Client/Server Application Using the JDeveloper Wizards

This practice will give you a feel for how to use the wizards to create a simple client/server–style Java application project. This practice also provides an introduction to working with JDeveloper 10*g* and gives you a basic understanding of its primary components. Although this practice introduces the main application development features of JDeveloper, Chapters 2 and 3 provide details about some of the features introduced in 10*g*. Detailed information about ADF Business Components may be found in Part II of this book. Chapter 7 and Part III contain detailed information about Java applications.

Since the focus in this chapter is to familiarize you with the overall JDeveloper 10*g* architecture, you will only use the higher-level wizards (that produce a complete code module) in this hands-on practice. Normally, you would modify the code created by the higher-level wizards or use the individual element wizards to create the code.

The two projects created in this practice could be partitioned across any number of application workspaces with any number of projects. For this practice, one workspace will be created to hold both projects; this is the default for most applications. Two separate projects will be used: a Model project for the business components and a View project for the Java application. Each project represents a number of files that will be deployed as a unit.

This practice consists of the following phases:

I. Create the application workspace and database connection

- Create the application workspace
- Create a database connection

II. Create the Model project

- Create ADF BC entity and view objects
- Test the Model project

III. Create the View project

- Create the Form

- Generate the JClient user interface components
- Test the application

As with most practices in this book, you will use ADF BC to build the business services (model) objects for the user interface layer.

I. Create the Application Workspace and Database Connection

If it is the first time you are opening JDeveloper 10*g*, you will see the welcome screen. Otherwise, the product will reopen to show the screen as it was the last time the product was closed.

The IDE window has several work areas as shown in Figure 1-1.

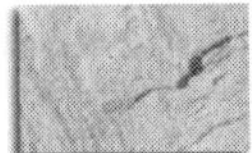

TIP
You can choose to view or hide each work area using the View menu. In addition, you can reposition the work areas in an arrangement different from the default described next. Chapter 2 contains details about how to manage the work areas and windows in the IDE.

- **The navigator area**, by default, contains tabs for Applications, System, Connections, and Run Manager. If the System and Run Manager tabs are not visible, you may display them using the View menu. The following navigators are available:
  - **The Application Navigator** displays the logical structure of your application including workspaces, projects, and files. Most of your time will be spent manipulating objects in this view.
  - **The System Navigator** displays the physical structure of your application, including workspaces, projects, and files. By expanding all of the nodes, you can view the contents of your projects.
  - **The Connection Navigator** is used to manage access to a database or other external resources.
  - **The Run Manager** navigator is used to display the processes that are running applications you started from JDeveloper. For example, running a web application will cause the Run Manager tab to appear and an entry placed in it for the Embedded OC4J Server.

Chapter 2 contains more information about the navigator windows.

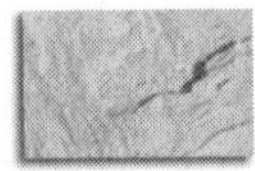

NOTE
As mentioned in Chapter 2, all navigator and other windows can be repositioned from their default location. This chapter describes the locations in which the navigators and other windows appear by default.

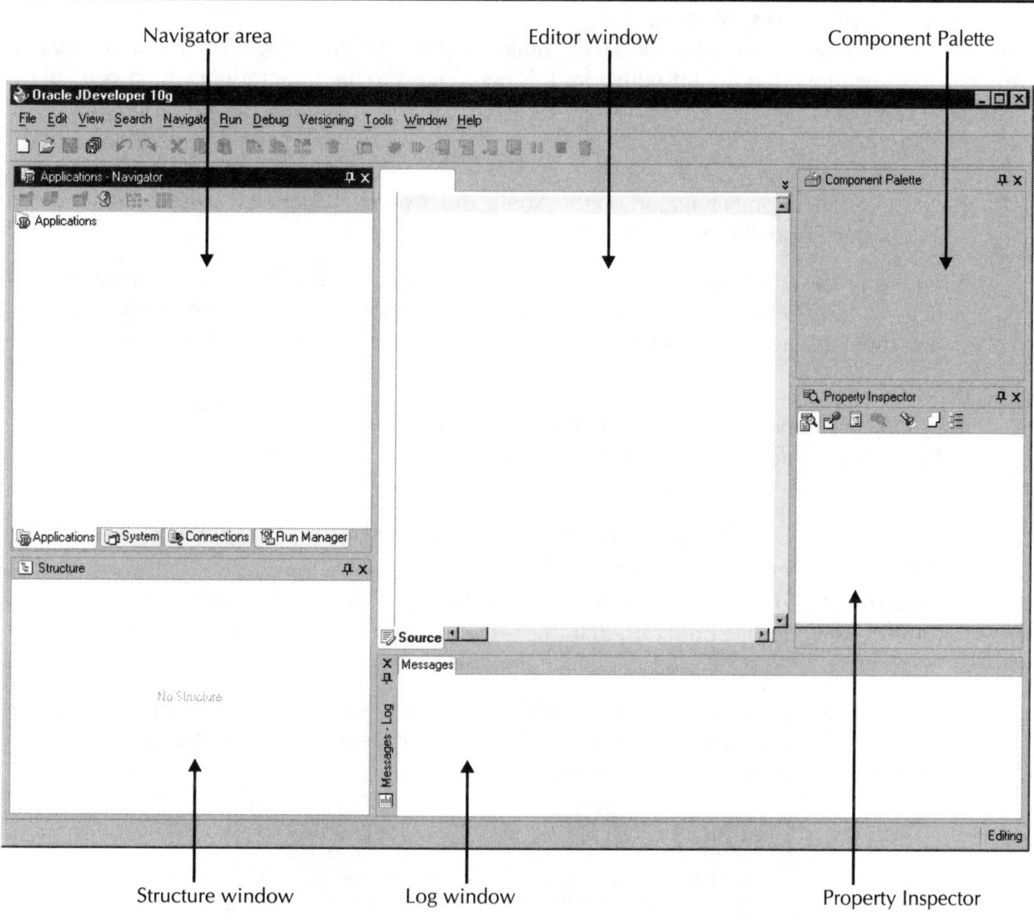

FIGURE 1-1. *JDeveloper 10g IDE window*

- **The Structure window** is used to display the contents of the object(s) selected in the Navigator.
- **The Log window** is used to display runtime messages including errors and system processing messages.
- **The editor window** is used to display the editors, visual editors, modelers, and viewers.
- **The Property Inspector** is used to view and change details of the selected object. It is activated when items selected in the navigator have associated properties that can be edited.
- **The Component Palette** is used to add elements to the file in the editor window.

Create the Application Workspace

By default, JDeveloper places all workspaces within the JDEV_HOME\jdev\mywork subdirectories structure. (As mentioned in the Introduction, this book refers to the directory in which you have installed JDeveloper, such as "C:\JDev10g," as "JDEV_HOME.") Use the following steps to create the application:

1. In the Application Navigator, on the Applications node, select New Application Workspace from the right-click menu.
2. In the Create Application Workspace dialog, change *Application Name* to "LocDept". (See Chapter 6 for a description of Naming Conventions). Note that the last part of the directory name automatically changes to "LocDept" as you type the name.

TIP
Dialogs in JDeveloper 10g contain a context-sensitive Help button. Use this button to get information about the fields and options in the dialog.

3. Enter "locdept" in the *Application Package Prefix* field. This prefix will then be automatically used for creating packages.

   Additional information: The *Application Package Prefix* field defaults to the last application package prefix used. If this is the first time you have used JDeveloper, this field will be blank. If not, replace the displayed value.

4. Change the Application Template pulldown to "Java Application [Default]" as shown next. Click OK to dismiss the dialog. Under the LocDept node in the navigator, you will now see Model and View nodes.

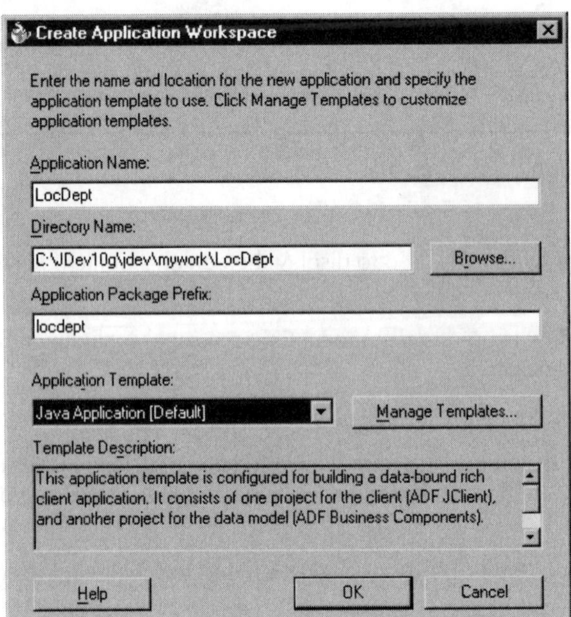

Additional Information: Different application templates will automatically build different projects for your application as explained before.

5. Click Save All (in the main toolbar).

Create a Database Connection

The Connection Navigator contains different types of connections such as Application Server, Database, Designer Workarea, Oracle SCM, SOAP Server, UDDI Registry, and WebDAV Server. More information about these connection types can be found in Chapter 2. For this hands-on practice, you will create a database connection to the HR schema.

The HR schema is one of the demonstration schemas supplied with the Oracle database. Details about setting up the HR database to work with the hands-on practices in this book can be found in the Introduction to this book.

1. Click the Connections tab in the navigator area. On the Database node, select New Database Connection from the right-click menu to access the Create Database Connection Wizard. Click Next if the Welcome page appears.

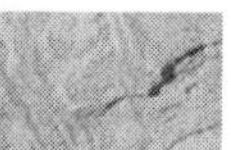

NOTE
The Welcome page appears by default in many wizards. This page explains the purpose of the wizard and is useful to read when you are learning the product. You can turn off the Welcome page for a particular wizard by checking the "Skip this Page Next Time" checkbox on the Welcome page.

2. On the Type page, name your connection. Since this practice will use the HR schema supplied with JDeveloper, enter "HR" in the *Connection Name* field. Leave the *Connection Type* as the default, "Oracle (JDBC)." Click Next.

3. On the Authentication page, type "HR" in both the *User Name* and *Password* fields since the practices in this book use the HR schema. Leave the *Role* field blank.

4. Check the *Deploy Password* checkbox. Click Next.

5. On the Connection page, you will need to explicitly set the *Host Name, JDBC Port,* and *SID.* Contact your network administrator or DBA if you are unsure of the appropriate settings. Click Next.

6. Click the Test Connection button on the Test Page to check your connection definition. If the settings were correct, you will see a "Success!" message in the status field. If you receive an error message, check the settings on the previous pages by clicking the Back button to return to those pages.

   Additional Information: A successful test does not necessarily mean that the database will allow you to build your application successfully. The connection will be successful even if you have no privileges to any table in the system. This test only verifies that you can connect to the specified account.

7. Click Finish. Check that the new connection is listed under the Connections\Database node in the Connection Navigator. The connection has been saved at this point. You do not need to explicitly save it.

   Additional Information: You can double click any connection you have created to view, edit, or test it at a later time. Explore the HR connection node. Examine the various objects to see what is contained in the Oracle-supplied HR schema. You also have the ability to drop existing objects or to create PL/SQL program units and database users. JDeveloper includes a simple and convenient utility, the SQL Worksheet, which you can use to enter SQL commands. This may save you from having to use another tool to work with database structures. You can access SQL Worksheet by selecting the Connection Navigator tab, expanding the Database and specific connection nodes. Right click the database connection (in this case HR) and select SQL Worksheet.

What Just Happened? You created an application workspace and database connection in preparation for building your JDeveloper application projects. The New Application Workspace dialog and Create Database Connection Wizard are typical of many of the dialogs and wizards you will encounter in JDeveloper.

Notice how the connection and application workspace are completely independent at this point. The workspace is a logical container for building your application and specifies the primary directory where that application will reside. The database connection is stored outside the workspace so that it can be referenced where appropriate. Therefore, any application workspace can use the connection that you just created.

II. Create the Model Project

Although the HR schema has numerous tables, you will only be defining objects for the tables necessary to make the practice applications run. This represents just one style of application development. An alternate approach would be to build the entity objects to support a large portion, if not all, of the database and then build separate view objects and application modules for each project.

Create ADF BC Entity and View Objects

Use the following steps to create the Model project:

1. Click the Applications tab of the Navigator area to switch to the Application Navigator.

2. If it is not already expanded, expand the LocDept application workspace node. On the Model node, select New from the right-click menu on the Model node.

3. The New Gallery is displayed. For this practice, leave the Filter By pulldown as "Project Technologies." Select the Business Tier\Business Components category. In the Items list, select Business Components from Tables as shown next.

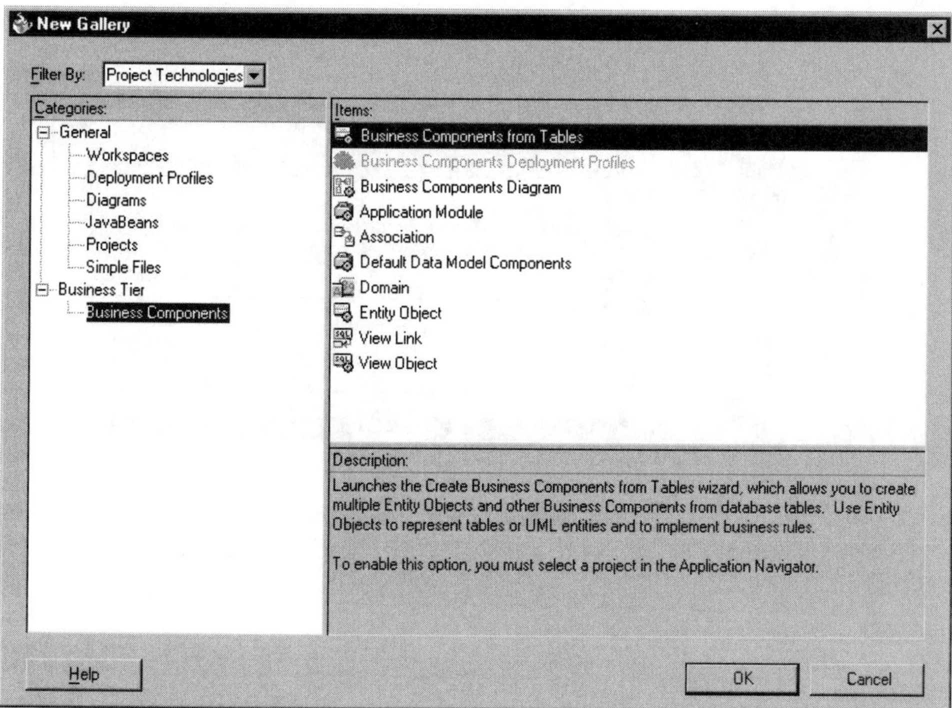

Additional Information: The Filter By pulldown at the top of the New Gallery allows you to choose between "Project Technologies" and "All Technologies." The filtered view ("Project Technologies") only displays items that are usually appropriate for the type of project you are creating. To see the entire list of options, select "All Technologies" from the pulldown.

4. Click OK. The Business Components Project Initialization dialog will appear. If you have multiple connections set up, you may not see HR in the *Connection* field. Make sure that HR is displayed. Leave the default *SQL Flavor* and *Type Map* settings. Click OK.

5. Click Next if the Welcome page of the Create Business Components from Tables Wizard appears.

6. On the Entity Objects page, since you specified the locdept application prefix when you created the applications workspace, the *Package* name should show "locdept.model." Ensure that "HR" appears in the *Schema* field. Select DEPARTMENTS. Hold down the

CTRL key and select LOCATIONS in the *Available* pane. Both tables will now be selected. Click the right arrow (">") to move these to the *Selected* pane as shown next.

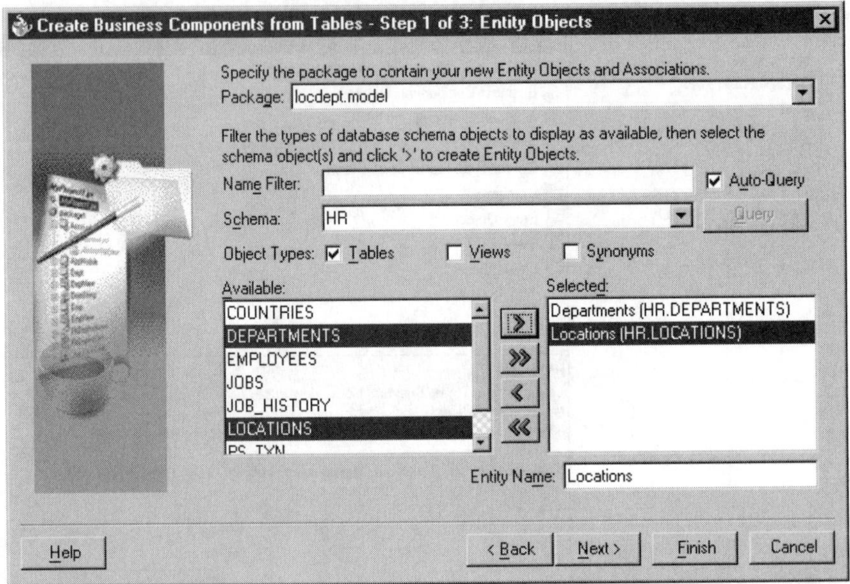

Additional Information: Since there are only a few tables in the HR schema, it is easy to scroll through them to find the one(s) you want. If you have a large number of tables or views on which to base your application, you can filter them using the *Object Types* field (Tables, Views, or Synonyms) and/or by using the *Name Filter* field. This will restrict the available objects list. You can also select different schemas and include database objects from those schemas if the connection you are working under has access to those objects.

TIP

The underscore ("_") and percent sign (%") characters in the "Name Filter" field will work as single- and multi-character wildcard filters, respectively. Each time you change a character in the name filter, the list is re-queried. If the list is long, this can take a long time unless you uncheck the Auto-Query checkbox; the Query button will then be enabled and you can click it to refresh the list.

7. Click Next. On the View Objects page, the *Package* field will default to "locdept.model." Leave this setting. Use the double arrows to move the entity object names to the *Selected* pane, which will declare view objects for both Departments and Locations. Leave the default *Object Name*. Click Next.

8. The locdept.model package name will already be entered in the *Package* field of the Application Module page. Change the application module *Name* to "LocDeptModule". Leave the *Application Module* checkbox checked. Click Next and Finish to complete the wizard.

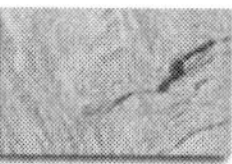

NOTE
A "package" is a logical container for a number of class files. It is represented in the file system by a single directory. Java code references this package name in the class file and in fully qualified names for a method. Chapter 6 contains more information about packages and how they are named.

9. Click Save All.

Test the Model Project

You now have ADF BC objects that can be used to connect the user interface to the database. This section shows how to test the ADF BC objects without creating a user interface project. It is useful to know that the model project objects work before creating the user interface code.

1. You will see the new entity objects and view objects under the Model node of the Application Navigator as shown here. On the LocDeptModule node of the Model project, select Test from the right-click menu.

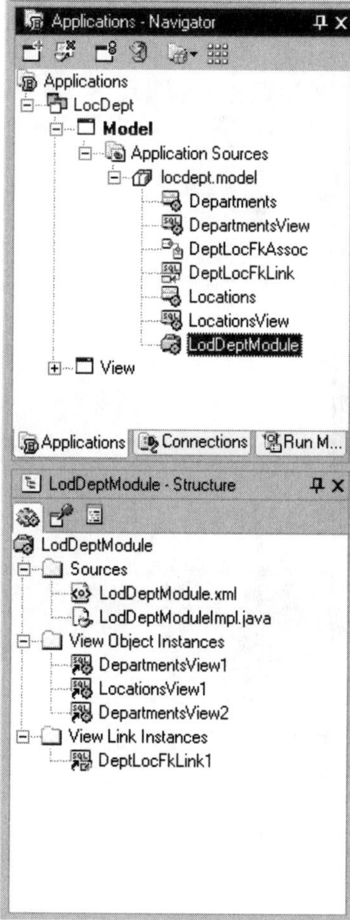

2. Click Connect on the Oracle Business Component Browser - Connect dialog. The Oracle Business Component Browser will open as shown in Figure 1-2. The Log window will display any error messages when the code is compiled.

3. On the LocationsView1 node, select Show from the right-click menu. Scroll through the records using the blue navigation arrows to test the database query.

4. If the Run Manager is not displayed in the navigator area, select Run Manager from the View menu. This will add a Run Manager tab to the navigator area. You can use this window to check on what processes are running.

5. Click the Run Manager tab. Select Terminate from the right-click menu on the Processes\ locdept.model.LocDeptModule node. This will close the Oracle Business Component Browser. This is one way to close the browser. You can also click the "X" icon in the top-right corner of the browser window or select **File | Exit**.

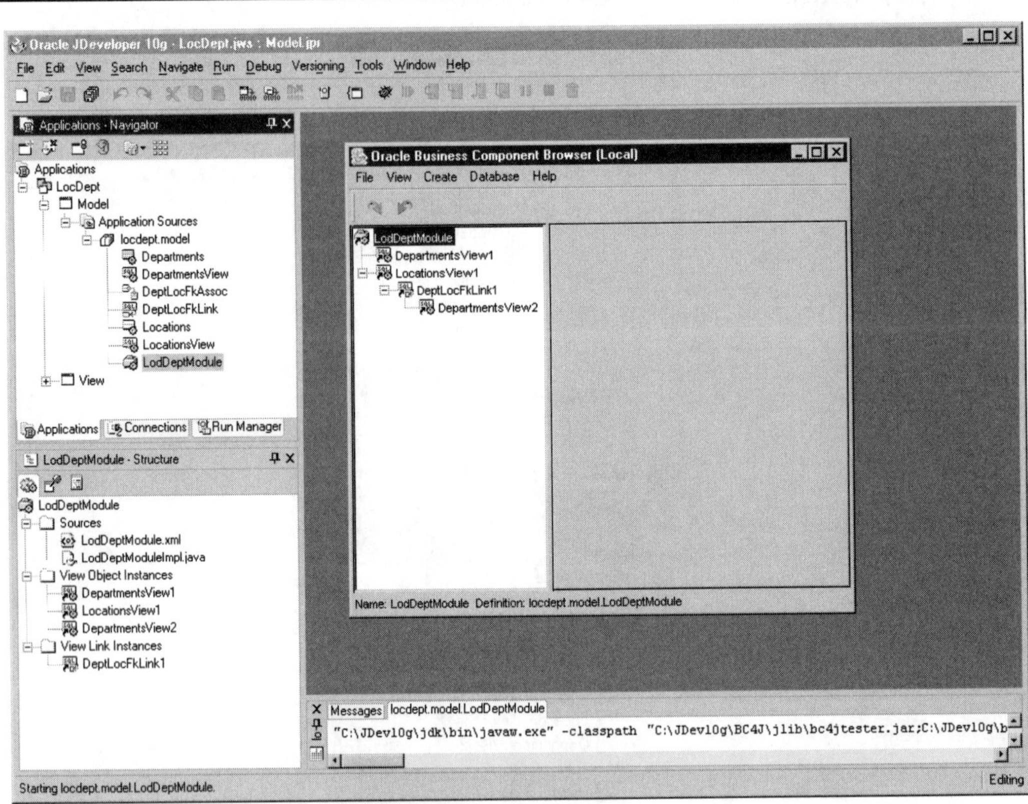

FIGURE 1-2. *Oracle Business Component Browser*

6. Click the Applications tab to return to the Application Navigator.
7. Click Save All to save your work.

What Just Happened? In this phase, you made a few simple selections and allowed the JDeveloper wizards to create an application project including information from the DEPARTMENTS and LOCATIONS tables of the HR schema. Using the high-level wizards, you created ADF business component objects that are exact images of the underlying DEPARTMENTS and LOCATIONS tables of the HR schema.

III. Create the View Project

In this phase, you will create a Java application form (a particular style of Java program) and link it to the Model project in the LocDept workspace created earlier. For more information about Java applications, see Chapter 7 and Part III of this book.

Create the Form

Use the following steps to create a simple Java application form:

1. In the Application Navigator on the View node, select New from the right-click menu.
2. In the New Gallery, under the Client Tier node, select Swing/JClient for ADF in the Categories list and Form in the Items list as shown here:

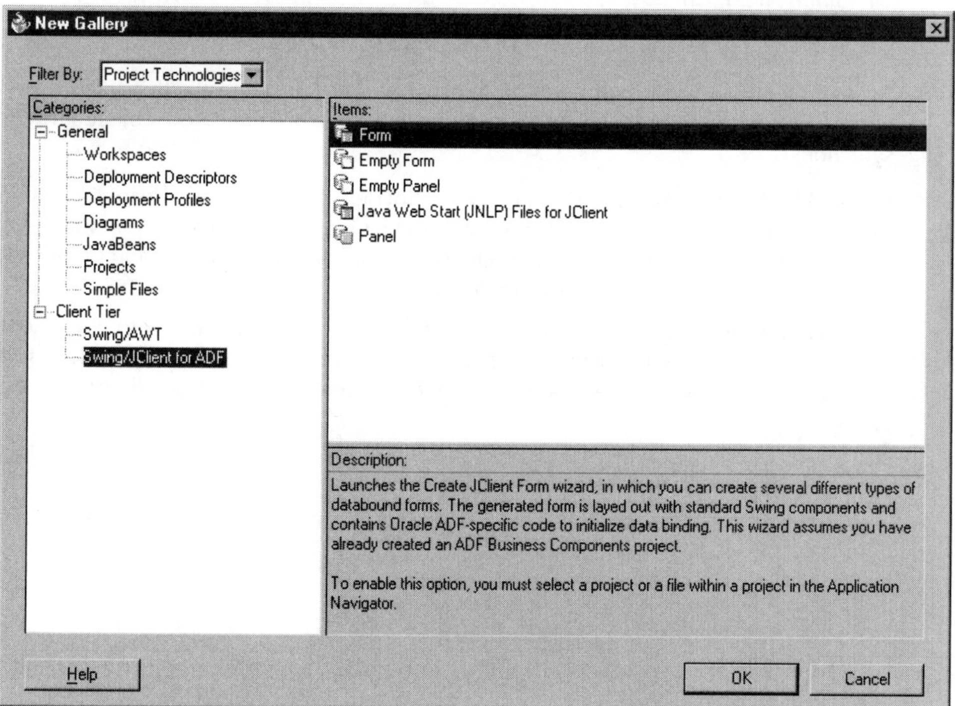

3. Click OK to start the Create JClient Form Wizard. Click Next to dismiss the Welcome page if it appears.
4. On the Form Types page, select the "Master-Detail Tables" radio group selection. Leave the default selection of "Form" for the implementation radio group. Click Next.
5. On the Form Layout page, leave the default for *Select a Master template* ("Single columns (label left)"). Change the *Number of columns* to "2." Leave the *Select a Detail template* set as "Table." Click Next.
6. To attach the View project to the Model project, on the Data Model page, click New to start the ADF Business Components Client Data Model Definition Wizard. Click Next to dismiss the Welcome page if it appears.
7. Since there is only one business components project created, leave the default settings for the Definition page. Click Next and Finish to complete the Client Data Model Definition Wizard.

Generate the JClient User Interface Components

These steps will create the files and Swing components to display the data in the application.

1. On the Data Model page of the JClient Form Wizard, the name of the model you just created (LocDeptModuleDataControl) will be displayed in the "*Select the Data Model Definition*" field. Click Next.
2. Leave the default settings on the Panel View page and click Next.
3. By default, all of the attributes will be selected on the Attribute Selection page. Click Next. Click Next again on the Attribute Selection page for detail view object attribute selections.
4. On the File Names page, the *Package name* "locdept.view" should already be filled in. Leave the other default settings. Click Next and Finish. You will now see a number of .java and .xml files under the View node in the Application Navigator and other window areas will become active as shown in Figure 1-3.

   Additional Information: You can now examine the Structure window to navigate the layout objects of the form. The Component Palette also opens to provide options for adding functionality and the Property Inspector for the PanelLocationsView1UIModel is displayed.
5. Click Save All.

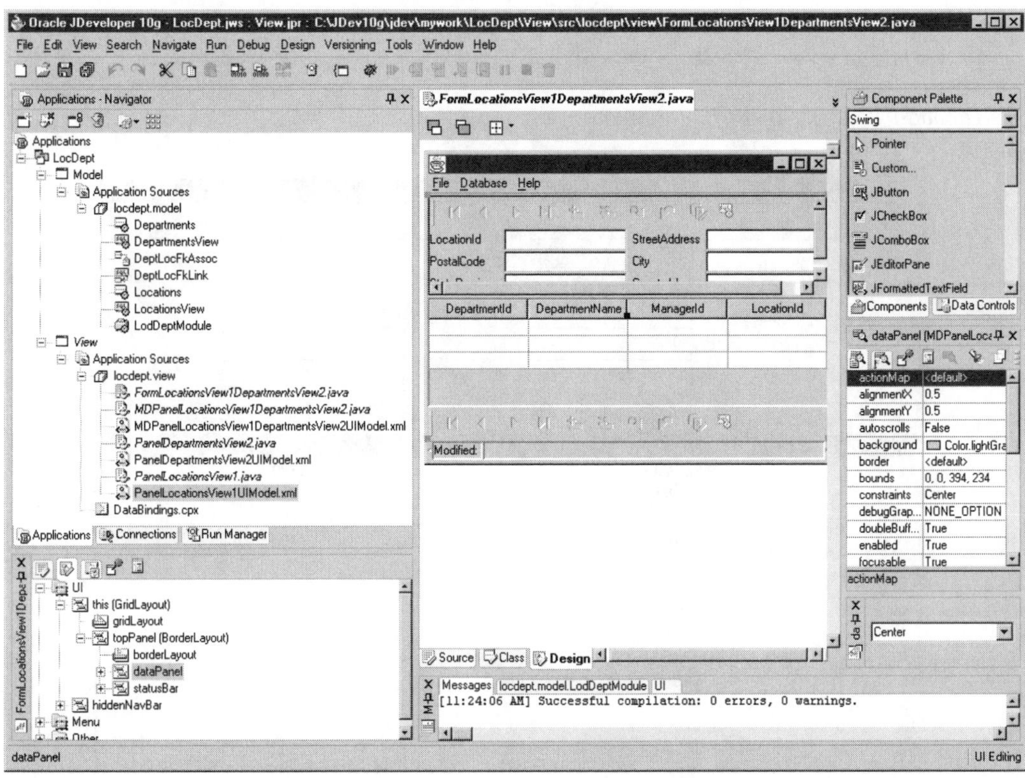

FIGURE 1-3. *Form created by JDeveloper wizards*

Test the Application

To ensure that the application is working at this point, you should test it using the following steps.

1. On the FormLocationsView1DepartmentsView2.java node under the LocDept\View\Application Sources\locdept.view node in the Navigator, select Run from the right-click

menu. Alternatively, you can click Run from the main toolbar to run the form shown here.

TIP
Location 1700 has many departments.

File Database Help

LocationId	1700	StreetAddress	2004 Charade Rd
PostalCode	98199	City	Seattle
StateProvince	Washington	CountryId	US

DepartmentId	DepartmentName	ManagerId	LocationId
10	Administration	200	1700
30	Purchasing	114	1700
90	Executive	100	1700
100	Finance	108	1700
110	Accounting	205	1700
120	Treasury		1700
130	Corporate Tax		1700
140	Control And Credit		1700
150	Shareholder Services		1700
160	Benefits		1700
170	Manufacturing		1700
180	Construction		1700
190	Contracting		1700
200	Operations		1700
210	IT Support		1700
220	NOC		1700
230	IT Helpdesk		1700
240	Government Sales		1700
250	Retail Sales		1700
260	Recruiting		1700
270	Payroll		1700

row 8 Modified:false Navigating: LocationsView1

2. Scroll through the records to see the data. Notice that the departments shown in the detail table are the details for the displayed location in the master area above. Close the form using the "X" icon in its upper-right corner or use **File | Exit**.

What Just Happened? In this phase, you created a simple Java application. You allowed the JDeveloper wizards to create all of the code and viewed the results of using the default settings for creating the application.

The first thing you did was to define an application workspace containing two projects for Model and View. You then set up the Model project using ADF BC components. You then ran the wizard to create a default user interface application. This is a fully functional application that you can use to select, insert, update, and delete records. It is not a production-level application, but if you carefully review the generated objects, you can use this code to get an idea of how you should structure a Java application that interacts with ADF BC.

To summarize the process of creating a Java application using the wizards, you would use these steps:

1. Create the application workspace with Model and View projects.
2. Create an image of the database using entity objects and associations.
3. Create a client data model for binding the ADF BC application module to the user interface.
4. Create the user interface application.

Hands-on Practice: Create a Simple JSP Page

This hands-on practice demonstrates how to create a simple JSP page to use a web browser such as Internet Explorer or Netscape to browse the Locations table of the HR schema. This project uses the same ADF BC project that you created for the earlier hands-on practice. JDeveloper 10*g* includes an easy-to-use visual editor with standard word processor editing capabilities and a drag-and-drop interface. For additional information about JSP technology, see Chapter 18.

This practice consists of the following phases:

I. Create the JSP project

II. Create the JSP file

I. Create the JSP Project

This project will reuse the ADF BC project built in the preceding practice and build an additional JSP project for an alternate user interface. If you have not completed the first practice in this chapter, complete through phase II before beginning this phase.

1. If not already displayed, click the Applications tab in the Application Navigator. Select New Project from the right-click menu on the LocDept node.
2. In the New Gallery, the Projects node will already be selected in the Categories list. Select Web Project from the Items list. Click OK.
3. If the Welcome page of the Create Web Project Wizard is displayed, click Next to display the Location page. Change the project name to "ViewController". Click Next.
4. On the Web Project Profile page, leave the default settings in all of the fields and check the *Add JSP Page* checkbox. Click Next and Finish.
5. The Create JSP dialog will open. Change the *File Name* to "Loc.jsp". Click OK.
6. Click Save All.

   Additional Information: You will now see a blank editor window for the JSP file in the center of the screen, the Structure window below the Application Navigator; and the Component Palette and Property Inspector on the right side of the screen.

What Just Happened? You just created a blank JSP project and an empty JSP file.

II. Create the JSP File

You now need to create the JavaServer Pages user interface components for the application, using the JSP/HTML Visual Editor. In terms of code, JSP files consist of HTML (or other language used to control page display and formatting) and Java tags (which supply data and processing). In JDeveloper, you will format the page and then add JDeveloper components to the layout.

1. Click at the top left of the blank editor page. Type "Locations Browser" as the JSP Page heading.

   Additional Information: Note that as you type, the words are added to the Structure window under the body node.

2. Select Heading 1 from the first (Block Format) pulldown. This will change the font of the line and add the appropriate HTML tag to the file. Press ENTER to move the cursor to the second line.

3. Select the Data Controls tab. In the Data Control Palette, select LocationsView1 under LocDeptModuleData Control. Select "Read-Only Form" from the *Drag and Drop As* pulldown and drag LocationsView1 onto the editor under Locations Browser. Your screen should look something like this:

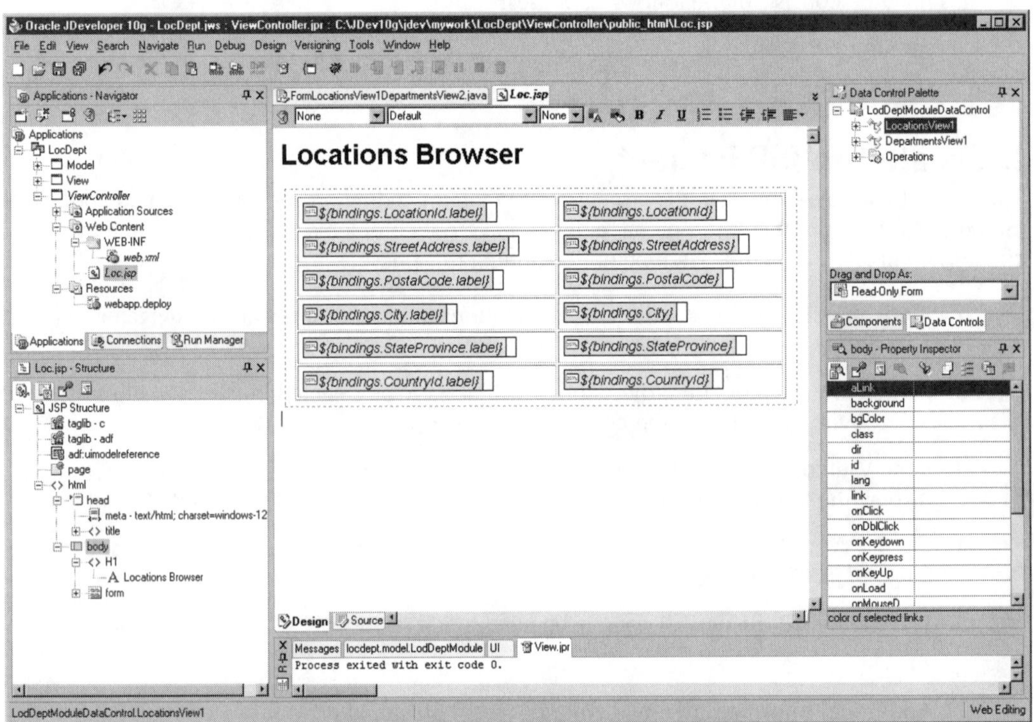

Additional Information: You can format a JSP file using HTML or other page formatting options. The Component Palette changes to show HTML components, but you could use cascading style sheets, JavaScript, or other technologies that are compatible with JavaServer Pages and HTML coding. You can also use the text editing features of this window to modify the font, type, size, style (bold, italic, underline), orientation (left, center, right), and so on.

5. Click above the top-left corner of the form inside the red dotted line. Press ENTER to create a blank line.
6. Select Navigation Buttons in the Drag and Drop As pulldown. Drag LocationsView1 to the cursor location.
7. Center the buttons using the alignment pulldown on the JSP page formatting toolbar and selecting Center or select "center" in the pulldown of the *align* property in the table Property Inspector. The visual design should look like the following:

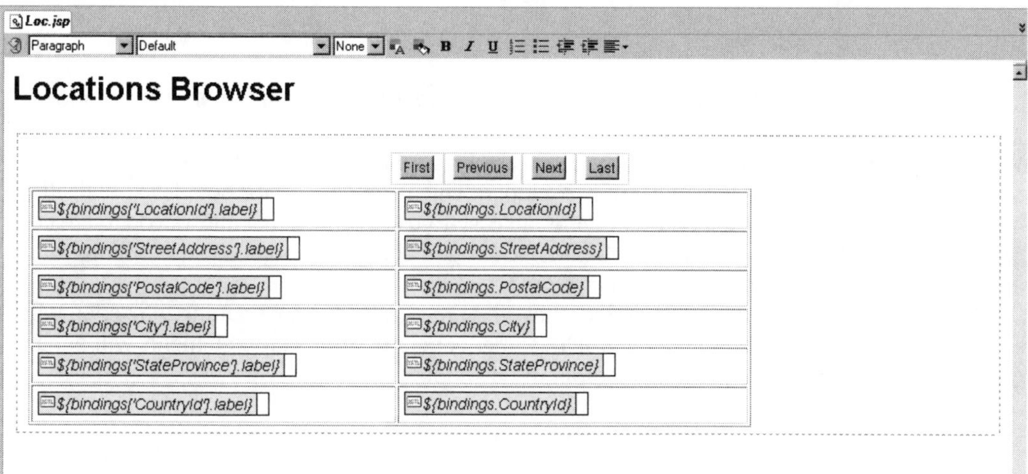

Additional Information: The alignment pull-down is on the far right of the formatting bar at the top of the design window. If it is not visible, expand the width of the window.

8. Apply a template to set the look and feel of your JSP page by selecting the Components tab. Select CSS from the pulldown.
9. Click JDeveloper in the CSS pulldown (you do not need to drag and drop this item) and note the changes in the editor window.
10. Click Save All.

11. Test the JSP by selecting Loc.jsp in the Navigator and clicking Run from the right-click menu. This will start the Embedded OC4J Server and open your default browser. The browser will display the Locations data as shown in the following portion of the browser screen:

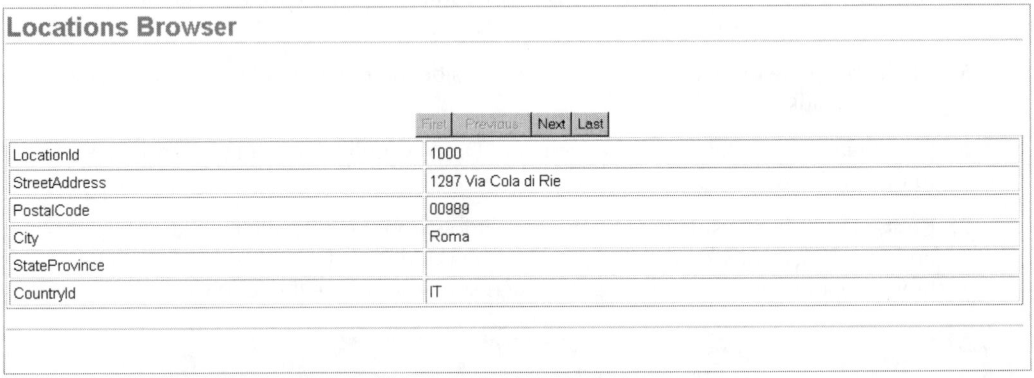

Locations Browser

First | Previous | Next | Last

LocationId	1000
StreetAddress	1297 Via Cola di Rie
PostalCode	00989
City	Roma
StateProvince	
CountryId	IT

12. Test the navigation buttons to browse the Locations table. Close the browser window.

What Just Happened? In this phase, you created a simple JavaServer Pages file. This demonstrates the power and flexibility of JDeveloper, which can be used for both Java applications and web pages. The new visual editor provides an easy-to-use interface that allows you to create more attractive JSP pages with foreground and background color, font, and text style options that were not possible in earlier versions of JDeveloper.

The authors suggest that you carefully follow the practice steps and examine the generated structures and code. Understanding how JDeveloper generates application elements will enhance your understanding of the rest of the material in this book.

CHAPTER 2

The Integrated Development Environment Overview

Beware the ides of March.

—William Shakespeare (1564–1616), *Julius Caesar* (I, ii, 18)

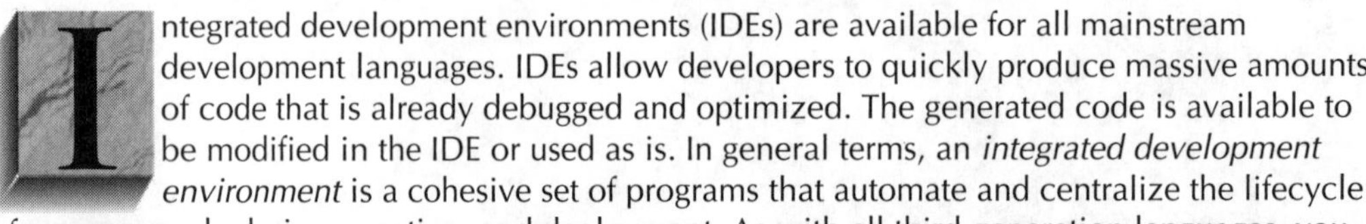

Integrated development environments (IDEs) are available for all mainstream development languages. IDEs allow developers to quickly produce massive amounts of code that is already debugged and optimized. The generated code is available to be modified in the IDE or used as is. In general terms, an *integrated development environment* is a cohesive set of programs that automate and centralize the lifecycle of program code design, creation, and deployment. As with all third-generation languages, you can create Java programs using a text editor, and there is no requirement to use an IDE for Java development. However, integrated development environments assist the development process by offering text editing tools that help create and format code. In addition, IDEs contain tools that greatly assist in the full lifecycle for application code including the ability to design, develop, debug, and deploy related files. Java IDEs are commonplace and several, including JDeveloper, offer sophisticated features that can greatly speed up application development. IDEs such as JDeveloper serve the following main functions:

- **Code generation** The IDE creates bug-free files from its internal templates that take care of much of the internal wiring required to make a set of files work together. This can speed up development significantly and make developers much more productive.
- **Code organization** Java projects contain hundreds of files and, for an application to work properly, the files need to be used together and must be located in certain directories or packages. IDEs automate the tedious tasks of keeping the files for an application in the proper locations and assembling them into deployment packages.

In addition to a description of the JDeveloper IDE, this chapter examines the following concepts as a background to the discussion of specific tools in Chapter 3:

- IDE window
- Customizing the IDE
- Main toolbar
- Main menu
- Help system
- Software configuration management

This chapter closes with a hands-on practice that explores installing Concurrent Versions Systems (CVS) support in JDeveloper.

Chapter 3 explains the tools that you use to create, view, and edit code. Since all of these tools appear within the main JDeveloper windows, the information in this chapter serves as the groundwork for using the tools in a productive way. The background topics in this chapter will assist you in understanding the more detailed information in Chapter 3 about operations and features within the IDE.

The JDeveloper 10*g* IDE

The key to working with the JDeveloper IDE is in knowing how it is organized and what facilities it offers. If you understand the major areas of the tool, you will be able to work more efficiently when creating code. While you can be productive in JDeveloper 10*g* without extensive preparation, a bit of time spent in learning about its features will be rewarded many times in time and effort saved.

The JDeveloper IDE is written in Java. The choice of Java means that JDeveloper may be run in the Java Virtual Machines (JVMs) of different operating systems with few, if any, changes. This makes JDeveloper extremely portable between operating systems.

The 10*g* release improves upon the solid foundation of the previous releases and offers an even more developer-friendly environment. This release features a facelift from its predecessor and has a "flat" look and feel (where internal window borders blend more seamlessly into the IDE window). If you are accustomed to JDeveloper release 9*i*, you will notice these differences immediately. Although the basic features remain the same, some operations have changed and you will need to adjust your development methods. Although you can perform development tasks in many different ways in JDeveloper, the IDE is oriented toward working with the Application Development Framework (ADF), which is discussed in Chapter 4.

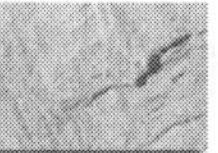

TIP
*JDeveloper will load faster if a reduced set of features is enabled. You can reduce the number of features loaded when JDeveloper is started by using the Extension Manager page of the Preferences dialog (**Tools | Preferences**). This page allows you to deselect features that you do not use or use infrequently. The Extension Manager page allows you to create and manage sets of extensions as named "profiles," and you can switch from one profile to another as needed.*

IDE Window

You can start JDeveloper from the executable file, jdevw.exe, in the JDEV_HOME\jdev\bin directory (where JDEV_HOME is specific to your installation). When you start JDeveloper, an IDE window such as the one shown in Figure 2-1 appears. (See the sidebar "About Monitor Resolution" for recommendations about display hardware. The Introduction to this book provides recommendations about other hardware.) As this figure shows, the IDE window contains a number of tools that are discussed in Chapter 3. These tools appear inside the IDE in locations called windows. Although these windows are docked to and are part of the main IDE window by default, you can drag them out as separate windows if needed. There are two types of windows, which exhibit different behaviors in the IDE —dockable windows and the editor window. These windows are described next in general terms.

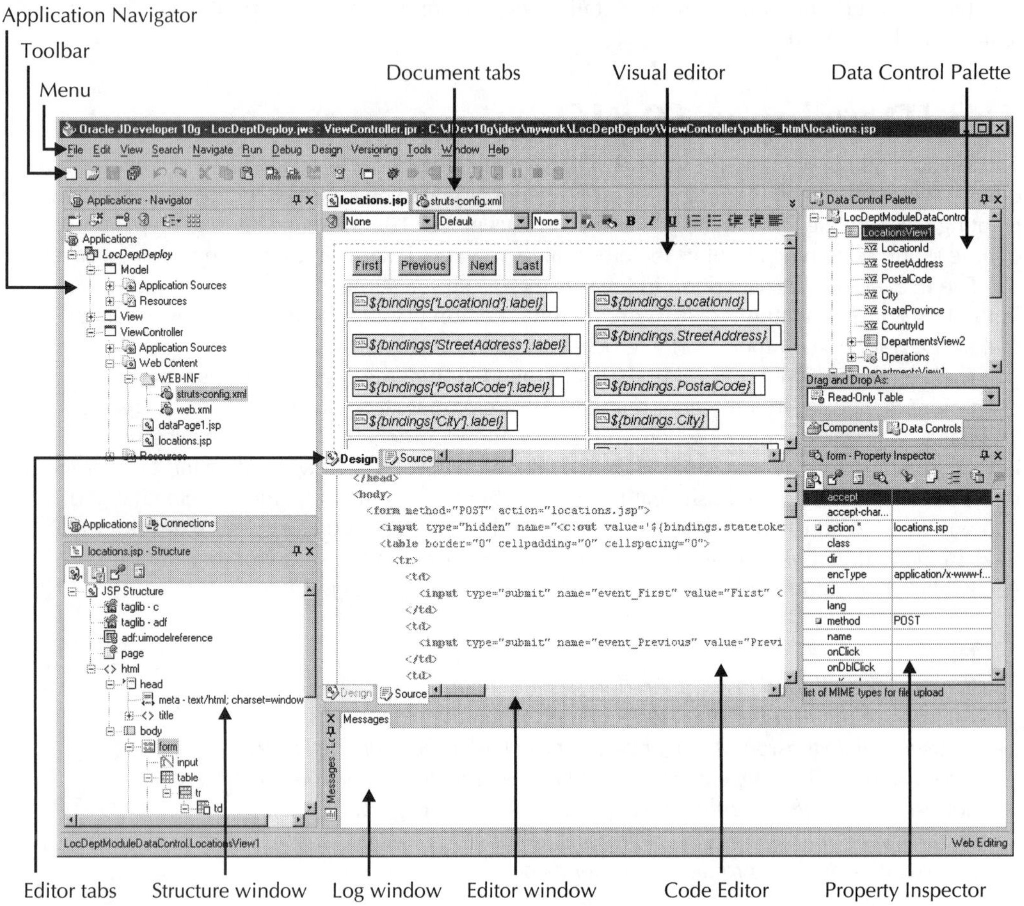

Application Navigator
Toolbar
Menu
Document tabs
Visual editor
Data Control Palette
Editor tabs
Structure window
Log window
Editor window
Code Editor
Property Inspector

FIGURE 2-1. *The JDeveloper IDE window*

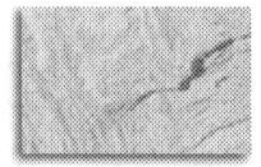

TIP

You can also start JDeveloper using jdev.exe from the same directory as jdevw.exe. Using jdev.exe will open a separate console window that displays any Java stack trace message. You can press CTRL-BREAK *in this console window to show information about the current running processes in the IDE. If JDeveloper freezes, it is easier to close the IDE by closing the console window than it is to stop the JDeveloper process in the Windows Task Manager.*

About Monitor Resolution

There are many work area windows in JDeveloper, and you usually need to have several of them open at the same time. Therefore, you need as much screen real estate as possible. The first rule of thumb for JDeveloper windows is to maximize the size of the IDE window. The next rule of thumb is to maximize screen real estate by using a monitor set to a high resolution such as 1280×1024 (or 1600×1200). Figure 2-2 shows JDeveloper running in a 1280×1024 resolution. Compare that with Figure 2-1, where the screen is running a 1024×768 resolution.

As in most modern GUI development tools, a large monitor and high resolution are best. Although most of the screenshots in this book use a 1024×768 resolution for clarity, you will be more productive with a higher resolution, because you will be able to open more windows and leave them arranged so they display the most content. With lower resolutions, you will spend time resizing windows so their contents are visible. This is time that could be better spent on other tasks. As a rule, a 19-inch monitor is a minimum size for 1280×1024 resolution. A resolution of 1600×1200 works on a good-quality, 21-inch monitor, but may not be comfortable for some people. If possible, it is optimal to split the IDE across multiple monitors (for operating systems such as Windows XP that support a split display), each of which shows different IDE windows.

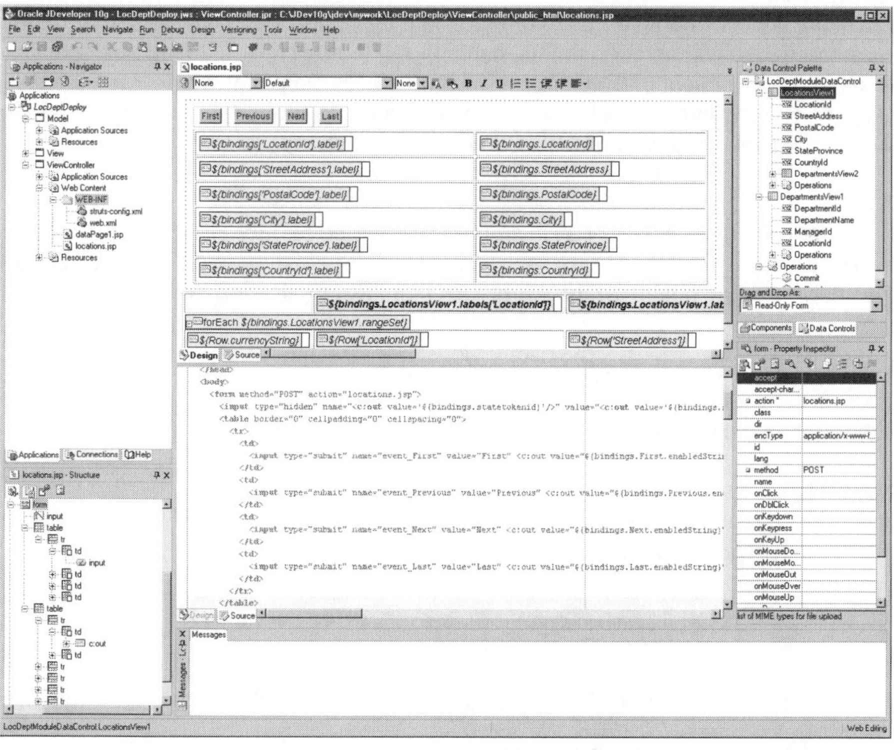

FIGURE 2-2. *JDeveloper running in a 1280×1024 resolution*

Editor Window

The *editor window* is an editing container in the center of the IDE window. It is the main window for most development and is normally used to display or edit a single file at a time. The name of the file that is active in the editor will be displayed in the IDE window title. Although the editor window normally shows only one file, it can be split to show multiple views of the same file or multiple files at the same time (as described later).

You can view and edit files in different ways. For example, you use the Code Editor to modify the source code for a Java application that displays Swing (windowed) controls; you use the Java Visual Editor to modify the visual aspects of the same file. Both editors appear in the editor window area. Chapter 3 discusses some details about the editors and viewers that can be displayed inside this window, but it is useful first to examine some of the features and operations available in this window.

TIP
You can resize any window inside the IDE frame by dragging an edge. Other windows will be resized, if needed, to accommodate the new window size. The IDE window will remain the same size.

Displaying the Editor Window

You display the editor window for a file selected in the Application Navigator either by selecting Open from the right-click menu on the file name or by double clicking the file in the navigator.

The default arrangement of JDeveloper windows places the editor window in the center, largest area of the IDE and the dockable windows containing support features around it. This is a logical arrangement and you probably do not need to change it.

Editor Tabs

You can display different editors for a single file using the *editor tabs* at the bottom of the editor window. For example, the Design tab displays the Java Visual Editor and the Source tab displays the Code Editor, as shown here for the editor tabs in a Java application file:

Editor tabs contain a name and an icon indicating the type of editor.

Document Tabs

The editor window can also hold more than one file. You switch back and forth between files using the *document tabs* at the top of the editor window as shown here:

Document tabs contain the name of the file and an icon indicating the type of file within the editor.

Splitting and Unsplitting the Editor Window

You can combine the use of editor tabs and document tabs to display more than one file at a time and to display more than one view of the same file at a time. Figure 2-3 shows an example of an

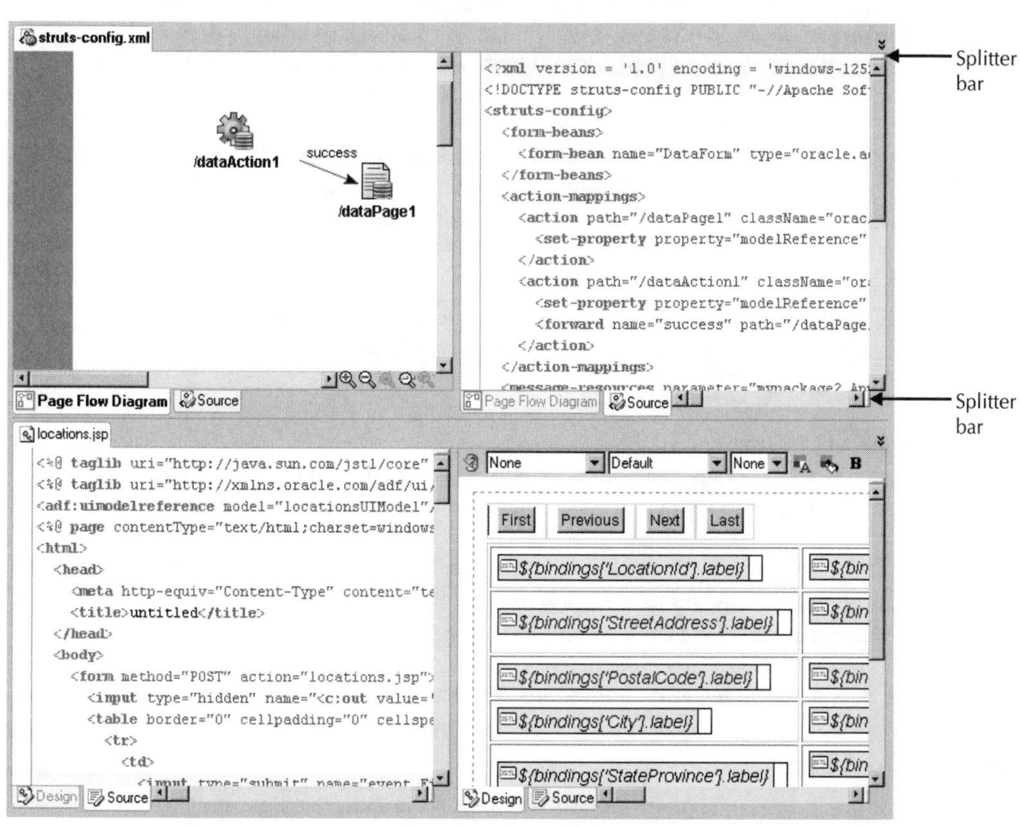

FIGURE 2-3. *Split editor window*

editor window containing the Page Flow Diagram of the struts-config.xml in the top left. The same file is displayed in the Code Editor in the top right. In addition, the editor window shows the locations.jsp file in split windows for the Code Editor (lower left) and the visual editor (lower right).

You can accomplish this type of arrangement using a combination of several techniques:

- **Window | Split Document** This menu selection automatically splits the active file in the editor window. Split Document is also available from the right-click menu on a document tab.
- **The splitter bars** The *splitter bars* allow you to divide or merge views of a file and are located next to the scroll buttons in an editor window (as shown in Figure 2-3). Dragging the splitter bar down or to the left will create another view of the same file. This technique is an alternative to the menu selection.

- **Window | New Tab Group** This menu selection will open the file in a separate pane in the editor window. Alternatively, you can grab an editor tab and drag and drop it inside another open file in the editor window. As you drag, an arrowed box icon will show where the window will end up when you drop it.

Unsplitting a window is just a matter of using the techniques in reverse (**Window | Unsplit Document**, dragging a splitter bar, and dragging and dropping, respectively). Use **Window | Collapse Tab Groups** to combine two document panes into one window.

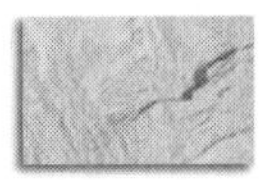

NOTE
As with all operations in JDeveloper, if you have more than one editor window open for a single file, changes in one editor will be immediately reflected in the other.

Closing an Editor Window

You can close a file that is open in an editor window by clicking the document tab's close ("x") icon or by selecting Close from the right-click menu on the corresponding document tab.

TIP
Clicking the double arrow at the right side of an editor window pane displays a pulldown list of open editor documents. Selecting a document from that list makes it the active document. You can also activate a document by selecting it from the Window menu.

Dockable Windows

Dockable windows typically contain support features and are arranged around the editor window. These windows may be anchored (docked) to the top, bottom, or sides of the outer IDE window. They can also be pulled out of the docked position to float inside or outside of the IDE frame. If docked windows share the same area, a tab control will allow you to switch between them. These windows can be displayed or navigated to using the View menu options. You manipulate the docking or floating operations by dragging the window title bar as described later in "Docking and Undocking a Window."

Arranging the Dockable Windows

By default, areas for dockable windows line the inside perimeter of the IDE window in an arrangement such as that shown in Figure 2-1. (By default, no window is assigned to the inside top perimeter of the IDE window.) You can change the positions taken by each area using the Dockable Windows page of **Tools | Preferences** (under the Environment node) as shown in Figure 2-4.

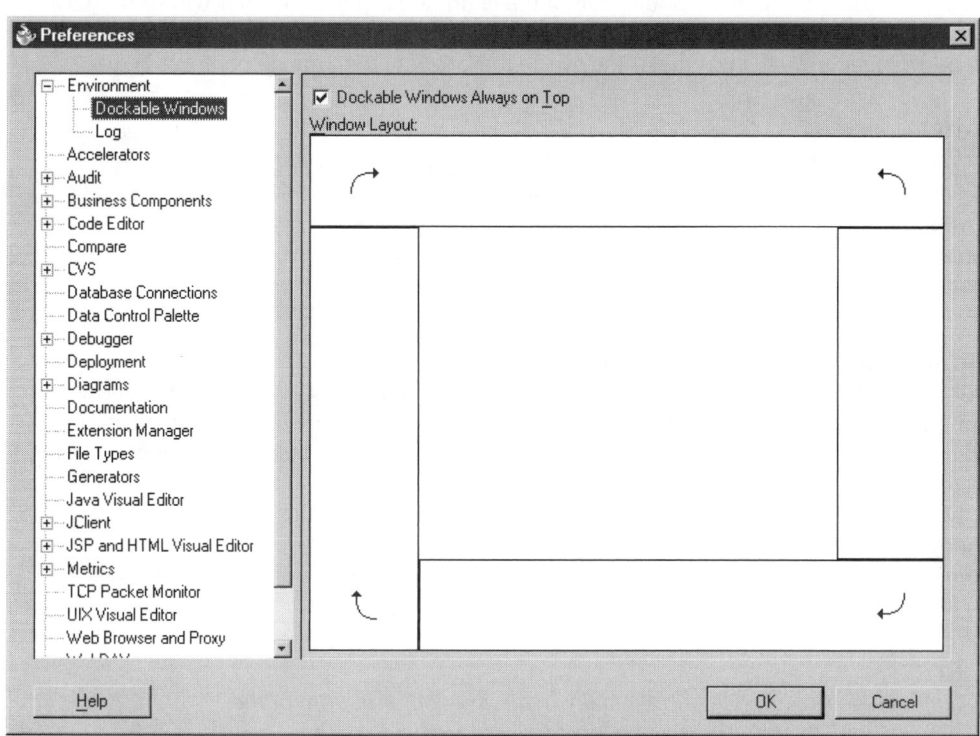

FIGURE 2-4. *Dockable Windows page of the Preferences dialog*

For example, if you click the curved arrow in the lower-left corner of this page, the arrangement will change so that the bottom area takes up the entire bottom border as shown in this snippet from the preferences page:

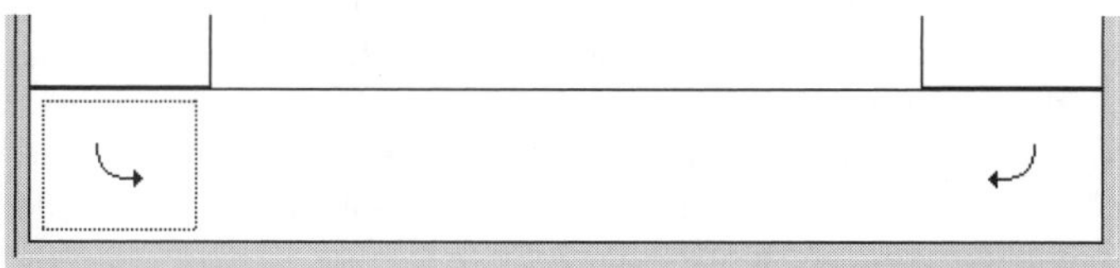

The contents and size of these areas vary based upon the type of work you are doing. The IDE displays the type of work in a "button" in the lower-right corner of the status bar. For example, the status bar will show the word "Editing" if you have opened the Code Editor for a

Java application file (using the Source tab of the editor area). The status bar will show "UI Editing" if you are viewing and interacting with the Design tab of the same file. The windows will be arranged in the same way as they were the last time the arrangement was active.

TIP
You can switch between arrangements by selecting from the right-click menu on that arrangement status "button." This can be handy in some situations. For example, you can switch to the Editing arrangement while working in the Java Visual Editor (UI Editing arrangement) if you need more space for the editor window.

Docking and Undocking a Window

Undocking a dockable window only requires dragging the title bar or tab of the window away from the docking edge of the IDE window to the center of the IDE window. When the window outline is over the center of the IDE window, releasing the mouse button will undock the window and make it float over the other windows.

Docking a dockable window requires grabbing the window's title bar and dragging the window until the mouse cursor reaches the border of the outer window. You will see the window outline snap into place on that side of the outer IDE window. Releasing the mouse button window will then dock the window.

NOTE
If the window is arranged horizontally across the top or bottom of the IDE window, the title bar may be located on the left side of the window.

Arranging Dockable Windows in the Same Space You can move a dockable window into the same space as another dockable window so that both windows share the same area. For example, if you had undocked the Structure window and wanted to dock it over the Application Navigator window, you would drag the Structure window over the navigator area and watch the outline as you position the window. If the window outline appears in the center of the Application Navigator window, releasing the mouse will dock the Structure window on top of the Application Navigator window; the two windows will share the same space and each will have a tab that you can click to bring the window to the foreground.

The tab will contain an icon and a title that indicates its contents. If the space within the window is insufficient for titles, only the tab icon will be displayed. For example, the following shows tabs in the navigator window area:

If this area is narrowed, one or more titles will not be displayed as shown here:

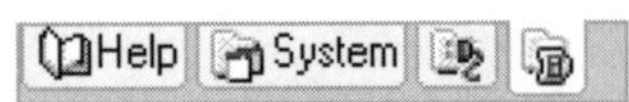

With some experimentation, you can see how a window can be docked under, over, to the left, or to the right of another window. The outline of the window you are dragging provides a visual clue as to where the window will dock when you release the mouse button.

Auto Hiding

When a window is docked, an Auto Hide icon (in the shape of a pin with the point of the pin down) appears in the window's upper-right or upper-left corner (next to the "x" close button). Clicking the Auto Hide icon causes the window to collapse and a tab with the window name to appear in the nearest margin. Clicking that tab (or just holding the mouse cursor over the tab) opens the window. Moving the mouse cursor over another window hides the hidden window. Clicking the pin button (which has its point to the left) again when the hidden window is displayed will display the window all the time. Since the navigator area is used infrequently, you may find it useful to auto hide it.

Displaying a Dockable Window

Dockable windows open automatically when they are needed for a particular task. If a window you want to see is not displayed, you can select it from the View menu (for example, **View | Log** to display the Log window). Alternatively, you can select the window from the right-click menu on any dockable window as shown here:

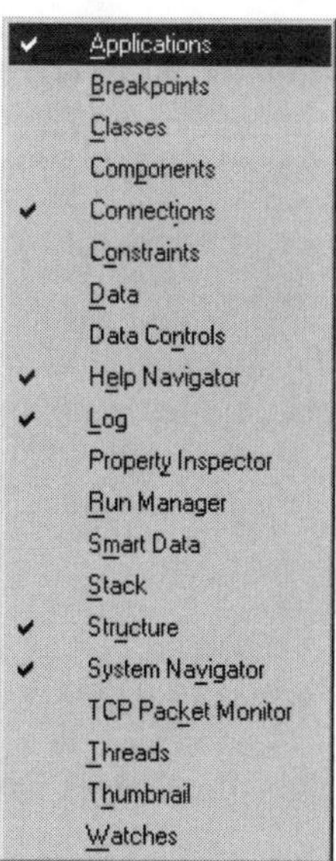

The right-click menu options toggle the display so that a window will be displayed if the menu item is checked. The window will be hidden if the menu item is unchecked. The View menu items will not hide a window but will navigate to or display it.

Customizing the IDE

You can employ several methods to modify how the IDE looks and works. You can resize and reposition the windows inside the IDE. You can also create JDeveloper extensions that present your own wizards and file creation dialogs using the Extension SDK documented in the JDeveloper help system. Some other customization methods (such as property editors, customizers, and keymaps) are mentioned in Chapter 3.

Preferences

The Preferences dialog (**Tools | Preferences)** is the main location for modifying the behavior of the tools (and many other IDE features). This dialog contains a navigator for different categories of settings. Changing a setting in this dialog changes the behavior in the tool. Most changes are immediate, although some require exiting and reloading JDeveloper. Examples of some of these preferences are mentioned throughout in this chapter and in Chapter 3.

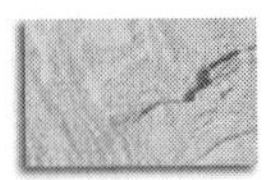

NOTE
As mentioned, the Extension Manager page of the Preferences dialog allows you to temporarily disable features you do not need. A reduced set of features can make finding a feature simpler and can speed up the JDeveloper startup time.

Look-and-Feel Preference

The ability to change the look-and-feel (aspects such as colors, fonts, and the treatment of window edges) of an application is a feature of Java. You can define the look-and-feel for your JDeveloper session using the Environment page of the Preferences dialog (**Tools | Preferences**). The options are "CDE/Motif," "Metal," "Oracle," and "Windows"; all but "Oracle" are supplied in Java base classes.

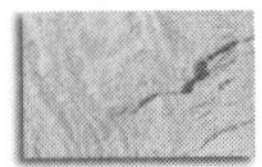

CAUTION
This book shows all screens using the default "Windows" look-and-feel definition. If you use another look-and-feel definition and the IDE does not work as you would expect, try switching to another look-and-feel such as "Windows" and try the feature again.

Main Toolbar

The IDE main toolbar contains frequently accessed commands in the following categories:

- **File operations** For opening the New Gallery, opening a file, saving a file, and saving all changed files.
- **Edit operations** For undo, redo, cut, copy, and paste.
- **Compile and run operations** For making a project, rebuilding a project, running a file, and running the Profiler. Making and rebuilding are explained further in the sidebar "Compiling with Make and Rebuild." The toolbar also contains an icon, Cancel Build, which stops a running compile process. This is useful for a long-running compile that has frozen or that you need to abort.
- **Debug operations** For running the debugger and stepping into, over, or out of code during a debug session.

Compiling with Make and Rebuild

The toolbar, main menu, and right-click menu for files contain options for two kinds of compiling. *Make* compiles modified files on the selected node as well as modified files that have been imported by those files (referenced in the import sections). *Rebuild* compiles all files in the selected node as well as files that have been imported by those files. Rebuild is useful when you want to force all files in that node to be compiled (for example, if you have replaced a file with an older file and that older file needs to be recompiled). Selecting a node in a navigator allows you to make or rebuild all files under it. Since Rebuild compiles all files in the selected node, it is slower than Make.

If you select the workspace node and select **Run | Make <workspace>**, all modified files (and modified imported files) in all projects within that workspace will be compiled. If you select a single file in a navigator and click the Rebuild button in the toolbar, only that file (and its imported files) will be compiled. The Run menu contains options for making and rebuilding the selected object, its project, and its workspace. You can also "make" a file that is open in the editor by selecting Make from the right-click menu in the editor.

When you make or rebuild files, check the Log window for messages. This window will indicate if the compilation has been successful or, if there were errors, what went wrong. Double clicking an error in this window will open the editor and select the problem line of code.

All toolbar buttons provide tooltip hints that appear when the mouse cursor is held over the button. All functions performed by the toolbar icons also appear in the main menu and some appear in the right-click menus.

Main Menu

The IDE main menu bar offers access to a large number of operations. In addition, JDeveloper uses right-click (context) menus extensively. Almost everything in the IDE offers right-click menu options for frequently used operations. Many of these options are also contained in the main IDE menu. Therefore, instead of listing and explaining all of the right-click menu selections here, it will be more useful to explore some of the unusual options in the main menu and provide the following tip.

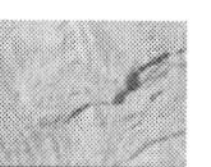

TIP
Always be aware that an operation you may want to perform on a particular object in the IDE may be more easily accessible in a right-click menu than in a pulldown menu.

File

This menu contains common operations such as opening and closing files. The open file dialog (**File | Open**) contains buttons that allow you to jump to directories defined for the JDeveloper home or current workspace, project, or user. The File menu also allows you to remove a file from the project but not delete it from the file system (Remove from <node>) or to delete the file from the file system (Erase from Disk). The New option (discussed in the "New Gallery" section of Chapter 3) creates a file or other element such as a connection. Revert closes the selected file without saving and reopens it from the file system.

A Rename option changes the name of a file. If you want to rename a class file that is used by other class files, use the **Tools | Refactor** menu items. *Refactoring* will rename the class and cascade the name change to all dependent classes. It will also change the class declaration code (for example, `public class TestClass`) so that it references the new file name. Renaming the file using the File menu will not automatically change the class declaration or other files that reference it. Refactoring will also delete the compiled .class file with the old name, but renaming will not.

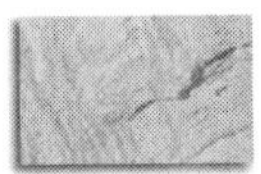

CAUTION
If you rename or erase a Java file that has already been compiled, the compiled .class file will not be renamed. This can cause side effects if other files reference the old file name. You will need to remove the compiled .class file with a file utility such as Windows Explorer. If you are just renaming a Java file, it is better to use the Refactor – Rename Class option than the Rename option to avoid this problem.

The Reopen menu item shows a list of all objects recently opened. You can select from that list and load projects into the IDE more quickly because you do not have to browse the file system.

You can load an existing file into an editor or viewer by selecting the Open item in this menu. This will open the file but not add it to the active project, in case you just want to edit, copy, or view the file's contents. Use the "Add to" menu item to add the file to the project.

To add a copy of (not just a reference to) an existing file into your project directory, use the Import menu option. You can include a file inside a WAR or EAR (types of Java archive files) as well as an existing file. The Import item can also just include the file without copying it.

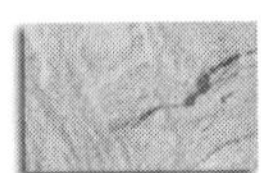

CAUTION
If you use Windows Explorer or another utility to change a file name listed in a project or a project file name in a workspace, that file name will not be updated automatically in JDeveloper. Although the old file name will show in the navigator, there will be no file in the file system to support it. Therefore, when you open that workspace or project, you must remove the old file and add the new file so that the project is properly updated.

File Comparisons The Compare With submenu of the File menu allows you to perform a file "diff" (comparison) between the selected file and another file as shown here:

Help Compare: 1

File on Disk - PanelLocationsView1.java

```
package locdept.view;
import java.awt.*;
import java.awt.event.*;
import javax.swing.*;
import javax.swing.table.*;
import javax.swing.text.*;
import oracle.jbo.uicli.jui.*;
import oracle.jbo.uicli.controls.*;
import oracle.jbo.uicli.binding.*;
import oracle.adf.model.*;
import oracle.adf.model.binding.*;
import java.util.ArrayList;



import oracle.jdeveloper.layout.*;



public class PanelLocationsView1 extends JPanel impl
{
  // Panel binding definition used by design time
  private JUPanelBinding panelBinding = new JUPanelB:

// Panel containing the data entry fields

  private JPanel dataPanel = new JPanel();
```

File on Disk - PanelLocationsView2.java

```
package locdept.view;
import java.awt.*;
import java.awt.event.*;
import javax.swing.*;
import javax.swing.table.*;
import javax.swing.text.*;
import oracle.jbo.uicli.jui.*;


import oracle.adf.model.*;
import oracle.adf.model.binding.*;
import java.util.ArrayList;
import java.lang.util.*;
import oracle.*;

import oracle.jdeveloper.layout.*;

/** this file displays fields for the LOCATIONS table.
*/
public class PanelLocationsView1 extends JPanel implem
{
  // Panel binding definition used by design time
  private JUPanelBinding panelBinding = new JUPanelBir

// Panel containing the data entry fields

  private JPanel dataPanel = new JPanel();
```

Compare

You can also compare project files using the Compare With submenu on the right-click menu on the project node. If you group projects in the same application workspace together (using CTRL click), you can select Each Other to compare the files. Comparing projects compares the XML code in the project files.

TIP

The OTN website contains a JDeveloper plugin that you can use to compare directories. At this writing, this extension is available for JDeveloper 9i. Navigate to the Extensions Exchange from the JDeveloper home page and look in the previous release extensions.

Edit

The Edit menu provides the standard Windows editing features. Many items here have keyboard shortcuts (such as CTRL-Z for Undo) that are faster to use than the menu selections. The Properties item allows you to modify the definitions of objects in the Connection Navigator. Properties for some other objects (including connections) are accessible using the Properties or Edit items in the right-click menu for the object. In addition, project properties are available from a menu item in the Tools menu.

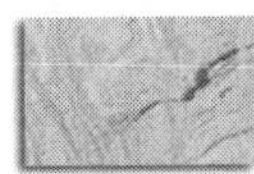

NOTE
The keyboard shortcuts mentioned in this book are based upon the default key assignments. You can modify the key assignment scheme by loading another scheme such as the key assignments for Visual C++. To reassign the keyboard shortcuts, select ***Tools | Preferences*** *and click the Load Preset button on the Accelerators page. This page contains a number of preset selections.*

View

Normally, the IDE displays the editors and windows appropriate to a certain task. The View menu allows you to override or supplement the choices that the IDE makes about which areas to display. You can display a window or make a window active by selecting items in this menu. You can also display or hide the status bar and toolbars using View menu selections.

Search

This menu contains standard find features for text searches in source code such as Find, Find Next, Find Previous, and Replace. Most items have shortcut keys (such as CTRL-F for Find). Selecting text to search will load it into the *Text to Search For* field in the Find Text dialog. Other items in this menu follow.

CAUTION
Pressing ENTER *in the Find Text window* (CTRL-F) *will find the specified text. Pressing* ESC *will cancel the dialog. You can also just use the OK and Cancel buttons to find the text or cancel the dialog, respectively.*

- **Clear Highlighting** If you check the *Highlight All Occurrences* checkbox in the Find Text dialog, all text that matches the search word or phrase will be highlighted throughout the document. This item removes the highlights from words or phrases highlighted by this mechanism.
- **Incremental Search Forward** and **Incremental Search Backward** These selections (CTRL-E and CTRL-SHIFT-E) are extremely handy for finding text in a large body of code. After selecting one of these options, you type into the Incremental Find Forward (or Incremental Find Backward) dialog, and the tool will find and highlight all occurrences of whatever you type. Exiting the dialog will navigate to the first occurrence of the text. Pressing F3 will repeat the find.
- **Search Files** This selection opens a dialog that allows you to search for files containing text that you specify, even if the text is within a .zip or .jar file. This is similar to the Windows Explorer file search feature. However, it is platform independent, so you can use this dialog regardless of the operating system in which you are working.

Navigate

This menu contains items to set, clear, and find bookmarks in a source code file. This is handy if you are frequently navigating back to the same lines of code. Setting a bookmark places a "bookmark" icon in the left margin of the Code Editor. "Go to Recent Files" shows a list of files you have recently opened in JDeveloper.

This menu also contains selections for navigating through messages in the Log window (Go to Next Message and Go to Previous Message). You can jump to a specific line number using Go to Line. The following are other items in this menu:

- **Select in Navigator** This selection will find the file node in the navigator that corresponds to a file that is open in an editor window.
- **Select in Structure** This item selects the node in the Structure window that corresponds to an object selected in an editor such as the JSP/HTML Visual Editor.
- **Go to Java Class** This selection (CTRL- –) displays a dialog where you enter or find a class name. When you click OK in that dialog, the source code file for that class is loaded into a Code Editor window (but not into the navigator). You can view the code and comments in read-only mode. The Structure window shows the contents of the source code file. The "Go to Java Class" feature is useful for determining which parent methods and attributes are available to a subclassed class. The Go to Java Class dialog also allows you to specify that you want to see the Javadoc instead of the source code for the class name you enter in the dialog.

The Go to Declaration option in the Code Editor's right-click menu has a similar effect, but loads the source file of the item at the cursor location. If the item is a class name, this option loads the source file for the class; if the cursor item is a primitive variable or object, this option displays the declaration of that variable or object; if the cursor item is a method, this option displays the method declaration.

NOTE
When JDeveloper navigates to a class file, it will try to reverse-engineer the code for a class that has no available source code. If it is not able to determine the code, it will display a message in the status bar of the IDE.

Run

The Run menu contains items for running the project or file that is selected. It also repeats the Make and Rebuild commands from the toolbar (see the sidebar "Compiling with Make and Rebuild" for more information). This menu also contains selections to run the *Profiler*, which provides details about runtime memory, events, and execution.

You can run the CodeCoach feature (which shows hints about how to improve your code) from this menu, to analyze the code and obtain suggestions for improvement. The Audit item runs a process that analyzes the code based on defined standards. The Measure item runs a metrics analysis of the code. The JDeveloper help system node "Working with Application Design Tools\Building and Tuning Applications\Optimizing Application Performance" contains more information about auditing, metrics, and CodeCoach.

The Javadoc item creates Javadoc for the selected file (see the sidebar "About Javadoc" later in this chapter). The Deploy item creates the installation files to be copied to a server based on a deployment profile you define. The Terminate item stops a running program.

NOTE
*When you run a file, all changed files in the project will be recompiled automatically. If you prefer to control compilation more closely, you can turn off this behavior by selecting **Tools | Project Properties** and unchecking the "Make Project" field in the Before Running section of the Profiles\Development\Runner\Options page.*

Debug

JDeveloper contains a fully featured debugger. It is accessible from items on the Debug menu. Debug <project> starts a debugging session and executes the code until the first breakpoint. In the debugging session, many of the items in this menu will become enabled.

Clicking the Debug toolbar icon or pressing SHIFT-F9 will also run the project in debug mode. Chapter 3 contains an introduction to the main features of the debugger. In addition, the JDeveloper help system contains more information about the debugger in the topics starting with the table of contents node "Working with Application Design Tools\Building and Tuning Applications\Debugging in JDeveloper."

About Javadoc

Javadoc is a standard feature of the Java language that allows you to generate an HTML help file from Java source code, as shown next. The help file will include any text contained within special code comments (delimited with a "/**" at the start and "*/" at the end). JDeveloper provides automated support of Javadoc viewing and creation.

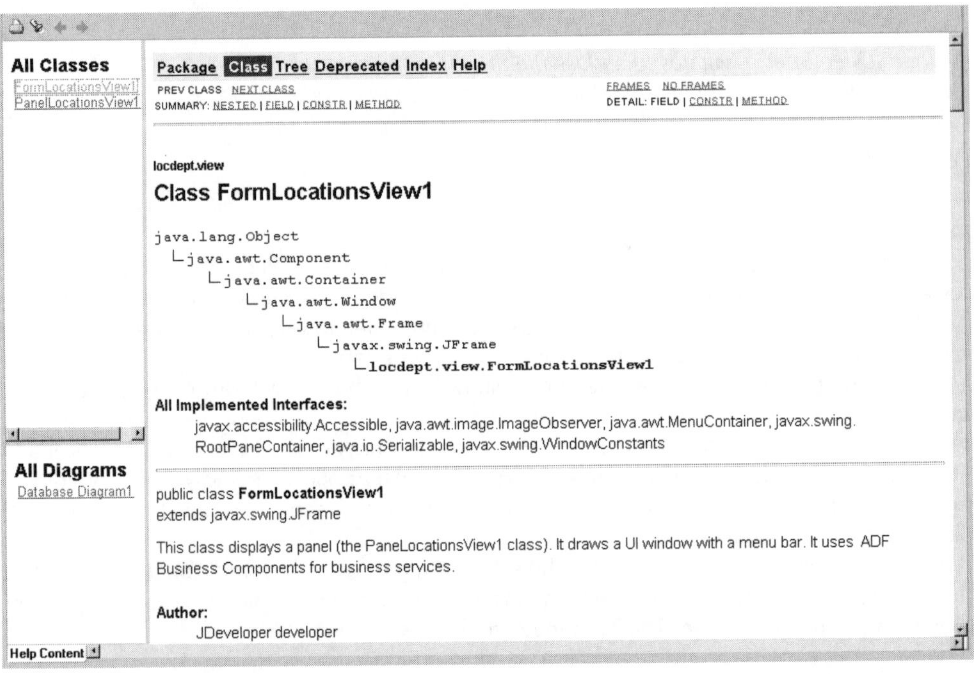

The first step for generating Javadoc is to be sure that your code contains Javadoc comments so that the output is useful. The Javadoc you create can become part of the deployment package that you provide to users. You can set properties for generating the Javadoc by using the Profiles\Development\Javadoc page of the Project Properties dialog (**Tools | Project Properties**).

To generate Javadoc for a project, select the project node in the System Navigator and select **Run | Javadoc <project>**. You can then review the Javadoc by clicking View Documentation in the Log window. The index.html file for the Javadoc is added to the navigator node Web Content\Miscellaneous Files under the project.

To view previously generated Javadoc for a library class or application class that you created, click the cursor on a class name in the Code Editor, and select Go to Javadoc from the right-click menu. You can also press the help key (F1) after placing the cursor in a class name. Alternatively, you can open the index.html file in the editor window and click the Preview editor tab.

Source

The Source menu appears when the Code Editor for a source code file is active in the editor window. It contains items that access the features of the Code Editor (described in Chapter 3) such as the following:

- **Widen Imports** changes imports for a specific class so that they reference the package that is the parent of the specific class.
- **Toggle Line Comments** modifies the source code by commenting or uncommenting a number of lines. You can also access this function by pressing CTRL-/.
- **Indent Block** and **Unindent Block** move blocks of code to the right or left, respectively.
- **Completion Insight** and **Parameter Insight** activate the code insight features described in Chapter 3.
- **Expand Template** to automatically insert a code snippet defined for a code abbreviation. (Code templates are described in Chapter 3.)
- **Quick Javadoc** displays a small box containing Javadoc for a single method or class referenced in the code.
- **Surround With** embeds the selected code inside a code structure, such as `if..else`.
- **Add Javadoc Comments** creates a Javadoc block that you can use as a starting point for your comments on a method or class.
- **Generate Accessors** displays a dialog that allows you to select class variables for which you would like to create getters and setters.

Model

The Model menu appears when a diagram is active in the editor window. This menu contains options that affect the UML modelers (class diagram, activity diagram, and use case diagram) and various class model variations (Java classes, business components, database objects, EJBs, and web services). The Publish Diagram item allows you to save the diagram as a .svg, .svgz, .jpg, or .png file.

Versioning

The Versioning menu offers items that you can use to manage files stored in an SCM tool. SCM in JDeveloper is described in the section "Software Configuration Management" later in this chapter.

Tools

The Tools menu contains a number of functions not found anywhere else such as the Preferences and Project Properties items already mentioned. The Tools menu contains a Default Project Properties item that you can use to set characteristics for new project files. This is useful if you need to change a particular setting for all projects. The sidebar "Project Properties Profiles" describes how to define multiple sets of project properties.

Other functions available in the Tools menu include wizards for installing the ADF runtime on a server (the ADF Runtime Installer submenu) and the following items:

- **Configure File Associations** This utility registers JDeveloper files with the file system so that when you double click a file outside of JDeveloper, JDeveloper will open and load that file.
- **Configure Palette** This item displays the Configure Component Palette dialog that allows you to add to or modify the contents of the Component Palette window (discussed in Chapter 3).
- **Implement Interface** This option displays a dialog where you can browse and select an interface file that your class will implement. After you select one or more interfaces and click OK, JDeveloper will add the `implements` clause to your class definition and will add method stubs for which you will need to write code. You can also use this to make an interface extend other interfaces.
- **Manage Application Templates** This menu selection opens the Manage Application Templates dialog where you can view, add, and remove the technology templates that you can apply to new application workspaces. This dialog also appears when you click the Manage Templates button in the Create Application Workspace dialog (New Application Workspace from the right-click menu on the Applications node in the Application Navigator).
- **Manage Libraries** This item opens the Manage Libraries dialog where you can create, modify, and remove groups of files that are organized into libraries. You can also manipulate libraries in the Libraries page (under the Profiles\Development node) of the Project Properties dialog.
- **Override Methods** You can use this menu item to add method stubs for methods in the parent that you want to replace or supplement. For example, you might want to override a parent `set()` method in your class file. This menu item adds a code stub for the parent `set()` method for which you can write code to replace (or supplement) the parent's method.
- **Plugin HTML Converter** This item calls a standard Java utility (Java Plug-in HTML Converter) that converts an HTML file containing applet tags to a file that supports a plugin (for Swing classes, for example). Since this is an external utility, it includes its own help text, which is not incorporated into the JDeveloper help system.

Project Properties Profiles

You can define project property *profiles* (called *configurations* in previous JDeveloper releases*)*, named sets of properties, and switch back and forth between them as required. The properties that you set for a profile are contained in the Paths, CodeCoach, Compiler, Debugger, Javadoc, Libraries, Profiler, and Runner nodes of the Profiles\<profile name> node of the Project Properties dialog. Multiple profiles can be useful if you often change the output directories or classpath directories for the same project (for example, for test and production environments). Instead of typing the new names into the Project Properties dialog, you can set up a profile to hold the special settings.

To define a new profile, open the Project Properties dialog, and click New on the Profiles page. You can copy an existing profile by checking the checkbox in the Create Profile dialog that appears. After you click OK, the Project Properties dialog tree area will contain a new profile under the old one. This new profile will contain all of the nodes mentioned earlier, and you can set the properties on those pages differently. The active profile name is shown in bold in the tree control. If you set up additional profiles in the default project properties dialog (**Tools | Default Project Properties**), those profiles will be available to all new projects.

To switch to a different profile, select it from the pulldown on the Profiles page. You can also delete and rename profiles on this page.

- **Refactor** (Rename Class, Move Classes, and Extract Method) These menu items solve the problem of renaming a class that has dependent classes. For example, normally if you reference Class1 in Class2 and rename Class1, the reference in Class2 will fail. The Rename Class option (available when you click a Java class node in the Navigator) changes the name of the file and modifies all dependent references to that file. The Move Classes option (available when you click one or more Java classes in the Navigator) allows you to change the package in which the classes are stored. This utility will change all references in dependent classes to point to the new package.
- **SQL Worksheet** This option opens a utility in the editor window that allows you to enter SQL commands in much the same way as in SQL*Plus, but this utility is part of JDeveloper so you do not need to install SQL*Plus. This feature is described in Chapter 3.
- **SQL*Plus** This option starts the SQL*Plus command-line SQL tool. You must select a database connection in the Connection Navigator before this menu item is enabled. If you have not defined the location of the SQL*Plus executable, a dialog will prompt you for the name and location. Then you enter (or browse to find) the name and path of SQL*Plus—usually in the ORACLE_HOME\bin directory file sqlplus.exe or sqlplusw.exe. If your directory names contain spaces, put the entire directory and file name string inside double quotes (for example, "C:\Program Files\oracle\bin\sqlplusw.exe" including the quotes). You can also define the SQL*Plus executable on the Database Connections page of the Preferences dialog.

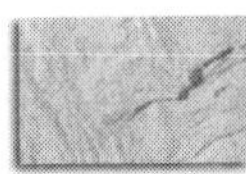

TIP

*You can also open SQL*Plus from the right-click menu on a specific Connections node.*

- **Show Dependencies** This item starts a utility that examines the parent and child classes to the file you have selected. The report of "Uses" and "Used by" appears in the Log window. This function is also available from the right-click menu on a Java class file in the navigator.
- **External Tools** This item allows you to add programs that are called for a selected file from the JDeveloper Tools menu, right-click menu, and IDE toolbar.
- **Embedded OC4J Server Preferences** This item opens the Embedded OC4J Server Preferences for <project> dialog where you manage the settings for the Oracle Containers for J2EE (OC4J) server that JDeveloper uses to run JSP and UIX files. This server is described further in Chapter 7. This dialog allows you to configure server properties so you can emulate a production OC4J server (which has full control over configuration settings).

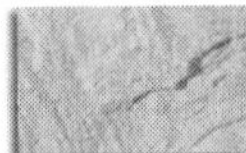

NOTE

In addition to using the External Tools feature to add items to the right-click menus, you can also add items to right-click menus and to the JDeveloper IDE menu using the Addin API. For more information, look in the "Working with Application Design Tools\Extending JDeveloper" node in the Contents page of the help system.

Window

The Window menu contains items for splitting and unsplitting documents and for creating and collapsing tab groups. Other items switch focus to one of the open windows so that you can activate a window that does not have focus. The "Go to" submenu contains options to navigate among the open windows or to create a list of files from which you can select. Use the Assign File Accelerator submenu to associate a shortcut (such as ALT-2) with the active window.

Help

Some items in the Help menu correspond to the tab pages in the Help window: Table of Contents, Index Search, and Full Text Search. The menu also contains an item that links to the Oracle Technology Network (OTN) website. Other items display the Release Notes, Welcome Page, and About dialog (for version information) as well as the Java API Javadoc, Tutorials, and Oracle Java Education topics. The Check for Updates item accesses the OTN website for new JDeveloper patches or add-ins.

The Help System

You start the JDeveloper help system by selecting from the Help menu (or pressing F1). The main help system interface appears in two windows: the Help window (in the navigator area) and a viewer for the help topic (in the editor window) as shown in Figure 2-5. Finding a topic in the help system is relatively easy for anyone who has used a modern help system such as those built using WinHelp or HTML Help. However, if the help engine is unfamiliar to you or if you are interested in some specific tips on how best to use it, it is worth spending some time reviewing some of its features. In addition, this book refers to help system topics, so a description of the help system structure will help you find the references quickly.

This help system was built using Oracle Help for Java. A benefit of this system is that it is platform independent, so the help system will work in any operating system that supports the JDeveloper IDE.

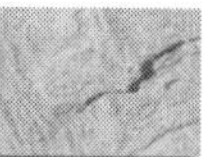

TIP

Oracle Help for Java has an open API and you can use it to create your own help system. The JDeveloper help system contains more information about Oracle Help for Java, starting at the table of contents node "Working with Application Design Tools\Extending JDeveloper\Developing Help With Oracle Help for Java."

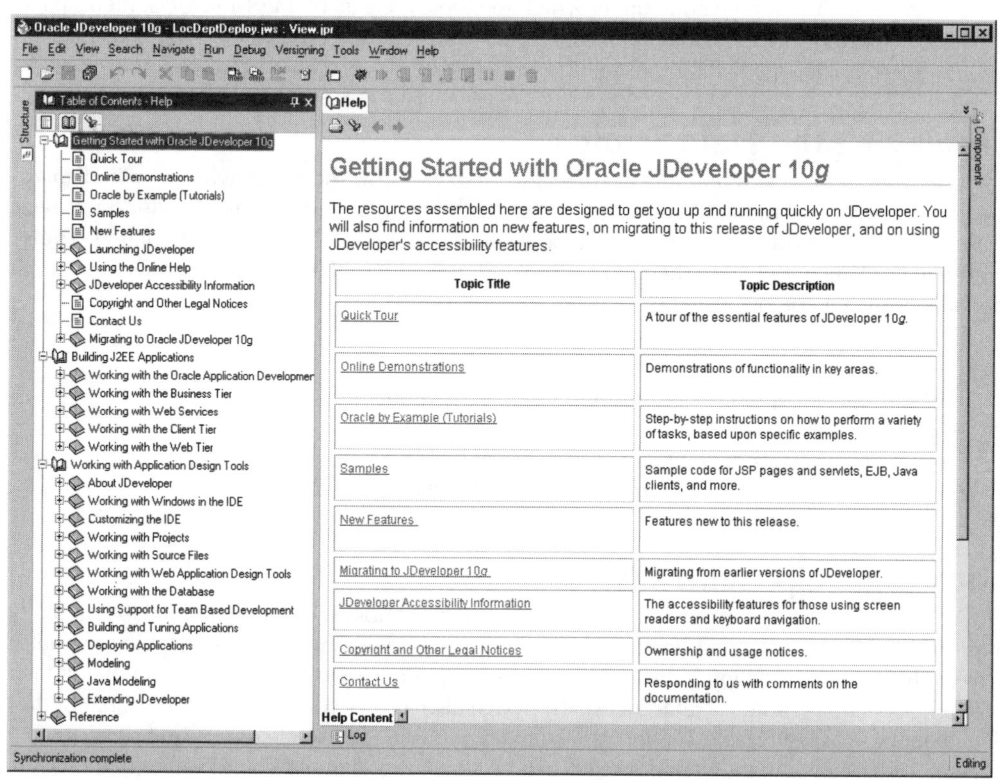

FIGURE 2-5. *Sample page from the help system*

Finding the Help Topic

In addition to the interface shown in Figure 2-5, the Help buttons in various wizards and dialogs in JDeveloper open the help system in a separate window that is attached to the dialog. You can view the help topic specific to the page you are viewing and then close the help topic window. You can also just move the help topic window to the side and continue to interact with the wizard or dialog, but the help topic window will close automatically when you exit the dialog.

Other than this context-specific help, you can find help topics using one of three pages, available as tabs in the Help window:

- **Table of Contents** This page displays a list of topics arranged hierarchically in books and in leaf nodes that represent topic pages.
- **Index Search** This page contains a list of keywords that are associated with one or more help topics. Typing the text navigates to a match in the keyword list.
- **Full Text Search** You can search for text strings in the entire help system using this page. When you click Search, the matching list of topics will appear in the list. The Source column displays the node under which the topic appears on the Table of Contents page. If you display a topic that has a source, you can return to the Table of Contents page, and the current page will be selected in the navigator.

Displaying the Help Topic

Once you find a topic and double click it in the Help window, the editor window will display the topic in read-only mode. If you want to display the help topic in a separate window, check the *Display in Window* checkbox in the Documentation page of the Preferences dialog (**Tools | Preferences**). When you close the help system and reopen it in the same JDeveloper session, the last open topic will be displayed or selected.

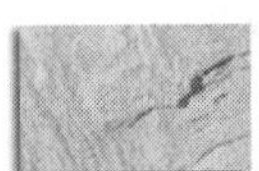

TIP
You can select text in the help system window (by dragging the mouse from left to right across the text), press CTRL-C *to copy, and press* CTRL-V *to paste the text into another editor. Line feeds and formatting will be removed but you will see all of the selected text.*

Locating Help Centrally

You can run the help system from a centralized server (for *hosted documentation*) so that the help files do not need to be loaded on each developer's hard drive. This requires installing the help files on the server and defining the location of the help files in the Documentation page of the Preferences dialog (**Tools | Preferences**). This page also allows you to define the source of the documentation as the Oracle Technology Network website (otn.oracle.com). Text searches in the hosted documentation environment can be slow, so weigh the convenience of this option with the need for developers to search for text using the Full Text Search tab.

Software Configuration Management

Developing software rarely involves one developer, a single application, and a one-time release. Typically, teams of developers produce many integrated applications with releases appearing regularly over time. A software configuration management system is designed to track and identify changes to development objects over time and to allow the developers to not only edit the latest version of a program, but also to go back to previous releases and work in parallel with a more current release.

JDeveloper addresses these requirements by providing access to source control systems such as Oracle Software Configuration Manager (Oracle SCM), Rational ClearCase, and Concurrent Versions System (CVS). You can also connect your own source control system to JDeveloper. More information is available in the help system node "Working with Application Design Tools\Using Support for Team Development\Using Source Control Support."

This section briefly explores the JDeveloper support for CVS, an open source version control solution (available at www.cvshome.org with a Windows version available at www.cvsnt.org). The concepts of other source control systems are similar, but other systems may have different steps and names for the operations as well as different details for how files are shared and maintained.

CVS Concepts

After you install the CVS client software, JDeveloper will allow you to connect to a server that is running the CVS server. You can then *import* (upload) into CVS a *module*, a predefined group of files that can correspond to a JDeveloper workspace with all of its files and directories. CVS stores files in the file system on a machine set up with the CVS server software. The module is the highest level of file organization in CVS. A CVS server connection can access multiple modules.

Once a module is set up in CVS, its files are available to other developers who have the CVS client. Others can *check out* the module to copy all files from that module to their local system. They can also add files to the module at any time. The CVS file *repository* will store all copies of the file throughout its lifecycle. These copies are called *versions* or *revisions* and are assigned an internal number. When you request an updated copy of a file, CVS returns the most recent version but all versions of a file are available.

Updating, Committing, and Concurrency Control

Once the files are copied locally, developers can make changes to the files and *commit* (save) them back to the CVS module using JDeveloper. Committing creates a new version in the CVS repository.

To obtain an updated version of a file from CVS, the developer *updates* the local copy of the file, which will download the current copy of the file to the developer's local machine. CVS maintains the internal version numbers for files so that changes one developer makes will not overwrite changes another developer makes.

For example, Developer 1 and Developer 2 update their copy of a file to download version 1.3 of the file to their local system. Developer 1 then makes a change and commits the file to CVS. The file version is incremented (in this example, to 1.4). Then Developer 2 makes a change to the 1.3 version of the file and tries to commit it to CVS. CVS will recognize that Developer 2's file was a change from 1.3, not from the current version (1.4), and will signal that the copy Developer 2 is committing is not up-to-date. Developer 2 then updates the local copy from CVS, which will merge the changes made by Developer 1 with the changes made by Developer 2. The merged lines will be marked in the source file so that Developer 2 can synchronize the changes before committing the final version.

Tags

JDeveloper also offers CVS support for *tags,* labels that you apply to a set of files at a particular moment. Other source control systems call these file sets "configurations." This is useful when you have a production release of an application that then requires enhancement. The files you are deploying to a production environment have all been tested and work together. As you move forward with the lifecycle of the files through enhancement and bug fix stages, you want to be able to recall the complete set of files in their production versions. You can add a common tag (short word or phrase) to a set of file versions and manipulate the set of files using that tag. The **Versioning | Sticky** submenu contains a Tag item that you can use to mark a number of files in this way.

Version History and Version Compare

When you have source control enabled, the JDeveloper editor window contains a History tab that allows you to view the version numbers, dates, and comments added to the versions of the file in the CVS repository. Double clicking any version file will open it in read-only mode in a new editor window.

The right-click menu on a particular file version in the History tab offers a Compare With submenu with items for different files you can compare. For example, you can compare one version of a file with another version of that file (or with another file on disk). After you select the file to be compared, the comparison window will display the differences.

Overlay Icons

By default, JDeveloper displays *overlay icons* that indicate the status of the file; the overlay icons appear in the navigator next to each file that is associated with CVS. Some of the icons are shown here:

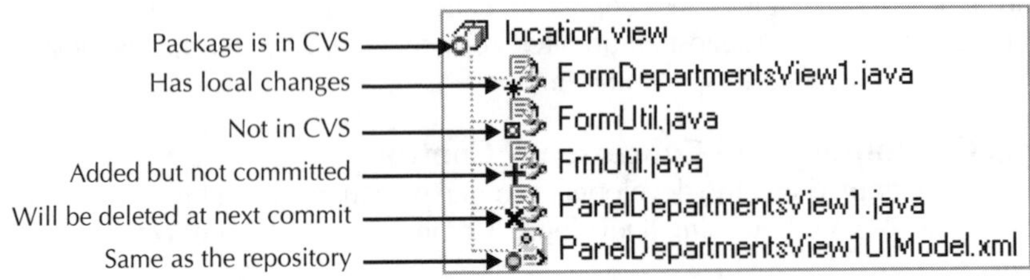

You can turn off the icon display by unchecking the *Use State Overlay Icons* checkbox in the CVS page of the Preferences dialog.

Hands-on Practice: Set Up CVS Locally

Before deciding upon CVS as the environment for your team, you might want to try out CVS locally to get a taste for how it works. This hands-on practice demonstrates a method for installing, configuring, and using a CVS server on a local machine. Of course, in a real team-development scenario, you would place the CVS repository on a network machine with an automatic file backup system to ensure that no work is lost. As with all other examples in the book, this hands-on practice assumes you are working with a Windows operating system.

This practice contains the following phases:

I. Install and set up the CVS server
II. Set up a CVS server connection
III. Import and check out a module

I. Install and Set Up the CVS Server

CVS is an open source project and requires no license. You can download the server software (for example, cvsnt_1.11.1.3.exe) from www.cvshome.org or www.cvsnt.org (for Windows only). After you obtain the installation software, use the following abbreviated steps to install it. Click the Help button in any dialog and use the JDeveloper help system node mentioned before if you need more information about a particular operation.

1. Run the .exe install file and accept all defaults.
2. Check your PATH environment variable to be sure that the installer added the CVS directory to the PATH. If it was not added to the PATH variable, add it at this stage and restart Windows.
3. Select **Programs | CVS for NT | Configure server** from the Windows Start menu. This will start the CVSNT dialog.
4. Click the Repositories tab and click the Add button to add a repository (the container for all files and directories).
5. In the path dialog enter the directory name where you want to store the CVS repository files, such as "c:/handson" (notice the use of "/" instead of "\"). Click OK. If you receive an error, try creating the directory first or follow any instructions in the error dialog. The dialog should appear as follows:

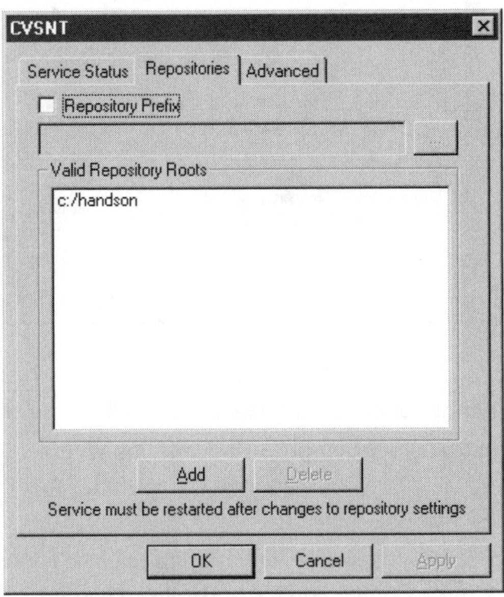

6. Click OK to dismiss the CVSNT dialog.

What Just Happened? You installed the CVS server software. As mentioned, in a multi-developer situation, you would locate the CVS server on a machine that was accessible by the entire team.

II. Set Up a CVS Server Connection

If you had not installed the server, you would need to install the client software before proceeding. This phase sets up a connection from JDeveloper to the CVS server.

1. By default, source control is not active in JDeveloper. You enable this feature using **Versioning | Select System**, which displays the Preferences dialog (also available using **Tools | Preferences**) as shown here:

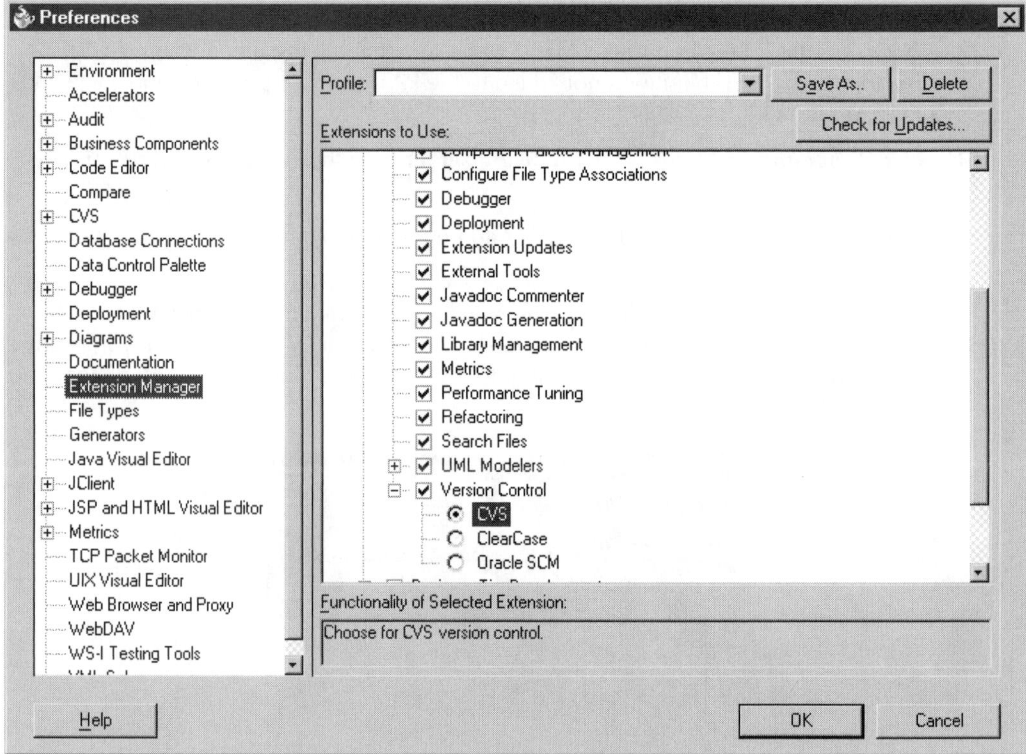

2. Select the CVS radio button and be sure the Version Control checkbox is checked. After you click OK, a number of items will be enabled in the Versioning menu.

   Additional Information: JDeveloper will determine whether a source control system is already installed. If a source control system is installed, the proper radio button will be selected in the Preferences dialog.

3. In the Connection Navigator, select New from the right-click menu on the CVS Server node to display the CVS Connection Wizard. Click Next if the Welcome page appears.

4. Enter a name for the connection and click Next. Set the *Access Method* to "Local" and the *Repository Path* to "c:/handson" or whatever you defined as the repository directory name in the last phase. Click Next.
5. Examine, but do not change, the CVSROOT string and click Next.
6. Click Test Connection. If you receive an error, return to the previous pages and check your settings.
7. Click Finish when the connection tests successfully.

What Just Happened? You set up JDeveloper for the CVS software and created a CVS server connection so that you can connect to the CVS repository.

III. Import and Check Out a Module

To proceed with the test, you need a JDeveloper application workspace with at least one project and one file. If you do not have a workspace open in JDeveloper, create one with a single file. Alternatively, you can use a workspace from any hands-on practice in this book. This phase creates a module in the CVS repository and then checks out that module.

1. Select the workspace node in the navigator. Select **Versioning | Import Module**. Click Next if the Welcome page appears in the Import to CVS dialog.
2. Ensure that the *Connection Name* is correct and enter a module name (the workspace name will be filled in by default, and you can use that as the module name). Click Next.
3. On the Tags page, click Next.
4. On the Sources page, the workspace directory should be displayed. This is correct for this example, so click Next.
5. On the Filters page, click Next. On the Common Operations page, click Next. These are more advanced options that you may want to explore later. Click Help on any of the wizard pages for a brief description of the options on the page.
6. On the Options page, be sure the *Perform Module Checkout* checkbox is checked.

   Additional Information: If this checkbox were unchecked, you would need to check out the module later (using **Versioning | Check Out Module**). Developers who access the CVS files will need to check out the module, but for the purposes of this test, you can take this shortcut.
7. Click Finish. The Log window will display the progress of the import and the CVS commands that are being used.

What Just Happened? You added a module to CVS and checked out the module. You can now explore CVS on your own. For example, change a file in the module and try committing it. Open another copy of JDeveloper, add the workspace to the navigator, make a change to a file and commit it, and then return to the first copy of JDeveloper, make a change and try committing that file. You can experiment with variations on team development and tags using this setup.

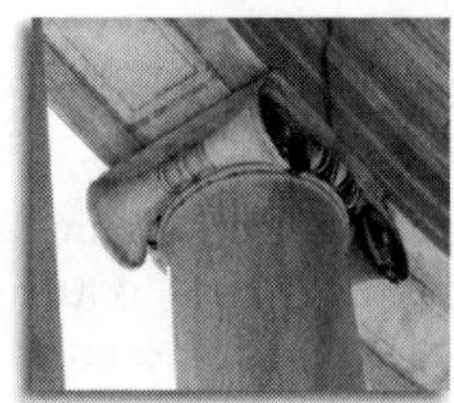

CHAPTER 3

IDE Tools

Intelligence … is the faculty of making artificial objects, especially tools to make tools.

—Henri Bergson (1859–1941),
L'Evolution Créatrice (Creative Evolution)

he preceding chapter provided an overview of the JDeveloper Integrated Development Environment (IDE). Since all JDeveloper tools appear within the IDE windows and you use the main menu and main toolbar to interact with files, the information in Chapter 2 serves as a solid foundation for understanding the best way to work with the tools.

This chapter builds upon the foundation from Chapter 2 by explaining details about the main JDeveloper tools that you use to create, view, and edit code. It introduces the major development features of the tools as they appear in the IDE. It addresses the subject differently than the JDeveloper help system, which is focused mostly on explaining one feature at a time. However, further details about the features mentioned in this chapter as well as features not explained in this chapter are supplied in the help system. The following main development tools and concepts are introduced in this chapter:

- Navigators
- Structure window
- Component Palette
- Property Inspector
- Log window
- Code Editor
- Debugger
- Visual editors
- HTML and UIX previewers
- New Gallery
- Data Control Palette
- Other editors
- Viewer windows
- SQL Worksheet
- Modelers and diagrammers

Exploring these tools will help you prepare for development work. You will experience the JDeveloper IDE features and concepts discussed in this chapter by following the hands-on practices throughout this book.

Navigators

The navigator is a standard interface tool in most IDEs. A *navigator* is a window that offers the user a hierarchical view of a group of objects as a series of indented nodes. This is a familiar interface style and needs little explanation because it is used by many other non-development tools, such as Windows Explorer. JDeveloper uses this interface style for two file navigators, the Application Navigator and System Navigator, and for the Connection Navigator.

Application Navigator and System Navigator

This release of JDeveloper offers two navigators that you can use to browse and interact with files—the Application Navigator and the System Navigator. (Since both navigators display files and the navigator you use is a personal preference, this chapter refers to both file navigators generically as "the navigator.") The Application Navigator and System Navigator appear, by default, in the dockable window in the top-left corner of the IDE. Since they share the same area, you switch between them by clicking the appropriate tab.

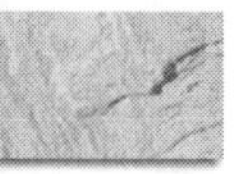

TIP
If a particular navigator is not visible, you can display it using the View menu.

Most work in JDeveloper starts in the *Application Navigator,* because this window is where you create, view, and interact with application workspaces, projects, files, and other components. As mentioned in Chapter 1, this navigator shows a view of the files you are working on using categories that are more logical than physical. For example, it shows all files that make up an Application Development Framework (ADF) business component entity object as one node. This type of view makes it easier to see the structure of the application but still have access to details about its component files.

The *System Navigator* offers a different view of the same files in a structure that more closely represents the file system. Figure 3-1 shows a view in both navigators of an ADF Business Components (ADF BC) project. You will notice that the Application Navigator summarizes some of the nodes (such as the Departments entity object node). You can still navigate to the files in this view using the right-click menu (for some nodes) or the Structure window list of the files comprising the component.

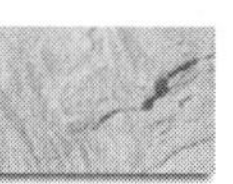

TIP
You can view more than one workspace in either navigator.

You can expand and collapse nodes as in any navigator. Both navigators show the same workspaces (collections of projects), which are termed "application workspaces" in the Application Navigator; and projects (collections of files). Nodes and files are distinguished by icons based on the file or node type. Both navigators use the same icons for the same nodes. If you hold the mouse cursor over the icon, a tooltip will pop up indicating the object type or file name, as shown here:

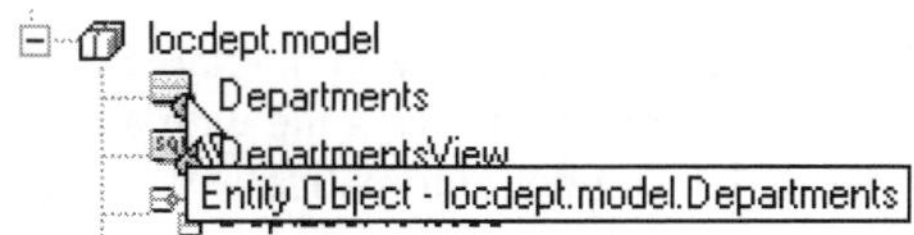

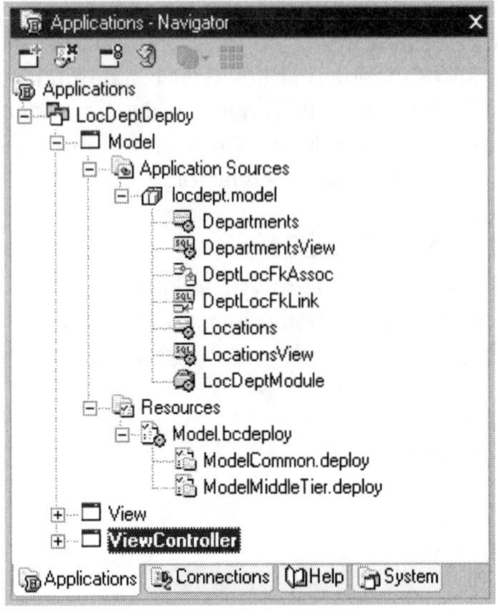

Application Navigator

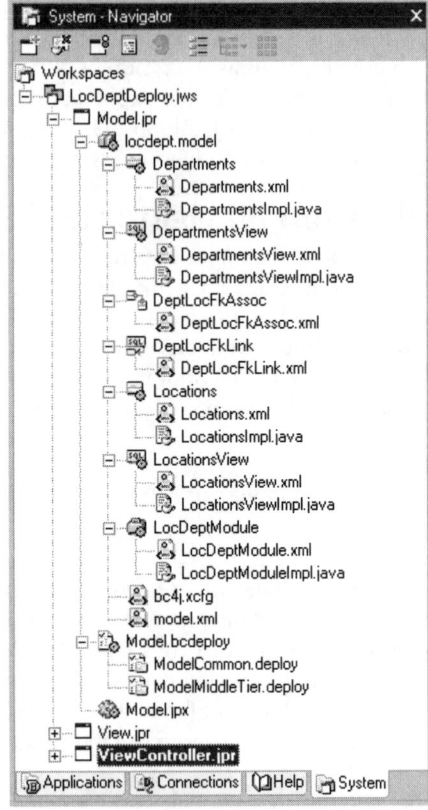

System Navigator

FIGURE 3-1. *JDeveloper file navigators*

The file name also appears in the IDE status bar when you select the file in the navigator.

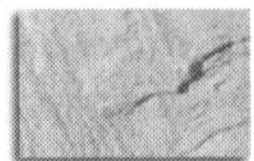

TIP
To load a file into JDeveloper temporarily (for example, just to view it), select ***File | Open*** *and uncheck the "Add to project" checkbox in the file open dialog. After you select the file and click Open, the file will be loaded into the editor without appearing under a project.*

Changed File Indicator

A modified or unsaved file is indicated by an italicized file name in the navigators and on the document tab in the editor window. When you save a file with an italicized name, JDeveloper removes the italics from the name. JDeveloper automatically saves files before compiling, so a name that was italicized may not be italicized after compiling. This behavior is controlled by the *Save Before Compiling* property on the Environment page of the Preferences dialog (**Tools | Preferences**).

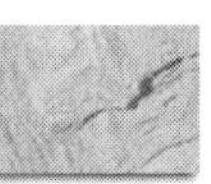

TIP
You can watch the italicization of file names when making a change to see which files are affected by an operation. The project file is sometimes italicized when you open its node even if no changes have been made because the project file saves information about the open navigator nodes as well as the names of the files.

Adding and Removing Files

You can use the "Add to" button in the navigator toolbar to load a file into a project or a project into an application workspace. The "Remove from" button hides the file from the navigator nodes. Removing a file from the IDE does not delete the file from the file system. A menu selection, **File | Erase from Disk**, deletes a file from the file system.

CAUTION
If you select Erase from Disk for an application workspace or project that has a dedicated directory, JDeveloper will remove the workspace or project file but not the directory or files in the directory. It is a good practice to manually remove the related directories after removing the workspace or project. This will prevent surprises from forgotten code later on.

Editing Items

Double clicking an item in any of the navigators opens it in the appropriate tool; for example, if you double click a .java file, the file will open in the Code Editor. If the item is a graphics file (such as a .gif or .jpg), the Image Viewer will display the file in read-only mode. If the item is a project file, the Project Properties dialog will be displayed.

You can also open a file by dragging it from a navigator (or from Windows Explorer) to the editor window.

Searching for Objects in the Navigators

If you need to search for a specific item in the navigator, click somewhere in the navigator and start typing the name of the item. The cursor will jump to the first occurrence of that name if the node that contains that item has already been opened. Press DOWN ARROW to find the next occurrence of the name in an expanded node. Press ESC or click in another window to exit search mode.

NOTE
*You can also search anywhere in the file system for files containing a text string by using the "**Search | Find in Files**" feature described in the section in Chapter 2 that covers the Search menu.*

Modifying the Display

When a project is selected, clicking the Show Categories button in the System Navigator toolbar toggles the display between a list of files and a list of file types. When you expand these categories, additional categories and files will appear. The categories allow you to easily find a file of a certain type and are useful if the project contains a large number of files.

You can modify the way files are displayed in these two navigators using other toolbar buttons, such as Package List (which switches between Directory Tree, File List, Package List, and Package Tree), Show All Files, and Sort By Type. Many of these items are also available in the **View | Options** menu. The buttons are context sensitive and are active only when an applicable node is selected.

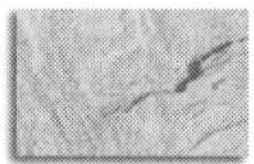

TIP
The navigator toolbar also has a Project Properties button. Clicking this button opens the Project Properties dialog for the project of the selected file. Using this button could save you a little time because it is not necessary to click the project node first as you must with the Tools menu and right-click menu methods of opening this dialog.

Connection Navigator

The Connection Navigator also appears, by default, in the same window as the file navigators. It contains a number of nodes as shown on the right:

These nodes allow you to create and edit definitions to the following external sources:

- **Application Server** This node lists the middle-tier servers that you use for Java services. You can define Oracle9*i*AS Containers for J2EE (OC4J), BEA WebLogic, Tomcat, or JBoss servers into which you can automatically deploy using the JDeveloper IDE. Deployment from JDeveloper to OC4J using an application server connection is discussed in Chapter 7.
- **CVS Server (or Oracle SCM)** Depending upon the type of software configuration management (SCM) code control you define, one of these two server names will appear. This node provides a connection to the SCM repository for file versioning, parallel development, and central storage of all JDeveloper code. You can also use ClearCase as a version control option, but it will not appear in the Connection Navigator. This feature is described further in the section "Software Configuration Management" in Chapter 2.
- **Database** You can define database connections using this node. Each connection uses a single database user's schema and allows you to browse the objects that the user owns or has access to. (The sidebar "About Database Connections" further explains which objects appear in this node.) When you are defining data access using ADF BC, you can select any object to which the user has been granted access, regardless of owner.

- **Designer Workarea** This connection type represents a link to an Oracle Designer repository. You can create ADF Business Components from Designer module, module component, and table definitions using this connection.
- **SOAP Server** This node allows you to define connections to Simple Object Access Protocol (SOAP) servers. *SOAP* is an XML-based protocol that accesses applications that have been set up as web services. You can define a connection to a SOAP server in this node so that JDeveloper can easily access the web service.
- **UDDI Registry** This node allows you to define a Universal Description, Discovery, and Integration (UDDI) connection that provides a location for lists of web services that you can use in your applications.
- **WebDAV Server** This node defines connections to Web-based Distributed Authoring and Versioning (WebDAV) servers that allow access to files stored on web servers. After you define the connection, you can use JDeveloper to open, edit, and save the files on these servers.

All connections can be created, tested, and edited using the right-click menu options on the Connections and specific server nodes. You can also open and close connections using the right-click menu options on a specific server name. Expanding the navigator node for the specific server name will also open the connection.

Run Manager

When you run a file such as a JSP page, a Run Manager tab appears in the navigator area. You can also display the Run Manager window by selecting **View | Run Manager**. The Run Manager is a separate window that displays the running process so that you can track the active processes. You can also terminate the process in the Run Manager window using the right-click menu option Terminate.

About Database Connections

By default, the Database connections node does not display objects in other schemas that are granted to the connection user. However, you can select Apply Filter from the right-click menu on a database connection node to display the Filter Schemas dialog. This dialog allows you to select which schemas the connection node will display. The user defined in the database connection's properties will only be able to view objects in other schemas that have been granted to that user or to PUBLIC.

You can also select Apply Filter from the right-click menu on a schema node under the connection node and define which object types will appear in the list (for example, Tables and Views only).

If you want to view public synonyms, select Apply Filters on the Synonyms node under any schema. After checking the *Show Public Synonyms* checkbox and clicking OK, you will be able to see all public synonyms (except public synonyms for sequences). However, you will not be able to view the object for which the synonym is defined.

Structure Window

The Structure window is a dockable window that appears by default in the bottom-left corner of the IDE. It is a type of navigator that displays a detailed view of the objects within or properties of the selected file or node. If an editor window has *focus* (is the window where the cursor is active), the Structure window displays the objects within the file in the active editor. The form that this view takes depends upon the selected file type and the editor that has focus. The following examples demonstrate some of the different displays for files and editors:

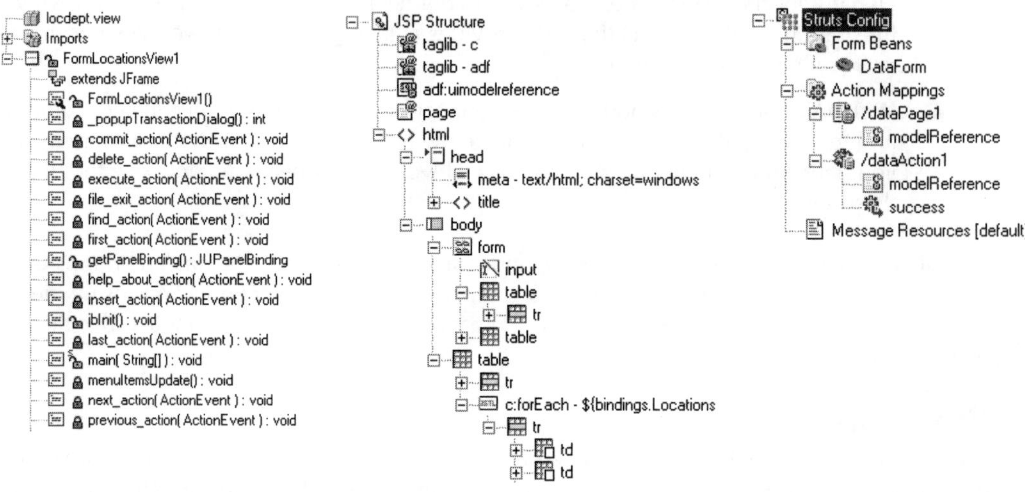

File type	Java application	JSP file	Struts configuration file
Editor	Code Editor	JSP/HTML Visual Editor	Struts Page Flow Diagram

When a Java application is open in the Code Editor, the Structure window displays details of the class, such as the imports, methods, superclass, and properties. When you are using the JSP/HTML Visual Editor to edit a JavaServer Pages (JSP) file, the Structure window displays a hierarchy of the HTML and JSP tags with their attributes. The Structure window for a Struts configuration file displays the hierarchy of tags in the XML document customized to the objects you would find in this file type. The Structure window for a database connection will display details about the connection such as the Type, Driver, User, and URL.

Structure Window Icons

As in the navigators, icons in the Structure window identify the type of object. For example, the following shows an excerpt from the Structure window display of a Java application:

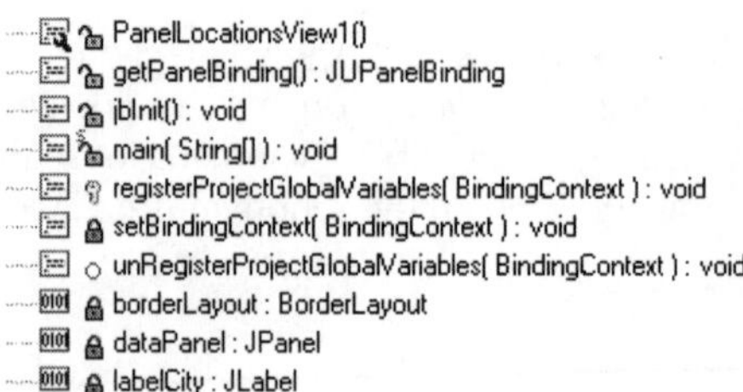

The icons on the left of each line indicate the type of code element; for example, PaneLocationsView1() is a constructor; jbInit()is a method; and borderLayout is a field. The icons next to the type icons indicate the access modifier. For example, jbInit() is public; registerProjectGlobalVariables() is protected; setBindingContext() is private; and unRegisterProjectGlobalVariables() has a default modifier. The "S" symbol added to the main() method modifier indicates that main() is a static method.

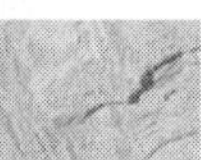

TIP
*You can open additional Structure windows by clicking the window title bar and selecting **View | Options | New View** in the menu. This feature is handy if you want to have more than one tab open at the same time, or if you need to freeze one structure view and compare it with the structure view for a different object. You can also use this technique for the System Navigator and Connection Navigator after you have selected a node that you would like to have as a root node in the new window.*

Other Structure Window Operations

The right-click menu in the Structure window offers rudimentary editing for some types of files. For example, the right-click menu in the Structure window for a JSP file allows you to cut, copy, paste, delete, and insert HTML/JSP. When you double click a node in the Structure window, the applicable editor will open if it is not already open, and the focus will be placed on the selected object or section of code. For example, double clicking an import node in the Structure window for a Java application file will open the Code Editor for that file and select the import statement. You can use the Structure window in this way as a table of contents to navigate through a large file.

If you are editing a file in the Code Editor, the Structure window will also show syntax errors such as mismatched tags and mismatched curly brackets. The errors are displayed as you move the cursor in the editor and do not require a compilation step. The following example shows how errors made while editing will be displayed in the Structure window:

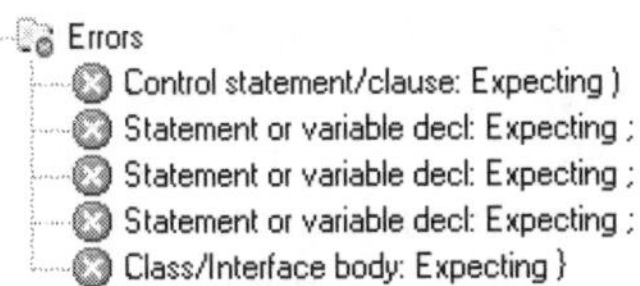

Double clicking an error opens the editor to the problem code line.

TIP
The Structure window toolbar for a Java file contains buttons to help sort or filter the display. You can use the "Sort by" button for ordering the contents. Other buttons allow you to hide or display methods, fields, static members, and public members.

Structure Window Views

The Structure window shows nodes appropriate to the active editor window. For example, if the Code Editor is active in the editor window, the Structure window will display nodes representing code elements, such as imports, methods, and variables. If a visual editor is active, the Structure window shows the visual element hierarchy (for example, the container hierarchy for a Java application file). These different Structure window views of the same file appear in different tabs and you can switch back and forth between them regardless of the active editor.

TIP
Normally, the Structure window displays details about the object selected in an editor or navigator. If you want to edit or navigate to other files but keep the view in the Structure window unchanged, click the Freeze View (red pin) icon in the Structure window toolbar. Click the button again to unfreeze the view.

Component Palette

The Component Palette window contains components you use in the visual editors for various styles of code such as Java client, JSP files, HTML files, or UIX files. You can switch between pages by selecting the page from a pulldown at the top of the Component Palette window. The pages that are available at any given time are based on the file that is active in the editor window.

The Component Palette contents change depending upon the file that is being edited. For example, if the cursor is in the Java Visual Editor for a Java application, the Component Palette contains applicable controls from the Swing and AWT libraries. If the cursor is in the Code Editor for a JSP file, the Component Palette contains applicable controls from the various JSP tag libraries supplied with JDeveloper. If a modeler is active, the Component Palette contains diagram components.

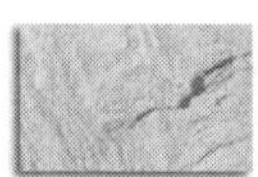

TIP
If you press SHIFT *before clicking an element in the Component Palette, the element will remain selected so that you can add more than one instance of the same element without reselecting the element. Click the Select (arrow) icon to release this selection.*

The tooltips for the icons in the Component Palette contain the library information for the class name (such as javax.swing) as well as the class name (such as JButton). By default, the palette shows an icon and a text label for each control, but you can hide the text label for each icon by selecting Icon View from the right-click menu on the Component Palette.

You can add to and modify the contents of these pages using Configure Component Palette dialog (**Tools | Configure Palette** or on the Component Palette, select Properties from the right-click menu on any control). A hands-on practice in Chapter 15 demonstrates how to add to the Component Panel.

NOTE
You cannot add to Component Palette pages for diagrams as you can to the other pages.

Code Snippets

The Component Palette contains a page called Code Snippets, which you can use to store frequently used blocks of code. The Code Snippets page is different for Java client applications (Java applications and applets) and for web client applications (JSP pages, HTML, and UIX). You can use selections from the right-click menu in the Code Snippets page of the Component Palette to add, edit, or remove snippets. Snippets are available to all projects. When you click a snippet icon in the Component Palette, the code stored in the snippet is added at the cursor location in the Code Editor.

TIP
You can also use Code Templates to quickly add frequently used code to the file you are editing. This feature is described in the "Code Templates" section later in this chapter.

Property Inspector

The Property Inspector window is automatically displayed when a visual editor is displayed. For Java client controls, this window contains two tabs—Properties and Events. For HTML, JSP, and UIX files, the window contains only the Properties tab.

Properties

The Properties tab shows a list of properties for the component that is selected in the visual editor or the Structure window. Selecting a property displays a description of that property in the lower pane of the Property Inspector window (if one is available for that property). When you modify the property value of a component, the code will be changed to reflect the new value.

The properties and events in these tabs appear in alphabetical order, but you can click the Categories button in the Property Inspector toolbar to order the properties by types (such as General and Visual). To set a property value, first click the property name; then type in a value, select from the pulldown, or click the ellipsis button for more options, as appropriate to the property. The toolbar for the Property Inspector changes based on the type of component it represents.

CAUTION
Press ENTER *or click another property to make the change on a property permanent. Clicking in another window may not record the change.*

Customizers and Property Editors

The standard editing interfaces in the Property Inspector, such as pulldown lists and text fields, are usually sufficient to handle property editing. However, if you would like a different interface for certain properties that you use often, you can create "customizers" for JavaBeans that handle a number of properties in a single dialog. You can define a customizer that works like a wizard or like a dialog with a set of properties. You can then access it by clicking the Customizer button in the Property Inspector.

You can also define your own "property editors" for editing individual properties in the Property Inspector. The help system contains further information about customizers and property editors ("Building J2EE Applications\Working with the Client Tier\Developing JavaBeans\JavaBeans Concepts").

Properties for Java Client Controls

The toolbar for the Properties tab for Java client controls, shown next, contains some of the same buttons as the navigators, such as Freeze View and New View.

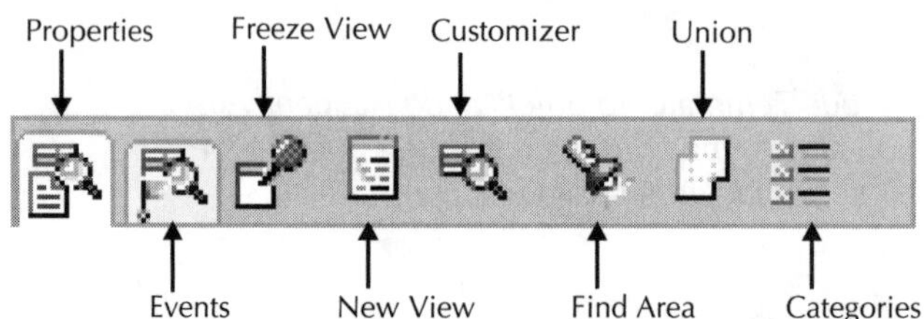

It also contains a Find Area button that opens a search field you can use to find a property by its name. If a property customizer is defined for a property, the Customizer button will be enabled.

You can group objects together in a visual editor using SHIFT-click and CTRL-click and examine the common properties of the group. Properties with different values will be displayed with the values italicized. You can modify simple (single-valued) properties of those objects as a group, and the modification will be applied to all objects in the group. If you need to see all properties for all grouped components, click the Union button.

Properties for Web Client Controls

The Property Inspector toolbar for web client controls (HTML, JSP, and UIX files), shown next, offers several additional features.

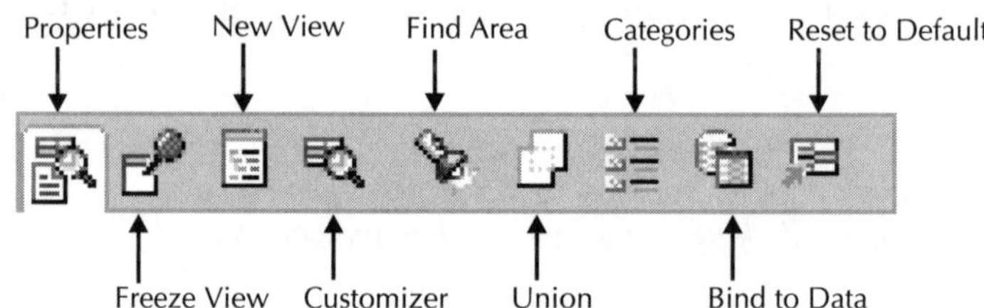

When you override a default property, a green square will appear to the left of the property name. To return the value to the default, select the property and click the Reset to Default button. You can convert a value in a property to a data-binding value by clicking the Bind to Data button. For example, you type the following in the *value* property of an item:

```
bindings.LocationId
```

After you click the Bind to Data button, the value changes to this expression language syntax:

```
${bindings.LocationId}
```

If the value is already in expression language such as the preceding code, the button will be called "Remove data binding." Clicking the button will remove the expression language syntax.

The Property Inspector for web components will also display links appropriate to the component over the property description pane as shown in the following Property Inspector window for an HTML table data cell:

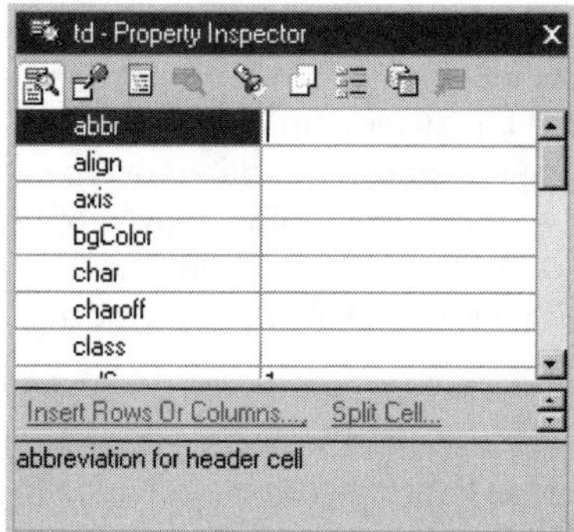

The links allow you quick access to actions for adding rows and splitting cells.

Events

The Events tab displays a list of JavaBean events for the component that is selected in the Structure window or the Java Visual Editor. You can add code to handle any event in this tab by typing an event name as the value for an event in the list and pressing ENTER. A code stub for the new event handler will be added in the source code. Instead of typing a name, you can click the "..." button in the event's value field. A dialog such as the following will open, allowing you to rename the event handler and showing the code stub that will be created:

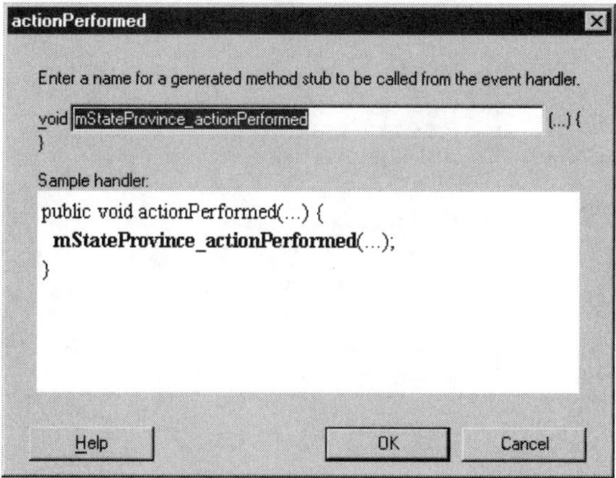

TIP

If you just want to create standard `actionPerformed` *event code, double click the component in the visual editor. This will insert a code stub and open the Code Editor to that stub. This is faster than any other method for creating the event code stub.*

Log Window

The Log window shows messages that are generated when you run, debug, or compile your code. If the message is an error, you can double click the error text, and the problem code will be highlighted in the Code Editor. This gives you a quick way to navigate to the problem area. The right-click menu in the Log window allows you to select and save the text into a file for later use. The messages are color-coded for easier reading.

The Log window area opens new windows for different types of activities. For example, generating Javadoc opens a new window. Compiling a Java application uses the window to present messages and errors. All of these windows appear as tabs in the Log window area and will move with the Log window if you undock it. You can close and clear them separately using options from the right-click menu.

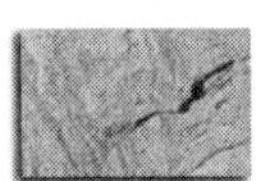

TIP

As described in Chapter 2 for the Javadoc comments, some log windows will provide links that lead to appropriate actions.

Code Editor

The Code Editor is a full-featured text editing area for all code files; it appears in the editor window. You open the Code Editor by double clicking any code file in the navigator or by selecting Open from the right-click menu for a file node.

Characteristics such as fonts, syntax colors, undo behavior, and tab size are customizable using selections from the Preferences dialog (**Tools | Preferences**) as shown in Figure 3-2.

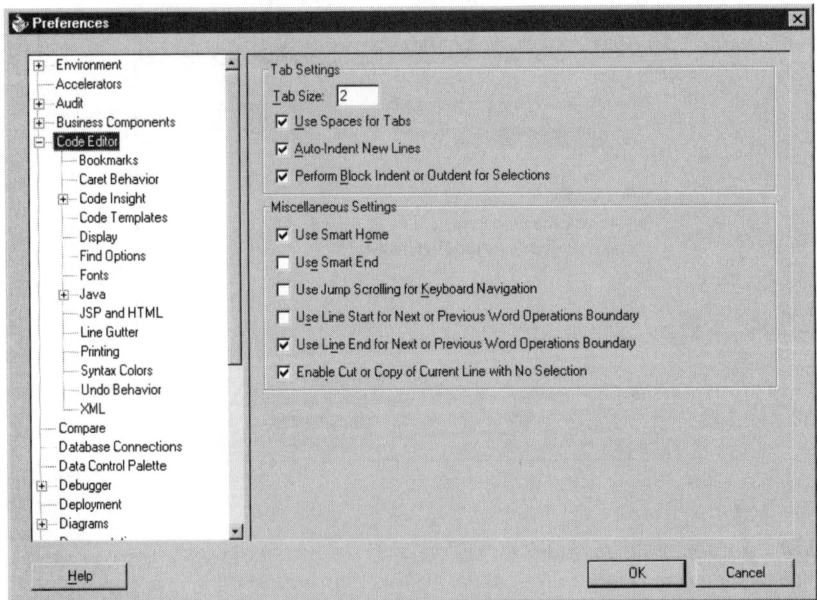

FIGURE 3-2. *Preferences dialog page for the Code Editor*

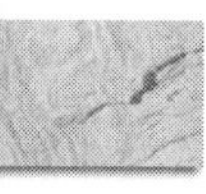

TIP
Use the "Preferred Open Brace Style" preference on the Code Editor\Java page of the Preferences dialog to set whether the opening curly bracket is entered on the same line or on a new line.

The Code Editor may be used to edit text files of various types such as Java, HTML, JSP, and UIX in similar ways. The Component Palette, Code Insight, syntax colors, and automatic completion features are specific to the file type.

The Code Editor uses standard Windows shortcut keys such as CTRL-C for Copy and CTRL-V for Paste. Search for "keymaps, list of available" in the Index Search tab of the help system to find the supplied key mappings. You can customize these keymaps if needed.

You can drag and drop selected text in the Code Editor by highlighting it with the mouse and dragging and dropping it into the new location. The right-click menu contains actions that you would use frequently (for example, Cut, Copy, Paste, and Undo). The right-click menu also contains a submenu for sorting import statements in a Java class file. For class files with many import statements, this can help make the code more readable.

Many of the Source menu items discussed in Chapter 2 are also available from the right-click menu in the Code Editor.

TIP
The file name and path of the file open in the editor are shown in the window title bar. You will also see the file name and path in the IDE status bar when you click the file node in a navigator. In addition, a tooltip containing the file name will appear when you hold the mouse above a file node in a navigator or above a document tab.

End Tag Completion

The *End Tag Completion* feature adds an ending tag for tag language files such as HTML, JSP page, and UIX. The editor determines the file type (by the file extension) and applies this behavior. For example, when you edit an HTML or JSP file in the Code Editor, the editor fills in ending tags (for example, for a starting tag such as "`<table>`") as you type the start of the ending tags. For example, after typing "</" that follows a table tag, the editor will fill the ending tag in as "</table>".

For XML files, the ending tag is filled in after you complete typing the starting tag. This behavior is defined on the Preferences dialog's "Code Editor\HTML and JSP" page.

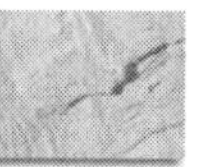

NOTE
Syntax highlighting is available for various types of files. You can modify the colors in the Preferences page "Code Editor\Syntax Colors."

Code Templates

The Code Template feature of the editor allows you to create shortcut text strings that can trigger a block of code to be entered automatically. For example, typing "for" in the Code Editor for a Java file and pressing CTRL-ENTER (using the default keymap) will replace "for" with the following code block:

```
for ( ; ; )
{

}
```

The word "for" is a shortcut for the code block *template* that was entered into the editor. The keypress CTRL-ENTER is called CodeTemplate.EXPAND in the keymap lists available in the help system (search for "keymap" in the index) and modified in the Accelerators page of the Preferences dialog. This keypress activates the shortcut and transforms it into the code template text. You can view, define, and modify shortcuts in the Preferences dialog (**Tools | Preferences**) Code Editor\Code Templates page as shown here:

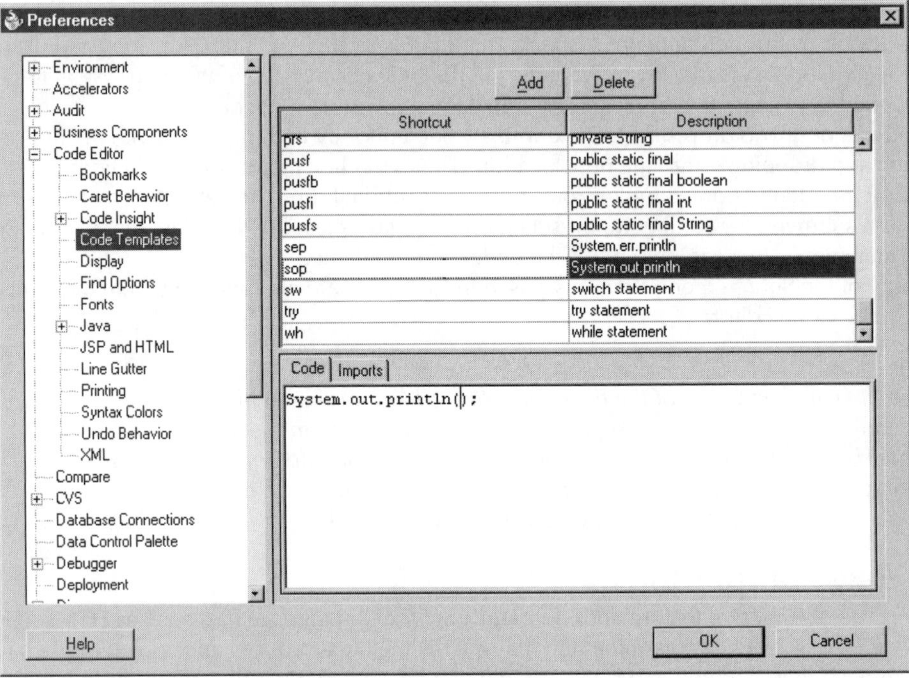

In addition to defining text blocks that will be inserted into the code, you can define import statements that will appear in the imports section. The Imports tab in the Code Editor\Code Templates page allows you to specify the import statements that will be inserted with the code in the Code tab. If your code already contains import statements for the parent package, the import code will not be inserted.

TIP

You can add an external editor using the ***Tools | External Tools*** *dialog, which allows you to save a file in JDeveloper and edit that file with another editor. When you save the file and return to JDeveloper, you can reload that file automatically (with or without a confirmation dialog) based upon settings on the Environment page of the Preferences dialog.*

Code Insight and Tag Insight

JDeveloper offers another feature to help you write code for Java, JSP, PL/SQL, HTML, UIX, and schema-based XML source files. This feature, called *Code Insight* (for Java and PL/SQL) or *Tag*

Insight (for tag languages), pops up context-sensitive lists of elements that are appropriate to the type of file you are editing in the context of the code you are typing. For example, for Java class files, Code Insight presents lists of methods, constants, imports, and method parameters. The list appears after you type a period and pause or press CTRL-SPACEBAR (in the default keymap). An example of a Code Insight list for a Java class file is shown here:

System.out.p

print(Object)	void
print(String)	void
print(int)	void
print(char[])	void
print(boolean)	void
print(float)	void
print(char)	void
print(double)	void

You can select from the list and press ENTER to enter the selected text. Alternatively, you can keep typing and navigate to a match in the list. Clicking outside the pulldown list (or pressing ESC) will dismiss the list. This style of Code Insight is called *completion insight* because it assists you in completing code that you are writing.

Another style of Code Insight, called *parameter insight,* presents a list of valid arguments for a method after you type an opening parenthesis "(" as shown here:

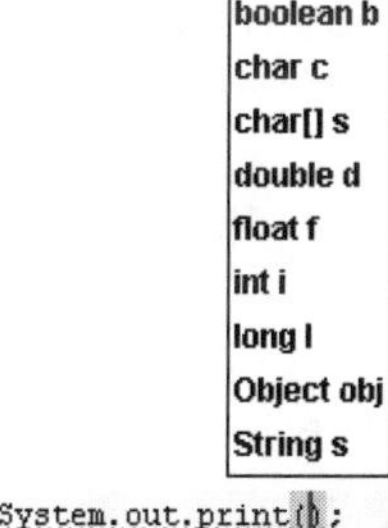

You do not select from this list but use it as a reminder of the types of objects or variables that can act as parameters to the method. This list will automatically appear when you type an opening parenthesis or if you press CTRL-SHIFT-SPACEBAR. Insight for tag languages works in a similar way.

Use the Code Editor\Code Insight page of the Preferences dialog to modify the time delay before Insight appears or to turn the feature off and on. Regardless of the settings in this dialog, Code Insight will appear if you press the appropriate key combinations (CTRL-SPACEBAR or CTRL-SHIFT-SPACEBAR).

CAUTION

The classes you want to provide Insight must be defined in the CLASSPATH of the project's settings. (The CLASSPATH is discussed further in Chapter 5.) You also need to compile your code if you want Code Insight to find its members. In addition, this feature may not work if the file has compile errors. If Code Insight is not available, an appropriate message will appear in the editor's status bar.

Other Text Editing Features

A number of features were added with the 10*g* release. Some have been mentioned already in the discussion about the main menu in Chapter 2. Other new features for the Code Editor are covered in the following sections.

Quick Javadoc

You can display the main Javadoc for a class, method, or member by selecting Quick Javadoc from the right-click menu (or from the Source menu) on an element in the Code Editor as shown here for the `JTextField` class:

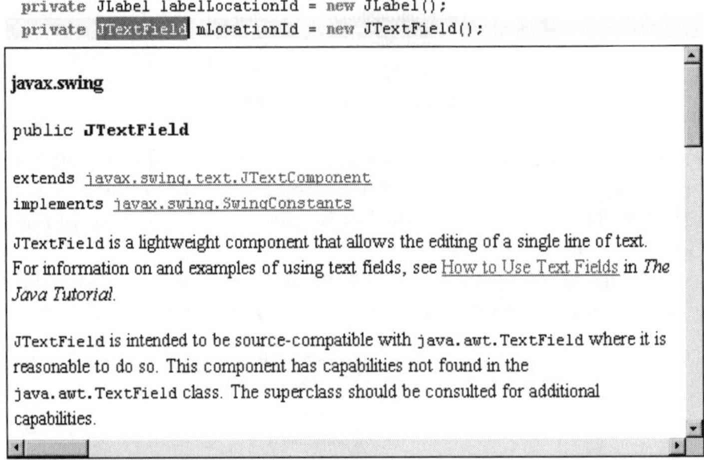

private JLabel labelLocationId = new JLabel();
private JTextField mLocationId = new JTextField();
javax.swing
public JTextField
extends javax.swing.text.JTextComponent
implements javax.swing.SwingConstants
JTextField is a lightweight component that allows the editing of a single line of text. For information on and examples of using text fields, see How to Use Text Fields in The Java Tutorial.
JTextField is intended to be source-compatible with java.awt.TextField where it is reasonable to do so. This component has capabilities not found in the java.awt.TextField class. The superclass should be consulted for additional capabilities.

Import Assistance

If a class you use in your Java source code is missing an import statement, a wavy line will appear under the class name as shown here:

```
import javax.swing.JPanel (Alt+Enter)

private JPanel dataPanel = new JPanel();
private BorderLayout borderLayout = new BorderLayout();
```

After a short time, a hint will pop up somewhere above the line of code, as shown in the previous example. This hint explains that you can press ALT-ENTER to create an import statement for that class. If the hint does not appear, press ALT-ENTER to see the hint, and ALT-ENTER again to add the import. The Source menu also contains an item for Import Assistance that will accomplish the same task (although this did not work from the Source menu in early production releases).

Syntax Error Highlighting

After you navigate the cursor off a line of code, the Code Editor will display a syntax or semantic error by placing a wavy line under the problem code. If you hold the mouse over that line of code, a hint will appear containing the error text as shown here:

```
dataPanel.etLayout(panelLayout);

Method 'etLayout(java.awt.GridBagLayout)' not found in javax.swing.JPanel
```

Editing PL/SQL

You can also use the Code Editor to edit PL/SQL database code. Navigate to the database object (function, procedure, package, or package body) that you want to edit in the Connection window Database node by expanding the <specific connection>\<user> nodes in the System Navigator. Double click the object to open it in the Code Editor.

You can create database code with the New <object> option from the right-click menu on a code object node (such as Package). After you name the object, an editor window will open where you can enter the code. You can also display the New Gallery (**File | New** or select New from the right-click menu on a database object node) and select the PL/SQL Subprogram item in the Database Tier\Database Objects category.

Compiling PL/SQL Code

To compile the code and save it to the database, select Compile from the right-click menu on the program name node in the Connection Navigator or on the editor window containing the code. Clicking the Save button will also compile and save the subprogram to the database. With either method, compile errors will be displayed in the Log window. Clicking the Make or Rebuild toolbar buttons will compile the project or workspace in addition to the PL/SQL subprogram. Errors for both project files and the PL/SQL subprogram will be displayed in the Log window.

Running PL/SQL Code

After creating and compiling PL/SQL subprograms, you can test them in standalone mode. Select the program unit in the Connection Navigator and click the Run button (or select Run from the right-click menu on the program's node or in the editor window). A window such as the following will appear:

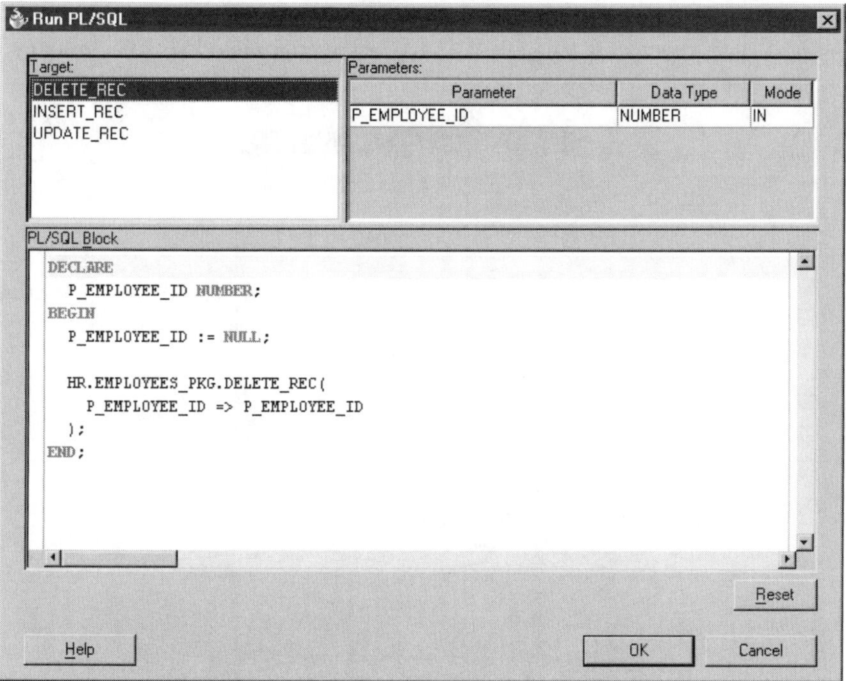

If you are running a PL/SQL package, you then select a subprogram in the Target area. A PL/SQL block that runs the subprogram will appear in the PL/SQL block area. You assign values to the variables declared in this block for the subprogram's parameters. When you click OK, the subprogram will be run with the parameter values passed to it in the variables. If the subprogram is a function, the output value from the function will be displayed in the log window by a call to DBMS_OUTPUT.PUT_LINE.

CAUTION
As of this writing, running a PL/SQL subprogram will compile the open project files. This could take unnecessary time if all you want to do is run the PL/SQL program. In addition, if any of the files contain compile errors, the run process will stop and you will need to fix the files before running the PL/SQL. An alternative is to close all open files and remove the workspace from the JDeveloper navigator (using the red "x" Remove button) and then run the PL/SQL subprogram. If this does not work, you will need to exit and restart JDeveloper after removing the workspace from the navigator.

Code Editor Style Sheet Support

Applying a cascading style sheet (CSS) to a JSP file or HTML file in JDeveloper is as easy as dropping a style sheet from the CSS page of the Component Palette. The CSS file is copied to your project directory when you drop it into a file. You can add your own style sheets to the Component Palette in the same way as you add other components (select Add Component from the right-click menu on any component on the CSS page of the Component Palette).

New in JDeveloper 10*g*, the Code Editor offers support for creating and modifying cascading style sheets. To use these features, open the CSS file in the editor window. The Structure window will display the list of styles as shown here:

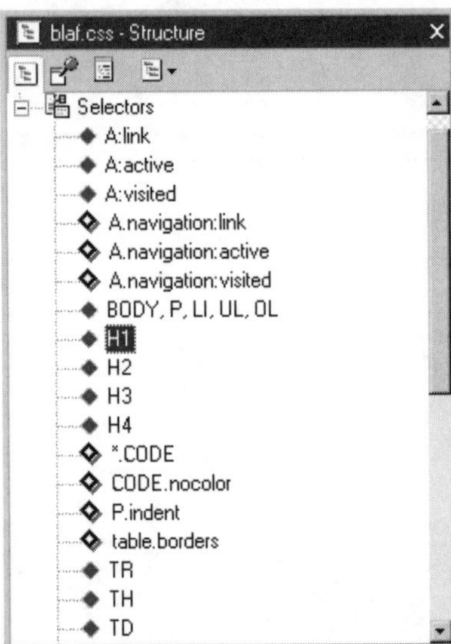

Double clicking a style name in the Structure window will navigate the cursor to the line of code where the style is defined. The Property Inspector will display all properties and values for that style as shown next:

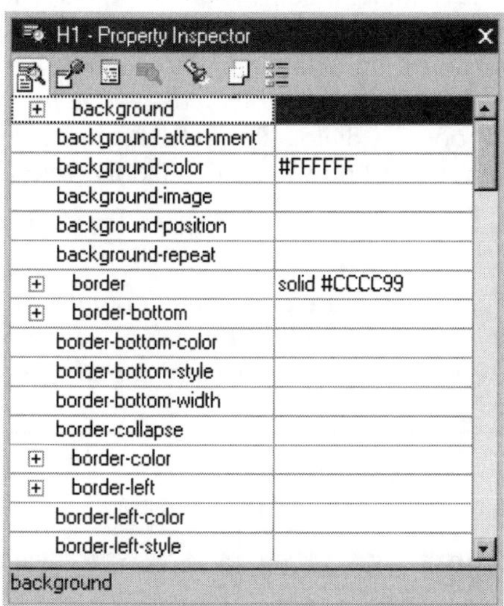

The Property Inspector contains color palettes for properties that set a color (such as *background color*). For these color properties, the property value field contains a pulldown palette and button that opens a color palette dialog. You can use either of these controls to set a color. You can make changes to properties in the Property Inspector or Code Editor. The Code Editor provides Code Insight for style attributes and values. For example, on a blank line inside a style definition, you can press CTRL-ENTER to show a list of properties that you can set for that style. After entering the property name and a colon, you can press CTRL-ENTER again to show a list of valid property values, such as the following list for a border property:

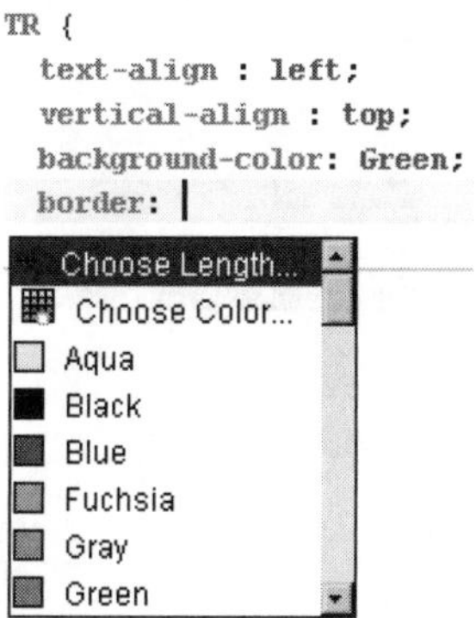

Notice that the first two entries in the list are "Choose" values that will display another dialog when you make a selection. The other property values are colors that you can select. Appendix C contains an introduction to and examples of using cascading style sheets.

Debugger

JDeveloper offers a full-featured debugger that you can use to examine the execution path and data values as a Java class file is running. It helps you find points where the code is in error by *tracing* (stepping through and stopping at) individual lines of code. It includes the ability to handle many JDK versions (version 1.2 and later), and to debug code on remote machines. To run a file in debug mode, you need to check the *Include Debug Information* checkbox on the Compiler page of the Project Properties dialog (**Project | Project Properties**). The file compiles with special debugging information and runs in a modified JDeveloper window such as that shown in Figure 3-3.

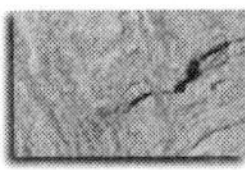

NOTE
The basic operations in the debugger are unchanged from the 9i release. A chapter describing the release 9i debugger is available from the authors' websites mentioned in the beginning of the book.

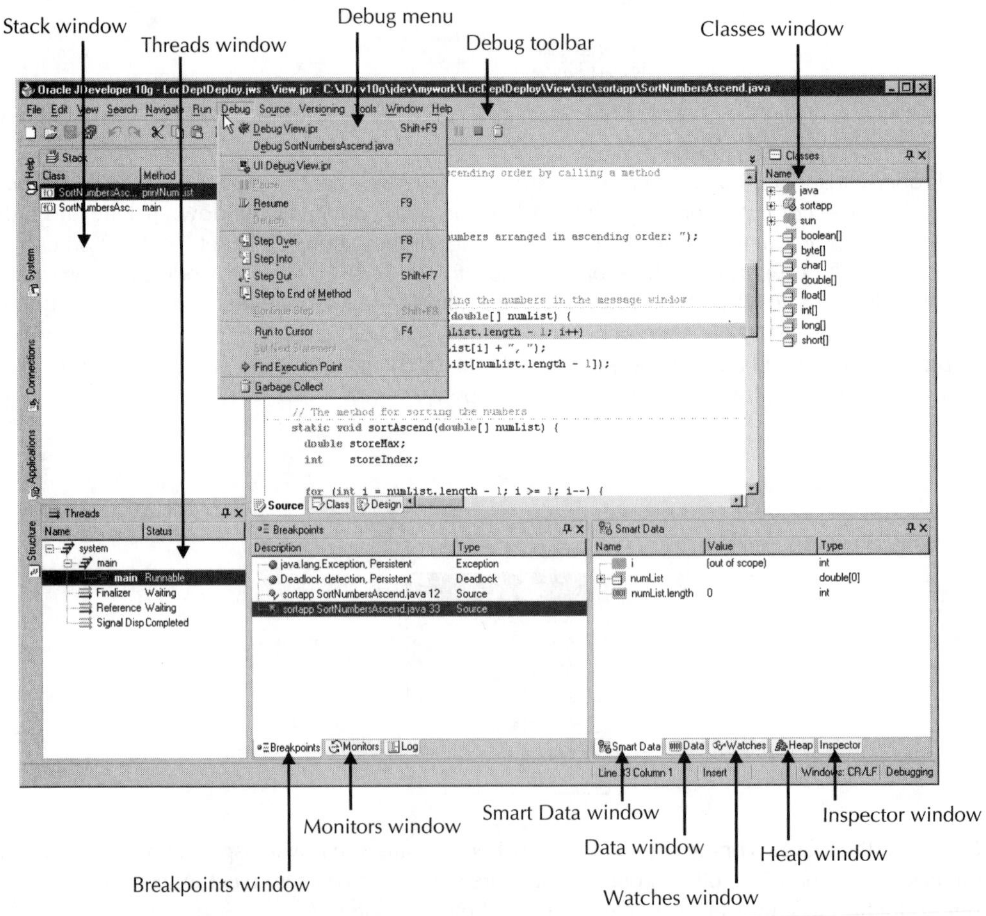

Stack window
Threads window
Debug menu
Debug toolbar
Classes window
Monitors window
Smart Data window
Inspector window
Data window
Heap window
Breakpoints window
Watches window

FIGURE 3-3. *JDeveloper running in debug mode*

Debugger Windows

Various windows appear by default in debug mode, but you can display or hide the following windows using the **View | Debugger** submenu:

- **Breakpoints** This window displays all *breakpoints* (program execution stopping points) that you have set or that are set by JDeveloper (such as exceptions and deadlocks). This window is viewable outside of debugging mode.
- **Classes** This window displays the packages and classes that will be traced in the debug session. You can include or exclude tracing of specific packages using the right-click menu.
- **Data** This window displays values of all variables, constants, and arguments that are in scope for the current execution point.
- **Heap** Use this window to examine the use of memory by objects and arrays in the program. This allows you to verify that an object is still in memory and to verify that garbage collection is occurring.
- **Monitors** This window tracks the synchronization of data and activities between threads of execution. For example, you can use this window to determine which thread is waiting for another thread to complete. This kind of check is helpful in detecting deadlocks.
- **Smart Data** This window shows variables, constants, and arguments that are used close to the execution point (the line of code that is being traced). The Smart Data window is more restrictive than the Data window because it shows only elements that are used near the point at which the code is stopped.
- **Stack** This window shows the sequence of method calls that preceded the execution point (the *stack*).
- **Threads** This window shows all program execution lines. Since you can write multi-threaded programs in Java, you may need to examine the state of the current simultaneously executing threads.
- **Watches** You use this window to display the current values of the expressions for which you have set *watches* (expressions that contain program variables or other data elements and their operators).
- **Inspector** This window is not available in the View menu, but is available as the Inspect option from the right-click menu after selecting a variable or expression (such as `storeMax * 100`) in the Code Editor, Watches window, Data window, or Smart Data window. You can open many Inspector windows and use each one to track a single variable or expression.

Debugging Java Code

You can set breakpoints at lines of code where you wish the program to stop by clicking the left margin of the editor window. The line of code will be highlighted in pink and a red dot will appear in the left margin.

You can start a debugging session from the IDE by clicking the Debug button, pressing SHIFT-F9, or selecting **Debug | Debug <file or project>** from the menu (where "*<file or project>*" is the name of the file you want to debug or the project you want to debug, respectively). When debug mode is in effect, you can use the Debug menu items or toolbar buttons to *step over* (execute the next method), *step into* (execute the program or go to the next line), *step out* (return to the calling method without stopping), *step to end of method* (execute the program to the end of the current method or to the next breakpoint), or terminate the debug session. More information on debugging local Java, remote Java, PL/SQL and stored Java, Swing and AWT, and web services programs is available starting in the JDeveloper help table of contents node "Working with Application Design Tools\Building and Tuning Applications\Debugging in JDeveloper."

Debugging PL/SQL

You can debug PL/SQL code in an Oracle database that is version 8*i* or beyond. For Oracle 9.2 (9*i*, release 2), the connection user must be granted the DEBUG CONNECT SESSION and the DEBUG ANY PROCEDURE system privileges. Before Oracle 9.2, no special privileges are required. You can set breakpoints by clicking in the left margin next to a line of code. When you run the subprogram using the Debug <program> menu item, the runtime session will stop at the breakpoint and you can examine variables, view the execution thread, and step through the code. Search in the help system Index page "PL/SQL, debugging programs" for a topic that explains more about PL/SQL debugging.

Other Tools for Improving Code

In addition to the debugger, you can apply the following tools (also described briefly in the section in Chapter 2 that discusses the Run menu) to assist in making your code more consistent and more efficient:

- **CodeCoach** This tool provides hints for how to optimize your code.
- **Profiler** This tool provides detailed information about the memory, events, and execution used by your code as it is running.
- **Auditing** This tool analyzes your code based on standards that you can tune. You would run this tool before compiling the code.
- **Measure** This tool provides statistics (metrics) about your code based upon a number of standard measurements.

Visual Editors

Visual editors provide a display of the user interface controls as they will appear at run time. You can modify the controls by dragging and dropping and using other familiar drawing operations. Changes you make in the visual editor, such as adding controls or containers, will be reflected immediately in the source code. JDeveloper offers three visual editors:

- **Java Visual Editor** This editor allows you to interact with Java client applications that use Swing and AWT controls. This editor also contains a Menu Editor to work with pulldown menus. You access the Menu Editor by double clicking an item under the Menu node in the Structure window UI Structure tab.

- **JSP/HTML Visual Editor** This editor works with JavaServer Pages (JSP) files and Hypertext Markup Language (HTML) files.
- **UIX Visual Editor** This visual editor is used to display and edit User Interface XML (UIX) files. UIX is a tag language that is optimized for display in different environments. UIX files can create standard HTML displays in a web browser.

The visual editors are responsible for showing the user interface controls. JDeveloper also includes modelers and diagrammers, which the developer can use to visually interact with code elements. These tools are described in the section "Modelers and Diagrammers" later in this chapter.

The editing environments for the JSP/HTML Visual Editor and the UIX Visual Editor are similar because both editors interact primarily with tag language code. All visual editors use the Structure window, Property Inspector, and Component Palette.

The visual editors have many common operations. You can open files by selecting Open from the right-click menu on the file in a navigator. If the file is open, clicking the Design tab will display the visual editor.

The visual editors also have a number of work area features in common such as the toolbar that is used for common operations on the particular file and the right-click menu that contains frequently needed operations for the type of file in the editor. Figure 3-4 shows views of the JDeveloper visual editors.

Many operations you perform in the visual editors, such as setting property values, are described in the discussions of other windows, the toolbar, and the main menu. Subsequent chapters in this book will provide hands-on practices that you can use to become familiar with the visual editors and how they are used to create data-aware files.

HTML and UIX Previewers

When you open an HTML or UIX file, you can edit the source code (in the Source tab) or work in a design mode with the tags (in the Design tab). The design mode contains extra layout elements that you manipulate when designing the page but which will not be displayed when you run the file. However, you can view the file as it will be displayed in the browser in the Preview tab as shown for an HTML page here:

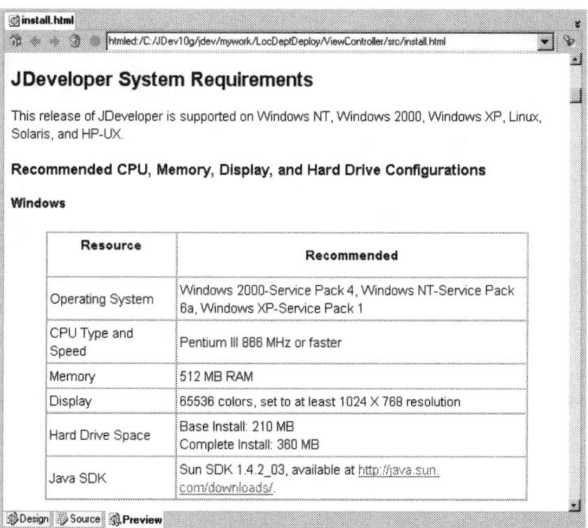

JDeveloper System Requirements

This release of JDeveloper is supported on Windows NT, Windows 2000, Windows XP, Linux, Solaris, and HP-UX.

Recommended CPU, Memory, Display, and Hard Drive Configurations

Windows

Resource	Recommended
Operating System	Windows 2000-Service Pack 4, Windows NT-Service Pack 6a, Windows XP-Service Pack 1
CPU Type and Speed	Pentium III 866 MHz or faster
Memory	512 MB RAM
Display	65536 colors, set to at least 1024 X 768 resolution
Hard Drive Space	Base Install: 210 MB Complete Install: 360 MB
Java SDK	Sun SDK 1.4.2_03, available at http://java.sun.com/downloads/.

Java Visual Editor

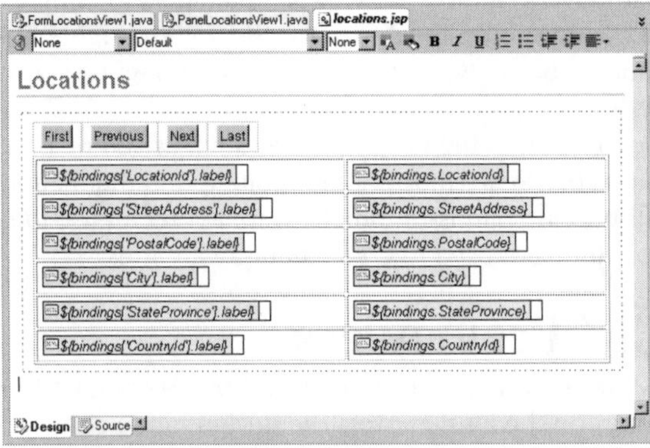

JSP/HTML Visual Editor

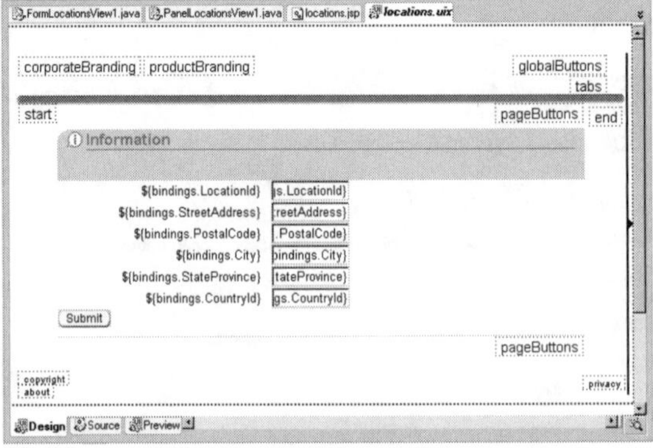

UIX Visual Editor

FIGURE 3-4. *JDeveloper visual editors*

When you preview a UIX page, no data will be displayed in preview mode, but you can check the layout elements that make up the page without layout-only elements. The previewers function as web browsers and will load pages that are linked through hypertext references.

New Gallery

The New Gallery offers dialogs that build starting code for a specific kind of new file. Wizards and new file dialogs are all started from the New Gallery. You access the New Gallery, shown in Figure 3-5, by using **File | New** or by selecting New from the right-click menu on various nodes in the navigator.

This window is divided into a categories navigator on the left and a list of items within that category on the right. The main nodes in the navigator roughly parallel the J2EE tiers (Business, Client, Database, Web). Normally, the New Gallery only displays items that are appropriate to the technology for the selected project. In case an item you need is not in the technology list for your project, you can set the *Filter By* pulldown to "All Technologies," which shows all items.

If you click a workspace node before displaying the New Gallery, only project items will be enabled. If you select a project node before displaying the New Gallery, only items that can be placed into a project will be enabled in the dialog. After you select an object from one of the categories and click OK, the file node will be created in the System Navigator under the project that you selected. Depending on the object, the appropriate wizard or dialog will appear and prompt you for properties.

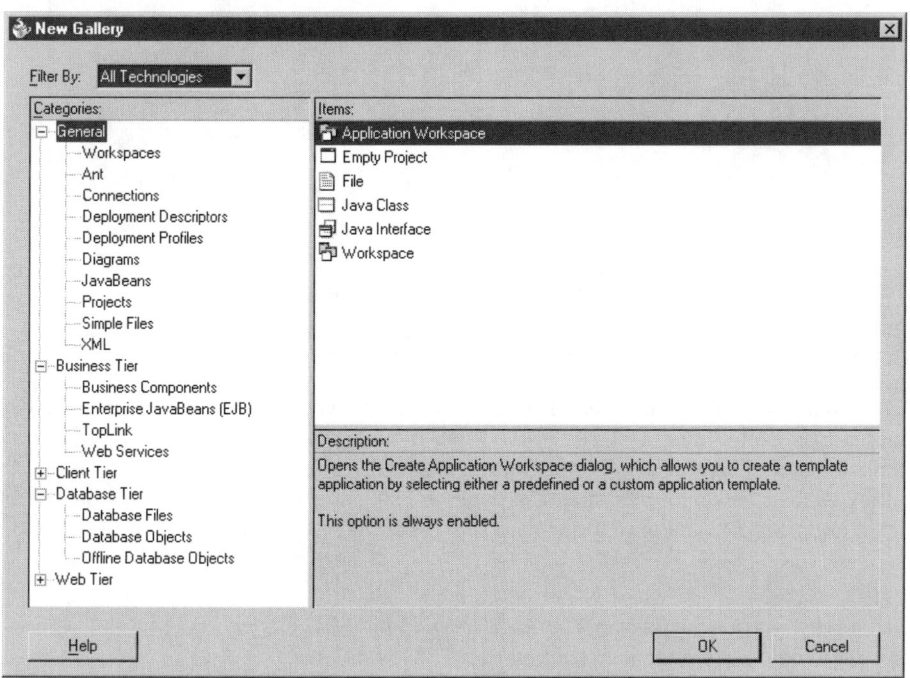

FIGURE 3-5. *The New Gallery dialog*

TIP

Instead of selecting New from the right-click menu to display the New Gallery, you can press CTRL-N.

Wizards

A *wizard* is a dialog (modal window) that leads you through the steps of creating a file or other object. Typically, a wizard presents the required properties in an easy-to-understand way, supplies default values where appropriate, and ensures that the values you enter are appropriate and complete.

The wizard usually presents a series of screens that step you through the process of creating an object. Next and Back buttons allow you to navigate between pages. A Finish button closes the wizard and accepts all values. A Cancel button exits the dialog, and a Help button presents specific instructions for the step you are performing. The following shows these features in the Create JClient Form Wizard:

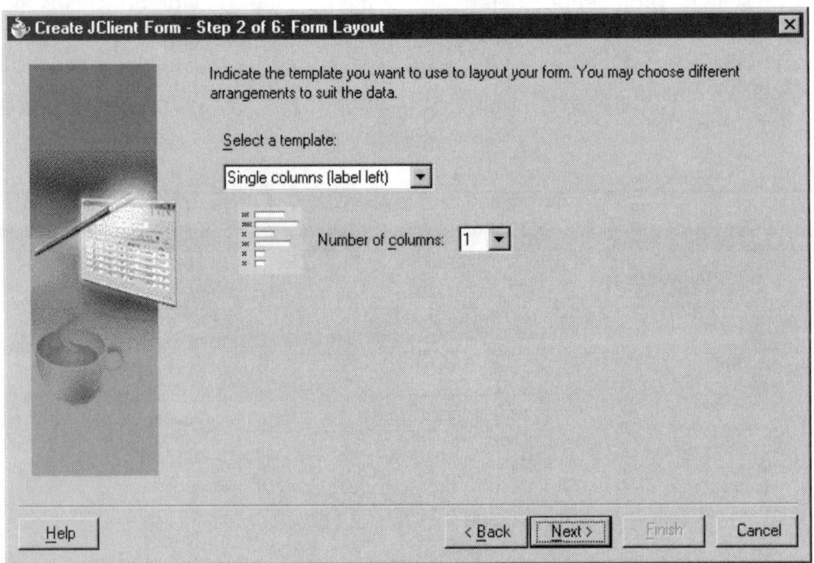

Many wizards are *re-entrant.* That is, once you run the wizard to create the file, you can also edit that file (using an Edit right-click menu option) by using the wizard. The edit version of the wizard does not offer Next and Previous buttons. Instead it allows you to navigate among the pages using a tab or navigator interface. The pages are usually the same in the creation version of the wizard and the edit version of the wizard, but there may be extra pages in one or the other.

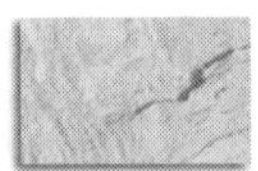

NOTE

You can define your own wizards and add them to the New Gallery. Start at the help system table of contents node "Working with Application Design Tools\Extending JDeveloper\Developing an Extension\Developing a New Gallery Wizard" for technical information about adding a wizard.

New File Dialogs

JDeveloper also offers *file dialogs (dialogs)*, single-page windows that allow you to specify characteristics of files you are creating. For example, the following is the Create Java Application dialog, where you can define the name and other properties of the application file. As with the wizards, settings in the dialog affect the code that is generated.

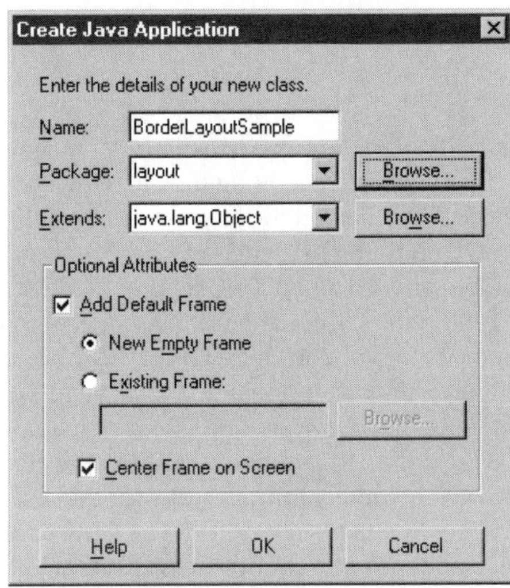

Sometimes a file dialog starts up another dialog based upon the settings. For example, in the previous illustration, the Optional Attributes area contains an option to create a new frame file. If you select that option and click OK, the New Application dialog will create the application file and automatically open the New Frame dialog where you define the frame file.

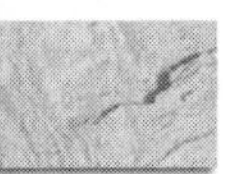

TIP
You can resize some wizards, dialogs, and user interface windows. In addition, some dialogs and wizards have multi-pane areas, which you can resize if something that you need to see is not visible.

Data Control Palette

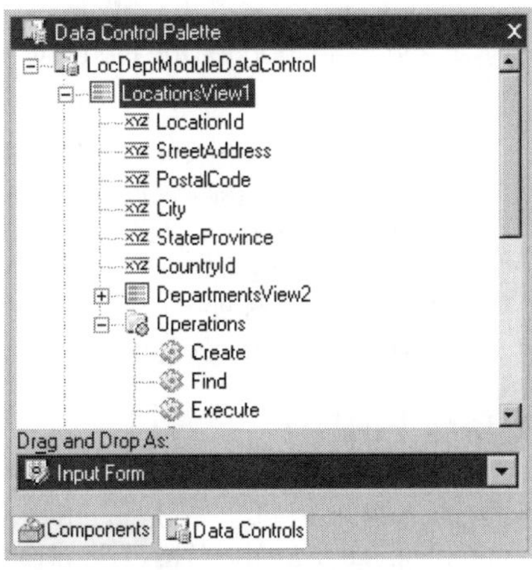

The Data Control Palette, new in JDeveloper 10*g*, allows you to transparently bind controls to data sources in the business services layer. This window, shown on the right, contains a view of the data elements, such as ADF business components, that are available in the application workspace.

In this example, the LocationsView1 view object is available in the workspace. The Data Control Palette allows you to expand the display to view sub-elements. A pulldown list appears in the bottom of the window and allows you to select a type of control. In this example an input form will be bound to the LocationsView1 data element.

To add a data-aware component, you select the data source or operation, select a component from the pulldown, and drag the data source or operation into the visual editor. The component will be added to the JClient form or panel, JSP file, or UIX page that is displayed in the editor and it will be bound to the proper source.

Other Editors

In addition to the Code Editor, JDeveloper offers several editors for creating source code files.

XML Editor

The Open option on the right-click menu for an XML file in a navigator opens the XML Editor. The XML Editor is a schema-driven editor for editing files in XML styles such as UIX XML, UIT, XSQL, XSL, XSD, XHTML, and WSDL. The editor offers syntax highlighting and is supported by the Structure window view, the Component Palette, and the Property Inspector.

If the tags in the XML file have an associated XML schema, Tag Insight and End Tag Completion are also available. *End Tag Completion* (where the ending tag is automatically inserted when you complete a starting tag) is controlled using the Code Editor\XML page of the Preferences dialog. *Tag Insight* is activated when you pause after opening a tag by typing a "<" character. Tag Insight pops up a list of available tags in the same way as Code Insight. It also pops up available attributes when you enter a space after a tag name. In addition, you can activate *Required Attribute Insertion* in the Preferences dialog. This feature adds attribute stubs for the required attributes of a tag (such as `name=""`) after you start typing that tag (such as `xsl:attribute`).

If the file is a read-only file (such as an ADF Business Components or other XML file that uses a dialog for editing), the right-click menu contains an option for Open. Selecting this option opens the editor in *protected* (read-only) mode as noted by "Protected" in the right-hand side of the IDE status bar. For example, editing an ADF BC view object XML file will run the XML Editor in protected mode; to edit this file, you select Edit <view object name> from the right-click menu on the view object parent node (for example, DepartmentsView) in the navigator. This opens a dialog with which you interact to change the contents of the XML file. You do not edit the code of this kind of XML file directly inside JDeveloper. The reason for this protection is that the XML structure is specific to the editors in JDeveloper. If you were able to edit the file and mistyped a value or tag, the editors might not work.

You can import an XML schema (.xsd file) for a specific file type using the Preferences dialog's "XML Schemas" page. If the schema is registered in this way, the XML Editor will provide Code Insight and validation for the elements that you enter.

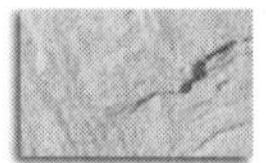

TIP

Syntax errors in XML files will be displayed in the Structure window. You can validate the syntax of an XML file by selecting Check XML Syntax from the right-click menu on an XML file in the navigator. You can also validate that the XML file uses the language specified in the XML schema by selecting Validate XML from the right-click menu on an XML file in the navigator.

Class Editor

Clicking the Class tab in an editor window for a Java file displays the Class Editor. This editor interacts with Java class code in a more declarative way than the Code Editor. Figure 3-6 shows a sample page from the Class Editor for a Java application file.

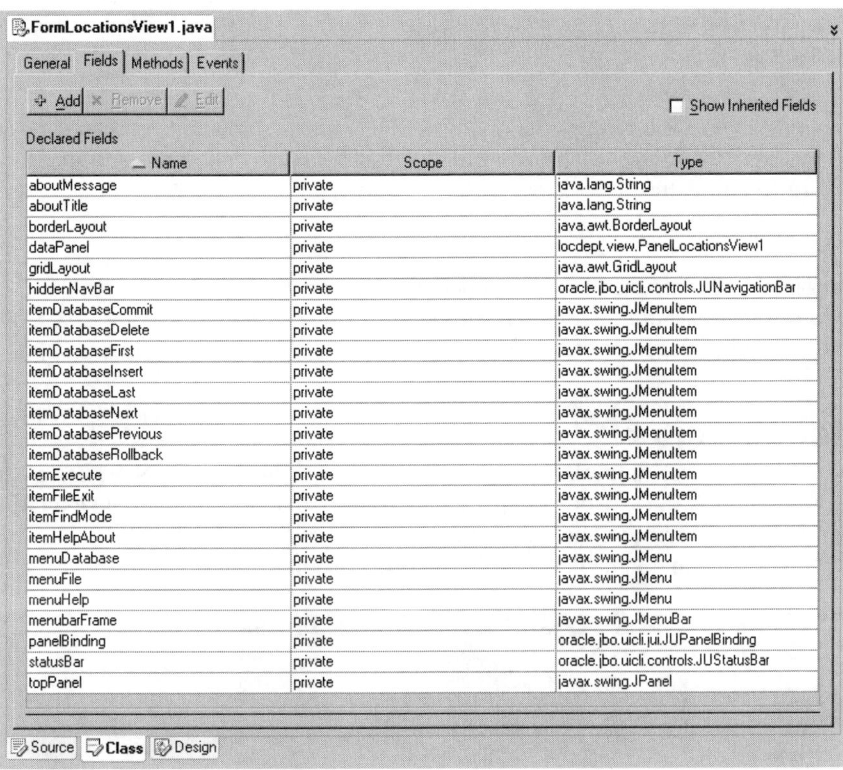

FIGURE 3-6. *Class Editor window*

You manipulate the file by entering definitions into the following tab pages:

- **General** Using the Generate Beaninfo button in this page, you can create a standard BeanInfo file from your class file so that the class can be used as a JavaBean.
- **Fields** This page allows you to enter and edit fields (attributes). When you edit fields using this page, you can declare that `get()` and `set()` accessor method stubs be created (or re-created) for a particular field.
- **Methods** You can declare methods in this class using this page. If you click the Add button, you enter details about the method such as the signature information, parameters, and exceptions. When you define a method on this page, a method stub will be added to the source file, and you can enter the code details in the Code Editor.
- **Events** This page is used to enter and modify the events in your class. There is an area to define the events that are fired and the event listeners that will be created.

NOTE
Chapter 5 contains an overview of Java elements such as fields, methods, and events.

The definitions you enter in this dialog immediately create code that you can view in the Code Editor. The Class Editor is handy for quickly entering basic definitions and structures of a class before you fill in the code using the Code Editor.

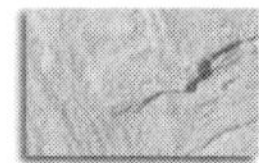

TIP
As mentioned, you can also use the Generate Accessors item (from the Source menu or from the right-click menu in a Code Editor window) to create accessor methods.

EJB Module Editor

You can create an Enterprise JavaBean (EJB) from the New Gallery (**File | New**) by selecting an EJB item from the Business Tier\Enterprise JavaBeans (EJB) category and clicking OK. After creating an EJB, you can access the EJB Module Editor by selecting Properties from the right-click menu on the EJB node in the navigator. This will open the EJB Module Editor shown here:

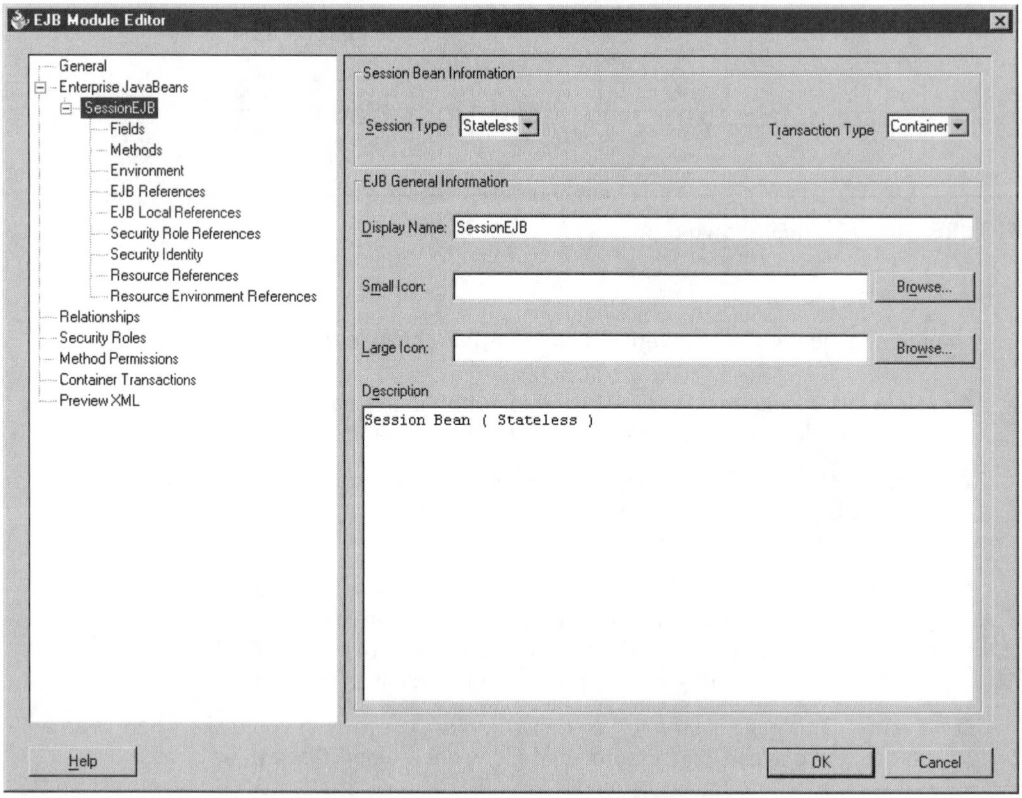

You can also open this editor by double clicking an EJB node in the navigator. This allows you to manipulate properties of the EJB without having to worry about which file in the EJB file set needs to be changed. When you accept the changes in this editor, the appropriate EJB class files will be updated.

TIP
You can check the code in an EJB by selecting Verify Enterprise Bean from the right-click menu on the EJB node in the navigator. This runs the EJB Verifier, which tests the EJB code against the EJB rules.

Viewer Windows

As mentioned, for most file types, double clicking the file name in the navigator will open the appropriate editor. For non-text files or objects, an appropriate viewer will open so that you can look at, but not edit, the item. As with editors, the file name and path appear in the window title. For files that require a viewer, you can select Open from the right-click menu on the file node in the navigator. The following sections describe some of the available viewer windows.

Image Viewer

Double clicking an image file (.gif, .jpg, .jpeg, or .png) in the navigator will display the image in read-only mode. The *Image Viewer* displays the image in a graphical format. If you just want to view an image but not load it into a project, you can drop the image file into the editor area from Windows Explorer.

Archive Viewer

You can view the contents of a .zip or .jar file using the same techniques (selecting Open from the right-click menu in the navigator, double clicking the file in the navigator, or dropping the file into the editor from Windows Explorer). The archive will be displayed in the *Archive Viewer* as shown here:

loc2.jar

Path	Date	Size	Compressed
.xdkjava_version_9.0.4.0.0_production	3/10/04 6:16 AM	0	0
DataBindings.cpx	3/17/04 9:47 PM	766	766
Loc/locdept5.cmd	3/1/04 1:05 AM	102	102
META-INF/MANIFEST.MF	3/17/04 9:47 PM	111	108
META-INF/application-client.xml	3/1/04 12:42 AM	300	300
Model.jpx	2/29/04 7:16 PM	629	629
com/sun/java/util/collections/AbstractCollection.class	3/10/04 6:16 AM	2.62 KB	2.62 KB
com/sun/java/util/collections/AbstractList$Itr.class	3/10/04 6:16 AM	1.69 KB	1.69 KB
com/sun/java/util/collections/AbstractList$ListItr.class	3/10/04 6:16 AM	1.88 KB	1.88 KB
com/sun/java/util/collections/AbstractList.class	3/10/04 6:16 AM	3.27 KB	3.27 KB
com/sun/java/util/collections/AbstractMap$1.class	3/10/04 6:16 AM	977	977
com/sun/java/util/collections/AbstractMap$2.class	3/10/04 6:16 AM	1.15 KB	1.15 KB
com/sun/java/util/collections/AbstractMap$3.class	3/10/04 6:16 AM	986	986
com/sun/java/util/collections/AbstractMap$4.class	3/10/04 6:16 AM	1.15 KB	1.15 KB
com/sun/java/util/collections/AbstractMap.class	3/10/04 6:16 AM	3.62 KB	3.62 KB
com/sun/java/util/collections/AbstractSequentialList.class	3/10/04 6:16 AM	1.77 KB	1.77 KB
com/sun/java/util/collections/AbstractSet.class	3/10/04 6:16 AM	956	956
com/sun/java/util/collections/ArrayList.class	3/10/04 6:16 AM	4.92 KB	4.92 KB
com/sun/java/util/collections/Arrays$ArrayList.class	3/10/04 6:16 AM	884	884
com/sun/java/util/collections/Arrays.class	3/10/04 6:16 AM	15.38 KB	15.38 KB

Archive

Clicking a column heading will sort the list by that column. The right-click menu on the column headings allows you to select which columns are displayed. You can double click a file name in this viewer, and the file will be opened in read-only mode in the appropriate viewer.

Tables Viewer

Using the Tables Viewer, you can display the structure of a database table or view as shown here:

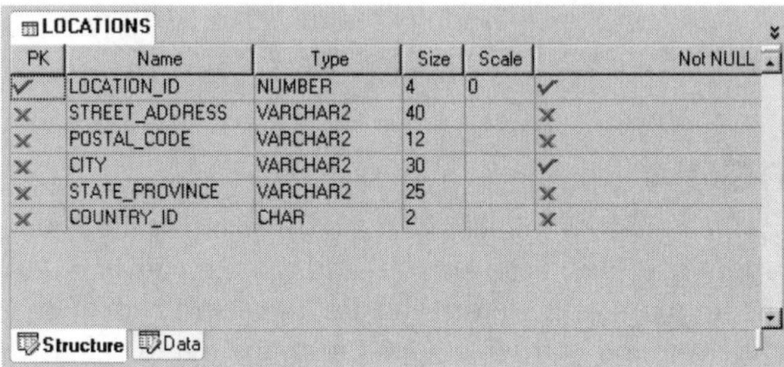

LOCATIONS

PK	Name	Type	Size	Scale	Not NULL
✓	LOCATION_ID	NUMBER	4	0	✓
✗	STREET_ADDRESS	VARCHAR2	40		✗
✗	POSTAL_CODE	VARCHAR2	12		✗
✗	CITY	VARCHAR2	30		✓
✗	STATE_PROVINCE	VARCHAR2	25		✗
✗	COUNTRY_ID	CHAR	2		✗

Structure | Data

You can also view some of the data for the table or view by clicking the Data tab, as shown next.

LOCATIONS

Fetch Size: 100 | Fetch Next | Refresh

LOCATION_ID	STREET_A...	POSTAL_CO...	CITY	STATE_PR...	COUNTRY_ID
1000	1297 Via Cola...	00989	Romas		IT
1100	93091 Calle d...	10934	Venice		IT
1200	2017 Shinjuk...	1689	Tokyo	Tokyo Prefect...	JP
1300	9450 Kamiya-...	6823	Hiroshima		JP
1400	2014 Jabberw...	26192	Southlake	Texas	US
1500	2011 Interiors ...	99236	South San Fr...	California	US
1600	2007 Zagora St	50090	South Brunsw...	New Jersey	US
1700	2004 Charade...	98199	Seattle	Washington	US

Structure | Data

The Data tab allows you to reorder columns by dragging and dropping the column headings, but the settings are not saved for the next time you open the viewer.

To view a table or view, navigate to the connection in the Database node of the Connection Navigator. Expand the user name and Tables node (or Views node for database views). Double click the name or select Open from the right-click menu on the object name.

TIP
When you select a table, view, or object type in the Tables node of the navigator, the Structure window will display a list of its columns and indexes. For the package specification (node under the Packages node), the Structure window displays a list of procedures and functions within the package. For the package body and for standalone procedures and functions, the Structure window also displays the parameters for each program unit.

Sequence Viewer

You can examine database sequences in the same way that you display tables and views. Double-click the sequence name in the navigator. The following dialog will appear:

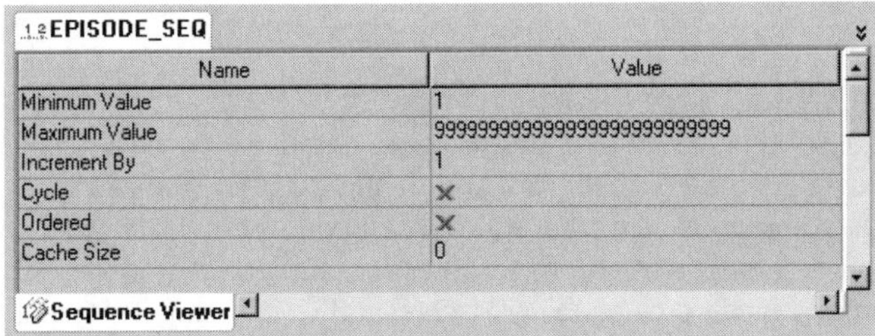

The viewer shows the standard properties for sequences such as the increment, minimum, and maximum values.

SQL Worksheet

The SQL Worksheet supplements the SQL*Plus option in the right-click menu of a database connection node but does not require an existing SQL*Plus installation. The SQL Worksheet presents a window (as shown in Figure 3-7) where you can enter and execute SQL statements through a database connection that you have defined in the Connection manager.

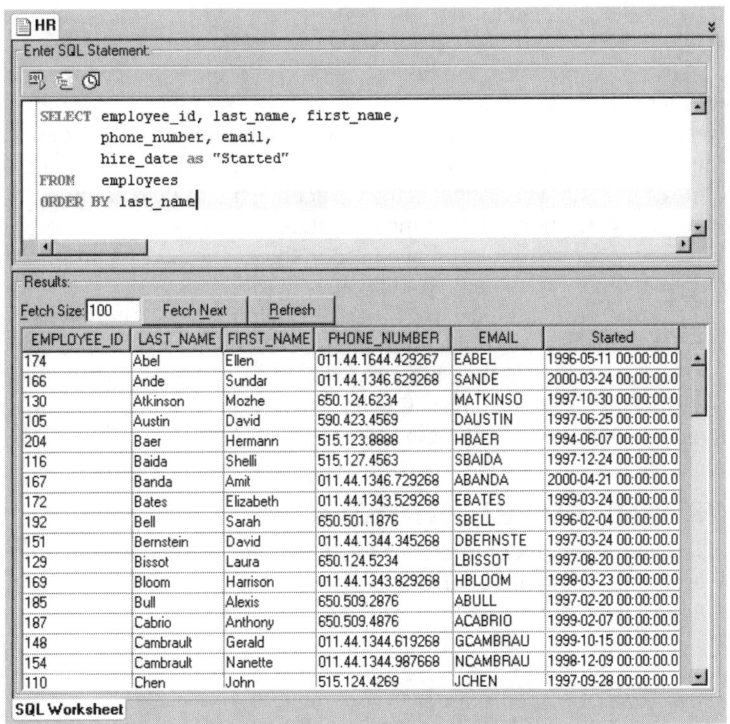

FIGURE 3-7. *SQL Worksheet*

Other Database Object Operations

This chapter has described how to view the structure of tables, views, and sequences. It also discussed how to create, edit, compile, run, and debug PL/SQL database code and how to enter and tune SQL commands using the SQL Worksheet. Another operation you can perform is to drop any database object that you have access to (and privilege to drop). In addition to PL/SQL subprograms, you can create tables, triggers, and views using items in the New Gallery or by selecting New <object type> from the right-click menu on the database object node.

You can create user accounts by selecting New from the right-click menu on a database connection node (the connection user must have privileges to create a user).

In addition, you can modify (but not create) object types and object collections. You can also define database objects that are not created in the database in "offline" mode. Look at the help system node "Working with Application Design Tools\Working with the Database\Working with Offline Database Definitions" for more information.

To open the SQL Worksheet, select SQL Worksheet from the right-click menu on a database connection name in the Connection Navigator. The top pane of the window allows you to enter SQL statements. When you click the "Execute SQL Statement" (the left-hand) button, the statement is executed and the results are displayed in the bottom pane. If the result is data (such as for a SELECT statement), the bottom pane will display the rows of data in a scrollable table. If the statement uses another SQL operator, the bottom pane will display the statement's results, for example, "1 row affected" for an update.

You can enter more than one command in the SQL Worksheet and execute them one at a time by selecting the command and clicking the "Execute SQL Statement" button.

Another feature of the SQL Worksheet is the "Execute Explain Plan" button (the middle button) that displays the execution path for the SQL statement. The "SQL History" (right-hand) button shows a list of the commands you have used in this session. You can select from the list and the text will be written into the command area.

Although you cannot create all database objects using the New Gallery, you can enter the creation command for any database object into the SQL Worksheet. As with all SQL, you need to be granted the privilege to create the object type for a particular creation statement to work.

See the above sidebar "Other Database Object Operations" for a description of some other operations that you can perform on database objects.

Modelers and Diagrammers

Although a detailed discussion about modelers (diagrammers) is out of scope for this book, it is useful to briefly examine what types of diagrams you can create in JDeveloper and to explain some of their common operations.

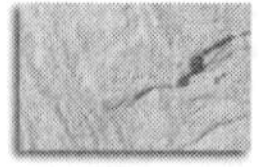

NOTE

The help system table of contents nodes "Working with Application Design Tools\Modeling" and "Working with Application Design Tools\Java Modeling" provide the starting points for help about the modelers and diagrammers.

Types of Diagrams

JDeveloper 10*g* includes the following Unified Modeling Language (UML) modelers:

- Class diagram
- Activity diagram
- Use case diagram

In addition, you can represent one or more of the following types of objects on a UML class diagram or use case diagram:

- Java classes
- ADF business components
- Database objects
- EJBs
- Web services

JDeveloper also offers the following non-UML modelers:

- XML Schema Editor
- Struts Page Flow Diagrammer

These diagrammers are not UML but they use many of the same diagramming techniques. These diagrams are discussed in the last two sections of this chapter.

Creating a UML Diagram

Each of the UML diagrams and each type of object just listed has a dedicated item in the General\Diagrams category of the New Gallery as shown in the following New Gallery excerpt. (You may need to select "All Technologies" in the *Filter By* pulldown to see all items.)

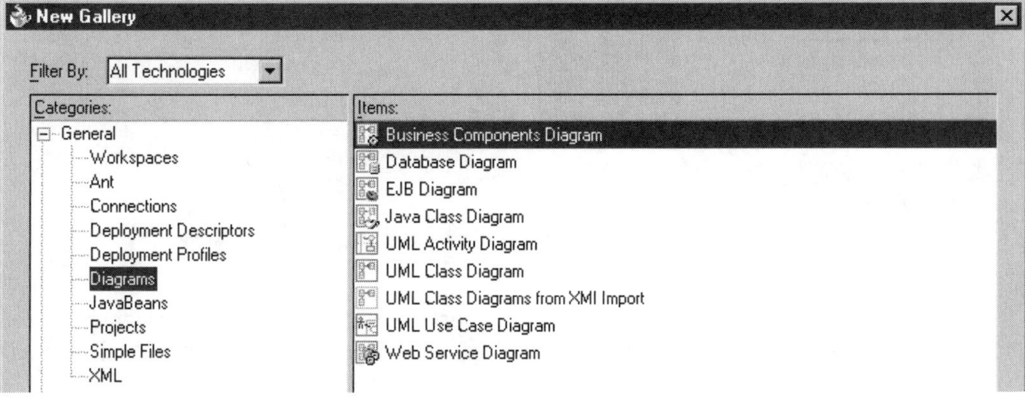

After you select a type of diagram and click OK, a dialog appears where you can name the diagram and indicate a package name where the diagram will be stored. Clicking OK on this dialog opens a new diagram window in the editor window. The selected page in the Component Palette contains elements specific to the item you selected in the New Gallery. However, all other symbol types will also be available from the Component Palette pulldown as shown on the right:

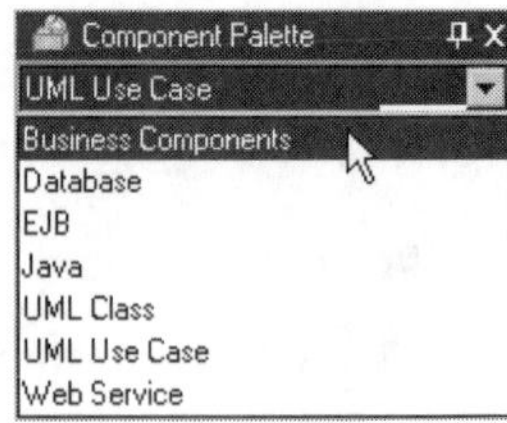

TIP

Except for Activity Diagram symbols, all diagram symbols should be available in all other diagrams as pages in the Component Palette. If a Component Palette page for a particular symbol set does not appear, create a blank diagram of the missing type and then close it without saving.

Some Diagramming Operations

The bottom-right corner of the diagram window contains a toolbar with zoom buttons (Zoom In, Zoom Out, Zoom to Selected, Fit to Window, and Zoom 100%). You can click these buttons to change the view of the objects on the diagram.

Another feature provided for navigation is the Thumbnail window. This window contains a small representation of the page with a rectangle indicating the current viewport of the page in the diagram window. For example, the following shows the Thumbnail window on the left displaying the location of the view in a business components diagram:

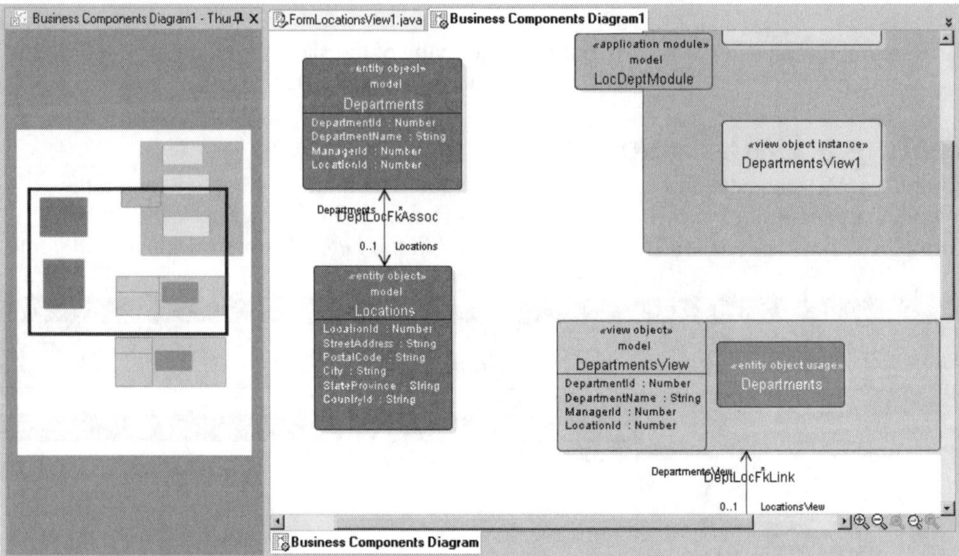

The diagrams provide the features you would expect for resizing and moving diagram elements. In addition, the right-click menu on diagram elements contains an item for Display Properties where you can modify the sub-elements displayed as well as the colors and fonts for a single or a selected group of elements. The Properties right-click menu item (or double clicking the object) opens the appropriate properties dialog or editor for that element; for example, when you select Properties from the right-click menu on a Java class file, the Code Editor will open (because this is where you define the contents of that object).

Some diagram elements allow you to generate code or database objects. For example, an ADF BC entity object contains a right-click menu "Generate" submenu item for Default Data Model Components (for ADF business component objects) and Database Objects (to create a table in the database).

The right-click menu on the diagram surface contains a Publish Diagram option that you can use to save the diagram to a file as mentioned in the Chapter 2 Model menu section. It also contains an Add to Diagram item that displays the Add to Diagram dialog as shown to the right: Selecting a file or object in this hierarchical display and clicking OK will add an element for that file or object on the diagram.

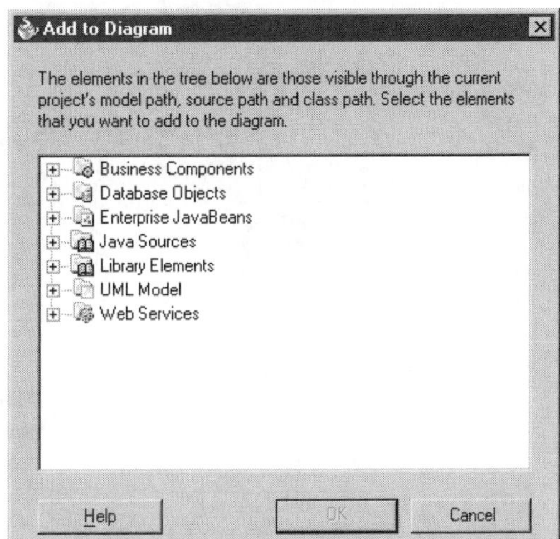

TIP
The Diagrams\Diagram page of the Preferences dialog allows you to change the default appearance of new objects drawn on the diagram. You can also select Display Properties from the right-click menu on a diagram element to change the colors and fonts of that element.

Activity Diagram

The Activity Diagram offers the same type of operations as the other diagrammers except that, as mentioned, you cannot use symbols other than Activity Diagram symbols. The diagram can be used by the (Oracle applications) E-Business Integration Wizard to generate coordination between application components in Oracle Workflow. The use of JDeveloper's activity model in the Oracle Workflow application is described starting at the help system node "Working with Application Design Tools\Modeling\Integrating Applications Using Oracle Workflow."

XML Schema Editor

JDeveloper 10*g* offers the XML Schema Editor for creating, viewing, and modifying XML schemas. An *XML schema* is an .xsd file that defines the structure, content, and language elements used in a set of XML files. (It is a replacement for the older concept of Document Type Definition files.) You associate XML files with the schema file so that the tags within the XML file can be validated and interpreted.

The Design tab of the XML Schema Editor is shown in Figure 3-8 for the base.xsd file in the schemas\ui directory of the JDEV_HOME\jlib\uix2-schemas.zip archive. The Source tab displays a text version of the code in the file. Using the Component Palette, you can drop elements into the design area and set their properties using the Property Inspector. You can also use the right-click menu on an object in the XML Schema Editor to add elements and modify the file. The Structure window will track the object hierarchy as you edit the file.

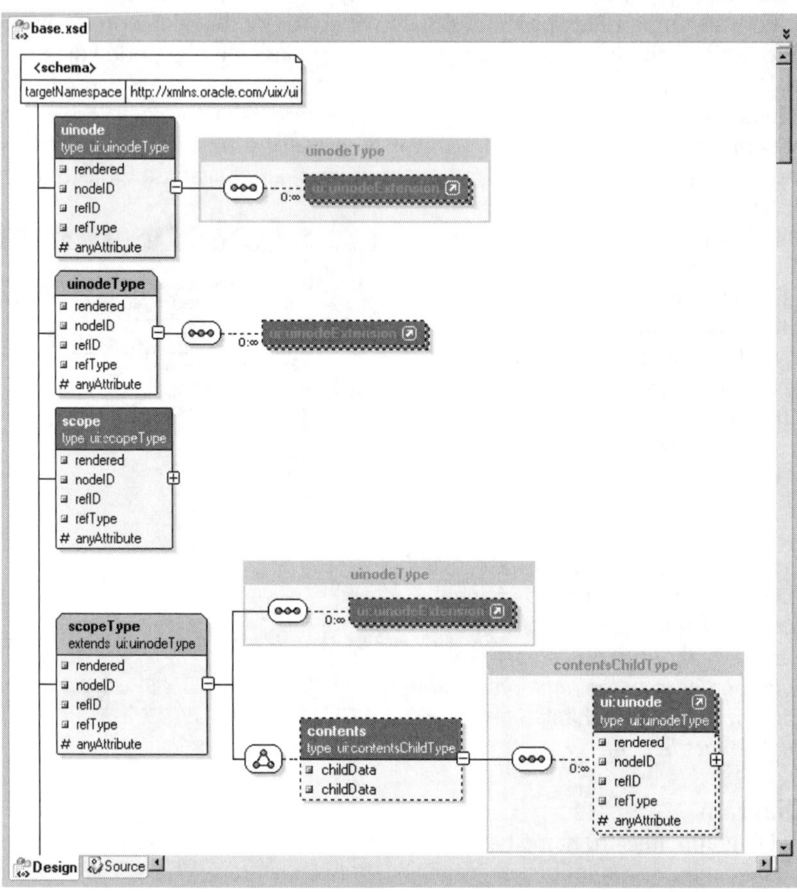

FIGURE 3-8. *XML Schema Editor*

More information about the XML Schema Editor is available starting at the help system Table of Contents node "Working with Application Design Tools\Working with Source Files\About Source Files\About Source Files\About the XML Schema Editor."

Struts Page Flow Diagrammer

The Page Flow Diagrammer is another diagrammer, new to JDeveloper 10*g*, that has less similarity to the modelers. It is primarily a visual representation of the Struts configuration file, struts-config.xml. You use this diagram to visually define actions, pages, and links that are written into the configuration file. Chapter 17 discusses Struts in more detail and several chapters in the book provide hands-on practices that use this diagrammer.

You can create a Struts Page Flow Diagram by selecting Struts Controller Page Flow from the Web Tier\Struts category of the New Gallery.

CHAPTER 4

Introduction to the Oracle Application Development Framework

Your scheme must be the framework of the universe;
all other schemes will soon be ruins.

—Henry David Thoreau (1817–1862),
A Week on the Concord and Merrimack Rivers

As use of the Java language matures and more and more technologies are based upon Java, designing, developing, and deploying Java-based applications becomes more and more complex. The use of Java has progressed from its early days, when Java programs were primarily command-line utilities, through the days of GUI windowed controls to today, when many new applications using Java are deployed on the Web. New technologies with Java at their core, such as those included in the Java 2 Platform, Enterprise Edition (J2EE, discussed in Chapter 7), offer many benefits to the enterprise, but require additional program components and introduce much additional complexity.

Although J2EE suggests and specifies high-level technologies (BluePrints) and low-level techniques (design patterns), it does not define a development method for business applications. Developers and architects are left with the task of selecting the appropriate method and making decisions about all of the choices.

Vendors have addressed the complexity of developing J2EE applications by creating Integrated Development Environment (IDE) tools, such as JDeveloper. IDEs can automate many of the tasks required to set up a particular style of development and deployment. A key part of a complex technology is the program files and code units that connect one component to another and to the appropriate application and database servers. Without the proper assistance, creating this part of the application, often called the "plumbing," takes a significant amount of time and effort.

To be more universally accepted, an IDE needs not only to assist with the plumbing but also to offer a clearly defined method for developing applications. JDeveloper 10*g* introduces an architecture mentioned in Chapter 1, called Oracle Application Development Framework (ADF), that assists in managing the complexity of developing and deploying applications, by addressing both these issues. This chapter explores the concept of frameworks and development frameworks; it then explains ADF further and provides a basis for understanding how ADF guides and assists in the development work you perform in JDeveloper 10*g*. This chapter contains a general set of steps for using ADF; other chapters contain hands-on practices that include more detailed steps for using ADF to create various types of code. Since ADF is the heart of JDeveloper 10*g*, it is important to understand its concepts. Therefore, throughout the chapter are references to where to look for more information.

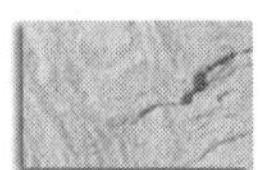

NOTE

JDeveloper allows you to create code without using the Application Development Framework, but ADF has many benefits in productivity and is a main reason to use JDeveloper over other Java IDEs.

What Is a Framework?

Programmers have long incorporated the principles of code reuse into their program designs. After you have created an application using a certain technology, you usually want to think about how to leverage the code you have written for the next project. Applications often have many aspects in common. If you can abstract and standardize common routines so that they can serve multiple applications, you can reduce the time and effort required to create new applications. Therefore, you end up collecting these common routines into code libraries that can be plugged into each new application. Over time, you make improvements and add features to make the code more flexible and useful for different types of applications. As the code grows, its complexity and size have the potential to overwhelm developers who use it. However, if the reusable code is well designed and well documented, it can become a solid foundation that saves significant development time.

A *framework* builds upon the idea of code reuse by offering well-designed code libraries, documentation, and often development tools. It supplies a complete system that accomplishes a specific task such as page flow (as with the Struts framework) or business services (as with the ADF Business Components framework). A framework provides (or simplifies) the implementation of a high-level architecture. You have limitless choices when developing applications; a framework applies a structure to the development process.

In the context of the Java environment, framework code consists of a complete set of interrelated, highly integrated Java classes. The base classes are written to perform in a certain way by default, and they handle the details of the architecture such as communication between objects, data access, and UI presentation. Some frameworks take custom information about your application primarily from metadata in XML files that use an *XML schema* (definition of the XML tag elements and their attributes) readable by the base classes. With this category of frameworks, the primary work that you perform in a framework consists of defining the metadata that will customize the behavior of the framework base classes for your needs. In addition, you can extend the base classes to add or override the functionality of the framework if defining metadata is not sufficient.

The proper way to use a framework is to stay as close as possible to its intention. This intention could include the definition of metadata that applies the framework to a particular business application, and defining this metadata can be considered working within the framework. However, writing massive customizations outside of the framework requires much time and effort and may even be less productive than writing the application from scratch without a framework.

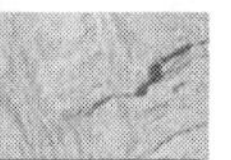

NOTE

A downside to using any framework, whether it is vendor-supplied or home-grown, is that it is proprietary in nature. Vendor-supplied frameworks usually offer support, documentation, and available developer talent that home-grown solutions do not offer. Migrating from one framework to another framework may be difficult but also is normally not necessary. Investing time in proven frameworks, such as those used by JDeveloper, will minimize the risks of obsolescence.

Why Use a Framework?

Applications that you develop with frameworks contain very little customized code compared to the code within the framework libraries, and most of this "code" is defined as XML metadata. You reuse the same framework base classes for each project. Therefore, the promise of code reuse making application programming easier and faster, often not realized in the past, is the major benefit of using frameworks. Developers are more productive when they use a framework properly.

A framework is a compromise between a 4GL and a 3GL. 4GLs (such as Oracle Forms Developer) are primarily declarative programming tools with which you create objects and assign property values. The runtime code is derived from metadata you define in the builder and you have no chance to see or modify the runtime code outside of the metadata. A 3GL requires you to write each line of code that creates the runtime program, but it gives you ultimate control because you directly manipulate the runtime code. A framework combines these two concepts and allows you to work in a declarative way but also allows you to modify the basic functionality of the system. In defining the framework metadata, you are working in a 4GL way; in modifying the framework base classes, you will be writing 3GL code.

In addition, a good framework delivers complete, working code as an infrastructure to your business code, as well as the flexibility to easily modify the framework's behavior. Maintenance and upgrades of a legacy application that uses a framework are, in concept, easier too because learning the system code is a matter of understanding the framework and examining a small amount of metadata and custom code.

The task of learning a framework may be non-trivial but the framework is likely to offer more documentation and to have more user community support than a custom-built code library. User community support is an important aspect to any product because the wider the use, the more examples of successful implementations and techniques will be available. Also, if the user base is strong, it is likely that there will be input based on experience that guides improvements in future versions of the framework.

NOTE
Well-built frameworks make clear distinctions between well-documented API code, which you can extend, and the internal "plumbing" code, which you do not call or extend.

What Is a Development Framework?

A *development framework* adds several layers around the idea of a framework and, in addition to base library classes of the framework, includes the following aspects:

- **A development method** The development framework defines a set of steps that you can use to create applications with the framework libraries. A method is implied when you are using frameworks, but a development framework documents the method explicitly.
- **A development tool** The development framework will be supported by a software tool that helps you complete the steps in the method.

As with a framework, working with a development framework consists mainly of following a set of steps in a tool to extend or customize the default behavior and mechanisms in the framework code libraries. Therefore, you need to learn its development method and adjust your development style to fit the framework.

Why Use a Development Framework?

The benefits of a development framework are the same as those for a framework in general. You benefit from using a base set of framework libraries that are easily extensible and flexible, and that save you from writing a large amount of foundation code for your application. You also benefit from the development method implied by the libraries because this method should be (and often is) easier than creating the application from scratch. The framework gives you a starting point for code and for the development method.

In addition to flexibility and extensibility of the code and ease of use of the development method, another important aspect of a development framework is that it saves time and effort, which makes the developer more productive. A key to productivity lies in a tool that supports the framework and makes learning and using the framework fast and relatively understandable. The tool must take care of the plumbing so the developer can concentrate on fulfilling the business requirements of the application. The tool must also assist in generating the customized, business-specific portions of the application.

Support for the Framework

Frameworks can be measured by the extent of user community support and the quality of information available. A framework without a clear definition of its development path will limit its adoption. Documentation about the development path as well as detailed descriptions and examples are keys to a successful framework.

Technical Support and User Community Support

It is also important that frameworks have good technical support other than documentation and tools. This can be supplied as formal product support through the framework vendor or a third party, but these sources are usually not enough. A broad user community is also essential. When you are in the middle of developing an application, you need to be able to ask questions of other framework users. This need can be fulfilled by Internet mail list servers, online discussion forums, and vendor and third-party white papers.

The Java community is a prime example of a broad, extensive user community. Technical support for Java is available on the Sun Microsystems website in user discussion forums, technical white papers, tutorials, and detailed specifications. In addition, third-party websites such as user groups extend this support by offering specialized views of a particular technology. A quick search for a Java technology in any web search engine will yield many available websites.

What Is Oracle Application Development Framework?

Oracle Application Development Framework is a full-featured development framework for creating application program code in JDeveloper. ADF contains all aspects of a true development framework as just discussed—highly integrated code libraries, a well-documented development method, and a full-featured IDE to support it. It also offers an architecture model that explains the concepts of the framework.

ADF combines a number of Oracle frameworks available in previous JDeveloper releases: ADF Business Components (ADF BC), formerly called Business Components for Java (BC4J); ADF UIX (formerly UIX or User Interface XML); and ADF JClient (used for Java client applications). Also, ADF includes built-in integration with the Struts framework for web controller functions and data binding. In addition, ADF supports work with JSP technology as a view alternative.

The primary strength and uniqueness of ADF is in its handling of business services (data sources). Much thought and effort have gone into providing a seamless method for connecting the various layers of an application to its data. ADF handles the complexity of binding the user interface components to various sources of data. In addition to the ADF BC framework for business services, ADF also integrates business services implemented as Enterprise JavaBeans (EJBs), web services, and Java classes.

Struts, JSP pages, EJBs, web services, and Java classes were all supported in Oracle9*i* JDeveloper, but ADF in JDeveloper 10*g* wraps them in a consistent architecture and development method. JDeveloper's visual editors, navigators, property inspectors, and modelers reduce the complexity of combining these different technologies and minimize the amount of code that you need to create.

The motto of this release is "Productivity with Choice." The choice comes from the many technologies, deployment platforms, and development styles that are supported. The productivity results from the ADF development method and architecture.

In addition to feedback received from expert user testing and months of feedback from a public preview release available on OTN, ADF has been road tested for over four years by more than two thousand of Oracle's E-Business Suite application developers. From that standpoint ADF is a mature product even though it was just released to the public in JDeveloper 10*g*.

Who Will Use ADF?

In the early days of Java, IDEs provided an easy way to compile, run, and debug code without having to use the command line. As Java evolved, IDEs evolved and included more tools such as navigators, visual editors for GUI code, property inspectors, and deployment wizards. The current trend in Java IDE tools is toward *model-driven architectures* (MDA), which allow a developer to graphically represent the underlying design of an application and then generate code from it. Until the recent tools came along, work in a Java environment has been difficult for the non-expert Java developer.

Today Java is a primary language taught in schools, which means that current graduates enter the workforce with Java skills. A Gartner study completed about two years ago ("Leading Languages for IT Portfolio Planning") placed the use of Java in IT shops at 70 percent. Visual Basic had the same penetration; COBOL and C++ both were in 45 percent of IT shops, and other languages were 20 percent or under. However, there is much talk that a skills gap exists in Java programmers and many Java "experts" do not know as much as they should about important concepts. Although the exact figures should only be used as guidelines, the trends are noteworthy. Vendors such as Oracle are paying attention. Tools such as JDeveloper are trying to fill the gap in skills and target the majority market.

ADF is aimed at all levels of Java developers. Developers who are in the expert category will find that the time-saving features of ADF (such as the data-binding mechanism) will assist their work. They will be able to perform their normal low-level code manipulation and use technologies with which they are familiar, such as EJBs.

ADF is also targeted at the not-so-expert Java developer who is new to development languages or who has migrated from another tool such as Visual Basic, PowerBuilder, or Oracle Forms Developer. JDeveloper 10*g* offers support for more development options than Oracle Forms Developer offers. Because of the flexibility, it is not yet as developer-friendly as a 4GL such as Oracle Forms Developer, but ADF is a step in the right direction toward a tool that is as easy to use as Forms Developer. ADF provides more of a 4GL wrapper on 3GL Java code than any other previous release.

NOTE
A help topic "About Oracle ADF Business Components: An Oracle Forms Developer's Perspective" explains ADF BC concepts in the context of their counterparts in Oracle Forms Developer.

Although developers familiar with tools such as Oracle Forms Developer will need study and training to understand the intricacies of the J2EE environment, they can still produce production-level code using JDeveloper and ADF. Those who have experience with Oracle Forms Developer will find many parallel tools in JDeveloper such as navigators, visual editors, and property inspectors. As ADF and JDeveloper mature further, the learning curve for non-Java developers will decrease and developer productivity will increase.

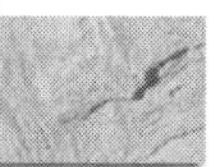

NOTE
As mentioned in other parts of the book, JDeveloper makes creating J2EE code possible for non-expert developers, but your project still needs one or more Java experts to act as architects and leaders for J2EE technology.

ADF User Community Support

As mentioned, one consideration for frameworks is the extent of support available in the user community and resources outside of the framework documentation. ADF is a new technology so you will see its third-party support grow over time. However, because many of the frameworks and options that were rolled into ADF had existed in previous releases, the Oracle OTN website (otn.oracle.com) already offers extensive community support and other resources for detailed technical information. Discussion forums on OTN supply the voice of the user community and already have many questions and answers about ADF technology and techniques. In addition, how-tos (detailed instructions for a specific technique), tutorials, product tours and demonstrations (including video clips of working in the IDE), code samples, white papers, Frequently Asked Questions (FAQs), overviews, code samples, specifications, and product sheets extend the range of technical information about ADF. In addition, OTN offers links to JDeveloper partner websites for ADF extensions and tools. These resources started growing during the JDeveloper 10*g* preview release period and expanded greatly after JDeveloper 10*g* was placed into production.

Development Frameworks in Previous JDeveloper Releases

Before fully exploring the concepts and features of ADF, it is useful to briefly examine the evolution of frameworks in JDeveloper. Previous releases of JDeveloper offered frameworks such as UIX, JClient, and BC4J. The BC4J framework contained base classes, wizards, and editor support in the IDE.

This method for creating BC4J was well supported and defined in the IDE wizards, Component Palette, Property Inspector, and editors. Other data access methods such as EJBs and web services were also supported but were not a major focus of the IDE. Other frameworks such as UIX and JClient had their own methods for developing the user interface part of the application. In JDeveloper 10*g*, all of these technologies are still separate components but have been reworked (refactored) to plug into the new ADF data-binding architecture (described in the "Model" section later in this chapter).

ADF Architecture Model

ADF is based on the J2EE design pattern Model-View-Controller (MVC). Chapter 7 explains MVC in the context of J2EE design patterns but a brief preview in this context is necessary as an introduction to the ADF architecture model.

MVC

For the purposes of this discussion, it is important to know that the *Model-View-Controller* design pattern defines three main layers of application code:

- **Model** This layer represents the data and values portion of the application.
- **View** This layer represents the screen and user interface components.
- **Controller** This layer handles the user interface events that occur as the user interacts with the interface (view), controls page flow, and communicates with the Model layer.

In concept, these layers are independent so that you can switch code in one layer to another technology and use the other two layers without modification. For example, if you build your view layer on JavaServer Pages technology, you could switch ADF UIX into the application and retain the same model and controller layers. In practice, completely separating layers is difficult, but MVC is still useful as a guide and a goal.

ADF Layers and Components

The ADF architecture divides its components into four layers as shown in Figure 4-1. The Model, View, and Controller layers in ADF correspond to the MVC layers with those names. However, ADF splits the MVC Model layer into two layers: Model and Business Services.

For the purposes of this discussion (and throughout the book), applications can exist in two main styles as follows:

- **Java client** This is a runtime alternative that runs code in a Java virtual machine on the client machine (such as for Java applications and applets). The Java Foundation Classes (JFC) Swing library (part of the Java Software Development Kit) provides components such as buttons, text items, containers, and windows for building the user interface. Although other component libraries exist, the examples in this book use the Swing library.
- **Web client** The web client style displays a user interface in the user's web browser and is run on a web tier server (as are servlets and JSP pages). The main idea of this type of client is that it is lightweight, so for the purposes of this book, mobile client (such as PDAs and cell phones) applications can be considered with this type of client.

Business Services

The Business Services layer of ADF provides a code layer for accessing data sources such as a database. Business services are responsible for *persistence*—the physical storage of data for future

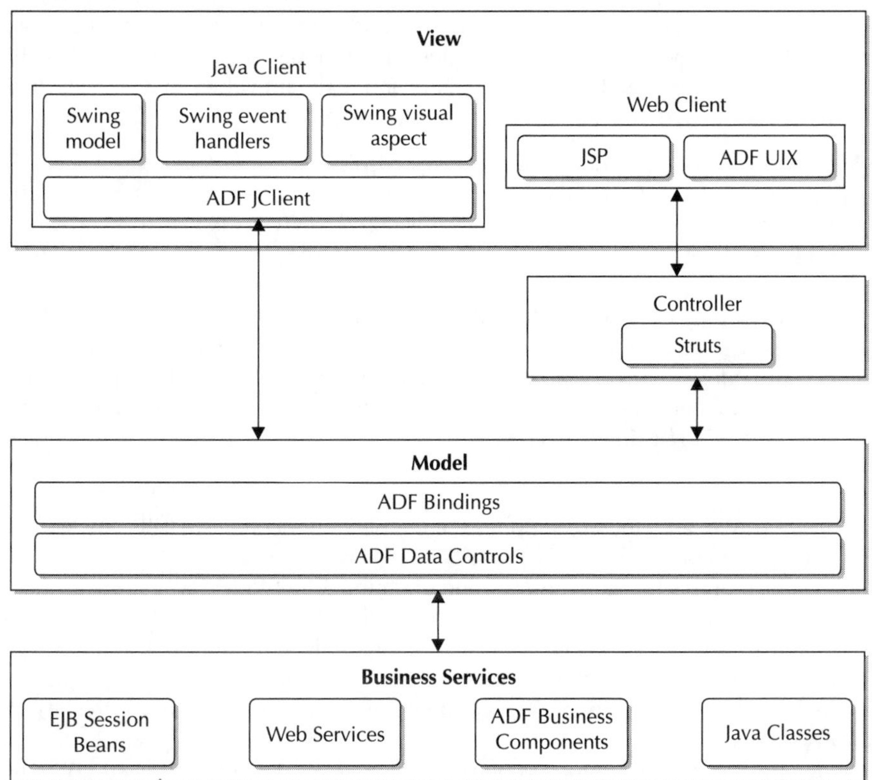

FIGURE 4-1. *ADF architecture model*

retrieval—and *object-relational mapping*—translating physical storage units such as rows and columns in relational database tables to object-oriented structures such as arrays of objects with property values. Business services code deployed into the J2EE Business Tier provides a place to code business logic for the application.

ADF was designed around the idea of flexibility. For example, if you are accustomed to working with business services delivered in Enterprise JavaBeans, you can develop EJBs to act as business services within the ADF method. ADF supports the following business services technologies:

- **EJB** A standard J2EE structure for managing data from within a runtime container, consisting of entity beans, session beans, and message-driven beans.
- **Web services** Utility functions and other resources written by a provider that are available through an Internet address and that you can incorporate into your application.

- **ADF Business Components** ADF BC is an evolution of BC4J, which provides components that allow developers to design and code business objects and business logic. It offers easy interaction with business data though SQL statements. ADF BC uses *declarative tools* (property editors to create and maintain values in XML files) that define functions for persistence and object-relational mapping.
- **Java classes** You can code Java class files, also called *Plain Old Java Objects* (*POJOs*) or JavaBeans, that supply data stored in files or in Java objects. JDeveloper's *TopLink* utilities (available in the New Gallery's Business Tier\TopLink category) provide flexible mapping and persistence services to these Java classes.

Chapters 8–13 of this book discuss ADF Business Components and Chapter 14 briefly explores other business services alternatives. The sidebar at the end of this chapter called "About ADF BC Code" provides an introduction to some concepts of ADF BC code. The upcoming sidebar "A Note About Service-Oriented Architecture" describes service-oriented architecture, which is closely related to business services.

Model

The Model layer in ADF architecture supplies the connection mechanism from the View layer to the data access components in the Business Services layer. It receives instructions from the Controller layer as requests for data retrieval and updating. The Model layer supplies data from the Business Services layer and sends a request to the View layer to update the display. For example, when the user submits a page in a web client application, the Controller layer requests an update of the data model through the Model layer. The Model layer communicates the data change to the View layer so the visual display can be updated when the page refreshes (in the case of a web client).

The Model layer in ADF is composed of two aspects—ADF Data Controls and ADF Bindings. Since these are core features of the new ADF development method and ADF architecture, they are worth a more detailed explanation.

ADF Data Controls *Data controls* are definitions used to abstract one or more business services into a common layer. For example, business services that use ADF BC, EJBs, and web services in one project will all be available through a common set of ADF data controls. This is the reason that ADF can support so many business services with a consistent interface. Data controls appear as a list of interface components available to data model components. A *data model* is a representation of the business service objects available to a project. For example, if

A Note About Service-Oriented Architecture

Current industry thoughts about business services are focusing towards service-oriented architecture (SOA), which generalizes the idea of business services to just "services." SOA services, like business services in ADF, provide a common interface to various service implementations (such as the different possible data sources in the ADF business services layer). SOA services can be data sources such as in ADF as well as any other code or data source. Although this concept is not used in ADF, it is primarily a widening of the ADF concept of business services.

you create a business services layer using ADF Business Components, you can define a data model in the application module definition using the Application Module Editor as shown here:

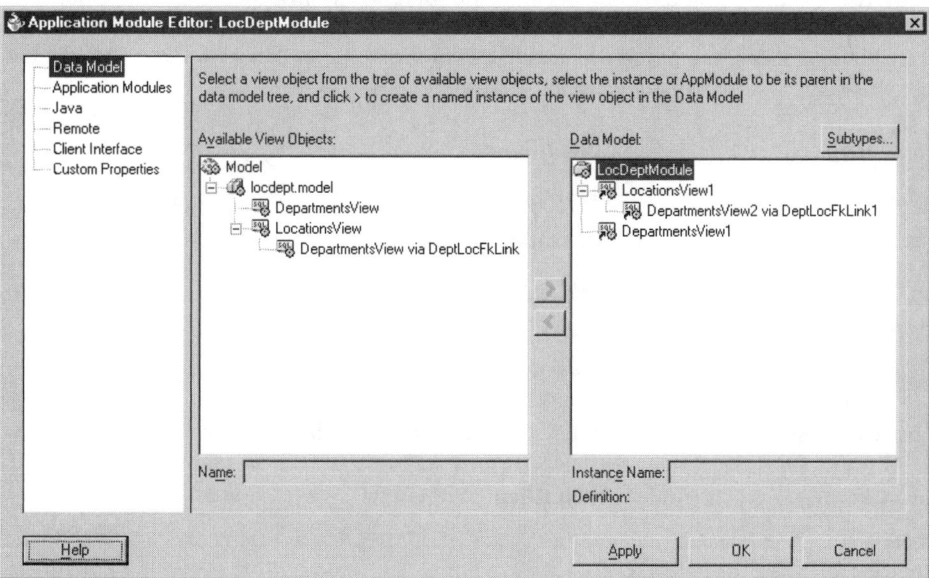

The left area of this editor shows the available data objects and the right side shows the data model—objects selected for this application module. You can also use the business components diagram to modify or display the application module data model as shown here:

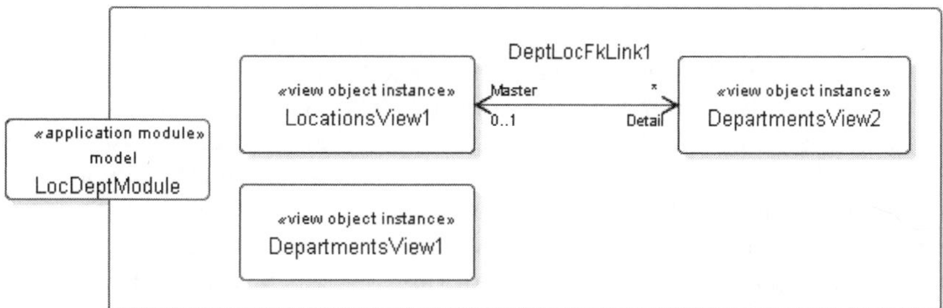

This data model contains two master view object instances—LocationsView1 and DepartmentsView1. It also contains a detail view object instance, DepartmentsView2, that links to LocationsView1. (You can change the names of the instances using the Application Module Editor.) The view object definitions and their attributes are available to the applications that reference the data model.

Data controls standardize the interface to business services other than ADF BC. The properties of a data control (if any) are usually collections of values (like row sets). The Data Control Palette offers user interface controls that are appropriate to the kind of page or panel you are working on (for a web client or Java client, respectively). The interface controls presented also depend upon whether the data source is a collection of data (such as an ADF view object instance with multiple rows), a single value (such as an attribute in a view object instance), or a single structure (such as a row). Different binding objects are supported depending upon the type of data and the controls available in the Data Control Palette will change based on these considerations.

The following lists some of the user interface components available for view object-level components such as LocationsView1 and DepartmentsView2:

Java Client	**Web Client**
Table	Read-Only Table
ComboBox	Navigation Buttons
Tree	Input Form
NavigationBar	Read-Only Form
ScrollBar	Select Row Link

The next list shows some data model components that are available for attributes:

Java Client	**Web Client**
TextField	Value
ComboBox	Label
CheckBox	Text Field
ScrollBar	Password Field
TextArea	List of Values

As you would expect, for each user interface style, different interface components are available for different types of data model components such as view object definitions and view object attributes.

Data controls are available from the Data Control Palette, which appears automatically when you display a visual editor (or when you select **View | Data Control Palette**). All data model objects defined for business services in the workspace will be available. When you select a data model object in this palette, the *Drag and Drop As* pulldown will display a list of available interface components. You add an interface component to the editor by selecting the data model component, such as DepartmentsView2 in the previous example, selecting an interface type from the pulldown, and dragging the data object node into the visual editor. After you release the mouse button, a component will appear in the editor. Figure 4-2 shows this action for a Read-Only Table built from the DepartmentsView2 detail view object definition.

In addition to data value components, the Data Control Palette also offers "operations" such as Commit and Rollback to send the current data in the Model to the Business Services layer. Other navigational operations such as Create, Find, First, Next, Last, and Delete appear on the data set (ADF BC view object definition) level. In addition, you can drag Data Control Palette components into the Page Flow Diagram to create controller-level operations as methods.

ADF Bindings *Bindings* are code or definitions that declare which data from a business service is connected to a user interface control or structure. One of the challenges in the classic definition

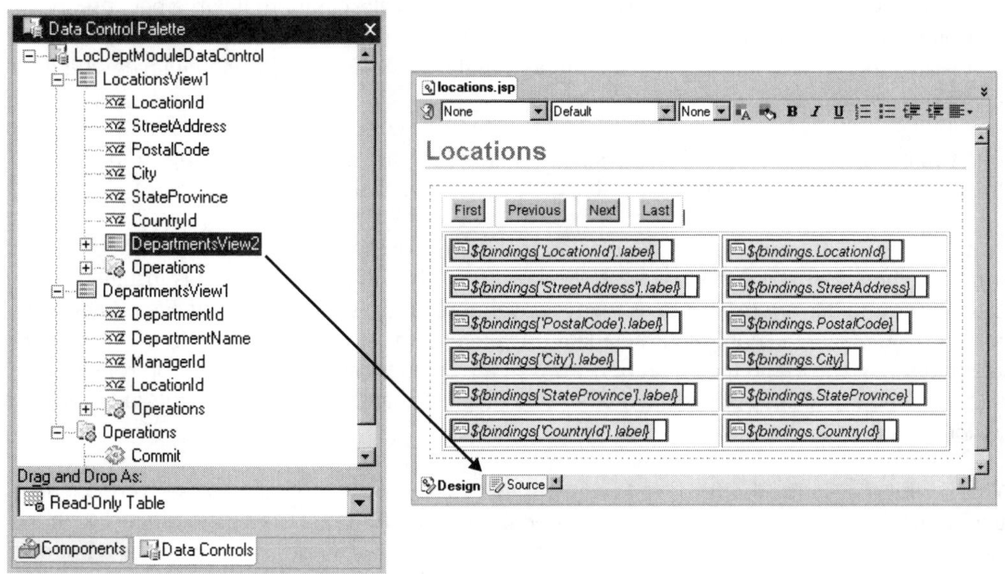

FIGURE 4-2. *Dragging a component to the visual editor*

of MVC has been where to place the data-binding functionality. ADF Bindings act as the connection layer from the View components to Business Services components. Bindings are defined using XML files, which are created and maintained automatically by actions in the JDeveloper IDE. The binding attaches to data both at design time and at run time.

When you drag a component from the Data Control Palette to a user interface surface, ADF binds the new interface component to the data control selected. For Java client controls, ADF sets the Swing component's *model* or *document* properties to the selected data control that connects to the business service component. For web client controls, ADF sets the appropriate data attribute for the element.

Chapter 12 discusses the ADF Model layer in depth. Chapter 15 contains examples of binding for Java client code. Chapter 18 contains examples of binding for web client code. A white paper on OTN, "Oracle ADF Data Binding Primer," discusses data bindings in more depth.

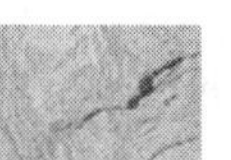

NOTE
Oracle has submitted the data-binding and data controls architecture to the Java Community Process as JSR-227 (www.jcp.org/en/jsr/detail?id=227).

Controller

The Controller layer in ADF is used only for web client code as shown in Figure 4-1. For a web client, the Controller layer defines *page flow*—which page is presented when an action occurs on another page—as well as the processing actions that occur between pages (such as a database query). Since the Controller handles the order in which pages appear, a page need not have a hard-coded link to the next page. This makes the page flow design more flexible because the Controller can apply conditional logic to determine the next page to be displayed. The Controller layer is also responsible for sending data entered in the View layer to the Model layer where it can be processed.

Although you can use any controller mechanism (even one you write yourself) for web client code you create in JDeveloper, the tools in the current release of JDeveloper 10*g* support the Struts controller framework the most fully.

Struts The Struts framework is an open source project of the Apache Software Foundation (struts.apache.org) that is used for Controller layer functionality. Struts support is installed with JDeveloper, and JDeveloper contains many powerful features, such as the Page Flow Diagram, that help you create the controller metadata (included in the struts-config.xml file). This metadata determines page flow and the chain of actions in a web application. The Struts controller layer interfaces well with existing view and model technologies. Chapter 17 discusses Struts in JDeveloper in more detail.

What About the Controller for Java Client Code? Java client applications use components such as those from the Swing library; these components perform the Controller functions on the client tier through event handlers. Event handlers are triggered by user events such as a button click or field navigation and can affect the component, the form (a collection of components), or the navigation between forms (a parallel concept to page flow in a web client).

Although the controller mechanism is built into the component event handlers and is not part of ADF, writing code for events is well supported in JDeveloper. ADF JClient provides the link from the Swing model layer to the Model layer's data bindings and data controls. Swing contains a visual aspect (View layer), event handlers aspect (Controller layer), and model aspect (Model layer). Figure 4-1 shows all Swing MVC layers, along with the ADF JClient binding API inside the View layer because the MVC layers use ADF JClient to communicate with the ADF Data Bindings and Data Controls that are part of the Model layer.

View

The View layer in ADF includes Java client and web client technologies that are used to render user interfaces.

Java Client As mentioned, Java client technology is a runtime alternative that runs code in a Java virtual machine on the client machine. It does not require application servers because all application code is stored and runs on the client machine (although it may access business services code such as ADF BC that is deployed on a web tier server as EJB session beans). A primary function of Swing controls is to present user interface objects—an MVC view aspect. As explained in the preceding section "What About the Controller for Java Client Code" Swing event handlers supply a controller function and JClient supplies a link from the Swing component model layer to the Model layer components in ADF (as shown in Figure 4-1).

Web Client ADF supports a number of web client view technologies that display in a browser. Although you can use any view technology, the following technologies are supported the most fully by the JDeveloper tools:

- **JSP technology** This is a popular J2EE coding style that combines HTML and JSP tags. You can also embed Java scriptlets that perform programming functions such as conditional processing and iteration. JSP files run on an application server and usually output HTML to the client browser.
- **ADF UIX** ADF UIX is an Oracle framework that defines a page using XML code. A unique feature of UIX is its rich container model, which allows you to easily create a standard look-and-feel for your application. Since the page definition is XML metadata, the page can be rendered using different viewers such as mobile devices or a desktop browser. Oracle's E-Business Suite (Oracle Applications) uses UIX technology for its self-service applications. UIX has many features in common with JSF technology.

For web client applications, the code is run on an application server and generates a page that is displayed in the client's display device (such as a web browser). These technologies are primarily coded with tag languages that are supported by various Java class libraries (called *tag libraries*). These libraries present the user interface using standard controls for the appropriate device (such as HTML in a web browser). When the user submits a web page that contains input values, the page is processed by the Controller layer.

JavaServer Faces Another view technology that deserves a mention (although it is not shown in Figure 4-1 because it has no native support yet in JDeveloper 10*g*), is *JavaServer Faces (JSF)* technology. JSF technology is a Sun initiative that developed from the Java community process as Java Specification Request (JSR) 127. This JSR has recently been released in its final form and has a reference implementation (code proving the specification can be built). Since it is a new technology, not all development frameworks support it yet.

JSF adds a cleaner separation between logic and HTML presentation to JSP technology. The JSF API and JSP tag libraries offer Controller functions that you can use instead of Struts as well as a standard way to manage the server-side processing of user interface components (for example, for data validation, page navigation, and events). JSF handles different client devices such as mobile clients and desktop clients more easily than JSP technology. Even though JDeveloper does not offer JSF support natively, you can still work with JSF using some of the JDeveloper tools as explained in the sidebar "A Word About JSF Technology in JDeveloper."

A Word About JSF Technology in JDeveloper

Although JSF is not automatically installed in JDeveloper, you can download the reference implementation from the Sun website (java.sun.com/j2ee/javaserverfaces) and register JSF tag libraries in JDeveloper. You can then develop JavaServer Faces code using some of the same tools you use for JSP and UIX files. The JDeveloper help system contains information about how to get started (search for "JSF" in the Index page) and a link to the OTN website where a "How To" white paper discusses details of using JSF in JDeveloper. The Sun Microsystems website also offers the *J2EE 1.4 Tutorial* (java.sun.com/j2ee/tutorial), which contains a thorough introduction to JSF. To learn more about the future of JSF in JDeveloper, refer to OTN for the white paper "Roadmap for the ADF UIX technology and JavaServer Faces."

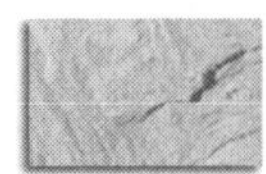

NOTE
View technology alternatives are discussed further in Chapter 7. Chapter 15 discusses Swing and JClient further, Chapter 18 describes JSP pages, and Chapter 19 discusses ADF UIX pages.

ADF Code Libraries

As with any framework, ADF provides a set of base libraries that you can extend and customize. These libraries are the core of the application that you create using JDeveloper tools and a specific development method. The application-specific code that you add in JDeveloper uses the ADF libraries for basic functionality. Therefore, you will very rarely need to know details about how the libraries work unless you need to replace or supplement a specific mechanism. However, you will need to know what functionality the libraries offer so that your code can take advantage of that functionality and so that you do not waste time writing code for functionality that the framework offers by default. Also, should you need to modify the way in which the libraries work, you will need to refer to the JDeveloper online documentation and Javadoc for the appropriate class.

The main libraries in ADF consist of many proven technologies. The code is based on J2EE design patterns and is deployable in any J2EE-compliant server or environment. The code, as with all Java code, is platform independent so it will run under any operating system. It is also non-specific to a particular database product, although ADF Business Components contain some features (like automatic sequence generators) that work best with an Oracle database. See the help system topic "Limitations of Developing Oracle ADF Business Components for Oracle9*i* Lite and Non-Oracle Datasources" for more information; in the table of contents node, navigate to "Building J2EE Applications\Working with the Business Tier\Developing Oracle ADF Business Components\Developing Oracle ADF Business Components for Oracle9*i* Lite and Non-Oracle Datasources."

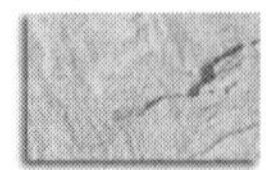

NOTE
ADF runtime libraries are included in the cost of the JDeveloper license. Deploying the runtime libraries to a J2EE server (for web client code) requires no additional runtime license.

Some ADF Libraries

Since the ADF libraries are automatically used by the IDE, a full list of the libraries and their contents would not be helpful outside the realm of a reference manual. However, the following is a list of some of the libraries available in the Libraries node of the Project Properties dialog:

ADF Controller Runtime	ADF Web Runtime
ADF Designtime API	BC4J Client
ADF EJB Runtime	BC4J EJB Client
ADF Model Runtime	BC4J EJB Runtime
ADF JSP Tag Library	BC4J HTML
ADF TopLink Runtime	BC4J Struts Runtime
ADF UIX Runtime	JClient Runtime

You can access the Project Properties dialog by double clicking a project node in the Application Navigator and selecting the Libraries page under Profiles\Development as shown here:

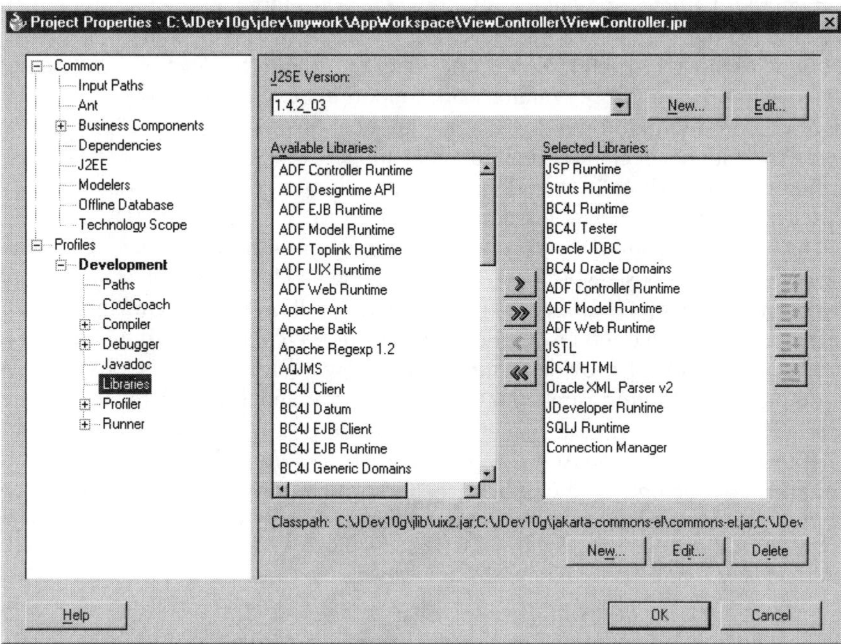

Selecting a library name shows the archive files that it is composed of under the *Available Libraries* area. You can also click the Edit button in this dialog to display the Edit Library dialog, which contains information about the library. The Edit Library dialog also contains a View button to the right of the *Class Path* field that shows the View Class Path dialog, which contains a list of archive files in the library as shown here:

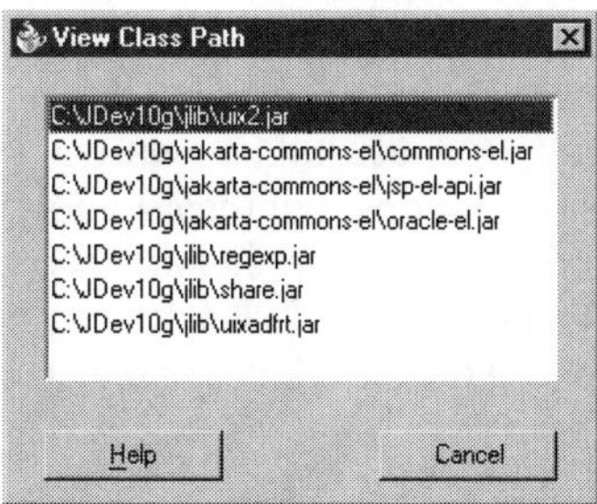

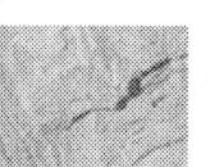

NOTE

Information about the ADF libraries can be found in the JDeveloper online help system. The table of contents node contains a Reference node (book) that contains Javadoc for a number of ADF libraries such as ADF BC (the library is called "Oracle Business Components for Java"), ADF UIX (the library is called "UIX"), and the ADF Controller.

ADF Development Method and IDE Support

Two major features of a development framework are the development method used to create applications and the IDE support for that development method. In JDeveloper, the development method is bound to the IDE. Therefore, it is necessary to explain the development method and IDE support together. The purpose of framework support in an IDE is to make the job of learning the framework easier and to allow you to create applications more quickly. Framework tools allow you to work within a declarative environment and let you focus on the business requirements instead of the details of writing 3GL code and the plumbing needed to connect application components. The objective is to use the declarative tools to create as much application code as possible and spend the least amount of time writing custom code. This will allow you to spend more time writing code that adds business value to the application and less time writing code for plumbing. The more you know about the framework, the closer you will be to achieving this objective.

This section provides an overview of these steps using ADF and a description of the tools that support these steps. Chapter 1 provides a summary of how to create applications in JDeveloper and hands-on practices to demonstrate the steps. Chapters 2 and 3 discuss the JDeveloper IDE more fully so this discussion will focus on how the IDE tools support ADF instead of all features of all tools. Individual tasks in the ADF development method are well documented in the online help system and in documents on the Oracle Technology website (otn.oracle.com). JDeveloper is oriented toward using ADF to create code and all tools support work within the ADF method.

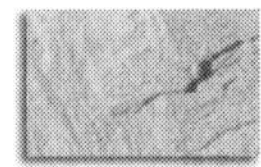

NOTE
Understanding a framework completely is not a prerequisite to producing workable code. You can start working in JDeveloper and ADF after a brief overview; however, the more you know about the framework, the better chance you have of using it in the right way and of being more productive.

All work in JDeveloper creates plain ASCII text files, some of which may need to be compiled but most of which will be deployed into a production environment. JDeveloper keeps track of all files (such as server configuration files) even if you are not aware of them so that the deployment package is complete. (Chapter 7 discusses details about J2EE deployment.)

Developers who use JDeveloper 10*g* must still be aware of how the plumbing works so that they can perform any required customizations, but they do not have to create or maintain the files that connect to or configure the client, the application server, and the database server. They do need to consider how the application should look and act and how it will implement business requirements. This is the most proper use of a developer's time and expertise—finding programmatic solutions for business problems.

The Steps

The steps for creating code are slightly different for each type of technology (for example, Java client or web client). However, the ADF development method is very similar for all. This section summarizes the high-level steps needed to create an ADF BC model and JSP view application. The general steps are similar for a Java client. Refer to the hands-on practices throughout this book for detailed steps. In addition to outlining the high-level steps you follow when creating such an application, this section also describes some of the tools and ADF concepts you will employ for each step. The method consists of the following general phases:

I. Create an application workspace using an application template
II. Create the Business Services and Model layers
III. Create the View and Controller layers
IV. Test, debug, and deploy the application

The steps for creating the Model layer are contained within the phase that creates the Business Services layer. The steps for creating the Controller layer are contained within the phase that creates the View layer. Details of how each project is created are specific to the type of code that you are building.

I. Create an Application Workspace Using an Application Template

As explained in Chapter 1, JDeveloper organizes code files into projects that contain similar types of code for an application. Projects are contained within application workspaces. When you start work on an application, you need to create an application workspace using the Create Application Workspace dialog shown next:

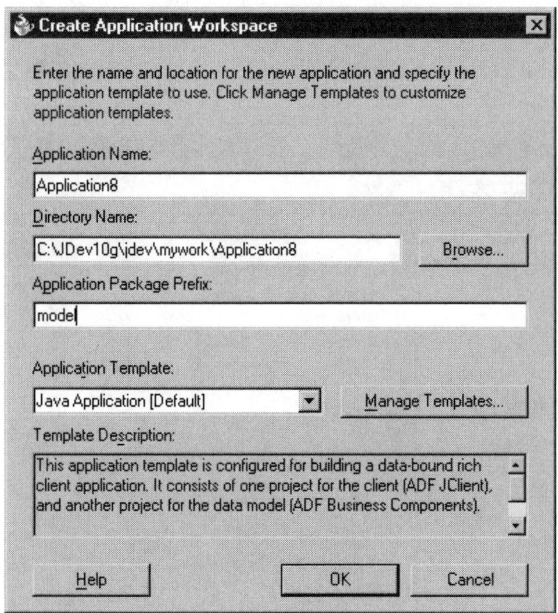

Application Template This dialog contains an *Application Template* pulldown where you select a specific application template. This pulldown contains pre-defined templates (described in Chapter 1). Using a specific template to create a workspace will create a set of projects, each of which is set up for a specific technology scope.

Technology Scope Each project created by an application template will be oriented toward a specific technology scope. Technology scopes are a way to reduce the enormous number of options available in the JDeveloper IDE to just the options that apply to the application you are developing. A technology scope in this context refers to the following behavior:

- **A set of code libraries** will be placed into the CLASSPATH for the application runtime and for coding the application.
- **Specific user interface and controller components** will be accessible using the Component Palette pages in a project.
- **A specific style of business services** will be available to the workspace.
- **Specific configuration files will be created** in the project, for example, a web.xml file for web client applications.
- **The New Gallery item list** will be filtered appropriately.

New Gallery Item Filtering As an example of filtering in the New Gallery, if you select the "Web Application [Default]" template, ADF will create a workspace containing a Model project for business services, and a ViewController project for the view (JSP or UIX code) and the controller (Struts) code. The New Gallery for the Model project will display items that are applicable to the technologies defined for the project, such as Business Components, as shown in the following illustration:

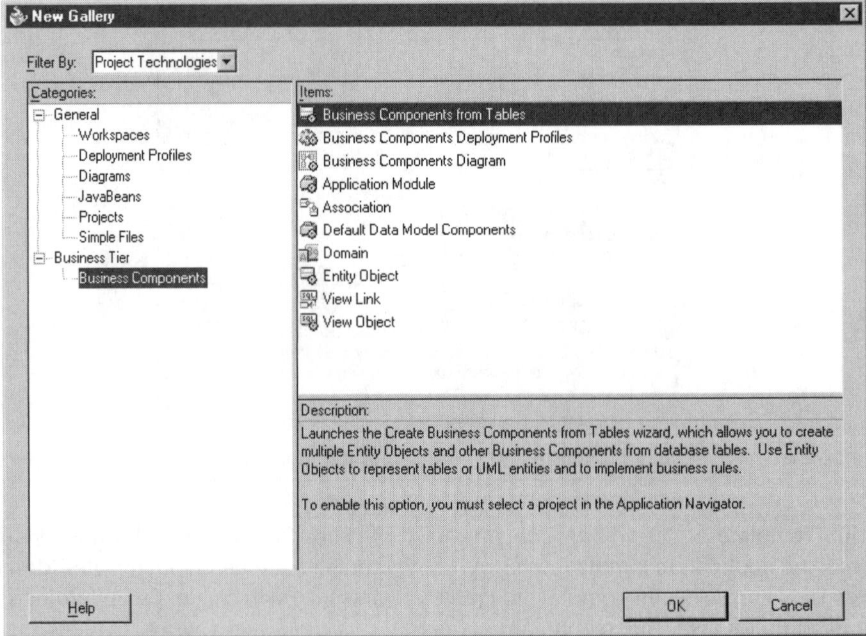

The list of categories is filtered to those that will likely be required for a model project. The ViewController project for this workspace would show New Gallery categories and items that are applicable to the technologies defined for the project as shown here:

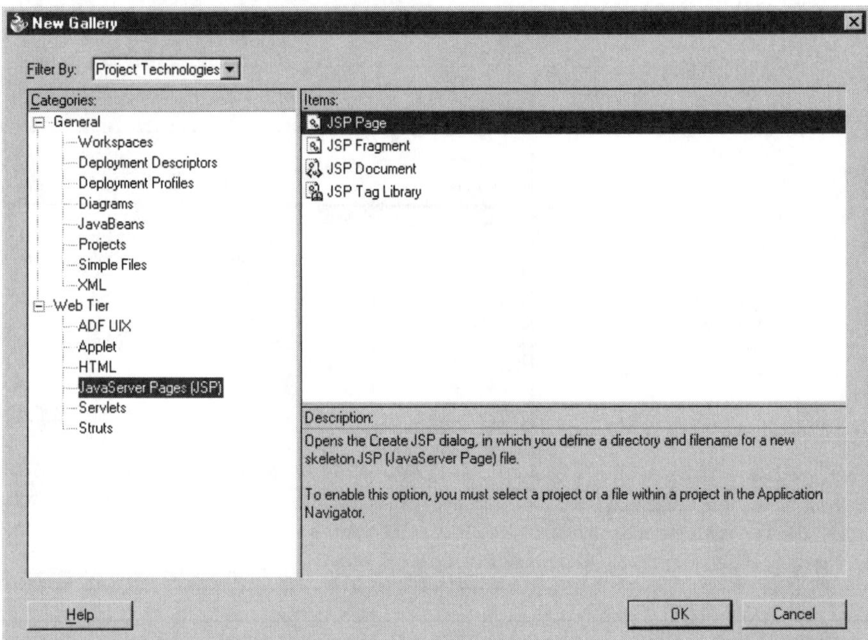

The *Filter By* pulldown at the top of the New Gallery allows you to select "All Technologies" in case an item you need to create does not appear. After you select an item or category outside the technology list and return to the New Gallery, that item or category will be available even if the pulldown in the New Gallery is "Project Technologies." You can add technologies to a project using the Technology Scope page of the Project Properties dialog (accessed by right-clicking the project node).

TIP
If in each project you create, you find yourself selecting the same New Gallery category or item that is outside of the project technology, you should create your own application template modeled after the default template that contains the appropriate technologies.

Managing Application Templates You can examine the definitions of the default templates and add your own templates by clicking the Manage Templates button (if the Create Application Workspace dialog is displayed) or by selecting **Tools | Manage Application Templates** to display the Manage Application Templates dialog shown in Figure 4-3.

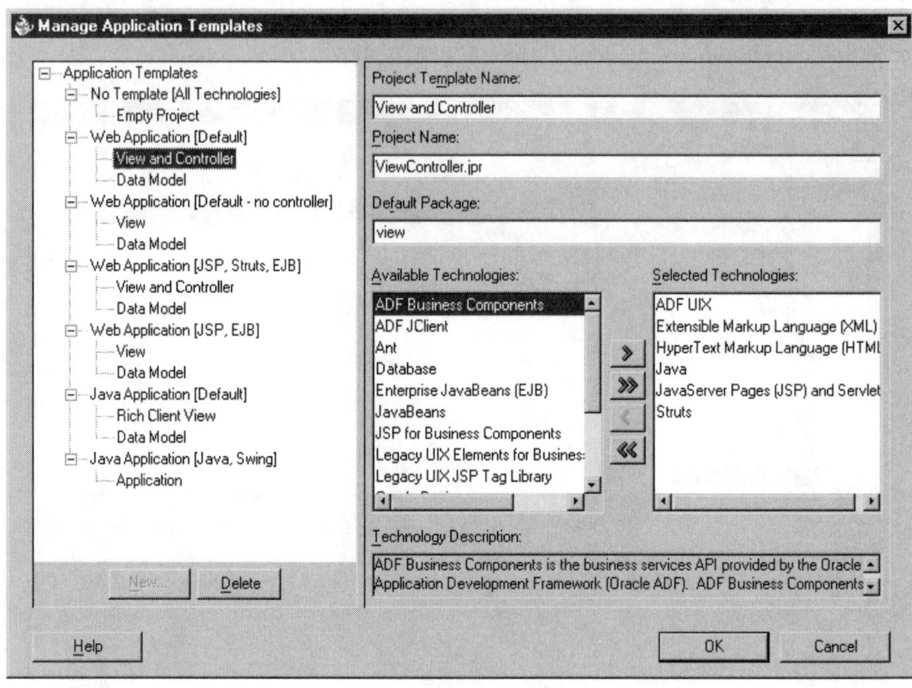

FIGURE 4-3. *Manage Application Templates dialog*

You can view the technologies that apply to a particular project within the application template by clicking the project node under a template name, as Figure 4-3 shows. Selecting the Application Templates node and clicking New allows you to define your own application template.

NOTE
*In addition to limiting the options available in the IDE by using technologies, you can use the Extension Manager to temporarily disable options that you will not use. You can access the Extension Manager using the Extension Manager page of the Preferences dialog (**Tools | Preferences**).*

II. Create the Business Services and Model Layers

After creating an application workspace with an empty Model project, you need to define the business services in that project. This task relies on ADF wizards, dialogs, or modelers to create default objects that you can modify. The following example describes a path for creating the default objects using ADF wizards. Part II of this book contains examples of using the Business Components Modeler to create ADF BC components.

Wizards and Editors The Model project created using the "Web Application [Default]" template shows ADF Business Components in the New Gallery. Selecting Business Components from Tables in this dialog starts the Business Components Project Initialization dialog shown here:

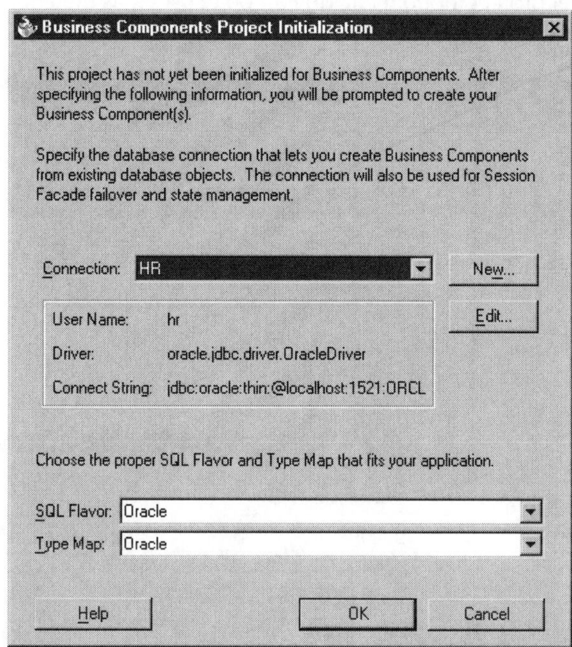

This dialog creates some ADF BC configuration files and starts the Create Business Components from Tables Wizard. This wizard steps you through the process of defining which tables will be the source of entity object definitions, which view object definitions to create from the entity object definitions, and how the application module is named. After running this wizard, you will see objects in the Application Navigator for the components you specified in the wizard such as the following for the DEPARTMENTS and LOCATIONS tables:

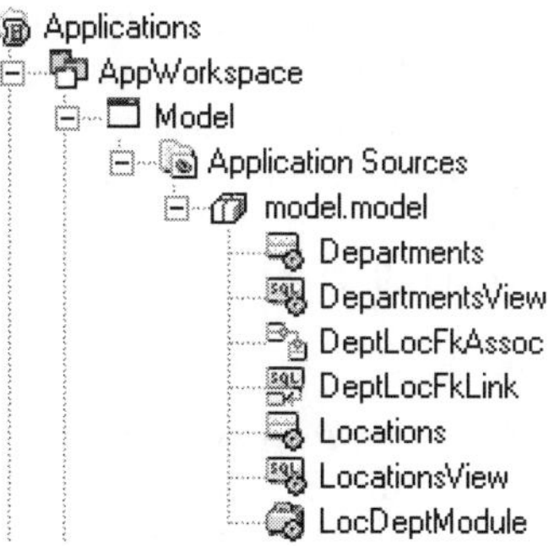

In addition to the objects shown in the Application Navigator, the wizard creates configuration and property files. For example, the Model project created using the Create Business Components from Tables Wizard will include the bc4j.xfcg, model.xml, and Model.jpx files. These configuration files are visible under the project's node in the System Navigator.

In addition to the wizards that create default code objects, ADF provides various editors. In this example of a Model project, double clicking an object such as the Locations entity object definition displays an editor such as the following:

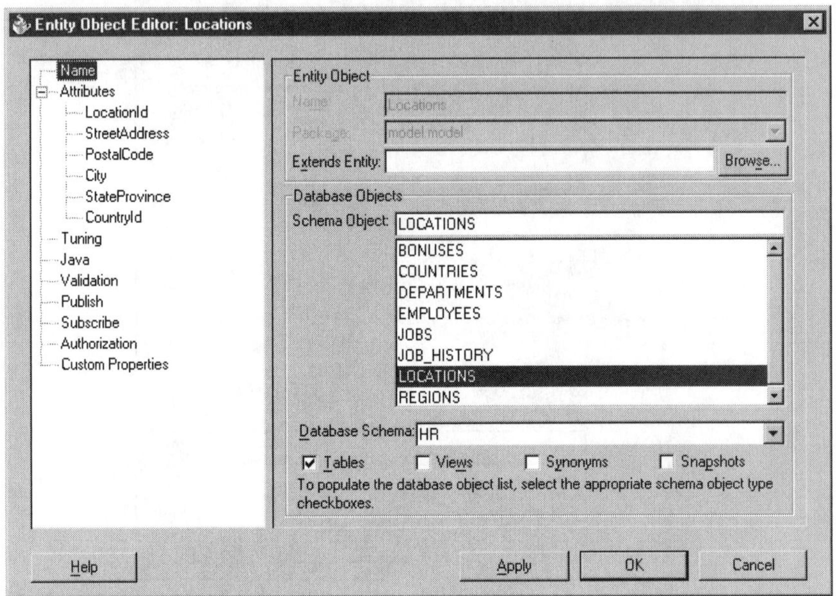

This editor modifies the XML file associated with the entity object definition. You cannot edit the XML file directly in a code editor within JDeveloper. This editor can also create Java class files that allow you to extend the default entity object behavior, and these Java files may be edited directly in the Code Editor. Chapter 10 discusses entity object definition editing.

Diagrams For model components, you can also create diagrams such as the business components diagram shown in Figure 4-4 for the Locations and Departments application module.

The Component Palette offers elements that you can add to the diagram as shown in the excerpt from the Component Palette for an ADF BC diagram in Figure 4-4. As with all diagrams, the Thumbnail window shows a version of the page you are editing and allows you to navigate around the window by dragging a viewport rectangle.

Other types of business services offer diagrams, wizards, and editors that are similar to this example.

Structure Window The Structure window displays the contents of business services objects such as the example in Figure 4-4 for an ADF BC entity object definition. You can view or edit most elements shown in the Structure window by double clicking the element or by selecting Edit from the right-click menu on the element's node.

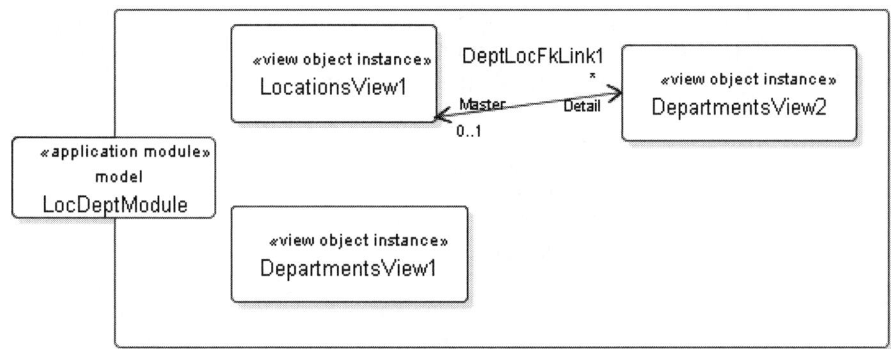

Business Components Diagram

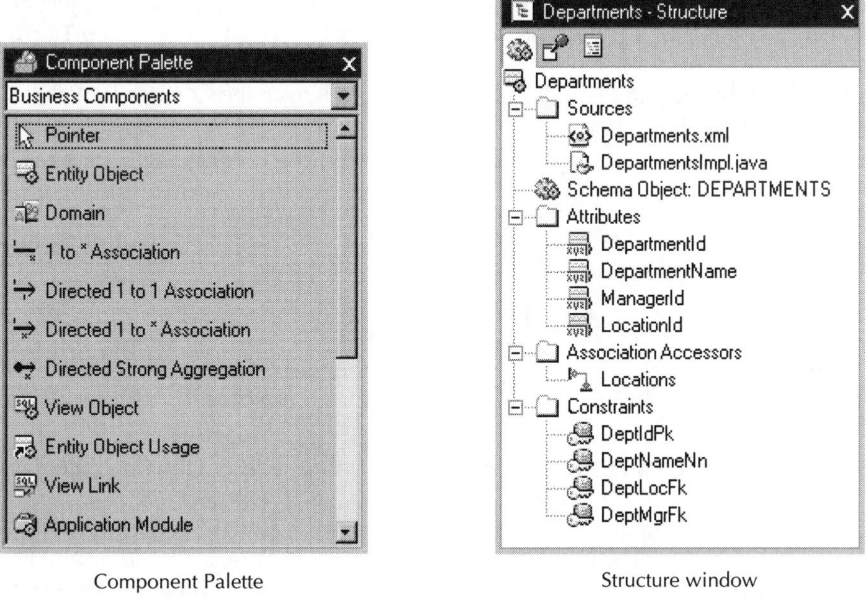

Component Palette

Structure window

FIGURE 4-4. *Some Business Services tools*

III. Create the View and Controller Layers

The ViewController project is the container for code in the View and Controller layers of the application. It uses the same Code Editor as the Model project objects. It also uses the same Structure window although the Structure window objects represent elements appropriate to the View and Controller components. The Component Palette contains the components appropriate to the View and Controller layers.

Page Flow Diagram ADF supports the Struts controller by default, and some Struts files are automatically created when you specify the "Web Application [Default]" application template. You can see these files, namely ApplicationResources.properties and struts-config.xml, in the Application Navigator as shown under the default ViewController project here:

The Page Flow Diagram is the starting point for creating user interface code such as JSP and UIX code. It is available by double clicking the struts-config.xml or by selecting Open Struts Page Flow Diagram from the right-click menu on the ViewController project. If the project does not contain a struts-config.xml file, you can create one using the New Gallery's Web Tier\Struts category.

After opening the diagram, you drop components on it from the Component Palette. A simple Page Flow Diagram is shown here:

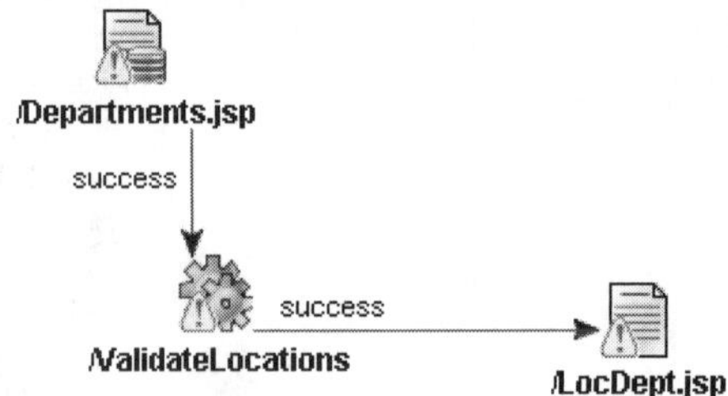

Notice that action components (cogwheel symbols) that represent the Controller layer as well as page components (rectangular box page symbols) that represent the View layer are displayed on the same diagram. The Component Palette for a Struts Page Flow Diagram contains all elements that would normally appear on this diagram. The Structure window and Property Inspector display the applicable elements and properties, respectively, for a selected component.

JSP/HTML Visual Editor and Data Control Palette The next step in creating a View project is to add user interface components to the pages defined in the Page Flow Diagram. Double clicking the page symbol opens a dialog that allows you to name the file associated with the Struts page symbol. The file extension you use in this dialog (.jsp or .uix) determines what type of editor will open when you click the OK button in the dialog.

For a JSP file, the JSP/ HTML Visual Editor will open as shown in Figure 4-5. (For a UIX file, the UIX Visual Editor will open.) As in other steps, you will also see the Component Palette and Structure window. In addition, the Data Control Palette will appear containing the business services objects and a pulldown listing the appropriate user interface components. (Data controls are explained earlier in this chapter, as well as in Chapter 17.)

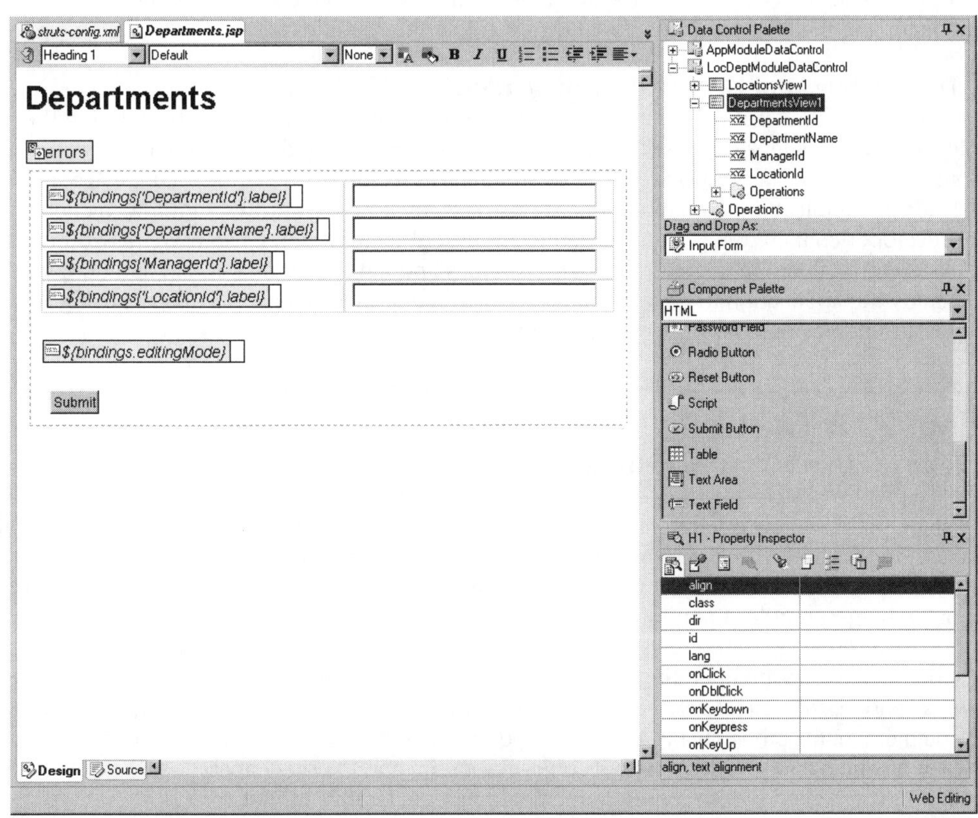

FIGURE 4-5. *JSP/HTML Visual Editor and supporting tools*

Next, you select a node in the Data Control Palette, select the appropriate component from the *Drag and Drop As* pulldown, and drop the component on the visual editor. This action binds the component to the selected business services object such as the LocationsView1 view object instance in this example. You can also add components using the Component Palette but this does not set the data-binding properties, so you will need to set them manually if the component represents business services data.

You can use the JSP/ HTML Visual Editor to edit the HTML portion of the JSP file including the style sheet (selected by clicking the visual editor and selecting the style sheet from the Component Palette), boilerplate text such as headings and labels, and other HTML elements such as tables. The visual editor allows you to view and edit the components (without data) in an emulation of the runtime display.

Property Inspector and Structure Window After dropping the required components onto the page, you can set details of an object by selecting it in the visual editor and using the Property Inspector.

As with other types of editors, the Structure window shows the elements for the selected component and the Property Inspector allows you to edit properties for the selected element.

IV. Test, Debug, and Deploy the Application

After you create the application using the JDeveloper tools, you can test it by running the application within JDeveloper. Selecting the Run option from the right-click menu on the struts-config.xml file starts a Java runtime session (in this example, the Embedded OC4J Server) and loads the application into an appropriate viewer such as a web browser for a web client.

JDeveloper contains a full-featured debugger (described further in Chapter 3) that you can use to step through problem code and identify values and the execution path. In addition, you can deploy the application to an appropriate archive file (as described in Chapter 7) using ADF wizards and deployment profile property editors.

About ADF BC Code

Before the release of BC4J framework in JDeveloper Release 3.0, connecting a Java-based application to the database was an extraordinarily difficult task. You needed to write Java Database Connectivity (JDBC) and/or SQL embedded in Java (SQLJ) code in order to coordinate a Java front-end with the database. In addition, you had to maintain your own data cache, batch your own updates, and keep track of table locks and commits. This complex interface with the database has proven to be one of the biggest hurdles to building web-based applications.

The ADF business components are built using a combination of Java and XML metadata. Since both languages are operating-system and platform independent, they interface well with networks and operate effectively across the Web. Each of these languages has unique strengths that complement the other. Java is a modular and portable language that is ideal for communicating between business applications due to its built-in security and Internet capabilities. Yet Java lacks a commonly accepted way to represent metadata in a declarative format.

This is where Extensible Markup Language (XML) becomes useful. *XML* is a tag or markup language that is similar to HTML; however, the XML tags are much more powerful because the basic tags can be extended to meet evolving needs. In HTML, you use tags to describe how you want things displayed; while in XML, you create tags to describe the structure and content of the text or data. It should be noted that XML is case sensitive just like Java.

From the developer's perspective, you will only need to think in terms of logical objects. You manipulate the Java classes only where complex validation or coding capability beyond what the visual environment can handle is required. You typically will not need to manipulate the XML documents in a text editor. Developers can edit the XML files indirectly using editor dialogs (such as the Entity Object Editor) and wizards.

CHAPTER 5

Java Language Concepts for JDeveloper Work

I love coffee, I love tea
I love the java jive and it loves me.

—The Ink Spots (1940), *The Java Jive,*
music by Ben Oakland, lyrics by Milton Drake

JDeveloper is primarily a Java development environment. It is a tool that helps you create and manage 3GL Java code and code written in supporting languages such as XML and HTML. Although you can create sophisticated application code using the declarative tools, a production system will always require extensive modification of this code. Therefore, you cannot avoid knowing about the Java language if you expect to produce a working production system using JDeveloper. The requirement of knowing the language is central to all IDEs. For example, Oracle Forms Developer requires you to be conversant in the PL/SQL language, but you do not need to be a PL/SQL expert to produce production-quality code in Forms. Similarly, with JDeveloper, knowledge of Java is essential, but you do not need to be a Java expert to produce high-quality code. However, unlike development with Forms, it is essential that you have a Java expert on your team when creating a production system with Java and JDeveloper.

One objective of this chapter is to provide a refresher (or introduction) to the Java basics that you will need to be productive in JDeveloper. Since a context is always important to those learning a language, the chapter starts by examining some of the reasons why the Java language is important for developing modern systems. Since Java is based upon object-orientation concepts, a review of those concepts is provided for those readers who are not using object orientation regularly. We expect that readers who are using Java now will be able to skim this chapter quickly or skip it altogether. Regardless of your level of Java expertise, you need to know how to create basic Java files in JDeveloper. The hands-on practice at the end of the chapter demonstrates some of the language principles discussed in the chapter as well as how to create a basic Java class file in JDeveloper.

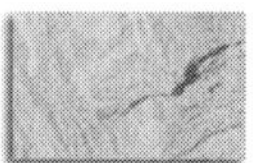

CAUTION
Although this book is aimed at those who may not be using Java as their main language for development, some code examples assume that you have already been trained in or have studied the Java language. If you expect to be creating production Java systems, you will need more formal training or study beyond the overview that this chapter provides. Appendix A contains some resources for further study.

Why Java?

Java is a relatively new, object-oriented language (officially launched in 1995) that provides many ways to deploy the code. Object orientation offers benefits in analysis and design because business concepts are more easily matched with objects than with standard relational structures. These concepts map easily to programming elements in an object-oriented language such as Java.

If you are in the process of evaluating the Java language for use in a production environment, you need to consider both its benefits and drawbacks as well as what you will need to make the transition.

Benefits

The IT industry is proceeding at a breakneck speed into Java technologies (primarily Java 2 Platform, Enterprise Edition) because of the perceived benefits. It is useful to examine some of the main strengths that Java offers.

Flexibility

Java is implemented as a rich set of core libraries that you can easily extend because the language is object oriented. Distributing these extensions is a normal and supported part of working with Java.

Java supports light-client applications (through technologies such as JavaServer Pages), which only require a browser on the client side. Running the client in a browser virtually eliminates runtime installation and maintenance concerns, which were a stumbling point with client/server application environments such as Forms (before it could be web deployed).

Java also supports deployment as a standalone application with a Java Virtual Machine (JVM) runtime on the client. It solves the problem of supporting different screen resolutions with layout managers (explained in Chapter 16) that are part of the core libraries.

The Java language is a core component of standards such as Java 2 Platform, Enterprise Edition (J2EE). It is used as the language in which basic libraries, such as those from which JavaServer Pages (JSP) code is built, are written. In addition, you can embed Java code snippets inside JSP files to perform actions specific to the web page. Chapter 7 contains further discussion on J2EE and the use of Java.

A popular J2EE design pattern, Model-View-Controller (MVC) defines layers of application code that can be swapped out when the needs of the enterprise change. With MVC, the view (presentation) layer can be implemented as a Java application running on the client with Swing components or as HTML elements presented in a browser. Although these views are different, they can share the same model (data definition and access) and controller (behavior and operation) layers. This kind of flexibility is a benefit.

Current strategies for deployment of Java code emphasize multi-tier architectures that provide one or more application servers in addition to client and database server tiers. Although this feature is not unique to Java environments, it is one of the main design features of current Java web architectures. The application server approach offers flexibility and better scalability as the enterprise grows. For example, to add support for more clients, it is only necessary to add application servers and software that distribute the load among servers. The client and database tiers are unaffected by this scaling. A multi-tier approach also offers a central location to support business logic that is common to many applications.

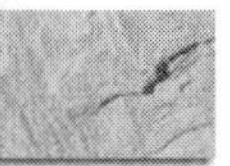

NOTE
Another characteristic that makes Java attractive is its relative ease of use. For example, the Java runtime automatically handles memory management and garbage collection. Also, Java supports multiple threads so that you can write a program in Java that runs in multiple simultaneous threads of execution.

Wide Support from Vendors

A compelling reason to use Java is that it is supported by many vendors. Instead of one main vendor, as with other technologies (for example, Microsoft .NET Framework), hundreds of companies produce and support Java products. Oracle is one of these companies. Oracle has a large stake in the Java world and continues to offer its customers guidance and robust product features for Java application development and deployment. Due to this wide support from vendors, the choice of Java as the language is not strongly tied to a single vendor who may not be viable or strong in the future.

Wide Support from Users

Another source of wide support is the user community. Java has a well-established user base that is not necessarily tied to a particular company. The Java community is reminiscent of the early days of Unix, when users made their work available to other users on a not-for-profit basis. The concept of *open source* (www.opensource.org) includes free access to the source code, no-cost licenses, and the ability for others to extend the product. For example, the Linux operating system started and continues to be enhanced through open-source channels.

Although the Java language is not an open-source venture, there are many Java products, such as the Apache web server, that are open-source products. Sample Java code is readily available from many sources on the Internet. In addition, many freeware (with no-cost licenses) or shareware (try before you buy) class libraries are available to Java developers.

Platform Independence

Java source code and runtime library and application files are not specific to a particular operating system. Therefore, you can create and compile Java class (runtime) files in a Windows environment and deploy the same files in a Unix environment without any changes. This aspect of Java, sometimes referred to as *portability,* is important to enterprises that find themselves outgrowing a particular operating environment but that need to support previously created systems in a new environment.

Drawbacks

Many of Java's drawbacks are derived from the same features as its benefits and result from the newness of the language.

Rapidly Changing Environment

The Java environment is less mature than traditional environments that access a relational database. This immaturity has two main effects: frequent updates that add significant new features, and shifts in technologies that occur more rapidly than in traditional environments. For example, when Java was first released, the main deployment environment was within a Java Virtual Machine (JVM) running on the client machine. As that environment matured, there were features added and features *deprecated* (supported, but specially marked as being removed or replaced in future releases).

In addition to updates in the language, additional technologies were added to the mix. Associated specifications such as Java Database Connectivity (JDBC), portlets and portals, and wireless Java guided how Java was used. Different environments were also developed. For example, in addition to the environment of Java running on the client, there are now many variations on web-deploying a system developed in Java. In fact, the Java web-deployment landscape is so complex that as part of the Java 2 Platform, Enterprise Edition (J2EE), Sun Microsystems has created *blueprints* (called BluePrints), which are descriptions of proven techniques and best practices for deploying applications. J2EE also includes descriptions of proven, lower-level coding techniques called *design patterns* that are used as additional guidelines for development.

Multi-Vendor Support

Although multi-vendor support was listed as one of Java's strengths, it can also be thought of as a drawback. You may need to merge Java technologies from different vendors, and each vendor is responsible only for their part. Oracle offers a complete solution for development (JDeveloper) and deployment (Oracle Application Server), but you may find yourself in a multi-vendor situation if Oracle products were not selected or were extended with components from other vendors. In addition, Oracle is not responsible for the base Java language. In that respect, a Java environment will always be multi-vendor because Sun Microsystems, which is responsible for the language, does not offer a complete solution including a database.

Significant Language Skills Required

Java developers need to think in an object-oriented way as well as to understand all aspects of the language and how the code pieces tie together in a production application. Java coding is largely a 3GL effort at this point. The IDEs assist by generating starting code and providing frameworks (such as Oracle's Application Development Framework, introduced in Chapter 4), but developers also need to have solid programming skills to effectively create production-level Java programs. Java is a popular language now with colleges and universities, so many new graduates are well trained in Java.

In addition, for web-deployed Java, developers need to have skills in other languages and technologies such as HTML, XML, JavaScript, and JSP tags. These skills are easily obtained, but are essentially prerequisites to effective work in the Java web environment.

If developers are to be completely effective, they must also have solid knowledge of database languages. Tools such as JDeveloper's Application Development Framework Business Components (ADF BC) and other technologies (such as Oracle Application Server TopLink) hide the SQL statements from the developers. However, developers must be aware of how the SQL statements are produced by the tools so that the statements can be as efficient as possible.

In addition, although database-stored code (packages, procedures, functions, and triggers) can be coded in Java, developers may still need to interface with existing code built in PL/SQL and, therefore, will need to understand some PL/SQL.

Transitioning to Java

Working in a Java environment is very different from working with traditional database development environments such as Oracle Forms Developer or Visual Basic (VB). If you are not already using Java but the benefits of Java have convinced you of the need to make the transition, you will need to plan that transition carefully.

It will take time to learn the nuances of a Java environment. If you are committed to creating an organization-wide Java environment, building a traditional client/server application using a local Java client (Java running on the desktop) may still make sense if your application is used in a small group or departmental situation. Coding and deploying the application locally on the desktop in this way postpones the complexities of working with web deployments and can give you a feel for how Java works. (Chapter 7 explains Java applications running on the desktop in more detail.)

If your development team has skills in other languages, Java will require retraining and ramp-up time. Building client/server applications directly in Java can be a good first step. This method leverages the improved flexibility of Java and its ability to build sophisticated applications. It also makes the transition of your business to the Web easier because Java is a primary language of the

Web. The smaller the application, the easier it will be to concentrate on the language and not the application. A prototype or internal administrative application that will not see extensive use might be a good candidate for this first effort.

Another variation on this transition advice is to develop a small web application in Java. This can be the next step after building a client/server application, or it can be the first step. Web applications add the complexity of application and web servers, and this will give you a taste of this extra layer of software. Chapters 17–19 will get you started with developing a web application.

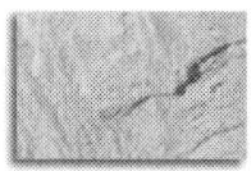

TIP
Be sure to take advantage of the many Java learning resources available on the Sun Microsystems website, java.sun.com. Appendix A contains a list of some of the applicable web pages.

Making the Leap

The transition to Java may not need to be (and probably should not be) a big bang where you move all new development to Java and start converting existing applications to Java. Although you want to minimize the number of tools and environments that you support, it is likely that you will have to support existing applications in the environments in which they were written. With all current development tools trying to improve their web-enabled capabilities, it becomes increasingly difficult to make a compelling argument for abandoning these technologies. For example, following a long evolution, Oracle Forms Developer running over the Web is now a stable and viable environment. Especially since you can extend Forms with Java plugins, there may be no reason to convert legacy Forms applications to Java.

Therefore, the best approach to transitioning into the Java environment is to leave core application development in whatever legacy environment you are comfortable with and to build a few systems of limited scope in Java using JDeveloper. Once you have some experience in building and deploying applications, you can make an informed decision about whether your organization is ready to make the transition to an entirely Java-based environment. There may still be good reasons to stay with a legacy environment for core applications and only to use a Java environment for e-commerce and other web-based applications.

As you become more comfortable with working in Java and have more Java projects under way, you can think about migrating current applications. However, some applications may never need to make the transition.

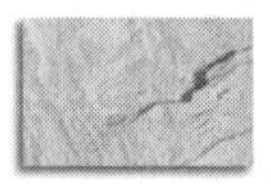

NOTE
As with many shops that support legacy COBOL-based programs, it is likely that you will have to support your current development environment for large enterprise-wide applications for some time.

Object Orientation Concepts

If you have experience in the C++ language, you will notice keyword and syntax similarities between Java and C++. However, there are enough differences between Java and C++ that it is worth reviewing the basics of the language even if you understand the concepts behind C++.

Java used C++ concepts as a springboard but was designed as an object-oriented language in its first incarnation (unlike C++). Understanding Java requires a comfort level with the concepts of object orientation (OO). If you have any experience with another object-oriented language, such as Smalltalk or C#, you may have already grasped the OO concepts you need to work with Java.

The fundamental building block of an object-oriented language like Java is a structure called a *class*. The class acts as a pattern or blueprint from which *objects* are built. In object-speak, "an object is an instance of a class." An object is built from a class and has an identity (or name). This means that, primarily, the class is actually not used as a programmatic element except to create other elements that you will manipulate (assign values to and query values from). For example, an object called "someBox" can be instantiated from a class called "Box." In this example, the someBox object is created from the pattern defined by the `Box` class.

The concept of a class and its object loosely parallels the concept of datatyping (and record variable definition) in programming languages such as PL/SQL. In PL/SQL, a datatype is a pattern upon which variables are built. If the datatype concept were expressed in object-oriented terms, a variable would be the object that instantiates the datatype (acting as a class). In fact, as you will see later in this chapter, Java objects are thought of as being typed from classes. In the Box example, you can say that "someBox is of type Box." In common Java parlance, you might also refer to "someBox" as "the Box" or "the Box object."

The parallel between a PL/SQL variable and a Java object is loose because, in addition to creating and initializing the Java object (as you do a variable in PL/SQL), you need code to "create" the Java object using code (you normally use the new operator to accomplish this creation). The creation operation runs constructor code to assign it some default data as well as to run code specific to the class. This concept will be discussed more a bit later in this chapter.

A class contains both data (values in variables, also called *attributes* or *fields*) and behavior or application code logic (in methods). This makes it different from anything in the world of relational databases. The closest concept to the class data and behavior characteristics is a relational table with a dedicated package of procedures that are used for SQL operations such as INSERT, UPDATE, DELETE, and SELECT. In this case, the combination of relational table and procedural package contains data (in the table) and behavior (procedures and functions in the package assigned to the table). Another example in the Oracle relational database paradigm is a database view with a procedural package run by INSTEAD OF triggers. The database view (the data) combines with the package and INSTEAD OF trigger (the behavior) to form a rough equivalent to an object-oriented class.

The difference between this example from the relational/procedural world and the object-oriented paradigm is that there is only a conceptual link or loose coupling between the table and the code package. The table and package exist as separate objects and can be used separately. (Although you could link the table and PL/SQL package using table triggers, this mechanism is not required by or native behavior of the language.) In object orientation, the class is inherently both data and behavior; the link is tight and perfectly integrated. The class is used as a pattern to create objects that contain data and pointers to the code in the class. Figure 5-1 depicts the coupling difference between data and application code for the relational/procedural and object-oriented paradigms.

Handling and Storing Data

The ways in which data is handled in an object-oriented language such as Java and in a relational database system are also fundamentally different. Data is not inherently *persistent* (permanently stored) in Java. Therefore, data is available only for the time in which the Java

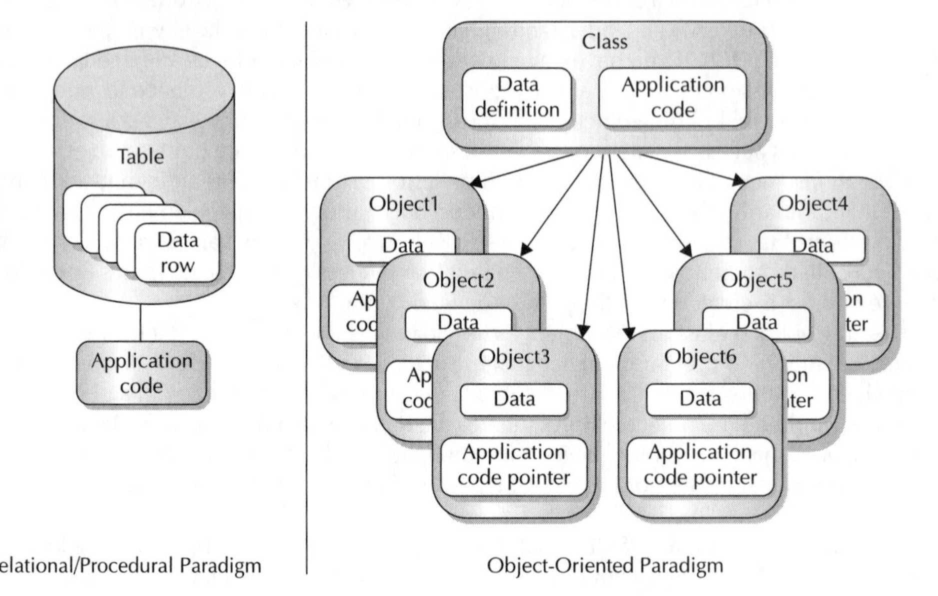

FIGURE 5-1. *Relational/procedural and object-oriented paradigms*

program is running. There are ways to store data in between program sessions; the method included as part of the base language is *object serialization*. Object serialization includes the ability to write object values to, and read object values from, a persistent stream (such as a file).

Object serialization is the built-in Java way to handle persistence. However, many programmers of Java and other languages have become accustomed to using a fully featured relational database management system (RDBMS) to handle data persistence. An RDBMS provides solid facilities for fast and safe storage, retrieval, backup, and recovery of mission-critical data. However, the RDBMS, by definition, is built around the concept of storing data in relational tables. This concept does not correspond to the way in which the Java language handles data in objects. Figure 5-2 shows a conceptual mapping that you can make between relational and object-oriented data storage.

This diagram shows how a row in a table roughly corresponds to the data in an object. You can describe a table in object-oriented terms as a collection of records representing instances of related data that are defined by the structure of the table. The problem is the difference in the way that data appears in the two paradigms. A table contains rows that are accessible using a relational database language such as SQL, which addresses requests for sets of data to the table. Objects contain data and you address requests for that data directly to the object. You cannot use SQL to access data in an OO environment because the source structure of the data is different; data is distributed across many objects. The standard solution to this mapping problem is to create an array object (often called a *row set*) of values that represents multiple rows in a database table. The row set is a single object with methods for retrieving individual rows and column values.

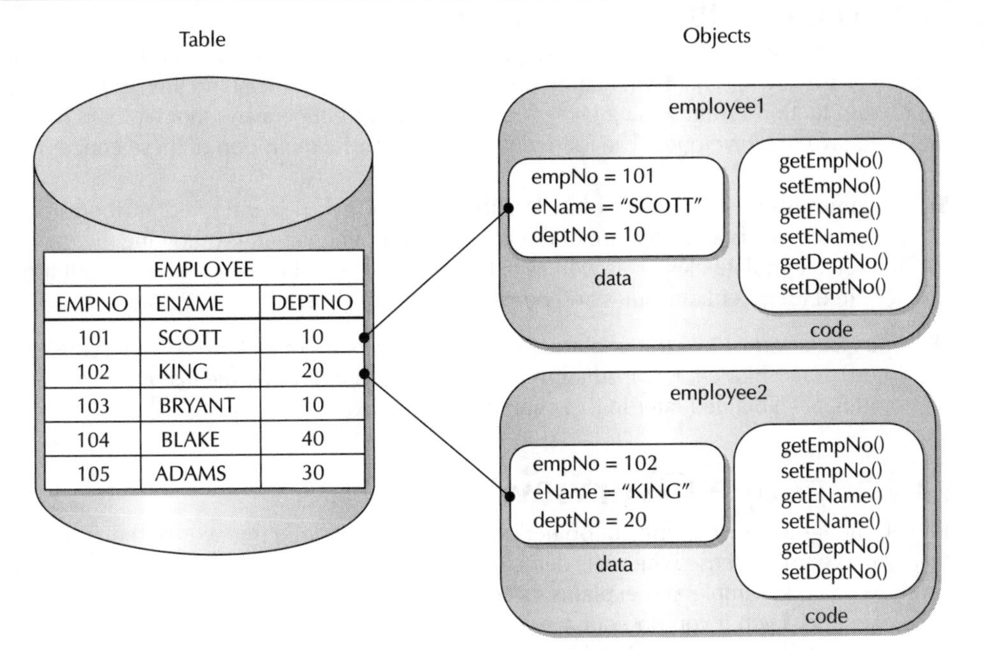

FIGURE 5-2. *Mapping between relational and object data storage*

Therefore, there are basic differences between the relational and the object paradigms in the areas of persistence, data structures and access code, and conceptual foundations. Using Java code to access a relational database is a common requirement, and there are many solutions to making an effective map between relational tables and objects. For example, architectures such as JDeveloper's ADF Business Components or Oracle Application Server TopLink hide the complexity of the relational-object mapping and provide programmers with object-oriented, Java-friendly structures that can be easily incorporated into application programs. Other strategies, such as JDBC, also ease the burden of accessing a relational database from an object-oriented language.

Inheritance

One of the key characteristics of object orientation is the ability of a class to automatically take on the attributes and methods of another class. This is the concept of *inheritance,* where one class is a parent of another. The parent, also called the *superclass* (base class or generalization), contains elements (data and behavior) that are available in the *subclass* (child class or specialization). The lines of inheritance can be deep, with one class acting as the grandparent or great-grandparent of another. To base a class on a parent class, you *extend* the parent class. The child class can then supplement, modify, or disable the attributes and behavior of the parent class. This kind of inheritance is shown in an annotated code example later in this chapter.

Other Primary Object-Oriented Concepts

Two other major concepts are inherent to object orientation—*polymorphism* and *encapsulation.* Although they are key to object orientation and it is necessary to understand them when you are developing production systems using Java, you do not need to understand them fully to begin working with Java in JDeveloper. The following provides a brief definition of these concepts:

- **Polymorphism** The ability of a class to modify or override inherited attributes or behavior. This is a key feature of the Java programming language allowing the developer to create template classes as well as extensions to these classes, which may (but are not required to) inherit attributes and behavior from the generalization (master) class.
- **Encapsulation** Only the important characteristics of an object are revealed; the internals are hidden. Encapsulation is accomplished in Java by means of access modifiers (explained later in this chapter).

Java Language Overview

High-level, theoretical discussions of object orientation often glaze the eyes of the audience. The theory makes more sense when it is demonstrated using some code examples. The following section shows a code sample and explains its contents to demonstrate object orientation and Java language concepts. Even if you do not have extensive Java experience but have been exposed to other programming languages, you will be able to identify some of the language elements as well as the structure of a typical source code file. The example also demonstrates, in the context of the Java language, some of the key object-oriented concepts just explained.

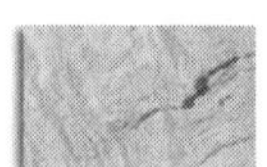

TIP
This chapter is not intended as a comprehensive overview of the Java language. If you do not have formal training or experience with the Java language, a good place to start is the free, self-guided Java Tutorial available online at java.sun.com.

Annotated Java Code Example

All Java code is contained in class files. A class file is made up of a number of standard elements. The following is a representative class file that contains standard elements. The hands-on practice at the end of this chapter shows how to create and work with this class in JDeveloper. The line numbers in the code listing serve as reference points and would not appear in the actual code file.

```
01: package shapes;
02: import java.lang.*;
03:
04: /*
05:    This class defines a shape with three dimensions
06: */
07: public class Box extends Shape {
08:   int height;    // override the Shape height
09:   int depth;     // unique to Box
```

```
10:
11:   public Box() {
12:     height = 4;
13:     width = 3;   // width is inherited from Shape
14:     depth = 2;
15:   }
16:
17:  public int getDepth() {
18:    return depth;
19:  }
20:
21:  public void setDepth(int newDepth) {
22:    depth = newDepth;
23:  }
24:
25:   // super.getWidth is the same as getWidth() here
26:   public int getVolume() {
27:     return height * super.getWidth() * getDepth();
28:   }
29: }
```

NOTE
All code in Java language is case-sensitive. Therefore, a class called "BOX" is different from a class called "Box." By convention, class names are mixed case, with each word in the name initial-capped. For example, a class that defines salary history would be called "SalaryHistory." Chapter 6 contains further guidelines for naming conventions.

Package Declaration

Line 01 identifies the location of this file. *Packages* are collections of class files in subdirectories in a file system. A package normally represents a directory in the file system. Packages of files can be archived into a .zip or .jar (*Java Archive* or *JAR*) file, and the Java runtime can search in this archive (sometimes called a *library*) for a specific class file. If a package is archived, the archive instead of the file system then contains the directory structure.

The *CLASSPATH* operating system environment variable contains a list of these archive files separated by colons (for Unix) or semicolons (for Windows), for example:

```
C:\JDev10g\jdk\jre\lib\rt.jar;C:\JDev10g\jdk\jre\lib\jce.jar;C:\JDev10g\
jdk\jre\lib\charsets.jar;C:\JDev10g\jdk\jre\classes;C:\JDev10g\jdev\lib\
jdev-rt.jar
```

(The path is a single variable value entered on one line.) Whether a particular file is inside a file system directory or a directory inside an archive file is irrelevant, but the CLASSPATH must include the archive file name if the file required is in an archived directory. The CLASSPATH must include the name of the file system directory if the file required is in a file system directory.

Line 01 ends with a semicolon, as do all Java statements.

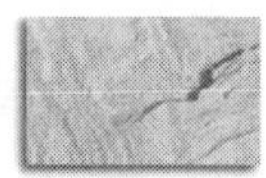

NOTE
You can view the contents of JAR files by using any file decompression utility. JDeveloper contains a ZIP- and JAR-file viewer that opens when you double click the file in the Navigator.

Import

Line 02 defines an *import* (called an "include" in other languages such as C++), specifying the external or library classes required for the code to compile and execute. Imports are identified by class name as well as by the package in which they reside. Many import statements may appear if more than one package structure or class is required. The import statement can reference a single class file or an entire package as in line 02. The directory is listed using fully qualified dot syntax (package.subpackage.subpackage*), with "*" indicating that all classes in that package will be available. Java libraries are often grouped by function into the same directory (package) so that associated functions can be called more easily. This example is provided for discussion purposes. The java.lang classes are automatically available without an import statement.

Comment

Lines 04–06 show a multi-line *comment* (using the beginning and ending symbols "/*" and "*/"). Line 08 shows a single-line comment (using the beginning symbol "//") at the end of the code line. As shown in line 25, this style of comment can be used on a line by itself. Java also offers special multi-line comments that start with "/**" and end with "*/" and are used to generate a type of documentation called "Javadoc." Chapter 3 contains a sidebar about Javadoc that describes these comments.

Class Declaration

Line 07 is the class declaration. It includes the keyword `public`, indicating that this class is available to all other classes. The keyword `public` is called an *access modifier* (or *access specifier*). Other choices for access modifiers are `private` (where access to the class member is limited to other members of the same class) and `protected` (where you cannot access the class from outside the package unless the calling class is a subclass). If you do not use a modifier keyword, this indicates the *default modifier,* where members are available only to code in the same package.

Code Block

The end of line 07 contains an opening curly bracket "{" indicating the start of a *block of code.* Between this and the matched closing curly bracket "}" are code elements and other blocks of code. The code blocks do not need to contain any code (unlike blocks in PL/SQL). Blocks of Java code may be nested. Blocks define the scope of variables and code structures such as `if` and `while`, as discussed later.

Using Brackets for Code Blocks It is good coding practice to always use curly brackets to contain code in code structures (such as `if` and `for`). Technically, you do not need curly brackets if there is only one statement to execute as in the following example:

```
if (width == 10)
  depth = 20;
```

However, it is easy to make the mistake of adding a line of code under an if statement that has no curly brackets and assume that it will execute conditionally. Since only the first line of code under the if statement is part of the conditional logic, the next statement would always be executed if no curly brackets contain the statements, for example:

```
if (width == 10)
   depth = 20;
   height = 30; // this will always execute
```

Always using curly brackets, even for single-line blocks, will prevent this type of error as in the following example:

```
if (width == 10)
{
   depth = 20;
}
```

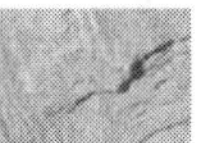

NOTE

*No recognized standard exists for whether to place the starting bracket for a block at the end of the line above or on a new line. This book shows examples of both techniques, but for consistency and readability, you will want to make a particular starting-bracket style a standard for your application code. Use the "Preferred Open Brace Style" property on the Code Editor\Java page of the Preferences dialog (**Tools | Preferences**) to specify the default for your editor work.*

Subclassing (extends)

This code defines a class called `Box` that is built (subclassed) from a class called `Shape`. The `extends` keyword declares that `Shape` is the parent of `Box` and defines the inheritance for `Box`. The `Shape` class might be defined as follows:

```
package shapes;

public class Shape  {
  int height;
  int width;

  public Shape() {
    height = 1;
    width = 1;
  }

  public int getHeight() {
    return height;
  }

  public void setHeight(int newHeight) {
```

```
      height = newHeight;
    }
    // getWidth() and setWidth() methods go here
}
```

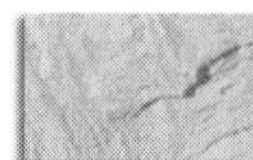

NOTE
A Java source code file can contain only one public class. The file name is the name of the public class in that file (with a .java extension).

Variable Declaration

Lines 08–09 (of the `Box` class) declare two variables (as `int` types). These constitute the data (attribute or field) for the class that was mentioned in the discussion of object-oriented concepts. Since the variables of the parent class are available in the child class, the `Shape` variables `height` and `width` are available to the `Box` class. In addition, the `Box` class declares its own `height` variable. This variable is available to objects created from the `Box` class. The parent's `height` variable is also available using the symbol `super.height` (the `height` variable of the `Shape` superclass). This code also declares a variable that is not in the parent: `depth`. Variable names are formatted with initial caps for all words except the first.

NOTE
The modifier "super" can be also be used in the child class to access methods from the parent class. For example, the `Shape` class contains a `setHeight()` method, which is available to the `Box` class (subclass) as `super.setHeight()`.

Technically, *variables* in Java are declared using primitive datatypes such as `int`, `float`, or `boolean`. Other data resides inside objects that are instantiations of classes such as `String` or `StringBuffer`. Datatypes are discussed in more detail later in this chapter.

Code Unit—Method and Constructor

Lines 11–28 define methods and constructors, which are the main containers for functional code in the class.

Method The standard unit of code in Java is called a *method.* The first line of the method is called the *method signature* or *signature* because it contains the unique characteristics of this code unit such as the arguments, access modifier, and return type.

You can use the same name for more than one method in the class if the methods with that name all have different argument lists (for example, `showWidth(int width)` and `showWidth(String widthUnit)`). Methods with the same name but different arguments are referred to as *overloaded methods.*

Methods implement the object-oriented concept of behavior in a class. Java does not distinguish between code units such as functions that return a value and procedures that do not return a value. It has only one unit of code—the method. Methods must declare a return type. They can return a primitive or class—as with functions in other languages—or they can return *void* (nothing)—as with procedures in other languages. Methods can only return one thing, but that thing could be an array or an object, which could be made up of many values.

Method names are, by convention, mixed case, with each word except for the first one initial-capped.

Constructor **Lines 11–15** define a unit of code called "Box," which has the same name as the class. This unit is called a *constructor* and is not a method. Constructors have a signature similar to methods, but do not return anything (not even `void`). If a return type is declared, the signature identifies a method not a constructor. Constructors are used to create an object that is based on the class (using the keyword `new`); in this case, the constructor just sets values for the variables in the object that is created from the class. The constructor code is contained within a block of code delimited by curly brackets. If you do not define a constructor, you can still create an object from the class because there is an implicit constructor that is available to calling programs.

Constructors must have the same name as the class. Since class names usually begin with an initial-capped word, the constructor also begins with an initial-capped word.

Accessor (Getter and Setter) **Lines 17–28** define getters and setters (also called *accessors* or *accessor methods*). A *getter* is a method that is usually named with a "get" prefix and variable name suffix. It returns the value of the variable for which it is named. Although this is a standard and expected method that you would write for each property or variable that you want to expose, it is not required for variables that you want to hide. Getters may include security features to restrict access to the values and may not be as simple as this example, which just returns the value of a single variable. In this example, the `getDepth()` method returns the value of the variable, and the `getVolume()` method calculates the volume based on the three dimensions of the box. As with the variable prefix "super." before, this method references the superclass methods `getWidth()` and `getDepth()`.

A *setter* is a method that is named with a "set" prefix and is normally used to change the value of the property for which it is named. As with the getter, it is normal and expected that you would write a setter for variables you want to expose to the caller; you would omit the setter if you did not want the variable changed. Setters can include validation logic (for example, not allowing the height to be set to a negative number), but they usually also assign a new value to the variable as in this example.

The object-oriented concept of encapsulation is implemented here by accessor methods that read and write to private variables in the class. Other code outside the class cannot see or manipulate the private variables in this class directly, but must go through the getters and setters to retrieve and change data values, respectively. The accessor methods can have specific logic that protects the variable values, for example, a setter called `setHeight()` could enforce the rule that the value for height may not be less than 0. If the variable were not private, the caller would be responsible for knowing and complying with the rule.

In this example, the `Box` class contains no setters and getters for the `height` and `width` variables. These would be defined in the parent class, `Shape`, and are available to `Box`.

Line 29 is the closing bracket for the class definition.

NOTE

Java is a case-sensitive language. If you are transitioning from a non-case-sensitive language, it is useful to keep reminding yourself of this fact.

Annotated Use of the Box Example Class

Code that uses a class such as `Box` demonstrates some other principles of the Java language. Consider the following example usage:

```
01: package shapes;
02:
03: public class TestBox  {
04:
05:   public static void main(String[] args) {
06:     // this creates an object called someBox
07:     Box someBox = new Box();
08:     someBox.setDepth(3);
09:     // getHeight() and setHeight() are from Shape
10:     // height shows the height variable from Box
11:     System.out.println (
12:       "The height of Shape is " + someBox.getHeight() +
13:       " and of someBox is " + someBox.height);
14:
15:     // getDepth and getVolume are from Box
16:     System.out.println (
17:       "The depth of someBox is " + someBox.getDepth() +
18:       " and the volume of someBox is " + someBox.getVolume());
19:   }
20: }
```

The output for the main method will be the following:

```
The height of Shape is 1 and of someBox is 4
The depth of someBox is 3 and the volume of someBox is 36
```

Lines 01–03 state the package and declare the class `TestBox`.

main() Method

Lines 05–19 define a method called `main()`. This is a specially named method that executes automatically when the JVM runs the class from the command line (for example: `java.exe client.TestBox`). The `main()` method can contain any accessible code; in this case, it shows messages in the Java console (that displays in the JDeveloper Log window).

The keyword `static` indicates that `main()` is a *class method* that can be run without declaring an instance of the class. Normally, you need to create an object and then call the method by prefixing it with the object name. With static methods, you can still run the method (in this example, `main()`) without having to create an object from the class.

The `main()` method signature also includes an argument within the parentheses that follow the method name. This argument is typed as a String and is named "args." The common parlance for expressing object type uses the datatype name, for example, "args is a String" or "args is [an instance] of the String type (or class)." (The words in square brackets are optional.)

The square brackets [ ] after args indicate that it is an array. *Arrays* are collections of similar objects. The String array args is used to pass any command-line arguments available when the class is executed. You can also use the expression "`String args[]`" to represent an array of strings.

Object Creation

Line 07 creates an object called someBox based on the `Box` class. The object is made from the `Box` class and, therefore, has the same variables (such as `someBox.width`) and methods (such as `someBox.getVolume()`) as the class. Line 07 accomplishes two tasks: it declares an object of type `Box` and creates the object by calling the constructor `Box()`. This line could also be expanded into the following two lines to separate the tasks:

```
Box someBox;
someBox = new Box();
```

Assign Values

Line 08 sets the value of the depth variable using the `setDepth()` method. This overwrites the value set in the constructor.

Console Output

Lines 11–13 output a message (using the `System.out.println()` method) that will be displayed in the Java console window. If you run a Java program from the command line, the Java console window will be the command-line window. If you run a Java program in JDeveloper, the message will appear in the Log window. You can concatenate literal strings (in quotes) and variables with the "+" operator regardless of type.

Variable and Accessor Usage

Line 12 references `getHeight()`, which is a method from the `Shape` class—the parent of `Box`, the class from which someBox is built. Since this method displays the value of the `height` variable in `Shape`, the value will be 1 (the default for that class). This demonstrates that you can call a method of a parent class from an object created from the subclass.

Line 13 references the `height` variable of `someBox` (which was built from the `Box` class). In this case, the `height` variable will be displayed as the default from the `Box` class ("4"). This output could be a bit confusing, and this system would probably not be used outside of demonstration purposes because the height of the parent class is set differently from the height of the subclass.

Lines 16–18 display the results of `someBox` method calls. Both `getDepth()` and `getVolume()` are declared in the `Box` class and will be output as 3 and 36, respectively.

Lines 19 and 20 close the method and class.

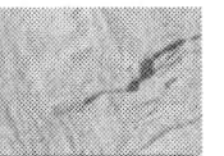

NOTE

When naming Java elements, you may use a combination of uppercase and lowercase letters, numbers, the underscore, and the dollar sign. However, you may not begin names with a number. There is no limit to the number of characters that you can use in a name.

Other Java Language Concepts

There are some other Java language concepts that were not demonstrated in the examples but that are useful to review.

The Code Development and Deployment Process

The typical Java development process, if you are not using an IDE such as JDeveloper, follows:

1. Write a source code file with a text editor, and name it using the name of the class that the file represents and a .java extension, for example, TestBox.java.
2. Compile the source code using the javac.exe executable (included in the Java SDK). If there are no syntax errors, the compiler creates a file with the same name and a class extension, for example, TestBox.class. This binary compiled file (called *bytecode*) is interpreted by the Java runtime engine when the program is executed. Java is compiled in this way, but it is considered an interpreted language. Java programs require a runtime interpreter—the JVM, a component of but often used synonymously with *Java runtime environment* or *JRE*.
3. Test the class file using the java.exe executable, the JVM (also included in the Java SDK). If the Java code is a Java application, the command line is as simple as the following example:

   ```
   java client.TestBox
   ```
4. Repeat steps 1–3 until the program performs as required.
5. Package the program file with the library files that it uses (libraries or classes declared in the import statements at the beginning of the program), and install the package on a client machine that has a Java runtime environment installed (containing the Java runtime engine—java.exe—and the base Java libraries such as java.lang.*).

Although an IDE such as JDeveloper automates many of these steps, the tasks are the same. Also, different types of Java programs have different requirements for the compile and runtime steps, but the concepts are the same. For example, working with JSP files requires the development of a .jsp file that is translated into a .java file and is compiled automatically into a .class file by a special Java runtime engine. The subject of JSP technology is further discussed in Chapter 7.

Control Statements

The idea of control statements is familiar to anyone who has written program code. Learning the Java control structures is usually just a matter of learning a different syntax (unless the other language is C++, which provided some of the syntax used in Java). This section reviews only the basic structures, since most structures are similar to those in other programming languages. You can refer to a standard Java language text to understand the variations and usage requirements for these control statements. (See Appendix A for Java language resources.)

Sequence One of the main concepts of control statements is sequence, and Java code is executed in the order in which it appears in the file. The method that is executed first varies with the style of Java program; for example, a Java application executes the `main()` method first; a Java applet executes the `init()` method first; JavaServer Pages applications execute a `service()` method first. The commands within these methods are executed in the order in which they appear in the code file. As in other languages, calls to other methods execute the method and return to the line of code after the method call. The keyword `return` jumps out of the current method and returns control to the statement in the calling unit after that method was called (or to the command line if the command line was the caller).

Conditional Branching Java uses the statements `if-else` and `switch` to branch the code based upon a condition as follows:

```
class ShowQuarter {

  public static void main (String args[]) {
    int taxMonth = 10;
    String taxQuarter;

    if (taxMonth == 1 || taxMonth == 2 || taxMonth == 3) {
        taxQuarter = "1st Quarter";
    } else if (taxMonth == 4 || taxMonth == 5 || taxMonth == 6) {
        taxQuarter = "2nd Quarter";
    // more conditions would appear here
    } else {
        taxQuarter = "Not Valid";
    }
    System.out.println("Your current Tax Quarter is: " + taxQuarter );
  }
}
```

This is a branching statement that uses multiple `if` statements. The "||" symbol is a logical OR operator ("&&" is a logical AND). Logical conditions are enclosed in parentheses. The "==" symbol is the equality comparison operator. Each condition is followed by a single statement or block of code. As mentioned before, it is a good idea to always define a block of code enclosed in curly brackets under the `if` statement.

The `switch` statement is an alternative to multiple `if` statements that test the same value. The following example could be used instead of the `if-then` example:

```
class ShowQuarter2 {
  public static void main (String args[]) {
    int taxMonth = 10;
    String taxQuarter;
    // The break statement jumps out of the conditional testing
    switch (taxMonth) {
      case 1:    case 2:    case 3:
        taxQuarter = "1st Quarter";
        break;
      case 4:    case 5:    case 6:
        taxQuarter = "2nd Quarter";
        break;
      // more conditions would appear here
      default:
```

```
            taxQuarter = "Not Valid";
        }    // end of the switch
        System.out.println("Your current Tax Quarter is: " + taxQuarter);
    }       // end of the main() method
}           // end of the class
```

Iteration or Looping There are three loop statements: `for`, `while`, and `do-while`. The `for` loop controls loop iteration by incrementing and testing the value of a variable as shown in the following example:

```
class TestLoops
{
  public static void main (String args[]) {
    for (int i = 1; i <= 10; i++) {
       System.out.println("Loop 1 count is " + i);
    }
  }
}
```

The `while` and `do-while` loops test a condition at the start or end of the loop, respectively. Refer to a Java language reference, such as the Java Tutorial at java.sun.com, for more examples of loop structures.

Exception Handling Exceptions can occur in the Java runtime environment when undefined conditions are encountered. To catch exceptions, you enclose the code in a block defined by the keywords `try`, `catch`, and (optionally) `finally` as in the following example:

```
public class TestException {
  public static void main(String[] args) {
    int numerator = 5, denominator = 0;
    int ratio;
    try {
      ratio = numerator / denominator ;
      System.out.println("The ratio is " + ratio);
    }
    catch (Exception e)  {
      // This shows an error message on the console
      e.printStackTrace();
    }
    finally {
      System.out.println("The end.");
    }
  }
}
```

If a `finally` block appears, it will be executed regardless of whether an exception is thrown. You may also raise an exception by using the keyword `throw` anywhere in the code.

NOTE
The preceding example shows how you can declare more than one variable (numerator and denominator in this example) of the same type on the same line.

Variable Scope

Variables can be declared and objects can be created anywhere in a class and are available within the block in which they are declared. For example, the following code shows a variable, `currentSalary`, that is available throughout the `main()` method. Another variable, `currentCommission`, is available only within the `if` block in which it is declared. The last print statement will cause a compilation error because the variable is out of scope for that statement.

```
class TestScope {

  public static void main (String[] args) {
    int currentSalary = 0;
    if (currentSalary < 0) {
      int currentCommission = 10;
      System.out.println("No salary but the commission is " + currentCommission);
    }
    else {
      System.out.println("Salary but no commission.");
    }
    // This will cause a compilation error.
    System.out.println(currentCommission);
  }
}
```

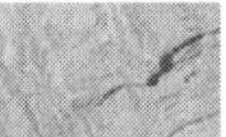

NOTE
Although Java does not use the concept of a variable declaration section (such as the DECLARE section of PL/SQL), Java variables have the scope of their enclosing curly brackets. It is good programming practice to put all variable declarations at the beginning of their scope. For example, if you are declaring method-wide variables, place their declarations at the beginning of the method. If you are declaring variables with a class scope, place their declarations under the class declaration statement. Positioning the variable declarations in this way makes the code easier to read.

In addition to the scope within a block, variable scope is affected by where and how the variable is declared in the class file. The following example demonstrates these usages:

```
class ShowSalary {
  static int previousSalary = 0;
```

```
  int commission = 10;

  public static void main (String[] args) {
    int currentSalary = 100;
    if (currentSalary == 0) {
      System.out.println("There is only a commission.");
    }
    else {
      System.out.println("Current salary is " + currentSalary);
    }
    System.out.println("{Previous salary is " + previousSalary);

    // The following would cause a compile error.
    // System.out.println(commission);
  }
}
```

This example demonstrates three usages for variables—instance variables (`commission`), class variables (`previousSalary`), and local variables (`currentSalary`). Both instance variables and class variables are categorized as *member variables* because they are members of a class (not within a method or constructor). Member variables are available to any method within the class. Methods are also considered members of a class because the class is the container for the method.

Instance Variables These variables are created outside of any method. In this example, the variable `commission` is an instance variable. It does not use the keyword `static` in the declaration and is not available to class methods (that are declared with the keyword `static`). Therefore, the variable `commission` is not available to the `main()` method in this example. Instance variables are available to objects created from the class. For example, you could create an object (instance) from this sample class using "`ShowSalary calcSalary` = `new ShowSalary();`", and the variable `calcSalary.commission` would be available. Each object receives its own copy of the class variable. Therefore, if you instantiate objects salary1 and salary2 from the `ShowSalary` class, `salary1.commission` and `salary2.commission` could contain different values.

Class Variables As with instance variables, class variables, such as `previousSalary` in this example, are declared outside of any method. The difference with class variables is that their declaration includes the `static` keyword and they are available to class methods that are also declared with the keyword `static`. The variable can be used without creating an instance of the class using the syntax "Classname.VariableName" (for example, ShowSalary.previousSalary). There is only one copy of the class variable regardless of the number of objects that have been created from the class. Therefore, if you create `salary1` and `salary2` from the `ShowSalary` class, the same variable `previousSalary` will be available from both objects (as `salary1.previousSalary` and `salary2.previousSalary`). If `salary2` changes the value of this variable, `salary1` will see that new value because there is only one variable. The following is an example that demonstrates this principle:

```
class TestShowSalary
{
  public static void main(String[] args)
  {
    ShowSalary salary1 = new ShowSalary();
    ShowSalary salary2 = new ShowSalary();
    //
    System.out.println("From salary1: " + salary1.previousSalary);
    salary2.previousSalary = 300;
    System.out.println("After salary2 changed it: " + salary1.previousSalary);
  }
}
```

The output from this program follows:

```
From salary1: 0
After salary2 changed it: 300
```

Local Variables This variable usage is declared inside a method. In the sample `ShowSalary` class, `currentSalary` is a local variable because it is declared inside a method (`main()`). The variable is available only within the scope of that method.

Constants and "final"

A variable can be marked as `final`, which means that its value cannot change. Since you cannot change the value, you must assign a value when you declare the variable. This is similar to the idea of a constant in other languages. The following is an example of a final "variable." Final variable names use all uppercase characters by convention (as mentioned in Chapter 6).

```
final int FEET_IN_MILE = 5280;
```

You can also mark methods as `final`, which means that you cannot override the method in a subclass. Thus, if class A has a `final` method b( ), and if class C extends A, then class C cannot override the inherited method b( ) in class C. For example:

```
final int getCommission() {
}
```

Classes may be marked with `final` to indicate that they cannot be subclassed. That is, no class may extend that class. For example:

```
class final CalcSalary {
}
```

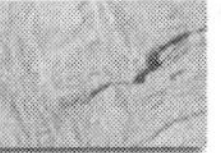

CAUTION
The keyword `final` stops inheritance (subclassing) of classes, but does not stop the overriding of a variable (constant).

Primitive Datatypes

Variable types fall into two categories: primitive and reference. *Primitive datatypes* can hold only a single value and cannot be passed by reference or pointers. Primitives are not based on classes and therefore have no methods. The primitive datatypes include `boolean` (for true and false values), several number types differentiated by the magnitude and precision of data they can represent (`byte`, `short`, `int`, `long`, `float`, `double`), and `char`.

A `char` is a single-byte number between 0 and 65,536 that is used to represent a single character in the Unicode international character set. A `char` datatype can be assigned in a number of ways as follows:

```
// decimal equivalent of the letter 'a'
char charDecimal = 97;
// using an actual character inside single quotes
char charChar = 'a';
// octal equivalent of the letter 'a'
char charOctal = '\141';
// Hex value for the letter 'a'
char charHex = 0x0061;
// Unicode (hex) value for the letter 'a'
char charUnicode = '\u0061';
```

NOTE
Assigning values to a byte can require surrounding the value in single quotes ('). This is the only time that single quotes are used in Java. Double quotes (") are used to surround a character string.

Reference Datatypes

Reference datatypes represent a memory location for a value or set of values. Since Java does not support pointers or memory addresses, you use the variable name to represent the reference. You can type an object using these reference datatypes, and the object instantiated in this way will have available to it the members in the class or referenced element (methods and variables). Reference datatypes may be arrays, interfaces, or classes.

Arrays *Collections* are programmatic groups of objects or primitives. There are various types of collections available in Java, such as arrays, sets, dynamic arrays, linked lists, trees, hash tables, and key-value pairs (maps). Java provides a type of collection appropriately called Collection that is extensively used by JDeveloper's ADF. This section discusses arrays. You will find information about the other categories of collections in Java language references.

Arrays in Java are collections of objects or primitives of similar type and may have one or more dimensions. Arrays are the only type of collection that can store primitive types. Elements within an array are accessed by indexes, which start at zero ([0]). To create an array, you declare it, allocate memory (size), and initialize the elements. These operations can be performed in two basic steps as shown here:

```
String animals[];
animals = new String[10];
```

The first line of code creates the array variable by adding a pair of square brackets to the variable name. The second line sets the size of the array (in this case, 10), which allocates memory, creates the object (animals), and initializes the elements. Arrays must be declared with a fixed number of members. This code could be condensed into the following line:

```
String animals[] = new String[10];
```

The next step is to store values in the array. In this example, the index numbers run from 0 to 9, and you store a value using that number as follows:

```
animals[3] = "Cat";
```

In Java, you can create arrays of arrays, more commonly known as *multi-dimensional arrays*. Since each array can be independently created, you can even create irregular combinations where array sizes vary within a given dimension. The more complex the array, the harder it is to keep track of, so moderation is advised. The following is a shorthand method for creating and assigning a two-dimensional array that stores pet owner names and the pet types:

```
class PetNames {
  public static main (String args[]) {
    String petFriends[ ][ ] = {
      {"George", "Snake", "Alligator"},
      {"Denise", "Butterfly"},
      {"Christine", "Tiger"},
      {"Robert", "Parrot", "Dove", "Dog", "Cat"}
    };
  }
}
```

Interfaces An interface is somewhat like a PL/SQL package specification because it lists method signatures and constants without any method code body. Classes that *implement* (or inherit) from the interface must include all methods in the interface. Interfaces are useful for providing a common type for a number of classes. For example, if you have a method that needs to return a type that will be manipulated by three different classes (that execute slightly differently), you can use an interface as the return type. Each of the three classes would implement the interface and, therefore, the classes could be used in the same way by the method.

You can base a class on one or more interfaces, and this also provides a form of multi-parent inheritance. For example, if you had interfaces called SalaryHistory and CommissionHistory, you could define a class as follows:

```
public class HistoryAmounts extends CalcSalary implements SalaryHistory,
  CommissionHistory {
}
```

The `HistoryAmounts` class is a subclass of the `CalcSalary` class and will implement (provide method code declared in) the SalaryHistory and CommissionHistory interfaces. If you did not want to provide the code for the methods, you could declare `HistoryAmounts` as abstract (for example, `abstract class HistoryAmounts`). An *abstract class* cannot be instantiated but can be subclassed.

Classes You can use any class to "type" an object (with the exception of abstract classes and classes with private constructors). The object becomes an instantiation of the class and has available to it the methods and member variables defined by the class. Therefore, classes can be used to create objects with the data and behavior characteristics defined in the class.

The Java language includes *wrapper* classes, such as `Boolean`, `Byte`, `Character`, `Double`, `Float`, `Integer`, `Long`, and `Number`, that implement the corresponding primitive datatypes and are commonly used as types for variables. These classes include methods that act upon the objects, such as a method that converts a `Long` to an `int`. For example, using a Long object called longVar, the `int` value is `longVar.intValue()`. The sidebar "About Wrapper Classes" at the end of this chapter describes wrapper classes further.

Two commonly used classes are `String` and `StringBuffer`.

String Class A String object can be declared and assigned a set of characters as follows:

```
String stringVar = "This is a Java test string";
```

Objects built from `String` can take advantage of the methods in the `String` class. The methods provide functions to create strings from literals, chars, char arrays, and other string reference objects. The following Java Strings store the value "Java" by assigning a value to one String object and concatenating that object to another string using the `concat()` method that is part of the `String` class.

```
String startingLetters = "Ja";
String newString = startingLetters.concat("va");
```

TIP

To view the Javadoc for a basic Java class such as `String`, type "String" into the Code Editor (or find the class name "String" in the file), place the cursor in the word, and select Quick Javadoc from the right-click menu. A window will pop up and display the documentation heading for that class. If you need to look at the entire Javadoc topic for the class including methods and other details, select Go to Javadoc. A window will appear with the full Javadoc topic containing methods and constants available to objects built from the class.

You can compare, concatenate, change the case of, find the length of, extract characters from, search, and modify strings. Strings in Java are considered *immutable,* that is, they cannot be changed. Whenever you alter a string through a string operation, the result is a new String object that contains the modifications. The old String object is no longer accessible because the object name points to the new object just created. You can take advantage of the overloading of the concatenation operator "+" to assign string values from number literals as in the following example:

```
// This assigns "The age is 235" to age.
String age = ("The age is " + 2 + 35);
```

```
// This assigns "The age is 37" to age.
String age = "The age is " + (2 + 35);
```

NOTE

In Java, the method `substring(int startIndex, int endIndex)` returns a portion of a string from the `startIndex` to the `(endIndex -1)`. As with arrays, the index numbers start with zero. The following example will assign "This is a Java" to the `newString` variable:

```
String baseString = "This is a Java string";
String newString = baseString.substring(0, 15);
```

StringBuffer Class `StringBuffer` is a sister class to `String` and represents character sequences that are *mutable,* that is, they can change size and/or be modified. What this means to the developer is that methods such as `append()` and `insert()` are available to modify a `StringBuffer` variable without creating a new object. Thus, the `StringBuffer` class is best if the character sequences being stored may need to be changed. The `String` class is good if the character sequence will not need to be changed.

The following shows an example usage of the `append()` method available to `StringBuffer`:

```
class StringAppend {
  public static void main (String args[]) {
    StringBuffer stringBuff = new StringBuffer("A string");
    stringBuff = stringBuff.append(" is added");
    System.out.println(stringBuff.toString());
  }
}
```

You could also append to a String variable using the String `concat()` method but, due to the immutable nature of String objects, that method would create a new String variable with the same name as the old variable. There is overhead and a bit of memory required by additional objects, so `StringBuffer` is better for concatenation.

Datatype Matching

Java is a semi-strongly typed language—every variable has a type, and every type is strictly defined. Type matching is strictly enforced in cases such as the following:

- The arguments passed to a method must match the argument types in the method's signature.
- Both sides of an assignment expression must contain the same datatype.
- Both sides of a Boolean comparison, such as an equality condition, must use matching datatypes.

There are few automatic conversions of one variable type to another. In practice, Java is not as restrictive as you might think, since most built-in methods are heavily overloaded (defined for different types of arguments). For example, you can combine strings, numbers, and dates using a concatenation operator (+) without formal variable type conversion, because the concatenation operator (which is, technically speaking, a base-language method) is overloaded.

In addition to overloading, an exact match is not always required, as shown in the following example:

```
public class TestCast {
  public static void main (String args[]) {
    byte smallNumber = 10;
    int largeNumber;
    largeNumber = smallNumber * 5;
    System.out.println("largeNumber is " + largeNumber);
    // smallNumber = largeNumber;
    smallNumber = (byte) largeNumber;
    System.out.println("smallNumber is " + smallNumber);
  }
}
```

The assignment starting with `largeNumber` assigns the `byte` variable `smallNumber` (times five) to the `int` variable `largeNumber`. In this case, there is a datatype mismatch (`byte` times `int`), but the code will compile without a problem because you are storing a smaller type (`byte`) in a larger type (`int`).

Rounding errors can occur from misuse of datatypes. The following shows an example of one of these errors:

```
int numA = 2;
int numB = 3;
System.out.println(numB/numA);
```

Although the division of these two variables results in "1.5," the print statement shows "1" because the output of the operator is the same type as the variables: `int`.

Casting Variables In the preceding example class (`TestCast`), the statement that is commented out will generate a compilation error because it tries to store a larger-capacity datatype (`int`) in a smaller-capacity datatype (`byte`), even though the actual value of 50 is within the range of the `byte` datatype.

You can *cast* (explicitly convert) one type to another by preceding the variable name with the datatype in parentheses. The statement after the commented lines in this example corrects the typing error by casting `largeNumber` as a `byte` so that it can be stored in the `smallNumber` `byte` variable. The disadvantage of casting is that the compiler will not catch any type mismatch as it will for explicit, non-cast types. Another disadvantage with older JDKs is performance—the cast takes time; the more recent JDKs minimize or eliminate this overhead.

Casting Objects You can also cast objects to classes and interfaces so that you can take advantage of the methods defined for the classes and interfaces. Casting allows you to match objects of different, but related, types. For example, the `Integer` class is a subclass of the `Number` class. The following code creates an object called numWidth as a Number cast from an Integer object. The cast is required because the `Number` class is abstract and you cannot instantiate it. The code then creates an object called width and assigns it the value of numWidth. Since numWidth is a Number object, which is less restrictive (or wider), this code needs to cast it to `Integer` to match the new object.

```
Number numWidth = (Number) new Integer(10);
Integer width = (Integer) numWidth;
```

If the example were reversed so that the Integer was created first and the Number second, casting would not be required. Consider the following example:

```
Integer width2 = new Integer(10);
Number numWidth2 = width2;
```

Explicit casting of the Integer (`width2`) into the Number (`numWidth2`) is not required because Number is less restrictive (or wider). Casting to interfaces works in the same way.

Casting Literals Floating-point literals (such as the value 34.5) default to the `double` datatype. If you want to assign a datatype of `float` to the literal, you must add an "F" suffix (for example, 34.5F). Alternatively, you may cast the literal using an expression such as `(float) 34.5`. Some examples for assigning datatypes to literals follow. ("L" is used for a `long` datatype, and "F" is used for a `float` datatype. It does not matter whether the suffix letters are upper- or lowercase.)

```
long population = 1234567890123456789L;
int age = 38;
float price = 460.95F;
float price = (float) 460.95;
double area, length = 3.15, width = 4.2;
area = length * width;
```

Non-floating literals (such as 38 in the example) will be assigned an `int` datatype. This can make an expression such as the following fail at compile time:

```
smallNumber = 5 + smallNumber;
```

The right side of the expression (`5 + smallNumber`) is assigned an `int` type because "5" is an `int` and `smallNumber` is implicitly cast up to match it. The right side does not match the left side because `smallNumber` is a `byte`. Explicit casting will solve the problem if you apply the cast to the entire side of the expression as follows:

```
smallNumber = (byte) (5 + smallNumber);
```

The Typesafe Concept *Typesafe* is an important type-matching concept in Java. At compile time, the compiler checks the type of a return with the method signature to ensure a match of types. Coding to a more specific (lower) level ensures that tighter matches are enforced by the compiler. For example, an object of type RowSet can be returned by a method that is declared to have a return of Object. However, that same method can return other class types and the method could lead to type problems in the calling program that the compiler will not catch. If the method were declared with a RowSet return, the compiler will ensure that the correct type is returned to the caller.

For example, the following code represents two different ways to declare an object and assign it a value from a view object attribute:

```
Number empId = (Number) newView.getAttribute("EmployeeId");
Number empId = newView.getEmployeeId();
```

The `getAttribute()` method returns an `Object` type. The first line shows a cast of the `Object` type to a Number. A runtime error would occur if `getAttribute("EmployeeId")` returned something other than a Number. The compiler cannot catch errors that occur because of the contents of quoted strings (`"EmployeeId"` in this case).

The second line requires no casting because `getEmployeeId()` returns a Number. The compiler will catch any mismatches of type, so this method is an example of a typesafe method.

Chapters 10 and 12 contain some more examples of typesafe methods. Using and creating typesafe methods will reduce the amount of casting needed for type matching. Since there is also some overhead associated with casting, the use of typesafe methods leads to better-performing code.

Hands-on Practice: Create Java Class Files

This practice demonstrates how to create three Java class files using JDeveloper. You can use this method to test the examples in this chapter and to experiment with variations on your own. Running examples that test aspects of the language is an excellent way to learn and absorb concepts. Also, actual working examples give you practice coding and formatting Java as well as interpreting and fixing syntax errors. The examples shown in this practice are the sample class, parent class, and test program shown in the "Java Language Review" section of this chapter. This practice contains the following phases:

I. Make an application workspace and project

II. Create and test Java class files

- Build the parent class file
- Build the subclass file
- Build the test program

I. Make an Application Workspace and Project

This phase builds an application workspace and an empty project for the class files. You will use the Create Java Class dialog as a starting point for most of the application program files in this practice. The right-click menus contain common operations for creating a workspace and project, and it can be faster to create some objects by using those menus.

As mentioned before, all files created in this and other practices are available for download from the authors' websites (mentioned in the author biographies at the beginning of the book).

1. On the Applications node in the Application Navigator, select New Application Workspace from the right-click menu.
2. In the Create Application Workspace dialog, enter the following:

Application Name as "JavaTest"
Application Package Prefix "shapes"
Application Template as "Java Application [Java, Swing]"

Additional Information: The directory name will be automatically typed in as the workspace name after JDEV_HOME\jdev\mywork (for example, "C:\JDev10g\jdev\mywork\JavaTest"). This creates a directory just for this workspace. It also creates a workspace file (.jws file) and a project directory and file (Client).

3. Click OK to create the workspace and Client project.
4. Click the Save All button in the toolbar.

What Just Happened? You created a workspace and project to hold the sample class files in this practice. If you want to test other files in the chapter, you can use the same workspace and project, or you can create additional projects in the same workspace. To create a project, select New Project from the right-click menu on the TestJava application workspace node, and select Empty Project from the General\Projects category in the New Gallery. Then enter the new project name in the Create Project dialog and click OK.

II. Create and Test Java Class Files

This phase creates the Java application files and allows you to test the interaction between a parent and a subclass. It is good practice to compile each file after creating it so that the final test will require less debugging.

Build the Parent Class File

The first class you need to build is the parent upon which the other files are based. This parent is the `Shape` class that contains some variables and basic methods.

1. On the Client project node, select New from the right-click menu. In the New Gallery, select the Java Class item in the General\Simple Files category and click OK. The Create Java Class dialog will appear as follows:

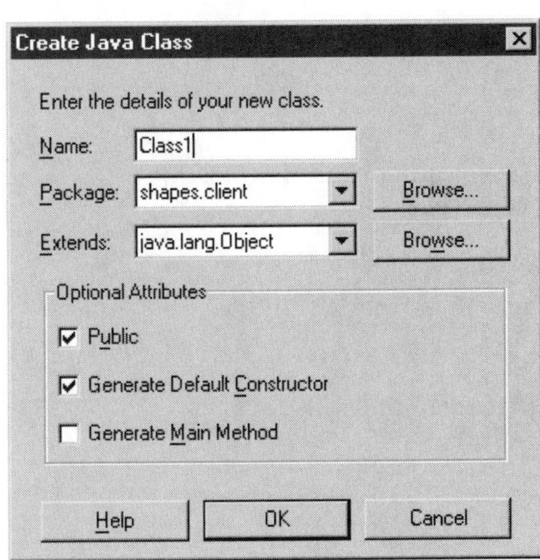

2. Fill in the field values as follows:

   Name as "Shape"
   Package as "shapes.client"
   Extends as "java.lang.Object"
   Public (checked)
   Generate Default Constructor (checked)
   Generate Main Method (unchecked)

   Additional Information: Adding a default constructor is standard practice even if it remains empty. You do not need a `main()` method for this example because the class only serves as a parent class and you will not execute it from the command line.

NOTE
Remember that Java is case sensitive, so you need to be careful of upper- and lowercase when entering class names and method names. For example, "Shape" and "shape" signify two different things in Java.

3. Click OK to create the file and open it in the Code Editor. Click Save All.
4. Replace the text in the file with the following:

```
package shapes.client;

public class Shape {
  int height;
  int width;

  public Shape() {
    height = 1;
    width = 1;
  }

  public int getHeight() {
    return height;
  }

  public void setHeight(int newHeight) {
     height = newHeight;
  }
  public int getWidth() {
    return width;
  }

  public void setWidth(int newWidth) {
     width = newWidth;
  }
}
```

5. Click Save All.

6. In the Code Editor, select Make from the right-click menu. The file will be compiled, and messages will appear in the Log window. If the Log window is not open, select **View | Log**. If you see errors or warnings, correct the code and repeat this step until you have no errors or warnings.

   Additional Information: Since this file has no `main()` method, you cannot run it, but compiling it successfully will suffice for now. The Log window shows error and warning messages when you compile. The messages usually include the number of the line in which the error occurred. If you double click an error message in the Log window, the cursor will jump to the appropriate line of code in the Code Editor.

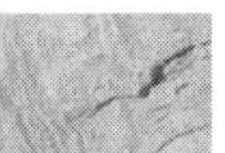

TIP
As you type code and before you try to compile, pay attention to the Structure window. It will display an Errors node if it finds syntax errors before you compile. Double clicking an error under that node will move the cursor to the problem line of code. In addition, the Code Editor will display red underscores for statements that contain errors. Holding the mouse above the red mark will display a hint box containing the syntax problem.

Build the Subclass File

This section creates a file that subclasses (extends) the `Shape` class. It demonstrates how some variables and methods in a parent can be overridden and how some variables and methods can be added.

1. On the Client project node, select New from the right-click menu. Select the Java Class item in the General\Simple Files category of the New Gallery. Click OK to display the Create Java Class dialog.

2. Fill in the field values as follows:

   Name as "Box"
   Package as "shapes.client"
   Extends: Click Browse and select Shape under the shapes\client node in the Class Browser. Then click OK to load "shapes.client.Shape" into the *Extends* field.
   Public and *Generate Default Constructor* (checked)
   Generate Main Method (unchecked)

3. Click OK to create the file and open the file in the Code Editor.

   Additional Information: The file contains code based on the fields you filled out in the New Class dialog. Using `shapes.client.Shape` as the superclass (in the *Extends* field) adds the `extends` clause to the class declaration. Checking the *Public* checkbox adds the keyword `public`; and checking *Generate Default Constructor* creates a code stub for the `Shape()` constructor.

4. Replace the text in the file with the following:

```
package shapes.client;

public class Box extends Shape {
  int height;    // override the Shape height
  int depth;     // unique to Box

  public Box() {
    height = 4;
    width = 3;    // the width from Shape
    depth = 2;
  }

  public int getDepth() {
    return depth;
  }

  public void setDepth(int newDepth) {
    depth = newDepth;
  }

   // super.getWidth is the same as getWidth() here
  public int getVolume() {
    return height * super.getWidth() * getDepth();
  }
}
```

5. Click Save All.
6. In the Code Editor, select Make from the right-click menu. If you see errors or warnings in the Log window, correct the code and repeat this step until you have no errors or warnings.

   Additional Information: You cannot run this file either, because it contains no `main()` method, but compiling it successfully will suffice for now.

Build the Test Program

This section builds a program that you can use to test the two class files and examine their inheritance and interactions. This file instantiates the `Box` class which, in turn, calls the `Shape` constructor (because `Box` is a subclass of `Shape`). It also contains a `main()` method so that you can run the class from the command line.

1. Repeat steps 1 and 2 in the previous section. In the Create Java Class dialog, specify a *Name* of "TestBox". The values in the other fields do not matter because you will be replacing the code completely.

Additional Information: If you were writing this class from scratch, you could specify the superclass name and package name as well as whether the class were public and should have a default constructor and main method.

2. Click OK to create the file and open it in the Code Editor.
3. Replace the text in the file with the following:

```
package shapes.client;

public class TestBox  {

  public static void main(String[] args) {
    // this creates an object called someBox
    Box someBox = new Box();
    someBox.setDepth(3);
    // getHeight() and setHeight() are from Shape
    // height shows the height variable from Box
    System.out.println (
      "The height of Shape is " + someBox.getHeight() +
      " and of someBox is " + someBox.height);

    // getDepth and getVolume are from Box
    System.out.println (
      "The depth of someBox is " + someBox.getDepth() +
      " and the volume of someBox is " + someBox.getVolume());
  }
}
```

4. Click Save All.
5. In the Code Editor, select Make from the right-click menu and correct errors or warnings.
6. In the Code Editor, select Run from the right-click menu to run the program. You will see a Client.jpr window (tab) appear in the Log window area.

   Additional Information: This tab displays the console messages about the code run in the Client project, such as the command line that runs the javaw.exe runtime. You will also see messages in the Client.jpr window that are output from the TestBox.java program.

7. Study the output carefully and verify that you understand how the values in the messages were assigned.

What Just Happened? You created three class files that represented a parent class, a subclass, and a test program. The first two files contained no `main()` method. You can compile this type of class but not test it without creating a `main()` method or another test program file. The test program you created contained a `main()` method that used the `Shape` class, so you could run it within the JDeveloper Java runtime (JVM). The JDeveloper Run button or menu option allows you to run a program in the same way you would if the program were deployed. In this case, the deployment environment would be as a command-line Java application.

This practice demonstrates the principles of class inheritance and instantiation as described in the "Annotated Java Code Example" and "Annotated Use of the Box Example Class" sections earlier in this chapter. It also shows how to build simple programs that you can use to test the syntax and principles of the Java language.

About Wrapper Classes

A *wrapper class* is a Java class that is created to control access to another Java class. A wrapper class can simplify the wrapped class' API, provide additional validation to the wrapped class, or change the access level of the wrapped class' methods. A wrapper class contains the wrapped class as an object member. For example, consider the following class:

```
 package sample;
public class WrappedClass {
  public WrappedClass() {
  }
  int sumNumbers(int number1, int number2, boolean reallySum) {
    int result = 0;
    if (reallySum){
      result = number1 + number2;
    }
    return result;
  }
}
```

Note that the sumNumbers() method is not public so many classes will not be able to access it. In addition, sumNumbers() accepts three arguments. This class could be wrapped by the following wrapper class:

```
 package sample;
public class WrapperClass {
  private final WrappedClass contents;
  public WrapperClass(WrappedClass newContents) {
    contents = newContents;
  }
  public int sumNumbers(int number1, int number2) {
    return contents.sumNumbers(number1, number2, true);
  }
}
```

Individual instances of WrappedClass are passed to the constructor and are stored in the `contents` field. The class exposes the API of WrappedClass, changing the number of arguments to `sumNumbers` and exposing it publicly. WrapperClass is said to wrap WrappedClass. In addition, instances of WrapperClass can be said to wrap the instances of WrappedClass that they contain.

CHAPTER 6

Naming Conventions

Today we have naming of parts. Yesterday, we had daily cleaning.
And tomorrow morning, we shall have what to do after firing.

But today, today we have naming of parts.

—Henry Reed (1914–1986), "Naming of Parts" (1.1–4),
Oxford Book of War Poetry, 1984

onsistently applied naming conventions are critical for the success of any system. Given the enormous number of elements available in the Java and JDeveloper environments, it is even more important to have a clearly defined set of conventions to follow. Unlike previous development environments that included a relatively finite set of components to name, the Java environment includes almost limitless possibilities. All of these possibilities are advantageous for development but pose special challenges for developing consistent naming standards. Using previously developed Java elements from different sources yields a hodgepodge of naming standards because the standards of those sources may be quite diverse. In addition, even elements from the same manufacturer may not be named consistently.

When formulating naming conventions for work in the 10*g* version of JDeveloper, it is important to decide in which environment you will be building applications. For example, names for Java applications are significantly different from those for JSP with Struts applications. If you are building a set of web services or some other isolated set of components, the naming conventions are less extensive.

JDeveloper 10*g* provides application templates that will automatically name many components for you. These templates generate and name projects and, depending upon the template selected, will automatically generate and/or name many other components as well. If you are just getting started with JDeveloper 10*g*, it is a good idea to use the templates provided; but as you develop your own development style, you may either modify the supplied templates or create your own.

When developing J2EE-compliant web applications in JDeveloper 10*g*, you will need to manage large groups of files that cross several programming languages. Integrating model, view, and controller functions in web applications often involves Java, XML, and HTML files. Careful consideration of naming conventions, storage locations, and deployment requirements will help you to maintain a structured approach to organizing and retrieving these files. Each language and technology has its own unique elements. Examining the code generated by JDeveloper will provide a starting point from which to formulate your own naming conventions. Whenever possible, you should use the default names generated by JDeveloper for the basis of your naming standards. JDeveloper usually generates reasonable names for components.

This chapter provides some insights into why standards are important. It also discusses guidelines and what standards have been used by others as well as some recommendations for structuring your own naming conventions when developing applications with Oracle JDeveloper. This chapter suggests the types of names you need to consider and provides examples to help in developing your own standards. JDeveloper supports many different areas of J2EE development spanning so many component types that this chapter can only provide naming conventions for a few sample components. However, you should be able to use the ideas presented in this chapter to create standards of your own for components specific to your applications.

The discussion of naming specific elements is divided into two sections: elements in the Java code and elements specific to JDeveloper. This separation is made for two reasons. First, a number of the objects discussed in the second section are unique to JDeveloper, and even experienced Java developers may be unfamiliar with these objects. Second, Java developers may already have their own consistent naming conventions for Java code.

The Importance of Using Naming Conventions

Creating naming conventions has several benefits. First, when you review your own or other people's code, you can quickly grasp the meaning of a particular element simply from its name. Also, by knowing how elements are named, you can locate specific elements more efficiently, making your applications easier to maintain. Another benefit of using a naming convention is that it frees you from having to re-create ways in which to name elements. By having a naming framework, you will not have to stop and think about how to name each new element.

Consistently named elements applied throughout an organization also make it easier for developers to work on each other's code. You should be able to scan through the code and easily identify specific element types. By using distinctive naming conventions with consistent prefixes or suffixes for the elements, you can quickly search all of the elements of a particular type by using an automated search routine.

Though elements imported from other sources may not adhere to these conventions, enforcing a naming standard for your own code makes it easier to identify those elements that are imported from outside sources and better organizes those created internally.

The standards you strive for should follow the four Cs adapted from *Oracle Developer Advanced Forms & Reports,* Koletzke and Dorsey (Oracle Press, 2000), as follows:

- **Consistent** The way in which you name elements should remain the same within an application and throughout all of your applications. You should try to create complete naming standards for all categories of development objects at the same time. For example, you should not create database-naming standards and then later create development standards since these two standards categories interact. The standards must be set for the entire development environment and lifecycle.
- **Concise** The names that you give elements should be short, but not so short that their meaning is not quickly understood. Short names make repeated typing easier and less prone to errors. Also, short names ease the burden on others who may need to read your code. If you use concise and consistent names, you will be able to scan through your code quickly, find the necessary elements, and determine their basic functions.

TIP
JDeveloper allows you to select classes, methods, and parameters from lists that pop up automatically (or by using a keypress such as CTRL-SPACEBAR *to display a list of available variables and methods for the class). You can save the typing necessary for long names by using these features. However, it is usually faster to type a shorter name than to browse or select from a list. If you use shorter names, you can still use the automatic completion features.*

- **Complete** If you use naming conventions at all, you should use them for every element type that needs a name. This means that you need to adopt or develop a naming standard before any coding begins. If you leave out a particular element from your standard, when it comes to your attention, you should develop a standard for that element before including it in your development effort.

- **Clear** Select meaningful names for variables to aid in the "self-documentation" of your programs. For example, when naming Boolean methods, use a name beginning with "is," such as "isOpen."

Naming conventions are an important part of an overall standards effort and, as such, should be included in your standards strategy. As with other components of your standards strategy such as code formatting and commenting, you have to consider how to document your naming conventions, train developers how and why to use them, and use code reviews to enforce the naming conventions that you develop.

The Consistency Issue

As you develop Java applications, you will use elements from libraries that someone else created. You will also use the JDeveloper wizards to generate code. Both of these sources use some type of naming convention. For consistency, it would make sense when you are writing your own code to use naming conventions that are similar to those employed by these sources. The good news is that there is some consistency regarding the general structure of a name. For example, a fully qualified name such as `java.lang.String.trim()` is consistent among all Java vendors. (This structure is discussed further in the section "Packages" later in this chapter.)

While most vendors try to be concise and clear when naming code elements, there is inconsistency among them as to how to name those elements. You will find naming inconsistencies in how code is generated, even within JDeveloper. In addition, there is inconsistency regarding how concise the names will be. For example, you will encounter the use of acronyms, full names, and abbreviations.

When you are creating your own naming conventions, you need to examine the names that are used for existing code and apply general rules that you create in order to come up with a fully defined naming convention of your own. It is useful to start your naming conventions with those that are generally recognized by Java programmers. This should be familiar territory if you have studied the Java language.

General Naming Convention Considerations and Guidelines

The task of defining and implementing any standard of your own can be formidable. It is easy to espouse the principle of using a naming standard, but attempting to encompass all of the possibilities can be very difficult if you try to create a list of naming methods for each element used in your development effort. Many developers attempting their first Java project have expressed their frustration when trying to apply what they have done in the past to the Java environment.

It is a good idea to learn and use the current conventions for the major items. To complete your naming convention, you need to add some general guidelines and specific rules to the conventions for naming all elements. By defining a simple naming structure that fits most situations, you will be free to add new components to your design without having to stop and think about how to name them. It is very difficult to create and validate your naming standards prior to building your first application. If you build a small sample application prior to finalizing your standards, you will be able to identify what types of components you will have to accommodate. Be prepared to evolve your standard over time as you add new component types to your development style.

The following sections include some general guidelines about how to create a workable naming standard.

Use Prefixes and Suffixes

Prefixes and suffixes imply type or help avoid naming conflicts. Some elements are more clearly named if they contain the name of the class or type to which they belong. For example, a panel that you create in the JDeveloper visual editor to hold information about the master table of a master-detail form would be called "masterPanel." The suffix indicates the type. This makes the code easier to read because you can distinguish the category that the component fits into by looking at the suffix. Without the type, you might have both a master panel and a master navigation bar that use the word "master" but do not imply the element type. A reader might be confused if the name has no suffix.

Using a suffix instead of a prefix is an arbitrary decision, but it follows the naming convention that JDeveloper most commonly uses when its wizards generate code. If you are using a combination of wizard code and custom-named code, there may be a disparity of suffixes and prefixes in your application. However, the reader will be able to rely on your code always using suffixes.

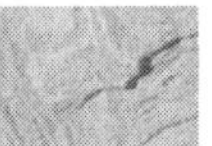

CAUTION
Naming elements with a suffix that denotes the component type, such as deptnoTextField, has a potential danger. If you decide to change the item type after you have written code based on the component name, you will either need to rename the item and update all of its references, or leave the item with a wrong and potentially confusing name. For Java client applications, JDeveloper will attempt to make all of the code changes automatically if you change the name in the Java Visual Editor unless you have embedded the name inside quotes. However, one of the authors has experienced problems with renaming components in complex applications.

File name conflicts sometimes occur. You can avoid this by adding something to the beginning of names of directories or folders containing shared libraries, such as the LD_LIBRARY_PATH or PATH environment variables.

There are several issues to consider when developing a set of naming conventions within an organization. It is useful to discuss the main categories of names and apply these general guidelines to describe how you might assign specific naming conventions to these categories.

Consider the Capabilities of the Language

When you are making decisions about what standards to create for naming Java elements, you will need to consider the capabilities of the language. For example, Java *identifiers* (names) are limited to strings that include characters, numbers, underscores (_), and dollar signs ($). These identifiers can be any length but cannot begin with a number or contain any blank spaces.

Be Aware of Case Sensitivity

In addition to establishing how things will be named, you also need to decide how they will be capitalized because of Java's case sensitivity. Even though Java is case sensitive, keep in mind that the Oracle database is not. "EMPLOYEES," "Employees," and "employees" refer to the same object in the Oracle database but different objects in Java. When dealing with Java objects that will be mapped into PL/SQL elements because of function calls to database tables or columns, remember that the Oracle database is case insensitive. However, Oracle string comparisons are case sensitive. If you query any system tables in Oracle, the names of the Oracle elements will usually be returned in uppercase. If you create a table using "CREATE TABLE "Employees" (col1.....)" the table name will be known as "Employees" (including the double quotes), so your SQL will need to format it that way, for example: SELECT * FROM "Employees".

Java developers should take special care with any elements that will be translated into Oracle elements. For example, if a developer created an entity object definition class called "Employee" and then generated an Oracle table from the entity object definition, the table would be called EMPLOYEE. If a command such as "update Employee..." is sent to the database, it would be successful. However, an investigation of the system view DBA_OBJECTS would not find an object named "Employee."

Use a Dictionary of Allowable Words

One of the simplest ways to ensure consistency of names is to start from a dictionary of allowable words. Therefore, you need to determine how this dictionary will be constructed, either using whole words or abbreviations. Code becomes much less readable if employees are referred to variously as "Employee," "EMPL," "EMP," or any other variations throughout a system rather than using the same term in all contexts.

Use Abbreviations Carefully

Because of the length limitation of Oracle object names, it is frequently impractical to use full words for Oracle objects, so some type of abbreviation mechanism is necessary. Names in Oracle must be from 1 to 30 bytes long with the following exceptions: names of databases are limited to 8 bytes and names of database links can be as long as 128 bytes. A useful standard is to select a fixed number of characters (usually five or six) as an abbreviation limit. Whenever possible, use the same number of characters, making exceptions only for industry standards such as "DEPT" for Department.

An alternative approach would be to maintain dual names for objects: Use a more abbreviated name for Oracle objects and spell out names for non-Oracle objects. A shorter name can be used in contexts where the name length is restricted and a more readable, verbose name is used where length is unrestricted. Although verbose names for code elements may make each element more readable, they may actually make it more difficult to read the entire code. Complex mathematical expressions can be hard to read if the variable names are particularly long. In addition, all of the developers have to know when to use each version of the name. The usage guidelines for long and short names should be written into the standards documentation. Use a naming convention that allows you to stay within the Oracle length limitations for all objects.

In order to enforce naming standards, all words and abbreviations that can be used in your code elements should be maintained in a list or database table. Developers can use this list to make sure that only accepted words are used for object names.

It is possible to write a program to check the code against the list and validate that only acceptable words are used in the code. Such a utility need not hinder programmer productivity. Words can be automatically added to the list when they are detected in the code. The utility can also help enforce that the same name is always used to refer to the same construct.

You must be somewhat careful about the abbreviations you select. Otherwise you may end up with undecipherable elements in your system. Under no circumstances should you adopt a naming standard with fewer than five characters per element since it is too hard to determine what some of these represent. One of the authors worked on a system where three- to four-character abbreviations had been used. By the time the developers creating the abbreviations got to the months of the year, "APR" and "DEC" had already been used for "Annual Percent Rate" and "Declined."

Recognized Naming Conventions in Java

Ultimately, consistent naming conventions in a Java environment are even more important than they were in traditional development environments such as Oracle Forms Developer. Not only is there a wider variety of elements from which to choose, but behind the scenes, you are working in a straight 3GL environment. This means that, at some point, you will be opening up large blocks of code to edit. All of your program elements may not be neatly organized into an object navigator. They might be organized into a structure navigator like the UI components in the JDeveloper Structure window. If you do not use precise naming conventions, you may end up spending time unnecessarily searching for a particular element.

Most Java professionals follow generally recognized conventions for naming basic Java elements. By following similar patterns in your own code, you will be able to produce a final product that is not only functional but also integrates well with established conventions.

The following sections examine basic Java code elements and explain the generally recognized naming conventions for those elements. Since names in Java can be any number of characters, you need no naming convention guideline for the number of characters in an identifier. Therefore, these conventions usually define case usage (uppercase or lowercase). There are a number of categories of elements, each of which has a recognized naming convention. Some naming conventions are imposed by the Java language. For example, constructor names must match the class name and reserved keywords are case sensitive (usually lowercase).

Constants (Final Variables)

Constants are identified by all uppercase letters. When the name of the constant contains more than one word, the words are separated using the underscore character (_), for example, `MAX_LOAD` and `MIN_SIZE`.

Classes

Class names are usually nouns. Classes use an initial capital letter for each word in the class name, for example, `JavaFirstClass`, `EmployeeHistory`, and `CustomerOrder`. Note that there are no spaces between the words in any Java element name.

Class Instances, Exceptions, Methods, and Variables

These elements use mixed case and always start with the first letter in lowercase. The remaining words use an initial capital letter. As mentioned, there are no blank spaces or underscores between words, for example, `javaFirstObject`, `printHistory()` and `customerName`.

NOTE
You should avoid starting names with an underscore because this is often used for internal operations. This applies to classes, class instances, exceptions, methods, and variables.

Some Java programmers use short, meaningless variable names such as "a" or "b1." This is not useful and violates the goal of clarity in naming elements. Meaningful names such as "price" or "totalPrice" can make the usage clear. An exception to this rule might be loop counter variables. A common practice in most languages is to use "i" as the name of an integer counter in a loop, for example, "(`int i=0; i < 10; i++`)". If there is a nested loop, you would use "j" as the counter for the inner loop. Although these variable names are uninformative, they are generally recognized in the programming community, and your standard could document them. Using descriptive counter names is a better idea. For example, if you are looping through all employee records, the loop counter could be named "countEmp."

Some methods are named to comply with standards in the language. For example, if you had a class called `Address` that contained methods for assigning a city name and retrieving a city name from an object instantiation, you would name the methods `getCity()` and `setCity()`, respectively. Method names are usually verbs. These implement a standard naming convention used by Java developers—getters and setters. The names of these methods use the "get" and "set" verbs combined with the attribute name (City). Chapter 5 discusses getters and setters (also called *accessor methods*) further.

Packages

In the JDeveloper development environment, a package is represented by a file folder. Programmatically, a "package" refers to a folder of grouped classes and related files that end up in deployed code. In JDeveloper, compiled class files (.class) are stored in folders referred to as "packages" usually in the default "classes" folder within each project.

Generally, packages are named using all lowercase letters, but you will find many exceptions to this convention because the package-naming standards have continued to change as the popularity of Java has grown. Follow the all-lowercase standard when you create code. There is also a recognized standard of how a fully qualified name is constructed. A *fully qualified name* contains the names of all elements that specifically locate it. For example, the qualified name `java.lang.String.trim()` points to the method `trim()` that is part of the class `String`. The class is contained in a package java.lang. The name also indicates (because of the word "java") that the vendor for this library is Sun Microsystems. The fully qualified name increases in precision from left to right. In the preceding example, "java" indicates the company, "lang" indicates a subsystem in the company, and "String" indicates a class within that subsystem. Fully qualified names may have many parts.

To avoid conflicts with packages created by other developers, the current convention is to use your reversed Internet domain name as the package root in the library. For example, if you wanted to store the `doJob()` method, from the class `BusTask`, in the businessutil package, use the following naming structure in your library: com.company.businessutil.BusTask.doJob(), where "com.company" is a reversed domain name such as "com.mcgrawhill."

This type of fully qualified name is logical and universally recognized. Since the Java naming standards just described are well established, the remaining topic of discussion is how you name the components you create in JDeveloper that make up the fully qualified name (for example, the actual object or method). A sensible strategy is to start with some general guidelines and to add specific rules for each type of element that needs to be named.

Objects can be grouped in packages in any way that the developer desires. For simple programs, a single package per application or project (using the same name) is adequate. For more complex development, a better way of managing objects is needed. One method is to nest the packages within the application. For example, the following table shows sample package names for the business services objects in the HR application.

Package Name Example	Components
hr.model.businessdomain	EJB entity beans or ADF BC entity objects
hr.model.datamodel	EJB session beans or ADF BC view objects and application modules
hr.model.services	Web services files such as WDSL documents and Java interfaces

JDeveloper-Specific Naming Conventions

There are some naming conventions to be aware of that are specific to JDeveloper. This section provides some guidelines to use in your work with JDeveloper.

When you create files in JDeveloper, the tool usually fills in the file extensions for you, so you do not need to type an extension such as ".java" for a Java class file.

Types of Objects to Name

Some of the objects you name in JDeveloper (such as packages) will be physically implemented as directory names in the operating-system file structure. When you are creating new application workspaces, the Create Application Workspace dialog includes a field for the *Application Package Prefix*. This prefix (when specified) is added to the beginning of the name of all packages associated with the application. Other objects such as class names will appear as file names within those packages.

Within the Java code, you may be creating Java elements that only exist within your code. Some objects such as connections will appear in the Connection Navigator, but are not visible or editable in any other context.

Application Development Framework Business Components (ADF BC) objects (such as entity object definitions and view object definitions) are visible and editable in several contexts. Therefore, in setting naming conventions, you need some understanding of how objects are physically implemented since you may want to identify the type of object clearly in whatever context it can be viewed.

If you are used to working in an Oracle environment, case sensitivity may be new to you. This leads to some complications. As mentioned, unlike Java, languages used with the Oracle database such as SQL and PL/SQL are not case sensitive. For example, in non-case-sensitive languages, "loc_dept" and "LoC_dePt" are all valid spellings of the same name. In Java and other case-sensitive languages this is not the case. The normal standard for naming objects in Oracle is to use all capitalized words with underscore separators such as the table "LOC_DEPT." In Java, the naming convention would use initial capital letter, mixed-case format to name the class representing the table, like this: LocDept. JDeveloper's wizards follow the Java convention. For example, when creating ADF BC entity object definitions, JDeveloper will alias Oracle tables and columns by removing underscores and changing the names to initial caps, mixed-case words. This convention is known as "camel-capping."

As long as you understand the algorithm behind the wizards, understanding the naming conventions will be less confusing. It is important to keep in mind that the name of a table or column in the database may not be exactly the same as the name of its associated entity object or view object. This may actually cause difficulties in some application coding since you cannot count on being able to directly map Oracle object names to ADF BC names.

If you rarely use underscores, dollar signs, and such in your column names, you may not even be aware that ADF BC strips them out. It may be tempting to write code using the ADF BC attribute name as the column name, erroneously assuming that they are always identical (with the exception of case). Your code would work, except when the database column name contained an underscore that was removed by the business components layer.

Workspaces

A workspace in JDeveloper is a container for projects. A workspace file should be stored in its own directory that has the same name as the file. Therefore, when naming a workspace, you are also naming the directory with the same name as the workspace. For example, when you use the Create Application Workspace dialog to create a workspace named "Layout", you are creating a directory named Layout that contains a file named "Layout.jws".

As mentioned earlier, when you are typing workspace and project names in the JDeveloper wizards, the appropriate file extensions are added automatically. (For example, ".jws" is added to all workspace files.) These workspace extensions will only be visible in the System Navigator.

Projects

In JDeveloper, projects are generally created and named by the application templates. Projects that you manually add should be made to be consistent with the template you already are using. For example, in JClient applications, the default project names are "Model" and "View." In web applications, they are "Model" and "ViewController."

Connections

For connection names, no suffix is needed. In this book, the authors use a descriptive, mixed-case name for the application or user such as "Scott" or "HR." If appropriate, you should include the associated role in the connection name such as HR_user, HR_admin.

There are a number of different types of connections such as Application Server, Database, SOAP Server, and UDDI Registry, but since they appear in separate nodes in the navigator, it is not necessary to use a special prefix or suffix to identify their type.

Class Source Files

JDeveloper's wizards create class files for you. If you need to create your own class file, the file name must have the same name and case as the class name. It is a well-established Java standard to use an initial capital letter, mixed case. For example, the employee history class file would be named EmployeeHistory.java.

Libraries

A *library* is a pointer to a collection of .zip and .jar files. Libraries are usually used to create reusable groups of Java classes or tags. Publicly available libraries are already named and should not be altered. If you create your own libraries, they should be stored in a handy location (not as a sub-sub-sub-directory in the application where they were created).

You may want to use the version number as part of the library name since you may need to keep several versions of a library. For example, a custom tag library could be named "ABC Corp Tag Lib V1.0".

Client Data Models

Client data models are internal JDeveloper objects used with ADF Business Components client applications. A file that JDeveloper by default names DataBindings.cpx contains the data model definition created by the Client Data Model Definition Wizard. There is no reason to modify this name.

UML Diagram Elements

No special naming convention is needed for elements appearing on UML diagrams. You are actually creating and naming already existing elements such as entity objects, Java classes, or packages. For example, when you create a diagram element that is a Java class, you will actually be creating a Java class file and not just the diagram element.

The only remaining naming standard is for the diagrams. You can use descriptive initial-capped names similar to the ones used for a class with a suffix of "CUML" for a UML class diagram or "AUML" for a UML activity diagram. For example, the class diagram for the Human Resources System might be called "HRCUML" or "HumanResourceCUML." An activity diagram modeling the process of hiring an employee might be called "HireEmpAUML."

ADF Business Components

The JDeveloper wizards create and automatically name the .xml and .java files for business components. There are several elements within ADF BC that require setting naming conventions if you are creating business components outside of the wizards. The following discussion uses the same kind of naming conventions that the wizards use so your code will be consistent with the wizard-generated code.

Entity Object Definitions

Entity objects in ADF BC correspond more or less directly to database tables and views. The same name as the database table is used, except that initial capital letters are used, and all underscores are removed. For example, the CUST_HIST table would be the CustHist entity object definition in ADF BC.

Entity Attributes

The entity object naming convention also applies to entity attributes. Use an initial capital letter and no underscores. For example, the column "EMP_NAME" becomes the attribute "EmpName".

Associations

The generated name for an association is a concatenation of the foreign key constraint name and "Assoc." Entity associations represent foreign-key referential integrity constraints at the ADF Business Components level. These should be named in the same way as foreign key constraints, that is, using the master entity/detail entity/Fk with an "Assoc" suffix (if that is your foreign key naming convention). You may have to shorten the entity names to keep the association name from getting too long. For example, the master-detail association between Location and Department would be LocDeptFKAssoc if the foreign key constraint were called LOC_DEPT_FK.

Domains

Domains are classes that can be used as datatypes for entity and view attributes. The ADF BC libraries include a number of domains; you can create others yourself. TelephoneNumber is an example of a commonly used domain. In JDeveloper, you can write validation code in the constructor to ensure that the values are correct. ADF BC allows you to use domains as the datatype of entity object and view object attributes in order to enforce validation checks on attribute values.

A sensible naming convention for domain definitions is to replace the default name "Domain" to reflect its intended usage. Use initial uppercase and a suffix of Domain, for example, MaxSalaryDomain.

Application Module Definitions

The generated name for an application module is "AppModule" by default. Application modules are named with a suffix of "Module" just like most other ADF BC objects. The base name is descriptive, such as LocDept, so the module would be "LocDeptModule."

View Object Definitions

The JDeveloper convention is used to name view objects. View objects should be named like the entity object with the suffix "View," for example, DepartmentsView, LocationsView, and so forth.

View Attributes

View attributes should be named the same as their associated entity attributes. If the column you are retrieving is not in a base table that is represented by an entity object, you need to construct a name. The name could be derived from a function or subquery embedded in the SELECT list. For example, you may have a business component that includes a query such as the following:

```
SELECT department_id,
       department_name,
       (SELECT city
        FROM   locations
        WHERE  locations.location_id = departments.location_id)
               as  dsp_location_name
FROM   departments
```

The "dsp" prefix for the last column denotes that this is a display-only column. The view attribute name for this column would be DspDeptName.

View Link Definitions

View links should be named the same as their corresponding entity associations with a "Link" suffix instead of "Assoc." For example, in the LocDept application used in Chapter 1, the view link that JDeveloper creates is called "DeptLocFkLink."

Java Client Application Files

Part of the naming convention document you create should list the names used to distinguish various files for a Java application. Some examples include the following:

- **Frame** DeptEmpFrame.java
- **Panel** DeptPanel.java
- **Master-detail panel** DeptEmpPanel.java

Java Client UI Components

Java has hundreds of pre-built classes available for your use. When the code generators (wizards) in JDeveloper add UI components to your project, they will include a default name that you should override. The default name is usually a number added to the component name, for example, jPanel1. After adding several components of the same type, you will find it nearly impossible to distinguish them unless you rename them.

As mentioned, it is good practice to use a suffix to define the type or class of object. This is particularly important for UI components. For example, if you were to add a button component from the Swing library as an "Exit" button, it would be named exitButton.

Web Client Components

When building web applications, there are numerous alternatives including JSP, UIX, or other tag libraries for the client portions of the applications. Struts or some other controller can also be selected or you can create your own. It is not possible to provide examples for all of the possible alternatives. Some examples of naming conventions for a Struts with JSP tags development environment will be discussed in this section.

Struts Components

JDeveloper provides the Struts Page Flow Diagram, a graphical environment for managing Struts components. The fact that these components will also be visible in the source code means that a coherent naming convention is a good idea. Some examples follow.

Data Actions For data actions, a DA suffix can be used, for example, editDeptDA. When the associated action class is created, JDeveloper automatically adds the word "Action" as a suffix. Using the Dept example, the action class would be named "editDeptDAAction."

Data Pages Data page names correspond to the names of their actions. A DP suffix can be used (editDeptDP, for example). The associated JSP page will be created with a .jsp extension, and .uix or .html is added if those application types are being created.

Forwards *Forwards* are lines represented on the Struts Page Flow Diagram that connect Data Actions and Data Pages. They should be named using the action associated with them. By default, JDeveloper names them "success." You can change this name to other words such as "browse" to correspond to the action followed by the forward arrow's path.

Page Forwards As with data actions, a PF suffix can be used (editDeptPF) to enable easy identification.

Other Components

In Struts, some user interface components, such as a value tag for an attribute, are not named.

Other objects such as buttons are named and these names are important. Buttons are named with the prefix "event," which signals the framework to associate the button with a "do" action. For example, a "First" button on the navigation bar will be named "event_First."

Components such as iterators are automatically created and named by JDeveloper. For example, the iterator for the Departments view object is DepartmentsViewIterator.

When creating your own components, you should try to follow JDeveloper's naming conventions for similar objects as closely as possible.

CHAPTER 7

J2EE Architectures and Deployment Alternatives

You pays your money and you takes your choice.

—*Punch* (1846), *X, 16*

After you create the application code and debug it, you need to install it into the production environment. The term *deployment* refers to the process of copying and installing the necessary application and configuration files into a specific server environment. When you develop an application, you choose the server architecture long before you write the code. Therefore, you will know ahead of time what server will be assigned to the database, what the client platforms will consist of, and what use you will make of web servers. In the past, the architecture decision was often made with little guidance from the industry. This kind of decision is now a bit easier because Sun Microsystems has published best practices as part of the Java 2 Platform, Enterprise Edition (J2EE). Once you decide upon an architecture, you can develop the system and deploy it.

This chapter provides an overview of the architectures of two popular types of front-end Java code. The first type of code, *Java client,* is a category that encompasses the Java application and applet styles. The second type is *web client,* a collection of the following styles of coding that can be used separately or together:

- **Java servlets (servlets)**, which are Java files run on an application server. Servlets can be written to output HTML to a browser.
- **JavaServer Pages (JSP) technology**, which is an extension of servlet technology that uses a code file containing HTML and other tag styles. This code file generates a servlet when the file is run. As with servlets, JSP files can (and usually do) send HTML to the browser.
- **ADF UIX**, which is an Oracle-specific framework in which you write extensible markup language (XML) code. This code is run within the framework environment and also outputs HTML to the browser.

All of these styles have Java at their core, either in library files or in the code files.

Servlet basics and the mechanics of the JSP and ADF UIX coding styles are further explored in Chapters 18 and 19. The material in this chapter serves as a foundation for the chapters in Part III of this book, which provide some details about how to develop Java client and web client applications.

For the purpose of this chapter, an application consists of code that needs to be packaged and copied to another machine to make it available for production use. This chapter considers that the application in this context includes all libraries and application code needed to implement the Application Development Framework (ADF) layers (explained in Chapter 4)—business services, model, controller, and view.

This chapter also provides an overview of the deployment process in JDeveloper. In addition, the hands-on practices in the chapter show one way to deploy a Java application and one way to deploy a JSP application. The practices should help you understand the deployment process and the many variations for deploying applications. They will also familiarize you with some of the necessary terminology. As with other practices in this book, the material in the practices is not a repeat of the introductory material in the chapter. Therefore, we recommend that you try the practices to enhance your understanding of the deployment process.

Before discussing the specific styles of application development and deployment, it is necessary to briefly examine the features of J2EE.

An Overview of J2EE

J2EE is not a product. It is a combination of technologies and specifications that is available on the Sun Microsystems website. Many vendors including Oracle have seen the value of the direction that J2EE provides and have developed products that supplement or, at least, comply with the basic features provided by Sun. Two other Java 2 platforms offer some of the features of J2EE—Java 2 Platform, Micro Edition (J2ME), and Java 2 Platform, Standard Edition (J2SE). To understand the "edition" part of the term J2EE, it is helpful to understand the features of the other platforms. Also, J2EE is built on top of J2SE. All specifications, guidelines, and Java language software included in these editions are available for browsing or download at the Sun Microsystems Java website (java.sun.com). The Sun website also includes free tutorials, quizzes, newsletters, and developer community forums that you can use to learn about the features of the Java 2 editions.

At the heart of all these editions is the Java language. At this writing, Java is available in version 1.4. Any version higher than 1.2 is considered "Java 2." The following sections describe the distinguishing features of the three editions.

J2ME

The *Java 2 Platform, Micro Edition* defines how applications are developed and deployed to "consumer and embedded devices" such as cell phones, pagers, and personal digital assistants (PDAs). The keywords for J2ME are "small" and "light." J2ME supports client applications that require less than one megabyte (MB) of memory and/or a lightweight processor. Applications built with J2ME can be run on many platforms. More information about J2ME is available on the Sun website java.sun.com/j2me/.

J2SE

The *Java 2 Platform, Standard Edition* is the foundation for J2EE and consists of components such as the following:

- **Java language libraries** for writing and compiling Java applications and applet code in Java using Java Foundation Classes (JFC) Swing and Abstract Windowing Toolkit (AWT) controls.
- **Java Database Connectivity (JDBC)** classes that provide a standard API to any database with a JDBC driver. Any Java class that needs access to database objects can use JDBC classes to accomplish the task. For example, ADF Business Components (ADF BC) and standard classes such as Enterprise JavaBeans (EJB) rely on JDBC classes.
- **Remote Method Invocation (RMI)**, which allows your program to call operations available in objects in a different program running under another Java Virtual Machine potentially on a separate machine.

J2SE is also documented on the Sun website java.sun.com/j2se/.

NOTE
AWT libraries are part of the JDK, but Swing controls are more fully featured and are the more popular choice for modern Java client application development.

J2EE

The J2EE environment is a superset of J2SE components that provides a corporation-wide (enterprise) strategy for distributing application code into a multi-tier architecture. Code may reside in the database, in application servers, or on the client. A variety of products and communication protocols enable these options. J2EE has several major components: blueprints, specifications, software, and an application architecture model.

J2EE BluePrints

The *J2EE BluePrints* provide guidelines and best practices for working with a specific environment such as enterprise, wireless, high-performance, and web services. These BluePrints are available online at java.sun.com. They discuss the considerations and requirements of the specific environment. BluePrints facilitate work within a particular environment by explaining the features and services required for effective deployments in that environment. BluePrints include *J2EE patterns* (or *design patterns*) each of which describes a low-level design solution to a common design problem (such as Session Façade, which is discussed in Chapter 14). One of the most pervasive and popular of all J2EE patterns is *Model-View-Controller* (MVC), which is actually inherited from the Smalltalk language. JDeveloper's ADF is built from the principles inherent in MVC and it is important to understand these principles when working in JDeveloper. Chapter 4 describes how MVC concepts are incorporated into JDeveloper 10*g* ADF.

Model-View-Controller (MVC) MVC defines a rigorous separation between these three components of application code:

- **Model** This layer represents the data and values portion of the application.
- **View** This layer represents the screen and user interface components.
- **Controller** This layer handles the user interface events that occur as the user interacts with the interface (view), controls page flow, and communicates with the Model layer.

The controller layer of MVC is often implemented in a centralized servlet that is responsible, among other things, for defining and implementing *page flow*—which page will be called from a specific action on another page. Before the incorporation of MVC principles into web technology, page flow was handled in a decentralized way; that is, each page would contain a hard-coded link to another page or would pass a parameter value to the next page, which processed the value to determine what would be displayed. The Java community refers to this decentralized method as *Model 1* and the centralized controller method as *Model 2*. Although those terms were only used in draft versions of the JSP specification, they are still in common use.

The separation between layers allows the switching of one code layer without affecting the other layers. For example, if your application were built using the MVC pattern, you could switch the user interface from a Java application to a mobile cell phone interface and still use the underlying controller and model layers. An extension of this principle is that a single model and controller layer can support more than one view at the same time, for example, in an application where some users accessed your application by cell phone and some by a desktop computer. This kind of flexibility is the key benefit of the MVC pattern.

The separation of layers also allows different developers to work on different parts of the application code. In addition, compartmentalized design work for data structures, interface screens, and processes affects code in different MVC layers—model, view, and controller, respectively.

Therefore, in theory, MVC offers many benefits. In practice, this separation is rarely achieved completely but it is viable as a goal and a design principle.

Specifications

The J2EE specifications (now at version 1.4) describe all features of the platform and provide details about standards for security, transaction management, naming, APIs, interoperability, application assembly and deployment, application clients, and service provider interfaces.

J2EE also contains specifications for Java servlet, JavaServer Pages, Enterprise JavaBean, JDBC, JavaMail, and other technologies. More information about J2EE is available on the Sun website java.sun.com/j2ee/.

Software

The software that comprises J2EE is primarily the J2SE Software Development Kit (SDK), formerly called the Java Development Kit (JDK). It contains development and runtime software for Java programming.

Application Architecture Model

J2EE provides a conceptual architecture model that is divided into multiple tiers, each of which is responsible for a specific function. Figure 7-1 depicts the architectural model. The model contains four logical tiers as follows:

- **Client Tier** This tier, also called the *Client-Side Presentation Tier,* contains code and processes that run on the client machine and with which the user interacts. For example, this tier can contain a Java application that runs in a Java Virtual Machine (JVM) on the client and presents a user interface.
- **Web Tier** This tier, also called *Server-Side Presentation Tier,* contains user interface code and processes that run on a common application server (J2EE server). For example, this tier can contain a JavaServer Pages application that constructs a user interface on the server and sends it to the browser on the client.
- **Business Tier** This tier, also called the *Server Business Logic Tier,* contains data access code and, optionally, validation and business rule enforcement. This tier also resides on a J2EE (web) server. There is no user interface function housed on this tier.
- **EIS Tier** The Enterprise Information System (EIS) Tier contains the persistent data storage mechanism—usually a relational database such as Oracle. The databases can be distributed across many servers, but all serve the function of an EIS server.

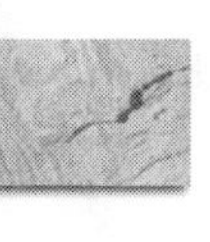

NOTE

The diagram in Figure 7-1 shows ADF Business Components in the Business Tier. ADF is a product of Oracle Corporation, not Sun Microsystems as is EJB. ADF Business Components (previously called BC4J) are part of the ADF Business Services layer, which also includes EJBs and web services.

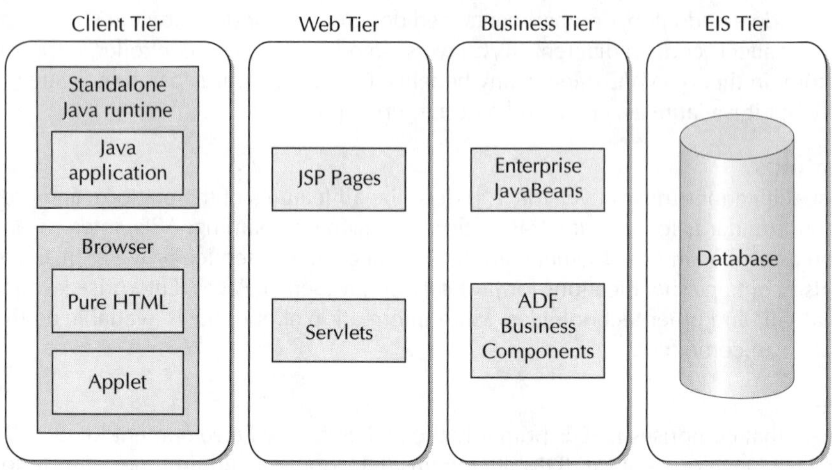

FIGURE 7-1. *J2EE application architecture model*

The J2EE tiers in Figure 7-1 show some examples of what the tier may contain. One application style will usually use at most one part from each tier. Some styles do not use all four tiers. The discussions in this chapter of Java clients and JSP pages will use this diagram as a basis for explaining the communications between tiers and the components used for each application style.

Technologies introduced in the future should fit into one of these tiers. The reason that this is considered a *conceptual* division of tiers is that a tier on the diagram does not necessarily represent a physical machine. One or more machines could be allocated to each tier. Alternatively, tiers can be combined on one machine.

NOTE
ADF is built on a variation of MVC. Chapter 4 shows the ADF architecture model and describes how it separates code into four layers.

Deploying a J2EE Application

As you have noticed, J2EE offers flexible choices for application architecture. Along with this kind of flexibility come the questions of how to manage all application files, where to place the files, how to notify the servers about their locations, and how the server should start and run the application. Fortunately, J2EE defines standards for file packages and locations and standard configuration files that help answer these questions. Using J2EE configuration and archive files, any J2EE-compliant server can find the proper files and process them in a standard way.

The first step in deploying an application is gathering together potentially thousands of application and library files that are located in various directories. J2EE defines standard *archive files,* single files that house more than one file and directory. Tools such as JDeveloper help you assemble the files into the archive. The next step in deployment is to copy the archive file to the proper directory on the server. The server either expands the file into individual files or runs the application by finding files inside the archive file.

J2EE Archive Files

Java archive files are usually one of four different types: Java archive (JAR), Enterprise JavaBeans JAR (EJB JAR), enterprise application archive (EAR, also called "enterprise archive"), and web application archive (WAR, also called "web archive"). Each file contains one or more files in one or more directories. A single archive file can contain the equivalent of one or more file system directories (with nested subdirectories) and files. The JVM can access files inside an archive file in the same way as if they were housed in a real file system directory. Archive files use extensions of .jar (for JAR and EJB JAR files), .war (for WAR files), and .ear (for EAR files). JVMs can also recognize JAR files that use a .zip extension. Any archive file can be viewed with an archive viewer (such as the Archive Viewer in JDeveloper) and manipulated with an archive file program (such as WinZip).

JAR File

A *JAR file* is an archive file used for deployment to a command-line JAR—an archive that can be run from the command line using a command such as `java -jar DeptEmp.jar`. JAR files can also act as repositories (libraries) for application or support code. EJB JAR files hold all files required to deploy EJBs.

WAR File

A *WAR* file is an archive file that contains all files required for the application's runtime. If the web application is a set of JSP pages, it will contain the JSP files in a root directory (that appears as a project subdirectory under the j2ee\home\applications directory). The WAR file also contains a number of files and directories inside a WEB-INF directory. These files are a combination of standard J2EE XML descriptor files (such as web.xml) and packages of ADF BC files. The deployment process expands the WAR file into its component files and directories. A copy of the WAR file is kept in the project root directory.

EAR File

The *EAR file* is an archive file used for standard J2EE deployments. It provides a single archive that contains all other archive and other files needed for an entire enterprise (many applications). The EAR file can contain one or more WAR files, JAR files, and EJB JAR files as well as several deployment descriptor files

Deployment Descriptor Files

Deployment descriptor files contain configuration information for a particular aspect of the server. One of these deployment descriptor files is *application.xml,* which provides the *context-root virtual directory* for one or more applications. You use this virtual directory to construct the URL for a JSP application. For example, the ViewController project is contained within the LocJSPDeploy workspace. The connection URL for files in the application directory is http://host:port/ LocJSPDeploy-ViewController-context-root/action.do, where "host: port" is the server name and JSP container port; "action.do" is the name of the Struts data action file that starts the JSP file or just the JSP file name (if Struts is not used); and LocJSPDeploy-ViewController-context-root represents the context-root (home) directory. For ADF BC projects, application.xml contains a list of runtime files.

Another configuration file in the EAR is *data-sources.xml,* which contains database connection information for the JDeveloper connection objects. The other deployment descriptor is *orion-application.xml,* which provides application information specific to OC4J.

More information about deployment descriptors is in the JDeveloper online documentation node "Working with Application Design Tools\Deploying Applications\Deploying Applications to J2EE Application Servers" in the help system Table of Contents tab.

Deploying Archive Files

Both WAR and EAR files may be created in the New Gallery's (**File | New**) General\Deployment Profiles node or from the right-click menu on a deployment profile (.deploy file). In addition, JDeveloper creates a default WAR and EAR when you select "Deploy to" from the right-click menu.

Java application and applet files contain .deploy file right-click menu options for JAR and EAR. The WAR file is not appropriate for a Java client deployment.

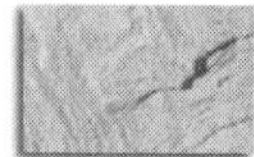

NOTE
Another important part of deployment is migrating database code and database objects to the production database. This subject is not unique to J2EE deployments and is discussed in many other books and websites.

JDeveloper and J2EE

JDeveloper provides rich support for all types of code that you can deploy into the J2EE tiers. In addition, some specific features of JDeveloper categorize it as a J2EE development tool:

- **The ability to create code** that complies with the latest Enterprise JavaBean, servlet, and JSP standards.
- **Full integration with Oracle Containers for J2EE (OC4J)**, a J2EE-compliant application server that is part of Oracle9*i*AS and Oracle Application Server 10*g*. This means you can develop and run code in JDeveloper in the same environment as you use for deploying the code. JDeveloper supports quick ("one-click") deployment to the application server as well.
- **Incorporation of MVC** as a coding standard for Java client as well as JSP applications.
- **Wizard support to generate J2EE deployment files**—Java Archive, Enterprise JavaBean Java Archive, web application archive, or enterprise application archive. (Archive files are explained in the earlier section "J2EE Archive Files".)

The JDeveloper wizards almost completely automate the time-consuming and error-prone task of packaging and installing the right application files in the right locations.

Deploying J2EE Applications in JDeveloper

Production Java projects contain many files that are dependent upon one another. Before there were tools to assist in deploying the proper files to the proper location, developers created *make scripts* (that automatically compile and package files in the right location) or used utilities such as Ant to compile and package all of the application files into a form that would run correctly on the server or client. Creating and maintaining these scripts took considerable time and effort.

The Deployment Profile

Tools such as JDeveloper now automate the deployment packaging process. Deployment using JDeveloper consists of creating and defining a *deployment profile* file that contains details about the files needed for the application and the locations into which the files should be placed. The deployment profile has different contents for each style of application and application server.

The Deployment Process

You can deploy a web application from JDeveloper by setting up an application server connection, creating the deployment profiles, and selecting Deploy in the right-click menu on the project node. In the case of a web deployment (applet or JSP page), a WAR file and JAR file will be created automatically. These files will then be automatically copied across the network to the correct location in the OC4J, Apache Tomcat, JBoss, or BEA WebLogic application server, and the server will be configured to recognize the application. The deployment process makes working with a J2EE server relatively simple. If your server is not one of those mentioned, you can deploy to an appropriate JAR, EJB JAR, WAR, or EAR file and then copy those files to the server manually. Since these are standard J2EE archives, any server that is J2EE compliant will be able to use them.

Now that the basics of J2EE and J2EE deployment have been explored, it is appropriate to examine the two popular deployment architectures—Java client and JSP applications. The hands-on practices in each section give you a feel for creating JAR, WAR, and EAR files in deployments created by JDeveloper.

Java Client Architectures

Java client is one of the possible J2EE development and deployment options supported by the J2EE architecture model. Java client refers to an application written in Java that is running in a JVM on the client's machine. There are two styles of Java client code: Java applications and applets. Chapters 15 and 16 provide some details about Java client development techniques.

Java Applications

The term "Java application" refers to a particular style of Java code. In Java terms, the code is considered just an "application," but since that term is a common one in the IT world, it is preceded by the word "Java" for greater clarity. A Java application runs on the client machine in a standalone JVM runtime process. The source code .java files are compiled into bytecode (.class) files and stored on the client machine, or on a local or wide area network server. No web server is required, and the runtime environment is located on the client machine without a browser. Therefore, a Java application runs using a typical client/server model.

Figure 7-2 shows one option for deploying a Java application into the J2EE tiers. As mentioned, other options exist for all of these styles of deployment. For example, the Java application could access data through EJBs instead of ADF BC. (As mentioned in Chapter 8, ADF BC can also be deployed as EJBs.) The arrowed lines between components represent the communication path. The Java application runs in a Java runtime (JVM) on the client presentation machine. The Java executables, application classes, and supporting libraries are all located on the Client Tier. The application communicates with ADF BC business logic in the Business Tier. ADF BC communicates with the database and sends data to the Client Tier.

The ADF Business Components code objects could alternatively be located on the client machine, but this strategy does not allow the ADF Business Components code to be shared among users.

Calling Sequence

Java applications have a method called `main()` (as shown in Figure 7-3). This method is automatically executed when the class is run from the command line and usually calls a constructor. The constructor creates the first object, such as a frame. All requests for data flow from the application's frame through the ADF BC layer.

To deploy a Java application, you install a Java runtime environment JDK, which contains java.exe (the Java runtime JVM) and supporting Java libraries on the client machine. You also install the .class files for the application objects and set up the client's CLASSPATH so that the JVM can find these .class files. ADF BC files are installed on the application server. To run the application, the user enters the following at the command line (or clicks a shortcut icon containing the following command line statement):

```
java deptemp.view.DeptEmpFrame
```

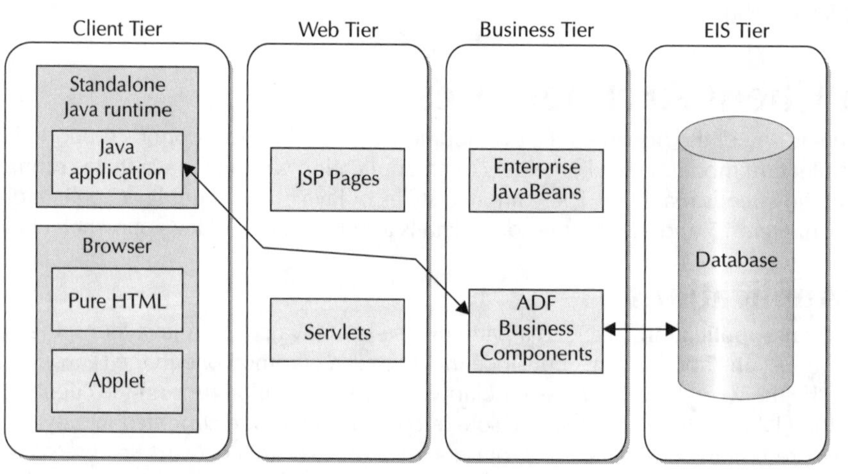

FIGURE 7-2. *Java application runtime architecture*

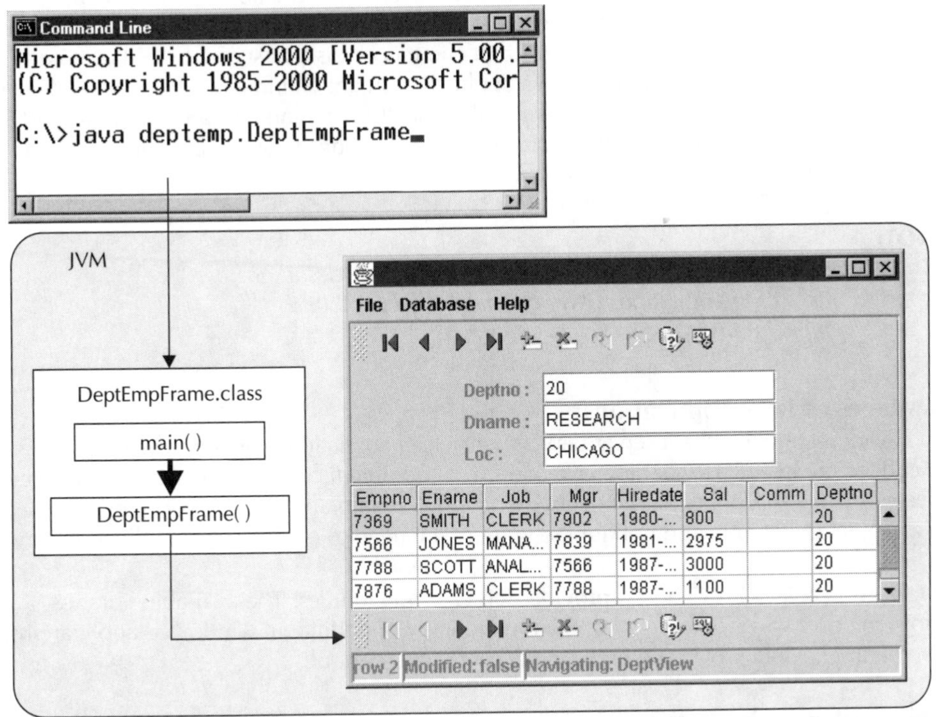

FIGURE 7-3. *Java application calling sequence*

In this example, "DeptEmpFrame" is the compiled .class file inside the deptemp package (directory). This class contains a `main()` method that runs the class' constructor, which draws the user interface.

NOTE
The deployment process in JDeveloper can use a dependency analyzer that determines which library files are required for the application. The deployment wizard will use this information to package the required libraries with the application.

When to Use Java Applications

Use Java applications for intranet, small-department, or small-scope solutions with a small number of clients. As the number of clients grows, you will experience all of the same problems and resource drains as encountered in client/server applications because, for each new client, a one-time Java runtime install and an application code install are required. If you do not want to worry about browser limitations and firewall restrictions and are able to easily manage local client installations, the Java application is the appropriate style.

In addition, if your application requires rich client controls that support rapid data entry and fast response from the user interface, a Java application might be indicated because it offers rich GUI controls in the Swing library that are installed locally. You can also add any third-party GUI controls library to further enhance the native features of Swing. A Java application also does not require a browser session as does an applet.

NOTE
The JDeveloper IDE runs as a Java application and provides a good example of the rich kinds of functionality you can build into Java applications.

Advantages of Java Applications

If you are accustomed to client/server deployments, Java applications provide you with a relatively easy architecture in which to deploy Java code. The user interface responds to user events quickly because the code is running on the client machine. You gain all the benefits of the Java language, such as object orientation and portability, without the need to configure an application server.

GUI Controls Java applications provide rich GUI possibilities. The available libraries of GUI controls, mainly Swing, provide all of the functionality of traditional windowed applications, but allow you the flexibility of modifying each aspect of the control.

Layout Managers In addition to the Swing components, you can also use a Java feature called *layout managers* to manipulate components at runtime. A layout manager is an object that you define and attach to a container (such as a panel) using the *layout* property. It is responsible for resizing and repositioning the components inside that container when the user resizes the outer window. This is useful because you can deploy the Java application on diverse platforms and be assured that the layout manager will maintain your design regardless of differences in the hardware or JVM used for display. Chapter 16 discusses layout managers in detail.

Disadvantages of Java Applications

Java applications have no inherent disadvantages if they are used in environments that can benefit from their advantages and are not affected by the limitations of client/server environments.

Limitations of Client/Server Environments Java applications run in either a pure client/server mode (where business logic is on the Client Tier) or in a variation on client/server mode (where business logic is on the application server, as in this example). Therefore, the characteristics of the client/server architecture must be taken into account when making the decision about whether to use the Java application style for deployment.

A significant problem is that runtime and application code must be maintained and installed on the client machine. WAN servers promise to ease this burden, but the reality is that they are often not responsive enough, so companies use LANs instead. The LAN solution for a large application is still not responsive enough and requires installation of the same code on more than one machine. This takes a lot of time and effort, as those who support client/server applications can attest. In addition, the client machine needs a large amount of resources because the application is running in its memory and using its disk space.

As the number of users grows, this architecture scales poorly. More users may require additional installations and further decentralization of the runtime code. Although the architecture does not take advantage of web server technology for centralized installation and maintenance, the Java Web Start technology (described in the sidebar "About Java Web Start") greatly mitigates the problems of client installation and configuration.

In addition, this architecture choice does not take advantage of the increased performance possible with a multi-tier architecture. With a multi-tier architecture, some processing (such as business logic stored on an application server) requires only communication between the web server and database server instead of between the client and the database server as with client/server architecture. Since server-to-server communication can be more efficient, the multi-tier architectures can offer better performance for those operations.

Terminal Server Variation

Java applications can be run in a client's browser using terminal server technology (such as Citrix MetaFrame). The terminal server strategy is essentially a mainframe model. The client is a dumb

About Java Web Start

The Sun Microsystems Java Web Start technology offers an alternative to other options for deploying Java applications. It is distributed with the Java runtime and SDK. Java Web Start relies on Java Network Launching Protocol (JNLP), a standard part of J2EE that uses an XML descriptor file on the server to specify details about how to start the application.

Once users install Java Web Start, they can download a Java application and its required support libraries by clicking a link in a web browser. This option provides Java applications with the ease of installation and code centralization that the applet strategy offers.

The user only needs a client browser to download the application. The JVM that runs the application is independent of the browser. Therefore, once the download is complete, the browser may be shut down, because the Java application will be running in a separate process, not within the browser process as is the case with applets. However, Java applications run using Java Web Start still execute in a restricted container that enforces the security model of the Java 2 platform just like applets.

JDeveloper supports deployment to the Java Web Start technology. Select "Java Web Start (JNLP) Files" from the Client Tier\Swing/AWT category of the New Gallery. If you are developing JClient code, select "Java Web Start (JNLP) Files for JClient" from the Client Tier\Swing/JClient category of the New Gallery. The Create Java Web Start-Enabled Application Wizard will open. You need to have a JAR file containing all of the application files before starting this wizard. The wizard steps through the creation of several XML files that are required for this alternative. The Java Web Start technology will probably serve most of your purposes for distributing, installing, and running client-side Java code. More information is available at the Sun website at java.sun.com/products/javawebstart/.

terminal that presents the interface for the application that is actually running on the application server. Software installed on the client emulates the runtime display. The user can interact with the application through this emulator, but a JVM runs the Java application on the server. That JVM is the actual runtime session. The terminal server strategy just displays (in a web browser) a Java application that is running on the application server.

Terminal server technology has all of the advantages of Java applications and the additional advantage that it can be run from a centralized server location. The biggest disadvantage is that this solution requires extra software on both the client and server. Another disadvantage is increased resource use on the server, since it also uses a server session for each client session, which could be impractical for a large number of users.

Applets

Before Java Web Start was introduced, applets offered an alternative to Java applications that leveraged the strength of centralized distribution. Since the main benefit of applets was easy deployment and installation (benefits now provided by Java Web Start), applets are not the preferred style for enterprise applications. They still have a use as plug-ins for a light client application that requires the power of a Java client (for example, a real-time stock ticker area inside the browser window). Since the use of applets is limited now, this section will describe them only briefly.

Applets are specified as a supported part of J2EE. You write applets using the same Swing and AWT classes that you use to create Java applications. An applet differs from the Java application only in the way in which it is started and in the initial location of the code. The steps in the applet startup and runtime processes are shown in Figure 7-4.

1. **The client browser requests an HTML startup file from the web server** through a standard URL. The HTML file may be static or dynamically generated from another

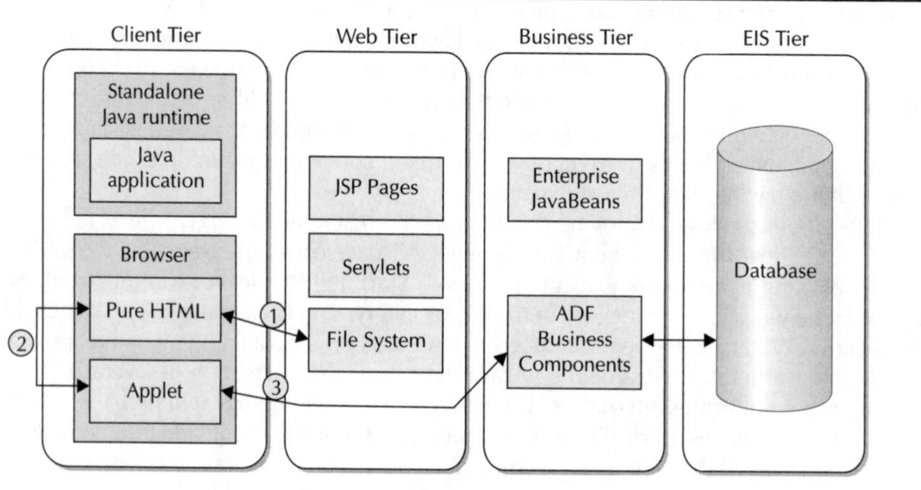

FIGURE 7-4. *Applet startup and runtime architecture*

application. It may or may not reside on the Web Tier, because the startup file is a normal HTML file. This HTML file contains a special applet tag such as the following:

```
<APPLET CODE = "dept.DeptEmp"
   CODEBASE = "/applet_code/"
   WIDTH = 250
   HEIGHT = 300
   ALIGN = middle >
</APPLET>
```

2. **The applet tag signals the browser to start an applet window** (within or outside of the browser window) for a JVM session and to load the application's .class file named by the CODE attribute. The applet tag's attribute CODEBASE specifies the location of the applet's .class files relative to the physical location of the HTML file. If the HTML file is in the same directory, the CODEBASE attribute is set to "." (the same directory). The CODE attribute finds a specific .class file in a directory listed in the CLASSPATH variable on the application server. The application's .class files and supporting libraries download from the application server and are presented in the applet window. After the initial download, the .class files are cached (in Java versions 1.3 and later) on the client's hard drive for use the next time that the applet is run.
3. **The applet .class file runs in the browser's JVM**. This is the difference between applets and Java applications. The applet JVM communicates with the database through the Business Tier (ADF BC components in this diagram) as with the Java application. As before, the applet could communicate to EJBs in the Business Tier. The applet runs an `init( )` method that draws the user interface in the same way as the `main()` method in a Java application.

When to Use Applets
Applets can be employed for an application that is used within an organization. An applet gives you rich user interface controls without the overhead of maintaining a client/server environment. An intranet environment may also provide adequate bandwidth to support a workable initial load time for large Java applets. Since an intranet system is a controlled environment, you will likely be operating behind the firewall, thus eliminating the security restrictions that are often applied to applets when they are accessed through a firewall.

Advantages of Applets
For the most part, the same advantages that apply to Java applications apply equally to applets. An applet has the additional advantage of allowing you to use the web application server to store the code. As mentioned, Java Web Start technology diminishes this advantage because it allows Java applications to be installed from a server using a browser.

Disadvantages of Applets
Java applets require an initial download that can be lengthy. Once the application loads, the performance will generally be excellent. For e-commerce purposes, the load time for the applet is likely to be unreasonable.

In addition, the actions that the Java applet can perform on the client machine are restricted by the built-in security mechanisms of the browser, because the applet is executing inside a browser session. If those features are circumvented with security strategies such as signature files, Java applets can be written to perform tasks on the client machine such as reading from and writing to the file system. In many organizations, client machines reside behind a firewall that prohibits the downloading of Java applets.

Inconsistent Browser Support Another disadvantage is that an applet uses an HTML browser to start the JVM and some browser versions do not support Java at all. Some browsers support only older Java releases. Other browsers do not support the Swing libraries, which have more functionality than AWT libraries. AWT classes are fully supported in browsers, but require much more coding to connect to the data layer. The amount of Java support in the browser is the responsibility of the browser vendor. The impact on your use of applet technology is in ensuring that your users can access and install the Swing library plugin offered by Sun Microsystems, which requires a one-time step to download and install.

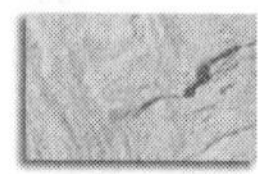

NOTE
Although Oracle Forms Developer presents its interface in a browser-run applet, this is not a true J2EE applet runtime environment because the Forms application runs in a non-JVM runtime on the application server, not in the client browser.

Hands-on Practice: Deploy a Java Application

As mentioned, deployment is the process of copying the proper application and runtime files to the correct location so they can be run by a user. The secret ingredient of a successful deployment process is a properly defined deployment profile. This practice demonstrates how to create a deployment profile for a Java application and deploy the resulting JAR file to a local machine. The ADF BC classes and other files are also copied into the same JAR file.

This practice contains the following phases:

I. Prepare a simple ADF BC Java application

II. Create a Java application JAR file

- Create the deployment profile
- Create and examine the JAR file

III. Create a batch file and run the JAR file

Although it is always good to practice working in the JDeveloper IDE, you can skip the first phase if you have completed the first hands-on practice (client/server application) in Chapter 1. Should you decide to use the Chapter 1 practice results, you will need to adjust the instructions in Phases II and III to the names of the projects and files used in Chapter 1.

NOTE
As mentioned in the Introduction, this book provides examples using the Windows operating system file and directory names. You will need to adapt the steps if you are running on another operating system.

I. Prepare a Simple ADF BC Java Application

This phase creates a Java application that you can use to test the deployment. It uses the JClient Form Wizard to generate a single table application. Since the point of this practice is to try a deployment, little explanation is given here for the steps you use to create the application. Other hands-on practices, such as those in Chapters 1 and 15, provide more details about these steps.

1. Create an application workspace (on the Applications node of the navigator select New Application Workspace from the right-click menu). Name the workspace "LocDeptDeploy" and use an *Application Package Prefix* of "locdept."
2. Select the Application Template "Java Application [Default]" and click OK to create the application workspace and two projects, Model and View. Click Save All.
3. Select New from the right-click menu on the Model project. In the New Gallery, select the "Business Components from Tables" item from the Business Tier\Business Components category. Click OK.
4. In the Project Initialization dialog, select the HR connection and click OK. The other defaults are sufficient. The Create Business Components from Tables Wizard will appear. Click Next if the Welcome page appears.
5. Move the DEPARTMENTS and LOCATIONS tables to the *Selected* list and click Next. On the View Objects page, move both entity object names to the *Selected* list and click Next.
6. On the Application Module page, be sure the *Application Module* checkbox is checked and enter a *Name* of "LocDeptModule." Click Next.
7. Review the objects you will create on the Finish page and click Finish. Click Save All.
8. Select New from the right-click menu on the View project node to display the New Gallery.
9. Select Form from the Client Tier\Swing/JClient for ADF category and click OK to display the Create JClient Form Wizard. Click Next if the Welcome page appears.
10. On the Form Types page, select the "Single Table" and "Form" radio buttons and click Next.
11. On the Form Layout page, select "Single columns (label left)" and "2" and click Next. On the Data Model page, click New to display the ADF Business Components Client Data Model Definition Wizard. Click Next if the Welcome page appears.
12. Click Next and Finish to create a default data model definition (LocDeptModuleDataControl) and return to the Create JClient Form Wizard. Click Next.

13. On the Panel View page, select LocationsView1 and click Next. Click Next on the Attribute Selection page. Click Next on the File Names page. Click Finish on the Finish page.
14. The Java Visual Editor will open and display the form. Drag the right side of the editor window to the right to widen it if you cannot see all of the fields.
15. Click Save All and run the form using the Run button after selecting FormLocationsView1.java in the navigator. You should see something like the following:

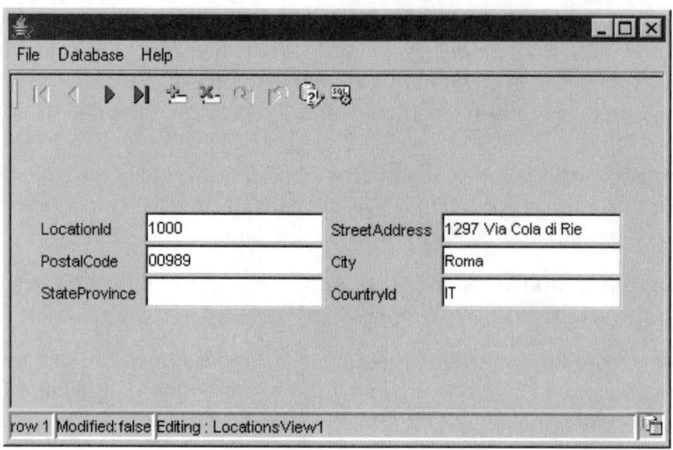

16. Close the window.

What Just Happened? You created a one-table Java application project and a default ADF BC project that you will use for the deployment practice. The ADF BC layer represents the DEPARTMENTS and LOCATIONS tables. Although this practice uses only the LOCATIONS table objects, you would use the same ADF BC project when you expand the application to include the DEPARTMENTS objects.

II. Create a Java Application JAR File

The next step in deploying the Java application is to create the JAR file that contains the required class files.

This section uses the approach of deploying the ADF BC project as part of the application's JAR file. This is called ADF BC *local mode* deployment and is fully viable in many situations. In production environments, you may choose to use *remote mode,* where the ADF BC files are deployed on an application server to allow multiple users access to the same business logic layer.

Create the Deployment Profile

JDeveloper creates deployment files by default for some styles of projects such as JSP pages. There is no deployment file created for this project, so this section will create the deployment file.

1. On the View project node, select New from the right-click menu. Select JAR File from the General\Deployment Profiles category and click OK.

2. Fill in the Deployment Profile Name as "locdept" and click OK. The JAR Deployment Profile Properties dialog will appear with the JAR Options page displayed as shown here:

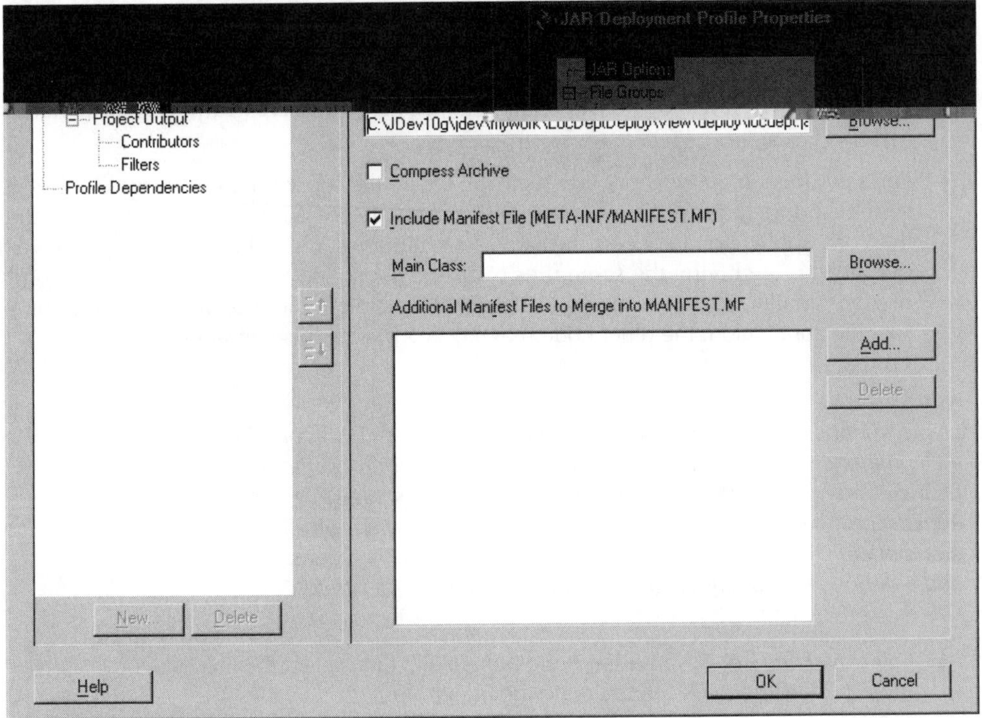

3. Change the *JAR File* field to "C:\Loc\locdept.jar". If you have no Loc directory, it will be created when you create the JAR file.

4. Be sure the *Include Manifest File* checkbox is checked and click the Browse button next to the *Main Class* field. In the Class Browser, expand the locdept\view nodes, and select FormLocationsView1 and click OK to return to the profile dialog.

   Additional Information: The *Main Class* field specifies the file name that starts the application. The *manifest file* (Manifest.mf) inside a JAR file contains information relevant to the JAR file contents. When the JVM runs or uses the JAR file, it can look up information in the manifest file. In this case, the JVM will look in the manifest file for the name of the class file to start when it runs the JAR file. This allows you to start the JAR file on the command line without specifying the name and location of the starting file.

5. On the File Groups node, click the New button to display the Create File Group dialog.

   Additional Information: *File groups* are collections of files that need to be deployed with the application files. Normally, JDeveloper groups the appropriate support files with the application automatically without requiring additional file groups. The deployment in this example is a bit different and therefore requires a new file group.

The reason that this example is out of the ordinary is that it includes with the application files all core support library (JAR and ZIP) files required for these applications. This will create a single JAR file that can be run on any machine that has a compatible JVM. This single, "monolithic" deployment file is a useful method if you want to ensure that the same versions of the library files used in development are also used at run time. This method also bypasses the need to install the support libraries on the client machine. It is used as an example to demonstrate file groups and how to create this type of standalone JAR file.

For a production application, you typically locate the supporting library files in the file system and include the library file names in the CLASSPATH. This would allow more than one application to access the same set of libraries. Using that method, you save the overhead of archiving the same files over and over, and the deployed application JAR files are smaller. However, if you change your version of the supporting libraries for a specific application, the older code may not work with those libraries.

NOTE
Deployment profiles created before JDeveloper 9.0.5.1 (10g) contain a Dependency Analysis page where you specify the libraries that will be included in your JAR file. After release 9.0.5.1, this page does not appear in the deployment profile dialog. The deployment profile automatically performs dependency analysis. In addition, you can add a dependency analysis group as this example demonstrates.

6. Enter the *File Group Name* as "Standalone JAR"; then select the Dependency Analysis radio button and click OK to create the file group.
7. On the Contributors node under Standalone JAR, click the Libraries tab. You can select which libraries to include in your JAR file on this page. Place a checkmark on the following library (top-level nodes):
   JClient Runtime
   Oracle XML Parser v2
   BC4J Runtime
   Oracle JDBC
   Connection Manager
   BC4J Oracle Domains

   Additional Information: As you select the library nodes, the file names in the library will be checked. If you do not know the files required by the application, select all libraries. After deploying and testing the file, you can return to the Libraries tab and try removing a library, deploying, and testing. By experimenting, you will find which libraries are required.
8. Under JClient Runtime, uncheck bigraphbean.jar and LW_PfjBean.jar. These files are not required by this application and they add significantly to the size of the JAR file.
9. Click OK to dismiss the JAR Deployment Profile Properties dialog.
10. Click Save All.

Create and Examine the JAR File

You now have defined the deployment profile that declares the name and location of the JAR file, the starting file, and the libraries that will be included in the file. This phase creates the JAR file and looks at its contents.

1. On the locdept.deploy node under the View project Resources node, select "Deploy to JAR file" from the right-click menu. You will see messages in the Log window that the dependency analysis is taking place and that the deployment process is creating the JAR file. The Log window will also show the location and name of the JAR file.

2. Click Save All when a message indicates that the deployment is finished. You will now examine the JAR file contents using the JDeveloper Archive Viewer.

3. Click the View project node and select **File | Open**. Uncheck the *Add to project* checkbox so that the JAR file will not be added to the project, but will open in editor area so you can browse the file.

4. Navigate to the C:\Loc subdirectory. Double click the locdept.jar file (not the locdept.jar folder). The file will appear in the *Archive Viewer* as shown here:

Path	Date	Size	Compressed
.xdkjava_version_9.0.4.0.0_production	2/17/04 3:17 AM	0	0
DataBindings.cpx	3/1/04 12:42 AM	766	766
META-INF/MANIFEST.MF	3/1/04 12:42 AM	111	108
META-INF/application-client.xml	3/1/04 12:42 AM	300	300
Model.jpx	2/29/04 7:16 PM	629	629
com/sun/java/util/collections/AbstractCollection.class	2/17/04 3:17 AM	2.62 KB	2.62 KB
com/sun/java/util/collections/AbstractList$Itr.class	2/17/04 3:17 AM	1.69 KB	1.69 KB
com/sun/java/util/collections/AbstractList$ListItr.class	2/17/04 3:17 AM	1.88 KB	1.88 KB
com/sun/java/util/collections/AbstractList.class	2/17/04 3:17 AM	3.27 KB	3.27 KB
com/sun/java/util/collections/AbstractMap$1.class	2/17/04 3:17 AM	977	977
com/sun/java/util/collections/AbstractMap$2.class	2/17/04 3:17 AM	1.15 KB	1.15 KB
com/sun/java/util/collections/AbstractMap$3.class	2/17/04 3:17 AM	986	986
com/sun/java/util/collections/AbstractMap$4.class	2/17/04 3:17 AM	1.15 KB	1.15 KB
com/sun/java/util/collections/AbstractMap.class	2/17/04 3:17 AM	3.62 KB	3.62 KB
com/sun/java/util/collections/AbstractSequentialList.class	2/17/04 3:17 AM	1.77 KB	1.77 KB
com/sun/java/util/collections/AbstractSet.class	2/17/04 3:17 AM	956	956
com/sun/java/util/collections/ArrayList.class	2/17/04 3:17 AM	4.92 KB	4.92 KB
com/sun/java/util/collections/Arrays$ArrayList.class	2/17/04 3:17 AM	884	884
com/sun/java/util/collections/Arrays.class	2/17/04 3:17 AM	15.38 KB	15.38 KB
com/sun/java/util/collections/Collection.class	2/17/04 3:17 AM	663	663
com/sun/java/util/collections/Collections$1.class	2/17/04 3:17 AM	2.50 KB	2.50 KB
com/sun/java/util/collections/Collections$10.class	2/17/04 3:17 AM	2.32 KB	2.32 KB
com/sun/java/util/collections/Collections$2.class	2/17/04 3:17 AM	2.97 KB	2.97 KB
com/sun/java/util/collections/Collections$3.class	2/17/04 3:17 AM	2.64 KB	2.64 KB
com/sun/java/util/collections/Collections$4.class	2/17/04 3:17 AM	2.08 KB	2.08 KB
com/sun/java/util/collections/Collections$5.class	2/17/04 3:17 AM	2.18 KB	2.18 KB
com/sun/java/util/collections/Collections$6.class	2/17/04 3:17 AM	2.27 KB	2.27 KB
com/sun/java/util/collections/Collections$7.class	2/17/04 3:17 AM	2.24 KB	2.24 KB
com/sun/java/util/collections/Collections$8.class	2/17/04 3:17 AM	2.33 KB	2.33 KB

Archive

Additional Information: The *Archive Viewer* allows you to see details about the contents of a JAR or ZIP file. In addition to viewing the name, size, and date of each file, you can also view the contents of some of the files. For example, if you double-click the

META-INF/MANIFEST.MF file in the archive, you will see the contents of the file including the definition of the JAR file main class (FormLocationsView1). In the Archive Viewer, click the Path heading at the top of the view to sort by the directory names. Then scroll down to the locdept directory to examine the list of files created in the project's package. If you double click a class file name, for example, locdept/view/FormLocationsView1.class, you will see a decompiled stub containing the imports and methods in the original file. The files are opened in read-only mode. You can view any ZIP or JAR file in JDeveloper using this same technique even if you did not create the file using JDeveloper.

5. This JAR file contains more than 2700 files, including your application files, the ADF BC project files, and all other required library files. Close the Archive Viewer (locdept.jar tab) when you are finished viewing.

   Additional Information: The file size is more than 14MB uncompressed. You can specify that the file be compressed by checking the *Compress Archive* checkbox on the JAR Options page of the deployment profile editor. (Access this editor by double clicking the file in the navigator.)

What Just Happened? This phase created a deployment profile containing configuration information about the project. This deployment example creates a single JAR file containing the Java application classes, ADF BC classes, and all supporting library files. This is a complete JAR file that only requires a Java runtime on the client. For production situations, the ADF BC code could be installed on a centralized server so it could be shared. In addition, the client may already have installed the support libraries, so they would not need to be included in the project's JAR file. If the support files were not included, the size of the JAR file would be greatly reduced.

III. Create a Batch File and Run the JAR File

Deploying the JAR file created it and placed it in the C:\Loc directory. You could copy the JAR file to any other directory to emulate installing the file on a client machine, but this phase will assume that the file has been copied to its final location ("C:\Loc"). You can now run the application by running the JAR file.

JDeveloper contains a copy of the Java runtime environment, so you already have a JVM available to you. If you were copying to another machine, that machine would need to have the Java SDK from Sun Microsystems (or another source) installed.

1. Select New from the right-click menu on the View project node in the Application Navigator. Select File from the General\Simple Files category. (Select All Technologies from the *Filter By* pulldown if you do not see this item.) Click OK.

2. In the Create File dialog, fill in the *Name* as "locdept.cmd" and the *Directory Name* as "C:\Loc". Click OK. The editor window will open.

3. Add the following code to this new file:

```
@echo off
echo Starting LocDept
set path=JDEV_HOME\jdk\bin
set classpath=

java -jar locdept.jar
```

Additional Information: This is a command-line script file that automates resetting the PATH and CLASSPATH and runs the JAR file. As before, substitute for "JDEV_HOME" the directory into which you installed JDeveloper (for example, C:\JDev10g). The CLASSPATH is set to null for this window so that an existing CLASSPATH will not be used.

4. Click Save All.
5. Start a command-line window by selecting **Start | Run** from the Windows start menu, entering "CMD" in the *Open* field, and clicking OK.

   Additional Information: As mentioned, this practice assumes that you are running a Windows operating system. Adjust these instructions if your operating system is different.
6. Change directories to C:\Loc. (Use the command "cd \loc" to accomplish this.)
7. Enter the following at the command line:

   ```
   locdept
   ```

   Additional Information: This should start the Java application that you developed earlier in this practice. The command file runs the Java Virtual Machine ("java.exe") whose directory you added to the execution path. This proves that you need no files other than those in the Java installation directory and in the JAR file. (You can even close JDeveloper to prove that it does participate in this session.) If you have problems, check your settings in the deployment profile and check the code in the batch file.
8. Close the application window.

What Just Happened? In this phase, you installed and tested the Java application using the JAR file. Running the program required setting the executable PATH and the Java library CLASSPATH environment variables. With the appropriate commands embedded in a command-line batch file, starting up the application is easy, but most users would not want to work on the command line. You can create a Windows shortcut that executes the batch file using the following steps:

1. Minimize all windows and select New | Shortcut from the right-click menu on the desktop. Enter the following:

   ```
   C:\Loc\locdept
   ```
2. Click Next and enter the name of your application (for example, "Browse Locations"). Click Finish.
3. Double click the new shortcut to test the application. The command-line window will open and display a message. The application will then start. When you close the application, the command-line window will close.
4. To hide the command-line window, select Properties from the right-click menu on the shortcut. Click the Shortcut tab and change the *Run* field to "Minimized." You can also change the icon associated with the shortcut in the Shortcut tab. Click OK.

The sidebar "How To Develop and Deploy Applets" describes the technical requirements for developing and deploying applets. As mentioned, Java Web Start can assist in installing and

How to Develop and Deploy Applets

Although the applet style of development is less common for new applications than are JSP pages and Java applications, it is useful to briefly examine how applets are developed and deployed. You can create an applet file using the same Form item in the New Gallery's Client Tier\Swing/AWT for ADF category. The Form Types page of this wizard allows you to select an applet style and it will lay out objects in the applet in the same way as in the Java application. You can also define a new applet without any items using the Applet item in the Web Tier\Applet category of the New Gallery.

The same category in the New Gallery contains an item for Applet HTML Page that you use to call the applet. This wizard contains an option for creating an applet deployment descriptor that you can use to define details about the applet JAR file in the same way as the Java application deployment descriptor.

You can deploy the files directly to the server by selecting "Deploy to | <name of server>" from the right-click menu on the deployment file. This deployment process follows the same path as a JSP deployment demonstrated in the next practice. One of the messages that appears in the Log window when you deploy an applet provides the *context root*—the starting virtual directory for the application files in the project. (The concept of a context root directory is also used for web application deployment.) You can then call the HTML file using that context root and the name of the HTML file. The HTML file will call the applet and display the interface you developed in the applet wizard. You may need to install the Java plugin for your browser by downloading it from the Sun website at java.sun.com/products/plugin/.

running Java applications and applets. The JDeveloper help system contains details about how to use this feature and the New Gallery contains items for Java Web Start wizards in the General\ Deployment Descriptors category.

JavaServer Pages Architecture

JSP technology offers another style of J2EE development and deployment that is supported by the J2EE architecture model. JSP technology is an extension of servlet technology, so it is useful to briefly examine what a servlet is before discussing JSP pages. Development techniques for JSP pages are discussed in Chapter 18 of this book.

Java Servlet Overview

A *Java servlet* is a Java class file that is stored and run on the application server and that extends the functionality of a server by providing extra services or application-specific logic. An *HTTP servlet* is a specific type of Java servlet (and a subclass of the Servlet class) that accepts requests from a client browser through an HTTP data stream (posted data or URL) and forms a response (usually in HTML format) that is sent to the browser. The servlet executes within a *container*—a service that can run code in a JVM. The *web container* (on the logical Web Tier) runs servlets and JSP code, and the *EJB container* (on the logical Business Tier) runs EJBs. Each container processes the target code in a specific way.

An HTTP servlet (often just called "servlet") can construct an HTML page by querying the database and outputting the HTML tags mixed with data from the query. The entire page is constructed dynamically by the program.

Before Java web technologies, a common way to present dynamic HTML content was to use a common gateway interface (CGI) program written in the Perl language. The advantage of servlets over CGI programs is that servlets only require a new thread, not an entirely new process like CGI programs. In addition, the memory and state of multiple threads are managed by the servlet runtime. This is a significant resource saver for the application server. In addition, unlike CGI output, servlets are cached, which provides performance benefits such as managing the state of database connections. Servlets are coded entirely in Java and are therefore portable and offer a bytecode "compiled" runtime version.

JSP Technology Overview

JSP technology is a variation on servlet technology that mixes HTML and Java in the same source file. JSP pages have both dynamic and static elements, usually represented by the Java and HTML code, respectively. This allows developers to easily code the parts of the application that do not change. For example, the JSP code would include the `<html>` tag at the beginning and the `</html>` tag at the end of the page. It would also include static links, boilerplate graphics, and boilerplate text.

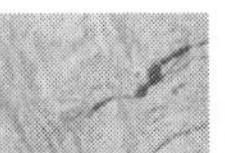

NOTE
Oracle offers the User Interface XML (ADF UIX) that allows you to code XML source files with special tags and run them in a J2EE servlet environment such as a JSP application. UIX is used extensively for the Oracle eBusiness Suite (Oracle applications) and you can develop UIX applications in JDeveloper. UIX is specific to Oracle so this chapter discusses JSP technology; Chapter 19 provides more information about UIX.

A servlet generates these tags using a `println()` statement each time the program is run, whereas a JSP program represents the static tag exactly as it will be output. In reality, the JSP page is compiled into a servlet .java file. The clarity of the JSP code provides developers with an advantage over the servlet style. In addition, because pure HTML code appears in the JSP page, you can use a visual HTML editor to work on the layout of the JSP page.

The following is an example of the default JSP code that JDeveloper creates when you select JSP Page from the New Gallery's Web Tier\JavaServer Pages (JSP) category:

```
<%@ page contentType="text/html;charset=windows-1252"%>
<html>
  <head>
    <meta http-equiv="Content-Type"
         content="text/html;
         charset=windows-1252">
    <title>untitled</title>
```

```
  </head>
  <body>
  </body>
</html>
```

This sample mixes standard HTML tags (delimited by "< >") for static content such as headings with servlet tags (delimited by "<% %>") for dynamic content created by running code. in Java classes. The file extension .jsp indicates to the web server that the page requested is a JSP file. The web server passes the interpretation of the page to a *JSP container* (web container) program that runs in a servlet process on the server. The JSP container acts as a *JSP translator* to convert the JSP file (.jsp) into a pure-Java, servlet file (.java) by adding `out.println()` statements for the HTML tags and adding print statements and other Java code for the JSP-specific servlet tags. The servlet is then compiled (to a .class file) and run in the container's JVM, and the servlet output is sent to the browser as HTML.

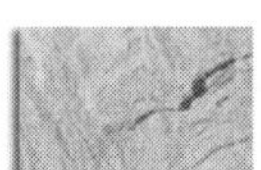

NOTE
Appendix D contains more information about the tags used in JSP code.

Figure 7-5 shows the main elements of the JSP runtime architecture. The Web Tier runs the JSP container process and waits for a request from the browser.

When the request for a JSP page appears, the web server determines that the request is for the JSP container because the file name has a .jsp extension. The JSP container process (JVM) runs the application file and accesses the application code as well as the controller code. These layers access code on the Business Tier (ADF BC in this example), which accesses the database. After

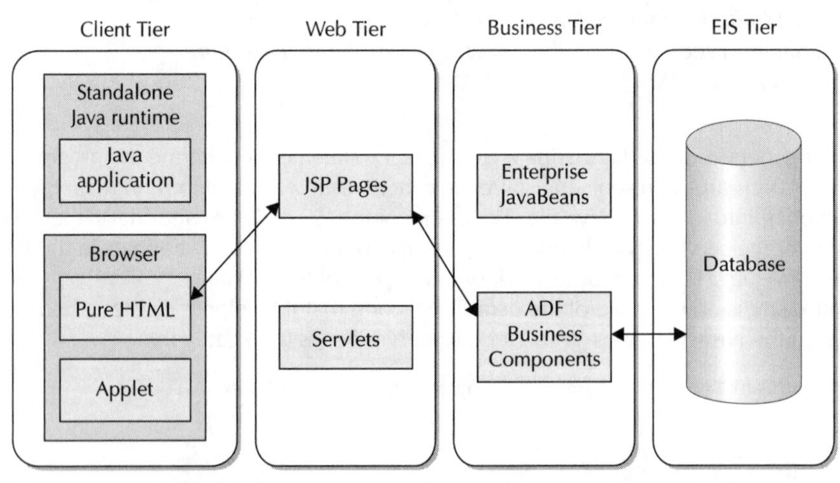

FIGURE 7-5. *JSP architecture*

the code is run and the HTML page is constructed, the server sends the page back to the browser, and the browser displays it as it would any other HTML page.

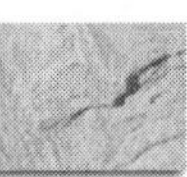

NOTE
Although Figure 7-5 shows JSP files and servlet files separately, when you use JSP technology, you are also using servlet technology because the JSP file is translated into a servlet. However, when speaking about the technology you are using, you would mention JSP technology because you do not code the servlet directly.

The first time a JSP page is accessed, the server process translates it into a Java servlet file and compiles that file into bytecode in a .class file. For subsequent accesses, the .class file is cached on the server so that this compilation is not required unless the code is changed. The JSP container runs the .class file in its JVM session. The Java and .class files are generated dynamically from the JSP source code file. The Business Tier layer sits on the application server and communicates with the database as in the other models. Figure 7-6 shows the various JSP code elements and the interaction with the browser. The dotted-line box represents a one-time compilation.

Therefore, JSP applications are different in two basic ways from Java client applications: They do not require a JVM on the client and they output HTML (or other types of content) that is displayed in a browser.

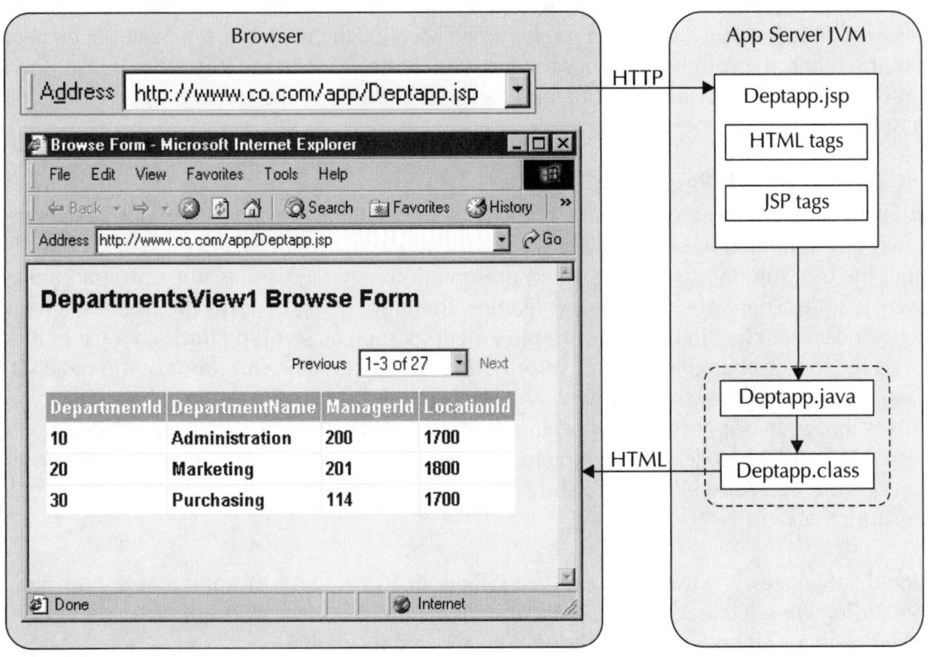

FIGURE 7-6. *JSP calling sequence*

When to Use JSP Pages

Use JSP pages when your requirement is a simple, lightweight user interface client. JSP pages are best used to display data and interact with the user in an HTML browser environment. Use them anywhere you would use standard CGI-generated or static HTML pages. If you can restrict your application to the limitations of the HTML and JavaScript languages, JSP pages are a logical choice. Since this solution is more efficient on the server side than is a Java client application, you can support a large number of users, such as for an e-commerce application. If you need a heads-down, high-volume data entry application, the standard HTML controls used in JSP pages might not be as efficient from the user's standpoint as a rich client solution that uses Swing controls. Also, JSP files are best at constructing a user interface. Business logic to validate data and to retrieve values displayed in the JSP file is best located in the Business Tier. This separation of user interface code and business logic code allows many types of client code to access the same business logic layer (one of the benefits of the MVC design pattern).

Advantages of JSP Pages

The main advantage of the JSP method is that the output is standard HTML and is therefore compact and universally readable in any browser. HTML only requires a compatible web browser on the client machine. There is no JVM running on the client, so there is no requirement for a set of Java runtime files or Java application files on the local machine.

The presentation look-and-feel of a page is embedded in HTML tags and *cascading style sheets* (an HTML facility for changing the appearance and formatting of common tags in a standardized way). Appendix C contains a brief introduction to cascading style sheets. Since the HTML tags are directly embedded in the JSP source file, you can split the development work. A web graphics designer can use HTML to create the look-and-feel for a page, while the dynamic JSP-specific sections would be developed by a Java programmer. Merging the work is just a matter of embedding one into the other. JDeveloper provides the tools to create and test the JSP code. It also provides a visual editor, toolbars, Component Palette pages, and Property Inspector support for the visual layout of the JSP file.

Disadvantages of JSP Pages

The main advantage of any web client technology including JSP pages—that they output lightweight HTML—is also a limitation because you do not use the feature-rich Swing (or AWT) controls to construct the user interface. HTML is a text presentation language and is not a programming language as such. Therefore, it has fewer features than the Swing controls for creating a highly interactive user interface. In addition, simple functions such as scrolling through a list of records, deleting a record, or changing the way information is sorted require a refresh of the page. This limitation is lessened somewhat by embedding JavaScript in the HTML page to enhance functionality if the users' browsers support JavaScript. In addition, the HTML limitation may not be important if you keep it in mind when deciding which technology to use for a certain application. Many HTML applications on the World Wide Web show reasonable complexity and suitability for complex business functions.

Additional Languages Developing robust JSP applications requires standard web development skills including knowledge of Java, HTML, and JavaScript. For developers accustomed to using a single language for all coding, this will feel like a step backward.

Web Technology Complexity Another disadvantage of any web solution including JSP pages is in the added complexity of the tags and the architecture. There is also added complexity in setting up the web server to support the servlet API and the JSP container. This extra complexity is not insurmountable and is made easier by standard tag libraries, Java tools such as JDeveloper, and J2EE architecture standards.

Where Does OC4J Fit?

As mentioned, a container is a process running on a server that is set up to run a particular style of Java code in a JVM. For example, the JSP container is responsible for translating JSP code into a servlet, compiling the servlet, and running the servlet class file. An EJB container is responsible for running EJB code.

OC4J is a Java program included with Oracle9*i* Application Server (Oracle9*i*AS) and Oracle Application Server 10*g*. It offers J2EE container services to the application server. An exact copy of OC4J from the Oracle Application Server is bundled with JDeveloper so that you can test JSP, UIX, and HTML code from within JDeveloper. The OC4J copy in JDeveloper is called the *Embedded OC4J Server.* You can also run the same copy of OC4J outside of JDeveloper as shown in the last practice in this chapter.

Since OC4J is available within JDeveloper, you can test your web client code in the same environment in which you will run the code (if you are running the code in the Oracle Application Server). In addition to testing your code, you can practice deploying your application to OC4J. The process of deploying to the Oracle Application Server is similar to the process for deploying to OC4J, although the deployment profile has some additional properties.

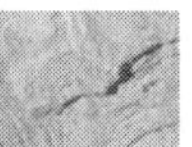

CAUTION

Standalone OC4J is included with JDeveloper to help you test J2EE applications. Although it is a complete solution for testing and debugging code, it is not a production-quality application server. If you want to use OC4J in a production environment, you should use the copy included with the Oracle Application Server. Other components of the application server provide security, scalability, and reliability features required by production deployments.

Hands-on Practice: Deploy a JSP Application

This practice shows how to distribute JSP code that you create using the JDeveloper deployment editor. The method described in this practice also deploys the ADF BC files required by the JSP application.

JDeveloper contains support for deploying files directly to an OC4J, Oracle Application Server, JBoss, Tomcat, or WebLogic server. You can run the standalone OC4J included with JDeveloper in two main ways. When you want to use the JDeveloper IDE to test JSP pages, servlets, or applications that use EJBs, you run them within the Embedded OC4J Server. Practices in other chapters in the book use this method. Alternatively, you can run these applications outside of JDeveloper using an OC4J (or other) server. This method allows you to access applications from outside of JDeveloper (even from across the network). This practice shows how to set up the standalone version of OC4J that is included with JDeveloper so that you can test your applications using the latter method.

This practice contains the following phases:

I. Create a JSP application

II. Set up OC4J

III. Deploy the JSP application

- Create the application server connection
- Examine the deployment files
- Deploy and test the application

This application starts with the workspace you created in the first practice in this chapter. If you have not completed Phase I of that practice, you can follow the steps in Phase I up through step 7. Alternatively, as with the earlier practice, you can use the workspace you completed in the second hands-on practice (JSP page) in Chapter 1. Should you decide to use the Chapter 1 practice results, you can skip Phase I, but you will need to adjust the instructions in Phase III to the names of the projects and files used in Chapter 1.

NOTE

You do not need to use the steps in this practice to test a JSP application during development because the Embedded OC4J Server is automatically started when you run a JSP page from JDeveloper. This practice demonstrates how to deploy and run the JSP application in a server outside of the JDeveloper IDE because this more closely emulates how the application will be run in a production environment.

I. Create a JSP Application

This phase creates s simple browse page that you can deploy to the OC4J server. As with the Java application deployment in the preceding practice, the point is not the application but the deployment method and steps. As mentioned, this practice starts with the workspace from the preceding practice. If you have not created the workspace, follow the steps in Phase I of the preceding practice through step 7. Alternatively, you can download a starting workspace from the authors' websites mentioned in the beginning of the book.

1. Select New Project from the right-click menu on the LocDeptDeploy workspace node in the navigator. In the General\Projects category, double click the Web Project item. The Create Web Project wizard will open. Click Next if the Welcome page appears.

2. In the Location page, enter the *Project Name* as "ViewController" and click Next.
3. On the Web Project Profile page, check the *Add JSP Page* checkbox and click Next. Click Finish. The Create JSP dialog will open.
4. Enter the *File Name* as "Locations" and click OK. The blank JSP file will open in the editor window.
5. Click the Data Controls tab in the window containing the Components Palette. (If the Data Control Palette is not displayed, select it from the View menu.)
6. Open the LocDeptModuleDataControl node and you will see something like the following:

Additional Information: This window contains a display of the view object instances in your application module. After selecting a view object or attribute under the view object, you can select a data control from the *Drag and Drop As* pulldown to drop into your application.

7. Select the LocationsView1 view object instance node. Then select "Read-Only Form" from the *Drag and Drop As* pulldown. Click the LocationsView1 node and hold down the left mouse button while you drag the data control onto the visual editor. Drop the control into the top-left corner of the editor. You will see a set of fields inside a box and an HTML table as shown here:

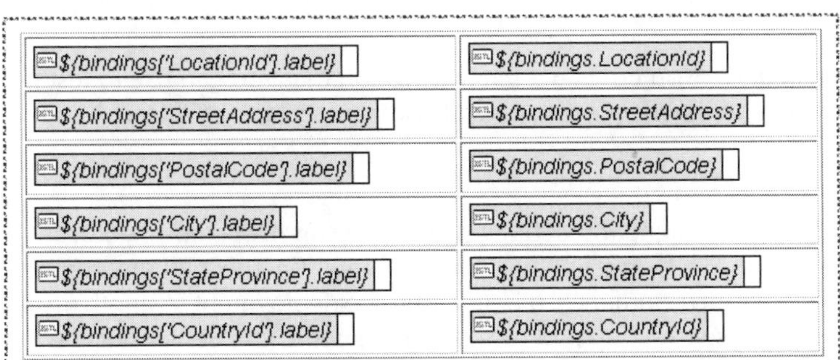

8. Select Navigation Buttons from the *Drag and Drop As* pulldown, drag the LocationsView1 data control to the page, and drop it just inside the upper-left corner of the dotted-line box surrounding the fields. The viewer should appear as follows:

First Previous Next Last

${bindings['LocationId'].label}	${bindings.LocationId}
${bindings['StreetAddress'].label}	${bindings.StreetAddress}
${bindings['PostalCode'].label}	${bindings.PostalCode}
${bindings['City'].label}	${bindings.City}
${bindings['StateProvince'].label}	${bindings.StateProvince}
${bindings['CountryId'].label}	${bindings.CountryId}

Additional Information: You need to drop the buttons between the dotted border (HTML form) and the HTML table border. If you dragged the buttons outside the box by mistake, press CTRL-Z to undo the change and try again.

9. Click Save All. With the cursor in the JSP editor window, click Run.
10. The OC4J server will start up and your browser will appear with the JSP file running. Click the Next and Previous buttons to test the application. Close the browser.
11. Click Save All.
12. Stop the Embedded OC4J Server in the Run Manager tab of the navigator by selecting Terminate from the right-click menu. Select **View | Run Manager** if this view is not displayed.

NOTE
You do not need to stop the Embedded OC4J Server every time you test an application. This practice stops the server so that you can test the application outside of JDeveloper.

What Just Happened? You created a JSP application that you can use to test the deployment operation. Part of the deployment package will contain the ADF BC files.

II. Set Up OC4J

As mentioned, for development and debugging purposes in JDeveloper, you can rely on the Embedded OC4J Server. This server allows you to test JSPs in an OC4J environment without leaving the JDeveloper environment. To better emulate deployment to another server, you can use the steps in this phase to set up and run the Embedded OC4J Server outside of JDeveloper. This allows you to test the deployment files in a real server environment. If you have an OC4J server already set up with ADF BC support, you can start it up and skip this phase.

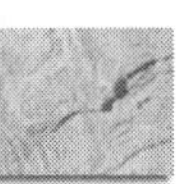

NOTE
As with the previous practice, this practice assumes that you are working in a Windows environment. The steps will need to be altered appropriately for other operating systems.

1. In a browser session, enter the following URL (location):

```
http://localhost:8888/
```

NOTE
You should receive an error stating that the page was not found. If you do reach a page, you already have an OC4J or other server running on the machine. Shut down the OC4J or other server instance before proceeding.

2. Start a command-line window by selecting **Start | Run** from the Windows start menu, entering "CMD" in the Open field, and clicking OK.

3. In the command-line window, change directories to the directory in which you installed JDeveloper. For example, if you installed JDeveloper into "C:\JDev10g," enter the following on the command line:

```
cd \JDev10g
```

4. Enter the following on the command line to set the environment variables to point to the JDeveloper installation of Java:

```
jdev\bin\setvars -go
```

   Additional Information: The `setvars.bat` batch file sets up a number of environment variables for this command-line session. If you had set variables for other installations of Java, this batch file would override them for the command-line session. You need to rerun this batch file each time you open a command-line window if you want to run OC4J. The batch file ensures that the correct JDK will be used for the OC4J runtime. OC4J is already configured (in its application.xml file) to read the ADF BC base library classes.

5. Change directories as follows:

```
cd j2ee\home
```

6. You should see the name of the directory (JDEV_HOME\j2ee\home) in the command-line prompt. Enter the following command:

```
java -jar oc4j.jar -install
```

7. This runs a Java program that configures an administration user for the OC4J server. Supply a password for the admin user, and confirm the password when prompted. The OC4J server can now be started from the command line outside of JDeveloper.

   Additional Information: You do not need to rerun this installation step again for the same installation of JDeveloper. To reset the administration password, run the Java command-line command again.

8. Start the OC4J server by entering the following at the command line:

```
start java -jar oc4j.jar
```

Additional Information: This command opens another command-line window (using the Windows `start` command) and starts the OC4J server. You will see a message indicating that the server is initialized, but no command-line prompt will appear in this window. Leave both command-line windows open.

9. Start your browser and connect to the following URL:

```
http://localhost:8888
```

The "localhost" portion of the URL points to your machine. (Alternatively, you can use the machine name instead of "localhost". You can also enter "//localhost:8888".) The "8888" portion represents the port number to which the server listener is assigned. You will see a page such as the following:

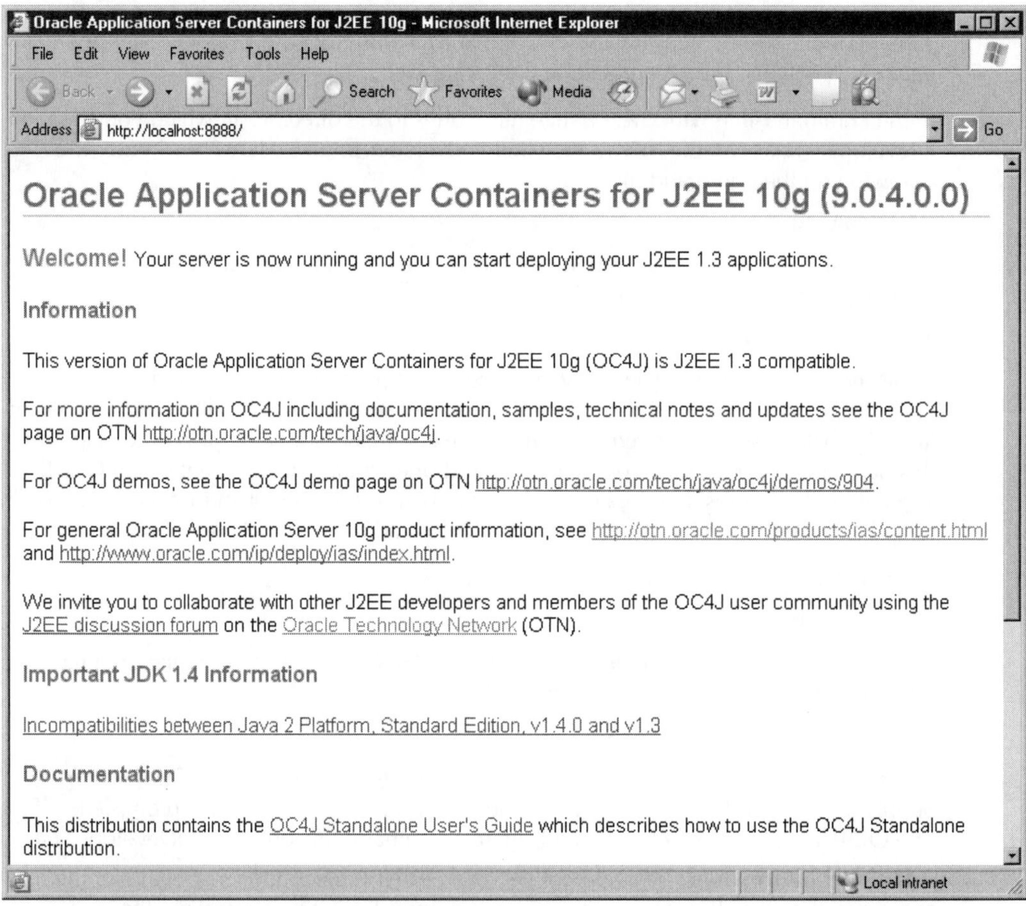

Additional Information: This is the default page for the OC4J server and proves that the server is running. The page is located in a file called index.html in the JDEV_HOME\j2ee\home\default-web-app directory. The index file contains links to a samples page for JSP pages and a samples page for servlets. These samples were developed by or for Sun Microsystems, and you can use them to test the server and capabilities of these styles of code. You can also view the source code from the links on the samples pages. A link on this page leads to the OC4J standalone server documentation. All of these files are located in the JDEV_HOME\j2ee directory structure.

Stopping the Standalone OC4J Server Although you want to leave the OC4J server running now so that you can deploy the JSP application, you may want to stop the OC4J server when you are finished with this practice. To stop OC4J, activate the command-line window that you left open and that has a command-line prompt. Enter the following at the command line:

```
java -jar admin.jar ormi://localhost admin admin_pwd -shutdown
```

In this command, "admin_pwd" represents the password that you entered when setting up the OC4J server (step 7). The command-line window that was running the OC4J server initialization should close. If the window does not close, switch to the OC4J initialization window, and press CTRL-C to stop the process and terminate the session. You can verify that the server has stopped by trying to connect to the welcome page.

Starting the Standalone OC4J Server When you want to rerun the OC4J server, use the following steps:

1. Open a command line and navigate to the JDEV_HOME\j2ee\home directory.
2. Enter the command to set up the environment variables (`..\..\jdev\bin\setvars -go`).
3. Start the server with the command: `start java -jar oc4j.jar`.
4. Wait for a message about OC4J initialization in a new command-line window. Test the server using the browser to connect to http://localhost:8888.

You can put these commands into a batch file that you run from the command line. You can also put the shutdown command in the previous section "Stopping the Standalone OC4J Server" into a batch file.

What Just Happened? You installed the OC4J server outside of the JDeveloper IDE. This will allow you to test your deployment method and runtime environment. As mentioned, you do not need to go through these steps if you are just doing development and testing the code within JDeveloper.

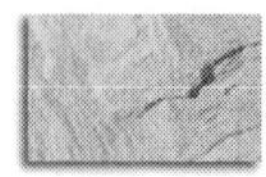

NOTE
You can check the version of OC4J by entering the following at the command line (after running `setvars`): "java -jar oc4j.jar -version". Be sure that the current directory is JDEV_HOME\j2ee\home. You can check the version even if OC4J is not running.

III. Deploy the JSP Application

Now that you have the OC4J server installed and running, you are ready to deploy the JSP application.

Create the Application Server Connection

The deployment features in JDeveloper require an application server connection. Like a database connection, setting up an application server connection is a one-time setup step that you can use for all deployments to the same application server.

1. If you have stopped the OC4J server at the command line (not the Embedded OC4J Server), start it again using the technique described in the preceding phase of this practice.
2. Click the Connections tab in the navigator area. (If the Connections tab is not displayed, select **View | Connection Navigator**.) On the Application Server node, select New Application Server Connection from the right-click menu. The Create Application Server Connection Wizard will appear.
3. Click Next if the Welcome page appears. In the Type page, enter the *Connection Name* as "LocalOC4J." Leave the *Connection Type* as "Standalone OC4J" and click Next.
4. Fill in the admin password you defined when you installed the server in Phase II of this practice, check the *Deploy Password* checkbox, and click Next.
5. Leave the defaults on the Connection page. The port number is not required because it is still the default of "8888."

   Additional Information: Your machine name may show instead of "localhost" in the *URL* field. In the case of a local installation, it will not matter which name you use here.
6. Click Next. On the Test page, click Test Connection. If you do not receive the Success message, return to the previous pages and check your settings. When everything works, click Finish.

Examine the Deployment Files

In this section, you examine the files used to deploy the application. The files described in the following two sections are required for a web deployment. JDeveloper created these files when you added the web project and the JSP file. The default settings in these files will work for the purposes of this practice but in a production situation, you would probably make changes to the files to suit your environment.

Web Deployment Descriptor The web deployment descriptor, web.xml, specifies details about how the web server will use the files in the WAR file. The JDeveloper deployment process also creates an EAR file that contains the WAR file. (The section, "J2EE Archive Files," earlier in this chapter describes the WAR file further.) This file is deployed with the application and is used at runtime. JDeveloper creates web.xml under the WEB-INF folder in the project when you create a JSP or other web content file. However, you can also create web.xml manually by selecting it from the New Gallery.

WAR Deployment Profile As with the JAR file deployment profile in the preceding practice, the deployment profile for a web application guides the process of deployment and specifies the files and locations of the files required by the application. It also specifies the names and locations of the WAR and EAR files that are created by the deployment. The WAR deployment profile is only used for the process of deployment and is not packaged into the WAR file. It is also not used at runtime. JDeveloper creates a WAR deployment profile file named "webapp.deploy" in the Resources folder when you create a web project. You can also use the New Gallery to create a WAR deployment profile.

1. In the Application Navigator, expand the Web Content\WEB-INF nodes under the ViewController project. On the web.xml file, select Properties from the right-click menu to display the property editor for the web.xml file. This property editor allows you to modify the file without having to know details about the XML syntax.

   Additional Information: You can also double-click the web.xml file to open it in the Code Editor, but you need to know details about the properties and the XML syntax.

2. The web.xml default values will work for this situation, but you can examine the various pages in this file to get a feeling for the types of properties that are available. Click the Help button if you need more information about a particular property. Click Cancel when you are finished examining properties.

3. Expand the Resources node under the ViewController project. Double-click the webapp.deploy file to display the WAR Deployment Profile Properties dialog.

4. Browse the pages of this dialog and notice that there are many more properties for deploying to the Web than for deploying a local Java JAR as in the preceding practice. If you would like more information about the properties, click the Help button.

5. The default values will work in this case. Click Cancel to dismiss the dialog.

Deploy and Test the Application

As mentioned, the application will run correctly with the default deployment files that JDeveloper creates. This section deploys the application to a WAR file (the EAR file that contains the WAR file is created automatically). Finally, you test the application in a browser.

1. On the webapp.deploy file node, select Deploy to | LocalOC4J from the right-click menu.

   Additional Information: This is the "one-click deployment" step mentioned in the JDeveloper product sheet. This process compiles the files, creates the WAR and EAR files, and copies the files to the web server, which expands the files and installs the application. The Log window will display messages about the progress of the deployment. One of the messages will provide the address that you can use to open the application in your browser. For example, "Use the following context root(s) to test your web application(s): http://localhost:8888/LocJSPDeploy-ViewController-context-root."

2. Copy the context root URL to the clipboard.
3. Open your browser if it is not already open, and paste the URL into the address field. Add the name of the JSP file ("/Locations.jsp") to the end of the URL, for example, you would use a URL such as the following (all on one line) and press ENTER:

```
http://localhost:8888/
   LocJSPDeploy-ViewController-context-root/Locations.jsp
```

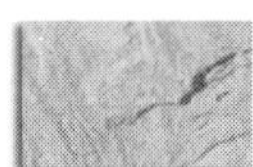

NOTE
The port number may appear as "????" if the deployment process could not determine the port. Substitute your port number (usually "8888") for the "????" characters when you connect to the page.

4. The browser should display the JSP page. Open Windows Explorer, navigate to the JDEV_HOME\j2ee\home\applications\webapp\webapp directory and notice the Locations.jsp file. The ADF BC files are located under this directory in the WEB-INF\classes\locdept\model subdirectory. The WAR and EAR files are created in the JDEV_HOME\jdev\mywork\LocDeptDeploy\ViewController\deploy directory. You can examine the EAR and WAR files (under the applications and webapp directories, respectively) using the Archive Viewer (described in the preceding practice).

   Additional Information: You can simplify the URL used by the application by selecting the *Specify J2EE Web Context Root* property (and filling in the name) on the General page of the webapp.deploy properties dialog. You can experiment with the URL by changing this property, redeploying the application, and testing the new context root.

5. Close the browser and stop the standalone OC4J server using the command provided in Phase II.

What Just Happened? You deployed the JSP application to an external standalone OC4J server. In JDeveloper, the process of deploying to an external OC4J server is really only one step. The deployment process and OC4J handle compiling the JSP pages, copying the WAR file to the server, expanding the WAR files, and configuring the application in the OC4J environment. Deploying to an Oracle Application Server, Apache Tomcat, JBoss, or BEA WebLogic server is a very similar process.

For servers other than those just mentioned, you can copy the WAR created in JDeveloper to the webapp directory of the server. When you stop and restart the server, the application will be active. Some servers can accept EAR files (that contain the WAR files) for deployment. WAR and EAR files are created using the same right-click menu that you used when deploying to OC4J.

If the files you are using do not have a deployment profile, you can create one using the New Gallery. Alternatively, you can select Create WAR Deployment Profile from the right-click menu on the web.xml (deployment descriptor) file that is copied into web application projects.

NOTE
This practice has shown how to deploy a JSP page to OC4J. There are many other variations on deploying JSP pages to different servers. The JDeveloper online documentation contains extensive information about deployment files and which files are required for which servers and application types. It also describes the process of creating the required files in JDeveloper. You can use these resources to better understand the contents and setup of the deployment profile and archive files required in a J2EE application at the Sun website, java.sun.com.

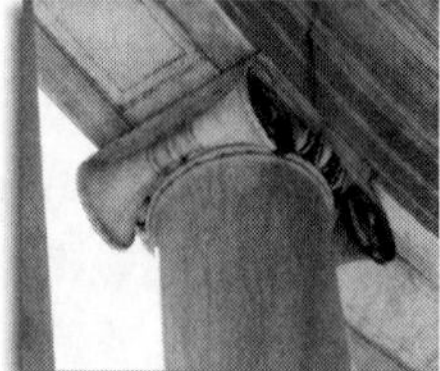

PART II

Business Services

CHAPTER 8

Introducing ADF Business Components

"If everybody minded their own business,"
the Duchess said, in a hoarse growl,
"the world would go round
a great deal faster than it does."

—Lewis Carroll [Charles Lutwidge Dodgson] (1832–1898),
Alice's Adventures in Wonderland

racle Application Development Framework Business Components (ADF BC, formerly called "BC4J") is JDeveloper's J2EE-compliant technology for creating business services. Business services provide business logic, including validation and default logic, queries, transaction handling, and data access, for an MVC application. (MVC applications were explained in Chapter 4.) Business services, including ADF BC, do not provide a user interface or control flow. They provide object/relational mappings and encapsulate business logic. The view and controller layers of an ADF application communicate with business services through the model layer and provide the user interface and control flow.

Chapters 1 through 4 provided an overview of the capabilities of JDeveloper and ADF. Part II discusses ADF BC (one of ADF's central technologies) in depth as well as how to expose it using the ADF model layer. Using ADF BC is the simplest way to design data-aware applications with JDeveloper and ADF. However, Part II will not teach you everything you need to write a complete ADF application. In addition to a business services layer (provided by ADF BC) and the ADF model layer, ADF applications require a view and controller, which you will learn to create in Part III.

This chapter provides an overview of ADF BC, describing its components and uses. Chapter 9 explains how to create business components to represent database objects, object types, and constraints. Chapter 10 explains how to use ADF BC to enforce complex business rules such as validation and defaulting logic.

Chapter 11 explains how ADF BC represents queries and relationships between query results and how it caches data. That chapter will show how to assemble the data your client needs while maintaining optimal performance. Chapter 12 explains how the ADF model layer exposes ADF BC to the view and controller. Chapter 13 explains how to write custom business services—methods that encapsulate complex business tasks. Chapter 14 provides an overview of some other business services technologies: EJB technology, Java classes with TopLink mappings, and web services.

NOTE
Many practices in Part II are sequential, but you can download starting and ending files for any chapter's practice from the authors' websites mentioned in the front of the book.

This chapter includes a brief discussion of the advantages of using ADF BC and a quick tour of the different business components: entity object definitions, associations, view object definitions, view link definitions, application module definitions, and domains. At the end of the chapter, a hands-on practice demonstrates how to create and explore a simple business components application.

Why Use ADF BC?

In previous releases of JDeveloper, two of the primary advantages of ADF BC (then called "BC4J") were that, unlike other business services technologies such as EJB, it automated mapping of Java objects to database objects (saving the developer the arduous task of coding JDBC) and provided easy hooks for binding user interface components. JDeveloper 10*g* mitigates both of these advantages somewhat. By making EJB technology easier to use, and by incorporating TopLink, JDeveloper now provides two other respectable ways of providing object/relational mapping without coding JDBC. And with the ADF model layer, JDeveloper now provides hooks, similar to those provided by ADF BC, for binding user interface components to EJB entity beans, Java classes with TopLink mappings, and web services (for more information about these business services technologies, see Chapter 14).

There are, however, still reasons why ADF BC is the simplest way to develop data-aware applications.

Automatic Implementation of J2EE BluePrints The components that make up ADF BC already implement many of Sun's J2EE BluePrints design patterns. These patterns make J2EE applications much more efficient, by reducing round-trips, reducing the amount of data that needs to be sent in each round-trip, and utilizing the cache more efficiently. Developers who do not use ADF BC and who want to create high-performance, scalable applications need to implement these design patterns, or something much like them, themselves. If you use ADF BC, you do not need to worry about these design patterns (Sun discusses them extensively on their website, java.sun.com); you will automatically be designing to them.

Hooks for Business Logic ADF BC provides convenient hooks for implementing business rules. Business rules can be implemented at multiple levels of an application—in the database, the view, or the business services layer. There are times when each of these locations is appropriate.

Adding business logic to the database, in the form of triggers or stored procedures, provides the maximum level of robustness. This business logic is guaranteed to be available and respected by any application, even by SQL commands run directly from a SQL*Plus prompt. However, business logic coded in the database is not highly responsive. It does not fire until data is posted to the database, which requires either waiting for an explicit post command or posting data after every change, which will degrade performance by requiring excessive JDBC round-trips. In addition, adding business logic to the database requires the database to perform tasks in addition to handling data, which reduces its efficiency and your application's modularity. Finally, adding business logic to the database requires you to integrate your Java or Web application with business logic written in PL/SQL code.

Adding business logic to the view layer, in Java for Java client applications or JavaScript for web applications, provides the maximum level of responsiveness. For example, business logic that triggers as each character is typed into a field, or as a mouse pointer passes over a graphical image, must be implemented at the view level. However, business logic added to the view layer is not robust. If users access the data through any other user interface, business logic added to the view layer will not be available or enforced.

Adding business logic to business services is a compromise between these alternatives. It is more responsive than business logic coded in the database, because it is enforced as soon as changes are made to Java objects in memory, and avoids the other disadvantages of adding business logic to the database. It is more robust than business logic coded in the view layer, because it will be enforced by any application that uses the business services.

Your most critical business logic should be implemented in the database, or redundantly in the database and business services (for increased responsiveness and easier Java integration at the cost of some productivity). Business logic that requires truly immediate responsiveness must be implemented in the view layer. The remainder of your business logic can be implemented at the business services layer. For this sort of business logic, the hooks provided by ADF BC are a distinct advantage over other business services technologies.

Deployment-Configuration Independence ADF BC is "deployment-configuration independent." A single set of ADF BC components can be deployed as local Java classes or as an EJB session bean, with no rewriting of code necessary. Applications using TopLink or standard EJB technology are locked into a single deployment configuration.

ADF Business Components, XML, and Java

As explained in Chapters 1 and 4, ADF is a Java framework, a set of Java class libraries that use XML metadata to provide most customization but are also extensible in Java. Using ADF technologies often does not involve writing much procedural code; instead, you can use wizards and visual tools to declaratively develop XML files that represent your components. The classes in the libraries contain code that handles the XML files to produce application behavior. However, if you want your XML files handled in a way other than the default, you can extend many of these classes to provide further customization.

ADF BC technology follows this general model. Each ADF BC component is primarily implemented as an XML file, which you can edit using wizards and visual tools. Classes in the ADF BC library read the information stored in these files and use it to provide application behavior. However, many business components can also have their own custom classes, which extend the classes in the ADF BC library to further customize application behavior. These custom classes are further described in Chapters 10 and 13.

ADF Business Component Groups

ADF BC components divide into two groups, business domain components and data model components, as shown next:

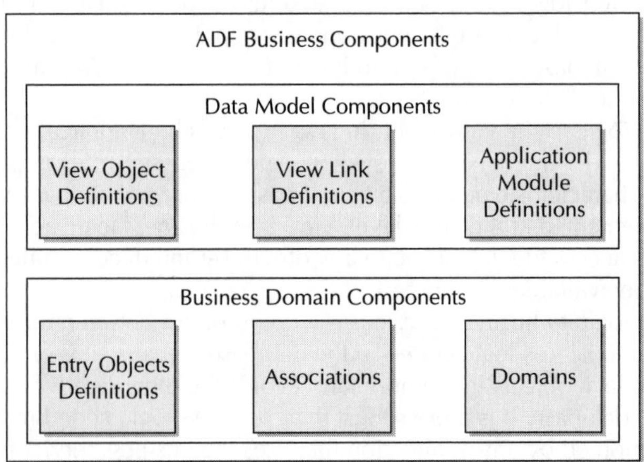

This section discusses the ADF business component groups and the components in them.

Business Domain Components

Business domain components are components that represent features of the database: tables and views, constraints, and relationships. Business domain components are the most reusable business components. They are designed based on the logical features of the data, rather than any specific application needs, so they can be used by any application that needs to access the same data. There are three kinds of business domain components: entity object definitions, associations, and domains.

Entity Object Definitions

An *entity object definition* typically represents a database table or database view. It handles all of the business rules for that table or view including validation, defaulting, and anything else that happens when a row is created, deleted, or changed.

One of the chief functions of any business service technology—including ADF BC—is to provide object/relational (O/R) mappings between Java objects that an application can use and entities in the database. A relational database consists of, among other objects, a set of tables, each of which contains columns. For example, consider the table DEPARTMENTS, with the following columns:

Column Name	SQL Datatype
DEPARTMENT_ID	NUMBER
DEPARTMENT_NAME	VARCHAR2
MANAGER_ID	NUMBER
LOCATION_ID	NUMBER

The ADF BC layer represents the database table as an entity object definition. An entity object definition has *entity attributes,* which typically represent the table columns, although the mapping is not always exactly one-to-one. (For more information about the mapping between table columns and entity attributes, see Chapter 9.)

The types of the attributes are Java classes that correspond to the SQL types of the columns. "Departments", the entity object definition for this table, might have the following entity attributes:

Attribute Name	Java Type
DepartmentId	`oracle.jbo.domain.Number`
DepartmentName	`java.lang.String`
ManagerId	`oracle.jbo.domain.Number`
LocationId	`oracle.jbo.domain.Number`

Java does not directly support SQL datatypes. However, each SQL datatype can be mapped to a Java type. Some of these Java types are classes in `java.lang` (such as `java.lang.String`), and others are in the package `oracle.jbo.domain` (which is discussed later, in the section "Domains").

As shown in Figure 8-1, an entity object definition is the template for *entity object instances,* which are single Java objects representing individual rows in a database table. For example, the entity object definition Departments provides a template for entity object instances that represent individual rows of the DEPARTMENTS table, such as the one with the following attribute values:

Attribute Name	Value
DepartmentId	A `Number` holding the value 10
DepartmentName	The `String` "Administration"
ManagerId	A `Number` holding the value 200
LocationId	A `Number` holding the value 1700

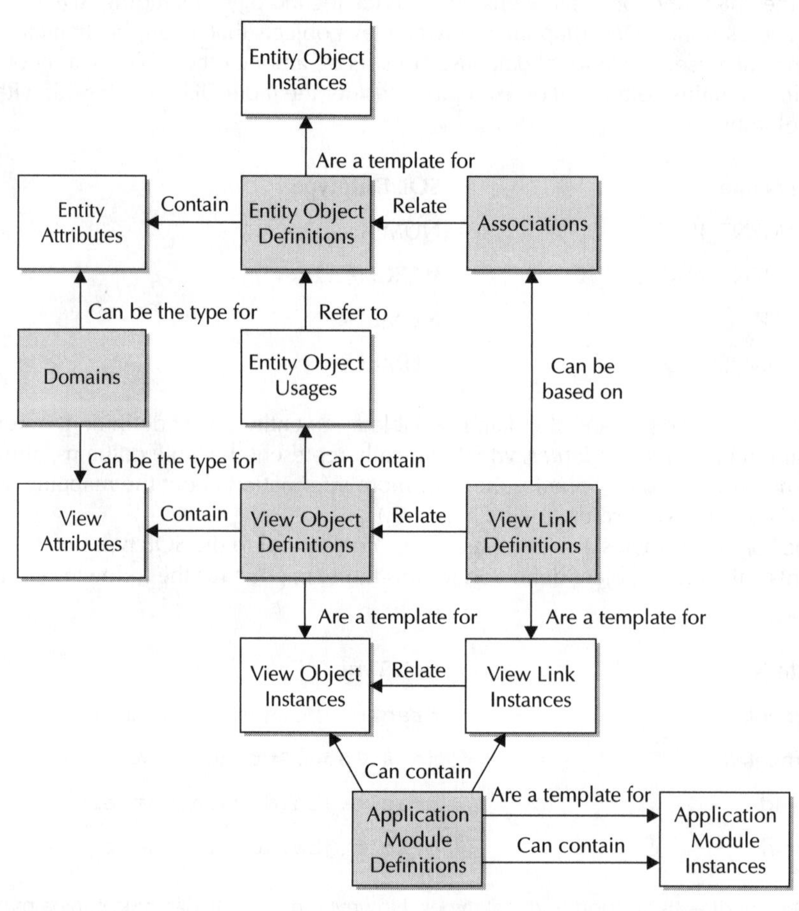

FIGURE 8-1. *ADF BC relationships*

An entity object definition consists of an XML file, which provides metadata, and between zero and three custom Java classes, which extend classes in the ADF BC library to modify their behavior. You will see the XML file and one of the Java classes in the hands-on practice.

Chapters 9 and 10 explain how to design entity object definitions.

Associations

Just as tables are often related to one another, entity object definitions are often related to one another. Relationships between entity object definitions are represented by associations, as shown in Figure 8-1. You can think of an *association* as the representation of a relationship such as a foreign key relationship. In the most common case, an association matches one or more attributes of one entity object definition with one or more attributes of another entity object definition, just as a foreign key constraint matches one or more columns of a parent table with one or more columns of a child table. If you are creating associations like this, you can (but do not need to) base them on foreign key constraints in the database. Associations, however, can also represent more complex table relationships than this. These relationships are explained in Chapter 9.

An association is implemented as an XML file, which provides metadata about the specific table relationship.

Domains

Domains are special Java classes that may be used by ADF BC as the types for entity and view attributes. Earlier, you learned that the Departments entity object definition has some entity attributes of type `oracle.jbo.domain.Number`. Entity attributes must be objects, not primitive Java types such as `int`.

For database columns of SQL datatype VARCHAR2, there is an obvious Java class for the entity attributes, namely `java.lang.String`. For other SQL types (such as NUMBER or BLOB), ADF BC provides domains to wrap the SQL datatype. Some domains, like `oracle.jbo.domain.Number`, are basically object wrappers for scalar types. Others, like `oracle.jbo.domain.BlobDomain`, are more complicated classes that store extensive data.

JDeveloper will also automatically create a domain for you if you base an entity object definition on a table with an Oracle object type column in it. This domain represents the Oracle object type, giving you Java wrappers for each of the object type's fields and methods. Domains that represent Oracle object types are discussed further in Chapter 9.

Finally, you may create your own domains. Suppose you have many database columns, possibly in different tables, that are all very similar. Not only are they of the same SQL type (for instance, VARCHAR2), but they all contain information in exactly the same form, such as a URL. You may have business logic that is simultaneously associated with multiple columns. For example, you may have validation logic that applies to any and all URLs—perhaps they must all begin with a protocol code, a colon, and two slashes. Rather than putting this logic in every entity object definition that contains one of these columns, you can create a URL domain that itself contains the validation code. Then you can apply the validation logic to all the relevant entity attributes by ensuring that the appropriate entity attributes are all instances of that domain rather than of type `java.lang.String`. Domains that enforce business logic will be discussed further in Chapter 10.

Data Model Components

Data model components are business components that collect data and present it to the view and controller through the ADF model layer. Data model components are not as reusable as business domain components: Their design is based on the data needs of particular client applications, so they can only be shared by applications with similar data needs. They are still independent of a user interface. A web application for self-service purchasing, a Java GUI application that allows sales staff to edit purchases, and a batch program to update purchases overnight could all use the same data model components, so long as they need to retrieve and update similar data. There are three kinds of data model components: view object definitions, view link definitions, and application module definitions.

View Object Definitions

An entity object definition usually represents a table or view in the database. But you generally do not present all of the information stored in a database object in one application interface. Also, you may want data taken from more than one database object. SQL has queries so that you can select exactly the data that you need from one or more tables. This is also the reason why ADF BC has *view object definitions,* which correspond to SQL queries. A view object definition actually stores a SQL SELECT statement. In this respect, it is much like a database view.

Just as an entity object definition has entity attributes, a view object definition has *view attributes,* which correspond to columns of the query result. For example, consider the view object definition, DepartmentsView, for the following query:

```
SELECT Departments.DEPARTMENT_ID,
  Departments.DEPARTMENT_NAME,
  Employees.EMPLOYEE_ID,
  Employees.FIRST_NAME,
  Employees.LAST_NAME,
  Employees.HIRE_DATE
FROM DEPARTMENTS Departments, EMPLOYEES Employees
WHERE Departments.MANAGER_ID=Employees.EMPLOYEE_ID;
```

This view object definition would have the following view attributes:

Attribute Name	Java Type
DepartmentId	oracle.jbo.domain.Number
DepartmentName	java.lang.String
EmployeeId	oracle.jbo.domain.Number
FirstName	java.lang.String
LastName	java.lang.String
HireDate	oracle.jbo.domain.Date

As shown in Figure 8-1, view object definitions may (but need not) contain one or more *entity object usages,* which are references to entity object definitions. View attributes can then be mapped to entity attributes within the entity usages. For example, the DepartmentsView view object definition could contain a usage of the entity object Departments. Then DepartmentsView's DepartmentId attribute could be mapped to Department's DepartmentId attribute, and similarly for other attributes.

As shown in Figure 8-1, a view object definition is the template for *view object instances,* which are particular caches of retrieved data. Your application may use several instances defined by the same view object definition; this is explained further in the section "Application Module Definitions" later in this chapter.

View Link Definitions

As shown in Figure 8-1, a *view link definition* represents a relationship, such as a master-detail relationship, between the query result sets of two view object definitions. It associates one or more attributes of one view object definition with one or more attributes of another view object definition. For example, you could create the following:

- A view object definition, DepartmentsView, containing the following query:

```
SELECT Departments.DEPARTMENT_ID,
  Departments.DEPARTMENT_NAME
FROM DEPARTMENTS Departments
```

- Another view object definition, EmployeesView, containing the following query:

```
SELECT Employees.EMPLOYEE_ID,
  Employees.FIRST_NAME,
  Employees.LAST_NAME,
  Employees.DEPARTMENT_ID
FROM EMPLOYEES Employees
```

- A view link definition, EmpDeptFkLink, that associates the DepartmentId attribute of EmployeesView with the DepartmentId attribute of DepartmentsView

EmpDeptFkLink represents a master-detail relationship between the query result sets of DepartmentsView and EmployeesView.

As shown in Figure 8-1, view link definitions between view object definitions can be, but do not need to be, based on associations between underlying entity objects.

A view link definition is a template for *view link instances,* which specify relationships between particular view object instances, as shown in Figure 8-1.

Application Module Definitions

An *application module definition* defines and aggregates all of the data and relationships that an application will need. As shown in Figure 8-1, application module definitions can contain view object and view link instances. An application module definition contains all of the view object instances that your application requires and the view link instances between them. This collection of view object instances in a hierarchical relationship is called an application module definition's *data model.* For example, an application module definition might contain an instance of DepartmentsView, called AllDepartments, and an instance of EmployeesView, called DepartmentEmployees, linked by an instance of EmpDeptFkLink, called DepartmentsToEmployees. The application module definition would use the data model shown here:

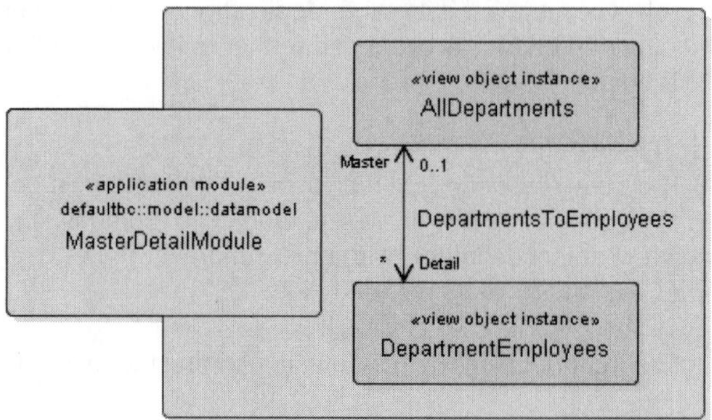

Using this application module definition, the two view object instances are tied together by a link (EmpDeptFkLink) representing a master-detail relationship between them. Through this application module definition, your application could select a row in AllDepartments, and ADF BC would immediately synchronize DepartmentEmployees so that it would only return employees from the selected department.

Alternatively, your application module definition could contain an instance of DepartmentsView and an instance of EmployeesView without using any instances of EmpDeptFkLink, as in the data model shown here:

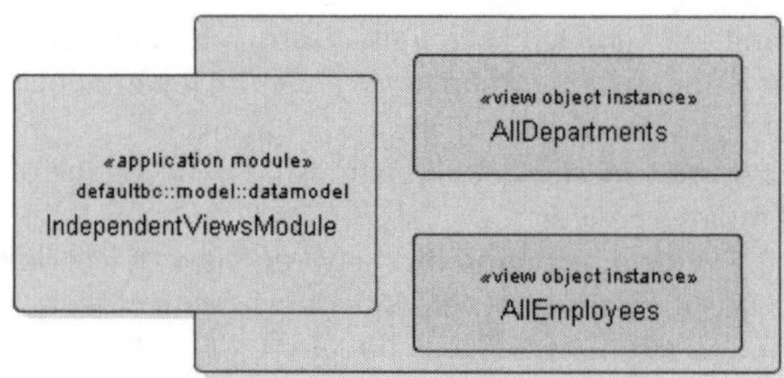

This application module definition provides instances of the same two view object definitions, but the instances are not linked. Through this application module definition, your application could select rows in AllDepartments and AllEmployees independently.

You could even include two instances of EmployeesView in your application module definition: one a detail of an instance of DepartmentsView and one independent, as in the data model shown here.

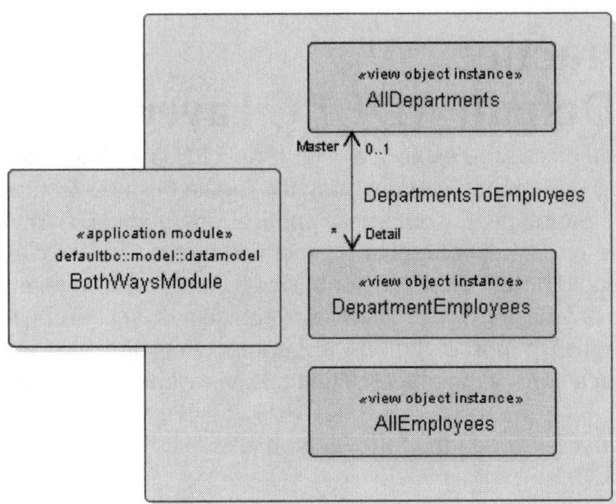

Through this application module definition, an application could select rows in DepartmentEmployees and have them automatically synchronized with AllDepartments. It could also select rows in AllEmployees independently.

An application module definition is a template for *application module instances,* which are individual copies of the data model used by particular instances of the application. Each application module instance represents an individual database transaction. For example, if you have five different users running the same application, there will generally be five different application module instances for them to use, representing five different transactions. (Actually, there may well be more or fewer because of application module pooling. For more information, see the sidebar "Application Module Pooling.")

Application Module Pooling

Creating an application module instance takes time, and storing all of the data contained in its view object instances takes space. In addition, it is rare that all the applications that are running at one time will really need access to data simultaneously. For example, in a web application, data can be retrieved and displayed, and then is not needed again until the user completes his or her "think time" and requests an update or refresh. ADF BC uses objects called *application module pools* to help maintain scalability by allowing multiple clients to share application module instances. The operation of the application module pool is completely transparent. The pool will write transaction logs to the database and refresh data whenever necessary to give users a consistent view of the data within their transactions.

Application module definitions can also contain instances of other application module definitions, as shown in Figure 8-1. For example, MasterDetailModule might contain an instance of IndependentViewsModule. This would allow clients that use an instance of MasterDetailModule to access the data model of IndependentViewsModule.

Hands-on Practice: Examine a Default ADF BC Layer

In this practice, you will create and explore a default ADF BC layer based on the HR schema. A *default ADF BC layer* is one created entirely using the Create Business Components from Tables wizard. It is basically a prototype. For enterprise applications, you can start with some wizard-generated components (or default components generated by the Class Modeler, discussed in Chapter 9), but you should design most of your business components by hand. A default ADF BC layer does not contain any business logic. However, the default ADF BC layer created in this practice contains examples of most of the business components discussed in this chapter: entity object definitions, associations, view object definitions, view link definitions, and an application module definition.

This practice steps you through the following phases:

I. Create an application workspace with a default ADF BC layer

- Create an application workspace
- Create a default ADF BC layer for the HR schema

II. Explore the business domain components

- Create a diagram of the business domain components
- Explore an entity object definition
- Explore an association

III. Explore the data model components

- Create a diagram of the data model components
- Explore a view object definition
- Explore a view link definition
- Explore an application module definition

IV. Test the default Business Components

- Open the Business Component Browser
- Test an independent instance of DepartmentsView
- Test two different instances of EmployeesView
- Test an instance of EmpDeptFkLink

I. Create an Application Workspace with a Default ADF BC Layer

This phase creates an application workspace with a default ADF BC layer in the Model project.

Create an Application Workspace

You can create a new workspace with a model project prepared for ADF BC using the following steps:

1. On the Applications node in the Application Navigator, select New Application Workspace from the right-click menu. The Create Application Workspace dialog opens.

2. Enter the following values:

   Application Name as "DefaultBC"
   Application Package Prefix as "defaultbc"
   Application Template as "Web Application [Default]"

   Additional Information: The *Application Package Prefix* tells JDeveloper that every package you create in this application should be a subpackage of `defaultbc`. For example, your ADF BC layer will be under the `defaultbc.model` package. The *Application Template* tells JDeveloper that you want to create an application using ADF BC as your business services, Struts as your controller, and JSP or UIX as your view. In this practice, the view and controller types are not important, but it is important to choose an application template that uses ADF BC.

3. Click OK. A new application workspace, DefaultBC, appears in the Navigator. This workspace contains two projects, Model and ViewController, as shown here:

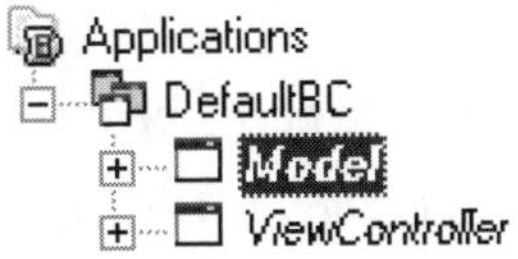

   Additional Information: The Model project will hold ADF BC components, and would also hold custom files for the ADF model, if any were required. The ViewController project would hold Struts, JSP, and/or UIX files, if you were creating a complete application.

Create a Default ADF BC Layer for the HR Schema

You can create a default ADF BC layer using the following steps:

1. On the Model node in the Navigator, select New from the right-click menu. The New Gallery opens.

2. In the Categories pane, select Business Tier\Business Components. In the Items pane, select Business Components from Tables.

3. Click OK. The Business Components Project Initialization dialog opens.

4. Select HR from the *Connection Name* dropdown and click OK. The Create Business Components from Tables Wizard opens. If the Welcome page appears, click Next.

5. On the Entity Objects page, type "defaultbc.model.businessdomain" in the *Package* field.

   Additional Information: This page will create business domain components. By putting business domain components in a separate subpackage of `defaultbc.model`, you can increase their reusability. If you later create another application that works with the same database schema but has different data needs, you can import `defaultbc.model.businessdomain` into that application and create a new set of data model components that use it.

6. Select DEPARTMENTS and EMPLOYEES and click the right arrow. This will create entity object definitions ("Departments" and "Employees") from each of those tables and create associations from each of the foreign keys between them.

7. Click Next. The View Objects page opens. Enter "defaultbc.model.datamodel" in the *Package* field.

   Additional Information: This page will create view object definitions and view link definitions. By putting these components in a subpackage distinct from `defaultbc.model.businessdomain`, you can reuse the business domain components without importing the data model components.

8. Click the right double-arrow.

   Additional Information: This will tell the wizard that you want to create default view object definitions ("DepartmentsView" and "EmployeesView") from each of the entity object definitions and one view link definition for each association. As you will see later, default view object definitions and view link definitions are not very useful for many real applications. (They correspond to "SELECT *" single-table queries and foreign-key–based master-detail relationships rather than the more complex queries and relationships that most applications need.) But they are useful for testing the functionality of the entity object definitions.

9. Click Next. The Application Module page opens.

10. Enter "defaultbc.model.datamodel" in the *Package* field, if it is not already there.

    Additional Information: This page specifies whether the wizard should create an application module definition. This will place the application module definition in the same package as the other data model components.

11. Leave the *Application Module* checkbox checked, with the name "AppModule" filled in.

    Additional Information: This will cause the wizard to create a default application module definition that contains the view object instances in every possible combination, both independent and joined by view link instances. Again, the default application module would not be that useful for developing a real application (it is generally too big and inefficient), but it is useful for testing a business components project.

12. Click Next. The Finish page appears.

    Additional Information: The Finish page lists the primary business components (entity object definitions, view object definitions, and the application module definition) that the wizard will create, as shown next:

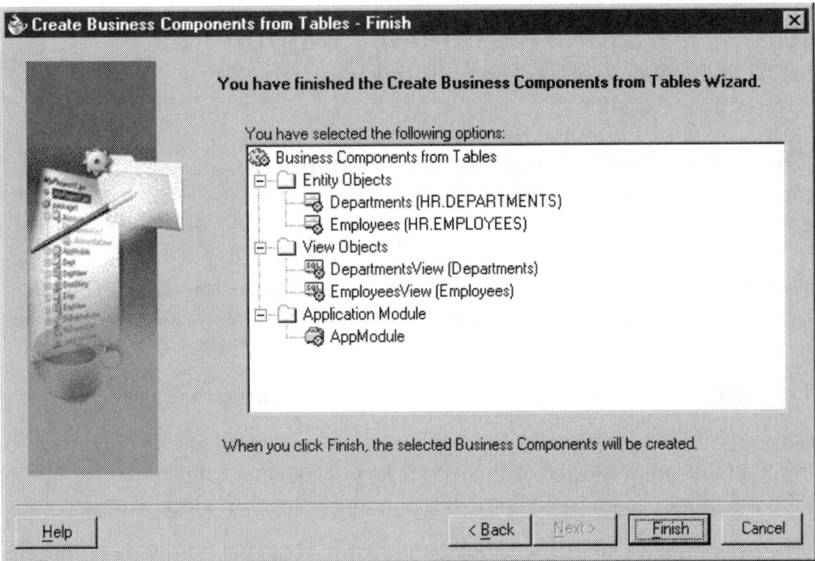

13. Click Finish.
14. Click Save All.

What Just Happened? You created a default ADF BC layer. JDeveloper creates business components (entity object definitions, associations, view object definitions, view link definitions, and an application module definition) based on the choices you made in the wizard. The business components are under the Application Sources node in the Application Navigator, as shown next:

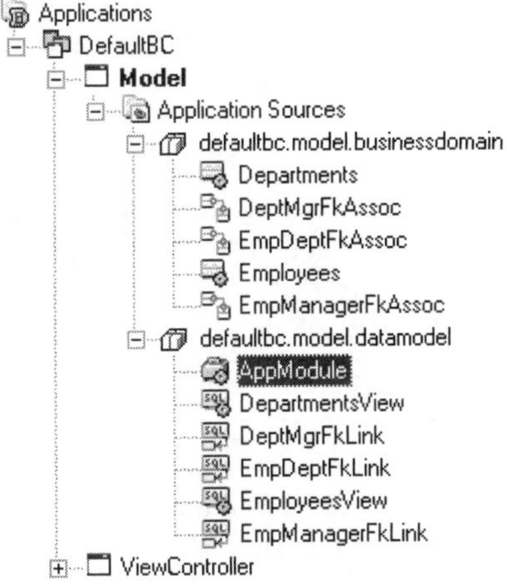

The icons next to the business components indicate the type of component. You can hold the mouse over an icon to display the object type and name.

II. Explore the Business Domain Components

This phase looks at the entity object definitions and associations in the package `hr.model.businessdomain`.

Create a Diagram of the Business Domain Components

You can create a UML diagram that provides a visual representation of the business domain components using the following steps:

1. In the Application Navigator, on the defaultbc.model.businessdomain node, select New from the right-click menu. The New Gallery opens. In the Categories pane, select General\Diagrams. In the Items pane, select Business Components Diagram.
2. Click OK to open the Create Business Components Diagram dialog.
3. Name the diagram "Business Domain Diagram" and click OK. A new node, Business Domain Diagram, is added to the Application Navigator under defaultbc.model.businessdomain, and an empty diagram window opens.
4. In the Application Navigator, group select (CTRL click) the following components and drag them onto the diagram:
   - Departments
   - DeptMgrFkAssoc
   - EmpDeptFkAssoc
   - Employees
   - EmpManagerFkAssoc

   Additional Information: JDeveloper creates a UML diagram of the business domain components, as shown in Figure 8-2. Entity object definitions are represented as boxes, and associations are represented as arrows.

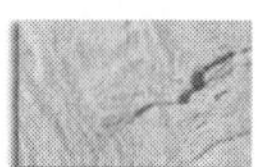

NOTE
You may need to resize the diagram and drag some diagram elements around slightly before your diagram exactly resembles Figure 8-2. In addition, for readability in print, Figure 8-2 and similar diagrams throughout this book do not show JDeveloper's default color scheme, which uses dark blue to represent entity object definitions.

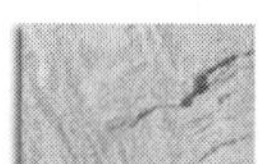

TIP
For maximum control while dragging lines in a diagram, hold down the SHIFT key and click and drag from any point on the line to bend it.

5. Click Save All.

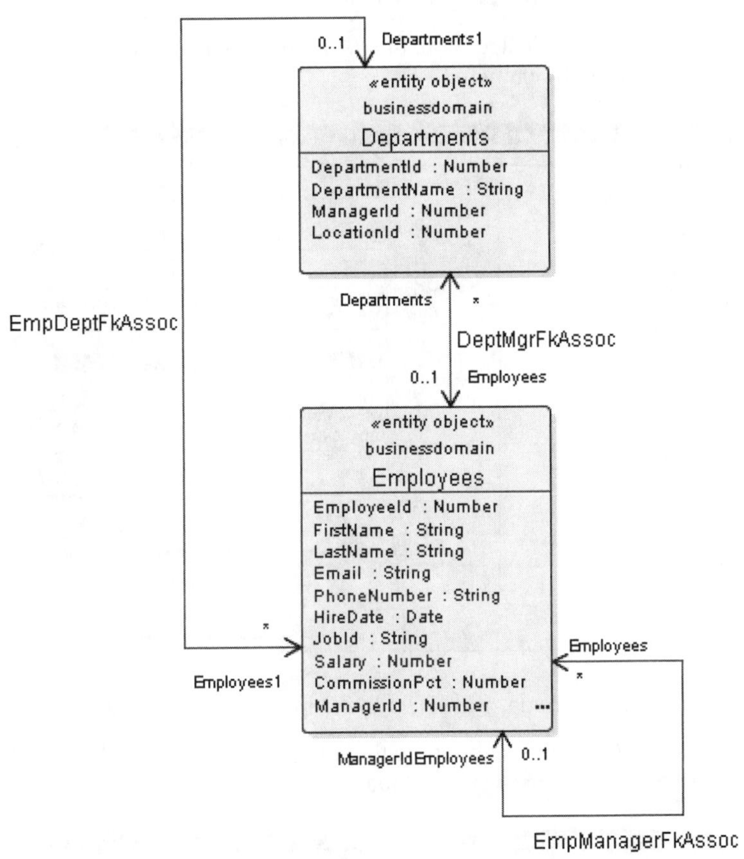

FIGURE 8-2. *A UML diagram of the business domain components*

Explore an Entity Object Definition

You can view an entity object definition's entity attributes and their types directly in the diagram, learn more about them using the Entity Object Editor (which you would use to fine-tune an entity object definition), and see the files that make up an entity object definition in the Structure window.

1. Find the Departments entity object definition on the UML diagram (in Figure 8-2, it is the upper box).

   Additional Information: Note that the entity attributes, with their Java types, are listed. DepartmentId, ManagerId, and LocationId are all of type `Number`, which is a domain. DepartmentName is of type `String`.

2. Double click either the Departments element in the diagram or the Departments node in the Application Navigator to open the Entity Object Editor.

3. With the Name node selected, note that Departments is based on the schema object DEPARTMENTS, as shown here:

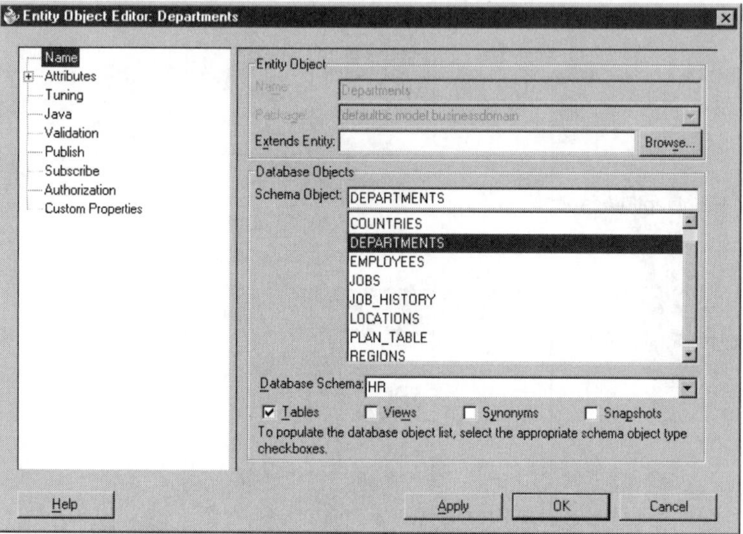

4. Expand the Attributes node, and select the DepartmentId attribute.

5. In the Database Column section, note that the DepartmentId attribute is mapped to the DEPARTMENT_ID column in the database, as shown here:

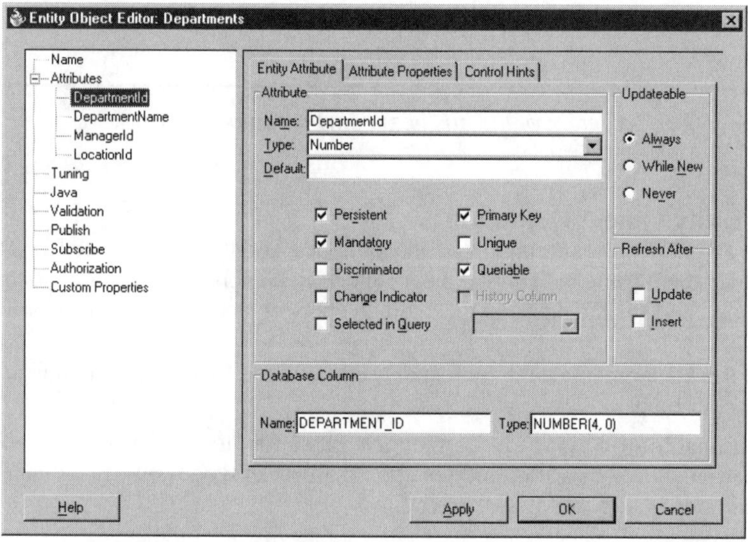

6. Click Cancel to close the editor without making any changes.
7. In the Application Navigator, select Departments.

   Additional Information: The Structure window displays a tree describing many features of the Departments entity object definition. In particular, under Sources, you can see two files, Departments.xml and DepartmentsImpl.java, as shown next:

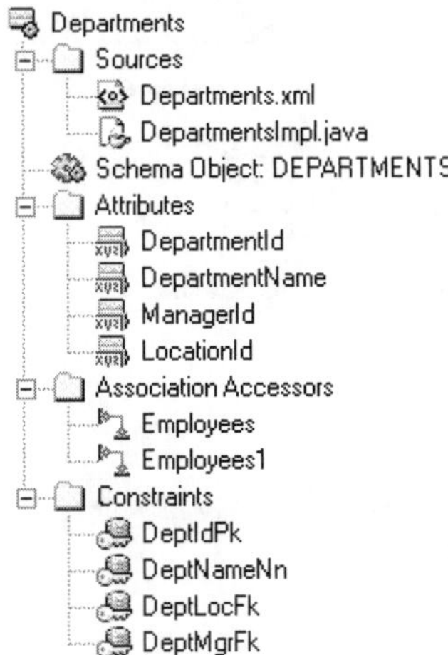

   These files constitute the Departments entity object definition. Departments.xml is the file that defines Departments' metadata, and DepartmentsImpl.java is a file that defines a custom class, the entity object class, that extends the ADF BC library's behavior. Entity object classes are discussed in Chapter 10.

Explore an Association

You can examine an association directly on the diagram, or in more detail using the Association Editor, which you would also use to fine-tune an association:

1. Find the EmpDeptFkAssoc association in the UML diagram (in Figure 8-2, it is the long arrow on the left).

   Additional Information: Note that this is an association between the Departments and Employees entity object definitions.

2. Double click either the arrow or the EmpDeptFkAssoc node in the Application Navigator to open the Association Editor.

   Additional Information: Note that the source entity object definition is Departments (which contains the primary key) and the destination entity object definition is Employees (which contains the foreign key). The wizard page shows the primary key attribute under the source entity object node and the foreign key attribute under the destination entity object node, as shown here:

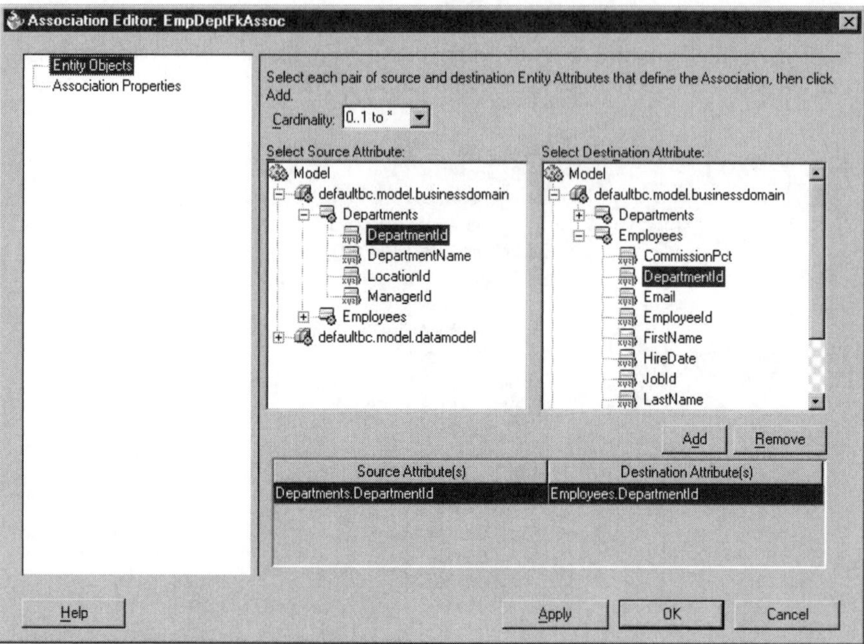

3. Click Cancel to close the wizard without making any changes.

What Just Happened? You created a graphical representation of the business domain components and looked at an entity object definition and an association. You saw that the entity object definition corresponds to a database table and that it has entity attributes, some of which have domain datatypes, that correspond to database columns. You also saw the files that made up a particular entity object definition. Finally, you saw that the association links two entity object definitions, just as foreign key relationships link two tables.

III. Explore the Data Model Components

This phase looks at the view object definitions, view link definitions, and application module definition in the package `defaultbc.model.datamodel`.

Create a Diagram of the Data Model Components

As with the business domain components, you can create a UML diagram that provides a visual representation of the data model components using the following steps:

1. In the Application Navigator, on the defaultbc.model.datamodel node, select New from the right-click menu. The New Gallery opens.
2. In the Categories pane, select General\Diagrams. In the Items pane, select Business Components Diagram.

3. Click OK. The Create Business Components Diagram dialog opens.
4. Name the diagram "Data Model Diagram" and click OK. A new node, Data Model Diagram, is added to the Application Navigator under defaultbc.model.datamodel, and an empty diagram window opens.
5. In the Application Navigator, group select the following components and drag them onto the diagram:
   - AppModule
   - DepartmentsView
   - DeptMgrFkLink
   - EmpDeptFkLink
   - EmployeesView
   - EmpManagerFkLink

   Additional Information: JDeveloper creates a UML class diagram of the data model components. This diagram will probably take up two pages, as shown in Figures 8-3 and 8-4. View object definitions are represented as boxes containing other boxes (entity object usages), view link definitions are represented as arrows, and application module definitions are represented as boxes containing other boxes (view object instances) and arrows (view link instances).

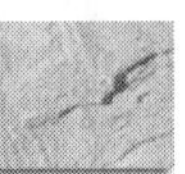

NOTE
You may need to drag some diagram elements around before your diagram exactly resembles Figures 8-3 and 8-4. In addition, for readability in print, Figures 8-3 and 8-4, and similar diagrams throughout this book, do not use JDeveloper's default color scheme, which uses light blue to represent view object definitions, dark blue to represent entity object usages, medium blue to represent application module definitions, and very light blue to represent view object instances.

6. Click Save All.

Explore a View Object Definition

You can examine a view object definition's view attributes and entity usages directly in the diagram, view its query using the View Object Editor (which you would use to fine-tune a view object definition), and see the files that make up a view object definition in the Structure window.

1. Find the DepartmentsView view object definition on the UML diagram (in Figure 8-3, it is the upper box).

   Additional Information: Note that the view attributes, with their Java types, are listed. Also note that the view object definition contains a usage of Departments.

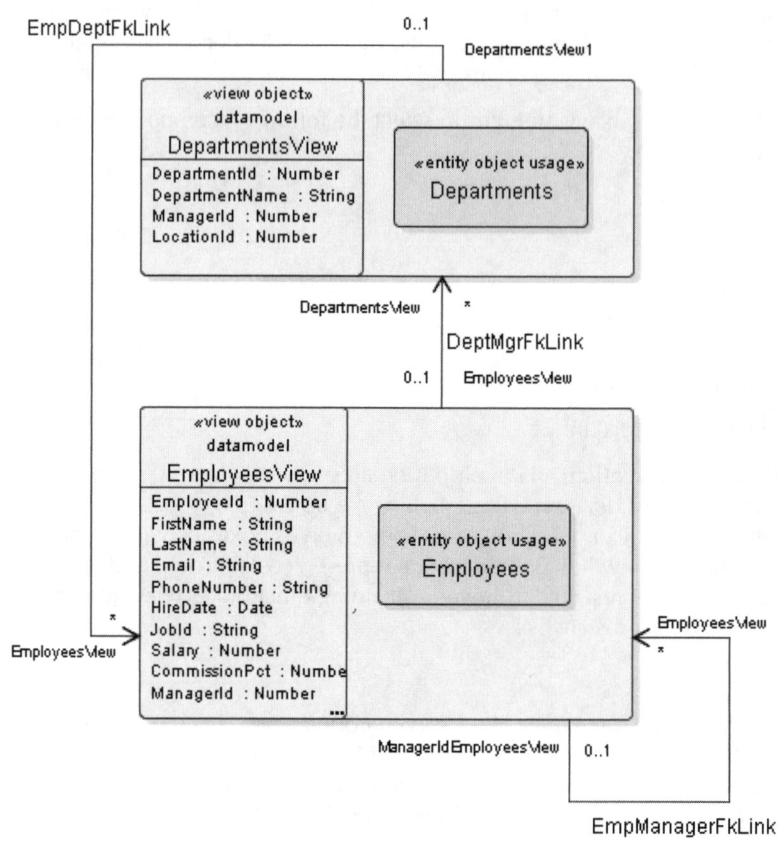

FIGURE 8-3. *A UML class diagram of the data model components showing view object and view link definitions*

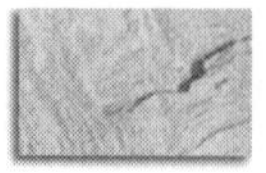

TIP

You can navigate around a large diagram like this one using the Thumbnail window. For example, if you manipulate the box in the Thumbnail window so that it resembles the following illustration, you will see the portion of the diagram containing Figure 8-3.

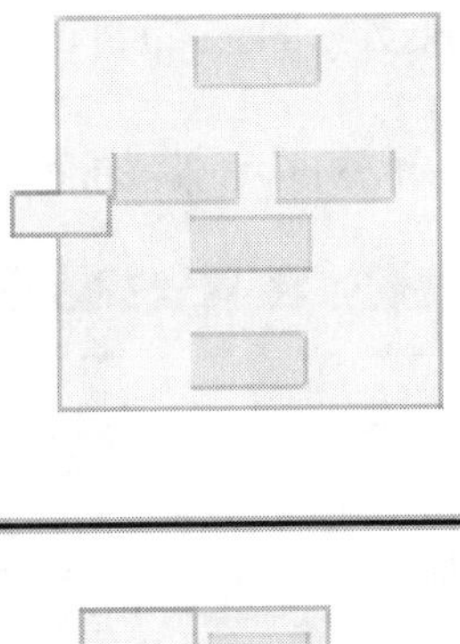

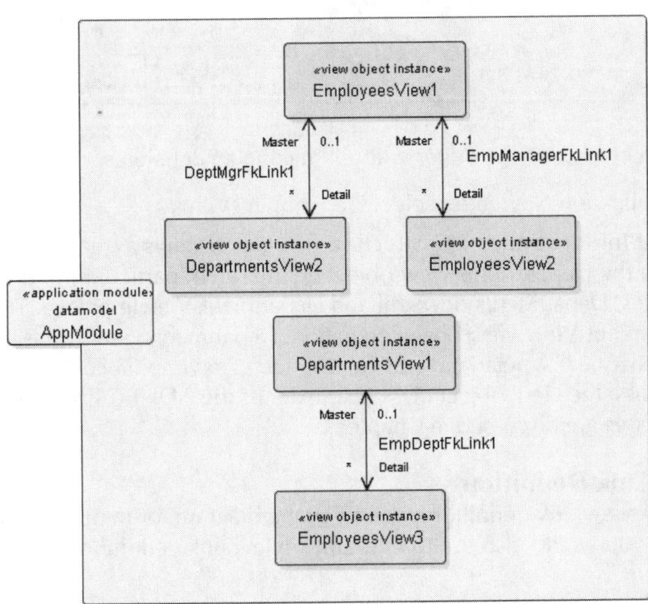

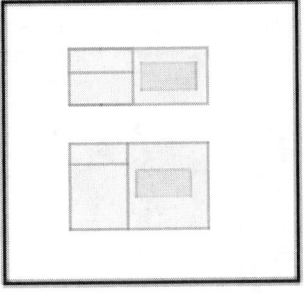

FIGURE 8-4. *A UML diagram of the data model components showing an application module definition*

2. Double-click the DepartmentsView element in the diagram to open the View Object Editor.

3. Select the Query node to see the view object definition's query, as shown next:

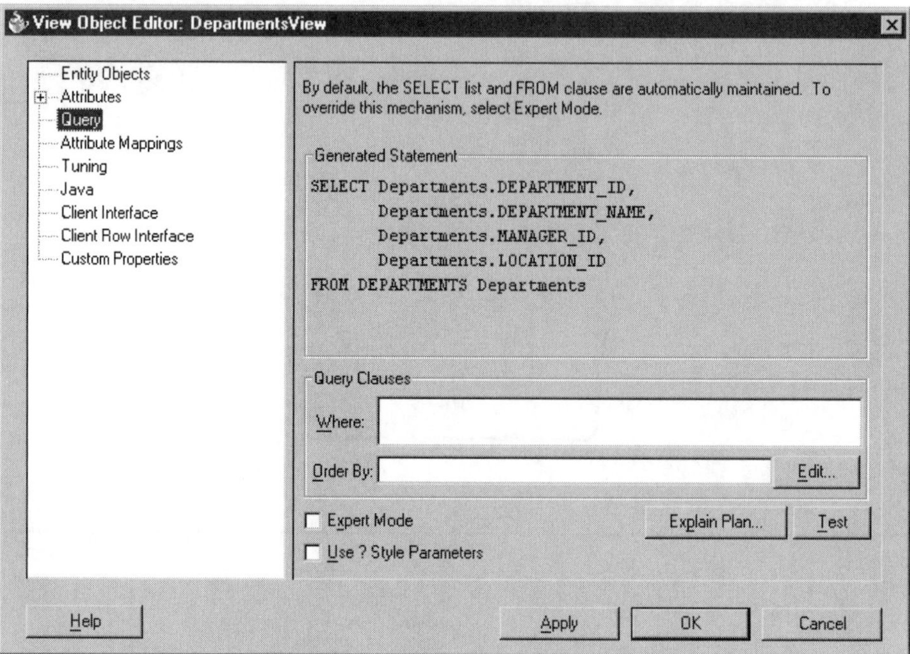

4. Click Cancel to close the editor without making any changes.

5. In the Application Navigator, select DepartmentsView.

   Additional Information: The Structure window displays a tree describing many features of the Departments view object definition. In particular, under Sources, you can see two files, DepartmentsView.xml and DepartmentsViewImpl.java. These files constitute the DepartmentsView view object definition. DepartmentsView.xml is the file that defines DepartmentsView's metadata, and DepartmentsViewImpl.java is a file that defines a custom class, the view object class, that extends the ADF BC library's behavior. View object classes are discussed in Chapter 13.

Explore a View Link Definition

You can examine a view link definition directly on the diagram, or in more detail using the View Link Editor, which you would also use to fine-tune a view link definition:

1. Find the EmpDeptFkLink view link definition in the UML diagram (in Figure 8-3, it is the long arrow on the left).

   Additional Information: This is a view link definition representing a master-detail relationship between the DepartmentsView and EmployeesView view object definitions.

2. Double-click the arrow to open the View Link Editor.
3. Click the View Link SQL node. In the *Query Clauses* box, you can see the WHERE clause that the view link will use to join Departments data to Employees data, shown next:

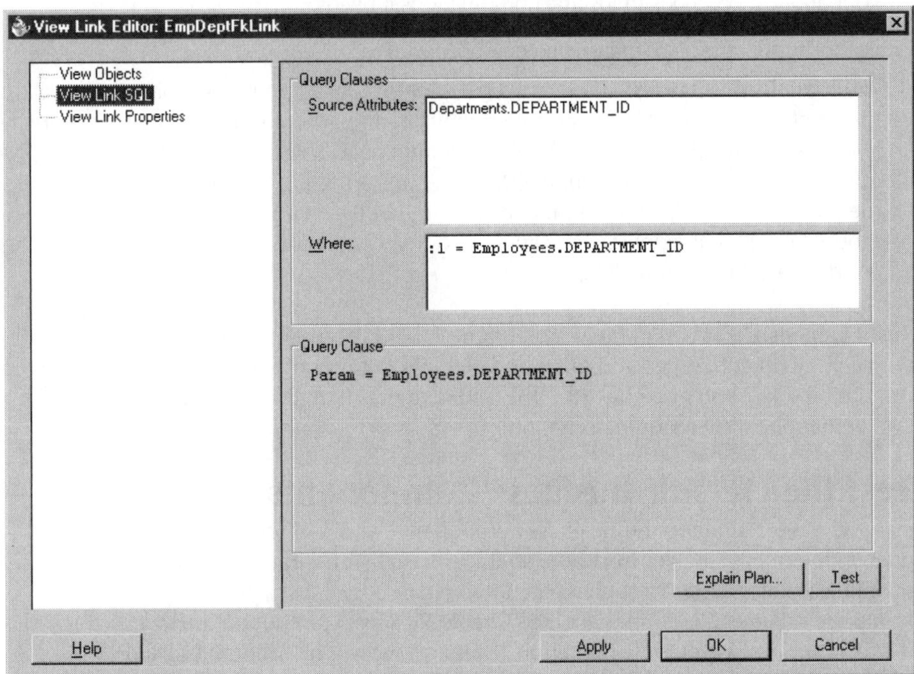

Additional Information: The attribute DepartmentsId from a row of a master instance of DepartmentsView will be substituted for the parameter :1 in the WHERE clause "WHERE :1=Employees.DEPARTMENT_ID" to limit the rows returned by a detail instance of EmployeesView. This definition is the reason why you will only be able to see employees for the selected department if you use this view link in your data model.

4. Click Cancel to close the editor without making any changes.

Explore an Application Module Definition

You can examine an application module definition's data model directly in the diagram and see the files that constitute it in the Structure pane:

1. Find the AppModule application module definition in the UML diagram, as shown in Figure 8-4.

   Additional Information: Note that the application module definition contains five separate view object instances, linked by three separate view link instances. DepartmentsView1 and EmployeesView1 are independent instances of DepartmentsView and EmployeesView, respectively. The other view object instances are linked to those instances, via view link instances, as details in master-detail relationships. The data model of a default application module contains all possible view objects in all possible combinations: both independent and joined by view links. When you create your own application modules, you probably will not want to do this. Instead, you will use just the view object and view link instances your application needs in just the combinations it needs.

2. In the Application Navigator, select AppModule.

   Additional Information: The Structure pane displays a tree describing many features of the AppModule application module definition. In particular, under Sources, you can see two files, AppModule.xml and AppModuleImpl.java. These files constitute the AppModule application module definition. AppModule.xml is the file that defines AppModule's metadata, and AppModuleImpl.java is a file that defines a custom class, the application module class, that extends the ADF BC library's behavior. Application module classes are discussed in Chapter 12.

What Just Happened? You created a diagram of the data model and looked at a view object definition's entity object usages and query, a view link definition's SQL code, and an application module's data model. You also saw the XML and Java files that constitute the view object definition and application module definition.

IV. Test the Default Business Components

Now that you have examined the business components, you can look at them in action. Business components do not have a user interface, so it is not really possible to see the business components working except through a user interface.

JDeveloper includes a user interface, the Oracle Business Component Browser, which can be run to test any application module definition. The browser will be used to test AppModule. Because AppModule contains instances of all view object definitions in all possible combinations, testing AppModule is really a way of testing the entire business components project.

NOTE
As mentioned earlier, default application module definitions are not generally suitable for production-quality enterprise applications because they are too big. They contain instances of every view object definition, linked together in every possible combination based on foreign key constraints in the database, instead of just the data model elements that the application needs. This leads to a needlessly large cache, which can degrade performance. However, they are excellent for testing all of your business components at once.

Open the Business Component Browser

You can open the Business Component Browser to test an application module definition and its associated business components using the following steps:

1. In the diagram, on the AppModule element, select Test from the right-click menu. The Business Component Browser starts up, showing the Connect dialog.
2. The defaults in the Connect dialog are fine for the purposes of this practice, so click Connect. The main dialog of the Business Component Browser appears. In the left-hand pane, you can see the AppModule's data model, as shown next:

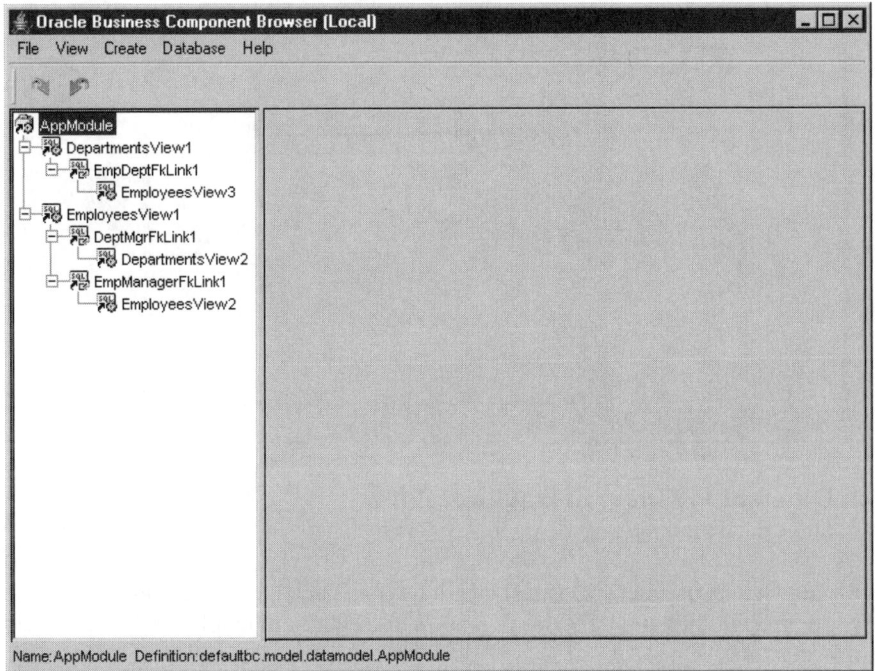

Test an Independent Instance of DepartmentsView

You can scroll through the query results for an independent view object instance using the following steps:

1. Double click DepartmentsView1. In the right-hand pane, you can now see the data from DepartmentsView's query, one row at a time.
2. Click the blue right arrow to scroll forward to Department 30 as shown next:

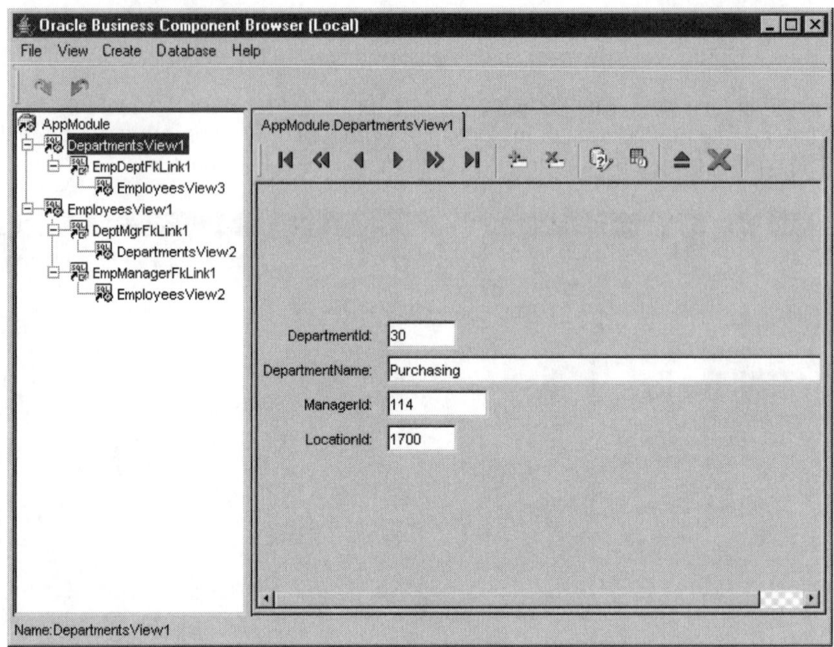

Test Two Different Instances of EmployeesView

You can contrast detail and independent view object instances using the following steps:

1. Be sure that Department 30 is displayed. Double click EmployeesView3 in the left-hand pane. In the right-hand pane, you can now see data from EmployeesView's query, one row at a time.

2. Scroll forward through the data. Notice that all the employees listed have DepartmentId 30. This is because ADF BC uses EmpDeptFkLink1 to automatically synchronize EmployeesView3 with DepartmentsView1. The current row of DepartmentsView1 is 30, so only employees with that department will show in EmployeesView3.

3. Double click EmployeesView1. The same kind of single-row browser is displayed.

4. Scroll forward through the data. Notice that EmployeesView1 contains all of the employees, not just those with DepartmentId 30. That is because the EmployeesView1 instance, unlike EmployeesView3, is not a detail of DepartmentsView1.

5. Click the red X in the toolbar to close each open window in turn.

TIP

If you want to pull a window out of the Oracle Business Component Browser's frame, click the blue up arrow in the toolbar.

Test an Instance of EmpDeptFkLink

You can view a split-screen display of view object instances in a master-detail relationship using the following steps:

1. Double click EmpDeptFkLink1. The right-hand pane is now split. In the top half, you can see rows from DepartmentsView1 one at a time, and in the bottom half, you can see a table of all rows currently showing in EmployeesView3. This is just another way the Oracle Business Component Browser lets you see view object instances in a master-detail relationship. Selecting a view link instance lets you view both view object instances at once, as shown next:

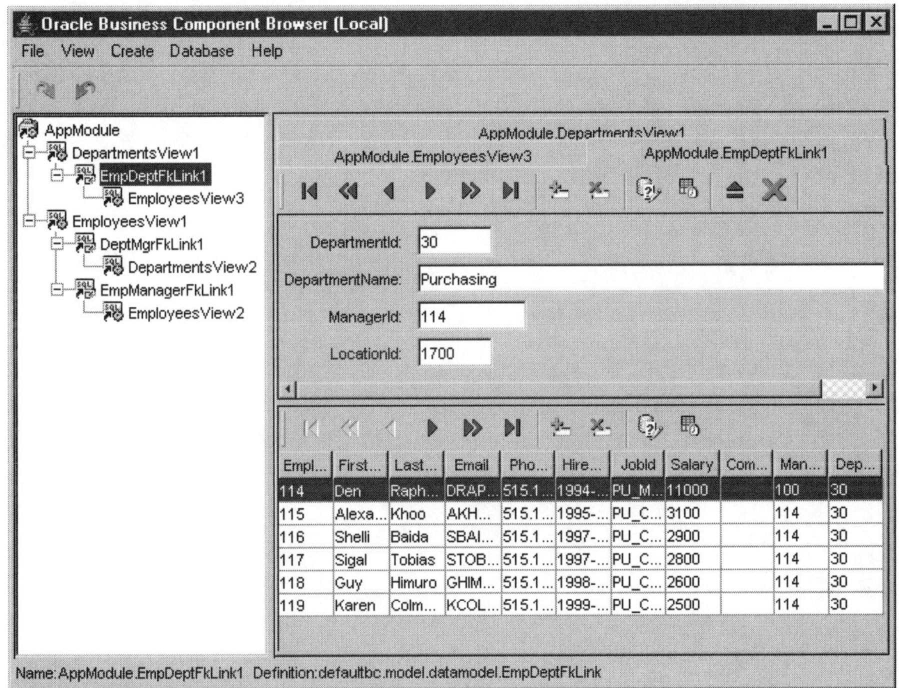

2. Scroll through the departments. The list of employees automatically synchronizes with the department in the top pane.

3. Close the Oracle Business Component Browser.

What Just Happened? You used the Business Component Browser to test your business components. You saw a display of all the view object and view link instances in your data model, two ways of displaying data in the Oracle Business Component Browser, and how view link instances synchronize detail view object instances with their master view object instances.

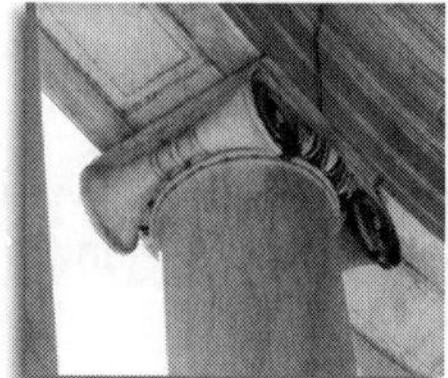

CHAPTER 9

Creating Business Domain Components

It is a capital mistake to theorize before one has data.

—Sir Arthur Conan Doyle (1855–1930),
A Scandal in Bohemia

he first step in building a database application is representing features of the database: tables and views, constraints, and relationships. Business domain components—entity object definitions, associations, and domains—were introduced in Chapter 8. In this chapter, you will learn how to do the following:

- Create entity object definitions from tables
- Edit entity object definitions to delete entity attributes representing database columns you do not need
- Add transient entity attributes to represent calculated values
- Represent primary key, not null, and foreign key constraints

In the hands-on practice, you will create, modify, and test business domain components to represent the HR schema.

Creating Default Business Domain Components

The first step in creating a business domain is creating default entity object definitions and associations for a database schema. These defaults have the following properties:

- Each entity object definition represents a table or view in the schema.
- There is a one-to-one correspondence between the entity attributes of the entity object definitions and the columns of the database tables.
- If two tables are represented by entity object definitions, there is a one-to-one correspondence between the foreign key relationships relating the tables and the associations relating the entity object definitions.

Although you may want more or fewer entity attributes or associations in your final business domain, these defaults are generally a good starting place.

There are two ways to create default business domain components. You can use the Business Components from Tables Wizard, as described in Chapter 8, or you can drag tables directly from the Connection Navigator onto a business components diagram, which you will do in the hands-on practice in this chapter.

Entity Attributes

Although default business domain components are a good starting place, you may not be satisfied with the number of entity object attributes in default entity object definitions, or with their properties. This section will discuss adding and deleting attributes from entity object definitions and changing those attributes' properties to add and remove constraints and affect their behavior.

Adding and Deleting Attributes

As mentioned earlier, in the case of default business domain components, there is a one-to-one mapping between columns in a table and attributes in the corresponding entity object definition. However, you may wish to change this. For example:

- The table may have columns that you know your business logic will never use. Entity attributes corresponding to these columns will just use up memory, so you may want to delete them.
- You may want to have *transient attributes*—attributes you calculate or set on a particular row that are needed for the duration of the transaction, but that are not stored in the database.

In these cases, you will need to add or delete attributes from an entity object definition. You might also need to add or delete attributes if your database table changes to include a new column or to drop an old one. The hands-on practice in this chapter will demonstrate how to add and delete attributes from an entity object definition.

Changing Datatypes

Chapter 8 explained that each database column (with its datatype) is mapped to an entity attribute (with its Java type). There are some restrictions on which Java types can correspond to particular SQL datatypes, but there is some flexibility as well. Table 9-1 lists some common mappings between Java types and SQL datatypes.

JDeveloper will select a default Java type appropriate to the database column datatype, but you can change it to any of the acceptable Java types listed in Table 9-1.

You can also change the Java type to synchronize the entity object with the database if you have changed the column definition in the table. To change the datatype, just click once on an attribute in the diagram to select it and again to edit its attribute type.

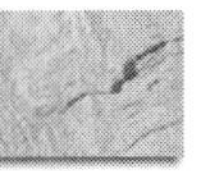

NOTE
To create ADF BC components that use a non-Oracle database, you will have to use a separate type map to associate datatypes with Java types—either JDeveloper's "Java" type map or a type map that you create. You can find information about using ADF BC with non-Oracle databases in the JDeveloper online help system.

Representing Column Constraints

Relational databases such as Oracle provide five constraints that can be applied to columns: not null, primary key, foreign key, check, and unique. As mentioned in Chapter 8, foreign keys are represented by associations, and this is discussed later in this chapter. Check that constraints are used to provide complex validation, which is discussed in Chapter 10. Unique constraints in the database are not used directly by ADF BC, although ADF BC can generate database tables with unique constraints. (This will be discussed in the section "Business Components and Database Object Generation").

Database Datatypes	Acceptable Java Types
NUMBER	Number, Boolean, Integer, BigDecimal, String
TINYINT, SMALLINT, INTEGER, BIGINT, INT, REAL, DOUBLE, FLOAT, DECIMAL, NUMERIC, BIT	Number, String
VARCHAR2, NVARCHAR2, CHAR, VARCHAR, LONG	String, Char, Character
DATE, TIME, DATETIME	Date
TIMESTAMP	Date, Timestamp
RAW, LONG RAW	Raw
CLOB	ClobDomain
BLOB	BlobDomain
BFILE	BFileDomain
STRUCT	Object
ARRAY, VARRAY	Array
REF	Ref
ROWID	Object

TABLE 9-1. *Common Type Mappings*

Not Null Constraints

When you create an entity object from a table, JDeveloper determines whether any column in the table has a not null constraint. If either of these constraints has been defined, JDeveloper automatically marks the corresponding attribute(s) as "Mandatory."

ADF BC allows you to represent not null constraints in entity object definitions to improve performance. Rather than posting data to the database every time the user changes a field value, the framework saves all changes until you request a post or commit. By representing the not null constraint in the entity object definitions, the framework can verify that the constraints are satisfied without making a round trip to the database.

Primary Key Constraints

When you create an entity object from a table, JDeveloper determines whether any column in the table is part of a primary key. If so, JDeveloper automatically marks the corresponding attribute(s) as "Primary Key."

ADF BC uses the entity attributes tagged as parts of the primary key in order to look up particular entity object instances. Without attributes tagged as parts of the primary key, the ADF BC would have no way of distinguishing between different entity object instances. If a table does not have a primary key, JDeveloper will create a RowId entity attribute, based on the pseudo-column ROWID, of type oracle.jbo.domain.RowId, and use it as a primary key. You can change the default behavior to mark any combination of entity attributes as "Primary Key," but these attributes must uniquely identify an entity object instance (database row).

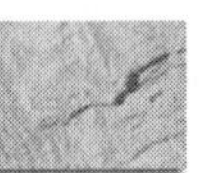

CAUTION
If you want to use entity object definitions to represent schema objects in a non-Oracle database, you must ensure that all of your tables have columns out of which you can construct a primary key.

Additional Constraints

You may want to define constraints in an entity object definition that do not correspond to any database constraint, if either of the following conditions hold:

- You need a constraint but do not have permission to perform DDL operations to change the table.
- The constraint applies only to your applications; other applications using the same tables do not need it.

In addition, you might want to enforce a constraint that has been added to a database table since you created the corresponding entity object definition. You will create column constraints in the hands-on practice.

Synchronizing Entity Object Definitions with the Database

In addition to manually adding and dropping attributes or constraints, you can use JDeveloper to automatically synchronize some or all of your entity object definitions with the database. On an ADF BC package node in the Application Navigator, select Synchronize with Database from the right-click menu, and use the Synchronize with Database dialog to select and make any desired updates to the entity object definitions.

Representing Relationships Between Tables

In Chapter 8, you learned that relationships between tables (such as foreign-key relationships) are represented by associations between entity object definitions. When you create default business domain components, JDeveloper will create an association corresponding to each foreign key constraint that occurs between tables you select. You may want to define associations that do not correspond to any foreign key constraint, if one of the following conditions hold:

- You need a relationship but do not have permission to perform DDL operations to change the table.
- The relationship applies only to your applications; other applications using the same tables do not need it.
- The relationship involves transient entity attributes.
- The relationship is a many-to-many relationship, which will be explained in the following section.

You will create associations in the hands-on practice.

Association Cardinality

Cardinality refers to the number of instances on each side of the relationship. The most common kind of relationship between tables is the one represented by a typical foreign key: a relationship where a row from the master table corresponds to any number of rows from the detail table. Each detail row has, at most, one master row, but a master row can have any number of detail rows (including zero). This kind of relationship has a cardinality of *one-to-many*. For example, the relationship between departments and the employees in those departments is one-to-many, as shown here:

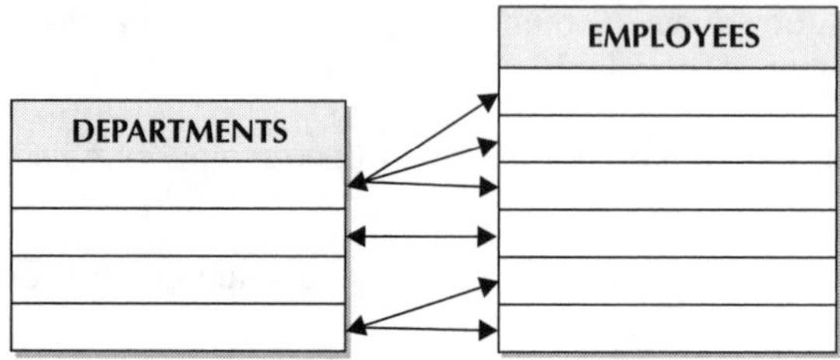

However, this is only one kind of relationship. Some relationships have a *one-to-one* cardinality, where there is a one-to-one correspondence between the rows of two tables. For example, you might have one table, DEPARTMENTS, containing basic information about departments, and another table, DEPARTMENTS_EXT, optionally containing more information for each row, as shown next:

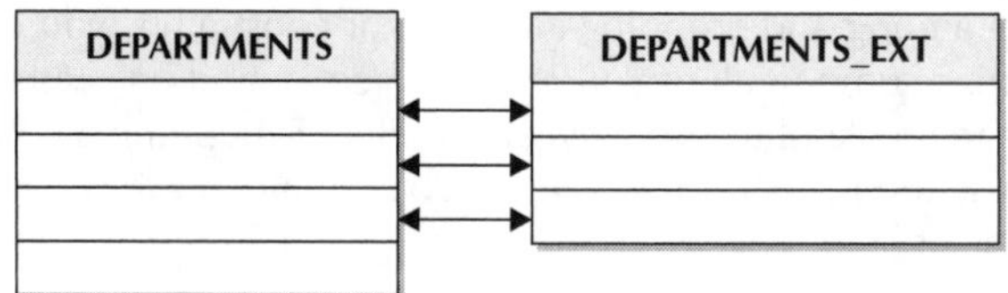

These relationships can also be represented by foreign keys.

The most complex kind of relationship is a *many-to-many* relationship, one where any number of rows from one table can be related to any number of rows from the other table. Consider the JOBS table, which lists all of the jobs in the company, and the EMPLOYEES table. A relationship exists between employees and all of the jobs they have held in the past.

This is not a one-to-one relationship, because an employee could have held any number of jobs. It is not a one-to-many relationship either, since either EMPLOYEES or JOBS could be considered the master. One possible relationship between the two tables is that a single employee may have held many jobs since joining the company. But another relationship is that every job has been held by a series of employees over the company's history. Each employee can correspond to many jobs, and each job can correspond to many employees, as shown here:

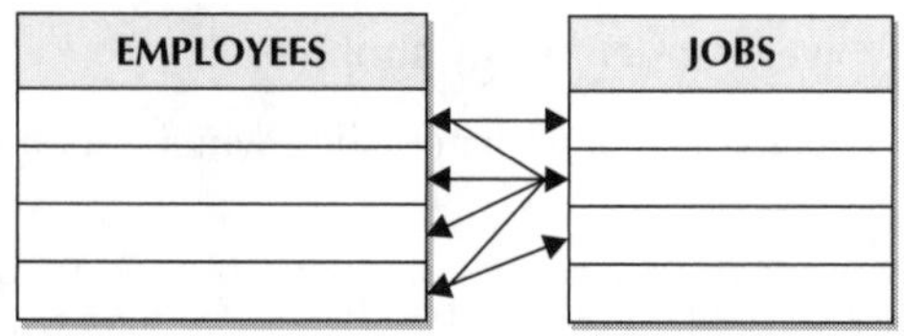

Unlike one-to-one and one-to-many relationships, implementing many-to-many relationships is not simply a matter of associating a foreign key in the detail table with a primary key in the master table. Instead, many-to-many relationships between two tables make use of a third table, called an intersection table.

An *intersection table* contains two foreign keys. One of them matches up with the primary key of one table, and the other matches up with the primary key of the other table as follows:

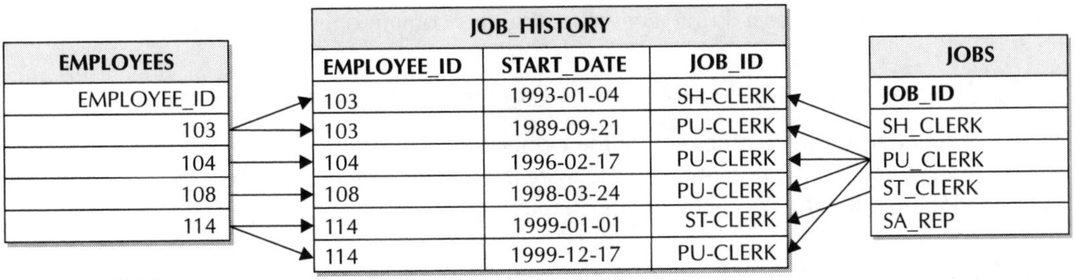

EMPLOYEES
EMPLOYEE_ID
103
104
108
114

JOB_HISTORY		
EMPLOYEE_ID	**START_DATE**	**JOB_ID**
103	1993-01-04	SH-CLERK
103	1989-09-21	PU-CLERK
104	1996-02-17	PU-CLERK
108	1998-03-24	PU-CLERK
114	1999-01-01	ST-CLERK
114	1999-12-17	PU-CLERK

JOBS
JOB_ID
SH_CLERK
PU_CLERK
ST_CLERK
SA_REP

This creates two one-to-many relationships. For example, in the EMPLOYEES-JOBS case, there is a one-to-many relationship with EMPLOYEES as the master and JOB_HISTORY as the detail, and another one-to-many relationship with JOBS as the master and JOB_HISTORY as the detail.

You can think of these two one-to-many relationships as representing a single many-to-many relationship, which relates rows from EMPLOYEES and JOBS if they share a JOB_HISTORY detail, as shown in the following illustration:

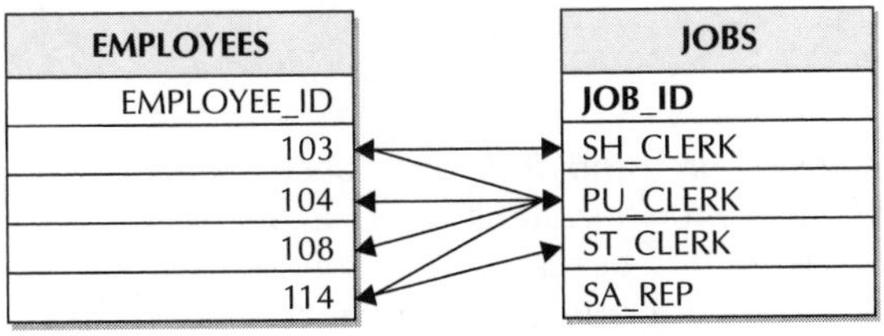

EMPLOYEES
EMPLOYEE_ID
103
104
108
114

JOBS
JOB_ID
SH_CLERK
PU_CLERK
ST_CLERK
SA_REP

Associations can represent relationships with any of these cardinalities: one-to-many, one-to-one, and many-to-many. You will create both a one-to-many and a many-to-many association in the hands-on practice.

Association Directionality and Accessor Attributes

The associations that JDeveloper automatically creates from foreign keys are *bi-directional*, meaning that they can be traversed in both directions. For any source (master) entity object instance, you can use the association to get its associated destination (detail) entity object instances, and from any destination entity object instance, you can use the association to get its corresponding source entity object instances.

You can also create associations that are uni-directional. *Uni-directional* associations can only be traversed in a single direction—most commonly from source to destination, although associations that can be traversed from destination to source are also possible. Directionality of associations is due to the presence or absence of accessor attributes. *Accessor attributes* are pseudo-attributes optionally created in entity object definitions when an association is created between them. An accessor attribute does not show up in the entity object definition's attribute list, but in all other respects it acts like another attribute. The purpose of the accessor attribute is to allow one entity object instance to retrieve associated entity object instances. For example, if you create the association EmpDeptFkAssoc between Employees and Departments, you can generate an accessor attribute in Employees that allows instances of Employees to retrieve associated instances of Departments, and/or an accessor attribute in Departments that allows instances of Departments to retrieve associated instances of Employees. Instead of containing a Domain or a common Java type such as a String, accessor attributes contain one of the following:

- **An associated entity object instance** if the other end of the association is a "one" end.
- **A row iterator** if the other end of the association is a "many" end. A *row iterator* is a kind of collection containing all the associated entity object instances. More information about row iterators is contained in Chapter 10.

If an accessor attribute exists only in the source entity object definition, the association is uni-directional, and can be traversed only from source to destination. If an accessor attribute exists only in the destination entity object definition, the association is also uni-directional, and can be traversed only from destination to source. If both entity object definitions have accessor attributes, the association is bi-directional.

The accessor attribute (if any) in the source entity object definition is called the *destination accessor attribute*, because it returns rows from the destination. The accessor attribute in the destination entity object definition is called the *source accessor attribute*, because it returns rows from the source.

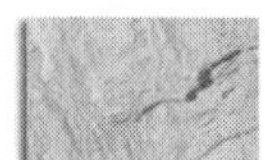

NOTE
Be careful not to confuse source and destination accessor attributes with the source and destination attributes for an association. Accessor attributes contain rows or sets of rows; the source and destination attributes of an association contain the keys that define the association.

On an ADF BC diagram, association directionality is represented by the presence or absence of arrows. A single arrow means a uni-directional association, with an accessor attribute in the entity object definition at the beginning of the arrow. A double arrow means a bi-directional association. The names of accessor attributes appear at either end of the association: The source accessor attribute near the source entity object definition, and the destination accessor attribute near the destination, as shown next:

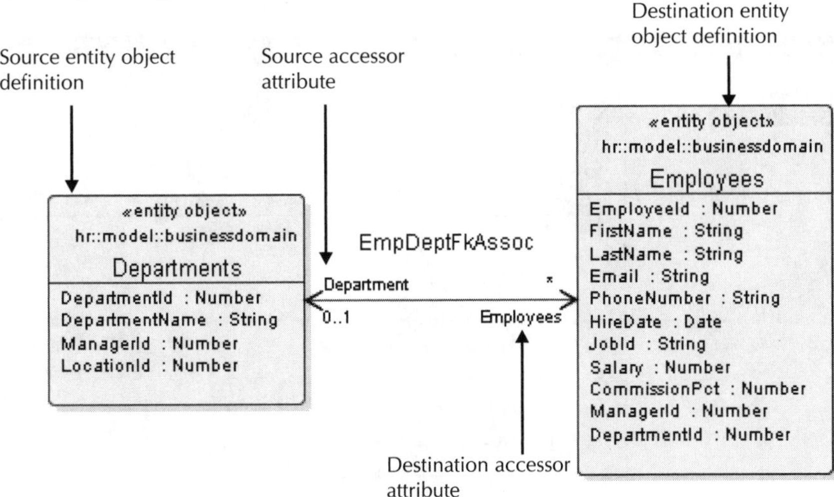

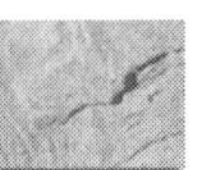

NOTE
Accessor attribute names will be displayed on both sides of the association, even if the association is uni-directional. These names indicate the name that the accessor attribute would have if it existed.

For a small application with a single developer, you can always create bi-directional associations. The primary reason to make an association uni-directional is if you do not have permission to change one of the associated entity object definitions. Making the association uni-directional allows you to create it without putting an accessor attribute in an entity object definition you cannot change.

Compositions

Consider two different sorts of foreign key relationships: relationships such as the one between employees and the departments that employ them, and those like the one between line items in a purchase order and the order itself. Certainly, most employees belong to a department, but an employee is not, strictly speaking, part of a department. Employees exist independently of their departments; a company could eliminate a department without necessarily eliminating its members. By contrast, a line item is part of a purchase order, rather than an independently existing thing. It makes no sense to delete an order without deleting all of its line items.

An association such as the one between line items and purchase orders, where the detail is part of the master, is called a *composition.* You cannot delete a master in a composition without deleting all of its details.

If JDeveloper detects that a database foreign key has ON DELETE CASCADE set, it will automatically create the corresponding association as a composition. You can also make an association into a composition on the Association Properties page of the Association Editor, as shown in Figure 9-1.

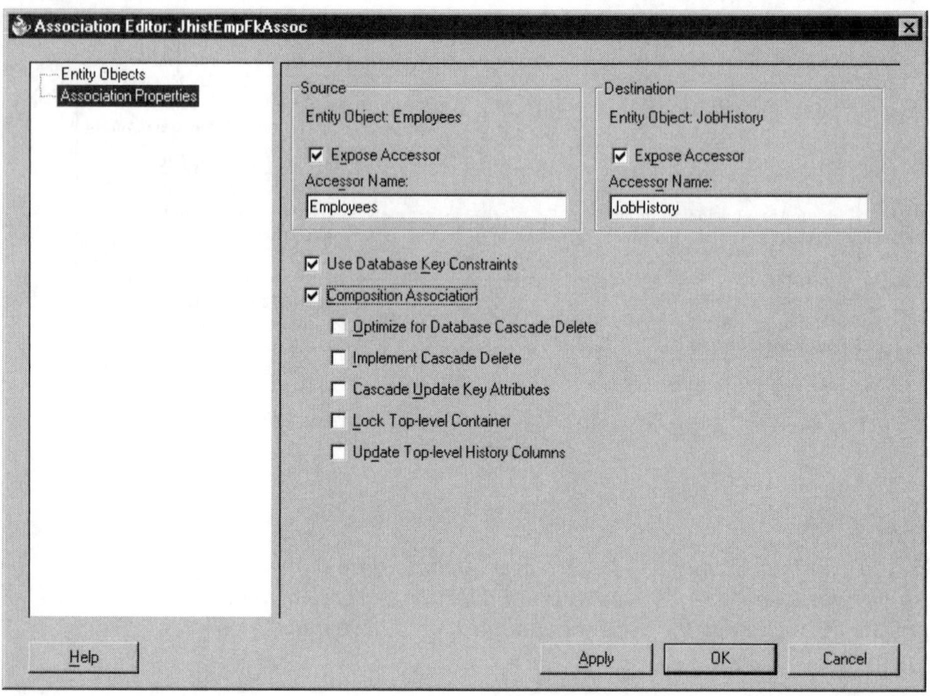

FIGURE 9-1. *The Association Properties page of the Association Editor*

Checking the *Composition Association* checkbox will make the association into a composition. The checkboxes below it affect the behavior of the composition:

- *Optimize for Database Cascade Delete* prevents the application from issuing explicit DML commands to delete detail rows when the master row is deleted. If the database is doing this automatically (because ON DELETE CASCADE is set), this will improve efficiency.
- *Implement Cascade Delete* deletes detail entity object instances when the master is deleted. If this checkbox is unchecked, attempting to delete a master entity object instance when it still has details will throw an exception rather than delete the details.
- *Cascade Update Key Attributes* makes destination attributes stay synchronized with source attributes. For example, consider the association EmpJhistFkAssoc. The source attribute is Employees' EmployeeId attribute. The destination attribute is JobHistory's EmployeeId attribute. If *Cascade Update Key Attributes* is checked, and an Employees instance's EmployeeId attribute is changed, the EmployeeId attributes of its detail JobHistory instances will change to the same value.

The other two checkboxes deal with ADF BC's locking and security mechanisms. For more information about these mechanisms, see the online help system topics, "Building J2EE Applications\Working with the Business Tier\Developing Oracle ADF Business Components\Managing Transactions" and "Building J2EE Applications\Working with the Business Tier\Developing Oracle ADF Business Components\Implementing Security in Oracle ADF Business Components."

Representing Oracle Object Types

As mentioned earlier in this chapter, ADF BC automatically associates standard SQL datatypes with Java classes. However, some table columns are of custom Oracle object types. As mentioned in Chapter 8, Oracle object type columns are represented as custom domains.

When you create an entity object definition based on a table with an Oracle object type column, JDeveloper automatically creates a custom domain for you and maps the column to an entity attribute with that domain as its Java type. If you have object types embedded in object types, JDeveloper recursively creates custom domains for all of them.

CAUTION
ADF BC does not support non-Oracle object types.

Like an entity object definition, a custom domain has a number of attributes (one for each column in the Oracle object type). All attributes have Java types, which can be either standard Java classes or other domains.

However, a custom domain is much simpler than an entity object definition. All of the features of tables that do not apply to Oracle object types are left out. Domains do not need (and cannot have) a primary key. They do not have column constraints. They are not the ends of associations (although they can be used to associate entity object definitions, just like any other entity attribute type).

Domains are not, however, used to represent Oracle object types that occur in object tables. If you create a table using CREATE TABLE <table> OF <object_type>, and you base an entity object definition on that table, JDeveloper will not create a domain to represent the object type; instead, it will simply create entity attributes for each of the object type's columns.

You can delete attributes from domains, add transient attributes to them, or change attribute properties (except for column constraints, which domains do not use), just as you can for entity object definitions.

For example, consider an Oracle object type called ADDRESS_TYP, with the following definition:

```
ADDRESS_TYP AS OBJECT
  (STREET_ADDRESS VARCHAR2(20),
   POSTAL_CODE VARCHAR2(12),
   CITY VARCHAR2(30),
   STATE_PROVINCE VARCHAR2(25),
   COUNTRY_ID VARCHAR2(2));
```

You could create a table called CUSTOMERS that uses this object type as follows:

```
CREATE TABLE CUSTOMERS
  ( CUSTOMER_ID NUMBER(6),
    CUST_FIRST_NAME VARCHAR2(20),
    CUST_LAST_NAME VARCHAR2(20),
    CUST_ADDRESS ADDRESS_TYP );
```

If you create an entity object definition from the table, the entity object definition will have attributes called CustomerId, CustFirstName, CustLastName, and CustAddress, and you will automatically get a domain, AddressTyp, with attributes StreetAddress, PostalCode, City, StateProvince, and CountryId.

On the other hand, you can create a table called ADDRESSES as follows:

```
CREATE TABLE ADDRESSES
  OF ADDRESS_TYP;
```

If you then create an entity object from ADDRESSES, the entity object will have attributes called StreetAddress, PostalCode, City, StateProvince, and CountryId, and no domain will be created.

Business Components and Database Object Generation

It is natural for a programmer with a database focus to think of entity object definitions and associations as representing database tables and constraints. For such a programmer, database objects are primary, and objects in the business services are used to represent these database objects in an application.

Some programmers, namely those with a UML modeling or J2EE focus, will think of this approach as backwards. To these programmers, objects in the business services (such as entity object definitions) and the relationships between those objects come first. Database objects are just used to handle persistence for these business service objects. Generally, these programmers do not want to design entity object definitions and associations to represent existing database tables. Instead, they want to design entity object definitions and associations from scratch and generate database tables and constraints to handle their persistence. JDeveloper supports this development style as well, allowing you to generate database tables from entity object definitions and foreign key constraints from associations.

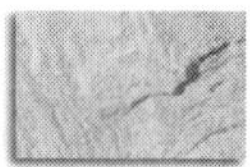

CAUTION

Although the JDeveloper table-generation features allow you to assign tablespaces and storage conditions, they are not a substitute for a full-featured database modeling tool such as Oracle Designer or the database diagramming capabilities of JDeveloper. In general, it is best to use generation from business domain components to create only a few relatively small tables needed by a single application. Even then, you should consult closely with your data architect and DBA to make sure you are not breaking rules of efficient database design.

Creating Entity Object Definitions for Table Generation

When you create an ADF BC diagram, the Component Palette displays a list of business components, as shown in Figure 9-2.

You can create a new entity object definition by clicking the Entity Object icon, and then clicking on your diagram. You can type the name of the entity object definition and a list of its attributes directly in the diagram. You will do this in the hands-on practice. When you generate a table from the entity object definition, the table will have one column for each entity attribute, except for attributes marked as transient.

NOTE
Do not add foreign key attributes (that is, the destination attributes for planned associations) to entity object definitions. JDeveloper will do this for you when you create the association.

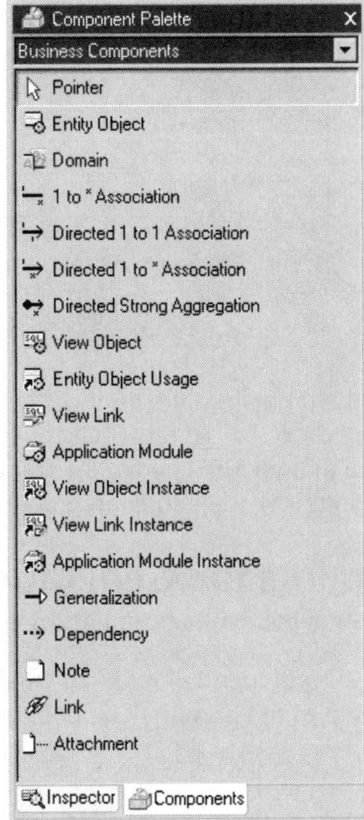

FIGURE 9-2. *The ADF BC Component Palette*

The table names generated by JDeveloper respect the conventions that JDeveloper uses for deriving entity object definition names from table names. For example:

- An entity object definition named EmployeeBonuses will correspond to a table named EMPLOYEE_BONUSES.
- An entity attribute named EmployeeId will correspond to a table column named EMPLOYEE_ID.

If you want to change the name of the table, you can do it on the Name page of the Entity Object Editor, as shown next:

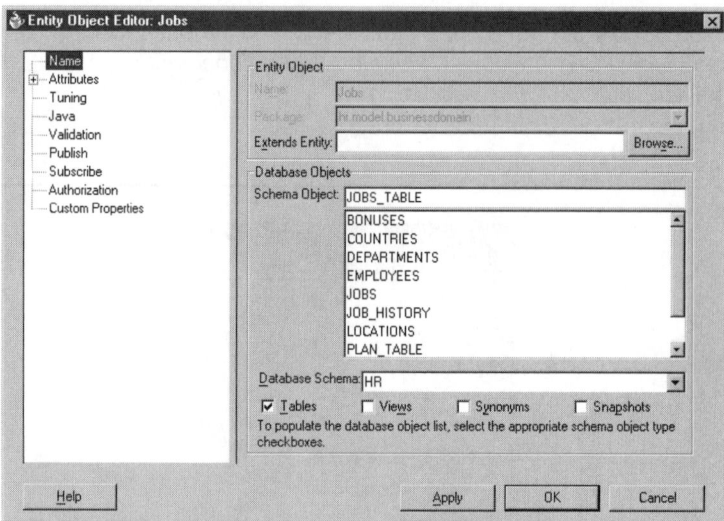

If you have already generated the table from the entity object, changing the *Schema Object* name in this property editor will not drop the old table. Changing the name of the entity object will not affect the name of the table that you will generate. You can also change the name of database table columns. You will do this in the hands-on practice.

Creating Table Constraints for Generation

You can generate the following types of database constraints by editing the entity object definition:

- **Primary Key** By default, JDeveloper will make the first attribute you type in the diagram the sole component of the primary key, but you can add other attributes to the primary key.
- **Not Null**
- **Unique** if the constraint applies to a single column.

You set these constraints directly in the Entity Object Editor or in the Attribute Editor, which you will do in the hands-on practice.

You can generate a foreign key constraint by creating an association and ensuring that *Use Database Key Constraints* is checked on the Association Properties page of the Association Editor, as shown in Figure 9-1.

More complex constraints require the creation of an entity object property called an *entity constraint*. Entity constraints can be defined by selecting the entity object definition and using the right-click menu option New Entity Constraint. They are listed and can be edited in the Business Components Project displayed in the Structure window when the entity object definition is selected in the Model project. You must create an entity constraint to generate the following types of database constraints:

- **Unique constraints** that are composed of more than one column
- **Check constraints**

You might also use this wizard if you want to generate primary key, not null, or single-column unique constraints, and have more fine-grain control over them than can be achieved by modifying entity attributes or creating associations. For example, you might want to be able to choose a name for the constraint (as opposed to accepting ADF's default name), or allow validation to be deferred until a COMMIT operation.

You can define entity constraints as follows:

1. On the entity object definition's node in the Application Navigator, select New Entity Constraint from the right-click menu to open the Create Entity Constraint Wizard. Click Next if the Welcome page appears.
2. On the Name page, in the *Name* field, enter a name that BC4J will use to identify the entity constraint. In the *Constraint Name* field, identify the name to use for the database constraint. Click Next.
3. On the Attributes page, select the entity attributes that correspond to the columns to which this constraint applies and click Next. For a check constraint, you do not need to specify attributes.
4. On the Properties page, select the type of constraint you want to create as shown here for a check constraint:

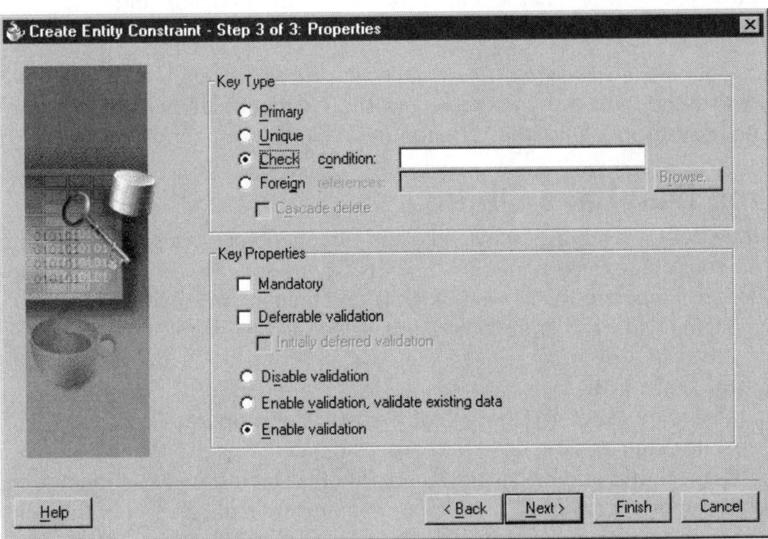

5. To create any constraint except not null, select the constraint type in the Key Type panel. To create a not null constraint, select the *Mandatory* checkbox in the Key Properties panel.
6. Still on the Properties page, select whether you want to allow the constraint check to occur only when a COMMIT is issued (the *Deferrable validation* checkbox) and, if so, whether you want it to be deferred by default (the *Initially deferred validation* checkbox).
7. Still on the Properties page, select whether you want the constraint to start as disabled (*Disable validation*), to be enabled for both new and existing data (*Enable validation, validate existing data*), or to be enabled for new data but not checked against existing data (*Enable validation*).
8. Click Finish to create the constraint.

The entity constraint will appear in the Structure window. You can edit or delete the constraint from its right-click menu in the Structure window. You will create a multi-column unique constraint in the hands-on practice.

Creating Domains for Oracle Object Type Generation

In addition to creating entity object definitions that will be used when you generate tables, you can create domains to generate Oracle object types. You can create a domain in much the same way as you create an entity object definition: Click the Domain icon in the component palette (as shown in Figure 9-2), and then click on your diagram to create a new domain. You can type the name of the domain and a list of its attributes by typing directly in the diagram, just as you would for an entity object definition. (Although you will not create a domain in the hands-on practice, you will create an entity object definition. The process is very similar.)

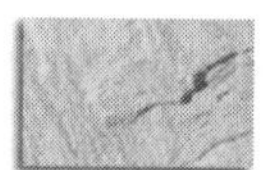

CAUTION
You can only name a domain when you first drop it onto a diagram. Once created, you cannot rename it later, but must instead delete and re-create it.

JDeveloper uses the same naming conventions to create Oracle object types from domains as it uses to create tables from entity object definitions.

Generating Database Objects

You can generate database tables, constraints, and Oracle object types for all of the business components on your diagram by right clicking outside any specific component (in the white space) and selecting Generate | Database Objects for Diagram. You can also generate a single table by right clicking within an entity object and selecting Generate | Database Objects.

Generating and Data Loss

If you select a table to be generated that already exists, JDeveloper will warn you that generating the table will first drop the existing table and any associated triggers. This will result in the loss of related database constraints and/or data. Triggers for other tables, views, and code that reference the table will have to be recompiled. If the table contains no data, and all of the constraints were generated from these business domain components, you can ignore this caution. However, because JDeveloper regenerates existing tables using DROP TABLE and CREATE TABLE commands rather than ALTER TABLE, you will lose existing data in the table, all triggers on the table, and any constraints not represented in the business domain components, by generating an existing table. If you need to alter a table with data or triggers, you should do so with SQL*Plus or another database tool.

Hands-on Practice: Represent the HR Schema

In this practice, you will create entity object definitions and associations to represent the tables in the HR schema. The package you create will involve a transient attribute, a column constraint, an entity object definition to generate a new table, and two new associations of different cardinality.

This practice steps you through the following phases:

I. Create an application workspace and default business domain components

II. Change entity attributes

- Add a transient attribute
- Make an attribute mandatory

III. Clean up accessor attribute names

IV. Create business domain components for table generation

- Create an entity object definition
- Create a one-to-many association
- Rename a table column
- Define not null constraints
- Define a multi-column unique constraint

V. Generate the new table and constraints

VI. Create a many-to-many association

VII. Test the business domain components

- Create default data model components
- Open the Business Component Browser
- Test a mandatory attribute
- Test transient and persistent attributes
- Test a many-to-many association
- Populate the BONUSES table

I. Create an Application Workspace and Default Business Domain Components

This phase creates an application workspace with default business domain components in the Model project.

1. On the Applications node in the Application Navigator, select New Application Workspace from the right-click menu. The Create Application Workspace dialog opens. Enter the following values:

   Application Name as "HR"
   Application Package Prefix as "hr"
   Application Template as "Web Application [Default]"

2. Leave the default directory name. Click OK. A new application workspace, HR, appears in the Navigator.
3. Click Save All.
4. On the Model node of the HR application workspace, select New from the right-click menu. The New Gallery opens.
5. In the Categories pane, select Business Tier\Business Components. In the Items pane, select Business Components Diagram.

   Additional Information: In Chapter 8, you created business components using the Business Components from Tables Wizard and then dragged them onto a diagram. Now, you will create them directly on the diagram by dragging them to the diagram from the database.

6. Click OK. The Create Business Components Diagram dialog opens.
7. Enter the following values:

   Name as "Business Domain Diagram"
   Package as "hr.model.businessdomain"

8. Click OK. An empty diagram opens.
9. Open the Connection Navigator.
10. Under Connections\Database\HR\HR\Tables, group select (CTRL-click) the following tables and drag them onto the diagram:

    - DEPARTMENTS
    - EMPLOYEES
    - JOB_HISTORY
    - JOBS

11. When the Create From Tables dialog appears, click OK.

    Additional Information: If your project had a different technology scope, different options (other than Business Components Entity Object Components) would be available. These options are described in Chapter 14.

What Just Happened? You created an application workspace with default business domain components, including entity object definitions for the DEPARTMENTS, EMPLOYEES, JOBS, and JOB_HISTORY tables. A rearranged version of the resulting diagram is shown in Figure 9-3.

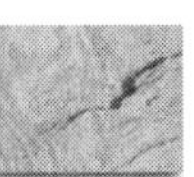

NOTE
If your diagram looks messy, and you want to redraw all or part of it, you can delete an entity object definition from the diagram. This will automatically also delete the associations to/from that definition. However, you have not deleted the definition or its associations from the Model project. If you now want to add them back to the diagram, click on the definition and its associations in the navigator and drag them all onto the diagram.

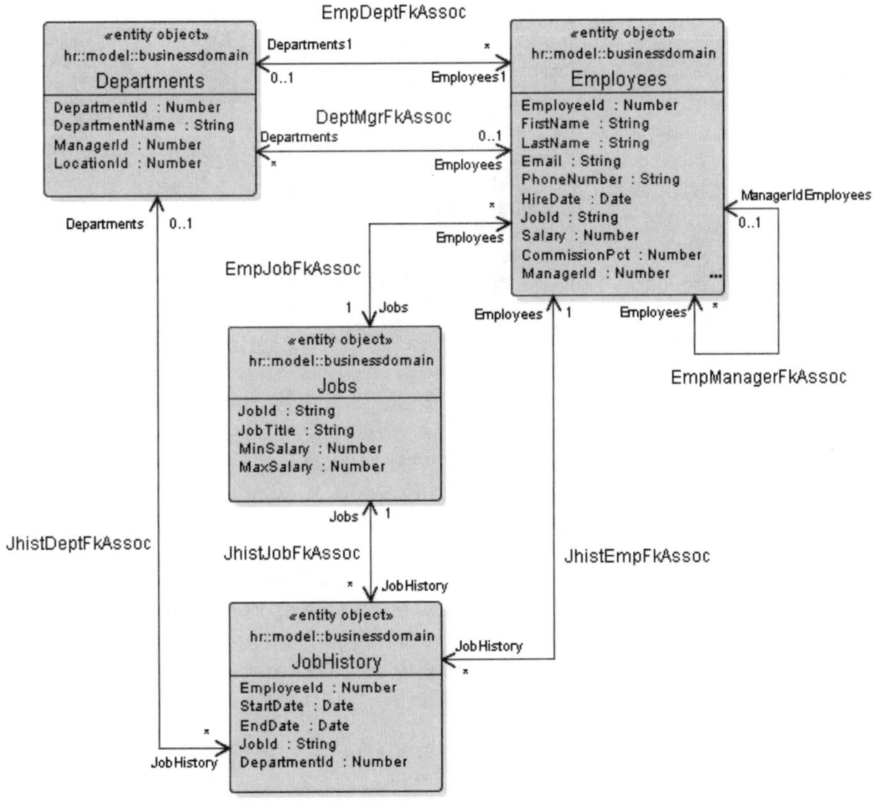

FIGURE 9-3. *The default business domain components*

II. Change Entity Attributes

In this phase, you modify the Employees entity object definition to add a transient attribute and make an existing attribute mandatory.

Add a Transient Attribute

You need to add a transient attribute for yearly pay. As mentioned, in contrast to persistent attribute values, a transient attribute holds a value that is not stored in the database. Use the following steps to accomplish this task:

1. On the diagram, select the Employees entity object definition. Small square drag handles will appear.
2. Use the drag handles to expand the Employees entity object definition so that you can see a dotted box at the bottom of the list of attributes, as shown here:

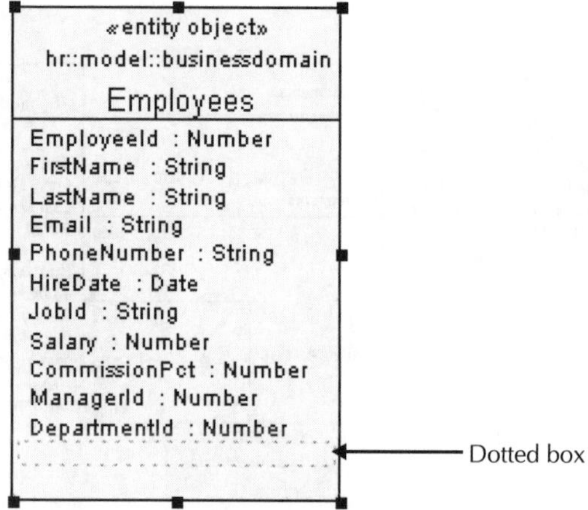

3. Click once to select the dotted box and then click again so that a text cursor appears at the left side of the box. Do not double click.
4. Enter "YearlyPay : Number" and press ENTER.

   Additional Information: This adds a new attribute, YearlyPay, to the Employees entity object definition. YearlyPay has the Number domain as its datatype. In Chapter 11, you will use this attribute to calculate an estimated yearly pay for an employee, based on that employee's monthly salary and commission. For now, it will be an uncalculated transient attribute.
5. Double click the YearlyPay attribute. The Attribute Editor opens.

Additional Information: The Attribute Editor allows you to change settings for a particular attribute. Most of these settings can also be accessed under the Attributes node of the Entity Object Editor. You can also access the Attribute Editor from the right-click menu on the attribute node in the Structure window.

6. Uncheck the *Persistent* checkbox. This makes the attribute transient. The dialog should look like this:

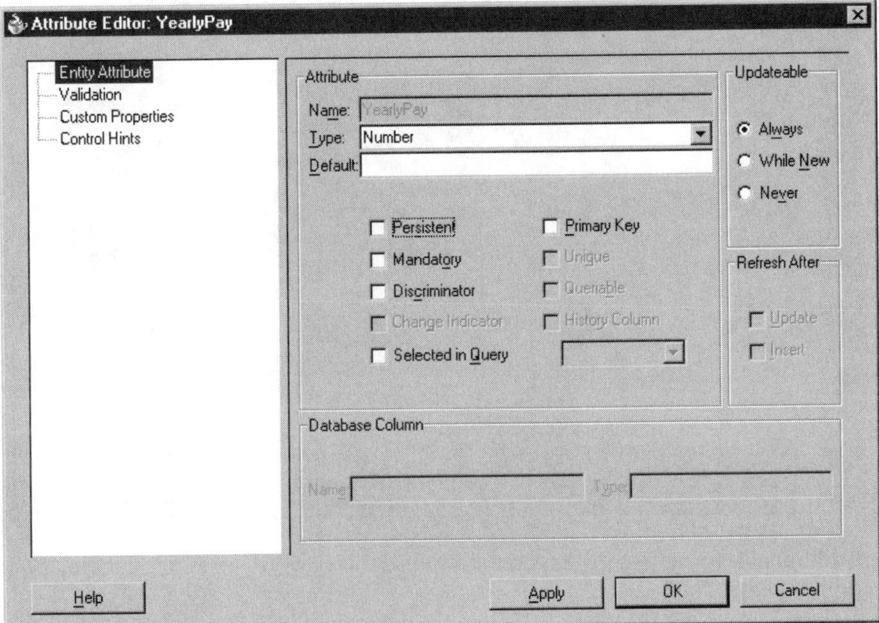

7. Click OK to close the editor.

Make an Attribute Mandatory

You can make an attribute mandatory using the following steps:

1. On the diagram, in the Departments entity object definition, double click the ManagerId attribute to open the Attribute Editor.

   Additional Information: You can also select Properties from the right-click menu on the attribute. The MANAGER_ID column does not have a not null constraint in the database, so dragging the tables from the database node to create the objects did not automatically make ManagerId a mandatory attribute. However, your business requirement for this application is that departments must have a manager.

2. Check the *Mandatory* checkbox, as shown in the following illustration:

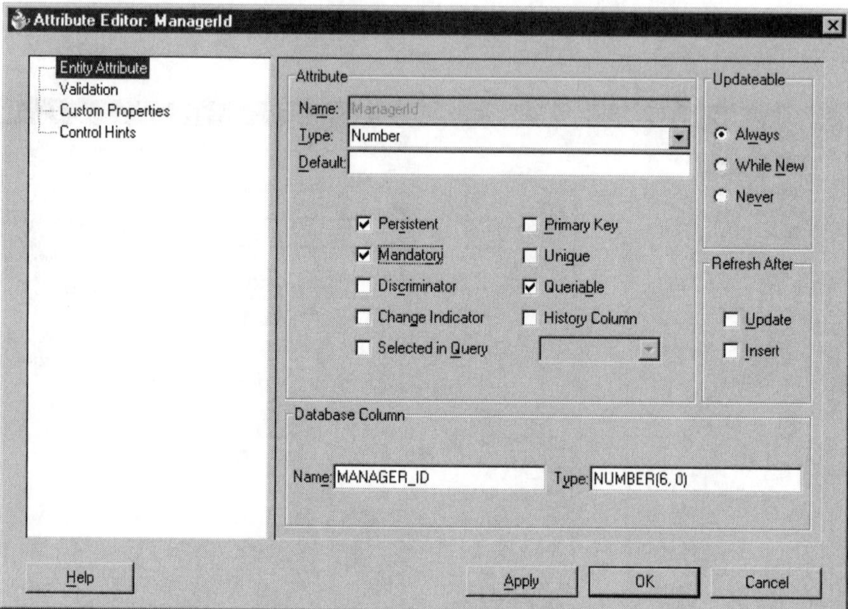

Additional Information: You could also use this page to mark an attribute as part of the primary key.

3. Click OK.

4. Click Save All.

What Just Happened? The transient YearlyPay attribute you just added will be stored in the ADF BC layer for as long as the application is running, but will not be stored in the database. In Chapter 10, you will use this attribute to store a calculated value. The mandatory ManagerId attribute will throw an exception if it is not populated when a record is inserted or updated.

III. Clean Up Accessor Attribute Names

In this phase, you will change the names of the accessor attributes for the automatically created associations. When you use these attributes in Chapter 10, user-friendly names will make the code much more readable.

1. In the diagram, on the association DeptMgrFkAssoc, click once on the source accessor attribute (it will be called "Employees" or "Employees1") to select it, and click again to make the name editable. Do not double click.

2. Change the name of the accessor attribute to "Manager".

3. Similarly, change the name of the destination accessor attribute to "ManagedDepartments".

4. In the diagram, make the following changes for other accessor attributes:

Association	Old Source Accessor Name	New Source Accessor Name	Old Destination Accessor Name	New Destination Accessor Name
EmpDeptFkAssoc	Departments or Departments1	Department	Employees or Employees1	Employees
EmpJobFkAssoc	Jobs	Job	Employees	EmployeesWithJob
EmpManagerFkAssoc	ManagerIdEmployees	Manager	Employees	Reports
JhistDeptFkAssoc	Departments	DeptDetails	JobHistory	History
JhistJobFkAssoc	Jobs	JobDetails	JobHistory	History
JhistEmpFkAssoc	Employees	EmployeeDetails	JobHistory	History

What Just Happened? You changed the names of the accessor attributes for seven associations to make them easier to understand. For example, within an Employee entity object instance, that employee's manager is now accessible through the accessor attribute "Manager." The people who report to the employee are now accessible through the accessor attribute "Reports." Your diagram should now look something like the one in Figure 9-4.

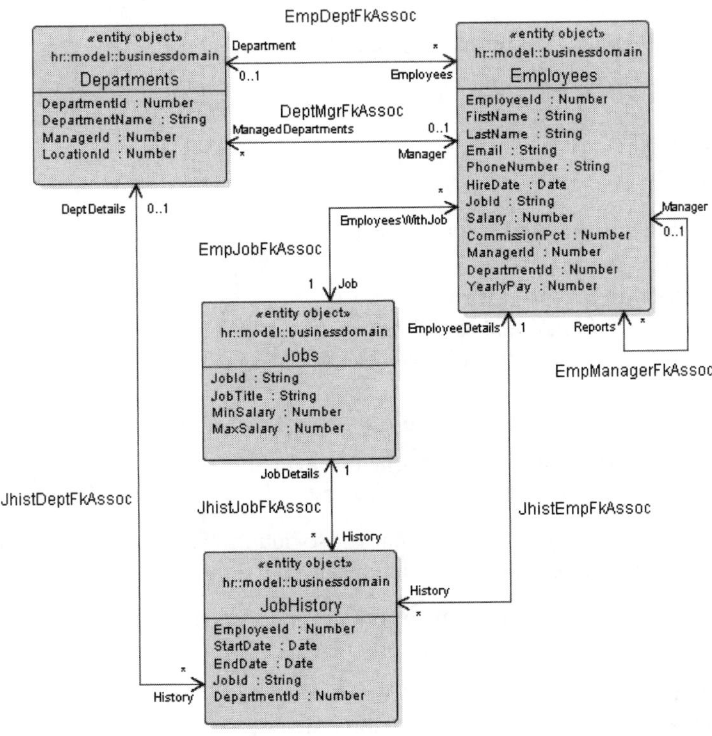

FIGURE 9-4. *The business domain components with changed accessor attribute names*

IV. Create Business Domain Components for Table Generation

In this phase, you will create an entity object definition that is not based on an existing table. Then, you will create an association, change attribute properties, and create an entity constraint, all of which will allow you to generate a table and its constraints.

Create an Entity Object Definition

Create an entity object to represent employee bonuses using the following steps:

1. In the Component Palette, Business Components should be listed. Click the Entity Object icon, and click a blank space in the diagram.

   Additional Information: JDeveloper creates an entity object definition and allows you to type in its name.

2. Enter "Bonuses" as the entity object's name and press ENTER to exit the edit field.
3. Click once on the dotted box to select it and again to begin to type in attributes.

   Additional Information: JDeveloper creates a default first attribute, attr, of type String. When you start typing, you will automatically override this choice.

4. Enter "BonusId : Number" as the first attribute and press ENTER.
5. Enter the following attributes, pressing ENTER after each:
   - Year : Number
   - Quarter : Number
   - Amount : Number
6. Click outside the entity object to finish entering attributes.

Create a One-to-Many Association

Create a one-to-many, bi-directional association between Employees and Bonuses, with accessor attributes on both sides, by using the following steps:

1. In the Component Palette, click the "Directed 1 to * Association" icon.

   Additional Information: The associations available on the Component Palette are not the ones you are most likely to need. The available associations follow:

   - **1 to * Association** A one-to-many association with no accessor attributes. As mentioned earlier, these associations are not directly useful.
   - **Directed 1 to 1 Association** A one-to-one association with an accessor attribute in the source entity object definition only.
   - **Directed 1 to * Association** A one-to-many association with an accessor attribute in the source entity object definition only.
   - **Directed Strong Aggregation** A one-to-many composition with an accessor attribute in the source entity object definition only.

Since you will create a bi-directional association, with accessor attributes in both the source and destination entity object definitions, none of these will suffice. However, it is easy to add an accessor attribute to the destination entity object.

2. Click once on the Employees entity object definition and once on the Bonuses entity object definition in that order to draw the association line.

   Additional Information: JDeveloper creates a one-to-many association, with Employees as the source and Bonuses as the destination. It also adds a destination attribute for the association, EmployeesEmployeeId, matching the name of the source entity object definition and source attribute. This is the equivalent of a foreign key column in a database table, and it will create that column if the entity object is used to generate a table.

3. Using the technique of selecting the name, clicking, and overtyping the default value, change the name of the association to "EmpBonusFkAssoc," the name of the source accessor attribute to "Employee," and the name of the destination accessor attribute to "Bonuses."

   Additional Information: The source accessor attribute name does not do anything yet, since there is no source accessor. However, JDeveloper will remember this name and use it for the accessor attribute if you decide to create it later.

4. Double click the association line to open the Association Editor.

5. Select the Association Properties node.

6. Check the *Expose Accessor* checkbox in the Source area to create the source accessor attribute and make the association bi-directional.

   Additional Information: Be sure the *Use Database Key Constraints* checkbox is checked. This defines a foreign key constraint that will be generated from the association if the entity object is generated to a table.

7. Click OK to close the editor.

   Additional Information: Note that the association in the diagram now has arrows at both ends, to indicate that it is bi-directional.

Rename a Table Column

This section renames the table column that will be generated by the entity attribute EmployeesEmployeeId.

1. In the diagram, on the Bonuses entity object definition, double click EmployeesEmployeeId to open the Attribute Editor.

2. In the Database Column area, change the value in the Name field to "EMPLOYEE_ID". Click Apply and OK.

3. Click Save All.

   Additional Information: EMPLOYEE_ID is a more natural name for a database column than EMPLOYEES_EMPLOYEE_ID.

Define Not Null Constraints

This section adds Mandatory flags to Year, Quarter, and Amount.

1. In the diagram, double click the Bonuses entity object definition, to open the Entity Object Editor. Expand the Attributes node.

   Additional Information: In addition to editing attributes with the Attribute Editor, you can edit them inside the Entity Object Editor.

2. Select Year and check the *Mandatory* checkbox.

   Additional Information: In addition to being enforced at the ADF BC level, this will generate a not null constraint when you generate the BONUSES table. BonusId is already marked as the primary key because it was the first attribute you entered.

3. Repeat step 2 for the attributes Quarter and Amount.

4. Click OK to close the editor.

Define a Multi-Column Unique Constraint

In this section, you will create an entity constraint to require the combination of YEAR, QUARTER, and EMPLOYEE_ID columns in the BONUSES table to be unique, that is, to prevent any employee from receiving two bonuses in the same quarter of the same year.

1. In the Application Navigator on the Bonuses entity object definition (under hr.model.businessdomain), select New Entity Constraint from the right-click menu to open the Create Entity Constraint Wizard. Click Next if the Welcome page appears.

2. On the Name page, enter the following values:

   Name as "BonusesUniqueKey"
   Constraint Name as "BONUSES_UK"

3. Click Next. On the Attributes page, select Year, Quarter, and EmployeesEmployeeId in the *Available* list, and click ">" to add them to the *Selected* list. Click Next.

4. On the Properties page, select Unique, leave the other settings as they are, and click Finish.

5. Click Save All.

What Just Happened? You created an entity object definition, Bonuses, and added attributes to it. Then, you defined a one-to-many association between Employees and Bonuses, renamed a table column for the BONUSES table (which you will create in the next phase), and defined not null constraints and a multi-column unique constraint.

V. Generate the New Table and Constraints

In this phase, you will generate the BONUSES table, the foreign key constraint based on the EmpBonusesFkAssoc association, the constraints you specified, and the primary key constraint JDeveloper specified for you automatically.

1. In the diagram on the Bonuses entity object definition, select Generate | Database Objects from the right-click menu.

   Additional Information: This generates the BONUSES table and its constraints.

2. In the Create Database Object Summary dialog, click Show SQL.

   Additional Information: This displays the DDL statements used to generate the table and constraints. This is for information purposes only. The table has already been created when you see this dialog.

3. Click OK and OK again to close the dialogs.

4. In the Connection Navigator, on Connections\Database\HR\HR\Tables, select Refresh from the right-click menu.

   Additional Information: The BONUSES table will appear in the tree.

What Just Happened? You generated the table and constraints.

VI. Create a Many-to-Many Association

This phase creates a many-to-many association between the Employees entity object definition and the Jobs entity object definition that links each employee with every job he or she has held.

1. In the Component Palette, click the "Directed 1 to * Association" icon.

   Additional Information: As mentioned before, the associations available in the palette are limited. You will change this association to a bi-directional many-to-many association later.

2. Click once on the Employees entity object definition and once on the Jobs entity object definition in that order to draw the association line.

   Additional Information: This creates the association and a destination attribute, EmployeesEmployeeId. You will actually use JobId as the eventual destination attribute and delete EmployeesEmployeeId. Do not delete it yet, since the association currently depends on it. Change the name of the association to EmpPastJobsAssoc.

3. Change the name of the source accessor to PastHolders and the name of the destination accessor to PastJobs.

4. Click the "1" beside the source end of the association twice to make it editable. Do not double click.

5. Change the value to "*" and click elsewhere on the diagram.

   Additional Information: This changes the cardinality of the association from one-to-many to many-to-many. You can also change the cardinality in the Association Editor.

6. Double click the association to open the Association Editor, and select the Entity Objects node.

7. If it is not already selected in the *Select Source Attribute* area, select hr.model.businessdomain\Employees\EmployeeId.

8. In the *Select Intersection Attribute* tree, select hr.model.businessdomain\JobHistory\EmployeeId.

9. Click the left-hand Add button to add the source/intersection attribute pair. The page should look as shown next:

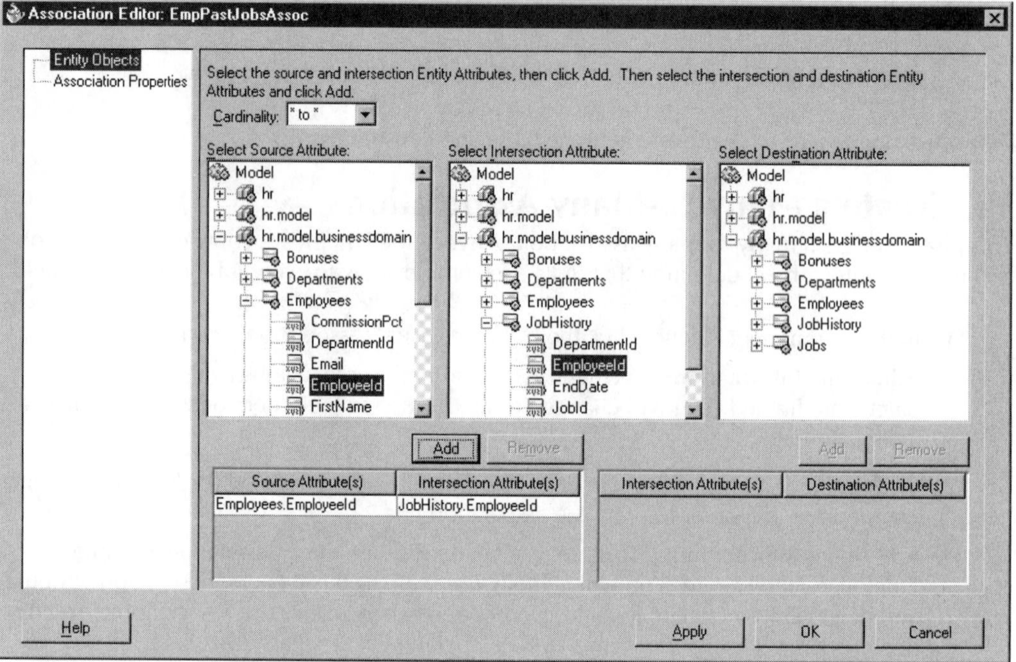

10. In the *Select Destination Attribute* tree, select hr.model.businessdomain\Jobs\JobId.

11. In the *Select Intersection Attribute* tree, select hr.model.businessdomain\JobHistory\JobId.

12. Click the right-hand Add button to add the destination/intersection attribute pair. The page should look as shown next:

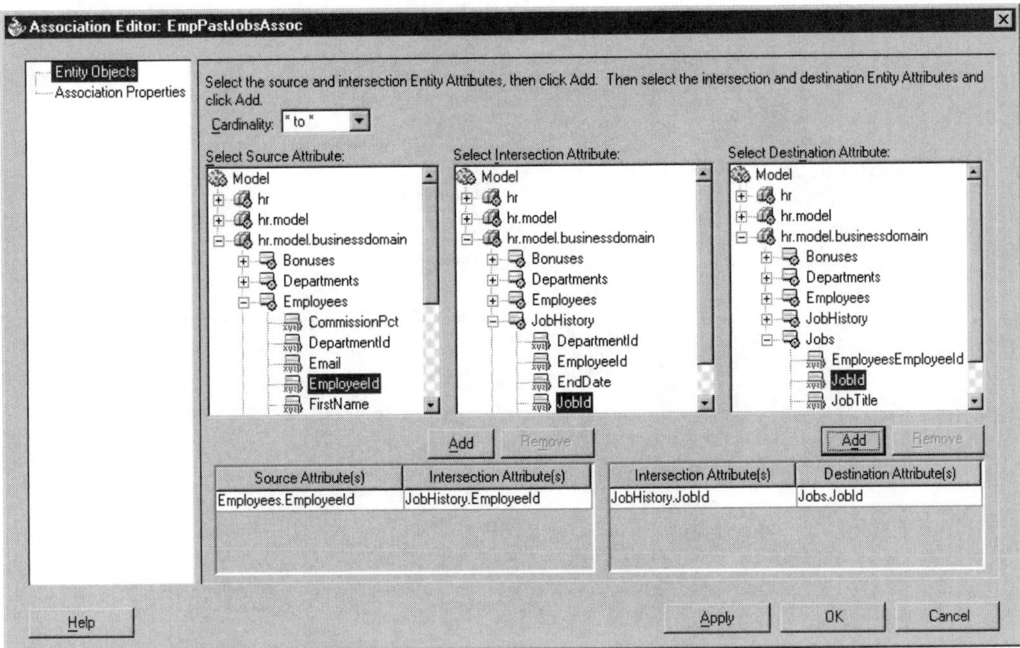

13. Select the Association Properties node.
14. In the Source area, check *Expose Accessor.*
15. Click OK.
16. In the Jobs entity object definition in the diagram, on the EmployeesEmployeeId attribute, select Delete from the right-click menu.
17. Click Save All.

What Just Happened? The association between Employees and Jobs was initially created as one-to-many. You changed this to a many-to-many association. The diagram should appear like the one in Figure 9-5.

VII. Test the Business Domain Components

In this phase, you will create default data model components and use them to test your business domain components.

Create Default Data Model Components

Create default data model components for your existing business domain components:

1. In a blank area of the diagram, select Generate | Default Data Model Components for Diagram from the right-click menu to open the Create Default Data Model Components Wizard.
2. Click Next if the Welcome page appears.

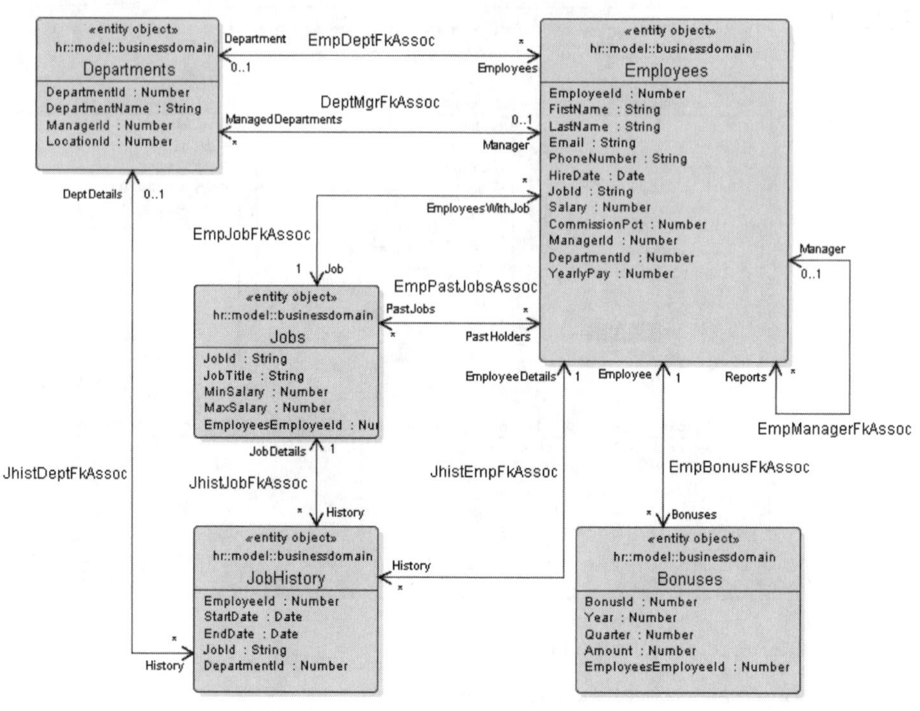

FIGURE 9-5. *The business domain diagram with the Bonuses entity object definition and EmpPastJobsAssoc association*

3. On the View Objects and View Links page, enter "hr.model.datamodel" in the *Package* field. Click Next.

4. On the Application Module page, enter "HrTestModule" in the *Name* field. Click Next.

5. Click Finish to generate the default data model components.

   Additional Information: Applications such as the Business Component Browser (introduced in Chapter 8) cannot interact directly with business domain components. By generating default data model components (one view object definition with a simple SELECT * query for each entity object definition, one view link definition for each association, and an application module with every possible combination of view object and view link instances), you can create a window into the functioning of your business domain components.

6. Click Save All.

Open the Business Component Browser

The Business Component Browser can be opened to test an application module and its associated business components using the following steps:

1. In the Application Navigator, select Test from the right-click menu on the HrTestModule node in the hr.model.datamodel package.
2. When the Oracle Business Component Browser – Connect dialog appears, click Connect. The main page of the Oracle Business Component Browser will appear, showing the data model for HrTestModule on the left.

Test a Mandatory Attribute

You can test a mandatory attribute using the following steps:

1. In the Business Component Browser, double click DepartmentsView1 to display the first row of DepartmentsView1 in the tester.
2. Erase Department 10's manager ID.
3. Click the blue right-arrow to scroll to the next department. You will get an error dialog, since the row now violates the mandatory constraint you added. Click OK to dismiss the dialog.
4. Add the manager ID ("200") back in (or click the Rollback the Changes button in the top toolbar).

Test Transient and Persistent Attributes

You can observe the differences between transient and persistent attributes using the following steps:

1. In the Business Component Browser, double click EmployeesView1 to display the first row of EmployeesView1 in the tester.
2. Click the blue right-arrow to scroll to the next employee.
3. Fill in the YearlyPay attribute for employees 101 and 102. Estimate their yearly pay at 100000 each. (In Chapter 11, you will populate this field automatically.)
4. Use the blue arrows to look at employees 101 and 102 again. Although the attributes are not persistent so the values will not be saved to the database, ADF retains the value of YearlyPay for both of these employees during this session.
5. Scroll to employee 103. Give Hunold a raise by increasing his salary to 9500.
6. Click the green arrow icon in the top-left toolbar of the tester to commit your changes.

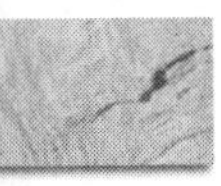

CAUTION
As mentioned in the Introduction of this book, you may have to disable the SECURE_EMPLOYEES trigger on the EMPLOYEES table if you are working after business hours.

7. Close the Business Component Browser.
8. Reopen the Business Component Browser and view EmployeesView1 as explained in the "Open the Business Component Browser" section.

9. Look at employees 101, 102, and 103. Note that the YearlyPay attribute values for Kochhar (101) and De Haan (102) are gone, but the change to Hunold's (103) salary is still there.

   Additional Information: This is the difference between a transient attribute that is not stored in the database and a persistent attribute that is stored in a database column. Transient attributes are only maintained for as long as the application module instance is active.

Test a Many-to-Many Association

The following steps explore the many-to-many association through an instance of the view link based on that association.

1. Double click the EmpPastJobsLink1 node in the Business Component Browser.
2. Scroll through the employees to view their past jobs.

   Additional Information: Note that some employees (like King) have had no jobs except their current job, and some (like Kochhar) have had more than one. Some employees share past jobs, as well. Since any number of employees can correspond to any number of past jobs, this is a true many-to-many relationship.

Populate the BONUSES Table

Use the Business Component Browser to add some rows to the new BONUSES table:

1. Double click EmpBonusFkLink1.
2. In the top pane, scroll back to King.
3. In the bottom pane, click the green plus sign to add a BONUSES row for King.

   Additional Information: The EmployeesEmployeeId attribute is automatically populated by EmpBonusFkLink.
4. Enter the following values:

   "100" for *BonusId*
   "2002" for *Year*
   "1" for *Quarter*
   "25000" for *Amount*
5. Scroll one Employees row to Employee 101, Neena Kochhar.
6. In the bottom pane, click the green plus sign to add a BONUSES row for Kochhar.
7. Enter the following values:

   "101" for *BonusId*
   "2002" for *Year*
   "1" for *Quarter*
   "10000" for *Amount*
8. Click the green plus sign again to add another BONUSES row for Kochhar.

9. Enter the following values:

   "102" for *BonusId*
   "2002" for *Year*
   "1" for *Quarter*
   "15000" for *Amount*

   Additional Information: This violates the unique constraint; there are now two bonuses for Kochhar in the first quarter of the year 2002. However, since unique constraints are only validated at the database level, ADF does not detect this violation yet.

10. Scroll to the next record to verify that the constraint is not checked when leaving the record.

11. Try to save your changes by clicking the commit button (green arrow in the top toolbar).

    Additional Information: The tester tries to post the changes to the database before committing, so you will get the following error message:

    ```
    (oracle.jbo.DMLConstraintException) JBO-26048: Constraint "BONUSES_UK" violated
    during post operation:"Insert" using SQL Statement "INSERT INTO
    BONUSES(BONUS_ID,YEAR,QUARTER,AMOUNT,EMPLOYEE_ID) VALUES (:1,:2,:3,:4,:5)".
    ```

12. Dismiss the error box, change Bonus 102's quarter to "2," and press ENTER.

13. Try again to save your changes. This time, the commit should be successful.

14. Close the Business Component Browser.

15. In the Connection Navigator, select SQL Worksheet from the right-click menu on the HR connection node.

16. Enter and run the following SQL command:

    ```
    SELECT * FROM BONUSES
    ```

17. Note that the data you entered in the Business Component Browser was saved in the database.

What Just Happened? You created default data model components and used them with the Business Component Browser to test your business domain components. You saw ADF enforce the *Mandatory* attribute setting, and saw a many-to-many association working. You also populated the new BONUSES table and tested the generated unique constraint.

CHAPTER 10

More Complex Business Rules

Let no act be done haphazardly, nor otherwise than according to the finished rules that govern its kind.

—Marcus Aurelius (A.D. 121–180), *Meditations*

hapter 9 discusses business domain components as representations of data and as enforcers of simple business rules, such as those implemented as foreign key constraints and mandatory attributes. Business domain components can also encapsulate more complex business rules pertaining to the data they represent. An entity object definition or domain can enforce validation rules for attribute values, calculate default values of attributes, and automatically calculate the values of transient attributes. This chapter explains how to use business domain components to implement business rules such as these. Other types of business rules can be implemented using a combination of these techniques or by using techniques related to those explained in this chapter. In the hands-on practices, you will change the business domain components you created in Chapter 9 to enforce rules governing data validation, defaulting, and calculated attributes.

Overview of the Entity Classes

In Chapter 8, you learned that ADF BC is a Java framework technology, which means that it has a library of classes that can use XML files to perform most customization but can also be subclassed to provide extra customization. Entity object definitions are handled by three classes in the ADF BC library, the *base entity classes*:

- **`oracle.jbo.server.EntityImpl`** Entity object instances are instances of this class—that is, each instance of this class represents a single row of a table. The class has all the methods you need to create, update, and delete rows.
- **`oracle.jbo.server.EntityDefImpl`** A single instance of this class acts as a wrapper for the entity object definition's XML file. The class contains methods that allow you to dynamically change the definition of the entity object itself—to add or remove entity attributes or to change the properties of those attributes.
- **`oracle.jbo.server.EntityCache`** A single instance of this class acts as an *entity cache*—a memory location holding instances of a particular entity object definition in use in a single transaction. The class contains methods that manipulate rows in the cache. For most purposes, you will not need to use these methods directly; they are used internally by ADF BC's caching mechanism. You will learn more about caching in Chapter 11.

Many applications can use these classes directly with an entity object definition's XML file. However, if you need further customization, you can also generate *custom entity classes* that extend one or more of them. For example, for a particular entity object definition, Departments, you could generate any or all of the following classes:

- **`DepartmentsImpl`** An entity object class, which extends `EntityImpl`
- **`DepartmentsDefImpl`** An entity definition class, which extends `EntityDefImpl`
- **`DepartmentsCollImpl`** An entity collection class, which extends `EntityCache`

You could then customize these classes for your particular application.

You will learn extensively about entity object classes in this chapter. This section contains an overview of all three kinds of classes, but a detailed discussion of entity definition classes and entity collection classes is beyond the scope of this book. The hands-on practice illustrates how to choose which entity classes to generate.

Entity Object Classes

An *entity object class* is a subclass of `EntityImpl` that a particular entity object definition can use to represent its instances. Entity object classes have the same name as the entity object definition with an "Impl" suffix (although JDeveloper allows you to specify different naming conventions, if you prefer—for more information, see the sidebar "Changing Class Naming Conventions"). For example, an entity object definition called "Departments" would have an entity object definition called "`DepartmentsImpl`."

Changing Class Naming Conventions

You can change all of the naming conventions ADF BC uses for custom classes in the IDE Preferences dialog (select **Tools | IDE Preferences**), as shown here:

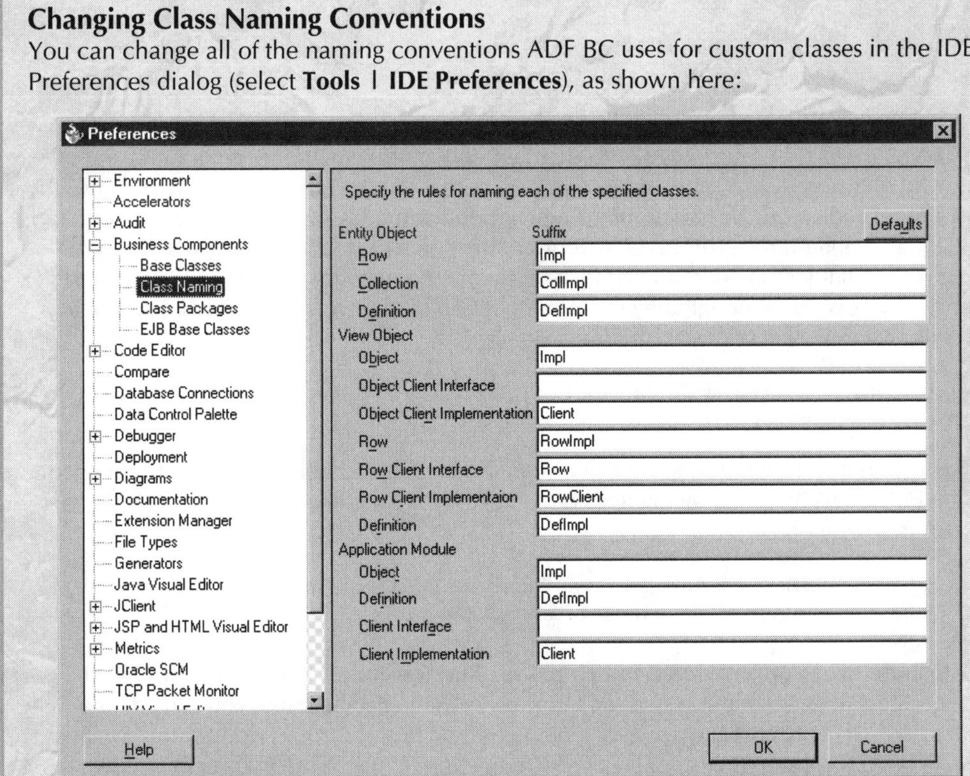

The *Entity Object* section contains the suffixes for the entity object class (*Row*), entity collection class (*Collection*), and entity definition class (*Definition*). For example, if you enter "Object" in the *Row* field, the entity object class for Departments will be `DepartmentsObject`. If you make the *Row* field blank, the entity object class for Departments will also be called "`Departments`".

Entity Attribute Accessors

The entity object class contains accessors (getters and setters) for each attribute. For example, `DepartmentsImpl` will by default contain `getDepartmentId()` and `setDepartmentId()` methods, which retrieve and change the value of the DepartmentId attribute, respectively. `EntityImpl` contains the methods `getAttribute()` and `setAttribute()`, which allow you to retrieve and change attribute values, but the accessors in the entity object class have the following two advantages.

Entity Attribute Accessors Are Typesafe Entity attribute accessors are *typesafe*, which means that they take fully typed objects as parameters and have fully typed return values. For example, `getDepartmentId()` has a return type of `Number`, and `setDepartmentId()` has a return type of `void` and takes a `Number` as a parameter. This can be very helpful when debugging. If you make a mistake with an attribute's Java type, you will get a compilation error that identifies the offending line. The following lines of code will cause compile-time errors because they assume the DepartmentId attribute has the wrong type (`String`, as opposed to `Number`).

```
String myDeptId=myDepartmentsImpl.getDepartmentId();
myDepartmentsImpl.setDepartmentId("25");
```

`EntityImpl.getAttribute()` and `EntityImpl.setAttribute()` are not typesafe. `EntityImpl.getAttribute()` takes a `String` (the attribute name) as an argument and has a return type of `java.lang.Object`; `EntityImpl.setAttribute()` takes a `String` (the attribute name) and an `Object` as arguments. If you forget the Java type of your attributes, you will not get a compile-time error. Instead, your application will throw an exception at run time, requiring substantially more work to debug. Neither of the following lines of code will cause compile-time errors (even though they make mistakes about the type of the attribute); instead, they will likely throw exceptions at run time.

```
String myDeptId=(String)myEntityImpl.getAttribute("DepartmentId");
myEntityImpl.setAttribute("DepartmentId", "25");
```

Using the entity attribute accessors can also make it easier to debug typos in attribute names. For example, the first of the following lines of code will yield a compile-time error; the second will throw an exception at run time:

```
Number myDeptId=myDepartmentsImpl.getDepqrtmentId();
Number myDeptId=myEntityImpl.getAttribute("DepqrtmentId");
```

Entity Attribute Accessors Provide Good Hooks for Business Rules Assuming you want to place business rules in the business logic tier and not in the database tier, you can edit the implementation of entity attribute accessor methods to add business rules. If you want to validate changes to data, you can put custom Java code in the body of these methods to enforce your requirements. If you want to trigger events whenever an attribute is changed, you can write Java code to do that as well. You do not need Java code for all business rules—validation, in particular, can often be implemented in other ways, which you will learn about later in this chapter. However, writing validation code directly in the setter methods is often the quickest way to implement validation code and matches standard practice for JavaBean technology. Additionally, more complex attribute-based business rules, such as events that trigger when an attribute is changed, must be implemented in accessor methods.

Overriding Methods in EntityImpl

In addition to the accessor methods, entity object classes also allow you to override various methods in the `EntityImpl` class to implement other sorts of business rules. For example, by overriding `EntityImpl.create()`, you can implement defaulting rules or trigger events whenever a row is created.

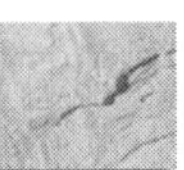

TIP

By default, JDeveloper will create an entity object class for every entity object you create. You can, however, remove entity object classes if you do not need them (you will do this in the hands-on practice); this will improve performance slightly. However, you may want to keep an entity object class to take advantage of the accessor methods or to override methods from `EntityImpl`.

Entity Definition Classes

An *entity definition class* is a subclass of `EntityDefImpl` that a particular entity object definition can use as a wrapper for its XML file.

JDeveloper does not generate entity definition classes by default. Unlike entity object classes, which many users will need to generate, entity definition classes only need to be created for two reasons:

- **You want to dynamically change the definition of an entity object** without writing code in every application that uses it. You can do this by overriding the method `EntityDefImpl.createDef()`, which is called as soon as the entity object definition is loaded into memory.
- **You need a place to put a custom method that affects an entire table**, as opposed to a single row (which should go in an entity object class) or all the rows returned by a particular query (which should go in a view object class).

In fact, not only can you usually avoid subclassing `EntityDefImpl`, but you may never have to call methods on it unless you need to dynamically change the structure of an entity object definition, for example, to dynamically add or remove entity attributes or dynamically change mappings between attributes and table columns.

Entity Collection Classes

An *entity collection class* is a subclass of `EntityCache` that a particular entity object can use for its entity caches. Although this book will not discuss directly using entity collection classes or `EntityCache`, it will return to the concept of entity caching in Chapter 11. You can also look at the `EntityDefImpl` and `EntityCache` Javadoc for more information on both entity definition classes and entity collection classes.

Manipulating Attribute Values

Most of the techniques described in this chapter involve the manipulation of entity attribute values. If you are working with attributes that have a standard Java class (such as `java.lang.String`) as their type, you can use the standard Java APIs (in the case of `String`, you have access to such methods as `length()` and `charAt()`). However, if you need to manipulate attributes with domain types, you must code to ADF-specific APIs.

If you are using domains from the package `oracle.jbo.domain`, you have two options. The first is to convert the domain to a standard Java type. You can then use methods and operators provided by Java itself. Table 10-1 lists the conversion methods for the most common domains.

After you are finished manipulating the domain value, you can re-create the domain by passing the standard Java type into the domain's constructor. For example, the following code will add one to the value of an object `salary` of type `Number`:

```
int salaryValue = salary.intValue();
salaryValue++;
salary = new Number(salaryValue);
```

Alternatively, you can work directly with the domains, using methods provided in the domain classes. Table 10-2 gives a partial list of useful methods on common domains.

Each of these alternatives has its own advantages:

- **Standard Java classes and primitives will likely be more familiar** to most Java programmers. By converting domains to standard Java types, you may make your code more readable and maintainable.
- **The operators on Java primitives (such as `double` and `int`) are very efficient.** If you are going to perform extensive manipulation of numeric types, it may be more efficient to convert the Number domain to a Java primitive.
- **Calling the domain manipulation methods may be more efficient** than first calling the method that converts the domain to a standard Java type, performing the operations, and then calling the constructor that converts the Java type back into a domain. This is particularly true if you are only going to perform a few operations on a domain.
- **Large arrays of bytes are very expensive to work with**, so if you are working with LOB types, you should not use the conversion methods. Use InputStreams and OutputStreams to work with the LOB's value. For more information on InputStreams and OutputStreams, see a beginning-to-intermediate Java text.

Domain	**Conversion Methods**
Number	`int intValue()`, `long longValue()`, `short shortValue()`, `float floatValue()`, `double doubleValue()`, `byte byteValue()`, `java.math.BigDecimal bigDecimalValue()`, `java.math.BigInteger bigIntegerValue()`
Date	`java.lang.Date toDate()`
Array	`java.lang.Object[] getArray()`
BFileDomain, BlobDomain, ClobDomain	`byte[] toByteArray()`

TABLE 10-1. *Domain Conversion Methods*

Domain	Methods
Number	`add()`, `subtract()`, `multiply()`, `divide()`, `increment()`, `abs()`, `exp()`, `sin()`, `cos()`, `tan()`, `compareTo()`
Date	`addJulianDays()`, `addMonths()`, `round()`, `lastDayInMonth()`, `diffInMonths()`, `getCurrentDate()`
BFileDomain	`getInputStream()`, `getOutputStream()`, `closeOutputStream()`
BlobDomain	`getBinaryStream()`, `getBinaryOutputStream()`, `closeOutputStream()`, `getBytes()`, `getLength()`
ClobDomain	`getCharacterStream()`, `getCharacterOutputStream()`, `getSubstring()`, `getLength()`

TABLE 10-2. *Domain Manipulation Methods*

Domains based on Oracle object types have accessor methods to retrieve and change values. For example, if the object myAddress is of AddressTyp (described in Chapter 9), you can append "-1234" to myAddress's PostalCode attribute with the following code:

```
String myPostalCode = myAddress.getPostalCode();
myPostalCode = myPostalCode + "-1234";
myAddress.setPostalCode(myPostalCode);
```

Attribute-Level Validation

The simplest kind of business rule is one that needs to fire whenever an attribute value is changed, to make sure the value passes some test. For example, you may want to implement a rule that email addresses must have a length of at most eight characters. Logic like this is called *attribute-level validation* because it is intended to check the value in a single attribute in a single row. ADF Business Components technology provides three ways to implement attribute-level validation:

- Validation rules
- Validation domains
- Setter method validation

Validation Rules

Validation rules are Java classes that can be attached to entity attributes or entire entity object definitions using the Entity Object Editor. (This section will only cover validation rules that attach to attributes; validation rules that attach to entire entity object definitions will be explained in the section "Entity-Level Validation.") A validation rule contains a method that throws an exception whenever a potential attribute value does not pass some test. The `EntityImpl` class will call this method whenever an application attempts to change the attribute value; the value is only changed if the exception is not thrown.

Built-in Validation Rules

JDeveloper provides four built-in validation rules for attributes, three of which you can use without writing a single line of code:

- **CompareValidator** This validation rule allows you to compare an attribute to a literal value, the first column of the first row of a query result, or a view object attribute value for a single view row.
- **ListValidator** This validation rule allows you to check whether or not an attribute is in a list of literal values, is in the first column of a query result, or is equal to a view object attribute value for any of a view object definition's view rows.
- **RangeValidator** This validation rule allows you to check whether or not an attribute is between a pair of literal values.
- **MethodValidator** This validation rule calls a method in the entity object class. The method must accept a value of the same type of the attribute and have a return type of `boolean`. Validation passes if the method returns "true."

If an application tries to set a value for an attribute, and the value does not pass the requirements of one of these validation rules, one of two things happens:

- **The entity object class throws an `oracle.jbo.ValidationException`** if the validation rule was a MethodValidator.
- **The entity object class throws an `oracle.jbo.AttrSetValException`** if the validation rule was not a MethodValidator.

You can catch these exceptions in your application, and handle them in whatever way you want. The exceptions contain error messages you can set when you apply the validation rule. You declare these validation rules using a property dialog such as the following, which is accessible from the Validation node of the Entity Object Editor. You will do this in the first hands-on practice in this chapter.

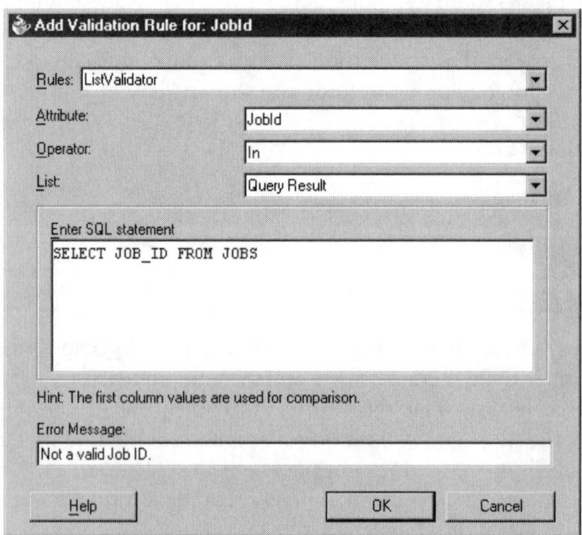

Custom Validation Rules

If the built-in validation rules do not satisfy your needs, you can create validation rules. Creating a validation rule involves some Java coding, but once you have created it, you can use it again and again on multiple attributes with no further coding required. One Java programmer in a large group of developers can create validation rules for the entire group; other developers in the group (including those with no Java knowledge) can customize and use these validation rules declaratively.

JDeveloper can create a skeleton validation rule class for you, which implements the interface `oracle.jbo.server.rules.JbiValidator`. All custom validation rules must implement `JbiValidator`, which has three requirements:

- **It contains a method, `validateValue()`**, which accepts a `java.lang.Object` (the new attribute value) as a parameter and returns a `boolean`, "true" or "false". Generally, you will use this method to return "true" if the attribute value is acceptable and "false" if it is not.
- **It contains a method, `vetoableChange()`**, which accepts a parameter of type `oracle.jbo.server.util.PropertyChangeEvent`. This is the method that `EntityImpl` calls when the attribute value is changed. Generally, you will use this method to extract the value from the `PropertyChangeEvent`, call `validateValue()`, and throw an exception if `validateValue()` returns "false". The skeleton class contains an implementation that already does this for you, although you can customize it further.
- **It contains a field named "description" (with accessor methods).** `EntityImpl` does not use this field in any way, but you can use it to provide instructions to people who use the validation rule, or they can customize it declaratively to write comments to themselves, or you can use it in your implementation of `validateValue()` or `vetoableChange()` (for example, to construct an error message in `vetoableChange()`).

In addition to these requirements, you can add additional fields to the validation rule. When you apply the rule to an entity attribute, you will have a chance to customize it by supplying values for the fields. For example, you could create a validation rule that requires data to be of a length less than n, where `n` is a number that can be filled in declaratively when the validation rule is applied.

After you create a validation rule, to reuse the rule in another project, you must register the rule with that project. Then you can apply it to an entity attribute using the Entity Object Editor.

You will also create, customize, and use a validation rule in the first hands-on practice in this chapter.

Validation Domains

In Chapter 9, you saw that custom domains could be used to represent Oracle object types. Custom domains can also be used to provide validation. These domains, called *validation domains*, wrap other domains or standard Java classes (such as `String`) that can be used as attribute types, but include validation code as well.

For example, consider the rule that an email address must contain at most eight characters. By default (since the EMAIL column has SQL type `VARCHAR2`), the Email attribute is of type `String`. However, you can create a validation domain, EmailDomain, that enforces your business logic and make Email of that type.

As with validation rules, you can reuse validation domains without writing any additional code. However, validation domains have more limitations on their reuse than do validation rules. This is for two reasons:

- **Validation domains must wrap a particular type.** For example, if you create a validation domain for String data (such as email addresses), you cannot reuse the logic in it to validate numerical data or data stored in Date format.
- **Validation domains cannot be declaratively customized.** You could write a validation domain to require that an email address be less than eight characters, but you could not write it in such a way that you could specify the maximum length declaratively when you apply the domain.

This does not mean that validation rules are always superior to validation domains; see the later section "Choosing a Validation Style" for recommendations.

The Java class for a validation domain is a bit different from the Java class for a domain that represents an Oracle object type. A validation domain's class is based on another class, either another domain or a standard Java class. There are actually two types of validation domains: those based on the Number or Date domains, and those based on all other classes.

Domains based on the Number or Date domains extend `oracle.jbo.domain.Number` or `oracle.jbo.domain.Date`, respectively, and they inherit the methods for manipulation and conversion listed in Tables 10-1 and 10-2. By contrast, domains based on other Java classes, such as `String`, do not extend those classes. Instead, they have a private field, `mData`, with a type matching the original class, and a public method, `getData()`, that returns `mData` cast to a `java.lang.Object`. (To work with the original class, you must cast it back.)

All validation domains have a `validate()` method. Whenever a new object of the domain's type is created, the ADF BC library classes call this `validate()` method. By writing code in this method to test the domain value and throw an exception if the value does not pass your requirements, you can block the instantiation of the domain.

Validation domains can also be used to represent column constraints. Chapter 9 mentioned that you can add properties to an entity attribute to represent not null, PRIMARY KEY, or single-column UNIQUE constraints, and that one of these properties—*Mandatory*—is enforced in the entity object. You can also add any of these properties to a validation domain. If you do so, the properties will be automatically set for any entity attribute of the domain type.

You will create a validation domain and apply it to entity attributes in the first hands-on practice in this chapter.

Setter Method Validation

If you generate the entity object class for an entity object definition, you can also write validation logic directly in attribute setter methods.

When JDeveloper generates an entity object class (such as `DepartmentsImpl`), it creates simple setters that do nothing but call a single method, `setAttributeInternal()`, as shown here:

```
public void setEmail(String value)
{
  setAttributeInternal(EMAIL, value);
}
```

`setAttributeInternal()` takes an `int` and an `Object` as arguments. The `int` is a constant that corresponds to a particular entity attribute. (If you examine the source code for `EmployeesImpl`, you will find a constant, EMAIL, defined with a value of 3.) The `Object` corresponds to a value to which you set the attribute.

The difference between `setAttributeInternal()` and `setAttribute()`—other than that `setAttributeInternal()` accepts an integer instead of a `String` to identify the attribute—is that `setAttribute()` calls the setter method (if setter methods have been generated), but `setAttributeInternal()` just sets the attribute's value (after checking for validation rules). In other words, when `EntityImpl.setAttribute()` is called, it calls a setter method (if one exists) in the entity object class, which in turn calls `setAttributeInternal()`, as shown in Figure 10-1.

To add validation logic to a setter method, wrap the call to `setAttributeInternal()` in an `if-then` block that tests for the condition you want and calls `setAttributeInternal()` only on success. The following is a trivial example of this. You will create a much more complex example in the second hands-on practice in this chapter:

```
public void setEmail(String value) throws oracle.jbo.JboException
{
  if (value.length <= 8)
  {
    setAttributeInternal(EMAIL, value);
  }
  else
  {
    throw new oracle.jbo.JboException(
      "An email address must have at most 8 characters.");
  }
}
```

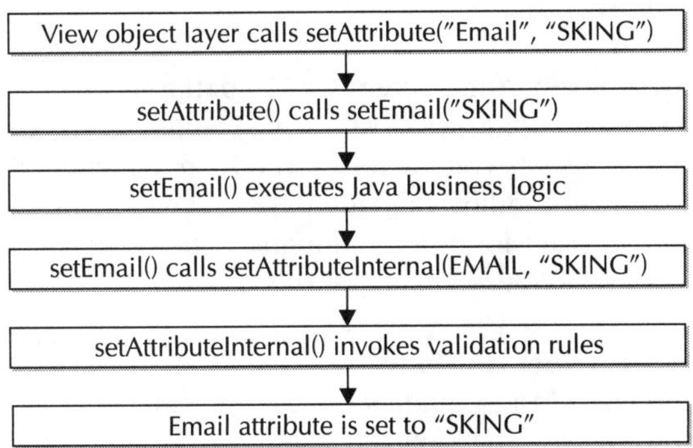

FIGURE 10-1. *setAttribute(), setEmail(), and setAttributeInternal()*

The main disadvantage of this method of writing validation code in setter methods is that it is not reusable. The preceding code will work only to validate the Email attribute of the Employees entity object definition. Enforcing similar validation logic for other attributes requires writing more code. However, this method of writing validation logic has its uses, which will be explained in the following section.

Choosing a Validation Style

For many cases of attribute-level validation, you could use validation rules, validation domains, or setter methods. However, some are more appropriate for certain uses than others. When choosing a validation style, you might want to take into account the following considerations.

Reusability As already mentioned, validation rules are the most reusable implementations of validation logic. They can be reused for attributes of different types and are declaratively customizable. Validation domains can be reused for multiple attributes of the same type but are not declaratively customizable. Validation logic in setter methods cannot be reused for other attributes.

Ease of Initial Creation On the other hand, custom validation rules and validation domains require more work to create. To create a custom validation rule, you must generate a skeleton class, implement the `validate()` and `vetoableChange()` methods, and register it with projects that need to use it. To create a validation domain, you must generate the domain and implement the `validate()` method. By contrast, validation logic can be added to setter methods in a single step.

When the Validation Logic Should Be Applied As shown in Figure 10-1, validation logic contained in setter methods is applied before validation logic contained in validation rules. Validation logic contained in validation domains is applied even earlier—the domain must be instantiated before it can be passed to `setAttribute()`. You can write code in setter methods with the assumption that it will only be executed if domain-level validation has been passed, and you can put code in validation rules with the assumption that it will only be executed if setter-level validation has been passed.

Whether You Need to Dynamically Add or Remove Validation Logic `EntityDefImpl` provides a method, `addVetoableChangeListener()`, that lets you dynamically add validation rules to attributes. This lets you decide, at run time, which methods to use to validate a particular attribute. (Dynamically adding validation rules is beyond the scope of this book. Look at the Javadoc for `EntityDefImpl` for more information.) If you need to dynamically add or remove validation logic, you should use validation rules.

Whether You Need to Access Other Attributes in the Validation Logic You can call the getter methods for other attributes inside validation logic implemented in a setter method. For example, if you need to implement validation logic that states that email addresses can have at most eight characters, except the email addresses for managers, you can call `getJobId()` within the `setEmail()` method to check the employee's JobId. In the second half of this chapter, you will learn to traverse associations to access attributes from different entity object definitions as well. You cannot access other attributes or traverse associations from within validation rules or validation domains.

Whether You Need Other Business Rules In the second half of this chapter, you will learn to implement other sorts of business rules (such as those required to maintain calculated attributes) in setter logic. Validation rules and validation domains are not suited for implementing business rules other than checking values and stopping the operation if the check fails. If you need to implement business rules other than validation, you will need to add code to setter methods. You may then wish to keep validation code in setter methods as well, so that all business rule code is in the same place.

Preferred Coding Style Many Java programmers are accustomed to putting validation logic in setter methods. Putting validation logic in attribute setters will bring your application more in line with typical Java practice and may make it easier for others to understand and maintain.

Entity-Level Validation

Some validation logic does not apply to a single attribute, but rather to multiple attributes in the same row. For example, you might want to require both that no executive (that is, no employee whose job title ends in "VP" or "PRES") has a salary less than 15,000 and that no non-executive employee has a salary of 15,000 or greater. You cannot apply this logic as attribute-level validation for the following reasons:

- **You cannot implement this validation on the Salary attribute alone**, since it has to be applied when users enter or change an employee's JobId.
- **You cannot implement this validation on the JobId attribute alone**, since it has to be applied when users enter or change an employee's Salary.
- **You cannot implement this logic twice**, as validation on both the Salary and JobId attributes, since it will then be impossible to promote an employee to an executive—if you try to promote him or her first, the JobId validation will fail because the salary is too low; if you try to give him or her a raise first, the Salary validation will fail because he or she is not yet an executive.

This kind of business rule requires *entity-level validation*, that is, value-checking logic that applies to an entire row, rather than to a single attribute. Entity-level validation is not invoked as soon as an attribute changes value. Rather, when an attribute changes value, the entity object instance is marked as needing validation. Entity-level validation is applied to entity object instances marked as needing validation in two cases:

- **Whenever the entity object instance loses currency**—that is, whenever an application is done looking at a particular row. If validation fails, the instance will not be allowed to lose currency. The sidebar "What Is Entity Object Instance Currency?" discusses what it is for an entity object instance to have or lose currency.
- **When an application attempts to commit a transaction.** If validation fails, the transaction will not be committed.

What Is Entity Object Instance Currency?
Entity object definitions do not maintain a pointer to a "current" row. What does it really mean to say an entity object instance "loses currency?"

As Chapter 11 discusses, view object instances do maintain pointers to a current view row. And as mentioned in Chapter 8, a view object definition can contain one or more entity object usages. When a view object instance points to a new row, any entity object instance the old row was based on "loses currency" and triggers entity-level validation. Chapter 11 discusses more about the relationship between entity object instances and view rows.

ADF Business Components technology provides two ways to implement entity-level validation:

- Entity-level validation rules
- The `validateEntity()` method

Entity-Level Validation Rules

You have already seen that validation rules can be applied to single attributes. They can be applied to entire entity object definitions, as well. Like attribute-level validation rules, an entity-level validation rule contains a method that throws an exception whenever an entity object instance does not pass some test. The `EntityImpl` class will call this method whenever entity-level validation is required.

Built-in Validation Rules

JDeveloper provides two built-in validation rules for entity-level validation:

- **MethodValidator** In addition to being applied to attributes, this validation rule can be applied to an entire entity object definition. When applied to an entity object definition, the rule calls a method in the entity object class that accepts no parameters and has a return type of `boolean`. Validation passes if the method returns "true." If validation fails, the rule throws an `oracle.jbo.ValidationException`.
- **UniqueKeyValidator** Chapter 9 explained that ADF does not enforce the *Unique* property on entity object attributes. This validation rule ensures that the primary key of the entity object instance is unique within the entity cache. If validation fails, the rule throws an `oracle.jbo.TooManyObjectsException`.

As with the exceptions thrown by attribute-level validation rules, the exceptions thrown by these rules contain error messages you can set when you apply the validation rule.

Custom Validation Rules

You can also create custom validation rules for entity-level validation. These validation rules must implement the same interface as attribute-level validation rules (`JbiValidator`) and can use the same skeleton class. The only difference is that when a validation rule is applied to an entity object definition (rather than an attribute), the parameter passed to `validateValue()` is the entity object instance (cast to an `Object`), rather than the attribute value.

Creating reusable entity-level validation rules is more complex than creating reusable attribute-level validation rules. If you want to use the validation rules on multiple entity object definitions, you will have to dynamically discover information about the entity object definition (such as which attributes it has). This generally involves the following steps:

1. Casting the parameter to the class `EntityImpl`.
2. Calling the method `EntityImpl.getEntityDef()` to retrieve the entity object definition's instance of `EntityDefImpl`.
3. Calling various methods on `EntityDefImpl` to discover facts about the entity object definition.

For more information about dynamically discovering facts about an entity object definition, see the Javadoc for `oracle.jbo.serverEntityDefImpl`.

The validateEntity() Method

The `EntityImpl` class contains a method, `validateEntity()`, that is called whenever the entity object instance needs to be validated. You can override `validateEntity()` to write entity-level validation logic. JDeveloper can generate a method stub in an entity object class to override `validateEntity`. The stub looks like the following:

```
protected void validateEntity()
{
  super.validateEntity();
}
```

You should always keep the call to `super.validateEntity()`, so that your entity object class will continue to exhibit `EntityImpl`'s default behavior (which includes invoking entity-level validation rules) in addition to your modifications. You can place code before or after the call to throw an exception if your requirements are not met. You will do this in the first hands-on practice.

Choosing a Validation Style

Most entity-level validation can be performed using either validation rules or the `validateEntity()` method.

When choosing a validation style, you might want to take into account the following considerations.

Reusability Entity-level validation rules can be reused for multiple entity object definitions and are declaratively customizable. Validation logic in the `validateEntity()` methods cannot be reused for other entity object definitions.

Ease of Initial Creation As described before, properly coding entity-level validation rules requires use of the `EntityDefImpl` class. Many developers will find it much easier to use the `validateEntity()` method.

When the Validation Logic Should Be Applied The `validateEntity()` method gives you more flexibility with when to apply validation logic. By throwing an exception before or after the call to `super.validateEntity()`, you can apply your logic before or after `EntityImpl` performs its validation tasks.

Whether You Need to Dynamically Add or Remove Validation Logic As with attribute-level validation rules, you can use `EntityDefImpl.addVetoableChangeListener()` to dynamically add validation rules to entity object definitions.

Preferred Coding Style If you have decided to implement all attribute-level validation in the entity object class, you may wish to use `validateEntity()` for consistency.

Entity-Level Validation and Compositions

Chapter 9 explained that compositions are associations between an entity object definition representing a whole and entity object definitions representing its parts—for example, between a purchase order and its line items. If a purchase order is changed, it is important to ensure that not only is the purchase order still valid, but all of its parts are valid as parts of this particular order. Similarly, if a line item in a purchase order is changed, it is important that the entire purchase order (including the other line items) be checked to ensure that the purchase order is still valid as a whole.

The ADF BC library classes act to ensure that this happens. If an entity object instance is marked as needing validation, the classes check to see whether its entity object definition is the destination of a composition. If it is, the classes recursively trace backward through compositions to find the top-level row. For example, if a line item is part of a purchase order, and a purchase order is part of a customer request sheet, the classes will find the customer request sheet containing the line item when there is a change to a line item. The customer request sheet is also marked as needing validation.

When `EntityImpl.validateEntity()` is called on an entity object instance (when that instance loses currency, or the transaction is committed), it checks to see if the entity object definition is the source of a composition. If it is, `validateEntity()` is called on the instance's destination entity object instances, which recursively call it on the destination entity object instances of any compositions they participate in. (For example, when `validateEntity()` is called on a customer request sheet, it will call `validateEntity()` on each purchase order in that sheet, which will in turn call `validateEntity()` on each line item in those purchase orders.)

Hands-on Practice: Add Validation to the HR Business Domain Components

In this practice, you will add validation logic to the business domain components `hr.model.businessdomain` package in four ways: using a built-in validation rule to enforce a minimum `salary` of 500, creating your own validation rule to enforce a maximum length on email addresses and department IDs, creating a validation domain to impose a format on job IDs, and writing code in a `validateEntity()` method to require that all executives, and only executives, have a salary above 15,000.

This practice builds on the HR application workspace created in the hands-on practice for Chapter 9. If you have not completed that practice, you can download the starting files for this practice from the authors' websites mentioned in the author information at the beginning of this book.

This practice steps you through the following phases:

I. Remove unneeded entity object classes

II. Apply a built-in validation rule

III. Create and use a custom validation rule

- Generate a validation rule skeleton class
- Add a customizable field to the class
- Implement the `validateValue()` method
- Implement the `vetoableChange()` method
- Apply the validation rule
- Test the validation rules

IV. Create and use a validation domain

- Generate a validation domain
- Implement the `validate()` method
- Use the domain to type entity attributes
- Test the validation domain

V. Provide entity-level validation

- Generate Implement `validateEntity()`
- Test the entity-level validation

I. Remove Unneeded Entity Object Classes

By default, JDeveloper generates an entity object class for each entity object definition you create. However, you will only need to use the `EmployeesImpl` class. In this phase, you remove the entity object class for the other entity object definitions.

1. Open the HR workspace and expand the Model project, Application Sources, and hr.model.businessdomain nodes.
2. Double click the "Business Domain Diagram" node to open the diagram you created in Chapter 9.
3. Double click the Departments entity object definition to open the Entity Object Editor.
4. Select the Java node.

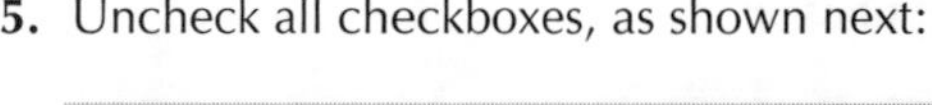

5. Uncheck all checkboxes, as shown next:

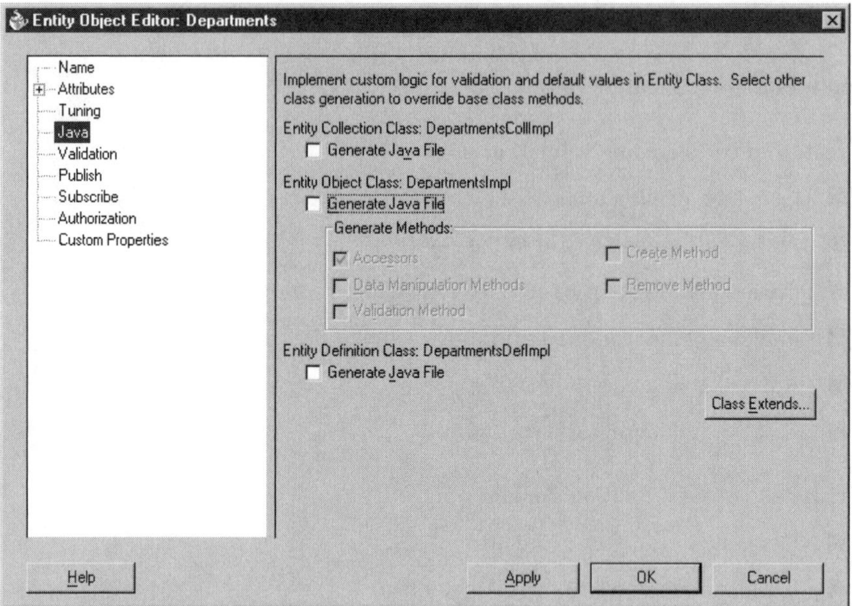

Additional Information: This page allows you to specify which custom entity classes the entity object definition needs. By default, the entity object class (with typesafe accessors) is generated. Since you will not be writing any code in `DepartmentsImpl`, you do not need to generate this class. You can always regenerate it if you decide you need it later.

6. Click OK to close the editor.

7. Repeat steps 3–6 for the Jobs, JobHistory, and Bonuses entity object definitions.

What Just Happened? You removed the entity object classes from the Departments, Jobs, JobHistory, and Bonuses entity object definitions. You will not need to use these custom classes, and removing them will improve performance.

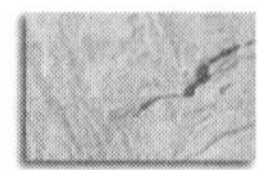

CAUTION

This will remove the classes from your project but will remove neither the source files nor the compiled class files from the disk. This can lead to confusion if you have other classes referring to these entity object classes; the referring classes will compile within JDeveloper but will cease to compile when deployed. We recommend occasionally deleting the contents of your output (classes) directory and rebuilding to prevent this from happening.

II. Apply a Built-in Validation Rule

In this phase, you will add a CompareValidator to the Salary attribute.

1. In the diagram, on the Employees entity object definition, double click the Salary attribute to open the Attribute Editor.
2. Select the Validation node.
3. Click New to add a validation rule for Salary. The Add Validation Rule dialog opens.
4. Verify that "CompareValidator" is selected in the *Rules* dropdown list.
5. From the *Operator* dropdown list, select GreaterThan.
6. Verify that "Literal Value" is selected in the *Compare With* dropdown list.
7. Enter "500" in the *Enter Literal Value* area.
8. In the *Error Message* field, enter "Salary must be over 500.", so the dialog resembles the following:

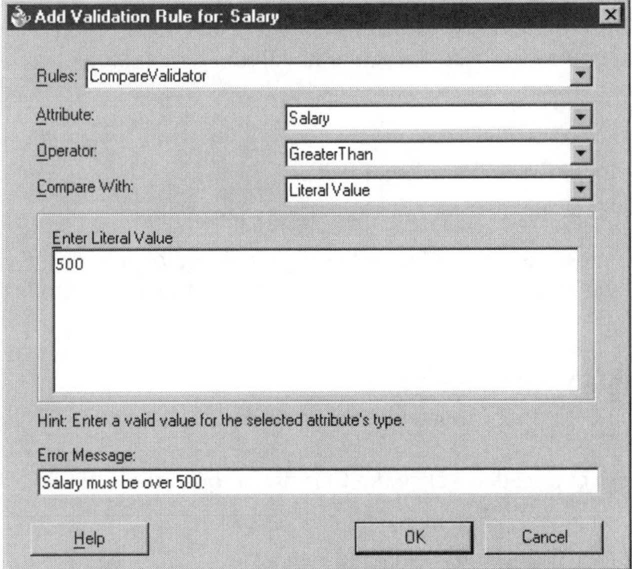

Additional Information: This creates an error message for this use of the validation rule and adds it to a resource bundle file called EmployeesImplMsgBundle.java. This file is shown in the Sources node in the Structure window for the Employees entity object definition.

9. Click OK to close the dialog.
10. Click OK to close the editor.
11. Build your project.
12. Click Save All.

What Just Happened? You added a CompareValidator to the Salary attribute. The validator will ensure that the salary is over 500. This validator is displayed in the Structure window under the Salary attribute node.

III. Create and Use a Custom Validation Rule

In this phase, you will create a validation rule that requires a data item's String representation to have a maximum length. You will then apply this rule to Employees' Email attribute and Departments' DepartmentId attribute.

Generate a Validation Rule Skeleton Class

You need to create a class file for the validation rule. You can create a validation rule skeleton class and register it with your project using the following steps:

1. In the Application Navigator, on the Model project node, select Project Properties from the right-click menu.
2. Select the "Common\Business Components\Registered Rules" node.
3. Click New to open the Create Validation Rule Class dialog.

   Additional Information: If you had already created a validation rule in a different project, you could click Add to register it with the Model project.
4. Enter the following values:
   Name as "MaxLengthValidator"
   Package as "hr.model.businessdomain"
5. Click OK to close the Create Validation Rule Class dialog.
6. Click OK to close the Project Properties dialog. JDeveloper adds the validation rule skeleton to the Model project, registers a class as a rule for the project, and opens it in an editor.

Add a Customizable Field to the Class

You can add and edit fields that can later be declaratively customized using the following steps:

1. At the bottom of the editor, click the Class tab to open the Class Editor for `MaxLengthValidator`.
2. At the top of the Class Editor, click the Fields tab.
3. Click Add to add a field. The Field Settings dialog opens.
4. Enter the following values:
   Field Name as "maxLength"
   Field Type as "int"
   Scope as "private"

   Additional Information: The dialog should appear as shown next.

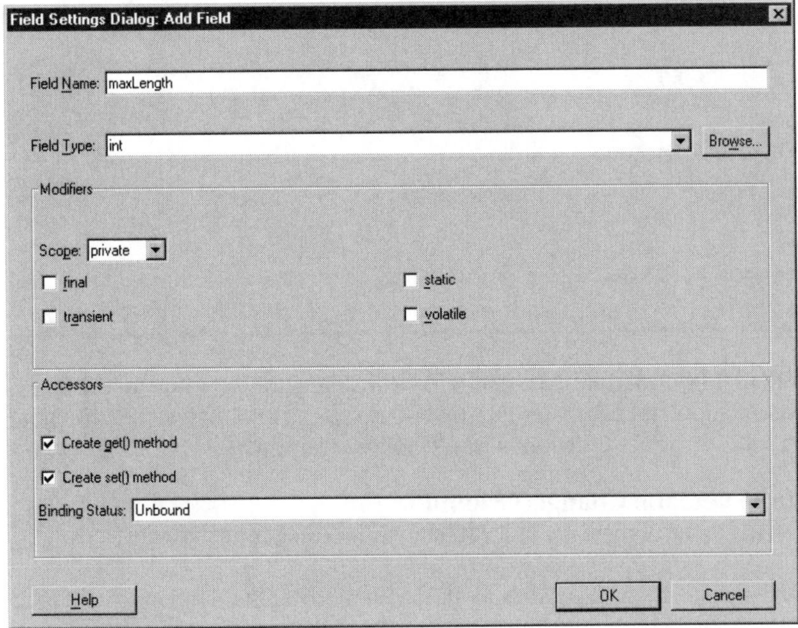

Users of this validation rule will be able to customize it to specify different maximum lengths.

5. Click OK to close the dialog.

Implement the validateValue() Method

You can add validation logic to a validation rule using the following steps:

1. At the bottom of the editor window, click the Source tab to reopen the Source Editor.
2. Find the `validateValue()` method. The body of the method should have a single command:

```
return true;
```

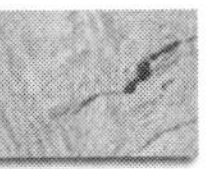

TIP
You can find the method in the Structure window, as shown on the right. If you double-click the method signature, JDeveloper will find the method in the source code.

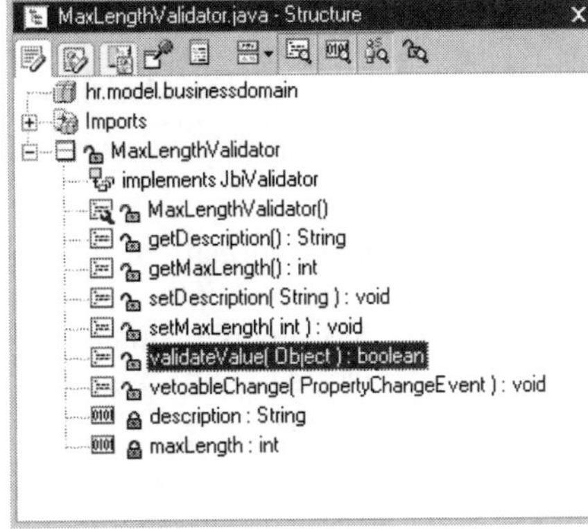

3. Change the body of the method so that it reads:

```
boolean returnVal;
if (value.toString().length() < getMaxLength())
{
  returnVal=true;
}
else
{
  returnVal=false;
}
return returnVal;
```

Additional Information: This code converts the attribute value to a String representation and compares its length to `maxLength`. If the value is longer than `maxLength`, validation fails; otherwise, it succeeds.

Implement the vetoableChange() Method

You can construct an error message in a validation rule using the following steps:

1. Find the `vetoableChange()` method. The body of the method should read as follows:

```
if (!validateValue(eventObj.getNewValue()))
{
  throw new ValidationException(
    "hr.model.businessdomain.MaxLengthValidator validation failed");
}
```

Additional Information: This code extracts the new attribute value from the eventObj, passes it to `validateValue()` (which you just rewrote), and throws an exception if `validateValue()` returns false.

2. Change the `throw` command so that it reads:

```
throw new ValidationException(getDescription());
```

Additional Information: This uses the customizable `description` field to construct an error message.

3. Click Save All.
4. Select **File | Add to Model.jpr**.
5. When the Add Files or Directories dialog opens, select "MaxLengthValidator.java" and click Open.

Additional Information: Although MaxLengthValidator.java appears in the application navigator as part of the `hr.model.businessdomain` package, it is not actually in the Model project until you add it. Adding it to the project ensures it will be compiled when the project is rebuilt.

Apply the Validation Rule

Now you are ready to use the validation rule. You can apply a custom validation rule to entity attributes using the following steps:

1. Rebuild the Model project.

   Additional Information: The Attribute Editor will not be able to pick up your customizable fields until the validation rule is compiled.

2. Reopen the editor for the diagram "Business Domain Diagram."
3. In the diagram, on the Employees entity object definition, double click the Email attribute to open the Attribute Editor.
4. Select the Validation node.
5. Click New to add a validation rule for Email. The Add Validation Rule dialog opens.
6. Select MaxLengthValidator from the *Rules* dropdown list.
7. Enter the following values. You must double click the fields to make them editable:

   description as "Email addresses must be at most eight characters."
   maxLength as "8"

   Additional Information: Custom validators only use the Error Message field if you write `vetoableChange()` in such a way that it consults the resource bundle file for the entity object definition. You can find information about manipulating resource bundles in the JDeveloper Help topic "Returning a Localized Error Message."

8. Click OK to close the dialog.
9. Click OK to close the Attribute Editor.
10. Repeat steps 3–9 for the DepartmentId attribute of the Departments entity object. Use the following values:

    description as "Department IDs must be at most three digits."
    maxLength as "3"

11. Click OK and OK. Rebuild your project.

Test the Validation Rules

You can see how the prebuilt and custom validation rules work by trying to violate them.

1. In the Navigator, expand hr.model.datamodel.
2. Select Test from the right-click menu on HrTestModule.
3. On the Connect page, accept the defaults and click Connect.
4. When the main window opens, double click EmployeesView1 in the data model to open it in the Business Component Browser.
5. Scroll forward to employee 104, Bruce Ernst.

6. Attempt to change Ernst's salary to "400." As soon as you click on another field or try to scroll off the row, you will get an exception dialog.

   Additional Information: The message you wrote in the CompareValidator validation that is attached to the Salary attribute will appear in the dialog. Validation is triggered when you navigate from that field to another field or from that record to another record.

7. Click OK to dismiss the dialog.
8. Press ESC to set Ernst's salary back to 6000.
9. Set Ernst's email address to "BRUCEERNST." As soon as you click on another field or try to scroll off the row, you will get an exception.
10. Click OK to dismiss the dialog.

    Additional Information: The message you wrote in the description field will appear in the dialog. Validation is triggered when you navigate from that field to another field or from that record to another record.

11. Press ESC to set Ernst's email back to BERNST.
12. Double click DepartmentsView1 in the data model to open it in the Business Component Browser.
13. Try to change the DepartmentId for the first department to "1000." As soon as you click on another field or try to scroll off the row, you will get an exception.

    Additional Information: Since you customized this application of the validation rule differently, it will trigger at a different length threshold and display a different message, based on the value you entered for the *description* field.

14. Press ESC to reset the value.

What Just Happened? You created a custom validation rule and applied it to attributes with two different types. You declaratively customized the validation rule for each attribute. The rule class is now registered with the project and available to all entity attributes in the project. Then, you tested both this validation rule and the prebuilt validation rule you used in Phase II.

IV. Create and Use a Validation Domain

In this phase, you will create a domain, `JobIdDomain`, to enforce a format for Job IDs: an underscore as the third character, and all other characters capital letters. This is just a simple example of a name validation and you would add more logic in a production situation.

Generate a Validation Domain

As with the validation rule class, you need to create a class file for the validation domain. You can generate a validation domain containing a `validate()` method stub using the following steps:

1. In the Component Palette, click the Domain icon, and click a blank space in the diagram.
2. Enter "JobIdDomain" as the domain's name and press ENTER to exit the edit field.

Additional Information: If you do not enter attributes for the domain, JDeveloper will assume it is a validation domain that wraps `java.lang.String`. If you want the domain to wrap a different type, you can double click it and change the wrapped type in the Domain Editor.

CAUTION
Be sure to enter the name of the domain right after clicking the diagram surface. If the edit field closes on the name, you will not be able to rename the domain. If you create a domain with the wrong name by mistake, you will need to re-create it as the correct name and delete the object with the incorrect name from the diagram and from the disk (using the right-click menu on the old object).

3. Click Save All.

Implement the validate() Method

Now that you have the domain files, you can add code to the `validate()` method to enforce the business rule:

1. In the Application Navigator, select JobIdDomain.
2. In the Structure window, double click JobIdDomain.java to open it in the Source Editor.
3. Find the `validate()` method by double clicking it in the Structure window.
4. Write the following code as the body of the method:

```
int length = mData.length();
char currentChar;
for (int i = 0; i < length; i++)
{
  currentChar = mData.charAt(i);
  if (
    (i == 2 && currentChar != '_') ||
    (i != 2 && (currentChar < 'A' || currentChar > 'Z')) )
  {
    throw new JboException(
      "Job IDs must have the format XX_XXXXXX.");
  }
}
```

Additional Information: This code cycles through the characters in `mData`. It throws an exception if the third character is not an underscore; it also throws an exception if any other character is not a capital letter. JDeveloper automatically imports `oracle.jbo.JboException` when it generates validation domain classes.

Use the Domain to Type Entity Attributes

Now you can use this domain instead of `String` as the Java type for any entity attribute to automatically enforce the business rule you added. You can use the domain as the type of various JobId attributes with the following steps:

1. Reopen the diagram in an editor.
2. On the Employees entity object definition, double click the JobId attribute to open the Attribute Editor.
3. On the Entity Attribute page, use the *Type* pulldown to select "hr.model.businessdomain.common.JobIdDomain" for the attribute's type.
4. Reset the database column type to `VARCHAR2(10)`.
5. Click OK to close the editor.

   Additional Information: You cannot change the type of attributes directly on the diagram when the attributes participate in associations, so you must use the attribute editor.
6. Repeat steps 2–5 for the JobId attribute of JobHistory.
7. Repeat steps 2–4 for the JobId attribute of Jobs.
8. Ensure that the *Primary Key* checkbox is still checked. Click OK to close the editor.
9. Rebuild your project and click Save All.

Test the Validation Domain

You can see how the validation domain works by trying to set a Job ID to a bad format.

1. In the Application Navigator, open the Business Component Browser for hr.model.datamodel\HRTestModule.
2. Double click JobsView1 in the data model to open it in the Business Component Browser.
3. Try to change the JobId for the first job to "PRESIDENT." As soon as you click on another field or try to scroll off the row, you will get an exception.
4. Press ESC to reset the value and then close the browser.

What Just Happened? You created a validation domain, `JobIdDomain`, that wraps a `String`. The `validate()` method of JobIdDomain throws an exception if the String does not have the right format. You changed the Java type of several entity attributes from `String` to `JobIdDomain`. Now, whenever one of those attributes is assigned, an exception will be thrown if the validation test fails.

V. Provide Entity-Level Validation

In this phase, you will use the `validateEntity()` method to implement entity-level validation. You will implement a rule that all executives, and only executives, have a salary of 15,000 or greater.

Implement validateEntity()

You can implement the `validateEntity()` method in the `EmployeesImpl` class file using the following steps:

1. In the diagram, double click the Employees entity object to open the Entity Object Editor.
2. Select the Java node.
3. Check the *Validation Method* checkbox in the Generate Methods section.
4. Click OK to close the editor.
5. In the Application Navigator, select the Employees entity object.
6. In the Structure window, double click EmployeesImpl.java to open it in the Code Editor.
7. Find the method `validateEntity()`.
8. After the call to `super.validateEntity()`, add the following code. (The authors' websites mentioned in the front of the book contain code snippets that you can use instead of typing the code.)

```
String jobIdString = (String) getJobId().getData();
if (

  jobIdString.endsWith("VP") ||
  jobIdString.endsWith("PRES") )
{
  if (getSalary().intValue() < 15000)
  {
    throw new oracle.jbo.JboException(
      "Executives must have a salary of at least 15,000.");
  }

}
else
{
  if (getSalary().intValue() > 14999)
  {
    throw new oracle.jbo.JboException(
      "Non-executives cannot have a salary of over 14,999.");
  }
}
```

   Additional Information: `jobIdString` holds the `String` value that JobId (now a `JobIdDomain`) wraps. The first `if` block throws an exception if an executive (whose Job ID ends with "VP" or "PRES") has a salary of less than 15,000; the `else` block throws an exception if anyone else has a salary of 15,000 or more.

9. Click Save All and rebuild your project.

Test the Entity-Level Validation

You can see how the `validateEntity()` method works by changing employees' salaries and jobs.

1. In the Application Navigator, open the Business Component Browser for hr.model.datamodel\HRTestModule.
2. Double click EmployeesView1 in the data model to open it in the Business Component Browser.
3. Scroll forward to Employee 104 (Bruce Ernst).
4. Try the following combinations for Bruce Ernst. Attempt to scroll off the row after you try each combination. The first combination is already set.

Salary	JobId
6000	IT_PROG
16000	IT_PROG
6000	AD_VP
16000	AD_VP

   Additional Information: You will get an exception when you try to scroll off the row in the second and third case. These are the cases that violate the rule that all executives, and only executives, have a salary of 15,000 or above.

5. Close the Business Component Browser.

What Just Happened? You created validation code to enforce a rule that applies at the level of an entity object instance, rather than at the level of an individual attribute.

Adding Default Values to Entity Attributes

The business rules discussed in the first part of this chapter are triggered at various times: when an entity attribute is set, when an entity object instance loses currency, or when a transaction is committed. You might also want to write business logic that applies to new rows in the database (in other words, to new entity object instances) as soon as they are created.

The most common case where you would want such business logic is *defaulting,* that is, giving an entity attribute a default value as soon as a row is created. Just as with validation logic, there are two ways to implement defaulting logic: in XML, or in Java code for cases too complex to handle in the XML. The primary distinction is that static default values (where you specify one default value at design time that always applies to that attribute) can be handled in XML; dynamically calculated default values (where the attribute can have different initial values in different rows) must be added to Java code.

Static Default Values

The BC4J framework stores static default values as XML attributes. You can set static default values using the *Default* field in the Attribute Editor, as shown here:

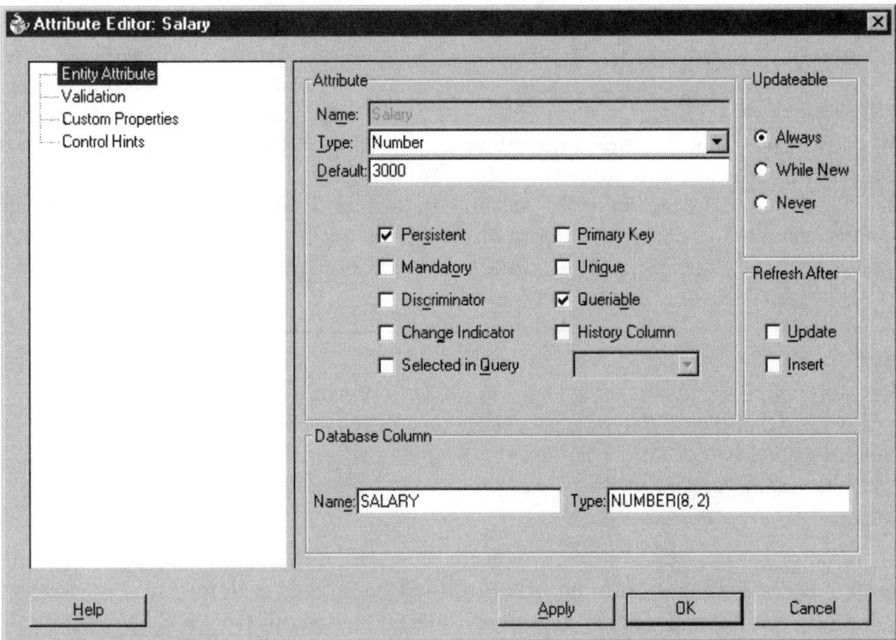

You can set static default values this way for any class with a String representation: `String`, as well as `Number`, `Date`, `Boolean`, and so on, and any validation domain based on one of these classes, but not, for example, `BlobDomain`, or a domain based on an Oracle object type. If you want to implement defaulting logic for these more complicated domains, you need to use Java as you would for dynamic default values.

Dynamically Calculated Default Values

Some attributes need to be automatically populated, but not necessarily with the same thing every time. To dynamically assign default values, you must write Java code.

The `EntityImpl` class contains a method, `create()`, that you can override to set defaults. This method is called whenever the entity object instance is created. JDeveloper can generate a method stub in an entity object class to override `create()`. The stub looks like the following:

```
protected void create()
{
  super.create();
}
```

You should keep the call to `super.create()`, but after that call, you can add any logic you want to calculate and set defaults. You will do this in the hands-on practice.

The SequenceImpl Class and the DBSequence Domain

One of the most common reasons to dynamically calculate a default value is to populate attributes in successive rows with a series of sequential numbers. The ADF BC libraries contain a class, `oracle.jbo.server.SequenceImpl`, that wraps Oracle database sequences.

The constructor for SequenceImpl requires that you pass in both the name of the sequence and a database transaction (so that ADF BC knows where the sequence is located). Fortunately, there is a method on EntityImpl, getDBTransaction(), that returns the current transaction. After calling getDBTransaction(), you can increment the sequence and extract the next value into a Number using getSequenceNumber(). You can find an example of this in the hands-on practice later in this chapter.

Instead of dynamically retrieving the attribute in Java, you can put a trigger in the database to update the value of the database column on which the attribute is based. If you do this, you should make the attribute of type DBSequence. DBSequence maintains a temporary unique value in the entity cache until the data is posted.

NOTE

When you create a client application, you should not expose to the user any field that uses DBSequence, except on rows that you can guarantee have been posted. The temporary value displayed in the cache has no relationship to the value that the database column will contain and may confuse users.

There are two advantages of using DBSequence over coding with SequenceImpl: It does not require Java coding, and you are guaranteed that sequence numbers will be sequential; that is, no sequence numbers would be generated in transactions that are rolled back before they are posted to the database. However, using DBSequence only works if the database contains a trigger to populate the attribute; SequenceImpl does not require a trigger.

Calculated Transient Attributes

Business rules can also be used to calculate values for transient attributes. The values in transient attributes exist only in the entity cache; they do not correspond to values in any database column. The most common use of such transient attributes is to hold values calculated from other attributes.

Implementing a calculated attribute consists of two parts: calculating it initially when rows are read from the database and updating its value when the attributes used in the calculation change. The former is done declaratively using SQL; the latter is written in Java in the setter methods for the attributes used in the calculation. You can find an example of this use in the hands-on practice.

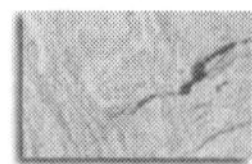

NOTE

Due to a bug in JDeveloper releases 9.0.5.1 and 9.0.5.2, transient entity attributes are not properly exposed to client applications. There is a workaround for this bug involving the view row class. You will use this workaround in the hands-on practice. View row classes are explained in Chapter 13. This bug is scheduled to be fixed in release 10.1.2.

Using Associations in Business Rules

Sometimes business rules do not simply apply to a particular entity object definition, but to relationships between entity object definitions. These relationships, as was discussed in Chapter 9, are implemented by associations, and using associations lets you implement cross-entity business rules.

Recall from Chapter 9 that you set association directionality by creating accessor attributes in the associated entity object definitions. If you create an accessor attribute in an entity object definition, you can use it to retrieve associated entity object instances just as you would use a regular attribute to retrieve attribute values, namely:

- **You can pass the name of the accessor attribute into `EntityImpl.getAttribute()`.** For example, since Departments has an accessor attribute called Employees, you can call `EntityImpl.getAttribute("Employees")` on a Departments entity object instance to retrieve the associated Employees entity object instances.
- **You can generate an entity object class, which will contain a getter method that returns the associated entity object instances.** For example, if you generate the `DepartmentsImpl` class, it will contain the method `getEmployees()`.

What these methods return depends on whether the other side of the association is a "many" side or a "one" side—that is, whether the returned data is guaranteed to be at most a single entity object instance or might be multiple entity object instances. You can use these methods within setters, `validateEntity()`, `create()`, or other methods to implement complex business rules. You will see an example of this in the next hands-on practice.

Getting a Unique Associated Entity

When the other side of the association has a cardinality of "one" (for example, the Department accessor attribute in the Employees entity object), the object returned by either of the methods is simply the associated entity object instance (for example, a single Departments entity object instance), or "null" if there is no associated instance).

Although the returned object is always an entity object instance, the return type can be one of three things:

- **`java.lang.Object`** `getAttribute()` has a return type of `Object`, so if you use this method, you must cast the returned value in order to use it.
- **An entity object class** If you have generated the entity object class for both associated entity object definitions, the getter method will have a return type of the appropriate entity object class. For example, if you have generated both `EmployeesImpl` and `DepartmentsImpl`, `EmployeesImpl.getDepartment()` will have a return type of `DepartmentsImpl`.
- **`EntityImpl`** If you have generated only the entity object class that contains the getter method, it will have a return type of `EntityImpl`. For example, if you have generated `EmployeesImpl` but not `DepartmentsImpl`, `EmployeesImpl.getDepartment()` will have a return type of `EntityImpl`.

Getting Many Associated Entities

When the other side of the association has a cardinality of "many" (for example, the Employees accessor attribute in the Departments entity object, which can return many Employees entity object instances), the object returned by either of the methods is an object called a *row iterator*, which is itself a collection of objects, called *row objects*, plus a pointer to one particular row object, the "current" row object. This pointer can be moved around, and data can be extracted from the current row object.

A row object is actually any object that implements the interface `oracle.jbo.Row`. In fact, `oracle.jbo.server.EntityImpl` implements `oracle.jbo.Row`, so entity object instances are, in fact, row objects. Other things can be row objects too, but the row iterators returned by association getter methods or the `getAttribute()` method contain only entity object instances.

Although the getter methods and `getAttribute()` both return the same thing, they have different return types. The getter methods have a return type of `oracle.jbo.RowIterator` whereas `getAttribute()` has a return type of `Object`. If you use `getAttribute()`, you must cast the return value to `oracle.jbo.RowIterator` before you can use it.

When a row iterator is first created, its pointer starts at a slot before the first row object it contains. You can then call the method `RowIterator.next()`, which has the following two effects:

- **It moves the pointer to the next row object in the RowIterator.** When the row iterator is first created, this is the first row object.
- **It returns that row object.**

`next()` has a return type of `oracle.jbo.Row`; you must cast the returned value to `EntityImpl` or the appropriate entity object class in order to use it. `next()` is most useful when used in conjunction with the method `RowIterator.hasNext()`, which returns true if the row iterator has at least one more row. Using `next()` and `hasNext()` together lets you write a loop that cycles through all the rows in the row iterator. You will see an example of this in the hands-on practice.

Integrating with Business Logic in the Database

You can place business logic in the business services layer, the database, or both; Chapter 8 contains some guidelines for making this decision (in the section "Why Use ADF BC?"). If you place business logic in the database, you must design your business components to integrate with this logic.

Integrating with Database Triggers

If your database contains triggers that fire when data is inserted or updated, you must ensure that changes made by those triggers are reflected in the entity cache. For example, if you use a database trigger to create default values for a table column, you must ensure that the corresponding entity attribute is populated with the database-created value whenever a new row is inserted. If you use a database trigger to maintain calculated attributes, you must ensure that the corresponding entity attribute is recalculated whenever a row is updated.

You can ensure that attribute values are synchronized with the database in this way by setting their *Refresh After* properties in the Attribute Editor, as shown next:

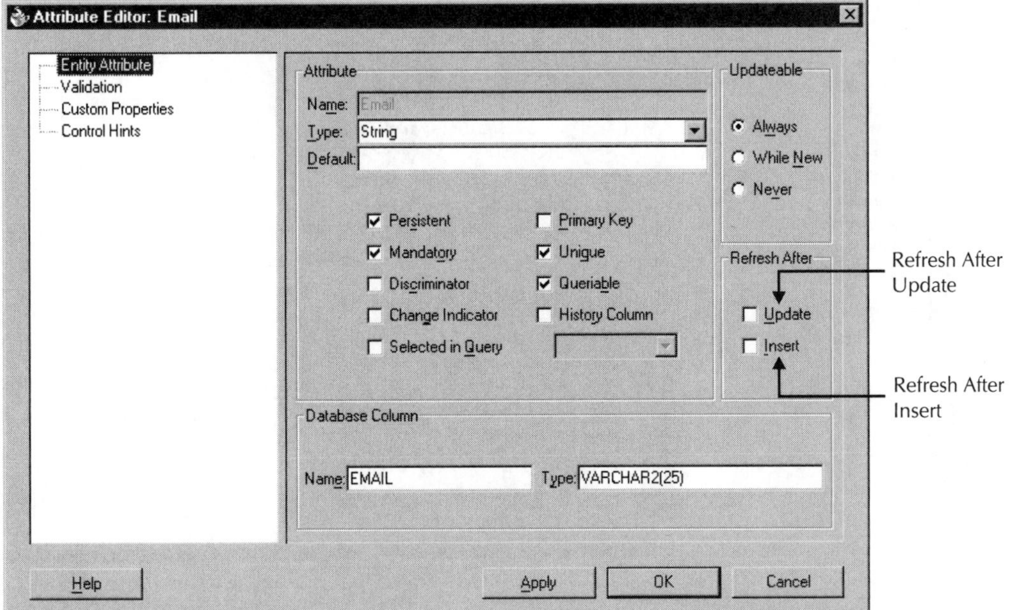

If an entity attribute's *Refresh After Update* property is set, the attribute will be repopulated for changed entity object instances as soon as the changes are posted to the database. You should set the *Refresh After Update* property if you have triggers that maintain calculated attributes in the database.

If an entity attribute's *Refresh After Insert* property is set, the attribute will be populated for new entity object instances as soon as they are posted to the database. You should set the *Refresh After Insert* property if you have triggers that create default attribute values in the database.

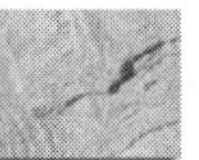

NOTE

As explained in Chapter 8, business logic in the database only fires when changes are posted. The "Refresh After" properties do not operate as soon as a new entity object instance is created or changed, but rather when the new instance or the changes are posted to the database.

Using Stored Procedures to Perform DML Operations

You may have stored procedures in the database that you want to invoke to perform DML operations. One way to do this is to create INSTEAD OF triggers and then set attributes' *Refresh After* properties, as described in the preceding section. The other way is to override `EntityImpl.doDML()`, a method called whenever ADF BC posts changes to the database.

If you create an entity object class, you can generate a stub to override `doDML()` by selecting the *Data Manipulation Methods* checkbox on the Java page of the Entity Object Editor, as shown next:

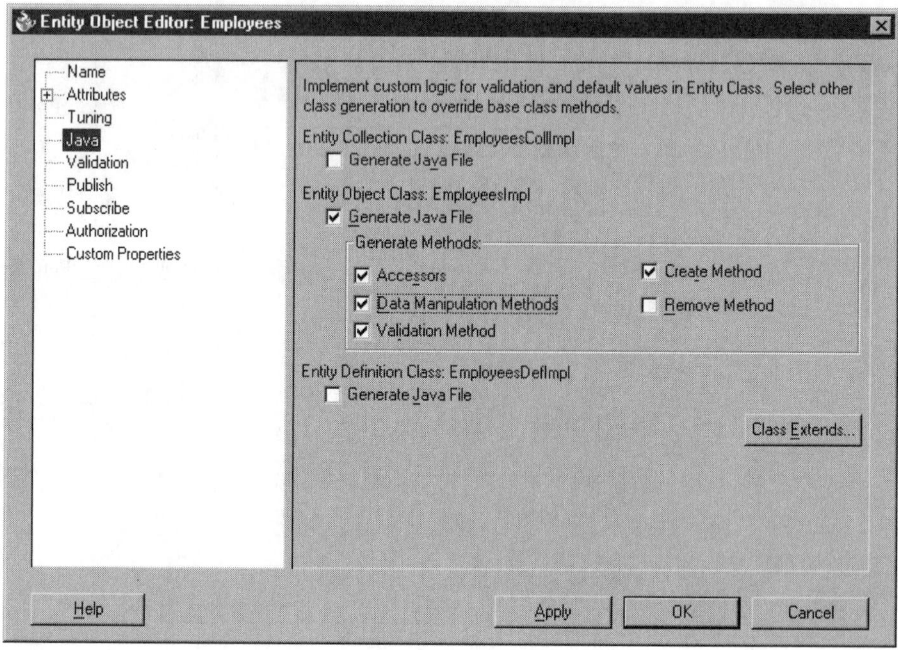

This will generate a stub like the following:

```
protected void doDML(int operation, TransactionEvent e)
{
  super.doDML(operation, e);
}
```

The `operation` parameter contains a value equal to one of the following constants:

- **`DML_INSERT`** if the requested operation is an INSERT
- **`DML_DELETE`** if the requested operation is a DELETE
- **`DML_UPDATE`** if the requested operation is an UPDATE

So, for example, you can write a method, `doCustomUpdate()`, that contains JDBC code to call a stored procedure to perform updates, and invoke it from `doDML()` by changing `doDML()`'s method body to the following:

```
protected void doDML(int operation, TransactionEvent e)
{
  if (operation == DML_UPDATE)
  {
```

```
      doCustomUpdate();
    }
    else
    {
      super.doDML(operation, e);
    }
  }
```

For information on writing JDBC code to call a stored procedure (for example, on implementing `doCustomUpdate()`), see the JDeveloper help topic "Calling Stored Procedures."

Hands-on Practice: Add More Business Rules to the HR Business Domain Components

In this practice, you will continue to refine the business components project you created in Chapter 9. In addition to the validation logic that you implemented in the last hands-on practice, when you have completed this practice, the business components in the `hr.model.businessdomain` package will automatically populate the EmployeeId attribute from a database sequence, calculate a value for YearlyPay, and enforce a requirement that managers make more money than their employees. It is this functional business domain that you will use to design data model components in the next two chapters.

This practice requires that you have completed the preceding practice in this chapter. Alternatively, you can download the starting files for this practice from the authors' websites mentioned in the beginning of the book.

This practice steps you through the following phases:

I. Add Defaulting Logic

- Generate the `create()` method
- Add defaulting code to the `create()` method
- Test the attribute defaulting

II. Calculate an attribute

- Calculate the initial attribute value
- Maintain the attribute value with setter methods
- Properly expose the calculated attribute to client applications
- Test the calculated attribute

III. Add validation logic that uses an association

- Add logic that retrieves the "one" end of the association
- Add logic that retrieves the "many" end of the association
- Test the validation logic

I. Add Defaulting Logic

In this phase, you will add logic populate two attributes of the Employees entity object definition with dynamically calculated default values. You will populate the HireDate attribute with the date the entity object instance was created. Then, you will populate the EmployeeId with a value taken from a database sequence, EMPLOYEES_SEQ, using the `SequenceImpl` class.

Generate the create() Method

The first step in dynamically calculating default attribute values is to generate a stub for the `create()` method. You can generate the `create()` method stub using the following steps:

1. On the Business Domain diagram, double click the Employees entity object definition to open the Entity Object Editor.
2. Select the Java node.
3. Check the *Create Method* checkbox in the Generate Methods section.
4. Click OK to close the editor and to generate a `create()` method stub in the EmployeesImpl.java class.

Add Defaulting Code to the create() Method

You can add code to retrieve a value from EMPLOYEES_SEQ and automatically populate EmployeeId using the following steps:

1. In the Application Navigator, select the Employees node.
2. In the Structure window, double click EmployeesImpl.java to open it in the Code Editor.
3. Double click the `create()` method in the Structure window.
4. After the call to `super.create()`, insert the following code:

```
Date currentDate = new Date(Date.getCurrentDate());
setHireDate(currentDate);
```

Additional Information: The this uses the static method `Date.getCurrentDate()` to create a new instance of `Date` based on the current date.

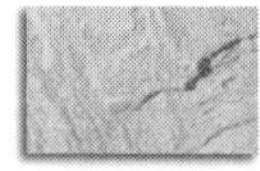

NOTE

In some versions of JDeveloper, the code editor will display a blue line, as for a syntax error, under the code "new Date(Date.getCurrentDate())". This is due to a bug and does not indicate an actual syntax error. The EmployeesImpl class will continue to compile properly.

5. Add the following code immediately after the lines you just entered:

```
SequenceImpl empSeq=new SequenceImpl(
  "EMPLOYEES_SEQ", getDBTransaction() );
setEmployeeId(empSeq.getSequenceNumber());
```

Additional Information: Note that `getDBTransaction()` is used to provide a DBTransaction for the `SequenceImpl` constructor.

6. The `SequenceImpl` type on the second line of code will show with a blue underline. This means that the class is not accessible. Hold the mouse cursor above the `SequenceImpl` word and press ALT-ENTER. A selection list will appear because there are two `SequenceImpl` classes. Double click the oracle.jbo.server.SequenceImpl item to add the import statement.
7. Rebuild the Model project.

Test the Attribute Defaulting

You can see how attribute defaulting works by adding a new row.

1. Test HrTestModule.
2. Double click EmployeesView1.
3. Click the Add Row button (shown on the right) to create a row. 
4. Note that the *HireDate* field is automatically populated with the current system date.
5. Note that the *EmployeeId* field is automatically populated with a new sequence number.
6. Roll back the transaction and close the Business Component Browser.

What Just Happened? You added code to the `create()` method to automatically populate HireDate and EmployeeId. Since the `create()` method is called whenever a new row is created, new employees will have their HireDate default to the current date and their EmployeeId default to a number picked from the database sequence. If the HR schema had contained a trigger to automatically populate EMPLOYEE_ID from EMPLOYEES_SEQ, you could have used the `DBSequence` domain instead, without writing Java code to populate EmployeeId.

II. Calculate an Attribute

In this phase, you add code to automatically calculate the value of the attribute YearlyPay, which you added to Employees in Chapter 9. When you have finished, YearlyPay will automatically be set to the estimated yearly pay for employees.

Calculate the Initial Attribute Value

You can use SQL to calculate the initial value for a calculated attribute using the following steps:

1. In the Business Domain Diagram, on the Employees entity object definition, double click the YearlyPay attribute to open the Attribute Editor.
2. Check the *Selected in Query* checkbox.

   Additional Information: This checkbox allows you to enter a SQL expression to calculate the initial value of the attribute. View object definitions with attributes based on the YearlyPay attribute (such as the default view object definition EmployeesView) will use this expression in their queries; the data returned will be stored in the YearlyPay entity object attribute. You will learn more about the relationship between view object queries and entity object attributes in Chapter 11.

3. Enter the following expression in the *Query Column Expression* text area:

```
(NVL(SALARY, 0) *
  (12 + (NVL(COMMISSION_PCT, 0) * .6)))
```

Additional Information: This calculates the initial value for YearlyPay based on the following rules:

- The base yearly pay is 12 times the monthly salary.
- Commission is estimated based on estimated sales of five times base yearly pay. The commission percentage, times .01 (since it is a percentage), times the monthly salary, times 12 (for 12 months), times 5 is (SALARY * COMMISSION_PCT * .6).
- Values of NULL for SALARY or COMMISSION_PCT are treated as zeroes.
- YearlyPay is the total of the base salary plus the commission calculated as described.

4. Click OK to close the editor. When a dialog appears asking you if you want to set the column type to `NUMBER`, click Yes.

Additional Information: The preceding expression returns a value of type `NUMBER`. Setting this in the attribute will improve performance of the JDBC mapping.

Maintain the Attribute Value with Setter Methods

You can maintain the value of a calculated attribute by adding code to the setter methods of the attributes used to compute the default value using the following steps:

1. Open EmployeesImpl.java in the Source Editor.
2. Add a new method, `calculateYearlyPay()`, to the Java class, as follows:

```
private void calculateYearlyPay(Number sal, Number commPct)
{
  int salValue=0;
  double commPctValue=0;
  if (sal != null)
  {
    salValue = sal.intValue();
  }
  if (commPct != null)
  {
    commPctValue = commPct.doubleValue();
  }
  int yearlyPayValue =
    (int) (salValue * (12 + (commPctValue * .6)));
  setYearlyPay(new Number(yearlyPayValue));
}
```

Additional Information: The preceding code repeats the calculation that was done in SQL. You will call this method whenever Salary or CommissionPct is changed.

3. Find the `setSalary()` method.

4. After the call to `setAttributeInternal()`, add the following line of code to the method body:

   ```
   calculateYearlyPay(value, getCommissionPct());
   ```

   Additional Information: The preceding code recalculates YearlyPay based on the new value for Salary and the value for CommissionPct.

5. Find the `setCommissionPct()` method.
6. After the call to `setAttributeInternal()`, add the following line of code to the method body:

   ```
   calculateYearlyPay(getSalary(), value);
   ```

7. Click Save All.
8. Rebuild the project.

Properly Expose the Calculated Attribute to Client Applications

Due to a bug in JDeveloper releases 9.0.5.1 and 9.0.5.2, calculated attributes are not properly exposed to client applications. If you are using a version of JDeveloper in which this bug has been fixed, you can skip these steps. If you are using releases 9.0.5.1 or 9.0.5.2, you can expose a calculated attribute using the following steps:

1. In the Application Navigator, double click hr.model.datamodel\EmployeesView to open the view object editor.
2. Select the Attributes node.
3. Remove YearlyPay from the *Selected* list.
4. In the *Available* list, select Employees\YearlyPay, and add it back to the *Selected* list.

   Additional information: This ensures that EmployeesView maintains the proper mapping between its query and Employees' YearlyPay attribute.

5. Select the Java node.
6. Select the *Generate Java File* checkbox in the View Row Class section. Leave the other checkboxes as they are.

   Additional information: The view row class implements view rows. For more information about this class, see Chapter 13.

7. Click OK.
8. When a dialog comes up asking you if you want to set default column types, click Yes.
9. In the Structure pane, double click EmployeesViewRowImpl.java to open it in the Source Editor.
10. Find the method `getYearlyPay()`.

    Additional information: This is the method that returns the value of the view attribute YearlyPay.

11. Replace the body of the method with the following:

```
return getEmployees().getYearlyPay();
```

Additional information: `getEmployees()` returns the entity object instance corresponding to this row. This ensures that, whenever an application retrieves a value for the YearlyPay view attribute, it gets the value for the YearlyPay entity attribute.

12. Click Save All.
13. Rebuild the Project.

Test the Calculated Attribute

You can see how your calculated attribute works by scrolling around and looking at its values on various rows. You will also test to make sure it stays in synch with Salary and CommissionPct.

1. Test HrTestModule.
2. Double click EmployeesView1.
3. Scroll forward to employee 104, Bruce Ernst.
4. Note that Ernst's YearlyPay is 72000, 12 times his Salary.
5. Change Ernst's salary to "7000". As soon as you click into another field or scroll off the row, Ernst's YearlyPay will change to 84000.
6. Give Ernst a CommissionPct of ".5" (one-half of one percent). As soon as you click into another field or scroll off the row, Ernst's YearlyPay will change to 86100. This is because 0.5 percent of five times Ernst's yearly salary is 2100.
7. Close the Business Component Browser.

What Just Happened? You specified SQL to calculate the YearlyPay attribute for rows queried from the database. Then you added code to `setSalary()` and `setCommissionPct()` to ensure that YearlyPay is recalculated after Salary or CommissionPct is changed.

III. Add Validation Logic That Uses an Association

In this phase, you add validation logic to ensure that no employee makes more than his or her manager does. The logic has to use the association EmpManagerFkAssoc in each direction: once to make sure no employee's salary is set higher than his or her manager's, and once to make sure no manager's salary is set lower than the salary of any of his or her employees.

Add Logic That Retrieves the "One" End of the Association

First, you must add code to `setSalary()` that uses EmpManagerFkAssoc to retrieve an employee's manager—that is, from the "many" end to the "one" end of the association. Since the "one" end is unique, this will involve retrieving a single entity object instance.

1. In the source code for EmployeesImpl.java, find the `setSalary()` method.
2. Add this code before the `setAttributeInternal()` statement:

```
boolean ok = true;
EmployeesImpl manager = getManager();
if (manager != null)
{
  if (manager.getSalary().intValue() < value.intValue())
  {
    ok = false;
  }
}
```

Additional Information: The Boolean variable "ok" is used to store the current validation state. The preceding code starts out by assuming the new value is acceptable. Then it uses an association accessor method to retrieve the manager of the current row, if any. If the manager exists and has a salary less than the new value, the current row is not acceptable.

3. Replace the existing call to `setAttributeInternal()` with the following `if-then-else` block:

```
if (ok)
{
  setAttributeInternal(SALARY, value);
}
else
{
  throw new JboException(
    "Managers' salaries cannot be lower than their employees'." );
}
```

4. Press ALT-ENTER and select `oracle.jbo.JboException` to import it.

6. Click Save All.

Add Logic That Retrieves the "Many" End of the Association

The code you just added to `setSalary()` ensures that an employee is not given a raise above the salary level of his or her manager. However, to really enforce the business rule, you must also ensure that no manager is given a pay cut below the salary level of any of his or her employees. This involves adding more code to `setSalary()` to use EmpManagerFkAssoc to retrieve a manager's reports, that is, from the "one" end to the "many" end of the association. Since the "many" end is not unique, this will involve retrieving a row iterator.

1. Add the following code to the body of `setSalary()`, right before the `if-else` block ("`if (ok)`") containing the `setAttributeInternal()` call:

```
RowIterator reports = getReports();
EmployeesImpl current;
while (reports.hasNext())
{
  current = (EmployeesImpl) reports.next();
  if (current.getSalary().intValue() > value.intValue())
  {
```

```
      ok = false;
    }
  }
```

Additional Information: The preceding code calls the accessor attribute getter method to return a row iterator. The loop cycles through the row iterator, using `next()` to step through the row objects and `hasNext()` to provide an exit condition. The variable "current" holds the current row object (cast to the type `EmployeesImpl`); at each step of the loop, the code tests to ensure that the salary for the current row object is no greater than `setSalary()`'s parameter. Note that this code will still work if the employee is not a manager. In that case, the row iterator will be empty, `hasNext()` will immediately be false, and the salary test will be skipped.

2. Click Save All. Build the project.

Test the Validation Logic

You can see how the `setSalary()` validation code works by trying to violate the rules: first, by setting an employee's salary too high and then by setting a manager's salary too low.

1. Test HrTestModule.
2. Double click EmployeesView1.
3. Scroll forward to employee 101, Neena Kochhar.
4. Try to set Kochhar's salary to "25000". As soon as you click into another field or scroll off the row, you will get an exception message.

   Additional Information: Kochhar reports to Steven King, the President, who has a salary of 24,000. This change would violate the first part of the validation code you placed in `setSalary()`—you cannot set an employee's salary to be higher than his or her manager's. The error message is not terribly informative. By writing more complex code (for example, keeping track of the EmployeeId and Salary of both the manager and the reporting employee that caused the test to fail), you could have passed a String to the JboException's constructor that contained more useful information.
5. Set Kochhar's salary to "18000". Notice that the change is accepted.
6. Scroll back to employee 100, Steven King.
7. Try to set King's salary to "16000". As soon as you click into another field or scroll off the row, you will get an exception.

   Additional Information: Because Kochhar has a salary of 18,000, this change would violate the second part of the validation code—you cannot set a manager's salary to be lower than any of his or her reporting employees.
8. Close the Business Component Browser.

What Just Happened? You added business logic to a setter method that will throw an exception whenever a client tries to assign a salary that would violate the rule "An employee's salary cannot be higher than his or her manager's." This involved using an association in each direction: once to retrieve a unique entity instance (an employee's manager) and once to retrieve a row iterator (a manager's employees).

CHAPTER 11

Creating Data Model Components

All is waste and worthless, till
Arrives the selecting will,
And, out of slime and chaos, Wit
Draws the threads of fair and fit.

—Ralph Waldo Emerson (1803–1882), *Wealth*

hapters 9 and 10 explained how to create business domain components to represent features of the database and encapsulate business logic. In this chapter, you will learn how to create data model components to collect data for use by MVC applications. Oracle ADF does not allow MVC applications to access entity object definitions and associations directly; instead, you select exactly what data you want clients to be able to access by exposing it through data model components. Data model components—view object definitions, view link definitions, and application module definitions—were introduced in Chapter 8.

The first part of this chapter will focus on creating view object definitions. There are many more choices involved in constructing view object definitions than there are in constructing entity object definitions. The chapter discusses the structure of view objects (including their relationship to entity objects) and how you can determine which structure will be most effective and efficient for your purposes. Later in the chapter, you will learn about using view link definitions to represent relationships between your view object definitions and using application module definitions to aggregate the data and relationships that your application will need.

This chapter contains two hands-on practices. In the first hands-on practice, you will create view object definitions to expose the data represented by the business domain components you created in Chapters 9 and 10, exploring a number of different view object definition structures. In the second hands-on practice, you will create view link definitions to represent relationships between the view object definitions and create an application module definition to aggregate and present data to the application.

View Attributes, Entity Attributes, and Caching

As mentioned in Chapter 8, view attributes can (but need not) be based on entity attributes. View attributes based on entity attributes are called *entity-derived view attributes*; other view attributes are *SQL-only view attributes.*

It is impossible to decide whether a particular attribute should be entity-derived or SQL-only without understanding the primary difference between entity-derived and SQL-only attributes—the way in which they are cached. *Caching,* in data processing, is holding copies of data in memory. The primary benefit of caching in general is optimizing performance. ADF BC's caching mechanisms optimize performance by holding the data in the middle tier, eliminating repeated trips to the database.

This section discusses how values for entity-derived and SQL-only view attributes are cached and then explains how to decide whether a particular attribute should be entity-derived or SQL-only.

How Entity-Derived View Attributes Are Populated

When a view object instance with entity-derived view attributes first executes its query, it sends the query to the database. The database returns a result, as shown in Figure 11-1.

The columns in the query result are mapped to view attributes and to the entity attributes they are based on, as shown in Figure 11-2.

Next, entity object instances are created, and the attributes are populated with the appropriate result column data, and inserted into entity caches (one for each entity object definition), as shown in Figure 11-3. There may not be as many instances in each entity cache as there are rows in the query result; the entity object definition's primary key attributes are used to determine how many rows are needed. For example, in Figure 11-3, there is only one Departments entity object instance (with a DepartmentId of 90) corresponding to all three rows of the query result. Note that only some of the entity attributes (those corresponding to query columns) are populated.

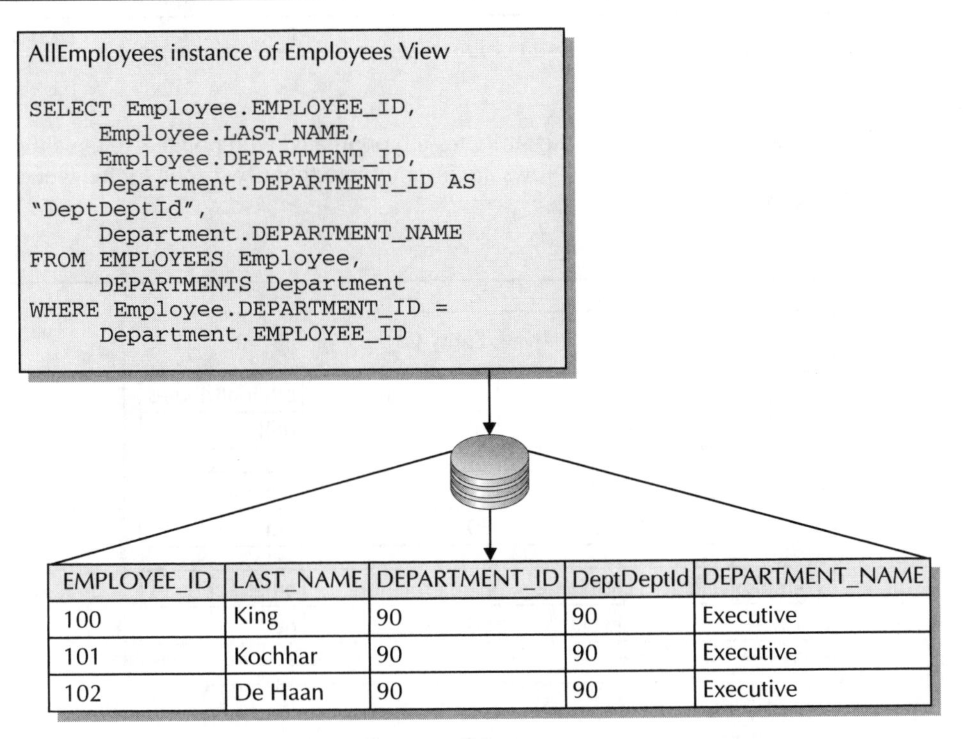
AllEmployees instance of Employees View
SELECT Employee.EMPLOYEE_ID,
Employee.LAST_NAME,
Employee.DEPARTMENT_ID,
Department.DEPARTMENT_ID AS
"DeptDeptId",
Department.DEPARTMENT_NAME
FROM EMPLOYEES Employee,
DEPARTMENTS Department
WHERE Employee.DEPARTMENT_ID =
Department.EMPLOYEE_ID

EMPLOYEE_ID	LAST_NAME	DEPARTMENT_ID	DeptDeptId	DEPARTMENT_NAME
100	King	90	90	Executive
101	Kochhar	90	90	Executive
102	De Haan	90	90	Executive

FIGURE 11-1. *Executing a query and returning a result*

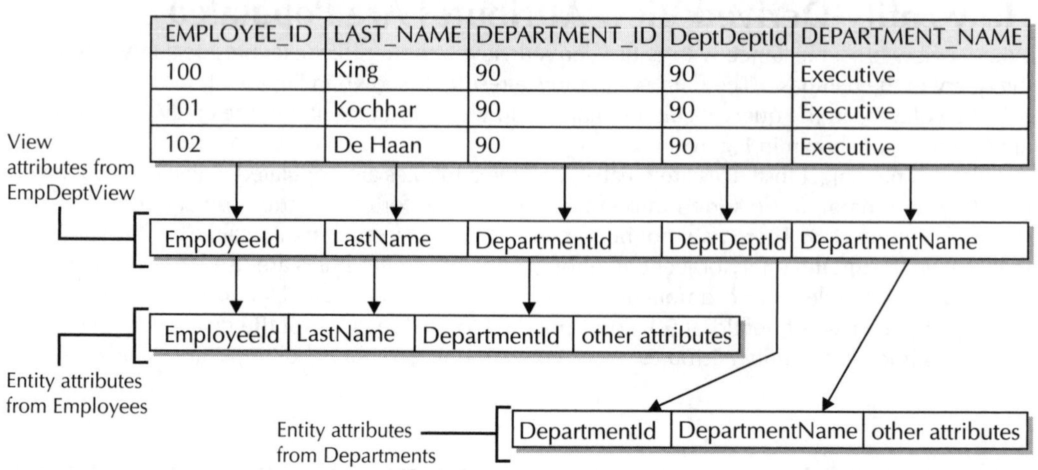

FIGURE 11-2. *Associating the query result columns with view and entity attributes*

Finally, view rows are created, and the attributes are populated with pointers to the entity attributes in the entity cache. These view rows are inserted into the view cache for the view object instance, as shown in Figure 11-4.

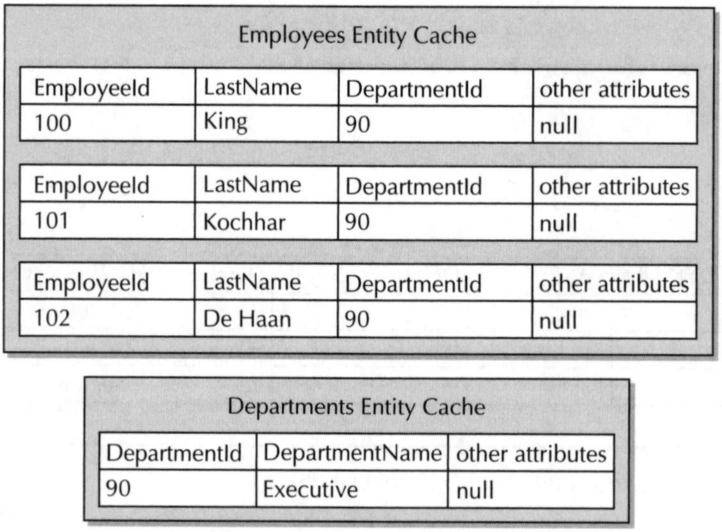

Employees Entity Cache

EmployeeId	LastName	DepartmentId	other attributes
100	King	90	null

EmployeeId	LastName	DepartmentId	other attributes
101	Kochhar	90	null

EmployeeId	LastName	DepartmentId	other attributes
102	De Haan	90	null

Departments Entity Cache

DepartmentId	DepartmentName	other attributes
90	Executive	null

FIGURE 11-3. *Populating entity caches*

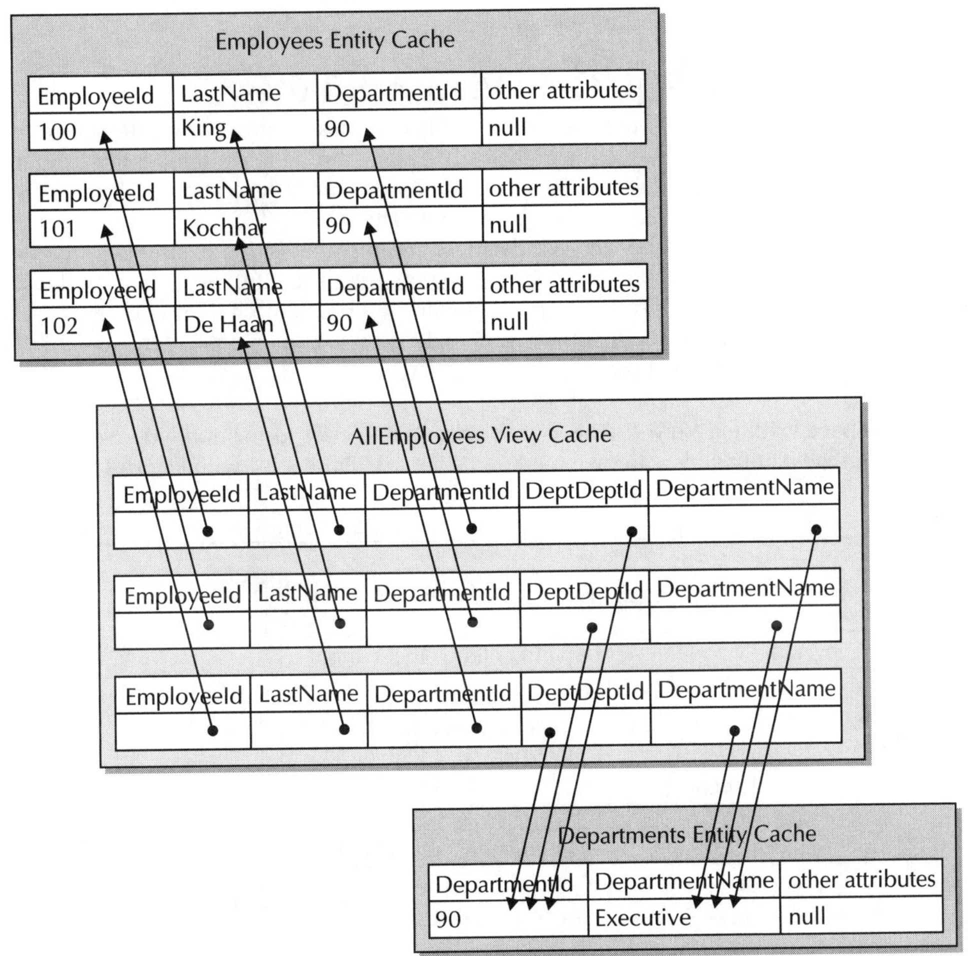

FIGURE 11-4. *Populating a view cache*

In summary, there are two sorts of caches: entity caches and view caches. In the case of entity-derived attributes, entity caches hold the data in those attributes, and view caches hold pointers to that data.

How SQL-Only Attributes Are Populated

SQL-only view attributes retrieve data from the database just as entity-derived view attributes do, as shown in Figure 11-1. After the data is retrieved, however, SQL-only view attributes are not added to any entity cache, because they have no corresponding entity attributes. Instead, when the view cache is created, the appropriate attribute is populated directly with the data, instead of a pointer to data in an entity cache, as shown in Figure 11-5.

Entity-Derived vs. SQL-Only View Attributes

The only reason you must use an entity-derived attribute is to make changes to a database column. As Chapter 9 mentions, all updates to the database are made through persistent entity attributes, so if your application needs to make changes to a database column, it must do so through an entity-derived view attribute based on a persistent entity attribute.

If you do not need to make changes to a database column, that is, if the attribute is read-only, a SQL-only attribute is usually more efficient than an entity-derived attribute because it skips the step of storing the data in the entity cache and maintaining a pointer to it. However, even if the attribute is read-only, there are a few reasons you might want to use an entity-derived attribute, as explained in the following sections.

It May Save Space Within a View Cache For some join queries, using entity-derived attributes for attributes of the parent table can save memory. Contrast Figure 11-4 with Figure 11-5. In

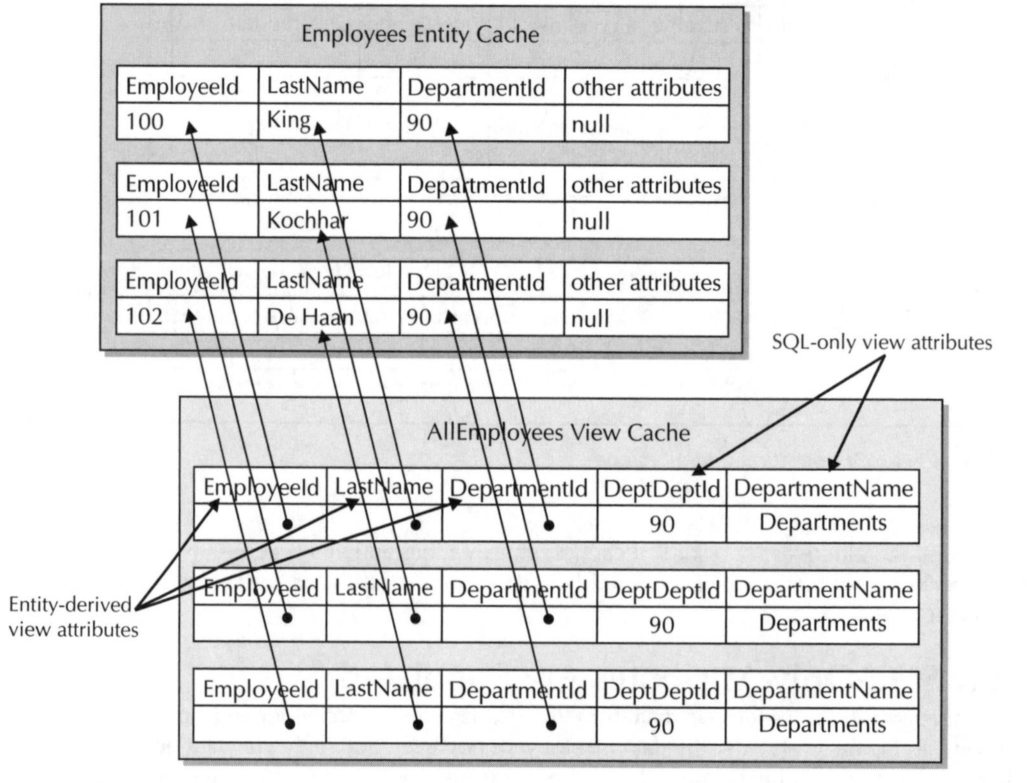

FIGURE 11-5. *Populating SQL-only attributes*

Figure 11-5, the data "90" and "Executive" is stored three times—once for each row of the query result. In Figure 11-4, a single entity object instance containing the data is created, and multiple view rows can point to that entity object instance.

This is only a significant consideration for join queries where there are many rows in the detail table for each average row in the parent table. Using entity-derived attributes for department information in situations where the average department has hundreds of employees is a significant savings; however, if the average department has only 10 or 20 employees, the relatively small savings in memory will generally not be worth the overhead of the two-level caching system.

It May Save Space Between View Caches If your data model contains multiple instances of the same view object definition, each instance will have its own view cache. For example, consider a data model with two instances of the EmpDeptView view object definition: AllEmployees and EmployeesInDepartment. The result sets of these instances may have many rows in common. For SQL-only attributes in EmpDeptView, all of the data will be stored twice—once in AllEmployees' cache, and once in EmployeesInDepartment's cache. For entity-derived attributes, only one copy of the data will be maintained (in the Employees and Departments entity caches), and both AllEmployees and EmployeesInDepartment can point at it.

Even instances of different view object definitions can share data. For example, consider the view object definition DeptMgrView, with the following query:

```
SELECT Department.DEPARTMENT_ID,
  Department.DEPARTMENT_NAME,
  Department.MANAGER_ID,
  Manager.EMPLOYEE_ID,
  Manager.LAST_NAME
FROM DEPARTMENTS Department, EMPLOYEES Manager
WHERE Department.MANAGER_ID = Manager.EMPLOYEE_ID
```

If AllDepartments is an instance of DeptMgrView, there will be a substantial overlap between its result set and the result set of AllEmployees. For example, both result sets will include a value of "Executive" as a department name. If DepartmentName is a SQL-only attribute in DeptMgrView and EmpDeptView, "Executive" (and other such values) will have to be stored in the view caches for both AllDepartments and AllEmployees. If it is an entity-derived attribute, it will only have to be stored once, in the entity cache for Employees.

This is only a significant consideration in cases where the data model contains many view object instances that return significantly overlapping query results. Otherwise, the space saved will not generally be worth the overhead of the two-level caching system.

It Ensures Synchronization As mentioned earlier, different view object instances can have result sets with overlapping data. For example, the result sets for the AllDepartments, EmployeesInDepartment, and AllDepartments view object instances might all include as data the name of Department 90.

If the DepartmentName view attribute of EmpDeptView and DeptMgrView is SQL-only, then the name of Department 90 will be stored separately in each of the three view caches. If the name is changed in AllEmployees' view cache, it will not automatically be changed in the others, as shown in Figure 11-6.

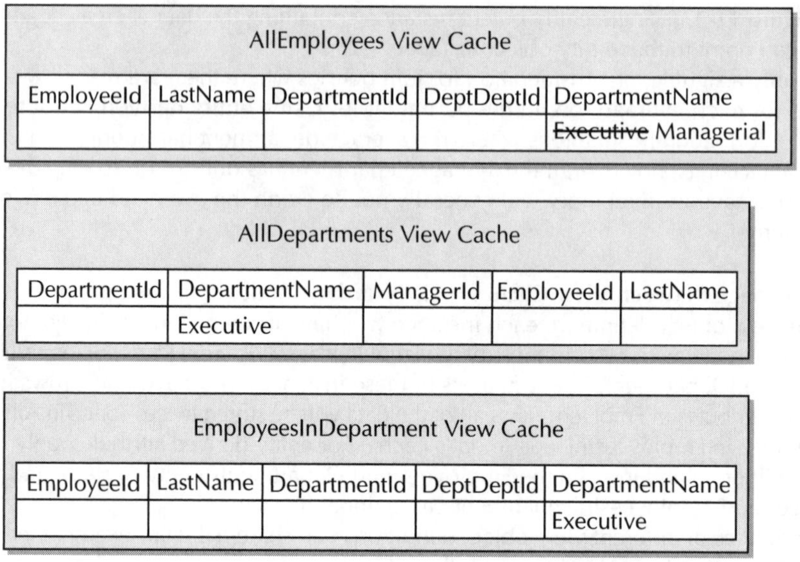

AllEmployees View Cache

EmployeeId	LastName	DepartmentId	DeptDeptId	DepartmentName
				~~Executive~~ Managerial

AllDepartments View Cache

DepartmentId	DepartmentName	ManagerId	EmployeeId	LastName
	Executive			

EmployeesInDepartment View Cache

EmployeeId	LastName	DepartmentId	DeptDeptId	DepartmentName
				Executive

FIGURE 11-6. *Synchronization and SQL-only view attributes*

Instead, if the DepartmentName view attribute is entity-derived, then the name of Department 90 will only be stored once, in the Departments entity cache. Consequently, making a change in one of the view caches really changes the data in the Departments entity cache, a change that is immediately visible in the other view caches, as shown in Figure 11-7.

It Allows You to Use the Attribute in a Many-to-Many View Link Many-to-many view links, discussed later in this chapter, must be based on associations. For this reason, their source and destination attributes must both be entity-derived.

SQL-Only View Object Definitions

A *SQL-only view object definition* is a view object definition with no entity usages. As described in Chapter 8, entity usages are references contained in view object definitions to entity object definitions. For example, the view object definition EmpDeptView in the preceding section may contain usages of the entity object definitions Employees and Departments. Entity usages are optional; view object definitions only need to include entity usages if they are going to use the entity cache. For example, EmpDeptView does not need to contain a usage of Departments if DepartmentId and DepartmentName are SQL-only attributes. If all of its attributes are SQL-only, it can be a SQL-only view object definition with neither Employees nor Departments entity object usages.

SQL-only view object definitions entirely bypass entity caching, saving not only the resources required to populate entity attributes but also those required to instantiate entity object instances.

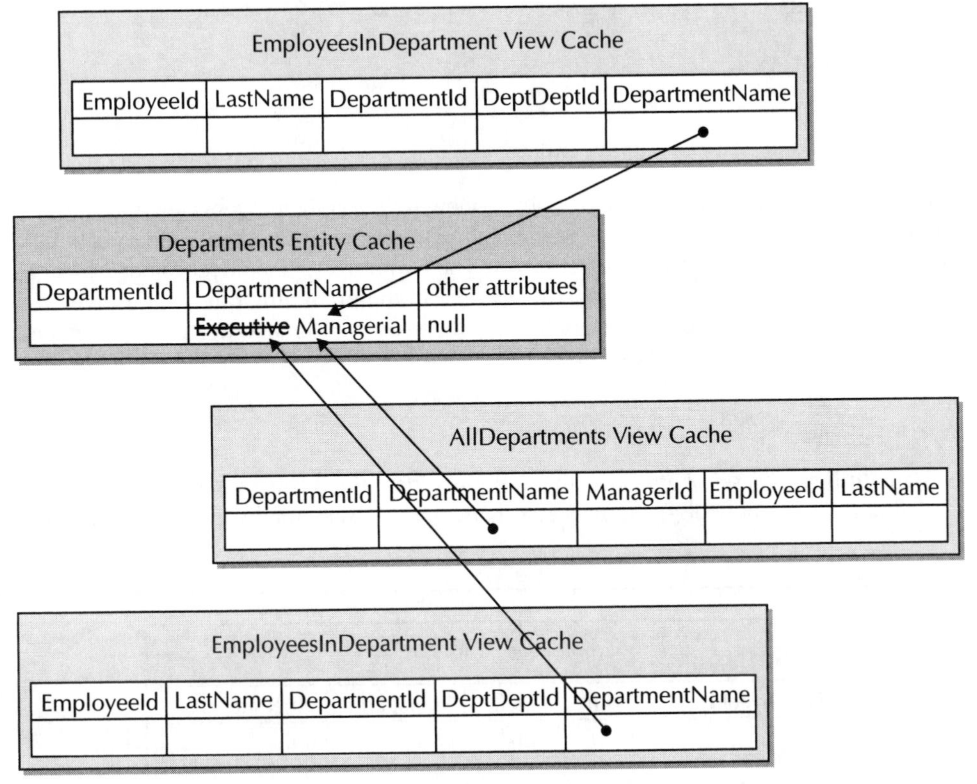

FIGURE 11-7. *Synchronization and entity-derived view attributes*

View object definitions that retrieve read-only data should almost always be SQL-only, because SQL-only view object definitions represent a substantial performance improvement over view object definitions that contain entity usages. The exceptions are those view object definitions that need to make use of the entity cache for the reasons discussed earlier in this section.

Entity Object Usages and Table Aliases

Consider a view object definition, EmployeesView, with the following query:

```
SELECT
  Employee.EMPLOYEE_ID,
  Employee.LAST_NAME,
  Employee.EMAIL,
  Employee.MANAGER_ID,
```

```
  Manager.EMPLOYEE_ID AS ManagerEmpId,
  Manager.LAST_NAME AS ManagerName
FROM
  EMPLOYEES Employee,
  EMPLOYEES Manager
WHERE
  Employee.MANAGER_ID = Manager.EMPLOYEE_ID;
```

If all the attributes are entity-derived, a single view row from EmployeesView must point at multiple entity object instances, as shown in Figure 11-8. This is accomplished by adding multiple usages of Employees to EmployeesView. The two usages, "Employee" and "Manager", correspond to the two table aliases for EMPLOYEES in the preceding query. EmployeeId, LastName, and Email will be derived from the Employee usage; ManagerId and ManagerName will be derived from the Manager usage.

Keys

A *key* is an attribute or a set of attributes that uniquely identifies a row in the view cache. A view object definition with entity object usages automatically has a key made up of all the attributes

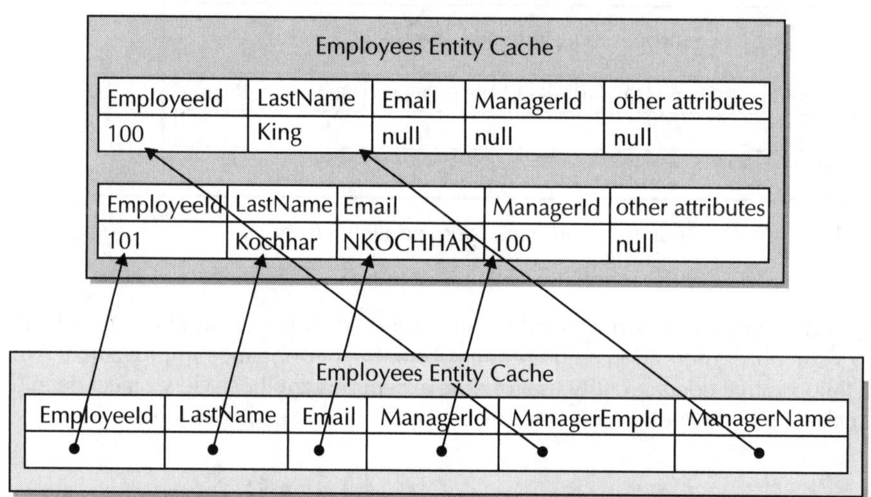

FIGURE 11-8. *Multiple entity object usages*

based on primary key attributes in those entity object usages. In addition, you can assign attributes in a SQL-only view object definition, or additional attributes in a view object definition with entity usages, to be part of the key. For this reason, if a view object definition contains any entity usages, it must contain view attributes based on the primary key attributes from each usage.

For example, consider the view object definition EmployeesView described in the preceding section. EmployeesView has a key made up of EmployeeId and ManagerEmpId, based on the primary key attributes (Employees.EmployeeId and Managers.EmployeeId) of its entity object usages.

It is important to ensure that every view object definition has a key whose values can uniquely identify rows. ADF BC uses keys to keep track of which row in the view cache is current. If you made EmployeesView a SQL-only view object, you would need to create a key containing at least EmployeeId (which uniquely identifies rows from EmployeesView). You will create a key for a SQL-only view object in the first hands-on practice in this chapter.

Refining a View Object's Query

Once you select the entity object usages and attributes for a view object, JDeveloper creates its query. The SELECT clause of the query is a list of all the database columns that correspond to the attributes. The FROM clause is a list of the tables and aliases that correspond to the entity object usages, plus any additional tables needed for SQL-only attributes. You can manipulate the query using the View Object Editor.

Setting the WHERE and ORDER BY Clauses

If a view object definition contains multiple entity object usages, you must set its WHERE clause to avoid returning a Cartesian product. The simplest way to do this is to base the WHERE clause on an association between the entity object definitions. For example, if the view object definition EmpDeptView contains usages of Departments and Employees, you can use the association EmpDeptFkAssoc to add the WHERE clause "WHERE Employee.DEPARTMENT_ID = Department.DEPARTMENT_ID". Alternatively, you could use the association DeptMgrFkAssoc to add the WHERE clause "WHERE Employee.EMPLOYEE_ID = Department.MANAGER_ID".

If you have multiple usages of the same entity object definition, you can use a recursive association to create a WHERE clause between them by specifying which entity object usage corresponds to each end of the association. For example, if the view object definition EmployeesView contains two usages of Employees called "Employee" and "Manager", you can use the association EmpMgrFkAssoc to add the WHERE clause "WHERE Employee.MANAGER_ ID = Manager.EMPLOYEE_ ID". You will use associations to specify WHERE clauses in the first hands-on practice in this chapter.

You can further change the WHERE clause (including changing the WHERE clause to do an outer join) or set an ORDER BY clause on the Query page of the View Object Editor, as shown here:

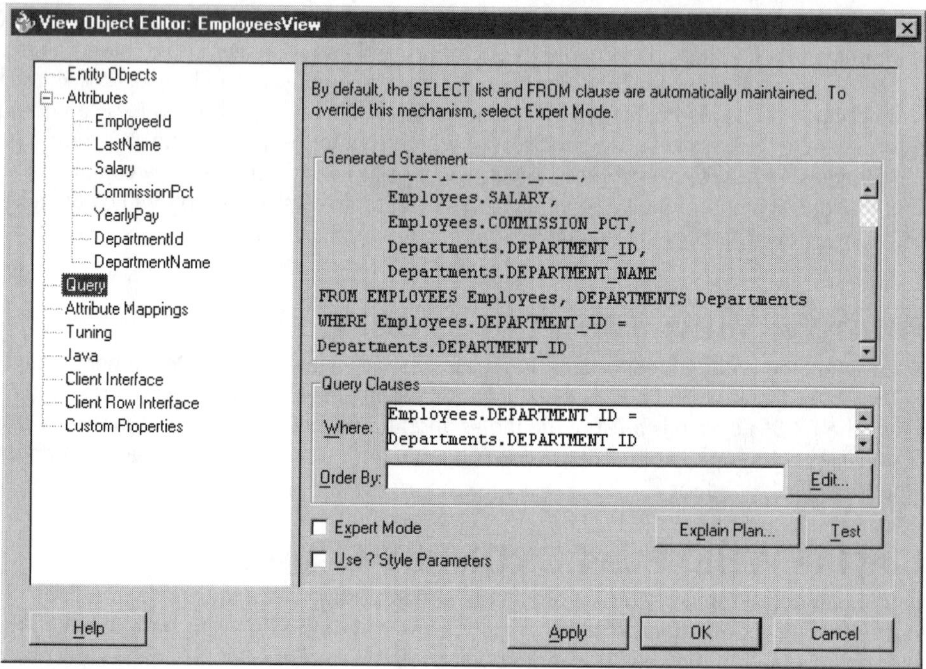

Do not type the words "WHERE" or "ORDER BY" in the fields; the editor adds those for you.

Expert Mode

Expert mode allows you to create view object definitions based on any valid SQL query. Not only do you have control over the WHERE and ORDER BY clauses of the query (as you do in regular view object definitions), but you can also type in the entire query and specify the SELECT clause, the FROM clause, and even other clauses such as GROUP BY. SQL-only view object definitions always use expert-mode queries, but you can also use expert mode with view object definitions that contain entity object usages.

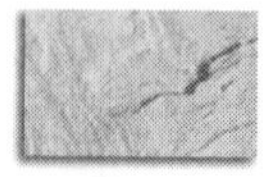

CAUTION
Expert-mode queries are not automatically updated when you add or remove attributes. To add or remove attributes in a view object definition that uses an expert-mode query, revise the query directly.

Expert Mode and SQL-Only View Object Definitions

When you create a SQL-only view object definition, you must fully specify its query yourself. JDeveloper will create view object attributes for each query column, using a convention much like the one it uses for making entity object attributes out of table columns:

- The first letter will be capitalized.
- Underscores will be removed, and the first letter after each underscore will be capitalized.
- All other letters will be lowercase.
- Symbols not valid for Java identifiers (such as parentheses) will be removed.

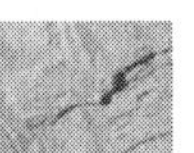

CAUTION
Use of $ is not removed but causes problems in the Java code.

For example, the query column EMPLOYEE_FULL_NAME will map to a view attribute called "EmployeeFullName", and the query column COUNT(Emp.EMPLOYEE_ID) will map to a view attribute called "CountempemployeeId". By using a column alias, you can define the name of the attribute. For example, COUNT(Emp.EMPLOYEE_ID) AS NUM_REPORTS will map to a view attribute called "NumReports".

Expert Mode with Entity Object Usages

Sometimes you need the query flexibility of expert mode, but you want or need to use entity object usages (either because you want to write to the database, or to take advantage of the synchronization and space-saving features that entity object usages can provide). In this case, you can use expert-mode queries with entity object usages, although it is more complicated.

As with SQL-only view object definitions, JDeveloper will create view object attributes based on the columns of the query you specify. However, you must then specify whether and how each query column maps to an underlying entity object attribute.

For example, consider a view object definition, ManagersView, with the following expert-mode query:

```
SELECT Manager.EMPLOYEE_ID,
  Manager.LAST_NAME,
  Manager.SALARY,
  Manager.JOB_ID,
  COUNT(Report.EMPLOYEE_ID) AS NUM_REPORTS
FROM EMPLOYEES Manager,
  EMPLOYEES Report
WHERE Manager.EMPLOYEE_ID = Report.MANAGER_ID
GROUP BY Manager.EMPLOYEE_ID,
  Manager.LAST_NAME,
  Manager.SALARY,
  Manager.JOB_ID
```

JDeveloper will create five view object attributes from this query: EmployeeId, LastName, Salary, JobId, and NumReports. If you want EmployeeId and Salary to be entity-derived attributes, you must specify that they map to the entity object attributes EmployeeId and Salary from the Manager entity object usage. You will use expert-mode queries with both a SQL-only view object definition and with a view object definition containing an entity object usage in the first hands-on practice in this chapter.

Hands-on Practice: Create View Object Definitions

In this practice, you will create a set of view object definitions to expose the data in the HR schema to an application. You can then use the view object definitions to display tables and forms in the UI and to allow users to modify data.

This practice builds on the results of the hands-on practices in Chapter 10. If you have not completed those practices, you can download the starting files for this practice from the authors' websites mentioned in the author information at the beginning of this book.

This practice steps you through the following phases:

I. Create an application workspace for the data model components

- Create an application workspace
- Import business domain components
- Create a diagram for the data model components

II. Create a simple view object definition

- Create a view object definition and add an entity object usage
- Select view attributes
- Check the SQL query
- Test the view object definition

III. Create a SQL-only view object definition

- Create a view object definition
- Write a query
- Test the view object definition

IV. Create a view object definition with multiple entity object usages

- Create a view object definition and add entity object usages
- Specify a WHERE clause
- Select view attributes
- Check the SQL query
- Test the view object definition

V. Create a view object definition with an entity object usage and an expert-mode query

- Create a view object definition and add an entity object usage

- Write a query
- Create attribute mappings
- Test the view object definition

I. Create an Application Workspace for the Data Model Components

In this phase, you will create an application workspace to hold your data model components and, eventually, an MVC application. You will create the MVC application in Chapter 12.

Create an Application Workspace

You can create an application workspace using the following steps:

1. On the Applications node in the Application Navigator, select New Application Workspace from the right-click menu. The Create Application Workspace dialog opens. Enter the following values:
   Application Name as "HRApp"
   Application Package Prefix as "hrapp"
   Application Template as "Web Application [Default]"

   Additional Information: You could create default data model components in the HR workspace from Chapter 10. However, as described in Chapter 8, business domain components are much more reusable than data model components. You will frequently need new data model components for each new application, whereas a single set of business domain components can often suffice for any application that uses a particular database schema. Although, in this book, you will not need to reuse your business domain components, making a new application workspace for every MVC application you need while reusing a single set of business domain components is a technique you may find useful for many real-world systems.

2. Leave the default directory name. Click OK. The new application workspace, HRApp, containing two projects, Model and ViewController, appears in the Navigator.

3. Click Save All.

Import Business Domain Components

You can import the business domain components you created in Chapters 9 and 10 using the following steps:

1. In the Application Navigator, double click the HRApp\Model node to open the Project Properties dialog.

2. Select the Profiles\Development\Paths node.

3. Click the Edit button beside the *Additional Classpath* field to open the Edit Additional Classpath dialog.

4. Click Add Entry.

5. Browse to the JDEV_HOME\jdev\mywork\HR\Model\classes directory.
6. Select the classes directory. Click Select to add the directory to the project's CLASSPATH. Click OK.

   Additional Information: This adds the output directory for the HR application's Model project to the CLASSPATH for the HRApp application's Model project. That gives the project access to the compiled business domain components you created in Chapters 9 and 10. Because the project only has access to the compiled files, you will not be able to change the business domain components from within HRApp. You could give the model project access to the source code by adding the business domain components to the source path rather than the CLASSPATH, but in general, this is not recommended: Allowing more than one project to edit the same files can lead to versioning problems.
7. Click OK to leave the Project Properties dialog.
8. Select **File | Import** to open the Import dialog.
9. Select "Business Components" and click OK.
10. Because your project is not yet initialized as an ADF BC project, the Business Components Project Initialization dialog opens. Make sure HR is selected as the database connection, and click OK.
11. In the Import Business Components XML File dialog, navigate to JDEV_HOME\jdev\mywork\HR\Model\classes\hr\model\businessdomain.
12. Select businessdomain.xml and click Open. When the confirmation dialog appears, click Yes to import the business domain components into your project.

    Additional Information: The businessdomain.xml file contains package information for the `hr.model.businessdomain` package. Selecting it will import all of the business components in that package, so that you can use them in your current project. The objects will appear under the Model project.
13. Repeat steps 8, 9, 11, and 12 to import HR\Model\classes\hr\model\model.xml.

    Additional Information: Due to a bug in some releases of JDeveloper, when you import a subpackage of a business components package, it is generally advisable to import the superpackage as well; otherwise, the JDeveloper design time may behave unpredictably. This will not import any additional business components.

Create a Diagram for the Data Model Components

In Chapter 9, you used a diagram to create and visualize business domain components. You can also create a diagram to create and visualize data model components, using the following steps:

1. On the Applications\HRApp\Model node, select New from the right-click menu.
2. Select the Business Tier\Business Components node.
3. Select Business Components Diagram and click OK. The Create Business Components Diagram dialog opens.

4. Enter the following values:
   Name as "Data Model Diagram"
   Package as "hrapp.model.datamodel"

5. Click OK. An empty diagram opens.

What Just Happened? First, you created a new application workspace to hold your data model components and an application that uses them. Then, you imported business domain components into the Model project for that workspace, so that you can base your data model components on those business domain components. Finally, you created an empty diagram. You will use this diagram to create and visualize data model components.

II. Create a Simple View Object Definition

In this phase, you will create a simple view object definition, JobsView, with one entity-derived and one SQL-only attribute.

Create a View Object Definition and Add an Entity Object Usage

You can create a view object definition and add a single entity object usage using the following steps:

1. On the Business Components page of the Component Palette, click the View Object icon. Then click a blank space in the Data Model Diagram.

   Additional Information: JDeveloper creates a view object definition and allows you to type in its name.

2. Enter "JobsView" as the view object definition's name and press ENTER to exit the edit field.

3. In the Application Navigator, find the hr.model.businessdomain\Jobs node, and drag it inside JobsView (on the diagram) to add an entity object usage to JobsView.

4. Rename the usage "Job".

Select View Attributes

You can select entity-derived and SQL-only view attributes for a view object definition using the following steps:

1. Double click JobsView to open it in the View Object Editor.

2. Select the Attributes node.

3. Multi-select (CTRL-click) all the attributes from the *Selected* list except JobId and use the left-arrow button to remove them.

   Additional Information: When you added the Job usage to JobsView, JDeveloper automatically added view attributes based on each entity attribute from the Job usage. You only need one entity-derived attribute, JobId, in JobsView, so you can remove the rest. You must make JobId an entity-derived attribute, because it will be the destination attribute for a many-to-many view link.

4. Still on the Attributes page of the View Object Editor, click New to open the New View Object Attribute dialog.

5. Enter the following values:
   Name as "JobTitle"
   Type as "String"

   Additional Information: The attribute JobTitle will not need to be changed, will not be shared between multiple view rows, and will not participate in a view link based on an association. Therefore, you can improve efficiency by making it SQL-only.

6. Check the *Selected In Query* checkbox.

7. Enter the following values:
   Alias as "JobTitle"
   Type as "VARCHAR2(35)"
   Expression as "Job.JOB_TITLE"

   Additional Information: This will make JobTitle correspond to "Job.JOB_TITLE" in JobsView's query.

8. Click OK to close the dialog.

Check the SQL Query

You can view a view object definition's SQL query using the following steps:

1. In the View Object Editor, select the Query node.

   Additional Information: The *Generated Statement* field should contain the following query:

```
SELECT Job.JOB_ID,
  Job.JOB_TITLE AS JobTitle
FROM JOBS Job
```

   Note that the table alias corresponds to the name of the entity object usage.

2. Click OK to close the editor.

   Additional Information: On the diagram, the JobsView view object definition should look like the following:

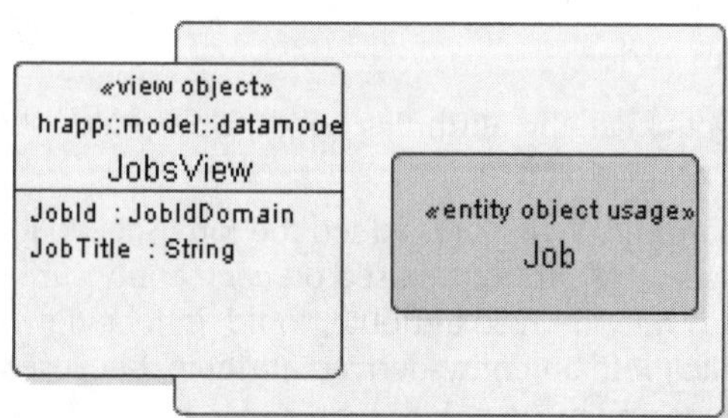

3. Click Save All.

Test the View Object Definition

You can test a simple view object definition using the following steps:

1. On the Business Components page of the Component Palette, click the Application Module icon. Then click a blank space in the Data Model Diagram.

   Additional Information: JDeveloper creates an application module definition and allows you to type in its name.

2. Enter "TestModule" as the application module definition's name and press ENTER to exit the edit field.

   Additional Information: This is not the application module definition you will use to expose data to the application; you will create that application module definition in the second hands-on practice in this chapter. This will be a very simple application module definition you can use to test the functionality of your view object definitions.

3. On the diagram, drag JobsView into TestModule to add a view object instance, JobsView1.
4. Select Test from the right-click menu on TestModule to open the Business Component Browser.
5. When the Connect dialog opens, accept the defaults and click Connect.
6. When the main window of the Business Component Browser opens, double click JobsView1.

   Additional Information: You can scroll through the rows of JobsView1 to see the query results.

7. Close the browser.

What Just Happened? You created a view object definition, JobsView, with a single usage of the Jobs entity object definition. The view object definition has two attributes: JobId, an entity-derived attribute, and JobTitle, a SQL-only attribute. Then, you created a simple application module definition with an instance of JobsView, and used the Business Component Browser to test JobsView's behavior.

III. Create a SQL-Only View Object Definition

In this phase, you will create a SQL-only view object definition, DepartmentsView.

Create a View Object Definition

You can create a view object definition with no entity object usages using the following steps:

1. In the Component Palette, select the View Object icon, and click a blank space in the diagram to create a view object definition.
2. Name the view object definition "DepartmentsView".

Write a Query

You can write an expert-mode query for a SQL-only view object definition using the following steps:

1. Double click DepartmentsView to open it in the View Object Editor.
2. Select the Query node.

   Additional Information: The *Expert Mode* checkbox is selected and disabled, because SQL-only view objects must have expert-mode queries.
3. Write the following query in the *Query Statement* area:

   ```
   SELECT Department.DEPARTMENT_ID,
     Department.DEPARTMENT_NAME,
     Department.MANAGER_ID,
     Manager.LAST_NAME
   FROM DEPARTMENTS Department,
     EMPLOYEES Manager
   WHERE Department.MANAGER_ID = Manager.EMPLOYEE_ID
   ```
4. Click Test to make sure the query is valid. When the confirmation dialog appears, click OK.
5. Click Apply to save the changes and generate SQL-only view attributes based on the query columns.
6. Select the Attributes\DepartmentId node.
7. Select the *Key Attribute* checkbox.

   Additional Information: In Phase II, when you created the JobsView view object, JDeveloper automatically created a key based on the primary key of the Job entity object usage. Because DepartmentsView is SQL-only, you must add a key yourself. DepartmentId uniquely identifies DepartmentsView view rows, so it can be the only key attribute.
8. Click OK to close the editor.

   Additional Information: On the diagram, the DepartmentsView view object definition should look like the following:

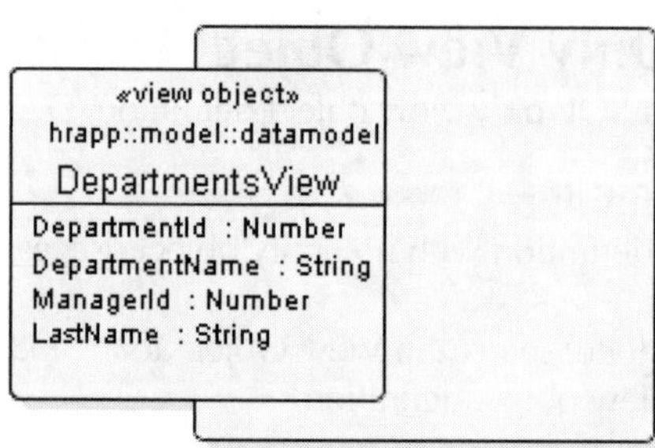

Test the View Object Definition

You can test a SQL-only view object definition using the following steps:

1. On the diagram, drag DepartmentsView into TestModule to add a view object instance, DepartmentsView1.
2. Select Test from the right-click menu on TestModule to open the Business Component Browser.
3. When the Connect dialog opens, accept the defaults and click Connect.
4. When the main window of the Business Component Browser opens, double click DepartmentsView1.
5. Find Department 90, and enter "Managerial" in the *DepartmentName* field.
6. Click Commit.
7. Close the Business Component Browser and reopen it.
8. Find Department 90.

   Additional Information: Note that the change was not saved to the database. ADF BC does not save changes to SQL-only attributes.
9. Close the browser.

What Just Happened? You created a view object definition, DepartmentsView, with no entity object usages, that is, a SQL-only view object definition. The view object definition has four attributes. Since the view object definition is SQL-only, all of its attributes are SQL-only as well. Then, you used the Business Component Browser to test the view object definition. You saw that changes to attribute values were not saved to the database. Despite this limitation, SQL-only view object definitions can be very useful, because they are generally much more efficient than view object definitions with entity object usages.

IV. Create a View Object Definition with Multiple Entity Object Usages

In this phase, you will create a view object definition, EmployeesView, with two usages of the Employees entity object definition.

Create a Definition and Add Entity Object Usages

You can create a view object definition with two entity object usages using the following steps:

1. In the Component Palette, select the View Object icon, and click a blank space in the diagram.
2. Enter "EmployeesView" as the view object definition's name and press ENTER to exit the edit field.
3. In the Application Navigator, find the hr.model.businessdomain\Employees node, and drag it inside EmployeesView (on the diagram) to add an entity object usage to EmployeesView.

4. Rename the usage "Employee".
5. Repeat steps 3–4 to add another entity object usage to EmployeesView.
6. Name the second usage "Manager".

Specify a WHERE Clause

You can use an association to specify a WHERE clause for a view object definition using the following steps:

1. Double click EmployeesView to open it in the View Object Editor.
2. Ensure that the Entity Objects node is selected.
3. In the *Selected* list, select the Manager entity object usage.
4. In the *Association End* dropdown, ensure that "Manager" is selected, rather than "Reports".

   Additional Information: The WHERE clause you are specifying is Employee .MANAGER_ID = Manager.EMPLOYEE_ID. That is, you want to maintain the relationship represented by EmpJobFkAssoc. EmpJobFkAssoc has two accessor attributes: Manager and Reports. You want the Manager entity object usage to represent the "Manager" side of the association, not the "Reports" side. If you selected "Reports," you would instead get the WHERE clause Employee.EMPLOYEE_ID = Manager.MANAGER_ID.
5. Select the *Reference* checkbox.

   Additional Information: Consider a row of EmployeesView's query result like the one shown in Figure 11-8. Suppose that the row's ManagerId attribute changes from 100 to 102. Making Manager a *reference entity object usage* ensures that the row's ManagerEmpId and ManagerName attributes will change to point to Employee 102.

Select View Attributes

You can select entity-derived view attributes based on multiple entity object usages using the following steps:

1. Still in the View Object Editor, select the Attributes node.
2. Click the double-left-arrow button to remove all attributes from the *Selected* list. Click OK on the confirmation dialog.
3. Still in the View Object Editor, select the following attributes from the *Available* list and use the right-arrow button to add them to the *Selected* list:
   - Employee (Employees)\EmployeeId
   - Employee (Employees)\LastName
   - Employee (Employees)\Email
   - Employee (Employees)\ManagerId
   - Manager (Employees)\EmployeeId
   - Manager (Employees)\LastName

Additional Information: The Available list includes the names of both the entity object usages (Employee, Manager) and the entity object definition they are based on (Employees), for reference. Note that the last two attributes you add will be added as EmployeeId1 and LastName1, respectively. You will change these defaults in the next step.

Because you marked Manager as a reference entity object, Employee.ManagerId and Manager.EmployeeId are guaranteed to be the same. However, you must add both of them, for separate reasons. You must add Employee.ManagerId to allow users to change an employee's manager (changing Manager.EmployeeId will not change an employee's manager, but rather the ID of that manager). You must add Manager.EmployeeId because it is the primary key of the Manager usage; it will be part of the key for EmployeesView.

4. Select the Attributes\EmployeeId1 node.
5. Enter "ManagerEmpId" in the *Name* and *Alias* fields. Click Apply.
6. Similarly, rename LastName1 to "ManagerName". Click Apply.

Check the SQL Query

You can view a view object definition's SQL query using the following steps:

1. In the View Object Editor, select the Query node.

   Additional Information: The Generated Statement field should contain the following query:

```
SELECT Employee.EMPLOYEE_ID,
  Employee.LAST_NAME,
  Employee.EMAIL,
  Employee.MANAGER_ID,
  Manager.EMPLOYEE_ID AS ManagerEmpId,
  Manager.LAST_NAME AS ManagerName
FROM EMPLOYEES Employee, EMPLOYEES Manager
WHERE Employee.MANAGER_ID = Manager.EMPLOYEE_ID
```

2. Click OK to close the editor.

   Additional Information: On the diagram, the EmployeesView view object definition should look like the following:

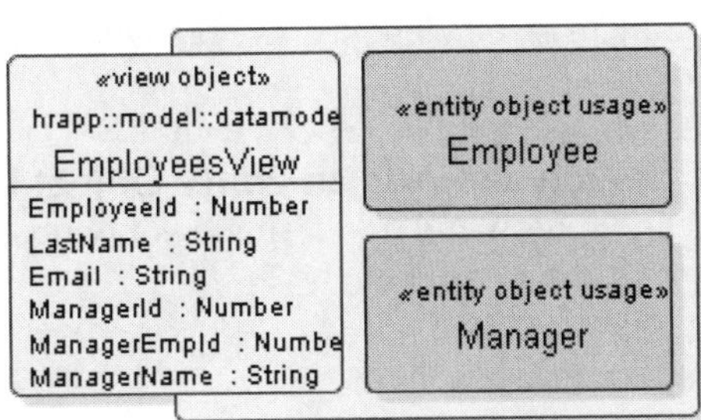

3. Click Save All.

Test the View Object Definition

You can test a view object definition with multiple entity object usages using the following steps:

1. On the diagram, drag EmployeesView into TestModule to add a view object instance, EmployeesView1.
2. Select Test from the right-click menu on TestModule to open the Business Component Browser.
3. When the Connect dialog opens, accept the defaults and click Connect.
4. When the main window of the Business Component Browser opens, double click EmployeesView1.
5. Find Employee 201, Hartstein.

   Additional Information: Information is displayed both about Hartstein and about his manager, King.
6. Enter "101" in the ManagerId field and press ENTER.

   Additional Information: The values of ManagerEmpId and ManagerName change to reflect the change in Hartstein's ManagerId.
7. Close the Business Component Browser.

What Just Happened? You created a view object definition with two usages of the Employees entity object. The view object definition has five attributes, all of them entity-derived. This is important because the attributes will be used to change data. It also has potential efficiency benefits, because the data will be reused: Kochhar, for example, will appear in her own row, in the rows of her direct reports, and in the rows from another view object definition, which you will create in the next phase.

V. Create a View Object Definition with an Entity Object Usage and an Expert-Mode Query

In this phase, you will create a view object definition, ManagersView, with an expert-mode query. ManagersView will not be SQL-only. It needs entity-derived attributes to participate in a many-to-many view link; in addition, it will share data with EmployeesView, so entity-derived attributes have the potential to increase efficiency. Therefore, you will have to create its attribute mappings yourself.

Create a View Object Definition and Add an Entity Object Usage

You can create a view object definition and add a single entity object usage using the following steps:

1. In the Component Palette, select the View Object icon, and click a blank space in the diagram.
2. Enter "ManagersView" as the view object definition's name and press ENTER to exit the edit field.
3. In the Application Navigator, find the hr.model.businessdomain\Employees node, and drag it inside ManagersView (on the diagram) to add an entity object usage to ManagersView.
4. Rename the usage "Manager".

Write a Query

You can write an expert-mode query for a view object definition using the following steps:

1. Double click ManagersView to open it in the View Object Editor.
2. Select the Attributes node, and remove all attributes except EmployeeId from the *Selected* list.

   Additional Information: Since you will be writing a query and managing attribute mappings yourself, you should remove as many pregenerated entity-derived attributes as possible to avoid confusion. You must leave the EmployeeId attribute, because, as the primary key of the Manager entity object usage, it is an essential part of ManagersView's key.
3. Select the Query node.
4. Select the *Expert Mode* checkbox to make the query editable.
5. Write the following query in the *Query Statement* area:

   ```
   SELECT Manager.EMPLOYEE_ID,
     Manager.LAST_NAME,
     Manager.SALARY,
     Manager.JOB_ID,
     COUNT(Reports.EMPLOYEE_ID) AS NUM_REPORTS
   FROM EMPLOYEES Manager,
     EMPLOYEES Reports
   WHERE Manager.EMPLOYEE_ID = Reports.MANAGER_ID
   GROUP BY Manager.EMPLOYEE_ID,
     Manager.LAST_NAME,
     Manager.SALARY,
     Manager.JOB_ID
   ```
6. Click Test to make sure the query is valid. When the confirmation dialog appears, click OK.

Create Attribute Mappings

You can create attribute mappings between query columns in an expert-mode query and entity attributes using the following steps:

1. Select the Attribute Mappings node.

   Additional Information: The table lists query columns in the left column, and attributes in the right column, as shown next:

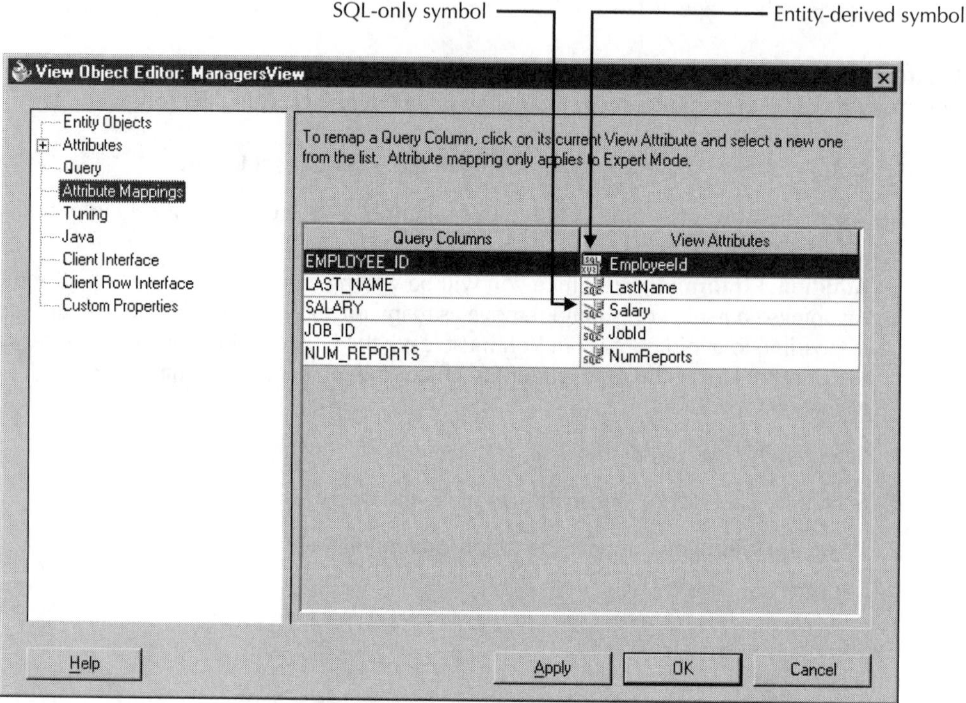

   The symbol beside EmployeeId indicates that it is an entity-derived attribute. The symbol beside the rest of the attributes indicates that they are currently SQL-only attributes, not mapped to any entity attribute.

2. Click the LastName view attribute to open a dropdown.
3. In the dropdown, select "Manager (Employees)\LastName", as shown next:

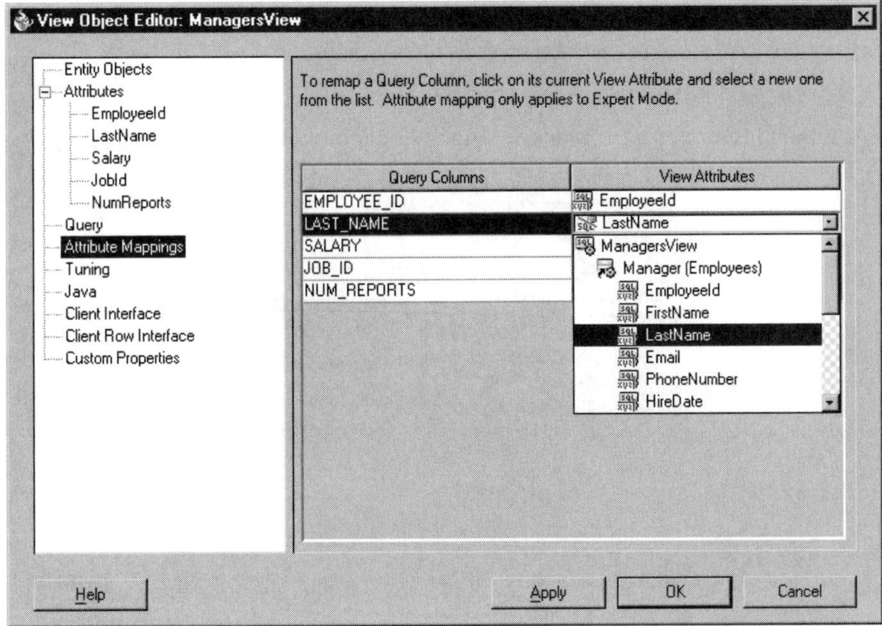

Additional Information: This creates a mapping between the LAST_NAME query column and the LastName attribute from the Manager entity object usage.

4. Repeat steps 2–3 to map JOB_ID to Manager's JobId attribute.

   Additional Information: The editor should now appear as shown next:

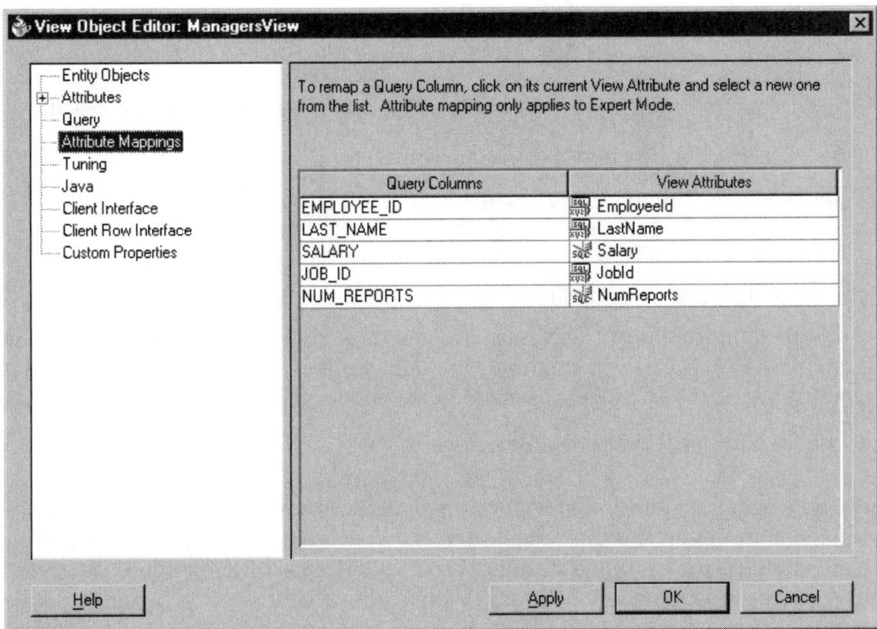

The symbol beside EmployeeId, LastName, and JobId means that they are entity-derived attributes. The other two attributes are still SQL-only.

5. Click OK to close the editor.

   Additional Information: ManagersView should look like the following:

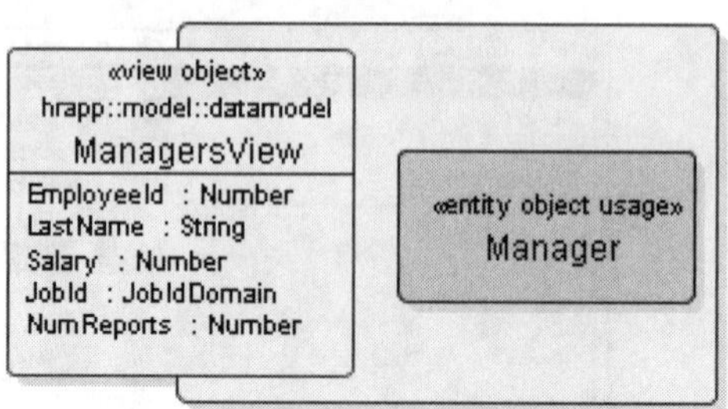

6. Click Save All.

Test the View Object Definition

You can test a view object definition with multiple entity object usages using the following steps:

1. On the diagram, drag ManagersView into TestModule to add a view object instance, ManagersView1.
2. Select Test from the right-click menu on TestModule to open the Business Component Browser.
3. When the Connect dialog opens, accept the defaults and click Connect.
4. When the main window of the Business Component Browser opens, double click ManagersView1.
5. Scroll through the managers, and note that NumReports is calculated correctly.
6. Find Manager 101, Kochhar.
7. Enter "Kochhar2" in the *LastName* field and press ENTER.
8. Double click EmployeesView1, and find Employee 101.
9. Note that the LastName field displays "Kochhar2".

   Additional Information: This is because ManagersView's LastName attribute and EmployeesView's LastName attribute are both entity-derived and based on the same entity attribute. The change was made in the entity cache.

10. Close the Business Component Browser.

What Just Happened? You created a view object definition with an expert-mode query and a usage of the Employees entity object definition. The view object definition has five attributes, three of them entity-derived and two of them SQL-only. Because this definition had an expert-mode query, you had to map query columns to entity object attributes for the entity-derived view object attributes. When you tested the view object definition, you saw how the entity cache provides synchronization between entity-derived attribute values.

Representing Relationships Between Query Result Sets

Relationships between query result sets are represented by view link definitions between view object definitions. A view link definition associates one or more attributes in one view object definition (called the "source" view object definition) with one or more attributes in another (the "destination" view object definition).

If both the source and the destination attributes are entity-derived, you can base the view link definition on an association. For example, if the source attribute for a view link definition is based on the DepartmentId attribute in Departments, and the destination attribute is based on the DepartmentId attribute in Employees, you can base the view link definition on EmpDeptFkAssoc.

View Link SQL

When you create a view link definition, JDeveloper creates a parameterized SQL expression called the *view link SQL*, which represents the relationship between the view object definitions. In most cases (see the section "View Link Definition Cardinality" for information about the most common exception), the view link SQL contains a bind variable for each source attribute, and sets each bind variable equal to the SQL expression for the corresponding destination attribute.

For example, consider a view link definition EmpDeptFkLink, which associates the DepartmentId attribute in DeptMgrView (the source) with the DepartmentId attribute in EmpDeptView (the destination). The SQL expression for the destination attribute is Employee.DEPARTMENT_ID, so JDeveloper creates an expression setting a bind variable (a stand-in for the source attribute) equal to Employee.DEPARTMENT_ID, as follows:

```
:1 = Employee.DEPARTMENT_ID
```

This expression is the view link SQL for EmpDeptFkLink. In this example, ":1" represents a value from the source view attribute.

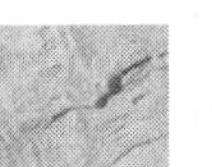

NOTE
If the tables in the destination view object definition are aliased, the view link SQL will use those aliases. Since EmpDeptView aliases EMPLOYEES to Employee, EmpDeptFkLink uses the alias in the view link SQL.

ADF BC uses the view link SQL to associate a row of the source view object definition with one or more rows of the destination view object definition. When a view link instance is used to create a master-detail relationship between instances of the source and destination view object definitions, the source view attributes from each row in the master view object instance are passed into the bind variable, and the resulting SQL is added to the WHERE clause of the detail view object instance to return a more restricted set of rows. This is the mechanism that implements the synchronization of detail rows with master rows in ADF BC.

For example, suppose an instance of EmpDeptFkLink is used to create a master-detail relationship between AllDepartments, an instance of DeptMgrView, and EmployeesInDepartment, an instance of EmpDeptView. Suppose the following row in AllDepartments' view cache is the current row:

DepartmentId	DepartmentName	EmployeeId	LastName
60	IT	103	Hunold

The value of DepartmentId in this row is passed as a bind variable to EmpDeptFkLink's view link SQL, yielding the following expression:

```
60 = Employee.DEPARTMENT_ID
```

This expression is appended to the WHERE clause of EmployeesInDepartment, restricting its cache to only those employees in Department 60.

You can view and change view link SQL on the View Link SQL page of the Create View Link Wizard, as shown here:

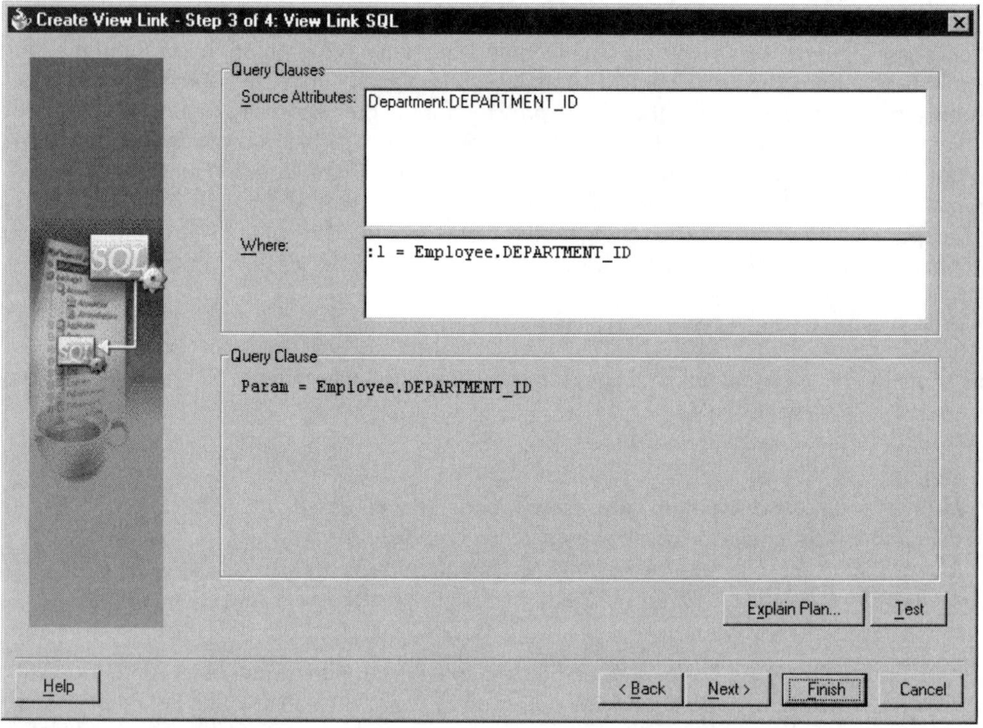

Changing the view link SQL has side effects, as described in the section "View Link Definition Directionality and Accessor Attributes."

View Link Definition Cardinality

Like associations, view link definitions have cardinality. View link definition cardinality has the following in common with association cardinality:

- View link definitions can be one-to-many, one-to-one, or many-to-many.
- For one-to-many view link definitions, a single row from the result set of the source view object definition's query can correspond to any number of rows (including no rows) from the result set of the destination view object's query.
- For one-to-one view link definitions, a single row from the result set of the source view object definition's query corresponds to one row (or no rows) from the destination view object definition's query.
- For many-to-many view link definitions, any number of rows (including no rows) from the result set of the source view object's query can correspond to any number of rows (including no rows) from the result set of the destination view object's query.

As with associations, many-to-many view link definitions are more complex than one-to-one or one-to-many view link definitions. First, unlike one-to-one and one-to-many view link definitions, which may or may not be based on associations, many-to-many view link definitions must be based on many-to-many associations. Second, many-to-many view link definitions contain more complicated view link SQL that makes use of an intersection table.

For example, consider a view link definition EmpPastJobsLink, between EmployeesView and JobsView, based on EmpPastJobsAssoc. Recall from Chapter 9 that EmpPastJobsAssoc represents a relationship between EMPLOYEES and JOBS, associating rows from each if they share a detail from JOB_HISTORY, as shown here:

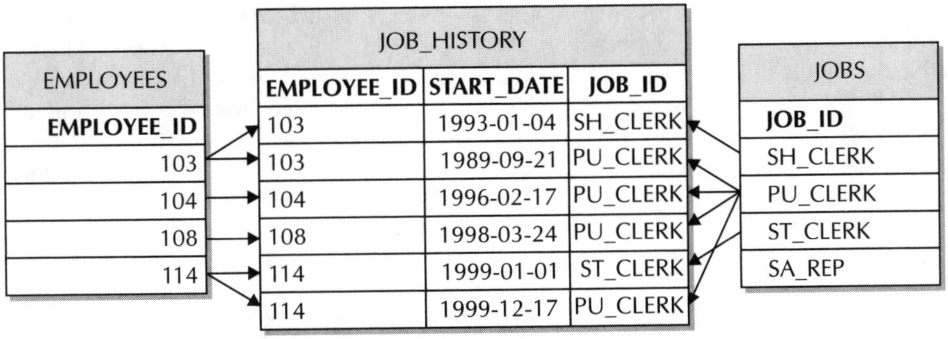

EMPLOYEES
EMPLOYEE_ID
103
104
108
114

JOB_HISTORY		
EMPLOYEE_ID	**START_DATE**	**JOB_ID**
103	1993-01-04	SH_CLERK
103	1989-09-21	PU_CLERK
104	1996-02-17	PU_CLERK
108	1998-03-24	PU_CLERK
114	1999-01-01	ST_CLERK
114	1999-12-17	PU_CLERK

JOBS
JOB_ID
SH_CLERK
PU_CLERK
ST_CLERK
SA_REP

EmpPastJobsLink will need to use this relationship to associate rows of EmployeesView's query result with rows of JobsView's query result. It can do this using the following view link SQL:

```
:1 = JobHistory.EMPLOYEE_ID AND JobHistory.JOB_ID = Job.JOB_ID
```

As with all view link definitions, when an instance of a many-to-many view link definition is used to create a master-detail relationship between instances of the source and destination view object definitions, the source view attributes from each row in the master view object instance are passed into the bind variable, and the resulting SQL is added to the WHERE clause of the detail view object instance to return a more restricted set of rows. In addition, the intersection table is added to the FROM clause of the destination view object instance.

For example, suppose an instance of EmpPastJobsLink is used to create a master-detail relationship between AllEmployees, an instance of EmployeesView, and EmployeePastJobs, an instance of JobsView. EmployeePastJobs' query will be modified at run time to add the view link SQL to the WHERE clause and the intersection table to the FROM clause, as follows:

```
SELECT JOB_ID,
  JOB_TITLE
FROM JOBS Job,
  JOB_HISTORY JobHistory
WHERE :1 = JobHistory.EMPLOYEE_ID AND JobHistory.JOB_ID = Job.JOB_ID
```

If the current row of AllEmployees has EmployeeId 101, the WHERE clause becomes

```
WHERE 101 = JobHistory.EMPLOYEE_ID AND JobHistory.JOB_ID = Jobs.JOB_ID
```

View Link Definition Directionality and Accessor Attributes

Typically, a view link instance is used to make an instance of the destination view object definition a detail of an instance of the source view object definition. However, you might also want to use a view link instance to make an instance of the source a detail of an instance of the destination. For example, in the preceding section, an instance of EmpPastJobsLink made an instance of JobsView a detail of an instance of EmployeesView; the JobsView instance contained only jobs previously held by the currently selected employee. However, you might also want to use it to make an instance of EmployeesView a detail of an instance of JobsView, so that the EmployeesView instance contains only employees who previously held the currently selected job.

To do this, you must make EmpPastJobsLink bi-directional. Just as associations can be uni-directional or bi-directional, view link definitions can be uni-directional or bi-directional. When a view link definition is bi-directional, ADF BC can reverse its view link SQL, replacing the parameters with source attributes and destination attributes with parameters. For example, if you make EmpPastJobsLink bi-directional, ADF BC will be able to automatically transform its view link SQL to the following:

```
Employees.EMPLOYEE_ID = JobHistory.EMPLOYEE_ID AND JobHistory.JOB_ID = :1
```

Because of this, you can use an instance of EmpPastJobsLink to create a master-detail relationship between AllJobs, an instance of JobsView, and JobsPastHolders, an instance of EmployeesView. In this case, a WHERE clause predicate containing the transformed view link SQL, plus a FROM clause containing the intersection table, will be added at run time to the query for JobsPastHolders, as follows:

```
SELECT
  Employee.EMPLOYEE_ID,
  Employee.LAST_NAME,
```

```
  Employee.EMAIL,
  Manager.EMPLOYEE_ID AS ManagerId,
  Manager.LAST_NAME AS ManagerName
FROM
  EMPLOYEES Employee,
  EMPLOYEES Manager,
  JOB_HISTORY JobHistory
WHERE
  Employee.MANAGER_ID = Manager.EMPLOYEE_ID AND
  Employee.EMPLOYEE_ID = JobHistory.EMPLOYEE_ID AND JobHistory.JOB_ID = :1;
```

Just like association directionality, view link definition directionality is determined by the presence or absence of accessor attributes. Accessor attributes for view link definitions appear in the view object definitions and contain one of the following:

- **An associated view row** if the other end of the view link definition is a "1" end.
- **A row iterator** if the other end of the association is a "many" end.

If both the source and destination view object definition contain accessor attributes, the view link will be bi-directional; if only the source contains an accessor attribute, the view link will be uni-directional.

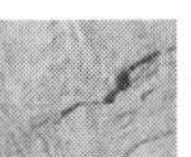

NOTE
You can only make a view link definition bi-directional if you have not changed the view link SQL. This is because ADF BC can only reverse view link SQL that JDeveloper generates.

Aggregating Data for Applications

Once you have created the view object definitions that will select the data your client needs and have created the view link definitions you need to create master-detail relationships, you can create an application module definition that aggregates the data needed by an MVC application. Chapter 8 covered the basics of application module definitions:

- An application module definition contains the view object instances an application needs for a single transaction.
- An application module definition contains view link instances that specify master-detail relationships between the view object instances.
- The relationships between these instances are represented by a tree, called the application module definition's data model.
- An application module definition acts as a template for application module instances.
- Application module definitions can access instances of other application module definitions, giving them access to the "nested" instance's data model.

- A single HTTP session (for a web application), or a single instance of a Java application accesses a single non-nested application module instance, which manages a single database transaction.

You will create an application module definition in the second hands-on practice in this chapter. You will learn more about application module definitions in Chapters 12 and 13.

Hands-on Practice: Create View Link and Application Module Definitions

In this practice, you will create view link definitions to represent relationships between the view object definitions you created in the first hands-on practice in this chapter. Then, you will create an application module definition to aggregate and present data. In Chapter 12, you will use the application module definition to provide an MVC application with data.

This practice builds on the results of the previous hands-on practice in this chapter. If you have not completed that practice, you can download the starting files for this practice from the authors' websites mentioned in the author information at the beginning of this book.

This practice steps you through the following phases:

I. Create view link definitions

- Create a one-to-many, uni-directional view link definition
- Create a many-to-many, bi-directional view link definition

II. Create and test an application module definition

- Create an application module definition
- Test the data model

I. Create View Link Definitions

In this phase, you will create two view link definitions: EmpManagerFkLink, a one-to-many, uni-directional view link definition between ManagersView and EmployeesView, which you can use to coordinate employees with their managers. Then, you will create EmpPastJobsLink, a many-to-many, bi-directional view link definition between EmployeesView and JobsView, which can be used to either coordinate employees with their past jobs or jobs with their past holders.

Create a One-to-Many, Uni-Directional View Link Definition

You can create a one-to-many, uni-directional view link definition using the following steps:

1. In the Component Palette, click the View Link icon.
2. In the diagram, click once on ManagersView and once on EmployeesView in that order to draw the view link definition line.
3. Click twice on the view link definition's name to make it editable. (Do not double click or the View Link Editor will appear).

4. Name the view link definition "EmpManagerFkLink". Press ENTER.

5. Double click the view link definition line to open it in the View Link Editor, and select the View Objects node.

   Additional Information: You will see that JDeveloper created a view link definition defined by the EmpManagerFkAssoc association, a recursive association on Employees.

6. Select the View Link SQL node to confirm that the view link SQL is ":1 = Employee.MANAGER_ID".

   Additional Information: When you create an instance of this view link definition, it will modify the query for an instance of EmployeesView so that it reads as follows:

```
SELECT Employee.EMPLOYEE_ID,
  Employee.LAST_NAME,
  Employee.EMAIL,
  Employee.MANAGER_ID,
  Manager.EMPLOYEE_ID AS ManagerEmpId,
  Manager.LAST_NAME AS ManagerName
FROM EMPLOYEES Employee, EMPLOYEES Manager
WHERE Employee.MANAGER_ID = Manager.EMPLOYEE_ID AND
  :1 = Employee.MANAGER_ID
```

7. Select the View Link Properties node.

8. In the Destination area, enter "ReportsView" in the *Accessor Name* field.

   Additional Information: This will change the destination accessor attribute's name to "ReportsView".

9. Click OK.

Create a Many-to-Many, Bi-Directional View Link Definition

You can create a many-to-many, bi-directional view link definition using the following steps:

1. In the Component Palette, click the View Link icon.

2. In the diagram, click once on EmployeesView and once on JobsView in that order to draw the view link definition line.

3. Name the view link definition "EmpPastJobsLink".

4. Double click the view link definition line to open it in the View Link Editor, and select the View Objects node.

   Additional Information: You will see that JDeveloper created a view link definition defined by the EmpPastJobsAssoc association, a many-to-many association between Employees and Jobs.

5. Select the View Link SQL node to confirm that the view link SQL is ":1 = JobHistory.EMPLOYEE_ID AND JobHistory.JOB_ID = Job.JOB_ID".

6. Select the View Link properties node.

7. Select the *Generate Accessor in View Object: JobsView* checkbox.

   Additional Information: This creates a source accessor attribute, making the view link definition bi-directional.

8. In the Source area, enter "PastHoldersView" in the *Accessor Name* field.

   Additional Information: This will change the source accessor attribute's name to "PastHoldersView".

9. In the Destination area, enter "PastJobsView" in the *Accessor Name* field.

   Additional Information: This will change the destination accessor attribute's name to "PastJobsView".

10. Click OK to close the editor.

11. Click Save All.

What Just Happened? You created a one-to-many, uni-directional view link definition and a many-to-many, bi-directional view link definition. You will use instances of these view link definitions to create master-detail relationships between view object instances in the data model. Your data model diagram should look something like Figure 11-9, which does not show the TestModule application module definition.

II. Create and Test an Application Module Definition

In this phase, you will create an application module definition to represent your data model to a client application. In Chapter 12, you will create an application that uses the application module definition.

Create an Application Module Definition

You can create an application module definition using the following steps:

1. On the diagram, on the TestModule application module definition, select Erase from Disk from the right-click menu.

   Additional Information: This application module definition existed only to help you test your view object definitions.

2. In the Component Palette, select the Application Module icon, and click a blank space in the diagram to create an application module definition.

3. Enter "HrAppModule" as the application module definition's name and press ENTER to exit the edit field.

4. On the diagram, drag ManagersView into HrAppModule to add a view object instance, ManagersView1.

5. Rename ManagersView1 to "AllManagers".

6. On the diagram, drag ManagersView into HrAppModule to add a second instance of ManagersView.

7. Name the new instance "ManagersForList".

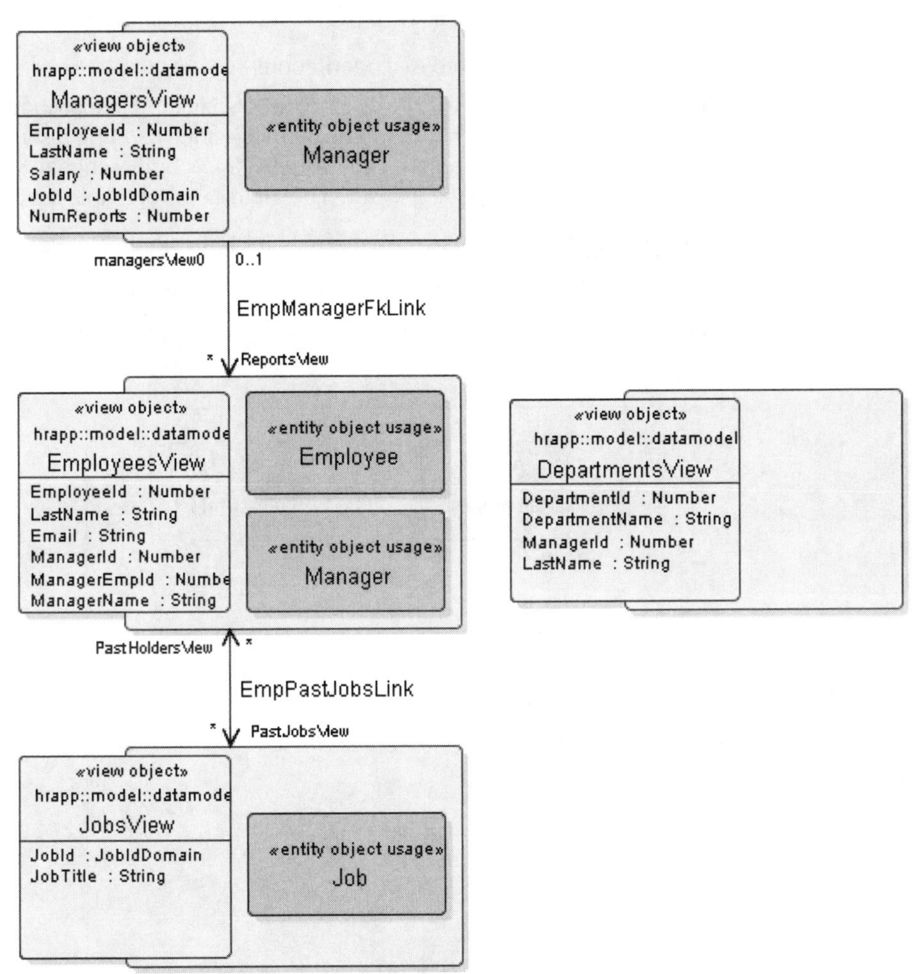

FIGURE 11-9. *View object definitions and view link definitions*

Additional Information: Although both of these are instances of the same view object definition, they will maintain separate view caches and separate master-detail relationships.

8. On the diagram, drag EmpManagerFkLink into AllManagers.

   Additional Information: This adds an instance of EmpManagerFkLink to HrAppModule. It also adds an instance of the other end of EmpManagerFkLink (that is, EmployeesView) to HrAppModule, and uses the view link instance to make it a detail of AllManagers.

9. Rename the view link instance from "EmpManagerFkLink1" to "ManagersToReports".
10. Rename the new view object instance from "EmployeesView1" to "ManagerReports".
11. On the diagram, drag EmpPastJobsLink into ManagerReports.

    Additional Information: This adds an instance of EmpPastJobsLink to HrAppModule. It also adds an instance of JobsView to HrAppModule, and uses the view link instance to make it a detail of ManagerReports. Because EmpPastJobsLink is bi-directional, you could also drag it into an instance of JobsView to add a detail instance of EmployeesView.
12. Rename the new view link instance from "EmpPastJobsFkLink1" to "ReportsToPastJobs".
13. Rename the new view object instance from "JobsView1" to "ReportPastJobs".

    Additional Information: The application module definition should look something like the following:

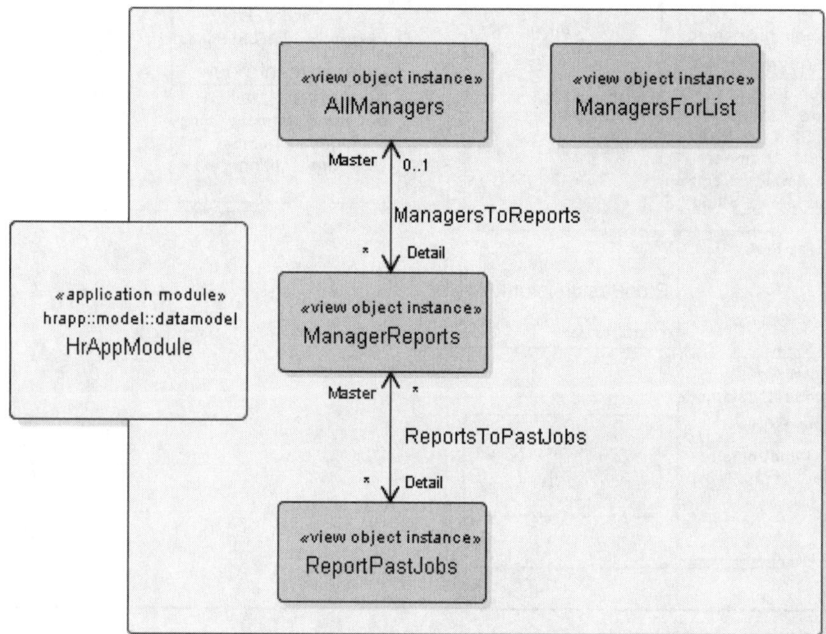

14. Click Save All.

Test the Application Module Definition

You can test an application module definition, including view object instances in master-detail relationships, using the following steps:

1. Select Test from the right-click menu on HRAppModule to open the Business Component Browser.
2. When the Connect dialog opens, accept the defaults and click Connect.
3. When the main window of the Business Component Browser opens, double click AllManagers to display Manager 100, King.
4. Double click ManagerReports and scroll through the employees shown. Note that all of the employees report to King.

   Additional Information: This is because the view link SQL of ManagersToReports is limiting ManagerReports' result set based on the current row of AllManagers.
5. Double click ManagersForList and scroll to manager 102, De Haan.
6. Check the rows displayed by AllManagers and ManagerReports. Note that they have not changed.

   Additional Information: ManagersForList is independent of AllManagers and ManagerReports. Changing its current row does not change the current row of AllManagers (even though they are based on the same view object definition), nor does it have any effect on ManagerReports' query.
7. Double click ReportsToPastJobs.
8. Scroll through the rows of ManagerReports in the top half of the window. Note that they are still restricted to reports of King.
9. In the lower half of the window, observe the past jobs held by each employee.
10. Close the Business Component Browser.

What Just Happened? You created an application module definition, HrModule, and added view object and view link instances to it. The data model represents a master-detail-detail relationship, with AllManagers as the master, ManagerReports as its detail, and ReportPastJobs as the detail of the detail. Then, you tested the application module definition and the view object and view link instances it contains.

CHAPTER 12

Exposing ADF BC to Applications

The knowledge of an unlearned man is living and luxuriant like a forest, but covered with mosses and lichens and for the most part inaccessible and going to waste.

—Henry David Thoreau (1817–1862)

An MVC model layer exposes business services to the rest of the application, receiving data change commands from the controller layer and providing data to the view layer for display. The *Oracle ADF model layer* (ADF Data Bindings and ADF Data Controls are described in Chapter 4) is JDeveloper's J2EE-compliant technology for creating a model layer for an MVC application. Ideally, the model layer provides an abstraction for business services, allowing the rest of the application to remain agnostic about whether the business services are implemented using ADF Business Components (ADF BC), Oracle Application Server TopLink, EJB beans, web services, or any other business service technology. In practice, however, the ADF model layer has slightly different functionality when it abstracts different business services.

Chapters 8–11 explained how to create business services using ADF BC technology. This chapter explains how to use the ADF model layer to expose business services to the rest of the application, with a particular emphasis on exposing ADF BC. (Chapter 14 describes the ways in which the ADF model layer differs when exposing other business service technologies.)

This chapter contains two hands-on practices. In the first, you will create a simple master-detail JSP application that uses the ADF model layer to interact with the ADF BC layer you created in Chapters 9–11. In the second hands-on practice, you will enhance the JSP application to provide list-based navigation, commit and rollback capabilities, and an edit page. The emphasis in these practices will not be on UI development (Part III focuses on UI development) but rather on the creation, customization, and use of ADF model layer components.

ADF Model Layer Architecture

Before you can use the ADF model layer effectively, it is important to understand the basics of its architecture. A single instance of an ADF application uses a single *binding context,* a container for all of the ADF model layer components that the application needs. A binding context contains data controls to access the business services, and binding containers to provide the data access needed for each page, form, or controller action. You can see the architecture of the ADF model layer in Figure 12-1. This figure shows a binding context interacting with JSP pages and ADF BC application module instances.

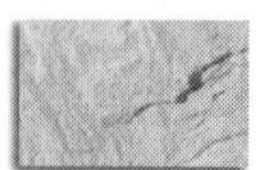

NOTE
The various layers of ADF including the model layer are introduced in Chapter 4.

Data Controls

A *data control* is a Java object in the ADF model layer that acts as an extra layer of code to abstract business services. Rather than reading data from or sending data to business services directly, the application will send requests through data controls.

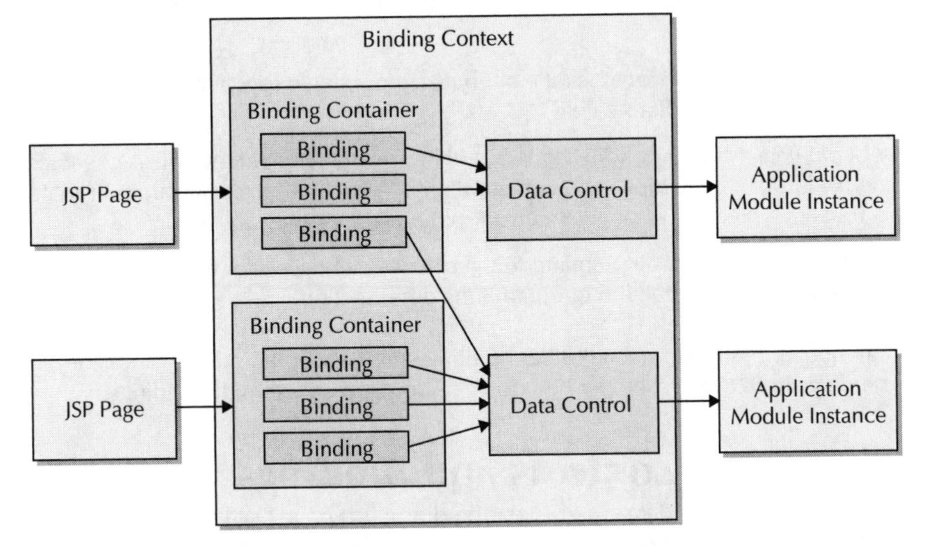

FIGURE 12-1. *ADF model layer architecture with JSP and ADF BC*

Without the use of data controls, ADF would need to use different APIs to communicate with ADF BC, EJB beans, and other diverse business services. Data controls provide a common API for the ADF, and convert calls to the common API into calls appropriate for each specific business services technology. As a result, JDeveloper provides a consistent development experience across business service technologies.

In an ADF BC application, a data control wraps a single top-level application module instance (that is, an application module instance not nested inside another application module instance). As discussed in Chapter 8, a top-level application module instance acts as a single point of contact between a set of ADF BC components and the rest of the application. The data control can go through the application module to access its data model, read and manipulate data, and manage database transactions.

Binding Containers

A *binding container* is a Java object in the ADF model layer that provides data access for a single page or form in an ADF application. For example, a page allowing a user to browse through a department's employees would have its own binding container, as would a separate page allowing a user to edit a particular employee. Binding containers contain *bindings*, which provide the interaction between a UI component in a page or form, or a single event in a controller action, and a data control. The ADF model layer provides a number of bindings. This chapter will discuss the following types of bindings:

- *Iterator bindings* identify a collection of data (hereafter called a "collection"—in the case of ADF BC, a view object instance) and keep track of its current row. Most other bindings must refer to an iterator binding.

- *Range bindings* gather together the data from a range of rows in a collection, for display in a tabular format.
- *Attribute bindings* present a single attribute from a single row in a collection, for display as a label or in an editable field.
- *List bindings* work with lists of values, either lists of literal values or lists of values derived from a collection. You can use them to simply display the values or to navigate through a collection or populate an attribute based on the values.
- *Action bindings* send a command to the business services—for example, changing the current row for a collection or committing a transaction.

You can obtain information about other bindings such as graph bindings, scrollbar bindings, and tree bindings from the JDeveloper help topic "About the Oracle ADF Bindings."

Creating Data Controls and Bindings

There are two ways to create data controls and bindings: using the Data Control Palette and using the UI Model tab of the Structure window. Both are available when you are editing a Struts page flow diagram, a JSP or UIX page, or a JClient form.

The Data Control Palette

The Data Control Palette contains a tree with the available data controls, the data models (data collections with their links as in the data model in an ADF BC application module) exposed by each data control, the attributes of their collections, and available operations (at both the data control and collection level). The Data Control Palette is shown in Figure 12-2.

The Data Control Palette and the Visual Editor

When you select an item in the Data Control Palette and you are editing a JSP page, UIX page, or JClient form, the *Drag and Drop As* dropdown list will be populated with a list of UI controls. The list of contents depends on two things:

- **The item selected** For example, a collection can generally be dropped as (among other UI controls) a table, an attribute as a value, and an action as a button.
- **What is being edited** The available UI controls differ depending on whether you are editing a Java application, a JSP page, or a UIX page. For example, you can drop trees into Java applications, but not into JSP or UIX pages.

After selecting an item and choosing an option from the *Drag and Drop As* list, you can drag the item onto the visual editor. This has the following effects:

- **Adding the appropriate data control** to the binding context, if it is not already there
- **Creating a binding container** for the page or form, if it does not already have one
- **Creating all data bindings** the UI control requires
- **Creating the code for the UI control** in the file

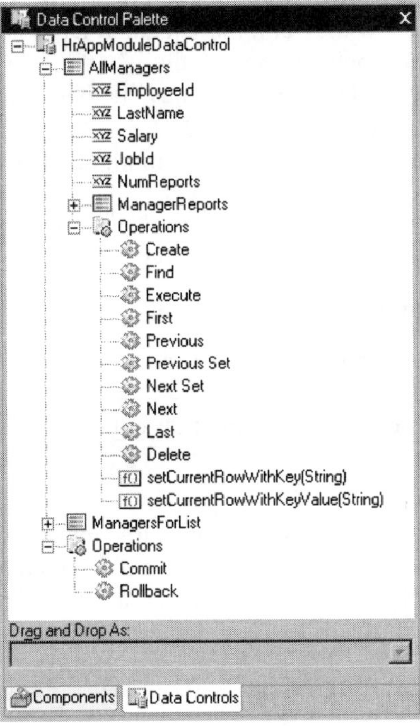

FIGURE 12-2. *The Data Control Palette*

For example, if you drag a collection onto a JSP page as a UI table, JDeveloper will do the following:

- Check to make sure that the binding context contains a data control for the application module definition that contains the view object instance; if it does not, it will add a data control to the binding context.
- Check to make sure that the page or form has a binding container; if it does not, it will create a binding container for the page and add it to the binding context.
- Check to make sure that the binding container already has an iterator binding for the view object instance; if it does not, it will create an iterator binding and add it to the binding context.
- Create a range binding for the UI table and add it to the binding context.
- Create the UI table and its rows and cells.

The binding container and its contents will be visible in the UI Model tab of the Structure window, as explained in the section "The UI Model Tab" later in this chapter. You will use the Data Control Palette in the hands-on practices for this chapter, and will learn many more details about creating UI controls in Chapters 14, 17, and 18.

The Data Control Palette and the Struts Page Flow Diagram

If you are editing a Struts page flow diagram, the *Drag and Drop As* list will only be available for operations, and will contain the single option "Method." After selecting an operation, you can drag it onto a Struts data action or data page. This has the following effects:

- **Adding the appropriate data control** to the binding context, if it is not already there
- **Creating a binding container** for the page or action, if it does not already have one
- **Creating an iterator binding**, if one is needed
- **Creating an action binding** for the operation
- **Creating an event** that invokes the operation

Chapter 17 explains how to create events for Struts data actions and data pages in more detail.

The UI Model Tab

The UI Model tab of the Structure window contains a tree representing the binding container for the page or form you are editing, or the selected data action or data page in the Struts page flow diagram. It displays all of the bindings in the container, as shown in Figure 12-3.

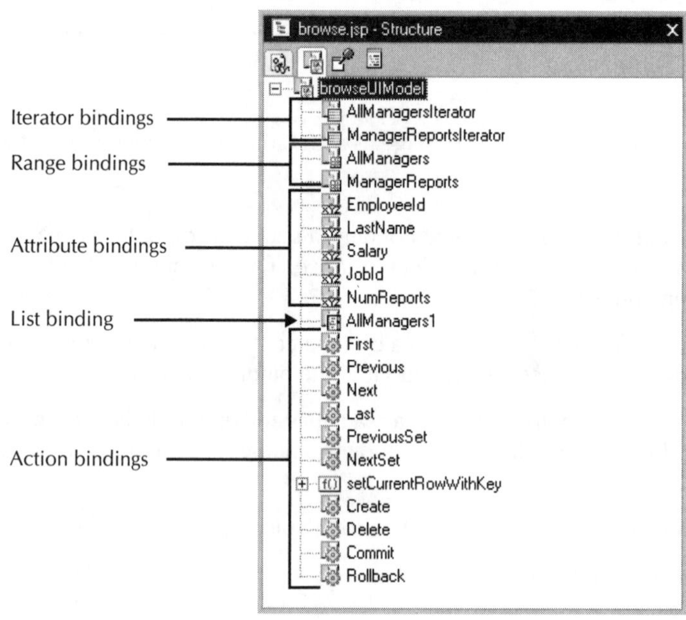

FIGURE 12-3. *The UI Model tab of the Structure window*

The UI Model tab allows you to do the following:

- **Create a binding container** for a page, form, or action, if one does not already exist, by selecting Create UI Model from the right-click menu on the root node
- **Create an iterator binding** for a collection, implicitly adding the appropriate data control to the binding context if it is not already there, by selecting Create Binding\Data\Iterator from the right-click menu on the root node
- **Create other bindings**, implicitly creating an appropriate iterator binding if one is needed and does not already exist, by selecting Create Binding and choosing the appropriate binding type from the right-click menu on the root node
- **Edit bindings**, including those created with the Data Control Palette, by selecting Edit from the right-click menu on the binding
- **View all bindings** for the selected file

The UI Model tab provides much more fine-grained control over bindings than does the Data Control Palette. However, it does not automatically create UI controls or events; if you create bindings using the UI Model tab, you must create UI controls or events by hand and hook them up to the bindings you have created.

Exposing a View Object Instance to an ADF Application

If an ADF application is to interact with a collection of data, it must do so through an iterator binding.

As mentioned earlier in this chapter, an iterator binding refers to a view object instance and keeps track of its current row. Other bindings use information in the iterator to know which row or rows to access. An iterator binding does not actually retrieve data from the view cache. It simply exposes the view object instance and specifies the current row; other bindings use that information to retrieve data. The iterator binding performs a function similar to that of the current row pointer in a PL/SQL cursor structure.

Ranges

Many applications, such as search engines, display only a small subset of a result set at a time. For example, a JSP application might display only the first ten results of a search and have a "Next" link to display the next ten results.

If an application will only display ten rows at a time, it should not retrieve hundreds or thousands of rows from the database at once. Iterator bindings use ranges to restrict the number of rows retrieved at one time. A *range* is a window into the result set of a query. If a view object instance is accessed through an iterator binding with a range size of `n`, only the first `n` rows will be retrieved into the view cache. You can use action bindings, as discussed in the section "Navigating Through Collections," to scroll the range set forward and retrieve more rows.

Iterator bindings have a default range size of 10, meaning that they will request that the view object instances to which they are bound retrieve ten rows at a time. You can raise or lower this number to retrieve more or fewer rows at once, or set the range size to -1 to retrieve all rows at once by setting the *rangeSize* property of the iterator binding. Bindings that use the iterator binding will only be able to access the rows currently in range; when the range is scrolled forward or backward, the new range will become available to those bindings.

Using Multiple Iterator Bindings

For many purposes, you can use a single iterator binding for each view object instance. However, there are reasons to use multiple iterator bindings.

As discussed in Chapter 11, a view object instance contains not only a cache of view rows, but a pointer to a "current" row. You can also keep two or more separate pointers to "current" rows by creating *secondary row set iterators,* which are extra pointers for a single view object instance.

Separate iterator bindings can use separate row set iterators for the same view object instance. Separate iterator bindings can also maintain different ranges and even have different range sizes. For example, Figure 12-4 shows two iterator bindings, AllManagersIterator and AllManagersIterator2, for a single view object instance, AllManagers. AllManagersIterator has a range size of 6, and AllManagersIterator2 has a range size of 5.

Accessing a Range of Data

The easiest way to access data for display in tabular format is by using a range binding. A range binding contains a *range set,* which is a collection of rows of data. Each row of data corresponds to a row currently in the associated iterator binding's range. The range set is stored in the range binding's *rangeSet* property. How you access the properties of bindings and how you extract rows from a range set depend on which client technology you are using. You will see how this is done in JSP pages in the first hands-on practice in this chapter.

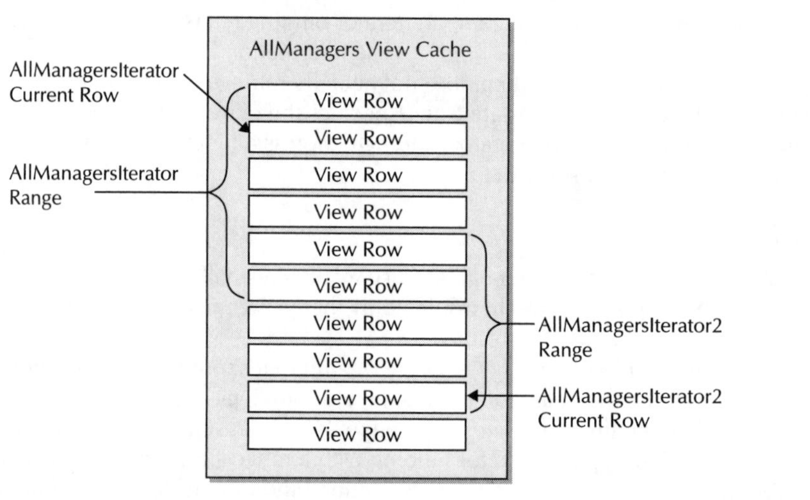

FIGURE 12-4. *Multiple iterator bindings*

A row in a range set does not necessarily contain all the data from its associated view row. When you define a range binding, you can specify a subset of the view attributes to include, as shown here:

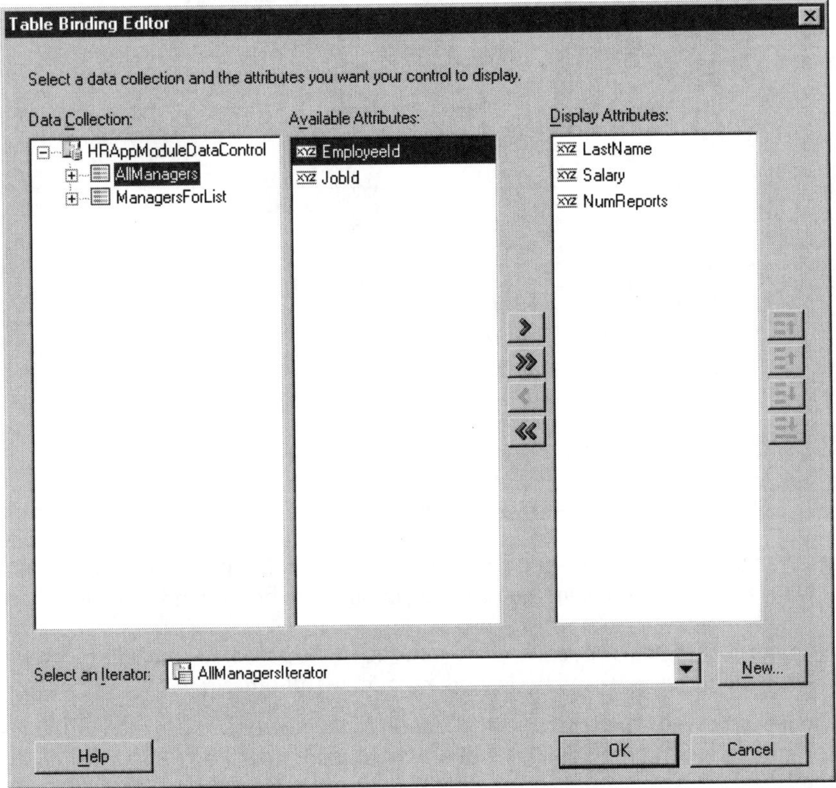

For example, you could create a range binding bound to an iterator binding for AllManagers with range size 10, and including only the following attributes:

- LastName
- Salary
- NumReports

You could use this range binding to display a 3×10 table, showing the LastName, Salary, and NumReports attributes for each of the ten rows in the iterator binding's range, as shown here:

LastName	Salary	NumReports
King	24000	14
Kochhar	17000	5
De Haan	17000	1
Hunold	9500	4
Greenberg	12000	5
Raphaely	11000	5
Weiss	8000	8
Fripp	8200	8
Kaufling	7900	8
Vollman	6500	8

The range binding would only retrieve the 30 values at a time required to display the table.

In addition to the row set, a range binding contains labels for each attribute it exposes. These labels are stored in the *labels* property of the binding. By default, the labels are the attribute names, but you can change the defaults by specifying Label Text control hints, as explained in Chapter 18.

Each row in the range set contains the following information beyond the attribute values, as well:

- **Whether it is the current row** This is stored in the row's *currencyString* property—it is "*" for the current row and " " (a single space) for all other rows.
- **The key object for the row** A serialization of the key object is stored in the row's *keyString* property—key objects will be explained in the "Key Objects" section later in this chapter.

Navigating Through Collections

You can navigate through a collection, moving the current row pointer or scrolling the range of an iterator binding, by using action bindings that invoke operations on collections. When you drag an operation to a page or Struts data action from under a collection in the Data Control Palette, JDeveloper creates a binding that invokes the operation on an iterator for that collection; when you create an action binding in the UI Model tab of the Structure window, you must choose an iterator binding that it will affect.

Moving the Current Row Pointer

You can advance an iterator binding's current row pointer forward one row using an action binding that invokes the Next operation. If a button bound to the operation is clicked, or an event bound to the operation is executed, the associated iterator binding will move its current row pointer one row forward. If this scrolls the current row pointer out of the iterator binding's current range, the entire range will be scrolled forward by a number of rows equal to the range size.

For example, suppose that AllManagersIterator is an iterator binding with a current row pointer at the first row, and a range of the first ten rows, and that AllManagersNext is an action binding that invokes Next on AllManagersIterator. The first nine times a button bound to AllManagersNext is clicked, the range of AllManagersIterator will not change; the current row pointer will simply advance within the current range. The tenth time the button is clicked, the range will scroll forward ten rows.

All action bindings have a property, *enabledString*, that has a value of "disabled" when the action should not be used. In the case of action bindings that invoke the Next operation, this will happen when the current row pointer of the iterator binding is on the last row. If you use the Data Control Palette to create a button bound to the Next operation, JDeveloper will create code to disable the button on the last row. If you create the control yourself, you will have to extract the value of *enabledString* and use it.

You can also use action bindings that invoke the following operations to move an iterator binding's current row pointer:

- **Previous** This operation moves the current row pointer backward one row. If this would put the current row outside of the current range, it will scroll the range backward a number of rows equal to the range size. *enabledString* will have a value of "disabled" when the current row pointer is on the first row.
- **First** This operation moves the current row pointer and the range to the beginning of the result set. *enabledString* will have a value of "disabled" when the current row pointer is already on the first row.
- **Last** This operation moves the current row pointer and the range to the end of the result set. *enabledString* will have a value of "disabled" when the current row pointer is already on the last row.

As with First, if you use the Data Control Palette to create a button bound to any of these operations, JDeveloper will automatically create code to disable the button when the *enabledString* property is "disabled".

Scrolling the Range

You can also explicitly move an iterator binding's range forward or backward using action bindings that invoke the following operations:

- **Next Set** This operation moves the range forward a number of rows equal to the range size, and moves the current row pointer to the beginning of the new range. If there are fewer rows remaining than the range size, Next Set will scroll the range forward as far as it can. *enabledString* will have a value of "disabled" when the range is at the end of the result set.
- **Previous Set** This operation moves the range backward a number of rows equal to the range size, and moves the current row pointer to the end of the new range. If there are fewer rows remaining than the range size, Previous Set will scroll the range backward as far as it can. *enabledString* will have a value of "disabled" when the range is at the beginning of the result set.

As with other action bindings, if you use the Data Control Palette to create a button bound to either of these operations, JDeveloper will automatically create code to disable the button when the *enabledString* property is "disabled".

Key Objects

As discussed in Chapter 11, a *key* is a collection of one or more view attributes that can be used to uniquely identify a row in a view object instance's cache. A *key object* is a Java object that aggregates the key values for a particular row.

As mentioned in the section "Accessing a Range of Data" earlier in this chapter, each row in a range set contains the key object for that row. You can extract the key object, in serialized form, and pass it to an action binding that invokes the setCurrentRowWithKey(String) operation. The iterator binding will move the current row pointer to that location.

The Data Control Palette works a bit differently with setCurrentRowWithKey(String) than it does with other operations. If you are editing a JSP page and select setCurrentRowWithKey(String) on the Data Control Palette, the *Drag and Drop As* list gives you a choice of creating a button or a link (as opposed to only a button). In fact, JDeveloper will extract the key from a row and pass it to the data action only if you drop the operation as a link. If you drop it as a button, you will have to do some manual coding to make the button work properly. To understand why JDeveloper does not provide this functionality, see the sidebar "Keys and Forms."

If you have a key made up of only one attribute, you can pass the value of that attribute to an action binding that invokes the setCurrentRowWithKeyValue(String) operation. JDeveloper does not provide an automated way of doing this; you must set it up by hand.

CAUTION
If you use setCurrentRowWithKeyValue(String) to navigate to a row, and the row is not in the iterator binding's current range, you will receive an exception. To ensure that this does not happen, you can either add code to check whether the value is within range or only use setCurrentRowWithKeyValue(String) with iterator bindings with a range size of –1.

Keys and Forms

If you drop setCurrentRowWithKey(String) as a link into a table created from the Data Control Palette, the operation will extract the key object from the row in the range set corresponding to the current table row. If you drop either setCurrentRowWithKey(String) or setCurrentRowWithKeyValue(String) as a button, JDeveloper creates a form with the button as a submit button. The key object or key value must come from the form, but you could create it in any number of ways, for example, by extracting it from a row in a range set, by using a parameter passed from another page, or by allowing a user to enter a value (for setCurrentRowWithKeyValue(String)). You must add code to use whichever source you need if you want to use a button instead of a link.

Creating and Deleting Rows

You can create a row and add it to a collection by using an action binding that invokes the Create operation. If a button bound to the operation is clicked, or an event bound to the operation is executed, the associated iterator binding will create a row directly before the current row, and will then move the current row pointer to point to the newly created row. The range will not move; this will often result in the last row being pushed out of the range.

For example, suppose an iterator binding's current row is Employee 102, and its current range contains Employees 100–109 (that is, a total of ten employees), in that order. If the Create operation is invoked, a new row will be inserted between Employee 101 and Employee 102. The range will then contain Employees 100–101, the new employee row (also the new current row), and Employees 102–108, in that order (again a total of ten employees). Employee 109 will no longer be part of the range.

Similarly, you can delete a row from the view cache (and mark associated entity object instances for deletion in the database) by using an action binding that invokes the Delete operation. If a button bound to the operation is clicked, or an event bound to the operation is executed, the associated iterator binding will delete the current row and move the row pointer to the next row. This will often result in rows being added to the range. For example, if the new row created in the preceding example is deleted, the current row pointer will return to Employee 102, and Employee 109 will be re-added to the range.

If the last row in a collection is deleted, the current row pointer will point to the new last row. If there are no rows in the collection, an action binding bound to the Delete operation will have an *enabledString* value of "disabled".

Accessing Individual Values

Many times, rather than displaying a range of data, you need to be able to access values from an iterator binding's current row individually. While it is possible to do this through a range binding, by determining which row in the range set is current and extracting data from that row, it is generally much easier to access values from the current row using an attribute binding. The Data Control Palette creates attribute bindings when you drop attributes onto a form or page to create labels, text fields, text areas, and most other controls that display or alter a single attribute value. (Select lists are a notable exception; they will be covered in the following section.) You can also use the Data Control Palette to create read-only or edit forms for a collection; JDeveloper will construct these using labels or text fields bound to attribute bindings.

An attribute binding contains both the value of the attribute (for the current row in the associated iterator binding), a label for the attribute (by default, the attribute name, but you can change the default using a Label Text control hint, as explained in Chapter 18), and the attribute's other control hints (as explained in Chapter 18).

You will use attribute bindings in the hands-on practices in this chapter.

Hands-on Practice: Create a Master-Detail JSP Application

In this practice, you will create a JSP application that uses the ADF Business Components you created in Chapters 9–11. This practice will not be concerned with the specifics of JSP development or Struts; those topics will be covered in detail in Chapters 17 and 18. This practice is primarily intended to demonstrate how the ADF model layer exposes business services to an MVC application.

NOTE
The results of both hands-on practices in this chapter are similar to the results of the practice in Chapter 18, and you will complete many of the same tasks in that practice. The focus, however, is different. In these practices, you will examine the ADF model layer more closely than in the Chapter 18 practice, whereas the Chapter 18 practice will be more concerned with UI development.

This practice builds on the results of the hands-on practices in Chapter 11. If you have not completed that practice, you can download the starting files for this practice from the authors' websites mentioned in the author information at the beginning of this book.

NOTE
JSP pages interact with the ADF model layer using a form of code called Expression Language (EL). This hands-on practice uses EL to interact with the ADF model layer, and will include the information necessary to understand those particular uses. Expression Language is covered in more detail in Appendix D.

This practice steps you through the following phases:

I. Create a read-only form with navigation

- Create a Struts data page and a JSP page
- Create a read-only form
- Add navigation buttons to the read-only form
- Test the read-only form

II. Create a UI table to display details

- Create a UI table
- Add navigation buttons to the table
- Add links to select a current row
- Add Create and Delete buttons
- Test the master-detail form

I. Create a Read-Only Form with Navigation

In this phase, you will use the Data Control Palette to create a read-only form that displays one view row from AllManagers at a time. You will use action bindings to provide navigation.

Create a Struts Data Page and a JSP Page

A *data page* is a Struts action that sets up a binding container for a page, displays the page, and responds to any UI events that occur on that page. You can create a Struts data page and a JSP page using the following steps:

1. Open the HRApp workspace if it is not already open.
2. On the ViewController node, select Open Struts Page Flow Diagram from the right-click menu.

   Additional Information: The page flow diagram allows you to map out the flow of control for the Struts controller. Chapter 17 explains the page flow diagram and Struts in more detail.
3. On the Component Palette, click the Data Page icon.
4. Click the diagram to create a data page.
5. Enter "browse" as the name of the data page.
6. Double click the data page to open the Select or Create Page dialog.

   Additional Information: This dialog allows you to create a page file that the data page displays.
7. Accept the defaults in the dialog and click OK to create a JSP page, browse.jsp, and open it in the visual editor.

Create a Read-Only Form

You can add a read-only data form to a JSP page using the following steps:

1. In the Data Control Palette, select HRAppModuleDataControl\AllManagers.
2. Select "Read Only Form" from the *Drag and Drop As* dropdown list.
3. Drag AllManagers onto the visual editor to create elements for a read-only form.

   Additional Information: A read-only form displays information from one row of a view object in an HTML table with two columns, as shown next:

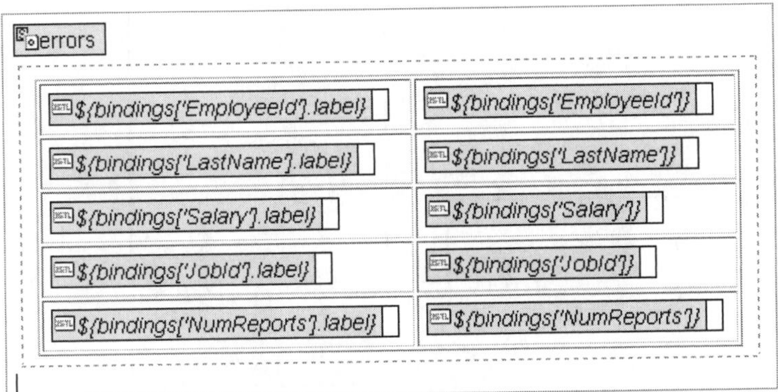

The left-hand column will display the labels for the view object instance's attributes, and the right-hand column will display values for a single row.

4. In the Structure window, select the UI Model tab to see the bindings in the binding container.

   Additional Information: JDeveloper has also added a data control for HRAppModule to the binding context and created a binding container, BrowseUIModel, for the data page. The binding container will look like the following:

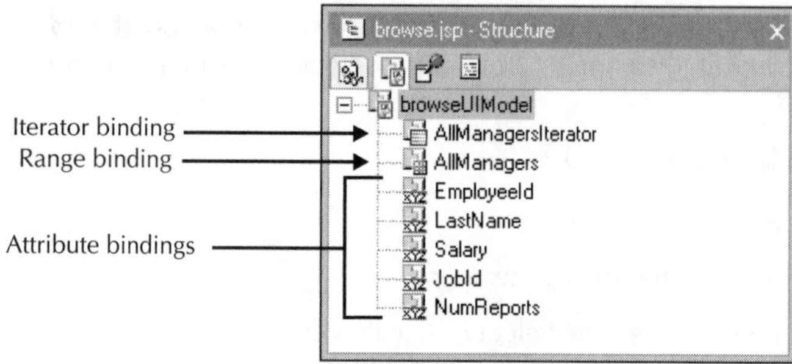

5. Double click the EmployeeId binding to open the Attribute Binding Editor.

   Additional Information: The binding is bound to the EmployeeId attribute of the AllManagers view object instance and is associated with the AllManagersIterator iterator binding, as shown here:

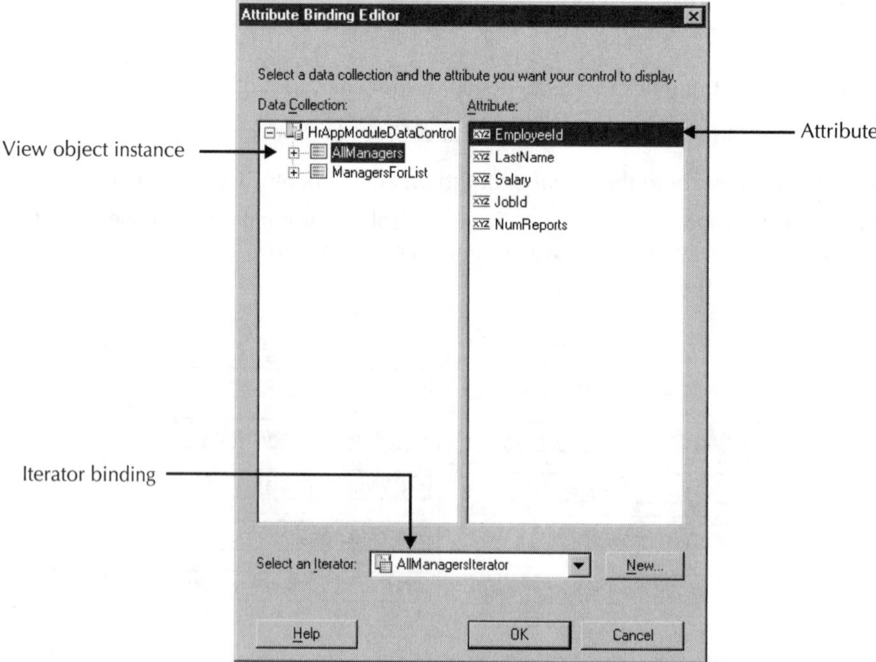

6. Click Cancel to close the editor without making any changes.
7. In the visual editor, examine the HTML table.

   Additional Information: Note that there are two columns in the HTML table. The left-hand column contains tags with expressions like the following:

   ```
   ${bindings['EmployeeId'].label}
   ```

   This is a value represented using EL. It returns the *label* property from the EmployeeId binding; in this case (because no control hints are specified) the attribute name, "EmployeeId".

   The right-hand column contains tags with expressions like the following:

   ```
   ${bindings['EmployeeId']}
   ```

   This is an EL expression that returns the value in the EmployeeId binding.

Add Navigation Buttons to the Read-Only Form

You can add navigation buttons to change the current row using the following steps:

1. In the Data Control Palette, select HRAppModuleDataControl\AllManagers\Operations\First.
2. Ensure that "Button" is selected in the *Drag and Drop As* list.
3. Drag the First operation onto the visual editor, below the table, but still inside the dotted box.

   Additional Information: The dotted box represents an HTML form. This form is already set up to send button clicks back to the browse data page. You could also add the button in a separate form (by selecting "Button with Form" from the *Drag and Drop As* list), but you would have to ensure that the form notified the correct data page or data action of the event.

4. Repeat steps 1–3 to drag the Previous, Next, and Last operations onto the form. The page should resemble the following:

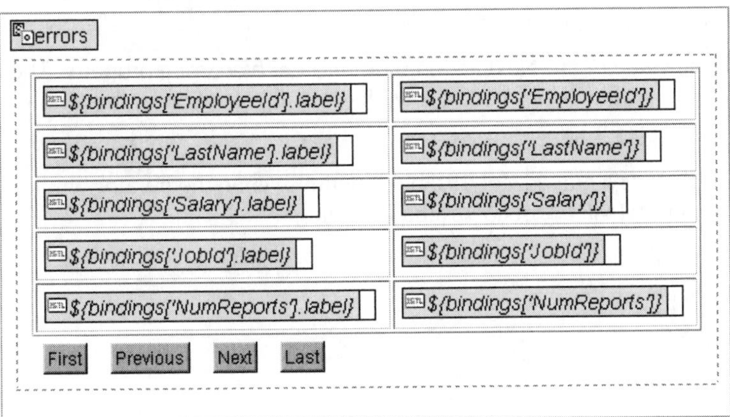

5. Note that the UI Model tab of the Structure window now contains action bindings for the navigation buttons, as shown here:

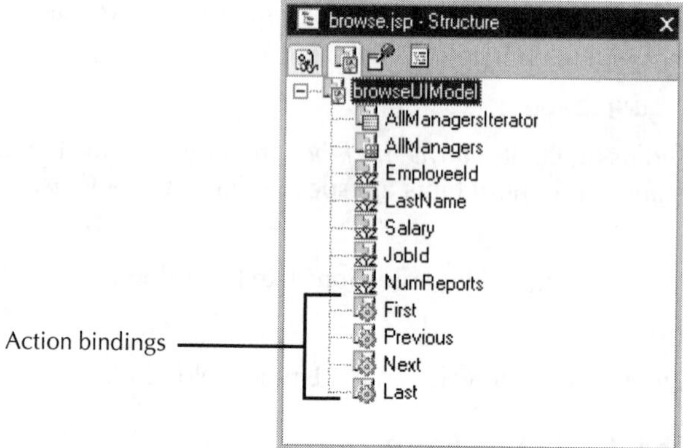

6. In the UI Model tab, double click the First binding to open the Action Binding Editor.

   Additional Information: You can see that the binding invokes the First operation and is associated with the AllManagersIterator iterator binding.

7. Click Cancel to close the editor without making any changes.

8. Select the Next button. In the visual editor, click the Source tab to view the source code for the JSP.

9. The following code will be selected (because you selected the button in the visual editor):

```
<input type="submit" name="event_Next" value="Next"
  <c:out value="${bindings.Next.enabledString}" />/>
```

   Additional Information: This is an HTML input tag with a type of "submit", which creates a button in HTML. HTML tags are discussed in more detail in Appendix C, but for now, note the <c:out> JSTL tag nested inside the HTML tag. This prints the value of the following expression:

```
${bindings.Next.enabledString}
```

   This is the value of the Next action binding's *enabledString* property. Therefore, when the iterator binding is on the last row, the HTML tag becomes the following:

```
<input type="submit" name="event_Next" value="Next" disabled />
```

   This displays as a grayed-out (disabled) button. When the iterator binding is not on the last row, the HTML tag becomes the following:

```
<input type="submit" name="event_Next" value="Next" />
```

   This displays an active button.

10. Save All.

Test the Read-Only Form

You can test a data page that uses the ADF model layer using the following steps:

1. Reopen the Struts page flow diagram.
2. On the browse data page, select Run from the right-click menu.

   Additional Information: After OC4J is initialized, a web browser window will open. The page displayed should look like the following:

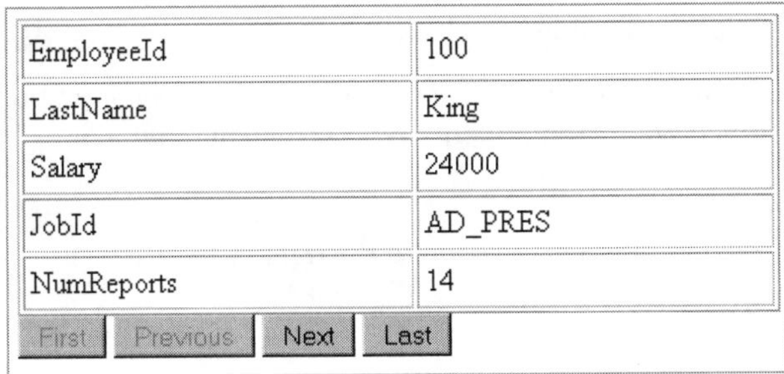

EmployeeId	100
LastName	King
Salary	24000
JobId	AD_PRES
NumReports	14

   Note that the First and Previous buttons are disabled, as they should be when the first row is the current row.

3. Use the navigation buttons to move through the result set.
4. Close the web browser window.

What Just Happened? You created a JSP page that displays a read-only form for AllManagers. The page's binding container includes the following:

- An iterator binding to keep track of AllManagers' current row
- Attribute bindings to access attribute labels and attribute values for the current row
- Action bindings to move the current row forward, backward, and to the first and last element of the view cache

This page is similar to other master-detail pages created in hands-on practices throughout this book, but in this practice, you also examined the contents of the binding container and saw how those contents were accessed through EL.

II. Create a UI Table to Display Details

In this phase, you will use the Data Control Palette to create an HTML table that displays the rows in ManagerReports, turning the form into a master-detail form. You will use action bindings to provide navigation and allow the creation and deletion of rows.

Create a UI Table

This section adds an HTML table containing ManagerReports rows (employees who work for a manager) that will show detail records for the master record displayed in the read-only form you created in the last phase.

1. Select the browse.jsp Design tab to reopen the visual editor.
2. In the Data Control Palette, select HRAppModuleDataControl\AllManagers\ManagerReports.
3. Ensure that "Read Only Table" is selected in the *Drag and Drop As* dropdown list.
4. Drag ManagerReports onto the visual editor, after the navigation buttons but still within that form (outlined with a red dotted line), to create a table.

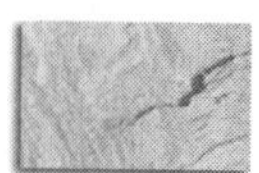

TIP
You can drop the component on the space to the right of the Last button.

5. In the Structure window, select the UI Model tab.

   Additional Information: Two new bindings have been added to the binding container: ManagerReportsIterator, an iterator binding for the ManagerReports view object instance, and ManagerReports, a range binding associated with ManagerReportsIterator.

6. Double click the ManagerReports binding to open the Table Binding Editor.

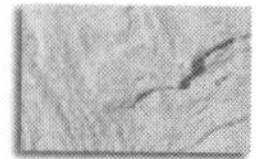

NOTE
The JDeveloper UI uses inconsistent terminology. In some places, range bindings are referred to as "table bindings."

   Additional Information: The binding uses all five attributes of the ManagerReports view object instance as its display attributes.

7. Click Cancel to close the editor without making any changes.
8. In the visual editor, examine the read-only table for ManagerReports rows.

   Additional Information: The table should look like the following (only the leftmost portion is shown):

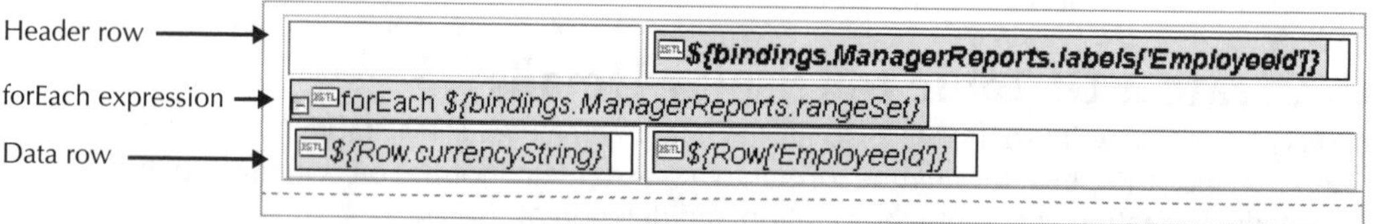

The header row contains seven cells. The left-hand cell is empty, but the rest of the cells in the header row contain tag boxes containing expressions like the following:

```
${bindings.ManagerReports.labels['EmployeeId']}
```

This is an EL expression that extracts the "EmployeeId" label from the *labels* property of the ManagerReports range binding.

The forEach tag is a representation of the JSTL iterator statement shown here:

```
<c:forEach var="Row" items="${bindings.ManagerReports.rangeSet}">
```

This statement creates a loop where the variable `Row` cycles through the elements in the collection supplied by the following expression:

```
${bindings.ManagerReports.rangeSet}
```

This expression returns the range set of the ManagerReports binding, so `Row` holds, in turn, each row in the range set.

The data row is inside the loop. The HTML row will create one HTML table row for each row in the loop. The leftmost cell of the data row contains the following expression:

```
${Row.currencyString}
```

This returns the *currencyString* property value from the current value of the `Row` variable. The rest of the cells contain expressions like the following:

```
${Row['EmployeeId']}
```

This returns the value of the EmployeeId attribute for the current value of the `Row` variable.

9. In the UI Model tab of the Structure window, select the ManagerReportsIterator binding.

10. In the Property Inspector, set the *Range Size* property to "8" and press ENTER.

    Additional Information: This sets the range size for the ManagerReportsIterator iterator binding to 8. Since the ManagerReports range binding uses ManagerReportsIterator, this limits its range set to eight rows.

Add Navigation Buttons to the Table

You can add navigation buttons to scroll an iterator binding's range using the following steps:

1. In the Data Control Palette, select HRAppModuleDataControl\AllManagers\ManagerReports\Operations\Previous Set.

2. Ensure that "Button" is selected in the *Drag and Drop As* list.

3. Drag the Previous Set operation onto the visual editor, after the detail table, but still inside the form.

4. Repeat steps 1–3 to drag the Next Set operation into the form.

   Additional Information: In addition to creating buttons, this adds two new action bindings to the binding container: PreviousSet and NextSet. These are visible in the UI Model tab of the Structure window.

5. In the UI Model tab of the Structure window, double click the PreviousSet binding to open the Action Binding Editor.

   Additional Information: You can see that the binding invokes the Previous Set operation and is associated with the ManagerReportsIterator iterator binding.

6. Click Cancel to close the editor without making any changes.

Add Links to Select a Current Row

As explained earlier in the chapter, the setCurrentRowWithKey(String) operation can be used to create links in a table that select a current row. You can do this using the following steps:

1. On the upper-right cell in the detail HTML table, select Table | Insert Rows Or Columns from the right-click menu.
2. Select the *Columns* and *After Selection* radio buttons and click OK.

   Additional Information: An extra cell is added to the end of both the header row and the data row.
3. In the Data Control Palette, select HRAppModuleDataControl\AllManagers\ManagerReports\Operations\setCurrentRowWithKey(String).
4. Select "Find Row Link" from the *Drag and Drop As* list.
5. Drag setCurrentRowWithKey(String) into the (blank) lower-right cell of the table.

   Additional Information: This creates a link and adds a new action binding, setCurrentRowWithKey, to the binding container.
6. In the UI model tab, expand the setCurrentRowWithKey node and select the param node.

   Additional Information: The setCurrentRowWithKey() operation requires a parameter (the serialization of the key object), which can be passed through action bindings that invoke it.
7. Examine the Property Inspector.

   Additional Information: The action binding will expect to see the parameter passed as `Arg0`. You could enter a static value for the parameter here, but instead, the value is dynamically constructed in the link, as you will see in the next step.
8. Select the "Select" link that you just added. Open the source view. The following tag will be selected:

```
<a href=
  "browse.do?
    event=setCurrentRowWithKey&
    Arg0=<c:out value='${Row.rowKeyStr}' />
  "
>
```

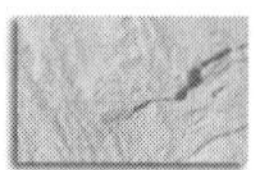

NOTE
We have added line breaks to the above code to make it easier to read. The actual tag will appear on one line.

Additional Information: This tag creates a link that goes back to the browse data action, passing two parameters: an event, which tells the data action which action binding to use, and a value for `Arg0`. This value is given by the following expression:

```
${Row.rowKeyStr}
```

This expression returns the `Row` variable's *rowKeyStr* property, that is, the serialized row key of each data row.

Add Create and Delete Buttons

You can add buttons to create and delete rows using the following steps:

1. Click the Design tab to reopen the visual editor.
2. In the Data Control Palette, select HRAppModuleDataControl\AllManagers\ManagerReports\Operations\Create.
3. Ensure that "Button" is selected in the *Drag and Drop As* list.
4. Drag Create onto the visual editor, immediately after the Next Set button.
5. Add a Delete button to the form next to the Create button.

   Additional Information: In addition to creating buttons, this creates action bindings that invoke the Create and Delete operations.
6. Click Save All.

   Additional Information: As expected, this action binding invokes the Commit operation. Note that it does not have an associated iterator binding because the Commit and Rollback operations apply to the entire data control.

Test the Master-Detail Form

You can test a data action and JSP page that use the bindings you created in this phase using the following steps:

1. Reopen the Struts page flow diagram.
2. On the browse data page, select Run from the right-click menu.

   Additional Information: A web browser window will open. The page displayed should look like the one in Figure 12-5.

   Note that the detail table displays eight rows, because its range binding is associated with an iterator binding of range size 8. Also note that the Previous Set button is disabled. The button is disabled because the detail iterator's range is already at the beginning of the result set.
3. Use the Next Set and Previous Set buttons to scroll the detail iterator's range forward and backward.
4. Click the "Select" link for Employee 120.

   Additional Information: When the page reloads, Employee 120 displays the *currencyString* "*".
5. Click Create to create a row.

EmployeeId	100
LastName	King
Salary	24000
JobId	AD_PRES
NumReports	14

First Previous Next Last

	EmployeeId	LastName	Email	ManagerId	ManagerEmpId	ManagerName	
*	101	Kochhar	NKOCHHAR	100	100	King	Select
	102	De Haan	LDEHAAN	100	100	King	Select
	114	Raphaely	DRAPHEAL	100	100	King	Select
	120	Weiss	MWEISS	100	100	King	Select
	121	Fripp	AFRIPP	100	100	King	Select
	122	Kaufling	PKAUFLIN	100	100	King	Select
	123	Vollman	SVOLLMAN	100	100	King	Select
	124	Mourgos	KMOURGOS	100	100	King	Select

PreviousSet NextSet Create Delete

FIGURE 12-5. *The Master-detail form*

Additional Information: The row is inserted before Employee 120 and becomes the new current row. ManagerId, the destination attribute of EmpMgrFkLink, is prepopulated to match the master view row. ManagerEmpId and ManagerName are prepopulated as well, because they come from a reference entity object usage and are determined by ManagerId. EmployeeId is prepopulated by business logic added in the Chapter 10 hands-on practice.

6. Click the "Select" link for Employee 121.
7. Click Delete to delete the row.
8. Close the web browser window.
9. Select **Run | Terminate | Embedded OC4J Server**.

   Additional Information: This terminates the server (and your HTML session) immediately and rolls back the changes you made.

What Just Happened? You turned the JSP page created in Phase I into a master-detail form. This involved adding the following bindings to the data page's binding context (some of which are represented by a control on the page):

- An iterator binding to keep track of ManagerReports' current row and range
- A range binding to display tabular data from ManagerReports
- Action bindings to scroll the detail range set
- Action bindings to move the current row pointer in the detail to a row based on its key object
- Action bindings to create and delete rows in the detail

Selecting from a List

The list binding is used for creating components that display a list of values or combinations of values, such as dropdown lists, multi-select lists, and radio button groups. There are three functions list bindings can perform:

- **Navigating to a particular row in a collection** This is handled by list bindings in navigation mode.
- **Updating an attribute value from a list of literal values** This is handled by list bindings in enumeration mode.
- **Updating an attribute value from a list of values derived from another attribute** This is handled by list bindings in LOV (list-of-values) mode.

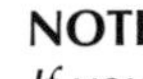

NOTE
If you create a list binding in enumeration or LOV mode, you can switch it between those two modes later. However, you cannot switch it to navigation mode, nor can you switch a list binding created in navigation mode into enumeration or LOV mode.

Much like range bindings, all list bindings contain a range set—a collection of rows of data. These rows are used to populate the UI control bound to the list binding.

Navigation Mode

List bindings in *navigation mode* allow a user to navigate within the current range of the associated iterator binding.

The range set for a list binding in enumeration mode has one row for each row in the associated iterator binding's range. Like range sets for range bindings, a row in the range set for a list binding in navigation mode does not necessarily contain all the data from its associated view row. When you create a list binding in navigation mode, you can select a subset of the view attributes to include; the list binding will retrieve only the values of those attributes into the binding container. For example, the following illustration shows a dropdown list bound to a list binding for an instance of DepartmentsView—only DepartmentName is included in the range set:

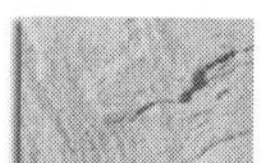

NOTE
It is very natural to use navigation buttons to scroll the range of a table, but considerably less natural to use them to scroll the range of a list. For this reason, we recommend basing navigation mode list bindings on iterator bindings with a range size of -1 (all rows).

Enumeration Mode

List bindings in *enumeration mode* allow a user to choose from a literal list of values; the chosen value will be used to populate an attribute in the current row of the associated iterator binding.

The range set for a list binding in navigation mode is not based on an iterator binding at all; instead, it is created from a literal list of values you define in the Set of Values pane of the List Binding Editor (opened when you create or edit a list binding), as shown here:

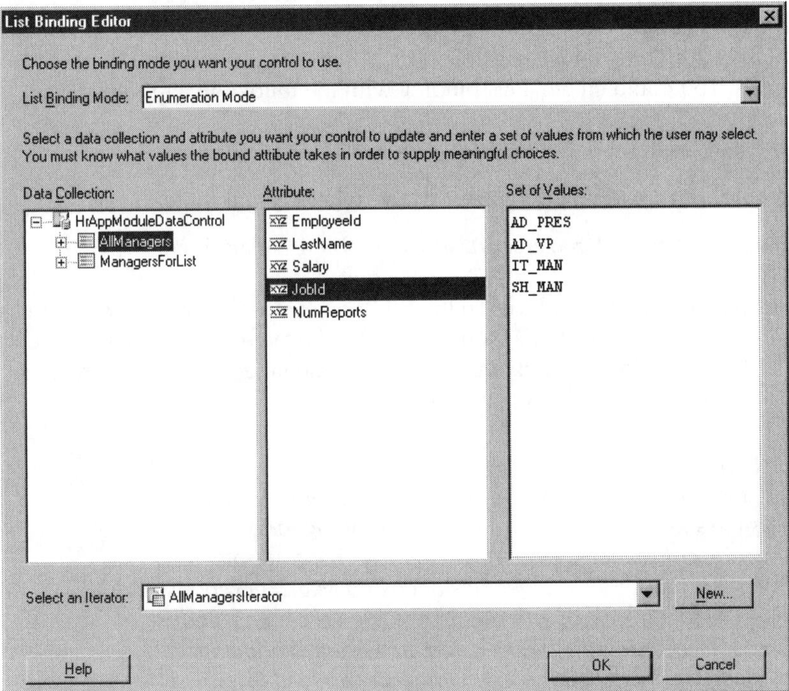

LOV Mode

List bindings in *LOV mode* allow a user to update an attribute value from a list of values derived from a collection. Unlike most bindings, list bindings in LOV mode are associated with two iterator bindings:

- **The source iterator**, which is an iterator binding used to populate the range set, as in a list binding in navigation mode
- **The target iterator**, which is an iterator binding used to determine which row gets updated, as in a list binding in enumeration mode

When you design a list binding in LOV mode, you must specify the following sets of attributes:

- **Display attributes** are the attributes included in the range set for display in the control
- **Target attributes** are the attributes to be populated by the list binding
- **LOV attributes** are the attributes from the source iterator to be used in populating the target attributes

LOV attributes need not be the same as target attributes. For example, suppose the source iterator is an iterator binding for ManagersForList, and the target iterator is an iterator binding for ManagerReports. You could create a list binding with the following attributes:

- **LastName (from ManagersForList)** as the sole display attribute
- **ManagerId (from ManagerReports)** as the sole target attribute
- **EmployeeId (from ManagersForList)** as the sole LOV attribute

Only LastName would be displayed in the list. However, selecting a particular LastName from the list (for example, "Kochhar") would populate the target attribute with the corresponding EmployeeId (102). This allows you to put user-friendly identifiers in your controls while maintaining numerical foreign key relationships.

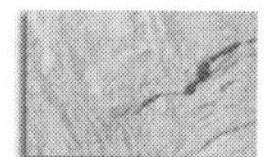

CAUTION
Do not attempt to use an iterator binding for a master view object instance as the source iterator and an iterator binding for one of its detail view object instances as the detail iterator. For example, if AllManagers is a master view object instance and ManagerReports is a detail view object instance, you should not use an iterator binding for AllManagers as the source iterator and an iterator binding for ManagerReports as the detail iterator. Doing so can lead to unpredictable application behavior.

Managing Transactions

The preceding sections described how to create and delete rows and manipulate attribute values. All these changes take place in the view and entity caches only. Posting changes to the database is a separate operation.

The easiest way to post changes to the database from ADF BC is to do so implicitly as part of a Commit operation. The Commit operation does the following:

- Fires entity-level validation on all entity object instances marked as needing validation
- Issues DML commands to the database to create rows corresponding to any new entity object instances, delete rows corresponding to entity object instances that are marked for deletion, and update rows corresponding to entity object instances that have been changed
- Issues a COMMIT command to the database

As with other operations, you can create an action binding that invokes the Commit operation. Unlike the action bindings discussed earlier in this chapter, action bindings that invoke the Commit operation do not require an iterator binding—they work directly on the data control.

You can also create action bindings that invoke the Rollback operation, which does the following:

- Issues a ROLLBACK command to the database
- Clears all the entity and view caches. If the data is needed again, the view object instances will re-execute their queries.

If there are no changed, new, or deleted entity object instances in the entity caches, action bindings that invoke the Commit and Rollback operations will have an *enabledString* value of "disabled".

Hands-on Practice: Refine the JSP Application

In this practice, you will add more functionality to the JSP application created in the first hands-on practice in this chapter. You will add a navigation list and transaction control to the master-detail form, and add an edit form for the detail view object instance. Like the first practice in this chapter, this practice will not be concerned with the specifics of JSP development or Struts; that will be covered in detail in Chapters 17 and 18. This practice is primarily intended to demonstrate how the ADF model layer exposes business services to an MVC application.

This practice builds on the results of the first hands-on practice in this chapter. If you have not completed that practice, you can download the starting files for this practice from the authors' websites mentioned in the author information at the beginning of this book.

This practice steps you through the following phases:

I. Refine the master-detail form

- Add a navigation list to the master portion of the form
- Add commit and rollback buttons
- Test the master-detail form

II. Create an edit form

- Create a Struts data page, forwards, and a JSP page
- Create an input form
- Create an iterator binding
- Use a list binding to populate an attribute
- Create a return forward
- Test the JSP application

I. Refine the Master-Detail Form

In this phase, you will use the Data Control Palette to enhance the master-detail form created in the first hands-on practice in this chapter. You will use a list binding to provide navigation and action bindings to provide commit and rollback capabilities.

Add a Navigation List to the Master Portion of the Form

You can add a list to move an iterator binding's current row pointer using the following steps:

1. Open the HRApp workspace if it is not already open.
2. In the Application Navigator, double click "HrApp\ViewController\Web Content\browse.jsp" to open the visual editor.
3. In the Data Control Palette, select HRAppModuleDataControl\AllManagers.
4. Select "Navigation List" from the *Drag and Drop As* list.
5. Drag AllManagers onto the visual editor, immediately after the Last button. Below the Data Control Palette, select the Components tab to display the Component Palette.
6. On the HTML page of the Component Palette, select the Submit Button icon and drag it onto the visual editor, immediately after the dropdown list.
7. In the UI Model tab of the Structure window, note that a new list binding, AllManagers1, has been added to the binding container.
8. Double click AllManagers1 to open the List Binding Editor.

   Additional Information: The binding is a list binding in navigation mode. It has all of the attributes from AllManagers as its display attributes and is associated with the AllManagersIterator iterator binding.
9. In the Display Attributes list, multi-select (CTRL click) the Salary, JobId, and NumReports attributes.
10. Click the "<" button to move these attributes to the *Available Attributes* list.

    Additional Information: This will make the dropdown list display only EmployeeId and LastName.
11. Click OK to close the editor.
12. In the UI Model tab of the Structure window, select the AllManagersIterator binding.
13. In the Property Inspector, set the Range Size property to "-1" and press ENTER.

    Additional Information: If you leave the range size as 10, only 10 rows of the iterator will be loaded into the list binding, making it impossible to use the navigation list to navigate to other rows. Setting the *Range Size* property to "-1" will display all rows.
14. Click Save All.

Add Commit and Rollback Buttons

You can add buttons to commit or roll back changes using the following steps:

1. In the Data Control Palette, select HRAppModuleDataControl\Operations\Commit.
2. Ensure that "Button" is selected in the *Drag and Drop As* list.

3. Drag Commit onto the visual editor, to the left of the master table but still within the form. The button will appear above the master table, as shown next:

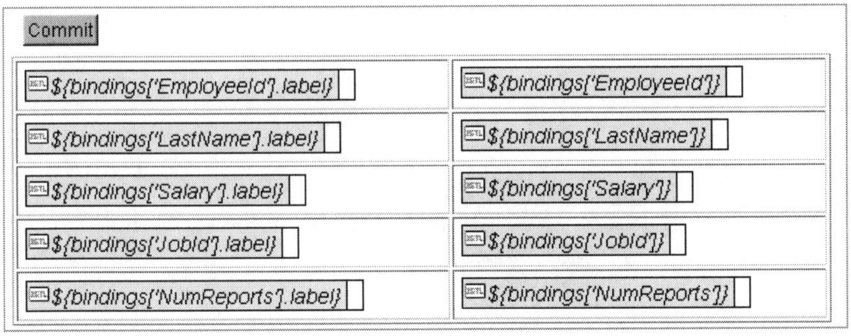

Commit

${bindings['EmployeeId'].label}	${bindings['EmployeeId']}
${bindings['LastName'].label}	${bindings['LastName']}
${bindings['Salary'].label}	${bindings['Salary']}
${bindings['JobId'].label}	${bindings['JobId']}
${bindings['NumReports'].label}	${bindings['NumReports']}

4. Add a Rollback button to the form, to the right of the Commit button.

   Additional Information: In addition to creating buttons, this creates action bindings that invoke the Commit and Rollback operations.

5. In the UI Model tab of the Structure window, double click Commit to open the Action Binding Editor.

   Additional Information: As expected, this action binding invokes the Commit operation. Note that it does not have an associated iterator binding because the Commit and Rollback operations apply to the entire data control.

6. Click Cancel to close the editor without making any changes.

7. Click Save All.

Test the Master-Detail Form

You can test a navigation list and Create and Rollback using the following steps:

1. Reopen the Struts page flow diagram.

2. On the browse data page, select Run from the right-click menu.

   Additional Information: After OC4J is initialized, a web browser window will open. The page displayed should look like the one in Figure 12-6. Note that the Commit and Rollback buttons are disabled. This is because no changes have been made to the data.

3. Select "145 Russell" from the dropdown list.

   Additional Information: The list shows the display attributes—EmployeeId and LastName. Note that, because the range size of the iterator binding is -1, all 18 managers are available in the list.

4. Click Submit to navigate to Russell.

5. Click the Create button to create a row. The Commit and Rollback buttons become enabled.

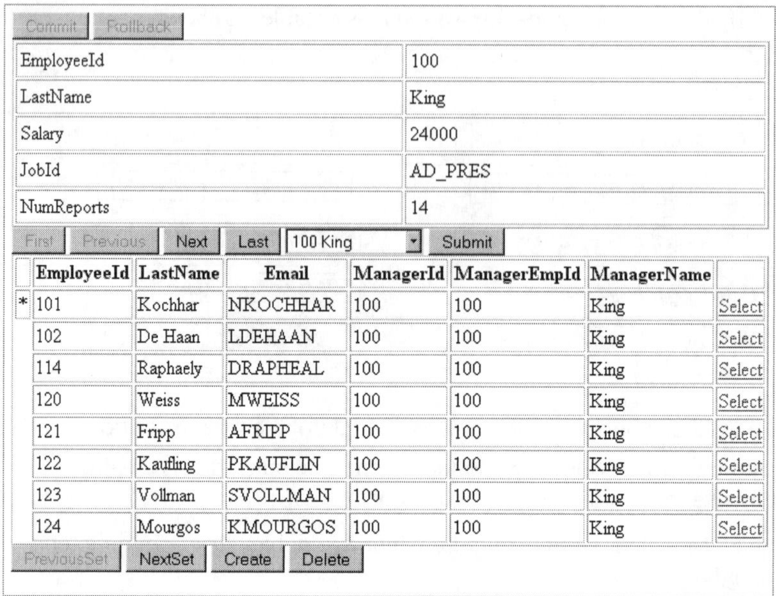

Commit | Rollback

EmployeeId	100
LastName	King
Salary	24000
JobId	AD_PRES
NumReports	14

First | Previous | Next | Last | 100 King | Submit

	EmployeeId	LastName	Email	ManagerId	ManagerEmpId	ManagerName	
*	101	Kochhar	NKOCHHAR	100	100	King	Select
	102	De Haan	LDEHAAN	100	100	King	Select
	114	Raphaely	DRAPHEAL	100	100	King	Select
	120	Weiss	MWEISS	100	100	King	Select
	121	Fripp	AFRIPP	100	100	King	Select
	122	Kaufling	PKAUFLIN	100	100	King	Select
	123	Vollman	SVOLLMAN	100	100	King	Select
	124	Mourgos	KMOURGOS	100	100	King	Select

PreviousSet | NextSet | Create | Delete

FIGURE 12-6. *The enhanced master-detail form*

6. Click Rollback to roll back the changes.

   Additional Information: This resets the transaction to its initial state, with no new row and with the master iterator pointing to King. You can navigate to Russell again to ensure that the new row is gone.

7. Close the web browser window.

What Just Happened? You added a navigation list and Commit and Delete buttons to the master-detail form. This involved adding the following to the page's binding context:

- A list binding in navigation mode to display a list of rows and allow direct navigation to any of them.
- Action bindings to commit and roll back the transaction. Since only the detail rows can be changed, these act only on the detail records.

II. Create an Edit Form

In this phase, you will use the Data Control Palette to create a form to enter and change values for rows of ManagerReports. Most values will be changed using attribute bindings, but one, ManagerId, will be changed using a list binding in LOV mode. The browse data page will forward to this form after using the Create or setCurrentRowWithKey action bindings.

Create a Struts Data Page, Forwards, and a JSP Page

You can create a Struts data page, forwards from one data page to another, and a JSP page using the following steps:

1. On the Component Palette, click the Data Page icon.
2. Click on the page flow diagram to add a data page to your controller.
3. Enter "edit" as the name of the data page.
4. On the Component Palette, click the forward icon.
5. Click once on the browse data page and once on the edit data page to add a forward between them.
6. Change the name of the forward from "success" to "Create" by clicking it once and then a second time (do not double click) and typing the new name. Press ENTER.

   Additional Information: This specifies that the browse data page forwards to the edit data page, rather than displaying browse.jsp, after it invokes the Create action binding. For more information about forwards, see Chapter 17.
7. Repeat steps 5–7 to add another forward from the browse data page to the edit data page, and rename this forward "setCurrentRowWithKey".

   Additional Information: Your page flow diagram should look something like the following:

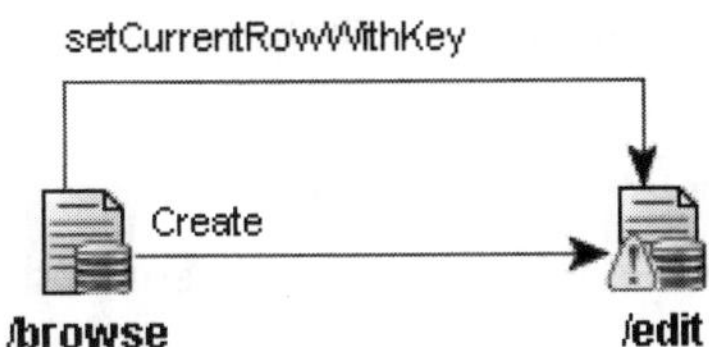

8. Double click the edit data page to open the Select or Create Page dialog.
9. Accept the defaults in the dialog and click OK to create a JSP page, edit.jsp, and open it in the visual editor.

Create an Input Form

You can create a form to edit a row using the following steps:

1. In the Data Control Palette, select HRAppModuleDataControl\AllManagers\ManagerReports.
2. Select "Input Form" from the *Drag and Drop As* list.
3. Drag ManagerReports onto the visual editor to create an input form.

Additional Information: JDeveloper creates an HTML table with two columns: The left-hand column will display the labels for ManagerReports' attributes, and the right-hand column will contain UI controls (HTML input fields) to update values for a single row. JDeveloper has also created a binding container for the edit data page, and created the bindings required to display the labels and edit data.

4. On the Structure window, select the UI Model tab to see the bindings in the binding container, shown here:

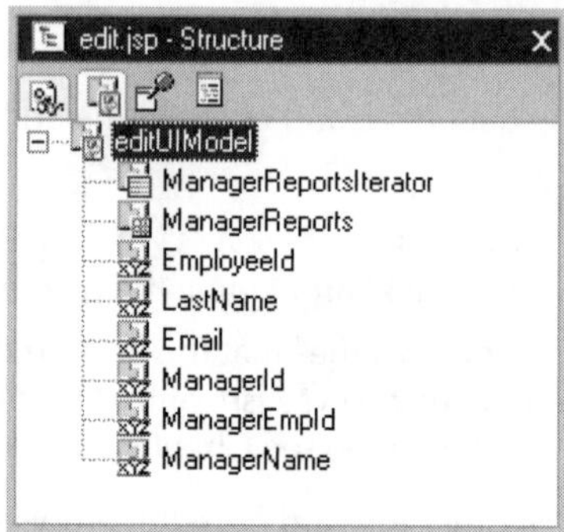

Additional Information: The binding container contains ManagerReportsIterator, an iterator binding for the ManagerReports view object instance; ManagerReports, a range binding associated with ManagerReportsIterator; and attribute bindings for each attribute in EmpMgrView. Although all of these bindings have the same name as bindings in the binding container for the browse data action, they are in fact different bindings, contained in a new binding container.

5. In the table, select the upper-right text field.

6. In the Property Inspector, find the *property* property and note the value.

   Additional Information: When this form is submitted, the value in this text field will be added to the URL as the parameter "EmployeeId". The data action will find the attribute binding with that name and use it to update the row.

7. On each of the last two rows of the table, select Table | Delete Row from the right-click menu.

   Additional Information: These rows would allow users to modify ManagerReports' ManagerEmpId and ManagerName attributes, which are entity-derived view attributes mapped to the Manager entity object usage. Since this form is intended to allow editing of reports, not editing of their managers, you should remove these rows. The page should resemble the following:

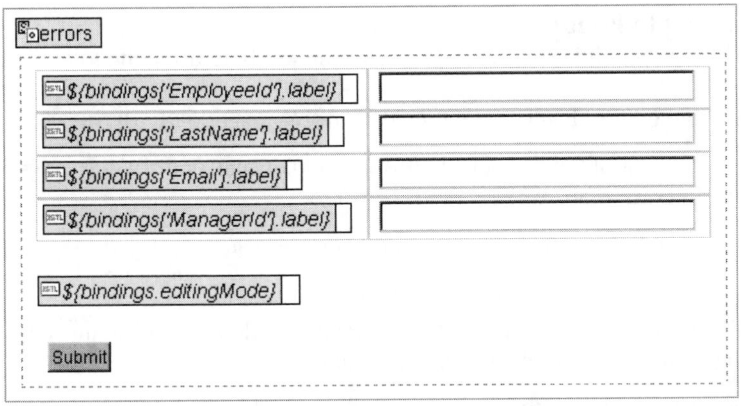

8. On the UI Model tab of the Structure window, on the ManagerEmpId attribute binding, select Delete from the right-click menu. Click Yes on the confirmation dialog.

9. Repeat step 8 to delete the ManagerName attribute binding.

   Additional Information: Since you are not displaying these attributes on the page, you can remove their bindings.

Create an Iterator Binding

Later in this phase, you will use a list binding in LOV mode to populate the ManagerId attribute. ManagerReportsIterator will be the target iterator, because the list binding will change a value for the current row of ManagerReports. The following steps allow you to create an iterator binding to act as the source iterator:

1. In the UI Model tab of the Structure window, on the editUIModel node, select Create Binding | Data | Iterator from the right-click menu to open the Iterator Binding Editor.

2. Enter "ManagerIterator" in the *Iterator Id* field.

3. In the *Data Collection* tree, select HRAppModuleDataControl\ManagersForList.

   Additional Information: This iterator binding will be the source iterator for a list binding in LOV mode, and ManagerReportsIterator will be the destination iterator. Because you cannot base source and destination iterators on master and detail view object instances, you must use ManagersForList rather than AllManagers.

4. Click OK to close the editor.

5. In the UI Model tab, select ManagerIterator.

6. In the Property Inspector, enter "-1" as the *Range Size*. Press ENTER.

   Additional Information: If you leave the range size as 10, only ten rows of the iterator will be loaded into the list binding, making it impossible to use the LOV list to populate the attribute with other managers. Setting the *Range Size* property to "-1" will display all rows.

Use a List Binding to Populate an Attribute

You can use a list binding in LOV mode to populate an attribute using the following steps:

1. In the visual editor, delete the text field for the ManagerId (third) row.
2. In the Data Control Palette, select HRAppModuleDataControl\AllManagers\ManagerReports\ManagerId.
3. Select "List of Values" from the *Drag and Drop As* list.
4. Drag ManagerId into the empty table cell.

   Additional Information: In addition to creating a dropdown list, this adds a list binding, ManagerId1, to the binding container.
5. On the UI Model tab of the Structure window, double click ManagerId1 to open the List Binding Editor.

   Additional Information: This binding defaults to LOV mode. It has ManagerReportsIterator preselected as the target iterator, but has no source iterator selected.
6. In the *Select LOV Source Iterator* list, select ManagerIterator.
7. Click Add to add an LOV attribute/target attribute pair.
8. Ensure that "EmployeeId" is selected as the LOV attribute.
9. Select ManagerId as the target attribute.

   Additional Information: When the user chooses a row from ManagerIterator, its EmployeeId attribute will be used to populate the ManagerId attribute for the current row of ManagerReportsIterator.
10. Still in the List Binding Editor, select the LOV display attributes tab.
11. Add EmployeeId and LastName to the *Attributes to Display* list.
12. Click OK to close the editor.
13. Click Save All.

Create a Return Forward

You can create a forward for when the edit form is submitted using the following steps:

1. Click the struts-config.xml tab to reopen the page flow diagram.
2. On the Component Palette, select the Forward icon.
3. Click once on the edit data page and once on the browse data page in that order to add a forward between them.
4. Name the forward "Submit".
5. Click Save All.

Additional Information: When a user clicks the Submit button on edit.jsp, the form is submitted to the edit data action, which posts the changes. This forward tells the controller to then forward to the browse data action instead of redisplaying edit.jsp. Your page flow diagram should look something like the following:

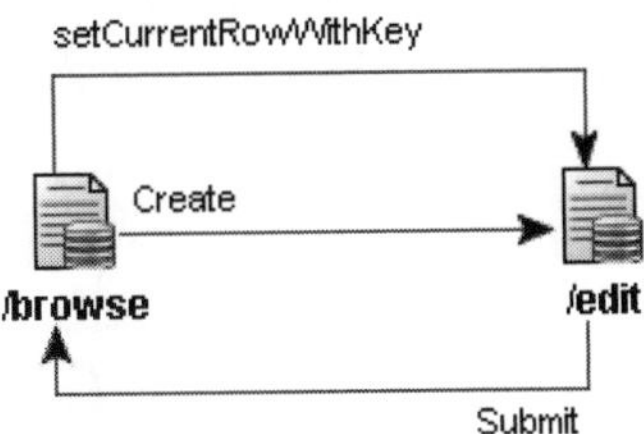

Test the JSP Application

You can test the edit form functionality using the following steps:

1. On the browse data action, select Run from the right-click menu.
2. When the page opens, click the "Select" link for Employee 124 to open the edit page for that row.
3. From the ManagerId dropdown, select Kochhar.
4. Click the Submit button.
5. Note that Employee 124 is no longer listed as reporting to King.
6. In the Master portion of the form, click the Next button.
7. Note that Employee 124 is now listed as reporting to Kochhar.
8. Close the web browser window.
9. Save All.

What Just Happened? You created a data page and a JSP that edit rows of ManagerReports, and you created forwards that tie its functionality to the browse page you created in Phases II and III. This page has its own binding container, containing the following bindings:

- An iterator binding to keep track of ManagerReports' current row for this page
- Attribute bindings to allow display and editing of ManagerReports' attributes
- A list binding in LOV mode to populate the ManagerId attribute
- An iterator binding to act as the list binding's source iterator

CHAPTER 13

Creating Custom Service Methods

"You know, Jeeves, you're by way of being rather a topper."
"I endeavor to give satisfaction, sir."
"One in a million, by Jove!"
"It is very kind of you to say so, sir."
"Well, that's about all, then, I think."
"Very good, sir."

—Sir Pelham Granville [P.G.] Wodehouse (1881–1975),
Jeeves Takes Charge

hapter 12 discussed how to use the ADF model layer to access ADF BC from applications. Although the ADF model layer provides a considerable amount of functionality for accessing ADF BC, you may need to perform specialized tasks that require writing code directly to the ADF BC API. You can write such code in *custom service methods*, methods you create within the ADF BC layer that can be accessed through action bindings in the ADF model layer.

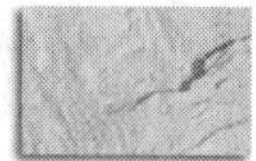

NOTE
Do not confuse custom service methods with web services (methods available over HTTP-based protocols such as SOAP). This chapter covers custom service methods; web services are discussed in Chapter 14.

Custom service methods allow you to perform complex operations in response to a single request from the client application. For example, you can create a custom service method that analyzes the sales records of all employees in the sales department and makes salary and commission adjustments based on these records. While all of the steps involved in this operation—navigating through the data in caches, retrieving data, and changing data—are possible using the techniques described in Chapter 12, creating a custom service method allows you to perform the entire operation in response to a single click of a button.

This chapter discusses creating custom service methods using the ADF BC API. You will learn to create custom service methods that navigate through the data in view caches, retrieve and change that data, and dynamically change the data model.

This chapter contains two hands-on practices. In the first practice, you will create a service method to perform a complex operation within the ADF BC layer you created in Chapters 9–11, and invoke it from the JSP application you created in Chapter 12. In the second practice, you will create service methods to maintain a dynamic master-detail relationship, and invoke them from the JSP application.

CAUTION
Oracle JDeveloper 10g contains a feature called "batch mode," which is intended to allow MVC applications to batch up requests to the ADF BC layer rather than contacting the ADF BC layer for every request. In releases 9.0.5.1 and 9.0.5.2 of Oracle JDeveloper 10g, batch mode contains a bug that makes it inadvisable to use batch mode if you are creating service methods. Tests have not indicated any performance difference between batch mode and "immediate mode" in these releases. The issue with batch mode and service methods is scheduled to be fixed in release 10.1.2, as are the issues that prevent batch mode from being more efficient than immediate mode.

Overview of Data Model Component Classes

Creating custom service methods involves writing code directly to the ADF BC API. This primarily involves using and extending the Java classes that implement data model components.

Overview of Application Module Classes

Chapter 8 explained that ADF BC is a framework technology, which means that it has a library of classes that can use XML files to perform most customization but can also be subclassed to provide extra customization. Application module definitions are handled by the following two classes in the ADF BC library, the *base application module classes*:

- **`oracle.jbo.server.ApplicationModuleImpl`** Application module instances are instances of this class—that is, each instance of this class is the point of entry to the view object instance usages and the transaction information for a single instance of the application. The class has all of the methods you need to find view object instances within the data model, dynamically change the data model for one application module instance, and manipulate database transactions.
- **`oracle.jbo.server.ApplicationModuleDefImpl`** A single instance of this class acts as a wrapper for the application module definition's XML file. The class contains methods that load the data model components into memory. For most purposes, however, you will not need to use these methods directly; they are used internally by ADF BC's metadata management mechanisms.

Although many applications can use these classes directly with an application module definition's XML file, you can also generate custom classes that extend one or both of them for further customization. For example, for a particular application module definition, HrAppModule, you could generate one or both of the following:

- An application module class, `HrAppModuleImpl`, which extends `ApplicationModuleImpl`
- An application module definition class, `HrAppModuleDefImpl`, which extends `ApplicationModuleDefImpl`

You can choose which of these classes to generate on the Java page of the Application Module Editor, as shown here:

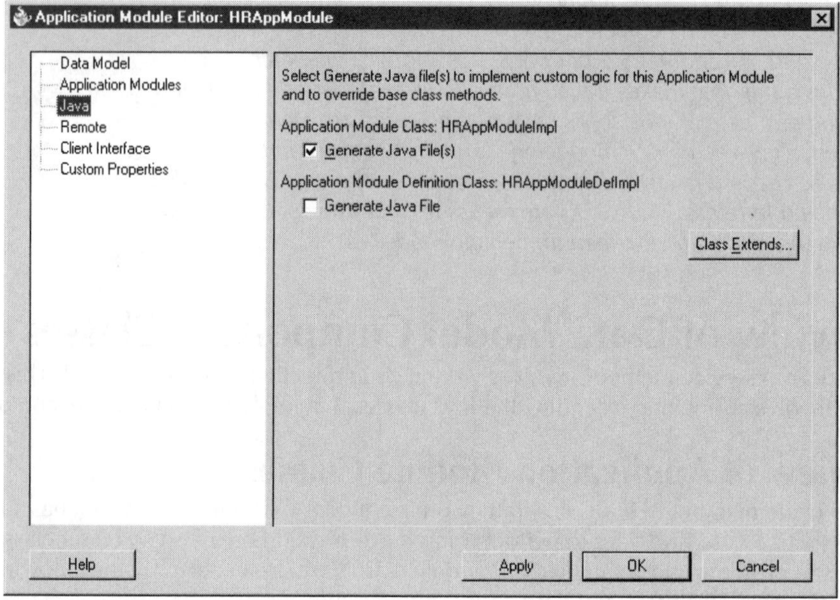

Application Module Classes

An *application module class* is a subclass of `ApplicationModuleImpl` that a particular application module definition can use to represent its instances. By default, application module classes have the same name as the application module definition with an "Impl" suffix. As with all other custom business component classes, JDeveloper allows you to specify different naming conventions, if you prefer. (For more information, see the sidebar "Changing Class Naming Conventions" in Chapter 10). For example, an application module definition called "HrAppModule" would have an application module class called "`HrAppModuleImpl`."

By default, JDeveloper will create an application module class for every application module definition you create. You can remove application module classes if you do not need them; this will improve performance slightly. However, all of the techniques in this chapter involve generating and using application module instance classes. This is because these classes are where you write custom service methods.

Application Module Definition Classes

An *application module definition class* is a subclass of `ApplicationModuleDefImpl` that a particular application module definition can use as a wrapper for its XML file. By default, application module definition classes have the same name as the application module definition with a "DefImpl" suffix. For example, an application module definition called "HrAppModule" would have an application module definition class called "`HrAppModuleDefImpl`." You can change this behavior, just as you can for application module classes.

JDeveloper does not generate application module definition classes by default. Unlike application module classes, which many users will want to generate, the only reason to generate an application module definition class is to override the way the ADF BC runtime handles application module XML files. Very few users will need to do this.

Overview of View Classes

View object definitions are handled by three classes in the ADF BC library, the *base view classes*:

- **`oracle.jbo.server.ViewObjectImpl`** View object instances are instances of this class—that is, each instance of this class manages a single view cache and is a single element of the data model for an application module instance. The class has methods to execute the view object instance's query, change the query dynamically, navigate through the results of the query, and create rows in the view cache. This can have the effect of creating rows in one or more tables, as described in the later section "Creating and Deleting Rows."
- **`oracle.jbo.server.ViewRowImpl`** View rows are instances of this class—that is, each instance of this class represents a single row from a query result. The class has all the methods you need to read and update the attribute values in a row, to remove existing rows, and to retrieve entity object instances on which the view rows are based.
- **`oracle.jbo.server.ViewDefImpl`** A single instance of this class acts as a wrapper for the entity object definition's XML file. The class contains methods that allow you to dynamically change the definition of the view object itself—to add or remove view attributes or to change the properties of those attributes—and to dynamically discover facts about the definition, such as the number and names of attributes.

As with application module definitions, many applications can use these classes directly with a view object definition's XML file, but you can also generate custom classes that extend one or more of them for further customization. For example, for a particular view object definition, EmployeesView, you could generate some or all of the following:

- A view object class, `EmployeesViewImpl`, which extends `ViewObjectImpl`
- A view row class, `EmployeesViewRowImpl`, which extends `ViewRowImpl`
- A view definition class, `EmployeesViewDefImpl`, which extends `ViewDefImpl`

View Object Classes

A *view object class* is a subclass of `ViewObjectImpl` that a particular view object definition can use to represent its instances. View object classes have the same name as the view object definition with an "Impl" suffix. For example, a view object called "EmployeesView" would have a view object class called `EmployeesViewImpl`. You can change this behavior, just as you can for application module classes.

By default, JDeveloper will create a view object class for every view object definition you create. You can, however, remove view object classes you do not need; this will improve performance slightly.

However, you may want to keep a view object class to write methods specific to that view object definition's query; these methods can be used by service methods in multiple application module classes. For example, suppose you have a common task that applies to EmployeesView's query result, such as promoting all employees that meet a particular criterion. You can generate a view object class for EmployeesView and add a method `promoteQualifiedEmployees()`. If you have instances of EmployeesView in two different application module definitions' data models, service methods in each application module class will be able to call it, allowing you to reuse the code.

View Row Classes

A *view row class* is a subclass of `ViewRowImpl` that a particular view object definition can use to represent its view rows. By default, view row classes have the same name as the view object definition with a "RowImpl" suffix. For example, a view object definition called "EmployeesView" would have a view row class called "`EmployeesViewRowImpl`."

JDeveloper does not generate view row classes by default. However, like entity object classes, view row classes can provide typesafe getters and setters for their attributes. `ViewRowImpl` provides only the non-typesafe methods `getAttribute()` and `setAttribute()`.

View Definition Classes

A *view definition class* is a subclass of `ViewDefImpl` that a particular entity object definition can use as a wrapper for its XML file. By default, view definition classes have the same name as the view object definition with a "DefImpl" suffix. For example, a view object definition called "EmployeesView" would have a view definition class called "`EmployeesViewDefImpl`."

JDeveloper does not generate view definition classes by default. Unlike view object and view row classes, which many users will want to generate, the only reason to generate a view definition class is if you need to override the way the ADF BC runtime handles view object XML files. Very few users will need to do this.

Custom Service Method Basics

When you write custom code to implement business rules, as discussed in Chapter 10, you primarily override methods already provided by the ADF BC library classes. Creating custom service methods is different in that you create a custom service method from scratch, specifying the return type and method signature. There are only four requirements for custom service methods:

- They must be written in the application module class.
- Their access level must be `public`.
- All of their parameters must be primitive Java types or Java classes that implement the `Serializable` interface. For most purposes, this means that the parameters should all be either Java primitives or Java classes that would be usable as attribute types (domains or standard Java classes such as `String`).
- Their return type should either be `void`, primitive Java types, or serializable Java classes.

Exposing and Accessing Service Methods

Once you have created a service method, you must expose it to the ADF model layer. You can do this by using the Application Module Editor to create a *client interface*, an interface that exposes service methods for an application module definition.

When a service method is exposed on the client interface, it will appear in the Data Control Palette and the Action Binding Editor as an operation. You can then create an action binding that invokes it, and use the action binding to bind buttons or events to the method. The action binding contains properties that allow you to set the method's parameters or access its return value, if it has parameters or a non-void return type. As with most bindings, the way you access these values depends upon the type of client application you are using; you will see this done for a client using Struts in the first hands-on practice in this chapter.

Finding View Object Instances in the Data Model

To manipulate data from within a custom service method, you need to gain access to the view object instances in the data model. Application module classes provide getter methods for each view object instance in the data model. These getter methods use the view object class as their return type, if a view object class has been generated. If no view object class has been generated, they use `ViewObjectImpl` as their return type. For example, suppose HrAppModule contains the following view object instances:

- AllManagers, an instance of ManagersView
- ManagerReports, an instance of EmployeesView
- ReportPastJobs, an instance of JobsView

Suppose that the view object class for EmployeesView, `EmployeesViewImpl`, has been generated, but that the other two view object classes have not been generated. Then, the application module class for HrAppModule will contain these three getter methods:

```
public ViewObjectImpl getAllManagers()
public EmployeesViewImpl getManagerReports()
public ViewObjectImpl getReportPastJobs()
```

You can call any of these methods to gain access to the appropriate view object instance; you can then manipulate its view cache as described in the following sections.

Finding View Object Instances in a Nested Application Module Instance

If your primary application module definition contains nested application module instances, the application module class will also contain getter methods for the nested application module instances. These getter methods use the application module class for the nested instance as their return type, if it has been generated, and use `ApplicationModuleImpl` as their return type, if there is no nested application module class. For example, suppose HrAppModule contains the following nested application module instances:

- **SalesEval,** an instance of SalesEvaluationModule
- **OrgChartAnalyze**, an instance of OrgChartAnalysisModule

Suppose that the application module class for OrgChartAnalysisModule, `OrgChartAnalysisModuleImpl`, has been generated, but that there is no application module class for SalesEvaluationModule. Then, the application module class for HrAppModule will contain the following getter methods:

```
public ApplicationModuleImpl getSalesEval()
public OrgChartAnalysisModule getOrgChartAnalyze()
```

If the application module class for the nested instance has been generated, you can then use the getter methods on that class to retrieve its view object instances. For example, if OrgChartAnalysisModule contains the view object instance TopLevelEmps, an instance of ManagersView, you could retrieve TopLevelEmps from a service method within `HrAppModuleImpl` using the following code:

```
OrgChartAnalysisModuleImpl orgChart = getOrgChartAnalyze();
ViewObjectImpl topEmps = orgChart.getTopLevelEmps();
```

If there is no application module class for the nested instance, you must retrieve view object instances using the method `ApplicationModuleImpl.findViewObject()`. This method accepts the name of a view object instance as a parameter, and has a return type of `oracle.jbo.ViewObject`, which is an interface `ViewObjectImpl` implements. You can then cast the returned view object instance to `ViewObjectImpl` or the appropriate view object class. For example, suppose SalesEvaluationModule contains the following view object instances:

- **SalesManagers**, an instance of ManagersView
- **SalesReports,** an instance of EmployeesView

You could retrieve SalesManagers and SalesReports from a service method within `HrAppModuleImpl` using the following code:

```
ApplicationModuleImpl sales = getSalesEval();
ViewObjectImpl managers =
  (ViewObjectImpl) sales.findViewObject("SalesManagers");
EmployeesViewImpl reports =
  (EmployeesViewImpl) sales.findViewObject("SalesReports");
```

Retrieving View Rows

Once you retrieve a view object instance, you can use it to retrieve specific rows of data. You should generally do this by creating a secondary row set iterator.

Secondary row set iterators were introduced in Chapter 12. They are objects of type `oracle.jbo.RowSetIterator` that function as additional current row pointers for the view object instance. Since the ADF model layer typically uses the primary row set iterator to keep track of the current row for the MVC application, creating a secondary row set iterator allows you to navigate through the cache and retrieve view rows without disturbing the current row pointer used by the MVC application. You will create a secondary row set iterator in the first hands-on practice in this chapter.

Secondary row set iterators are row iterators; that is, `RowSetIterator` extends the `RowIterator` interface first described in Chapter 10. Like other row iterators, a secondary row set iterator is a collection of row objects (the view cache) and a pointer to one particular row object, the "current" row object. The pointer can be moved around, and data can be extracted from the current row object.

As described in Chapter 10, a row object is actually any object that implements the interface `oracle.jbo.Row`. The row objects in the row iterators discussed in Chapter 10 were all entity object instances, which was possible because `EntityImpl` implements the `Row` interface. The row objects in secondary row set iterators are view rows—`ViewRowImpl` implements the `Row` interface as well. This section describes how to retrieve row objects within a view cache. Like the row objects retrieved from row iterators in Chapter 10, you can cast these row objects to particular classes—in this case, `ViewRowImpl` or view row classes.

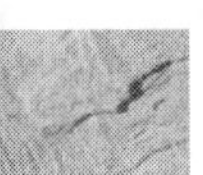

TIP
`ViewObjectImpl` has a method, `executeQuery()`, that will issue the SELECT statement associated with the view object instance and populate the entity and view caches. However, you do not need to explicitly call `executeQuery()` before navigating through view rows. If you call a row navigation method on a secondary row set iterator for a view object instance that has not had its query executed, ADF BC will call `executeQuery()` automatically. Later in this chapter, you will see some uses for calling `executeQuery()` explicitly.

Stepping Through a View Cache

As discussed in Chapter 10, the `RowIterator` interface contains methods called `next()` and `hasNext()`. The `next()` method advances the row iterator's current row pointer and returns the new current row, and the `hasNext()` method tests whether there is a next row. Chapter 10 showed how to write loops like the following to cycle through a row iterator's rows:

```
Row current;
while (someRowIterator.hasNext())
{
  current = someRowIterator.next();
  /* do something */
}
```

Row Keys

As explained in Chapter 12, a key object is a Java object that aggregates a key, a set of view attributes whose values uniquely identify a view row. Within a custom service method, you can create a key object, containing values for some or all of the attributes in the key. You can use this key object to retrieve an array containing some or all of the rows that match the appropriate values.

Creating a Key Object

Before you create a key object, you must create an array of objects that corresponds to it. Each object in the array should correspond to one of the attributes in the view object definition's key, in the order in which those attributes appear in the view object definition. For example, if you are trying to create a key for EmployeesView, with a key containing EmployeeId and ManagerEmpId, the array of objects should contain a value for EmployeeId and a value for ManagerEmpId, in that order. The following code creates an array for a key object with EmployeeId 102 and ManagerEmpId 100:

```
Object[] empKeyValues = new Object[]
{
  new Number(102),
```

```
  new Number(100)
};
```

To create a partial key, for example, a key that will find all rows with ManagerEmpId 100, the array should still have objects for each key attribute but with "null" used for the attributes you are not interested in. The following code creates such an array:

```
Object[] empPartialKeyValues = new Object[]
{
  null,
  new Number(100)
};
```

After you create and load the object array, you can pass it to the `Key()` constructor to create a key object, as in the following code:

```
Key empKey = new Key(empKeyValues);
```

If you have already navigated to a row through other methods, you can also retrieve its key object using `getKey()`, as follows:

```
Key currentEmpKey = current.getKey();
```

This can be useful if you want to remember the location of a row for retrieval later.

Retrieving Rows

After you create a key object, use the method `ViewObjectImpl.findByKey()` to retrieve an array containing matching rows. `findByKey()` takes two arguments: the key and a maximum number of rows to return (or –1 if you want to return all the rows). For example, if `emps` is a variable containing the view object instance ManagerEmployees, and `empPartialKey` is a variable containing a key object created from `empPartialKeyValues`, the following code returns an array containing the first ten rows with ManagerEmpId 100:

```
Row[] partialKeyRows = emps.findByKey(empMgrPartialKey, 10);
```

If fewer than ten rows match the key, the extra elements of `partialKeyRows` will be null.

Changing the Current Row Pointer

Calling `findByKey()` only returns row objects. It does not change the current row pointer in the view object instance. If you want to set the current row pointer, pass one of the rows to `RowSetIterator.setCurrentRow()` as follows:

```
secondaryIterator.setCurrentRow(partialKeyRows[0]);
```

Manipulating Data

You can use methods on `ViewObjectImpl`, `ViewRowImpl`, and view row classes to retrieve and modify the data in your tables.

Reading and Changing Attribute Values

Just like the `EntityImpl` class, the `ViewRowImpl` class has `getAttribute()` and `setAttribute()` methods that you can use to retrieve and set values for the attributes of a particular row. As described for entity object instances in Chapter 10, you can call these methods on view rows to manipulate specific attribute values.

As discussed in Chapter 11, SQL-only view attributes store their values directly, whereas entity-derived view attributes store pointers to values in the entity cache. For this reason, the behavior of `getAttribute()` and `setAttribute()` differs for SQL-only and entity-derived view attributes:

- **If the attribute is SQL-only**, the methods will read and change the value in the view cache.
- **If the attribute is entity-derived**, the methods will call `EntityImpl.getAttribute()` or `EntityImpl.setAttribute()` on the appropriate entity object instance.

If you are working with a view row class instead of directly with `ViewRowImpl`, you can use the typesafe getter and setter methods instead of `getAttribute()` and `setAttribute()`. You will manipulate attribute values in the first hands-on practice in this chapter.

Creating and Deleting Rows

`RowSetIterator` contains three methods that let you insert and delete rows from the view cache: `createRow()`, `insertRow()`, and `removeCurrentRow()`.

If the view object definition contains entity object usages, the relevant entity object instances will be created or marked for deletion. When a Commit operation is called, these rows will be added to or deleted from the database.

`createRow()` returns a new view row (its return type is `Row`), and `insertRow()` inserts that row into the view cache right before the current row, as in the following example:

```
Row newEmp = secondaryIterator.createRow();
secondaryIterator.insertRow(newEmp);
```

It is important to call both of these methods. Creating a row will not, by itself, mark it as needing to be posted to the database; only rows that have been inserted into view caches will be posted.

`removeCurrentRow()` does not return anything or change the current row pointer; you will have to execute `next()` to get the next undeleted row. Here is an example that deletes a row and sets the current row pointer to the next row:

```
secondaryIterator.deleteCurrentRow();
Row nextEmp = secondaryIterator.next();
```

Until you navigate off the row, the current row pointer points to null.

You can also delete a view row by calling `remove()` directly on the row object. The row deleted in this way does not need to be current. The following example deletes a view row called `badEmp`:

```
badEmp.remove();
```

NOTE
Remember that creating and deleting rows in this way does not affect the database until you issue a COMMIT or POST statement.

Restricting a View Object Instance's Cache

Sometimes, you need to further restrict the rows in a view object's cache within a service method. You may need to do this because you are restricting it based on user input, or because you only want a temporary filter for the duration of the service method. One way to restrict the view cache within a service method is using dynamically created view link instances, which will be explained in the section "Dynamically Creating Master-Detail Relationships" later in this chapter. There are, however, several other ways to restrict the view cache.

Using setWhereClause()

By using the method `ViewObjectImpl.setWhereClause()`, you can add a WHERE clause to a particular view object instance. The WHERE clause you pass as an argument to `setWhereClause()` will be conjoined with the WHERE clause, if any, specified in the view object definition. For example, suppose `richEmployees` is a variable containing a particular instance of EmployeesView. Recall that EmployeesView already contains the following WHERE clause:

```
WHERE Employee.MANAGER_ID = Manager.EMPLOYEE_ID
```

You can use `setWhereClause()` to change richEmployees' WHERE clause to the following:

```
WHERE (Employee.SALARY > 3000) AND
  (Employee.MANAGER_ID = Manager.EMPLOYEE_ID)
```

You can do this using the following code:

```
richEmployees.setWhereClause("Employee.SALARY > 3000");
```

If the view object definition does not contain a WHERE clause, the argument is used by itself. For example, if EmployeesView did not contain a WHERE clause, the preceding code would add the following WHERE clause to `richEmployees'`:

```
WHERE Employee.SALARY > 3000
```

In no case do you include "WHERE" in the string passed to `setWhereClause()`.

NOTE
If the tables in the view object definition are aliased, the SQL you pass to `setWhereClause()` should use those aliases. Since EmployeesView aliases EMPLOYEES to Employee, you should use that alias in the argument passed to `setWhereClause()`.

Parameterized WHERE Clauses

A *parameterized WHERE clause* is a WHERE clause in a view object definition that contains bind parameters. You can set these parameters at run time. For example, suppose you know that you will want to restrict the caches of instances of EmployeesView to include only those employees making over a certain amount of money, but you want to be able to change that amount of money for specific instances at run time. You can do this in the View Object Editor by providing a parameterized WHERE clause in the *Where* field as shown here:

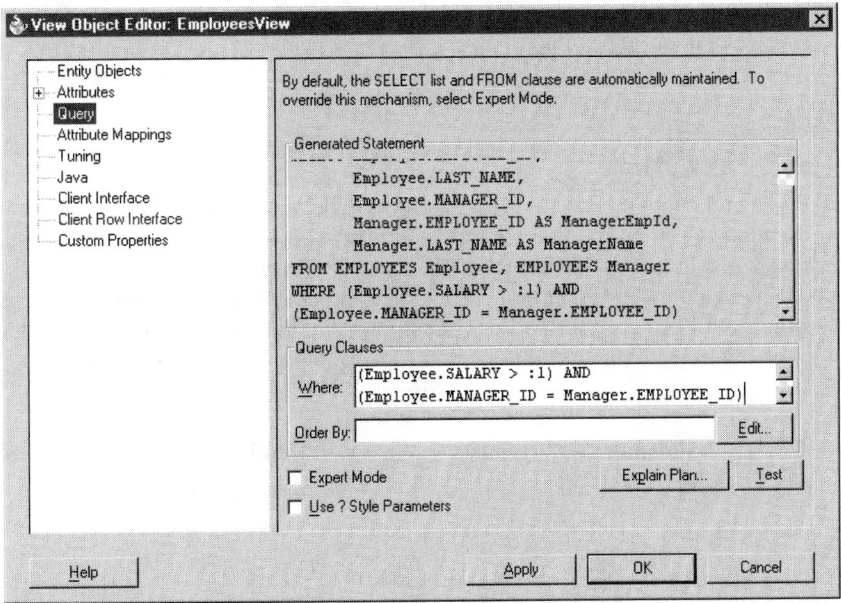

The parameter ":1" stands in for the attribute you will set at run time. You can have WHERE clauses with multiple bind parameters. You can name these parameters in increasing order (":1", ":2", ":3" and so on), but this is for readability purposes only; the parameters are filled from left to right, irrespective of their names.

If your view object has a parameterized WHERE clause, you can fill in the parameters at run time by calling `ViewObjectImpl.setWhereClauseParams()`. This method takes, as an argument, an array of `Object` instances containing values for the bind parameters, as shown next:

```
Object[] bindParamValues = new Object[]
{
  new Number(3000)
```

```
};
richEmployees.setWhereClauseParams(bindParamValues);
```

The order of the array members is significant because the bind parameters will be filled using that order.

`setWhereClauseParams()` is more efficient than `setWhereClause()`. Therefore, if you just need to change individual values in your WHERE clause, instead of changing the WHERE clause's entire structure, you should use a parameterized WHERE clause rather than calling `setWhereClause()`.

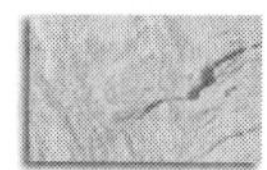

CAUTION
If a view object instance's query is executed while it has unbound parameters, it will throw an exception. Therefore, if you are going to use parameterized queries, it is important to initialize those queries before any data is retrieved from the view object. In particular, if you bind the view object instance to an iterator binding, you should call a service method that binds all the bind parameters earlier in your page flow.

View Criteria Objects

The most flexible and efficient way to restrict a view cache at run time, but also the one that takes the most effort to set up, involves using *view criteria objects,* which are Java objects that provide a structured way to represent a WHERE clause expression.

You can think of a view criteria object as a table. The table has columns that correspond to the view object attributes, but instead of containing data, the columns contain conditions that apply to the corresponding attributes, such as the following view criteria object for ManagersView:

EmployeeId	LastName	Salary	JobId	NumReports
null	null	> 8000	LIKE '%MAN'	<5
null	null	> 12000	null	< 3

Each row of the table, called a *view criteria row,* represents a conjunction of conditions on attributes. For example, the first row in the table represents the following condition:

```
Employees.SALARY > 8000 AND
  Employees.JOB_ID LIKE '%MAN' AND
  Employees.NUM_REPORTS < 5
```

The view criteria object as a whole represents the disjunction of all the individual rows; that is, view criteria rows are joined using the OR operator to create the full view criteria object. For example, the entire preceding table represents the following condition:

```
(
  Employees.SALARY > 8000 AND
  Employees.JOB_ID LIKE '%MAN' AND
  Employees.NUM_REPORTS < 5
)
OR
(
  Employees.SALARY > 12000 AND
  NUM_REPORTS < 3
)
```

When the view criteria object is applied to a view object instance, the condition is added to the instance's current WHERE clause.

View criteria objects allow you to manipulate query conditions in a structured fashion, adding and removing individual requirements and possibilities.

Re-Executing the Query

After you make any change to a view object instance's WHERE clause, using any of the techniques described in this section, you must call `ViewObjectImpl.executeQuery()` to re-execute the view object instance's query against the database.

Using View Link Definitions in Service Methods

Chapter 10 explained that you could use an entity object instance's association accessor attributes to retrieve associated entity object instances. You can also use a view row's view link accessor attributes to retrieve master or detail view rows.

Recall from Chapter 11 that you set view link directionality by creating accessor attributes in the associated view object definitions. If you create an accessor attribute in a view object definition, you can use it in one of the following ways to retrieve associated view rows just as you would use a regular attribute to retrieve attribute values:

- **Pass the name of the accessor attribute into `ViewRowImpl.getAttribute()`.** For example, since ManagersView has an accessor attribute called ReportsView, you can call `ViewRowImpl.getAttribute("ReportsView")` on a ManagersView view row to get the associated EmployeesView view rows.
- **Use the getter method that returns the associated view row instances.** These are available, if you generate a view row class for the view object definition. For example, if you generate the `ManagersViewRowImpl` class, it will contain the method `getReportsView()`.

As with association accessor attributes, these methods return either a single view row (if the other side of the view link definition has a cardinality of one) or a row iterator (if the other side of the view link definition has a cardinality of many).

Hands-on Practice: Create and Invoke Service Methods

In this practice, you will add a business service method to the ADF Business Components you created in Chapters 9–11, and invoke them from the JSP application you created in Chapter 12. The method will fire all managers who meet specified view criteria.

This practice builds on the HR and HRApp workspaces created in the hands-on practices in Chapters 9 through 12. If you have not successfully completed those practices, you can download the starting files for this practice from the authors' websites mentioned in the author information at the beginning of this book.

NOTE
As with the hands-on practice in Chapter 12, this practice makes some use of JSP and Struts technology. While this is not the focus of the practice, it is necessary to invoke the custom methods you will create. You will learn more about JSP and Struts technology in Chapters 17 and 18.

This practice steps you through the following phases:

I. Turn off batch mode

II. Choose view classes

III. Create a view object method stub and a service method

- Create the view object method stub
- Create the service method
- Expose the service method

IV. Access the service method from a JSP application

- Add controls to a JSP page to accept method parameters
- Add a data action to execute the custom method
- Create a JSP page to display method results
- Test the method

V. Add navigation code to the view object method

- Add navigation code
- Test the method

VI. Add code to filter data

- Create and apply a view criteria object
- Test the method

VII. Add code to change data

- Add code to cycle through detail rows
- Add code to change attribute values
- Add code to delete a row
- Test the method

I. Turn Off Batch Mode

As mentioned in the introduction to this chapter, batch mode does not work properly with service methods. In this phase, you turn off batch mode for the HRApp application.

1. Open the HRApp workspace, if it is not already open.
2. In the Application Navigator, select "Applications\HRApp\ViewController\Application Sources\DataBindings.cpx".

   Additional Information: This file contains information about all the components in the binding context, including the data controls.
3. In the Structure window, select "Data Controls\HrAppModuleDataControl".
4. In the Property Inspector, select "Immediate" from the *Synch Mode* dropdown list.
5. Click Save All.

What Just Happened? You configured the data control in the ADF Model's binding context to use immediate mode rather than batch mode.

II. Choose View Classes

By default, JDeveloper generates a view object class for each view object definition you create. However, you will use only EmployeesView's view object class, and will use accessor methods from the view row classes for ManagersView and EmployeesView. In this phase, you remove the view object class for EmployeesView and JobsView, and generate view row classes for ManagersView and EmployeesView.

1. In the Application Navigator (under "Applications\HRApp\Model\Application Sources\hrapp.model.datamodel") or on the "Data Model Diagram" diagram, double click ManagersView to open the View Object Editor.
2. Select the Java node.
3. Under *View Row Class,* check the *Generate Java File* checkbox as shown here:

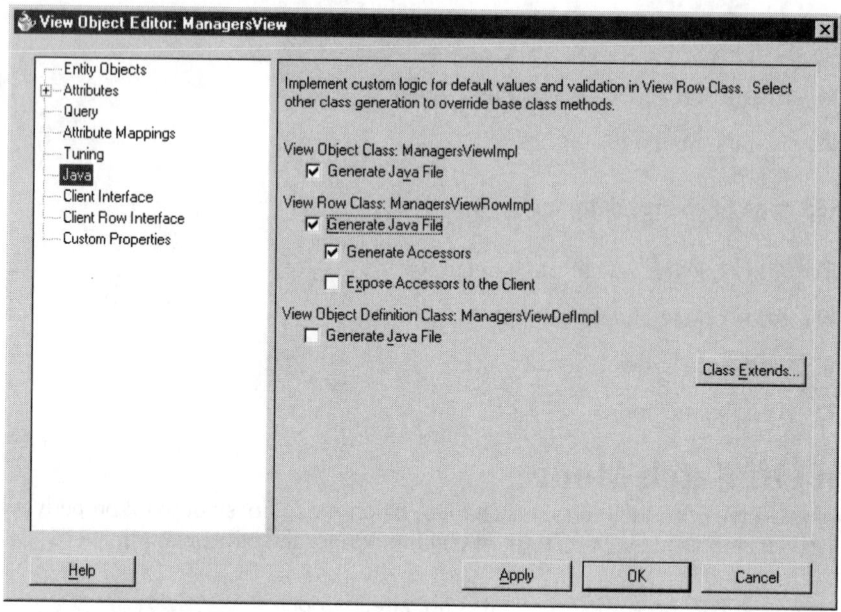

4. Click OK to close the editor.
5. Double click EmployeesView to open the View Object Editor.
6. Select the Java node.
7. Under *View Row Class,* check the *Generate Java File* checkbox as before.
8. Under *View Object Class,* uncheck the *Generate Java File* checkbox.

CAUTION
If you uncheck the "Generate Java File" checkboxes in a subsequent editor session, the corresponding source code files (and any corresponding compiled .class files) will be removed from the project but they will not be deleted from disk. This can cause unwanted side effects later so it is best to remove the source and compiled files manually if you do not need them.

9. Click OK to close the editor.
10. Remove the view object class for JobsView. Do not generate a view row class. Click OK.
11. Rebuild the project. Click Save All.

CAUTION
*In some releases of JDeveloper, there is an intermittent bug that causes view row classes to be improperly generated. If the project fails to compile, edit the view row class that contains errors and remove all copies of the class definition (including the package and import statements) by hand except for the final copy. For example, if `ManagersViewRowImpl` produces compile errors, edit `ManagersViewRowImpl.java` and find the **final** occurrence of the following line of code:*

```
package hrapp.model.datamodel;
```

Erase everything before that line and rebuild the project.

What Just Happened? You removed the view object classes for EmployeesView and JobsView. They were added to the project by default when you created the view object definitions. You will not need any of these classes, and removing them will yield a slight increase in application performance. You also generated view row classes for ManagersView and EmployeesView. The typesafe accessors on those classes will be useful.

III. Create a View Object Method Stub and a Service Method

In this phase, you will add the stub for a method to the view object class for ManagersView. This is the method you will use to perform the audit of managers. You will then add a service method to the application module class for HRAppModule that calls the view object method.

Create the View Object Method Stub

You can add a method to a view object class using the following steps:

1. In the Application Navigator, select "Applications\HRApp\Model\Application Sources\hrapp.model.datamodel\ManagersView".
2. In the Structure window, double click ManagersViewImpl.java to open its source code.

   Additional Information: This is the view object class for ManagersView.
3. Add the following line to the import block:

   ```
   import oracle.jbo.domain.Number;
   ```

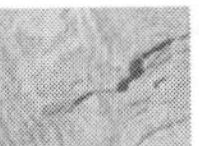

NOTE
You cannot use Import Assistance to import `oracle.jbo.domain.Number`, because JDeveloper will assume references to "`Number`" are references to `java.lang.Number`.

4. Add a method, `audit()`, before the closing curly bracket in the Java class, as follows:

```
public Number audit(Number salaryThreshold, Number reportsThreshold)
{
  int managersFired = 0;
  return new Number(managersFired);
}
```

Additional Information: Later in this practice, you will use `salaryThreshold` and `reportsThreshold` to establish job criteria for managers, and `managersFired` to keep track of how many managers have been fired in the audit.

5. Rebuild the project.

Create the Service Method

You can add a service method to an application module class using the following steps:

1. In the Application Navigator, select "Applications\HRApp\Model\Application Sources\hrapp.model.datamodel\HRAppModule".
2. In the Structure window, double click HrAppModuleImpl.java to open its source code.

   Additional Information: This is the application module class for HRAppModule.
3. Add the following line to the import block:

```
import oracle.jbo.domain.Number;
```

4. Add a method, `auditManagers()`, before the closing curly bracket in the Java class, as follows:

```
public Number auditManagers(Number salaryThreshold, Number
reportsThreshold)
{
  return getAllManagers().audit(salaryThreshold, reportsThreshold);
}
```

Additional Information: This method calls `getAllManagers()`, which finds the AllManagers view object instance (an instance of ManagersView); then this method wraps the view object instance in its `audit()` method (which you added in the preceding section). Rebuild the project. This will automatically save the changes.

Expose the Service Method

You can expose a service method on an application module definition's client interface using the following steps:

1. In the Application Navigator or on the Data Model Diagram, double click HRAppModule to open the Application Module Editor.
2. Select the Client Interface node.

3. Move "auditManagers(Number, Number)" from the *Available* list to the *Selected* list. Click OK.

   Additional Information: The *Available* list contains the signatures of methods that meet the requirements for service methods: They are public and have simple or serializable attributes and return types. The *Selected* list contains methods exposed on the client interface.

4. Click Save All.

5. Rebuild the project.

What Just Happened? You created a method on a view object class. Then, you created a custom service method that retrieves a view object instance and calls the view object method. Finally, you added the service method to the client interface. Currently, the view object method does nothing except return the value "0". You will add code to fire managers who do not meet certain requirements in Phases V–VII.

IV. Access the Service Method from a JSP Application

In this phase, you will add code to the JSP application you created in Chapter 12 to invoke the service method.

Add Controls to a JSP Page to Accept Method Parameters

You can add controls to a JSP page to accept parameters for a custom service method using the following steps:

1. In the Application Navigator, under "HRApp\ViewController\Web Content", double click browse.jsp to open the visual editor.

2. Click after the final row of buttons, still within the HTML form, and press ENTER to add a line.

3. Type the text: "Managers must have a salary at most " with a trailing space.

4. Select the Components tab to open the Component Palette.

5. From the HTML page, click the Text Field icon to add a text field.

6. In the Property Inspector, enter the following values, pressing ENTER after each one:
   name as "salaryThreshold"
   size as "10"

   Additional Information: The value the user enters in the text field will be submitted as a parameter called "salaryThreshold". In a later step, you will pass this parameter to an action binding.

7. After the text field, type the text: " or at least " with a leading and trailing space.

8. Click the Text Field icon to add another text field.

9. In the Property Inspector, enter the following values, pressing ENTER after each one:
   name as "reportsThreshold"
   size as "5"

10. After the text field, type the text: " direct reports." with a leading space.

11. Click the Submit Button icon in the Component Palette to add a submit button.

12. In the Property Inspector, enter "event_Submit" in the *name* field. Press ENTER.

    Additional Information: When the user clicks the button, the button's value ("Submit") will be submitted as a parameter called "event_Submit". This will allow the data page to forward the request appropriately. You have created all other submit buttons using the Data Control Palette, which assigns the proper name for you. The prompts and UI components you have just added should resemble the following:

    Managers must have a salary at most or at least
    direct reports. Submit

Add a Data Action to Execute the Custom Method

You can create a data action to invoke a custom method using the following steps:

1. In the Application Navigator, expand "HRApp\ViewController\Web Content\WEB-INF".

2. Double click struts-config.xml to open the Page Flow Diagram for the ViewController project.

3. In the Component Palette, click the Data Action icon.

4. Click on the diagram to add a data action to your controller.

   Additional Information: A data action is a Struts action that communicates with the ADF Model and has its own binding container. You will learn more about data actions in Chapter 17.

5. Enter "invokeAudit" as the name of the data action.

6. On the Component Palette, click the Forward icon.

7. Click once on the browse data page and then on the invokeAudit data action to add a forward between them.

8. Name the forward "Submit", replacing the default name "success".

9. Click the Data Controls tab to reopen the Data Control Palette.

10. In the Data Control Palette, select "HRAppModuleDataControl\Operations\auditManagers(Number, Number)".

    Additional Information: The auditManagers(Number, Number) operation was added when you exposed the service method on the application module definition's client interface. It works on the data control level (for the application module definition) as do the Commit and Rollback operations.

11. Drag auditManagers(Number, Number) onto the invokeAudit data action.

    Additional Information: This creates an action binding in the binding container for invokeAudit that invokes the `auditManagers()` service method, and binds an event in the data action to that binding.

12. In the Struts Structure tab of the Structure window, select "Struts Config\Action Mappings\/invokeAudit\paramNames[0]".

    Additional Information: `paramNames` is an array containing the parameter values that will be passed to the service method. The two parameters with index numbers 0 and 1 were created because the service method takes two arguments.

13. In the Property Inspector, enter "${param.salaryThreshold}" as the *value* property and press ENTER.

    Additional Information: "${param.salaryThreshold}" is an EL expression that extracts the value of the HTTP request parameter named "salaryThreshold". Since this matches the name property of one of the text fields on browse.jsp, the value entered in that text field will be used for the `paramNames[0]` parameter.

14. In the Structure window, select "Struts Config\Action Mappings\/invokeAudit\paramNames[1]".

15. In the Property Inspector, enter "${param.reportsThreshold}" as the *value* property and press ENTER.

16. Click Save All.

17. Rebuild the ViewController project.

Create a JSP Page to Display Method Results

You can create a JSP page to display the return value of a service method using the following steps:

1. On the Component Palette, click the Data Page icon.

2. Click on the diagram to add a data page.

3. Name the data page "auditResults".

4. Create a forward from the invokeAudit data action to the auditResults data page. You do not need to rename the forward.

5. Double click the auditResults data page to open the Select or Create Page dialog.

6. Accept the defaults in the dialog and click OK to create a JSP page, auditResults.jsp, and open it in the visual editor.

7. On the Data Control Palette, select "HRAppModuleDataControl\Operations\auditManagers(Number, Number)\return" and drag it onto the JSP page. Be sure to select the line containing "return," not the line containing the method signature.

    Additional Information: This adds a `c:out` tag to the JSP page, which displays the expression ${bindings.auditManagers.result}. This expression extracts the return value from the auditManagers action binding. Since `auditManagers()` is invoked before the page is displayed, the expression will contain a value; if `auditManagers()` had not been invoked, attempting to display the value would throw an exception.

8. On the JSP page, after the expression, type " managers were fired." and press ENTER to add a line.

9. Reopen the Component Palette, and click the Submit Button icon to add a submit button to the page. When asked if you want to add a form element, click Yes.

   Additional Information: This adds a submit button, within an HTML form, to the JSP page. The form element (the button) must be within a form, and there was no other form already defined on the page. The page should resemble the following:

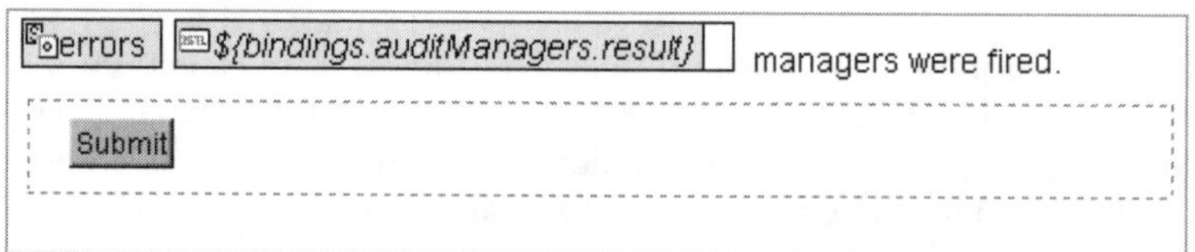

10. In the Property Inspector, enter "event_Submit" for the button's *name* property.

11. With the cursor anywhere inside the form, select "Form\Select Form Tag" from the right-click menu.

12. In the Property Inspector, select "auditResults.do" from the *action* dropdown.

    Additional Information: This adds the attribute `action"/=auditResults.do"` to the form tag.

13. Reopen the Page Flow Diagram.

14. Create a forward from auditResults back to browse.

15. Name the forward "Submit".

    Additional Information: Your page flow diagram should resemble the following:

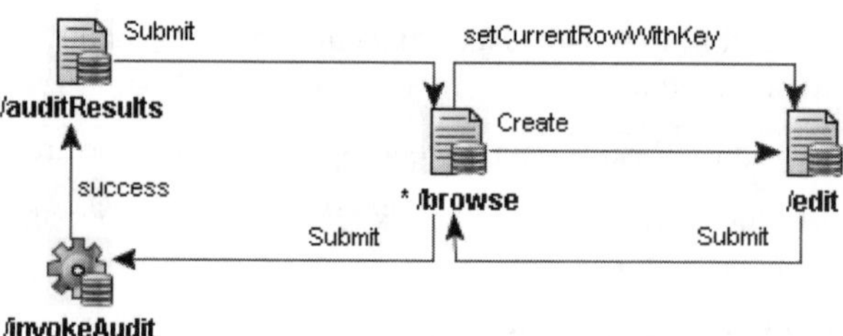

16. Click Save All.

17. Rebuild the project.

Test the Method

You can run a JSP application to test a custom service method using the following steps:

1. On the browse data page, select Run from the right-click menu.
2. When browse.jsp opens, enter "8000" in the first text field at the bottom of the page and "5" in the second.
3. Click Submit.
4. When auditResults.jsp opens, note that no managers were fired.

   Additional Information: The return value of the method will change as you add code.
5. Click Submit to return to browse.jsp.
6. Close the browser window.

What Just Happened? You created some skeleton code for a method on a view object class, and a service method that retrieved a view object instance and called the view object method on it. Then, you exposed the service method on the client interface, created JSP form elements to accept parameters for the method, and created a data action with an action binding to invoke the service method. Currently, the method does nothing except return "0". You add code to the method in the remainder of the hands-on practice.

V. Add Navigation Code to the View Object Method

In this phase, you will add code in your method to create a secondary iterator and cycle through all the rows.

Add Navigation Code

1. Open `ManagersViewImpl`.
2. Find the method `audit()`.
3. Add the following code immediately before the `return` statement:

   ```
   RowSetIterator secondaryIterator = createRowSetIterator(null);
   ```

   Additional Information: This creates a secondary row set iterator that you can use to cycle through the rows in `ManagersViewImpl` without disturbing the current row pointer.
4. Press ALT-ENTER to import `oracle.jbo.RowSetIterator`.
5. Add the following code immediately before the `return` statement:

   ```
   ManagersViewRowImpl currentMgr;
   while (secondaryIterator.hasNext())
   {
     currentMgr =
       (ManagersViewRowImpl) secondaryIterator.next();
   ```

```
  managersFired++;
}
```

Additional Information: This loop uses `next()` and `hasNext()` to cycle through all the rows in the view cache, incrementing `managersFired` for each row.

6. Add the following line immediately after the block you just entered and before the `return` statement:

```
secondaryIterator.closeRowSetIterator();
```

Additional Information: This cleans up the secondary row set iterator before leaving the method.

7. Click Save All.
8. Rebuild the project.

Test the Method
You can test the navigation code in the method using the following steps:

1. Reopen the Page Flow Diagram.
2. On the browse data page, select Run from the right-click menu.
3. When browse.jsp opens, enter "8000" in the first text field and "5" in the second.
4. Click Submit.
5. When auditResults.jsp opens, note that the page claims that 18 managers were fired.

   Additional Information: Currently, the method is counting all rows in AllManagers' cache. The return value of the method will change to reflect the actual rows that meet the query criteria, and the managers will actually be fired, as you add code in the next two phases.
6. Close the browser window.

What Just Happened? You added code to the view object method to create a secondary row set iterator, and used a `hasNext()/next()` loop on that iterator to cycle through the rows in the view cache.

VI. Add Code to Filter Data
In this phase, you will add code to the service method to create a view criteria object based on the method parameters, and apply it to the view object instance to filter the data in the view cache. The view criteria object will limit the cache to only those managers that do not obey the test for maximum salary or minimum number of direct reports; in the next phase, you will add code to fire these managers.

Create and Apply a View Criteria Object
You can create a view criteria object for a view object instance and apply it to filter data in the instance's view cache using the following steps:

1. Reopen the `ManagersViewImpl` class in the editor.
2. At the very beginning of the `audit()` method body, add the following code:

   ```
   ViewCriteria mgrCriteria = createViewCriteria();
   ```

   Additional Information: This creates an empty view criteria object with a structure to match the attributes in ManagersView.
3. Press ALT-ENTER to import the `ViewCriteria` class.
4. Immediately after the line that creates the view criteria object, add the following code:

   ```
   ViewCriteriaRow manRow = mgrCriteria.createViewCriteriaRow();
   manRow.setAttribute("Salary", "> " + salaryThreshold);
   manRow.setAttribute("NumReports", "< " + reportsThreshold);
   mgrCriteria.addElement(manRow);
   ```

   Additional Information: This creates a view criteria row, `manRow`. If the value passed into the method for `salaryThreshold` is "8000", and the value passed into the method for `reportsThreshold` is "5", the view criteria row represents the following expression:

   ```
   Employees.SALARY > 8000 AND Employees.NUM_REPORTS < 5
   ```

   The last line of code adds the view criteria row into the view criteria object. As this is the only row in the view criteria object, the entire object represents the same expression as the row.

   The view criteria object selects exactly those managers who do not meet the requirements the user specifies on the browse page. Those managers will be removed in the next phase.
5. Use ALT-ENTER to import the `ViewCriteriaRow` class.
6. Add the following code immediately after the code block that creates and inserts the view criteria row:

   ```
   applyViewCriteria(mgrCriteria);
   executeQuery();
   ```

   Additional Information: This applies the view criteria object to the view object instance and re-executes its query.
7. Add the following code immediately before the `return` statement:

   ```
   applyViewCriteria(null);
   executeQuery();
   ```

   Additional Information: After the method has cycled through the rows in the view cache, this removes the view criteria object and re-executes the query to bring in all rows again.
8. Click Save All.
9. Rebuild the project.

Test the Method

You can test the navigation code in the method using the following steps:

1. Reopen the Page Flow Diagram.
2. On the browse data page, select Run from the right-click menu.
3. When browse.jsp opens, enter "8000" in the first text field and "5" in the second.
4. Click Submit.
5. When auditResults.jsp opens, note that the page claims that four managers were fired.

   Additional Information: This time, only those managers with a salary over 8000 and fewer than five direct reports were counted. You will add code to actually fire the managers in the next phase.
6. Close the browser window.

What Just Happened? You created a view criteria object and used it to add a WHERE clause onto a view object instance. This reduced the number of rows iterated through in the loop to those that actually matched the query criteria.

VII. Add Code to Change Data

In this phase, you will add code to fire the managers who appear in the filtered view cache, and reassign their reports to Employee 100, King.

Add Code to Cycle Through Detail Rows

You can add code to cycle through the rows in a detail view object instance using the following steps:

1. Reopen the `ManagersViewImpl` class in the editor.
2. Find the following line of code inside the `audit()` method body:

   ```
   ManagersViewRowImpl currentMgr;
   ```
3. Immediately after that line of code, add the following code:

   ```
   RowIterator reportsIter;
   EmployeesViewRowImpl currentRpt;
   ```

   Additional Information: You will use reportsIter to hold the employees that report to each manager in turn, and use `currentRpt` to cycle through those employees.
4. Press ALT-ENTER to import `oracle.jbo.RowIterator`.
5. Find the following line of code inside the `while` loop in the `auditManagers()` method body:

   ```
   managersFired++;
   ```
6. Immediately before that line of code, add the following code:

   ```
   reportsIter = currentMgr.getReportsView();
   ```

Additional Information: This uses EmpMgrFkLink's view link accessor to retrieve the detail rows for `currentMgr`.

7. Immediately after the line you just added, insert the following code:

```
while (reportsIter.hasNext())
{
  currentRpt = (EmployeesViewRowImpl) reportsIter.next();
}
```

Additional Information: This uses a `next()/hasNext()` loop to cycle through the rows of reportsIter.

Add Code to Change Attribute Values

You can write code to change a view attribute value using the following step:

- Right before the end of the inner `while` loop (the loop you just added), add the following line:

```
currentRpt.setManagerId(new Number(100));
```

Additional Information: For each employee reporting to the current manager, this sets the report's ManagerId to 100, moving the report to King.

Add Code to Delete a Row

You can add code to delete a view row using the following steps:

1. Right after the end of the inner `while` loop, add the following line:

```
currentMgr.remove();
```

2. Click Save All.
3. Rebuild the project.

Test the Method

You can test the code to reassign detail rows and remove master rows using the following steps:

1. Reopen the page flow diagram.
2. On the browse data page, select Run from the right-click menu.
3. When browse.jsp opens, use the dropdown list or Next button to note that the following managers have salaries greater than 8000 and less than five direct reports:
   - 102 (De Haan)
   - 103 (Hunold)
   - 201 (Hartstein)
   - 205 (Higgins)
4. Enter "8000" in the first text field and "5" in the second.

5. Click Submit.
6. When auditResults.jsp opens, note that the page claims that four managers were fired.

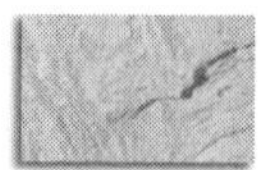

NOTE
If the page reports a record lock, close the browser and terminate the process using the Processes node in the Run Manager (View | Run Manager). Then rerun the browse page.

7. Click Submit to return to browse.jsp.

   Note that managers 102, 103, 201, and 205 have disappeared, and that their employees have been reassigned to King.
8. Close the browser window.

What Just Happened? You used a view link accessor to retrieve detail rows, changed attribute values in those rows, and then deleted the master row.

Dynamically Creating Master-Detail Relationships

Chapter 11 explained how view link instances in the data model could restrict the view cache of view object instances based on the current rows of other view object instances, setting up a master-detail relationship. You learned to add view links to the data model at design time to maintain these relationships.

However, you can also add view link instances to the data model within a service method, making an independent view object instance into a detail of another view object instance. Deferring view link instance creation as long as possible can yield a much more efficient application.

Consider two view object instances, ManagerReports and ReportPastJobs, and a view link instance, ReportsToPastJobs, that creates a master-detail relationship between them. As the application cycles through the rows of ManagerReports, it must query the detail rows for ReportPastJobs each time. If there are many detail instances, this can entail a serious performance hit. In the case of multi-level master-detail-detail relationships, the hit increases exponentially with the number of levels.

In some cases, it is impossible to tell whether an application will ever need access to the details for one particular row. For example, rather than using a traditional master-detail form, with a master row in the top pane and a table of detail rows in the bottom pane, the application could contain just one pane, showing master rows, with a button that opens up a separate display of detail rows. The application will need access to the detail rows if a user clicks the button, but not otherwise.

If you add ReportsToPastJobs to the data model at design time, the application will query the detail rows for ReportPastJobs each time the current row of ManagerReports changes, whether or not the application needs the rows. By only adding ReportsToPastJobs in a service method that responds to the button click, you can defer the detail queries until they are needed.

You can dynamically create view link instances by calling the method

`ApplicationModuleImpl.createViewLink(). createViewLink()`

takes four arguments:

1. A name for the view link instance
2. The package-qualified name of the view link definition
3. The master view object instance
4. The detail view object instance

You can later remove the view link instance by calling `ApplicationModuleImpl.findViewLink()` to retrieve the view link, and then calling `oracle.jbo.ViewLink.remove()` to remove it from the data model.

You will dynamically create and remove a view link instance in the following hands-on practice.

Hands-on Practice: Create and Invoke Service Methods to Maintain a Dynamic Master-Detail Relationship

In this practice, you will add two business service methods to the ADF Business Components you created in Chapters 9–11, and invoke them from the JSP application you created in Chapter 12. These methods will maintain a dynamic master-detail relationship between ManagerReports and ReportPastJobs.

This practice builds on the results of the previous hands-on practice, although it will also work if you start with the results of the second hands-on practice in Chapter 12. If you have not completed one of those practices, you can download the starting files for this practice from the authors' websites mentioned in the author information at the beginning of this book.

This practice guides you through the following phases:

I. Remove a view link instance from an application module definition

II. Create service methods to maintain a dynamic master-detail relationship

- Create a service method to dynamically add a view link instance
- Create a service method to dynamically remove the view link instance
- Expose the service methods

III. Use the dynamic master-detail relationship

- Add a button to start the method invocation
- Create a data action to add the view link instance

- Create a page to display the detail data
- Create a data action to remove the view link instance

IV. Test the service methods

I. Remove a View Link Instance from an Application Module Definition

In this phase, you will remove a statically defined view link instance from an application module definition. The master-detail relationship it defines is not always used by your client application, so you can make the application more efficient by maintaining the view link instance dynamically.

1. Open the HRApp workspace, if it is not already open.
2. Double click "Applications\HRApp\Model\Application Sources\hrapp.model.datamodel\Data Model Diagram" to open it.

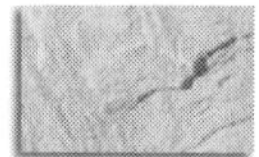

CAUTION
You must use the diagram for this operation. If you use the Application Module Editor, you might also delete the view object instance for ReportsToPastJobs, which is required later.

3. On the diagram, find HRAppModule.
4. On the ReportsToPastJobs view link instance, select Delete from the right-click menu.
5. Click Save All.
6. Rebuild the project.

What Just Happened? You removed the ReportsToPastJobs view link instance. Its detail view object instance, ReportsPastJobs, is now an independent view object instance. Whenever you need to access ReportsPastJobs, you will add the view link instance back to the data model at run time, making ReportsPastJobs a detail again.

II. Create Service Methods to Maintain a Dynamic Master-Detail Relationship

In this phase, you will create service methods to dynamically add and remove a view link instance, and expose them on the client interface.

Create a Service Method to Dynamically Add a View Link Instance

You can create a service method to dynamically add a view link instance to the data model using the following steps:

1. In the Application Navigator, select "Applications\HRApp\Model\Application Sources\hrapp.model.datamodel\HRAppModule".
2. In the Structure window, double click HrAppModuleImpl.java to open its source code.

3. Add a method, `addReportsToPastJobs()`, to the end of the Java class, as follows:

```
public void addReportsToPastJobs()
{
  createViewLink(
    "ReportsToPastJobs",
    "hrapp.model.datamodel.EmpPastJobsLink",
    getManagerReports(),
    getReportPastJobs() );
}
```

Additional Information: This creates a view link instance named "ReportsToPastJobs", based on the view link definition EmpPastJobsLink in the package `hrapp.model.datamodel`, creating a master-detail relationship between the ManagerReports view object instance and the ReportPastJobs view object instance.

4. Click Save All and rebuild the project.

Create a Service Method to Dynamically Remove the View Link Instance

You can create a service method to dynamically remove a view link instance from the data model using the following steps:

1. Add a method, `removeReportsToPastJobs()`, to the `HrAppModuleImpl` Java class, as follows:

```
public void removeReportsToPastJobs()
{
  ViewLink linkForRemoval =
    this.findViewLink("ReportsToPastJobs");
  linkForRemoval.remove();
}
```

Additional Information: The first statement finds the view link instance ReportsToPastJobs (note that calling this method when ReportsToPastJobs is not in the data model will throw an exception). The second command removes the view link instance from the data model.

2. Select the `ViewLink` class name and press ALT-ENTER to import `oracle.jbo.ViewLink`.
3. Click Save All.
4. Rebuild the project.

Expose the Service Methods

You can expose service methods on an application module definition's client interface using the following steps:

1. In the Application Navigator double click HRAppModule to open the Application Module Editor.
2. Select the Client Interface node.

3. Move "addReportsToPastJobs()" and "removeReportsToPastJobs()" from the *Available* list to the *Selected* list.
4. Click OK to close the editor.
5. Click Save All.
6. Rebuild the Model project.

What Just Happened? You created a service method, `addReportsToPastJobs()`, that will, when invoked, create a view link instance to create a master-detail relationship between ManagerReports and ReportPastJobs. Then, you created a service method, `removeReportsToPastJobs()`, that will, when invoked, remove that view link instance. Finally, you exposed both methods on the client interface.

III. Use the Dynamic Master-Detail Relationship

In this phase, you will create Struts data actions and a Struts data page to use the dynamic master-detail relationship to optionally display past jobs information for a selected employee.

Add a Button to Start the Method Invocation

You can add a button to a JSP page to invoke a service method using the following steps:

1. In the Application Navigator, expand "HRApp\ViewController\Web Content".
2. Double click edit.jsp to open it in the visual editor.
3. Click after the button, but still inside the form.
4. In the Component Palette, on the HTML page, click the Submit Button icon to add a second submit button.
5. In the Property Inspector, enter the following values:
   name as "event_Invoke"
   value as "View Past Jobs"

Create a Data Action to Add the View Link Instance

You can create a data action to invoke a custom method using the following steps:

1. Reopen the Page Flow Diagram.
2. In the Component Palette, click the Data Action icon.
3. Click on the diagram to add the data action.
4. Enter "addMasterDetail" as the name of the data action.
5. Add a forward from the edit data page to the addMasterDetail data action.
6. Name the forward "Invoke".
7. In the Data Control Palette, select HRAppModuleDataControl\Operations\addReportsToPastJobs().

8. Drag addReportsToPastJobs() onto the addMasterDetail data action.

9. Click Save All.

10. Rebuild the project.

Create a Page to Display the Detail Data

You can create a page to display the detail data using the following steps:

1. In the Component Palette, click the Data Page icon, and click on the diagram to add a data page.

2. Name the data page "displayPastJobs".

3. Add a forward from the addMasterDetail data action to the displayPastJobs data page. You do not need to rename the forward.

4. Double click the displayPastJobs data page to open the Select or Create Page dialog.

5. Accept the defaults and click OK to create displayPastJobs.jsp and open it in the visual editor.

6. In the Data Control Palette, select HRAppModuleDataControl\ReportPastJobs.

   Additional Information: On the Data Control Palette, this appears to be an independent view object instance, rather than a detail of ManagerReports. However, since this page will only be displayed after `addReportsToPastJobs()` has been invoked, ReportPastJobs will function as a detail view object instance.

7. Ensure that "Read Only Table" is selected in the *Drag and Drop As* list.

8. Drag ReportPastJobs onto the page to create an HTML table to display the jobs, an iterator binding for ReportPastJobs, and a range binding.

9. In the Structure window, select the UI Model tab.

10. Select displayPastJobsUIModel\ReportPastJobsIterator.

11. In the Property Inspector, enter "-1" as the *Range Size* property and press ENTER.

    Additional Information: This range size value will ensure that all past jobs are displayed in the table, without a need for navigation buttons. Most employees have not had many past jobs, so a limited range size is not necessary.

12. Ensure that the cursor is not inside the table, reopen the Component Palette, and click the Submit Button icon to add a submit button to the page. When asked if you want to add a form element, click Yes.

    Additional Information: Users will click this button to remove the view link instance and return to edit.jsp.

13. In the Property Inspector, enter "event_Submit" for the button's *name* property. Press ENTER.

14. Inside the form, select "Form\Select Form Tag" from the right-click menu.

15. In the Property Inspector, select displayPastJobs.do from the *action* dropdown.
16. Click Save All.
17. Rebuild the project.

Create a Data Action to Remove the View Link Instance

You can create a data action to invoke a custom method using the following steps:

1. Reopen the Page Flow Diagram.
2. In the Component Palette, select the Data Action icon.
3. Click on the diagram to add a data action to your controller.
4. Enter "removeMasterDetail" as the name of the data action.
5. Add a forward from the displayPastJobs data page to the removeMasterDetail data action.
6. Name the forward "Submit".
7. Click the Data Controls tab to reopen the Data Control Palette.
8. In the Data Control Palette, select HRAppModuleDataControl\Operations\removeReportsToPastJobs().
9. Drag removeReportsToPastJobs() onto the removeMasterDetail data action.
10. Add a forward from the removeMasterDetail data action back to the edit data page. Leave the name as "success." Your page flow diagram should resemble the following:

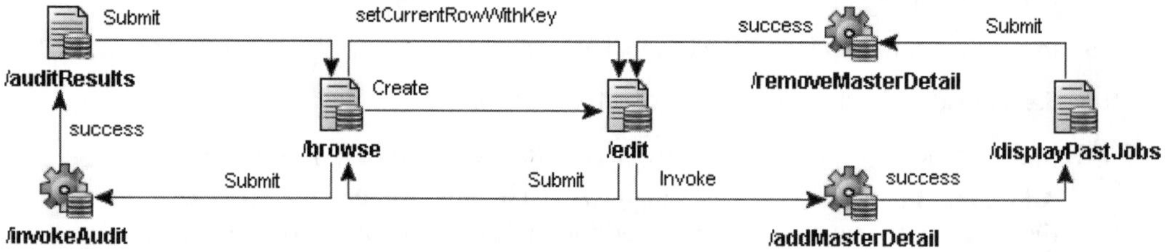

11. Click Save All. Rebuild the project.

What Just Happened? You created a data action to invoke `addReportsToPastJobs()`, a data page to display detail data based on the dynamically added view link instance, and a data action to invoke `removeReportsToPastJobs()`. Because the view link instance is only used on one page, displayPastJobs.jsp, this ensures that it will only be active when that page is being viewed.

IV. Test the Service Methods

You can test the service methods you created using the following steps:

1. On the browse data action, select Run from the right-click menu.
2. When the browser window opens and displays browse.jsp, click the Select link for Employee 102.
3. When edit.jsp opens, click View Past Jobs.
4. Note that Employee 102 had exactly one past job, IT_PROG.
5. Click Submit to return to edit.jsp.
6. Test other employee records. Close the browser when you are finished.

What Just Happened? You tested the dynamic view link instance.

CHAPTER 14

Business Service Technology Alternatives

Give no decision 'till both sides thou'st heard.

—Phocylides of Miletus (6th century B.C.)

Throughout Part II of this book, you have learned about ADF Business Components, ADF's technology for creating business services. ADF BC is the simplest way to provide business services for J2EE applications, but it is by no means the only way. The ADF model layer can also use Enterprise JavaBeans (EJB) technology, ordinary Java classes, or web services as business service providers. Each of these options has important use cases; by understanding them you can decide when to use ADF BC and when to use another technology.

This chapter introduces each of these technologies and explains how and when to use them as business services for J2EE applications. You will learn to create and use EJB beans, how to use TopLink to provide object-relational (O/R) mappings between Java classes and the database, and how to retrieve data from web services.

NOTE
This chapter provides an introduction to some alternative business services technologies. It is not intended to be a complete explanation of EJB, TopLink, or web services. For more information about these technologies, see the references listed in Appendix A.

This chapter contains three hands-on practices, covering each of the alternative business services technologies. In the first practice, you will create EJB beans and a simple master-detail form that uses them. In the second practice, you will create Java classes, use TopLink technology to map them to database objects, and create another simple master-detail form. In the third practice, you will create an application that accesses a web service.

Enterprise JavaBeans Technology

Enterprise JavaBeans technology is Sun Microsystems' official technology for creating business services. EJB is historically a very popular choice for interfacing with a persistence layer. EJB is not a framework technology; unlike ADF BC, EJB components do not use a vendor-specific library of classes to provide their behavior.

There are several reasons why you might use EJB technology:

- **Independence** You need to develop business services without using vendor-specific libraries.
- **Existing code base** Your organization has made a commitment to EJB technology; you have substantial amounts of code already in EJB beans.
- **In-house skill set** You or other developers in your organization are comfortable with EJB technology.

In the past, developing EJB applications was extremely time-consuming. Developers had to spend considerable amounts of time working with EJB protocols such as Remote Method Invocation (RMI) and Internet Inter-ORB Protocol (IIOP). The ADF model layer, described in

Chapter 12, makes creating clients that use EJB technology substantially simpler than before. However, developing an EJB application is still not as simple as developing an application using ADF BC, as discussed in Chapter 8.

As with ADF BC, EJB technology essentially divides into two parts:

- There are features of EJB technology that represent features of the database (equivalent to ADF BC's business domain components).
- There are features of EJB technology that collect data and present it to the rest of the application.

This section will cover both parts and then briefly return to the ADF model layer to explain the most important ways in which its handling of EJB business services differs from its handling of ADF Business Components.

Table 14-1 pairs some of the EJB concepts discussed in this section with the corresponding ADF BC concepts with which you may be more familiar. The EJB concepts will be explained at greater length throughout this section.

EJB	ADF BC	What It Does
Container-managed persistence (CMP) entity bean	Entity object definition	Represents a database object that stores data
Entity bean instance	Entity object instance	Represents a single row of data from a database object
Container-managed relationship (CMR)	Association	Represents a relationship between database objects
CMR field	Association accessor attribute	Allows access from one entity bean/entity object instance to related instances
EJB finder method	View object definition WHERE clause	Returns a set of rows
Data Transfer Object (DTO)	View object definition attribute list	Exposes a set of attributes
DTO CMR field wrapper	View link accessor attribute	Allows access from one view row/DTO instance to related view rows/DTO instances
Session Façade	Application module definition	Aggregates the data needed by an application
Session Façade DTO collection	Master view object instance	Accesses the view rows/DTO instances that are not details in master-detail relationships

TABLE 14-1. *EJB and ADF BC Concepts*

EJB Technology and the Business Domain

Like ADF BC, EJB technology must represent database tables, views, synonyms, and relationships among them. There are two ways EJB technology does this: with EJB entity beans and EJB relationships.

EJB Entity Beans

EJB entity beans are EJB components that represent database tables, views, and synonyms. Just as entity object definitions have entity attributes to represent columns in the database, entity beans have *fields* that represent database columns (although, as with entity attributes, the correspondence is not always one-to-one).

There are two types of EJB entity beans: bean-managed persistence (BMP) entity beans, and container-managed persistence (CMP) entity beans. *BMP entity beans* implement their own O/R mappings. The developer who creates them is responsible for writing the JDBC code necessary to communicate with the database. *CMP entity beans* rely on a *CMP provider*, a component of the application server that implements O/R mappings and persistence. While BMP entity beans allow you the greatest flexibility and control over the object/relational mappings, they are vastly more difficult to develop than CMP entity beans, requiring extensive knowledge of JDBC. This chapter focuses on CMP entity beans. You can find more information about BMP entity beans in the references listed in Appendix A.

An EJB entity bean consists of some or all of the following parts.

An Element in an EJB Deployment Descriptor An *EJB deployment descriptor* is an XML file that describes a set of EJB components. In particular, each entity bean corresponds to an element in an EJB deployment descriptor that describes its O/R mappings.

A Bean Class An entity bean's *bean class* is a class that represents instances of the entity bean—that is, individual rows in the database table. It contains getters and setters for the bean's fields.

In the case of CMP entity beans, the bean class is *abstract*, meaning it cannot be directly instantiated. All of the getters and setters are abstract as well, which means that they are merely method declarations (as in an interface), rather than actual implementations. This is because the EJB container will automatically extend the EJB class to provide a true implementation of entity bean instances, automatically writing the JDBC required for the getters and setters.

A Local Interface It is a violation of EJB specifications for other components to directly use the bean class. Instead, they must use interfaces that the bean class implements. This allows you to expose exactly the fields you want to other components, reserving the remaining fields for bean-internal use. As shown in Figure 14-1, one interface implemented by an entity bean's bean class is the entity bean's local interface.

An entity bean's *local interface* is the interface used by other classes in the same EJB container. Client applications will never access the local interface directly. Strictly speaking, local interfaces are optional. If an EJB entity bean will only be accessed from outside of the container, you do not need to generate a local interface for it.

A Remote Interface There are two ways that client applications can access an EJB entity bean. One is through another interface implemented by the bean class, the entity bean's *remote interface*. ADF applications do not generally use entity beans' remote interfaces to access entity beans. Rather, they use the Session Façade design pattern, which is explained later in this chapter.

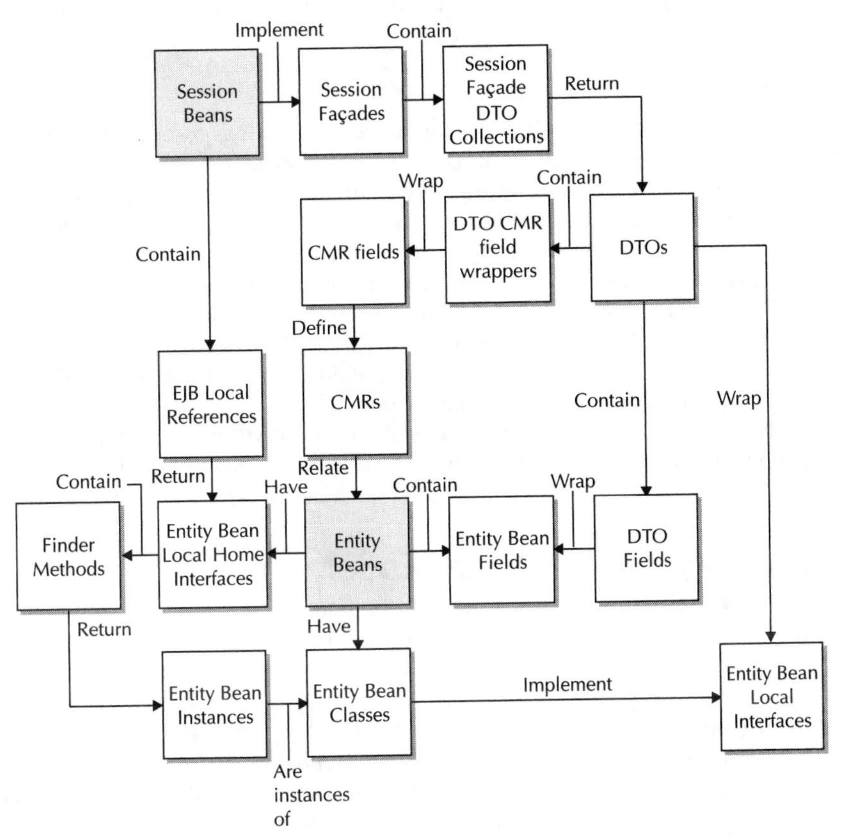

FIGURE 14-1. *EJB component relationships*

Like local interfaces, remote interfaces are optional. If you use the Session Façade design pattern, you will generally not need to create remote interfaces for entity beans.

A Local Home Interface The EJB class and the interfaces it implements are only responsible for retrieving and changing data in a single row. Creation and retrieval of entity bean instances are handled through different interfaces.

An entity bean's local home interface is used by other classes in the same EJB container to create and retrieve entity bean instances. Like local interfaces, local home interfaces are optional; if you will only be creating and finding entity bean instances directly from the client, you need not generate them. Later in this chapter, the section "Finder Methods" explains more about local home interfaces.

A Home Interface An entity bean's home interface is used by clients in the same way that its local home interface is used by other classes in the same EJB container: to directly create and retrieve entity bean instances. As with remote interfaces, most ADF applications use the Session

Façade design pattern, rather than EJB home interfaces, to create and retrieve entity bean instances.

EJB Relationships

EJB relationships define relationships between entity beans, much as associations define relationships between entity object definitions. Much like associations with their accessor attributes, EJB relationships are defined through fields, in the source and destination entity bean, which can contain instances (typed to the entity bean's local interface) or collections (typed to `java.util.Collection`) of the entity bean at the other end of the relationship.

As with entity beans themselves, there are two sorts of EJB relationships. *Bean-managed relationships (BMRs)* require the source and destination beans to maintain the relationship; the developer is responsible for writing code to ensure the fields return the related instance or instances. *Container-managed relationships* let the container maintain the relationship based on foreign-key or other attribute-matching relationships. The container will implement code to ensure that the fields on either side of the relationship, called *CMR fields* (as shown in Figure 14-1), will return the related instance or instances. You will use CMRs in the hands-on practice; more information about BMRs can be found in the references listed in Appendix A.

EJB Technology and the Data Model

Like ADF BC, EJB technology must also collect data and present it to the view and controller through the model layer. There are three parts to doing this: with EJB finder methods, Data Transfer Objects, and Session Façades.

EJB Finder Methods

As shown in Figure 14-1, an *EJB finder method* is a method on an EJB entity bean's local home interface or a home interface that retrieves entity bean instances matching some condition. (This section focuses on finder methods on the local home interface.) An EJB finder method can either retrieve a single entity bean instance (typed to the bean's local interface if the finder method is on the local home interface) or an entire collection (typed to `java.util.Collection`) of entity bean instances, depending on whether the condition uniquely identifies an entity bean instance.

For example, suppose Employees is an EJB entity bean representing the EMPLOYEES table, with a local interface called "`EmployeesLocal`" and a local home interface called "`EmployeesLocalHome`". `EmployeesLocalHome` could expose either or both of the following methods:

- `findRichestEmployee()`, which returns the employee with the highest salary. This method would have a return type of `EmployeesLocal`.
- `findRichEmployees()`, which returns all employees with salary higher than 10,000. This method would have a return type of `Collection`.

EJB local home interfaces offer two pre-generated finder methods:

- `findAll()`, which takes no arguments and returns a collection containing entity bean instances for each row in the database object

- `findByPrimaryKey()`, which takes one argument for each primary key field in the entity bean, and returns the entity bean instance matching that primary key

You can also create finder methods to find entity bean instances according to other criteria. These methods will be added to the local home interface.

Because the local home interface is an interface, containing only method declarations, rather than a class containing method implementations, you cannot implement the finder methods in Java. Instead, the EJB container will implement the methods for you based on your declarative descriptions. There are two ways this can happen.

Find-By-Field Methods Suppose Employees is an EJB entity bean representing the EMPLOYEES table, with a field, `departmentId`, of type `java.lang.Long`. To create a method that returns all Employees instances with a particular `departmentId`, all you have to do is create a finder method called `findByDepartmentId()`, which accepts a parameter of type `java.lang.Long`. The EJB container will automatically implement the method for you.

In general, if a finder method is called `findByFoo()`, where "Foo" is the initial-capped name of a field (for example, "DepartmentId" if the field is "`departmentId`"), and has a parameter of the appropriate type, the EJB container will automatically assume that the method should return instances with the appropriate attribute value, and implement it to do so.

EJB Query Language For more complex requirements, you can write a query and add it to the EJB deployment descriptor. The EJB container will use the expression to implement the finder method.

These queries are not in SQL. Rather, they are in a query language called *EJB Query Language (EJB QL)*. This section will provide a brief introduction to EJB QL. For more information, see the references listed in Appendix A.

An EJB QL query, like a SQL query, has two mandatory clauses: a `select` clause and a `from` clause. For queries in EJB finder methods, these have a single format:

```
select distinct object (e) from Employees e
```

The letter "e" is just used as an example here. Any legal Java identifier is acceptable as an alias. "Employees" is the entity bean's abstract schema name, a property in the EJB deployment descriptor that uniquely identifies the bean (by default, it is the same as the bean's name).

You can also specify a `where` clause in an EJB QL query. Most simple `where` clauses, like the one that follows, have the same syntax as a SQL WHERE clause, except that parameters are specified with question marks followed by numbers:

```
select distinct object (e) from Employees e
where e.salary > ?1 and e.salary < ?2
```

The parameters ("?1" and "?2") in the query correspond to parameters in the method. The method for the preceding query would accept two parameters, which would form the range for the salary field.

You can write an EJB QL query on the Methods page of the EJB Module Editor, as shown in Figure 14-2. You can access the EJB Module Editor by double clicking a bean in the Application Navigator or on an EJB diagram.

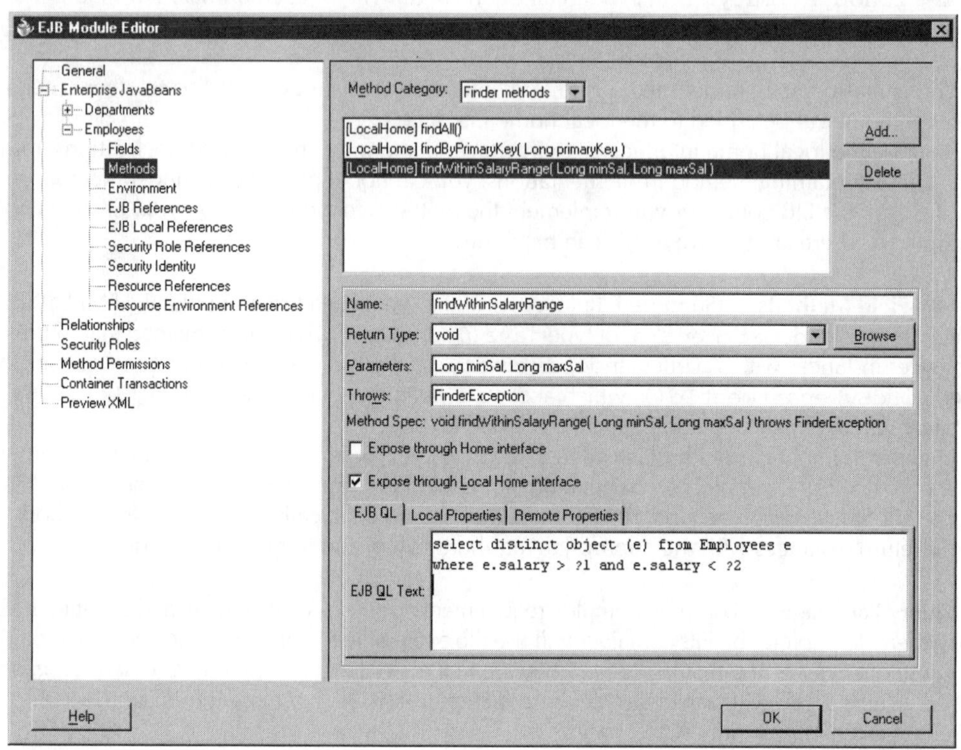

FIGURE 14-2. *The EJB Module Editor*

Data Transfer Objects

An EJB finder method, unlike a view object definition's query, can only limit the rows presented to the application. It cannot limit the fields in each row that the application sees. You can remove some fields from an entity bean's local or remote interfaces, but since different applications need to see different fields, removing all fields an application does not need will limit the reusability of the entity bean.

As shown in Figure 14-1, a *Data Transfer Object (DTO)* (also called a *Transfer Object*) is a lightweight Java class that wraps an EJB local or remote interface for use by a particular application. A DTO is not actually part of the EJB specification; rather, it is one of the J2EE BluePrints design patterns. A DTO contains fields that wrap some or all of the entity bean's fields. Because a DTO is lightweight, and has only the needed classes, marshalling it across the network through EJB protocols such as IIOP is more efficient than marshalling the entity beans.

When a DTO instance is created (based on an entity bean instance), its fields are immediately populated. Most of these fields are populated directly with the value of the corresponding entity bean field. The exception is fields that wrap CMR fields. The bean's CMR fields contain single entity bean instances or collections of entity bean instances from the associated entity bean; the DTO's CMR field wrappers return instances or collections of other DTOs.

For example, suppose Departments and Employees are two entity beans, and `DepartmentsLocalDTO` and `EmployeesLocalDTO` are DTOs for those beans. Departments contains a CMR field, `employees_departmentId`, that contains all Employees entity bean instances with the appropriate `departmentId`. `DepartmentsLocalDTO` will contain a field (unless it is removed), `employees_departmentIdDTO`, which contains DTO instances for all of those Employees entity bean instances, as shown next:

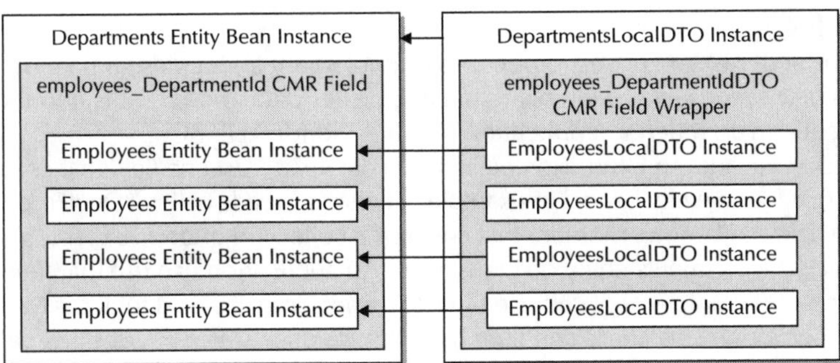

JDeveloper allows you to automatically generate a default DTO, exposing all fields, for any entity bean. This DTO includes the code to wrap the CMR fields. You can remove any unneeded fields yourself.

EJB Session Beans

EJB session beans are EJB components that are instantiated by client applications. Unlike entity beans, EJB session beans are not persistent. They do not represent data; they exist solely to process client requests.

Session beans have all the same components as entity beans.

An Element in an EJB Deployment Descriptor Each session bean has an element in the EJB deployment descriptor. Unlike the elements for entity beans, which contain O/R mapping information, these elements contain only the bean's name.

A Bean Class A session bean's bean class contains session-wide fields and service methods. Unlike the bean class for entity beans, this class is not abstract. It is directly instantiated when a session bean instance is created.

A Local Interface A session bean's local interface is the interface to the bean class used by other classes in the same EJB container. Unlike entity beans, which primarily use the local interface for ADF applications, most simple applications do not require the use of a session bean's local interface.

A Remote Interface A session bean's remote interface is the interface to the bean class used by client applications. Most ADF applications will primarily use this interface to the bean class.

A Local Home Interface A session bean's local home interface is used by other classes in the same EJB container to create new instances of the bean. Like the local interface, most ADF applications will not use the local home interface.

A Home Interface A session bean's home interface is used by clients to create new instances of the bean. Most ADF applications will primarily use this interface to create new bean instances.

Session Façades

The most common use of an EJB session bean is to implement a J2EE design pattern, the Session Façade. A *Session Façade* is a session bean that aggregates data and presents it to the application through the model layer, much as application modules do for ADF BC.

To be a Session Façade, an EJB session bean must contain at least one field that contains a collection of DTOs for an entity bean. For example, a Session Façade called "DeptEmpSessionBean" might contain a field, `allDepartments`, that contains a collection of `DepartmentsLocalDTO` instances for every Departments entity bean instance. An application can use that field to access both departments and employees. It can use the `allDepartments` field to access a collection of `DepartmentsLocalDTO` instances and then use each instance's `employees_departmentId` field to access the detail collection of `EmployeesLocalDTO` instances.

EJB Technology and the ADF Model Layer

The ADF model layer, described in detail in Chapter 12, provides a largely consistent way to develop databound applications using any business services technology. However, there are a few differences.

Data Control Definition Files

The most important difference is that if you use EJB technology to provide your business services layer, you must create data control definition files. *Data control definition files* are XML files that specify metadata for data controls created by the binding context. ADF Business Components XML files provide all the metadata the ADF model layer needs to create data controls, but the ADF model layer requires additional metadata to create data controls for other technologies, including EJB technologies. EJB technology uses three sorts of data control definition metadata files, as follows:

- **Bean model definition files** There is one bean model definition file for each DTO. The bean model definition file describes the fields and methods on the DTO.
- **Data control metadata files** There is one data control metadata file for each session bean. The data control metadata file describes the fields and methods on the session bean's remote interface; it allows the binding context to create a data control that accesses the session bean.
- **Data control description files** There is one data control description file for each package containing session beans. The description file lists the data control metadata files in the project; the binding container uses it to find particular data control metadata files when it needs to create data controls.

In addition to the metadata files, creating data controls for EJB applications requires the following two Java files:

- **Data control implementation files** These Java files wrap the data control metadata files.
- **Data control BeanInfo files** These Java files are BeanInfo classes for the data control implementation files. BeanInfo classes expose methods to provide descriptions of JavaBean properties. These classes provides methods used by the ADF model layer to discover the properties of the corresponding data control implementation files.

Creating defaults for all the data control definition files is straightforward. For most purposes, the only change you need to make to these files is to provide bean class properties for collections. A *bean class property* is a metadata property that describes, for a field of type `Collection`, what class the collection is a collection of. For example, `allDepartments` might be a field of type `Collection` that is a collection of `DepartmentsLocalDTO`s. Providing a bean class property allows the ADF model layer to determine how to cast individual rows in `allDepartments`.

Operations

The second difference between how the ADF model layer handles EJB technology and how it handles ADF BC technology is in the operations it provides. Recall that, for ADF BC applications, the ADF model layer provides the following operations:

- For collections:
  - Next
  - Previous
  - First
  - Last
  - Next Set
  - Previous Set
  - setCurrentRowWithKey()
  - setCurrentRowWithKeyValues()
  - Create
  - Delete
- For data controls:
  - Commit
  - Rollback
  - Any exported service methods

If you are working with EJB technology, the operations will be a bit more limited; Create, Delete, Commit, and Rollback operations are not provided by default. You can write methods on the session bean class to create and delete DTO instances and to commit and roll back transactions; if you expose them on the bean's remote interface, they will appear as operations, much like ADF BC service methods.

Collections

When the ADF model layer exposes ADF BC components, details are always exposed as collections, with the attendant operations, even if they are a "one" side in a one-to-many or one-to-one relationship. For example, suppose a one-to-many, bidirectional view link is created between ManagersView and DepartmentsView, and in the data model, an instance of that link is used to make DepartmentManagers, an instance of ManagersView a detail of AllDepartments, an instance of DepartmentsView. The Data Control Palette will show both view object instances as collections, as shown here:

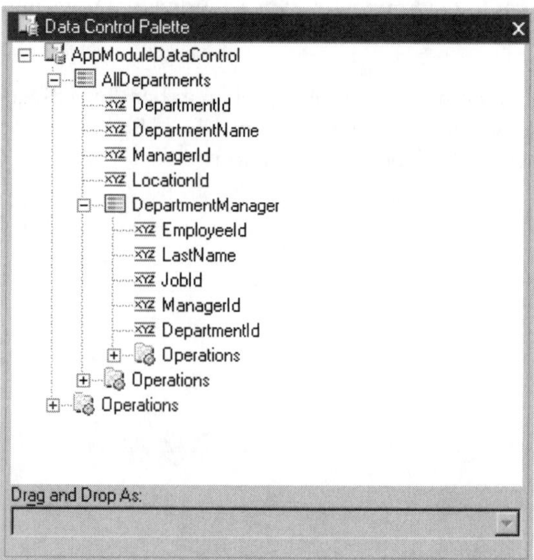

The detail collection even provides navigation operations, although, as it is guaranteed to hold only a single row, these operations will not do anything.

When the ADF model layer exposes EJB beans, by contrast, details are exposed as collections or single rows, depending on the return type of the CMR field wrappers in the master DTO. If the detail is in a one-to-one relationship or on the "one" side in a one-to-many relationship, the detail will appear as a single row, without navigation operations, as shown for the employees_managerIdDTO node here:

Hands-on Practice: Build a Simple EJB Application

In this practice, you will create a simple EJB application that displays a master-detail form.

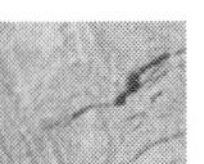

NOTE
This practice uses a number of code snippets. Instead of entering them by hand, you can download them from the authors' websites mentioned in the introduction.

This practice guides you through the following phases:

I. Create an application workspace and EJB diagram

II. Create the business domain

III. Create the data model

- Create an EJB finder method
- Create and refine DTOs
- Create an EJB session bean
- Implement a Session Façade

IV. Create data control definition files

- Generate default data control definition files
- Set bean classes for collections

V. Create a master-detail form

- Create a data page
- Create and add controls to a JSP page
- Test the application

I. Create an Application Workspace and EJB Diagram

In this phase, you create an application workspace with the proper technology scope for an EJB application and an empty EJB diagram. You will use the diagram to create entity beans, DTOs, and a session bean in Phases II and III.

1. On the Applications node in the Application Navigator, select New Application Workspace from the right-click menu. The Create Application Workspace dialog opens.
2. Enter the following values:
   Application Name as "HREJB"
   Application Package Prefix as "hrejb"
   Application Template as "Web Application [JSP, Struts, EJB]"

   Additional Information: The application template is the same as the "Web Application [Default]" used in the hands-on practices in Chapters 8–13, except that it uses EJB technology for the business services and does not include ADF UIX in the technology scope of the ViewController project.
3. Click OK. A new application workspace, HREJB, appears in the navigator.

   Additional Information: As with application workspaces created using the default template, this workspace holds a Model project, which will contain your business services and data control definition files, and a ViewController project, which will contain your view, controller, and data bindings.
4. On the Model node in the navigator, select New from the right-click menu to open the New Gallery.
5. Select the "Business Tier\Enterprise JavaBeans (EJB)" category and the "EJB Diagram" item and click OK.
6. When the Create EJB Diagram dialog appears, name the diagram "EJB Diagram" and click OK.
7. Click Save All.

What Just Happened? You created an application workspace for your EJB application, and an empty EJB diagram to help create your EJB beans and DTOs.

II. Create the Business Domain

In this phase, you create EJB entity beans and CMR relationships to act as the business domain for your application. The EJB entity beans will represent the DEPARTMENTS and EMPLOYEES tables, and the CMR relationships will represent the foreign key relationships between those tables.

1. Open the Connection Navigator. (Choose **View | Connection Manager** to display the Connections tab if it is not already displayed.)
2. Under Connections\Database\HR\HR\Tables, group-select (CTRL-click) DEPARTMENTS and EMPLOYEES and drag them onto the diagram
3. When the Create From Tables dialog appears, ensure that "EJB 2.0 Entity Beans (OC4J Native persistence)" is selected and click OK.

   Additional Information: The two technologies listed are those available in the project's technology scope. EJB 1.1 entity beans correspond to an earlier version of the EJB specification—an option provided for backward compatibility. The option you selected is for a newer version of CMP entity beans, using OC4J as their CMP provider. As explained later in this chapter, you can also create EJB 2.0 entity beans that use the TopLink runtime as a CMP provider.

What Just Happened? You created two EJB entity beans, Departments and Employees, and CMR relationships between them representing the foreign key relationships between the corresponding tables in the database. Your diagram should resemble the one shown in Figure 14-3. You can see the following features in that figure:

A. EJB fields

B. Methods on the EJB's home and local home interfaces

C. Departments - Employees, a CMR representing DEPT_MANAGER_FK

D. Employees - Departments, a CMR representing EMP_DEPT_FK

E. Employees - Employees, a CMR representing EMP_MANAGER_FK

F. `employees_managerId`, a CMR field for Departments - Employees

G. `departments_managerId`, a CMR field for Departments - Employees

H. `employees_departmentId`, a CMR field for Employees - Departments

I. `departments_departmentId`, a CMR field for Employees - Departments

J. `employees_managerId` and `employees_managerId1`, CMR fields for Employees - Employees

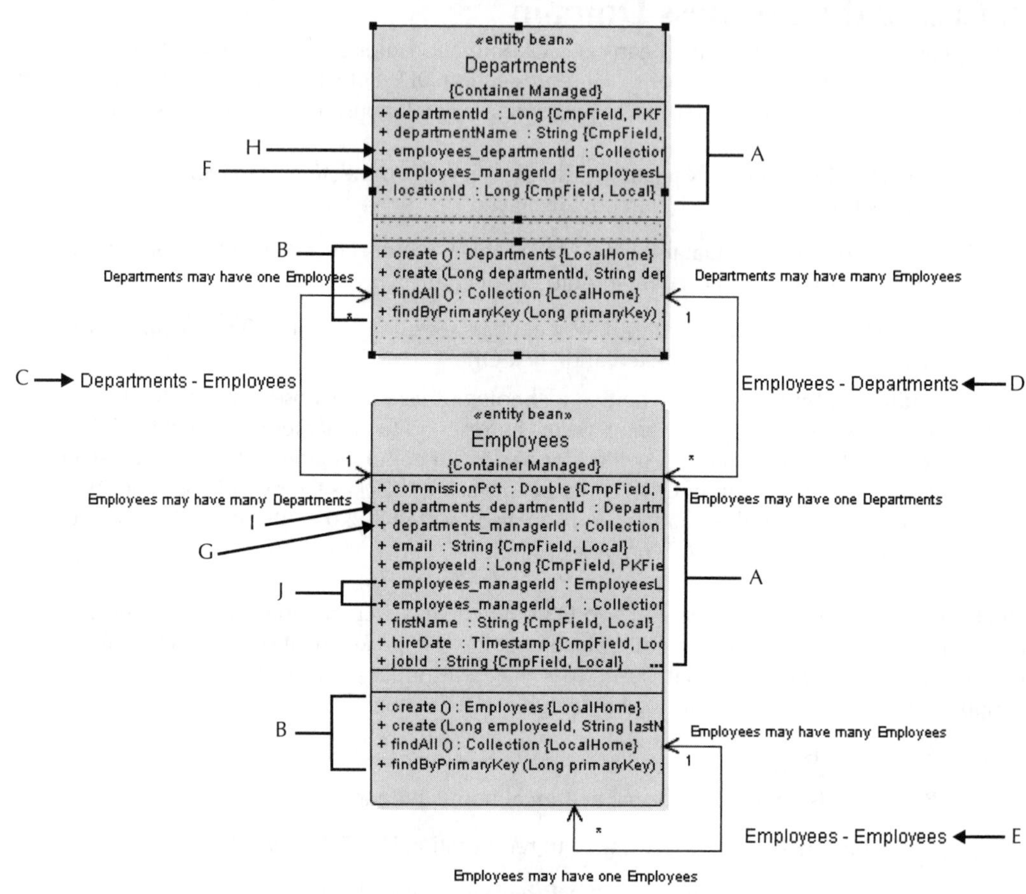

FIGURE 14-3. *Entity beans and CMRs*

III. Create the Data Model

In this phase, you will create an EJB finder method, DTOs, and a Session Façade to aggregate data for use by an MVC application.

Create an EJB Finder Method

You can add a simple finder method to an EJB's home interface using the following steps. The EJB finder method will accept a location ID as a parameter and return a limited set of instances of the Departments entity bean, namely those in the specified location.

1. On the diagram, click the diagram background to deselect the objects; then select the Departments entity bean. Several dotted boxes will appear inside the bean's representation.

2. Find the dotted box inside the area containing the local home interface methods for Departments, as shown here:

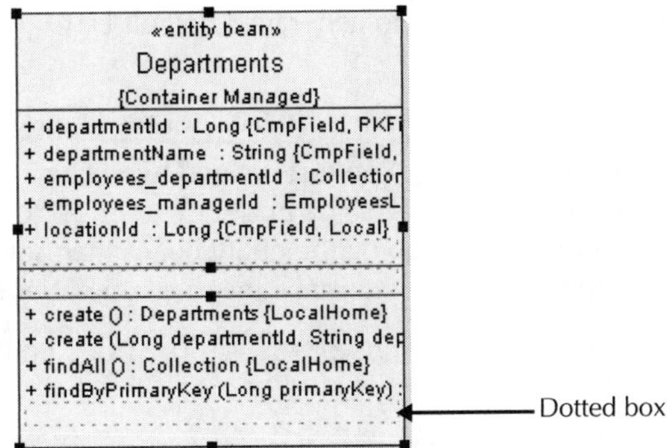

3. Click the dotted box twice to make it editable. Do not double click.

4. Type the following and press ENTER:

```
+ findByLocationId(Long locationId) : Collection {LocalHome}
```

Additional Information: This creates a public method called `findByLocationId()` on the local home interface. Because of the method's name and parameter type, the CMP provider will treat it as a find-by-field method and implement it to return a collection of all entity bean instances with a `locationId` matching the method parameter. The bean should resemble the following (note that after you press ENTER, the methods will be rearranged in alphabetical order):

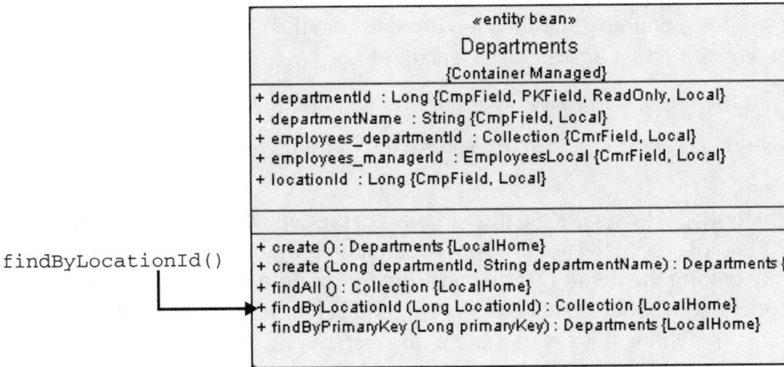

5. Click Save All.

6. Rebuild the project.

Create and Refine DTOs

Rather than requiring your application to marshal instances of the Departments and Employees entity beans across the network, you can generate and customize Data Transfer Objects that expose only the needed attributes from the entity beans.

1. On the diagram, on the Departments entity bean, select Generate | Data Transfer Object from the right-click menu to generate a default DTO. A box representing the DTO will appear on the diagram.
2. Repeat step 1 to generate a default DTO for the Employees entity bean.

   Additional Information: You just created two Data Transfer Objects as wrappers to entity bean local interfaces: `DepartmentsLocalDTO` and `EmployeesLocalDTO`. These will appear overlapping the entity beans themselves; you may want to drag them away from the entity beans to make the diagram easier to read.
3. Double click `DepartmentsLocalDTO`. The Code Editor will open and display the corresponding class code.
4. Click the Class tab to open the Class Editor. You can use this editor to generate and remove fields and default accessors automatically.
5. Select the Fields tab of the Class Editor.
6. Select the field *employees_managerIdDTO*, and click Remove. When the confirmation dialog appears, click OK.

   Additional Information: This application will only use the Employees - Departments CMR, which represents the EMP_DEPT_FK foreign key relationship. This field is a wrapper for the CMR field `employees_managerId`. The `employees_managerId` field maintains the CMR Departments - Employees, which represents the DEPT_MGR_FK relationship. Therefore, it can be removed to make the DTO smaller and simpler.
7. Click the Source tab to open the Code Editor.
8. In the Structure window, double click the DepartmentsLocalDTO(DepartmentsLocal) constructor, to navigate to the constructor's declaration.
9. Uncomment the following line in that constructor by deleting the "//":

   ```
   // _loadEmployees_departmentIdDTO(departmentsLocal.getEmployees_
   departmentId());
   ```

   Additional Information: As explained earlier in this chapter, the default DTOs contain code to wrap CMR fields. For CMR field wrappers containing a single instance, this can be handled simply by calling the detail DTO's constructor. For field wrappers containing a collection, the code is somewhat more complicated, and is handled in methods with the prefix "_load". Uncommenting this line populates the `employees_departmentIdDTO` field with a collection containing DTO instances for the employees assigned to the department.
10. Switch back to the EJB Diagram tab and repeat steps 3–5 to open the Fields tab for `EmployeesLocalDTO`.

11. Remove the following fields:

   - `email`
   - `firstName`
   - `hireDate`
   - `phoneNumber`

   Additional Information: This application will not use these values, so you can remove them. Doing so will make the DTO more efficient.

12. Still on the Fields page, remove all of the bean's CMR field wrappers:

   - `departments_departmentIdDTO`
   - `departments_managerIdDTO`
   - `employees_managerIdDTO`
   - `employees_managerId1DTO`

   Additional Information: You only need CMR field wrappers if you want the DTO to act as a master in a master-detail relationship. Since this application will only use one relationship, with `EmployeesLocalDTO` as the detail, `EmployeesLocalDTO` does not need CMR field wrappers. The page should appear as shown here:

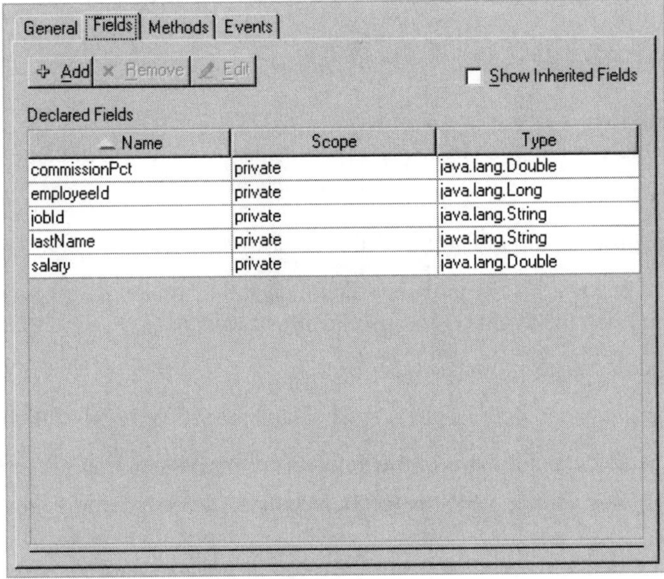

13. Select the Methods tab of the class editor.

14. Remove the following methods:

    - `_load_departments_managerIdDTO`
    - `_load_employees_managerIdDTO`

    Additional Information: Since you have removed the CMR fields, you must also remove the methods that load them. There are no comparable methods for `departments_departmentIdDTO` and `employees_managerId1DTO` because these CMR fields contain single entity-bean instances rather than collections and so are populated using constructors rather than specialized methods.

15. Click the Source tab to switch back to `EmployeesLocalDTO` in a source editor.

16. Find the constructor with the following declaration:

```
public EmployeesLocalDTO(EmployeesLocal employeesLocal)
```

17. Remove the following lines from the constructor method:

```
firstName = employeesLocal.getFirstName();
email = employeesLocal.getEmail();
phoneNumber = employeesLocal.getPhoneNumber();
hireDate = employeesLocal.getHireDate();
```

    Additional Information: Since you have removed these fields, you must remove the lines of the constructor that initialize them.

18. Click Save All.

19. Rebuild the project.

Create an EJB Session Bean

You can create an EJB session bean to process requests from a client application using the following steps:

1. Select the EJB Diagram tab in the editor window.
2. On the EJB page of the Component Palette, click the Session Bean icon, and click the diagram to open the Create Enterprise JavaBean Wizard.
3. If the Welcome page appears, click Next.
4. On the EJB name and options page, enter "DeptEmpSessionFacade" in the *EJB Name* field.
5. Click Finish to accept the rest of the defaults on this page and in the rest of the wizard.

   Additional Information: The session bean will be added to your diagram, as shown here:

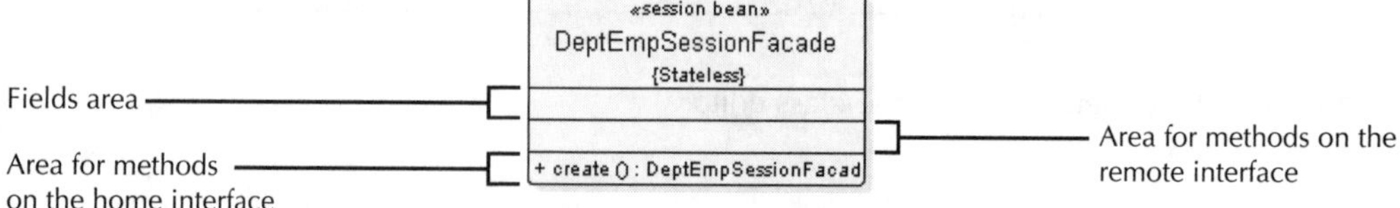

6. Click Save All.
7. Rebuild the project.

Implement a Session Façade

You can use an EJB session bean to implement the Session Façade design pattern using the following steps:

1. On the Component Palette, click the EJB Local Reference icon.

   Additional Information: An *EJB local reference* is a relationship between two EJB beans in the same EJB container, which allows the first bean to retrieve the second bean's local home interface.

2. Click once on the DeptEmpSessionFacade session bean and once on the Departments entity bean to create an EJB local reference from DeptEmpSessionFacade to Departments.

   Additional Information: This adds a method, `getDepartmentsLocalHome()`, to DeptEmpSessionFacade's bean class (it will not appear on the diagram, because it is not exposed on any of the bean's interfaces). You will use this method to add a master collection field to DeptEmpSessionFacade.

3. Click in the top empty box (the fields area) on DeptEmpSessionFacade twice to make it editable. Do not double click.
4. Enter the following field:

   ```
   + seattleDepartments : Collection {Remote}
   ```

   Additional Information: You will implement this field to contain DTO instances for all departments in location 1700 (Seattle). The field will be exposed on the session bean's remote interface.

5. Click the diagram outside of the session bean to stop entering fields.
6. On DeptEmpSessionFacade, select "Go to Source\'DeptEmpSessionFacadeBean.java' Bean Class" from the right-click menu.
7. Using the Structure window, find the method `getSeattleDepartments()`.

   Additional Information: When you added the `seattleDepartments` field, JDeveloper automatically added getter and setter methods to the bean class.

8. Remove the `return` statement from the body of the method.
9. Add the following `try/catch` block to the method:

   ```
   try
   {
   }
   catch (Exception e)
   {
     System.out.println(e.toString());
     throw new javax.ejb.EJBException(e);
   }
   ```

Additional Information: You will write code to return the collection of DTOs inside the `try` portion of the block. This code will require you to use `getDepartmentsLocalHome()` and `findByLocationId()` to retrieve the entity bean instances corresponding to departments in Seattle. Since EJB local reference accessors and finder methods both throw exceptions, you must wrap the code in a `try/catch` block. The `catch` portion of the block consolidates the exceptions, prints information to the console, and throws a single exception in their place.

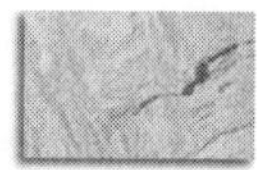

TIP
Do not forget code templates when working with the Code Editor. For example, you can type "sop" (without quotes) and press CTRL-ENTER *to add the* `println()` *method.*

10. Add the following line of code to the `try` portion of the block:

```
ArrayList dtoList = new ArrayList();
```

Additional Information: `ArrayList` is an implementation of `java.util.Collection` that you will use to assemble the collection of DTOs.

11. Press ALT-ENTER to import `java.util.ArrayList`.
12. Add the following code immediately after that line:

```
Collection beanList =
  getDepartmentsLocalHome().findByLocationId(new Long(1700));
Iterator beanIter = beanList.iterator();
DepartmentsLocal currBean;
```

Additional Information: The collection `beanList` contains all the entity bean instances with `locationId` 1700. `beanIter` is an iterator over `beanList` that will allow you to cycle through it, and `currBean` will hold each entity bean instance in turn, typed to Departments' local interface. Of course, in a production application, you would not hard-code the location ID in the method, but this practice does so for simplicity.

13. Press ALT-ENTER to import `java.util.Iterator`.
14. Add the following code immediately after the preceding:

```
while(beanIter.hasNext())
{
  currBean = (DepartmentsLocal) beanIter.next();
  DepartmentsLocalDTO deptsDTO =
    new DepartmentsLocalDTO(currBean);
  dtoList.add(deptsDTO);
}
```

Additional Information: This loop cycles through the entity bean instances in beanList, wrapping each one in a new DTO instance and adding the DTO instance to dtoList.

15. Add the following line of code after the end of the `while` loop:

```
return dtoList;
```

16. Click Save All.
17. Rebuild the project.

What Just Happened? You created components to filter and aggregate data for an MVC application. First, you created a finder method to return rows from DEPARTMENTS matching a particular condition. Then, you created DTOs for the Departments and Employees entity beans to expose some of their fields, and maintained a wrapper for a single CMR field to allow access of detail employee DTO instances from master department DTO instances. Finally, you created a session bean and used it to implement the Session Façade design pattern by adding a field and implementing its getter method to return a collection of department DTOs.

IV. Create Data Control Definition Files

In this phase, you will create data control definition files to expose your Session Façade and Data Transfer Objects to the ADF model layer.

Generate Default Data Control Definition Files

You can generate a default data control metadata file, a data control implementation file, and a data control BeanInfo file for a session bean, as well as a data control description file for its package, using the following steps:

1. In the Application Navigator, select "Applications\HREJB\Model\Application Sources\hrejb.model\DeptEmpSessionFacade".
2. On DeptEmpSessionFacade, select "Create Data Control" from the right-click menu.

   Additional Information: JDeveloper creates the following files, which appear in the Application Navigator:

   - **DeptEmpSessionFacadeDataControl.xml**, the data control metadata file for DeptEmpSessionFacade
   - **DeptEmpSessionFacadeDataControl.java**, the data control implementation file for DeptEmpSessionFacade
   - **DeptEmpSessionFacadeDataControlBeanInfo.java**, the data control BeanInfo file for DeptEmpSessionFacadeDataControl.java
   - **DataControls.dcx**, the data control description file for the `hrejb.model` package

   Bean model definition files will be automatically created as you set bean classes.

Set Bean Classes for Collections

You can set bean classes for collections, allowing the ADF model layer to determine how to cast individual rows in collections, using the following steps:

1. In the Application Navigator, select DeptEmpSessionFacadeDataControl.xml.
2. In the Structure window, select seattleDepartments.
3. In the Property Inspector, select the *Bean Class* field and click the ellipsis button to open the Bean Class dialog.

4. Click Browse.
5. Navigate to hrejb\model\DepartmentsLocalDTO and click OK.

   Additional Information: `getSeattleDepartments()` returns a collection of `DepartmentsLocalDTO` instances. However, the return type of `getSeattleDepartments()` is simply `java.util.Collection`; the method returns no information about the type of object in the collection. Setting the bean class tells the ADF model layer that the collection contains `DepartmentsLocalDTO` instances so that it can create bindings appropriately.
6. Click OK to close the Bean Class dialog.

   Additional Information: In addition to setting the bean class for the Session Façade's `seattleDepartments` collection, this creates a bean model definition file for `DepartmentsLocalDTO`, DepartmentsLocalDTO.xml.
7. In the Application Navigator, select DepartmentsLocalDTO.xml.
8. In the Structure window, select employees_departmentIdDTO.

   Additional Information: This is the CMR field wrapper that contains the employees in each department.
9. Repeat steps 3–6 to set the bean class to `EmployeesLocalDTO`.

   Additional Information: In addition to setting the bean class for the collection of detail employees, this creates a bean model definition file for `EmployeesLocalDTO`, EmployeesLocalDTO.xml.
10. Click Save All.
11. Rebuild the project.

What Just Happened? You created data control definition files for your Session Façade and Data Transfer Objects, and set the bean classes for the two collections they contain. This will give the ADF model layer access to your business services' metadata.

V. Create a Master-Detail Form

In this phase, you create a very simple Struts application with a JSP page that displays a master-detail form, using your EJB beans and DTOs to provide business services.

Create a Data Page

You can create a Struts data page using the following steps:

1. In the Application Navigator, on the ViewController project, select "Open Struts Page Flow Diagram" from the right-click menu.
2. Drag a data page from the Component Palette onto the diagram.
3. Name the data page "masterDetailEJB".

Create and Add Controls to a JSP Page

You can create a JSP file corresponding to the Struts data page and add databound controls to it using the following steps:

1. Double click the masterDetailEJB data page to open the Select or Create Page dialog.
2. Click OK to create a JSP page and open it in the visual editor.
3. In the Data Control Palette, select DeptEmpSessionFacadeDataControl\seattleDepartments.
4. In the *Drag and Drop As* dropdown list, select "Read-Only Form".
5. Drag seattleDepartments onto the visual editor to create a read-only form and the needed bindings.
6. In the Data Control Palette, select DeptEmpSessionFacadeDataControl\seattleDepartments\Operations\First.
7. In the *Drag and Drop As* dropdown list, ensure that "Button" is selected.
8. Drag First onto the visual editor, after the table but still inside the form, to add a button to the form and an action binding to the binding container. Drop the button between the lower-right corner of the HTML table and the right side of the form outline.
9. Repeat steps 6–8 to add Previous, Next, and Last buttons.
10. In the Data Control Palette, select DeptEmpSessionFacadeDataControl\seattleDepartments\employees_departmentIdDTO.
11. In the *Drag and Drop As* dropdown list, ensure that "Read-Only Table" is selected.
12. Drag employees_departmentIdDTO onto the visual editor, to the right of the buttons but still inside the form, to add a detail table to the form.
13. In the Data Control Palette, select DeptEmpSessionFacadeDataControl\seattleDepartments\employees_departmentIdDTO\Operations\Previous Set.
14. In the *Drag and Drop As* dropdown list, ensure that "Button" is selected.
15. Drag Previous Set onto the visual editor, after the table but still inside the form. Drop the button between the lower-right corner of the HTML table and the right side of the form outline.
16. Repeat steps 13–15 to add a Next Set button.
17. Click Save All.
18. Rebuild the project.

Test the Application

The application now has a JSP view, Struts controller, and EJB business services layer. You can test it using the following steps:

1. Select the struts-config.xml tab to access the Struts page flow diagram.

2. On the masterDetailEJB data page, select Run from the right-click menu.
3. When masterDetailEJB.jsp opens, use the buttons to navigate through the master and detail collections.
4. Close the browser window.

What Just Happened? You created a simple master-detail form that uses the EJB beans, DTOs, and data controls you created in Phases I–IV, and ran the form to test the business services.

TopLink Technology

Oracle Application Server 10g TopLink is an Oracle technology for providing O/R mappings, persistence, queries, and transaction management for Java classes. JDeveloper includes support for creating and editing TopLink code. Unlike ADF Business Components, which provide a library of classes that your own components extend or use, or Enterprise JavaBeans technology, which provides a set of specifications that your components must implement, TopLink does not require you to use any specific sort of Java class to implement your object model. Instead, TopLink maps arbitrary Java classes to the database tables and provides functionality for creating instances of those classes based on database queries and saving instances of those classes as database rows.

TopLink technology can work in two ways: as a CMP provider for EJB entity beans, and as a mapping provider for Java classes. This chapter focuses on the latter use, called *TopLink Plain Old Java Objects (TopLink POJO).*

The primary reason to use TopLink POJO is if your organization has already created, or wants to create, its own framework of Java classes to serve as the object model. If you have your own systems or requirements for representing business objects, implementing business logic, and aggregating the data for clients, you may not be able to use ADF BC components or EJB beans. TopLink POJO allows you to create classes fulfilling your requirements and map them to database tables without directly coding JDBC.

It is important to note that TopLink POJO's flexibility is both an advantage and a disadvantage. TopLink POJO allows you to develop your own Java framework, but in order to create efficient and maintainable applications, it also requires you to develop such a framework. If you do not have your own framework and do not need to develop one, ADF BC technology (if you are willing to use Oracle's framework) or EJB technology (if you do not want to use any framework) are easier alternatives for creating efficient, maintainable, scalable applications.

Like ADF BC and EJB technology, TopLink POJO contains functionality both to help you represent your business domain and to create a data model for clients. This section discusses both features, and then turns briefly to the ADF model layer, to explain the ways in which its handling of POJO with TopLink mappings is unique.

Table 14-2 pairs some of the TopLink POJO concepts discussed throughout this section with the corresponding ADF BC concepts with which you may be more familiar.

TopLink POJO and the Business Domain

As explained previously, if you use TopLink POJO, it is your responsibility to implement Java classes that represent database objects. However, TopLink provides functionality to help you map Java classes to database objects, and to maintain relationships between Java classes.

As shown in Figure 14-4, a package of Java classes uses an XML file called a *TopLink deployment descriptor* to provide metadata about the ways in which its classes are mapped to

TopLink POJO	ADF BC	What It Does
Java class with TopLink descriptor	Entity object definition	Represent database objects that store data
Field with TopLink direct mapping	Entity attribute	Represent a database column
Field with TopLink relationship mapping	Association accessor attribute	Allow access from one instance of the Java class/entity object to related instances
TopLink Query	View object definition query	Access a particular set of rows and attributes
TopLink Session	Application module instance	Exposes queries, manages the cache, and handles transactions

TABLE 14-2. *TopLink POJO and ADF BC Concepts*

the database. Each mapped Java class corresponds to a *descriptor*, an element in the TopLink deployment descriptor that describes the mappings for that individual class. The TopLink runtime uses the deployment descriptor to create instances of your classes based on queries and save the classes as database rows. Mappings for particular attributes are sub-elements of the descriptor. They come in two forms: direct mappings and relationship mappings.

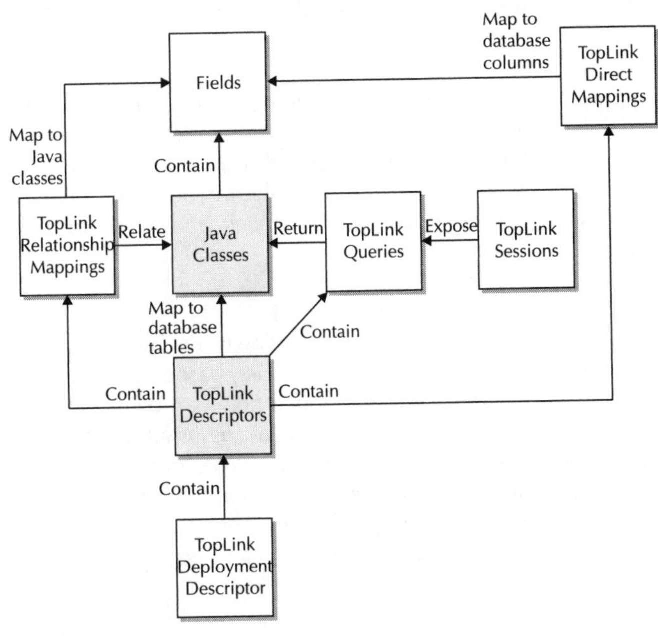

FIGURE 14-4. *TopLink POJO component relationships*

Direct Mappings

As shown in Figure 14-4, a TopLink *direct mapping* is a mapping between a field in a Java class and one or more database columns. TopLink provides a wide variety of direct mappings; a detailed discussion of all of them may be found in the TopLink documentation, available at otn.oracle.com/products/ias/toplink. In addition, this section provides a brief description of the most common mappings.

Direct-to-Field Mappings *Direct-to-field mappings* are the simplest type of direct mapping, which allow you to map a field onto a database column of corresponding type: a numerical type (either a primitive such as `int` or a class such as `java.lang.Integer`) onto a NUMBER, or a `String` onto a VARCHAR2, for example.

Object Type Mappings An *object type mapping* allows you to represent data differently in the Java object's field and in the database column. For example, you could store genders in the database as "M" and "F" and represent them within the Java object as "male" and "female", respectively.

Type Conversion Mappings *Type conversion mappings* allow you to perform more complex conversions between the Java type of the field and the SQL type of the database column. For example, you could use a type conversion mapping to map a `String` onto a NUMBER or DATE according to a format mask.

Serialized Object Mappings A *serialized object mapping* efficiently maps a large database type, such as a LOB or multimedia type, onto a field of a Java type that implements the `Serializable` interface. Rather than being stored in memory, the field value will be stored in the file system.

Transformation Mappings A *transformation mapping* is a mapping between fields in the class and columns in the database table with which the class is associated that is not one-to-one. For example, it could map two database columns, LAST_NAME and FIRST_NAME, into one field, `name`. Methods must handle the transformation, in both directions: *attribute transformation methods* derive the fields from the database column values, and *field transformation methods* derive database column values from the fields.

Relationship Mappings

As shown in Figure 14-4, a TopLink *relationship mapping* is a mapping between a field in one Java class and one or more instances of another Java class, based on one or more foreign key relationships in the database. The relationship-mapped field can be used to retrieve instances of the related Java object, just as, in ADF BC, association accessor attributes can be used to retrieve associated entity object instances. Just as there are many types of direct mappings, there are many types of relationship mappings; a complete discussion may be found in the TopLink documentation, available at otn.oracle.com/products/ias/toplink. In addition, this section provides a brief discussion of the three most common mappings.

One-to-One Mappings A *one-to-one mapping* represents a one-to-one relationship based on a foreign key. Fields mapped using one-to-one mappings return a single instance of the related Java class.

One-to-Many Mappings A *one-to-many mapping* represents a one-to-many relationship based on a foreign key. Fields mapped using one-to-many mappings return collections of instances of the related Java class.

Many-to-Many Mappings A *many-to-many mapping* represents a many-to-many relationship, based on two foreign keys and an intersection table (just as ADF BC many-to-many associations are based on two one-to-many relationships and an intersection table). Fields mapped using many-to-many mappings, like those mapped using one-to-many mappings, return collections of instances of the related Java class.

TopLink POJO and the Data Model

Like ADF BC and EJB applications, TopLink applications must also collect data and present it to the view and controller layers through the model layer. If you use TopLink, as with the business domain, it is your responsibility as a developer to create a framework for aggregating and presenting data to the ADF model layer. However, TopLink provides two tools to make this task considerably easier: TopLink queries and TopLink sessions. In fact, for simple applications, queries and sessions allow you to reuse your business domain components as data model components, without creating specialized components to aggregate and present the data at all.

TopLink Queries

As shown in Figure 14-4, a *TopLink query* is a sub-element of a descriptor that specifies a query the TopLink runtime can use to create instances of the descriptor's Java class. TopLink provides considerable flexibility in the way you can specify these queries: You can use SQL, EJB QL, or specialized TopLink expressions. TopLink expression language is explained in the TopLink documentation, available at otn.oracle.com/products/ias/toplink.

To understand TopLink queries, consider a Java class, `Departments`, that contains fields with direct mappings to each column in the DEPARTMENTS table. You could define a TopLink query, departmentsQuery, with the following SQL:

```
SELECT DEPARTMENT_ID, DEPARTMENT_NAME
FROM DEPARTMENTS
WHERE LOCATION_ID=1700
```

When the TopLink runtime executes departmentsQuery, it will create one instance of `Departments` for every row returned, and populate the fields mapped to DEPARTMENT_ID and DEPARTMENT_NAME, leaving the rest of the fields unpopulated. It will cache those rows and create a collection containing them. If the runtime executes another query in `Departments`' descriptor later, it can reuse instances of `Departments` already stored in the cache, populating additional fields if the second query returns additional columns.

TopLink will automatically create one query for each mapped Java class which acts as a SELECT * query. The query has the same name as the Java class, with a "readAll" prefix: For example, the default query for Departments is called "readAllDepartments".

TopLink Sessions

A *TopLink session* is a Java object, created by the TopLink runtime, that exposes TopLink queries, manages the cache, and handles database transactions. You can use JDeveloper to create metadata files that help you customize sessions, but for most applications, you do not need to do so; the TopLink runtime will automatically create a session that uses the TopLink deployment descriptor to expose queries and connect to the database, and provides transaction management and caching adequate to the vast majority of purposes.

TopLink Technology and the ADF Model Layer

As mentioned earlier in this chapter, the ADF model layer provides a largely consistent way to develop databound applications against any business services technology. However, there are a few ways in which the ADF model layer handles TopLink POJO business services uniquely.

Candidates for Data Controls

Unlike ADF BC or EJB technology, where only specific components (application modules and session beans, respectively) can be wrapped with data controls, any class in a TopLink project can be wrapped with a data control. If you have implemented separate data model components, you can expose them as data controls, and collection fields will be exposed as collections (much the same way view object instances or Session Façade DTO collection fields are exposed).

However, you can also create data controls to directly wrap business domain components. If you do so, each SQL query will be available as a method that returns a collection. For example, to create a read-only table for the query findManagers, you would select its return value in the Data Control Palette, as shown here:

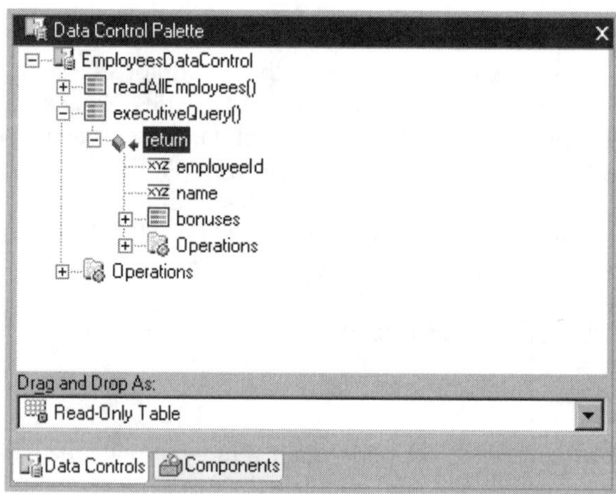

Data Control Definition Files

As with EJB applications, you must create data control definition files for TopLink applications. However, there are fewer files created for TopLink applications than for EJB applications. Two sorts of metadata files are required to create data controls for TopLink applications, as follows:

- **Bean model definition files** *Bean model definition files* describe the fields and mappings for a class. There is one bean model definition file for each class in the project.

- **Data control description files** *The data control description file* lists the bean model definition files for some of the classes in the project; these are the classes exposed as data controls. The binding container uses this file to find particular bean model definition files when it needs to create data controls. There is one data control description file for each package.

Unlike EJB applications, TopLink applications do not require any specialized Java files to create data controls. If you generate data controls directly for TopLink persistent business objects, you will also not need to specify bean classes.

Operations

The ADF model layer provides the same operations for TopLink technology that it does for ADF BC:

- For collections:
  - Next
  - Previous
  - First
  - Last
  - Next Set
  - Previous Set
  - setCurrentRowWithKey()
  - setCurrentRowWithKeyValues()
  - Create
  - Delete
- For data controls:
  - Commit
  - Rollback

If you create separate data model components, you will need to provide service methods to perform Create, Delete, Commit, and Rollback operations, just as you do for EJB technology.

Collections

When the ADF model layer exposes TopLink components, it distinguishes between relationship-mapped fields that return collections and those that return single class instances, just as it distinguishes between "many" and "one" sides of EJB relationships.

Hands-on Practice: Build a Simple TopLink Application

In this practice, you will create Java classes to represent departments and employees. Then, you will use TopLink POJO to map these Java objects to database tables. In addition to direct-to-field mappings, you will use a transformation mapping. Next, you will use a relationship mapping to implement a relationship between the classes, and create a TopLink query for one of the classes.

Finally, you will create data control definition files and a JSP and Struts application to display a master-detail form.

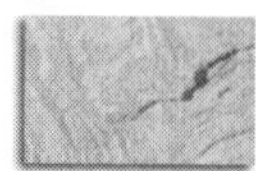

NOTE
Instead of creating a complete object framework, the practice uses two simple Java classes as business domain components, and rather than creating separate data model components, the practice exposes one of the business domain classes directly to the model layer. This is fine for simple applications, but in an enterprise application environment, we strongly recommend using TopLink POJO with an object framework. For more information on framework design, see the resources listed in Appendix A.

This practice guides you through the following phases:

I. Create an application workspace

II. Create Java classes

III. Create descriptors and direct mappings

- Create descriptors
- Create direct-to-field mappings and generate a TopLink deployment descriptor
- Create a transformation mapping

IV. Create a relationship mapping

V. Create a TopLink query

VI. Create data control definition files

VII. Create a master-detail form

- Test the application

I. Create an Application Workspace

In this phase, you create an application workspace with the proper technology scope for a TopLink POJO application.

1. On the Applications node in the Application Navigator, select New Application Workspace from the right-click menu.
2. Enter the following values in the Create Application Workspace dialog:
   Application Name as "HRTopLink"

Application Package Prefix as "hrtoplink"
Application Template as "Web Application [Default]"

Additional Information: There is no predefined template for TopLink applications. The default application template, as you learned in Chapter 8, configures the application to use ADF BC as its business services technology. You will reconfigure the application to use TopLink technology in steps 4–8.

3. Click OK. A new application workspace, HRTopLink, appears in the navigator, containing a Model project and a ViewController project.
4. On the Model node in the navigator, select Project Properties from the right-click menu.
5. Select "Common\Technology Scope".

   Additional Information: This node allows you to specify the technologies that should be available in the project.
6. Remove "ADF Business Components" from the *Selected Technologies* list.
7. Move "TopLink" from the *Available Technologies* list to the *Selected Technologies* list.

   Additional Information: JDeveloper adds the "Database" technology to the Selected Technologies list as well, as shown here:

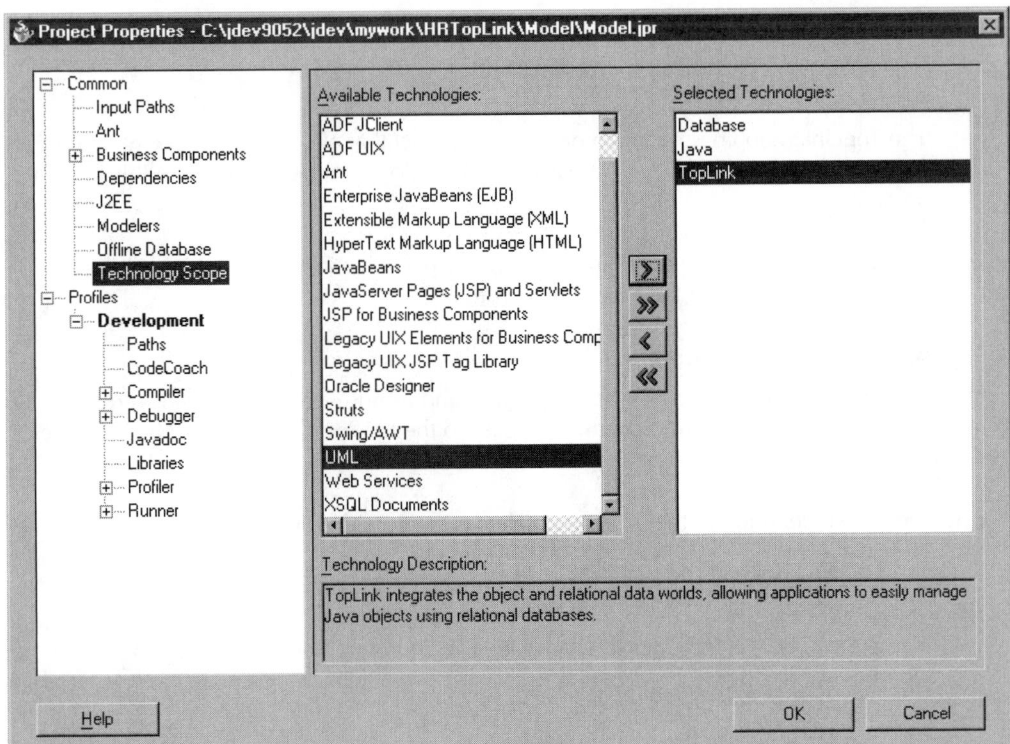

This is because JDeveloper's TopLink development tools, unlike its ADF BC or EJB development tools, work against offline database tables, which are part of the "Database" technology. *Offline tables* are copies, stored in JDeveloper, of database tables' metadata.

8. Click OK.

Additional Information: JDeveloper adds a TopLink package, containing a TopLink Mappings node, to the Model project, as shown next:

The TopLink Mappings node is a design-time object that allows you to specify descriptors for your objects; you can generate a TopLink deployment descriptor from this node at any time.

What Just Happened? You created an application workspace for your TopLink application and set the technology scope of the Model project to use TopLink.

II. Create Java Classes

In this phase, you will create two classes, Employees and Bonuses, to act as business domain components. In Phase III, you will map these classes to the EMPLOYEES and BONUSES tables, respectively.

1. On the Model node in the navigator, select New from the right-click menu to open the New Gallery.
2. Select General\Java Class. Click OK.
3. Name the class "Departments". Click OK. The Source Editor opens.
4. Click the Class tab to open the Class Editor.

5. Select the Fields tab.
6. Click Add to create a field.
7. Enter the following values:
   Field Name as "departmentId"
   Field Type as "int"
8. Click OK.
9. Repeat steps 6–8 to create the following fields:
   - `departmentName`, a `java.lang.String`
   - `employees`, a `java.util.Collection` (Use the browse button to find the java\util\Collection node in the Class Browser.)

   Additional Information: The class editor should appear as shown here:

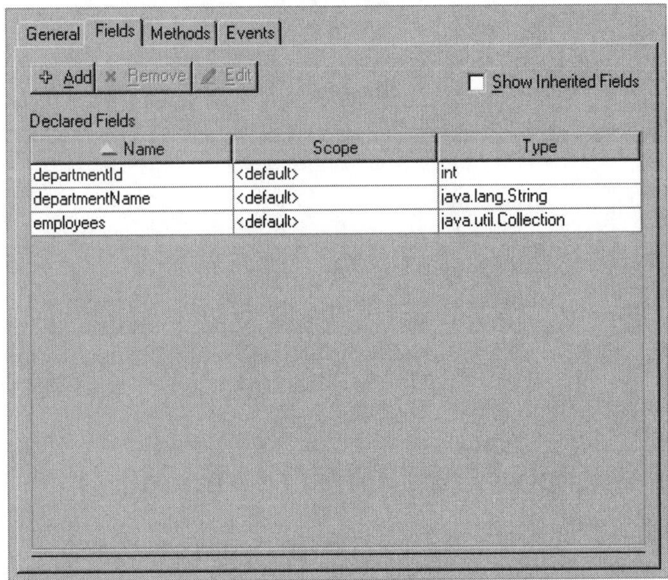

10. Create another class, named "Employees".
11. Using the Class Editor, add the following fields to `Employees`:
    - `employeeId`, an `int`
    - `name`, a `java.lang.String`
    - `departmentId`, an `int`

Additional Information: The class editor should appear as shown here:

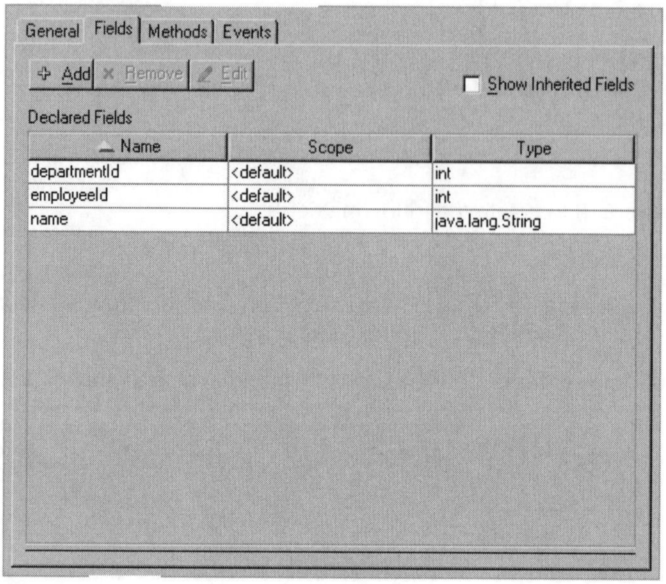

12. Click Save All.
13. Rebuild the project.

What Just Happened? You created two Java classes, `Departments` and `Employees`, which will act as your business domain components. As you will see in the next section, these Java objects are not isomorphic to the DEPARTMENTS and EMPLOYEES tables, but you can create mappings between the objects and those tables.

III. Create Descriptors and Direct Mappings

In this phase, you will create descriptors for your Java classes, and direct mappings between their fields and columns in the database tables DEPARTMENTS and EMPLOYEES.

Create Descriptors

In this section, you will create offline tables for DEPARTMENTS and EMPLOYEES, and use them to create TopLink descriptors for the `Departments` and `Employees` classes you created in Phase II.

1. In the Application Navigator, select "Applications\HRTopLink\Model\Application Sources\TopLink\TopLink Mappings".
2. In the Structure window, on the TopLink Mappings node, select "Add or Remove Descriptors" from the right-click menu. The TopLink Descriptors dialog will appear.
3. Expand the hrtoplink.model node and click the double right arrow (>>) to add both Java classes to the *Selected Classes* list.

4. Click OK. The TopLink Mappings editor opens in the editor window.
5. In the *Deployment Connection* dropdown, select "HR".
6. In the Structure window, select "TopLink Mappings\hrtoplink.model\Departments".

   Additional Information: The TopLink Mappings editor changes to allow you to edit high-level information in the Departments descriptor.
7. In the *Associated Table* dropdown, select "Import Database Objects" to open the Import Offline Database Objects Wizard.

   Additional Information: Because the TopLink design time utilities work with offline database tables, you will have to create offline versions of the DEPARTMENTS and EMPLOYEES tables.
8. If the Welcome page appears, click Next.
9. On the Select Target Schema page, enter "HR". Click Next.
10. On the Select Source Connection pages, ensure that "HR" is selected and click Next.
11. On the Select Objects page, shuttle "DEPARTMENTS" and "EMPLOYEES" from the *Available* list to the *Selected* list.
12. Click Finish to create the offline tables.

    Additional Information: The tables will now appear in the *Associated Table* dropdown.
13. Ensure that "TopLink Mappings\hrtoplink.model\Departments" is selected in the Structure window. Select "HR.DEPARTMENTS" from the *Associated Table* dropdown.
14. In the Structure window, select "TopLink Mappings\hrtoplink.model\Employees".
15. In the TopLink Mappings editor, select "HR.EMPLOYEES" from the *Associated Table* dropdown.
16. Click Save All.

Create Direct-to-Field Mappings and Generate a TopLink Deployment Descriptor

You can create direct-to-field mappings between fields and database columns, and generate a TopLink Deployment Descriptor to contain mapping information for the package, using the following steps:

1. In the Structure window, on the "TopLink Mappings\hrtoplink.model\Departments\departmentId" node, select Map As | Direct to Field from the right-click menu.

   Additional Information: The TopLink Mappings editor changes to allow you to specify a direct-to-field mapping.
2. In the TopLink Mappings editor, select "DEPARTMENT_ID" from the *Database Field* dropdown.
3. Similarly, create a direct-to-field mapping between `departmentName` and the database column "DEPARTMENT_NAME".

Additional Information: You will create a one-to-many relationship mapping for the remaining field, `employees`, in Phase IV.

4. In the Structure window, expand "TopLink Mappings\hrtoplink.model\Employees".
5. Similarly, create direct-to-field mappings between the following fields of `Employees` and columns of EMPLOYEES:
   - `employeeId` and EMPLOYEE_ID
   - `departmentId` and DEPARTMENT_ID

   Additional Information: You will create a transformation mapping for the remaining field, `name`, later in this phase.
6. In the Application Navigator, on the TopLink Mappings node, select "Generate toplink-deployment-descriptor.xml" from the right-click menu.
7. When the Generate TopLink Deployment Descriptor dialog shows you the status, verify that there are no errors and that the descriptors have been generated. Click OK in the Generate TopLink Deployment Descriptor dialog.

Create a Transformation Mapping

This section creates a transformation mapping between a single field and multiple database columns using the following steps:

1. In the Application Navigator, double-click Employees.java to open it in the editor. If the Code Editor is not displayed, click the Source tab to open it.
2. Add the following method skeleton at the bottom of the Java class:

```
public String calculateName(DatabaseRow row)
{
}
```

3. Press ALT-ENTER to import `oracle.toplink.publicinterface.DatabaseRow`.

   Additional Information: TopLink uses this class to wrap database rows.
4. Add the following code to the body of the method:

```
String firstName = (String) row.get("FIRST_NAME");
String lastName = (String) row.get("LAST_NAME");
return firstName + " " + lastName;
```

   Additional Information: This attribute transformation method will calculate a value for the `name` field, based on the values of the FIRST_NAME and LAST_NAME table columns. The `DatabaseRow.get()` method returns values from the database row. The attribute transformation method concatenates them, using a space as a separator.
5. Add the following method at the bottom of the class:

```
public String nameToFirstName()
{
```

```
  int spacePosition = getName().indexOf(' ');
  return getName().substring(0, spacePosition);
}
```

Additional Information: This field transformation method calculates a value for FIRST_NAME based on the value of the `name` field: the value of FIRST_NAME is the substring of the `name` field ending before the space.

6. Add the following method at the bottom of the class:

```
public String nameToLastName()
{
  int spacePosition = getName().indexOf(' ');
  return getName().substring(spacePosition + 1);
}
```

Additional Information: You will use this field transformation method to calculate a value for LAST_NAME: the substring of `name` field starting after the space.

7. Click Save All.
8. Rebuild the project.
9. In the Application Navigator, select "TopLink Mappings".
10. In the Structure window, on the "TopLink Mappings\hrtoplink.model\Employees\name" node, select Map As | Transformation from the right-click menu.

    Select the TopLink Mappings tab to reopen the TopLink Mappings editor.
11. In the *Database Row -> Object Method* dropdown, select "calculateName(oracle.toplink.publicinterface.DatabaseRow)".

    Additional Information: This field allows you to specify the attribute transformation method that calculates the field value from the database columns.
12. Click the Add button to add a row to the *Object -> Field Methods* table.

    Additional Information: This table allows you to specify field transformation methods that calculate database column values from the field.
13. Select the following values from the pulldowns:
    Database Field as "FIRST_NAME"
    Method as "nameToFirstName()"
14. Click the Add button again to add another row.
15. Select the following values from the pulldowns:
    Database Field as "LAST_NAME"
    Method as "nameToLastName()"

Additional Information: The editor should resemble the following:

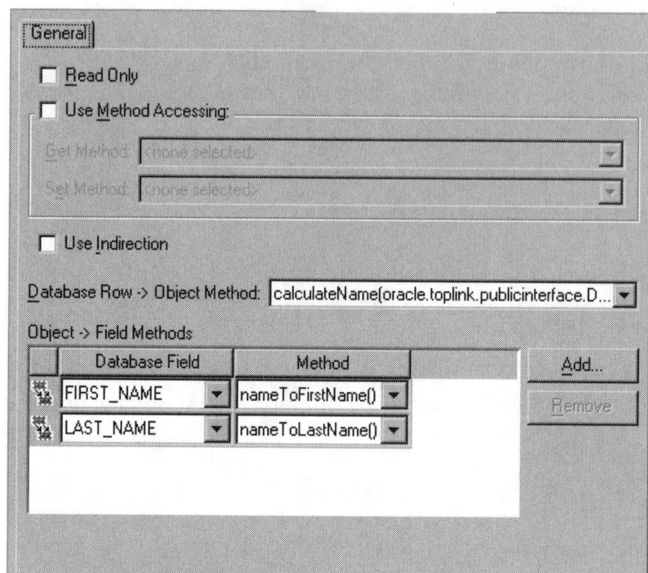

16. In the Application Navigator, on the TopLink Mappings node, select "Generate toplink-deployment-deiscriptor.xml" from the right-click menu.
17. When the Generate TopLink descriptor dialog asks you whether to overwrite the existing deployment descriptor, click Yes.
18. Click OK.

What Just Happened? You mapped all but one of your Java object fields to database columns using direct mappings. You used direct-to-field mappings to map most of those fields to corresponding single database columns, and used a transformation mapping to map the `name` field of `Employees` to two database columns. You will map the last field, `Departments.employees`, using a relationship mapping in the following phase.

IV. Create a Relationship Mapping

In this phase, you will create a relationship mapping between the `Departments.employees` field and the `Employees` class, based on a foreign key relationship between DEPARTMENTS and EMPLOYEES.

1. In the Structure window, on the "TopLink Mappings\hrtoplink.model\Departments\employees" node, select Map As | One-to-Many from the right-click menu.

   Additional Information: The TopLink Mappings editor changes to allow you to specify a one-to-many relationship mapping.

2. In the *Reference Descriptor* dropdown, select "Employees (hrtoplink.model)".

Additional Information: This indicates that the field is a collection of instances of `Employees`.

3. Select the Table Reference tab.
4. In the *Table Reference* dropdown, select "EMP_DEPT_FK".

   Additional Information: This tells the TopLink runtime to base the relationship on the EMP_DEPT_FK foreign key constraint. Each instance of `Departments` corresponds to a row of DEPARTMENTS. Its `employees` field will be populated with a collection of `Employees` instances corresponding to the detail rows from EMPLOYEES.

5. In the Application Navigator, on the TopLink Mappings node, select "Generate toplink-deployment-descriptor.xml" from the right-click menu.
6. When the Generate TopLink Deployment Descriptor dialog asks if you want to overwrite the existing deployment descriptor, click Yes.
7. Click OK.

What Just Happened? You created a relationship mapping to allow you to access department's employees through the `Departments.employees` field. This will allow you to maintain a master-detail relationship between `Departments` and `Employees`.

V. Create a TopLink Query

In this phase, you will create a TopLink query to create and populate instances of `Departments`.

1. Select "TopLink Mappings" in the Application Navigator. In the Structure window, select "TopLink Mappings\hrtoplink.model\Departments".
2. In the TopLink Mappings editor, select the Queries tab, as shown here:

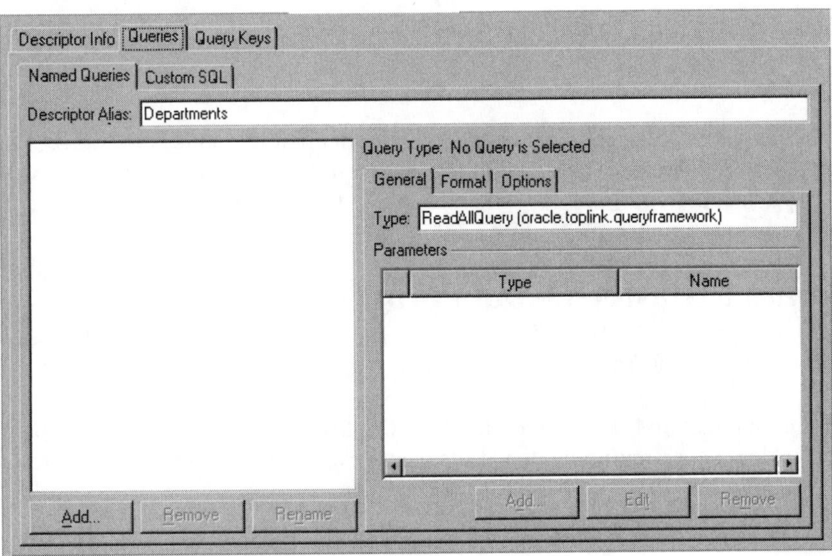

3. Click Add to open the Add dialog.
4. Name the query "seattleQuery" and click OK.
5. Select the Format tab.
6. Select the *SQL* radio button.
7. Enter the following query in the *Query String* text area:

```
SELECT DEPARTMENT_ID,
  DEPARTMENT_NAME
FROM DEPARTMENTS
WHERE LOCATION_ID = 1700
```

   Additional Information: Location ID 1700 corresponds to Seattle, so this query returns all departments in Seattle.

8. Generate the TopLink deployment descriptor. Click Yes to overwrite the existing deployment descriptor, then click OK.

What Just Happened? You created a TopLink query to return a selected set of departments and create the appropriate `Departments` instances. You will use the results of this query as a master collection; the detail collection will be accessed through the relationship mapping created in Phase IV.

VI. Create Data Control Definition Files

In this phase, you will create data control definition files to allow the ADF model to create a data control that wraps the `Departments` class.

1. In the Application Navigator, select "Applications\HRTopLink\Model\Application Sources\hrtoplink.model\Departments.java".
2. Select "Create Data Control" from the right-click menu.
3. Click Save All.

What Just Happened? JDeveloper created bean model definition files for `Departments` and `Employees`, and a data control definition file that indicated that `Departments` should be exposed in a data control. The bean model definition for `Employees` was generated because of the relationship mapping from `Departments`.

VII. Create a Master-Detail Form

In this phase, you create a Struts application with a JSP page that displays a master-detail form, using your Java classes and TopLink deployment descriptor to provide business services.

1. In the Application Navigator, on the ViewController project node, select Open Struts Page Flow Diagram to open the Struts page flow diagram for the ViewController project.
2. Drag a data page from the Component Palette onto the diagram.

3. Name the data page "masterDetailTopLink".
4. Double click the masterDetailTopLink data page to open the Select or Create Page dialog.
5. Click OK to create a JSP page and open it in the visual editor.
6. In the Data Control Palette, select DepartmentsDataControl\seattleQuery()\return.

   Additional Information: seattleQuery is the TopLink query you created in Phase V. Its return value is the collection of `Departments` instances corresponding to Location ID 1700.
7. In the *Drag and Drop As* dropdown list, select "Read-Only Form".
8. Drag the return value onto the visual editor to create a read-only form and the needed bindings.
9. In the Data Control Palette, select DepartmentsDataControl\seattleQuery()\return\Operations\First.
10. In the *Drag and Drop As* dropdown list, ensure that "Button" is selected.
11. Drag First onto the visual editor, after the table but still inside the form, to add a button to the form and an action binding to the binding container.
12. Add Previous, Next, and Last buttons to the right of the First button.
13. In the Data Control Palette, select DepartmentsDataControl\seattleQuery()\return\employees.
14. In the *Drag and Drop As* dropdown list, ensure that "Read-Only Table" is selected.
15. Drag employees onto the visual designer, after the buttons but still inside the form, to add a detail table to the form.
16. In the Data Control Palette, select DepartmentsDataControl\seattleQuery()\return\employees\Operations\Previous Set.
17. In the *Drag and Drop As* dropdown list, ensure that "Button" is selected.
18. Drag Previous Set onto the visual designer, after the table but still inside the form.
19. Add a Next Set button.
20. Click Save All.
21. Rebuild the project.

Test the Application

You can test this application with a JSP view, Struts controller, and TopLink POJO business services using the following steps:

1. Reopen the Struts page flow diagram.
2. On the masterDetailTopLink data action, select Run from the right-click menu.

3. When masterDetailTopLink.jsp opens, use the buttons to navigate through the master and detail collections.

   Additional Information: The page should resemble the following:

departmentId	10
departmentName	Administration

First | Previous | Next | Last

	departmentId	employeeId	name
*	10	200	Jennifer Whalen

PreviousSet | NextSet

4. Close the browser window.

What Just Happened? You created a simple master-detail form that uses the Java classes, TopLink mappings, and data controls you created in Phases I–VI, and ran the form to test the business services.

Web Services

Web services is a term used to describe applications that make APIs available over any of a number of HTTP-based protocols. One developer or organization can create a web service and publish it on the Internet; anyone with access to the URL can invoke methods on the web service.

JDeveloper contains a number of tools to help you create web services from ADF Business Components, EJBs, Java classes, or even stored procedures in a database. You can find an article on using JDeveloper to develop and deploy web services at otn.oracle.com/products/jdev/collateral/papers/10g/jdev10g_ws.pdf.

This section will focus on the other side of web services, that is, creating ADF applications that use existing, published web services as their business services. Unlike other business services technologies, where developing and using the business services are two parts of the same development process, developing a web service and developing an application that uses a web service are completely separate processes, usually undertaken by separate organizations.

WSDL, SOAP, and Web Service Stubs

Most web services are published as an XML document using a format called *Web Services Definition Language (WSDL).* A WSDL document contains metadata describing the operations and values the web service makes available. For example, if a WSDL document is publishing a Java class as a web service, it will describe the methods (including their parameters and return types) and fields that the developer has chosen to expose.

An application can parse a WSDL document and use its information to invoke the web service's operations and access its values using the *Simple Object Access Protocol (SOAP),* a lightweight protocol based on HTTP. If you use JDeveloper to build applications that access web services, you do not need to be able to parse WSDL or use SOAP. Instead, you can use JDeveloper to create a web service stub based on the WSDL document. A *web service* stub is a class that provides Java methods and fields to wrap some or all operations and values published by the web service; JDeveloper automatically generates code into the stub that generates the SOAP requests and parses the service's responses.

Sometimes a web service's values or operations will be of a complex type. When they are, JDeveloper will also automatically generate auxiliary Java classes to represent those types.

After you create a web service stub, it will often be useful for you to create an extra class to wrap the stub and expose exactly the API you want.

Web Services and the ADF Model Layer

The ADF model layer, described in detail in Chapter 12, provides a largely consistent way to develop databound applications against any business services technology. However, web services technology is a slightly special case. Projects based around web service stubs generally do not have specialized components (like application module definitions or Session Façades) designed to aggregate data; nor do they have specialized services (like TopLink queries or sessions) that perform tasks above and beyond the generated Java. They are, from the perspective of the ADF model layer, simply a collection of classes.

As with TopLink projects, you can create data controls for any of these classes. Most commonly, you will create data controls either for the stub itself or for a wrapper class you create to use the stub. The data control will expose the fields and methods on the class as-is. Collection fields will be exposed as collections; fields containing single Java objects (with fields of their own) will be exposed as single rows; methods will be exposed as operations (possibly themselves returning collections or rows).

As with the other technologies described in this chapter, you must create data control definition files for applications that use web services. The files created are the same as those for TopLink applications, that is, bean model definition files that describe all classes in the project, and data control description files that indicate which classes are exposed as data controls.

Hands-on Practice: Create an Application That Uses a Web Service

In this practice, you will create an application that uses the *Google Web APIs*, a web service published by Google to provide access to their search engine. This web application will accept a search string and allow you to browse through the first ten Google web search results.

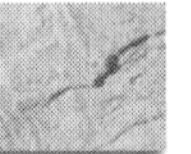

CAUTION
The use of the Google Web APIs in this practice is for educational purposes only. If you are planning on using the Google Web APIs in your own applications, please read Google's terms of service at www.google.com/apis/api_terms.html.

This practice guides you through the following phases:

I. Register to use the Google Web APIs

II. Create an application workspace

III. Create a web service stub

IV. Create a wrapper class for the stub

V. Create data control definition files

VI. Create a search application

- Create a data page and JSP page to submit a search string
- Create a data action to execute the search
- Create a data page and JSP page to display search results
- Test the application

I. Register to Use the Google Web APIs

Before you can develop against the Google Web APIs, you have to create a developer's account with Google and obtain a license key. You will need to pass the license key to the web service whenever you access it.

1. In a web browser, navigate to www.google.com/apis/.
2. Click the link in the section "Create a Google Account".
3. Follow the instructions on the page that appears.
4. In a web browser, navigate to www.google.com/apis/download.html and download the Google Web APIs Developer's kit.

   Additional Information: Among other files, this contains the WSDL document that defines the Google Web APIs.
5. Unzip the file into your JDEV_HOME/jdev/mywork directory.
6. When the verification email from Google arrives, click the enclosed link and log in to your account. Google will send you a second email, containing your license key.
7. When the second email from Google arrives, note your license key. You will use it in Phase IV.

What Just Happened? You created an account with Google that will allow you to use the Google Web APIs. Again, be careful to read Google's terms of service.

II. Create an Application Workspace

In this phase, you create an application workspace with the proper technology scope for a web application that uses a web service.

1. On the Applications node in the Application Navigator, select New Application Workspace from the right-click menu. The Create Application Workspace dialog opens.

2. Enter the following values:
   Application Name as "GoogleWSApp"
   Application Package Prefix as "googlewsapp"
   Application Template as "Web Application [Default]"

   Additional Information: There is no predefined template for applications that use web services. As mentioned in Chapter 8, the default application template configures the application to use ADF BC as its business services technology. You will reconfigure the application to use web services technology in steps 4–8.

3. Click OK. A new application, GoogleWSApp, appears in the navigator, containing a Model project and a ViewController project.
4. On the Model node in the navigator, select Project Properties from the right-click menu.
5. When the Project Properties dialog opens, select "Common\Technology Scope".
6. Remove "ADF Business Components" from the *Selected Technologies* list.
7. Move "Web Services" from the *Available Technologies* list to the *Selected Technologies* list.
8. Click OK.
9. Click Save All.

What Just Happened? You created an application workspace for your application and set the technology scope of the Model project to use web services.

III. Create a Web Service Stub

In this phase, you create a web service stub for the Google Web APIs.

1. On the Model node in the navigator, select New from the right-click menu to open the New Gallery.
2. Select the "Business Tier\Web Services" category and the "Web Service Stub/Skeleton" item. Click OK to open the Generate Web Service Stub/Skeleton Wizard.
3. If the Welcome page appears, review the information and click Next.
4. On the Select Web Service Description page, click Browse, and browse to JDEV_HOME\jdev\mywork\googleapi\GoogleSearch.wsdl. Click Open.

   Additional Information: This is the Google Web APIs' WSDL document. If you open this document in an XML-enabled browser, you can view the WSDL metadata.

5. Click Next.
6. On the Select Stubs/Skeletons to Generate page, uncheck the *doSpellingSuggestion()* and *doGetCachedPage()* checkboxes. Be sure to leave the other checkboxes checked.

   Additional Information: These methods allow you to retrieve Google's spelling suggestions for potentially misspelled search strings, and web pages stored in Google's cache, respectively. Your application will only use the remaining method, `doGoogleSearch()`, which executes a Google search. Removing the other methods will make your code simpler and more maintainable.

7. Click Finish to generate the web service stub and auxiliary classes.

What Just Happened? You generated a web service stub for the Google Web APIs and the auxiliary classes it requires. JDeveloper automatically created the following classes, visible in the Application Navigator:

- **GoogleSearchServiceStub.java**, the web service stub.
- **GoogleSearchResult.java**, the return type of `GoogleSearchServiceStub.doGoogleSearch()`, which contains the results of the search.
- **ResultElement.java**, an object representing a single web page found in the search.
- **DirectoryCategory.java**, a representation of a page's category in the Open Directory Project. This practice will not use DirectoryCategory.java; for more information on the Open Directory Project, see the project website at dmoz.org.

IV. Create a Wrapper Class for the Stub

In this phase, you create a wrapper class with a method to wrap `GoogleSearchServiceStub.doGoogleSearch()`. The parameters passed to `doGoogleSearch()` are quite complex and include your license key; this wrapper will have a simple API that only requires a search string.

1. On the googlewsapp.model node in the navigator, select New from the right-click menu to open the New Gallery.
2. Select the General category.
3. Select Java Class and click OK to open the Create Java Class dialog.
4. Name the class `Search` and click OK to create the class and open it in the code editor.
5. Add the following field declaration to the class:

   ```
   private final GoogleSearchServiceStub stub;
   ```

6. Add the following line to the `Search()` constructor body:

   ```
   stub = new GoogleSearchServiceStub();
   ```

   Additional Information: This creates an instance of the web service stub for this class to wrap.

7. Add the following method to the class. Replace XXXX with your license key.

   ```
   public GoogleSearchResult doSearch(String searchString)
     throws Exception
   {
     return stub.doGoogleSearch(
       "XXXX",              // license key
   ```

```
            searchString,         // search string
            new Integer(0),       // start at
            new Integer(10),      // results returned
            new Boolean(true),    // filter results
            "",
            new Boolean(true),    // SafeSearch
            "",
            "",
            ""
        );
    }
```

Additional Information: The `doGoogleSearch()` method accepts ten parameters. Most of these parameters are not used by this application, but six are. The following table identifies the parameters your application will use by the corresponding comments in the preceding code:

Comment	Description
license key	Your Google Web APIs license key.
search string	The search string to use in the search.
start at	Where to start returning results. A value of "0" returns the first and following results; a value of "10" returns the eleventh and following results.
results returned	How many results to return. Note that the Google Web APIs do not allow you to return more than ten results at a time.
filter results	A value of "true" tells the Google search engine to filter out results it considers similar to those already returned.
SafeSearch	A value of "true" turns on Google's SafeSearch content filter.

8. Click Save All.
9. Rebuild the Model project.

What Just Happened? You created a Java class to wrap the web service stub, and added a method to the class. This method accepts a single parameter, the search string, and passes it with several fixed values to the `doGoogleSearch()` method. When you design your web application, you will not need to pass these fixed values to execute a search.

V. Create Data Control Definition Files

In this phase, you create data control definition files to allow the ADF model to create a data control that wraps the `Search` class.

1. In the Application Navigator, select "Applications\GoogleWSApp\Model\Application Sources\googlewsapp.model\Search.java".

2. Select "Create Data Control" from the right-click menu.
3. Click Save All.

What Just Happened? JDeveloper created a data control definition file (DataControls.dcx) that indicates that `Search` should be exposed in a data control. It also created a bean model definition for Search.java, and recursively created bean model definitions for all classes Search.java depends on (which are, in fact, all classes in the project).

VI. Create a Search Application

In this phase, you create a Struts application with two JSP pages: The first accepts a search string, and the second uses that string and the Google Web APIs to display search results.

Create a Data Page and JSP Page to Submit a Search String

This section creates a Struts data page and JSP page to accept a method parameter, the `String` to be passed to `Search.doSearch()`.

1. In the Application Navigator, on the ViewController project, select Open Struts Page Flow Diagram to open the Struts page flow diagram.
2. Drag a data page from the Component Palette onto the diagram.
3. Name the data page "search".
4. Double click the search data page to open the Select or Create Page dialog.
5. Click OK to create a JSP page named search.jsp and open it in the visual editor.
6. Type "Enter search string: " on the page.
7. On the HTML page of the Component Palette, click the Text Field icon and drag it onto the diagram.
8. When the Add Form Element Confirmation dialog appears, click Yes to add a form and text field.
9. In the Property Inspector for the text field, enter the following values:
   name as "searchString"
   size as "30"
10. On the Component Palette, click the Submit Button icon to add a submit button to the form. (This cursor should be to the right of the searchString text field, within the form.)
11. In the Property Inspector, enter "event_Submit" in the *name* field.
12. Inside the form, select Form | Select Form Tag from the right-click menu.
13. In the Property Inspector, select "search.do" from the *action* dropdown.
14. Click Save All.
15. Rebuild the ViewController project.

Create a Data Action to Execute the Search

You can create a data action to invoke a custom method using the following steps:

1. Reopen the Page Flow Diagram.
2. In the Component Palette, select the Data Action icon.
3. Click the diagram to add a data action to your controller.
4. Enter "executeSearch" as the name of the data action.
5. On the Component Palette, click the forward icon and draw a forward from the search data page and to the executeSearch data action.
6. Name the forward "Submit", as shown here:

7. In the Data Control Palette, select SearchDataControl\Operations\doSearch(String).
8. Drag doSearch(String) onto the executeSearch data action.

   Additional Information: This creates an action binding that invokes the `doSearch()` method, and binds an event in the data action to that binding.
9. In the Structure window, select "Struts Config\Action Mappings\/executeSearch\paramNames[0]".
10. In the Property Inspector, enter the *value* property as "${param.searchString}" and press ENTER.
11. Click Save All.
12. Rebuild the project.

Create a Data Page and JSP Page to Display Search Results

This section creates a JSP page to display the query results returned by the web service after the Submit button is clicked.

1. On the Component Palette, click the Data Page icon.
2. Click the diagram to add a data page.
3. Name the data page "searchResults".
4. Create a forward from the executeSearch data action to the searchResults data page. You do not need to rename the forward.

5. Double click the searchResults data page to open the Select or Create Page dialog.
6. Click OK to create a JSP page named searchResults.jsp and open it in the visual editor.
7. On the Data Control Palette, select SearchDataControl\Operations\doSearch(String)\return\resultElements.

   Additional Information: This is a field of the returned `GoogleSearchResult` instance containing an array of `ResultElement` instances.
8. In the *Drag and Drop As* dropdown list, select "Read-Only Form".
9. Drag resultElements onto the visual editor to create a read-only form and the needed bindings.
10. On the HTML form, select the JSTL tag that displays {$bindings['directoryTitle']}, as shown here:

${bindings['URL'].label}	${bindings['URL']}
${bindings['cachedSize'].label}	${bindings['cachedSize']}
${bindings['directoryTitle'].label}	${bindings['directoryTitle']}
${bindings['hostName'].label}	${bindings['hostName']}
${bindings['snippet'].label}	${bindings['snippet']}
${bindings['summary'].label}	${bindings['summary']}
${bindings['title'].label}	${bindings['title']}

11. In the Property Inspector for that tag, select "false" in the *escapeXML* dropdown.

    Additional Information: Some information from Google is returned in HTML format and puts your search terms in boldface. By default, JSTL escapes XML and HTML special characters (such as "<"), resulting in XML and HTML being displayed as source code. By setting `escapeXML` to "false", you can override this behavior, allowing the page to render the returned HTML normally.
12. Repeat steps 10 and 11 for the JSTL tags that display the {$bindings['snippet']} and {$bindings['title']} expressions.
13. In the Data Control Palette, select SearchDataControl\Operations\doSearch(String)\return\resultElements\Operations\First.
14. In the *Drag and Drop As* dropdown list, ensure that "Button" is selected.
15. Drag First onto the visual designer, after the table but still inside the form, to add a button to the form and an action binding to the binding container.
16. Drag the Previous, Next, and Last operations onto the form as buttons.
17. After the Last button, insert a carriage return.

18. Reopen the Component Palette, and click the Submit Button icon to add a submit button to the form.

    Additional Information: Your application will use this button to return to the search page. The form should resemble the following:

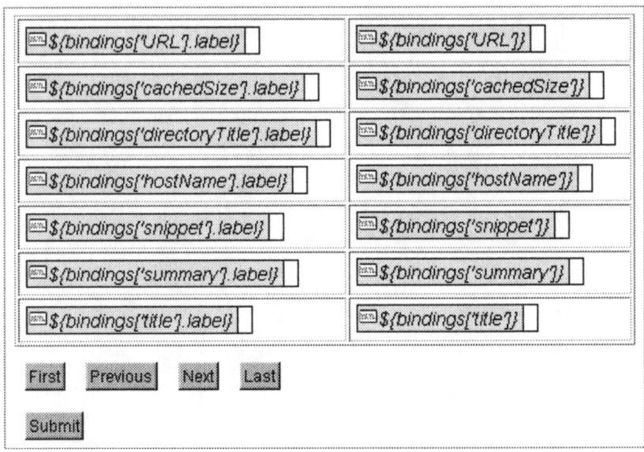

19. In the Property Inspector, enter "event_Submit" for the button's *name* property.
20. Reopen the page flow diagram.
21. Create a forward from searchResults back to search.
22. Name the forward Submit, as shown here:

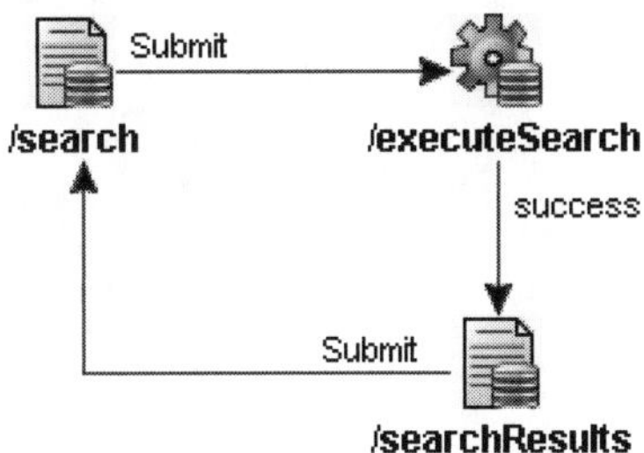

23. Click Save All.
24. Rebuild the project.

Test the Application

You can test the web application based on the Google Web APIs using the following steps:

1. On the search data action, select Run from the right-click menu.
2. When search.jsp opens, enter a search string, such as "Oracle JDeveloper", and click Submit.

3. When searchResults.jsp opens, use the navigation buttons to explore the search results.
4. Click Submit and try another search string.
5. Close the browser window.

What Just Happened? You created a web application that invokes the Google Web APIs to perform searches.

PART III

Java Client and Web Applications

CHAPTER 15

Creating Java Client Applications

For me, the creative process, first of all, requires a good nine hours of sleep a night. Second, it must not be pushed by the need to produce practical applications.

—William N. Lipscomb Jr., *NY Times,* 7 December, 1977

Java *client applications* are standalone programs that run in a Java Virtual Machine (JVM) on the Client Tier. The user interface portion is usually written using Sun's Swing components and other third-party components (for example, for graphs and charts). As described in Chapter 7, this book concentrates on two styles of applications where the JVM runs on different machines, namely *Java applications* (Java code run in a standalone JVM process) and *applets* (Java code run in a web browser's JVM).

Java client applications can be deployed in the same way as applications built for traditional two-tier client/server architectures. In order to make deployment and installation easier, Sun created Java Web Start, which allows client machines to automatically download and install newer versions of an application as they become available.

A Java application provides data-entry performance and graphical quality of the user interface unmatched by using a JSP or similar web application. For critical internal applications, there are still situations where you need the rich user-interface components available to Java client applications rather than the limited controls available in HTML or XML environments.

Java applications can be fully featured, since your code primarily uses the Java language, as opposed to JSP pages, which use a combination of tag languages and Java. Chapter 5 contains more detailed information about Java and how it is used in web development.

The chapters in this part of the book focus on Java client and web applications (which run in a JVM on the Web Tier). This chapter provides an overview of the architecture decisions and discusses Swing components and Java client applications. The uses and functions of the layout managers that dictate the positioning of Swing components are discussed in Chapter 16. Chapter 17 describes the role of Struts in application development with JDeveloper 10*g*. JSP and UIX development is explored in Chapters 18 and 19, respectively.

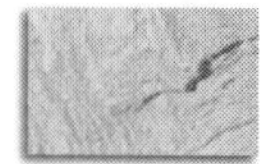

NOTE
Since applets use the same programmatic elements as Java applications, all techniques mentioned for Java applications in this chapter can also be applied to applets.

The JDeveloper IDE for Java Client Development

The rule of thumb when working with any Java IDE is to try to reduce the amount of hand coding. Expert Java programmers may produce code nearly as quickly as a generator; however, generated code is consistent, predictable, and error free. Although it is not possible to create an enterprise-class application using only the wizards and existing components, these features give you a big head start and greatly minimize the supplemental code that you have to write. If you are careful about how elaborate your GUI becomes, the amount of code you need to write will be very small. The technical, architectural details that Java requires to make the code work, such as imports and constructors, can all be handled by the code generators and property inspectors.

One of the key features that the JDeveloper IDE offers is quick access to commonly used Java components. A Java component corresponds to what other languages or environments (such as Windows) call a "control," and the words "component" and "control" are often used interchangeably. Typically, a *component* represents a visual object, but the term can be extended to cover non-visual data control objects. The IDE allows you to drag and drop components and data controls into your project, set most properties, and define events, all without writing code. The code that is generated from these actions is ready to run, error free, and can be edited using the Java Visual Editor, Structure window, Code Editor, and Property Inspector.

Both web applications and JClient applications now make use of a common technology, the ADF Model, to provide data bindings. Although the examples shown in Chapter 12 involve accessing the ADF Model from within web applications, the process is essentially the same in databound web applications as it is in JClient applications. You access binding properties using the components' *model* property instead of using expression language. JClient is not interacting directly with application module instances, view object instances, and such. It is interacting with data bindings, which are themselves interacting with data controls that wrap Application Module instances. This is explained in more detail in Chapter 12.

An especially powerful feature of JDeveloper is the way in which the Data Control Palette manages interaction with the data model. You can now drag and drop data-bound components (from view objects and attributes) as well as row set operations (create, first, and so forth) into your application.

The Component Palette offers the ability to create components and generate code. The available pages of the Component Palette depend upon which type of file is open in the Java Visual Editor. When you are editing a .java file, the Component Palette allows you to toggle between Swing or Abstract Windowing Toolkit (AWT) components, JClient controls, and other sets of components relevant to Java client applications. The hands-on practices in this chapter include examples of how to work with these components to create simple, data-aware Java client applications. With this knowledge, you will be better able to explore the other components and understand where to get information about developing Java client applications.

Building Java Client Applications

The first step in application development is to build or add the ADF business services (usually ADF BC) Model project. The Model project must be open in the same workspace as your application. Next, you build the user interface (View) portion of the program. This will usually reside in its own project or projects within the same workspace as the Model project. Projects in JDeveloper 10*g* are usually created automatically when you select the proper template but projects can also be added manually. This chapter focuses on business services examples in ADF BC.

Deployment is based on the packages associated with the various objects in your program. Packages also help organize your work in the development directories. In the preceding example, the Model project is associated with a package called "model" and the View project is associated with the package "view" as shown here.

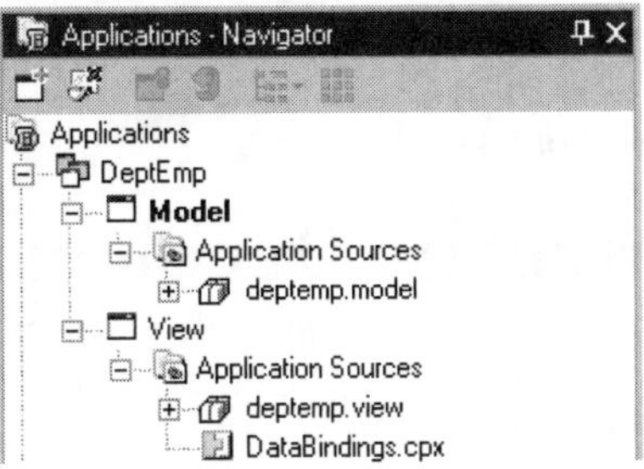

By default, JDeveloper places the project directories under the application workspace directory. This structure provides an easy way to delete (or back up) an entire program by just deleting (or backing up) the workspace directory and all of its subcomponents. See the sidebar "Directory Organization for a Java Client Application" for more information about this topic.

Directory Organization for a Java Client Application

Developers should be aware of the organization of directories for a Java client application. The following example will help to illustrate the default organization for a Java client application. (JSP or other applications may have additional directories, but the basic structure is the same.) Assume that you are building a simple application with an ADF BC model project and a view project in the same application workspace. The application workspace will be stored in a named directory under the "JDEV_HOME\jdev\mywork" directory (or whatever you might have named the default work directory) and the Model and View projects are stored in their own project subdirectories.

If you navigate to the operating system, the complete directory structure will be as shown here:

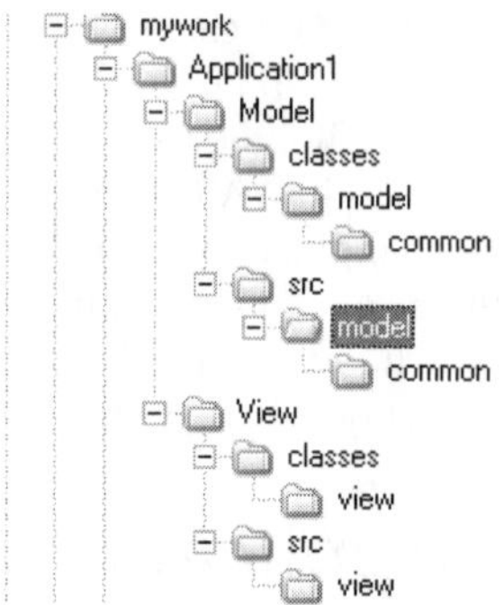

By default, subdirectories called "src" and "classes" are automatically added to each project subdirectory. The "src" directory stores the source code files for your classes, and the "classes" directory stores the compiled code files. These directory names will be familiar to developers and should not be changed, although JDeveloper supports changing the names used for these directories when you create the project or in the project properties. Notice how the package name is used for subdirectories under the src and classes directories. It is in these package subdirectories that your files will be stored.

Building Java client applications requires careful planning. You need to decide how your program will be structured before you start building it. It is a bad idea to just start building the application and then allow it to "evolve." You have many alternatives in structuring your application. The next section will discuss some of these decisions.

Java Client Architecture Decisions

This section describes the decisions that have to be made when building a Java application or applet. These decisions can be quite difficult to change after the development process is well under way, so they should be considered from the start.

How Many Independent Programs Will You Use?

One of the temptations when writing programs in Java is to write very complex, graphics-intensive programs just because it is possible. The dream of building a "super program" that can support a major portion of a complex system can be realized. But this capability can lead to programs that are so large that they suffer from poor performance and are difficult to maintain.

There is no restriction on the number of physical programs that make up a Java client application. One advantage of a 3GL environment is that you can partition your code any way you like. Very large programs take longer to load and may consume enough memory resources that the program runs slowly. It is easier to manage a few programs of moderate size than one giant program. Programs should be partitioned into manageable chunks.

Breaking Java Client Applications into Separate Classes

One example of breaking up class files is found in the JDeveloper wizards. When you build a master-detail Java application using the Create JClient Form Wizard (as in the LocDept application in the Chapter 1 hands-on practice), JDeveloper creates four classes, which you can verify by expanding the application in the System Navigator (the form file, the formUIModel.xml file, master panel view, detail panel view). You can break your program into classes any way that you like. In building this Java application by hand, it would be logical to combine the first two classes into a container class, but it is recommended that you keep the master and detail classes separate. Using one class for each table usage is a good way to organize your code.

How Many Directories, Workspaces, and Projects Will You Create?

You have a lot of flexibility in how you manage your program within JDeveloper. Application workspaces and projects are merely logical folders where you place your work. You can place many programs in the same application workspace or split a single program across multiple application workspaces. You can build reusable components that can be used by several programs, and you can store your work in multiple folders/directories in the operating system.

JDeveloper is well suited to manage up to a few dozen classes in a single project and can support several projects in the same application workspace. For very large programs, developers can significantly improve the readability and manageability of the code by partitioning the code into several projects, and perhaps even several workspaces. JDeveloper 10*g* allows you to have multiple application workspaces open at the same time so that you can work on many logically distinct application areas simultaneously.

Another mechanism available to help manage your work is to partition your files within the projects. You can easily partition your work into packages or nested sets of file folders using a "dot" notation.

Where Will the Data Validation Take Place?

There are several possible strategies for business services (such as ADF BC) usage. The main architecture-level ADF BC–related decision to be made is where the data validation will take place.

Data validation can be supported in many places in a Java application. The selection of the validation location is the same kind of decision that had to be made in a 4GL environment where you decide whether the validation should take place in the database or in the application. In a

Java application, data validation can be implemented in three places: in the database, within the business services layer, or in the user interface portion of the application.

For ADF BC, in addition to using entity object definitions, data validation can take place in the view object definitions, but that is only recommended when multiple view objects share the same entity object and there are specific validation requirements for a particular view object. Some complex validation involving the interactions at the row level is best handled in the ADF BC application module, but that is beyond the scope of this discussion.

What Type of Container Layout Should Be Used?

Laying out the containers (frames, panes, and panels) in a Java application or applet should be accomplished before you get very far into the application. It is quite easy to change your mind about the container structuring at any time during development if you are a skilled Java developer. If you want to rely on the JDeveloper wizards to lay out the containers for you, you should think through the structure before launching into work with the wizards. Chapter 16 provides information about many of the layout options available.

How Many Packages Will You Create and How Will You Name Them?

Packages govern the deployment, internal .jar file structure, and the work area subdirectory names for projects. They are also the logical internal storage area names for project components. The point is that the package names are used in many places. Changing package names after development has started can be quite difficult. Similarly, going from a single-package structure to a multiple-package structure after significant development has been completed is difficult to implement for existing objects.

You can set the package structure for new objects in JDeveloper quite easily using the default settings or through the interactive dialogs when creating new objects. This is particularly helpful when organizing objects by logical types (that is, entity objects in one package and web services in another). Anything already created will belong to the original package/file-folder structure under which it was created.

Other Issues

As in any new product, the first time you try to do something, it will take some time to figure it out and get it to work. With JDeveloper and Swing components, you will quickly need to go beyond the default behavior generated by the wizards. For example, you will definitely want to control column widths in `JTables`, so that data presented in tabular format is displayed consistently. This requires working outside of the defaults

TIP

You can place a large number of objects on a single page and use the page's navigation arrows to access the components. However, the most developer-friendly interfaces usually do not require scrolling. Therefore, you should limit yourself to the number of components that may be viewed without scrolling when the window is maximized.

Because the possibilities are virtually limitless, you will need to figure out more little tricks than it is possible to keep in memory. Fortunately, with JDeveloper 10*g*, it is very easy to look up syntax and details about classes that you use. There is a wealth of information on numerous Java development websites and online forums. Some additional resources are listed in Appendix A and in the "Getting the Right Information" section later in this chapter.

ADF JClient

ADF JClient (JClient) technology is used with Java client applications such as Java applications and applets. With Java applications and applets, you usually use *Swing components*, which are UI Java classes supplied by Sun that present user interface controls such as text fields and buttons. In Part II, you learned that ADF BC architecture offers business services that support interaction with the database. The ADF JClient framework is the glue that connects the Swing components to ADF business services (described in Chapter 4) such as ADF BC, EJBs, and web services. ADF JClient is a thin layer used to set up and manage communication between the Swing components and the underlying data sources through the Model layer.

The issue of connecting standard Java components to database objects is one that requires much thought and effort. The traditional solution is to write many lines of code that act as a *binding* (connection) layer from user interface objects to the database tables and columns. Oracle has solved this using the JClient architecture. JClient sets up a code layer that performs the binding of Java user interface components (Swing JavaBeans such as JTextField and JCheckBox) to ADF BC objects. This allows developers to easily bind the interface elements to data. For example, to connect a text field to an ADF BC attribute (that represents a column in a table), the only required action is using the Property Inspector to set the text field's *document* property.

Recall that in ADF BC, you specify an application module that is a collection of view object and view link instances. (In this book, the majority of examples of business services use ADF BC.) This application module defines how the view objects and view links will be visible to the application. All interaction with the user interface portion of the application to ADF BC is accomplished by using this application module. Swing panels and frames can be bound to view object usages in the application module, and UI Swing components such as text fields can be bound to view object attributes.

A diagrammatic representation of JClient architecture for a form based on EmployeesView is shown in Figure 15-1. The Swing components are bound to attributes in the Client Data Model using the *document* property. These components are then bound to attributes and view objects in the application module of the ADF BC project. The empPanel container is bound to the EmployeeView view object using the *model* property.

Chapter 4 contains information about where ADF JClient fits into ADF architecture. In addition to the JDeveloper help system, you can find an article called "Developing Swing-based Java Clients using Oracle JDeveloper 10g and Oracle ADF JClient" in the JDeveloper area of otn.oracle.com.

Swing UI Architecture

Swing components contain both the Model and View layer within them in a structure called the *UI Delegate*. This provides the functionality to handle interaction with the Model. For example, with a JCheckBox Swing component, the act of checking or unchecking the checkbox needs to be detected so that an appropriate value can be passed to the model. Attaching a Swing component to the Model layer in Oracle's JClient architecture is handled declaratively with

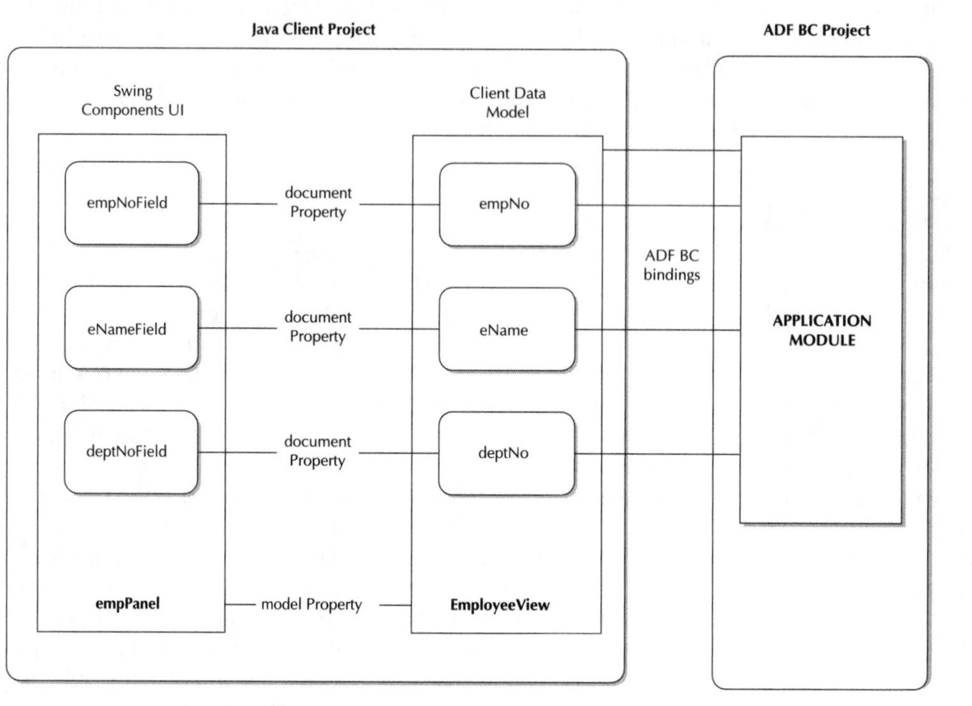

FIGURE 15-1. *Panel components and data-binding layers*

a single setting in the *model* property. Outside of the JClient context, binding Swing components to models is a tedious task.

Developing a Client Data Model

ADF JClient (as well as JSP pages built with the ADF BC Data Tags Library) requires a client data model to connect to ADF BC. The *client data model* definition describes the ADF BC application module to which the application will connect. When you use the wizards to add components to a user interface project, the ADF framework automatically creates or updates the client data model. In addition, there are a number of wizards that allow you to manipulate options such as column order. The order of columns is changed in the data-binding container UIModel.xml file.

You can have only one ADF BC client data model file per project. JDeveloper names the file "DataBindings.cpx." This file only contains references to the available data controls.

Binding Swing Components to ADF BC

The easiest way to bind a Swing component to business services such as ADF BC is by dragging and dropping the component from the Data Control Palette to the Java Visual Editor. This automatically assigns the data source for the component.

If you need to bind components to data sources manually, you can use the Property Inspector. Different Swing components bind differently to ADF BC. The *model* property is used for ADF BC binding to view object-level components such as navigation bars. For attribute-level components such as text fields, the Swing-named *document* property is used for binding. You can edit the current value by clicking the "…" button. For example, the following code will be created after setting the *document* property of the Department Name text field (the code will appear all on one line in the editor):

```
departmentNameTextField.setDocument((Document)
panelBinding.bindUIControl("DepartmentName", departmentNameTextField));
```

The `setDocument` method sets the data source of the field. The `bindUIControl` method passes the binding information to the JTextField. As depicted in Figure 15-1, the *model* property is used for ADF BC binding of a container (such as a `JTable` or navigation bar) to a view object usage. The binding of components such as text fields uses the property *document*. After clicking the button labeled "…" next to the *model* property in the Property Inspector for a JClient panel, you will see the JClient property editors. You can select an editor from the pulldown list. Some components have more than one JClient property editor, since they support more than one type of binding to the middle tier. You can edit the current value by clicking the "…" button. If you are going to make significant edits to component binding, it may be easier to directly edit the UIModel.xml file in the View\Application Sources nodes under the view package.

In summary, binding Swing components available to ADF BC in JDeveloper is best accomplished by dropping the component into the visual editor from the Data Control Palette. Alternatively, you can set the data binding manually by simply filling in a property on the Property Inspector. You will have little reason to manipulate the binding other than through the Property Inspector properties *document* or *model*. You can inspect the underlying binding code to see how Java handles the binding.

Binding Panels

As you create frames and add supporting panels, you usually set the binding context of the parent panels for each of your program areas to the ADF BC data model. You can set the binding context of your containers to the appropriate model component. In the JClient wizards, this is done when you generate the program. You can set the binding context for most of the containers with the exception of `JFrames` and `JInternalFrames`. Once you set the binding context of a container, its nested containers are automatically bound.

The JDeveloper Form wizards set the binding context of the top-level `JPanel` container in the project. Then in each additional class, they pass that binding context using a call to setBindingContext in the called panel.

The original binding context of the top panel is accomplished by the code shown next. First, the BindingContext is declared and retrieved from the panelBinding in the `jbInit()` method as follows:

```
/* the JbInit method
   */
  public void jbInit() throws Exception
  {
```

```
BindingContext _bctx = panelBinding.getBindingContext();
ArrayList varList = new ArrayList(1);
varList.add(hiddenNavBar);
_bctx.put(JUUtil.PROJECT_GLOBAL_VARIABLES, varList);
dataPanel.setBindingContext(_bctx);
this.getContentPane().setLayout(gridLayout);
topPanel.setLayout(borderLayout);
```

Alternatively, you can simply create an empty panel in your application. When you drag and drop the first data component from the Data Control Palette onto your panel (such as DepartmentName), the panel will be automatically bound as well.

First the panel binding is associated with the data model as in the following code:

```
private JUPanelBinding panelBinding = new JUPanelBinding("DeptPanelUIModel");
```

Next, in the "main" routine, the binding context is set to the panel.

```
DeptPanel panel = new DeptPanel();
panel.setBindingContext(JUTestFrame.startTestFrame("DataBindings.cpx",
  "null", panel, panel.getPanelBinding(), new Dimension(400, 300)));
```

Further discussion of ADF Data Binding may be found in an excellent white paper that explains the data-binding advanced features; it is available in the JDeveloper "How To" section of OTN called "Oracle ADF Data Binding Primer and ADF Struts Overview" (otn.oracle.com/products/jdev/collateral/papers/10g/ADFBindingPrimer/index.html).

Working with Swing Components in JDeveloper

Swing components are Java program units written to conform to a specific (JavaBean) protocol. Swing components are added to a project to control the layout and visibility of your data. This section describes how to work with these components in JDeveloper and how applications built with Swing components can be structured.

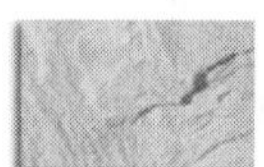

NOTE

Chapter 4 discusses how features of Swing fit into the layers of ADF and MVC.

The Data Control Palette

The Data Control Palette is a wonderful addition to JDeveloper for user interface application development. The Data Control Palette displays the available data model components for the application module. The central function of the Data Control Palette is to allow you to drag and drop data model components already associated with an appropriate user interface object into the visual editor, creating the object and binding it to the data model component in a single step.

The first hands-on practice in this chapter provides some experience with how to use the Data Control Palette as well as the data controls. The user interface components available in the data controls are the same as those contained on the Component Palette.

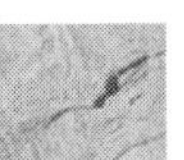

NOTE
Some of the components in the Data Control Palette have slightly different names from their Component Palette counterparts.

The Component Palette

The Component Palette for Java client components is normally located on the upper-right side of the JDeveloper window when the Java Visual Editor is open. A pulldown allows you to select from a number of different component sets as follows:

- AWT
- Code Snippets
- JClient Controls
- Swing
- Swing Containers

Remember that you are not bound by the components installed by default. You can add or remove pages in the Component Palette and add, remove, or move components as described in the second hands-on practice later in this chapter.

The Component Palette offers controls that are appropriate to the file that you are editing in the Java Visual Editor. This chapter refers to only the Component Palette pages that appear when a Java application or applet is active in the Java Visual Editor. Appendix B contains a description of the Component Palette elements available to Java client applications.

Using Swing Components

It is simple to use Swing components in JDeveloper 10*g*. Objects can be added in several ways. They can be placed into the Structure window in a tree structure, dragged and dropped directly into the Java Visual Editor from the Component Palette or the Data Control Palette, or added in the code. Getting the components on the screen and coupling them to business services is very straightforward. With practice, you can quickly be as productive at adding components as in any 4GL tool such as Oracle Forms Developer.

Trying to control the objects you have created reveals both the blessing and the curse of using Java. Java is almost limitlessly flexible. You can do just about anything you want. However, almost anything you might want to do other than dropping a Swing component into your application and setting properties in the Property Inspector requires a good deal of work to figure out how to achieve the desired result. JDeveloper 10*g* makes the binding of Swing components to the data model effortless. Even a simple-sounding task such as making a field wider, adding a double-click event, or changing the color of a field in a specific context may be a frustrating experience if you do not have some guidance or a tool such as JDeveloper. Using the right layout manager may help. It may take you a few tries until you find the right clue in the right Java book or find the answer to your question on an Internet mail list server.

Adding Swing Components to a Program

Swing components are the most often used Java UI components. Adding Swing components to a program is simple because of the new Data Control Palette, which makes binding much easier. If the component you want to add needs to be bound to data elements, drag and drop it from the Data Control Palette onto the Java Visual Editor.

If the component you want to add is in the Component Palette (while the Java Visual Editor is open) and you do not need to bind it to data, you can select it and click either the place on the Java Visual Editor where you want the component to appear or in the Structure window in the desired position. You can add many components at once by using the wizards or one at a time by using the Java Visual Editor. Of course, you can also add them by editing the code itself. It is important to have each component in its correct logical place. Sometimes it is hard to position an object in the correct place (usually in a particular `JPanel`) by using the Java Visual Editor, because a layout manager imposes a particular behavior; therefore it is best to start with a "null" layout and then apply a specific Layout Manager as described in Chapter 16.

When you add a Swing component using the Component Palette or the Data Control Palette, JDeveloper inserts code into your program. For example, when you add a button (JButton) to the Java Visual Editor, the editor adds a line of code that declares the button as shown here:

```
private JButton jButton1 = new JButton();
```

Next, in the `jbInit()` method of the code, the wizard will typically set one or more properties of the component. In this case it only sets a single property as shown next:

```
jButton1.setText("jButton1");
```

Also, it adds the component to the container in a specific position as shown here:

```
dataPanel.add(jButton1, BorderLayout.CENTER);
```

Finally, it adds the appropriate import statements so that the proper class files are available. In this example, JDeveloper adds the following code:

```
import javax.swing.JButton;
```

If you rename the component or modify its properties, the code will be updated to reflect the changes.

Categories of Swing Components

The Swing components can be loosely grouped as follows:

- **Container** Windows, frames, panes, and panels that act as areas on the screen into which you place visual objects such as fields and labels
- **Data** Text fields, checkboxes, tables, trees, charts that display data
- **Action** Buttons, sliders, free-standing scrollbars, and so on, that control other components, generate actions, generate a value, or respond to events
- **Static** Labels and graphic items that are not data related
- **Non-visual** Timers and similar components that are not displayed
- **Dialog** Help messages, modal alert boxes, and similar components

Appendix B contains a list of the Swing container objects available by default in the Component Palette. Using most of these components is fairly straightforward. Containers are a bit more complex and require a bit of explanation.

Container Objects

Container objects are typically the first Swing components you add to a user interface application. They act as the windows and canvases on which to place other objects. As discussed earlier, you need to bind container components to ADF BC so that the data components within the containers will be able to access data.

Most of the common Swing containers are described in the "Swing Containers" section in Appendix B (`JPanel`, `JTabbedPane`, `JScrollPane`, and `JSplitPane`). Other common containers follow.

- **`JFrame`** This is the main container frame for the program. It appears as a window on the screen. There is usually only a single `JFrame` in a program.
- **`JInternalFrame`** This appears as a window in the user interface. It is used to support Multiple Document Interface (MDI).
- **`JDesktopPane`** This is an enclosing panel to support the `JInternalFrame` windows.

Container Layout Guidelines Laying out panels and frames is a critical and challenging step in the UI design of a program. Creating frames, panels, and panes can be accomplished in the three following ways:

- **Use the wizards.** This is typically where you start your development. Until you are comfortable with the code that wizards generate, this is the easiest way to create working code that you can modify to meet your needs.
- **Use the Java Visual Editor, Data Control Palette, Component Palette, and Property Inspector.** The visual tools are easy and more flexible to work with and create error-free code.

- **Write code manually in the Code Editor.** You can use the Java Visual Editor or Structure window to add panels more quickly, easily, and reliably than in the Code Editor. However, if you are more comfortable and efficient in typing your own code, JDeveloper provides this option.

What Containers Should Be Used Where? If you look closely at the layout generated by the Form Wizard, you will see that the container structure in Java is very logical. The following describes some of the container classes and their use.

- **JFrame and JPanel** For a Java application, you always start with a `JFrame` as the outside container (the window). Then you access its contentPane and place a `JPanel` directly inside it. This is just like the primary window and the main content canvas in Oracle Forms. The `JPanel` acts as your main container to partition the screen into different areas. You may add other containers for specific purposes. For all containers, you need to make decisions about the layout manager (as described in Chapter 16).
- **JScrollPane** The next most common type of container is the `JScrollPane`. This is a special container used whenever you want a scrollbar to traverse large quantities of data or images that will not fit on the available screen size. There is also a scrollbar Swing component, but usually it is more convenient to use the `JScrollPane` and take advantage of its default behavior. The JDeveloper wizards create a scrollbar to scroll through a set of records just by placing a `JTable` (providing a multi-record display) inside a `JScrollPane` (which provides the scrollbar).
- **JTabbedPane** To make a tab container, you create a `JTabbedPane` in your program. You then add a `JPanel` for each tab page. Each tab page in the tab container is a `JPanel`.
- **JSplitPane** A `JSplitPane` contains exactly two `JPanels` that share the area defined for the `JSplitPane`. `JSplitPanes` can divide a given area either horizontally or vertically.
- **JDesktopPane** If you want to have multiple independent or floating windows in your program, you can add a parent container called a `JDesktopPane` and then add child `JInternalFrame` containers for each window you wish to display.

Container Layout Example The following is a simple example of how the Create JClient Form Wizard in JDeveloper builds the frame and panel containers for a standard master-detail application to interact with the LOCATIONS (master) and DEPARTMENTS (detail) tables. This discussion is based on the structure of the files that are generated in the Chapter 1 Java application hands-on practice. An examination of the four classes that the wizard generates reveals the container structure described here.

- **The Frame Class** The first class generated by the wizard is the program-level container class represented by the diagram shown here:

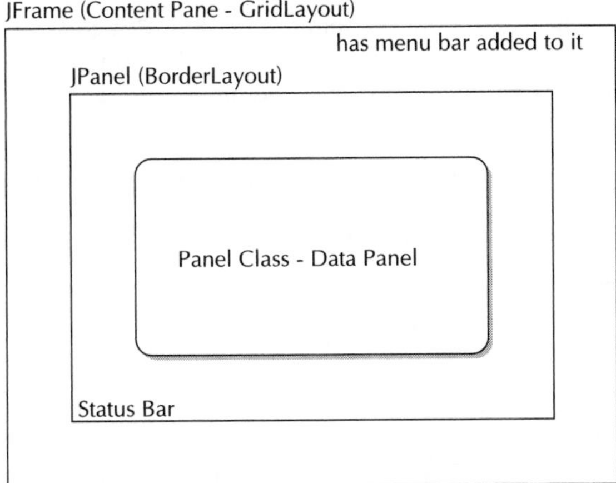

This class is the outside container, so it starts with a `JFrame` (with a `GridLayout` layout manager) as is expected. Inside the `JFrame` is a menu bar. Also inside the `JFrame` is a `JPanel` with a `BorderLayout` layout manager that encloses the panel class. Layout managers and ADF BC bindings are designed to work with panels, so this container is required. Finally, inside the main `JPanel` is the data panel, which is just an instance of the panel class (described next) and has the purpose of controlling the layout for the remaining components.

- **The Panel Class** The second class extends a `JPanel` and has a BorderLayout as shown here:

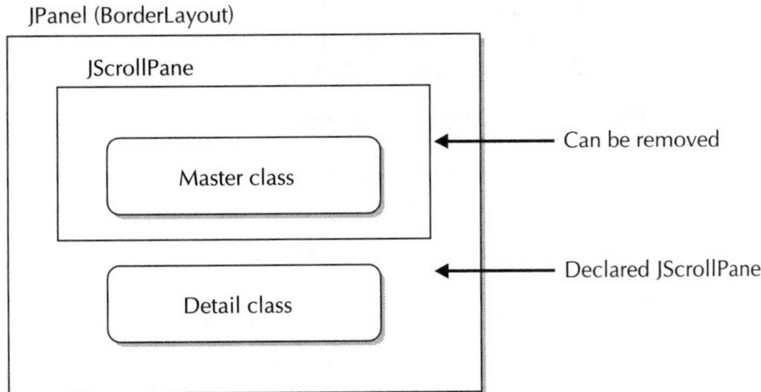

A `JScrollPane` encloses the master class. A second `JScrollPane` is declared but never used and is not visible in the diagram. Neither of these panes is necessary and either can be removed manually without affecting the functionality of this type of master-detail application. The `JScrollPanes` are added by the wizards for use in some of the other layout options. Within the master `JScrollPane` is an instance of the master class. An instance of the detail class is also added to the main `JPanel`. This effectively divides the `JPanel` class into two areas: one for the master class, one for the detail class.

- **The Master Class** The third generated class is the master class for Locations as shown here:

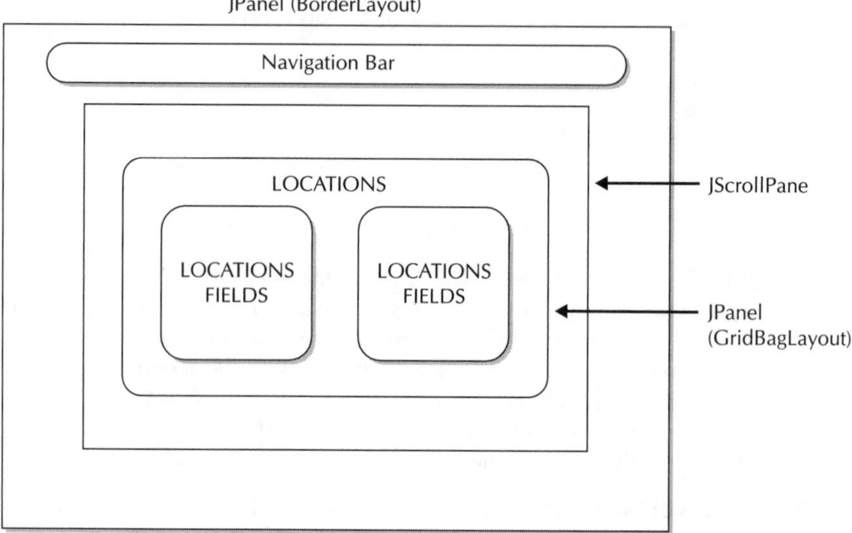

The master class is a `JPanel` with a `BorderLayout` layout manager. Inside this panel are a navigation bar and a `JScrollPane`. Inside the `JScrollPane` is a `JPanel` with a `GridBagLayout` manager that holds the data fields.

- **The Detail Class** The fourth class in the application is also a `JPanel` as shown here:

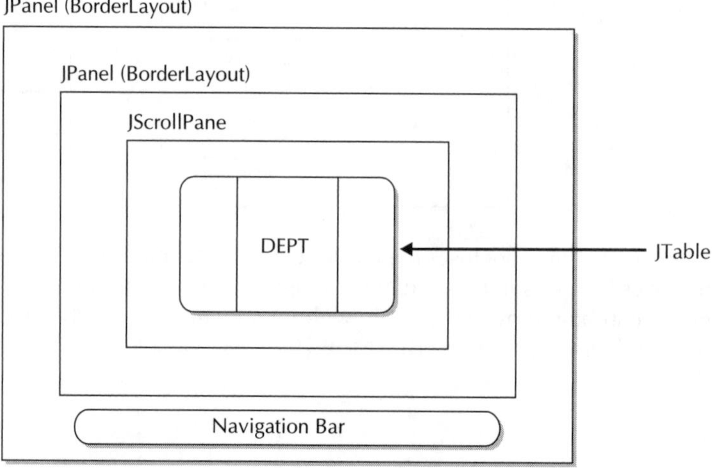

This class is a `JPanel` used for the Departments area (the detail in the master-detail). Inside the class is another `JPanel`. Inside that is a `JScrollPane` to hold the `JTable` (which provides the multi-column, multi-row grid display of the DEPT information). Just like the `Locations` class, it contains a navigation bar.

Modifying Swing Components

Most common properties of a Swing component can be modified using the Property Inspector, which, in turn, modifies your program code and the display in the visual editor. For example, if you access the properties of a button and change the *border* property of the button to be a raised bevel border, you will find the following line in your code:

```
jButton1.setBorder(BorderFactory.createBevelBorder(BevelBorder.RAISED));
```

The following imports are also added to support the bevel border:

```
import javax.swing.BorderFactory;
import javax.swing.border.BevelBorder;
```

Alternatively, you can directly modify the component by calling the appropriate method. You can see a list of the methods available for each component by using the JDeveloper Code Insight feature introduced in Chapter 3. To activate this feature, type the name of the component followed by a period ("."). After a short pause, a list will appear containing the available methods, classes, variables, and constants. For a simple button, there are hundreds of items in the list. You can also activate Code Insight by pressing CTRL-SPACEBAR after typing the period ("."). Code Insight is also available for packages and attributes.

Component objects can be manipulated without restriction at run time. In addition, objects are created at run time without restriction. For example, if you wrote the code for adding a button in an event handler somewhere in your code, the button would be created dynamically even though it was not "physically" represented in the Java Visual Editor.

Defining Events

Swing components are JavaBean classes that include the ability to fire events. An example of an event is the action performed when the user clicks a button. Events allow you to execute code based on user interaction with your application. Events can be anything from detecting that a button has been clicked, to more complex events such as detecting that a component has been moved.

Events require two types of code as follows:

- **An event listener** to detect the event and to call an event handler
- **A method** (event handler) with code that executes when the listener determines that the event has occurred

Event code is most easily created using the Java Visual Editor. Double click the component in the visual editor. This will create the actionPerformed listener and event handler method stub and open the Code Editor to the method stub.

If you want to create an event type other than actionPerformed (the default event for a component such as a button click for a button component) or want to use something other than the default name of the method stub, you can use the Property Inspector to create the event code. After you select the object in the Java Visual Editor, the Property Inspector will show a Properties tab with properties applicable to that component and an Events tab with a list of events offered by that component, as shown in Figure 15-2.

You select the event in the Events tab and click the "..." button for that event. A dialog such as the one shown here for the actionPerformed event will appear where you can name the event handler method stub:

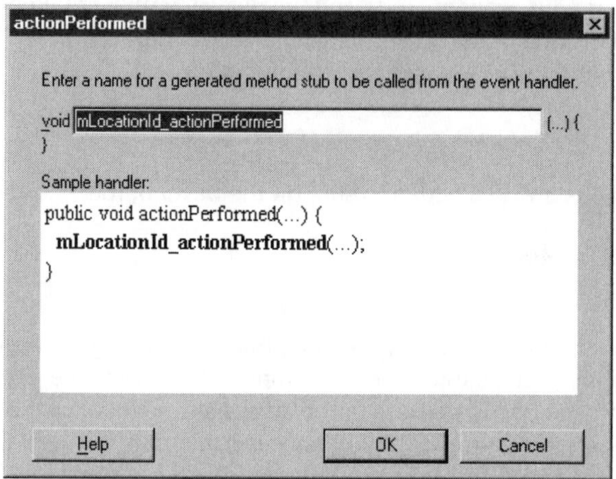

When you click OK, the dialog will create both the listener and the method code stub for you, and place the cursor in the code stub so you can add the event code. You cannot add the code directly in the Property Inspector. However, you can type the name of the code stub into the event field in the Property Inspector and press ENTER. The Property Inspector will create the code stub and pass the focus to the Code Editor. The event dialog will not appear in this case.

The second hands-on practice in this chapter shows how to build a button with a an actionPerformed event.

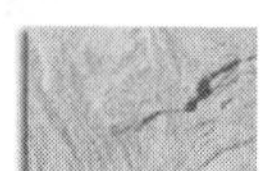

TIP

For more advanced users, when editing Java source code, there are a number of code template shortcut keys accessible. For example to add an action listener, type "aal" and press CTRL-ENTER. *More information about the code templates is available in Chapter 3 and under the help topic "JDeveloper Code Templates."*

Getting the Right Information

What is the critical success factor for building Java applications and applets quickly and efficiently using JDeveloper? Information, information, information. You can find tips and techniques from

FIGURE 15-2. *Events tab of the Property Inspector*

a wide variety of sources. In trying to manipulate a specific component in a certain way, the best way may be found only in one of many sources or may need to be gleaned from a combination of sources.

It would take many hundreds of pages to describe in detail all of the components included for use in JDeveloper, along with their methods and properties. In addition, these components are the more common of the thousands of components available. Describing all of them goes far beyond the scope of this book. The good news is that many components are fully documented in reference form within the JDeveloper help system. Browse under the Reference node in the Table of Contents page, or look for the library using a full text search. You will also find some examples and techniques in the help system.

In addition, many reference books provide details about the Swing components and show even more examples of their use. For more information about the Oracle components, look for examples and descriptions on the Oracle Technology Network website (otn.oracle.com). Appendix A provides a list of resources for many subjects in this book including Java applications and applets.

Hands-on Practice: Create a Tabbed User Interface Application

This hands-on practice shows how to create a tabbed application. Tabbed user interfaces are familiar to most developers and users. This practice will create an application that gives you practice in using some of the most common Swing components and Swing containers.

This practice includes the following phases:

I. Create the ADF BC project

II. Create the Java application project

III. Create a three-tab user interface

- Create the main panel and three tabs
- Create labels and fields on Tab 1
- Create a table on Tab 2
- Add a tree structure on Tab 3

If you need help or more detailed explanations for any of the basic steps, refer to the more detailed descriptions in the first hands-on practice in Chapter 1.

I. Create the ADF BC Project

In this phase, you create a workspace and two projects and select the business components that will be used in the Java application that you will create in Phase II.

1. On the Applications node in the Navigator, select New Application Workspace from the right-click menu.
2. In the Create Application Workspace dialog, change the *Application Name* to "DeptEmp." Change the *Application Package Prefix* to "deptemp."
3. Ensure that the *Application Template* pulldown is set to "Java Application [Default]." Click OK to dismiss the dialog and create the workspace and projects. Under the DeptEmp node, you will now see Model and View nodes.

4. Click Save All.
5. On the DeptEmp\Model node, select New from the right-click menu. Select Business Components from the Business Tier category and Business Components from Tables in the Items list and click OK.
6. The Business Components Project Initialization dialog will be displayed. Ensure that HR appears in the *Connection* field. Click OK.
7. Click Next if the Welcome page of the Create Business Components from Tables Wizard appears.
8. On the Entity Objects page, ensure that "deptemp.model" is shown in the *Package* field. Select DEPARTMENTS and EMPLOYEES, and move them to the *Selected* pane by using the right-arrow button. Click Next.
9. Click the double arrow to select the Departments and Employees view objects. Click Next.
10. On the Application Module page, ensure that the *Package* name is deptemp.model. Change the *Name* to DeptEmpModule. Click Next and Finish. The wizard will create default ADF BC objects in the new project.
11. Rebuild the Model project, which automatically saves all changed nodes.

What Just Happened? You used the wizards to create an application workplace including a View project and a default ADF BC project containing department and employee objects. The ADF BC project includes the package and module needed for the application project to be created in the next phase.

II. Create the Java Application Project

The application you use for this practice can be relatively basic, but it needs some specific elements. The following abbreviated steps will create a minimal application that you can use as a foundation. You will use the Create JClient Empty Form Wizard to build an application based on the business components you defined before.

1. Select New from the right-click menu on the View node to display the New Gallery. Select Swing/JClient for ADF under the Client Tier node and Empty Form from the Items list. Click OK to open the Create JClient Empty Form Wizard. Click Next if the Welcome page appears.
2. On the Form name page leave the *Package name* as "deptemp.view". Change the *Form name* to "DeptEmpForm". Leave the *Generate a menu bar* checkbox checked as shown here.

Additional Information: See the sidebar "Renaming Project Elements" for some important information about naming objects.

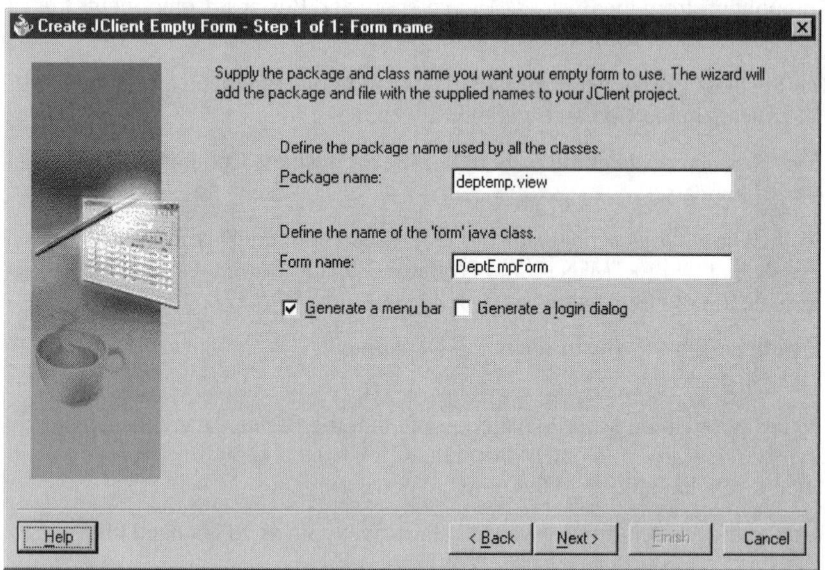

3. Click Next and Finish. You will now see the DeptEmpForm.java, DeptEmpFormUIModel .xml, and DataBindings.cpx files added to the Navigator under the Application Sources node of the View node, and the Java Visual Editor will open to display a user interface like the one shown in Figure 15-3.
4. Click Save All.

Renaming Project Elements

Be careful about naming objects. If you need to rename something as you are developing, the following is an example of the correct way to do this.

1. Be sure that the file compiles successfully. You will not be able to refactor a file that does not compile.
2. Select the file to be renamed in the navigator, and select **Tools | Refactor | Rename Class**. In the Rename Class dialog, enter the new name and click OK.
3. If the Rename Class option is disabled, click something else in the Navigator, select the file again, and select **Tools | Refactor | Rename Class**.

   Additional Information: The .java file extension will be added automatically. You may receive a confirmation dialog about the Refactor/Rename action not being able to be undone and an *Update Imports* property in the project settings. Click "Yes" on both of these dialogs.

4. Click OK on the final Operation Complete dialog and click Close. The file will be renamed, and all references to the file in that file and other code files will be modified.

5. Rebuild the project to verify that the code was correctly modified.

   Additional Information: Using **File | Rename** to rename the file will not properly update the references to this file in other files.

The Application Navigator already separates the files by package name. Renaming a class may cause problems because the UIModel.xml file names will no longer be in synch with the Class names.

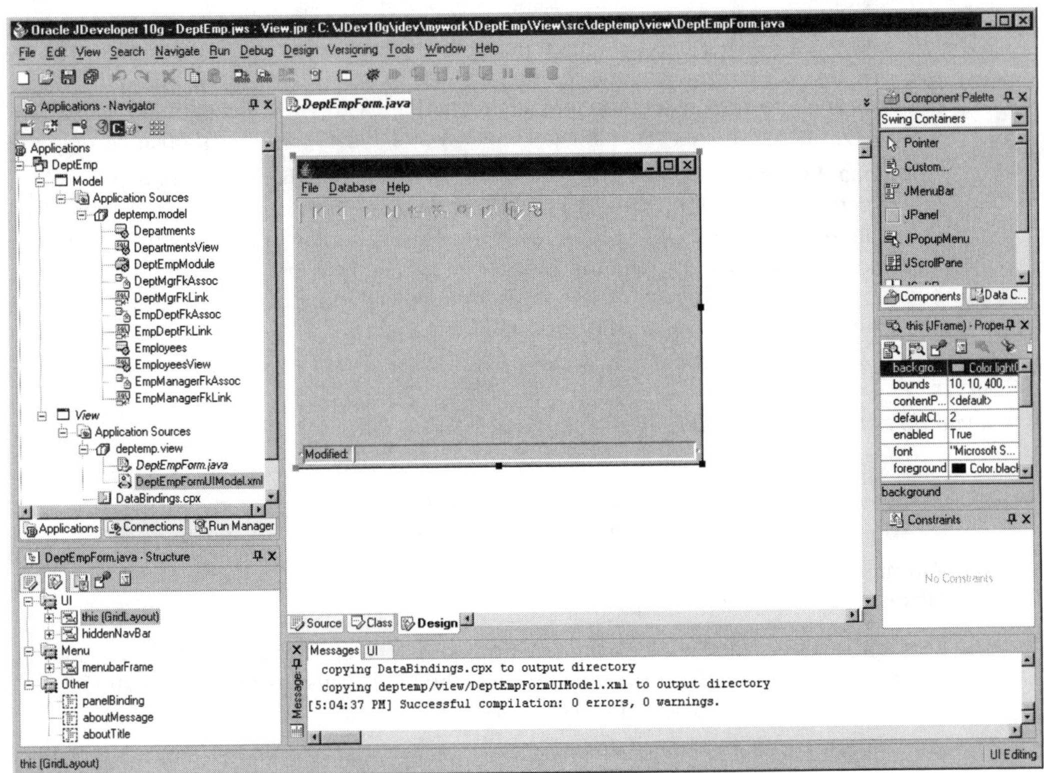

FIGURE 15-3. *Java Visual Editor and JDeveloper IDE view for DeptEmpForm.java*

What Just Happened? You created a simple Java application form that will serve as the basis for adding more user interface components in the following phases. This application already has the JClient data binding available so that components created in the panel will be able to bind to the ADF BC objects. You can run the DeptEmpForm.java file at this point to test that the empty form displays. Close the application after testing it.

III. Create a Three-Tab User Interface

In this phase, you will add three tabs to display the data in the form you just created.

Create the Main Panel and Three Tabs

This section adds a tab container and three tab pages.

1. If the Java Visual Editor is not displayed, double click the DeptEmpForm.java node in the Application Navigator.
2. In the Structure window, expand the UI, "this," and topPanel nodes.
3. On the dataPanel node, select Cut from the right-click menu to remove the dataPanel. This will leave you a space in the layout to add a `JTabbedPane` component.
4. Select JTabbedPane from the Swing Containers Component Palette. Drag the mouse over the layout and watch the lower-left corner of the IDE status bar. Click the mouse when you see "topPanel (BorderLayout): Center," which indicates that you will drop the tab pane inside the center area of the topPanel container. Verify that the pane is placed under the TopPanel node in the Structure window and that its *constraint* property is Center.

   Additional Information: The tabbed pane serves as a container for multiple panels and is perfectly suited for a standard multi-tabbed user interface common to many applications. The `JTabbedPane` serves as the outside container for all of the tab pages. It provides the tab "buttons" and the logic for navigating between tab pages, only showing one tab page at time. The actual tab pages are regular `JPanels`. When a `JPanel` is placed inside a `JTabbedPane`, it appears as a tab page.

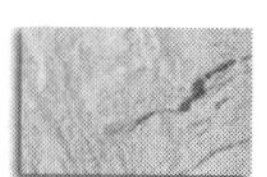

NOTE
*If you do not see the IDE status bar, select **View | Status Bar**.*

5. In the Property Inspector for jTabbedPane1, change the *name* property to "mainTab" and press ENTER. You will see mainTab under topPanel in the Structure window.

   Additional Information: This mainTab pane will serve as the container for the multiple tabs you will create for this application.
6. Select JPanel from the Swing Containers Component Palette, and watch the IDE status bar as you move the mouse over the layout. When the status bar indicates "mainTab z: 0," click the layout to add the first tab.
7. In the JPanel1 Property Inspector, change the *name* property to "tab1Panel," and change the *constraints* property to "Tab 1" to set the visual label on the tab. Be sure to press ENTER after changing the properties. If you change the constraints property in the Constraints window, click Apply.

8. Repeat steps 6 and 7 twice to create tab2 and tab3 by clicking JPanel in the Swing Containers Component Palette and then clicking mainTab in the Structure window. Use the *name* values of "tab2Panel" and "tab3Panel," respectively, and *constraints* of "Tab 2" and "Tab 3," respectively.

   Additional Information: When dragging the new components to the layout, hold the mouse between the navigation bar and Tab 1 to see "mainTab z: 0" (indicating the container into which you will drop the panel). Alternately, you can click the mainTab node in the Structure window after selecting the JPanel component.

9. Click Save All.

10. Run the DeptEmpForm.java file to make sure that everything is working. The application should look like the following:

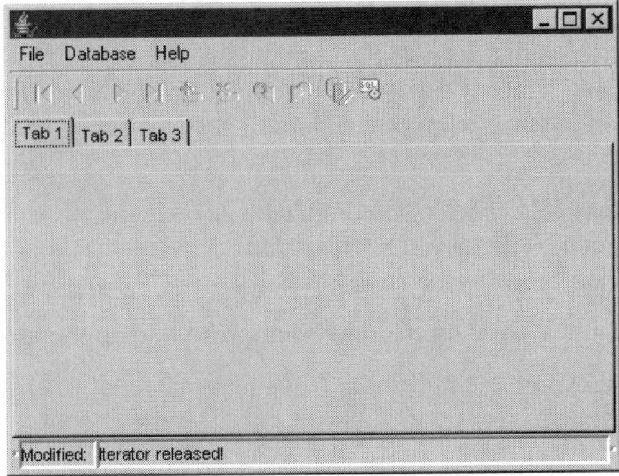

11. Close the application.

Create Labels and Fields on Tab 1

Use these steps to create a basic user interface showing labeled fields and a status bar.

1. On the Property Inspector for tab1, change the *layout* property from "<default>" to "null."

2. Click the Data Controls tab and expand the DeptEmpModuleDataControl and DepartmentsView1 nodes as shown here:

3. Select DepartmentId above and "Label For" from the *Drag and Drop As* pulldown. Drag the DepartmentId node to Tab 1. This creates a JULabel object.
4. Select the new label in the visual editor. On the Property Inspector, change the *name* property to "departmentIdLabel" and the *text* property to "ID:". Press ENTER.
5. Repeat steps 3 and 4 to place a second label on Tab 1 by dragging the DepartmentName node onto the visual editor. Use "departmentNameLabel" and "Name:" for the *name* and *text* properties respectively.
6. Select DepartmentId in the Data Control Palette and TextField in the *Drag and Drop As* pulldown. Place the text field to the right of the ID label on Tab 1.
7. On the Property Inspector for jTextField1, change the *name* property to "departmentIdTextField." Press ENTER.
8. Select DepartmentName in the Data Control Palette and "TextField" in the *Drag and Drop As* pulldown. Place the text field to the right of the Name label. Drag the name field out horizontally to accommodate longer names or you can do this later when running the form.
9. If it is not already selected, select the jTextField1 node in the Structure window. Change the *name* property for the control you just added to "departmentNameTextField." Press ENTER.
10. Select the ID label in the Java Visual Editor and SHIFT click the Name label. Click the Align Left icon in the Java Visual Editor window to line up the labels.
11. Select the ID label and SHIFT click the DepartmentID field. Click the Align Bottom icon to line up the labels.
12. Repeat Step 11 with the Name label and DepartmentName field.
13. Select the two text fields, and click the Align Left icon. Your screen should look something like this:

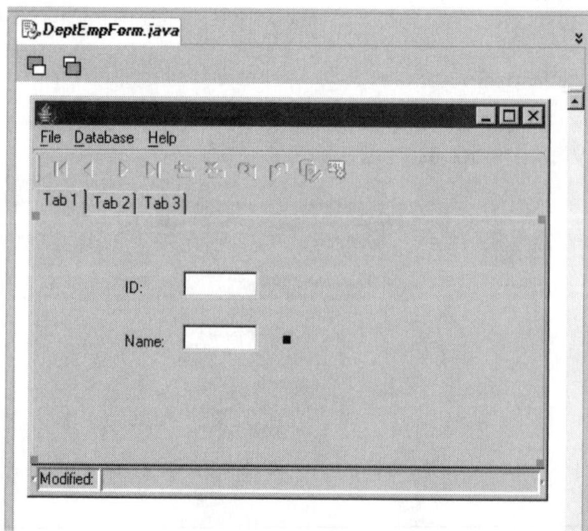

14. Click Save All.

15. Rebuild and run DeptEmpForm.java. Test Tab 1 to make sure that it is working correctly. Place the cursor in one of the fields, and then click the navigator buttons. Close the form.

    Additional Information: If the *Name* field is too small for some of the data, return to the Java Visual Editor. Use the center drag handle on the right side of the *Name* field to make it long enough so that department names will not be truncated.

Create a Table on Tab 2

These steps demonstrate how to create a table UI control to show data in a multi-column, multi-row form.

1. Select the Tab 2 tab in the Java Visual Editor. This displays the second JPanel surface.

2. Use the Property Inspector to set the *layout* property for the tab2Panel to BorderLayout.

   Additional Information: You may see the following message in the Log window: "Unable to instantiate anonymous inner classes at design time. Using base class oracle.jbo.uicli.controls.JUNavigationBar as placeholder." This will not affect the application.

3. On the Swing Containers page of the Components tab, select JScrollPane, and drag and drop it in the visual editor when the IDE status bar indicates "tab2Panel (BorderLayout): Center."

4. Change the *name* property of jScrollPane1 to "tableScrollPane." Press ENTER.

5. In the Application Navigator, expand the DeptEmp\Model\Application Sources\demtemp.model nodes. Select Edit EmployeesView from the right-click menu on the EmployeesView node to display the View Object Editor.

6. In the View Object Editor, select the Attributes node. Move the Email, PhoneNumber, HireDate, JobId, Salary, and CommissionPct attributes out of the *Selected* pane using the left arrow. Click Apply and OK.

7. Click the Data Controls tab, expand the DeptEmpModuleDataControl if needed. Expand the DepartmentsView1 node and select the EmployeesView3 node under it.

   Additional Information: Setting the EmployeesView3 allows the information on the Tab 2 table to reflect what is selected on Tab 1. As discussed in previous chapters, the way in which ADF BC views links work means that EmployeesView1 is a view of all employees, but EmployeesView3 restricts the employees to the selected department.

8. Select "Table" in the *Drag and Drop As* pulldown and drag the EmployeesView3 onto tableScrollPane on Tab 2. You will see the jTable1 component added under tableScrollPane in the Structure window.

9. Change the *name* property of jTable1 to "empTable." Press ENTER.

10. Click Save All.

11. Rebuild and Run DeptEmpForm.java.

12. If Department ID 10 is selected on Tab 1, then Tab 2 should look like this.

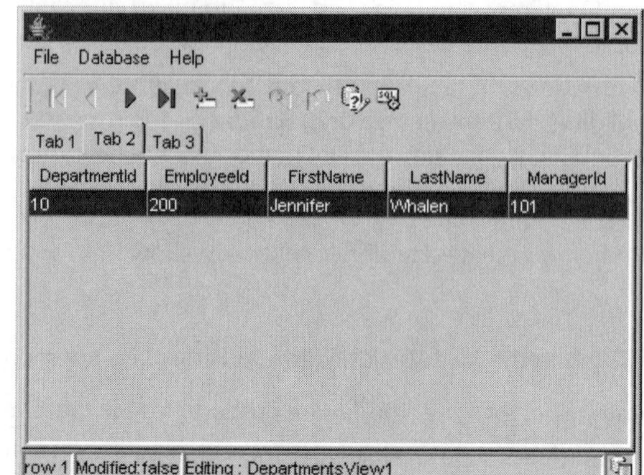

13. The table display on Tab 2 will change depending upon what Department is selected on Tab 1. (Department 50 has many employees if you want to test the scrollbar for Tab 2.) Close the application.

Add a Tree Structure on Tab 3

The following steps demonstrate how to add a tree structure to the third tab of the UI.

1. Click Tab 3 of DeptEmpForm in the Visual Editor. In the Property Inspector for tab3Panel, change the *layout* property to FlowLayout.

   Additional Information: If you have trouble setting the *layout* property to FlowLayout, select another layout and then re-select FlowLayout again.

2. Click JScrollPane from the Swing Containers page of the Component Palette. Move the mouse over the Tab 3 panel (the status bar will read "tab3Panel (FlowLayout) z: 0") and click to add the scroll pane.

3. Change the *name* of the new component to "treeScrollPane." (Select it in the Structure window if it is not already selected.) Press ENTER.

4. Use the Property Inspector to change the *preferredSize* of treeScrollPane to 200,170. Press ENTER.

5. In the Application Navigator, expand the DeptEmp\ Model\Application Sources\ deptemp.model nodes. Double click the DeptEmpModule node to display the Application Module Editor. In the Data Model pane, examine the EmployeesView1 node. You do not need the two view object instances created under this node (EmployeesView2 and DepartmentsView2). Move these view objects back to Available Views using the left arrow. The Application Module Editor should look like this:

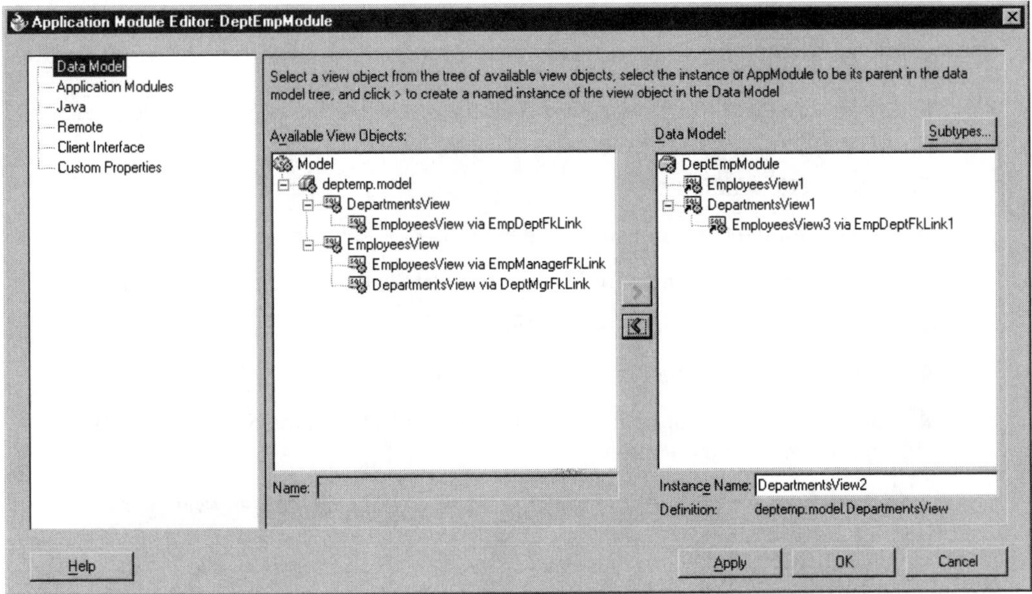

6. Click Apply and OK to close the editor.

   Additional Information: The two view object instances you just removed would allow the program to retrieve an employee's manager or the manager of a department. Since this functionality is not needed in this module, you can delete the view object instances from the application module. You should always try to have only the ADF BC objects that are really needed. All objects consume resources and even though each object's impact is negligible, they can eventually add up to have a significant performance impact. This is especially true in web applications with large numbers of users.

7. Switch to the Data Controls tab. Select DepartmentsView1 under the expanded DeptEmpModuleDataControl node. Use the *Drag and Drop* As pulldown to select "Tree" and drag DepartmentsView1 onto the treeScrollPane in the center of Tab 3 in the Java Visual Editor.

8. Select jTree1 in the visual editor if it is not already selected. Change the *name* property to "deptEmpTree".

9. Click Save All.

10. Now you need to set the bindings for the tree. Click the UI Model tab (the third tab) in the Structure window and expand the node to display the list of bindings. On the DepartmentsView1 node, select Edit from the right-click menu to display the Tree Binding Editor.

11. In order to populate the tree with employee information, make the following selections on the Edit Rule tab:

    - Select deptemp.model.EmployeesView in the *Data Collection Definition* pane.

- Select LastName in the *Display Attribute* pane.
- Leave the *Branch Rule Accessor* set to <none>.
- Make sure that DepartmentsView1Iterator is selected in the *Select an Iterator* drop-down.

12. Click Modify Current Rule.
13. Select the Edit Rule tab again and make the following selections:
    - deptemp.model.DepartmentsView in the *Data Collection Definition* pane.
    - DepartmentName in the *Display Attribute* pane.
    - EmployeesView in the *Branch Rule Accessor* pane.
    - Make sure that DepartmentsView1Iterator is selected in the *Select an Iterator* drop-down as shown here:

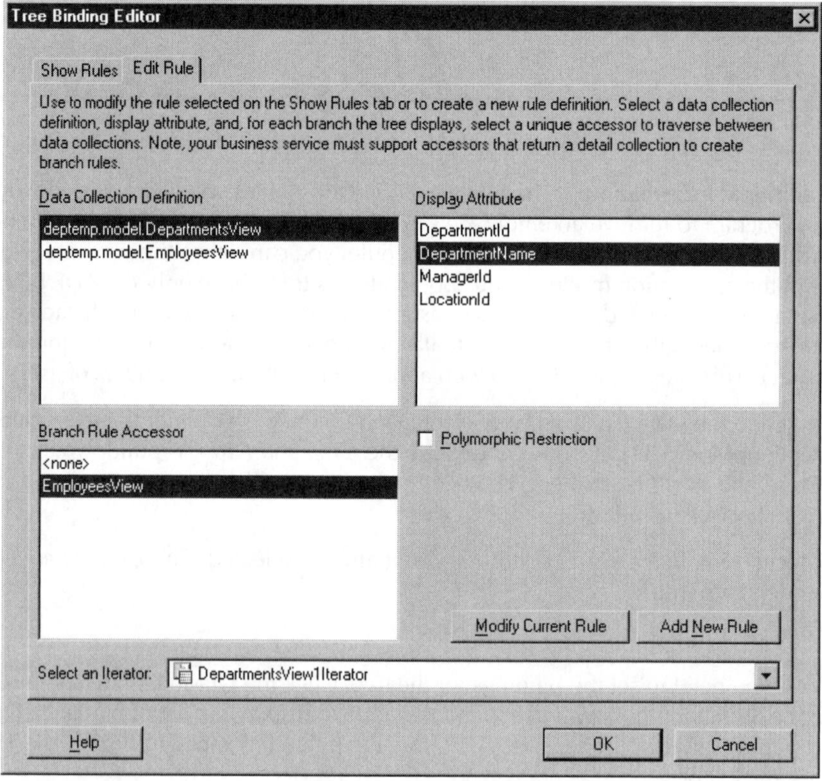

14. Click Add New Rule. Switch to the Show Rules tab to see that the two new rules have been added to the list. Click OK.

Additional Information: Rules identify the parent-child relations in the tree. At each level you select the parent view and the accessor (the child view object usage in the data model) to the child view. Then you select the appropriate iterator. Theoretically there could be more than one, but you will rarely encounter that situation. See the "Working with Tree Controls in ADF-Enabled Web Pages" topic in the help system for more information (use the Full Text Search tab to look for "tree control").

15. Click Save All.
16. Rebuild and run the DeptEmpForm.java file. Tab 3 should look something like the following. You can expand the nodes and scroll as needed to view the information. The navigation bar does not affect the data on this tab because you are viewing all records in the DEPARTMENTS table.

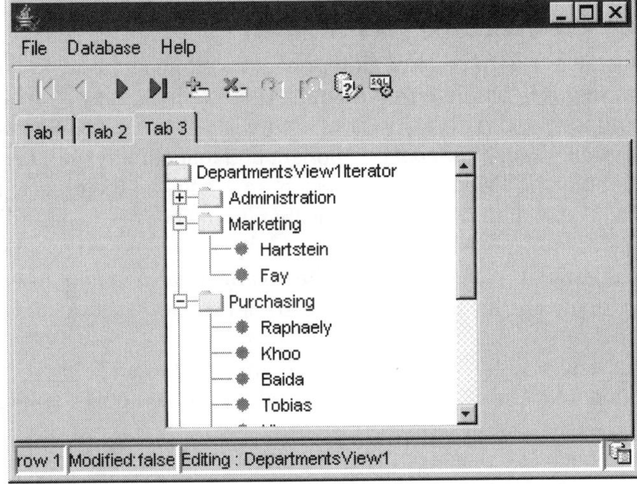

17. Note that the name on the top tree folder is DepartmentsView1Iterator. Close the form. To change this to a more user-friendly name, navigate to the UI Model tab in the Structure window. Select DepartmentsView1Iterator and select Edit from the right-click menu. Change the *Iterator Id* to "Departments." Click OK.
18. Rebuild and run the DeptEmpForm.java file and check Tab 3 to see the change in the tree.
19. Click Save All and close the form.

What Just Happened? In this phase, you added a tree structure to Tab 3 to display the Departments information in another format. Because of the way the binding is made, you can control the structure and order of the parent and child tree nodes as well as the number of tree levels in the hierarchy. You manually specified the binding for each level of the tree. You also removed extraneous view object instances from the application module.

This completes the practice. You created a form with three tabs. Each tab displayed the information in a different format:

- Labels and fields
- Table
- Tree structure

These UI components are typical of the types of user interfaces you will use in creating applications with JDeveloper.

Hands-on Practice: Customize the Component Palette and Create a JavaBean

This practice demonstrates how to create a Component Palette page, how to add components to the page, and how to reorder components within the preinstalled pages. In this practice, you will create a JavaBean component and library to contain the JavaBean. A *JavaBean* is one or more classes that form a reusable (usually visual) component and that comply with certain coding standards such as the ability to be rendered at design time. Most of the objects on the Component Palette are JavaBeans. The benefit of a JavaBean is that it offers ease of reusability and enables you to take advantage of introspection, which allows a tool like JDeveloper to display a list of its properties. Once you design, create, and debug the JavaBean (also called a *bean*), you can reuse it in a tool like JDeveloper. The JavaBean hides the complexity of its code and offers an interface that you can control.

This practice also steps you through adding the component to an "Other" page that you create for the Component Palette. Finally, you will build a simple application to test the new component.

You can add components to pages of the Component Palette as well as reorder components within the preinstalled pages. You can even delete existing pages. For example, you could remove the AWT component page. While you are learning the tool, it is probably best to keep the preinstalled pages intact and add components that you need to new pages. You will be able to find components more easily when they are referenced in examples and documentation. After you learn the product and components better, you will be better able to customize the pages to match your style.

For ordering the components on the page, you can either choose a logical organization or an alphabetical organization (which requires you to know the names of the items). By default, JDeveloper ships with the components arranged alphabetically from top to bottom. You should probably keep this configuration. This will make it easier for developers coming from other environments to find the components for which they are looking.

This practice consists of the following phases:

I. Create and deploy a JavaBean

- Create the JavaBean

- Deploy the JavaBean

II. Create a library for the JavaBean

III. Add a Component Palette page and add the custom JavaBean

- Create a Component Palette page
- Add the custom JavaBean to the page

IV. Test the custom component

I. Create and Deploy a JavaBean

The easiest way to manage custom JavaBeans is to store them in a separate workspace and project. This way you can keep them in an isolated area and deploy them as necessary in your projects. This practice will familiarize you with the steps required to create and add your own customized Beans for reuse in JDeveloper projects.

Create the JavaBean

This section creates a JavaBean by extending an existing component.

1. On the Applications node in the navigator, select New Application Workspace from the right-click menu. Change the *Application Name* to "CustomBeans" and the *Application Package Prefix* to "custombeans." Change the Application Template to "No Template [All Technologies]" using the pulldown. Click OK to create the workspace and project.
2. On the Project node, select New from the right-click menu. Expand the General Category node and select JavaBeans and the Bean item. Click OK to display the Create Bean dialog.
3. Enter "DemoJOptionBean" in the *Name* field and "custombeans" in the *Package* field. If this package is not available in the *Package* pulldown, type it into the field.
4. Ensure that the *Extends* pulldown is set to java.lang.Object as shown here:

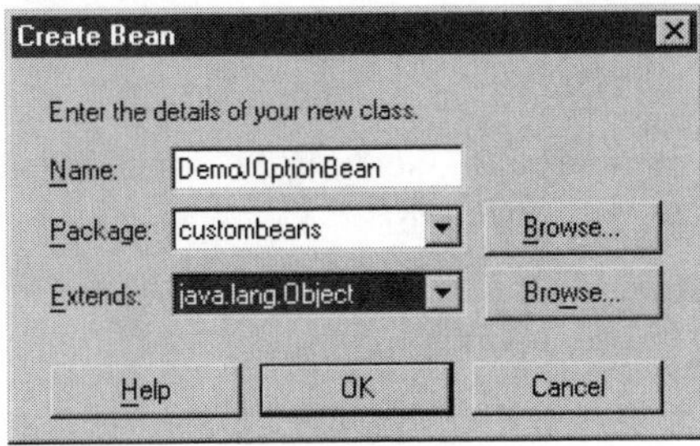

5. Click OK. Click Save All.

6. If the file does not open in the code editor, double click DemoJOptionBean.java in the navigator to open the code editor. Select the Source tab.

7. Replace the default public `DemoJOptionBean( )` constructor with the following code:

```
public DemoJOptionBean(JPanel inPanel)
{
  JOptionPane.showMessageDialog(
      inPanel,
      "This is a modal dialog box",
      "Sample Information Dialog",
      JOptionPane.INFORMATION_MESSAGE);
}
}
```

   Additional Information: You will notice blue underlines on some of the statements, which indicates that you are missing import statements. Although you can type in the imports, JDeveloper can automatically add them as shown in the next step.

8. Click once anywhere in the code editor. Hold the mouse cursor over the blue underline under JPanel. You will see a hint indicating which import statement is required. Press ALT-ENTER to automatically add the import. Repeat this step for the JOptionPane import.

9. This code shows a message dialog (alert or message box) with a default message and title within a specific panel referenced by the input argument `inPanel`. Right click anywhere in the code editor and select Make.

10. Click Save All.

Deploy the JavaBean

The following steps are used to define a deployment profile and to deploy your bean. (Chapter 7 contains more information about deployment profiles and the deployment process.)

1. Right click the CustomBeans\Project node in the Application Navigator and select New.

2. In the New Gallery, select General\Deployment Profiles under Categories and Client JAR File under Items. Click OK.

3. In the Create Deployment Profile–Client JAR File dialog, change the *Deployment Profile Name* to "demojar.deploy." Click OK.

4. Accept the default settings in the Client JAR Deployment Profile Properties dialog, and click OK to generate the deployment profile.

5. Click Save All. The top part of the navigator should look like the following:

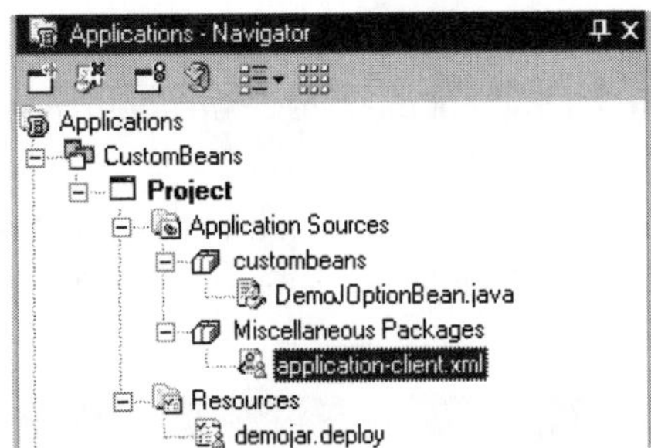

6. Select the demojar.deploy node in the navigator, and select "Deploy to JAR file" from the right-click menu. You should see a message such as "Deployment finished" in the Log window.

What Just Happened? You created a JavaBean that can be an instantiatable (as opposed to static) class and deployed it to a JAR file. The name of the JAR file appears in the Log window. You can open this JAR file (**File | Open**, uncheck "Add to project") to see its contents in the Archive Viewer. In the next phase, you will reference this JAR as a library in order to reuse the bean.

II. Create a Library for the JavaBean

You need to make the new JavaBean available to JDeveloper by including it in a library. A *library* is a name for one or more JAR and/or Zip files (Java archives) that contain code required to run an application. You can add libraries to a project in two ways. The first way is to add the library to the default project settings (**Tools | Default Project Properties**) so that every project created from that moment on will be able to use the library. You can also add the library to the settings for a specific project (after selecting the project, select **Tools | Project Properties**) so that only that project will use the library.

This phase creates the library and adds it to the default project settings area so that any new project will be set up to use it. When you or a JDeveloper wizard adds a library to a project, the files in the library are added to the CLASSPATH when running the project in JDeveloper. When you deploy the project, the libraries attached to the project can be added using the deployment profile dialog. Since this particular library will not be used for development after this practice, a later phase will remove it from the default project properties.

1. Select **Tools | Default Project Properties** from the menu.
2. In the Default Project Properties dialog, select Libraries under the Profiles\ Development node.
3. In the lower-right corner, click New to create a library.

4. In the Create Library dialog, change the *Library Name* to "CustomJOptionBeans."
5. Click the Edit button to the right of the *Class Path* field. Then click Add Entry in the Edit Class Path dialog.
6. In the Select Path Entry dialog, navigate to CustomBeans\ Project\deploy directory. Select (do not double-click) demojar.jar. Click Select and OK. The Create Library dialog should look like this:

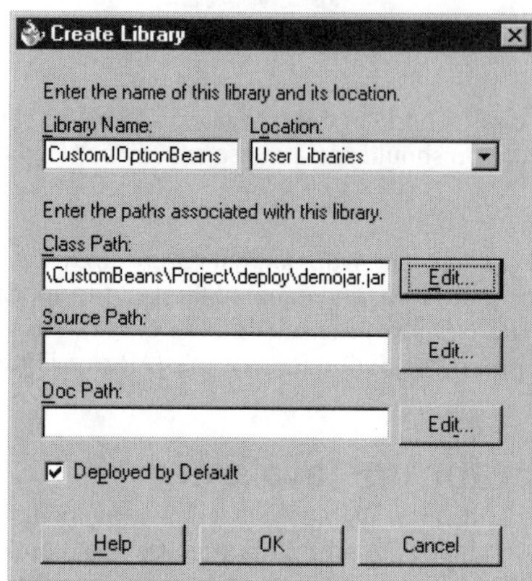

7. Click OK to close the Create Library dialog. You will see the new library listed in the Selected Libraries pane. Click OK to close the Default Project Properties dialog.

What Just Happened? In this phase, you created a library to reference the JAR file containing the JavaBean from Phase I. You also made the modifications to the default project setting, so that the library will be available to all future projects. A later phase will reverse this default project setting.

III. Add a Component Palette Page and Add the Custom JavaBean

In this phase, you create a page on the Component Palette and add the custom bean you created in Phase I. You will also learn how to add predefined and user-defined components to the palette.

Create a Component Palette Page

You can easily create pages to hold additional components using steps such as the following:

1. Open the Java Visual Editor for the DemoJOptionBean.java file by double clicking it in the navigator. In this case, you can use the bean created in Phase I. You may need to select the Design tab. The Java Visual Editor will be blank. You need to display the visual editor so that the Component Palette is available.
2. To create a Component Palette page, select Add Page from the right-click menu on the Component Palette.
3. On the Create Palette Page dialog, enter "Other" in the *Page Name* field. Leave "java" as the *Page Type*. Click OK.
4. You will now see "Other" in the Component Palette pulldown and the Pointer and Custom item icons on that page.

   Additional Information: You can also accomplish this task using the Configure Component Palette dialog (select Palette Properties from the right-click menu on a palette page or select **Tools | Configure Palette**). You will use this dialog later in the practice to add components.

TIP
You can add, rearrange, or remove any of the components or component pages installed with JDeveloper.

Add the Custom JavaBean to the Page

The following steps will add the DemoJOptionBean component to the Other page you just created. The only information needed to add a component to a page is its name, a library location, and the icon file name. The DemoJOptionBean is located in the CustomJOptionBeans library.

1. To add the component, select "Other" in the Component Palette pulldown. Select Add Component from the right-click menu on the Component Palette to open the Add JavaBeans dialog.
2. Using the Library pulldown, select CustomJOptionBeans.
3. Expand the custombeans node. Select DemoJOptionBean.

4. The path name and name of the default icon will be shown in the *Icon* field, and the icon will be displayed under *Preview* as shown here. Click OK to dismiss the Add JavaBeans dialog.

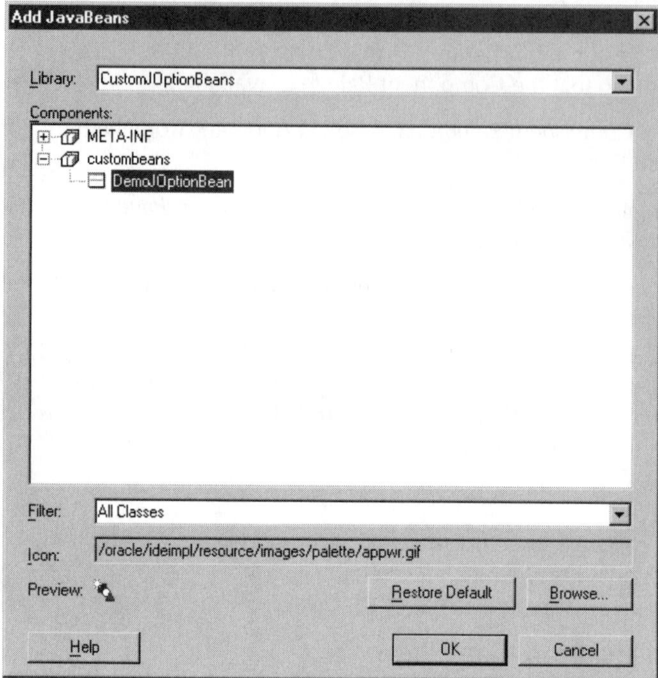

5. Click Yes in the Confirm JavaBean Installation dialog and OK to confirm. You will see the generic icon on your Other Component Palette page.

   Additional Information: The icon that is added to the project is the default icon that is used when you add any component to the Component Palette. If you want to deploy a different icon with the JAR file, you can use **File | Import** to select a different one, such as "Container.gif," in the directory and have the import utility copy it to the project file. Then be sure it is deployed with the JAR file (you will have to experiment with deployment profile settings to include the icon file). Then, in the Add Component dialog, browse for the icon file, find the bean JAR file that contains the icon, and use that as the icon for the Component Palette.

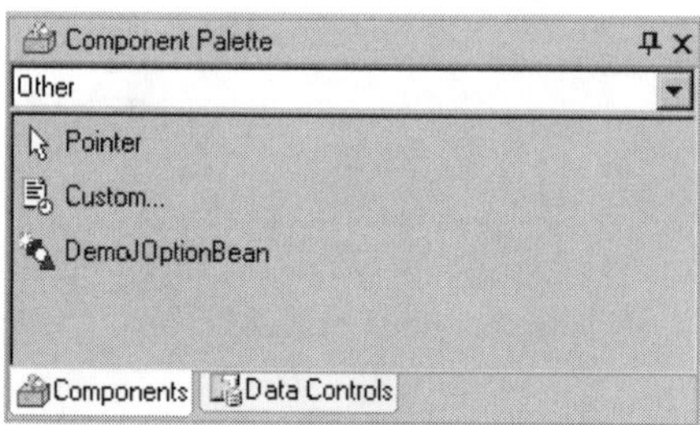

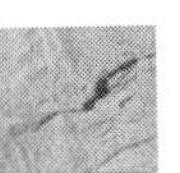

NOTE
Archive files for libraries should be placed in a common directory that is outside of all project directories.

6. Hold the mouse cursor over the icon, and you will see the name of the class that the icon represents.

What Just Happened? You created a page on the Component Palette and added the DemoJOptionBean component to it. This component will be available for use in the Java Visual Editor for any Java class file. Dropping this component to a class file will add the component to the frame or panel, although no visual component will be visible until you run the application.

IV. Test the Custom Component

This phase creates a simple application that uses DemoJOptionBean to create a message dialog.

1. Select New Project from the right-click menu on the Custom Beans workspace node. Select Java Application Project from the General\Projects category in the New Gallery and click OK to display the Create Java Application Project Wizard.
2. Click Next if the Welcome page appears. Use "TestOptionPane" for the *Project Name*. Click Next.
3. Change the *Default Package* name to "beantest", and leave the *Java Source Path* and *Output Directory* selections. Click Next.
4. Leave the default settings on the Libraries page. Click Finish to open the Create Java Application dialog.
5. Enter "TestOption" in the *Name* field. Ensure that beantest is the package. Leave the other default selections and click OK.
6. In the Create Frame dialog, enter "TestOptionFrame" in the *Name* field, and accept the other default settings. Click OK to create the files.
7. Click Save All.
8. Select TestOptionFrame.java in the navigator window and click the Make icon.
9. Double click TestOptionFrame.java to open the Java Visual Editor. Click the Design tab. Expand the UI node in the Structure window and select the "this" node. Change the *layout* property to "BorderLayout."
10. From the Swing Containers page of the Component Palette, click the JPanel icon, move the mouse cursor over the visual editor until "this (BorderLayout): Center" appears in the IDE status bar, and click the mouse to drop the component.
11. Using the jPanel1 Property Inspector, change properties as shown here:
    name property to "mainPanel"
    layout property to "BorderLayout"

12. From the Swing page of the Component Palette, select the JButton icon, move the mouse over the visual editor until you see "mainPanel (BorderLayout): South," and click the mouse to drop the component. The button will appear in the bottom of the panel.

13. Change the following JButton properties:
    name to "testButton"
    text to "Test"

14. Click Save All.

15. The Java Visual Editor should look something like the following:

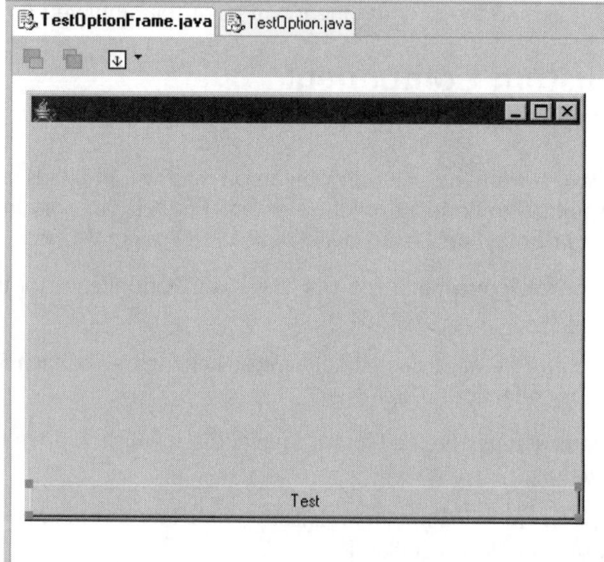

16. Select the DemoJOptionBean component that you created earlier from the Other page of the Component Palette, move the mouse over the visual editor until the IDE status bar indicates "mainPanel (BorderLayout): North," and click the mouse to add the component.

    Additional Information: The bean is added under the Other node at the bottom of the Structure window. The Java Visual Editor window will go blank because the focus has shifted to the Other node in the Structure window and the new component has no visual design aspect. Disregard the warning to that effect in the Log window.

17. In the Property Inspector for the demoJOptionBean1 object, change the name to "demoJOptionBean".

18. Click "this" in the Structure window to redisplay the frame in the visual editor. Double click the testButton in the Java Visual Editor to add the actionPerformed event and open the Code Editor to the event handler stub.

19. Find the following line of code that instantiates the DemoJOptionBean:

```
private DemoJOptionBean demoJOptionBean = new DemoJOptionBean();
```

Additional Information: This line was added when you dropped the component into the visual editor.

20. Cut this line of code, and paste it between the curly brackets after this line of code at the end of the file:

```
private void testButton_actionPerformed(ActionEvent e)
```

21. Modify the line of code in the new position to look like the following. (Note that you will be deleting the word "private" and adding a parameter to the constructor call.)

```
DemoJOptionBean demoJOptionBean = new DemoJOptionBean(mainPanel);
```

22. Rebuild the project and click Save All.

    Additional Information: Navigate to the top of the file, and look for the import statement for DemoJOptionBean. This line was also automatically added when you dropped the component into the Structure window.

23. Run the TestOption.java application and click the Test button to try the dialog. The dialog window title will be "Sample Information Dialog," and the message will appear in the dialog as shown next:

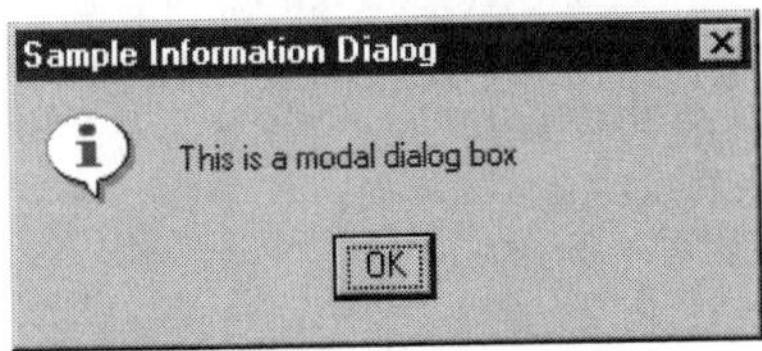

24. Click OK and close the window.

    Additional Information: The reason that the Java application found the new component is that you included its library in the project settings information. Select Project Properties from the right-click menu on the TestOptionPane node and check that the Selected Libraries pane in the Libraries page contains the CustomJOptionBeans library that you added to the default project settings before you created the project. Check the project settings for the project in this workspace; the new library is not available because you modified the default project properties after creating this project. All new projects will include that library as well so that your new component will be available.

NOTE
The code that JDeveloper writes for you in this case is minimal if you do not modify properties in creating the JavaBean. However, by using this framework, you can pass parameters to your custom class and return reusable custom components of almost any complexity.

25. This practice showed how to add a library to all new projects. Since this demonstration JavaBean is not required in future work, you can remove it from the default project

settings by selecting **Tools | Default Project Properties** to display the Project Settings dialog.

26. Select the Libraries node in the navigator. Select CustomJOptionBeans and click the left-arrow button to remove it from the selected list. Click OK. New projects will not include this library in their Selected Libraries list.

NOTE
If you also want to restore the Component Palette to its default, display the Other page of the Component Palette, and select Remove Page from the right-click menu. You can also remove the Other page by selecting Remove Page from the right-click menu on the Other page of the Component Palette. This will return your setup to the default.

What Just Happened? You created a small test application and tested adding and running the new component. You may want to try some other variations, such as using ERROR_MESSAGE instead of INFORMATION_MESSAGE. This will change the dialog's icon. You can also try other methods, such as showConfirmDialog, showInputDialog, or showOptionDialog. You will have to redeploy the JAR file after making these changes, but you will not need to change your test Java application file to take advantage of the changes. Study this example carefully before trying to branch out to other components.

CHAPTER 16

Layout Managers

Mad world! mad kings!
mad composition!

—William Shakespeare (1564–1616),
King John (II, i, 561)

ne of the strengths and principal objectives of the Java language is platform independence—the ability of applications built with Java to be deployed to diverse operating systems and platforms. One manifestation of platform independence is in the area of user interface design. When applications are deployed on different platforms, the windows and the objects within them are not always rendered in the same size and position. In addition, users may resize the windows in an application to match their preferences. Developers grapple with this problem in many programming languages and often develop their own solutions. However, these solutions are often very code-intensive and time-consuming.

Another problem that developers grapple with is the actual positioning of objects in the user interface. As development tools evolved through the following features, the developer was able to place components on the user interface more easily:

- **Programmatic functions** that developers could use to set an exact X (horizontal) and Y (vertical) coordinate and size. This method required typing many lines of code but allowed exact placement of objects on the screen.
- **Property palettes** that contained a list of property names and values. The positioning properties allow the developer to set the component position and size without writing lines of code. In some development environments, setting properties in this way would generate lines of code that the developer could still manipulate. In other environments, the property values were held in internal code that the developer could not modify outside of the property palette.
- **Visual layout editors** that set the placement properties after the developer dragged in, resized, and placed the component onto a visual representation of the runtime window. Since exact alignments and placements are difficult using drag and drop, visual editors usually provide only an approximation of the desired layout. Therefore, development tools offer alignment and sizing tools that the developer uses to place components more precisely relative to each other.

The first method was used exclusively by earlier programming environments. Most current windowing development environments allow the developer to use all methods to place the components on the page. However, they all take some time and effort to use and a certain amount of trial and error is required to create the desired layout.

Java offers a feature—layout managers—that directly addresses the layout problems that occur when displaying applications on different platforms and that assists the developer in creating a desired layout more quickly. When working with Java client applications (Java applications and applets), a *layout manager* is a class (in the Swing library) that you instantiate and attach to a container (such as a JPanel object). This class defines how objects within the container are positioned and sized at run time both initially and when the container is resized.

You can take advantage of the layout manager features in a Java application (or the older-style applet) by associating the layout manager with a container and by setting a few properties.

The layout manager handles the calculations and functions necessary to perform the positioning and sizing manipulations. Java supplies a number of layout managers and JDeveloper supports them. In addition, you can add layout managers to JDeveloper that you or a third party create. To work effectively with layout managers, you need to be aware of what is available and how each of the managers works.

This chapter explains the concepts of layout managers and the details about each layout manager that JDeveloper provides. It also includes a hands-on practice to show you how to apply some of the more commonly used layout managers.

How Does This Work in a J2EE Web Application?

The concept of layout managers extends beyond the realm of Swing classes in Java client applications. As described in Chapter 19, User Interface XML (UIX) is an XML-based tag language that can generate a light-client, browser-based HTML page at run time. When creating components for a user interface in UIX, you define nested containers, as you do with nested panels in Java client applications. Like Swing layout managers, these containers (called *layout elements*) define how components within them will be placed and how the container will react when the window is resized.

For example, the `BorderLayout` Swing layout manager class has a UIX counterpart layout element called "borderLayout." Both `BorderLayout` and `borderLayout` define similar placement and layout behavior for the components within them (as described for `BorderLayout` later in this chapter).

Java layout managers are currently more mature and more feature-rich than their UIX counterparts, but the philosophy is similar. Therefore, learning about and practicing how to code Java client layout managers as described in this chapter will serve you well even if you do not intend to code for the Java client environment.

NOTE
Table 16-2 contains a summary of layout managers and their uses.

Layout Manager and Container Concepts

A layout manager instance (or "layout" for short) is a separate object built from a layout manager class that exists within the context of a container. A *container* is an object that can hold other objects (usually user interface objects). The container's layout manager determines how objects inside the container will be placed and sized both at design time and at run time. In Java, objects are organized into three main levels in what is called the *containment hierarchy*:

- **Window** A window is a top-level container that supplies the visual root for all objects in a Java application. It appears as a standard GUI window on the user's desktop. Classes such as `Frame`, `JFrame`, `Dialog`, and `JDialog` are examples of windows.

- **Non-Window Container** Within the window are other non-window containers. Classes such as `Panel`, `JPanel`, `ScrollPane`, `JScrollPane`, and `JSplitPane` are all non-window containers. Non-window containers have no visible border by default although you can add a visible border by assigning a border object as described later in the "Borders" sidebar. Non-window containers house atomic components or other containers as children. It is common practice to embed panels within panels to more easily and precisely manage portions of the frame or dialog.

- **Atomic components** These are objects such as buttons and text fields that cannot contain other objects. If a component cannot contain another object, it is an *atomic component*; otherwise, it is a container.

Laying Out a User Interface

The standard procedure in JDeveloper for creating a user interface layout consists of the following steps:

1. **Create a window.** The top-level window is formed from a `Window` class or an `Applet` class (that runs in a browser session).
2. **Add a non-window container.** The non-window container is placed as a child object within the Window container and serves as the layout area for user interface objects. It houses all other components except the toolbar and status bar, which are also direct children of the window. JDeveloper creates this intermediate container when you use the New Frame dialog to create a frame. The following illustration shows how a non-window container panel (mainPanel) would appear in the UI tab of the Structure window:

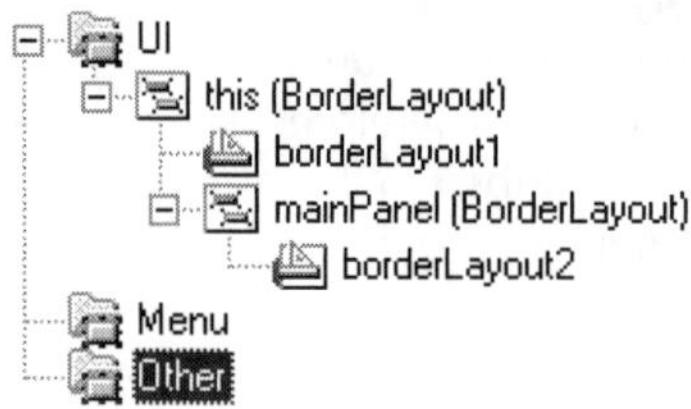

3. **Assign a layout manager and set layout manager properties.** These tasks are described further in the next sections.

Borders

Although toolbars, scroll panels, and tab panels include visible borders, some components such as JPanel do not show a visible border by default. You can create a border for these components using a border object. A *border object* supplies a visual aspect to the panel. The examples in this chapter that use a panel also assign a border so that you can see the panel's edges. A property editor dialog associated with components makes assigning the border easier. Select Swing Border from the *border* property pulldown to display this dialog. You can use this dialog to select from various styles of borders such as BevelBorder, EmptyBorder, EtchedBorder, LineBorder, and TitledBorder.

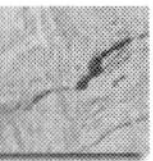

TIP

You can make a container that uses a layout manager (other than "null") resize automatically to its contents using the `pack()` *method. The following example could be used in the constructor method for a frame file so that the frame will compress to surround its contents when it is initialized:*

```
try {
   jbInit();
   pack();
}
```

4. **Add components.** When you drop components from the Component Palette into a container in the Structure window or Java Visual Editor, JDeveloper creates the code to call the `add()` method on the container. The `add()` method takes as arguments the component and a constraint that is specific to the layout. For example, the code JDeveloper creates for adding a button (jButton1) to a panel (jPanel2) with a `FlowLayout` or `GridLayout` (which have no *constraints* property to assign) would be the following:

   ```
   jPanel2.add(jButton1, null);
   ```

   For a panel that uses `BorderLayout`, the code would be something like the following:

   ```
   jPanel2.add(jButton1, BorderLayout.SOUTH);
   ```

NOTE

For some layout managers, such as GridBagLayout, you might find it easier to add components to a container using a "null" layout and then assign the layout manager after aligning the components. For other layout managers, such as `BorderLayout`*, you will find it easier to assign the layout manager and then add the components. Both techniques are demonstrated in the hands-on practice in this chapter.*

5. **Set the component constraints.** The *constraints* property appears in the Property Inspector window for each component. This property (assigned for a particular object) specifies how the component will behave, for example, the location of the component within the container. The *constraints* property takes different values depending upon the selected layout manager.

6. **Set component properties.** Other properties of the component, such as *preferredSize,* manage other aspects of the component's behavior and appearance. With some layouts, you can set the size and placement properties of a component (such as a button) by dragging and resizing it in the Java Visual Editor. If you just drop the component onto the Structure window, you may have to set the properties afterward.

The Default Layout Manager

When you set the *layout* property for a container component (such as jPanel1), the code that is created sets a layout manager on the container. The layout assignment is shown in the Structure window as a child object of the container. The layout type will be indicated in parentheses in the container object label. If no layout has been assigned to the container, the *default layout* for that container will be in effect. For example, JPanel has a default layout manager of `FlowLayout`. If the default layout is in effect, the layout manager child node under the container will show the default layout style (enclosed in "< >", for example, "<FlowLayout>") as in the following example:

The default layout manager is only a placeholder to indicate the style of layout that the object will use unless you change it. This default layout has no properties to manipulate. You will need to assign an actual layout manager to the container if you need to change the layout manager properties.

Setting Layout Manager Properties

Since it is an object, a layout manager has properties. When you click the layout object in the Structure window, the Property Inspector will show the layout properties, as shown in the following example:

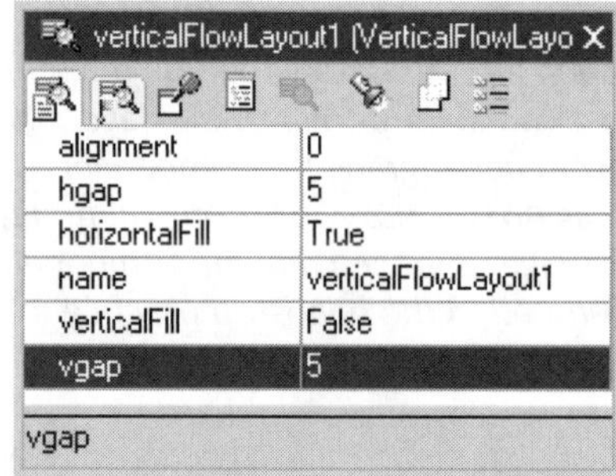

Some layout managers use gap properties to define how much space (in pixels) will appear between components that are inside the container. There are horizontal gap (*hgap*) and vertical gap (*vgap*) properties. Some layout managers have a property, *alignment,* to specify whether the components within the container will be left justified, centered, or right justified. The value for this property is an integer ("0," "1," or "2," respectively).

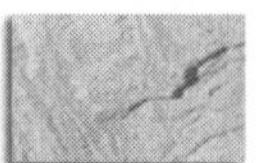

TIP

To verify that the layout manager is working properly, check the effect of resizing the window at run time. You may want to test your application on different resolutions, different browsers (if it is an applet), and different operating systems (such as Macintosh and Windows). You can also resize the frame window in the Java Visual Editor to check the layout manager behavior. Press CTRL-Z *to restore the window size.*

Java Visual Editor Tools

To assist with layout, the Java Visual Editor toolbar performs some of the common operations on components within the container. The operations are specific to the layout manager style. For example, if you use no layout manager (the *layout* property is "null"), whenever components within that container are selected, the Java Visual Editor toolbar contains buttons for alignment such as Align Left, Align Center, Align Right, Align Top, Align Middle, and Align Bottom. It also contains buttons for Make Same Size Width and Make Same Size Height that are enabled after grouping components within a common container together. All layout managers also offer Send To Back and Bring To Front buttons that change the *z-order* (layering and ordering of components explained in the sidebar "A Word About Z-Order"). JDeveloper uses the term *order* for z-order.

Some of the toolbar items are also displayed in the right-click menu on a component in the Java Visual Editor. In addition to Undo, Redo, Cut, Copy, Paste, and other standard operations, the right-click menu may offer Order, Align, Make Same Size, or Space Evenly options, depending on the layout type, to assist in layout. The Design main menu item contains a number of the same layout operations. The Design menu is only enabled when the visual editor has focus.

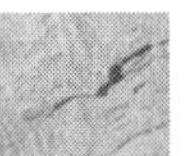

NOTE
The Java Visual Editor displays a grid of dots when you draw or move a component inside some layout manager containers. These dots assist you when lining up components. The Java Visual Editor page of the Preferences dialog contains grid settings.

A Word About Z-Order

Z-order defines the order in which components are layered, which is important if components overlap and you need to define which one overlays another. Overlapping components is not the normal situation, but z-order is also used as the default *tab order*, because it also defines the sequence of cursor navigation for components in the application. For example, a form might contain three items and a button. By default, when the user presses the TAB key when the cursor is in the first item, the cursor will pass to the second item. The next TAB key press moves the cursor to the next item in the z-order. You can set the tab order explicitly (using the *nextFocusableComponent* property on a component) to define the cursor navigation through the components on the window.

The first item that the cursor moves to when the form starts will be the first item listed under the first container in the Structure window. You can move objects around in the Structure window using the Order | Bring To Front or Order | Send To Back options in the right-click menu of the Java Visual Editor. These options also appear in the Java Visual Editor toolbar for all layout managers. The Structure window immediately shows changes you make in z-order using the Java Visual Editor menu items and toolbar buttons. You can also cut an item in the Java Visual Editor and paste it into the Structure window.

Layout Managers in JDeveloper

Most work with the layout managers is accomplished in the JDeveloper Java Visual Editor and the Structure window. Table 16-1 contains a list of layout managers supplied by JDeveloper and indicates whether they represent the standard Java Foundation Classes (JFCs), have been modified to work with the JDeveloper Java Visual Editor, or are specific to JDeveloper. The list does not include the "null" layout manager described later because it has no source and is not really a layout manager.

Each of these layout managers are described in this chapter. It is possible to add layout managers from other sources to this set, and it is also possible to create your own layout managers. The JDeveloper help system contains information about how to add to this set, but the group in Table 16-1 should suffice for most purposes.

TIP
Regardless of which layout manager you select, you can prevent the user from resizing the window by setting the "resizable" property on the "this" frame to "False."

Layout Manager	Source
`BorderLayout`	Standard
`BoxLayout2`	Modified version of the JFC `BoxLayout`
`CardLayout`	Standard
`FlowLayout`	Standard
`GridBagLayout`	Standard
`GridLayout`	Standard
`OverlayLayout2`	Modified version of the JFC `OverlayLayout`
`PaneLayout`	Specific to JDeveloper
`VerticalFlowLayout`	Specific to JDeveloper (a modified version of the JFC `FlowLayout`)
`XYLayout`	Specific to JDeveloper

TABLE 16-1. *JDeveloper Layout Managers and Their Source*

Overview of the Layout Managers

The following discussion provides some details about the layout managers that JDeveloper offers. The information in this chapter will get you started; however, as you progress with your Java work, you will want to refer to other Java books for further examples and explanations.

The layouts are explained in alphabetical order. Table 16-2, at the end of this section, summarizes the key uses for each layout. The hands-on practice at the end of this chapter further explains two commonly used layout managers—`BorderLayout` and `GridBagLayout`. In addition, Appendix A contains references to online sources of Swing class information including layout managers.

Although panels are used in some examples as components within the container, you can place any component type in a container. Panels are used in the examples as generic objects with no implied functionality.

It is important to understand how layout managers behave. The easiest way to achieve this understanding is to look at sample layouts. The examples in this chapter demonstrate a layout manager by setting the layout of a JPanel object inside the frame container. The frame container layout manager is left at its default setting (`BorderLayout`). The JPanel object is assigned to the center area of the parent frame container. Since the panel is the only container under the frame, it fills the frame. Therefore, when you resize the window (frame) at run time, you are essentially resizing the inner JPanel container that manages the layout.

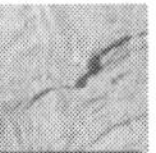

NOTE
Although the hands-on practice in this chapter focuses on two commonly used layout managers, you can apply similar techniques to experiment with any other layout manager. Experimenting with layout managers with simple test cases is the best way to learn the features.

A Word About the *"null" Layout*

In addition to "default" and the layout managers shown in Table 16-1, the *layout* property offers a value of "null." This value indicates that no layout manager will be used. (This chapter refers to this setting as the *"null" layout.*) The "null" layout is different from the default layout manager; the default layout manager implies that some layout manager behavior is applied to the container, whereas the "null" layout means that no behavior is defined for the container. The "null" layout manager allows you to arrange its child components using X and Y coordinates and specific, fixed sizes. For example, you can place or size components in any way (including overlapping components) and the components will retain their position and size when the container is resized. In this way, it is the same as the `XYLayout` described later in this chapter, but `XYLayout` is different from the "null" layout as described in the XYLayout section.

BorderLayout

The `BorderLayout` manager divides the container into five areas that are named geographically: North, South, East, West, and Center, as shown in Figure 16-1. Each area may contain more than

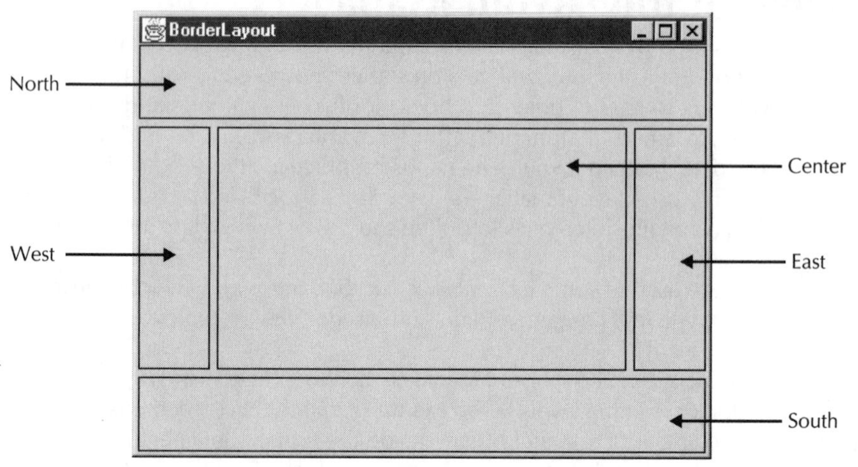

FIGURE 16-1. *BorderLayout sample*

one object but only one object (the topmost object) will be displayed at a time in each area. If you need to place more than one component in a BorderLayout area, use a panel as the single displayed object for that area and add components as children of the panel. `BorderLayout` takes care of sizing the components within each area.

If the user resizes the window so that it is shorter, the Center, East, and West areas will shorten, as shown here:

Increasing the height will expand the Center, East, and West areas in the same way. If the user narrows the window, the Center, North, and South areas will narrow. Increasing the width will expand the same areas. Components inside the areas will resize accordingly.

The heights of the North and South areas and the widths of the East and West areas are calculated based upon the size of the components. If the user moves the sides of the window inside the limits that those areas define, some areas will be partially or completely hidden. The hands-on practice later in this chapter allows you to experiment with resizing the container and watching what happens to the enclosed objects.

Layout Properties

The BorderLayout manager has the following two properties:

- **vgap** The amount of vertical space between the North, Center, and South areas.
- **hgap** The amount of horizontal space between the East, Center, and West areas.

Both properties are measured in *pixels* (picture elements that correspond to dots on the screen). You will be able to see the effect of a change in these values in the Java Visual Editor.

Component Constraints and Properties

The *constraints* property of the component specifies in which of the five areas the component will be placed. Although you can set more than one component constraint to the same area, only one component will be visible at any given moment. As mentioned, you can get around this limitation by using a panel as the single component and placing objects inside the panel.

The heights of the North and South areas are managed by the *preferredSize* property of their contents. Thus, if you place a toolbar object in the North area and a status bar object in the South area, the heights of those areas will be determined by the heights of the objects. If the object height needs to be expanded, reset the second number in the *preferredSize* property of the component. This property is assigned a pair of numbers that indicates the width and height. For example, if the property value is "50, 50" and you need a 100-pixel height, change the value to "50, 100." The first number sets the width; `BorderLayout` ignores this number for North and South areas because it determines the width based upon the container's size.

Similarly, the widths of the East and West areas are managed by the *preferredSize* property of their contents. The height number in the *preferredSize* value is ignored for East and West areas. The Center area ignores the *preferredSize* property completely.

Uses for BorderLayout

`BorderLayout` is a popular layout manager. It is useful for UI designs where one or more edges of the window contain objects and the edges need to be resized automatically when the window resizes. Normally, you would combine this layout with others, as described in the later section "Multiple Layouts."

This layout style is commonly used for placing toolbars or button areas and a status bar. Since these objects are normally fixed to the top and bottom of the window, the `BorderLayout` manager would be used on the frame (window). The toolbar would be placed in the North area and the status bar would be placed in the South area. If you need a vertical toolbar, you could use the West area.

A hands-on practice at the end of this chapter steps through creating an example of this layout.

BoxLayout2

The `BoxLayout2` manager (an Oracle version of the Swing BoxLayout manager) arranges multiple components within it in a vertical or horizontal layout. The *axis* property of the layout manager specifies whether the component layout will be vertical or horizontal. If *axis* is set to "X_AXIS", all components placed in the container will be arranged horizontally side by side. If the *axis* is set to "Y_AXIS," all components placed in the container will be stacked vertically. The layout will attempt to give each component the amount of space defined by its *preferredSize* property. If more than enough space is available, each component will be expanded up to the setting of their *maximumSize* property.

The layout also attempts to make all components as large as the largest component in the dimension opposite of the axis. For example, if the axis is set to "X_AXIS," all components will have the same height; if the axis is set to "Y_AXIS," all components will have the same width. Any remaining space after all components have been allocated their maximum size is left unfilled. If not enough space is available to display the component based on its *preferredSize* property, the component will be reduced in size. The setting of the *minimumSize* property of the component is respected in the dimension of the axis of the layout (horizontal for "X_AXIS" and vertical for "Y_AXIS").

The "X_AXIS" arrangement only allows a single row for each container and will not wrap if the container is not sufficiently large enough to display all of its components. Figure 16-2 shows this arrangement using three panels inside a container managed by the BoxLayout2 manager. As with other examples in this chapter, the example shows panels inside the container, but this layout manager is often used for containers that hold buttons in a toolbar.

At run time, child components will be constrained (limited to resizing) by their *minimumSize* and *maximumSize* properties in the direction of the layout axis (horizontal for "X_AXIS" and

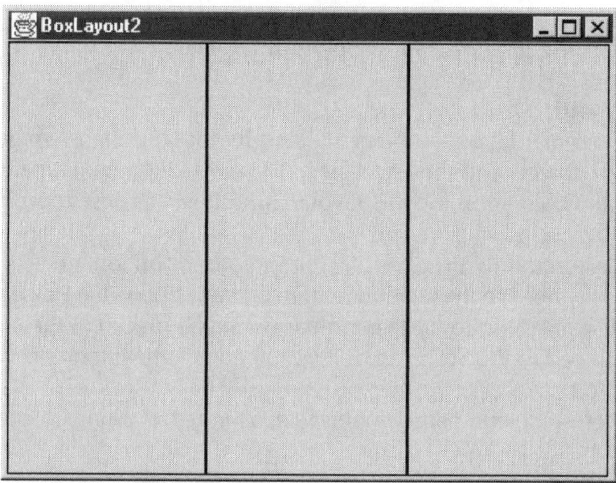

FIGURE 16-2. *BoxLayout2 sample*

vertical for "Y_AXIS"). The components will be constrained based on their *maximumSize* property and the size of the container in the opposite direction from the axis. The following shows the result when an "X_AXIS" arrangement container is resized vertically and horizontally:

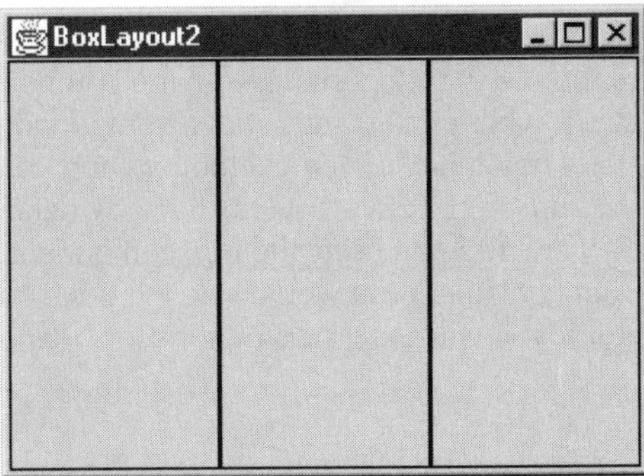

If you specify that the layout is vertical (components arranged on the Y axis), the components will be stacked top to bottom. With both arrangements, you can alter the sizes of the components and maintain the stacking effect that this layout offers. This is described in the "Component Constraints and Properties" section.

Layout Properties

The layout has only one property—*axis*. You set this to "X_AXIS" to specify a horizontal arrangement of components or to "Y_AXIS" to specify a vertical arrangement of components.

Component Constraints and Properties

The component *constraints* property is not used by the BoxLayout2 manager. A number of properties affect the layout:

- **maximumSize** As with most size properties, this is a pair of numbers indicating width and height. For a vertical arrangement, the width number (first number) of this property affects the width of the component. For a horizontal arrangement, the height (second number) of this property affects the height of the component. The component will take up as much space as the layout manager can provide up to its *maximumSize* setting. Set the *maximumSize* to less than the size of the container to make the component take less than the available space and to be centered in the space.
- **minimumSize** The layout respects this property only in the dimension of the layout axis. It will not make the component smaller than the minimum size in the direction of the layout axis. In the direction opposite to the axis, the component may be reduced to fit within the container.
- **preferredSize** The layout uses this property as a starting point to which additional size will be added to the maximum for each component. Size will be removed down to the minimum based on the actions of the layout.

- **alignmentX and alignmentY** These properties align the component within the space allocated to it. They require a bit of thought and experimentation. Refer to the Javadoc for `BoxLayout2` if you require alignment other than the default.

Uses for BoxLayout2

Unlike other layout managers, `BoxLayout2` can preserve the component alignment and size. Therefore, it is useful in situations where you want to have components stack together in a single row or column (for example, for a horizontal or vertical toolbar) and you do not want the wrapping effect offered by `FlowLayout` and `VerticalFlowLayout`. By default, there is no gap between components. You can, however, define a gap using the Box component as an empty but additional component inside the BoxLayout container. You would size the Box component according to your needs for the gap. This is useful if you want to group buttons together and separate the groups with a gap.

CardLayout

The CardLayout manager allows you to place components on top of one another. Only one component is visible at any given time, but you can use the `show()` method of the layout manager to display it. For example, `jPanel1` contains multiple panels and is defined with a CardLayout object called cardLayout1. Only one panel will be displayed at a time and it will fill the entire container, but you can programmatically display the next panel using "`cardLayout1.next(jPanel1);`". The name "CardLayout" evokes a stack of cards, where one card is piled upon another and only one is showing.

For example, you might have an interface such as the one in Figure 16-3. This example has two panels—one for the top and one for the bottom of the display. The top panel contains a combo box, and the bottom panel is assigned the CardLayout manager and contains two more panels. One of these panels contains a button, and the other contains a text field. The application displays one panel or another based on code executed when the combo box element is selected.

Layout Properties

`CardLayout` has the following gap properties:

- **hgap** The distance in pixels between the left and right sides of the container and the component within the container
- **vgap** The distance in pixels between the top and bottom of the container and the component within the container

Component Constraints and Properties

The component *constraints* property is not used by this layout manager. There are no other component properties that affect the layout manager.

Uses for CardLayout

`CardLayout` provides functionality similar to that of a tab control but does not have a tab interface. The Swing tab component (JTabbedPane) is easier to use because it is a single component instead of several components that are required for this layout. However, if you need to control the display with a component other than the tab interface (such as with a push button, radio button,

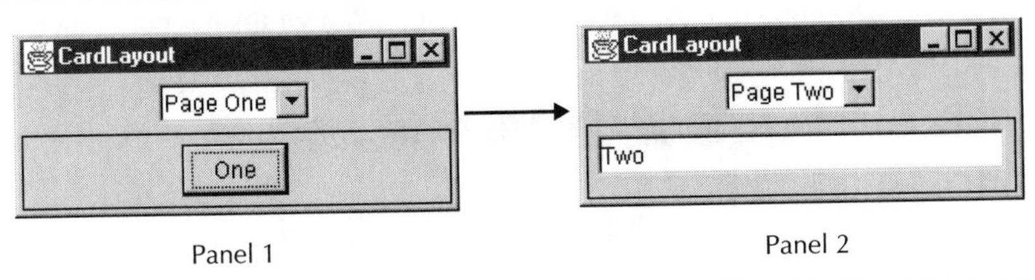

FIGURE 16-3. *CardLayout sample*

or combo box), this layout manager will provide the correct functionality. This layout manager can also be used to switch fields or explanation text that appears in a display area based on placing the cursor in a field or radio group item.

FlowLayout

The FlowLayout manager arranges components inside it in a row. If the row is filled and there are more components to display, the layout starts another row, as Figure 16-4 shows. This layout manager works in the same way as the word-wrap feature in word processors. Rows span the entire width of the container and are as high as the highest component on a particular row. The contents are centered on the row by default, but they can be right or left justified as well.

The actions that this layout offers are similar to the `BoxLayout2` manager defined with a horizontal (X_AXIS) axis setting. This layout offers the wrapping feature that `BoxLayout2` does not. `FlowLayout` does not restrict the container from being sized smaller than the minimum size of the components.

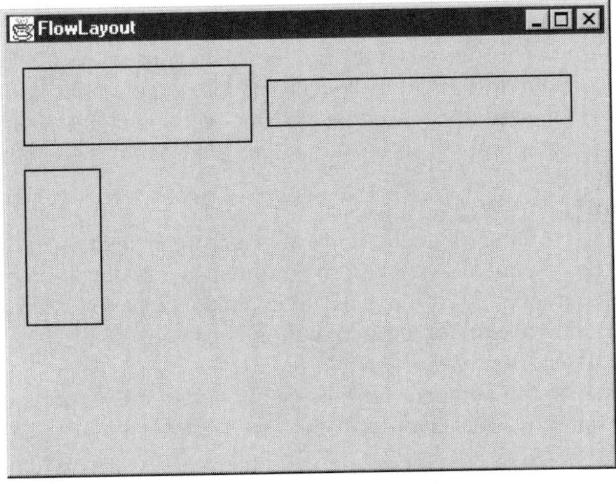

FIGURE 16-4. *FlowLayout sample*

When the user resizes the width of the container, the layout wraps the components so they will fit in the horizontal space, as shown here:

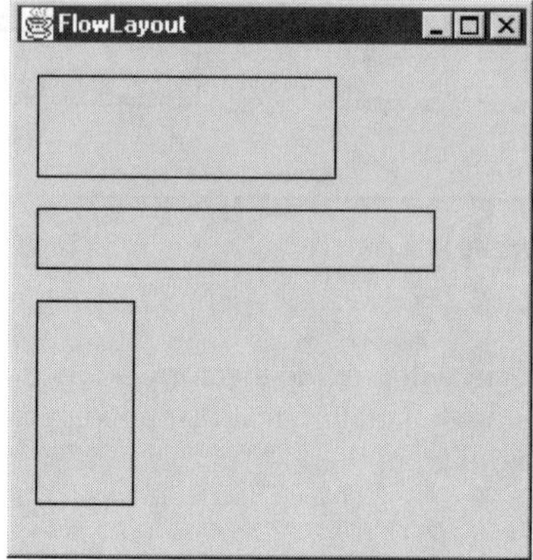

Layout Properties

A FlowLayout object uses the following properties:

- **alignment** This property is set to "0" to left-justify the components, "1" to center components within the horizontal space, or "2" to right-justify the components.
- **hgap** This property sets the number of pixels of horizontal space between components that are on the same line.
- **vgap** This property sets the number of pixels of vertical space between a row and the row underneath it. The row height is the same as the tallest component in that row.

Component Constraints and Properties

The component *constraints* property is not used by this layout manager. The component's *preferredSize* property determines the row's height and the component's width. The row height is equal to the height of the highest component (the one with the largest value in the second number of the *preferredSize* property). The row's width is based on the width of the container.

Uses for FlowLayout

Panels created with classes such as JPanel use this layout as the default. As mentioned, you cannot assign properties to a default layout manager, so a normal step in development is to explicitly assign a layout manager (such as `FlowLayout`) to containers that you want to manipulate. `FlowLayout` is particularly useful for a row of buttons that you want to have wrap to another line if the window width is decreased.

A hands-on practice on the authors' websites mentioned in the author biographies steps through creating an example of this layout.

GridBagLayout

The GridBagLayout manager creates container cells that contain components. Unlike the `GridLayout` discussed later, cells in a GridBagLayout container may be different sizes and the components within the cells may span several cells or be less than the area of a single cell. Unlike `FlowLayout` and `VerticalFlowLayout`, this layout uses both preferred heights and widths of components to determine both the cell's height and width rather than one of the two sizes. For example, the height of a cell is determined by the largest preferred height of components in that row; the width of the cell is determined by the largest preferred width of components in that column.

Figure 16-5 shows a complex layout with a number of components demonstrating the cell and component size concepts. When the user resizes this container, the contents shift and resize according to the values of the component *constraints* property.

The layout manager object does not include any properties to modify its behavior. However, it offers a high level of control through the *constraints* property of the components within the container. With this level of control comes complexity, and the `GridBagLayout` is the most complex of the layout managers to set up. However, because of its flexibility, `GridBagLayout` is the most commonly used layout manager.

Working with GridBagLayout

As you might expect with a complex layout manager such as `GridBagLayout`, there are many ways to manipulate it in the JDeveloper Java Visual Editor.

Using Drag Handles When you add a component to the container managed by this layout, a cell is created. The cell borders are visible in the Java Visual Editor, although they will not be

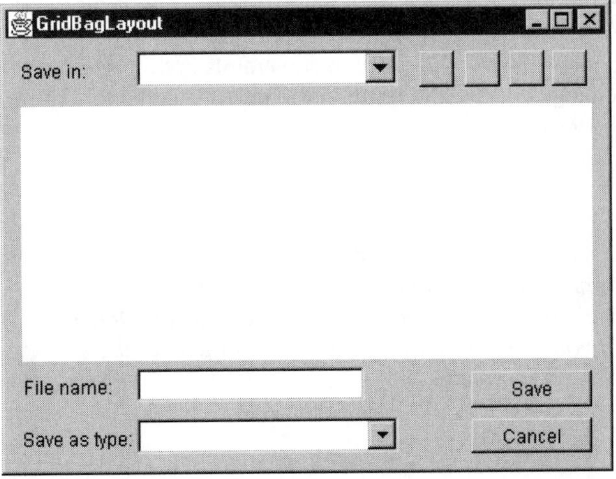

FIGURE 16-5. *GridBagLayout sample*

visible at run time. You can turn the grid display on and off using **Design | Show Grid**. When you select the component in the Structure window or Java Visual Editor, two sets of drag handles will appear on the component inside the cell, as shown here:

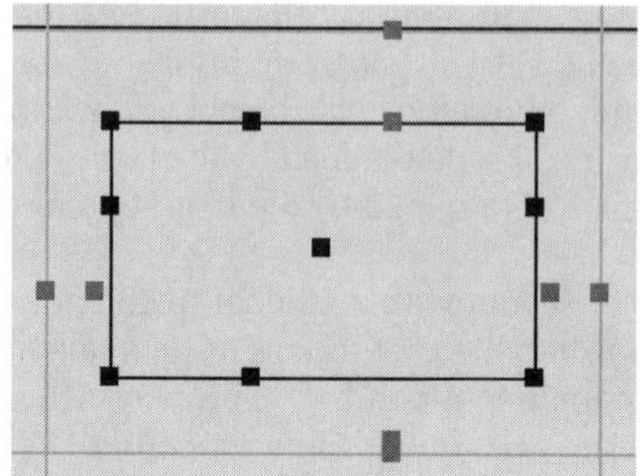

You can resize the component insets and padding (described later) separately using these drag handles. You can resize the insets using the blue handles and resize the padding using the black handles. The sizes you set in this way change the *constraints* property of the component. When you are first learning about this layout manager, this may help you achieve a layout that requires less manual tuning of properties. Experienced developers who understand the GridBagLayout constraints may prefer setting the constraints values manually.

Using the Constraints Window In addition to dragging and positioning components, you can set the *constraints* values precisely for each component using the Constraints window, as shown in Figure 16-6. This window will appear under the Property Inspector by default when you have selected a component inside a container, which is assigned a layout of `GridBagLayout`, `PaneLayout`, or `XYLayout`. The fields and values in this window will vary based upon the layout that is assigned to the component's container. If the Constraints window does not appear, you can select **View | Constraints** or select Constraints from the right-click menu on a component in the Java Visual Editor. You set values for the constraints in this window and click the Apply button to make the change and see the result in the Java Visual Editor. The window can stay open while you work in the visual editor.

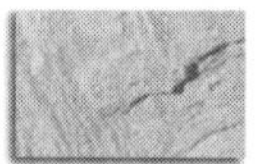

NOTE
The Constraints property editor dialog (available by clicking the "…" button in the Property Inspector's "constraints" property) also allows you to edit the same constraints for a component, but this window is modal, so you need to dismiss it before continuing to work. Oracle recommends that you use the Constraints window instead of the Constraints property editor dialog.

You can also just write code to precisely set the constraints' values. Using either the Constraints window or code, you have to be fairly certain of the exact values and how they will affect the interaction with other components. Setting the precise values is definitely more scientific than dragging and dropping in the visual editor to change the constraints, and you have to be fairly

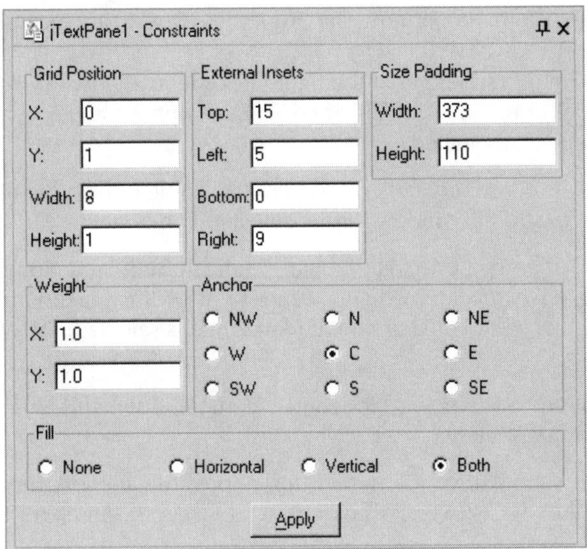

FIGURE 16-6. *Constraints window for GridBagLayout*

accurate in estimating how large an area (for example, 100 pixels) will be in the layout. `GridBagLayout` offers the largest number of constraint properties for a component, so setting constraints manually can require a lot of manual calculation and take some time when you are first working with this layout manager.

NOTE
The "constraints" property for GridBagLayout components is actually an object with properties of its own, such as "anchor" and "fill." For consistency and because the constraints object shows in the Property Inspector as a property, you can think of it as a single property when working in the Java Visual Editor.

Using the Java Visual Editor Toolbar and Right-Click Menu In addition to the Bring To Front and Move To Back items in the Java Visual Editor toolbar, a container with the GridBagLayout manager attached to it offers toolbar selections for Weight, Fill, Anchor, Padding, and Inset properties (described in the "Component Constraints and Properties" section). Clicking the Weight, Fill, and Anchor toolbar items display pulldown menus that provide a number of options for the specific constraints property.

The right-click menu on a component within a GridBagLayout container contains the same options as the toolbar. Where the toolbar has a pulldown for different items in a group (such as weight), the menu has a submenu. You can group components (using CTRL click) and apply properties to the group using the toolbar and menu. The following briefly describes the toolbar, main menu, and right-click menu options. The properties they set are discussed later.

- **Order** This item (a submenu in the right-click menu and two buttons in the toolbar) offers the usual Bring To Front and Send To Back options and is enabled only when a single component is selected.
- **Constraints** As described earlier, this item (available only in the right-click menu) displays the Constraints window for the selected component.
- **Weight** This submenu offers Horizontal, Vertical, Both, and None items and sets the appropriate *weightx* and *weighty* values to "1.0" (the maximum weight) or "0.0" (the minimum weight). For example, if Horizontal is selected, the *weightx* value is set to "1.0."
- **Fill** This option also contains Horizontal, Vertical, Both, and None items and sets the *fill* property appropriately.
- **Anchor** This submenu contains items for all possible *anchor* property settings (North West, North, North East, West, Center, East, South West, South, or South East).
- **Remove Padding** This item sets the values of the selected component's *ipadx* and *ipady* properties to the default value of "0."
- **Remove Insets** This item sets the Top, Bottom, Left, and Right inset properties to "0."
- **Show Grid** This check menu item (available in the Design main menubar) displays or hides the cell border lines in the Java Visual Editor. The grid will not show at run time regardless of this setting. This does not depend on which components are selected.

Converting from *"null" Layout* Another way to work with this layout when you are first learning about it is to set the container to a "null" layout initially, place and size the items, and then assign a `GridBagLayout` to the container. While you are working with the "null" layout, you can place and size the components visually without having the layout manager apply rules to the layout. When you assign the layout to `GridBagLayout`, the Java Visual Editor will set the *constraints* values based on the layout. You will need to adjust some of the values, but you may find this less work than other methods.

When using this method, carefully consider which objects really require the benefits of `GridBagLayout` and which objects could be placed in other layouts. The idea is to reduce the complexity of constraints by placing as many objects as possible in simpler layouts and leaving the GridBagLayout manager to handle only the components that require its features.

For example, a typical application uses a toolbar and status line. The `BorderLayout` is perfectly suited for managing these types of components, so the top-level container should be defined with a `BorderLayout`. You would assign the toolbar *constraints* property to "North" and the status bar *constraints* to "South." You could then place another panel in the Center area of the `BorderLayout`.The new panel could be set up initially as a "null" layout container and converted to `GridBagLayout` after the objects inside it were positioned.

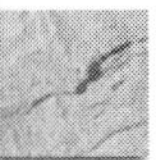

NOTE
As with all editors and wizards in JDeveloper, setting or modifying "constraints" attributes in the Constraints window modifies code that you can manipulate in the Code Editor.

Layout Properties

A GridBagLayout object has no properties other than *name*.

Component Constraints and Properties

The component constraints, as described earlier, are the heart of this layout manager. The component size properties (minimum, maximum, and preferred) are used to set default initial sizes and are used when the layout manager does not specify a dimension. It is useful to examine each value briefly. The JDeveloper help system and the Java Tutorial (online at java.sun.com) contain further descriptions and examples. As mentioned, the Constraints window appears if you select Constraints from the right-click menu on a component. The Constraints window may already be displayed in the Property Inspector (right side) of the IDE.

As with other properties in Java that manage size, the unit of measurement is the pixel. The main areas of the Constraints window shown in Figure 16-2 and their values follow. Each description includes the actual name of the property behind the value in the window.

Grid Position These values manipulate the grid cell around the component:

- **X** The *gridx* property specifies in which column the component is located. A value of "0" indicates the first column, and "1" indicates the next column.
- **Y** The *gridy* property specifies in which row the component is located. A value of "0" indicates the first row, and "1" indicates the next row.
- **Width** The *gridwidth* property specifies how many columns the component spans. The default is "1."
- **Height** The *gridheight* property specifies how many rows the component spans. The default is "1."

Here is an example showing part of the layout of a frame. The combo box (poplist) component is located in cell "1, 0" and spans two columns and one row. Therefore, the values of X, Y, Width, and Height are "1, 0, 2, 1."

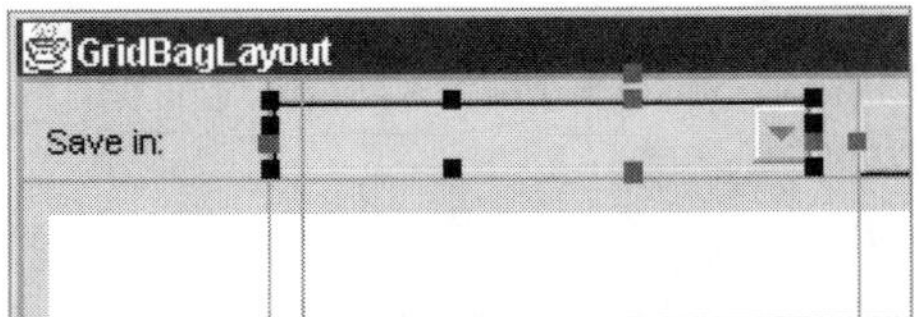

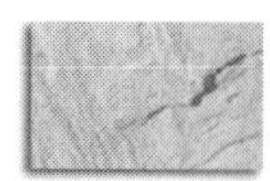

TIP
Dragging the component to a new position in the Java Visual Editor will also modify the "gridx" and "gridy" values. It is best to drag the component by its upper-left corner and to watch the IDE status bar and the gray outlines for visual feedback.

External Insets This area of the Constraints window specifies four values that are used in a single property called *insets.* The values specify the number of pixels that act as a margin (inset) between the cell border and the component (the space is external to the component). Each value specifies a component side: Top, Left, Bottom, and Right. The following is part of a frame layout. The text item has a blank space between the cell borders and three of its sides. The bottom of the component rests on the cell border, but other sides are inset, which creates the blank spaces. The Top, Left, Bottom, and Right values for this example are "11, 10, 0, 9."

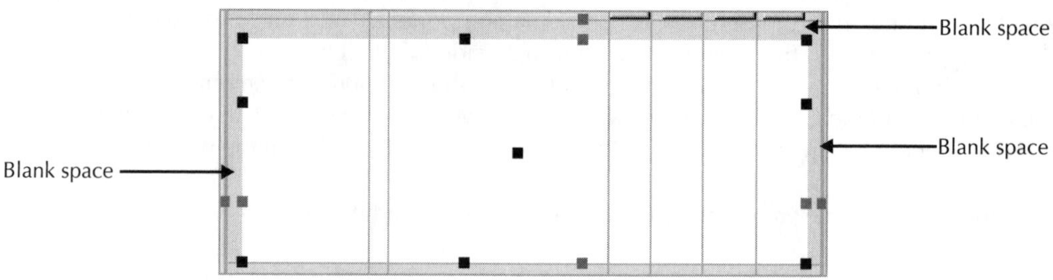

TIP
You can modify the insets in the Java Visual Editor by moving the blue reshape handles. As before, watch the status bar of the JDeveloper IDE window for additional information.

Size Padding The padding properties, *ipadx* and *ipady* (for Width and Height, respectively), define an amount of space in pixels that is added to the preferred size of the component. Therefore, a component will require a cell that is wider than its preferred width if you have defined a padding width. A padding width of "0" indicates that the component property sizes will be used. You can set the values to be negative, which will make the component smaller than its preferred size.

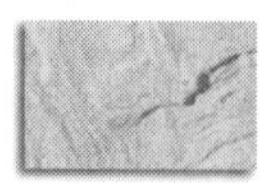

TIP
You can modify the "ipadx" and "ipady" values in the Java Visual Editor by moving the black reshape handles. The status bar will provide information during this operation.

Weight When a user resizes a container, there may be extra space into which cells can expand. The weight properties (*weightx* and *weighty* for the X and Y values in this window, respectively) specify a rule by which the expansion occurs. The value (between "0" and "1" with decimals allowed) represents a percentage of the extra space that the cell will take ("1" represents "100%").

For example, you have a layout with three buttons in a row. The constraints for the first and second have an X (width) weighting of "0.2," and the third has an X weighting of "0.6." If the container is widened, the cells for the first two buttons will each widen by 20 percent of the additional space, and the cell for the third button will widen by 60 percent of the additional space.

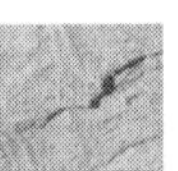

NOTE
Weight applies to cells that contain components.
Fill applies to the component's size within the cells.

Cells in the same row will be allocated extra width based on their X weight property. If all cells in a particular row use a weighting of "1," they will all receive the same amount of extra width. If all cells in the row have a weighting of "0," none will be resized. The concepts apply similarly to the Y weighting and the heights of the cells.

For example, the following frame contains three cells that have X weightings of "0.2," "0.2," and "0.6." As the user widens the container, the cells widen according to their relevant weighting. If the container were widened by 100 pixels, the first two cells would widen by 20 pixels each, and the third cell would widen by 60 pixels.

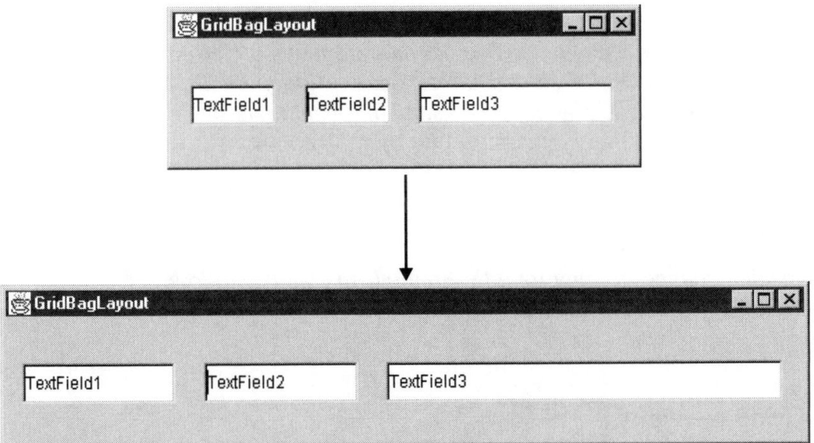

Anchor This is actually a single property (*anchor*) with one of the following values: "NORTHWEST," "NORTH," "NORTHEAST," "WEST," "CENTER," "EAST," "SOUTHWEST," "SOUTH," or "SOUTHEAST." (The right-click menu selections show these options in mixed case and the Constraints window abbreviates the values.) This value specifies the region to which the component is fixed inside the cell. For example, the following shows part of a frame in the Java Visual Editor. The field inside the cell is set to an anchor of "WEST." Changing the value to "EAST" makes the component move to the right side of the cell.

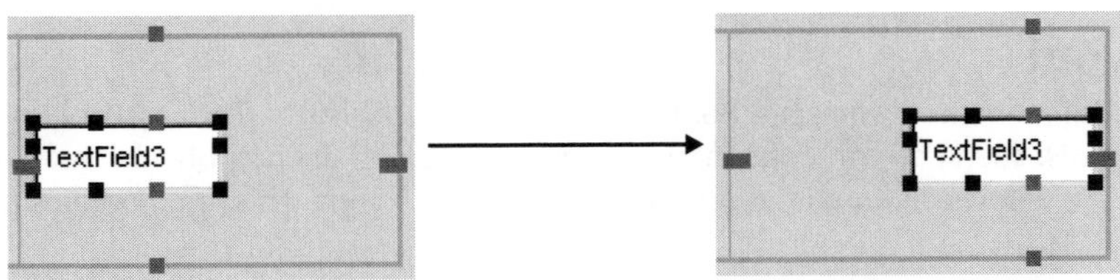

Fill This is also a single property (*fill*) with one of the following values: None, Horizontal, Vertical, or Both. If the value is "Horizontal," the component fills the width of the cells it occupies (less the inset X value). If the value is "Vertical," the component fills the height of the cells it occupies (less the inset Y value).

If it is "Both," the component's width and height expand to fill the cells it occupies. If the container resizes and the cells resize, the component will resize accordingly. A value of "None" means that the component will be sized using only its size properties. The following is a component from a layout that uses horizontal fill on the field and a left and right inset of "10":

NOTE
The fill properties take precedence over the component's preferred size. Padding increases cell size and cannot be overridden by fill, which just fills the cell. Therefore, if you set a fill of "Horizontal," the component will fill the width of its cells, and the component preferred width will be disregarded.

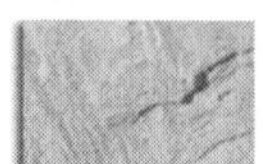

TIP
When making changes to the properties in the Constraints window, you can check the results of a change in the Java Visual Editor by clicking the Apply button.

Uses for GridBagLayout

Use `GridBagLayout` when complex layout is required and you cannot find any other way to place the objects. In many cases, you can accomplish the desired layout using the other layout managers by themselves or in combination. (See "Multiple Layouts" later in this chapter for an example.) However, if you get stuck and cannot find a way to implement a specific design, you can turn to the GridBagLayout manager. The JDeveloper wizards use this layout manager for containers in data forms and panels. Once you master the interactions of its attributes, this layout manager will give you much flexibility in the user interface design.

A hands-on practice at the end of this chapter steps through creating an example of this layout and provides more details about property and constraint settings and how they interact.

GridLayout

The GridLayout manager creates a set of layout areas that consists of rows and columns of equal-sized cells. Each cell can contain one component, and that component fills the entire cell. Figure 16-7 shows a grid with three rows and three columns. This grid contains properties

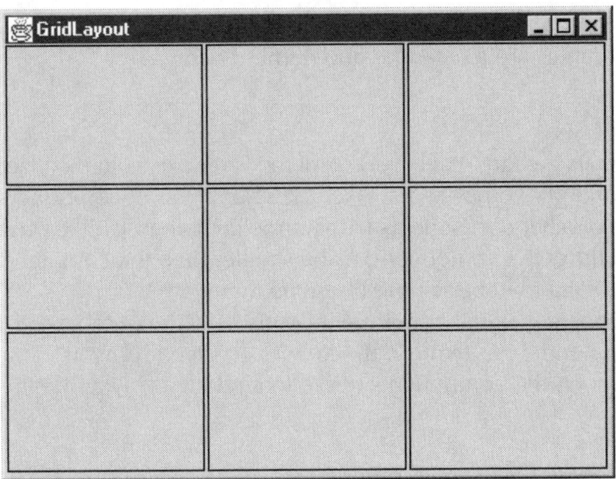

FIGURE 16-7. *GridLayout sample*

defining a two-pixel horizontal and vertical gap. When the user resizes the container, the cells automatically resize and retain their equal size.

After declaring this layout manager for a container, you set the number of rows and columns. As you add components to the container, the layout manager arranges them into equal-sized cells based on the maximum number of rows or columns specified.

Layout Properties

The GridLayout manager object uses the following properties to define its behavior:

- **columns** This sets the maximum number of columns that will appear in the grid.
- **hgap** This property specifies the number of pixels between columns.
- **rows** This sets the maximum number of rows that will appear in the grid.
- **vgap** This property sets the number of pixels that will appear between each row.

If there are more cells than the maximum (the number of rows times the number of columns), the layout manager will add columns but retain the maximum number of rows. All cells will still be of equal size.

Component Constraints and Properties

No component constraints or other component properties are used. The sizes of the cells are taken purely from a calculation of the available space divided by the number of cells (less any defined gaps). The ordering of the components in the container determines in which cell the component appears.

Uses for GridLayout

This layout is perfect for an application that requires same-sized cells that will resize when the container resizes. Examples are a calendar and number pad.

OverlayLayout2

The OverlayLayout2 manager (an Oracle version of the OverlayLayout manager) allows components to be placed on top of other components. Like `CardLayout`, all components in the container will be placed on top of other components in the same container. Unlike `CardLayout`, however, `OverlayLayout2` allows the components to be smaller than the container, which means that more than one component may be seen at the same time.

The alignment properties of the component define how the overlap occurs. Figure 16-8 shows an example of a container that is defined with an OverlayLayout2 manager. When the user resizes the container, the components resize in a relative way and retain their overlap.

Layout Properties

`OverlayLayout2` containers have no properties.

Component Constraints and Properties

The *constraints* property of the component is not used for this layout. The layout manager uses the size properties (*minimumSize, preferredSize,* and *maximumSize*) to determine how large to make the area that holds the component. The layout will respect the minimum size and not allow the outer container to resize so that the component would be smaller than that value. The layout uses the *alignmentX* and *alignmentY* properties to position the component relative to the other components within the container. These properties use the values "0" (for left or top), "0.5" (for center), and "1" (for right or bottom) to set the alignments.

In the example shown in Figure 16-8, the following property values are set on the two components of this panel:

Property	**Large Panel**	**Small Panel**
alignmentX	0.5	0.5
alignmentyY	0.0	0.5
maximumSize	300, 200	200, 50
minimumSize	100, 100	10, 10
preferredSize	10, 10	10, 10

The order in the Structure window determines which component will be visible on top. In this example, the small panel appears before the large panel in the Structure window list. You can change the order using the right-click menu's Order options in the Java Visual Editor. If you set the *opaque* property to "False" for any or all components, the entire image of the underlying component will be displayed.

Uses for OverlayLayout2

Although this layout is rarely used, there are some situations where you need to place all components on top of all other components in the same container and view them all at once. For example,

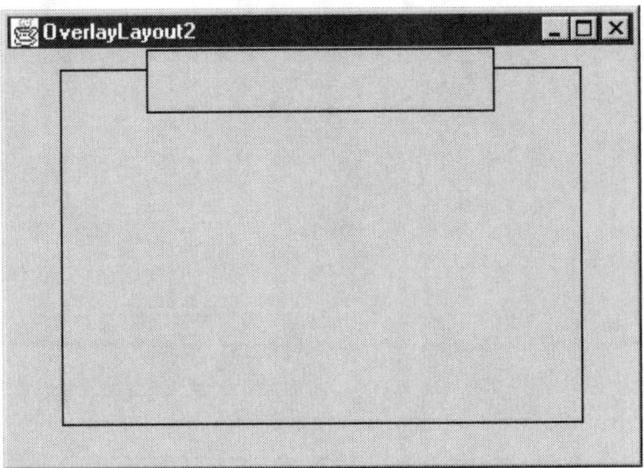

FIGURE 16-8. *OverlayLayout2 sample*

you may need to attach a scrollbar to a component and have that scrollbar appear on top of the component. This layout would help in this situation. It would also help if you had separate graphical elements that needed to be overlaid. For example, you might have an image that you want to use as a watermark (behind items and labels on the screen). This layout would allow you to place the image in back of the other objects.

PaneLayout

The PaneLayout manager allows you to place multiple components in the container and size them proportionally to each other. The logical areas that are created are called *panes,* and the component inside a pane fills the pane completely. The first pane you lay out (by dropping a component into the container) becomes the "root," and all other panes are specified in relationship to that pane. Figure 16-9 shows a container with a PaneLayout manager and four components inside the container. A gap of two pixels has been defined to better show the components within the container.

When the user resizes the container, the layout maintains the placement of one component to another and resizes the components proportionally based on their properties.

The steps for adding components to an empty container with this layout follow:

1. Add a component. It will fill the entire container. This component becomes the root component.
2. Add another component. It will split the container with the root component.
3. Open the Constraints window for this component if it is not already open, by selecting Constraints from the right-click menu on the component. Set the position relative to the component being split and specify the percentage.
4. Repeat steps 2 and 3 for each additional component.

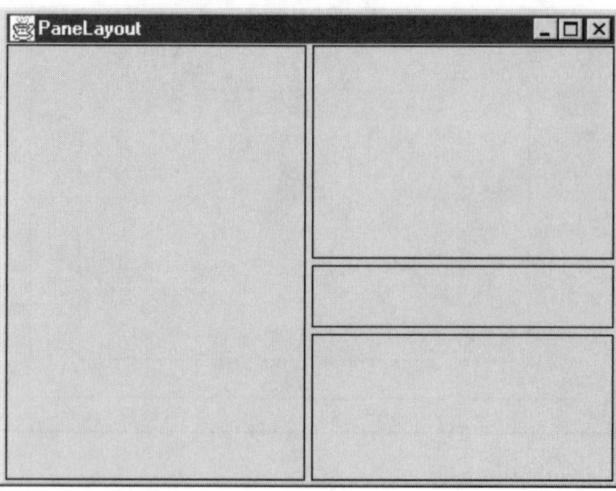

FIGURE 16-9. *PaneLayout sample*

Layout Properties

The only property offered by `PaneLayout` is *gap*, which specifies the number of pixels between components.

Component Constraints and Properties

You specify the *constraints* property using a window that contains the following fields:

- **Name** This is the name of the component upon which you are setting the constraint.
- **Splits** This is the name of the component that you have just split by adding this component. Think of the "splits" component as the object whose area is being reduced to accommodate the new component.
- **Position** You can specify where you want this component to appear relative to the split component (Top, Bottom, Left, or Right). If you select "Top," for example, the new component will take over the top part of the area formerly used by the "splits" component and the splits component will be positioned under it.
- **Proportion** This is a number between 0 and 1. A value of "0.5" indicates that 50 percent of the space formerly taken by the split component will be taken by the new component.

Uses for PaneLayout

You can use this layout whenever you need the "diminishing boxes" effect, where each additional component splits the one before it, and the relative proportions of those panels are maintained when the user resizes the container.

If you are just using two panes, you could use the Swing component JSplitPane. JSplitPane allows the user to dynamically resize the panes.

VerticalFlowLayout

The `VerticalFlowLayout` works in the same way as the `FlowLayout` except that it arranges components in a column. If there is not enough space in the column, the layout wraps the other components to the next column. Figure 16-10 shows an example of this layout.

When the user resizes the container to make it shorter, the components reposition themselves, as shown here:

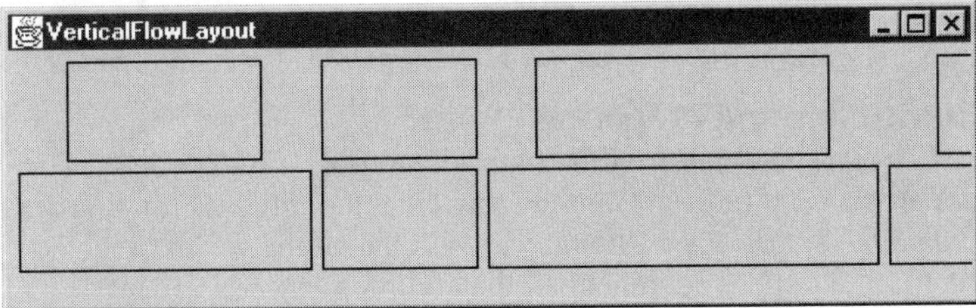

In this example, the user would also widen the window so the components on the right would be visible.

Layout Properties

The `VerticalFlowLayout` offers the following properties:

- **alignment** This is set to "0" by default, which indicates that the components are aligned at the top of the container. A value of "1" indicates that the components will be centered vertically. A value of "2" means that the components will be bottom justified.

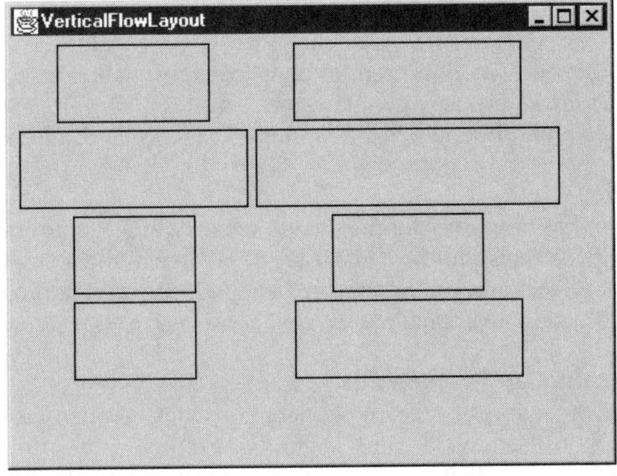

FIGURE 16-10. *VerticalFlowLayout sample*

- **hgap** This sets the amount of space in pixels between columns of components.
- **horizontalFill** This is set to "True" by default, indicating that the components will expand to the width of the container. Set this to "False" if you want to set the width using the component's *preferredSize* property.
- **verticalFill** This is set to "False" by default, which indicates that extra space at the bottom of the last component will be left intact. Setting this to "True" indicates that if there is empty space after the last component, the last component will expand to fill the space.
- **vgap** This sets the amount of vertical space in pixels between a component and the component underneath it.

Component Constraints and Properties

`VerticalFlowLayout` does not use the component *constraints* property. The component's *preferredSize* property is used to determine the row height and the width. Be sure that the layout manager *horizontalFill* is set to "False" if you want to change the width of the component.

Similar to the FlowLayout layout manager, the column for `VerticalFlowLayout` is sized on its width dimension based on the widest component (the one with the largest value in the first number in the *preferredSize* property). The column's height is based on the height of the container.

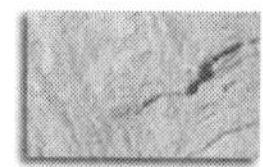

CAUTION
Changing the first number (the width) of the component's "preferredSize" property will have no impact if the layout's "horizontalFill" property is set to "True."

Uses for VerticalFlowLayout

This layout has the same kind of uses as `FlowLayout`, except that it applies to applications where you need a column layout style with wrapping. Vertical button bars are a good use for this layout.

XYLayout

The XYLayout layout manager imposes no rules on its contents. In that respect, it acts similarly to the "null" value for the *layout* property mentioned earlier. It is a JDeveloper-specific layout that was inherited originally from Borland when JDeveloper used Borland's JBuilder code base.

XYLayout Properties

The XYLayout manager has properties for *height* and *width*, which act as hints for the desired size of the container. However, the surrounding container may ignore these sizes. For example, if the surrounding container were managed by `BorderLayout`, setting these properties would have no effect because the surrounding container would impose a size.

Component Constraints and Properties

As with some other layout managers, the component *constraints* property is made up of four numbers: X position, Y position, width, and height. For example, a *constraints* property value of "270, 140, 75, 100" specifies that the component appears 270 pixels to the right and 140 pixels down from the upper-left corner of the container and is 75 pixels wide and 100 pixels high. You can change the numbers manually or drag-and-drop in the UI Designer to resize and reposition the component. Setting the width or height properties to a value of "-1" indicates that the preferred width or preferred height should be used. Other component properties do not affect the *constraints* property assignment.

XYLayout or "null" Layout

The main differences between "null" layout and `XYLayout` follow:

- **`XYLayout` participates in hierarchical size negotiations.** For example, if the XYLayout container were housed inside a JScrollPane container and the *preferredSize* of a component in the XYLayout container were set to "-1,-1," the component will grow if its contents (for example, the *text* or label value of a button) grows. In this example, the pane would display a scrollbar if the component were outside the border of the visible pane. The "null" layout does not recognize preferred sizes and does not have this capability. The authors' websites mentioned at the beginning of the book contain an example of this effect.
- **`XYLayout` is a real class.** The "null" layout is merely an assignment of "null" to the *layout* property. The assignment of "XYLayout" to the *layout* property creates a layout object that has properties. XYLayout properties are limited to constraints that specify the component's position and size.
- **`XYLayout` is specific to JDeveloper.** The "null" layout is a standard Java option and, therefore, has more universal support.

Since it is not a class, the "null" layout does not allow you to set a width and height for the layout. You can set these properties for a "null" layout by manipulating the size properties (*minimumSize, maximumSize,* and *preferredSize*) of the parent container.

Uses for XYLayout

Both `XYLayout` and "null" layout are useful for initial layouts of components in the Java Visual Editor because you can take advantage of the Java Visual Editor's drag-and-drop mouse support. For applications that may safely use fixed locations and sizes, the `XYLayout` is superior to the "null" layout since it will participate in size negotiations during resizing of the container hierarchy. However, neither of these layouts is well suited for applications that need to support international text. Such applications need to adjust the size and locations of controls based on the lengths of the captions that vary because of language differences.

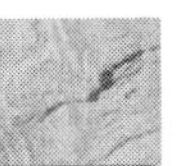

CAUTION
Since the XYLayout does not impose any resizing logic, it is best to change the container to another layout manager before deploying to take advantage of automatic sizing and positioning features.

Layout Manager Usage

Table 16-2 summarizes the main uses for each layout manager.

Layout Manager	Usage
`BorderLayout`	Used to place components in five areas. It is particularly useful for a window that contains a main interface area between a status bar and a toolbar.
`BoxLayout2`	Used to cleanly align components in a row or column without wrapping, for example, in a toolbar.
`CardLayout`	Used to change the contents of an area. Components take the entire space, and you write code to display one component at a time. Useful for explanation text that appears based on placing the cursor in a field or radio group item.
`FlowLayout`	Used to align components in a row, with the ability to wrap to the next row, if required. Useful for horizontal button bars.
`GridBagLayout`	Used when complex and flexible layouts are required. Useful in situations where you cannot use another layout manager.
`GridLayout`	Used whenever cells of the same size are required, for example in a calendar window.
`"null"`	Used for prototypes and applications where automatic resizing and placement are not required. Rarely used in production environments because it does not manage anything.
`OverlayLayout2`	Used to place components on top of one another and allow all of the multiple components to be visible. Rarely used.
`PaneLayout`	Used to define panes for layout that need to keep their proportional size and placement when the container is resized.
`VerticalFlowLayout`	Used to align components in a column with the ability to wrap to the next column if required. It is useful for vertical button bars.
`XYLayout`	Used for the same purposes as the "null" layout except that it will additionally participate in size negotiations within the container hierarchy. Its use is not recommended for applications that require international language support.

TABLE 16-2. *Uses for JDeveloper Layout Managers*

Multiple Layouts

When you are designing an application, one of the key considerations is how to best use the layout managers. Keep in mind that a single layout manager will probably not suffice for a particular application. It is common practice to nest containers that have different layouts and to take advantage of the strengths of each layout manager. To get an idea of the possibilities, it is useful to look at an example. Chapter 15 presents a similar example in the context of Swing containers. A master-detail application could contain instances of different layout managers. The running form is shown here:

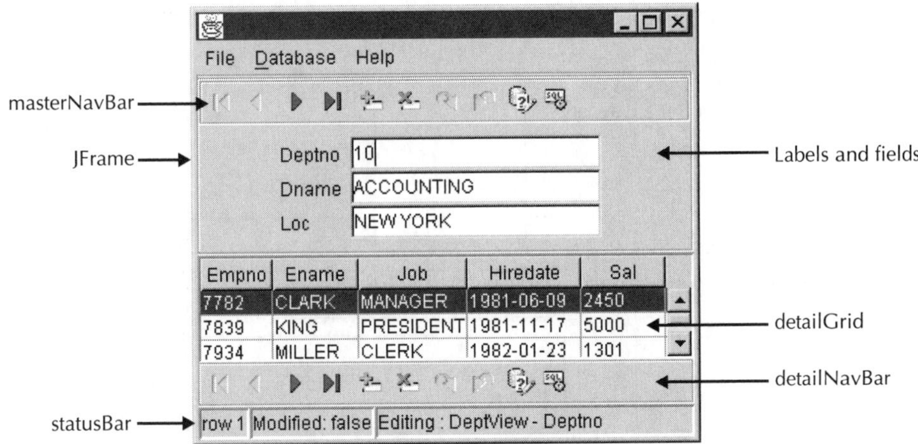

The JFrame area is the overall frame class file that is represented by the "this" node in the Structure window.

Figure 16-11 is a diagrammatic representation of the frames and major objects with a designation of the assigned constraints and layouts where applicable. Most of the objects in this diagram are containers (created from the JPanel object). The interplay of objects is best explained by describing the contents of this application as follows:

- **The JFrame container is assigned a BorderLayout layout.** This frame will contain a South area for the status bar. It will also contain a Center area for the major user interface containers and components.
- **A status bar assigned to the South area appears inside the JFrame.** The `BorderLayout` ensures that the status bar always appears at the bottom of the frame, that the status bar height will be maintained, and that the status bar width will resize as the window width is resized.
- **The formPanel object is assigned to the Center area**, and there are no other objects directly within the JFrame container. Therefore, the formPanel fills the rest of the frame, and its height and width are resized as required when the outer window is resized. The East, West, and North regions of the layout manager are not used.
- **The formPanel is assigned a GridLayout manager.** It contains two equal-sized panels (specified as one column and two rows) for the master and detail views (called "masterTable" and "detailTable," respectively). The layout manager ensures that the panels are always the same size regardless of the size of the window.
- **The masterTable panel uses a BorderLayout manager** and contains a navigation bar (masterNavBar) assigned to the North area of the layout and a panel (masterPanel) assigned to the Center area of the layout. If the window is resized, the cells in the grid will resize, causing the BorderLayout areas to resize according to the BorderLayout rules. The navigation bar will retain its height and allow its width to resize. The masterPanel area will resize along its height and width because it is assigned to the Center area.

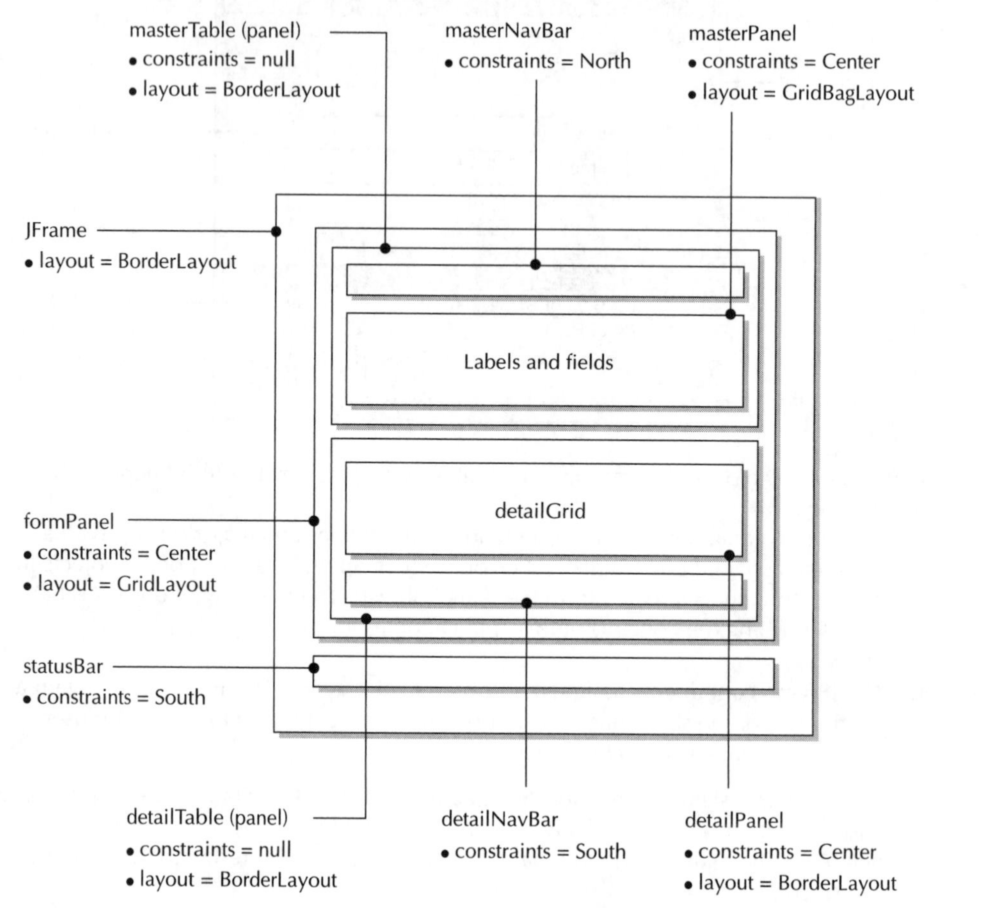

FIGURE 16-11. *Master-detail form panels and major components*

- **The masterPanel is assigned a GridBagLayout manager** that contains the labels and text fields for the DEPARTMENTS table. The `GridBagLayout` causes its contents to retain their relative positions and centering within the panel if the window is resized.
- **The detailTable panel uses a BorderLayout manager** and contains a navigation bar (detailNavBar) assigned to the South area of the layout and a panel (detailPanel) assigned to the Center area of the layout. As the detailTable's cell area is resized, it imposes the BorderLayout rules on the contents so that the navigation bar retains its height, and the panel resizes on both height and width dimensions. The detailPanel's component, detailGrid, represents the grid (table) display of EMPLOYEES table fields.

This application demonstrates a number of principles. The first is that you can nest containers. The second is that you can assign different layout managers to different containers depending on the behavior that you want their contents to adopt. The last principle is that the layout managers offer an easy way to achieve complex functionality and ease of layout that would otherwise require many lines of code and much effort to implement.

Hands-on Practice: Work with Layouts

This practice creates applications that use two layout managers—`BorderLayout` and `GridBagLayout`. Each practice creates a separate application and frame to run it. There is no database connection required, as the objective is to practice a user interface feature.

After setting up a sample application, this practice shows how to do the following:

I. Set up an application workspace and two projects

- Create the application workspace and projects
- Create blank Java application and frame files

II. Use the BorderLayout manager

- Add components
- Resize the side panels
- Try some variations

III. Use the GridBagLayout manager

- Add components
- Align and size the components and convert the layout
- Set the *constraints* property

Phases II and III are independent so, after completing the application workspace setup, you can follow either or both phases of this practice.

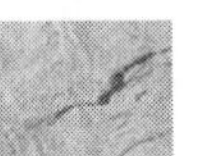

NOTE
In addition to this practice, the authors' websites contain a practice for implementing an application using a FlowLayout layout manager.

I. Set up an Application Workspace and Two Projects

The phases in this practice use a basic application workspace that contains a separate project for each layout manager sample. Use the following steps to create a starting application workspace. The project file names are different for each phase as described in later steps.

Create the Application Workspace and Projects

The first section sets up a new application workspace and two projects within the workspace.

1. On the Applications node in the Application Navigator window, select New Application Workspace from the right-click menu.
2. In the Create Application Workspace dialog, fill in the following fields:

   Application Name as "LayoutManagers"
   (leave the default *Directory Name*)
   Application Package Prefix as "layout"
   Application Template as "Java Application [Java, Swing]"
3. Click OK to create the LayoutManagers application workspace and Client project. Click Save All.

   Additional Information: The Application Navigator will now show a new application workspace and a project called "Client."
4. On the LayoutManagers node in the Application Navigator, select New Project from the right-click menu. In the General\Projects category, select the Empty Project item and click OK.
5. In the Create Project dialog, enter the *Project Name* as "Client2" and click OK to create the second project.

Create Blank Java Application and Frame Files

This section creates Java application and frame files inside the projects you set up in the preceding section.

1. On the Client project node, select New from the right-click menu. The New Gallery will appear.
2. Select the Client Tier\Swing/AWT category. Select the Java Application item and click OK to display the Create Java Application dialog.

   Additional Information: The application file is used to run the project. It calls a frame file, which creates the window. You will be using the frame file to place components and practice layout managers.
3. Fill in the *Name* field as "BorderLayout". Ensure that the Package field contains "layout.client" and *Extends* contains "java.lang.Object.". Leave the remaining fields as their default to request a new frame file. Click OK.
4. In the Create Frame dialog, fill in the *Name* field as "BorderLayoutFrame" and the Title as "BorderLayout." Click OK.

   Additional Information: The application and frame files will be created and displayed in the Application Navigator. The *title* value will add a call to `setTitle()` for the frame file so that the window title bar will display the text at run time.
5. Click Save All.
6. Repeat steps 1–5 for the Client2 project. Name the application file "GridBagLayout" and the frame file "GridBagLayoutFrame." Title the frame file with "GridBagLayout." The package name should be the same as before ("client.layout").

What Just Happened? You set up an application workspace for the practice in this chapter. Creating separate application workspaces for new projects is not a requirement but gives you better control over working with a set of files. These steps also created two projects containing a Java client (Java application) file that displays the JFrame (window) object. Each project has two files—one for the application and one for the frame. You can run the application file in each project and verify that it displays correctly. You will add objects in the frame file to demonstrate layout manager features.

II. Use the BorderLayout Manager

This phase steps through creating a layout using the BorderLayout manager. You can place any component inside the areas of this layout manager, but this practice will lay out panels to illustrate the technique. Since panels are normally not visible, you will also assign a border to the panels so you can see them. As mentioned, this phase is optional.

Add Components

The following steps add components to the frame file that you created in the preceding phase.

1. In the Client project, double click the BorderLayoutFrame file in the Application Navigator to open it in the editor. The Editor will open to the Design tab and display a frame window in the Java Visual Editor. (Click the Design tab if the visual editor does not appear.)

NOTE
If a window such as the Property Inspector does not display as indicated, select it from the View menu of the main menu. The Property Inspector normally appears automatically when you display the Java Visual Editor.

2. Click the "this" node in the Structure window. Check that the title of the Property Inspector window is "this (JFrame)" and change the *layout* property from "null" to "BorderLayout." The layout name nested under "this" in the Structure window will change to "borderLayout1."

   Additional Information: The default layout manager for an application frame is "null," which signifies no layout manager. By applying a real layout manager, you can take advantage of the behavior that it offers. In this example, the `BorderLayout` will automatically size areas in the panel that you will add next to fill the frame.

3. Select the "this" node in the Structure window. Click the JPanel component icon in the Swing Containers page of the Component Palette to select the panel component. Watch the lower-left corner of the IDE status bar as you drag the mouse over the "this" window in the visual editor. When the status bar reads "this (BorderLayout): Center," click the mouse button. This will add the component into the center area of the BorderLayout container.

   Additional Information: You selected the "this" node first so that the new panel would be placed as a child of the frame. The status bar shows exactly where the component will be placed when you drop it into the visual editor. The JPanel you just added will act as the main user interface area for the application. If you were finishing the application, you would also add a toolbar (in the North area) and a status bar (in the South area) to the frame. All of the main user interface components would be placed into the JPanel you just added.

4. Set the *layout* property of this panel (jPanel1) to "BorderLayout." Since you dropped the component into the center area of the container, the *constraints* property will be set to "Center" so that the panel will fill the "this" frame. This property will be shown in the Property Inspector list and in the Constraints window below the Property Inspector.

   Additional Information: This creates a layout manager object for this container that you can manipulate. If you expand the JPanel1 node in the Structure window, you will see the following:

   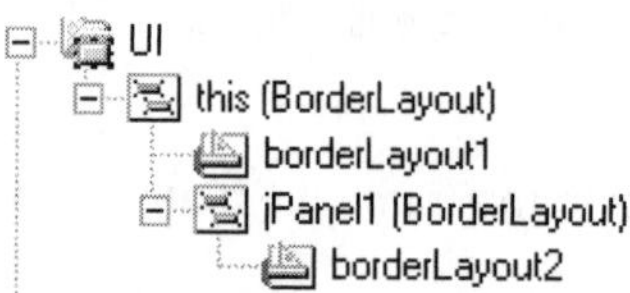

5. Click the JPanel component in the Swing Containers page of the Component Palette. Watch the status bar until it indicates the center area of the jPanel1 ("jPanel1 (BorderLayout): Center"). Click the visual editor to add the component.

   Additional Information: This adds a panel called "jPanel2" under the jPanel1 object. The layout manager assigns a *constraints* value of "Center" to this panel so that it fills the parent container.

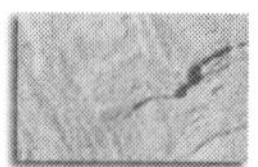

TIP
As mentioned in Chapter 2, it is best to run JDeveloper in a full-screen window so that the internal windows are as large as possible.

6. Click jPanel2 to select it in the Structure window, and in the Java Visual Editor drag the center drag handle to the South area of jPanel1. Drop the component when the IDE status bar reads "jPanel1 (BorderLayout) South".

   Additional Information: The status bar lets you know to which area the component will be assigned if you release the mouse button after dragging the component.

TIP
Normally, it is easy to select an object by clicking it in the visual editor. However, selecting containers in the visual editor can be more difficult because the container borders may not be visible. Therefore, it is usually easier to select containers by clicking their node in the Structure window.

7. Practice repositioning the panel to other areas by dragging and dropping it in the Java Visual Editor. Check the *constraints* property in the Constraints window after dragging to ensure that the assignment is correct. Move the panel back to the center area of jPanel1.

8. Click the jPanel2 object in the Structure window and apply a border by selecting Swing Border in the Property Inspector's *border* property. A dialog will open where you can select "EtchedBorder" (and click the "LOWERED" radio button). Click OK to apply the border.

9. Click jPanel2 in the Structure window and press CTRL-C (to copy). Click jPanel1 (the parent) and press CTRL-V (to paste).

   Additional Information: An additional panel, jPanel3, will appear under jPanel2 in the Structure window. This shows how you can copy objects using the Structure window. You have to be careful that the proper parent object is selected before you paste.

10. Repeat the sequence of selecting the jPanel1 node and pasting the panel until you have five panels as child containers under jPanel1 as shown here:

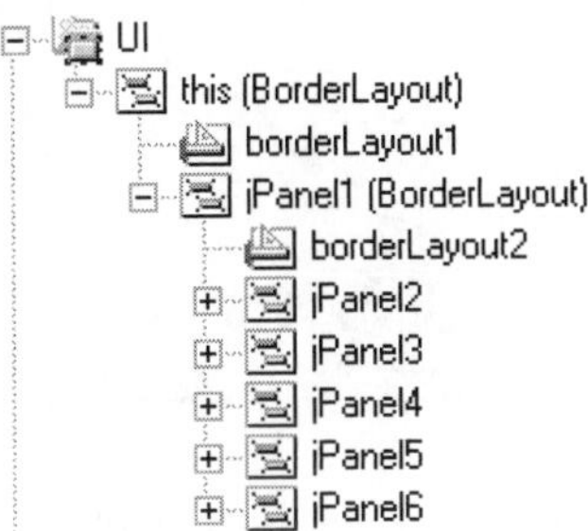

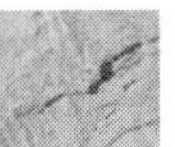

NOTE
If your arrangement looks different, delete the misplaced panels and be sure to select jPanel1 before pasting.

11. Using the Property Inspector, change the *name* property of jPanel1 to "mainPanel".

12. Check the *constraints* property for each panel in the Property Inspector to make sure that you have a panel in each of the areas. As you are checking, change the other panel names to "northPanel," "southPanel," "centerPanel," "westPanel," and "eastPanel" to match the area to which they are assigned.

13. Change the *border* property of northPanel to "BevelBorder" and "RAISED" so that you can see the effect of a different border style.

14. Click Save All.

Resize the Side Panels

Panels are laid out in a `BorderLayout` with default sizes. You can change these most easily in the Property Inspector.

1. Click westPanel (in either the Structure window or Java Visual Editor) and CTRL click eastPanel to group the two panels. Set the *preferredSize* property to "50, 14" (for width

and height, respectively). Press the ENTER key to commit the change. This increases the width of both panels.

2. Click the northPanel and CTRL click southPanel to group the panels. Set the *preferredSize* property to "14, 50". The Java Visual Editor should appear as follows:

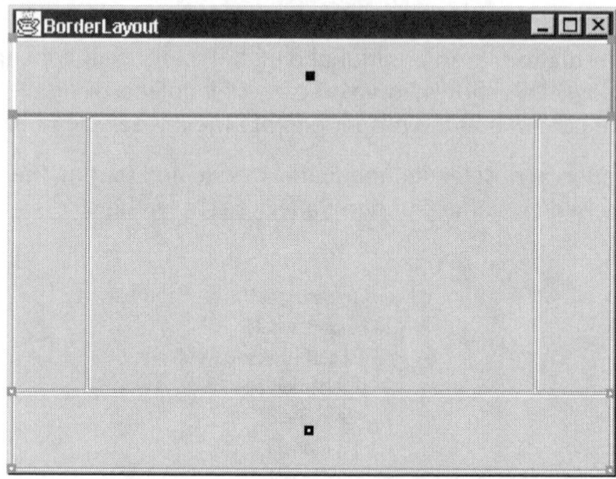

3. Click Save All. Select Make from the right-click menu on the BorderLayoutFrame.java file. On the BorderLayout.java node of the Application Navigator, select Run from the right-click menu to run the application. Select the `BorderLayout` file if a dialog appears requesting the run target.
4. Try resizing the frame's height and width to test the effect of the BorderLayout manager. You will notice the following behavior:

   The North and South panels resize only their widths.
   The East and West panels resize only their heights.
   The Center panel resizes both its height and width.
5. Close the window using the window close button in the top-right corner of the window.

Try Some Variations

You can set properties of the layout manager to add gaps between components.

1. Click the borderLayout2 node (the layout manager object) under mainPanel in the Structure window. Set the following properties:

   hgap to "5"
   vgap to "5"

TIP
Press the ENTER *key after changing a property to commit the change. That way, when you select another component, the cursor will be in the same property for a component of the same type.*

2. The layout will show the gaps between components.

3. Rebuild the project and run `BorderLayout.java`. Try resizing the window to check the effect on the gaps. You will notice that the gaps are not resized when you resize the window.

4. Close the application.

NOTE
When you select a file in the Application Navigator, the Structure window changes to the Code Structure tab. Click the Design tab of the visual editor if you need to return to the UI view in the Structure window. You can perform layout work in either the Structure window or Java Visual Editor, or both.

What Just Happened? You defined a BorderLayout manager for a panel and added other panels inside it. You also made the panels visible by adding border objects and resized the areas by adjusting properties of the components assigned to them.

NOTE
In a BorderLayout container, an area can display only one object at a time. As mentioned, you can make that object a container such as a panel, which contains other objects. The container would require a layout manager of its own that is appropriate to its contents. Figure 16-11 shows how containers with different layout managers can be nested in this way.

III. Use the GridBagLayout Manager

This practice demonstrates how to work with the GridBagLayout manager by building a simple application with components and a layout similar to the Save As file dialog that is common to many programs. Usually, the Save As dialog is not resizable, but for the purposes of demonstration, you will create a window that is resizable (although it will have no functionality). This phase shows how to create and position components using the "null" layout and how to convert the "null" layout to GridBagLayout when all components are positioned. It also gives you experience with some of the GridBagLayout *constraints* properties.

Add Components

The following steps start with the Client2 project created in Phase I. The first section of this phase places objects on the frame in their approximate positions. The exact positions and sizes are set in the next section.

1. Display the Java Visual Editor for the frame file. (Double-click the GridBagLayoutFrame.java node in the Application Navigator and click the Design tab if the visual editor does not appear.)

2. Change the JFrame ("this") window's *layout* property to "BorderLayout." As shown in the preceding phase, this layout manager will change the height and width of the intermediate containers when you resize the outer window.

3. Add a JPanel object from the Swing Containers page of the Component Palette into the center area of the window. Check that the panel's *constraints* property is set to "Center." Change the jPanel1 object's *layout* property to "null." Its default is `FlowLayout`.

   Additional Information: This gives you a full-frame container (jPanel1) that will allow you to place and size objects in any way that you want without imposing any layout manager behavior.

4. Create the following objects (ordered left to right and top to bottom) using the layout in Figure 16-12 as a guide to placement. All components are from the Swing page of the Component Palette. Add them by clicking the component in the Component Palette and then clicking on the frame in the visual editor. Do not worry at this stage about exact placement, sizing, or how to assign the label text.

   Additional Information: Also, remember that you can copy and paste objects in the Structure window. This is a good technique to use for the four buttons at the top; after adding and sizing one button, you can copy and paste it, then drag it off the top of the button you copied (the paste operation also copies the position so the buttons will be in the same location). The order in which the objects are displayed in the Structure window may not match the order in which the objects are displayed in the Java Visual Editor.

UI Object	Component
Label	JLabel
Combo box	JComboBox
Four buttons	JButton
Multiline text area	JTextPane
Label	JLabel
Single-line text field	JTextField
Button	JButton
Label	JLabel
Combo box	JComboBox
Button	JButton

5. Change the *text* property of the labels to match the text in the sample.

TIP
You can hold the SHIFT *key when you click a component in the Component Palette to pin the button. This allows you to add more than one of the same object (such as more than one button) to the Java Visual Editor without having to reselect the component's button.Click the Select (arrow) button to unpin the button. Change the text property of the text pane and text field to blank (no text) so that nothing appears inside the fields when running the application.*

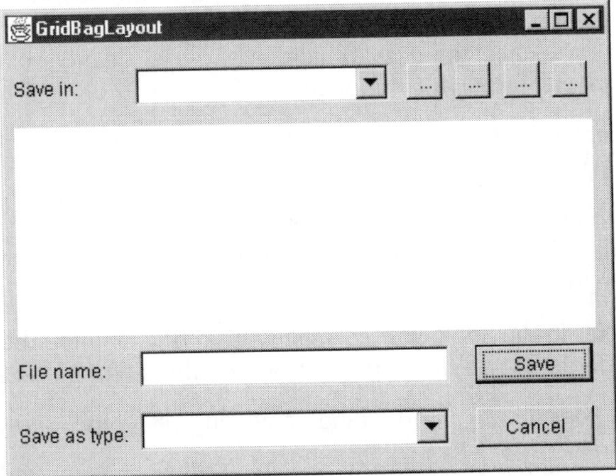

FIGURE 16-12. *Save As dialog using Swing components*

6. Change the *text* property of the buttons in the bottom of the screen to match the sample. Do not worry about the icons in the buttons on the top of the screen.
7. Click Save All.

Align and Size the Components and Convert the Layout

Before converting the layout to `GridBagLayout`, you need to place and size the objects as closely as possible to the design. The reason is that the conversion process calculates grid cells for the components, and if a component is slightly out of alignment with another component, two rows or columns will be created even if one would suffice. Although you will tune the *constraints* properties later, if the objects are aligned, the conversion process will use fewer cells, which makes the layout easier to manipulate.

1. Precisely size the leftmost button on the top of the screen by setting the last two numbers in its *bounds* property to "23," for example, "238, 7, 23, 23". Press ENTER.

   Additional Information: This explicitly sets the button's height and width to 23 pixels but leaves the X and Y positions alone.

2. Select the rightmost button and CTRL click the other buttons at the top of the frame from right to left to select them as a group. Be sure to select the leftmost button last because this button will be used as the pattern to set the group.
3. Select the following from the right-click menu on a button in this order:

   Make Same Size | Both
   Align | Top
   Space Evenly | Horizontal

Additional Information: This step aligns and spaces the buttons. It also accomplishes the same height and width operation as the explicit *bounds* setting in step 1. This method allows you to set the sizes as a group and may be more efficient than setting the *bounds* property for each component.

4. Set the last number in the *bounds* property of the top combo box (the height) to "23".
5. Select the bottom combo box and CTRL click the text field and top combo box (to group the three components), and on the top combo box, click the Make Same Size Height button in the Java Visual Editor toolbar. This copies the height value in the *bounds* property of the top combo box ("23") to the other controls.
6. Select all objects in the first row (the label, combo box, and four buttons) and click Align Middle in the toolbar. This lines up all objects on the top of the screen.
7. Select both buttons at the bottom of the frame, and select the following from the right-click menu:

   Make Same Size | Both
   Align | Left

8. Select the text field and combo box on the bottom of the frame, and click the following toolbar buttons:

   Make Same Size Width
   Align Left

9. If any of the label text is hidden, manually drag the right side of the label or resize the fields until all of the text is visible.
10. Select all labels (select the "Save as type" label last), and select the following from the right-click menu:

    Make Same Size | Width
    Align | Left

11. Click Save All.
12. Rebuild the project and run the application file (`GridBagLayout`). When you resize the window, no resizing or repositioning occurs because the container is managed by the "null" layout, which imposes no resizing behavior. Close the application.

    Additional Information: Before proceeding, be sure that you used the alignment tools in the previous section to line up and size the components. The better aligned the components are, the fewer cells you will create when you convert to `GridBagLayout`.

13. Be sure that the *constraints* property of jPanel1 is "Center," which will ensure that both horizontal and vertical sizes will be affected when the window is resized.
14. Set the *layout* property of jPanel1 to "GridBagLayout."

    Additional Information: Some components may resize or reposition. Although it is not essential for this practice, you may switch back to the "null" layout, reposition, and realign the objects, then reset the layout to `GridBagLayout`. Alternatively, to alter the layout, you could try working with the cell and component drag handles while the layout is set to `GridBagLayout`.

15. Click Save All.
16. Rebuild and run the application, and notice the difference in component behavior when you resize the window.
17. Close the application.

Set the Constraints Property

Now that the layout is a `GridBagLayout`, you can set the *constraints* properties of the components to fine-tune the behavior. This is an application that you can use to experiment with the *constraints* settings.

1. Select a component in the Java Visual Editor, and you will see the grid borders of the cells that were created when you converted to `GridBagLayout`, as in the following illustration:

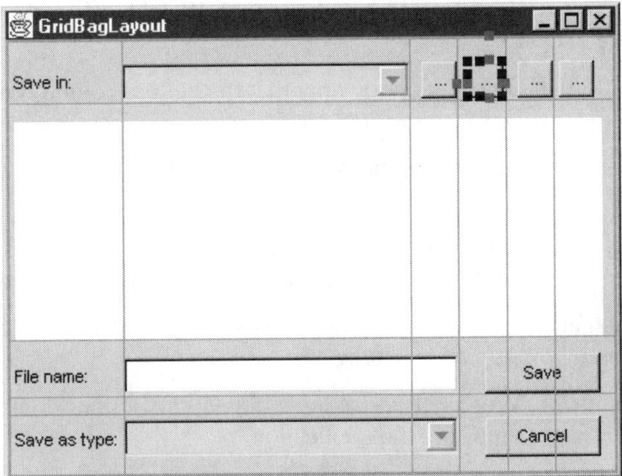

Additional Information: The following instructions refer to this setup, and you may need to adjust the steps slightly if your grid is different. In this section the effect of the properties is more important than the exact layout.

2. The button in the upper-right corner may not be spaced evenly with the other buttons. If the Constraints window is not visible, on that button, select Constraints from the right-click menu (do not display the constraints dialog from the Property Inspector's ellipses button).

Additional Information: The Constraints window will usually appear in the same frame as the Property Inspector, but it may appear outside that frame as a separate window (not a free-floating dialog). If you scroll to the bottom of the Constraints window, you will see an Apply button. Resize the window so you can reach the button without much or any scrolling.

NOTE
The Constraints window is available from the right-click menu on all components, but constraints only apply to components inside containers that use the BorderLayout, GridBagLayout, PaneLayout, and XYLayout.

3. Change the *External Insets – Left* value to a smaller number. Remember that negative numbers are allowed. Click the Apply button and check the layout.

   Additional Information: The insets modify the space between the edge of the cell and the component.

4. Adjust the number and check the effect until the spacing of the top buttons is even.
5. When you run this application, the combo boxes may resize in a horizontal direction but not in a vertical direction when you resize the window. Run the application to verify this effect. Close the application.
6. To see the effect of the *Fill* property, change the value of this property to "Both" for the bottom combo box. You also need to change the *Weight – Y* property to "1.0" so that the fill will be activated.
7. Click Apply. Run the application to verify that the bottom combo box resizes vertically as well as horizontally. Close the application.
8. For the combo box, reset the *Fill* property to "Horizontal" and the *Weight – Y* property to "0". Click Apply.
9. Select the right-hand button at the top of the frame. If the Constraints window is not visible under the Property Inspector, select Constraints from the right-click menu.
10. The horizontal and vertical weights should be set to "0". Verify that all buttons in the top of the frame have the same setting.
11. Run the application. When you resize the window, the buttons do not resize because they have no weighting. Close the application.
12. Group the buttons on the top of the frame together. Change the horizontal weighting of the group of buttons by selecting **Weight | Horizontal** from the right-click menu. With the buttons grouped, select **Fill | Horizontal** from the right-click menu.

    Additional Information: These operations set the horizontal fill so that the buttons will resize horizontally when the window is resized. The weighting settings are required so that the fill will take effect.

13. Rebuild, run, and watch the effects on the buttons of resizing the window. The buttons will resize horizontally when the window is resized horizontally. Close the application.
14. Click the bottom combo box and display the Constraints window. Change the *Grid Position – Width* property to one more than the current setting. (For example, if it is "2", change it to "3".) Click Apply and watch the effect on the component.

Additional Information: Setting the width property determines how many cells the component will span horizontally. The *Grid Position – Height* property works the same way for the component's height in one or more cells.

15. The easiest way to move a component to another cell is to adjust the X and Y positions. Note the setting for the *Grid Position – X* property of the bottom combo box and change it to "0". Click Apply and watch the effect.

    Additional Information: The component will move horizontally to the leftmost cell (the "0" column). The X position sets the column in which the component will appear. The *Grid Position – Y* property works in the same way for the component's row assignment. Since a component may span cells, these two properties define the position of the top-left corner of the component.

16. Reset the combo box X position. Click the text field at the bottom of the frame in the Java Visual Editor and display the Constraints window.

17. Change all external insets to "0" if they are not set that way and click Apply. If the *Anchor* property is set to "C", you will see the component reposition to the center of the cell. Set the *Anchor* property to "N" and click Apply. You will see the component attach to the top (North) border of the cell, as in the following:

    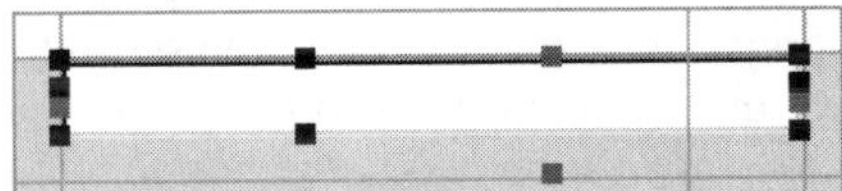

18. Set the anchor to "S" and apply the change. You will see the component reposition to the bottom (South).

19. Verify that the *fill* property is set to "Horizontal," and select an anchor of "W". Click Apply.

    Additional Information: The component may center itself vertically, but it will not move horizontally because the *fill* property indicates that the component will fill the horizontal space within the cell. Therefore, it is already attached to the left border of the cell, which is what the anchor of "W" would accomplish. This shows the interaction between the *fill* property and the *anchor* property.

20. In the Constraints window for the same text field, set the *Size Padding – Height* to "0" and click Apply. The height will change if the padding was more than zero.

21. Change the *Size Padding – Width* to "0" and click Apply. If the setting is already "0", set it to "4" and apply the change. Then set it to "0" and apply the change.

    Additional Information: As before, the width will not change relative to the cell because the *fill* property is set to "Horizontal," which means that the component fills the width of the cell regardless of sizes or other properties.

22. Change the *Fill* to "None" and click Apply. The component width will change (and may become very narrow) because it is no longer set to fill the width of the cells to which it is assigned.

23. Modify the *Size Padding – Width* to 20 more than the current value (for example, "100" if the current setting is "80") and click Apply. Experiment with different padding widths to see the effect that they have on the component.

    Additional Information: You should see the padding increase the component width because the *fill* property is no longer set and allows the padding to take effect. This demonstrates the interaction between the fill and padding properties.

24. Click Save All if you want to save the changes in this section. Otherwise, close the editor and discard the changes when the change dialog appears.

What Just Happened? You added components to a frame and set their properties. You then converted the "null" layout to the GridBagLayout manager. The GridBagLayout is influenced mostly by the *constraints* values. For proper understanding of the power of this layout, you might want to take some time to further explore other constraint properties such as Grid Position (X, Y, Width, and Height). Watch how the settings interact with one another and how they affect the runtime behavior.

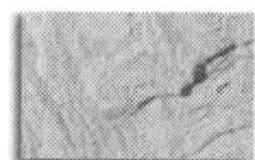

NOTE
The GridBagLayout layout manager uses complex logic to determine the interaction and precedence of components. However, while you are initially learning about this layout, use common sense to determine how the interactions will occur. For example, common sense would dictate that if the "fill" property is set to horizontal, the component's width properties will be ignored because the component must "fill" the cell's horizontal space. Using this approach will help you quickly come to an understanding of the logic used by this component and be able to better predict the effect of a change in properties.

CHAPTER 17

Working with Struts

...to strut before a wanton ambling nymph...

—William Shakespeare (1564–1616),
King Richard III (I, i)

truts is a framework of reusable components used in J2EE web applications built with various J2EE technologies such as JavaServer Pages (JSPs), JavaBeans, and servlets. Incorporating Struts into your application development provides solid support for the Controller layer in the Model-View-Controller (MVC) design pattern.

The Struts framework is part of the Apache Software Foundation's Jakarta Project (http://struts.apache.org/), where you can find the latest standards and tools for web-based J2EE design. The Jakarta Project maintains free, open-source solutions on the Java platform for distribution to the public.

Although Struts can be used to manage any J2EE (or Java) development effort, its primary use is for web development. This includes applications built using JSP pages, HTML, and Oracle's ADF UIX framework. Struts is used for building and managing page flow. Struts logic will manage how pages are connected, what happens before the page is called, and what happens when you submit the page. In addition, with ADF, the Struts controller manages the communication of data from the Model layer to the View layer.

As with all frameworks, Struts provides both an architecture and a library of elements to support that architecture. Struts includes a number of tag libraries that are designed to simplify the interaction between your page elements and Struts controller functionality.

In JDeveloper 9*i*, Oracle introduced a controller-level framework for UIX called UIX Controller (now called UIX servlet). Oracle Consulting created and uses a framework called JHeadstart, which utilizes the Oracle Application Server MVC controller. These controllers do many of the same things that Struts does. In JDeveloper 10*g*, Oracle clearly shifted its focus to supporting Struts rather than trying to build a proprietary solution.

This chapter includes a brief overview of the Struts technology and how Oracle modified it to work more efficiently with their ADF service layer. It is not an exhaustive overview of Struts because Struts is a popular framework and much detailed information exists in other places. Entire books have been written about the Struts framework. The authors recommend that that you add one or more Struts books to your J2EE library (see Appendix A for some suggestions). This chapter also discusses how Struts is implemented in JDeveloper.

The hands-on practices in this chapter use JSP pages, although Struts is equally applicable to Oracle's proprietary UIX architecture (see Chapter 19). Struts can even be used with Java applications. The practices in this chapter will demonstrate Oracle's ADF extensions of Struts, although JDeveloper can also be used to build traditional Struts-based applications that do not use ADF. The practices will provide both a basic implementation of Struts using the ADF extensions, followed by a more complex implementation to handle the types of situations that you may encounter in production applications.

Chapters 12 and 18 complete the picture of web application development using JSP pages by discussing the ADF Model layer and View layer.

Struts Architecture

Traditionally, in JSP (or any) development the user interface controls all of the application logic. There is no separation between the application components and how they interact. The navigation from one page (or screen) to another is handled through code attached to the user interface elements (such as hard-coded links on the page). This type of development uses what is called "*Model 1* architecture." The problem with this kind of development is that the logic is not separated from the UI components. This usually means that quite a lot of Java code gets embedded in the HTML code in the JSP page. These pages can be hard to develop, debug, and maintain, requiring a web developer who is conversant with Java, JavaScript, and various tag libraries.

In order to separate much of the logic from user interface development, various controller technologies have been developed. The idea is to use a framework that separates the display code from the page flow control code. This results in what is termed "*Model 2* architecture." In Model 2 architecture, servlets, running in the application server, control the page flow with any necessary logic. In JSP pages, developers only write minimal display logic (using JSTL or Struts tags) that is designed to interact with the controller implementation. Struts is the most popular of the available controller technologies that promote Model 2 architecture.

Struts has its own vocabulary to describe the logical flow of an application. It provides a well-structured approach to application development. Struts also uses a state transition engine (STE) metaphor for page control. Struts uses pages (like JSP or HTML pages) that are obvious STE nodes, but you might also want to have STE nodes that are not associated with displayed pages to perform some programmatic function, so Struts also includes *actions*, which also act as STE nodes. *Forwards* are the transitions (or links) between nodes in Struts.

Struts Elements

Various elements are included within the Struts architecture. In a traditional environment, you would have to maintain all of these elements by hand. In JDeveloper 10*g*, most of the complexity is handled for you using graphical drag-and-drop tools. However, it is still important to understand these traditional elements. After brief descriptions of these elements, this section will describe how JDeveloper 10*g* has extended this framework to make applications that use Struts easier to build and maintain.

Action and Forward Tags

A Struts *action* is a tag used to change control in an application. This tag may have a number of properties and other tags nested inside of it. An action may also have many forward tags defined within it. Each forward tag provides an alternative place to which the action can branch. Forward tags can point to other action tags for more processing, or displayable pages to continue the application flow.

A *forward* tag actually changes control based on a parameter passed from the application. A forward tag has two parameters: `name` and `path`. The forward's `name` parameter represents the expected value of the passed parameter (for example, "success" or "failure"). The `path` parameter indicates where control will be passed (to another action or another page). The action tag may also have a property that points to a Java file for more complex control. This file is called the *action class.*

Action Class

An *action class* is any custom Java class that extends the Struts class `org.apache.struts.action.Action`. Each Struts action may have an action class associated with it. The most common use of an action class is to support complex page flow logic. You can place the necessary Java code in your action class to help implement any business logic needed between pages. For example, you can execute a stored procedure and use the results to decide on an appropriate branch page. Implementing an action class allows developers to add custom functionality to their applications.

The Struts action class includes a method called "execute." This method is where you place custom code to be executed. Traditionally, Struts developers also write complex data validation in the action classes, although in JDeveloper 10*g*, you are more likely to write such logic in ADF BC entity objects, in the business services layer.

ActionForm Class

An `ActionForm` *class* (also called a `FormBean`) is a Java class that caches data as you move from to page to page. It also handles the persistence requirements of the application within the session. Traditionally, Struts developers place simple validation, such as checking for mandatory fields that have been left blank, in the `ActionForm` class.

Custom `ActionForm` classes are not usually used in JDeveloper 10*g*. If you are using ADF BC, the ADF framework generates code to replace the `ActionForm` class dynamically. If you look behind the generated code, you will find that Oracle has done all of the work for you. You can simply use your business services layer to implement your validation and persistence requirements. The ADF Model layer bolts the business services to the Struts framework automatically. `ActionForms` are Java classes referenced within form-beans tags in the struts-config.xml.

How Struts Elements Interact

The following sample sequence of steps, diagrammed in Figure 17-1, help explain the concepts described earlier, using a hypothetical Struts application that needs to display data from the database:

1. The action class requests information from the database.
2. The database returns the data to the action class.
3. The action class passes the data to the `DataForm` class.
4. The `DataForm` class passes the data to the JSP page.
5. If there are any edits, the page passes them back to the `ActionForm` class, which may perform simple validation. If that validation fails, the application control returns to the page to allow the user to correct the data.
6. If validation succeeds, the data is passed back to the action class. The action class then executes any complex validation and then decides where to pass control.
7. The control is passed via the forward tags to other action tags or another viewable page.
8. Finally the action class will send any updated data back to the database.

ApplicationResources.properties Files

Files with .properties extensions contain key-value pairs. When the key is encountered in the view page, it is replaced with the associated value. These files act as a central place in which to store string values and global variables for your application, including items such as text values for the screen. You can also place initialization parameters for the application in the file. One advantage of using .properties files is that it makes it very easy to change properties that are referenced in many places in the page. You can also have multiple files for different languages. For example, one page could give the values in English, another in German. This is a

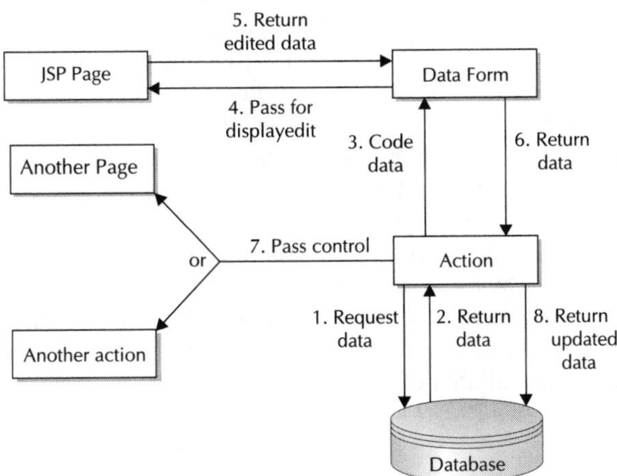

FIGURE 17-1. *Action class path*

formalization of the standard coding practice of not having hard-coded string values in your application code. Struts provides an explicit container for all string values in a file typically called "ApplicationResources.properties."

Multiple property files benefit the developer by permitting division or delegation of programming tasks; relevant properties can be farmed out in "sections" to appropriate parties or phases of application construction. Different properties files may be loaded on domain (class path) or property names. As an example, a property fragment for a Norwegian-language application might appear under com.yourapp.utils.ApplicationResources.properties.no, whereas the English-language version "app" master might be found in a file that uses the basic name com.yourapp.ApplicationResources.properties.

You can place any text as the value of the property. If you are working in a JSP environment, you can place HTML code in the value. When an element is encountered, the appropriate HTML code is substituted.

JDeveloper will automatically create a file called "ApplicationResources.properties" when you specify a project containing Struts support. Other .properties files can be added as needed. Initially, JDeveloper places some values in the files to support error handling. Values will automatically be added where appropriate, for example, when you create a link. However, you will need to edit the file manually to add application-specific keys and values.

The struts-config.xml File

The core of Struts is the struts-config.xml file. This XML file is where all of the Struts action tags, form-bean tags, and message resources tags are defined. The action tags include references to the forward tags that define the possible paths to which the controller can send the application. But, as already mentioned, it is the job of the action classes to select the appropriate forward for any given situation in the page flow.

The struts-config.xml file is divided into several sections. The form-bean area, at the top of the file, lists all of the `ActionForm` classes in the application. In Oracle ADF, the form-bean area of the struts-config.xml file becomes a single line that interfaces with the UIModel.xml files, forming Oracle's ADF databinding. The second section is the action-mappings area. This section lists all of the action tags, what action class (if any) is called when the action is called, and the possible forward tags for a given action tag. ADF adds an element called a data action. A *data action* is similar to a generic action, but it extends the `oracle.adf.controller.struts.actions.DataAction` class. In this class, Oracle has provided a number of methods that automatically connect to data controls. You can override these methods to incorporate any necessary code needed to control your application. You will get some experience using this technique in the practices later in this chapter.

Examine the following file fragment based on Oracle's ADF (the line numbers have been added for reference purposes and are not part of the code):

```
01: <struts-config>
02:   <form-beans>
03:     <form-bean name="DataForm"
04:       type="oracle.adf.controller.struts.forms.BindingContainerActionForm"/>
05:   </form-beans>
06:   <action-mappings>
07:     <action path="/browseDeptDA
08:         className="oracle.adf.controller.struts.actions.DataActionMapping"
09:         type="view.BrowseDeptAction" name="DataForm">
10:       <set-property property="modelReference" value="browseDeptDPUIModel"/>
11:       <forward name="success" path="/browseDeptDP.do"/>
12:     </action>
13:     <action path="/browseDeptDP"
14:         className="oracle.adf.controller.struts.actions.DataActionMapping"
15:         type="oracle.adf.controller.struts.actions.DataForwardAction"
16:         name="DataForm"
17:         parameter="/browseDeptDP.jsp">
18:       <set-property property="modelReference" value="browseDeptDPUIModel"/>
19:     </action>
```

In the preceding code, note that the ADF binding class (line 04) that replaces the traditional `ActionForm` class is referenced in the form-beans tag (oracle.adf.controller .struts.forms.BindingContainerActionForm). Following that section, there are two action tags (lines 07 and 13) with their associated action classes. Note that these tags are being created as data actions from ADF. These action tags automatically bind themselves back to the ADF Model layer via the property references (*className*, *type*, and *name*).

Notice the ".do" in the sample code (in the path property of the forward tag on line 11). The *path* property in the forward tag acts like a method on the item that it suffixes (/browseDeptDP, in this example). When the Struts controller encounters a ".do" reference, it acts as an internal "go to" for the Struts controller and executes the matching action tag that has the path value with the same name as the ".do" item. For example, consider this code:

```
    <forward name="success" path="/browseDeptDP.do"/>
```

The forward tag indicates that the following should be executed:

```
<action path="/browseDeptDP" ...>
    </action>
```

What Is the Real Page Flow for Your Application?

It is an oversimplification to think that the struts-config.xml file contains the page flow and that the action classes contain additional called program code. The struts-config.xml contains the definition of some of the page flow but the real situation is a bit more complex. First, the struts-config.xml file does not contain the complete page flow logic. It does contain the "nodes" (pages and action tags) of the page flow, and the forward tags that represent transitions, but the struts-config.xml file explicitly does not contain the logic to choose which forward tag should be selected when there is more than one defined in a particular action tag. That logic is always contained in the action class.

Second, it is possible to circumvent the implied flow in the struts-config.xml file. This practice should be avoided because the external link is not contained within the struts-config.xml file and this fragments the page flow definition.

Most of the transitions between nodes are represented as forward tags within the action in the struts-config.xml file, but other transitions may be executed in the code (such as in the JSP pages) that do not appear in the struts-config.xml file.

Finally, if any action tag has more than one forward tag associated with it, the logic to determine which forward to use must be written in the action class associated with the action tag. Therefore, if you want to know what the complete page flow for your application is, you will need to look at the struts config.xml file, in the code in the action classes, and in the code in your pages.

View-Level Struts Tag Libraries

As mentioned earlier, Struts is used mainly in the controller level. However, many Struts library tags can be implemented in the view layer. These tags can be used to simplify page construction and tie the view elements to the rest of the framework.

There are six different Struts custom JSP tag libraries that can be referenced at the View level:

- **HTML** This library is used to generate standard HTML elements.
- **Bean** Beans are used to provide a number of utility-like operations such as access data in a cookie.
- **Logic** This library provides conditional and iterative logic support.
- **Nested** This library is used to support nested elements such as an address embedded in an Edit Person page.
- **Templates** This library helps create pages based on a template.
- **Tiles** Tiles allow you to partition pages into areas that can be loaded from reusable components.

Creating an application in the JDeveloper 10*g* visual editor automatically generates tags from these libraries.

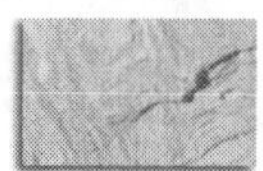

NOTE
More information about the Struts tags can be found in any book about the Struts framework. See Appendix A for some suggestions. There are also numerous resources available on the web. A good place to start is jakarta.apache.org/struts/api.

JDeveloper's Implementation of Struts

JDeveloper has done much more than provide a graphical user interface to write Struts code. ADF has extended and simplified the framework to assist developers in building Struts applications. This section discusses Struts from the perspective of a JDeveloper user.

In Oracle 9*i* JDeveloper, developers learned how to work with Struts like any J2EE developer. It was necessary to write much of your own code and it was often difficult to get things working properly. Moving to 10*g*, development became much easier, but also very different. JDeveloper 10*g* extends the base Struts functionality and binds it closely to Oracle ADF.

Assuming that you use ADF business services, you will have little need to worry about Struts while you are building your ADF BC project. The Struts components are automatically configured to interact with the business services you are creating. Your Struts development really begins after you build the business services project. JDeveloper 10*g* has extended many traditional Struts elements to give you the ability to develop code faster and make it more maintainable. Table 17-1 shows the traditional Struts elements and the associated JDeveloper 10*g* elements.

In traditional Struts development, you build pages, action classes, and `ActionForm` classes using the code editor of your choice. In JDeveloper 10*g* Struts development, you will use a visual

Traditional Struts	JDeveloper 10*g* Struts
`<action />` tag	`<action />` tag
Action Class - xxxx.java - execute()	`DataAction` (with ADF) (`<action/>` + xx.java) - Validation in ADF BC Action (static content)
Action Form -get/set -reset() -validate	Hidden `DataForm` and ...UIModel.xml `<form-bean .../>`
Forward	Forward
Page	DataPage (with ADF) Page (static content)
Combined element (`<action/>` + forward)	PageForward

TABLE 17-1. *Traditional vs. JDeveloper Struts Elements*

page-flow editor to define pages, data actions, and forwards using a drag-and-drop interface. Most of the code is generated for you; however, you can modify the source code at any time by switching to the source code tab located at the bottom of the screen. This approach lets you concentrate on the page flow logic while JDeveloper handles the drudgery of coding the struts-config.xml file.

As you build Struts applications, control passes to pages or data actions in a way similar to that of a state transition engine. This is an excellent way to think about development, and JDeveloper implements this philosophy brilliantly.

Working in the Page Flow Diagram

The main work area for Struts development in JDeveloper is the Page Flow Diagram. It is accessed by double clicking on the struts-config.xml file in the Navigator window. A sample diagram is shown here.

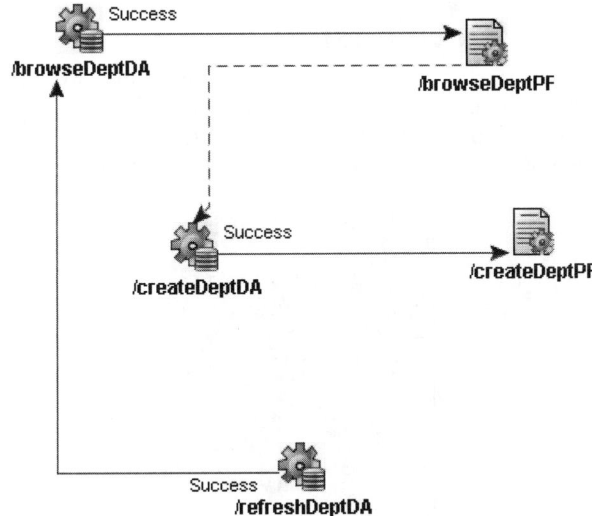

As with all visual editors in JDeveloper, any work you do in the Page Flow Diagram will automatically be reflected in the struts-config.xml code. The Page Flow Diagram appears with two tabs: one for the diagram (labeled "Page Flow Diagram") and one for the source code (labeled "Source"). You can toggle between these two areas and modify the struts-config.xml file using either a graphical or text approach.

As you build your application, you will drag and drop objects from the Component Palette onto the Page Flow Diagram. You can open the diagram by double clicking on the struts-config.xml node in the Application Navigator. As each object is added, you will see its visual representation appear on the screen. By toggling between the Source and Page Flow Diagram tabs, you can see the generated tags for each object you have added.

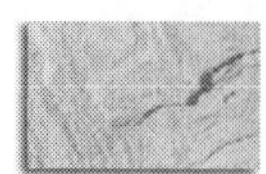

NOTE
The actual X,Y coordinates of the visual elements and non-code elements such as notes are stored in a file called StrutsPageFlow.oxd_struts that cannot be edited in JDeveloper.

The label on each element actually corresponds to a particular property of the element; it is not just a display name. For example, the display name for a data page corresponds to the *path* property. You can edit that property directly on the diagram by clicking the data page symbol twice.

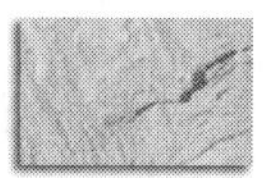

TIP
To add nodes to any Forward or Page Link lines on the Page Flow Diagram, use SHIFT *click where you want the node to appear. Similarly, use* SHIFT *click on an existing node to delete it.*

Struts Elements in JDeveloper

The primary tools you will use when creating Struts applications in JDeveloper are the Page Flow Diagram, the Component Palette, and the Data Control Palette. This section briefly describes the Struts components available for use on the Page Flow Diagram. These are accessed by selecting the Struts Page Flow page of the Component Palette pull-down shown here:

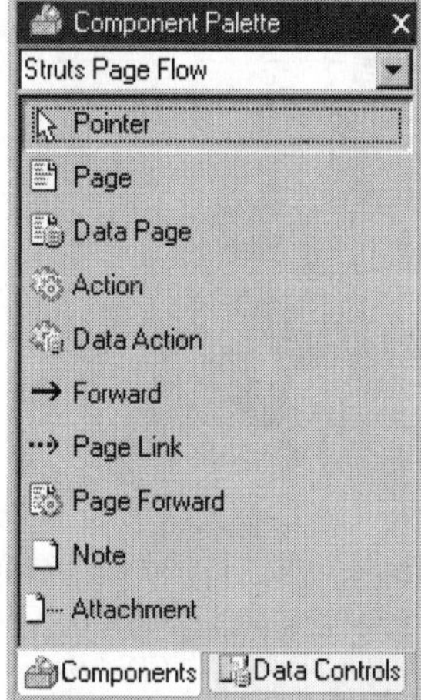

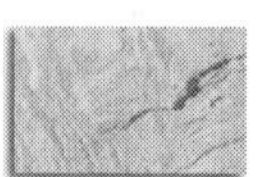

TIP
When the pointer is selected you can drag an area around multiple elements to select them. This allows you to move more than one visual component at the same time.

Page

The *Page* component allows you to create a JSP page on the diagram. It has no effect on the struts-config.xml file until you draw a forward line to it. The Page component will not be needed if you are using ADF and is only included for developers who want to use JDeveloper for traditional Struts development and pages that do not interact with any business service. When you double click the page icon on the diagram, JDeveloper will create the JSP file and navigate to the visual editor view of that file.

Data Page

A *Data Page* component extends the Struts idea of a user interface page. A *data page* is a user interface page (JSP page or UIX file) that is enabled to use ADF. It contains the functionality of both a data action (discussed later) and a Struts page. You can drop data page components onto a data page and the framework will take care of binding them to the ADF business services components such as ADF BC. The strength of this element is its compact structure in which only simple data binding and page flow are required. However, the separate data action class must be used when more complex logic is required.

It is customary to create one data page for each unique screen in your application. Typically you will have one page for a multi-record display and a separate page to edit a single record. When you create a data page, JDeveloper generates the following code:

```
<action path="/dataPage1"
className="oracle.adf.controller.struts.actions.DataActionMapping"
type="oracle.adf.controller.struts.actions.DataForwardAction"
name="DataForm"
parameter="unknown"/>
```

The *path* attribute designates the name of the data page. The generated user interface page will use this name. For example, if you generate a JSP page in this example, it would be called "dataPage1.jsp."

The *className* and *name* attributes connect the data page to ADF business services. These properties need never be modified.

Action

The *Action* element, mentioned earlier in this chapter, defines how the incoming HTTP request will be handled by the Struts controller. This includes interaction with the data model and page navigation. It represents the org.apache.struts.action.Action element contained in the struts-config.xml file. When you first place an action icon on the Page Flow Diagram, it will display with an information (exclamation point) icon. This means that information defining the action class for that action has not yet been entered. Once you double click the action to associate it with an action element, the indicator will disappear.

Data Action

A *Data Action* tag contains properties set so that it uses the ADF framework. A data action is frequently used to query data. The default behavior of the framework passes the data to the path defined in the forward tag (named "success" by default) for the given data action tag. A data action can also navigate from one element or another based upon some condition. An example of using conditional logic is included in the hands-on practices in this chapter.

In simple applications, ADF makes it unnecessary to use data actions very often. You can build applications with quite a lot of functionality using only a few components. When building more complex applications, you will frequently need to go beyond what the framework provides by default.

In very complex applications, data actions are a common element type in your Page Flow Diagram. You can have separate data actions for creating a record, deleting a record, editing a record, querying data for display in a multi-record block, and so on.

It is possible to query data and display it in a single data page; however, using this strategy means that the additional control that a data action provides is lost because you lose ability to override the default behavior of the data action class. This is because the data page tag is of type "DataForwardAction," where the "DataAction" type is used for the data action tag. For this reason, you might consider using a data action for each data page in your Page Flow Diagram where complex logic may be needed.

When you drop a data action onto a Page Flow Diagram, the following code is placed in the action mapping area of the struts-config.xml file:

```
<action path="/dataAction1"
  className="oracle.adf.controller.struts.actions.DataActionMapping"
  type="oracle.adf.controller.struts.actions.DataAction"
  name="DataForm"/>
```

This entry creates a Struts action tag called "dataAction1" and prepares it to be associated with an ADF element because of the reference to "DataForm" in the name attribute. *DataForm* is a JavaBean that is part of the ADF Struts framework. The DataForm is a reference to the class (DataActionMapping) that creates the automatic bindings between ADF BC and Struts. This will allow data to be passed to and from the business service layer.

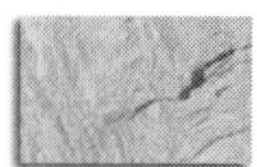

CAUTION
JDeveloper uses the "/" slash at the start of the path name for data actions and data pages. In later releases of JDeveloper 10g, if you type a path name without the slash into the Page Flow Diagram or Property Inspector, JDeveloper will add the slash for you. It is a good idea to be sure the "/" is added because a missing "/" will create bugs that are hard to locate and debug.

The clause `type="oracle.adf.controller.struts.actions.DataAction"` is the Oracle default data action and causes the other ADF-related properties to be correctly interpreted. Once you create the Struts action, you can double click it to generate an associated data action class. You can use a data action class to override or extend any of the ADF default behavior.

Forward

The *Forward* component is a standard Struts element that links any two data actions, data pages, or page forwards. A forward can form a link between components whether they are of the same type or not. A forward is a name-destination pair that resides within the source component. The name represents the name of the link between the components and the destination (path) is the name of the component to which the forward link navigates.

A forward represents a change of control in the program logic. It is the Struts equivalent of a "goto" or a hyperlink. If you draw a forward named "success" from a component called "A" to one called "B," the following code is added to the struts-config.xml file within the declaration of the "A" component.

```
<forward name="success" path="/B.do"/>
```

Page Link

A *Page Link* is a Struts element that corresponds to the standard Struts HTML link tag that calls a separate component. Page links always start in a page (or data page) and the destination is either a data page (or page) or a data action. Page links do not impact the struts-config.xml file, but they are frequently used when building web applications.

If you add a page link in the Page Flow Diagram between two pages "A" and "B", the following code will be added to the user interface page for "A" (assuming you are using JSP technology):

```
<html:link page="/B.do">
    <bean:message key="link.B"/>
</html:link>
```

The link page tag tells the page where to go and the message tag indicates where to find the label text (the key) for the link in the .properties file. You will see examples of this in both hands-on practices.

Page Forward

A *page forward* is a simple link to a page. When you drag a Page Forward onto the diagram, the following code is created:

```
<action path="/page1" forward="unknown"/>
```

When you double click the component to create a user interface file (for example, a .jsp file), JDeveloper will add the name of the file to the forward attribute.

It may seem confusing to use both forwards and page forwards. A forward is a simple link to a page or data action. You can have multiple forwards in an action. A page forward is just an action tag with a single forward with no additional properties specified. It is usually associated with a JSP page.

Note

You can place text on the diagram to annotate your diagram. Notes have no impact on the functionality of your code and do not appear in the struts-config.xml file. Text in a note can be resized, moved, or deleted.

Attachment

An attachment is a line that connects a note to any other element (even another note) so you can associate the note with a particular element on the diagram. Notes do not appear in the struts-config.xml.

Data Controls

When you place components on the Page Flow Diagram, you can modify or extend them using the Data Control Palette. This is the same tab that is used for standard JSP page or JClient development. In the Struts context, the generated code is somewhat different since it relies on the Struts tag libraries for its implementation.

As in other contexts, the Data Control Palette contains collections and their attributes as shown here in the HR schema Departments table used in the hands-on practices later in this chapter.

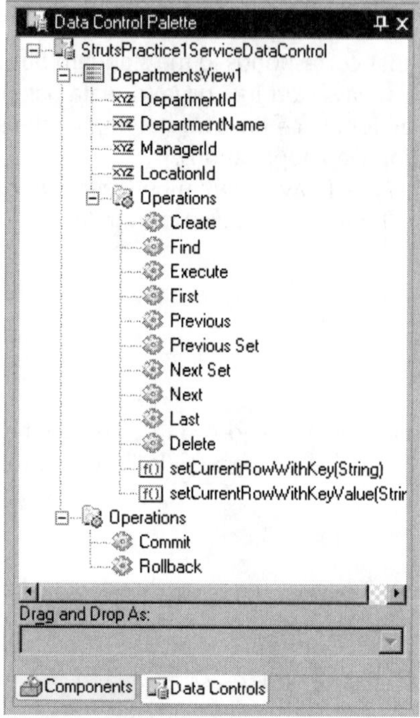

At the data control level, the operations `Commit` and `Rollback` are available. For example, you might want to create a data action and then apply a `Commit` operation to it so that if your application navigated to that data action, it would commit the data. When you drag and drop `Commit` onto a data action called dataAction1, the following code will be added to the struts-config.xml file under the action tag:

```
<set-property property="modelReference" value="dataAction1UIModel"/>
<set-property property="methodName" value="dataAction1UIModel.Commit"/>
<set-property property="resultLocation" value="${requestScope.methodResult}"/>
<set-property property="numParams" value="0"/>
```

The "dataAction1UIModel" value is a reference to the dataAction1UIModel.xml file as shown here:

```
<?xml version='1.0' encoding='windows-1252' ?>
<DCContainer
   id="dataAction1UIModel"
   xmlns="http://xmlns.oracle.com/adfm"
   Package="view"
   FindMode="false"
   EnableTokenValidation="true" >
   <Contents >
      <DCControl
         id="Commit"
         SubType="DCAction"
         DTClass="oracle.adf.dt.objects.JUDTCtrlDataControlAction"
         Action="100"
         RequiresUpdateModel="true"
         DataControl="AppModuleDataControl" >
      </DCControl>
   </Contents>
</DCContainer>
```

For page flow diagrams, the only things you can select from the Data Control Palette are operations. These can only be dragged and dropped as methods onto the Struts components. The following operations are available:

- **`Create`** to insert a blank record
- **`Find`** to support filter criteria for parameterized queries
- **`Execute`** to force execution of the query for the view object
- **`First`** to navigate to the first object in the query range (not necessarily the whole query)
- **`Previous`** to navigate to the previous object in the query range
- **`Previous Set`** to query the previous range of records when you are retrieving a range of records at one time
- **`Next Set`** to query the next range of records
- **`Last`** to navigate to the last object in the current query range
- **`Delete`** to remove the current data object

When using the Data Control Palette for a user interface file such as a JSP page, you can select the data object from the list and then select what you want to create when you drag and drop the component using the *Drag and Drop As* pulldown. This is a great time saver and will make your Struts development much easier.

You can drag and drop elements onto data pages and data actions. It only makes sense to drag and drop elements onto components that are associated with ADF. Attempting to drag and drop ADF data elements onto non-ADF components will be ignored by JDeveloper.

Using the Struts Elements

There are always multiple ways of building any application. You can use different combinations of Struts components to accomplish the same goals. In general, you will mainly use data actions and data pages. You will use standard pages when there is no data interaction. You will use a page forward when you are creating "child" data pages (for example, a new or edit record page connected to a browse data page).

You will connect components using a forward when you want to associate the transition with a button or program logic. You will use a page link when you want to transition using a link on the page. See the first hands-on practice in Chapter 12 for an example of flexible page links.

There are many different elements in the Struts framework. Even with the support from Oracle's ADF framework, it can still be confusing when building your first few applications. The best advice is to go through the following hands-on practices a few times to help you understand the structure of the applications you are building.

Introduction to the Hands-on Practices

The hands-on practices in this chapter build a simple single-table maintenance application to support the insert, update, and delete functions for department records.

The first practice illustrates how you can take full advantage of the ADF Struts environment. You will be able to build the application with just a few steps. This practice shows that in a complex application, generic actions will provide the basic functionality but may not allow adequate control over the logical flow of the application. For this reason, the second practice pairs custom data actions with each page and operation. Data actions can have data action classes associated with them to allow for the addition of complex logic.

The second hands-on practice will give you experience building an application using the same style of development that you will need for building complex applications. You will create a page flow diagram for managing department records in the HR schema including two data actions, a data page, and a page forward to maintain department records. This type of structure is best suited for complex page control. In the first hands-on practice, which takes full advantage of ADF, you will create a similar application with limited extendability using two data pages and three data actions. Page flow diagrams frequently start with a data action. You can optionally use additional data actions for each data page and anywhere it is necessary to control the flow of your application.

For simple applications, the first practice might serve as your guide. If you find that you need more complex control, you might consider implementing the style demonstrated in the second practice.

NOTE
The practices in this chapter build much of the same functionality as practices in Chapters 12, 13, 18, and 19. However, the focus of the practices in this chapter is on explaining how Struts components work, which is different from the focus in other chapters.

Hands-on Practice: Create a Simple Struts Application

This practice uses the full power of ADF to rapidly build an application. It is similar to the one available in the JDeveloper help system under the topic "Creating JSP Browse and Edit Forms" under the node "Building J2EE Applications\Working with the Oracle Application Development Framework\End-to-End Solutions for Struts, JSP, Business Components, and Oracle ADF" but contains more detailed steps. In this practice, you will create a page flow diagram for managing department records in the HR schema. The application will consist of two data pages. The first page will display data from the department table and allow users to scroll through the rows and select a particular department for an edit or delete operation. The second page will allow users to edit data from the selected record.

The phases for this practice are as follows:

I. Create the application workspace and ADF BC project

II. Create browse and edit JSP data pages

- Create the browse page
- Add an edit page

III. Add the ability to save edits

IV. Add the ability to create records

V. Add delete functionality to the application

VI. Add a logic tag to highlight the current record

VII. Shade every other row

VIII. Test for a value in the table

I. Create the Application Workspace and ADF BC Project

This phase creates a web application workspace containing two projects. One project will hold ADF BC objects; the other will hold two JSP pages that you can use to browse and edit the Departments table in the HR schema. This phase also creates the ADF BC objects.

1. In the Application Navigator, on the Applications node, select New Application Workspace from the right-click menu. In the Create Application Workspace dialog enter or select the following:

   Application Name as "StrutsPractice1"
   Application Package Prefix as "strutspractice1"
   Application Template as "Web Application [Default]"

2. Click OK. Under the StrutsPractice1 node, you will now see Model and ViewController project nodes.
3. Click Save All.
4. On the Model node, select New from the right-click menu. In the New Gallery, select the Business Tier\Business Components category. Select the "Business Components from Tables" item. Click OK.
5. Ensure that the HR connection is selected in the Business Components Project Initialization dialog and click OK.
6. Click Next if the Welcome page of the Create Business Components from Tables Wizard appears.
7. On the Entity Objects page, the package name will default to "strutspractice1.model." Ensure that HR appears in the *Schema* field. Select DEPARTMENTS in the *Available* pane and move it to the *Selected* pane. Click Next.
8. On the View Objects page, click the double right arrows to specify the Departments view object definition. Click Next.
9. On the Application Module page, change the *Name* to "StrutsPractice1Module." Click Finish to create the ADF BC objects.
10. Click Save All.

What Just Happened? You created an application workspace and ADF BC Model project containing objects for the DEPARTMENTS table. You also created a ViewController project that will contain the Struts and UI code for your application. This second project contains the basic Struts folders and default files for your application. You will add custom pages and page flow logic to this project during the next phase.

II. Create Browse and Edit JSP Data Pages

In this phase, you will build the data pages for browsing and editing. To do this, you will interact with the Page Flow Diagram, which updates the struts-config.xml file.

Create the Browse Page

1. On the ViewController node, select Open Struts Page Flow Diagram from the right-click menu. The Page Flow Diagram will open in the editor window.
2. Click the Components tab if it is not already in focus. The Struts Page Flow page should be selected. Drag a Data Page onto the Page Flow Diagram.

   Additional Information: The right-click menu for the data page gives you access to a Display Properties option that displays a Display Properties dialog where you can change the color, font style, and size.

3. Immediately type "browseDeptDP" to change the `path` parameter of the data page. If you do anything else before typing the path, you will need to click once to select the name and a second time to type in the new name. Click elsewhere in the diagram to save your entry.

   Additional Information: Remember to watch for the leading forward slash "/". JDeveloper adds this character automatically but it is good practice to ensure that the "/" is added. This character helps to identify that this element also represents an action. Alternatively, you can change the *path* property in the Property Inspector.

4. Double click the browseDeptDP data page icon in the Page Flow Diagram. In the Select or Create Page dialog, accept the default page name to create the associated JSP file "browseDeptDP.jsp." Click OK.

   Additional Information: The browseDeptDP.jsp file will be added under the Web Content node under the ViewController project and the blank JSP page will open. If the Source page opens, click the Design tab to switch to the visual editor.

5. Type the text "Departments Application". Select "Heading 1" from the first pull-down (*Block Format*) to apply the HTML `<H1>` style.

6. If it is not already displayed, click the Components tab. Select CSS from the *Component Palette* pull-down. Click JDeveloper to apply the JDeveloper style sheet. (You do not need to drag the style sheet onto the page.) Note the font and color changes in the visual editor (in addition to a horizontal rule line) that were applied from the style sheet.

   Additional Information: As you type in the visual editor, you will see your changes in the Structure window. Notice the link tag for the css/jdeveloper.css file that was added under the JSP-Structure\html\ head node. To view or edit the style sheet, on the style sheet name in the Structure window, select Open from the right-click menu. See Appendix C for more information about cascading style sheets (CSS).

7. To set the insertion point for the form tag, click just below the "Departments Application" heading. Select Struts Html from the *Component Palette* pull-down and click form. The JavaServer Page Tag Editor will appear. This dialog allows you to set properties for the form tag before it is added to the page.

   Additional Information: The next step is to add the Departments table data to the page. Since there may be a larger number of departments to view, first you need to add a form tag from the Struts library so that later you can include navigation buttons to access all departments.

8. Select the browseDeptDP.do value from the *action* property pulldown in the form Property Inspector. Click OK. Now you will see the form as a box in the visual editor.

9. Click the Data Controls tab and expand the StrutsPractice1ModuleDataControl node. Select DepartmentsView1 and verify that Read-Only Table is selected in the *Drag and Drop As* pulldown. Drag and drop DepartmentsView1 inside the form (box) that you just created.

10. Select DepartmentsView1 in the Data Control Palette and drag and drop as Navigation Buttons between the top-left side of the form box and the left side of the HTML table as shown here.

11. Click Save All.

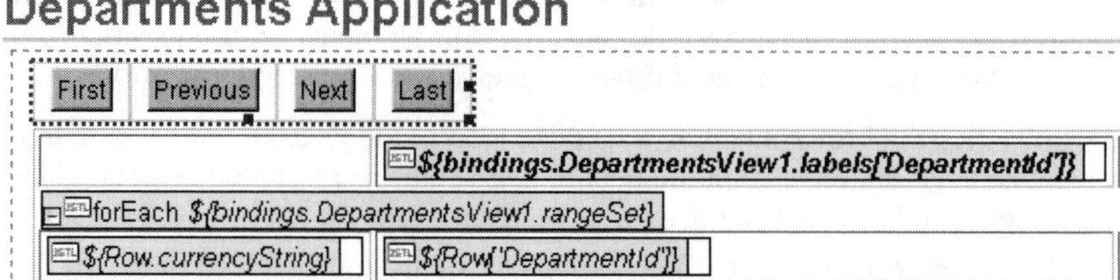

Add an Edit Page

In this phase, you will add a page to edit the departments for your application.

1. Click the struts-config.xml tab in the editor window to reopen the Page Flow Diagram. Click the Components tab and drag a second Data Page onto the Page Flow Diagram, placing it to the left of the /browseDeptDP.

2. Change the label (path) to "editDeptDP" and press ENTER.

3. Double click editDeptDP in the Page Flow Diagram. In the Select or Create Page dialog, accept the default page name "/editDeptDP.jsp." Click OK to create the associated JSP file.

4. In the Design tab for the newly opened editDeptDP.jsp, type the heading "Edit Department" and select "Heading 1" from the *Block Format* pulldown.

5. Click the Components tab. Apply the JDeveloper cascading style sheet from the CSS page. Note the changes in the visual editor.

6. Click the Data Controls tab. Select DepartmentsView1 and drag and drop it as Input Form under the Edit Department heading.

   Additional Information: Most of the items available in the *Drag and Drop As* list are self-explanatory, but Chapter 18 provides a brief explanation of each option. An *Input Form* provides a single-record display with updateable fields for the associated ADF view object attributes.

7. To modify the browse page to add a link to the edit page for the selected department, select the browseDeptDP.jsp tab in the editor. On the tag labeled "${Row.currencyString}" select Table | Insert Column from the right-click menu. A small blank cell is created just to the left of the Row.currencyString and to the left of the blank cell in the top-left corner of the HTML table.

Additional Information: By default, JDeveloper uses an asterisk ("*") as a current row indicator for a read-only table. This indicator is dynamically added using the tag labeled "${Row.currencyString}". Later in this practice, you will use this value to make the current row a different color.

8. Add an Edit link for each row adjacent to the current row indicator by dragging and dropping DepartmentsView1 from the Component Palette as a "Select Row Link" into the lower-left corner HTML table cell. This adds a "Select" link to each row in the table.

9. On the "Select" link, select Edit Tag from the right-click menu. In the Edit Link dialog, change the *URL* to point to the editDeptDP data page by changing only the first word in the string (change "browseDeptDP" to "editDeptDP").

   Addtional Information: See Chapter 12 for an alternative way to accomplish this.

10. Change the *Text* field from "Select" to "Edit" to change the visual display of the link.

    Additional Information: The value after the equals sign in the URL ("rowKeyStr=<c:out value='${Row.rowKeyStr}'") is a JavaServer Pages Standard Tag Library (JSTL) tag that uses "c" as the alias for the core tag library. The "c" alias is specified in the `taglib` directive in the first line of the JSP page.

11. Click OK.

    Additional Information: The leftmost portion of the visual editor should look like the following. Note that the fields are very wide (the display is not very WYSIWYG) and you may not see all of them without scrolling to the right.

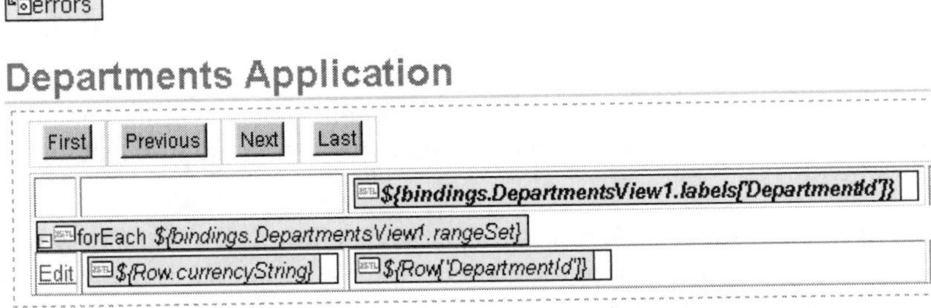

12. Switch to the struts-config.xml Page Flow Diagram. Switch to the Data Control Palette and expand the DepartmentsView1\Operations node. Drag and drop the operation "setCurrentRowWithKey(String)" as a Method onto the editDeptDP page so that it will pick up the passed current row indicator.

    Additional Information: The Page Flow Diagram offers no visual confirmation of what you just did, although the change is recorded in the struts-config.xml file. To review the effects of this action, click the Source tab on the Page Flow Diagram; you will find that the following method property will be added under the editDeptDP action:

```
<set-property property="methodName" value=
  "editDeptDPUIModel.setCurrentRowWithKey"/>
```

13. Click the Page Flow Diagram tab. To establish where you want the application to go after you update the department's data in the Edit Page, select Forward in the Component Palette, then click /editDeptDP and click /browseDeptDP. This adds a forward from the edit data page that returns the user to the browse data page when they click Submit in the edit page. The flow from the browse page to the edit page is handled by the Edit link you added before.

14. You will now see a line drawn from the Edit page back to the Browse page with the word "success" above the line. To take advantage of the automatic page flow framework, click the word "success" once; then click a second time, type "Submit", and press ENTER.

Additional Information: This matches up the name from the submit button on the Edit Page with the forward name. If you inspect the source code for the edit page, you will discover that the submit button has a *name* property of "event_Submit". By default, the framework uses the prefix "event_" to match up forward names with button names, requiring no further coding on your part to implement your navigation logic.

Your page flow diagram should look like the following:

Additional Information: By default, JDeveloper names the forwards in the struts-config.xml file with the word "success."

15. Select the ViewController project node in the Application Navigator and click Rebuild to save and recompile the code. Check the Log window to make sure that the files compile with no errors.

16. Test the partially constructed browse page by selecting Run from the browseDeptDP right-click menu. This will start the Embedded OC4J Server if it is not already running and open your default browser.

17. You should be able to see the list of departments as shown here (after clicking the Next button several times) and to click any of the Edit links to navigate to the Edit Department page for the selected record. Click the Submit button to return to the browse page from the Edit page.

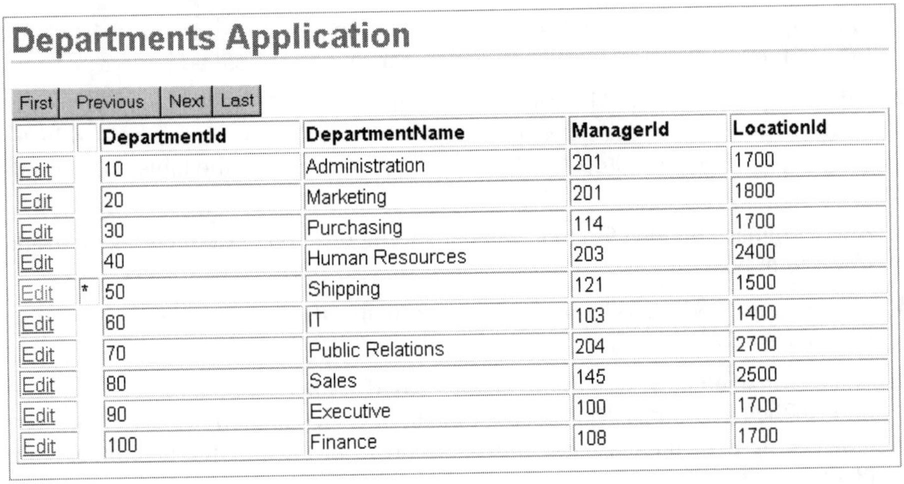

Departments Application

First | Previous | Next | Last

		DepartmentId	DepartmentName	ManagerId	LocationId
Edit		10	Administration	201	1700
Edit		20	Marketing	201	1800
Edit		30	Purchasing	114	1700
Edit		40	Human Resources	203	2400
Edit	*	50	Shipping	121	1500
Edit		60	IT	103	1400
Edit		70	Public Relations	204	2700
Edit		80	Sales	145	2500
Edit		90	Executive	100	1700
Edit		100	Finance	108	1700

Additional Information: On the Browse page, hold the mouse cursor over any Edit link and notice the URL in the status bar of the browser. Then move the mouse to another row's Edit link and notice the change in the key value. The key values are used by the controller to retrieve the current row's data from the ADF BC cache. This key value is constructed by the SetCurrentRowWithKey(String) data control you used as a basis for the link.

18. Close the browser window.

What Just Happened? You used the Struts Page Flow Component Palette to create two pages in the Page Flow Diagram. Note that there is no visible indication of the page links that provide navigation to the edit page. Recall that you connected the pages using an operation data control, which provided a hyperlink from the edit page to the browse page. When you complete the edit page and click Submit, you are returned to the browse page via the submit button tag with the name "event_Submit".

You can interact with the edit page you created, but you will not yet be able to save changes made to a record. The next phase will add code for this functionality.

III. Add the Ability to Save Edits

This phase cleans up the labels and adds a Commit button to save the updated Department information.

1. In the struts-config.xml Page Flow Diagram, double click /editDeptDP to display the visual editor. Select the "Submit" button to access its Property Inspector and change the

value property from "Submit" to "Update." This only changes the visible label on the button. Press ENTER. The button label will change in the visual editor.

2. Click the browseDeptDP.jsp tab to display the visual editor. In the Data Control Palette, under the StrutsPractice1ModuleDataControl\ Operations node, select Commit and drag and drop as a "Button with Form" below the table and form that you created earlier.

3. Add a Rollback button ("Button" without a form) next to the Commit button inside the lower form box.

4. Rebuild the ViewController project. Make sure that the file compiles with no errors. Click Save All.

5. There is an alternative way to run a Struts-based application. On the ViewController node in the navigator, select Run from the right-click menu. In the "How should the target be started?" dialog, select "browseDeptDP" and click OK. The browse page will be displayed.

6. You can now save the changes made on the Edit page. Test this by clicking the Edit link for department 90, changing the *DepartmentName* value to the plural form "Executives", and then clicking Update. The browser page will be reloaded and you will see the change you just made. Click Rollback to discard your changes or click Commit to save your changes to the database and then close the browser.

   Additional Information: If you committed the data, you can verify the database changes by viewing the table data in the Connection Navigator. Navigate to the Database\HR\HR\ Tables node and double click the DEPARTMENTS table node. Click the Data tab to view data before performing the update and commit. After performing the update and commit, in the Connection Navigator Database\HR node, select Refresh from the right-click menu. Then navigate to and double click the DEPARTMENTS table node again and click the Data tab to view the refreshed data.

TIP
For testing, it can be handy to start from different points in the Page Flow Diagram. You do not necessarily have to run the program from the logical beginning of the flow. You might want to test a portion of the application by starting from a different element in the diagram.

What Just Happened? You added a Commit button in its own form, to your browse page. You also added a Rollback button next to the Commit button to allow you to roll back any changes. In general when adding buttons to a JSP, you will embed them in a Struts form. The *value* property determines the displayed label (as with any HTML button), and the *name* property, by default, will begin with the prefix "event_" and end with the name of the forward you wish to use, which is specified in the action called from the Struts form tag. This gives you the ability to add any number of buttons to a given form.

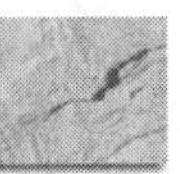

TIP

*If you make errors when building your application, you may find that record-locking errors occur when running your application. If this happens, you will need to stop the embedded OC4J server to release the locks. To do this select the Run Manager tab in the navigator (select **View | Run Manager** from the menu), and select "Terminate" from the Embedded OC4J Server node right-click menu.*

IV. Add the Ability to Create Records

In this phase, you will add the functionality to create a department in your application. This is easy to do using the operations made visible in the Component Palette. If you add a data action to your Page Flow Diagram and drop a `Create` operation from the Data Control Palette, the appropriate code will be added to your struts-config.xml file to tell the ADF BC to create a row in the Departments table when the data action is called. After creating the row, you can use the same edit page that you have already created by adding a forward on the browse page to the edit page. Then you can update the information for the new department.

1. If it is not already showing, open the struts-config.xml Page Flow Diagram. Add a Data Action from the Component Palette and rename it "createDeptDA".
2. Switch to the Data Control Palette and expand the DepartmentsView1\Operations node Select Create, and drag and drop as a Method onto createDeptDA.
3. From the Component Palette, add a Forward from createDeptDA to editDeptDP.
4. The final step is to add a link from your browse page that will point to the create Data Action. Add a Page Link from browseDeptDP to createDeptDA. Your page flow diagram should look something like the following.

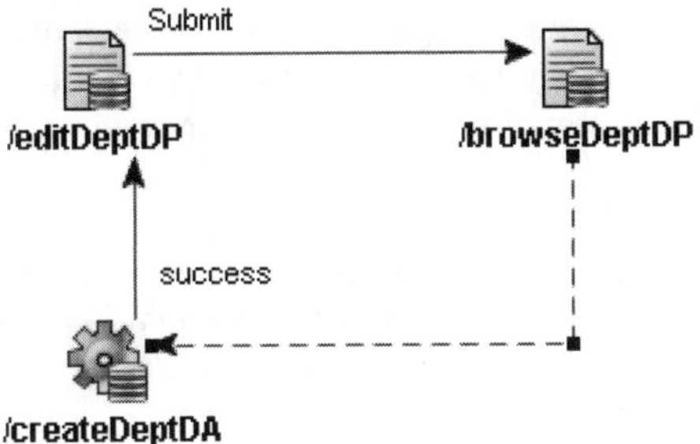

Additional Information: This adds a tag on the browse page that links to the edit page. When the user clicks the Create link, the Create Row data action will be called and you will be shown the edit page to fill in the data for a new department. This step could also be accomplished with a Button and a Struts form (or with a link that passes the event, as described in Chapter 12). The form would need a data action and associated forward to point to the Create data action. The link option was selected in this example for simplicity.

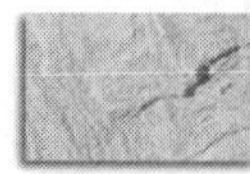

TIP

When drawing lines, you can hold down the right mouse button and drag to a turning point, then release and continue in a new direction. Drawing nodes can be added or deleted from a line using SHIFT *click. To add a drawing point to an existing line, hold* SHIFT *while dragging the line from a midpoint.*

5. To change the link to display the more user-friendly message "Create a department," double click /browseDeptDP to switch to the visual editor for that page. You will see the new tag box containing the link at the bottom of the page. The box is labeled "message *link.createDeptDA*". On this tag, select "Go to Source" from the right-click menu to navigate to the source code in the browseDeptDP.jsp file where you will see the following:

```
<html:link page="/createDeptDA.do">
    <bean:message key="link.createDeptDA"/>
</html:link>
```

Change the code to read:

```
<html:link page="/createDeptDA.do">
    Create a department
</html:link>
```

Additional Information: By default, the label for this link is stored in the associated properties file. To change the label you would normally edit the key (link.createDeptDA) in the ApplicationResources.properties file (that is, "link.createDeptDA= Create a department"). Such labels are accessed via the `<bean:message key="xxx"/>` tag. This file can be used for multi-lingual support, or even as a central location to store all your labels. Such text can be easier to maintain if it is centrally located. This step replaces the reference to ApplicationResources.properties with a hard-coded string.

6. Switch back to the Page Flow Diagram, select browseDeptDP, and click the Run icon. You should now be able to create a department by clicking the "Create a department" link and entering the information in the Edit Departments screen fields.

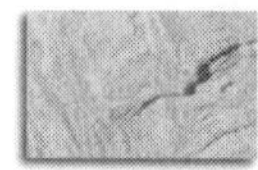

TIP

In order to avoid having to always specify the starting point of your application, you can fix a default start page for an application using "Set as Default Run Target" from the right-click menu on the appropriate page icon in the diagram.

7. Test the Create function by clicking the "Create a department" link and entering the following in the Edit Department screen:

   DepartmentId as "11"
   DepartmentName as "Packaging"
   ManagerId (leave blank)
   LocationId (leave blank)

8. Click Update and view the newly added department, which will appear at the top of the list. Close the browser. Click Save All.

NOTE
Do not use the Refresh or Back buttons in your browser. These buttons will result in an error.

What Just Happened? You added a data action that will allow the user to create a department by clicking the hyperlink to access the Edit Department page where they can enter new information. Clicking the Commit button will send the new row to the database and will commit the data if no errors occur. Note that there is no ORDER BY clause in the query; thus if you close and reopen your application, you may find your new Department 11 at the bottom of the table.

V. Add Delete Functionality to the Application

In this phase, you will add the ability to delete a department record to the application. You will need to set the current row for deletion and then delete the row. Since you can only perform a single operation in each data action, you will need to create two data actions to implement the delete functionality. The new Delete data actions are called from links just like those you used earlier to support editing departments.

1. If the Page Flow Diagram is not already open, double click the struts-config.xml file in the Application Navigator and click the Page Flow Diagram tab.
2. From the Struts Page Flow page of the Component Palette, select Data Action and drag it onto the Page Flow Diagram below browseDeptDP.
3. Rename the Data Action path to "setCurrentDeptDA".
4. Click the Data Controls tab and expand the StrutsPractice1ModuleDataControl\DepartmentsView1\Operations node and drag a setCurrentRowWithKey(String) operation onto the setCurrentDeptDA data action. This action will now interact with ADF BC to set the current row using the row key that will be sent via the link to be built shortly.

   Additional Information: You will see the setCurrentDeptDAUIModel.xml file added under the "ViewController\Application Sources\strutspractice1.view" node in the Application Navigator. The UIModel.xml files are the glue the framework uses to bind the application components to the ADF BC service layer. If you inspect their contents, you will see the tags that represent your data.
5. Create another data action above setCurrentDeptDA and rename the path "deleteDeptDA".
6. Expand the StrutsPracticeModuleDataControl\DepartmentsView1\Operations node in the Data Control Palette and drag a `Delete` operation onto the deleteDeptDA data action. This action signals to ADF BC to delete the current row set by the previous action.
7. From the Component Palette, add a Forward from setCurrentDeptDA to the deleteDeptDA data action. This means that the `Set Current Row` operation will occur before the delete occurs.

8. Add a Forward from the data action deleteDeptDA to the data page browseDeptDP. Your diagram should contain elements and connectors as shown here (the exact arrangement of the elements is not important):

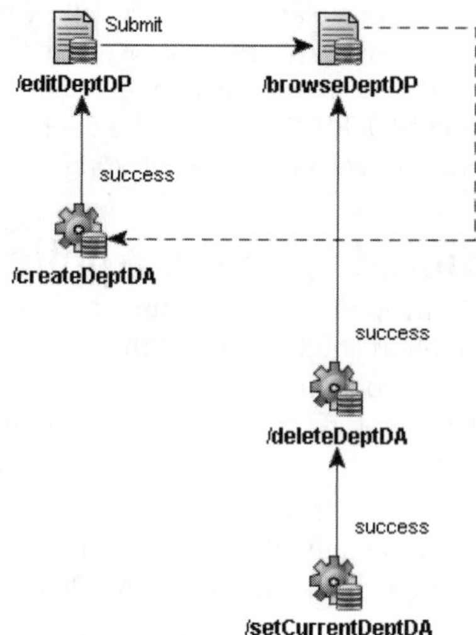

9. To add Delete links to the Browse Departments screen, open the browseDeptDP.jsp file in the visual editor. On the Edit tag cell, select Table | Split Cell from the right-click menu. Accept the default of 2 Columns in the Split Cell dialog and click OK. The new column will be inserted to the right of the Edit cell.
10. From the Data Control Palette, drag and drop DepartmentsView1 as a Select Row Link into the new cell.
11. On the Select link, select Edit Tag from the right-click menu. In the Edit Link dialog, make the following changes:

    URL: Change the beginning of the string so it reads "setCurrentDeptDA.do?rowKeyStr=<c:out value='${Row.rowKeyStr}'/>"
    Text: Delete
12. Click OK.
13. Select the ViewController node in the navigator and click Rebuild. Make sure that the file compiles with no errors.
14. Click the struts-config.xml tab and on the browseDeptDP icon, select Run from the right-click menu. The application should look like Figure 17-2.
15. Test the new link by selecting Delete for Department 40. Use the Rollback button to undo the delete.
16. Close the browser.

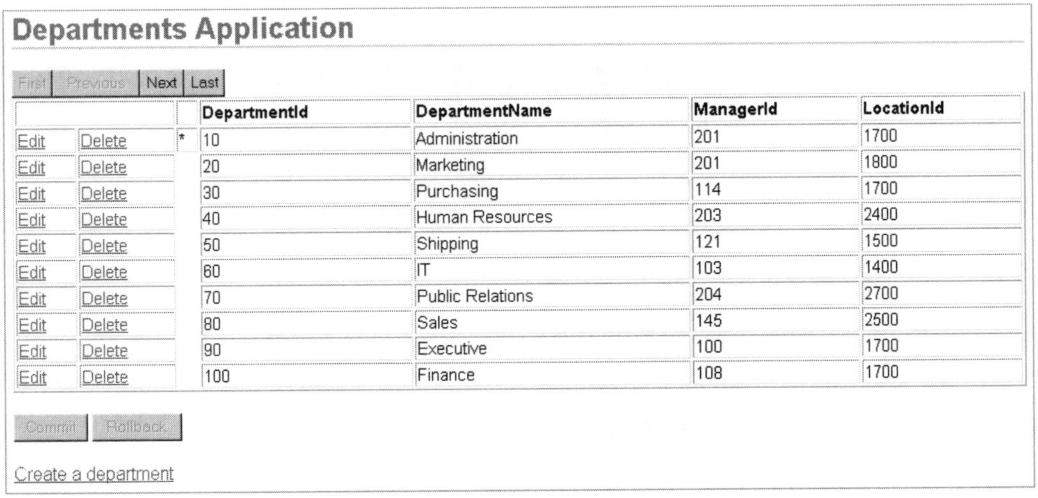
Departments Application
First
Previous
Next
Last
DepartmentId
DepartmentName
ManagerId
LocationId
Edit Delete * 10 Administration 201 1700
Edit Delete 20 Marketing 201 1800
Edit Delete 30 Purchasing 114 1700
Edit Delete 40 Human Resources 203 2400
Edit Delete 50 Shipping 121 1500
Edit Delete 60 IT 103 1400
Edit Delete 70 Public Relations 204 2700
Edit Delete 80 Sales 145 2500
Edit Delete 90 Executive 100 1700
Edit Delete 100 Finance 108 1700
Commit
Rollback
Create a department

FIGURE 17-2. *Departments application*

What Just Happened? You added the ability to delete a department from the application. This was accomplished by adding two data actions. The first action used a key set from the browse page to tell the ADF BC which row was to be set as the current row. The second action signaled to ADF BC to delete the current row. You tested the Delete link and Rollback button in the Departments application.

VI. Add a Logic Tag to Highlight the Current Record

In this phase, you will change the application to display a yellow background for the current record in the multi-record page.

1. You need to add conditional logic within the HTML table row loop. In the browseDeptDP.jsp visual editor, find the second row in the HTML table, which includes the "forEach ${bindings.DepartmentsView1.rangeSet}" tag. This defines the multi-row block for Departments. Click this tag and select "Go to Source" from the right click menu.

2. Find the `<tr>` tag right below the selected `<c:forEach>` tag. Place the cursor inside or after the `<tr>` tag and in the Property Inspector, set the property *bgColor* to "White" using the pulldown. You will see the added attribute code pop into the editor.

3. Add a line below the <tr> tag. With the cursor in the new line, select JSTL Core from the Component Palette pulldown and click choose. As described in Appendix D, the JSTL choose tag allows you to perform if...the...else conditional testing.

4. In the c:choose construct dialog, click New to create the test attribute. Doubleclick the *Value* field and fill in the *Value* as "${Row.currencyString=='*'}" (without the starting and ending double quotes).

5. Check the *Add c:otherwise* checkbox. This will create the otherwise clause for the choose element. The dialog should appear as follows:

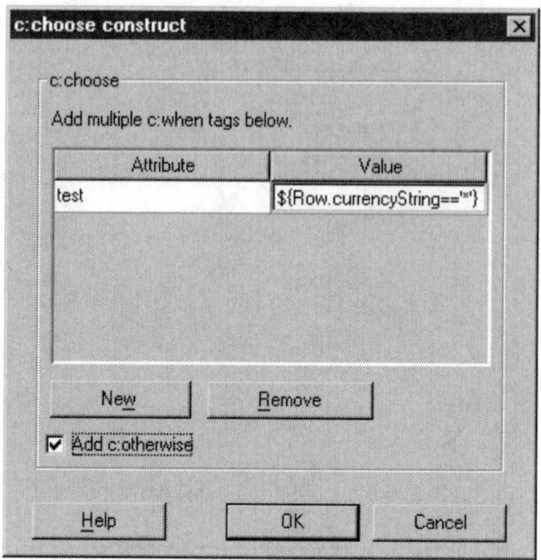

6. Click OK to create the choose tag set in the code.

7. For readability, spread out the tags so they appear as follows:

```
<c:choose>
  <c:when test="${Row.currencyString=='*'}">
  </c:when>
  <c:otherwise>
  </c:otherwise>
</c:choose>
```

8. Add a line between `<c:otherwise>` and `</c:otherwise>`. Highlight the `<tr bgcolor="White">` tag and drag it into the new line. (This demonstrates how you can drag code as well as visual elements.)

9. Add a line between the `when` tags and copy the `<tr>` tag into that new line. Change the background color to "Yellow". The new code under the forEach tag should appear as follows:

```
<c:choose>
  <c:when test="${Row.currencyString=='*'}">
    <tr bgcolor="Yellow">
  </c:when>
  <c:otherwise>
    <tr bgcolor="White">
  </c:otherwise>
</c:choose>
```

Additional Information: The Struts Logic library also contains conditional tags but the JSTL conditional tags allow you to code multiple conditions. Recall that the current row on the browse page is always marked with an "*". This comes from a property called "currencyString". When you test the currencyString for the notEqual to value="*", you can set the not-current rows to a background color of white.

10. Select the ViewController node and click Rebuild. Be sure that the file compiles with no errors.

11. Select browseDeptDP in the struts-config.xml Page Flow Diagram and select Run from the right-click menu.

    Additional Information: The Departments application will now show the selected department in yellow as shown in Figure 17-3. When you click an Edit link for a record, this page will change the current record to that record. When you return from the edit page, that record will appear with the yellow background.

NOTE
If all rows show as yellow, the `taglib` directive for the struts-logic tag library may be missing. To add that tag, select the Struts Logic page in the Component Palette. Drop in any of the tags, which will add the `taglib` directive. Then delete the new tag, leaving the `taglib` directive.

12. Close the browser.

Departments Application

First | Previous | Next | Last

		DepartmentId	DepartmentName	ManagerId	LocationId
Delete	Edit	10	Administration	200	1700
Delete	Edit	20	Marketing	201	1800
Delete	Edit	30	Purchasing	114	1700
Delete	Edit	40	Human Resources	203	2400
Delete	Edit	50	Shipping	121	1500
Delete	Edit	60	IT	103	1400
Delete	Edit	70	Public Relations	204	2700
Delete	Edit	80	Sales	145	2500
Delete	Edit	90	Executive	100	1700
Delete	Edit	100	Finance	108	1700

Create a department

Commit | Rollback

FIGURE 17-3. *Departments application with selected row highlighted*

What Just Happened? You made the current record appear in yellow by adding JSTL logic tags to the code. The logic tags require more manual attention than other tags. This practice includes a few more opportunities to work with these tags to give you some additional experience before searching the Internet or reference books for more complex examples.

VII. Shade Every Other Row

In this phase, you change the application to make every other row a gray background color for ease of reading. This phase was inspired by a technique described in the article "How To Color Alternate Lines in JSP Databound Table" on the OTN website.

1. Click the browseDeptDP tab and select the Design tab to display the corresponding JSP file in the visual editor. Once again find the tag containing "forEach ${bindings.DepartmentsView1.rangeSet}". Click that tag. In the Property Inspector, set the property *varStatus* to "currentStatus" by typing it. Press ENTER.

   Additional Information: You just created a local variable "currentStatus" to reference the current row number.

2. On "forEach ${bindings.DepartmentsView1.rangeSet}", select Go to Source from the right-click menu. The `<c:forEach...` tag will be selected in the Code Editor. Notice that `varStatus="currentStatus"` appears at the end of the tag.

3. Add a JSTL tag to handle colors for alternate rows. Add a blank line after the `</c:when>` closing tag several lines below. With the cursor in that blank line, from the JSTL Core page in the Component Palette add a `when` tag.

4. In the JavaServer Page Tag Editor dialog, for the *Value* column opposite "test," double click the field and type in the value "${currentStatus.count%2==0}" (without the opening and closing quotes). Click OK to close the dialog and add the tag. Move the ending `</when>` tag to a new line.

   Additional Information: The currentStatus.count variable obtains the current row number. Then using the modulus operator ("%"), you can test for even rows.

5. Add a line after the tag `c:when test="${currentStatus.count%2==0}">` and type in the tag

   ```
   <tr bgColor="#EEEEEE">.
   ```

   Your code fragment should look like the following:

```
<c:choose>
  <c:when test="${Row.currencyString=='*'}">
    <tr bgcolor="Yellow">
  </c:when>
  <c:when test="${currentStatus.count%2==0}">
    <tr bgcolor="#EEEEEE">
  </c:when>
  <c:otherwise>
    <tr bgcolor="White">
  </c:otherwise>
</c:choose>
```

Additional Information: You added a test for every other row that uses the JSTL expression language syntax to test for the two modulus of the current record number. (Appendix D discusses JSTL and expression language in more detail.)

6. In the Page Flow Diagram, click /browseDeptDP and select the Run icon. If the "How should the target be started?" dialog appears, select /"browseDeptDP" and click OK.

   Additional Information: You do not have to rebuild the application at this point (although you should save it) since you have not changed any Java code. You have only changed the JSP tags, but the browser renders the HTML tags. If there is an error, you may get strange output, but still not receive any compilation errors.

   The finished application should look something like Figure 17-4.

7. Close the browser.

What Just Happened? You defined conditional logic so that the row of the table that contained data for a department was displayed either white or grey. You did this by embedding two `<tr>` commands within conditions, so that only one of them is executed for any given row.

VIII. Test for a Value in the Table

In this phase, you will obtain more practice with the tag libraries by changing the way data in a table cell is displayed. It demonstrates how you can programmatically interact with cell values. You will use conditional logic (in a Struts logic tag) to apply formatting to a cell of a table

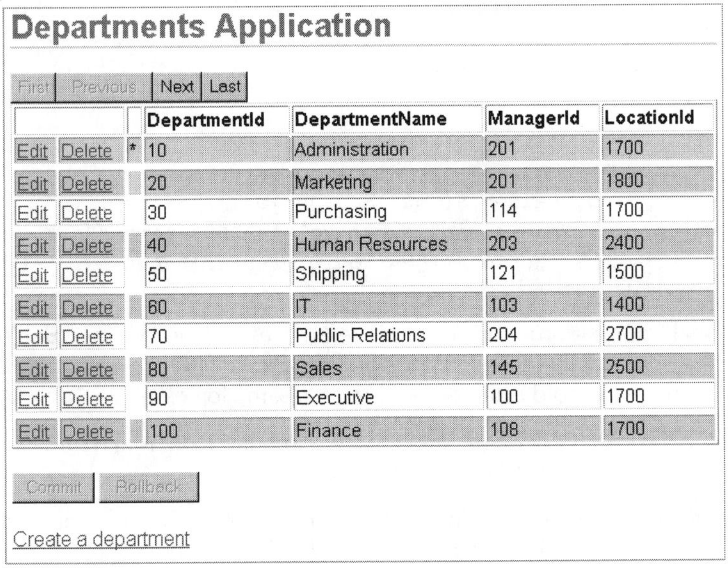

Departments Application

First | Previous | Next | Last

			DepartmentId	DepartmentName	ManagerId	LocationId
Edit	Delete	*	10	Administration	201	1700
Edit	Delete		20	Marketing	201	1800
Edit	Delete		30	Purchasing	114	1700
Edit	Delete		40	Human Resources	203	2400
Edit	Delete		50	Shipping	121	1500
Edit	Delete		60	IT	103	1400
Edit	Delete		70	Public Relations	204	2700
Edit	Delete		80	Sales	145	2500
Edit	Delete		90	Executive	100	1700
Edit	Delete		100	Finance	108	1700

Commit | Rollback

Create a department

FIGURE 17-4. *Departments application with alternating color rows*

(contents of the `<td>` tag). For this example, you will make all Manager IDs with a value greater than 200 turn bold. Although this particular example is a bit contrived, this technique is very useful in highlighting exceptions.

1. In the Design tab for browseDeptDP.jsp, on the ${Row['ManagerId']} tag (you may have to scroll right to see it), select Go to Source from the right-click menu. This will navigate to the Manager ID tag in the code. Add a blank line above this line:

   ```
   <c:out value="${Row['ManagerId']}"/> 
   ```

2. From the Struts Logic page of the Component Palette, click the greaterThan tag and enter the following values in the JavaServer Page Tag Editor dialog:

   scope as "page"
   value as "200"
   name as "Row"
   property as "ManagerId"

3. Click OK to close the dialog and add the tag.

   Additional Information: The JavaServerPage Tag Editor added the following code:

   ```
    <logic:greaterThan scope="page" value="200" name="Row"
   property="ManagerId"></logic:greaterThan>
   ```

   If you want to make changes to the parameters, you can now directly edit the code or place the cursor anywhere in the tag and edit the properties in the Property Inspector.

4. Add a <b> (the bold tag) right before the closing tag </logic:greaterThan>.

5. Right after the <c:out value="${Row['ManagerId']}"/> tag, copy the same <logic:greaterThan ... line, but change the <b> tag to a closing </b>. The resulting code should look like the following

   ```
   <td>
     <logic:greaterThan scope="page" value="200" name="Row"
       property="ManagerId"><b></logic:greaterThan>
             <c:out value="${Row['ManagerId']}"/> 
     <logic:greaterThan scope="page" value="200" name="Row"
       property="ManagerId"></b></logic:greaterThan>
         </td>
   ```

   Additional Information: This example references a value in a row. Bold is turned on (using the bold tag) if the logic detects that the ManagerID is greater than 200. The value is then printed and bold is turned off using the same logic.

6. Select the ViewController node and click the Rebuild icon. Make sure that the file compiles with no errors. Click Save All.

7. In the struts-config.xml Page Flow Diagram, click browseDeptDP and select the Run icon. If the "How should the target be started?" dialog appears, select /"browseDeptDP."

   The revised application should look like Figure 17-5, with the Manager IDs higher than 200 shown in bold.

8. Close the browser.

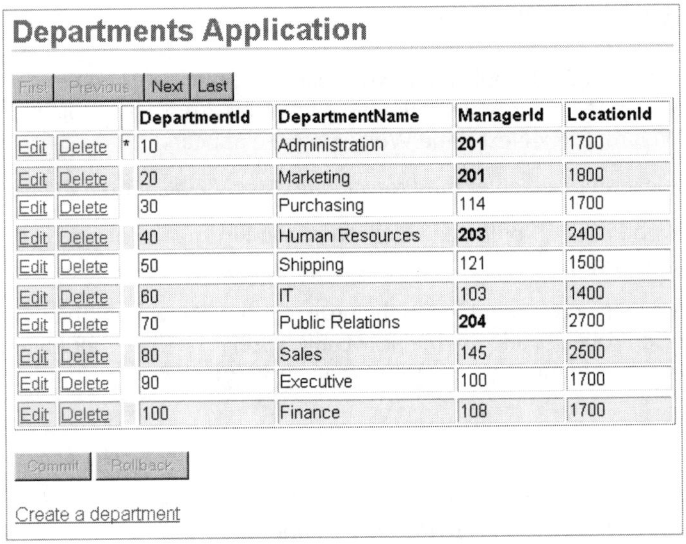

Departments Application

First | Previous | Next | Last

		DepartmentId	DepartmentName	ManagerId	LocationId
Edit Delete	*	10	Administration	**201**	1700
Edit Delete		20	Marketing	**201**	1800
Edit Delete		30	Purchasing	114	1700
Edit Delete		40	Human Resources	**203**	2400
Edit Delete		50	Shipping	121	1500
Edit Delete		60	IT	103	1400
Edit Delete		70	Public Relations	**204**	2700
Edit Delete		80	Sales	145	2500
Edit Delete		90	Executive	100	1700
Edit Delete		100	Finance	108	1700

Commit | Rollback

Create a department

FIGURE 17-5. *Departments application showing certain manager IDs in bold*

What Just Happened? This example actually interacted with values in a table row. It showed how JDeveloper refers to the column values that are displayed in a JSP page. It also showed how to use the Struts Logic tag library to change the look and feel of the rows based on cell data.

Hands-on Practice: Create a Struts Application with Data Actions for Custom Logic

This hands-on practice builds an abbreviated version of application as in the preceding practice. However, this practice provides for more complex control of the application and uses additional data actions, based on a framework that gives you complete control between pages to do anything you may need. This type of architecture will most likely be used for your production-level application design.

The phases for this practice are as follows:

I. Create another ViewController project

II. Create a data action and a JSP data page

III. Add edit and update functionality

I. Create Another ViewController Project

This phase reuses the Model project from the previous practice and adds another ViewController project for the user interface objects in this practice. If you have not completed the first phase of the preceding practice, you can complete it now and start with this phase of this practice.

Alternatively, you can download the starting files for this practice from the authors' websites mentioned at the beginning of this book.

1. On the StrutsPractice1 application workspace node, select New Project from the right-click menu. In the New Gallery, double click Web Project to display the Create Web Project Wizard. Click Next if the Welcome page appears.
2. On the Location page, enter the *Project Name* as "ViewController2" and click Next.
3. On the Web Project Profile page click Next and Finish. The project will be added to the application workspace.
4. To add the struts-config.xml file to the project, select New from the right-click menu of the ViewController2 node. In the New Gallery, select "All Technologies" in the *Filter By* pulldown. Then in the Web Tier\Struts category, select Struts Controller Page Flow and click OK.

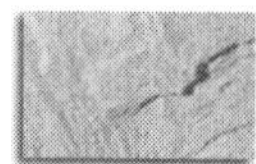

NOTE
An alternative way to include a struts-config.xml file in a web project is to open the Project Properties dialog and move Struts from Available Technologies to Selected Technologies under the Common Technology scope node. Select the Common\Input Paths node and change the "Default Package" field to the desired package name. This will be the main package directory for the files you will create in this project. Click OK. Since you selected the Struts technology, Struts files will be created in the project. This method allows you to change the package name, if desired.

What Just Happened? You created a second project and added the default Struts files using the JDeveloper wizards.

Expand the new ViewController2 node if it is not already expanded to examine what is created when you add the default Struts files. Expand the Application Sources\mypackage1 folder and locate the ApplicationResources.properties file. This file includes message text and parameter values, which can be used for customization or multi-lingual support. Text and parameters for the new application will be included in this file as the practice proceeds.

The bean:message tag in a JSP file uses the ApplicationResources.properties file. For example, you might use the following tag in a page:

```
<bean:message key="errors.header"/>
```

This tag will actually send the following tag to the browser:

```
<h3><font color="red">Validation Error</font></h3>You must correct the following
error(s) before proceeding:<ul>
```

The message tag looks up the value for the `errors.header` parameter in ApplicationResources.properties and substitutes the value that it found in the .properties file.

The Web Content\WEB-INF folder includes a struts-config.xml file and a web.xml file. The web.xml file sets application-specific parameters for the servlet runtime environment. The one parameter that you might want to change is the following:

```
<session-timeout>35</session-timeout>
```

This means that your sessions will time out (be dropped) after 35 minutes with no activity. For external standard Internet users (for example, customers purchasing products), this is probably fine. Many commercial websites drop sessions in as little as 10–20 minutes. However, internal users (such as salespersons entering orders) may be entering a large amount of information, or be interrupted during their work, so being disconnected after 35 minutes may be inconvenient.

CAUTION
You might decide that you can increase the timeout limit to 480 (8 hours to correspond to the length of a normal workday). However, with this setting, as soon as your application is put into production, you will start running out of sessions because the number of sessions is limited. Determining the proper timeout setting can be a difficult problem. You need to balance the amount of time you can afford to leave sessions open with your users' application usage patterns.

The struts-config.xml (also under the WEB-INF folder) is the core Struts configuration file. When you create page flow diagrams, you are really editing this file. Consider this excerpt from struts-config.xml:

```
<struts-config>
     <message-resources parameter="view.ApplicationResources"/>
</struts-config>
```

This code points to the ApplicationResources.properties file in the view package (the ".properties" extension on this file is implied and required).

II. Create a Data Action and a JSP Data Page

Now, you can edit the struts-config.xml file using the Page Flow Diagram.

1. Select "Open Struts Page Flow Diagram" from the ViewController2 right-click menu to open the Page Flow Diagram in the editor window.
2. Click the Components tab. Struts Page Flow should show in the pulldown. Drag a Data Action onto the Page Flow Diagram and immediately type in the path as "browseDeptDA". Press ENTER.

   Additional Information: The data action you just added refers to a Struts Java class that you can extend to perform any complex steps that you might need between displaying your pages. Some examples of how you can use this functionality are included in this practice. If you click the Source tab you can examine the code that was added to the struts-config.xml file. The following code is an excerpt from what was added by dragging the data action onto the Page Flow Diagram:

```
<action-mappings>
  <action path="/dataAction1"
    className="oracle.adf.controller.struts.actions.DataActionMapping"
    type="oracle.adf.controller.struts.actions.DataAction"
    name="DataForm"/>
</action-mappings>
```

This code represents a default `DataAction` class that is now being referenced in your project. You can override the default class by double clicking the data action in the Page Flow Diagram. Also, the first time you drag a Data Page or Data Action onto the diagram you will also see the form-bean and message-resources tags being added.

3. Return to the page flow diagram by selecting the Page Flow Diagram tab.

4. To create an override for the default class, double click the browseDeptDA data action to open the Create Struts Data Action dialog. Leave the default name of BrowseDeptDAAction and click OK. You will see the BrowseDeptAction.java file added in the Application Navigator, under the ViewController2\Application Sources\mypackage1 node.

   Additional Information: After adding the override class for the data action, you will see the following modified code in the struts-config.xml file:

```
<action path="/browseDeptDA"
className="oracle.adf.controller.struts.actions.DataActionMapping"
type="strutspractice.view.BrowseDeptDAAction" name="DataForm"/>
```

   When this action tag is called, it will call the class `BrowseDeptDAAction`, which extends the default `DataAction` class. You will use this technique later in this practice to override several methods in the default class, though no custom code is shown in this instance. The BrowseDeptAction.java file contains the following code stub:

```
package my package1;
import oracle.adf.controller.struts.actions.DataAction;
public class BrowseDeptDAAction extends DataAction
{
  // To handle an event named "yourname" add a method:
  // public void onYourname(DataActionContext ctx)

  // To override a method of the lifecycle, go to
  // the main menu "Tools/Override Methods...".
}
```

5. Return to the Page Flow Diagram by clicking the struts-config.xml tab and then the Page Flow Diagram tab. In the Struts Page Flow page of the Component Palette, select Data Page and drag it onto the Page Flow Diagram. Rename it "browseDeptDP". The following code will be added to the struts-config.xml file:

```
<action path="/browseDeptDP"
  className="oracle.adf.controller.struts.actions.DataActionMapping"
  type="oracle.adf.controller.struts.actions.DataForwardAction"
  name="DataForm" parameter="unknown"/>
```

6. Double click browseDeptDP in the Page Flow Diagram. Uncheck the *Edit this page now* checkbox (you do not need to modify the page at this point) and click OK to create the associated JSP file. The browseDeptDP.jsp file will be added to the ViewController2/ Web Content node in the Application Navigator.

7. Click Save All. Select the ViewController2 node in the Application Navigator and click the Rebuild icon. Be sure that the project compiles with no errors.

8. Select the Forward component on the Struts Page Flow Component Palette page and make a connection from browseDeptDA to browseDeptDP. This points the data action to the data page so that when the data action is run successfully, it will pass control to the data page.

9. Double click the browseDeptDP.jsp file in the Application Navigator. The blank JSP page will open.

10. Type the heading "Departments Application 2" and select "Heading 1" from the *Block Format* pulldown.

11. Select the CSS page on the *Component Palette* pulldown and click JDeveloper to apply the JDeveloper cascading style sheet.

12. Click the visual editor under the line. Type "List of Departments". Select Heading 3 on the *Block Format* pulldown to format the new text. Press ENTER again to move the cursor to a new line.

13. To add a form that will be used to hold your table, select the Struts Html page of the Component Palette and click form.

14. In the Java Server Page Tag Editor select "browseDeptDP.do" from the action pull-down (be sure that the "/" is included in the tag) for the value of the action attribute in the JavaServer Page Tag Editor and click OK. Now you will see the form as a box in the visual editor.

15. Switch to the Data Controls tab and expand the StrutsPractice1ModuleDataControl node. Select DepartmentsView1 and verify that Read-Only Table is selected in the *Drag and Drop As* pulldown. Drag and drop DepartmentsView1 inside the form box you just created.

    Additional Information: Switch to the Source tab and view the code to see the HTML formatting tags and the `<html:errors>` tag. Note that the errors and form tags (and the `taglib` directive for the Struts library) are the only Struts-specific part of the code. The messages tag enables the display of any errors thrown. You do not have to code a special error handler because it is built into Struts.

16. Switch back to the Design tab and drag and drop DepartmentsView1 as navigation buttons between the top-left corner of the box for the table and the box representing the form as shown here:

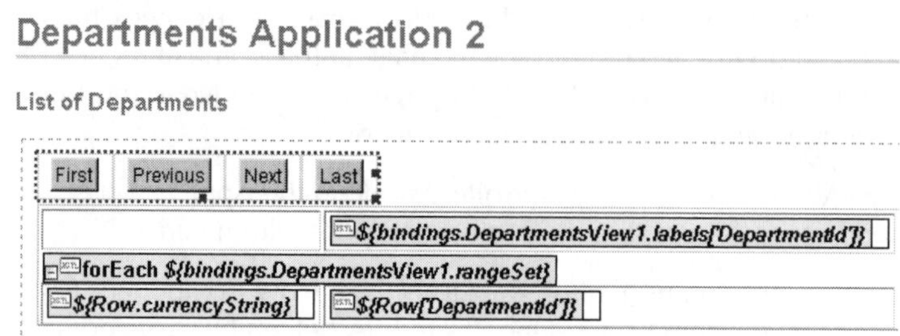

17. Select the ViewController2 node and click the Rebuild icon. Be sure that the files compile with no errors.

18. Test the application by clicking the struts-config.xml file tab. Select Run from the right-click menu of the browseDeptDA icon in the Page Flow Diagram. You will see the Departments Application 2 page as shown here:

Departments Application 2

List of Departments

First | Previous | Next | Last

	DepartmentId	DepartmentName	ManagerId	LocationId
*	10	Administration	201	1700
	20	Marketing	201	1800
	30	Purchasing	114	1700
	40	Human Resources	203	2400
	50	Shipping	121	1500
	60	IT	103	1400
	70	Public Relations	204	2700
	80	Sales	145	2500
	90	Executive	100	1700
	100	Finance	108	1700

19. Note that only 10 rows are displayed. To display more rows, you can change the range size number. To do this, select browseDeptDP.jsp in the Application Navigator and select the UI Model node (the second tab) in the Structure window.

20. Expand the browseDeptDPUIModel to select the DepartmentsView1Iterator in the Structure window to access the Property Inspector.

21. Change the *Range Size* property to 100. Press ENTER. The next time you run this file, you will see up to 100 records.

22. Close the browser.

What Just Happened? You used the Struts Page Flow Component Palette to add to the diagram a data action, a data page, and a forward; these additions automatically added the appropriate code to the struts-config.xml file. You implemented the ability to browse department data. You made some simple modifications to the JSP page including heading information and a cascading style sheet.

III. Add Edit and Update Functionality

This phase creates a data action to edit and update the department information on the JSP page.

1. Switch to the Page Flow Diagram. Select Data Action from the Struts Page Flow Component Palette and drag it onto the Page Flow Diagram. Rename the path to "editDeptDA."
2. Select Page Forward from the Struts Page Flow Component Palette and drag it onto the struts-config.xml page. Rename the path to "editDeptPF".
3. Draw a Forward from editDeptDA to editDeptPF.
4. Draw another Forward from editDeptDA to browseDeptDA. Change the name "forward1" to "browse". Your Page Flow Diagram should now look something like the following:

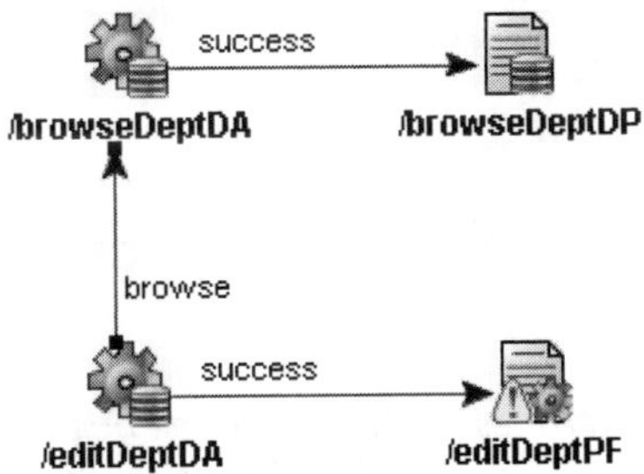

5. From the Data Control Palette, expand the DepartmentsView1\Operations nodes and select the setCurrentRowWithKey(String). Drag and drop it as a Method on top of the editDeptDA data action.

   Additional Information: The setCurrentRowWithKey that you just dropped added code to the struts-config.xml file. If you set properties for the data action, the Struts framework will set ADF BC to the current row (passed from a link in the Browse page). The following code was added within the editDeptDA component to set these properties:

```
<set-property property="methodName"
    value="editDeptPFUIModel.setCurrentRowWithKey"/>
<set-property property="resultLocation"
    value="${requestScope.methodResult}"/>
<set-property property="numParams" value="1"/>
```

6. In the Page Flow Diagram, double click the editDeptDA data action to create the override `DataAction` class. In the Create Struts Data Action dialog, accept the default EditDeptDAAction name and click OK. This will open the EditDeptDAAction.java source file.

7. JDeveloper provides an easy way to override the methods from the default class. Be sure that the cursor is in the editor window (Source tab) for the EditDeptDAAction.java file. Select **Tools | Override Methods** and check the *findForward(DataActionContext): void* checkbox on the Override Methods dialog as shown here. Click OK. This will add a method stub to the class file.

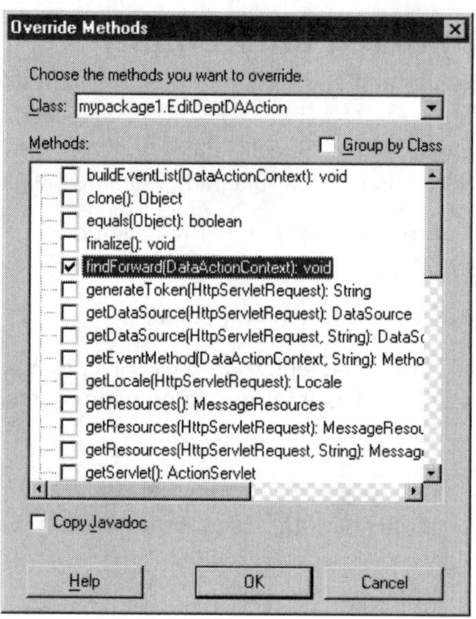

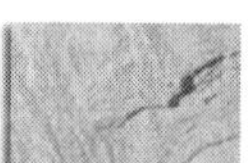

NOTE
Remember that the authors' websites mentioned at the beginning of the book contain sample solutions and code snippets for the hands-on practices in this book.

8. In the EditDeptDAAction.java source code, the following code will be used to override the logic for finding the correct Struts forward. Since you have not built the edit form and associated submit button, you can use the value "Update" for the button when you do build it. Replace the code inside the `findForward()` method (two lines consisting of a comment and call to `super.findForward()`) with the following. The backslash "\" at the end of two lines here indicates that the line below the line with the backslash should replace the backslash, making one continuous line. If you do not remove the "\" and append the `findForward` to the previous line, your code will not compile correctly.

```
HttpServletRequest request = actionContext.getHttpServletRequest();

//"Update" will be the value of the "name" property on the Submit button
Object s = request.getParameter("Update");
if (s != null)
```

```
{

  //Now test to see if update has errors
  if (this.hasErrors(actionContext))
  {
    //if Update has Errors, return to the edit page to correct data
    actionContext.setActionForward(actionContext.getActionMapping().\
      findForward("success"));
  } else
  {
    // if Update is successful, go back to the browse page
    actionContext.setActionForward(actionContext.getActionMapping().\
      findForward("browse"));
  }
}
//Finally - if not an "Update" from the Edit page
//use default code from parent class to control the forward action
super.findForward(actionContext);
```

Additional Information: The code will look for the existence of the value "Update" in the request. If it exists, you know that an edit has occurred. Then you can test to see if the proposed edit has errors. If it does you will return the application to the Edit page to correct the errors. Otherwise you will pass control back to the Browse page if the update was successful.

9. Hold the mouse cursor over the `request.getParameter()` call (which has a blue wavy underline) and press ALT-ENTER to automatically enter the three required import statements.

10. Select the ViewController2 node and click Rebuild. Make sure that the project compiles with no errors.

11. Open the struts-config.xml Page Flow Diagram. Double click the editDeptPF page forward to open the Select or Create Page dialog. Accept the default "editDeptPF.jsp" *Page Name*. Click OK.

12. Ensure that you are on the Design tab for editDeptPF.jsp. Select DepartmentsView1 in the Data Control Palette and drag and drop it as an Input Form onto the visual editor.

13. Now you must update the range size to match your browse page. To do this, make sure that editDeptPF.jsp is selected in the Application Navigator, select the UI Model tab in the Structure window, and select the DepartmentsView1Iterator in the Structure window. In the Property Inspector, change the *Range Size* property to 100. Press ENTER.

14. Place the cursor before the errors tag and press ENTER to insert a line. Type "Edit Departments" and select Heading 1 from the *Block Format* pulldown.

15. Apply the JDeveloper cascading style sheet from the CSS page of the Component Palette.

16. On the Submit button select Edit Tag from the right-click menu. Change the *Name* property to "Update" and the *Value* property to "Update". Click OK. The button label will change in the visual editor.

    Additional Information: In this step, the "Update" *Name* property matches the value in the code you entered in the previous section for the custom DataAction. A parameter called "Update" is added to the HTTP request when this button is clicked so the preceding code can detect that this button was clicked and react in any way you wish. Also note that you could have set the *Name* property on the submit button to "event_browse" and then you would not need the override code presented here for the data action to work correctly. Using the "event_browse" *Name* property with a forward named "browse" or any number of submit buttons and named forwards is sufficient for most applications. However, subclassing the custom `DataAction` class provides the ultimate, customizable solution.

17. Click the browseDeptDP.jsp tab. Select the Design tab.
18. On the tag labeled "${Row.currencyString}", select Table | Insert Column from the right-click menu. You will see a small blank box that is created just to the left of the Row.currencyString.
19. Select DepartmentsView1 in the Data Control Palette and drag and drop it as a Select Row Link into the blank box.
20. On the Select link in the visual editor, select Edit Tag from the right-click menu and change the fields as follows:

    URL (change "browseDeptDP" to "editDeptDA" so the field reads "editDeptDA.do?rowKeyStr=<c:outvalue='${Row.rowKeyStr}'/>"

    Text Type "Edit" in the field.

21. Click OK.
22. In the Data Control Palette, under the StrutsPractice1ModuleDataControl\Operations node select Commit and drag and drop it as "Button with Form" onto browseDeptDP just below the existing visual elements.
23. Select the Rollback operation and drag and drop as "Button" (not "Button with Form") onto browseDeptDP just to the right of the Commit button within the same form box.
24. Select the ViewController2 node and click Rebuild. Make sure that the file compiles with no errors. Click Save All.
25. Test the application by running browseDeptDA from the Page Flow Diagram. You will see the Departments Application 2 page with many departments as shown in Figure 17-6.

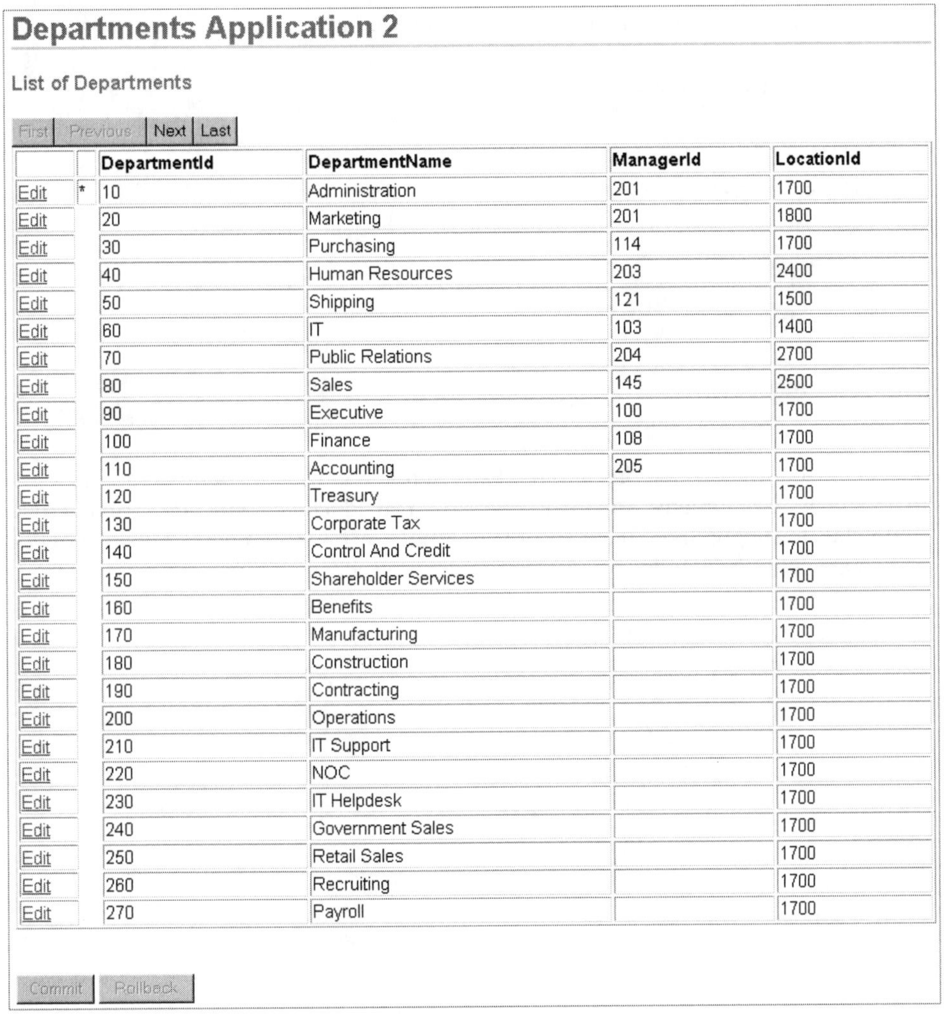

Departments Application 2

List of Departments

First | Previous | Next | Last

		DepartmentId	DepartmentName	ManagerId	LocationId
Edit	*	10	Administration	201	1700
Edit		20	Marketing	201	1800
Edit		30	Purchasing	114	1700
Edit		40	Human Resources	203	2400
Edit		50	Shipping	121	1500
Edit		60	IT	103	1400
Edit		70	Public Relations	204	2700
Edit		80	Sales	145	2500
Edit		90	Executive	100	1700
Edit		100	Finance	108	1700
Edit		110	Accounting	205	1700
Edit		120	Treasury		1700
Edit		130	Corporate Tax		1700
Edit		140	Control And Credit		1700
Edit		150	Shareholder Services		1700
Edit		160	Benefits		1700
Edit		170	Manufacturing		1700
Edit		180	Construction		1700
Edit		190	Contracting		1700
Edit		200	Operations		1700
Edit		210	IT Support		1700
Edit		220	NOC		1700
Edit		230	IT Helpdesk		1700
Edit		240	Government Sales		1700
Edit		250	Retail Sales		1700
Edit		260	Recruiting		1700
Edit		270	Payroll		1700

Commit | Rollback

FIGURE 17-6. *Departments Application 2*

26. You can click an Edit link to navigate to the Edit page for Department 40, as shown next. Change the DepartmentName value and click Update.

Edit Departments

DepartmentId	40
DepartmentName	Human Resources
ManagerId	203
LocationId	2400

Update

What Just Happened? You added another Data Action and Page Forward component to allow users to update the Departments Application records. You added custom code in an overridden data action class to support the "success" forward. You now have a framework that gives you a place to add any additional code you may require to control page flow.

CHAPTER 18

Working with JSP Pages

And hangs this web in the sky
Or finds it hanging, already hung for him,
Written as a path for him to travel.

—Carl Sandburg (1878–1967),
Webs (Good Morning, America)

As with many innovations in the Java community, the concept of lightweight web applications gained ground quickly. Web Tier technologies such as servlets and JSP pages offer developers a powerful method for coding applications that have Java at the core and HTML output for the client. Providing HTML output from a programming language is an old concept that has taken many forms. JSP code is attractive in the same way that Perl and the PL/SQL Web Toolkit are—it offers the powerful combination of development using a full-featured programming language (Java) with presentation using HTML in the browser.

This chapter discusses how to build basic JSP applications using JDeveloper 10*g*. The necessary background for the discussions in this chapter is the description of the architecture, advantages, and disadvantages of the JSP technology presented in Chapter 7. Another prerequisite to proper assimilation of the material in this chapter is an understanding of Hypertext Markup Language (HTML), JSP core tags, JSP Standard Tag Library (JSTL), and JSP expression language (EL). These concepts are introduced in Appendixes C and D. This chapter focuses on the view technology of JSP. Chapters 12 and 13 discuss details about the data controls and data bindings that are used in JSP development. To complete the picture of how JSP code is developed, the discussion of the Struts controller in Chapter 17 is necessary.

The practice in this chapter steps you through the process of creating and modifying basic JSP pages. It provides experience with JSP coding and how it is accomplished in JDeveloper.

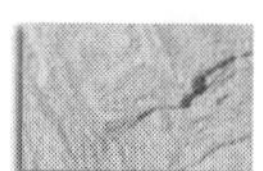

TIP
The JDeveloper help system contains a wealth of information about JSP pages. Examine the folders and topics under the Table of Contents node "Building J2EE Applications\Working with the Web Tier."

JSP Development Requirements

Although routine work in JSP code does not require deep skill in Java, a working knowledge of the language is helpful. Moreover, if you need to extend Struts action classes, you will need basic Java skills. If you need to create or extend a JSP tag library, you will use Java at an expert level. In addition to familiarity with JSP coding, compilation, and runtime as discussed in Appendix D, other programming language skills are necessary.

NOTE
The Sun Microsystems website is the starting place for learning about JSP pages (and any other Java technology). Start your search for material at java.sun.com/products/jsp.

Required Language Skills

Working with JSP applications requires not only a working knowledge of Java (as well as SQL), but also requires familiarity with HTML, JavaScript, cascading style sheets, and tag language syntax. All of these are very approachable languages or concepts, but may require a bit of study and a good reference book before you become fully fluent and comfortable with them.

When developing JSP pages in JDeveloper 10*g*, it is also essential to have a working knowledge of JSTL and EL. The JDeveloper tools generate code using these two tag library sets. In addition, the JDeveloper Component Palette, Property Inspector, and JSP/HTML Visual Editor natively support work with these tags.

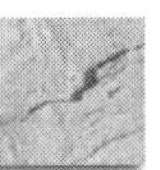

NOTE
Cascading style sheets are used to modify the display of standard HTML tags and can assist you in creating and using look-and-feel standards. It is important to spend time creating the styles that you will apply to the tags in your application.

Understanding JSP Compilation and Runtime

While working with JSP pages, it is helpful to keep in mind the mechanism used to run the JSP page. As a review of the JSP architecture introduced in Chapter 7, the application server (Web Tier) accepts an HTTP request from a browser (diagrammed in Figure 18-1). It interprets the type of file (using the file extension or type information embedded in the file) and sends the file to the JSP container (running a Java Virtual Machine or JVM). The first time the JSP page is run, the JSP container translates the JSP file into a *servlet*—a standard .java (Java source code) file that does not contain any raw HTML—and compiles it into a .class (bytecode) file. The transformation and compilation takes a bit of time. When the JSP page is requested again, the server finds the compiled code and does not need to generate the .java and .class files, so the JSP page will start up a bit faster. The JSP container then runs the .class file, which outputs HTML that is sent back to the browser.

The JSP container generates a Java servlet with the same name as the JSP file (except with an underscore "_" prefix and a .java extension). The servlet contains one main method, _jspService(). Like the `main()` method in a Java application, this method is automatically executed when the class file is called. The servlet contains all of the code that is required to interact with the HTTP session and to assemble a complete HTML page that is sent to the browser.

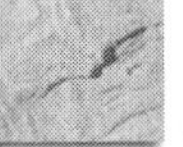

NOTE
When you run a JSP file inside JDeveloper, the Embedded OC4J Server plays the roles of the Application Server and JSP container. It creates virtual ports that handle the HTTP requests and HTML return. It also processes the JSP file as just described.

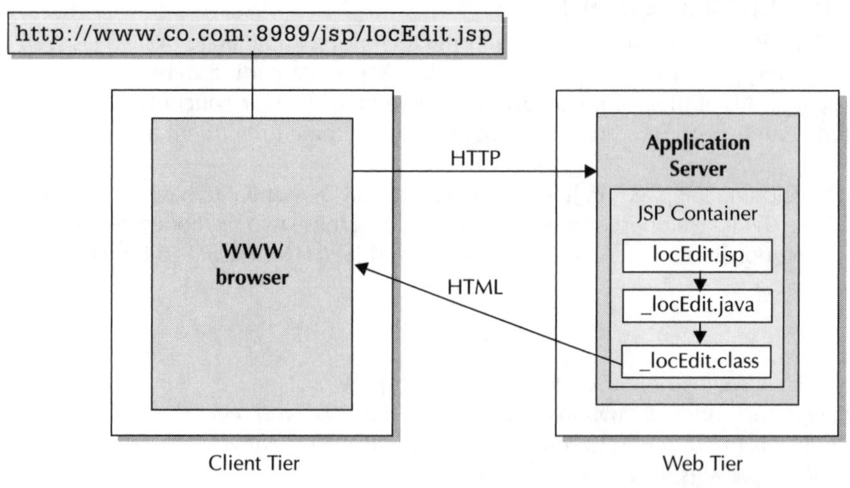

FIGURE 18-1. *JSP compilation and runtime*

Additional Information Sources

In addition to the discussion of basic JSP, JSTL, and EL tags in Appendix D, you can read an introduction to HTML, cascading style sheets, and JavaScript in Appendix C. In addition, free online resources are readily available from the originators of the languages, as follows:

Language	Resource	Online Location
HTML and cascading style sheets	World Wide Web Consortium	www.w3c.org
Java	Sun Microsystems	java.sun.com
JSP, JSTL, and EL tags	Sun Microsystems	java.sun.com
JavaScript	Netscape	devedge.netscape.com/central/javascript

To supplement the information from the originator of the language, use your favorite Internet search engine to find other online reference guides. You can find extensive information about these languages on the Internet. You can also search in the JDeveloper product area on the Oracle technology website (otn.oracle.com) for white papers, how-tos, sample code, and documentation that serve as valuable reference material. In addition, many books on the market discuss JSP technology, and you will want to refer to one or more for additional material.

NOTE
JDeveloper 10g supports the JSP 1.2 specification that is part of J2EE 1.3.1. This specification is available for download from java.sun.com/products/jsp.

JSP Application Development in JDeveloper

JDeveloper contains rich support for developing JSP applications. It provides wizards, component palettes, code libraries, and editor features that help you create JSP pages. In addition, when you develop JSP applications in JDeveloper, you use many of the same tools as when you develop Java client applications (Java applications and applets) in JDeveloper including the Component Palette, Data Control Palette, visual editor, Property Inspector, Structure window, and the Code Editor. These tools are introduced in Chapters 2 and 3 and used and referred to in discussions and hands-on practices throughout the book. However, it is useful to examine the key features of each tool used for JSP page development and the steps for creating a JSP application.

JSP/HTML Visual Editor

The JSP/HTML Visual Editor (shown in Figure 18-2) allows you to perform HTML editing in an environment that emulates the appearance of the JSP page at run time. Double clicking a JSP file in the navigator or Page Flow Diagram will display this editor. In addition, if you are working with the Code Editor for the file, clicking the editor's Design tab will display the visual editor.

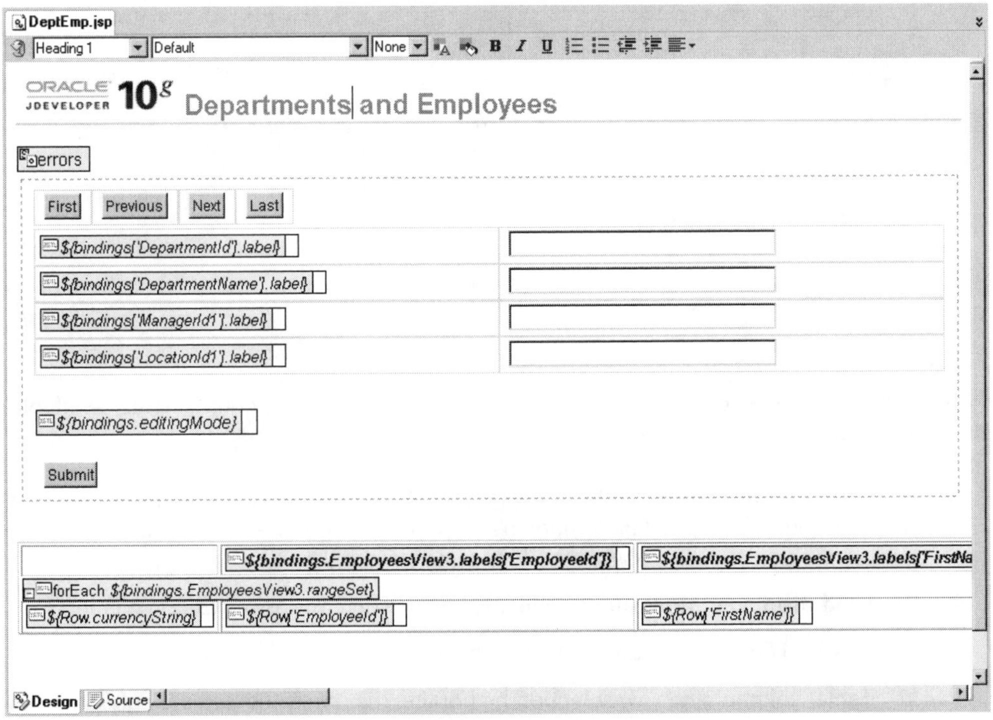

FIGURE 18-2. *JSP/HTML Visual Editor*

This visual editor displays fonts, colors, graphics, and all HTML tags as they will be displayed in the browser. In addition, tag library tags, such as the Struts errors tag shown in Figure 18-2, will be represented by gray boxes labeled with the tag name or value and an icon indicating the tag library where the tag is defined (such as JSTL). As with all tools in JDeveloper, the visual editor is synchronized with the Structure window, Property Inspector, and Code Editor so that changes in any of the tools will be reflected immediately in the other tools. This selection effect is shown in the following excerpt from the IDE window:

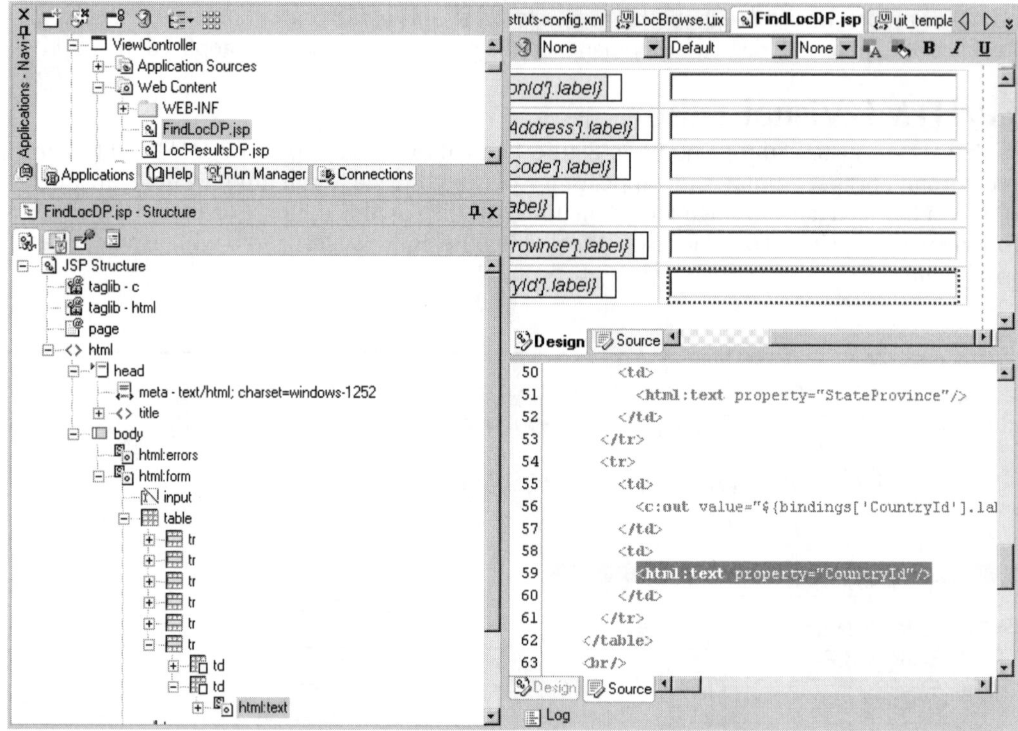

The JSP/HTML Visual Editor contains the same features as separate, commercially available HTML editors such as the following:

- **A toolbar with formatting tools** for applying HTML styles, fonts, font sizes, colors, text attributes (bold, italic, and underline), paragraph styles (numbered list, bulleted list, indent, and outdent), and alignment (left, center, and right).
- **Drag-and-drop operations on its elements** so that you can easily position elements.
- **Features for HTML table editing** such as the following:
  - **Table, column, and row selection** by holding the mouse next to the column or row as shown next and clicking the mouse button.

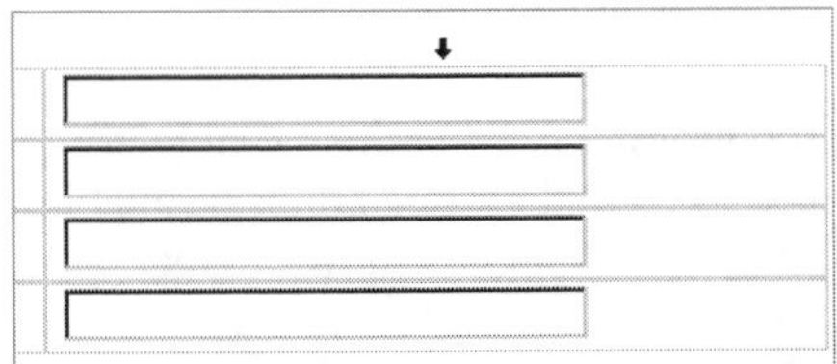

- **Right-click menu options** as shown next that appear when the cursor is in an HTML table in the Table submenu.

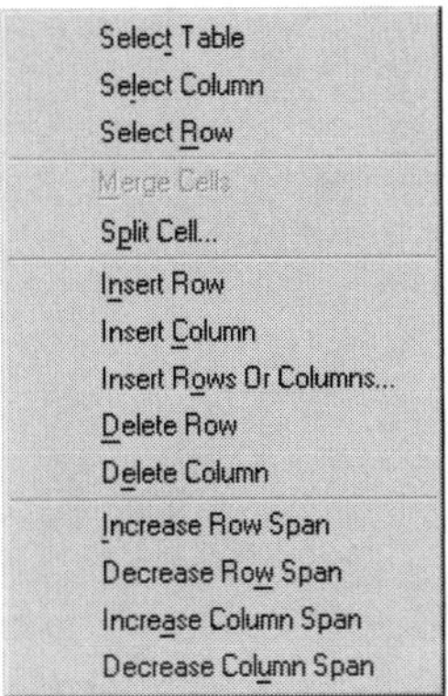

- **Smart delete actions** so that when you select a row or column in an HTML table and press DELETE, the HTML representation of the row or column will be deleted along with its contents.
- **Manual addition of any tag** by typing in the tag using the Insert HTML/JSP dialog, which appears as follows after you select Insert HTML/JSP from the right-click menu:

- **Tag editing** using the editor dialog available for a tag by selecting Edit Tag from the right-click menu.
- **HTML form actions** in the right-click menu for selecting, deleting, or changing the form method (`Get` or `Post`).
- **The ability to accept images** dropped in from a file system utility (such as Windows Explorer), from the navigator, or from a web browser.

TIP

To add image (and other types of) files to a project, you can drag the file from another program such as Windows Explorer or Internet Explorer and drop it onto the project node in the navigator. This operation does not move the file, but if you subsequently drag the image onto a page, a dialog will appear asking if you want to copy the file to the project directory.

Code Editor

Although most of the work you perform will be in the visual editor or Page Flow Diagram, you can and will probably need to edit text in the Code Editor (available by clicking the Source tab in the editor window after a JSP file is opened) as shown here:

DeptEmp.jsp

```
%@ taglib uri="http://xmlns.oracle.com/adf/ui/jsp/adftags" prefix="adf"%>
%@ taglib uri="http://java.sun.com/jstl/core" prefix="c"%>
%@ taglib uri="/WEB-INF/struts-html.tld" prefix="html"%>
%@ page contentType="text/html;charset=windows-1252"%>
html>
head>
meta http-equiv="Content-Type" content="text/html; charset=windows-1252">
title>Departments and Employees</title>
link href="css/blaf.css" rel="stylesheet" media="screen"/>
/head>
body>
  <H1>
    <img height="39" width="142" src="jd_clr_rgb_sm.gif"/>Departments and Employees
  </H1>
  <html:errors/>
  <html:form action="/dataPage3.do">
    <input type="hidden" name="<c:out value='${bindings.statetokenid}'/>" value="<c:out value='${bindi
    <table border="0" cellpadding="0" cellspacing="0">
      <tr>
        <td>
          <input type="submit" name="event_First" value="First" <c:out value="${bindings.First.enabled
        </td>
        <td>
          <input type="submit" name="event_Previous" value="Previous" <c:out value="${bindings.Previou
        </td>
        <td>
```

Design Source

As mentioned in Chapter 3, the Code Editor is a configurable text editor with extensive support for 3GL coding. In addition to standard text editing, the Code Editor offers features for JSP editing such as the following:

- **Code highlighting** that shows tags, attributes, comments, and user-defined values in different colors.
- **Syntax checking**, which is performed as you are editing. Errors are displayed in the Structure window before compiling.
- **End Tag Completion** fills in tag endings (such as "</h2>") for HTML and JSP tags after you type "</".
- **Tag Insight** for tags presents a list of valid attributes for the tag element and for Java code inside *scriptlets* (Java fragments inside JSP tags).
- **Dragging and dropping of tags** from the Component Palette and Data Control Palette into any location in the JSP file.
- **Attribute editing** in the Property Inspector, which is available after you place the cursor anywhere inside a tag in the Code Editor.

Many of these features are configurable in the Preferences dialog (**Tools | Preferences**).

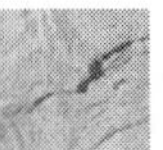

TIP
Context-sensitive help is available in the Code Editor for the custom JSP tags supplied with JDeveloper. For example, if you place the cursor inside a Struts tag such as "<html:errors/>" and press F1*, the help topic for the errors tag will be displayed.*

Structure Window

The Structure window works with the Code Editor to display organizational information about the file. As mentioned in Chapter 3, the Structure window contains two tabs: the UI Model tab, which shows the contents of the UIModel.xml file and the data model elements used in the file; and the JSP Structure tab (shown in Figure 18-3), which displays the hierarchy of HTML and other tag elements in the file.

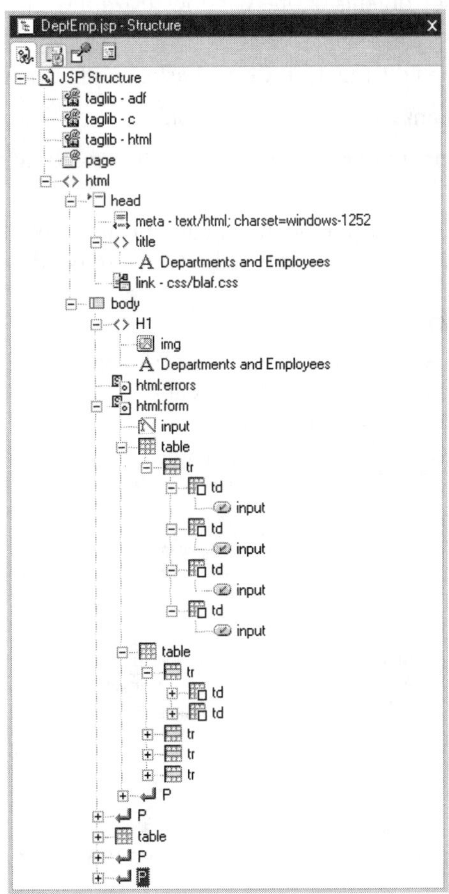

FIGURE 18-3. *JSP Structure tab for a JSP file*

The Structure window also shows a representation of the tag attributes and their values. This gives you an accurate picture of how the JSP page is constructed. As with other types of files, you can click a node in the Structure window to navigate to its code in the Code Editor or its visual representation in the visual editor. The Property Inspector shows and allows you to edit the properties of the element selected in the Structure window.

TIP
The JSP Structure tab of the Structure window allows you to drag and drop nodes to change the code.

The Structure window also offers the following features:

- **Toolbar buttons for Freeze and New Value**. The Freeze button allows you to prevent the Structure window from highlighting a selected element and New Value allows you to open a new Structure window. Freezing and showing new views are useful if you want to compare the contents of one window (frozen) with another (unfrozen) window that shows a selected element.
- **Tag editing** using the Edit Tag, Cut, Copy, Paste, and Delete right-click menu options.
- **Table and form actions** as in the visual editor.
- **Dragging and dropping of tags** within the Structure window so that you can easily restructure the JSP file.
- **Addition of tags** from the Component Palette or Data Control Palette by dragging and dropping to, above, or below a node in the Structure window.

Page Flow Diagram

The Page Flow Diagram, shown next, is a key tool for JSP applications that use the Struts controller (the preferred style in JDeveloper 10*g*) because it allows you to quickly build and modify the struts-config.xml file in a graphical way.

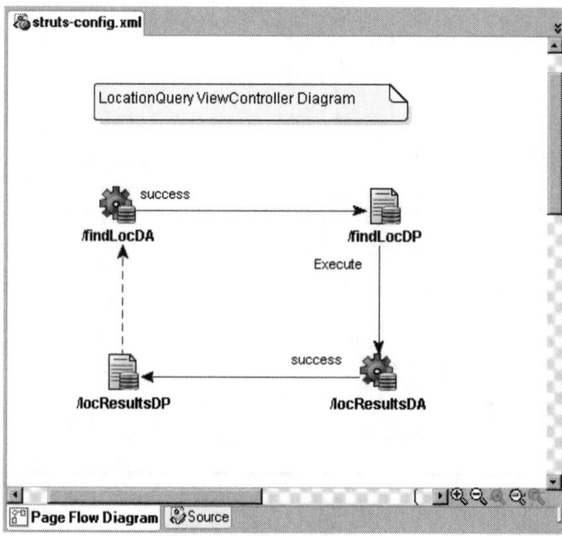

The Page Flow Diagram, unlike most windows, is not available from the View menu, but you can display it by double clicking a struts-config.xml file in the navigator, by selecting Edit Struts-Config from the right-click menu on that file, or by selecting Open Struts Page Flow Diagram from the right-click menu on the project node in the navigator.

The Thumbnail window (described in Chapter 3), a separate window that automatically appears when you open a page flow diagram, shows a miniature picture of the diagram. It allows you to quickly navigate a large diagram by dragging a view window box around the Thumbnail window.

The Page Flow Diagram is described further in Chapter 17 and is used in practices throughout the book.

Property Inspector

The Property Inspector, shown next, allows you to edit properties or attributes of tags in the file.

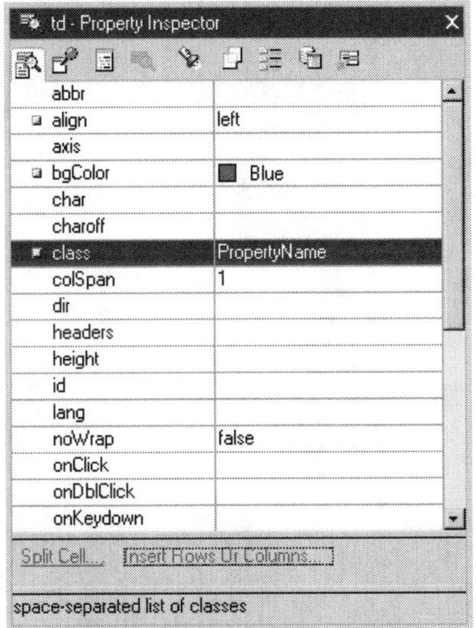

You can access the properties of an object by selecting it in the Structure window, JSP/HTML Visual Editor, or Code Editor. Grouping elements together allows you to apply property values to all elements at the same time. Toolbar buttons allow you to find properties and display the properties with category headings. For a group of selected elements, the Union button displays the intersection (only common properties) or the union (all properties in all elements). As with the Structure window, you can use buttons in the toolbar to freeze the property list or to create another window containing properties.

For JSP file editing, the Property Inspector contains the following features:

- **Property editors** that facilitate editing. For example, color properties such as *bgcolor* contain a color palette selector as well as a color pulldown, both of which facilitate finding the desired color.
- **Change indicators** that appear as green squares to the left of the property name. The change indicator signals that a value was changed from the default (as with the *align* property in the preceding illustration). The Reset to Default button restores the property to its original value.

- **Split and Insert links** that appear in the links area under the property list for an HTML table element such as `<td>`. These links allow you to access editors that quickly enter table tag elements.
- **Property hints** in the bottom pane of the Property Inspector window. These hints briefly describe the property.
- **Bind to Data toolbar button** that allows you to access the value dialog shown next. This dialog provides a list of possible data sources for the element. Selecting a data source in this dialog inserts the JSTL tag that will bind the element to that source.

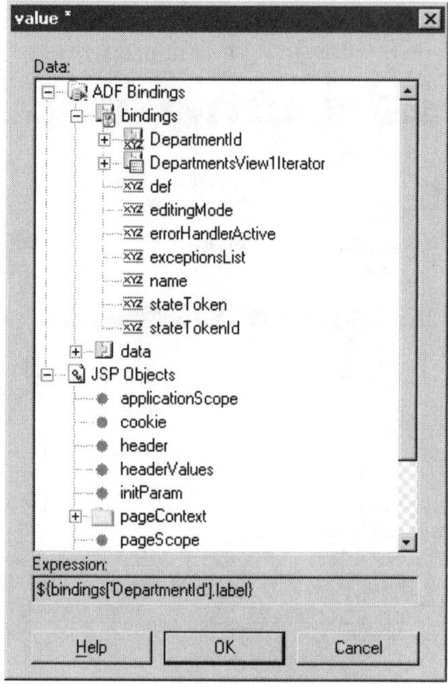

The window title of the Property Inspector shows the type of element whose properties you are viewing.

Component Palette

The Component Palette (shown in Figure 18-4) allows you to drop tags into the visual editor, Code Editor, or Structure window. After selecting a page from the Component Palette pulldown, you can select an element and place it in the proper place in one of those three tools. If the tag requires property settings, the appropriate property dialog will appear so that you can type in values before the tag is created.

When you create a JSP file, the appropriate Component Palette pages will be available. If needed, you can add tags to the Component Palette as described in the last hands-on practice in Chapter 15. However, the tag libraries available to a JSP should offer enough functionality for

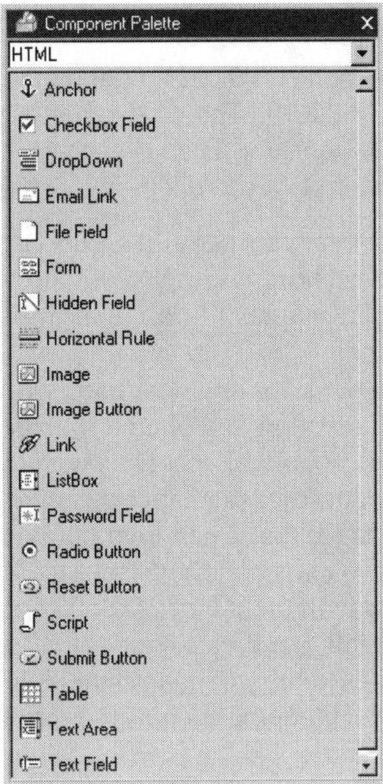

FIGURE 18-4. *Component Palette page for HTML tags*

most requirements. The following Component Palette pages (and groups of pages) are available by default when you work with JSP pages:

- **ADF Data Access** The tags in this page draw HTML form elements such as fields for text (`inputrender` tag) and complex data such as images (`render` tag); another tag facilitates building a page that does not use a controller layer but still binds elements to the available ADF business services (`uimodelreference` tag).
- **CSS** This page contains three cascading style sheets that you can drop into a JSP file. Cascading style sheets are described in Appendix C.
- **Code Snippets** This page (described in Chapter 3 and Appendix B) is blank by default, but you can add components to define a block of code that will be inserted when you drag the component into a file.
- **HTML** This page, shown in Figure 18-4, contains choices for Hypertext Markup Language tags (described in Appendix C) such as `<html>`, `<body>`, and `<table>`.
- **JSP** This page contains standard JSP tags such as scriptlets, expressions, declarations, directives, and standard action tags as discussed in Appendix D.

- **JSTL tag libraries** JSTL Core, JSTL FMT, JSTL SQL, JSTL XML. These libraries provide access to the JSP Standard Tag Library tags described in Appendix D.
- **OJSP tag libraries** OJSP Cache, OJSP EJB, OJSP Email, OJSP File Access, OJSP JESI, OJSP SQL, OJSP Utility, OJSP XML. These J2EE-compliant libraries are supplied with the OC4J server. They offer elements for database access, email and file manipulation, web object cache maintenance, and web services invocation.
- **Struts tag libraries** Struts Bean, Struts Html, Struts Logic, Struts Nested, Struts Templates, Struts Tiles. These libraries implement Struts data pages, data actions, and other elements in a JSP. Chapter 17 describes these libraries further.

Generally, you decide on one type of tag library or framework for a particular project because each implies a specific method of operation and often a specific look-and-feel. All of the data-aware frameworks and libraries are capable of accessing data through ADF business services, and JDeveloper makes binding to data sources relatively simple.

One of the main strengths of a tag is that it can incorporate a large amount of functionality. Since a custom tag is based on a Java class file, the base class file can encapsulate complex functionality into a single line of code in the JSP page. You can adapt or create tags to fit the needs of your project. Custom tags fall into the category of JSP action tags. Therefore, they are just single-line calls to Java class files, rather than tags that include low-level Java code (as are the standard tags included with the JSP engine such as the scriptlet, expression, and declaration).

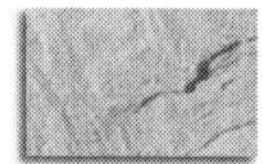

NOTE
All elements in the Component Palette offer tooltip hints that you can use to get an idea of the purpose of the tag. Although some hints are briefer than others, they should all help you determine which tag is best for a specific purpose.

Data Control Palette

The Data Control Palette, shown in Figure 18-5, provides components that are bound to business services objects. The mechanics of inserting components from this tool are similar to the drag-and-drop operation you use with the Component Palette. The difference with the Data Control Palette is that you select the data control model element first from the list at the top of the window. Then you select a component from the *Drag and Drop As* pulldown at the bottom of the window. Finally, you drag the model element into the Code Editor, JSP/HTML Visual Editor, or Structure window.

The result of dragging components from both palettes is similar—a tag or set of tags appear in the code. However, the Data Control Palette binds the component automatically to the data model, whereas you need to manually bind the components you drop in from the Component Palette.

The Data Model

The data model in the Data Control Palette is based upon the business services (in this example, ADF BC application modules) in the Model project. The hierarchy of the data model will be displayed in the palette as shown with EmployeesView3 under DepartmentsView1 in Figure 18-5.

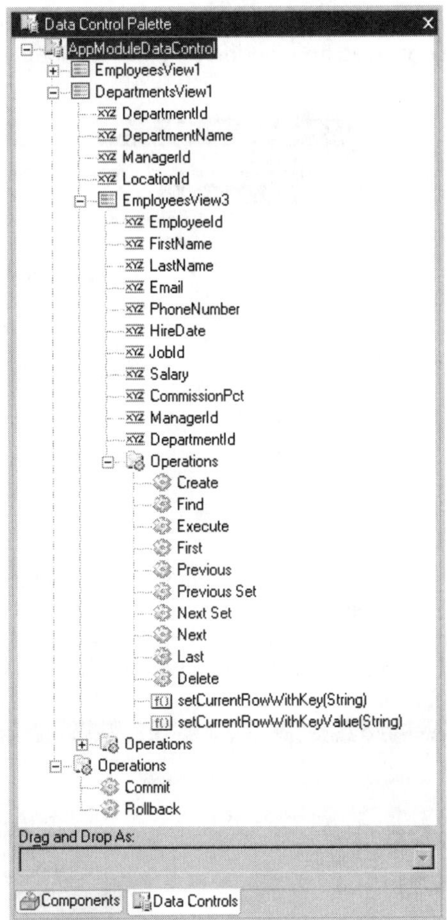

FIGURE 18-5. *The Data Control Palette*

This data model also contains an EmployeesView1, which is not linked to DepartmentsView1. When selecting the data model node, it is important to keep in mind which view object instance (linked or independent) is required for a specific page.

The Data Control Palette offers tags at three main levels: data model level (for business services), data collection level (for example, ADF view object definitions such as DepartmentsView1 in Figure 18-5), and attribute level (such DepartmentId in Figure 18-5). In addition, the Data Control Palette offers *operations*—actions that work on the collection level (for example, view object operations such as `Create`, `Find`, `Delete`, `Execute`, `First`, `Last`, `Next`, `Previous`) or on the model level (application module operations such as `Commit` and `Rollback`).

Data Binding Editors

When you drag a data control into a JSP file, the tools set a data binding for each tag that requires data. This data binding can be viewed and modified in the UI Model tab of the Structure window as shown here:

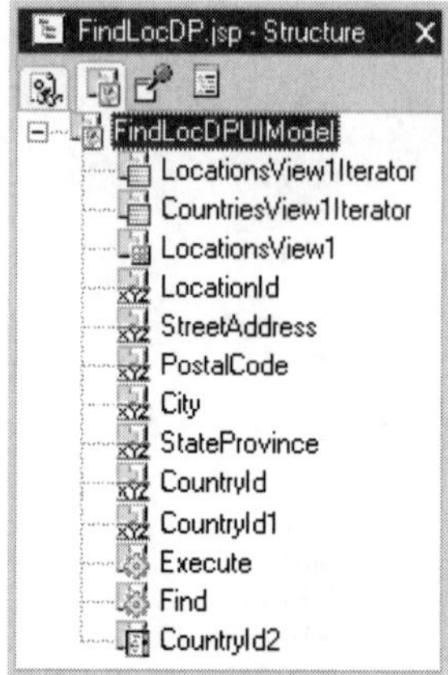

In most cases, the binding created by the tools will work without modification. However, some controls require more complex settings and you will need to use the binding editors available in the Structure window. Various editors exist for various binding types (for example attributes, tables, iterators, actions, and lists). For example, the following shows the binding editor for a table control:

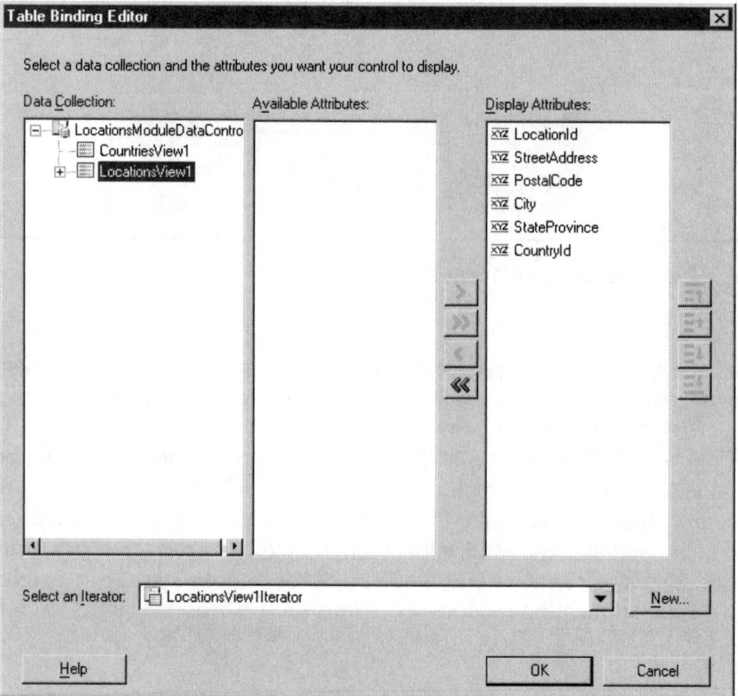

This control identifies the view object instance and view attributes that will be displayed in the table. Each binding is given a name and this name is referenced in the tag that displays the data.

Data Controls for Struts JSP Pages

The hands-on practices in Chapter 17 and in this chapter give you experience with using this tool for elements and operations. Although the *Drag and Drop As* list changes based upon what element is selected and what type of file is being built, it is useful to examine the controls available for different levels of the data model.

Model Level The model level for an ADF BC project is named with the application module name and the suffix "DataControl." Use these controls when you need to act on the database transaction. The controls available when selecting the `Commit` or `Rollback` operations under this node appear in Table 18-1.

An HTML form is required to process any HTML button. If you drag a button into a location in the JSP file that is not surrounded by an HTML form, you will see the following dialog:

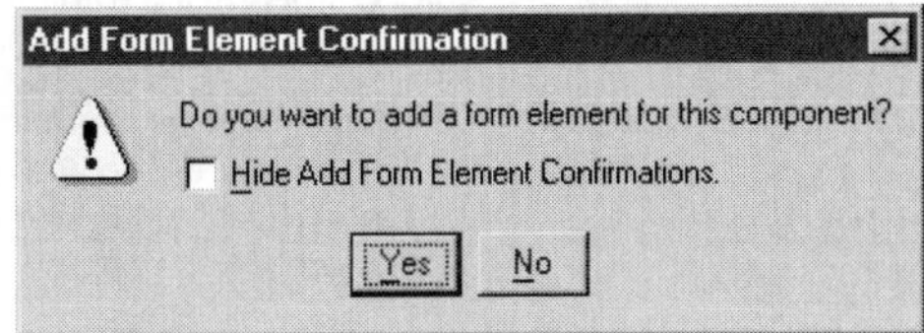

Clicking Yes in this dialog will add a form element around the button you are dropping.

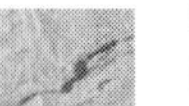

NOTE
`Commit` and `Rollback` can also be dropped as a method onto a component in a page flow diagram.

Control	HTML or JSP Element	Description
Button	Submit button	This button would be dropped inside an existing HTML form. The button is named "event_Commit" or "event_Rollback" (depending upon the operation selected). The name signals a database operation to the business services layer. You can change the "value" attribute of this tag to replace the button label.
Button with Form	Submit button and form	This control is the same as the Submit Button control except that it includes the HTML form element surrounding the button.

TABLE 18-1. *Model-Level Data Controls*

Data Collection Level The collection level for an ADF BC application module corresponds to the view object instance in the data model of an ADF BC application module. These controls are used when you need a representation of a row from the data source. The data controls listed in Table 18-2 are available when a collection level (such as DepartmentsView1 in Figure 18-5) is selected.

Control	HTML or JSP Element	Description
Read-Only Table	Table with column headings, data cells, and a current row indicator	The HTML table contains column headings populated by control hints (discussed later in this chapter) or attribute names. It also contains multiple rows of data from the collection. Values are placed in the cells of the table from the attributes (such as the view attributes) for each row of the collection. The values are not displayed in fields, so they are not editable.
Read-Only Dynamic Table	Table with column headings, data cells, and a current row indicator	The table is built in the same way as the Read-Only Table from multiple rows from the collection. The difference with this control is that the columns are built at run time based on the attributes in the collection.
Navigation Buttons	A table with submit buttons for the `First`, `Previous`, `Next`, and `Last` operations	As with all buttons, a form must surround the HTML table so that the actions can be submitted to the controller. The buttons navigate to the starting row in the collection (First), row before the current row (Previous), row after the current row (Next), and final row of the collection (Last).
Graph	A Graph tag from the Oracle Business Intelligence Beans library	After dropping in this control, you need to set its binding details in the UI Model tab of the Structure window. See the help system topic "Working with Graphs in ADF-Enabled Web Pages" for more information about graphs.
Input Form	A form containing a table with labels in one column, fields in the other column, and a submit button	This control allows editing of a single row from the collection. The field labels in the first column are derived from the attribute names or control hints (discussed later). Submitting the form submits the changes made to the collection but does not commit the changes to the database.
Read-Only Form	A form containing a table with labels in one column and non-editable values in the other column	This control is similar to the Input Form but does not include the submit button and displays the attribute values as text, not inside text fields.
Select Row Link	An anchor tag containing a link to the page "do" method	The link contains a reference to the current row key so that the row selected in the link can be acted upon. Chapter 17 builds an application where this link is used to navigate from a read-only row in an HTML table to an edit page with fields containing the same row values.
Navigation List	A Struts select tag	This control displays a pulldown list for each record in a collection. This can be useful for a master-detail form where the master collection would be represented by the pulldown and the detail collection would be represented by a table. After you select a master record, the detail records for that master would be displayed. The control requires a form action (for example, the page do method) to be set.

TABLE 18-2. *Collection-Level Data Controls*

Operations under the collection level fall into several categories:

- **Navigation actions** for `First`, `Previous`, `Previous Set`, `Next Set`, `Next`, `and` `Last`, which move the current row displayed or selected to a different record or set of records. `Previous Set` and `Next Set` are only available for ADF BC.
- **Record-level actions** for `Create` and `Delete`, which insert and remove the current row from the collection. These operations will not be saved to the database until a `Commit` is issued on the model level.
- **Current row actions** for *setCurrentRowWithKey(String),* which sets the current row with an internal row key (RowId) value (best used if the unique identifier is made of multiple attributes or you do not want to see the key value in the URL bar of the browser); or *setCurrentRowWithKeyValue(String)*, which uses an attribute value from the collection (best used if the unique identifier is only one attribute and you do not mind seeing the key value in the URL bar of the browser).

The controls listed in Table 18-3 are available when selecting one of these operations on the collection level.

Attribute Level The final level for data controls is the attribute level of the collection. This level represents a single data value within the collection (such as LocationId under DepartmentsView1 in Figure 18-5). The data controls listed in Table 18-4 are available to the attribute level of the model.

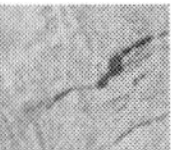

NOTE
The help system topic "About UI Components in Oracle ADF Web Pages" shows how these controls will be displayed in a JSP page and further describes the ADF binding. This topic is available by searching for "About UI Components" in the help system's Full Text Search tab.

Control	HTML or JSP Element	Description
Button	Submit button	This is the same as the Button in the model level.
Button with Form	Submit button and form	This is the same as the Button with Form in the model level.

TABLE 18-3. *Collection-Level Operation Data Controls*

Control	HTML or JSP Element	Description
Value	JSTL out tag	This control displays the data in a single attribute.
Label	JSTL out tag	This control displays the attribute name as a label for a field or column of data. If a control hint is defined for an attribute, the label text will be generated from the control hint (discussed later in this chapter).
Input Render	ADF inputrender tag	This displays a text field with an attribute value.
Input Field	Input tag	This control is a standard text field that must be contained within a form. It will contain a single row's attribute value.
Text Area	Text area tag	This control will also contain a single row's attribute value but the value is displayed in a multi-row text area used for editing long text strings. The text area will also display a scrollbar for navigating the text in the field.
Hidden Field	Struts hidden field tag	This control holds the value of an attribute but does not display that value to the user. The value can be examined using **View | Source** in the browser menu. The hidden field needs to be contained in a form so that its value will be submitted with other field values.
File Input Field	Struts file field	This control displays a field and a button used to browse the file system. When the user selects a file, the path and name of the file are loaded into the field. This can be used for `put` requests where the user needs to upload a file to the web server. As with all other fields, this control must be placed within a form.
Password Field	Struts password field tag	This control displays a standard HTML field that represents an attribute value. When the user inputs characters into the field, each character is displayed inside the field as an asterisk "*". The value that is retrieved from the data collection is visible using **View | Source** in the browser menu, but the value typed by the user will not be visible until the form is submitted and the page is redisplayed.
Render Value	ADF render tag	This control displays a field used for complex data such as images, video, and audio.
Single Select List	Struts select tag	This control displays a list from a collection that is assigned in the List Binding Editor (described further in the hands-on practice in this chapter). The list binding is available for the element in the UI Model tab of the Structure window. This type of list element is assigned an *Enumeration Mode* binding where you type in a static list of values that form the collection. You need to enter these values in the List Binding Editor.
List of Values	Struts select tag	This control displays the same selection list as the Single Select List. The only difference is that the binding for this control is assigned as *LOV Mode* where the list of values is derived from a data collection (such as a view object definition). List of Values and Single Select List are equivalent except for the default mode, and the mode can be reassigned in the List Binding Editor.
Radio Button Group	A JSTL forEach iterator enclosing a Struts radio tag and a JSTL out tag	This control displays a radio group whose selections are built dynamically from a data collection or a static list. Assigning the collection or static list follows the same process as with the Single Select List and List of Values just described. If you substitute the Struts multibox tag, the available options will be rendered as checkboxes instead of radio buttons.

TABLE 18-4. *Attribute-Level Data Controls*

Steps for Creating a Struts JSP Application

JSP applications that use the Struts controller and ADF BC business services use the following general steps to create the application:

1. Create a business services project containing the data collections required for the pages.
2. Create a Struts page flow diagram containing the actions, pages, and forwards.
3. Drop the required data controls from the Data Control Palette onto each page.
4. Modify the layout of the elements by dragging and dropping them in the Structure window or visual editor.
5. Adjust properties as required using the Property Inspector.
6. Modify or define the data binding for elements if needed.
7. Adjust the visual display by adding cascading style sheets and graphics, applying styles, and changing colors and fonts.
8. Test the application by selecting Run from the right-click menu on the starting file in the Page Flow Diagram. This starts up the Embedded OC4J Server, which is a "real world" container process for JSPs. This server is the same one used to run JSP pages within the Oracle Application Server. Therefore, running it in JDeveloper replicates the production environment.

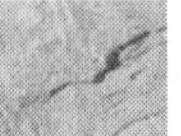

NOTE
Although code based upon the Struts controller is the focus of this book, ADF also supports "Model 1" JSP code that is not based on a controller.

Some ADF BC JSP Coding Techniques

If you are using ADF BC for business services, you can use several unique options (as demonstrated in the hands-on practice in this chapter).

Find Mode

Query functionality requires the page to be in Find mode. A page in "normal" mode (not in Find mode) either displays, creates, or updates records. A page in *Find mode* does not present data by default and is processed in a special way when it is submitted to the controller. The controller assembles WHERE clause predicates based upon the values on the page (for example, "COUNTRY_ID = 'US'"); it then issues a query to the business services layer that includes the new predicates. After a page in Find mode is processed and the query is returned, the page reverts from Find mode to normal mode. Find mode may not be cancelled if an error occurs in the processing. If the page needs to be restored to Find mode, a data action is required. The JSP hands-on practice in this chapter builds a page that uses Find mode.

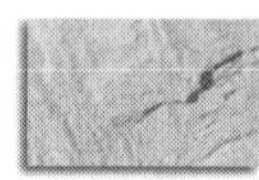

NOTE
Find mode in an ADF-built web page is similar to Enter Query mode in Oracle Forms Developer. The data action triggered by the Find button on the JSP page is similar to the EXECUTE_QUERY process in Forms. In both environments, the form is returned to "normal" mode (the opposite of Find mode or Enter Query mode) after the query is successfully executed.

ADF Business Component Properties

You can specify the interface behavior of ADF BC entity attributes and view attributes in various technologies (such as JSP and UIX) using properties available in the editors. You can display the editors by double clicking the entity object or view object node in the navigator.

TIP
When deciding on which level to set attribute properties, remember that the entity object definition is used for database INSERT, UPDATE, and DELETE operations whereas the view object definition is used for SELECT operations.

Updateable Property

The *Updateable* property on the attribute page of the View Object Editor provides control for disabling the attribute in several situations. It may be set to the following values:

- **Always** This value means that the user can fill in the attribute's field when inserting a record and can modify the attribute's field when updating the record.
- **While New** This value means that the attribute will be disabled during updates. This is a useful setting for primary key attributes.
- **Never** This setting means that users cannot fill in the attribute's field during inserts or updates. This setting has the same restriction as hiding the attribute; if the attribute is mandatory, the user needs to be able to enter a value into it while inserting a record unless the value is provided by business components code or by the database.

A setting of "While New" or "Never" of the entity object attribute property forces the same setting on the view object attribute.

Queriable Property

This property, also on the attribute page of the Attribute Editor, hides the attribute from the find components as demonstrated in the UIX hands-on practice in Chapter 19. This property is also available from the attribute page of the Entity Object Editor, but unchecking this property on the entity object will disable the *Queriable* property in all view objects built from the entity object.

Mandatory Property

This property, on the attribute page of the Entity Object Editor, will affect a prompt that is built from the ADF BC attribute. If this property is checked in the Entity Object Editor, some libraries (such as the UIX tag libraries demonstrated in Chapter 19) will precede the attribute name with an asterisk ("*") indicating that it is required.

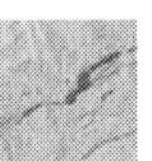

NOTE
As mentioned, the techniques in this section are only available when using ADF BC for business services.

Using Control Hints for Labeling and Formatting

Normally, attributes that affect the display are stored in properties on UI objects. ADF Business Components allows user interface objects (such as JSP elements) to read and use properties called "control hints." *Control hints* are properties of ADF BC entity object attributes and view object attributes. Control hints alter the display behavior for all attributes displayed from the ADF BC objects where they are defined. Since they are set on the entity object or view object level, they provide a way to make all pages built from the same business services layer consistent.

For example, if you set control hints for the Employees entity object attributes, all user interfaces that use view objects based upon the Employees entity object will take advantage of the settings on the entity object. You can also set control hints on the view object level, which is more specific to an application usage. Control hints are used by JSP pages and ADF UIX code as well as by rich-client Java applications and applets. You can test control hints without developing a view layer by using the Oracle Business Component Browser introduced in Chapter 8.

Accessing Control Hints

You can edit control hints from the View Object Editor or the Attribute Editor. The View Object Editor is available by double clicking the view object node in the navigator; each attribute edit page includes a Control Hints tab where you can specify Control Hints.

If you want to set the properties using the Attribute Editor (which is faster for a single attribute because it does not load the entire view object into the editor), select the entity object or view object node in the Model project. Then, on an attribute node in the Structure window, select Edit from the right-click menu (or double click the attribute node). Click the Control Hints node in the editor, and you will see something like the following:

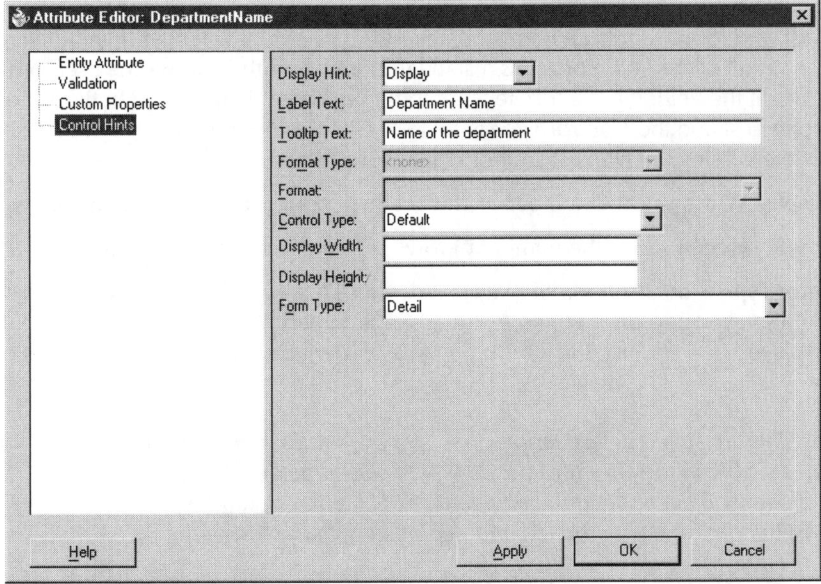

Control Hints

The control hints offered for attributes in the entity object or view object follow:

- **Display Hint** defines whether the attribute will be displayed in the user interface. Set this to "Hide" for attributes such as those for ID columns. If an attribute is set to be hidden, when you drag data controls into the page from the Data Control Palette, no user interface control will be created for that attribute.
- **Label Text** is displayed as a prompt for the attribute item.
- **Tooltip Text** is displayed when the mouse pauses over an item. It will be written into the HTML *title* attribute for UIX files so the text will appear when the user holds the mouse over a field. The Tooltip Text acts the same way in a Java client (Swing) application. It is ignored for JSP files.
- **Format Type** shows which formatter will be used to display the item. A *formatter* is a set of format masks each of which define a different style of output for a date or number field.

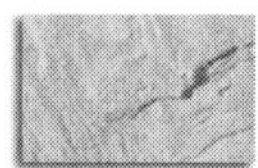

TIP
You can define your own formatters as described in the online help topic "Defining a Formatter and Format Masks for Business Components Clients." (On the Index tab, select "control hints: setting formatters.")

- **Format** is the format mask from the formatter's set that will be used for the attribute (such as "dd-MMM-yyyy" for a date). Formats are described further in upcoming sections.
- **Control Type** declares what type of *renderer* (user interface object) will be used for the field based upon the attribute type. "Default" means that a renderer appropriate to the item will be selected. For example, an item based on a character attribute will be displayed using a text field (single line) if it is short; a text area (multiline field) will be displayed for the attribute if the character Display Width is longer than 30 characters. The "Edit" control type presents a standard input field that allows the user to type into and edit the field. If the attribute is set to non-updateable (in the ADF BC attribute properties) and the *Control Type* is set to "Edit," the input field will still be displayed (whereas using the Default control type will display a non-editable area).
- **Display Width** sets the number of characters of horizontal space that a field will take.
- **Display Height** stores the number of rows of vertical space that the field will take.
- **Form Type** is not used for JSP pages. It defines Detail mode (long form where attributes are displayed as a prompt and text field) or Summary (short form where attributes are displayed in a grid) for the attribute in a Java client program (Java application or applet).

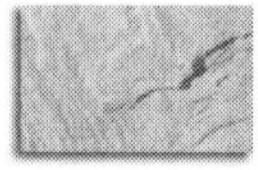

NOTE
Control hints are stored as text strings in a Java class (message bundle) file that is visible in the Structure window after selecting the entity object or view object node in the navigator. This file has a suffix of "ImplMsgBundle" and is compiled and deployed with the rest of the Model files.

Formatting Date Fields

You can specify a format for a date component on the Control Hints page of the attribute or domain object using the following steps:

1. Select the entity object or view object node in the Model project (for example, Employees, which you can add to an existing project).
2. On the attribute node (for example, HireDate) in the Structure window, select Edit from the right-click menu (or double click the attribute) to display the Attribute Editor.
3. Select the Control Hints node. Select "Simple Date" in the *Format Type* field, and enter the format mask in the *Format* field as shown here:

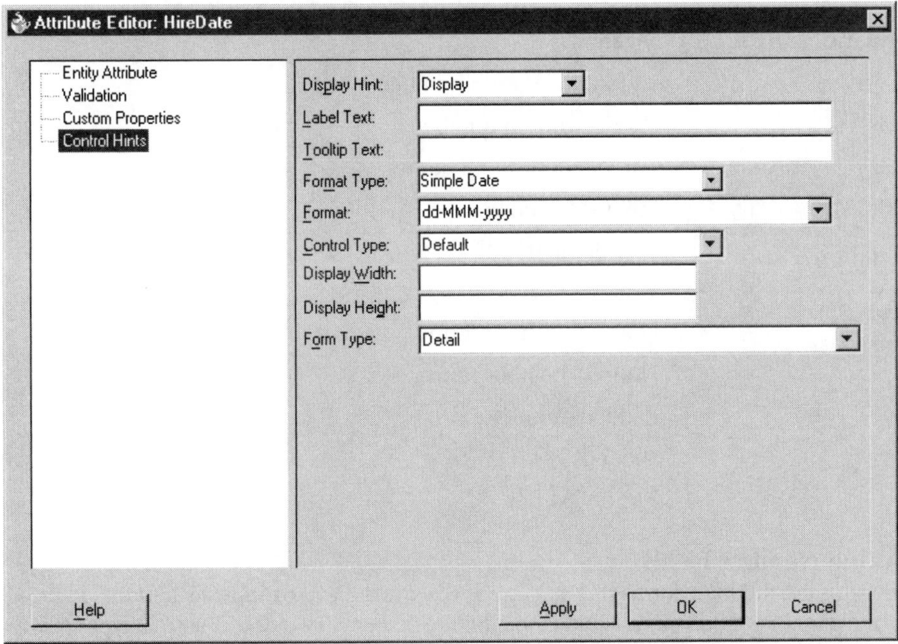

4. Click OK to dismiss the dialog. This writes the control hints into the message bundle class file.

   Additional Information: If the `MsgBundle` class has compile errors, you will not be able to dismiss this dialog. Cancel the dialog and fix the errors before continuing. You can open this file by double clicking its name in the Structure window after selecting the appropriate entity object or view object in the navigator.

5. Test the new Model project using the Business Component Browser. You will be able to see the new format in the browser.

When you run a JSP page built from this business service, the new date format will appear as in the following example:

HireDate
17-Jun-1987
21-Sep-1989
13-Jan-1993

Date Format Strings The format strings used for a date object are documented in the Javadoc for the `java.text.SimpleDateFormat` class. Some of the valid format characters follow. All format masks are case sensitive.

Format Character	Meaning
M	Unpadded month number
MM	Padded month number
MMM	Three-letter month name
MMMM	Full month name
dd	Day of the month
yyyy	Year
kk	Hour in 24-hour form
hh	Hour in 12-hour form
mm	Padded minute
ss	Second
aa	AM or PM

Formatting Number Fields

Number fields use the same formatting strategy as date fields. You can specify a format in the Control Hints of the attribute or domain to which the attribute belongs. Two default format types (Currency and Number) have several default masks as shown in the following example from the Attribute Editor:

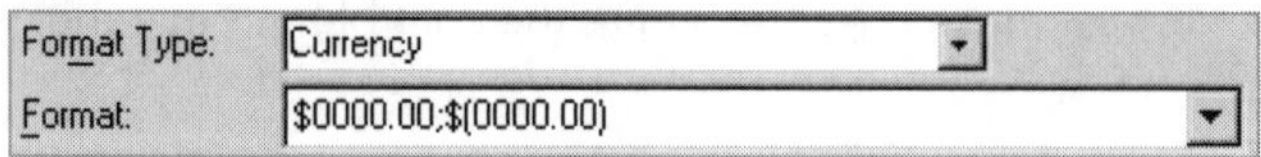

For this example, the Salary field will appear as follows in a JSP page:

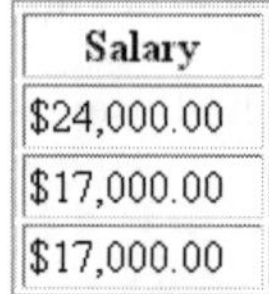

Salary
$24,000.00
$17,000.00
$17,000.00

The group separator (",") is optional for this use of the number format mask.

Number Format Strings The format strings used for a number field are documented in the Javadoc for java.text.DecimalFormat. Some of the valid format characters follow:

Format Character	Meaning
0	Padded single number
#	Unpadded number that will not show if it is zero
%	Multiply by 100 and show with percentage symbol
;	Separates negative and positive format masks
.	Decimal separator
,	Group separator
E	Separates the two parts of a scientific notation number

Hands-on Practice: Build JSP Query and Results Pages

Several chapters in this book demonstrate JSP development techniques. Hands-on practices in Chapters 1 and 7 use the JDeveloper tools to build basic JSP applications that browse one record at a time. The practices in Chapters 12 and 13 concentrate on data binding and data control concepts and build multi-row browse and single-row edit JSP pages. The practices in Chapter 17 demonstrate Struts techniques by building similar browse and edit JSP applications. Web applications frequently use these styles of pages. Another commonly used interface style contains one page to enter query conditions (a *find page*) and another page to display the records that match those conditions (a *results page*).

This practice demonstrates JSP development by building a JSP application containing a find page and a results page. Although this practice uses similar techniques for creating the Struts controller code and JSP view code as the practices in 12, 13, and 17, the focus is different in each chapter. The practices in Chapters 12 and 13 concentrate on details about the ADF BC bindings; Chapter 17 concentrates on details about the controller code; and this practice concentrates on details of the JSP code. The practices in all these chapters build components that perform all of the basic database operations (SELECT, INSERT, UPDATE, and DELETE). Building web page code that interacts with the database is a main strength of JDeveloper and ADF.

In addition to components that interact with the database, a production-level application would need a look-and-feel that has been carefully designed to reflect the content and corporate or product identity. This design would be built with an HTML editor such as JDeveloper's JSP/HTML Visual Editor, Macromedia Dreamweaver, or Microsoft FrontPage. The design components and database components can be developed together in any order, or they can be developed separately and then merged at some point in the development process.

The application you build in this practice is used to find locations based on query parameters for City, StateProvince, and CountryId. This practice is divided into the following phases:

I. Create the application workspace and business services

II. Create the JSP pages and controller actions

- Build the find data action and data page
- Build the results data action and data page

III. Modify the Data Elements

- Remove unnecessary fields
- Add a list of values
- Add navigation controls

IV. Modify the Visual Aspects

- Add text and apply styles
- Add an image and change the link message
- Specify control hints for the field prompts

I. Create the Application Workspace and Business Services

This phase builds the application workspace and project containers for the code in this application. If you have followed other practices in this book, the steps will be familiar and are, therefore, somewhat abbreviated in this phase. Refer to Chapters 1 and 4 for more information about application workspaces and projects.

1. On the Applications node in the Application Navigator, select New Application Workspace from the right-click menu. In the Create Application Workspace dialog, specify the following:

   Application Name as "LocationQuery"
   Application Package Prefix as "location"
   Application Template as "Web Application [Default]"

2. Click OK to create the application workspace and projects. Click Save All.
3. On the Model project node, select New from the right-click menu. In the New Gallery, select the Business Tier\Business Components category and double click the "Business Components from Tables" item. The Business Components Project Initialization dialog will appear.
4. Ensure that the *Connection* field specifies "HR" and click OK to start the Create Business Components from Tables Wizard. Click Next if the Welcome page appears.

5. In the Entity Objects page, select the COUNTRIES and LOCATIONS tables and move them to the *Selected* area. You will use the LOCATIONS table as the main data source and the COUNTRIES table to provide a list of values. Click Next.
6. Click the ">>" button to specify that view objects will be created for both entity objects. Click Next.
7. On the Application Module page, enter the application module *Name* as "LocationsModule" and click Next and Finish. This will create default ADF BC objects in the Model project.

   Additional Information: This application uses the default business components generated by the wizard. Normally, you would build the business components one at a time to ensure that no extra objects were created. Alternatively, you can remove objects that are not required in the application. This practice will not use the association and view link, but the practice in Chapter 19 will use these objects for a master-detail link.
8. Click Save All.

What Just Happened? You created the application workspace and projects for a web application. You also added ADF BC objects for the COUNTRIES and LOCATIONS tables. You may test this project now if desired. (On the LocationsModule node, select Test from the right-click menu). The data model for this application module contains two top-level objects for the tables and a Locations detail object under the top-level Countries object. Naturally, this example is a bare-bones version of a data model that you would use in a production system. Close the browser when you are satisfied that the business components work.

II. Create the JSP Pages and Controller Actions

This phase builds a struts-config.xml file using the Page Flow Diagram. The main objects you create are the JSP find page and results page. The page flow diagram you will create in this practice looks something like the following:

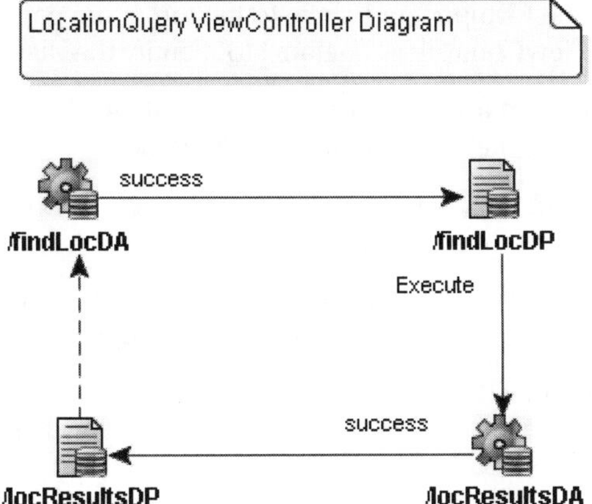

More About the Data Page

A *data page* represents the combined functionality of a data action, a forward, and a web page. If you are using the default functionality of a component, a data page by itself will suffice. Using data pages alone simplifies the Struts application because one element represents many functions. Using data actions is necessary when you need functionality that does not forward to a page (for example, a series of actions that set the current row and query the page). Although data pages simplify the diagram and reduce the number of elements included, some developers prefer to see a data action for each data page so that the diagram represents the page and action flows more explicitly.

The first data action (findLocDA) places the find data page (findLocDP) in Find mode (described earlier). The find data page contains input fields and a Find button that issues an Execute message based upon the conditions entered by the user in those fields. The find page forwards to the results data action (locResultsDA), which executes the query and forwards to the results data page (locResultsDP). The results page then displays the data from the query. The above sidebar "More About the Data Page" describes details about the data page. Introductory information about data pages and data actions may be found in Chapter 17.

Build the Find Data Action and Data Page

The data page alone is not sufficient for placing the page into Find mode. This section adds a data action and data page for the find page functionality. Most of the work in this section occurs in the Page Flow Diagram, which adds code to the struts-config.xml file.

1. On the ViewController node, select Open Struts Page Flow Diagram from the right-click menu. The diagram will open and the Component Palette will show the Struts Page Flow component page.

2. Add a Note from the Component Palette to the top of the page and type the text "LocationQuery ViewController Diagram" to identify the diagram.

3. Add a Data Action item from the Component Palette to the diagram. Name it "findLocDA". Add a Data Page and name it "findLocDP".

4. Draw a Forward from the data action to the data page. This forward declares that when you execute the data action, the data page will be called.

5. Double click the findLocDP data page and click OK when the Select or Create Page dialog appears. The Design tab of the JSP/HTML Visual Editor will be displayed.

6. In the Data Control Palette, select LocationsModuleDataControl\LocationsView1. Select "Input Form" in the *Drag and Drop As* pulldown and drag and drop LocationsView1 to the visual editor.

   Additional Information: This adds to the page an HTML form containing an HTML table with fields, labels, and a button. It also adds an errors (html:errors) tag outside of the form. The html:errors tag is used to display error messages that are returned from the Struts controller.

7. In the Data Control Palette, expand the LocationsView1\Operations node. Select the `Execute` operation and select Button in the *Drag and Drop As* pulldown.

8. Drop the `Execute` operation next to the Submit button on the form. An Execute button will appear.

   Additional Information: This button will submit the query conditions on the find page and requires the Execute action binding for that functionality. The `Find` operation in the Data Control Palette would be used to create a button that places the page into Find mode. Although you could change properties of the existing button, dragging the `Execute` operation into the diagram also adds the Execute action binding to the page's UI model. This binding could also be added manually, but it is faster to drop in the appropriate operation and change the value.

9. In the Property Inspector, with the Execute button selected, change the *value* property to "Find" and press ENTER.

   Additional Information: The button label will change. Look at the value of the *name* property: event_Execute. This value is sent to the controller as an identifier for the button that was clicked. The prefix indicates a user action and the suffix indicates the action that will be performed ("Execute"), which is the forward on the page flow diagram.

10. Delete the Submit button.

    Additional Information: When building a Struts-based application, it is a good idea to test each page separately, if possible, so you are certain that each part of your application performs correctly.

11. Switch back to the Page Flow Diagram. Although the page is not complete you can test it. On the findLocDA data action icon, select Run from the right-click menu.

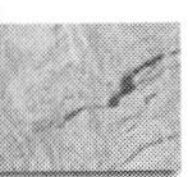

TIP
When working with Struts, it is important to run the data action that forwards to the page rather than the running the data page. The data action performs operations necessary to make the page work.

    Additional Information: The data action will execute and load the data page. The data page appears with data, because the default mode for the page is to display data from the view object. You will change the page to Find mode next.

12. Close the browser. With the Page Flow Diagram displayed, under the Data Control Palette's LocationsView1\Operations node, select "Find." Be sure that "Method" is selected in the *Drag and Drop As* pulldown. Drag the Find node to the diagram, and drop it on the data action (findLocDA) icon.

    Additional Information: Nothing visible will change. This sets the operation of the data action to the Find method, which will place the page into Find mode. It also modifies the model file (findLocDPUIModel.xml). If you select this file in the navigator (under the ViewController\Application Sources\location.view node), you will notice that the Structure window UI Model tab contains `Execute` and `Find` operations in addition to elements from the view object instance. You can also view and modify these action bindings using the struts-config.xml file. However, the next steps show how to display the contents of this file in a structured way using an editor dialog.

13. On the struts-config.xml node (under Web Content\WEB-INF) in the navigator, select Edit Struts-Config to display the Struts Configuration Editor. Select the Action Mappings node to display the current elements as shown in Figure 18-6.

    Additional Information: The *Struts Configuration Editor* allows you to view and modify the properties and elements in the struts-config.xml file without typing XML code. Although you can view these elements in the Code Editor, Structure window, and Property Inspector, you may prefer to use the more declarative view presented by the Struts Configuration Editor for editing and viewing the struts-config.xml file.

14. Select the "findLocDA" item in the *Action Mappings* area. Click the Properties tab and notice that the *methodName* property is set to "findLocDPUIModel.Find." This value is the Find action binding you saw in the UI Model tab. You are just exploring this editor, so click Cancel to return to the Page Flow Diagram.

15. Run the page again (by running the data action). You will see something like the following:

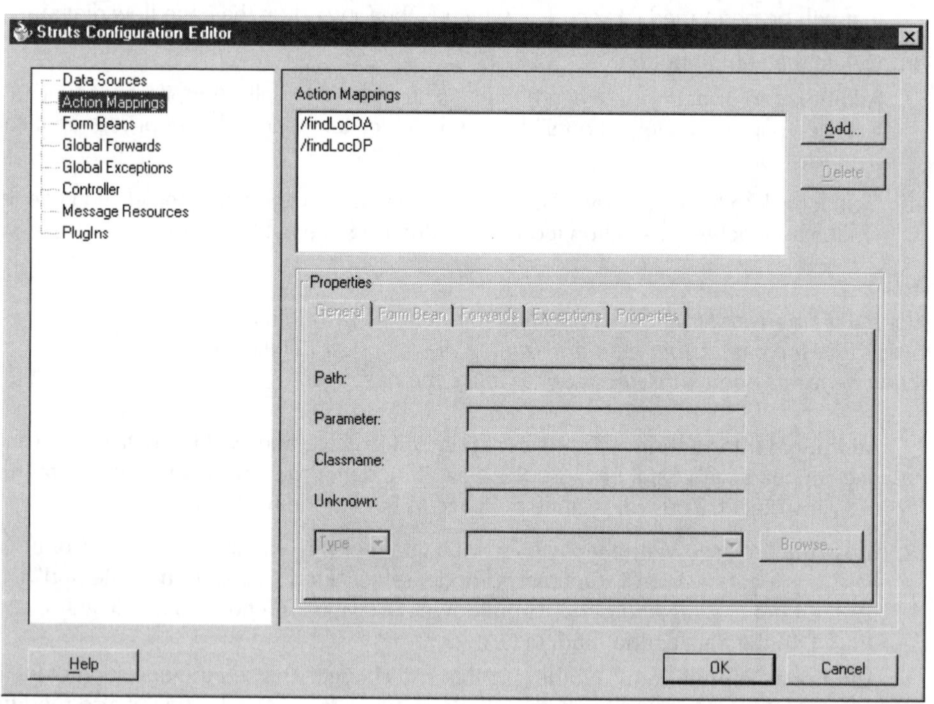

FIGURE 18-6. *Struts Configuration Editor*

LocationId
StreetAddress
PostalCode
City
StateProvince
CountryId

*Find Mode

Find

Additional Information: This time, the fields do not contain data and a message appears above the button indicating that the page is in Find mode. This message is a result of the Find method you added to the data action that calls the page.

16. Click Refresh in the browser toolbar (or Go next to the Address field). The page will revert to normal mode and the "*Find Mode" message will disappear. This shows how the page cycles between Find mode and normal mode.
17. Click Refresh again. The page will return to Find mode.
18. Close the browser.

    Additional Information: The code that was created when you dropped elements into the editor worked without much modification, and you do not need to verify the structure or contents of the actual code. However, taking some time now to browse the contents of the source code for the JSP page (by clicking the Source tab) will familiarize you with the elements used by the tools. At the beginning of the file, you will see taglib directive tags that identify the tag libraries used in the file. You will then see standard html, head, title, and body tags. You will also notice a Struts tag html:form that creates an HTML form. Within the form is an HTML table containing rows and cells. The column for the labels contains a JSTL out (c:out) tag for each attribute name. The column for the fields contains a Struts field (html:text) tag for each attribute value. Before the end tag of the form, an input tag displays the button.

Build the Results Data Action and Data Page

Now that you have created the first page in the sequence and this page is in Find mode, you can add the second data page for the query results.

1. On the Page Flow Diagram, add a data action called "locResultsDA" and a data page called "locResultsDP".
2. Add a Forward from locResultsDA to locResultsDP.

3. Draw a Forward from findLocDP to locResultsDA. Change the forward name to "Execute". This will cause the Find button on the Find page to call the results data action's `Execute` method. The diagram will look something like this:

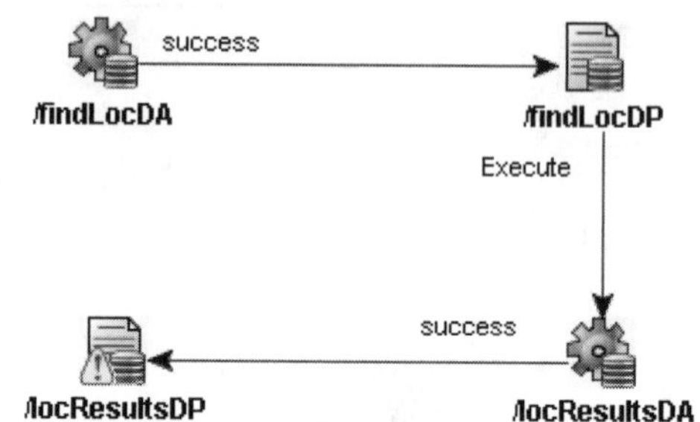

4. Double click locResultsDP and click OK to open the JSP file in the visual editor.
5. Select the Struts Html page of the Component Palette and drop a form onto the page. The JavaServer Page Tag Editor will appear.
6. In the *action* property, select "locResultsDA.do" from the pulldown.

   Additional Information: This property defines the page's data action as the process that will be executed when the page is submitted. At this point, you will not be submitting the results page, but in a later section, you will add navigation buttons that are processed as submit buttons.
7. Click OK. A box representing the HTML form will appear on the page.
8. In the Data Control Palette, drag and drop LocationsView1 as a Read-Only Table inside the form box on the page.
9. Click Save All.
10. Return to the Page Flow Diagram and run the locResultsDA data action. The browser will open and display a page with ten rows from the LOCATIONS table. This shows the results page in a default mode querying records from the page's data model. Close the browser.
11. Run the findLocDA data action. On the input form, enter "US" in the CountryId field and click Find. The results page will appear showing data with country IDs of "US."

    Additional Information: To enter another a query, you need to rerun the findLocDA data action. Just clicking the Back button in the browser will not rerun this action. Notice that the URL in the Address field of the browser points to findLocDP.do even though you are viewing the locResultsDP.jsp because findLocDP.do represents the data action that you ran originally to reach the results page. The controller has displayed the results page from the Find button on the find page, but that button is not a link with a URL. You need a way to rerun the find page data action from this page, and a page link can fulfill this navigation requirement.
12. Close the browser.

13. With the Page Flow Diagram displayed, select Page Link in the Component Palette and draw the link from the locResultsDP data page to the findLocDA data action. Click Save All.

14. Run the find data action again. Enter "CA" for the country and click Find. When the results page appears, you will see an additional link (shown next) that returns you to the find page. Hold the mouse above the link and view the URL in the browser's status bar (findLocDA.do without any parameters).

	LocationId	StreetAddress	PostalCode	City	StateProvince	CountryId
*	1800	147 Spadina Ave	M5V 2L7	Toronto	Ontario	CA
	1900	6092 Boxwood St	YSW 9T2	Whitehorse	Yukon	CA

link to /findLocDA.do

15. Test this link and you will be returned to the find page.

16. Close the browser.

What Just Happened? In this phase, you created data actions and data pages to place a page into Find mode and to display query results. You also saw how you can view and edit the struts-config.xml file using an editor dialog instead of changing the diagram or the XML code. As your struts-config.xml file grows, familiarity with this editor can be helpful for finding and changing properties.

III. Modify the Data Elements

Now that you have implemented the basic functionality of the query pages, you can make the files more production-ready. This phase changes the fields with which the user interacts and adds components that assist with navigation.

Remove Unnecessary Fields

The default data controls such as the input form and read-only table supply interface objects for all attributes in the view object definition. In most cases, you do not need to show the user all of these attributes. You can remove an attribute in several ways as follows:

- **Delete or omit them from the ADF BC layer.** If the view object does not have the attribute, the Data Control Palette drag-and-drop operation will not create a user interface item for that attribute.
- **Set the *Display Hint* control hint to "Hide".** User interface libraries such as those that render Java client or JSP tags will not display an item for the attribute. This could be useful if you want to access the value programmatically but do not want to display it (such as for an internal ID column that would not be shown to the user). With the preceding technique, you will not be able to access the attribute's value.
- **Remove the item after it is created in the visual editor.** You can delete the item, an associated label, and an HTML cell that encloses the item using tools in the visual editor.

The first two techniques change the underlying business services layer so that any user interface created from the view object (or entity object if the properties are set at that level) will not display the attribute. This may be viable in some situations, but sometimes you just want to remove the item for a limited number of pages. This section shows how to remove items from the page. It is really as simple as deleting the applicable components.

In this case, you do not want the user to be able to query using the LocationId, StreetAddress, and PostalCode attributes. In addition, the user does not need to see the PostalCode attribute in the query results.

1. In the visual editor for the findLocDP.jsp page, drag the mouse from the top-left cell to the right-hand cell of the third row (the rows for LocationId, PostalCode, and City). The selected rows will be outlined with dotted lines as shown here:

   ${bindings['LocationId'].label}
   ${bindings['StreetAddress'].label}
   ${bindings['PostalCode'].label}
   ${bindings['City'].label}
   ${bindings['StateProvince'].label}
   ${bindings['CountryId'].label}

2. Press DELETE. This will delete the fields, their prompts, and the enclosing HTML cells.

   Additional Information: You can also use the Cut option on the right-click menu to remove the objects. Removing individual objects can be accomplished in the same way (selecting and pressing DELETE).

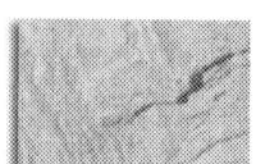

NOTE
All operations described in this section can also be performed in the Code Editor. However, HTML layouts can be quite complex with many nested tables and reading them is challenging. Therefore, the visual tools such as the JSP/HTML Visual Editor and the Structure window are usually easier to work with than the Code Editor.

3. Click Save All.

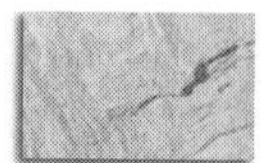

NOTE
Remember that CTRL-Z, *the toolbar Undo icon, or* ***Edit | Undo*** *will reverse the last change (even after you save the file). You can keep undoing if you want to go back to a previous state.*

4. Open the visual editor for the locResultsDP.jsp file. On the postal code label tag ("${bindings.LocationsView1.labels['PostalCode']}"), select Table | Delete Column from the right-click menu. The label and field below it will be deleted. This demonstrates the technique of manipulating the HTML table using right-click menu options.

5. Return to the Page Flow Diagram and run the findLocDA data action. The first page should appear as follows:

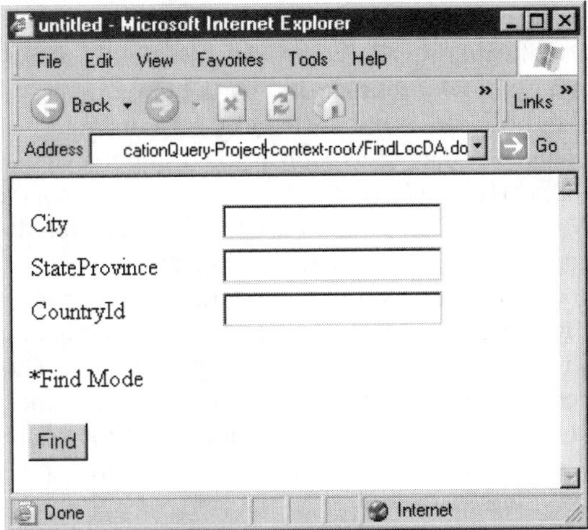

6. To demonstrate the query capabilities of the fields in a find page, enter the following (including the intentional typographical error for "LIKE") in the CountryID field:

```
US' or country_id LIK 'JP
```

7. Click the Find button and you will see the results page with the following error message at the top of the page:

Validation Error

You must correct the following error(s) before proceeding:

- JBO-27122: SQL error during statement preparation. Statement: SELECT Locations.LOCATION_ID, Locations.STREET_ADDRESS, Locations.POSTAL_CODE, Locations.CITY, Locations.STATE_PROVINCE, Locations.COUNTRY_ID FROM LOCATIONS Locations WHERE (((Locations.COUNTRY_ID LIKE 'US' or country_id LIK 'JP')))
- ORA-00920: invalid relational operator

Additional Information: This error message is rendered by the Struts errors tag at the top of the page in the visual editor. The typographical error was made intentionally so that you could see the query created by the data action. You can see how the value entered is enclosed in single quotes and is preceded by the LIKE operator. Knowing this will allow you to enter conditions other than a simple value. This technique also shows an easy way to check the SQL statement that is being executed.

8. Fix the spelling error in the query condition. Click Find and notice that the query results contain records from both US and JP. Also notice that the postal code column is not displayed.

9. Close the browser.

Add a List of Values

The user may not know the country codes required for this application. A friendlier interface would use a list of values to offer the user a selection list of names for code values such as the country code. Although the term *list of values* (LOV) is used by Oracle Forms Developer to refer to a separate window, a list of values in ADF is, by default, a pulldown (combo box) control. This section creates an LOV as a pulldown using Struts HTML components.

The *LOV binding* defines how data is connected to the pulldown. The LOV binding defines a *source data collection*—a source of data rows such as the result of a view object query. The LOV binding also declares the *target data collection*—the view object attribute and row into which the value returned by the LOV is placed. The target is usually the collection that contains the row being displayed. (Refer to Chapter 12 for an extensive discussion about the LOV list binding.)

In this example, the source data collection will be the CountryId in the CountriesView view object definition. The selected value will be placed into the CountryId attribute in the LocationsView target data collection. An LOV for a JSP file can be built from two data controls with similar functionality: a Single Select List or a List of Values. As mentioned before, the Single Select List is best for a hard-coded set of values and the List of Values is best for a list that is dynamically built from a data collection. Since this practice needs to load values from the Countries view object, this section uses the List of Values data control.

The LOV example presented in the second hands-on practice in Chapter 12 demonstrates and describes the LOV from the standpoint of data binding and how to use the LOV in an input form. The example in this practice focuses on the JSP presentation aspects and how to use the LOV in a query form.

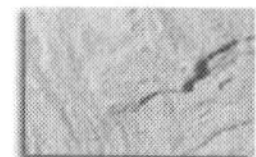

NOTE
You will use this technique often and you can find samples outside this book. For example, another version of this technique is described in the help topic "Creating a List of Values with an ADF LOV Binding" (search for "Creating ADF LOV" in the Full Text Search tab of the help system). This technique also appears in the "How To's" page available from the "How-To's" link on the OTN JDeveloper home page. The technique is currently called "How To Create a Databound Pop-list with Oracle JDeveloper 10g."

1. In the visual editor for findLocDP.jsp, select the CountryId field (in the bottom-right cell of the HTML table) and press DELETE. You will substitute a pulldown control for the text field.

2. In the Data Control Palette, select LocationsModuleDataControl\LocationsView1\CountryId node. Select "List of Values" from the *Drag and Drop As* pulldown and drag CountryId into the empty cell in the HTML table. A narrow combo box control will appear.

   Additional Information: This action adds the selection HTML control to the JSP file. Select the control if it is not selected and click the Source tab in the editor window. In the Code Editor, the line of code that displays this control is displayed ("`<html:select property="CountryId1">`"). Since a CountryId attribute existed before in the binding (for the field that you deleted), the second instance is suffixed with a number. You still need to specify that the CountriesView view object definition will be the source data collection.

3. Click the UI Model tab in the Structure window to display the model details for the findLocDP file. You will see both CountryId (for the field you deleted) and CountryId1 (for the List of Values you just added).

4. In the Structure window, on the CountryId node (for the original attribute), select Edit from the right-click menu. This will display the Attribute Binding Editor dialog, which is used to map the UI binding definition to a data collection attribute in the data model.

   Additional Information: Notice that this editor contains the collection, attribute, and iterator that are used to bind CountryId.

5. Click Cancel to dismiss this dialog without making a change.

6. On the CountryId1 node, select Edit from the right-click menu. A different editor, the List Binding Editor, will appear. This is a different editor because the element was added when you dragged in the List of Values data control, which allows you to map the source and target data collections. You will return to this dialog to set its properties, but click Cancel for now.

7. In the navigator, on the findLocDPUIModel.xml node under the LocationQuery\ViewController\Application Sources\location.view node, open the right-click menu. Among other options, this menu contains items you can use to create bindings of different types. Select the Open item. The data model file will open in the Code Editor in "protected" (read only) mode.

8. Search for "CountryId1". Under the id element, you will see a reference to the data control subtype of "DCListSingleSel" indicating that you dragged in a (single selection) List of Values data control.

9. Double click the CountryId1 attribute in the Structure window to display the binding editor. In the List Binding Editor, be sure that "LOV Mode" is selected in the *List Binding Mode* pulldown as shown next:

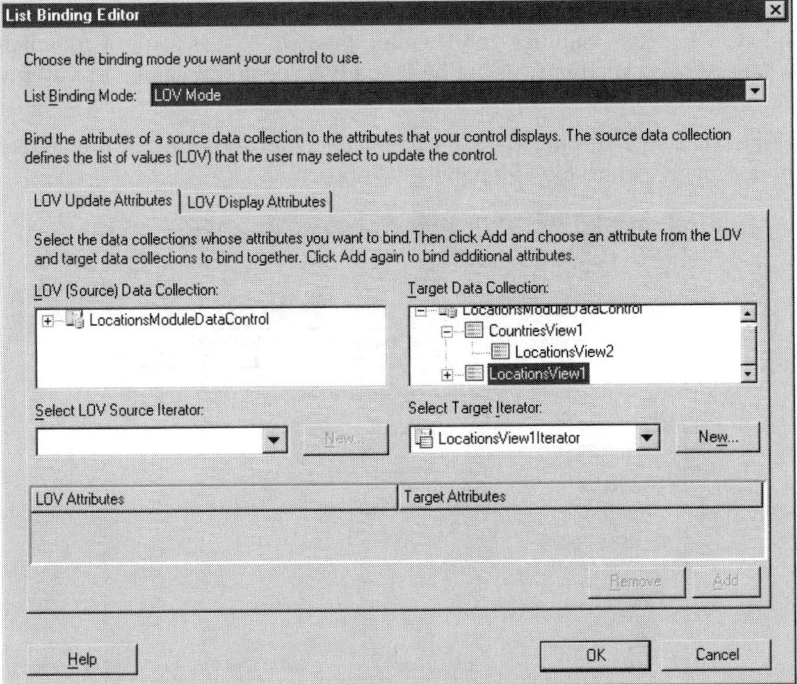

Additional Information: This selection allows you to define the list as the data collection returned by a view object query.

11. In the LOV Update Attributes tab, select LocationsModuleDataControl\CountriesView1 in the *LOV (Source) Data Collection* area. This area contains a list of all available data collections.
12. Click the New button to the right of the *Select LOV Source Iterator* pulldown. Be sure the Iterator Id field reads "CountriesView1Iterator" and click OK to dismiss the Iterator Id dialog. This defines the name of the *iterator,* a "cursor" object that will navigate through the rows in the data collection.
13. Click the LOV Display Attributes tab and move CountryName to the *Attributes to Display* area. This defines the attribute value that will be shown to the user in the pulldown.
14. Click the LOV Update Attributes tab and click Add at the bottom of the dialog. This area defines the attribute mapping between an attribute in the LOV data collection and an attribute in the target data collection (that is shown on the form).
15. In the *LOV Attributes* pulldown, be sure that "CountryId" is selected. In the *Target Attributes* pulldown, select "CountryId." Click OK to dismiss the List Binding Editor.
16. Click the findLocDPUIModel.xml tab if the file is not displayed in the visual editor from step 7. Notice that a number of additional elements for the CountryId1 List of Values data control were added since you viewed it in step 7. These elements define the data collections, attributes, and iterator.
17. Click Save All. The default query returns ten rows. You now need to specify that all rows from the CountriesView view object will be displayed.
18. Click the findLocDP.jsp tab in the editor window. In the UI Model tab of the Structure window, select the CountriesView1Iterator (the iterator that you just added) and change the *Range Size* property to "-1" in the Property Inspector (meaning that all rows will be retrieved). Press ENTER.
19. Test the pages by returning to the Page Flow Diagram and running the findLocDA data action. A page such as the following will appear:

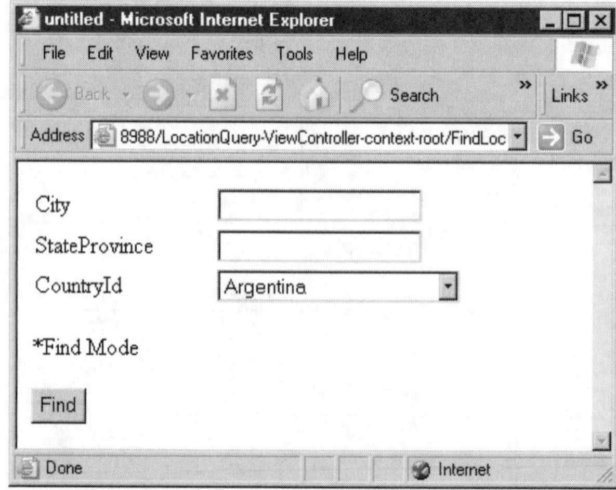

20. Notice that the CountryId pulldown contains all country names from the CountriesView view object query. Select "Canada" and click Find. The results page will appear with the Canadian locations.

NOTE
Instead of using the mouse to select a value from a pulldown, you can press the first letter of a value in a pulldown to select that value. If more than one row appears with the same first letter, press the letter as many times as required to select the desired value. This is standard behavior for an HTML select control.

21. Close the browser.

    Additional Information: The pulldown contains a list of all countries, but it does not allow the user to query all countries by leaving the CountryId field blank. The next steps add a value to the pulldown that represents all countries.

22. Navigate to the visual editor for the findLocDP.jsp file. Click the JSP Structure tab of the Structure window if it is not displayed. You will see something like the following:

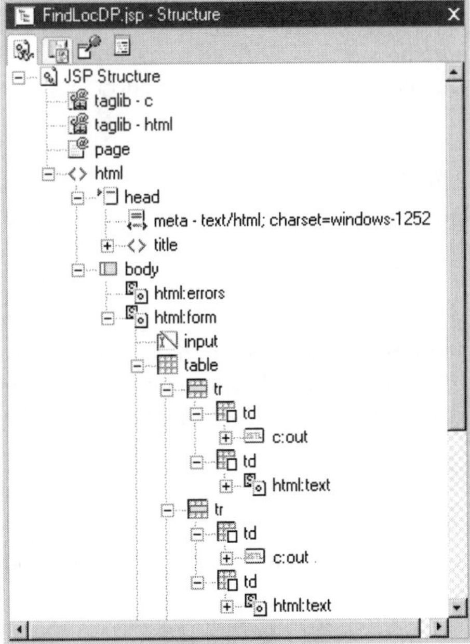

23. Select the new CountryId pulldown component in the visual editor. The Structure window will select the corresponding tag (html:select). (If it does not show the selection, on the pulldown in the visual editor, select "Select in Structure" from the right-click menu.)

    Additional Information: This tag displays an HTML selection list (pulldown). The values within the list are created by the html.optionsCollection tag (a tag from the Struts HTML tag library) nested under the option tag.

24. Expand the html:select node and select the html:optionsCollection tag under the select tag in the Structure window. The Property Inspector shows the *property* attribute set to the name of the collection from which the list values are derived (in this case, the CountryId1.displayData data collection). You need to add an option that displays a null value so that you can select locations from all countries.

25. From the Struts Html page of the Component Palette, click the option (not "options") tag and drag it into the Structure window above the html:optionsCollection tag as shown here:

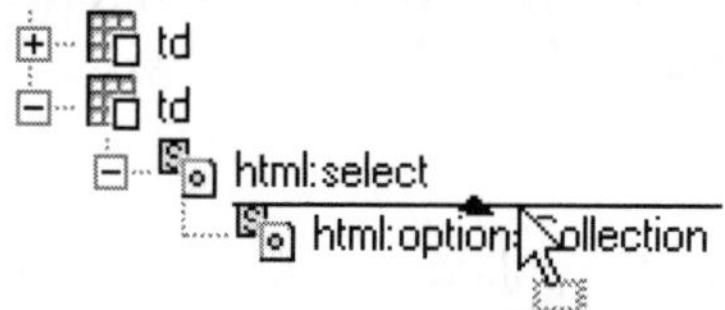

Additional Information: Notice that during the drag-and-drop operation, a line with an arrow shows where you will drop the tag in the structure. Be sure the arrow is pointed up so that the tag is added above the current option collection tag. You may have to move the mouse cursor horizontally to trigger the up arrow.

26. When the element is positioned correctly, drop it. The JavaServer Page Tag Editor will appear. Enter the *value* property as "-1" (all rows) and click OK. Click the Source tab if the Code Editor is not displayed and view the option tag, shown here:

```
<html:option value="-1" />
```

27. Change this tag so it appears as follows.

```
<html:option value="-1">All Countries</html:option>
```

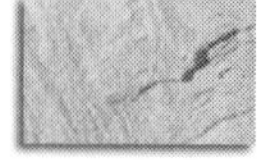

NOTE
If you know the exact syntax, or part of the syntax and want to rely on Tag Insight to assist, you can more easily type in this tag instead of using the Component Palette and Structure window. The steps were provided to demonstrate the Component Palette method for adding tag code.

28. Click Save All. Run the findLocDA data action from the Page Flow Diagram. Try the "All Countries" option and click Find. Records from more than one country will appear.

29. Close the browser.

Add Navigation Controls

The next user-friendly feature to add is a set of navigation controls for the query results page. At this point, the user can only see ten records. However, the query may return more than ten records and the user might want to scroll through the query results. This section adds navigation buttons and a selection list for a set of records. Button actions must be contained within an HTML form and this form was added earlier in this practice. However, if you did not know to add the form tag beforehand, you could also add it at this point and place the HTML table inside the form.

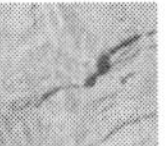

NOTE
Since the sample data set for Locations is small, this section will change the displayed records to three to better demonstrate record set navigation. Often, the page will have room for more than three records.

1. Open the locResultsDP.jsp file in the visual editor.
2. In the Data Control Palette, select the LocationsView1\Operations\Previous Set node, select a Button from *Drag and Drop As,* and drag the operation to between the top-left corner of the form box (shown with a dotted line) and the left side of the HTML table as shown here:

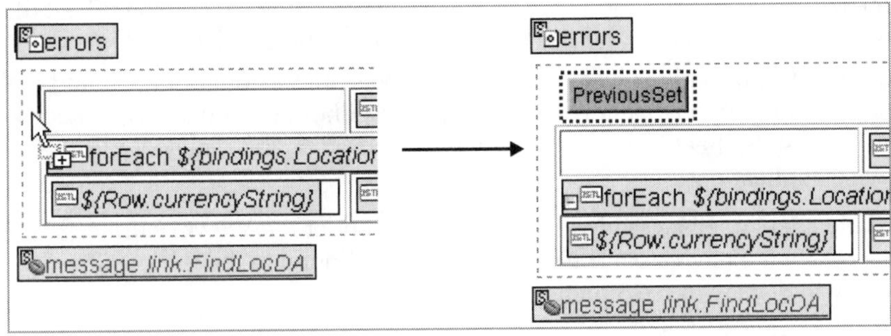

Dragging Dropped

3. Drag a `Next Set` operation as a button in the same way and drop it to the right of the PreviousSet button. Change the *value* property for NextSet to "Next Page" and for PreviousSet to "Previous Page".
4. With the locResultsDP.jsp file displayed, click the UI Model tab of the Structure window. Select the LocationsView1Iterator and change the *Range Size* property in the Property Inspector to "3".

   Additional Information: As mentioned, this smaller return set will allow you to test the navigation capabilities better for this small number of rows. Normally you would return as many rows as are appropriate for the page layout.
5. Click Save All. Run the findLocDA data action from the Page Flow Diagram. Leave "All Countries" selected and click Find. You will see the first three records of the results. The Previous Page button is disabled because this is the first record set in the query. (Chapter 12 discusses row set, current row, and record set scrolling extensively.)
6. Click Next Page to display the next three records. Return to the query page and select "United States of America" in the CountryId pulldown. Click Find. The query results will be reduced to locations in the US.
7. Close the browser.

What Just Happened? You modified the data elements on the pages so that unnecessary fields would not appear. You also added an LOV for CountryId and saw how LOV binding works. The last section added navigation controls so the user can scroll through the query results.

IV. Modify the Visual Aspects

The main functionality is now created for the query pages and you can spend time on modifying some of the visual aspects. This section demonstrates techniques you can use to manipulate the visual aspect of the application.

Add Text and Apply Styles

This section applies the style sheet and adds text and styles to the two pages.

1. Open the visual editor for the findLocDP page. From the Component Palette CSS page, click Blaf. This action adds a link tag for the Oracle Browser Look-and-Feel (BLAF) cascading style sheet and copies the blaf.css file to the project directory.

   Additional Information: Cascading style sheets offer a common look-and-feel and are discussed further in Appendix C. Chapter 3 describes code editor style sheet support. The BLAF style sheet is the primary style sheet used by the Oracle E-Business Suite self-service applications.

2. Double click the blaf.css file that now appears under the ViewController\Web Content\css node in the navigator. The style sheet file will open in the Code Editor and the list of styles will display in the Structure window.
3. Double click the H1 style in the Structure window to view its properties in the Property Inspector and navigate to its code in the Code Editor. Also look at the "*.smalltext" style definition and notice that it reduces the font size.
4. Click the findLocDP.jsp tab in the editor window. Add a blank line above the errors tag at the top of the file and type the heading "Find Locations".
5. In the *Block Format* pulldown of the visual editor toolbar, select "Heading 1." The font, color, and border will change to those of the H1 tag style defined in the BLAF style sheet.
6. Select the Find button. In the Property Inspector, click the down-arrow button in the *class* property to display the style pulldown as shown next. This is a list of global styles (and those applied to the <p> tag) available in the BLAF style sheet.

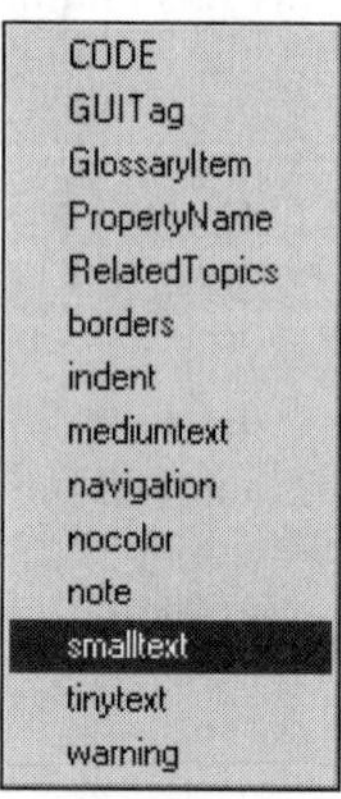

7. Select "smalltext." The font of the button label will reduce in size. While the Find button is still selected, select Go to Source from the right-click menu and you will see the input tag selected, which contains the *class* attribute for this style.
8. Click the Design tab. Add a blank line between the bottom of the HTML table and the editing mode message tag. Click the cursor on the new line.
9. Type the text "Enter query conditions and click Find." and, in the Property Inspector *class* property select "tinytext." (This style is applied to the paragraph tag created when you added a blank line.)
10. In the Structure window, find the title tag in the JSP Structure tab. (It will appear under the html\head node.) On the title node, select Edit Tag from the right-click menu. The Title Editor dialog will appear.
11. Replace the existing text with "Find Locations" and click OK. This text will appear in the window title when you run the application in the browser.
12. In the visual editor for the locResultsDP page, add the same style sheet (Blaf). Add a heading before the errors tag for "Location Search Results" and apply the Heading 1 style using the visual editor toolbar.
13. Add title text of "Location Search Results" as in steps 10 and 11.
14. Click the Previous Page button and change the *class* property to "smalltext." Repeat this setting for the Next Page button.
15. Click Save All.
16. Run the findLocDA data action from the Page Flow Diagram and notice the window title, page title and button fonts and colors, and new message on the find page.
17. Close the browser.

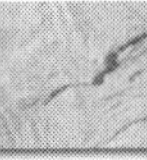

TIP
Some changes you make to visual elements (and most data elements) can be viewed in the same browser session after saving the modified JSP file. Upon rerunning the JSP file, the server will recompile the modified file and display the changes. Some changes only require that you close the browser but not stop the server. Since there are so many objects that can be changed, learning what needs to be closed to test a modification is mostly a matter of trial and error.

Add an Image and Change the Link Message

This section adds a logo to the pages and changes the link text on the results page.

1. Display the visual editor for the findLocDP file and select the HTML page of the Component Palette. Drag an Image tag to the visual editor and drop it before the "Find Locations" heading. The Insert Image dialog will appear.
2. Click the Browse button and navigate to JDEV_HOME\jdev\doc\welcome\welcomeImages directory.

3. Select the jd_clr_rgb_sm.gif file. You will see a preview of the file appear on the right of the Select Image Source dialog.
4. Click Open. In the Image Location Problem dialog, click Yes and click Save in the Save Image dialog to copy the file to the project public_html directory.
5. Click OK to dismiss the Insert Image dialog. The file will appear in the navigator's WEB-INF node and the JDeveloper 10*g* logo will appear next to the title as shown here:

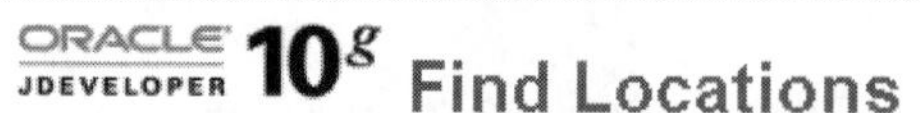

6. Display the visual editor for the locResultsDP page. Now that the image file is part of the project, you can drag it from the navigator and drop it before the heading "Location Search Results." Do so now.

TIP
You can also drag images into the project or the JSP file from Windows Explorer or even from Internet Explorer.

7. You now need to make the page link text more user friendly. In the visual editor, notice that the message tag at the bottom of the search results page reads "link.findLocDA." This is the key value that is contained in the ApplicationResources.properties file.
8. Double click the ApplicationResources.properties in the navigator (under the Application Sources\location.view node) and change the link.findLocDA value (after the "=" sign) to "Return to Find Locations".
9. Click Save All.
10. Run the find page from the Page Flow Diagram. You will see the new logos and page link.
11. Close the browser.

Specify Control Hints for the Field Prompts

The prompts for all fields and columns are derived from the view object attribute names. Since many of the attributes are named descriptively, the prompts sufficiently identify the fields for testing purposes, but you do not want to present even slightly cryptic prompts to users. Although you could remove the references to the attributes and hard-code text for each prompt, you would need to change all occurrences of all attribute prompts. On these two pages, the fields are repeated, so changing one attribute prompt could require changing two labels. This section shows a technique for using control hints to modify the attribute prompt in a central location so that all applications can display the same prompt.

1. Click the Run Manager tab. (If Run Manager is not displayed, select it from the View menu.) Expand the Processes node and, on the Embedded OC4J Server node, select Terminate from the right-click menu.

   Additional Information: This section changes ADF BC properties and the server cannot dynamically read modifications to ADF BC objects. You need to restart the server for these changes to take effect. The server will start automatically when you run the application in the IDE.

2. Click the Applications tab. Under the Model project location.model node, double click the Locations entity object definition to open the Entity Object Editor.

3. Select the Attributes\LocationId node and click the Control Hints tab.

   Additional Information: As mentioned earlier, control hints are properties of attributes stored in a *message bundle* (resource) file that is used by the base classes. If you needed to supply different prompts for another language, you can code another resource file with the same entries but different text strings.

4. Enter the *Label Text* field as "ID" and the *Tooltip Text* field as "Location ID".

5. Repeat steps 3 and 4 for the other attributes and values listed next:

Attribute	Label Text	Tooltip Text
StreetAddress	Street	Street address for this location
StateProvince	State or Province	State or province for this location
CountryID	Country ID	Country for this location

6. Click OK.

7. With the Locations entity object definition selected in the navigator, double click the LocationsImplMsgBundle.java file in the Structure window. The file will be displayed in the Code Editor. You will see the labels and tooltip text you entered in the sMessageStrings array. The tooltip text is not used by the Struts tags, but these will be useful to the hands-on practice in Chapter 19 that builds from this Model project.

8. Rebuild the Model project.

9. Return to the Page Flow Diagram and run the findLocDA data action. The application will appear as shown next:

ORACLE JDEVELOPER 10g Find Locations

City

State or Province

Country ID — All Countries

Enter query conditions and click Find.

*Find Mode

Find

Additional Information: Notice the new prompts for the fields on the find page. Click the Find button and notice that the prompts are the same for the column headings on the results page.

NOTE
You can specify control hints on the view object definition level as well as the entity object level. However, control hints on the view object level will override control hints on the entity object level. Normally, you would want the same prompts for the same attributes regardless of the number of view objects created from the entity object. You would, therefore, place the control hints on the entity attributes. However, you can use the view object control hints to override the normal entity object control hint for a specific purpose.

10. Close the browser.

What Just Happened? You changed the visual aspects of the application by applying a style sheet to each page and using the styles in the style sheet for headings, text, and buttons. You added some text to the page and specified window titles. You also added a logo to both pages and made it part of the project files (so that it can be deployed with the project). The link text on the results page was reworded in the ApplicationResources.properties file. You then used the ADF BC control hints feature to define prompt and tooltip text.

The next steps for an application such as this would be to add the other visual elements needed for it to comply with the look-and-feel of the rest of the web pages in the application. You can easily add a link from the search results page to an edit or new record page as described in the Chapter 17 practices. A combination of query, browse, edit, and create pages would make this an application that could perform all basic data manipulation to the table.

CHAPTER 19

Working with ADF UIX Pages

Let us go then, you and I,
When the evening is spread out against the sky
Like a patient etherized upon a table;
Let us go, through certain half-deserted streets,
The muttering retreats
Of restless nights in one-night cheap hotels
And sawdust restaurants with oyster-shells:
Streets that follow like a tedious argument
Of insidious intent
To lead you to an overwhelming question...
Oh, do not ask, "What is it?"
Let us go and make our visit.

—T. S. Eliot (1888–1965),
The Love Song of J. Alfred Prufrock

DF UIX (UIX) is an Oracle-specific web-tier view framework that acts as an alternative view technology in the ADF framework. It is J2EE-compliant and it has many of the same benefits and considerations as JSP technology. However, UIX offers a streamlined design and development model and has unique aspects that make it preferable for applications that require support for multiple output devices (such as mobile and desktop).

Initially, the UIX framework, formerly called User Interface XML (uiXML), was used by developers of the Oracle E-Business Suite (Oracle Applications) for front-end, self-service applications and by customers of the E-Business Suite to develop extensions to those front ends. In addition, Oracle uses UIX as a front end to products such as Oracle iLearning, Enterprise Manager (EM), and Oracle9*i* Internet File System (iFS). Now, JDeveloper offers the ability to easily create UIX applications inside or outside of the Oracle application products.

This chapter discusses how to build basic ADF UIX applications using JDeveloper 10*g*. As with Chapter 18, the prerequisite to proper assimilation of material in this chapter is an understanding of web client technology, introduced in Chapter 7. In addition, knowledge of JSP Standard Tag Library (JSTL) and JSP expression language (EL) is helpful (and is introduced in Appendix D). A basic knowledge of the Struts controller (the subject of Chapter 17) is also recommended.

The hands-on practice in this chapter builds a set of ADF UIX pages that perform basic browse, edit, and query functions.

ADF UIX Overview

Before describing how to develop UIX code in JDeveloper, a brief discussion of the features that ADF UIX offers will help you to better understand this framework.

NOTE

More information about ADF UIX is available in the Online Demos, Tutorials, Code Samples, and How-To's sections from the JDeveloper home page on OTN (otn.oracle.com/products/jdev). Additional overview and reference material is contained in the JDeveloper help system. In the Search tab, look for "oracle adf uix developer's guide" and double click "Oracle ADF UIX Developer's Guide," which explains the framework in detail. In the Table of Contents tab, look under the Reference book node for "UIX Reference" topic, which describes the UIX tags.

UIX Features

ADF UIX offers many features that distinguish it from traditional J2EE technologies.

Platform Independence

UIX code files use a .uix extension and are built with XML syntax using the ADF UIX tags. The use of XML means that the code is interpreted at run time (in contrast with JSP code, which is translated and compiled before it is run). It also allows the language to support deployment to different platforms. If the display device does not support HTML, UIX can be instructed to render the display in a form that the device can accept. This allows UIX files to be displayed in multiple output devices, such as desktop computer browsers or mobile devices. Naturally, the UIX design must take the device type into account, so a particular UIX file will be designed for a particular output device. For example, the page must be much simpler if the output will be on a PDA because the screen is smaller than on a desktop monitor.

NOTE
JDeveloper offers a UIX JSP tag library that allows you to include many UIX features in a normal JSP file. This tag library is not recommended for new applications because of planned obsolescence and because it requires an extra layer in the runtime library process.

Integrated into ADF

UIX is completely integrated into the view layer of the ADF framework. This means that UIX code can be developed in JDeveloper in the same way as other types of code that ADF supports. It also means that UIX code can share the controller and business services layers with other types of code. UIX can bind to any ADF data source.

Internationalization Support

UIX supports *internationalization* (abbreviated as *i18n*)—the application is adaptable to any language. Image files are created dynamically (as described in a later section) so that they can be built for a particular language at run time. In addition, styles are defined in XSS (XML Style Sheet Language). At runtime, UIX generates a locale-specific CSS (cascading style sheet) based on the definitions. This style sheet can be defined specifically for a language, if needed.

UIX and J2EE

Although UIX is an Oracle-specific technology, it is J2EE-compliant, proven, and mature. It shares with JSP technology the ability to render an HTML page from Web Tier code. In addition, UIX shares design principles with JavaServer Faces (JSF) technology, which was recently ratified by the Java Community Process as Java Specification Request 127 (jcp.org/en/jsr/detail?id=127). Future releases of UIX will implement JSF principles and act as extensions to JSF functionality. For more information about JSF and ADF, refer to the white paper "Roadmap for the ADF UIX technology and JavaServer Faces" currently available in the Technical Papers section of JDeveloper's home page on OTN (otn.oracle.com/products/jdev).

Standardization

UIX uses a page design model (described later) that provides consistency within the application. The template use in UIX enforces standards use as well. In addition, the concept of *look-and-feel,* a standard set of fonts and colors, is integrated into the page display. All of these features help make application pages appear in a consistent way.

Rich Component Set

UIX contains a large variety of user interface components with rich functionality such as the shuttle control that you can use to move items between lists or reorder items in a list. Components are divided into the following categories:

- **Simple components** are low-level, user input controls such as fields, buttons, and links. Many of these controls offer features more powerful than those offered by normal HTML controls. For example, the `messageDateField` tag displays a field and a button; when the user clicks the button, a calendar appears in a separate window and allows the user to select a date, which is then passed back to the field.
- **Layout components** act as containers for other components. These components correspond roughly to Java client containers such as JPanel and their layout managers such as BorderLayout and FlowLayout. Each UIX layout component that contains other components defines a layout style such as `borderLayout` or `flowLayout`. In fact, the UIX layout components often have an exact counterpart in the Swing layout managers (described in Chapter 16).
- **Composite components** are higher-level collections of simple and layout components. These collections are prebuilt to perform a special operation, such as the `tree` element that displays a hierarchical data in a navigator format.

As with any tag in a tag library, the rich functionality of these components makes developing basic modules for each new application easier. Developers do not need to think in terms of HTML coding. Rather, they think in terms of larger units. In addition, templates and look-and-feel attributes aid in creating a pleasing and user-friendly page design. Although you can code JSP tags to implement virtually any look-and-feel, the default UIX templates and tags are richer-looking out of the box.

UIX Dynamic Images

UIX creates image files on the fly for objects such as buttons and tabs. The text property value of the tag (such as the tag for a button) is derived from the object at run time and the graphic is generated accordingly. This dynamic image generation further facilitates internationalization because the text value for an object can be customized to the locale or language in which the page is displayed. Also, developers need not worry about creating or properly locating graphics files for the design objects such as tabs.

Easy Look-and-Feel Swapping

UIX ships using the Oracle Browser Look-and-Feel (BLAF) design layout, which was developed for the Oracle E-Business Suite. You can switch the look-and-feel to another Oracle look-and-feel or to one of your own design. A single UIX can be displayed in any look-and-feel available by setting a single property in the UIX configuration file. This is demonstrated in the hands-on practice later in this chapter.

Extensibility

You can extend the capabilities of UIX using these two facilities:

- **Templates (UIT)**, which are reusable files with a .uit extension that combine standard components to create a new component. A template will be displayed as a tag in the UIX file and, when run, it will be included in the UIX page. After creating a template, you will see it automatically appear in the Component Palette. JDeveloper offers no visual editor for templates but does offer two template wizards and support in the Code Editor. Templates are a powerful feature for standardizing the content or look-and-feel of an application.
- **Extensions**, which are custom renderers (display controls) that fulfill complex requirements. You would develop these custom tags if templates were not sufficient or if no existing component is usable. Extensions require low-level coding and this should not be necessary often.

Partial Page Rendering

UIX offers the ability to perform *partial page rendering* (PPR), a refresh of part of the page. No custom JavaScript is required, although JavaScript is used to perform the contents update. The mechanism starts with a partial page event that results in only part of the page contents being sent back to the browser. PPR uses inline frames (*iframes*) to communicate between the browser and the web application. The UIX controls that support PPR are hGrid, hideShow, hideShowHeader, lovInput, processing, subTabLayout, and table.

In addition to these distinctive features, UIX uses a special tag structure that is useful to explore before starting to learn about developing UIX pages.

UIX Page Design Structure

Unlike JSP tags, which are often closely coupled with the HTML tags shown in the browser, a component in a UIX file usually translates into more than one HTML tag; the UIX tag places the HTML tags on the page in the order in which they appear in the code according to a specific page design structure. This structure is organized around a hierarchy of *user interface nodes,* nodes arranged in a hierarchical tree represented in XML by nested components.

User Interface Nodes

User interface nodes are logical structures that identify a particular part of the page or components within those areas. Figure 19-1 shows a design structure (from the Structure window) of the search page you will create in the hands-on practice in this chapter.

In this example, the page node is the parent user interface node for all other nodes defined for the page. The content and handlers nodes act as children of the page node and parents to their nested elements. Following the hierarchy down through the content node, you will see the form node representing the HTML form; under the pageLayout node, you will find a flowLayout node containing all components for the page.

The pageLayout node contains a number of preset *named children* slots (placeholders for specific components) including copyright, corporate branding, global buttons, pageHeader, product branding, and tabs as shown later in this section. It also includes named child nodes not being used in this file (those which have no "+" symbol next to them).

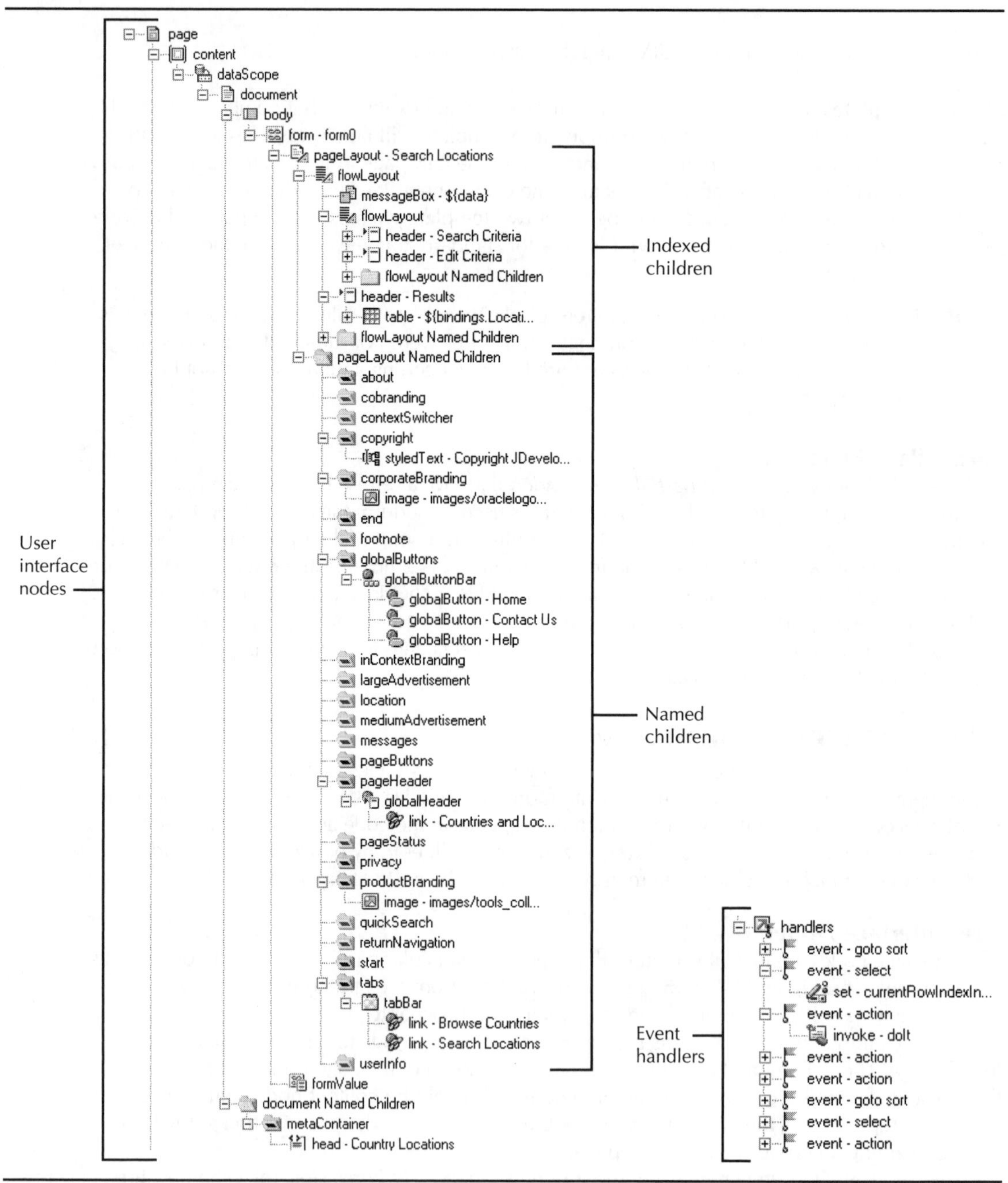

FIGURE 19-1. *Sample UIX design structure*

Therefore, you can place components in the named children nodes that will correspond to a specific location on the page. You can also stack components separately (as *indexed children*) outside of the named child nodes. The "pageLayout -Search Locations" node in Figure 19-1 shows examples of indexed children.

Event Handlers

In addition to page elements, the right-hand hierarchy shown in Figure 19-1 lists the events defined for the page. (This hierarchy appears under the page design hierarchy in the Structure window.) *Event handlers* define what happens for a specific user interaction. After defining the *event* property of an object, you create the event in the Design Structure tab and link the event to a specific controller action. In a project that uses Struts as the controller, this action could be a data action or a data page.

UIX Component Example

Named child nodes have recommended contents, but there is no requirement to place a particular component inside a particular node. For example, the named child, globalButtons, usually contains a `globalButtonBar` tag that, in turn, contains `globalButton` tags.

The component tags render the HTML elements. For example, when you display a single UIX tag, `globalButtonBar`, in a browser, the tag translates into an HTML table containing the links and images defined inside the named child tag borders (from `<globalButtons>` to `</globalButtons>`). The code for such a structure in UIX would look like the following snippet from a page you will create in the hands-on practice in this chapter:

```
<globalButtons>
  <globalButtonBar>
    <contents>
      <globalButton source="images/www_home.gif"
                    text="Home" destination="#"/>
      <globalButton source="images/www_contact.gif"
                    text="Contact Us" destination="#"/>
      <globalButton source="images/www_help.gif"
                    text="Help" destination="#"/>
    </contents>
  </globalButtonBar>
</globalButtons>
```

This code is rendered by the *UIX Servlet* (the runtime process that processes UIX code) in the following way:

The translation of code tag to HTML display is the same as with a high-level JSP tag that can display an HTML table with two rows and three columns including graphics and text labels. UIX, however, also places this object in the position assigned to the globalButtons named child node (in this example, the top-right corner of the page). In addition, the same tag can be used to display the same component in a different output device such as a PDA.

Named Children Example

Figure 19-2 shows the UIX Visual Editor with the edit page from the hands-on practice in this chapter. This figure identifies the following page design areas, and Figure 19-1 shows the hierarchy nodes (for the search page) that correspond to some of these areas:

- **Page header** This area contains the *corporate branding* (a graphic that identifies the company or a top-level entity) and the *product branding* (a graphic that identifies the application or low-level entity). The corporate branding and product branding can also be stacked.
- **Global buttons** This area holds buttons that appear on all pages. The buttons link to other pages or websites.
- **Tabs and navigation** This area shows the tab control that allows users to quickly navigate to another page. In addition, the page can contain an additional navigation bar control (usually on the left side of the page) that contains links to more pages.
- **Data component area** This area is reserved for *data components,* controls that interact with data, for example, input forms or browse tables. You drop components from the Data Control Palette into this area to place data on the page.
- **Page footer** This area shows the *copyright* (a message at the bottom of the screen), the *privacy message* (the statement to the user about information sharing), and a *privacy statement* (the privacy text). In addition, the links from the tab area and global buttons are repeated in text in this area.

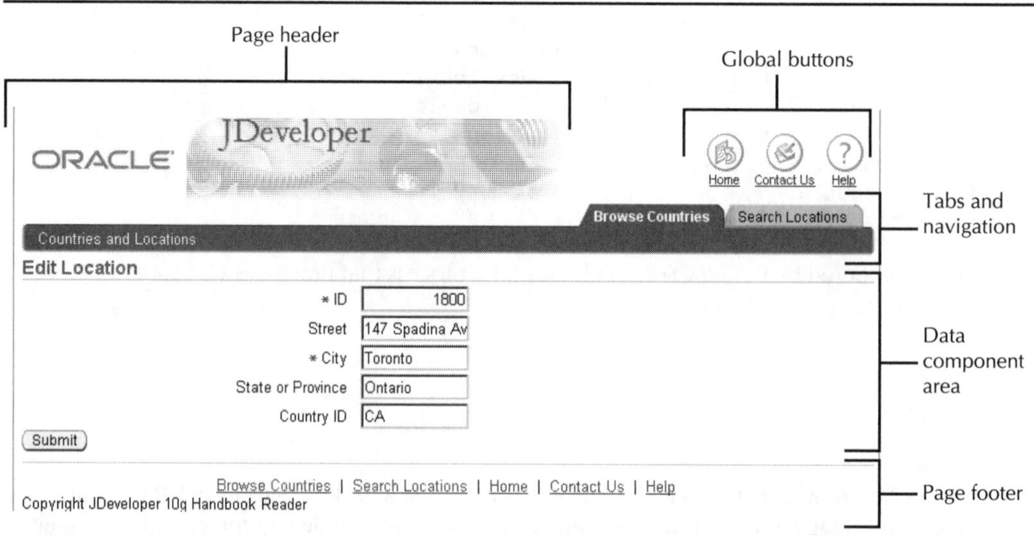

FIGURE 19-2. *UIX Visual Editor with layout areas*

UIX Application Development in JDeveloper

JSP and ADF UIX technologies both use code deployed in the Web Tier and a user interface displayed in a web browser. The tools that are used for JSP file creation and modification are used in a similar way with both technologies. Therefore, additional discussion about the basic tools and operations for using those tools is unnecessary.

The JDeveloper tools assist in the creation of UIX code and for much of the time, you will not need to type XML code in the Code Editor. The UIX Visual Editor, Property Inspector, Structure window, Data Control Palette, and Component Palette allow you to work in a declarative way. In addition, wizards help create files containing templates or standard named child container elements.

TIP
If you know JSP technology and would like to read about UIX in the context of JSP technology, on the Search tab of the help system, look for "about jsp pages and uix xml" and review the topic "About JSP Pages and UIX XML Similarities and Differences."

Wizards and File Creation Dialogs

The following list describes the New Gallery items for creating ADF UIX files. In some cases, the item displays a file dialog where you enter the name of the file and click OK. In other cases, a wizard appears and you fill out the wizard pages to define the file. Finishing the wizard creates the file.

- **Empty UIX XML Page** This item opens a dialog that creates a UIX file containing basic tags such as providers (data sources), body (content), and handlers (for events).
- **UIX XML Page Based on Existing UIX XML Template (UIT)** This item starts the "Create UIX XML Page Based on UIT Wizard," which creates a file by including a template for common objects such as images, copyright text, and header text. The wizard is relatively simple because all common page design areas have been defined in the template.
- **UIX XML Page with Header, Footer, and Navigation** This item starts the "Create UIX XML Page Wizard," which allows you to define the major page design areas (title, branding images, navigation elements, and footer element). It does not use a template.
- **UIX XML Page with pageLayout** This item starts a dialog where you specify a file name and click OK. The file that is created contains the same objects as the empty UIX XML page described before; in addition, a pageLayout tag and related tags are added so that you can add content without having to worry about many of the components.
- **UIX XML Template (UIT)** This opens a dialog that creates a basic template (UIT) file with no objects.
- **UIX XML Template (UIT) with Header, Footer, and Navigation** This dialog opens the "Create UIX XML Template (UIT) Wizard," which creates a UIT file containing tags for tab pages, footer text, global buttons, corporate branding, product branding, and page title. Once you define a template, you can use it as the basis for a UIX file with the New Gallery item "UIX XML Page Based on Existing UIX XML Template (UIT)."

UIX Visual Editor

The UIX Visual Editor (shown in Figure 19-2) allows you to view the components of a UIX page. As with the JSP/HTML Visual Editor, the UIX Visual Editor accepts drag-and-drop operations from the Component Palette and Data Control Palette. You do not type text directly into the visual editor; instead, you select an object and set its properties in the Property Inspector. The hands-on practice provides experience with the process of modifying content using property values.

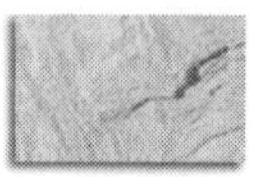

NOTE
You can add, move, and delete objects in the UIX Visual Editor but you cannot perform inline editing (direct typing into the editor). Inline editing is planned for a future JDeveloper release.

UIX Preview

The UIX Preview is available by clicking the Preview tab. Although you cannot make changes to the file in this mode, you will see the page in the way that it will appear in the browser. The UIX Visual Editor shows the page in a similar way but it also shows named child areas that are empty.

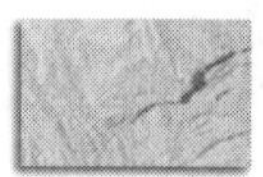

NOTE
JSP files have no preview capability such as that available to UIX.

XML Editor

The XML Editor is available from the Source tab of the editor window when a UIX or UIT file is displayed. This editor contains the usual code-editing features including syntax highlighting, syntax error evaluation (errors appear in the Structure window), Tag Insight, and Tag Completion. Remember that tag completion for an XML file works differently from tag completion for an HTML or JSP file. The XML ending tag will fill in automatically after you type the ">" character for the starting tag. For example, as soon as you type "`<pageLayout>`" in the Code Editor, the "`</pageLayout>`" tag will pop in. For JSP and HTML files, you need to type the entire starting tag and the "</" characters of the ending tag (for example, "`<body></`") before the ending tag is completed automatically.

TIP
As in the JSP code editor, pressing F1 *after placing the cursor in a tag will display the help system topic or Javadoc for that tag.*

Structure Window

The Structure window for UIX files contains the following tabs:

- **XML Structure** This tab shows the hierarchy of XML tags (like the hierarchy of JSP tags in the JSP Structure tab for a JSP file).

- **UI Model** This tab displays the data binding to business services components and allows you to access the binding editors for each node. This works the same way as for a JSP file.
- **Design Structure** This tab, which is shown next (Figure 19-1 shows an expanded view), displays the nested page layout elements in the UIX file. It is unique to UIX files.

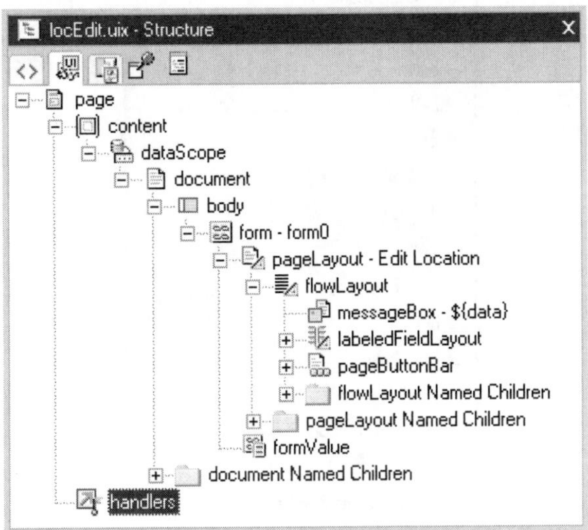

The Design Structure tab allows you to see the possible named children that you can add to the page. It also allows you to use right-click menu options to add elements to user interface nodes. The right-click menu options "insert before," "insert inside," and "insert after" allow you to specify the relative position of the added element inside the hierarchy.

Page Flow Diagram

The Page Flow Diagram represents the struts-config.xml file and acts the same for a UIX application as it does for a JSP application. If you define a data page and double click its icon, the Select or Create Page dialog will appear. If the file name you fill in for this dialog uses a .uix extension, a UIX file will be created with standard UIX page tags. If the file name you fill in uses a .jsp extension, a JSP file will be created.

Property Inspector

The Property Inspector for UIX files looks and works the same way it does for JSP files although, in this release of JDeveloper, you cannot select a tag in the XML Editor and have the properties appear in the Property Inspector as you can in the code editor for JSP files.

Component Palette

The Component Palette for UIX files, shown next, looks and works the same way as the Component Palette for JSP files.

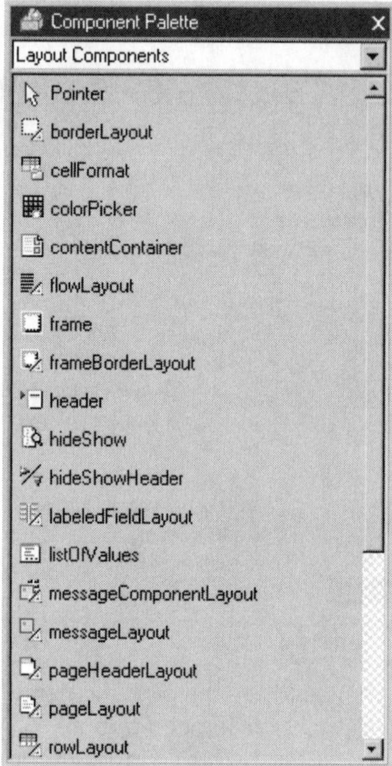

The following pages appear in the Component Palette for a UIX page:

- **All UIX Components**, which lists all available UIX tags.
- **Code Snippets**, which allows you to create a Component Palette element for your own code.
- **Form Components**, which contains elements that will be placed in the HTML form for user input, such as messageDateField, messageLovChoice, and messageTextInput.
- **Include Components**, which allows you to insert content from other UIX or non-UIX pages, for example, include, servletInclude, and urlInclude.
- **Layout Components**, which displays the container components such as borderLayout, flowLayout, header, pageLayout, and stackLayout.
- **Miscellaneous Components**, which includes components that do not fit into other categories, such as colorPalette, icon, and switcher.
- **Navigation Components**, which contains elements used to move to other pages, such as button, globalButtons, and tabBar.

- **Preferred Components**, which contains a list of recommended components for the selected component or named child. For example, you can select the Preferred Components page, click a globalButton element in the visual editor, and the element will be available to this palette page. Then select another Component Palette page and click any other component. When you return to the Preferred Components page, the globalButton item will still be available for use.
- **Simple Components**, which contains text and other basic components, such as formattedText, link, and styledText.
- **Simple Form Components**, which contains basic components used inside the HTML form, such as checkBox, lovChoice, and textInput.
- **Table Components**, which defines HTML tables or their child tags, such as column, sortableHeader, and table.

In addition to the pages just described, other pages will appear for each template that you add to the project. The tab page will be created from the targetNamespace attribute of the templateDefinition tag and the element name will be formed from the localName attribute of the same property.

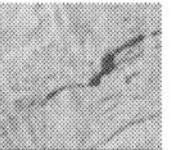

NOTE
More information about these groups of components is available in the JDeveloper help system "Building ADF UIX User Interfaces" topic. Search for those words in the Search tab and sort by Topic Title to find this topic.

Data Control Palette

The Data Control Palette for UIX pages looks the same and works in a similar way as the Data Control Palette for JSP pages. However, the contents of the *Drag and Drop As* pulldown are slightly different because different controls are available in UIX. Table 19-1 lists the elements available. Most of the controls on the collection level have a parallel control in the JSP data control set so descriptions are omitted. The attribute level contains many controls that correspond to UIX tags. Refer to the UIX Reference in the JDeveloper help system for descriptions of these controls.

On the collection level, master collections (such as DepartmentsView1) have different controls from detail collections (such as EmployeesView3, which is linked to DepartmentsView1). Therefore Table 19-1 shows both sets of controls.

Steps for Creating a Struts UIX Application

The following hands-on practice demonstrates how to create a set of working pages that perform basic data manipulation and querying. The following describes the general steps for creating a UIX application in JDeveloper. Many of these steps are the same as the steps used to create JSP applications.

1. Create a business services project containing the data collections required for the pages. For example, the hands-on practice that follows uses an ADF BC project.

2. Run the UIX wizard to create a file either by using a prebuilt template or by specifying the page design areas in the wizard pages. Templates provide the most reusability. Create all pages required for the application in this way. As a shortcut, the following hands-on practice copies the wizard-generated file instead of taking the time to create a reusable template.
3. Create a Struts page flow diagram containing the data actions and data pages linked by forwards. Link the UIX pages to the data pages in the diagram.
4. Drop the high-level data controls (such as Input Form or Search Form) from the Data Control Palette onto each page.
5. From the Component Palette, drop onto the page all required navigation buttons or other interface objects not in the default, high-level component.
6. Connect the navigation and action buttons and links to events and specify the data action or data page that will be called for each event.
7. Adjust properties as required using the Property Inspector.
8. Modify or define the data binding for elements if needed.
9. Test the application by selecting Run from the right-click menu on the startup file in the page flow diagram. As with the JSP runtime in JDeveloper, this starts up the Embedded OC4J Server.
10. Adjust the code and repeat the development steps.

Level	**Control**
Model operations	SubmitButton
Master collection	Read-Only Table, Read-Only Form, Input Form, Input Form (With Navigation), Search Form, Master Detail (Self)
Detail Collection	Read-Only Table, Read-Only Form, Input Form, Input Form (With Navigation), Search Form, Master Detail (Self), Master Detail (Many to Many), Master Detail (Many to One), Master Detail (One to Many), Master Detail (One to One)
Master and detail collection operations	SubmitButton
Attribute (master or detail)	Column, MessageTextInput, MessageStyledText, MessageCheckBox, MessageChoice, MessageRadioSet, MessageList (Select One), MessageList (Select Many), MessageLovInput, Shuttle, TextInput, StyledText, FormattedText, CheckBox, Choice, List, RadioSet, FormValue, LOV Table

TABLE 19-1. *UIX Data Controls*

Hands-on Practice: Build a UIX Application

This practice uses ADF UIX to create an application that provides basic browse, edit, and find operations on the same data objects used in the JSP practice in Chapter 18—Countries and Locations. The resulting application will perform the find and results functions in the Chapter 18 practice as well as the browse and edit functions developed in the Chapter 17 practice.

This practice contains the following phases:

I. Prepare the projects

- Create a UIX ViewController project
- Modify business services properties

II. Create the Browse Page using a wizard

III. Add data and action components to the browse page

IV. Create and link the edit page

V. Create and link the search page

VI. Modify the look-and-feel

As with other practices in this book, this practice uses Struts for the controller layer and ADF business components for the business services layer. This practice uses the LocationQuery workspace and the Model project created in the JSP practice in Chapter 18. If you have not completed the JSP practice in Chapter 18, finish phase I and the phase IV section "Specify Control Hints for the Field Prompts" in that practice before starting. Alternatively, you can download starting files for this practice from the authors' websites mentioned at the beginning of the book.

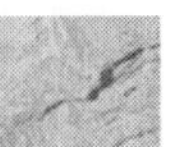

NOTE
*Cookies are enabled by default in most browsers, but if you have disabled cookies in your browser you will need to enable them for this practice. Setting cookie preferences can be accomplished in Internet Explorer by selecting **Tools | Internet Options** and clicking the Advanced button in the Privacy tab.*

I. Prepare the Projects

This phase adds a project for the UIX code and modifies some of the ADF BC properties in the Model project.

Create a UIX ViewController Project

This section creates a project into which you will place the UIX pages. If you were creating an application workspace using the "Web Application [default]" template, this project would already be created. However, you used this ViewController project in the JSP practice, and the UIX files need to be kept in a project separated from the JSP files and their page flow.

1. On the LocationQuery application workspace node, select New Project from the right-click menu.

2. In the New Gallery, select Web Project and click OK. Select Next if the Welcome page appears. Specify the Project Name as "ViewControllerUIX" and click Next. Click Next and click Finish to create the project.
3. You need to change the technology scope to include Struts and ADF UIX. Double click the ViewControllerUIX node to open the Project Properties dialog.
4. Select the Common\Technology Scope node and move ADF UIX and Struts from *Available Technologies* to *Selected Technologies.*
5. Select the Common\Input Paths node and change the *Default Package* field to "locationuix". This will be the main package directory for the files you will create in this project.
6. Click OK. Since you selected the Struts technology, Struts files will be created in the project.

Modify Business Services Properties

This section updates components in the Model project to demonstrate how some ADF BC properties can change the way an application works.

1. Expand the Model\Application Sources\location.model node. Double click the LocationsView node to open the View Object Editor, and navigate to the Attributes\PostalCode node. Click the Control Hints tab and set the *Display Hint* to "Hide."

   Additional Information: This setting specifies that data controls built from this view object will not contain an item for Postal Code. For this application, the Postal Code will be loaded from another process and the user does not need to view this information. You set the control hint on the view object level so that you can build another view object from the same entity object and not hide the Postal Code for that usage.
2. Click OK. You do not want the user to query using the Location Id. Open the Entity Object Editor for Locations and select the Attributes\LocationId node. Uncheck the *Queriable* property and click OK to rewrite the entity object definition.
3. Click Save All.

What Just Happened You added a project for the UIX files and set up its technology scope. You also modified an ADF BC control hint to hide the PostalCode attribute. You also set an entity object property so that LocationId is not queriable.

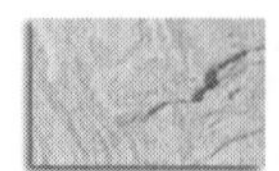

NOTE

As mentioned in Chapter 18, unchecking the "Queriable" property in the Entity Object Editor will disable the "Queriable" property in all view objects built from that entity object.

II. Create the Browse Page Using a Wizard

When you create a UIX application, you can use a wizard to create a page that contains locations for the named child page design areas but no specific components loaded into those areas. You can also use a wizard that creates a page with components in all of the named child locations. This practice uses the latter wizard. This phase runs the Create UIX XML Page Wizard, which requires graphics files for the page header area and for the global buttons. The first four steps copy sample graphics files from a JDeveloper installation directory into the project directories.

1. Select the ViewControllerUIX node. Select **File | Import**. In the Import dialog, select Existing Sources and click OK. Click Next if the Welcome page appears.

2. On the Add Source Files and Directories page, click the Add button. Navigate to the JDEV_HOME\jdev\multi\system\templates\uixwebapp directory. Using CTRL click, select oraclelogo.gif, tools_collage.gif, www_contact.gif, www_help.gif, and www_home.gif. Click Open. The files will be listed and checked.

3. Check the *Copy Files to Project Directory* checkbox and click Browse. Click the public_html directory once and click Select. At the end of the *Copy Files to Project Directory* field, add "\images" (including the backslash).

   Additional Information: This step will place the image files you are adding into a new images directory under the public_html directory, which contains the UIX files. It is customary to place graphics files in a separate directory called "images."

4. Click Finish. The images directory will be created under public_html and the graphics files will be copied into it. The files will also appear in the navigator.

5. On the ViewControllerUIX node, select New from the right-click menu. In the Web Tier\ADF UIX category, select "UIX XML Page with Header, Footer, and Navigation" and click OK. Click Next if the Welcome page appears.

   Additional Information: The Create UIX XML Page Wizard contains a number of pages and fields that you can use to specify the contents of the standard page design areas. Although it takes some time to fill out the fields in the wizard, this process is much faster than hand-coding the XML. If you were basing the page on a template, you could select the "UIX XML Page Based on Existing UIX XML Template (UIT)," which requires less input.

6. Specify the *File* name as "locBrowse.uix" and click Next. Specify the *Title* as "Country Locations" and click Next.

7. On the Corporate Branding page, click Select Image, navigate to the images directory, and select oraclelogo.gif. Click Open. You will see the image appear in the wizard page. In the *URL* field, enter "http://www.oracle.com" (the link behind the graphic file) and click Next.

8. On the Product Branding page, click Select Image, navigate to the images directory, and select tools_collage.gif. Click Open. Click Next.

9. On the Tab Bar page, click Add Tab. Specify the *Tab Text* as "Browse Countries" and the *Tab Destination* as "#" (which specifies the current page).

   Additional Information: The *Tab Destination* defines a link that will be activated when the user clicks the tab. You will set the links later. This application will contain two pages, each of which will be identified by tab text you define on the Tab Bar page.

10. Repeat step 9 and specify *Tab Text* as "Search Locations" (with the same *Tab Destination*). Notice the tab numbers ("0" and "1"), which will be used to identify the tabs.

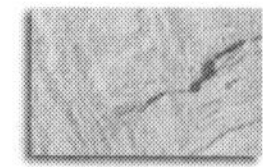

NOTE
Even though you will create three pages—browse, edit, and search—the edit page will only be run from a button on the browse page. Therefore, no tab is required for that page.

11. Enter "0" in the *Selected tab index* field. This field specifies that the Browse Countries tab will be displayed when the application starts. Click Next.
12. On the Page Header page, click Add Page Header and specify the *Page Header Text* as "Countries and Locations". This text will appear at the top of the page. You will not be linking the page header text, so you can leave the *Page Header Destination* empty. Click Next.
13. On the Global Buttons page, click Add Button three times to create three rows. Enter the following details for the global buttons:

Text	Destination URL	Image Location
Home	#	images/www_home.gif
Contact Us	#	images/www_contact.gif
Help	#	images/www_help.gif

Additional Information: Instead of typing the image path and name, you can use the browse ("...") button in the *Image Location* field to find and select the file.

14. Click Next. On the Footer page specify the Copyright message as "Copyright JDeveloper 10g Handbook Reader". Remove the *Privacy message* value. (Later, you can create another page with the privacy statement and link to it using the *Privacy Statement URL*).
15. Click Next and Finish to create the page and open it in the visual editor. You will see something like the layout shown in Figure 19-3. Identify the elements and the contents based upon the entries you made in the wizard.

    Additional Information: Notice that the graphics files for the global buttons in the top right corner are displayed inside circles. This is an example of the way that UIX dynamically generates image files. The tab graphics are another example of dynamic image generation.
16. Click Save All.

What Just Happened? You used a wizard to create a UIX page containing named child areas that contain components. Although this wizard takes a bit of time to complete, the result is a page that contains useful objects in all design areas. You can use this file as a starting point for other pages you need to create in this project.

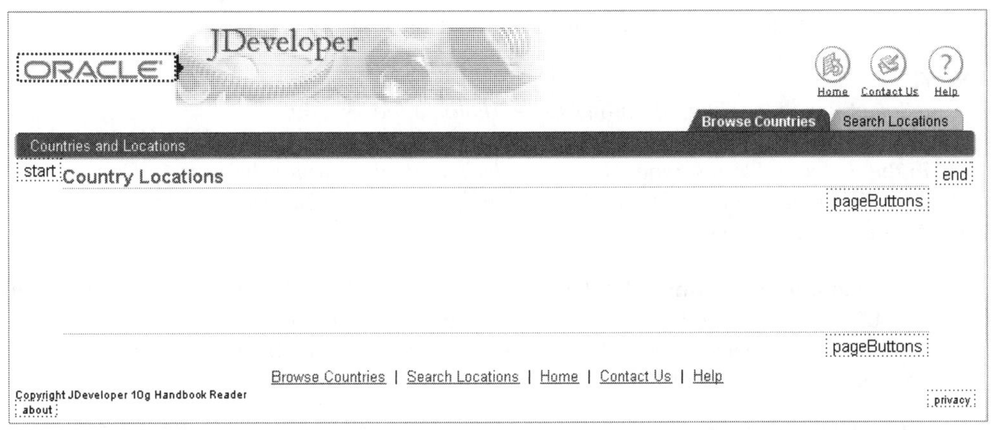

FIGURE 19-3. *Empty UIX page created by the wizard*

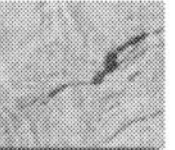

NOTE
To minimize the number of steps, this practice does not complete some of the default components such as the global buttons (and footer) links that would navigate to another web page. These navigation links could be added later.

III. Add Data and Action Components to the Browse Page

This phase copies the UIX file you just created so you will have a starting point for the other files you need in this practice. This saves you from the process of filling out the same fields in the UIX wizard and will ensure that the same layout can be used in all three pages in this application. After copying the files, you will add data elements to the page and define the page flow diagram.

1. On the locBrowse.uix node in the navigator, select **File | Save As**. In the Save As dialog, specify the name as "locEdit.uix" and click Save. The locEdit.uix file will appear in the navigator.

2. Repeat step 1 and name the new file "locSearch.uix". Repeat again for the file name "UIX_backup.uix". (This file will be used as a backup in case you need to delete a file and start again from the wizard-generated file.)

3. Double-click struts-config.xml in the navigator and add a Data Page from the Component Palette. Change the name (path name) to "locBrowse".

   Additional Information: In the JSP application practice, you created data pages before creating the files. This practice creates the files from a wizard and then links them to data pages in the Page Flow Diagram. You can use either method for JSP and UIX pages but JSP pages do not offer wizards to create the files.

4. Double click the icon and, in the Select or Create Page dialog, select "locBrowse.uix" from the pulldown. Click OK to display the visual editor for this page.

NOTE
If the Select Page Flow Data Binding Option dialog appears, you probably created a Page instead of a Data Page on the diagram. Click OK in the dialog without saving, close the editor, and click No for the file save dialog that appears. Delete the page in the Page Flow Diagram and try steps 3 and 4 again.

Additional Information: The data page icon on the Page Flow Diagram now represents the UIX file. Click the Preview tab in the editor. You will see a representation of the runtime for the page without data elements (which have not been added) and without layout markings such as layout area borders. Click the Design tab.

5. Be sure you have the Design tab open. In the Data Control Palette, expand the LocationsModuleDataControl\CountriesView1 node and select the LocationsView2 node (the detail of the CountriesView1 master). Select "Master-Detail (Many to Many)" in the *Drag and Drop As* pulldown and drag the data control and drop it in the center of the layout area.

Additional Information: This will display both master and detail data areas with labels and navigation buttons as shown next.

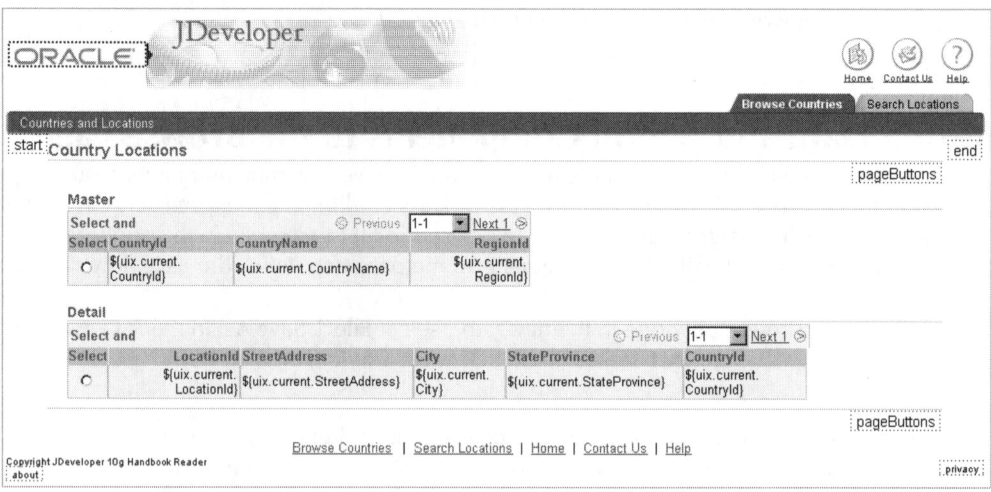

The UIX data controls for master-detail pages are not available in the same way for JSP pages. For a JSP version of this one control, you would need to drop in controls for the master collection, the detail collection, navigation buttons, and navigation pulldowns; then you would need to add the style sheet and labels. The UIX data controls contain a number of options for master-detail layouts: Many to Many, Many to One, One to Many, and One to One. The names indicate how many records are shown for the master and detail respectively. For example, "Many to Many" indicates that many master records will be displayed and many detail records will be displayed; "One to Many" indicates that one master record will be displayed for many detail records. This example uses the "Many to Many" option, which allows faster scrolling through master records.

6. Select the master area by clicking the word "Master." The entire master area will be surrounded by a selection box. A vertical bar with an arrow will appear, and the Property Inspector title bar will show "header - Master - Property Inspector." Change the *text* property to "Countries" and press ENTER. Change the detail *text* property to "Locations" in the same way. The visual editor will show the changes.

   Additional Information: Remember that when you are editing a UIX page, you do not type text into the visual editor; all text in a UIX file is entered in properties.

7. The column CountryId repeats the information in the master record and is not required. Select the CountryId column heading in the Locations area so that a selection box surrounds the heading and field. (You may need to CTRL-click the field to cause the selection box to appear on both header and field.) Press DELETE to remove this column.

8. Click Save All. Return to the Page Flow Diagram, and on the locBrowse icon, select Run from the right-click menu. The page will load into your browser.

9. Select different country records using the Select radio group in the Countries area.

   Additional Information: The detail records are synchronized with the master records as they are in the Business Component Browser because the Model project contains a view link between the view object definitions. Also, notice that the PostalCode column is not displayed because you set the control hint *Display Hint* to "Hide."

10. Click the "Next 10" link at the top of the Countries area. If you watch carefully, you will notice that the page does not refresh—only the record data changes.

    Additional Information: This step demonstrates the partial page rendering (PPR) feature that redisplays only part of the page. Also notice that the "Next 10" link changed to "Next 5" because only five records remain in the collection. Click the ">" link. This performs the same action as the "Next 5" link. Notice that you still see ten records, even though you clicked "Last 5" because the range size of this control is ten records (in this case, the last five from the previous set plus the last five in the collection).

11. Select the US country record. Click the heading for the State or Province column in Locations. You will see a sort indicator appear in the column heading that indicates you have sorted the records by that column in ascending order. PPR is active when you sort records, too, so you do not see the page refresh.

12. Click the State or Province column heading again and you will see the records reordered and the arrow reversed, indicating descending order.

13. Close the browser. Examine the locBrowse.uix code in the Code Editor (Source tab). You will see a number of tags with familiar names such as pageHeader, globalButton, copyright, corporateBranding, and productBranding (values you filled in using the wizard). The Structure window's XML Structure tab contains a summary of the tags in this file.

What Just Happened? You added data-aware components to the empty page and refined the page by setting properties and deleting an attribute. You also tested the application and looked at the functionality supplied by UIX. In short order, you have created a fully-functional, nearly production-ready browse page with a useable look-and-feel. Features such as the navigation =links and partial page rendering make the page easier and faster to use. Controls such as the UIX master-detail component make UIX useable for simple prototyping and limited rapid application development (RAD).

IV. Create and Link the Edit Page

Now that the browse page is available, you can create an edit page for modifying location records. This phase starts with the copy of the wizard-created page and adds components to it for the edit functionality.

1. In the Page Flow Diagram, add a data page to the right of the locBrowse. Change its path name to "locEdit." Double click the icon and specify the file name as locEdit.uix. Click OK to open the visual editor for this page.

   Additional Information: You created this file as a copy of the wizard-generated page. The file contains the page design areas but no data elements.

2. Click the middle of the page. The Property Inspector title bar should indicate that you have selected the pageLayout element. Change the *title* property to "Edit Location" and press ENTER.

3. Click a tab (such as Browse Countries) in the tab bar. The Structure window will open the nodes to the selected tab (under the tabBar node). Select the tabBar node if it is not already selected. This node represents the container for the tabs.

4. In the Property Inspector, change the *selectedIndex* property to "1". Press ENTER and notice that the second tab (with an index of 1) is selected (highlighted). Change the property back to "0" and press ENTER. The first tab will show as active in the editor. The edit page will only be accessible from the browse page, so it shares the same tab.

5. In the Data Control Palette, select the LocationsModuleDataControl\CountriesView1\LocationsView2 node and select "Input Form" in the *Drag and Drop As* pulldown. Drop the data control into the center of the page. A number of controls and prompts will appear.

   Additional Information: A row ID must be passed to this page so that it can display the correct row in the edit fields. Therefore, the technique used in this practice passes the current row ID (for the selected record) from the browse page. This technique will be implemented with a button in the Locations area of the browse page.

6. Click Save All.

7. Return to the Page Flow Diagram. Draw a Forward from locBrowse to locEdit and name the link "editLink". The Page Flow Diagram should look like the following illustration:

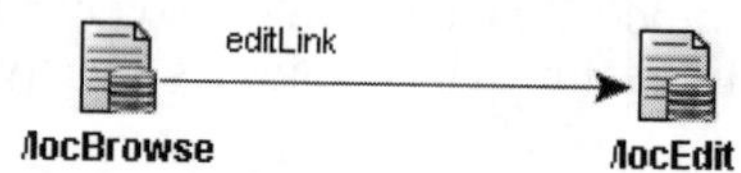

8. Open the visual editor for locBrowse.uix. In the Form Components page of the Component Palette, drag a submitButton and drop it onto the *Select* radio button in the *Locations* data area. The button will appear next to the words "Select and" under the Locations heading.

9. Change the *text* property of this button to "Edit" and the *event* property to "editLink" (the name of the forward).

   Additional Information: If you match the *event* property to the forward path name, you do not need to define events or event handlers.

10. Click Save All. Return to the Page Flow Diagram and run locEdit. You will see no data or fields because no row ID is passed to the page, but the prompts will be displayed. The first tab is active because the selectedIndex was set to "0" for this page. The Postal Code is hidden because you set the control hint.

11. Close the browser. Run locBrowse from the Page Flow Diagram. Select Canada as the country. Select one of the locations and click Edit.

    Additional Information: The edit page will appear with all values loaded from the record as shown next. Notice that the ID and City prompts are prefixed with an asterisk indicating the entity attribute property *Mandatory* is checked and the user must enter a value in that field. This is a feature of the UIX control.

12. Close the browser. Next you will add a link from the edit page back to the browse page.

13. In the Page Flow Diagram, draw a Forward from locEdit to locBrowse and name it "updateBack". This defines the page flow to the browse page. You now need to define the action from the button.

14. Open the edit page in the visual editor. In the Data Control Palette, select LocationsModuleDataControl\Commit and drag it as a SubmitButton to the visual editor. Drop it to the right of the Submit button.

15. Select the Commit button.

    Additional Information: This button contains a `Commit` operation but does not go forward to any page. You need to define a forward for the controller.

16. In the Property Inspector, set the *text* property to "Update". Set the *event* property to "action" if it is not set that way. Select "false" for the *disabled* property.

NOTE
If you have problems setting the "disabled" property to "false," select "true" first, then select "false."

Additional Information: This is the default event for the `Commit` operation. You now need to insert an action after the `Commit` operation to move back to the browse page.

17. With the Update button selected, in the Design Structure page of the Structure window, expand the "handlers\event - action" node. On the "invoke - doIt" subnode, select Insert after invoke -doIt | UIX Servlet | go from the right-click menu.

18. The Insert go dialog will appear. Select "updateBack" in the *name* pulldown and click OK. An event step ("go - updateBack") will appear under the event handler node as shown here:

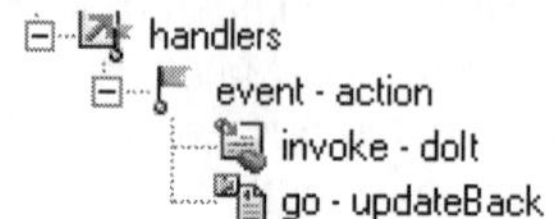

19. Select the Submit button and press DELETE to remove the button

20. Click Save All. Run locBrowse page from the Page Flow Diagram.

21. Select China in the *Countries* area and click Edit in the *Locations* area to load the edit page. Add several characters to the end of the city name and click Update.

    Additional Information: The change will be committed and the browse page will reload. Notice that the change you made in the edit page is now visible in the browse page.

22. You can confirm that the new value is in the database. Leave the browser open and, in JDeveloper's Connection Navigator (the Connections tab in the navigator area), double click LOCATIONS under the Database\HR\HR\Tables node. The Table Viewer will appear for the LOCATIONS table.

23. Click the Data tab and look for the country "CN" record. The city value will show the change you made. If you want to return the database to its initial state, return to the browser, edit the same record, remove the characters, and click Update. In the JDeveloper Table Viewer, click the Refresh button to view the change.

24. Close the browser.

What Just Happened? You added data controls for a locations edit page. You also added a button to call the edit page. Setting the event for the button to the name of the Struts forward defined the page flow sufficiently that the edit page was loaded with the selected record. You also defined a buttonand an event handler for the page flow back to the browse page.

V. Create and Link the Search Page

This phase completes the basic pages for the application by adding a page containing a UIX search component. This component has the ability to perform searches using OR logic as well as AND logic.

1. In the Page Flow Diagram, add a data page and name the path "locSearch". Double click the locSearch icon and specify the file name as "locSearch.uix". Click OK to open the page that was copied earlier from the wizard output.

2. Change the *title* property of the pageLayout to "Search Locations". As before, you can click the middle of the layout to select the pageLayout.

3. Select a tab in the tab bar. The Structure window will open the nodes to the selected tab. Select the tabBar node if it is not already selected. In the Property Inspector, change the *selectedIndex* property to "1" so that the second tab will be active. Press ENTER. The second tab will display as active.
4. In the locSearch visual editor, drag LocationsView1 (the non-linked version of the Locations view object) into the center of the layout as a "Search Form." The page will look similar to the example in Figure 19-4.
5. This page needs to start in Find mode so that the user can enter query criteria immediately. Click the UI Model tab in the Structure window.
6. Select the locSearchUIModel node (the page-level binding node) and set the *Find Mode* property to "True" (the property value may display as "true"). Press ENTER. This will initialize the page in Find mode.
7. On the Page Flow Diagram, run locSearch.
8. Enter a Country ID of "US" and State or Province of "W%". Click Submit. The values will be added to the Search Criteria row above the query.
9. Click Create to create another criteria conditions row. Enter a CountryId of "JP" and City of "T%". Click Submit. The Search Criteria area will appear as follows:

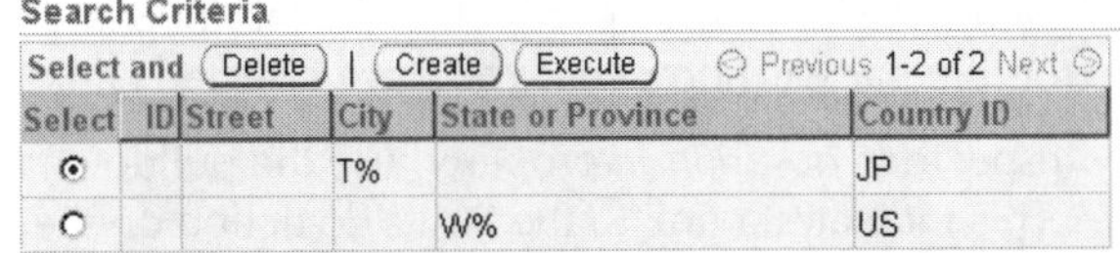

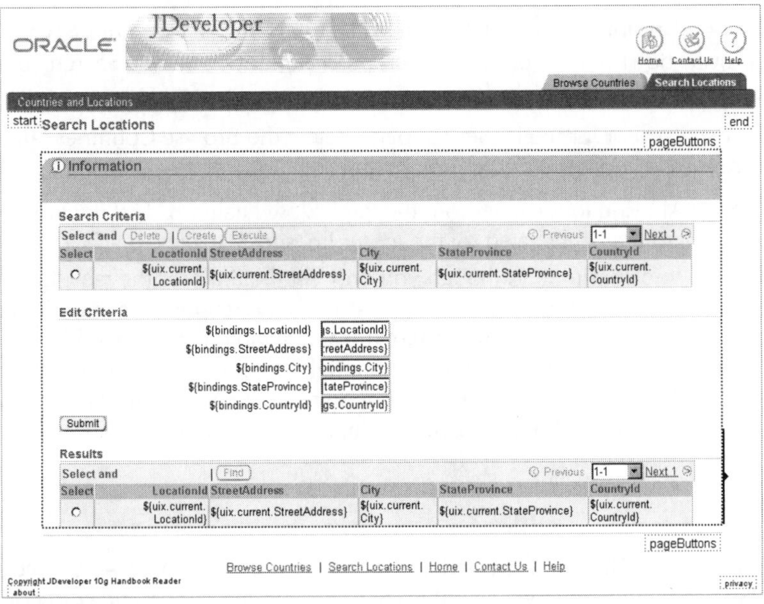

FIGURE 19-4. *Search control for locations*

Additional Information: Values within each row of the criteria will be joined with an AND operator. Rows will be joined with an OR operator. In this example, the following WHERE clause would be used for this query:

```
WHERE (city LIKE 'T%' AND country_id = 'JP')
OR    (state_province LIKE 'W%' AND country_id = 'US')
```

Notice that the ID field is queriable although you set the view attribute property to non-queriable. The control does not read the *Queriable* property (as of the 9.0.5.2 release). Not all tag libraries implement all control hints.

10. Hold the mouse over the ID field and you should see a tooltip that you defined for this attribute in the JSP exercise in Chapter 18.

11. Click Execute to execute the query based on the two Search Criteria rows. The results will appear in a Results page.

12. Close the browser.

    Additional Information: Now all that is left is to set up a method to navigate between the browse and search pages. The tab controls at the top-right side of the page are set up to perform this kind of navigation. This is a familiar, user-friendly way for the user to perform page navigation between application functions.

13. In the visual editor for the locBrowse page, click the tab for Search Locations. The Property Inspector title bar will show that you have selected "link - Search Locations."

14. In the Property Inspector's *destination* property, use the pulldown to select "locSearch.do." This indicates a link to the Struts do action on the search data page. The Browse Countries tab already contains a link to the current page ("#"), so no modification is needed for that tab.

15. In the visual editor for the locEdit page, select the Browse Countries tab and select "locBrowse.do" from the *destination* property pulldown. Set the Search Locations tab destination to "locSearch.do."

16. In the visual editor for the locSearch page, select the Browse Countries tab and select "locBrowse.do" from the *destination* property pulldown.

17. Click Save All. Run locBrowse from the Page Flow Diagram. Test the tab navigation between the three pages. Also try the footer links for the same pages.

    Additional Information: Although you only set the links for the tabs, the footer links also work from the same definition. Tab controls are rendered as graphics that include fonts and colors. When you click a tab, the active tab changes to a darker color (blue in this case) and the inactive tab changes to a lighter color (grey-green in this case). UIX automatically generates graphics based upon text property settings in the XML file. You do not need to worry about creating, linking, sizing, and maintaining separate graphics files for these text graphics.

18. Close the browser.

What Just Happened? This phase created a search page and results page—the same functionality as the entire JSP hands-on practice in Chapter 18. However, the JSP practice did not contain the feature of being able to enter multiple criteria sets that would be combined with OR operators in the WHERE clause for the query. This type of page is much easier to generate using the native UIX components than with JSP tags. You also set up navigation for the tabs.

VI. Modify the Look-And-Feel

This phase demonstrates how to change the look-and-feel (fonts, colors, decoration images, and design) using a single property on the project level. This is another strength of UIX that allows it to be displayed on different platforms such as desktops and PDAs. Two look-and-feel options are distributed with JDeveloper—BLAF (Oracle Browser Look and Feel) and minimal.

1. Open the visual editor for the locBrowse.uix file. Keeping a page visible will allow you to see the changes to the look-and-feel immediately.
2. Select (do not open) uix-config.xml in the navigator (in the ViewControllerUIX\ Web Content\WEB-INF folder). In the Structure window, expand the configurations\ default-configuration node.

   Additional Information: The *uix-config.xml* file, deployed into the WEB-INF directory, defines information about global properties for the application, default properties that can be overridden, and specific overrides to the defaults. The look-and-feel property modified in this phase is an example of a default property.
3. Double click the look-and-feel folder node to open the "look-and-feel Properties" dialog shown here:

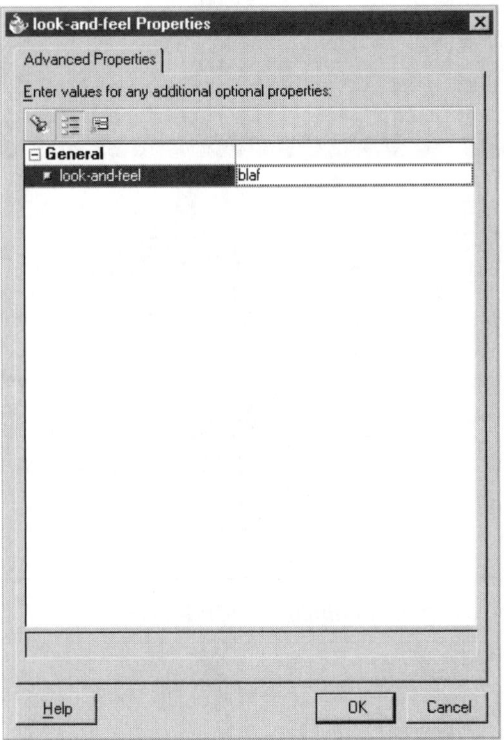

4. Change the value to "minimal" and click OK. You will see the visual editor update to the new look-and-feel as shown in Figure 19-5.

What Just Happened? You changed the look-and-feel of the application. You can define your own look-and-feel templates as described in the help topic "About UIX Look and Feels." In addition, a How-To on OTN ("How To create a Look and Feel for ADF UIX") provides an example of developing a custom look-and-feel.

Additional actions you would need to work into this application to make it production-ready follow:

- **Create and Insert functionality** for Location records.
- **Commit and Rollback actions** so changes other than location edits can be saved to the database or reverted.
- **Links for the global buttons**
- **Reducing the number of rows displayed** in the countries list on the browse page. This is accomplished the same way as with a JSP page: using the *Range Size* property after selecting CountriesView1Iterator in the UI Model tab in the Structure window for that page.

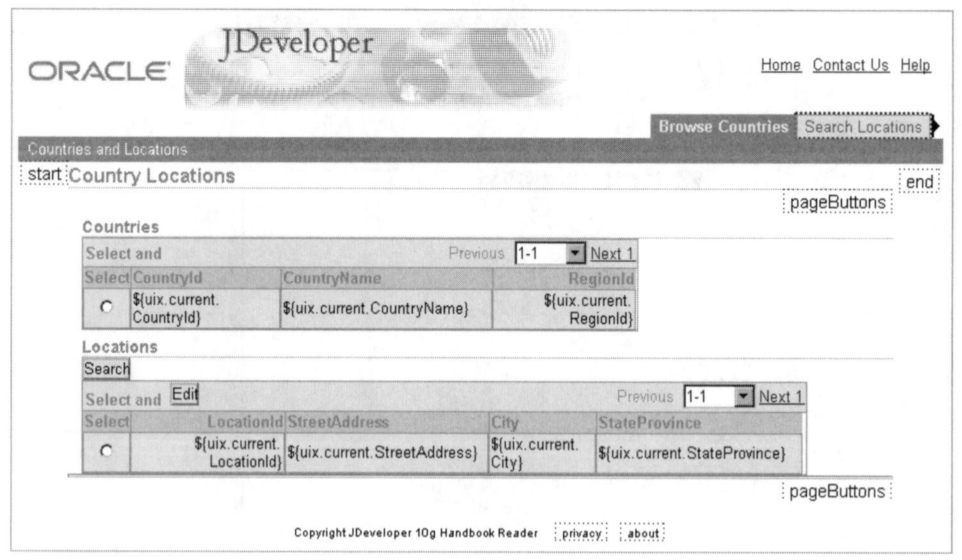

FIGURE 19-5. *UIX page using the minimal look-and-feel*

PART IV

Appendixes

APPENDIX A

Other Resources

I cannot say that I am in the slightest degree impressed by your bigness, or your material resources, as such.

—Thomas Henry Huxley (1825–1895)

Using JDeveloper effectively requires many resources beyond those available from Oracle and this book. While the following is by no means a comprehensive list, the authors have found these resources to be helpful when working in the JDeveloper environment. Many of these resources are mentioned in context throughout the book.

The best advice is to do both of the following:

- **Build a Java- and J2EE-related library** You should not scrimp on the book budget in this area. Collect a library of Java and J2EE reference books. Since each book focuses on different subjects and explains techniques in a different way, you will need at least three books for each of the major subjects.
- **Use the Internet** There are now many useful websites, and more spring up all the time. Use your favorite search engine to find them. Be sure to take advantage of the tutorials on the Java website (java.sun.com).

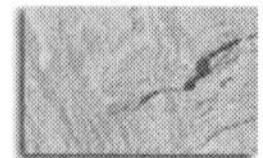

CAUTION
Always be skeptical of what you read. Many white papers from scholarly sources are out of date or inaccurate. This is particularly true of information on the Internet, where anyone can publish information on a website.

Books

The following books are useful references when working with JDeveloper:

- *Building Application Frameworks: Object-Oriented Foundations of Application Design.* Edited by Mohamed E. Fayad, Douglas C. Schmidt, and Ralph E. Johnson. Wiley, 1999.
- *Building Oracle XML Applications.* Steve Muench. O'Reilly, 2000.
- *Core J2EE Patterns: Best Practices and Design Strategies, Second Edition.* Deepak Alur, John Crupi, and Dan Malks. Prentice Hall PTR, 2003.
- *Domain-Specific Frameworks: Frameworks Experience by Industry.* Edited by Mohamed E. Fayad and Ralph E. Johnson. Wiley, 1999.
- *Enterprise JavaBeans, Fourth Edition.* Richard Monson-Haefel, Bill Burke, and Sasha Labourey. O'Reilly and Associates, 2004.
- *Expert One-on-One J2EE Design and Development.* Rod Johnson. Wrox, 2002.

- *Implementing Application Frameworks: Object-Oriented Frameworks at Work.* Edited by Mohamed E. Fayad, Douglas C. Schmidt, and Ralph E. Johnson. Wiley, 1999.
- *The Java Class Libraries – Volumes 1, and 2,* Patrick Chan and Rosanna Lee. Addison-Wesley, 1999, 1998.
- *Java 2: The Complete Reference, Fifth Edition.* Herbert Schildt. McGraw-Hill/Osborne, 2002.
- *The Java Tutorial: A Short Course on the Basics, Third Edition.* Mary Campione and Kathy Walrath. Addison-Wesley, 2000.
- *The Java Tutorial Continued.* Mary Campione, Kathy Walrath, Alison Huml, et al. Addison-Wesley, 1998.
- *The JFC Swing Tutorial: A Guide to Constructing GUIs (Second Edition).* Kathy Walrath, Mary Campione, et al. Addison-Wesley, 2004.
- *Oracle8 Design Using UML Object Modeling.* Dr. Paul Dorsey and Joseph Hudicka. Oracle Press, 1998.
- *Oracle9iAS: Building J2EE Applications.* Nirva Morrisseau-Leroy. Oracle Press, 2002.
- *Oracle9*i *Application Server Portal Handbook.* Steve Vandivier and Kelly Cox. Oracle Press, 2001.
- *Oracle9*i *JDBC Programming.* Jason Price. Oracle Press, 2002.
- *Oracle9*i *JDeveloper Handbook.* Peter Koletzke, Dr. Paul Dorsey, and Dr. Avrom Faderman. Oracle Press, 2002.
- *Oracle9*i *XML Handbook,* Ben Chang, Mark Scardina, and Stefan Kiritzov. Oracle Press, 2001.
- *Oracle9*i *Web Development.* Bradley D. Brown. Oracle Press, 2001.
- *Oracle JDeveloper 10*g*: Empowering J2EE Development.* Harshad Oak. APress, 2004.
- *Programming Jakarta Struts, Second Edition.* Chuck Cavaness. O'Reilly, 2004.
- *Refactoring: Improving the Design of Existing Code.* Martin Fowler et al. Addison-Wesley, 1999.
- *Struts Kick Start.* James Turner and Kevin Bedell. Sams, 2002.
- *Thinking in Java, Third Edition.* Bruce Eckel. Prentice Hall PPR, 2002.

Websites

Free online resources are readily available for various J2EE development subjects. Table A-1 contains a summary of many of the websites listed throughout this book.

URL	Website Description
devedge.netscape.com/central/javascript	Netscape JavaScript developer's website.
Dmoz.org	Website of The Open Directory Project. The Open Directory Project is the largest, most comprehensive human-edited directory of the Web. It is constructed and maintained by a vast global community of volunteer editors.
dynapi.sourceforge.net	Open source product DynAPI, cross-browser JavaScript libraries.
jakarta.apache.org	Apache Jakarta Project website for open source Java solutions such as JSTL, Tomcat, Apache HTTP Server, and Struts.
java.sun.com	Sun Microsystems website for Java and JSP, JSTL, and EL tags.
java.sun.com/developer/Books/javaprogramming/MasteringJava/Ch17/	Sun website page that discusses Java collections including advice about Vectors.
java.sun.com/developer/onlineTraining/index.html	Sun website page containing a list of tutorials, for example, Java, J2EE, and web services.
java.sun.com/products/jfc/tsc/articles/architecture/	Sun website discussion about Swing architecture including how MVC is implemented.
java.sun.com/docs/books/jls/second_edition/html/conversions.doc.html	Sun website page from the Java Language Specification explaining type conversions.
java.sun.com/docs/books/tutorial	Sun website location for the *Java Tutorial,* which provides an introduction to the language. It is the online version of the book listed earlier and is downloadable so that you can run it without being connected to the Internet.
java.sun.com/docs/books/tutorial/uiswing/layout/visual.html	Visual Guide to Layout Managers, a page from the Java Tutorial describing and showing Swing layout managers.
developers.sun.com/events/techdays/codecamps/index.html	Sun website containing a list of *code camps*—slides, demo code, and lab manuals.
Java.sun.com/blueprints/patterns/MVC-detailed.html	Sun website page describing the MVC design pattern.
java.sun.com/features/1998/05/birthday.html	Information about the release announcement of the Java language.
java.sun.com/j2ee/ java.sun.com/j2se/ java.sun.com/j2me/	Sun website information about Java 2 Platform, Enterprise Edition; Java 2 Platform, Standard Edition; and Java 2 Platform, Micro Edition, respectively.

TABLE A-1. *Useful Websites for J2EE Work in JDeveloper 10g*

URL	Website Description
java.sun.com/j2ee/1.4/docs/tutorial/doc/index.html	Sun website for a J2EE 1.4 tutorial including JSP technology and JSTL.
java.sun.com/j2ee/javaserverfaces/	Sun website for information about JavaServer Faces technology.
java.sun.com/jsp/	Sun website information about JavaServer Pages.
java.sun.com/jstl	Sun website with information about JSTL.
java.sun.com/products/javawebstart/	Sun website information about and downloads of Java Web Start.
java.sun.com/products/plugin/	Sun website information about and downloads of plugins for browser Swing class support.
java.sun.com/products/jlf/ed1/dg/higm.htm	Sun website information about menus and toolbars in Java applications and applets.
java.sun.com/reference/codesamples/index.html	Sun website page containing a list of code samples and applications.
otn.oracle.com	Oracle Technology Network, which includes white papers, how-tos, sample code, and documentation that serve as valuable reference material.
otn.oracle.com/products/ias/toplink	TopLink home page on the Oracle Technology Network
otn.oracle.com/products/jdev	JDeveloper home page on the Oracle Technology Network.
struts.apache.org	The Apache Software Foundation website page describing the Struts project.
www.bradsoft.com	TopStyle CSS editor.
www.cvshome.com	Source of Concurrent Versions System (CVS), an open source version control solution available for Unix and Linux.
www.cvsnt.org	Official home of CVSNT, a version of CVS for Windows platforms. CVSNT is an open source product.
www.google.com/apis	Website for Google Web APIs for creating a developer's account and obtaining a license key.
www.ioug.org	Website of the International Oracle Users Group, which contains discussion forums and a technical repository of tips and white papers from users of Oracle technology.
www.jcp.org	Website of the Java Community Process with the goal of developing and revising the Java technology specifications, reference implementations, and test suites.

TABLE A-1. *Useful Websites for J2EE Work in JDeveloper 10*g (continued)

URL	Website Description
www.odtug.com	Website for the Oracle Development Tools User Group, which focuses on Oracle development tools. The website contains a page to sign up for electronic mailing lists as well as presentations and white papers from conferences.
www.omg.org	Website for the Object Management Group, which developed and provides specifications for UML and other object-oriented technologies.
www.opensource.org	The website for Open Source Initiative, which promotes the concept of free access to source code, no-cost licenses, and the ability for others to extend products that are built upon open source concepts.
www.quest.com	Commercial website featuring products to support the Oracle database development environment such as TOAD.
www.rational.com	Contains a full discussion of UML and all of its diagrams; see the UML documentation on the Rational website.
www.sitepoint.com/print/xml-dtds-xml-schema	An article explaining the differences between XML DTDs and XML schemas.
www.sys-con.com/java/	Java Developer's Journal website, which contains numerous archived articles from past issues of the printed version of this popular journal.
www.theserverside.com	A news source and developer community centered on J2EE and middleware issues.
www.uddi.org	This website contains information about the standards of the Universal Description, Discovery, and Integration (UDDI) protocol.
www.w3c.org	The website for the World Wide Web Consortium (W3C), which developed and maintains standards for, among others, HTML and Cascading Style Sheets.
www.w3c.org/TR/SOAP	Provides information about the Simple Object Access Protocol (SOAP).
www.ws-i.org	The website for the Web Services-Interoperability Organization (WS-I) formed by Oracle and other industry leaders to promote the interoperability of web services technologies across a variety of platforms, operating systems, and programming languages.

TABLE A-1. *Useful Websites for J2EE Work in JDeveloper 10*g (continued)

Many websites offer information about building computer applications with Java and other technologies. Use your favorite web search engine to gain access to these websites.

APPENDIX B

Java Client User Interface Components

Good design keeps the user happy, the manufacturer in the black and the aesthete unoffended.

—Raymond Loewy,
Time Magazine, October 31, 1949

This appendix provides some details about the components available in the JDeveloper Component Palette that you can use in your Java client programs. Dozens of visual components are available, providing much more flexibility than the 25 or so components in Oracle Forms Developer. Beyond the dizzying array of components, each Java component has much greater flexibility than its correlate in Oracle Forms Developer or similar products. Each component also has many methods and supports many different listeners and events used to trigger other program behavior.

This appendix lists and briefly describes the Java client components that are included by default in JDeveloper so that you can get a sense of the wide range of functionality that they offer. (You can also add components from other libraries to the Component Palette.) When you decide to use one of these components, you can obtain more information from the JDeveloper online help system. In addition, Chapters 15 and 16 contains details about using JDeveloper to create Java client applications that use these components.

AWT

The components on the AWT (Abstract Windowing Toolkit) page of the Component Palette shown in Figure B-1 are JavaBeans distributed as part of the Java SDK from Sun Microsystems. Currently, developers prefer Swing over AWT for new applications. One of the reasons not to use AWT components is that they are heavyweight components that require the developer to handle issues when combining them with Swing components. Further, AWT components are less flexible than their Swing counterparts. Therefore, it is recommended that you use Swing components instead to help ensure better consistency across platforms.

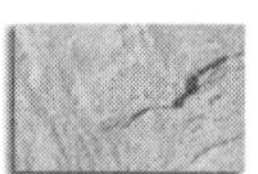

NOTE
You can choose to hide the component names by selecting Icon View from the right-click menu on the Component Palette.

Table B-1 lists the default components on the AWT Component Palette page and a brief description of each (except for the Pointer icon that appears in all pages).

For more details about the AWT components available in JDeveloper, see the help topic "About AWT JavaBeans" by entering "About AWT JavaBeans" in the Full Text Search tab.

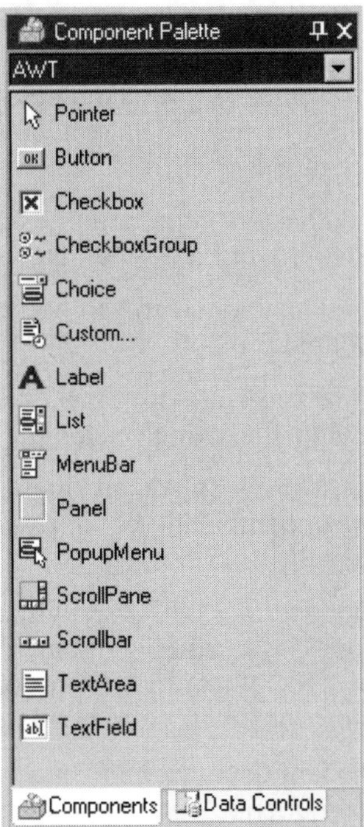

FIGURE B-1. *AWT Page of the Component Palette*

Component	**Description**
`Button`	A standard pushbutton that you can label with text or an icon or both.
`Checkbox`	A box that toggles between checked and unchecked. The value changes from "true" to "false" when a checkbox is unchecked. You can set the *icon* property to use a graphic other than the check mark.
`CheckboxGroup`	This component does not have a visual representation. It is a container for `Checkbox` components.

TABLE B-1. *AWT Components*

Component	Description
`Choice`	A pulldown list that presents multiple values for the user to select from. You can allow the user to enter a value by setting the *editable* property to "True."
`Custom`	You can add custom components using this selection. Depending upon the context, this will access the Class Browser, Package Browser, or both.
`Label`	This is a text label to which you can also attach an icon. Normally, you use this for field prompts.
`List`	A control that presents a list of text strings. The AWT control supplies a scrollbar, while the Swing version (JList) does not.
`MenuBar`	A component to which you add menus and menu items. The menu bar appears under the title bar of a window and offers a pulldown menu system.
`Panel`	This component does not have a visual representation, although you can set properties to visually display the border. This is a panel into which you place other objects. This control is responsible for layout manager functionality (as described in Chapter 16).
`PopupMenu`	This component defines a menu that appears when the user right clicks a component.
`ScrollPane`	This pane allows you to define horizontal and vertical scrollbars. The user moves the scrollbars to access objects in the pane that are outside the pane's borders.
`Scrollbar`	A vertical or horizontal bar with a button that moves the display or manipulates a value.
`TextArea`	A text editing area that shows text strings ending in newline characters. This control has no scrollbar, but you can place it in a `JScrollPane` container if the user will need to scroll.
`TextField`	A single-row text editing area. Some of the hands-on practices in this book use the Swing version of this control (JTextField).

TABLE B-1. *AWT Components* (continued)

Code Snippets

You can create a reusable *code snippet* (a small amount of code that you may want to use over and over in your projects), and store it on the Code Snippets Component Palette.

Although Code Snippets is one of the Component Palette pages, most code snippets are non-visual, and you cannot add them in the Java Visual Editor. You must use the Code Editor. Clicking a snippet inserts text in the Code Editor.

As an example, the snippet shown next in the Add Code Snippet dialog could be reused to set the column widths on forms that include a Departments view object. You can do this by right clicking anywhere on the Code Snippets Component Palette and selecting Add Component. Another way to add components and snippets is using the Configure Component Palette dialog. This dialog is accessed by selecting **Tools | Configure Palette** from the menu. You then enter the name and code for your snippet in the Add Code Snippet dialog as shown here:

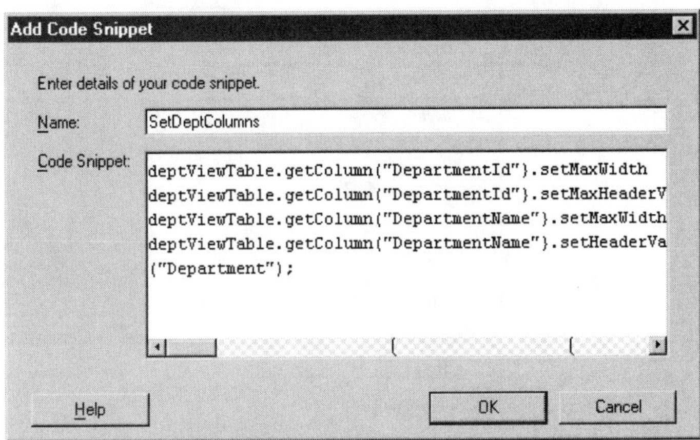

The Code Snippets page of the Component Palette is shown here with the added SetDeptColumns snippet:

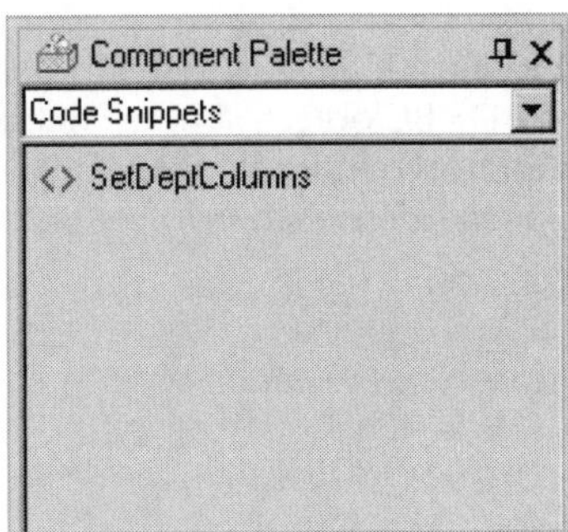

NOTE
The Code Templates feature described in Chapter 2 also allows you to add code blocks easily by typing in an abbreviation such as "sop" and pressing CTRL-ENTER.

JClient Controls

JDeveloper includes a set of controls to supplement the standard Swing components, as shown next:

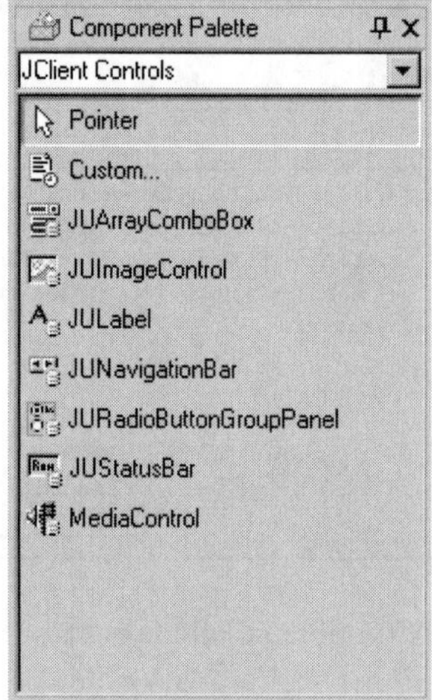

These controls implement the JClient facility discussed in Chapter 15 and allow normal Swing components to be bound to ADF BC objects. These controls are accessible in the Java Visual Editor by selecting JClient Controls on the Component Palette pulldown.

You can select from the components described in Table B-2.

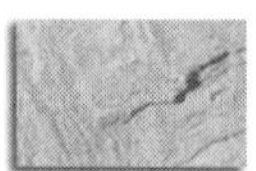

NOTE
interMedia support in JDeveloper 10g is included only for backward compatibility.

More information about the functionality of each of these components can be found by searching for "JClient controls" in the help system Full Text Search tab and examining the topic "About JClient-Specific Controls."

Component	Description
`Custom`	You can add any component using this selection. This is useful for components not included on a Component Palette page. Depending upon the context, this will access the Class Browser, Package Browser, or both.
`JUArrayComboBox`	This control can be bound to an array-type business service. The ADF attribute binding uses the data collection attribute to access the data. This control is limited to numbers, strings, or date values.
`JUImageControl`	This is a display control that can be bound to business service collection attributes to support BLOB datatypes and interMedia.
`JULabel`	This field, similar to `JLabel`, binds to a business service collection attribute to retrieve data and display the attribute value as a label.
`JUNavigationBar`	A toolbar with database-related actions such as commit. This can be bound to a view object usage, to control items in the same panel, or to a `JUPanel` to control items in child panels.
`JURadioButtonGroupPanel`	This panel can be used with an LOV to show attribute values when a selection made by the user causes the LOV binding to update the attribute value. The `RadioButtonGroupPanel` can only display values from a single attribute.
`JUStatusBar`	A container that displays the status of data items in a panel that is bound to a business service data collection or `JUPanel`. The `JUStatusBar` displays the status of controls in the same panel or any child panels on an empty `JClient` form.
`MediaControl`	This control can be used to load, clear, or render multimedia content into interMedia objects, or save it into a file. The data itself cannot be edited. The `MediaControl` Component consists of a panel with a display area and these four buttons: * The *Change* button accesses an Open dialog box to select the multimedia file to load. * The *Clear* button deletes content from the database. * The *Launch* button opens the window used to render the multimedia data. * The *Save* button saves the contents to a file.

TABLE B-2. *JClient Controls*

Swing

The Swing components in the Swing page of the Component Palette shown in Figure B-2 are part of the Java Foundation Classes library in the Sun Java SDK.

The Swing component class names usually start with the letter "J" and are contained in the javax.swing package. Many Swing controls are extensions of the AWT controls described earlier, but Swing components offer a more complete set of properties.

The items in the Swing page of the Component Palette are described in Table B-3.

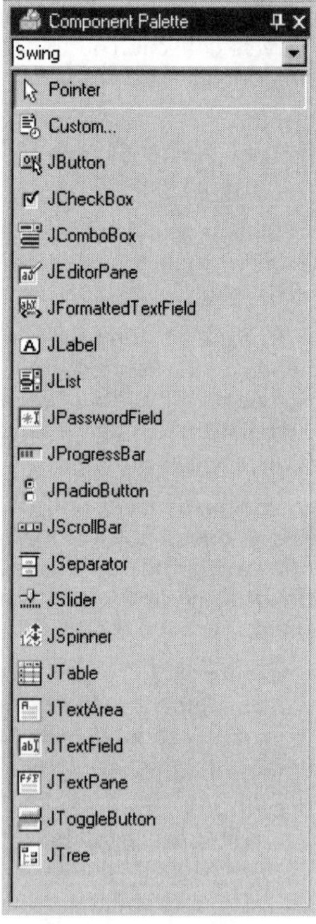

FIGURE B-2. *Swing page of the Component Palette*

Component	Description and Example
`Custom`	You can add any component using this selection. Depending upon the context, this will access the Class Browser, Package Browser, or both.
`JButton`	A standard push button that you can label with text or an icon or both.
`JCheckBox`	A box that toggles between checked and unchecked. The value changes from "true" to "false" when a checkbox is unchecked. You can set the *icon* property to use a graphic other than the check mark.
`JComboBox`	A pulldown list that presents multiple values for the user to select from. You can allow the user to enter a value by setting the *editable* property to "True." This control is also called a "poplist" (as in Forms Developer) or a "popup menu" (although there is a different control with the same name that displays a right-click menu). The term that refers to this control with the least confusion and that is generally accepted by Java experts is "combo box."
`JEditorPane`	A box that can display text formatted in HTML or RTF. It can be used for formatted displays such as that in a help system.
`JFormattedTextField`	A richer text field than `JTextField` that allows independent formatting for insert and edit modes.
`JLabel`	This is a text label to which you can also attach an icon. Normally, you use this for field prompts.
`JList`	A control that presents a list of text strings without a scrollbar. Use the `JScrollPane` container if you need a scrollbar for this control.
`JPasswordField`	The same type of control as `JTextField`, except that this field hides the input by displaying an asterisk (*) for each character typed.
`JProgressBar`	A control that graphically displays the completion percentage for a process.
`JRadioButton`	A single selection button that will be part of a set of buttons in a radio group (`ButtonGroup` class). Only one button in the group may be selected.
`JScrollBar`	A vertical or horizontal bar with a button that moves the display or manipulates a value.

TABLE B-3. *Swing Components*

Component	Description and Example
`JSeparator`	This component is used in menus to separate menu items with a horizontal line. It can also be used as a horizontal or vertical straight line or as a spacer in toolbars.
`JSlider`	A control that is visually and functionally similar to the scrollbar. This control is used more often to change values than is the scrollbar.
`JSpinner`	This component is a visual control that allows you to scroll through the available values using an up or down button.
`JTable`	A spreadsheet-like (grid) display of data. The user can modify column widths at run time.
`JTextArea`	Another text box that shows text strings ending in newline characters. There is no scrollbar on this component, but you can place it in a `JScrollPane` container if the user will need to scroll.
`JTextField`	A single-row text editing area. Some of the hands-on practices in this book use this control.
`JTextPane`	A subclass of `JEditorPane` that allows you to edit formatted text and embed images and other components within that text. (`JEditorPane` only allows images within HTML or RTF text.) This means that you can embed other frames or window components as in a Multiple Document Interface (MDI) window.
`JToggleButton`	This component looks like a `JButton` control, but when clicked, it sets the selected state to "True" until clicked again (similar to the way checkboxes work).
`JTree`	Use this to display hierarchical data in a form that emulates the Windows Explorer. A hands-on practice in Chapter 15 includes techniques for working with this component.

TABLE B-3. *Swing Components* (continued)

For specific information about each of these components, see the help topic "About Swing JavaBeans Components" by searching for "Swing" in the Index Search tab.

Swing Containers

This page of the Component Palette (shown next) contains Swing components that are used as *containers,* or areas into which other components are placed:

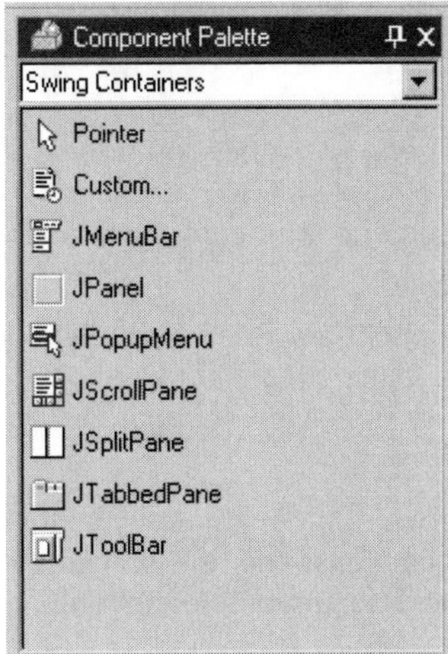

Technically, many Swing controls are containers because they are subclassed from the `java.awt.Container` class. For example, `JButtons` and `JTextField` are both subclassed from `Container`, although you do not use them as receptacles for other components. The components on this page are more commonly used to hold other components.

Table B-4 lists the Swing containers and a brief description of each.

Component	Description
`Custom`	You can add any component using this selection. Depending upon the context, this will access the Class Browser, Package Browser, or both.
`JMenuBar`	A component offers a pulldown menu system to which you add menus and menu items. The menu bar appears under the title bar of a window.
`JPanel`	This component does not have a visible border by default, although you can set properties to display the border. `JPanel` is the main container that is used by the application to hold other objects. It is used in the `JTabbedPane` to represent each of the tabs. This control is also responsible for layout manager functionality.
`JPopupMenu`	This component defines a menu that appears when the user right clicks a component.
`JScrollPane`	This container allows you to define horizontal and vertical scrollbars. The user moves the scrollbars to access objects in the pane that are outside the pane's borders, for example, multi-record data items. Another example is a window that may need scrolling, such as a large navigation tree.

TABLE B-4. *Swing Containers*

Component	Description
`JSplitPane`	This highly useful container component provides the user with two work areas and a movable bar to manipulate the width of the panes. The panes can contain other components and can be split either horizontally or vertically.
`JTabbedPane`	This component offers a standard tab folder interface with multiple pages. You can define the edge that the tabs appear on, and use any `Container` component for the pages. A hands-on practice in Chapter 15 shows how this control works.
`JToolBar`	This pane provides a container for buttons and other components. The toolbar is floatable, so the user can drag it out of the window into its own window. You can define the toolbar with a horizontal or vertical orientation.

TABLE B-4. *Swing Containers* (continued)

For specific information about the container components, see the help topic "About Containers" by searching for "Swing containers" in the Full Text Search tab.

APPENDIX C

Overview of HTML, JavaScript, and Cascading Style Sheets

An author arrives at a good style
when his language performs
what is required of it without shyness.

—Cyril Connolly (1903–1974),
Enemies of Promise

ork in browser-centric technologies requires skills with Hypertext Markup Language (HTML), JavaScript, and cascading style sheets (CSS). This appendix introduces these subjects. A complete discussion of these subjects is the topic of entire books and websites. You can refer to those sources for additional and more complete information. The discussion in this appendix is intended to start you thinking about these subjects with an assumption that you will continue to study them using other resources.

HTML

HTML is a tag language that is responsible for presenting text in a web browser. "Hypertext" in the name of the language refers to the ability to click a word or phrase and open a new page. You navigate hypertext pages in a nonlinear way as your interest dictates. This navigation method differs from the linear way in which you read printed information such as this book. "Markup" in the name of the language refers to the process of adding tags to plain text. The tags are separated from the text with angle brackets ("<" and ">"), and each tag designates a specific format for the text within it. HTML is not a procedural language; it only formats plain text in a way that the browser can use to transform the text into a more graphical format with fonts, colors, and layout characteristics.

HTML is a product of the World Wide Web Consortium (W3C) and has become a standard for all web browsers. Complete information about the language, including links to tutorials and examples, is available on the W3C website, www.w3c.org.

Editing HTML

HTML files are standard ASCII text files that you can edit using any text editor. Many visual HTML editors, such as JDeveloper's JSP/HTML Visual Editor, allow you to view and modify the page as it will look when it is presented in the browser. In addition, the JDeveloper JSP/HTML Visual Editor allows you to code J2EE-style applications that are displayed inside an HTML page. Other commercially available editors such as Macromedia Dreamweaver and Microsoft FrontPage offer more features for HTML editing, such as template support, but may not provide the level of support for database-centric J2EE development that you require. A number of low-cost shareware editors are also available; a quick search on the Web will give you a starting point for such shareware. In addition, some standard word processing tools, such as Microsoft Word, will save files in an HTML format and allow rudimentary visual editing. You will probably find that the visual editor in JDeveloper will suffice for most purposes.

HTML Tags

HTML tags are usually paired to have a starting tag and an ending tag, inside of which you embed text or other content such as graphics or JavaScript. The starting and ending tags have the same name and are distinguished with the ending tag containing a slash "/." For example, the starting tag used to apply the bold style to text is "<b>," and the ending tag is "</b>." The tag delimiters "< >" set the tag apart from the text that is inside it. The tag name is not case sensitive, so "<B>" is the same as "<b>." Tags define how the browser should display the content as shown here:

```
<b>This is bold. </b>This     is not bold.
```

The browser will interpret the <b> tag and display everything between it and the matching closing tag </b> in boldface as in the following illustration:

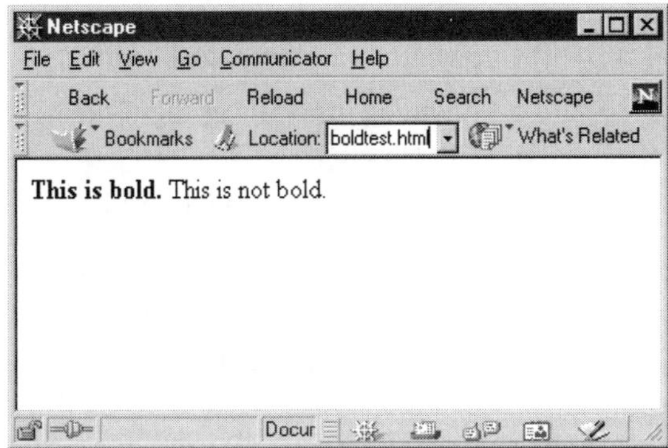

Extra spaces in the body section are ignored. For example, the five spaces between "This" and "is" in the preceding example are compressed to one space. You can specify the display of a space character using the special characters " " (nonbreaking space). There are other special characters called "character entity references" that you can use to display symbols such as "<" (less than), ">" (greater than), "&" (ampersand), and copyright. The special characters are "<", ">", "&", and "©" respectively.

Table C-1 lists some common tags, in roughly the order in which they would appear in a file. An example containing these tags appears later in Figure C-1. As mentioned, tags are not case sensitive, so "<b>" and "<B>" will produce the same results.

Well-Formed Tags

HTML browsers are sometimes forgiving if an ending tag is missing, but an HTML file is considered *well-formed* when all starting tags that can have ending tags actually do have ending tags. Browsers may display code improperly if it is not well-formed. This is especially true for table, row, and cell tags that are not well-formed. Well-formed HTML code is a goal to strive for.

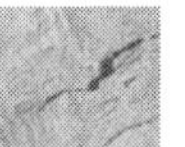

TIP

If you want to code well-formed tags but a specific tag has no contents (for example an <hr> tag), you can close the tag within the opening tag (for example, "<hr />").

Opening Tag	Ending Tag	Purpose
`<html>`	`</html>`	Declares the beginning and end of the page. Anything outside of these tags will not be placed on the page.
`<head>`	`</head>`	Page heading that will not print on the page. This section of the page can contain code such as JavaScript and a reference to the cascading style sheet. The text in this section is not printed on the page.
`<title>`	`</title>`	Displays the text inside the tags as the window title. It is placed inside the page heading "`<head>`" tags.
`<body>`	`</body>`	Anything inside these tags is treated as display content for the page.
`<h1>`	`</h1>`	Heading level 1, which displays text in a larger font. There are also `<h2>` through `<h6>` tags (with corresponding closing tags) for nested heading levels. You can align the heading (left, right, or center) with the `align` attribute.
`<p>`	`</p>`	The paragraph tag. Hard returns in HTML code are ignored, so you need to define the paragraph by enclosing the text in paragraph tags (or by placing a "`<p>`" at the end of the paragraph).
` `	(none)	Inserts a line break. Line breaks insert a smaller vertical space between lines than do paragraph tags.
`<b>`	`</b>`	Displays the text in boldface.
`<i>`	`</i>`	Displays the text in italics.
`<a>`	`</a>`	An anchor that links to another file, page, or location on the same page. The most common attribute for this tag is `href`, which defines a hyperlink to another page or to another location on the same page as shown in the section "Sample HTML Code."
`<!--`	`-->`	Comments, which are not processed. Comments, as well as other tags, are displayed when the user selects View Source from the right-click menu on the browser page.
`<ul>`	`</ul>`	An unordered list. These tags surround a list of paragraphs that are bulleted and surrounded by a `<li></li>` (list item) tag pair. Use `<ol>` and `</ol>` for an "ordered list," where list items are numbered.
`<hr>`	`</hr>`	A horizontal rule (line). Code in the section "Sample HTML Code" shows two `<hr>` attributes: `align` and `width`.

TABLE C-1. *Common HTML Tags*

Attributes

Many tags have documented *attributes* whose values refine how the tag is interpreted. Attributes appear in the opening tag just before the closing ">". For example, the heading tag "`<h1 align="center">`" contains an `align` attribute with a value of "center" that signals the browser to center the heading text within the browser window. When the window width is changed, the text is re-centered within the new size. Although some tag languages and browsers can interpret attribute values without surrounding quote marks, it is safest to always enclose attribute values inside quote marks. You can use single or double quotes as long as they are paired correctly. The attributes for each tag are documented in the HTML language reference manuals available on the Web or in many books.

The HTML Form

The *HTML form* is a construct that allows users to input values and click a Submit or Reset button. It is a standard HTML feature. Form tags contain input fields and buttons. When a button is clicked, the form information is sent to the process or procedure defined in the form tag (which is typically code in a language such as Java, Perl, or another language). The form is useful for HTML pages that accept input from the user (for example, an edit or input page). A page can contain more than one form.

NOTE
Different versions of HTML offer different tags and attributes. The W3C website discusses HTML versions (www.w3.org/MarkUp/#previous) and the elements available for each.

Sample HTML Code

The following is a sample of HTML code that demonstrates the tags in Table C-1:

```
<html>
  <head>
    <title>Sample HTML Tags</title>
  </head>
  <body>
    <h1 align="center">Samples of Basic HTML Tags</h1>
    The font for plain body text depends on the browser settings.
    <b>This is bold. </b>
    <i>This is italic. </i>This is not.
    <i><b>This is both.</b></i>

    <p/>New paragraph before this sentence.<br/>Line break before this sentence.

    <br/>Extra spaces            without special characters are ignored.

    <p/>Line breaks
    in
    the code are ignored.
    <p/>
```

```
    <!-- A comment: the anchor tag has several attributes.
         HREF is one -->
    JDeveloper is a product of
    <a href="http://www.oracle.com">Oracle Corporation </a>&copy;2004.

    <hr width="80%" align="center" />
    <b>Unordered List</b>
    <ul>
       <li>An item in a list </li>
       <li>Another item in a list </li>
       <li>Yet another item in a list </li>
    </ul>
  </body>
</html>
```

Notice that the `<hr>` tag does not surround text, so it can be closed within the opening tag by using the "/" character preceded by a space. The `<hr>` line is equivalent to "`<hr width="80%" align="center"></hr>`." As with any programming language, you can indent HTML code to show its structure. This makes the code more readable and maintainable. Since the browser will ignore hard returns and extra spaces, the code formatting will not be displayed.

Figure C-1 shows how this code will display in the browser.

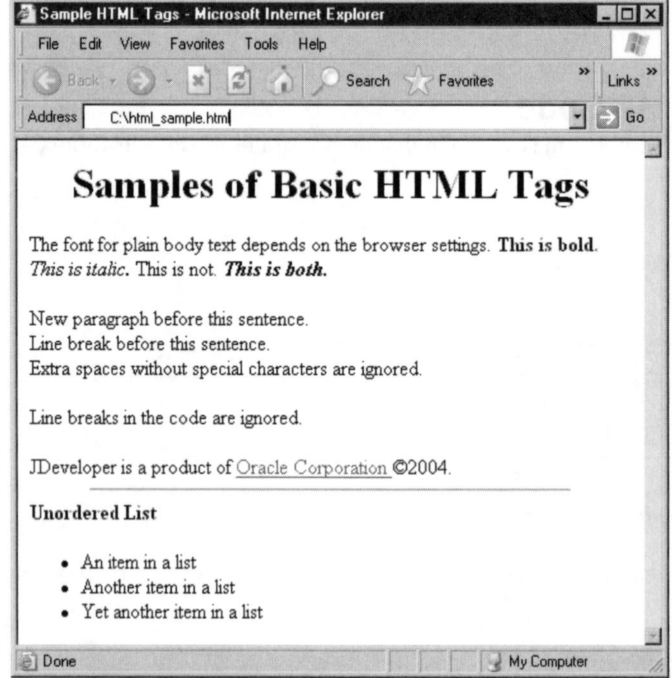

FIGURE C-1. *Output of sample HTML code*

JavaScript in HTML

You can extend the functionality of HTML by embedding code written in *JavaScript*, an object-based scripting language created by Netscape but supported in all browsers. For example, you can use JavaScript to perform data validation on the client side, which saves network traffic. Although it is beyond the scope of this book to describe any of the basics of JavaScript, the following sample will help you become familiar with what JavaScript looks like. You will then be able to recognize it in the code that JDeveloper creates. As mentioned earlier, the Web is an excellent source of information. Start with the information pages on the Netscape JavaScript developer's website, devedge.netscape.com/central/javascript.

```
<html>
<head>
  <script language="JavaScript">
  <!--
  function checkRequired(which) {
    if (which.fname.value == '') {
      alert("The Name field is required.");
      return false;
      }
    else {
      alert("The Name = \"" + which.fname.value +"\"");
      which.fname.value = which.fname.value.toUpperCase();
      return true;
      }
    }
  -->
  </script>
</head>

<body>
   <form onsubmit="return checkRequired(this)">
   First Name:  <input type="text" name="fname">
   <p><input type=submit value="Save">
   </form>
</body>
</html>
```

The HTML tags in the body section display a label, a text item, and a button, as shown here:

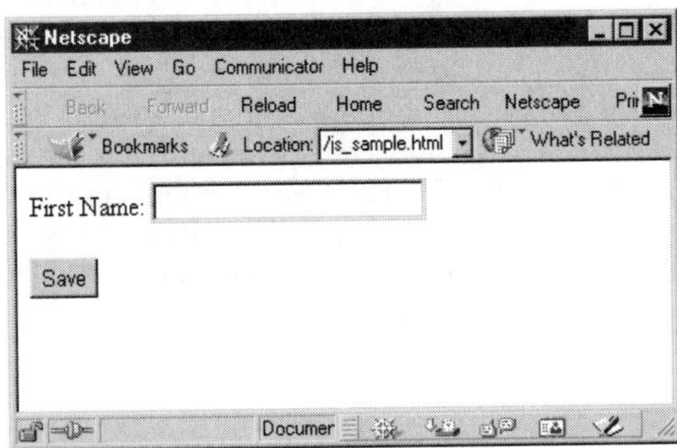

In this example, the source code for JavaScript appears in a comment in the heading section. Alternatively, you can refer to a central JavaScript source code file in the heading using the script tag as shown in the following example:

```
<script src="jdevscript.js" language="JavaScript"></script>
```

In the preceding example, the <form> tag defines the form as well as what happens when the button that is labeled "Save" (and defined by the 'input type="submit"' tag) is clicked. When the button is clicked, the JavaScript function checkRequired() is executed. If a value is input into the field, the checkRequired() function converts the value to uppercase and returns a Boolean "true"; the submit feature of the form calls the page again and passes it a parameter of the field value. (This value will appear in the URL.)

If no value is input, the checkRequired() function displays an error message and returns a Boolean "false"; the form is not submitted in this case. This demonstrates one way that JavaScript is defined and called, but you will need to consult a JavaScript reference for further information.

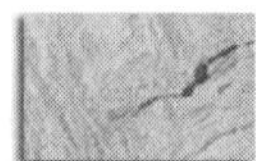

CAUTION
JavaScript is not supported equally by all browsers, and it is important to test your application using the same browsers that your users will employ to access your application. If you do not know which browsers your users have, you need to test your application in the most popular browsers (such as Internet Explorer, Mozilla, Opera, and Netscape). This is good advice to follow even if you do not use JavaScript because even HTML is not handled consistently by all browsers. An option that you might pursue is JavaScript libraries that are designed to be cross-browser–compliant (for example, the open source product DynAPI at dynapi.sourceforge.net).

Cascading Style Sheets

A cascading style sheet provides another way of extending HTML by enabling a set of common definitions to serve multiple uses within an HTML document. A *cascading style sheet* is a set of named style definitions each of which has a list of visual attributes. The styles can be applied to text or tags in the HTML document to change the default appearance presented by the browser. You can define styles that change the appearance of a tag every time it appears in the page. You can also define styles that you can explicitly apply to a tag when needed. These styles can be limited to a particular tag or set of tags or can be *global* styles that are available to all tags.

The cascading style sheet styles can be embedded in the page heading of each HTML file. They can also be placed in a separate file (normally with a .css extension) that can be used by many pages. JDeveloper uses the separate file strategy because it is the most flexible and maintainable for multi-page applications. That strategy also reduces the size of the HTML page.

The JDeveloper sample .css files (bc4j.css and blaf.css) are located in the JDEV_HOME\jdev\multi\system\templates\common\misc directory (where JDEV_HOME is the JDeveloper installation directory, for example, C:\JDev10g). Each style sheet has a different set of fonts and colors.

Building a Cascading Style Sheet

A cascading style sheet is a standard ASCII text file that you can edit using a text editor. The JDeveloper Code Editor and Structure window offer basic style sheet editing as described in Chapter 3. Some HTML editing tools provide assistance with this task and allow you to view samples of the style as you are editing it. There are also dedicated CSS editors such as TopStyle (www.bradsoft .com).

A cascading style sheet allows you to define and name a set of attributes that you want to apply to HTML tags. The following is a sample of a small cascading style sheet file named demo.css:

```
<!--
/*
||  demo.css style sheet
*/

H2 {
  font-family: Arial;
  font-style: italic;
  color: BLUE;
}

BODY
{
  background-color:#DDDDDD;
}

.emphasis
{
  color: black;
  font-weight: bold;
  font-style: italic;
}

P.codeText{
  font-family: Courier;
  color: BLACK;
  font-weight: BOLD;
  font-size: 10pt;
}

TH {
  color:WHITE;
  background-color:#888888;
  font-weight: BOLD;
}

TD {
  color:BLACK;
  background-color:WHITE;
}
-->
```

This example defines three types of style sheet entries as follows.

Standard HTML Tag Styles You can define styles to replace the default display characteristics of standard HTML tags (such as H2, BODY, TH, and TD in the example) so that each time the tag is used, the style will be applied. This simplifies the HTML coding a great deal because you do not have to keep applying the same style to the same tag. In the preceding example, the `<h2>` and `<body>` tags will always be shown as defined in the style sheet.

Global Styles A global style may be applied to any tag as a value of the `class` attribute (for example, '`<p class="emphasis">`'). The name of a global style is preceded in the CSS file by a period ("."). In the preceding example, "emphasis" is a global style that would display the contents of the tag to which it is applied as bold, black, and italicized.

Tag-Specific Styles Tag-specific styles may only be applied to a specific tag (for example, `codeText` in the style sheet example). The style name (`codeText`) is prefixed with the tag name (P) so that only the `<p>` tag may use the `codeText` style.

Using a Cascading Style Sheet

Using the cascading style sheet file is a matter of referencing the file location in the heading section of the HTML page and using the styles in the HTML tags by specifying the style name in the `class` attribute. The following HTML file uses the styles defined in the demo.css style sheet:

```
<html>
  <head>
    <title>CSS Demo</title>
    <link rel="stylesheet" type="text/css" href="demo.css">
  </head>
  <body>
    This is normal body text. The body background is gray.
    <p class="emphasis">
      This uses the EMPHASIS style.
    </p>
      <p class="codeText">// Java code sample comment</p>
    <P>
    <h2>An H2 header is blue by default.</h2>
    <table border=0>
      <tr>
        <th>ID<th>
        <th>Name<th>
      </tr>
      <tr>
        <td>101<td>
```

```
        <td>Tiger<td>
      </tr>
      <tr>
        <td class="emphasis">102<td>
        <td class="emphasis">Dragon<td>
      </tr>
    </table>
  </body>
</html>
```

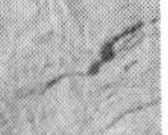

NOTE
This example shows an "HTML table" structure that represents rows and columns of data. It is useful to be familiar with this structure because it is used extensively for formatting pages in most applications.

The `<link>` tag references the style sheet file. The heading 2, body, table heading, and table data cell tags (`<h2>`, `<body>`, `<th>`, and `<td>`, respectively) default to the styles defined in the style sheet and do not require anything additional in the HTML file. Both a line in the top of the body and the table data (cells) in the second row of the table apply the global style "emphasis" by specifying a `class` attribute. The nature of the global style allows it to be used in two different tags. The text at the top of the file also applies the tag-specific style `codeText`. The following illustration shows how this HTML file will appear in the browser:

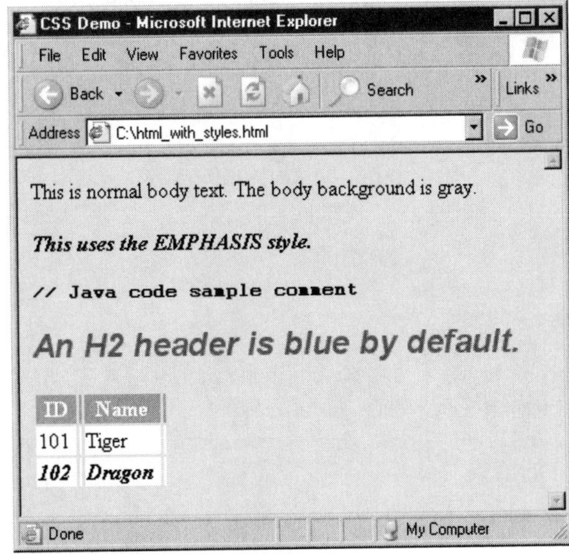

If you were to remove the link tag so the style sheet was not used, the results would appear as follows:

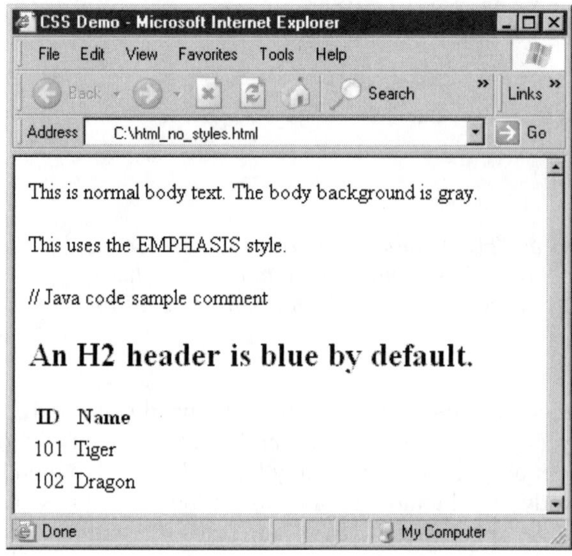

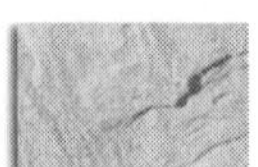

NOTE

The W3C group is also responsible for the creation of cascading style sheet language, and more information is available on the W3C CSS website, www.w3c.org/ Style/CSS.

APPENDIX D

Overview of JSP, JSTL, and EL Tags

A spear, a spike,
A point, a nail,
A drip, a drop,
The end of the tale…
It's the wind blowing free
It's the curve of the slope
It's an ant, it's a bee
It's a reason for hope

— Antonio Carlos Jobim (1927–1994),
The Waters of March

Although you can create basic JavaServer Pages (JSP) files in JDeveloper without extensive knowledge of JSP tags, you will be most effective with knowledge of those tags. In addition, since developing JSP files in JDeveloper uses the JSP Standard Tag Library (JSTL), an understanding of these tags is helpful. JDeveloper also uses expression language (EL), which is integrated with JSTL 1.0, to represent values in JSTL tags. This appendix provides an introduction to JSP, JSTL, and EL tags.

Basic JSP Tags

A *JSP tag* is a piece of code that encapsulates a repeatable process (coded in Java) and serves as a small program within the JSP page. The purpose of a JSP tag is to reduce redundant coding, increase code legibility, and provide features that can be applied to multiple JSP pages with minimal alteration. JSP tags use a syntax similar to that of other tag languages such as HTML. Like the tags in these languages, JSP tags are bracketed by "< >" symbols, and many have *attributes* that supply information to the tag and customize its behavior for a particular requirement. The mechanics and syntax of JSP tags are a bit different from those of tags in other languages and need a more detailed description. Therefore, the following discussion presents details about standard JSP tags and examines how they are processed to the servlet and HTML page. It also explains the basics of JSTL and how it can be used in JSP files.

Two types of files have a .jsp extension, and both can be created in JDeveloper. The JSP file types follow:

- **JSP page** A JSP page contains HTML and JSP tags and uses JSP tag syntax.
- **JSP 1.2 document** A JSP 1.2 document is an XML file with a .jsp extension. The code in this document mixes XML tags and normal JSP and HTML tags.

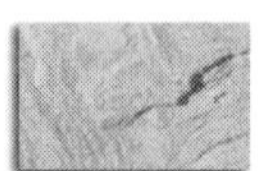

NOTE
As of this writing, the JavaServer Pages specification version 2.0 has been ratified. JDeveloper 10g supports work within JSP version 1.2 so this section discusses JSP elements for that version.

Where to Put the Code?

Although JSP files support embedding as much Java code as needed, the preferred location for application logic is within a centralized controller layer or business services layer; this makes the code more maintainable and reusable. In addition, application logic that customizes the behavior of a standard HTML element such as a text field can be moved to a tag library for the same reasons.

Beginning and Ending Tags

As with all well-formed tag languages, when using JSP, JSTL, or EL tags, you need to provide an ending tag for each starting tag. The ending tag can be written using one of the following syntax examples:

```
<tag>body of tag</tag>
<tag></tag>
<tag />
```

The first example shows body text between the beginning and ending tags. The second example is the same but without the body text. (Some tags do not require or use the text within the beginning and ending tags.) The last example ends the tag within the starting tag.

Processing of Standard Tags

Working effectively with JSP pages requires an understanding of how the code you write is processed. How the code is processed (compiled into a servlet and rendered in HTML) depends on the type of tag. JSP tags can be categorized as one of the following types:

- Scripting elements
- Directives
- Actions

NOTE
The main reference for native JSP tags is the "JavaServer Pages Specification, Version 2.0" file accessible online at java.sun.com/jsp.

Scripting Elements

Scripting elements are tags that the JSP container converts to Java code in the servlet that it generates from the JSP file. There are three kinds of scripting elements: expressions, scriptlets, and declarations. In addition, you can add different kinds of comments to a JSP file. Their descriptions follow.

Expressions Expressions produce values that are output directly in the HTML page. The expression takes the following form:

```
<%= expression %>
```

The expression will be embedded inside a print statement in the servlet and can be as simple as a hard-coded value or mathematical expression such as the following:

```
<%= 450 %>
<%= 50*6 %>
```

The first expression displays "450" and the second expression displays "300." More often, the expression will be the return value from a Java method call or a variable value such as the following:

```
<%= new java.util.Date() %>
<%= salAmount %>
```

The first expression displays the current date and the second displays the value of the variable `salAmount`.

Scriptlets *Scriptlets* are snippets of standard Java code that you want the JSP container to insert into the servlet. Scriptlets are designated using the delimiters "`<% %>`", as in the following syntax:

```
<% Java code; %>
```

The JSP container pulls the code from inside the tag delimiters and embeds it as is into the Java servlet when the JSP page is translated. Unlike expressions that are just values, scriptlets must be syntactically correct and must be combined into complete Java code statements. Syntax problems in the Java code will be caught when the servlet is compiled. IDEs such as JDeveloper will provide compile error messages for the Java code inside scriptlet tags.

You use scriptlets if you want to do something that JSP tags or related tag libraries do not offer. One reason to use scriptlets is to incorporate constructs such as loops or conditional tests. For example, the following scriptlets conditionally test for a value and present an `<h2>` title if the value matches; if the value does not match, a scriptlet formats an HTML table with an error message. (The variable value is hard-coded in this code example. Normally, it would be loaded dynamically in the code.)

```
<%
  int salAmount = 3000;
  if (salAmount > 0) {
%>
<h2>The salary is positive.</h2>
<%
  }
  else  {
%>
<table border="1">
  <tr align="center">
    <td><b>Warning!</b></td>
  </tr>
  <tr align="center">
    <td>Salary is negative or zero.<br />
```

```
        Contact your Financial Advisor.
    </td>
  </tr>
</table>
<%
}
%>
```

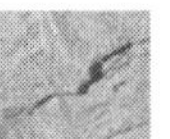

NOTE
Notice the `<br />` tag in this example. Although `<br>` needs no ending tag, this syntax makes the break tag well-formed. The space before the slash ("/") is required so the browser can interpret this as a self-contained start and end tag.

The preceding code displays the following if `salAmount` is positive:

The salary is positive.

It will display the following if `salAmount` is zero or negative:

Warning!
Salary is negative or zero. Contact your Financial Advisor.

The scriptlet code is contained in the sections surrounded by "`<% %>`" delimiters.

The preceding code example may be a bit difficult to read at first because of the mixture of Java code and HTML tags. The JavaServer Pages Standard Tag Library (JSTL or "JSP Standard Tag Library") eases this confusion by providing iteration ("`forEach`") and conditional evaluation ("`if`" and "`choose`") tags, among other functions. JSTL is currently packaged as part of the Java Web Services Developer Pack and, as with all JSP efforts, is well documented on the Sun website at java.sun.com/jstl.

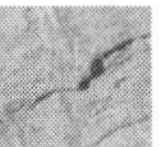

NOTE
Tag libraries such as JSTL (discussed later in this appendix) and Struts provide conditional and iteration code structures in tags that could perform the same type of logic as the preceding example. The benefit of using code structures in tag libraries is that they do not require context switches between Java and tag languages. Using tag library code structures can make the code more readable.

Sometimes expressions and scriptlets can be used for the same purpose. The following two tags will each display the same amount in the HTML page:

```
<%= salAmount %>
<% out.println(salAmount); %>
```

Scriptlets are best used where there is a unique logic requirement for a JSP page. They do not promote the idea of reusable code because they are written specifically for a single JSP page. If you use a large scriptlet in more than one JSP page, you should consider embedding the logic in a class that you call from a scriptlet or in a custom JSP tag.

CAUTION
When embedding Java logic constructs (such as "`if`" and "`for`") in a scriptlet, be sure to enclose the code that follows the keyword within block delimiters ("{ }"), as shown in the "`if...else`" construct in the preceding code example, because the JSP container may generate code under the "`if`" statement. If you were to have only one line of code under "`if`," you could normally avoid using the block symbols. However, if the JSP container were to generate an additional line under yours, the resulting logic would be incorrect.

Declarations The JSP container inserts expressions and scriptlets into the `_jspService()` method of the servlet. This is the method that starts automatically when the JSP page is run. If you want to insert code outside this method, you can use a *declaration*, which is delimited by "`<%! %>`" symbols. As with the scriptlet, you need to use valid Java code. Declarations do not cause any output in the browser.

Declarations are particularly useful if you need to declare a servlet-specific method that you will call more than once in scriptlets or expressions. For example, the following would create code for a method in the servlet class that is outside of the `_jspService()` method:

```
<%!
  public static double calcRaise(int salary) {
    return(salary * 1.3);
  }
%>
```

This method could be called from any expression or scriptlet inside the JSP page, for example:

```
<%= calcRaise(empSalary) %>
```

You can also declare class variables (that are outside of any method) in this same way. By combining scriptlets and declarations, you can add almost any type of code to the servlet class file.

Types of Comments A Java comment inside scriptlet tags will appear in the Java servlet file. For example, the scriptlet "`<% // this is a comment %>`" will be written as "`// this is a comment`" into the Java code. (You can also use the multi-line Java comment, delimited by "/*" and "*/", in this same way within a scriptlet.)

The JSP file can contain a JSP comment (also called a *page comment*) that is not copied into the servlet file. It is used only for documentation in the JSP file. This comment uses the delimiters "<%-- --%>".

Although it is not a JSP tag, you can embed HTML comments using the normal HTML form "<!-- -->". These will appear as is in the browser's View Source window. The JSP container prints all HTML (including HTML comments) using a call to out.write().

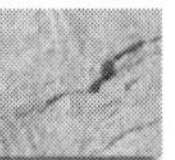

TIP
You can dynamically generate an HTML comment by embedding an expression within the comment using the format "<!-- static comment <%= expression %> static -->".

Scripting Elements in the Servlet When the JSP container creates a Java servlet from a JSP file, it translates the JSP tags into pure Java. Different types of scripting elements appear differently in the servlet. For example, consider the following code, an excerpt from a JSP page called DemoTag.jsp. (The line numbers are added for reference purposes and do not appear in the JSP file.)

```
<!-- Salary display -->
<%-- scriptlets --%>
<%
  int salAmount = 3000;
  if (salAmount > 0) {
%>
<h2>The salary is positive.</h2>
<br>
<%
  out.write("The new salary is " + calcRaise(salAmount));
%>
<%
  }
  else {
%>
<h1>The salary is
<%-- expression --%>
<%= salAmount %>
</h1>
  <%
  }
  %>

<br>
<%// expression %>
<%= "Salary is " + salAmount %>

<%-- declaration --%>
<%!
  public static double calcRaise(int salary) {
    return(salary * 1.3);
  }
%>
```

The JSP container will convert this JSP code to Java code in a servlet file called DemoTag.java. It will also compile the Java file into a .class file.

The JSP page excerpt corresponds to the following lines in the Java servlet. The line numbers refer to the lines in the JSP file that was the source for the code. The "`\n`" symbol creates a new line in the HTML page. Notice that lines 2 and 17 do not appear in the servlet because they are page comments that do not create code outside of the JSP page.

```
01: out.write("<!-- Salary display -->\n");
04:  int salAmount = 3000;
05:  if (salAmount > 0) {
07-08:    out.write("<h2>The salary is positive.</h2>\n<br>\n");
10:    out.write("The new salary is " + calcRaise(salAmount));
13:  }
14:  else {
16:    out.write("<h1>The salary is \n");
18:    out.print( salAmount );
19:    out.write("\n</h1>\n");
21:  }
24:    out.write("<br>");
25:    // expression
25:    out.write("\n");
26:    out.print ( "Salary is " + salAmount );
27: out.write("\n");
30: public static double calcRaise(int salary) {
31:  return(salary * 1.3);
32: }
```

Lines 01–27 are written into the `_jspService()` method. Lines 30–32 appear in the servlet before the `_jspService()` method because the JSP lines that created them were written inside a declaration tag. The code uses both `out.print()` and `out.write()` to output text into the HTML that is displayed in the browser. Both methods are equivalent.

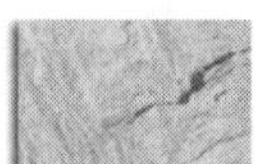

NOTE
The servlet code listing is simplified somewhat for understanding. The text strings that appear in the JSP file are actually loaded into a String array, which is used in the servlet code. The details of this implementation are not important to an understanding of how JSP files are processed, but you can examine the generated servlet file if you are interested in the actual code.

This converted code reflects the following rules for the different types of JSP code:

- **Scriptlets** are written as Java code into the `_jspService()` method.
- **Expressions** are embedded into `out.write()` Java statements.
- **Declarations** are written as Java code outside the `_jspService()` method.
- **Page comments** are not copied into the servlet file.

If you view the source on the HTML page that this JSP produces, the following will be shown:

```
<!-- Salary display -->
<h2>The salary is positive.</h2>
<br>
The new salary is 3900.0
<br>
Salary is 3000
```

Neither page comments ("`<%-- --%>`") nor Java comments ("`<%// %>`") are displayed in the HTML page or in the View Source window.

Directives

The *directive* tag allows you to affect the structure of the Java servlet that is generated from the JSP file. A directive appears in the format "`<%@ directive_name %>`" where "*`directive_name`*" is `page`, `include`, or `taglib`.

page The `page` directive allows you to specify file-level commands such as the imported classes or the page content type. Here are some examples:

```
<%@ page contentType="text/html;charset=windows-1252" %>
<%@ page import="java.util.*, oracle.jbo.*" errorPage="errorpage.jsp" %>
```

The first `page` directive specifies to the servlet the type of content—in this case, HTML ("text/html"). This generates the following servlet line in the `_jspService()` method:

```
response.setContentType( "text/html;charset=windows-1252");
```

The second line specifies the addition of the following to the servlet import section:

```
import java.util.*;
import oracle.jbo.*;
```

It also designates which file will be displayed if an error occurs. The `errorPage` attribute adds the page name to the assignment of the `pageContext` variable in the servlet's `_jspService()` method, as shown here:

```
PageContext pageContext = JspFactory.getDefaultFactory().getPageContext( this,
  request, response, "errorpage.jsp", true, JspWriter.DEFAULT_BUFFER, true);
```

include The `include` directive inserts the text from another file (for example, a JSP or an HTML page fragment) into the generated .java file. This is useful for a design element that will be shared by many pages. The following example inserts the output of a JSP file:

```
<%@ include file="TimeInfo.jsp" flush="true" %>
```

The TimeInfo.jsp file consists of the following:

```
<!-- Current Time is here -->
<br>The current time is: <%= new java.util.Date() %></p>
```

The JSP container inserts the entire file into the main JSP page before the page is translated into a servlet. The tags and text within the included file are treated in the same way as other tags and text in the main JSP page.

The code from the included file (in this case, a JSP page) is embedded into the servlet that is generated from the JSP page and therefore does not need to be compiled as a separate file. The included file is not run along with the main JSP page and does not need to be present at run time. The source code to be included must be present when the JSP is compiled.

If the included file changes, the JSP page must be recompiled to incorporate the changes. If the included source file is not available when the JSP page is compiled, you will receive a compile error.

Another way to include a page inside another page is by using the <jsp:include /> tag. This is technically an action tag (discussed next), but it accomplishes a task similar to that of the `include` directive even though the mechanism is different.

taglib The `taglib` directive specifies the name (alias) and location of the *tag library descriptor* (.tld) file—an XML file that contains a list of tags, their attributes, and the classes that implement the tags. The `uri` (*uniform resource identifier* or URI) attribute identifies the location of the tag library definition. The `prefix` attribute provides an alias for the tag library that will be used in action tags. An example follows:

```
<%@ taglib uri="/WEB-INF/struts-html.tld" prefix="html"%>
```

There is no corresponding code generated in the servlet for the `taglib` directive. However, the JSP container looks in the tag library identified in this tag for information about the class names of the action tags that are used in the JSP page. For example, the JSP page might have a call such as the following:

```
<html:form action="/Dept.jsp.do">
```

The JSP container looks in the tag library definition file identified by the prefix "html" specified in the `taglib` directive for a reference to the class and path that represents the form tag (in this case, using FormTag.class). It then generates code in the `_jspService()` method to instantiate the class (the `form` tag in the JSP page) and pass it parameters based on the attributes of the tag.

Actions

Actions allow you to specify a component from a tag library or a standard tag. Actions may display output in the HTML page or may just write code into the servlet without showing output. The syntax for an action includes the tag prefix and the name of the action component as follows:

```
<prefix:tag_name  attribute=value />
```

The tag_name is the actual tag used in the code and the tag has attributes with values. It is mapped to a Java class in the tag library as mentioned before and as shown in this example used earlier, in the preceding section:

```
<html:form action="/Dept.jsp.do">
```

Much of the work you do in JDeveloper with JSP pages uses action tags such as this for the components.

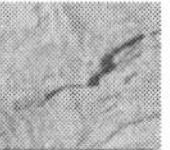

NOTE
An action in the case of standard JSP tags is different from an action in the Struts controller. The JSP action is a tag that indicates a call to a library class whereas the Struts action is a definition used to change the flow of an application.

Other Standard Action Tags JSP pages support a set of standard action tags. There are no extra libraries to specify in the code to access these tags although the JSP container needs to have CLASSPATH information that points to the core JSP JAR files. Table D-1 provides a brief summary of the standard action tags. All of the standard tags are documented in the Sun Microsystems "JavaServer Pages Specification, Version 2.0" file, available at java.sun.com. Standard tags use a prefix of "jsp," which is automatically known by the JSP container and needs no taglib directive. You will notice that some tags in Table D-1 support applet and bean plugins.

Tag	Description and Example
<jsp:fallback>	The fallback action must appear inside a plugin action tag (described later). It defines what will happen if the plugin fails to load. The following example loads the CalcErrorLoad.html page if the CalcSalary applet cannot be started: <jsp:plugin type=applet code="CalcSalary.class" > <jsp:fallback> http://www.download.com/CalcLoadError.html </jsp:fallback> </jsp:plugin>
<jsp:forward>	The forward action passes a request to another JSP page, servlet, or HTML file. The target location may be an expression that is dynamically loaded by other actions or Java code. The request may include parameters and values. A simple example follows: <jsp:forward page="EmpCalc.jsp" />
<jsp:getProperty>	The getProperty tag returns the value of a bean property. The bean must be used before this tag (for example, using a useBean action) so that it has been instantiated. In the following example, the *value* property of the item called "newItem" will be printed on the page: <jsp:getProperty name="newItem" property="value" />

TABLE D-1. *JSP Standard Action Tags*

Tag	Description and Example
<jsp:include>	This tag embeds a file inside the JSP page at run time. It is similar to the include directive, but the included file (JSP or HTML) does not need to be available when the main JSP page is compiled. However, it does need to be available when the main JSP page is run. If the included file is a JSP page, it needs to be compiled for the main JSP page to run correctly. But if the included JSP page is not compiled, compilation will occur when the main JSP page is run. For example: <jsp:include page="TimeInfo.jsp" flush="true" /> This tag can specify a page dynamically if you embed an expression in the page attribute. This kind of functionality is not possible with the include directive. For example, you assign the page file name to a variable, includePage, based upon some condition. The include tag would appear as follows: <jsp:include page="<%= includePage %>" flush="true" />
<jsp:param>	The param action specifies a name/value pair that is embedded in (and must appear within) the fallback, include, and params tags. The params tag description contains an example of the param action.
<jsp:params>	The params action, like the fallback action, can only occur inside of a plugin action tag. It surrounds the <jsp:param> actions inside a plugin block. For example: <jsp:plugin type=applet code="CalcSalary.class" > <jsp:params> <jsp:param name="id" value="101" /> <jsp:param name="name" value="Tiger" /> </jsp:params> </jsp:plugin>

<jsp:plugin>	The plugin tag runs an applet or bean that may require a browser extension (plugin). The JSP engine returns an HTML tag ("embed" for Internet Explorer or "object" for Netscape). A number of attributes specify the plugin name, the type (bean or applet), the size of the display window, the directory that contains the plugin, and so on. A short example follows:
	<jsp:plugin type="applet"
	  code="ShowSalary.class" codebase="/devices/"
	  name="MainSalaryDisplay" align="bottom"
	  height=400 width=600>
	</jsp:plugin>

<jsp:setProperty>	The setProperty tag, like the getProperty tag, works with beans. It assigns the property of an existing bean object. The object must be instantiated before you call the setProperty tag. The following example sets the *value* property of the newItem object to "Harry": <jsp:setProperty name="newItem" property="value" value="Harry" />.
<jsp:useBean>	The useBean tag allows you to make a Java class available inside a JSP page. You can pass attributes to the object to alter its functionality and define its use. Here is an example for a file access bean from the OJSP library: <jsp:useBean id="fileBean" scope="page" class= "oracle.jsp.webutil.fileaccess.HttpUploadBean"> </jsp:useBean>.

TABLE D-1. *JSP Standard Action Tags* (continued)

An Action Tag Example

The following code is an example JSP action tag used to specify an HTML form that is processed by the Struts controller:

```
<html:form action="/Dept.jsp.do">
```

The parts of this tag are processed in the following way (as shown in Figure D-1).

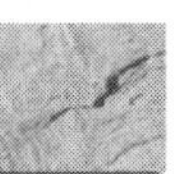

NOTE

In this example, keep in mind the difference between a tag and its attributes. The action tag called "html:form" just happens to have an attribute called "action." However, a tag and its attribute are two separate syntax elements, so the use of the word "action" for both does not indicate a link of any kind.

1. The *tag prefix* (html) refers to the alias given to the tag library, which contains a reference to the action tag class. The tag library's prefix is specified in the taglib directive that also appears in the JSP file.
2. The taglib directive specifies the location (*uniform resource identifier* or uri) of the tag library descriptor (struts-html.tld in this example) that contains a list of tags from the Struts HTML tag library.
3. The tag (form) refers to the tag element in the tag library descriptor (in this example, "<tag><name> form</name></tag>").
4. The tagclass attribute of the tag element contains the name of the class file that will be run by the container when this tag is processed. (The class name is embedded in the servlet that is generated by the JSP translation process.) The class file name is fully qualified (with its directory names). The class file appears in the library (struts.jar).
5. The attributes of the form tag are defined in the tag library descriptor. Each attribute refers to an argument that is passed to the constructor of the class file. In this example, the form attribute action specifies the name of the process that is run when the form is processed.

JDeveloper copies a tag library descriptor (struts-html.tld) into the project directory's \public-html\WEB-INF subdirectory when you specify a project configured for Struts. The class library is defined in the project libraries so that it will be added to the class path and the container runtime will be able to find the tag's class.

Summary of JSP Tag Delimiters

The following table summarizes the tag format introduced in this appendix:

Type of Tag	Format
Action	<prefix:action_name />
Declaration	<%! %>

Type of Tag	**Format**
Directive	`<%@ directive_name %>`
Expression	`<%= %>`
Page comment	`<%-- --%>`
Scriptlet	`<% %>`

Other than the action tag type, the delimiters are self-closing and do not require a separate tag to close them. Action tags can use the single tag form where one tag includes both opening and closing tags ("< *tag* />"). If you use this form, be sure to include a space right before the end symbol "/>".

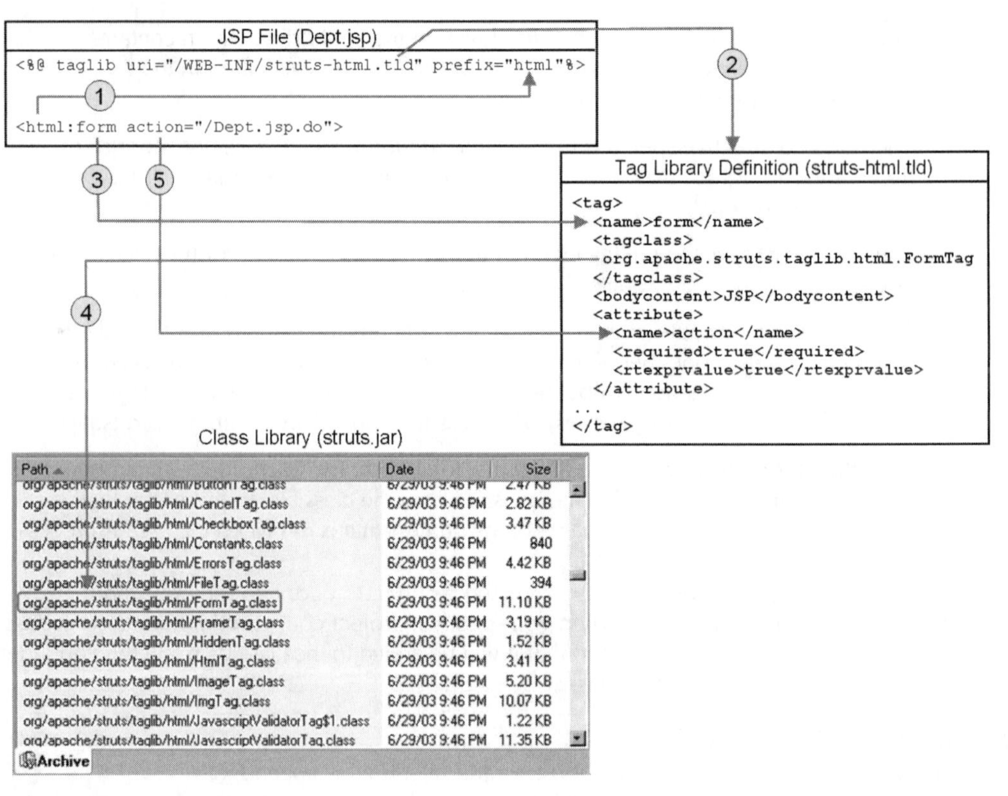

FIGURE D-1. *JSP file references to the tag library descriptor and class library*

NOTE
It is important to remember that the code you are including in JSP pages will be written into a Java servlet. Remembering how scriptlets, expressions, directives, and action tags are converted to code in the servlet will help you avoid or fix syntax errors. The JDeveloper Code Editor features for tag completion help with this task as do curly brace and parenthesis matching.

JSP Standard Tag Library

As described in the preceding section, you can extend the non-procedural functionality of HTML by embedding Java logic inside a JSP file using scriptlets and expressions. However, extensive use of those elements has the following drawbacks:

- **The code is difficult to maintain.** Application logic is contained within each JSP file, so a change to logic that affects more than one page requires a change to more than one file.
- **The code is not easily reusable.** Although you can use mechanisms such as `include` action tags to incorporate portions of a page, a solution coded into a JSP file cannot be easily reused if it becomes required in another file.
- **The code is difficult to read and write.** You need to switch back and forth between Java code and HTML tags in the same file.

For an example of the readability concern, consider a frequently used HTML structure—an HTML table—that needs to be coded so that it can display a variable number of columns and rows. Using scriptlets and expressions, you could code such a table in the following way:

```
<table border="1">
<% for (int i = 1; i <= 3; i++) { %>
  <tr>
    <% for (int j = 1; j <= 4; j++) { %>
       <td>
       <%= i %>:<%= j %>
       </td>
    <%} %>
  </tr>
<% } %>
</table>
```

Although this example uses hard-coded values for the number of rows (3) and number of columns (4), the number of rows and columns would be based on variables determined by the data retrieved from the query. The data values (represented by the expression tags "`<%= i %>:<%= j %>`" would be replaced by the actual data retrieved from the query. This example shows how mixing scriptlets and expressions with HTML tags can create a file that is difficult to read. Much of the readability problem results from the code switching between HTML and Java-oriented tags (scriptlets and expressions).

The Java code requires curly brackets to define blocks of code, and these symbols must be embedded within scriptlets. Therefore, if HTML needs to appear conditionally or iteratively (as in the preceding example), the scriplet tag symbols appear frequently.

Developers and vendors have addressed these drawbacks by writing their own tags in custom libraries. These custom tags moved some of the application logic to the tag library code. These tags can then be mixed with HTML and other action tags to make a more homogeneous file that is easier to read and write.

The problem with vendor and developer solutions such as these is that they require each organization to create and maintain custom tag libraries. The Jakarta Apache Project (jakarta.apache.org) created JSTL out of the need to have a standard way to embed basic logic in a JSP file using tags. JSTL is extensible and you can add custom tags to its standard set. It also includes an expression language that you can use when coding JSP files in JDeveloper. You refer to a JSLT tag in the same way as any other action tag—with a standard prefix and a tag name (for example, `c:forEach`).

NOTE
You can obtain a more detailed overview of JSTL in the J2EE 1.4 Tutorial at java.sun.com/j2ee/1.4/docs/tutorial/doc/index.html. The JSTL libraries are housed at the Jakarta Project web page: jakarta.apache.org/taglibs/doc/standard-1.0-doc. In addition, the JDeveloper help system documents the JSTL 1.0 tags (search for "JSTL reference" on the index page).

JSTL Example

The following code shows how to use JSTL to define the same HTML table as in the preceding example:

```
<table border="1">
  <c:forEach begin="1" end="3" var="i" >
    <tr>
    <c:forEach begin="1" end="4" var="j">
      <td>
        <c:out value="${i}" />:<c:out value="${j}" />
      </td>
    </c:forEach>
    </tr>
  </c:forEach>
</table>
```

This example mixes JSTL and HTML tags to create the HTML table in the same way as the preceding example mixed Java and HTML. The JSTL version contains more characters. However, most developers will find it much easier to write and read because the code uses only well-formed tags instead of a mixture of HTML tags and Java. Instead of having to embed HTML inside a Java loop (which requires switching in and out of scriptlets), the loop functionality is supplied by the `forEach` JSTL tag.

The Java class that implements the forEach tag in the second example is contained in a custom code library that is referred to by the prefix "c." The tag class contains the same Java logic as the scriptlet in the previous example, but the internals of this logic are hidden from the developer. The developer only needs to work with tags and tag attributes, not with Java.

Tag Libraries

JSTL 1.0 (for JSP 1.2) is divided into four libraries, each of which uses a standard prefix. You need to include a taglib directive in the JSP file for each library whose tags you use in that file. The taglib directive includes a URI for the appropriate library and the prefix. The following section lists the tags in each library and shows the taglib directive required in the JSP file when you use tags in each library.

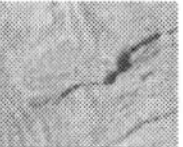

NOTE
In addition to the libraries discussed here, an additional library that contains functions (such as endsWith, indexOf, length, replace, toUpperCase, and trim) was released with JSTL 1.1. JSTL 1.1 requires a Web Tier container (runtime) that supports JSP 2.0. Since JDeveloper supports JSP 1.2, it also natively supports JSTL 1.1, but you need to register the JSTL 1.1 libraries if you want to use JSTL 1.1 with JDeveloper.

Core

The core JSTL library includes basic tags for the following functionality:

- **Variable scope:** remove, set
- **Miscellaneous:** catch, out
- **Flow control:** choose, forEach, forTokens, if, otherwise, when
- **URL management:** import, param, redirect, url

You reference this library using the following directive:

```
<%@ taglib uri="http://java.sun.com/jstl/core" prefix="c" %>
```

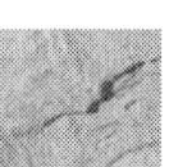

NOTE
The JDeveloper Component Palette provides pages for the tags in these libraries. When you drag a component into your code from one of these pages, JDeveloper also adds the appropriate taglib directive if it is not already in the file.

XML

The XML library tags access and process the contents of XML documents and data streams. XML tags fall into the following categories:

- **Core:** `out, parse, set`
- **Flow control:** `choose, forEach, if, otherwise, when`
- **Transformation:** `transform, param`

Use the following `taglib` directive when including XML JSTL tags:

```
<%@ taglib uri="http://java.sun.com/jstl/xml" prefix="x" %>
```

NOTE

Many tag libraries contain tags that are used as subtags. That is, the tag must appear within the context of another tag. For example, `param` *must be contained within the start and end tags of another tag, such as* `transform`*.*

Internationalization

The internationalization (abbreviated as *i18n* because the word "internationalization" contains 18 characters between the "i" and the "n") tags allow you to set a specific locale for messages in the application. Based on the locale, the messages will be taken from a resource bundle file that is specific to the locale. The internationalization tags also allow you to format number, date, and time data. These tags fall into the following categories:

- **Setting locale:** `setLocale`, `requestEncoding`
- **Messaging:** `bundle`, `message`, `param`, `setBundle`
- **Number and date formatting:** `formatNumber`, `formatDate`, `parseDate`, `parseNumber`, `setTimeZone`, `timeZone`

The following `taglib` directive points to the internationalization tags:

```
<%@ taglib uri="http://java.sun.com/jstl/fmt" prefix="fmt" %>
```

SQL

The SQL tags allow you to embed basic Structured Query Language statements. Although these statements are fully functional for database queries (SELECT) and updates (INSERT, UPDATE, DELETE, and DDL operations), the SQL operations are better placed inside other frameworks such as ADF BC so that they can take advantage of features such as caching. The following SQL tags are available in this library:

- **General:** `setDataSource`, `transaction`
- **Query operation:** `query`, `param`, `dateParam`
- **Update operation:** `update`, `param`, `dateParam`

Use the following `taglib` directive to reference the SQL library:

```
<%@ taglib uri="http://java.sun.com/jstl/sql" prefix="sql" %>
```

Expression Language

As with other tags, attribute values for JSTL tags can be specified as character strings, for example:

```
<c:forEach begin="1" end="3" var="i" >
```

In this example, the `begin`, `end`, and `var` attributes contain static character strings, "1," "3," and "i," respectively.

For dynamic attribute values derived from beans or other Java code in the JSP, JSTL uses an *expression language* that provides implicit objects and operators to manipulate and access the values of code objects and variables. EL is regarded to be simpler than the expressions used for dynamic values in JSP tags. Consider the following example:

```
<c:forEach begin="1" end="${param.columns}"  var="i">
```

In this example, the value of the `end` attribute is based on a parameter that is loaded dynamically in an HTTP request (which might be input using an HTML form). The standard markers for an EL value are the "$" sign prefix and curly brackets "{ }" enclosing the expression.

NOTE

Expression language can be used in static text as well as in tag attribute values. You can mix EL and static character strings in a single attribute value.

Implicit Objects

Expression language assumes that the identifiers used inside the expression are user-defined variables unless they are one of the following:

- `applicationScope`
- `cookie`
- `header`
- `headerValues`
- `initParam`
- `pageContext`
- `pageScope`
- `param`
- `paramValues`
- `requestScope`
- `sessionScope`

Each of these identifiers has a specific meaning within the context of the JSP runtime session. For example, the `pageContext` object sets the scope for the JSP page and includes access to values in the servlet, session, HTTP request, and HTTP response. The `param`, `cookie`, and `header` objects access a single value by name. The other objects are Map (collection) types that contain arrays of values.

In the `forEach` example shown earlier, the expression contains "`param.columns`", which refers to the value of an HTTP request variable called "`columns`."

HINT
The J2EE tutorial mentioned before contains details about these implicit objects and operators.

Operators

EL offers the standard Java operator for property access ("."). Instead of using the "." syntax, you can also use square brackets. For example, the following two lines of code are equivalent:

```
<c:out value="${param['columns']}" />
<c:out value="${param.columns}" />
```

The square bracket syntax is useful if you want to dynamically construct the name of the property. In the preceding example, the word "columns" could be assigned dynamically in code before the `out` tag. Then, an expression or variable name would be used inside the square brackets to represent the value "columns."

Other operators offered by EL follow:

- **Arithmetic** `+`, `-`, `*`, `/` (or `div`), `%` (or `mod`)
- **Relational** `==` (or `eq`), `!=` (or `ne`), `<;` (or `lt`), `>` (or `gt`), `<=` (or `le`), `>=` (or `ge`)
- **Logical** `&&;` (or `and`), `||` (or `or`), `!` (or `not`)
- **Validation** `empty`

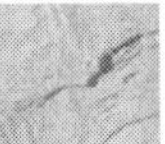

NOTE
Expression language was developed as part of JSTL 1.0 (JSP 1.2) but has been incorporated into the JSP 2.0 specification. As mentioned, JDeveloper supports JSP 1.2 and therefore also supports JSTL 1.0.

An Annotated Example

The best way to demonstrate how JSTL can be used in a JSP is by showing a simple example. The following code presents a basic HTML form containing two input fields. When the JSP page first appears, it looks like the following:

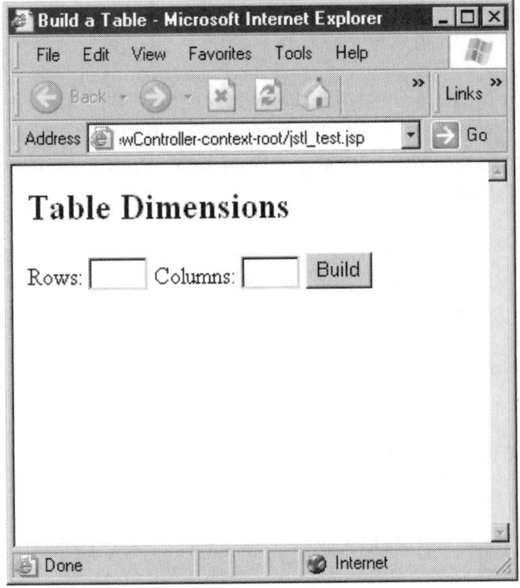

After the user enters a value for each field and clicks Build, the JSP file processes the input and draws an HTML table above the fields; the table is sized as the user requested, and its cells contain the row and column number as shown here:

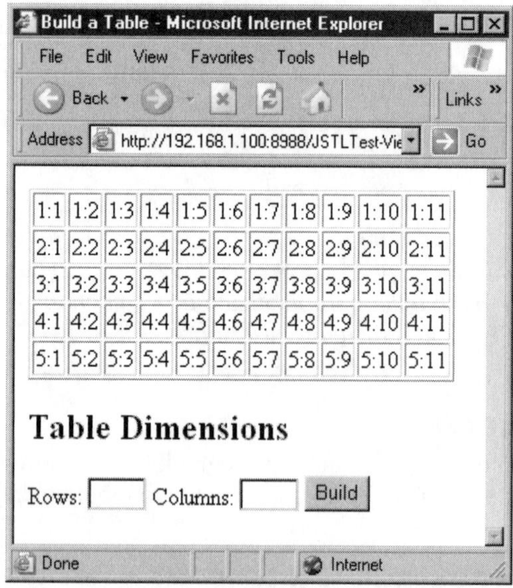

The Sample Code

The following code listing implements one solution for the JSP page just shown. This code is not a full production-level solution and therefore does not contain all possible validity checks on the values entered by the user. The line numbers shown here are for reference purposes only and would not be part of the JSP file.

```
<%@ page contentType="text/html;charset=windows-1252"%>
<%@ taglib uri="http://java.sun.com/jstl/core" prefix="c" %>
<html>
  <head>
    <title>Build a Table</title>
  </head>
  <body>
    <c:if test="${pageContext.request.method=='POST'}" >
      <c:set var="varName" value="rows" />
      <c:choose>
        <c:when test="${param[varName]=='0' or param.columns=='0'}" >
          Both Rows and Columns must be greater than 0.<br />
        </c:when>
        <c:otherwise>
          <table border="1">
            <c:forEach begin="1" end="${param.rows}" var="i" >
              <tr>
```

```
18:               <c:forEach begin="1" end="${param.columns}"  var="j">
19:                 <td>
20:                   <c:out value="${i}:${j}" />
21:                 </td>
22:               </c:forEach>
23:               </tr>
24:             </c:forEach>
25:           </table>
26:         </c:otherwise>
27:       </c:choose>
28:     </c:if>
29:
30:     <h2>Table Dimensions</h2>
31:     <form method="POST">
32:       Rows: <input type="text" name="rows" size="3" />
33:       Columns: <input type="text" name="columns" size="3" />
34:       <input type="submit" value="Build" /><br />
35:     </form>
36:
37:   </body>
38: </html>
```

The following provides a brief explanation of this code:

- **Lines 01 and 02** set up the page type and the reference to the JSTL core library. This JSP file only contains core tags so it only needs one `taglib` directive.
- **Lines 03 and 38** define the boundaries of the HTML page.
- **Lines 04–06** display the browser window title.
- **Lines 07 and 37** define the visible page contents (the body).
- **Lines 08 and 28** define a block of code inside an `if` conditional test. This conditional tests whether the HTML page has been called by a POST operation (for example, from the result of an HTML form submission). If it has not, the JSP does not process any of the code inside the `if` block. The request object within the context of the page contains a property, `method`, which exposes the type of request (POST or GET). This request type is specified in the form tag (line 31 in this JSP file).
- **Line 09** creates a variable, `varName`, which stores the name of a variable. In this case, `varName` is included only as an example of how you can embed a dynamic name in a value reference (in line 11). Instead of hard-coding the value as in this code line, the value of `varName` would be loaded dynamically in other code or in a request parameter.
- **Line 10** starts another conditional block that ends at line 27. JSTL does not offer an `else` clause for the `if` tag, but the `choose` tag provides a way to create a multi-condition block of code (like a nested `if` in Java). The conditional blocks are embedded within the `choose` tag by using `when` tags. The last block uses an `otherwise` tag that acts as an `else` condition (and is executed when other `when` conditions are false).

- **Lines 11–13** define the first condition, which checks if either the row or the column numbers entered by the user are "0." If so, it displays a message and then exits the `if` block. The expression within the test attribute checks if the `rows` variable is "0" using the square bracket syntax for property statements. The `varName` variable is evaluated and its value substituted as the name of the property. The second part of the condition is joined to the first using the `or` operator; it checks whether the columns entered by the user have a value of "0" using the "." property syntax.

- **Lines 14 to 26** define the `otherwise` block that occurs if the other `when` conditions (of which there is only one in this case) fail. This block draws the HTML table based on the row and column values entered by the user.

- **Lines 15 and 25** specify an HTML table with a visible border.

- **Line 16** defines a loop that iterates between one and the number of rows in the parameter passed from the HTTP request. It defines a variable, "`i`", that will contain the value of the iterator. The loop block ends at line 24. Although this example uses a beginning and ending counter value, you can alternatively define the iterator for a `forEach` loop using an `items` attribute that allows you to loop over a number of members of a Map collection. This type of iterator is used for processing multiple rows from a result set of a database query.

- **Line 17 and 23** uses the `tr` tag to define the boundaries of the HTML table row.

- **Line 18** begins a loop for the columns in the row. It specifies a different iterator variable ("`j`") and uses the columns parameter value as its last iteration number. The loop block ends at line 22.

- **Lines 19–21** add a `td` tag that defines the table cell. The columns loop continues to add columns until the iterator reaches the value of the columns parameter.

- **Line 20** displays the counter values, `i` and `j`, separated by a colon ":" using the core library `out` tag. In this example, the expressions contain only variable names and are concatenated with the colon using implicit string concatenation (no operator is required for string concatenation in JSTL).

- **Lines 30–35** define the HTML form for this page. The form is processed using the POST method and contains two input fields (called `rows` and `columns`) and a submit button. When the user fills in the fields and clicks Build, the JSP file calls itself and passes the values of the fields in the HTTP request. These parameters are then available to the JSTL code in the `param` object properties `param.rows` and `param.columns`.

Since JDeveloper uses JSTL and EL extensively when generating databound JSP files, the concepts introduced here should help you understand and make changes to the code that JDeveloper generates with ADF. Refer to the information resources mentioned throughout this appendix for more information.

Index

!--, 736, 741, 751
& HTML tag, 735, 765
> HTML tag, 765
< HTML tag, 735, 765
  HTML tag, 735
<% = expression %>, 747–748, 758, 759
<% Java code %>. *See* Scriptlet
<% ! %> 750, 757. *See also* Declarations, JSP
<%@ directive_name %>, 753, 758
< >, 206, 548, 735, 746. *See also* HTML, tags
3GL, xxxvi, 106, 108, 120, 132, 173, 505, 644
4GL, 7, 9, 11, 106
1 to *, 276
1 to 1, 276

A

<a> HTML tag, 736
Abbreviations, 172, 173, 726
Abstract Windowing Toolkit. *See* AWT
Accelerators, 48, 78
Access modifier, 71, 142
Access specifier. *See* Access modifier
Accessor attributes, 259–260, 360–361
    destination, 260
    renaming, 274–275
    source, 260
Accessor methods, 145, 174
Accessors
    generate menu item, 51
    See also Getters, Setters
Action bindings, 372, 374, 378, 379, 382, 386, 387, 390, 393, 397, 408
Action tags, 595, 596
    JSP, 650, 754, 755–756, 758
ActionForm class, 594, 596, 598
actionPerformed, 75, 517, 518, 540
Actions, 503, 593, 601
    class, 593–594
    JSP tags, 754–757
Activity Diagrammer. *See also* Modelers, Activity
Activity diagrams, 101
Add CodeSnippet dialog, 725
Add JavaBeans dialog, 538
Add Javadoc Comments, 51
Add to
    Diagram dialog, 101
    menu item, 46
Add to Diagram, 101
Add to project checkbox, 66, 201
Add Validation Rule dialog, 305
Addin API, 54
ADF, 4, 10, 104–130
    and EJB technology, 454–456
    architecture model, 110–118
    bindings, 114–115
    business components, 112
    Business Services layer, 110–112
    code libraries, 118–119

data controls, 112. *See also* Data controls
development method, 120–130
JClient, 507
layers and components, 110–118
model layer, 382, 454–456, 474–475, 489
UIX integration, 687
user community support for, 109
ADF BC, xxxvii, 112, 255, 263, 447
and TopLink POJO, 471
binding Swing components to, 508–509
Component Palette, 265
default layer, 234
JDeveloper implementation of, 598
prepare a simple Java application, 197–198
project, 520–521
relationships, 228
why use, 225–226
See also ADF Business Components
ADF Business Components, 9, 10, 107, 112, 118, 130, 175, 185, 190, 224–251
groups, 226–234
naming, 177–179
properties, 658
See also ADF BC
ADF Data Access, Component Palette page, 649
ADF JClient, 116, 507, 508
ADF UIX, 6, 9, 117, 182, 205, 686–712
and J2EE, 687
application development in JDeveloper, 693–698
component example, 691
data controls, 698
dynamic images, 688
extensibility, 689
features, 687–689
hands-on practice: Build an Application, 699–712
JDeveloper support for applications, 7
overview, 686–693
page design structure, 689–692
standardization, 687–688
steps for creating Struts application, 696–698
Aggregation, 276, 361–362
Aliases, table, 337–338
Align, 526, 549, 574, 585
Alignment, 31, 548, 558, 571
align property, 549, 550, 568, 571, 647
alignmentx, 556
alignmenty, 556
All UIX Components, Component Palette page, 696
ALTER TABLE, 269
anchor, 561, 562, 565, 589
Apache Software Foundation, 10, 116
append( ), 157
Applets, 194–196, 502
develop and deploy, 204
Application architecture model for J2EE, 185–186
Application code, creating in JDeveloper, 13–15
Application Development Framework, xxxvii, 8, 9, 10. *See also* ADF
Application module classes, 409–410

Application module definitions, 178, 231–234, 447
  classes, 410
  create and test, 365–367
  exploring, 247–248
  hands-on practice: creating, 362–367
  testing, 366–367
Application Module Editor, 113, 410, 529
Application module pooling, 233
Application Navigator, 16, 65–68, 237
Application Package Prefix, 175, 235
Application. *See* Applications
Application server, connection, 68, 216
Application Templates, 121
  managing, 123–124
Application Workspaces, 13, 65
  creating, 16–18, 121–124, 160–161, 235, 270–272, 343, 458, 476–478, 490–491, 577–578, 607–608, 664–665
  See also Workspaces
application.xml, 187
ApplicationModuleDefImpl, 410
ApplicationModuleImpl, 410
ApplicationResources.properties, 594–595
Applications. *See also* Java Applications
Archive Viewer, 95–96, 201
Archive
  deploying files, 188
  files, 186
Arrays, 146, 154
  multi-dimensional, 155
Association accessor attribute, 447
Association Editor, 242, 261–262, 280, 281
Associations, 229, 447
  1 to *, 276
  bi-directional, 259
  cardinality, 258–259
  directed 1-to *, 276, 279
  directed 1-to-1, 276
  directionality, 259–261
  exploring, 241–242
  naming, 178
  uni-directional, 259
  See also Relationships
Attachment element on Component Palette, 603
Attribute Binding Editor, 384, 675
Attribute bindings, 372, 381
Attribute Editor, 273, 274, 314–315, 319, 659
Attributes, 137
  accessor, 259
  adding and deleting, 255
  calculating, 323
  controls, 655
  display, 395
  HTML, 737
  LOV, 395
  mandatory, 273–274, 283

manipulating values, 291–293
mapping, 354–357, 472
persistent, 283
reading and changing values, 417
target, 395
transient, 255, 283, 316–318
validation, 293–299
Auditing, 86
Auto Hiding, 43
AWT, 183, 722–724
axis, 555

B

<b> HTML tag, 736
Base application module classes, 409
Batch files, 202–204
Batch mode, 409
turn off, 423
BC4J, 5, 6, 109
Bean class, 448
property, 455
BeanInfo, 93, 455
Bean-managed relationships (BMRs), 450
Bean-model definition files, 454, 474
Bi-directional associations, 259
view-link definitions, 360, 361
Bind to Data button, 74
Bind to Data toolbar, 648
Binding containers, 370–372, 402
Binding context, 370
Bindings, 371–375, 402, 507
ADF, 114–115
panels, 509–510
Swing components to ADF BC, 508–509
blaf.css, 680, 688, 711
BluePrints, 134, 184, 225
Body HTML tag, 736
Bookmarks, 48
Boolean, 327
datatype, 154, 157
Border object, 546
border, 517, 581
BorderLayout, 515, 550, 551–553, 574, 576
Manager, 579–583
borderLayout, 545
Borders, 546
bounds property, 586
BoxLayout2, 550, 554–556, 574

 HTML tag, 736
Brace, open style, 77, 143, 759
Brackets, 142–143
Breakpoints window, 84, 85
Breakpoints, 86
Bring to Front, 549
Browsers
HTML, 735
support, 196, 699, 739
Build. *See* Rebuild
Business Component Browser, opening, 248–249, 282–283
Business Components Client Data Model Wizard, 26
Business Components for Java. *See* BC4J
Business components
and database object generation, 264–269
creating default, 264
testing, 249–251
Business domain components, 227–229, 236, 459

creating, 253–285
exploring, 238
for table generation, 276–278
importing, 343–344
testing, 281–285
Business logic, 225–226, 319–321
default, 314, 322
Business rules
complex, 288–328
hands-on practice: Add to HR Business Domain Components, 321–328
using associations in, 317
Business Services, 12, 110–112
creating, 124–127
Business Tier, 185, 186, 190, 206
Button, 653, 655, 702, 723. *See also* JButton
Button with Form, 385, 653, 655
byte, 154, 158
bytecode, 148, 189, 639

C

c:out, 386, 429–430, 669
C++, 136–137
Caching, 330
Calling sequence, 190–191, 207
Cardinality
association, 258–259, 279
changing, 279–280
view link definition, 359–360
CardLayout, 550, 556–557, 574
Cascade Delete, 262
Cascading style sheets, 609, 649, 680, 740–744
building, 741–742
using, 742–744
See also CSS
Case sensitivity, 141, 162, 172, 175–176
Casting
literals, 159
objects, 158–159
catch, 465, 466
Categories
button, 73, 74
navigator, 89, 121
Character entity references, 735
Check constraints, 267
Checkbox component, 723
Checkbox Group, 724
CheckRequired( ), 740
Choice, 724
Class diagrams, 11, 99
Class Editor, 92–94, 479, 480
Class instances, naming, 174
Class Path, 119. *See also* CLASSPATH
Class variables, 152, 750
Classes, 137, 140, 146, 156
debugging, 85
detail, 516
entity collection, 291
entity definition, 291
entity object 289–291
Java, 112
master, 516
moving, 53
naming, 173, 177

renaming, 53
string, 156
variables, 152
wrapper, 156
Checkboxes
Add c:otherwise, 620
Add to Project, 66, 201
Application Module, 236
Auto-Query, 22
Cascade Update Key Attributes, 262
Composition Association, 262
Compress Archive, 202
Copy Files to Project Directory, 701
Data Manipulation Methods, 320
Deferrable Validation, 268
Display in Window, 56
Enable Validation, 268
Expert Mode, 348
Expose Accessor, 277
Generate Default Constructor, 163
Generate Java File, 325, 424
Highlight All Occurrences, 48
Implement Cascade Delete, 262
Include Debug Information, 84
Include Manifest File, 199
Initially Deferred Validation, 268
Key Attribute, 348
Mandatory, 274
Optimize for Database Cascade Delete, 262
Perform Module Checkout, 61
Persistent, 273
Public, 163
Refresh After Insert, 319
Refresh After Update, 319
Skip this Page Next Time, 19
Selected in Query, 323
Show Public Synonyms, 69
Use Database Key Constraints, 266
Use Database Key Constraints, 277
Use State Overlay Icons, 58
Version Control, 60
CLASSPATH, 79, 122, 141, 344. *See also* Class Path
Clear Highlighting, 48
Client Data Models
developing, 508
naming, 177
Client interface, 412
Client tier, 185, 186, 190, 206
Client/server
hands-on practice: Building Applications, 15–29
environment limitations, 192–193
CMP entity beans, 448
CMR, 447, 450, 460
field wrappers, 463, 464
fields, 452
CMR field, 447
Code
block, 142
deployment, 148–151
development, 148–151
Code Coach, 49, 86
Code Editor, 76–83, 644–645, 724
style sheet support, 82–83
Code generation, 34
Code Insight, 78–79
Code organization, 34
ADF libraries, 118–119
Code Snippets, 72–73, 649, 696, 724–725

Code stub, 75, 518
Code templates, 73, 77–78
CodeCoach, xxxviii, 49, 86
Coding techniques, ADF BC JSP, 657–663
Collections, 154, 371, 456–457, 475
  navigating, 378–380
Column constraints, 255–257
Columns, 567
Comment, 142, 750
Commit, 391, 396, 398, 455
Common Gateway Interface. *See* CGI
CompareValidator, 294
CompareWith, submenu of File menu, 46–47
Compiling, 45
Completion Insight, 79
  menu item, 51
Component Palette, 17, 25, 72–73, 127, 511, 547, 648–650, 696–697, 722–732
  add a page to, 536–539
  customizing, 532, 536–539
  Struts Page Flow page, 600, 762
Components, 503
  atomic, 546
  Swing, 512–513
Composition Association checkbox, 262
Compositions, 261–263, 302
Compress Archive checkbox, 202
concat( ), 156, 157
Concurrent Versions System, 9, 57–58. *See also* CVS
Conditional branching, 149
Configuration management, xxxix
Configurations, 53
Configure File Associations, menu item, 52
Configure Palette, menu item, 52
Connection Navigator, 16, 19, 68–69
Connections
  application server, 68
  CVS Server, 60, 68
  Designer workarea, 69
  naming, 176
  SOAP Server, 69
  UDDI Registry, 69
  WebDAV server, 69
Consistency, 170
Console, 36, 146, 147, 165, 466
Constants, 153
Constraints
  additional, 257
  check, 267
  entity, 267, 547
  not null, 256
  primary key, 256–257
  unique, 266, 267, 285
  window, 561
constraints property, 524, 547, 553, 555, 560, 562, 587–590
Constructor, 145
Container managed persistence entity bean (CMP), 447
Container-managed relationships. *See* CMR
Containers, 204, 513–517
  concepts, 545–551

EJB, 205
layout, 506
web, 204–205
Containment Hierarchy, 545
Context menus, xlii, 45
Control hints, 659–663, 682, 684
Control statements in Java, 148–149
Control type, 660
Controller, 115–117
layer, 127–128
Core JSTL library, 761
Create Application Workspace dialog, xliii, 18
Create Business Components Diagram, 270
Create Business Components from Tables Wizard, 125, 234, 237
Create Entity Constraint Wizard, 267
Create JClient Empty Form, 522
CREATE TABLE, 269
Create UIX XML Page Wizard, 701
Create View Link Wizard, 358
create( ), 322, 605, 608
operation, 455, 655
createRow( ), 417
CSS, 649, 687, 734. *See also* Cascading style sheets
Curly brackets (brace style), 71, 77, 142, 143, 149
Current row pointer, 378–379
changing, 416
Custom service methods, 408–443
Custom, 724, 727, 729, 731
Customizers, 73
button, 74
Customizing, 73
IDE, 43–44
CVS
concepts, 57–58
server, 59
setting up locally, 58–61
See also Concurrent Versions System
CVS Server, 68

D

Data, 513
debugger window, 85
handling and storing, 137–139
validation, 505–506
Data actions, 601–602
creating, 495, 627–631, 667
naming, 179
Data binding editors, 652–653
Data bindings. *See* Bindings
Data collection level, 654–655
Data control BeanInfo files, 455
Data control definition files, 454, 486
create, 493–494
Data control description files, 454, 475
Data control implementation files, 455
Data control metadata files, 454
Data Control Palette, 91–92, 113–114, 128–129, 372–374, 381, 456, 474, 509–511, 605, 650–657
Data Controls, 112–114, 370–371, 604–605
definition files, 467–468, 474
for Struts JSP pages, 654–655

UIX, 704–705
See also ADF data controls
Data Manipulation Methods checkbox, 320
Data models, 650–651
and TopLink POJO, 473–474
application module, 113
client, 6
components, 114, 344–345
components, 230–234
creating an EJB Finder, 460–464
creating defauly components, 281–282
diagram, 242–243
Data Pages, 180, 383, 468, 494, 495–496, 601, 666, 667, 703
Data sources, 91, 92, 112, 508, 509, 648
Data Transfer Objects. *See* DTOs
Database
connections, 69
datatypes, 256
generating objects, 268–269
triggers, 318–319
versions, xlii
Database connection, 19
Database Modeler, 11
Database, xl, xli, xlii, 5, 6, 13, 137–138, 172, 225, 331
connection, 16, 19, 68, 69
data-sources.xml, 188
datatypes, 256
integrating with business logic, 318–321
non-Oracle, 255
object generation, 264–269
object operations, 98
TopLink mapping, 470–472
Datatypes, 154–155
changing, 255
matching, 157
primitive, 154
reference, 154
See also Variables
Date fields, 661
Date format strings, 662
DBSequence, 315–316
Deadlocks, 85
Debug
button, 86
menu, 86
Debugger, 84–86
Debugging, xxxviii, 130
Java code, 85–86
PL/SQL, 86
Declarations, JSP, 750, 752, 757
Default layout, 548
Default modifier, 142
Default values
adding to entity attributes, 314–316
dynamically calculated, 315
static, 314–315
Deferrable validation checkbox, 268
Delete, 455, 605, 655. *See also* Erase from Disk
Dependency
analysis, 200
analyzer, 191
Deploy
application, 130
J2EE applications, 186–188

Java applications, 196–204
menu item, 49
Deployment, 182
archive files, 188
descriptor files, 187–188, 470
J2EE alternatives, 182–219
process, 189
profile, 189, 198–200
Deprecated features, 12, 134
Descriptors, 471
create, 480–484
Design patterns, 134, 184. *See also* BluePrints
Design structure tab, 695
Designer Workarea, 69
Desupported features, 12
Detail class, 516
Development frameworks, 106–107
in previous JDeveloper releases, 109–110
Development process, 8, 105, 148
Development steps, 14–15
Diagrams, 98–102, 126
activity, 101
business components, 127
business domain, 282
Create Business Components, 270
UML, 99–100
Dialogs
Add JavaBeans, 538
Add to Diagram, 101
Add Validation Rule, 294, 305
Business Components Project Initialization, 125
Create Application Workspace, 121
Create Bean, 533
Create Business Components Diagram, 270
Create Java Class, 101
Create Library, 536
Field Settings, 307
Insert HTML/JSP, 643
Project Properties, 53
View Class Path, 119
Directed Association 1 to *, 276
Directed Association 1 to 1, 276
Directed Strong Aggregation, 276
Directives in JSP pages, 753, 758
Directories, xliv, 14, 53, 67, 171, 504, 505
Directory Structure, 14
Disable validation, 268
Display, modifying, 68
Display Height control hint, 660
Display Hint control hint, 660, 671
Display Width control hint, 660
DML operations, 319–321
Dockable windows, 35, 40–43
Docking, windows, 40–43
Document, tabs, 38
document property, 115, 507, 509
Domains, 229, 263
conversion methods, 292
creating for Oracle object type generation, 268
custom, 263
DB Sequence, 315–316
manipulation methods, 293
naming, 178
validation, 295–296, 310–312
do-while, 150

Drag and Drop As, pulldown, 114, 129, 372, 380, 605, 650
Drag handles, 558–560
DROP TABLE, 269
DTO CMR field wrapper, 447
DTOs, 447, 462–464, 466

E

EAR file, 187, 188
Edit menu, 47–48
Edit Rule tab, 529
Editing
  items, 67
  PL/SQL, 81–82
  text, 80
Editor tabs, 38
Editor window, 17, 38–40
  splitting, 38–40
  unsplitting, 38–40
Editors
  Application Module, 113
  Class, 92–94
  Code, 81–83
  Entity Object, 126
  JSP/HTML Visual, 128
  Property, 73
  Visual, 86–87
  XML, 92
EIS tier, 185, 186, 190, 206
EJB, 111, 94–95
  and ADF Model layer, 454
  component relationships, 449
  hands-on practice: Build a Simple, 458–470
  local reference, 465
  relationships, 450
  session beans, 453
  See also Enterprise JavaBeans
EJB Deployment Descriptor, 448
EJB entity beans, 448
EJB finder method, 447, 450
EJB Query Language, 451
EJB session beans, 453, 464–467
EJB Module Editor, 94, 451
EL. *See* Expression Language
Embedded OC4J Server, 392, 639
  menu item, 54
  See also OC4J Server
Empty UI,X XML Page, 693
Enable validation, 268
Encapsulation, 140
EndTag Completion, 77, 92, 644. *See also* Code Completion
Enterprise application archive. *See* EAR
Enterprise Information System. *See* EIS tier
Enterprise JavaBeans, 446–457
  hands-on practice: Build a Simple EJB Application, 458–470
  See also EJB
Entity associations, 178, 179
Entity attribute accessors, 290–291
Entity attributes, 178, 227, 254, 330–337
  adding default values, 314–316
  transient, 254, 272–274
  typing, 312
  See also attributes

Entity bean instance, 447, 449
Entity Bean, 447, 448
Entity cache, 288
    populating, 332, 333
Entity classes
    base, 288
    custom, 288
    overview, 288–291
Entity collection classes, 291
Entity constraints, 267
Entity definition classes, 291
Entity derived view attributes, 2, 334–337
    populating, 331–333
Entity object classes, 289–291, 317
    removing unneeded, 303–304
Entity object definitions, 227–229, 254
    creating for table generation, 265, 276
    exploring, 239–242
    naming, 177, 447
    synchronizing with database, 257
Entity Object Editor, 126, 240, 266, 304, 320
Entity object instances, 228, 447
    currency, 300
Entity object usages, 337–338
    reference, 350
    with expert mode, 341
Entity objects, 23, 177
EntityImpl, 290, 291, 301, 315, 317
Entity-level validation, 302, 312–314
    rules, 300–301
Enumeration mode, 394–395
Erase from Disk, 67
Errors, 71, 76, 81, 92
Event handlers, 116, 690, 691
Event listener, 517
event_Execute, 667
event_Submit, 428, 429
Events, 75
    button, 74
    defining, 517–518
    submit, 428
    tab of Property Inspector, 519
Exception handling, 150
Exceptions
    handling, 150
    naming, 174
Execute, 605, 667
executeQuery( ), 415
Expand Template, menu item, 51
Expert mode, 340–341
ExplainPlan, 98
Expose Accessor checkbox, 281
Expression Language (EL), 639, 763–765
Expressions in JSP pages, 752, 758
Extension Manager, 35, 44, 124
Extensions, UIX, 689
External Tools, menu item, 54

F

Fields
    remove unneeded, 671–672
    transformation methods, 472
File
    change validator, 66–67
    comparisons, 46–47
    dialogs, 91
    diff, 46–47

groups, 199
menu, 45–47
navigators, 66
struts-config.xml, 595–597
File input field, 656
Files
adding, 67
ApplicationResources.properties, 594–595
class source, 177
class, 140
create Java class, 160–166
data control definition, 467–468, 474–475
deploying archive, 188
deployment descriptor, 187–188
frame, 578–579
removing, 67
search, 48
support for JSP, 7
fill property, 562, 566, 589
Filter By pulldown, 10, 21, 89, 122, 123
Filters
applying, 69
multi-character, 22
name, 22
single character, 22
final
class, 153
keyword, 153
method, 153
finally, 150
Find Area button, 74
Find, 595
mode, 657–658
First, 379, 455, 605, 655
Fit to Window icon, 100
float, 159, 276
Flow control
JSTL tags, 761
XML, 762
FlowLayout, 550, 557–558, 574
for loop statement, 150
Foreign key
attributes, 242, 265
constraints, 255, 266
relationships, 178, 229, 261, 472–473
Form components, Component Palette page, 696
Form elements, 653
Form Type control hint, 660
form, HTML tag, 737, 739–740
Format, 660
Format masks, 660, 661
Format Type control hint, 660
Formatters, 660
See also Format masks
Forms, 380
edit, 400–405
input, 401, 610
master-detail, 468–470, 486–488
read-only, 382–387
Forms Developer. *See* Oracle Forms Developer
Forwards, 180, 401, 404, 593, 602–603

Frame, 179, 190, 547
class, 514, 575
container, 551
files, 578
New dialog, 91, 546
Frameworks, 104–105
development, 106–107
Freeze view button, 74, 646

G

Gallery. *See* New gallery
Generate Accessors, menu item, 51, 94
Generate Default Constructor checkbox, 162
Generate Javadoc, 51
Generate Java File checkbox, 424
Generate Main Method checkbox, 162
getAttribute( ), 160, 290, 317, 318, 417
Getters, 145, 174, 290, 318, 421, 448. *See also* get( )
Global style, 680, 740, 742, 743
globalButtonBar, 691
Go to declaration, 49
Go to Java Class, menu item, 49
Google, Web APIs, 490
Graph, 654
GridBagLayout, 516, 547, 550, 559–566, 574, 576
manager, 583–590
gridheight property, 563
GridLayout, 550, 566–568, 574
gridwidth property, 563
gridx property, 563
gridy property, 563
GROUP BY, 340
GUI controls, 192

H

<h1> HTML tag, 736
Hands-on practices, xxxix, xlii-xliv, 15–32, 58–61, 160–166, 196–203, 209–215, 269–285, 302–314, 321–328, 342–357, 362–367, 381–393, 397–405, 422–436, 437–443, 457–470, 475–488, 439–498, 520–532, 532–542, 577–590, 607–625, 625–636, 663–684, 699–712
hasNext( ), 415
<head> HTML tag, 736
Heap debug window, 84, 85
Help
button, 90
context-sensitive, 18, 645
displaying topic, 56
finding topic, 56
locating centrally, 56
menu, 54
system, xlii, xliv, 54–56
hgap property, 548, 553, 556, 558, 567, 572
Hidden field, 656
Highlighting, clear, 48
Home interface, 449–450, 454
horizontalFill property, 572
Hosted documentation, 56
<hr> HTML tag, 736, 738

HR schema, xl-xli
hands-on-practices:
Representing, 269–275,
Add Validation, 302–314
<html> HTML tag, 736
HTML
and applets, 204
Component Palette page, 649
editing, 734
end tag completion, 47
form, 737
in JSPs, 31, 205–206, 208
JavaScript in, 739–740
JSP/HTML Visual Editor, 87, 88, 128–129
Plugin Converter, 52
Previewers, 87, 89
sample code, 737–738
tags, 734–740
HTML DB, 5, 8
HTML Previewer, 87–89
HTTP Servlet. *See* Servlet
HTML tags, 386, 734–737
style, 742
well-formed, 735

I

<i> HTML tag, 736
I18n. *See* Internationalization
Icons
overlay, 58
Structure window, 70–71
IDE, 17
customizing, 43–44
for Java Client development, 502–503
overview, 34–61
support for ADF development, 120–130
tools, 64–102
windows, 35–43
if else statement, 149
iframes, 689
Image files, 643
dynamic, 688
Image Viewer, 95
Immutable, Java strings, 156, 157
Implement Interface, menu item, 52
Import, 142
Import Assistance, 80
Imports tab, 78
Include Components, Component Palette page, 696
Include Debug Information checkbox, 84
include directive, 753–754
includes. *See* Import
Incremental Search, 48
Indent Block, menu item, 51
index.html file, 51, 215
Indexed children, 691
Inheritance, 139, 153
init( ), 148, 195
Input field, 656
Input form, 610, 654, 706
InputRender tag, 656
Insert HTML/JSP dialog, 643
insertRow( ), 417
insets property, 564

Inspector
debugger window, 85
See also Property Inspector
Instance variables, 152
INSTEAD OF triggers, 137
int datatype, 144
Integrated Development Environment, 9–10. *See also* IDE
Interfaces, 155
interMedia, 726, 727
Internationalization (i18n), 687
JSTL library, 762–763
Intersection table, 259, 360, 473
ipadx property, 564
ipady property, 564
Iteration, 150
Iterator Binding Editor, 403
Iterator bindings, 371, 396
create, 403
multiple, 376
Iterators
source, 395
target, 395

J

_jspService( ), 639, 750, 752
J2EE, xxxv, 4, 8, 104, 183–186, 640
and UIX, 687
architectures, 182–219
archive files, 187
BluePrints, 184–185
deploying, 189
deployment alternatives, 182–219
JDeveloper and, 187–189
specifications, 185
J2ME, 183
J2SE, 183
Jakarta Project, 592
JAR Deployment Profile Properties dialog, 199
JAR files, 141, 187, 188
creating a file, 198–202
run file, 202–204
Java, xxxvi, 226
application support, 8
applications, 189–194
benefits, 133
classes, 112, 161–166, 478–480
drawbacks, 134–135
flexibility, 133
language concepts, 132–166
language libraries, 183
language review, 140–160
recognized naming conventions, 173–175
runtime architecture, 190
transitioning to, 135–136
Java 2 Platform, Enterprise Edition. *See* J2EE
Java 2 Platform, Micro Edition. *See* J2ME
Java 2 Platform, Standard Edition. *See* J2SE
Java Application [Default] template, 10
Java Application [Java, Swing] template, 10
Java applications, 189–194
advantages, 191–192
disadvantages, 192–193

when to use, 191–192
See also Applications
Java archive. *See* JAR files
Java client, 110, 182
applications, 502–542
architectures, 189–196, 504–507
controller, 116
controls, 74
data model components, 114
directory organization for application, 504
naming application files, 179
naming UI components, 179
user interface components, 114
user interface components, 722–732
Java Community Process (JCP), 8
Java Database Connectivity. *See* JDBC
Java Development Kit. *See* JDK
Java Network Launching Protocol. *See* JNLP
Java Platform, Micro Edition. *See* JME
Java Platform, Standard Edition. *See* JSE
Java Runtime Environment (JRE), 148
Java Server Faces, xxxix, 8, 117. *See also* JSF
Java Servlets. *See* Servlets
Java Virtual Machines, 35
See also JVMs
Java Visual Editor, 86, 549, 561
Java WebStart, 193, 194, 195, 203–204, 502, 719
java.lang.object, 317, 533
java.lang.String, 174, 229, 311
JavaBeans
creating and deploying, 532–535
custom, 537–539
Javadoc, 50–51
menu item, 49
Quick menu item, 51, 80
Add Comments menu item, 51
JavaScript, in HTML, 739–740
JavaServer Pages, 6, 182
architecture, 204–209
See also JSP
jbInit( ), 509–510, 512
JBuilder, 4
JButton, 729. *See also* Button
JCheckBox, 729
JClient Controls, 726–727
JClient. *See* ADF JClient
JComboBox, 729
JDBC, xxxvii, 183
JDesktopPane, 513
jdev.exe, xl, 36
JDEV_HOME, xl, 18, 35
JDeveloper 10*g*, xxxv, xxxvii, 4, 6–9
and J2EE, 188–189
development steps, 14–15
directory structure, 14
help system, xliv
history, 4–6
IDE window, 17, 36
IDE, 34–61
installing, xl
modeling, 11–12

release notes, xlv
running, xl
specific naming conventions, 175–180
vision, 6–7, 8–9
what's new, 9–12
why use, 6
JDeveloper9*i*, 5, 6
jdevw.exe, xl, 35, 36
JDK. *See also* SDK
JEditorPane, 729
JFormatted Text Field, 729
JFrame, 513, 514, 515, 575
JInternalFrame, 513
JLabel, 729
JList, 729
JMenuBar, 731
JNLP, 193
JPanel, 514, 515, 731
JPasswordField, 729
JPopupMenu, 731
JProgressBar, 729
JRadioButton, 729
JScrollBar, 729
JScrollPane, 514, 515, 516, 731
JSeparator, 730
JSF, 7. *See also* JavaServer Faces
JSlider, 730
JSP applications, 207, 638, 639, 641, 663
JSP comment, 751
JSP pages, 7, 747, 755, 757
JSP Standard Tag Library. *See* JSTL
JSP, 9, 117, 746
1.2 document, 746
advantages of, 208
application development, 641–657
architecture, 206
build query and results pages, 663–684
calling sequence, 207
compilation and runtime, 639–640
Component Palette page, 649
container, 206
create data page, 637–631
creating, 29–32, 210–212, 383, 469, 494
deploy an application, 209–219
development requirements, 638–640
disadvantages of, 208
hands-on practice: Create Master-Detail, 381, 393
hands-on practice: Refine the Application, 397–405
Standard Tag Library, 759–768
Structure tab, 646
support in JDeveloper, 7
tag delimiters, 757–758
tags, 446–759
technology overview, 205–209
translator, 206
when to use, 208
working with, 638–684
See also JavaServer Pages
JSP/HTML Visual Editor, 30, 87, 88, 128–129, 641–643, 734
JSpinner, 730
JSplitPane, 514, 732
JSTL, 639, 746
example, 760
tag libraries, 650, 749, 759–763

JTabbedPane, 514, 524, 732
JTable, 230
JTextArea, 730
JTextField, 730
JTextPane, 730
JToggleButton, 730
JToolBar, 732. *See also* Toolbars
JTree, 730
JUArrayComboBox, 727
JUImageControl, 727
JULabel, 727
JUNavigationBar, 727. *See also* Navigation bar
JURadioButtonGroupPanel, 727
JUStatusBar, 727
JVMs, 35. *See also* Java Virtual Machines

K

Key objects, 380, 415–416
Keyboard shortcuts, 48
Keymaps, 77
Keys, 338–339, 380
Keywords, final, 153

L

Label, 656, 724
Label Text control hint, 660
LAN, 192
Last, 379, 455, 605, 655
Layout components
    Component Palette page, 696
    UIX, 688
Layout managers, 544–590
layout property, 548, 551, 555. *See also* Layout managers
Layouts, 192, 544–590
    hands-on practice: Work With, 577–590
    multiple, 573–577
    setting properties, 548
    sources, 550
    See also Layout managers
Libraries, 141
    ADF code, 118–119
    creating, 535–536
    naming, 177
    view-level Struts tag, 597–598
Links
    insert, 648
    split, 648
List, 724
List Binding Editor, 395, 404, 675
List bindings, 372, 393, 398
List of Values, 650, 674–678. *See also* LOVs
ListValidator, 294
Literals, Casting, 159
Local home interface, 198, 448, 449, 453, 454
Locking, 263, 615
Log window, 17, 76
LONG, 256
Look-and-feel, 44
    modifying, 711–712
    swapping, 688
    UIX, 687–688
Looping, 150

LOV
- attributes, 395
- binding, 674
- mode, 395–396

M

Machine resources, xli
Main menu, 45–54
main( ), 146, 165, 190, 191
Make, 45, 49, 81
Make Project checkbox, 50
Manage Application Templates, menu item, 52
Manage Libraries, menu item, 52
Mandatory checkbox, 274
Mandatory, 256, 273–274, 296
- attribute testing, 283
- property, 658

manifest.mf, 199, 202
Many to Many, 705
Many-to-many, 258, 279–281, 284
- mappings, 473
- view link, 336, 359
- view link definition, 363–364

Mappings, 139
- datatype to Java, 256
- direct, 480–484
- direct-to-field, 472, 481–482
- many-to-many, 473
- object type, 472
- one-to-many, 473
- one-to-one, 473
- relationship, 472, 484–485
- serialized object, 472
- TopLink direct, 472
- transformation, 472, 482

Master class, 516
Master-detail panel, 179, 576
Master-detail
- relationships, 436–437, 440–443
- UIX layout, 704

maximumSize property, 554, 555
MDA. *See* Model-Driven Architecture
MDI, 513, 730
Measure, 49, 86
MediaControl, 727
Member variables, 152, 156
Menu Editor, 86
MenuBar, 724
Menus, xxxviii
- Debug, 50–51
- Edit, 47–48
- File, 46–47
- Help, 54
- Main, 45–54
- Model, 51
- Navigate, 48–49
- Run, 49–50
- Search, 48
- Source, 51
- Tools, 52–54
- Versioning, 52
- View, 48
- Window, 54

Message bundle, 660, 683
Methods, 144, 517
- attribute transformation, 472, 482
- class, 146
- createRow( ), 417

creating custom, 408–443
custom service, 412
EJB finder, 450
exposing and accessing service, 412
field transformation, 472, 483
find-by-field, 451
getAttribute( ), 160
hasNext( ), 415
insertRow( ), 417
main( ), 146, 165
naming, 145, 174
next( ), 415
overloaded, 144
overriding, 291, 632
pack( ), 547
removeCurrentRow( ), 417
signature, 144
substring, 157
System.out.println( ), 147
validateEntity( ), 301
validation( ), 296
MethodValidator, 294, 300
minimumSize property, 554, 555
Miscellaneous
Component Palette page, 696
core JSTL tags, 761
Miscellaneous Components, Component Palette page, 696
Model
layer, 112, 124–127, 370
menu, 51
project, 13, 20
Model 1 architecture, 184, 593, 657
Model 2 architecture, 184, 593
model property, 115, 503, 507, 509
Model-Driven Architectures (MDA), 108
Modelers, 98–102
Modeling, xxxix, 8, 11–12
Model-View-Controller (MVC), 6, 110, 133, 184–185, 592
Modifiers, 71
access, 142
default, 142
super, 144
Monitors
debugger window, 85
resolution, 37
Move Class, menu item, 53
Multiple Document Interface. *See* MDI
mutable, 157
MVC, 110, 184. *See also* Model-View-Controller

N

name property, 429, 667
Named children
example, 692
slots, 689
Naming conventions, 167–180
ADF business components, 177
application module definitions, 178
associations, 178
changing class, 289
class instances, 174
class source files, 177
classes, 173

client data models, 177
connections, 176
constants, 173
data actions, 179
data pages, 180
domains, 178
entity attributes, 178
entity object definitions, 177
exceptions, 174
forwards, 180
fully-qualified, 174
guidelines, 170–171
Java, 173–175
Java Client application files, 179
Java Client UI components, 179
Java elements, 147
libraries, 177
methods, 174
packages, 174
page forwards, 180
projects, 176
Struts components, 179
UML diagram elements, 177
variables, 174
view attributes, 178
view link definitions, 179
view object definitions, 178
Web client components, 179
workspaces, 176
Navigate menu, 48–49
Navigation bar, 516, 531, 575, 576, 692
Navigation components, Component Palette page, 696
Navigation
add a list, 398
add code, 431
buttons, 385, 654
controls, 678–680
list control, 654
mode, 393–394
Navigators, 16, 65–69
Application, 237
Connection, 68–69
See also System Navigator
New Class dialog, 163
New Gallery, 21, 25, 89–90, 122–123
New TabGroup, 40
New View button, 74, 646
Next Set, 379, 455, 605, 655
next( ), 415, 455, 655
NOT NULL, constraint, 256, 266, 277–278, 296
Note, 603
null layout, 547, 551, 562, 573, 574
Number class, 158
Number fields, formatting, 662–663
Number format strings, 663

O

Object orientation, concepts, 136–137
Object serialization, 138
Object-relational mapping, 111, 112, 446
Objects, 137
casting, 147
creating, 158–159
implicit, 764
serialization, 138
OC4J, 188, 209
server, 215, 615

set up, 212–216
startup, 214
stopping, 215
Offline tables, 478
OJSP tag libraries, 650
ON DELETE CASCADE, 261
One-click deployment, 217
One-to-many relationship, 258, 276
mappings, 473
view link definition, 362–363
view link definition
cardinality, 341
One-to-one relationship, 258
mappings, 473
view link definition
cardinality, 359
Operating systems, supported, xli
Operations, 114, 379, 455–456, 475, 650–651, 655
rollback, 397
Operators, 292, 764–765
Oracle Application Development Framework. *See* ADF
Oracle Business Component Browser, 24, 248, 251
Oracle Forms Developer, 5, 7, 8, 13
Oracle Help for Java, 55
Oracle object types, 263–264
Oracle Portal, 5, 8
Oracle SCM, 9, 57, 68
Oracle Technology Network. *See* OTN
Oracle user groups, xlv, 107
oracle.jbo.AttrSetValException, 294
oracle.jbo.domain, 292
oracle.jbo.JboException, 312
oracle.jbo.server.ApplicationModule DefImpl, 409
oracle.jbo.server.ApplicationModule Impl, 409
oracle.jbo.server.EntityCache, 288
oracle.jbo.server.EntityDefImpl, 288
oracle.jbo.server.EntityImpl, 288
oracle.jbo.server.ViewDefImpl, 411
oracle.jbo.server.ViewObjectImpl, 411
oracle.jbo.server.ViewRowImpl, 411
oracle.jbo.ValidationException, 294
ORDER BY clause, 339–340
org.apache.struts, 593
orion-application.xml, 188
Other node, 540
OTN JDeveloper resources, xlv
Overlay icons, 58
OverlayLayout2, 550, 568–569, 574
Overloaded methods, 144, 157
Override Methods, menu item, 52

P

<p> HTML tag, 736, 739
Packages, 23, 141, 174, 175, 506
Page
component, 601
directive, 753
page comment, 762, 758. *See also* JSP comment
Page Flow Diagram, 116, 128, 401, 646–647, 665, 695, 706
Page Flow Diagrammer, 102
Page Forwards, 180, 603

Page Link, 593
Pageflow, 115, 184, 597
Panel, 724. *See also* JPanel
PaneLayout, 550, 569–571, 574
Panels, binding, 509–510
Parameter Insight, menu item, 51, 79
Parameterized WHERE clauses, 419–420
Partial Page Rendering (PPR), 689, 705
Password field, 656
PATH, 59, 203
Persistence, 110–111, 137–138
Pinning, 584
PL/SQL, 135
  compiling, 81
  debugging, 86
  editing, 81–82
  running, 81–82
PL/SQL Server Pages, 5
PL/SQL Web Toolkit, 5
Plugin HTML Converter, menu item, 52
Polymorphism, 140
PopupMenu, 724
Portability of Java, 134
Post, 643
Preferences, xli, 48
  class names, 289
  diagram, 101
  dialog, 41, 44, 76
  look-and-feel, 44
  Required Attribute Insertion, 92
Preferred Components, Component Palette page, 697
preferredSize, 553, 554, 555, 558
Prefixes, 171
Previous event, 379, 455, 605, 655
PreviousSet event, 379, 401, 455, 655
Primary Key Constraints, 256–257, 266, 296
private, 142, 145
Profiler, 86
Profiles
  deployment, 189
  project properties, 53
Project Properties, 477, 626
  button, 68
  dialog, 53, 119
  profiles, 53
Project Settings, 542. *See also* Project Properties
Projects, 14, 505
  model, 20
  naming, 176
  view, 25
Properties, 73–75
  anchor, 562
  button, 74
  constraints, 580
  currrencyString, 378
  document, 115
  enabledString, 379, 380, 381, 386
  fill, 562
  keyString, 378
  labels, 378
  layout, 580
  model, 115
  order, 562
  project profiles, 53, 477
  rangeSize, 376
  Remove Insets, 562
  Remove Padding, 562
  Save Before Compiling, 67
  show grid, 562

Specify J2EE Web Context Root, 218
value, 614
weight, 562
Property Editors, 73–75
Property Inspector, 17, 26, 129–130, 73–75, 83, 519, 647–648, 695
Protected mode, 92
protected keyword, 92, 142, 675
public keyword, 142, 144
Public synonyms. *See* Show Public Synonyms
public_html directory, 682, 701
Publish Diagram, menu item, 51, 101

Q

Queriable checkbox, 658
Queries
parameterized, 420
result set relationships, 357–361
TopLink, 473
Query columns, 354
Query page, 340
Quick Javadoc, 80, 156
menu item, 51

R

Radio button group, 656
Range bindings, 372
Range set, 376
Ranges, 375–376
scrolling, 379–380
rangeSet, 376
RangeSize attribute, 376, 389, 398, 403, 676
RangeValidator, 294
RDBMS, 138
Read-only dynamic table, 654
Read-only form, 211, 654
Read-only table, 654
Rebuild, 45
Refactor, menu item, 53
Refactoring, 46, 522–523
Reference entity object usage, 350–351
References, xliv, 596, 716–717
Relational database system. *See* RDBMS
Relationships, 228, 229, 257, 258, 259, 261, 357, 436, 450. *See also* Associations
Remote Interface, 448–449, 453
Remote Method Invocation. *See* RMI
Remote mode, 198
Remove insets, 562
Remove padding, 562
removeCurrentRow( ), 417
Rename, 46, 522–523
Rename class, 53
Renderer, 660
RenderValue tag, 656
Reopen, 46
RequireAttribute Insertion, 92
Reset to Default button, 74
Resolution, monitor, 37

Resources, xliv
books, 716–717
websites, 717–720
Result sets, 335, 357
Right-click menu, xlii
RMI, 183
Rollback, 400, 455
Row keys, 415–416
Row objects, 318, 414, 415, 416
RowIterator, 260, 318
Rows, 567
creating and deleting, 381
RowSet iterators, 417
Run menu, 337–50
Run Manager, 16, 24, 69
Runtime, 49, 86, 106, 130, 148, 194, 202. *See also* JVM

S

Save As dialog, 583, 585
Schemas, 19, 22, 69
HR, xl
XML, 92, 101
SCM, 6, 9, 57–58, 68. *See also* Software Configuration Management
Scope of variables, 142
Scripting elements, 747, 751–753
Scriptlets, 748–750, 752, 758
Scrollbar, 724
ScrollPane, 724
SDK, xl, 148, 185, 193, 722, 728. *See also* JDK
Search
files, 48, 67
for object in Navigators, 67
incremental Backward, 48
incremental Forward, 48
menu, 48
Search Files dialog, 48
Secondary rowset iterators, 376, 414
Select in Navigator, menu item, 49
Select in Structure, menu item, 49
Select Row Link, 654
Selected in Query checkbox, 323, 346
Send to Back, 549, 562
Sequence, 148
Sequence Viewer, 96–97
SequenceImpl, 315–316
Server-side Presentation Tier, 185
Service Methods, 426–427, 337–443
access from JSP application, 427–431
hands-on practice: Create and Invoke, 422–436
Service Oriented Architecture, 112. *See also* SOA
Service( ), 148
Servlets, 7, 182, 639, 751, 752
HTTP, 204
Java, 204–205
Session Facade DTO Collection, 447
Session Facades, 447, 454, 467
implementing, 465–467
set( ), 93
setAttribute( ), 297
setAttributeInternal( ), 296–297
setCurrentRowWithKey(String), 380, 390, 455, 613, 655
setCurrentRowWithKeyValue( ), 455, 655

Setters, 145, 174, 290, 324–325
  method validation, 296–298
  See also set( )
setvars.bat, 213
setWhereClause( ), 418–419, 420
setWhereClauseParams( ), 420
short, 292
Shortcuts, keyboard, 47, 48, 78
Show Categories button, 68
Show Dependencies, menu item, 54
Show Grid, 560, 562
Show Public Synonyms checkbox, 69
Show rules tab, 530
Signature, 145, 159
Simple Components, Component Palette page, 697
Simple Form Components, Component Palette page, 697
Simple Object Access Protocol server, 69, 488–489, 720. *See also* SOAP server
Single select list, 656
Size padding, 564, 589
Smart Data, debugger window, 84, 85
Snippets. *See* Code Snippets
SOA, 112. *See also* Service-Oriented Architecture
SOAP Server
  connection, 69
  See also Simple Object Access Protocol
Software Configuration Management. *See* SCM
Software Development Kit. *See* SDK
Software, J2EE, 185
Source menu, 51
Source Control, 57, 58, 60. *See also* Software Configuration Management
Source data collection, 674
Source iterator, 395, 396, 403
Specialization, 139
Specifications, J2EE, 185
Specify J2EE Web Context Root, 218
Split Document, 39
Splits, 570
Splitter bars, 39
SQL, 137
  JSTL library, 763
SQL Worksheet, 20, 53, 97–98
SQL*Plus, xli, 53, 54
SQL-only view attributes, 330, 333–334
SQL-only view object definitions, 336–337
  and expert mode, 340
  creating, 347–349
SQL-only view objects, 348
src subdirectory, 14, 504
Stack debug window, 84, 85
static keyword, 513
Step Into, 86
Step Over, 86
Step to End of Method, 86
Stored procedures, 319–321
String class, 144
StringBuffer class, 144, 157
Structure window, 17, 26, 70–72, 96, 126, 127, 129–130, 163, 239, 243, 307, 384, 583, 584, 645–646
  for UIX files, 694–695

UI model tab, 374–375
views, 71–72
Struts Configuration Editor, 668
Struts page flow diagram, 374, 599–600, 611–612
Struts, 6, 9, 10–11, 116, 128, 592–636
architecture, 592–598
data page, 383, 401
elements, 593–594, 600–603
hands-on practice: Create a Simple Application, 607–625
hands-on practice: Create Application with Data actions for Custom Logic, 625–636
JSP application steps, 657
libraries, 597, 621, 650
naming components, 179
Page Flow Diagrammer, 102
struts-config.xml, 116, 128, 595–597, 695
Stubs
web service, 491–492
wrapper class for, 492–493
Style sheets, 31, 640–83, 208, 639, 649. *See also* CSS
Subclass, 139, 143–144
building file, 163–164
Suffixes, 171
Superclass, 139
Surround With, menu item, 51
Swing
binding components, 508–509
components, 510–518, 728–730
controls, 183
modifying components, 517
UI architecture, 507–508
Swing containers, 730–732
switch statement, 149
Synchronization, 335–336, 337
Synonyms. *See* Show Public Synonyms
Syntax errors, highlighting, 80
System Navigator, 16, 65–68, 71
System.out.println( ), 147

T

Tab Destination, 701
Table Binding Editor, 377, 388, 652
Table Components, 697
Tables Viewer, 96
Tables
aliases, 337–338
creating constraints for generation, 266–268
intersection, 259
renaming columns, 277
representing relationships between, 257–263
Tabs, 36, 42, 692
Document, 38
Editor, 38
Help, 56
Property Inspector, 73
Tag Completion, 296
Tag Insight, 78–79, 92, 644, 694
Tag libraries, 117, 749, 759–763
Tag library descriptor (.tld), 754
tagclass, 757
taglib directive, D10, 762
Tags
action, 593
beginning and ending, 747

CVS support for, 58
forward, 593
prefix, 757
processing, 747–759
See also JSP Action tags
Target data collection, 674
Target iterators, 395
Technology scope, 122
Technology Templates, 9–10
Java Application[Default], 10
Java Application[Java, Swing], 10
Web Application[Default], 9
Web Application[Default-no controller], 9
Web Application[JSP, EJB], 10
Web Application[JSP, Struts, EJB], 10
Templates, 597
application, 121, 168
code, 73, 77–78, 466, 518, 726
Expand, 51
Manage Application, 52, 123
UIX, 689
Web Application[Default], 125
Terminal server, strategy for running Java applications, 193–194
Terminate, menu item, 49
Testing
application, 27–29, 130
class files, 164–166
connection, 19
model project, 23
Text area, 656, 724
text property, 584, 688, 710
TextField, 724
this node, 575, 579
Threads, debugger window, 85
throw statement, 150
Thumbnail window, 100, 126, 244
<title> HTML tag, 736
Toggle Line Comments, menu item, 51
Toolbars, xxxviii
main, 44–45
See also JToolbar
Tools menu, 53–54
Tooltip Text, 660
Tooltips, 65
TopLink Plain Old Java Objects (TopLink POJOs), 470–474
component relationships, 471
TopLink, 446, 470–475
and ADF Model layer, 474–475
deployment descriptor, 470, 481–482
hands-on practice: Build a Simple Application, 475–488
mappings node, 478
queries, 473, 485–486
sessions, 474
Tracing classes, 84
Transactions, managing, 396–397
Transfer objects. *See* Data Transfer Objects
Transient attributes, 255
Tree Binding Editor, 530
Tree structure, 528–532
Triggers, 316, 318–319

Troubleshooting, hands-on practices, xlii-xliv
try keyword, 150
Typesafe, 159–160, 290

U

UDDI Registry Connection, 69
UI Delegate, 507
UI Model, 373, 378, 386
    .xml files, 617, 667
    tab, 374–375, 558, 695
UI, 7, 179, 507, 512, 532, 736. *See also* User Interface
UIT, 689, 693
UIX JSP tag library, 687
UIX preview, 694
UIX Previewer, 87–89
UIX Visual Editor, 87, 88, 692, 694
UIX XML Page Based on Existing UIX XML Template (UIT), 693
UIX XML Page with Header, Footer, and Navigation, 693
UIX XML Page with pageLayout, 693
UIX XML Template (UIT), 693
UIX XML Template (UIT) with Header, Footer, and Navigation, 693
UIX. *See* ADF UIX
uix-config.xml file, 711
UML, 6, 11
    diagrams, 99–100, 243–245
    naming diagram elements, 177
Undocking windows, 42
Uni-directional associations, 259, 261
Unified Modeling Language. *See* UML
Uniform resource identifier (uri), 757
Unindent Block, menu item, 51
Union button, 74
Unique constraints, 266, 278
UniqueKey Validator, 300
Universal Description, Discovery and Integration. *See* UDDI
Updateable property, 658
URL management, JSTL tags, 761
Use Active Project Source Path by Default checkbox, xl
Use Case Modeler, 11–12
Use Cases, 11
User interface nodes, 689–691
User Interface. *See also* UI

V

validate( ), 311
validateEntity( ), 301
validateValue( ), 295
Validation
    attribute-level, 296–299
    choosing a style, 298–299, 301–302
    custom, 295, 306–310
    domains, 295–296, 310–312
    entity-level, 299–301
    logic, 326–328
    rules, 293–295, 300–301, 305–306
    setter method, 296–298
Value, 656
Variable scope, 151
    JSTL tags, 761

Variables
- casting, 158
- class, 152–153
- declaration, 144
- final, 153
- instance, 152
- local, 153
- member, 152
- naming, 174
- scope, 151–153

veotableChange( ), 295, 308
Version Compare, 58
Version control. *See* SCM
Version History, 58
Versioning, 52, 60, 61, 68, 344
verticalFill, 572
VerticalFlowLayout, 550, 571–572, 574
vgap, 548, 553, 556, 558, 567, 572
View attributes, 230, 330–337
- entity derived, 330
- naming, 178
- selecting, 350–351
- SQL-only, 330

View cache, 333, 334–335
- stepping through, 415

View criteria objects, 420, 432
View criteria row, 420, 433
View definition classes, 412
View link definitions, 231, 357, 421
- cardinality, 359–360
- directionality, 360–361
- exploring, 246–247
- hands-on practice: Creating 362–367
- naming, 179

View Link Editor, 246, 247
View link instances, 439
- removing, 438

View link SQL, 357–358
View object classes, 411–412, 423–425
View object definitions, 178, 230–231, 357, 365
- attribute list, 447
- creating, 345–357
- exploring, 243–246
- hands-on practice: create, 342–347
- SQL-only, 336–337, 347–349
- testing, 347, 349, 352, 356
- WHERE clause, 447

View Object Editor, 246, 247, 340, 354–355, 419, 424
View Object Instances, 411, 413
- exposing to ADF application, 375–376
- restricting cache, 419–421

View objects, refining query, 11
View row classes, 412
View rows, 414–416
View usages, 232
View
- layer in ADF, 116, 127
- menu, 48
- project, 13, 25

ViewController, project, 13, 122, 127, 128, 176, 235, 699
ViewDefImpl, 412
Viewers
- archive, 653–96
- Image, 95

Sequence, 96–97
Tables, 96
ViewObjectImpl, 411, 415, 417
ViewRowImpl, 411, 412, 415
ViewRowImpl.getAttribute( ), 421
Views
splitting, 39
Structure window, 71–72
Visual Editor, 86, 372, 523
tools, 549
See also Java Visual Editor, JSP/HTML Visual Editor, UIX Visual Editor
void keyword, 145

W

W3C group. *See* World Wide Web Consortium
WAN, 192
WAR Deployment Profile, 217, 218
WAR files, 187, 188
deployment profile, 217
Watches, debugger window, 85
Web Application [Default – no Controller] template, 9
Web Application [Default] template, 9, 128
Web Application [JSP, EJB] template, 10
Web Application [JSP, Struts, EJB] template, 10
Web Client, 110, 116–117, 182
controls, 74
data model components, 179
naming components, 179
user interface components, 114
Web container, 204
Web deployment descriptor, 216–217
Web Forms. *See* Oracle Forms Developer
Web Services Definition Language. *See* WSDL
Web Services Interoperability Organization (WS-1), 8
Web Services, 12, 111, 487–489
and ADF model layer, 489
stub, 488–489, 491–493
hands-on practice: Create an Application Using, 489–498
Web Tier, 185, 186, 190, 206
web.xml, 216, 217, 627
Web Application Archive. *See* WAR files
WebDAV Server, 19, 69
Websites, 717–720
weight property, 564
Welcome page, 19
WHERE clauses, 339–340, 350, 451
while loop statement, 150
Widen Imports, 51
Window, 545
focus, 70
menu, 54
Windows
arranging, 330–343
debugger, 85
displaying dockable, 43
dockable, 40–43
Editor, 38–40
resizing, 38

thumbnail, 100
viewer, 653–655
Wizards, 90
Create Business Components from Tables, 125, 237
Create Entity Constraint, 267
Create UIX XML Page, 701
Create View Link, 358
Workspaces, 505
application, 13
creating, 16–19
naming, 176
World WIde Web Consortium (W3C), 734, 737, 744
Wrapper classes, 156, 166, 492
WSDL, 488–489
WYSIWYG, 6, 7

X

XML, xxxvii, 126, 130, 226
core library tags, 762
schema, 105
XML Editor, 92, 694
XML Schema Editor, 99, 101–102
XML structure tab 694
XSS, 687
XYLayout, 550, 572–574

Z

.zipfiles, 141, 142
Zoom, 100
in, 100
out, 100
Z-order, 549

INTERNATIONAL CONTACT INFORMATION

AUSTRALIA
McGraw-Hill Book Company
Australia Pty. Ltd.
TEL +61-2-9900-1800
FAX +61-2-9878-8881
http://www.mcgraw-hill.com.au
books-it_sydney@mcgraw-hill.com

CANADA
McGraw-Hill Ryerson Ltd.
TEL +905-430-5000
FAX +905-430-5020
http://www.mcgraw-hill.ca

GREECE, MIDDLE EAST, & AFRICA (Excluding South Africa)
McGraw-Hill Hellas
TEL +30-210-6560-990
TEL +30-210-6560-993
TEL +30-210-6560-994
FAX +30-210-6545-525

MEXICO (Also serving Latin America)
McGraw-Hill Interamericana Editores
S.A. de C.V.
TEL +525-1500-5108
FAX +525-117-1589
http://www.mcgraw-hill.com.mx
carlos_ruiz@mcgraw-hill.com

SINGAPORE (Serving Asia)
McGraw-Hill Book Company
TEL +65-6863-1580
FAX +65-6862-3354
http://www.mcgraw-hill.com.sg
mghasia@mcgraw-hill.com

SOUTH AFRICA
McGraw-Hill South Africa
TEL +27-11-622-7512
FAX +27-11-622-9045
robyn_swanepoel@mcgraw-hill.com

SPAIN
McGraw-Hill/
Interamericana de España, S.A.U.
TEL +34-91-180-3000
FAX +34-91-372-8513
http://www.mcgraw-hill.es
professional@mcgraw-hill.es

UNITED KINGDOM, NORTHERN, EASTERN, & CENTRAL EUROPE
McGraw-Hill Education Europe
TEL +44-1-628-502500
FAX +44-1-628-770224
http://www.mcgraw-hill.co.uk
emea_queries@mcgraw-hill.com

ALL OTHER INQUIRIES Contact:
McGraw-Hill/Osborne
TEL +1-510-420-7700
FAX +1-510-420-7703
http://www.osborne.com
omg_international@mcgraw-hill.com

ORACLE

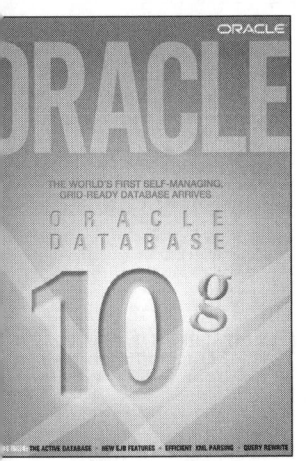